Presents

The World of Professional Golf 2015

Founded by
Mark H. McCormack

IMG

Editor: Jan Davis
Publication Coordinator: Sarah Wooldridge
Contributors: Andy Farrell, Doug Ferguson, Donald (Doc) Giffin, Marino Parascenzo
Official World Golf Ranking Statistician: Tony Greer

First published 2015

Designed and produced by Davis Design

ISBN-13: 978-0-9914858-1-9

Printed and bound in the United States.

Contents

APPENDIXES

Introduction

Rolex has done so many things over the years that were and are good for golf. Sponsorship of this publication is a prime example. My friends at Rolex, recognizing the historic and research value *The World of Professional Golf* has provided to the game continuously since the middle 1960s, stepped up in 2005 with the support necessary to continue its existence and the service it extends to the world of golf.

I well remember my conversations with my close friend and business manager, the late Mark McCormack, when he outlined his concept of filling a written gap in the game's history with an annual book carrying detailed stories and statistics covering every organized national and international tournament during that particular calendar year. The idea made complete sense to me and I encouraged him to proceed. He did, recruiting a group of talented golf journalists to work with him in producing the first edition that covered the 1966 season worldwide. Its publication has continued and grown in size and scope ever since, keeping pace with the tremendous growth of the game throughout the world.

Mark McCormack passed away in 2003, but his contribution to the historical record of golf did not die. Credit for this goes to IMG executives and others within the organization who considered the book an important continuing tribute to Mark and to the executives at Rolex, whose support has kept the literary chain intact.

Arnold Palmer
Orlando, Florida

Foreword
(Written in 1968)

It has long been my feeling that a sport as compelling as professional golf is deserving of a history, and by history I do not mean an account culled years later from the adjectives and enthusiasms of on-the-spot reports that have then sat in newspaper morgues for decades waiting for some patient drudge to paste them together and call them lore. Such works can be excellent when insight and perspective are added to the research, but this rarely happens. What I am talking about is a running history, a chronology written at the time, which would serve both as a record of the sport and as a commentary upon the sport in any given year—an annual, if you will....

When I embarked on this project two years ago (the first of these annuals was published in Great Britain in 1967), I was repeatedly told that such a compendium of world golf was impossible, that it would be years out of date before it could be assembled and published, that it would be hopelessly expensive to produce and that only the golf fanatic would want a copy anyway. In the last analysis, it was that final stipulation that spurred me on. There must be a lot of golf fanatics, I decided. I can't be the only one. And then one winter day I was sitting in Arnold Palmer's den in Latrobe, Pennsylvania, going through the usual motions of spreading papers around so that Arnold and I could discuss some business project, when Arnold happened to mention that he wanted to collect a copy of each new golf book that was published from now on, in order to build a golf library of his own. "It's really too bad that there isn't a book every year on the pro tour," he said. "Ah," I thought. "Another golf fanatic. That makes two of us." So I decided to do the book. And I have. And I hope you like it. If so, you can join Arnold and me as golf fanatics.

Mark H. McCormack
Cleveland, Ohio
January 1968

Mark H. McCormack
1930 – 2003

In 1960, Mark Hume McCormack shook hands with a young golfer named Arnold Palmer. That historic handshake established a business that would evolve into today's IMG, the world's premier sports and lifestyle marketing and management company —representing hundreds of sports figures, entertainers, models, celebrities, broadcasters, television properties, and prestigious organizations and events around the world. With just a handshake Mark McCormack had invented a global industry.

Sean McManus, President of CBS News and Sports, reflects, "I don't think it's an overstatement to say that like Henry Ford and Bill Gates, Mark McCormack literally created, fostered and led an entirely new worldwide industry. There was no sports marketing before Mark McCormack. Every athlete who's ever appeared in a commercial, or every right holder who sold their rights to anyone, owes a huge debt of gratitude to Mark McCormack."

Mark McCormack's philosophy was simple. "Be the best," he said. "Learn the business and expand by applying what you already know." This philosophy served him well, not only as an entrepreneur and CEO of IMG, but also as an author, a consultant and a confidant to a host of global leaders in the world of business, politics, finance, science, sports and entertainment.

He was among the most-honored entrepreneurs of his time. *Sports Illustrated* recognized him as "The Most Powerful Man in Sports." In 1999, ESPN's Sports Century listed him as one of the century's 10 "Most Influential People in the Business of Sport."

Golf Magazine called McCormack "the most powerful man in golf" and honored him along with Arnold Palmer, Gerald Ford, Dwight D. Eisenhower, Bob Hope and Ben Hogan as one of the 100 all-time "American Heroes of Golf." *Tennis* magazine and *Racquet* magazine named him "the most powerful man in tennis." Tennis legend Billie Jean King believes, "Mark McCormack was the king of sports marketing. He shaped the way all sports are marketed around the world. He was the first in the marketplace, and his influence on the world of sports, particularly his ability to combine athlete representation, property development and television broadcasting, will forever be the standard of the industry."

The London *Sunday Times* listed him as one of the 1000 people who influenced the 20th century. Alastair Cooke on the BBC said simply that "McCormack was the Oracle; the creator of the talent industry, the maker of people famous in their profession famous to the rest of the world and making for them a fortune in the process ... He took on as clients people already famous in their profession as golfer, opera singer, author, footballer, racing car driver, violinist—and from time to time if they needed special help, a prime minister, or even the Pope."

McCormack was honored posthumously by the Golf Writers Association of America with the 2004 William D. Richardson Award, the organization's highest honor, "Given to recognize an individual who has consistently made an outstanding contribution to golf."

Among McCormack's other honors were the 2001 PGA Distinguished Service Award, given to those who have helped perpetuate the values and ideals of the PGA of America. He was also named a Commander of the Royal Order of the Polar Star by the King of Sweden (the highest honor for a person living outside of Sweden) for his contribution to the Nobel Foundation.

Journalist Frank Deford states, "There have been what we love to call dynasties in every sport. IMG has been different. What this one brilliant man, Mark McCormack, created is the only dynasty ever over all sport."

Through IMG, Mark McCormack demonstrated the value of sports and lifestyle activities as effective corporate marketing tools, but more importantly, his lifelong dedication to his vocation—begun with just a simple handshake—brought enjoyment to millions of people worldwide who watch and cheer their heroes and heroines. That is his legacy.

The year 2014 marked another exciting season for professional golf, characterized by the commitment to excellence and superior performance that have distinguished the sport since its inception.

Among the many accomplishments, Rolex was especially thrilled to celebrate Rolex Testimonee Martin Kaymer's victories at The Players Championship, the U.S. Open and the PGA Grand Slam, as well as top-level play from two of the younger Rolex Testimonees, Rickie Fowler and Jordan Spieth. Spieth performed extremely well and captured both the Australian Open and the Hero World Challenge title at the end of the season.

In team events, the highlights included the return of The Ryder Cup to Scotland, the home of golf. Gleneagles hosted the first unofficial Ryder Cup back in 1921. The 40th edition of the tournament in 2014 brought immense pride for Rolex, whose role as one of the leading supporters of golf is renowned worldwide.

Rolex reinforced its long-standing support for women's golf with the 10-year extension of its LPGA and Rolex Rankings partnerships, and also contributed to the creation of the new Rolex Annika Major Award, named after Swedish golfing legend Annika Sorenstam, and presented to the player who performs the best on all five of the women's Majors in the same year.

Another high point included welcoming New Zealand golfer Lydia Ko to the Rolex family of Testimonees. During her first season as a professional, Lydia not only became the youngest player ever to win a professional tour event; with three wins this season, she also finished runner-up in the Rolex Rankings, earning her the 2014 Louise Suggs Rolex Rookie of the Year award.

Rolex has been at the heart of golf for over half a century and we are proud to present the 2014 edition of *The World of Professional Golf*, a retrospective of the highlights and results of the year's golf championships and tours worldwide.

Gian Riccardo Marini
Rolex SA
Chief Executive Officer

Rolex and Golf

Rolex is proud to be a major force at play behind the finest events, players and organizations in golf. The company's involvement began with Arnold Palmer in 1967. He, along with fellow Rolex Testimonees Jack Nicklaus and Gary Player — otherwise known as The Big Three — contributed to modernizing golf and giving it a worldwide dimension. Since 1967, the relationship between Rolex and golf has continuously grown and prospered. At present, Rolex is golf's leading supporter and is associated with the most important and prestigious entities governing the sport worldwide, as well as with golf's principal professional tours, competitions and athletes.

As a supporter of the USGA and the U.S. Open Championship, Rolex is proud to have Martin Kaymer, the 2014 champion, as one of its Testimonees.

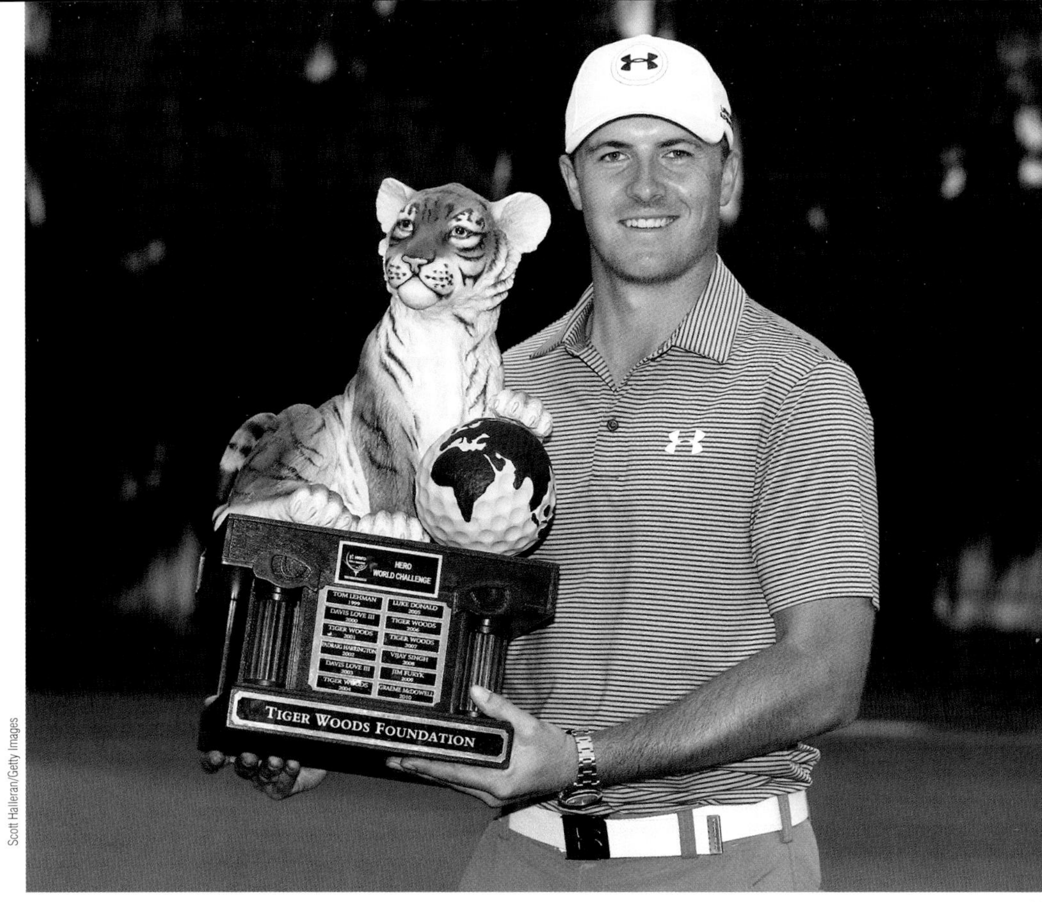

Scott Halleran/Getty Images

Jordan Spieth, winner of the Hero World Challenge

©Rolex/Chris Turvey

Bernhard Langer, winner of The Senior Open Championship presented by Rolex

©Rolex/Chris Turvey

Lexi Thompson, winner of the Kraft Nabisco Championship

Adam Scott

Rickie Fowler

Tiger Woods

Harry How/Getty Images

The Ryder Cup

©Rolex/Chris Turvey

Tom Watson and Paul McGinley

©Rolex/Chris Turvey

Martin Kaymer and Thomas Bjørn

Jason Day

Brooks Koepka's victory in the Turkish Airlines Open helped him secure the European Tour's Rookie of the Year Award.

Thorbjørn Olesen at the DP World Tour Championship

Lydia Ko at the Evian Championship

Annika Sorenstam poses with the five ladies major trophies at the Rolex ANNIKA Major Award ceremony.

The 2014 Rolex Rankings Top Three

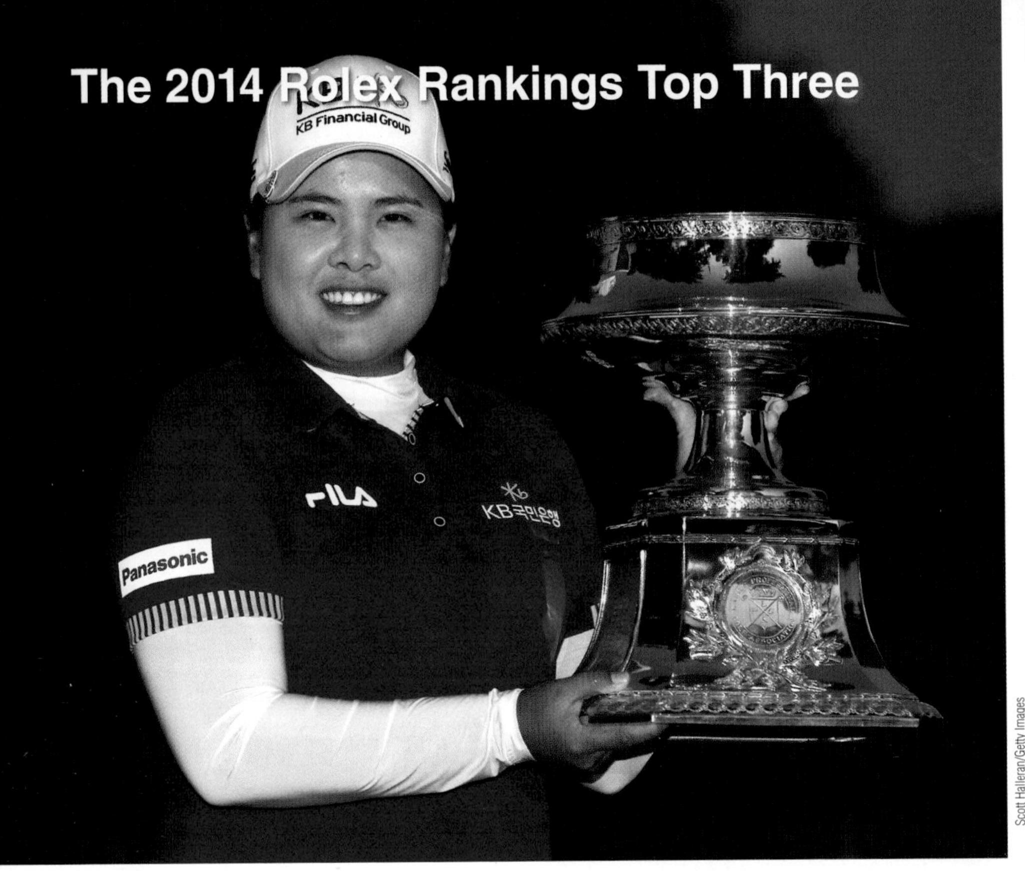

Scott Halleran/Getty Images

1. Inbee Park (Korea) 10.82 points

Sam Greenwood/Getty Images

2. Lydia Ko (New Zealand) 9.80 points

Victor Fraile/Getty Images

3. Stacy Lewis (USA) 9.74 points

Rolex Rankings

A fierce battle raged throughout 2014 for the top spot on the Rolex Rankings, although Inbee Park ended the year as she started it as the World No. 1. For much of the season the crown of being the best woman golfer seemed to be up for grabs, however. Stacy Lewis won twice to claim the No. 1 position for the second time in her career in June, but by retaining her title at the LPGA Championship and winning two other LPGA events and once on the Ladies European Tour, Park resumed possession of the top spot in October.

Park's average dropped slightly to 10.82, while Lewis improved hers in a season in which she did the triple crown by topping the LPGA money list, the stroke average and the Player of the Year points table. However, by year's end she had been pushed down to third spot on the Rankings by Lydia Ko, who won three times in her first full season as a professional, including the CME Tour Championship. Ko, who started the year as No. 4, finished it with an average of 9.80, just marginally ahead of Lewis. There were weeks when the identity of the World No. 1 could have changed in a three-way battle and Ko's turn in the top spot appears only a matter of time.

Eight players retained their positions in the top 10, including Kraft Nabisco champion Lexi Thompson, while two players won major championships to force their way into that elite company — Michelle Wie at the U.S. Women's Open at Pinehurst after starting the year 61st, and Hyo-Joo Kim, who was 24th at the end of 2013, at the Evian Championship. Despite an injury-curtailed season, Wie finished in sixth position with Kim eighth. American Mo Martin was ranked 99th in the world when she won the Ricoh Women's British Open at Royal Birkdale, her maiden LPGA victory.

The Rolex Rankings — which was developed at the May 2004 World Congress of Women's Golf — is sanctioned by eight women's professional golf tours: the Ladies Professional Golf Association (LPGA); Ladies European Tour (LET); Ladies Professional Golfers' Association of Japan (JLPGA); Korea Ladies Professional Golf Association (KLPGA); Australian Ladies Professional Golf (ALPG); Symetra Tour; China Ladies Professional Golf Association Tour (CLPGA) and the Ladies European Access Series (LETAS) - as well as the Ladies' Golf Union (LGU) and the United States Golf Association (USGA).

The major golf tours developed the rankings and the protocol that governs the ranking, while R2IT, an independent software development company, was retained to develop the software and to maintain the rankings on a weekly basis. The official events from all of the tours are taken into account and points are awarded according to the strength of the field, with the exception of the five major championships on the LPGA Tour and the Symetra Tour, CLPGA and LETAS events, which have a fixed points distribution. The players' points averages are determined by taking the number of points awarded over a two-year rolling period and dividing that by the number of tournaments played, with a minimum divisor of 35.

The Rolex Rankings are updated and released following the completion of the previous week's tournaments around the world.

Rolex Rankings
(As of December 31, 2014)

Rank	Player	Country	No. of Events	Average Points	Total Points
1	Inbee Park	Korea	54	10.82	584.52
2	Lydia Ko	New Zealand	43	9.80	421.52
3	Stacy Lewis	USA	55	9.74	535.46
4	Suzann Pettersen	Norway	49	7.01	343.55
5	Shanshan Feng	China	57	6.94	395.33
6	Michelle Wie	USA	49	6.39	312.92
7	So Yeon Ryu	Korea	55	6.11	335.98
8	Hyo-Joo Kim	Korea	54	6.07	327.67
9	Karrie Webb	Australia	43	5.67	243.87
10	Lexi Thompson	USA	49	5.41	265.20
11	Kyu Jung Baek	Korea	33	4.93	172.69
12	Anna Nordqvist	Sweden	57	4.61	262.83
13	Cristie Kerr	USA	46	4.30	197.70
14	Azahara Munoz	Spain	56	4.17	233.64
15	Sun Ju Ahn	Korea	54	4.02	217.21
16	Mi Rim Lee	Korea	42	3.99	167.48
17	Na Yeon Choi	Korea	55	3.79	208.26
18	Brittany Lincicome	USA	50	3.68	183.88
19	Paula Creamer	USA	48	3.55	170.47
20	In Gee Chun	Korea	49	3.53	172.83
21	Ha-Na Jang	Korea	52	3.47	180.32
22	Angela Stanford	USA	50	3.43	171.69
23	Amy Yang	Korea	44	3.39	148.97
24	Jessica Korda	USA	47	3.36	157.87
25	Lizette Salas	USA	48	3.27	157.01
26	Chella Choi	Korea	63	3.20	201.69
27	Pornanong Phatlum	Thailand	54	2.96	159.67
28	Catriona Matthew	Scotland	48	2.90	138.98
29	I.K. Kim	Korea	46	2.82	129.90
30	Lee-Anne Pace	South Africa	43	2.76	118.67
31	Jung Min Lee	Korea	42	2.74	115.27
32	Yoon-Kyung Heo	Korea	50	2.74	137.06
33	Mo Martin	USA	51	2.74	139.75
34	Teresa Lu	Taipei	60	2.74	164.34
35	Julieta Granada	Paraguay	55	2.68	147.55
36	Jiyai Shin	Korea	60	2.65	158.73
37	Bo-Mee Lee	Korea	62	2.64	163.61
38	Charley Hull	England	40	2.61	104.40
39	Sei Young Kim	Korea	50	2.50	124.95
40	Gerina Piller	USA	52	2.49	129.55
41	Jin-Young Ko	Korea	29	2.45	85.65
42	Jenny Shin	Korea	57	2.37	135.29
43	MinYoung Lee	Korea	51	2.37	121.02
44	Shiho Oyama	Japan	50	2.36	117.79
45	Karine Icher	France	54	2.35	126.87
46	Carlota Ciganda	Spain	56	2.35	131.53
47	Sakura Yokomine	Japan	62	2.31	143.26
48	Hee Young Park	Korea	58	2.29	133.08
49	Min Sun Kim	Korea	30	2.28	79.66
50	Sandra Gal	Germany	56	2.24	125.47

Rank	Player	Country	No. of Events	Average Points	Total Points
51	Meena Lee	Korea	54	2.20	118.83
52	Morgan Pressel	USA	54	2.20	118.59
53	Christina Kim	USA	51	2.18	110.99
54	Caroline Masson	Germany	57	2.11	120.47
55	Caroline Hedwall	Sweden	48	2.08	99.76
56	Mi Hyang Lee	Korea	48	2.04	98.11
57	Ha Neul Kim	Korea	49	2.04	99.87
58	Ilhee Lee	Korea	58	2.01	116.61
59	Se-Ri Pak	Korea	37	1.99	73.58
60	Misuzu Narita	Japan	65	1.95	126.74
61	Beatriz Recari	Spain	54	1.91	103.25
62	Gwladys Nocera	France	43	1.91	82.14
63	Eun-Hee Ji	Korea	56	1.88	105.05
64	Mi Jung Hur	Korea	49	1.83	89.82
65	Momoko Ueda	Japan	56	1.75	98.00
66	Brittany Lang	USA	58	1.75	101.45
67	Rikako Morita	Japan	69	1.70	117.47
68	Na-Ri Lee	Korea	69	1.68	115.67
69	Ai Suzuki	Japan	31	1.62	56.69
70	Jennifer Johnson	USA	48	1.61	77.41
71	Line Vedel Hansen	Denmark	39	1.61	62.70
72	Seung Hyun Lee	Korea	45	1.60	72.01
73	Miki Sakai	Japan	73	1.57	114.54
74	Jodi Ewart Shadoff	England	49	1.57	76.84
75	Austin Ernst	USA	49	1.54	75.49
76	Erina Hara	Japan	65	1.48	96.19
77	Kotono Kozuma	Japan	33	1.47	51.62
78	Minjee Lee	Australia	18	1.47	51.39
79	Su Yeon Jang	Korea	45	1.43	64.15
80	Yumiko Yoshida	Japan	70	1.41	98.83
81	Xi-Yu Lin	China	42	1.40	58.85
82	Mika Miyazato	Japan	48	1.40	67.09
83	Yani Tseng	Taipei	49	1.39	68.30
84	Haeji Kang	Korea	51	1.37	69.92
85	Mariajo Uribe	Colombia	50	1.35	67.53
86	Harukyo Nomura	Japan	55	1.35	74.04
87	Nikki Campbell	Australia	41	1.30	53.41
88	Ayaka Watanabe	Japan	70	1.29	90.44
89	Mina Harigae	USA	53	1.28	67.62
90	Yuki Ichinose	Japan	45	1.26	56.65
91	Ji Hyun Kim	Korea	46	1.25	57.42
92	Kim Kaufman	USA	35	1.24	43.24
93	Pernilla Lindberg	Sweden	63	1.22	77.04
94	Sun Young Yoo	Korea	52	1.22	63.21
95	Bo Kyung Kim	Korea	48	1.21	58.01
96	Hee-Kyung Bae	Korea	48	1.20	57.79
97	Holly Clyburn	England	33	1.20	41.87
98	Soo-Jin Yang	Korea	44	1.18	51.83
99	Seul A Yoon	Korea	47	1.17	55.11
100	Valentine Derrey	France	39	1.17	45.62

Rank	Player	Country	No. of Events	Average Points	Total Points
101	Esther Lee	Korea	72	1.17	83.94
102	Stephanie Meadow	N. Ireland	7	1.14	40.07
103	Hee Kyung Seo	Korea	31	1.14	39.75
104	Ai Miyazato	Japan	47	1.12	52.46
105	Ji-Hee Lee	Korea	58	1.11	64.54
106	Onnarin Sattayabanphot	Thailand	64	1.11	70.80
107	Ariya Jutanugarn	Thailand	24	1.10	38.50
108	Ritsuko Ryu	Japan	72	1.07	76.92
109	Hae Rym Kim	Korea	48	1.07	51.19
110	Yeon Ju Jung	Korea	43	1.06	45.68
111	Moriya Jutanugarn	Thailand	54	1.05	56.61
112	Danielle Kang	USA	51	1.05	53.35
113	Belen Mozo	Spain	51	1.04	53.07
114	Yoo Lim Choi	Korea	49	1.04	50.98
115	Jane Park	USA	40	1.04	41.59
116	Yea Lin Kang	Korea	27	1.03	35.92
117	Ran Hong	Korea	46	1.03	47.21
118	Thidapa Suwannapura	Thailand	53	1.02	53.82
119	Lala Anai	Japan	69	1.01	69.99
120	Yoon Ji Cho	Korea	45	1.01	45.43
121	Katherine Kirk	Australia	54	1.00	53.75
122	Hyun Soo Kim	Korea	51	0.99	50.68
123	Chae-Young Yoon	Korea	47	0.99	46.69
124	Erika Kikuchi	Japan	72	0.98	70.27
125	Junko Omote	Japan	73	0.97	70.66
126	Mi Jeong Jeon	Korea	61	0.97	58.90
127	Miki Saiki	Japan	61	0.94	57.45
128	Ji Hyun Kim	Korea	45	0.94	42.31
129	Dewi Claire Schreefel	Netherlands	55	0.94	51.53
130	Mamiko Higa	Japan	67	0.92	61.73
131	Jeong Eun Lee	Korea	47	0.91	42.97
132	Asako Fujimoto	Japan	69	0.91	62.87
133	Kylie Walker	Scotland	36	0.91	32.80
134	Ayako Uehara	Japan	61	0.90	55.14
135	Joanna Klatten	France	42	0.90	37.95
136	Soo-Yun Kang	Korea	57	0.90	51.09
137	Saiki Fujita	Japan	62	0.89	55.04
138	Sarah Jane Smith	Australia	57	0.88	49.93
139	Laura Davies	England	56	0.87	48.63
140	Hee Won Jung	Korea	46	0.87	39.86
141	Florentyna Parker	England	37	0.85	31.53
142	Hikari Fujita	Japan	37	0.84	30.94
143	Ji Hee Kim	Korea	46	0.83	38.26
144	Hsuan-Yu Yao	Taipei	52	0.83	43.14
145	Trish Johnson	England	34	0.82	28.65
146	Yoko Maeda	Japan	35	0.81	28.46
147	Camilla Lennarth	Sweden	33	0.81	28.43
148	Marina Alex	USA	43	0.81	34.62
149	Stacy Lee Bregman	South Africa	33	0.80	28.16
150	Malene Jorgensen	Denmark	29	0.80	28.02

Rank	Player	Country	No. of Events	Average Points	Total Points
151	Beth Allen	USA	44	0.80	35.13
152	Juli Inkster	USA	35	0.78	27.28
153	Candie Kung	Taipei	51	0.77	39.48
154	Ssu-Chia Cheng	Taipei	11	0.77	26.89
155	Ju Young Park	Korea	45	0.77	34.46
156	Yukari Baba	Japan	66	0.76	50.23
157	Char Young Kim	Korea	45	0.76	34.14
158	Ji-Young Oh	Korea	44	0.75	33.18
159	Hye-Youn Kim	Korea	47	0.75	35.27
160	Sydnee Michaels	USA	44	0.75	32.89
161	Ashleigh Simon	South Africa	35	0.73	25.72
162	Seonwoo Bae	Korea	37	0.73	26.92
163	Amy Boulden	Wales	22	0.72	25.10
164	Yuri Fudoh	Japan	43	0.72	30.82
165	Hannah Burke	England	43	0.71	30.44
166	Na Ri Kim	Korea	66	0.70	46.42
167	Giulia Sergas	Italy	51	0.70	35.45
168	Rumi Yoshiba	Japan	41	0.69	28.35
169	Da-Ye Na	Korea	68	0.69	46.63
170	Mayu Hattori	Japan	72	0.68	49.20
171	Alison Walshe	USA	48	0.68	32.78
172	Sung Hyun Park	Korea	28	0.68	23.83
173	Kaori Ohe	Japan	71	0.68	48.28
174	Tiffany Joh	USA	45	0.68	30.39
175	Liz Young	England	39	0.67	26.31
176	Mami Fukuda	Japan	62	0.67	41.77
177	Kris Tamulis	USA	43	0.67	28.67
178	Hae Jung Kim	Korea	27	0.66	23.23
179	Laura Diaz	USA	41	0.66	27.08
180	Haruka Morita-WanyaoLu	China	17	0.65	22.86
181	Song Yi Ahn	Korea	48	0.65	31.11
182	Katie M. Burnett	USA	45	0.64	28.97
183	Vikki Laing	Scotland	33	0.64	22.53
184	Dori Carter	USA	49	0.64	31.51
185	Natsuka Hori	Japan	70	0.64	44.52
186	Soo Hwa Jang	Korea	48	0.63	30.38
187	So Yeon Park	Korea	45	0.63	28.27
188	Connie Chen	South Africa	35	0.63	21.98
189	Hye Jung Choi	Korea	45	0.62	28.06
190	Amelia Lewis	USA	55	0.62	34.22
191	Sarah Kemp	Australia	60	0.62	37.25
192	Christel Boeljon	Netherlands	46	0.62	28.43
193	Sophie Giquel-Bettan	France	33	0.61	21.51
194	Rebecca Artis	Australia	46	0.61	27.89
195	Rui Kitada	Japan	67	0.61	40.61
196	Ji Ram Kweon	Korea	45	0.60	27.15
197	Megumi Kido	Japan	70	0.60	41.92
198	Rye Jung Lee	Korea	48	0.59	28.44
199	Jing Yan	China	18	0.59	20.68
200	Klara Spilkova	Czech Rep.	28	0.59	20.54

Official World Golf Ranking
(As of December 31, 2014)

Ranking		Player	Country	Points Average	Total Points	No. of Events	2014 Points Lost	2014 Points Gained
1	(6)	Rory McIlroy	NIr	11.04	541.10	49	-345.11	567.77
2	(3)	Henrik Stenson	Swe	8.13	422.93	52	-334.37	279.26
3	(2)	Adam Scott	Aus	7.71	323.82	42	-317.70	248.09
4	(28)	Bubba Watson	USA	7.27	349.16	48	-211.61	398.45
5	(10)	Sergio Garcia	Esp	6.70	334.81	50	-246.10	315.61
6	(4)	Justin Rose	Eng	6.69	327.75	49	-317.52	272.77
7	(19)	Jim Furyk	USA	6.62	291.41	44	-206.96	280.17
8	(11)	Jason Day	Aus	5.81	232.44	40	-201.58	201.37
9	(22)	Jordan Spieth	USA	5.75	298.88	52	-161.57	296.42
10	(40)	Rickie Fowler	USA	5.47	284.30	52	-146.66	297.94
11	(7)	Matt Kuchar	USA	5.11	265.54	52	-289.13	234.98
12	(39)	Martin Kaymer	Ger	4.86	252.84	52	-152.06	265.03
13	(41)	Billy Horschel	USA	4.48	232.84	52	-120.91	217.90
14	(5)	Phil Mickelson	USA	4.45	200.09	45	-283.04	137.21
15	(14)	Graeme McDowell	NIr	4.16	199.54	48	-224.51	163.74
16	(23)	Hideki Matsuyama	Jpn	4.12	210.16	51	-132.67	187.80
17	(32)	Victor Dubuisson	Fra	4.02	185.05	46	-108.79	161.64
18	(9)	Zach Johnson	USA	3.83	198.99	52	-229.31	145.11
19	(16)	Dustin Johnson	USA	3.78	158.96	42	-208.84	137.25
20	(60)	Chris Kirk	USA	3.76	195.73	52	-108.84	198.82
21	(47)	Jimmy Walker	USA	3.72	193.39	52	-148.38	213.00
22	(31)	Hunter Mahan	USA	3.61	187.74	52	-156.51	176.12
23	(73)	Patrick Reed	USA	3.51	182.68	52	-103.15	210.97
24	(26)	Jamie Donaldson	Wal	3.44	178.84	52	-152.14	151.71
25	(233)	Kevin Na	USA	3.31	135.69	41	-61.01	164.07
26	(25)	Lee Westwood	Eng	3.28	170.49	52	-175.32	154.18
27	(12)	Ian Poulter	Eng	3.23	151.90	47	-196.29	91.52
28	(20)	Keegan Bradley	USA	3.16	164.51	52	-205.33	142.96
29	(49)	Joost Luiten	Ned	3.16	164.21	52	-102.76	147.19
30	(33)	Ryan Moore	USA	3.08	154.14	50	-131.90	125.07
31	(18)	Charl Schwartzel	SAf	3.02	157.30	52	-209.68	120.21
32	(1)	Tiger Woods	USA	3.01	120.28	40	-368.94	9.73
33	(17)	Luke Donald	Eng	2.99	146.67	49	-208.47	121.67
34	(86)	Brooks Koepka	USA	2.97	154.63	52	-60.75	150.68
35	(66)	Stephen Gallacher	Sco	2.91	151.49	52	-115.61	170.12
36	(24)	Thomas Bjorn	Den	2.86	148.88	52	-139.09	96.13
37	(46)	Thongchai Jaidee	Tha	2.83	147.14	52	-122.49	136.51
38	(15)	Jason Dufner	USA	2.82	135.40	48	-214.62	91.18
39	(29)	Bill Haas	USA	2.81	146.12	52	-155.35	128.04
40	(37)	Miguel Angel Jimenez	Esp	2.81	129.05	46	-113.28	111.37
41	(8)	Steve Stricker	USA	2.74	109.65	40	-181.12	61.84
42	(126)	Ryan Palmer	USA	2.74	134.15	49	-84.24	153.49
43	(21)	Webb Simpson	USA	2.71	141.03	52	-182.53	104.57
44	(76)	Shane Lowry	Irl	2.66	138.08	52	-83.69	132.22
45	(34)	Louis Oosthuizen	SAf	2.64	118.81	45	-169.61	134.34
46	(72)	Marc Leishman	Aus	2.60	135.23	52	-99.82	140.41
47	(84)	Mikko Ilonen	Fin	2.60	129.82	50	-77.82	133.54
48	(56)	Gary Woodland	USA	2.56	132.93	52	-90.72	110.50
49	(108)	John Senden	Aus	2.48	129.08	52	-89.67	140.53
50	(116)	Danny Willett	Eng	2.47	125.87	51	-64.99	123.06

( ) Ranking in brackets indicates position as of December 31, 2013.

Ranking		Player	Country	Points Average	Total Points	No. of Events	2014 Points Lost	2014 Points Gained
51	(118)	Tommy Fleetwood	Eng	2.45	127.36	52	-61.06	118.11
52	(44)	Kevin Streelman	USA	2.44	127.05	52	-120.83	113.44
53	(226)	Alexander Levy	Fra	2.44	126.90	52	-35.15	124.85
54	(186)	Brendon Todd	USA	2.40	124.68	52	-59.90	136.14
55	(38)	Francesco Molinari	Ita	2.35	121.99	52	-127.52	104.70
56	(67)	Koumei Oda	Jpn	2.34	119.58	51	-74.19	95.34
57	(36)	Graham Delaet	Can	2.30	119.78	52	-126.98	98.12
58	(13)	Brandt Snedeker	USA	2.30	119.50	52	-226.61	92.22
59	(42)	Jonas Blixt	Swe	2.29	118.84	52	-118.43	101.05
60	(89)	Russell Henley	USA	2.24	116.32	52	-100.16	135.10
61	(90)	Marcel Siem	Ger	2.23	115.85	52	-75.06	109.05
62	(69)	Tim Clark	SAf	2.22	113.22	51	-74.94	103.66
63	(27)	Ernie Els	SAf	2.21	115.06	52	-165.60	95.20
64	(111)	Anirban Lahiri	Ind	2.08	93.44	45	-51.13	82.18
65	(157)	Ben Martin	USA	2.06	107.19	52	-51.57	103.29
66	(475)	J.B. Holmes	USA	2.02	80.99	40	-35.05	102.87
67	(461)	Hiroshi Iwata	Jpn	2.02	95.08	47	-17.43	97.80
68	(71)	Ross Fisher	Eng	2.02	104.95	52	-75.33	85.86
69	(114)	Marc Warren	Sco	2.01	104.52	52	-64.00	94.65
70	(113)	Kevin Stadler	USA	1.97	102.64	52	-88.24	117.81
71	(101)	Pablo Larrazabal	Esp	1.96	101.88	52	-86.32	108.67
72	(52)	Bernd Wiesberger	Aut	1.92	99.59	52	-98.96	79.63
73	(64)	Angel Cabrera	Arg	1.91	93.53	49	-83.00	81.78
74	(102)	Charley Hoffman	USA	1.87	96.99	52	-75.96	94.36
75	(87)	Paul Casey	Eng	1.85	96.45	52	-68.87	85.33
76	(133)	Matt Every	USA	1.85	96.06	52	-82.96	111.97
77	(53)	Harris English	USA	1.81	94.31	52	-103.37	79.44
78	(88)	Matt Jones	Aus	1.81	93.98	52	-79.13	94.12
79	(77)	Shingo Katayama	Jpn	1.81	79.51	44	-56.54	48.34
80	(65)	Thorbjorn Olesen	Den	1.78	92.66	52	-105.57	94.62
81	(98)	George Coetzee	SAf	1.78	92.56	52	-92.63	107.10
82	(50)	Branden Grace	SAf	1.75	90.80	52	-115.10	83.16
83	(58)	Brendon de Jonge	Zim	1.73	90.04	52	-94.11	76.06
84	(139)	Sang-Moon Bae	Kor	1.73	89.90	52	-61.90	83.27
85	(198)	Cameron Tringale	USA	1.71	88.83	52	-55.99	99.18
86	(173)	Brian Harman	USA	1.65	86.03	52	-61.11	93.01
87	(51)	Richard Sterne	SAf	1.61	75.85	47	-97.63	56.52
88	(94)	Hideto Tanihara	Jpn	1.61	79.00	49	-56.68	58.11
89	(342)	Steven Bowditch	Aus	1.60	83.37	52	-34.71	91.54
90	(220)	Tomohiro Kondo	Jpn	1.60	76.84	48	-29.71	67.19
91	(356)	Robert Streb	USA	1.59	82.50	52	-32.63	89.41
92	(136)	Richie Ramsay	Sco	1.57	67.31	43	-55.99	65.60
93	(140)	Rafa Cabrera-Bello	Esp	1.56	81.08	52	-73.70	87.22
94	(122)	Geoff Ogilvy	Aus	1.55	78.79	51	-62.20	78.66
95	(362)	Erik Compton	USA	1.52	79.27	52	-40.63	94.98
96	(123)	Scott Hend	Aus	1.52	71.31	47	-49.58	55.62
97	(172)	Romain Wattel	Fra	1.51	78.67	52	-49.64	76.75
98	(276)	Robert Karlsson	Swe	1.51	73.98	49	-34.58	76.57
99	(514)	Fabrizio Zanotti	Par	1.50	76.54	51	-26.07	87.81
100	(245)	Russell Knox	Sco	1.50	77.76	52	-46.11	87.29

( ) Ranking in brackets indicates position as of December 31, 2013.

Ranking		Player	Country	Points Average	Total Points	No. of Events	2014 Points Lost	2014 Points Gained
101	(125)	Hennie Otto	SAf	1.50	76.25	51	-51.13	59.58
102	(83)	Ryo Ishikawa	Jpn	1.48	76.90	52	-80.52	64.66
103	(285)	Edoardo Molinari	Ita	1.47	64.88	44	-32.03	71.92
104	(35)	Gonzalo Fdez-Castano	Esp	1.47	76.65	52	-117.95	45.84
105	(176)	Seung-Yul Noh	Kor	1.47	76.57	52	-59.57	83.39
106	(121)	Yuta Ikeda	Jpn	1.47	75.00	51	-49.24	55.16
107	(92)	Freddie Jacobson	Swe	1.46	68.81	47	-65.44	70.30
108	(81)	Chris Stroud	USA	1.46	76.12	52	-70.76	57.14
109	(317)	Will Mackenzie	USA	1.46	74.36	51	-38.27	85.25
110	(62)	Hyung-Sung Kim	Kor	1.46	75.70	52	-78.53	53.76
111	(110)	Kevin Chappell	USA	1.44	74.95	52	-66.26	65.72
112	(615)	Andrew Johnston	Eng	1.42	56.83	40	-12.11	60.37
113	(145)	Hiroyuki Fujita	Jpn	1.42	72.19	51	-64.14	70.00
114	(275)	George McNeill	USA	1.41	67.82	48	-41.67	77.41
115	(288)	Shawn Stefani	USA	1.39	68.05	49	-36.96	73.82
116	(134)	K.J. Choi	Kor	1.37	71.17	52	-71.33	76.51
117	(171)	Simon Dyson	Eng	1.36	70.79	52	-50.53	66.85
118	(54)	Boo Weekley	USA	1.36	70.62	52	-91.42	45.04
119	(1180)	Benjamin Hebert	Fra	1.35	54.14	40	-4.18	56.83
120	(103)	Chesson Hadley	USA	1.34	69.86	52	-52.68	62.19
121	(748)	Seung-Hyuk Kim	Kor	1.33	65.33	49	-7.22	66.82
122	(1074)	Justin Thomas	USA	1.31	52.58	40	-11.35	61.98
123	(212)	Jerry Kelly	USA	1.31	64.20	49	-47.65	68.62
124	(175)	Morgan Hoffmann	USA	1.31	67.89	52	-43.46	68.70
125	(106)	Scott Stallings	USA	1.30	67.75	52	-83.37	75.02
126	(138)	David Hearn	Can	1.29	67.22	52	-59.85	62.31
127	(30)	Nick Watney	USA	1.28	66.51	52	-143.74	39.49
128	(277)	Emiliano Grillo	Arg	1.27	66.21	52	-38.03	72.32
129	(211)	Prom Meesawat	Tha	1.27	57.10	45	-34.22	48.89
130	(272)	Stuart Appleby	Aus	1.27	65.89	52	-36.11	67.92
131	(93)	David Howell	Eng	1.26	65.61	52	-63.24	48.20
132	(376)	Tyrrell Hatton	Eng	1.26	61.77	49	-20.59	64.09
133	(519)	David Lipsky	USA	1.26	57.88	46	-15.11	60.12
134	(59)	Kiradech Aphibarnrat	Tha	1.26	65.27	52	-80.80	41.86
135	(78)	Charles Howell	USA	1.25	64.91	52	-86.14	62.03
136	(160)	Prayad Marksaeng	Tha	1.25	62.30	50	-47.41	52.23
137	(146)	Jason Bohn	USA	1.24	64.45	52	-47.46	49.61
138	(132)	Yoshinori Fujimoto	Jpn	1.24	60.54	49	-47.86	44.35
139	(136)	Daniel Summerhays	USA	1.23	63.88	52	-60.58	58.78
140	(68)	Nicolas Colsaerts	Bel	1.23	63.73	52	-87.49	52.00
141	(74)	Chris Wood	Eng	1.22	57.31	47	-81.14	48.34
142	(1508)	Carlos Ortiz	Mex	1.20	48.16	40	-13.11	61.28
143	(63)	Peter Uihlein	USA	1.20	62.59	52	-70.36	30.16
144	(236)	Ben Crane	USA	1.19	56.12	47	-43.34	63.32
145	(292)	Camilo Villegas	Col	1.19	61.87	52	-32.32	62.11
146	(1216)	Tony Finau	USA	1.18	47.15	40	-4.71	50.65
147	(43)	Matteo Manassero	Ita	1.16	60.33	52	-120.23	45.21
148	(239)	Wade Ormsby	Aus	1.15	52.85	46	-25.93	49.57
149	(187)	William McGirt	USA	1.14	59.40	52	-48.86	59.89
150	(364)	Andy Sullivan	Eng	1.14	59.22	52	-30.75	65.70

( ) Ranking in brackets indicates position as of December 31, 2013.

Ranking		Player	Country	Points Average	Total Points	No. of Events	2014 Points Lost	2014 Points Gained
151	(256)	Eddie Pepperell	Eng	1.13	55.57	49	-26.91	52.94
152	(184)	Brendan Steele	USA	1.12	58.09	52	-50.17	60.17
153	(159)	Thomas Aiken	SAf	1.11	57.93	52	-65.18	66.05
154	(423)	Katsumasa Miyamoto	Jpn	1.10	52.92	48	-16.72	50.64
155	(231)	David Horsey	Eng	1.09	52.14	48	-37.30	50.26
156	(161)	Jason Kokrak	USA	1.08	53.13	49	-54.49	50.54
157	(284)	Antonio Lascuna	Phi	1.08	43.27	40	-22.15	40.37
158	(164)	Felipe Aguilar	Chi	1.07	53.73	50	-52.86	51.16
159	(142)	Thaworn Wiratchant	Tha	1.07	53.58	50	-56.12	45.77
160	(223)	Satoshi Kodaira	Jpn	1.07	49.14	46	-23.34	40.17
161	(528)	In-Hoi Hur	Kor	1.06	55.02	52	-8.88	52.48
162	(150)	Alejandro Canizares	Esp	1.04	46.82	45	-53.59	40.18
163	(124)	Darren Fichardt	SAf	1.03	53.76	52	-66.22	54.17
164	(507)	Oliver Wilson	Eng	1.03	48.40	47	-10.73	44.00
165	(216)	Kristoffer Broberg	Swe	1.03	53.34	52	-42.40	62.44
166	(178)	Yusaku Miyazato	Jpn	1.02	52.19	51	-37.21	40.07
167	(99)	John Huh	USA	1.02	52.98	52	-71.20	42.32
168	(185)	Greg Chalmers	Aus	1.02	52.96	52	-45.83	51.42
169	(115)	David Lingmerth	Swe	1.02	52.95	52	-67.71	48.08
170	(85)	Martin Laird	Sco	1.01	48.63	48	-71.13	37.00
171	(1000)	Derek Fathauer	USA	1.00	48.22	48	-7.77	53.20
172	(97)	Marcus Fraser	Aus	1.00	39.90	40	-63.79	22.64
173	(105)	Carl Pettersson	Swe	1.00	51.82	52	-79.69	54.39
174	(104)	Wen-Chong Liang	Chn	0.99	51.51	52	-55.91	29.76
175	(117)	David Toms	USA	0.99	39.61	40	-50.00	34.10
176	(75)	Brett Rumford	Aus	0.99	50.48	51	-70.16	32.74
177	(181)	Brian Stuard	USA	0.98	50.99	52	-50.59	52.89
178	(251)	Andrew Svoboda	USA	0.98	50.89	52	-33.00	45.75
179	(444)	Byeong-Hun An	Kor	0.98	49.73	51	-15.24	48.71
180	(622)	Adam Hadwin	Can	0.97	49.54	51	-17.31	56.12
181	(127)	Rory Sabbatini	SAf	0.95	49.33	52	-54.53	36.34
182	(417)	Billy Hurley	USA	0.95	49.30	52	-26.04	54.74
183	(487)	Sang-Hyun Park	Kor	0.95	39.72	42	-15.40	42.29
184	(55)	Scott Piercy	USA	0.94	40.60	43	-100.61	23.94
185	(261)	Justin Hicks	USA	0.94	48.69	52	-37.47	51.55
186	(129)	Ashun Wu	Chn	0.93	44.78	48	-44.59	24.80
187	(100)	Gregory Bourdy	Fra	0.93	48.50	52	-59.79	30.95
188	(229)	Jbe' Kruger	SAf	0.93	48.45	52	-38.43	43.81
189	(155)	Brad Kennedy	Aus	0.93	42.58	46	-39.99	30.22
190	(899)	Cameron Smith	Aus	0.92	36.80	40	-6.97	40.22
191	(602)	Danie van Tonder	SAf	0.92	47.80	52	-20.98	57.97
192	(730)	Hao-Tong Li	Chn	0.92	36.68	40	-5.50	36.18
193	(165)	Stewart Cink	USA	0.91	45.71	50	-44.44	40.22
194	(70)	Roberto Castro	USA	0.91	47.42	52	-71.23	24.20
195	(1018)	Moritz Lampert	Ger	0.91	38.92	43	-9.28	45.89
196	(162)	Scott Brown	USA	0.90	46.93	52	-50.34	45.23
197	(321)	Chapchai Nirat	Tha	0.90	36.06	40	-22.46	31.06
198	(592)	Blayne Barber	USA	0.89	35.55	40	-12.82	39.10
199	(1508)	Yoshitaka Takeya	Jpn	0.89	35.44	40	-3.26	38.71
200	(600)	Rashid Khan	Ind	0.88	35.37	40	-11.93	38.42

( ) Ranking in brackets indicates position as of December 31, 2013.

Age Groups of Current Top 100 World Ranked Players

Under 25	25-28	29-32	33-36	37-40	Over 40
		Kaymer			
		D. Johnson			
		Kirk			
		Mahan			
		Na			
		Moore			
		Schwartzel	Scott		
		B. Haas	B. Watson		
	McIlroy	Simpson	Garcia		
	Day	Oosthuizen	Rose		
	Fowler	Leishman	Kuchar		
	Horschel	Woodland	McDowell		
	Luiten	Todd	Walker	Stenson	
	K. Bradley	F. Molinari	Ilonen	Z. Johnson	Furyk
	Lowry	DeLaet	Streelman	Donaldson	Mickelson
	Willett	Blixt	K. Oda	Poulter	Westwood
	Lahiri	Holmes	Snedeker	Woods	Bjorn
Spieth	Martin	Larrazabal	Siem	Donald	Jaidee
Matsuyama	English	Wiesberger	Iwata	Gallacher	Jimenez
Dubuisson	G. Coetzee	Every	R. Fisher	Dufner	Stricker
Reed	Olesen	Sterne	Warren	Palmer	Senden
Koepka	Grace	Bowditch	Stadler	T. Clark	Els
Fleetwood	S-M Bae	Ramsay	M. Jones	C. Hoffman	Cabrera
Levy	Tringale	Cabrera-Bello	de Jonge	Casey	Katayama
Henley	Harman	Zanotti	Tanihara	Ogilvy	Hend
Wattel	Streb	Knox	Compton	Kondo	Karlsson

2014 World Ranking Review

Major Movements

Upward

Name	Net Points Gained	Position 2013	Position 2014
Rory McIlroy	222	6	1
Bubba Watson	187	28	4
Rickie Fowler	151	40	10
Jordan Spieth	135	22	9
Martin Kaymer	113	39	12
Patrick Reed	108	73	23
Kevin Na	103	233	25
Billy Horschel	97	41	13
Chris Kirk	90	60	20
Brooks Koepka	90	86	34
Alexander Levy	90	226	53
Brendon Todd	76	186	54
Jim Furyk	73	19	7
Sergio Garcia	70	10	5
Ryan Palmer	69	126	42

Downward

Name	Net Points Lost	Position 2013	Position 2014
Tiger Woods	359	1	32
Phil Mickelson	146	5	14
Brandt Snedeker	134	13	58
Jason Dufner	123	15	38
Steve Stricker	119	8	41
Ian Poulter	105	12	27
Nick Watney	104	30	127
Charl Schwartzel	89	18	31
Luke Donald	86	17	33
Zach Johnson	84	9	18

Highest-Rated Events of 2014

	Event	No. of World Ranked Players Participating					World Rating Points
		Top 5	Top 15	Top 30	Top 50	Top 100	
1	The Open Championship	5	15	29	49	94	828
2	PGA Championship	5	14	28	48	98	819
3	U.S. Open Championship	4	14	28	48	66	720
4	Masters Tournament	4	14	29	49	68	699
5	The Players Championship	4	13	27	46	72	704
6	WGC-Bridgestone Invitational	5	15	29	49	67	730
7	WGC-Cadillac Championship	4	14	29	49	65	700
8	The Barclays	5	14	23	37	68	678
9	WGC-Accenture Match Play	2	12	27	47	64	634
10	BMW Championship	5	14	22	33	57	595
11	Deutsche Bank Championship	3	12	20	32	60	582
12	WGC-HSBC Champions	3	9	22	40	58	564
13	Memorial Tournament	3	11	16	25	55	496
14	BMW PGA Championship	1	4	11	17	34	301
15	Honda Classic	4	8	14	24	47	455
16	Shell Houston Open	2	8	15	23	48	419
17	The Tour Championship	4	12	18	25	28	409
18	Northern Trust Open	1	5	16	26	48	405
19	DP World Tour Championship	2	6	10	19	37	348
20	Arnold Palmer Invitational	2	6	12	21	42	377
21	Crowne Plaza Colonial	2	6	10	20	40	360
22	Farmers Insurance Open	2	5	11	19	37	340
23	AAM Scottish Open	0	3	11	18	39	310
24	Waste Mgmt. Phoenix Open	1	3	9	22	46	340
25	Valspar Championship	0	3	9	15	41	305
26	Wells Fargo Championship	0	4	10	21	40	315
27	RBC Heritage	0	4	10	20	37	307
28	Travelers Championship	2	5	8	16	33	288
29	Omega Dubai Classic	2	3	6	11	29	262
30	Quicken Loans National	1	4	8	13	35	274
31	Turkish Airlines Open	1	3	6	13	30	242
32	Abu Dhabi HSBC Champ.	2	4	7	12	31	252
33	BMW Masters	0	1	6	13	29	224
34	Hero World Challenge	2	9	16	18	18	275
35	Hyundai Tourn. of Champions	1	5	9	14	24	228
36	Alfred Dunhill Links	1	2	4	9	27	218
37	HP Byron Nelson Champ.	1	3	9	14	25	228
38	AT&T Pebble Beach	1	4	7	13	25	224
39	CommercialBank Qatar Masters	1	3	6	10	27	210
40	FedEx St. Jude Classic	0	3	7	12	30	222

World Golf Rankings 1968-2014

Year	No. 1	No. 2	No. 3	No. 4	No. 5
1968	Nicklaus	Palmer	Casper	Player	Charles
1969	Nicklaus	Player	Casper	Palmer	Charles
1970	Nicklaus	Player	Casper	Trevino	Charles
1971	Nicklaus	Trevino	Player	Palmer	Casper
1972	Nicklaus	Player	Trevino	Crampton	Palmer
1973	Nicklaus	Weiskopf	Trevino	Player	Crampton
1974	Nicklaus	Miller	Player	Weiskopf	Trevino
1975	Nicklaus	Miller	Weiskopf	Irwin	Player
1976	Nicklaus	Irwin	Miller	Player	Green
1977	Nicklaus	Watson	Green	Irwin	Crenshaw
1978	Watson	Nicklaus	Irwin	Green	Player
1979	Watson	Nicklaus	Irwin	Trevino	Player
1980	Watson	Trevino	Aoki	Crenshaw	Nicklaus
1981	Watson	Rogers	Aoki	Pate	Trevino
1982	Watson	Floyd	Ballesteros	Kite	Stadler
1983	Ballesteros	Watson	Floyd	Norman	Kite
1984	Ballesteros	Watson	Norman	Wadkins	Langer
1985	Ballesteros	Langer	Norman	Watson	Nakajima
1986	Norman	Langer	Ballesteros	Nakajima	Bean
1987	Norman	Ballesteros	Langer	Lyle	Strange
1988	Ballesteros	Norman	Lyle	Faldo	Strange
1989	Norman	Faldo	Ballesteros	Strange	Stewart
1990	Norman	Faldo	Olazabal	Woosnam	Stewart
1991	Woosnam	Faldo	Olazabal	Ballesteros	Norman
1992	Faldo	Couples	Woosnam	Olazabal	Norman
1993	Faldo	Norman	Langer	Price	Couples
1994	Price	Norman	Faldo	Langer	Olazabal
1995	Norman	Price	Langer	Els	Montgomerie
1996	Norman	Lehman	Montgomerie	Els	Couples
1997	Norman	Woods	Price	Els	Love
1998	Woods	O'Meara	Duval	Love	Els
1999	Woods	Duval	Montgomerie	Love	Els
2000	Woods	Els	Duval	Mickelson	Westwood
2001	Woods	Mickelson	Duval	Els	Love
2002	Woods	Mickelson	Els	Garcia	Goosen
2003	Woods	Singh	Els	Love	Furyk
2004	Singh	Woods	Els	Goosen	Mickelson
2005	Woods	Singh	Mickelson	Goosen	Els
2006	Woods	Furyk	Mickelson	Scott	Els
2007	Woods	Mickelson	Furyk	Els	Stricker
2008	Woods	Garcia	Mickelson	Harrington	Singh
2009	Woods	Mickelson	Stricker	Westwood	Harrington
2010	Westwood	Woods	Kaymer	Mickelson	Furyk
2011	Donald	Westwood	McIlroy	Kaymer	Scott
2012	McIlroy	Donald	Woods	Rose	Scott
2013	Woods	Scott	Stenson	Rose	Mickelson
2014	McIlroy	Stenson	Scott	Watson	Garcia

(The World of Professional Golf 1968-1985; World Ranking 1986-2014)

Year	No. 6	No. 7	No. 8	No. 9	No. 10
1968	Boros	Coles	Thomson	Beard	Nagle
1969	Beard	Archer	Trevino	Barber	Sikes
1970	Devlin	Coles	Jacklin	Beard	Huggett
1971	Barber	Crampton	Charles	Devlin	Weiskopf
1972	Jacklin	Weiskopf	Oosterhuis	Heard	Devlin
1973	Miller	Oosterhuis	Wadkins	Heard	Brewer
1974	M. Ozaki	Crampton	Irwin	Green	Heard
1975	Green	Trevino	Casper	Crampton	Watson
1976	Watson	Weiskopf	Marsh	Crenshaw	Geiberger
1977	Marsh	Player	Weiskopf	Floyd	Ballesteros
1978	Crenshaw	Marsh	Ballesteros	Trevino	Aoki
1979	Aoki	Green	Crenshaw	Ballesteros	Wadkins
1980	Pate	Ballesteros	Bean	Irwin	Player
1981	Ballesteros	Graham	Crenshaw	Floyd	Lietzke
1982	Pate	Nicklaus	Rogers	Aoki	Strange
1983	Nicklaus	Nakajima	Stadler	Aoki	Wadkins
1984	Faldo	Nakajima	Stadler	Kite	Peete
1985	Wadkins	O'Meara	Strange	Pavin	Sutton
1986	Tway	Sutton	Strange	Stewart	O'Meara
1987	Woosnam	Stewart	Wadkins	McNulty	Crenshaw
1988	Crenshaw	Woosnam	Frost	Azinger	Calcavecchia
1989	Kite	Olazabal	Calcavecchia	Woosnam	Azinger
1990	Azinger	Ballesteros	Kite	McNulty	Calcavecchia
1991	Couples	Langer	Stewart	Azinger	Davis
1992	Langer	Cook	Price	Azinger	Love
1993	Azinger	Woosnam	Kite	Love	Pavin
1994	Els	Couples	Montgomerie	M. Ozaki	Pavin
1995	Pavin	Faldo	Couples	M. Ozaki	Elkington
1996	Faldo	Mickelson	M. Ozaki	Love	O'Meara
1997	Mickelson	Montgomerie	M. Ozaki	Lehman	O'Meara
1998	Price	Montgomerie	Westwood	Singh	Mickelson
1999	Westwood	Singh	Price	Mickelson	O'Meara
2000	Montgomerie	Love	Sutton	Singh	Lehman
2001	Garcia	Toms	Singh	Clarke	Goosen
2002	Toms	Harrington	Singh	Love	Montgomerie
2003	Weir	Goosen	Harrington	Toms	Perry
2004	Harrington	Garcia	Weir	Love	Cink
2005	Garcia	Furyk	Montgomerie	Scott	DiMarco
2006	Goosen	Singh	Harrington	Donald	Ogilvy
2007	Rose	Scott	Harrington	Choi	Singh
2008	Karlsson	Villegas	Stenson	Els	Westwood
2009	Furyk	Casey	Stenson	McIlroy	Perry
2010	McDowell	Stricker	Casey	Donald	McIlroy
2011	Stricker	D. Johnson	Day	Schwartzel	W. Simpson
2012	Oosthuizen	Westwood	B. Watson	Dufner	Snedeker
2013	McIlroy	Kuchar	Stricker	Z. Johnson	Garcia
2014	Rose	Furyk	Day	Spieth	Fowler

World's Winners of 2014

U.S. PGA TOUR

Hyundai Tournament of Champions	Zach Johnson
Sony Open in Hawaii	Jimmy Walker
Humana Challenge	Patrick Reed
Farmers Insurance Open	Scott Stallings
Waste Management Phoenix Open	Kevin Stadler
AT&T Pebble Beach National Pro-Am	Jimmy Walker (2)
Northern Trust Open	Bubba Watson
WGC - Accenture Match Play Championship	Jason Day
Honda Classic	Russell Henley
WGC - Cadillac Championship	Patrick Reed (2)
Puerto Rico Open	Chesson Hadley
Valspar Championship	John Senden
Arnold Palmer Invitational	Matt Every
Valero Texas Open	Steven Bowditch
Shell Houston Open	Matt Jones
Masters Tournament	Bubba Watson (2)
RBC Heritage	Matt Kuchar
Zurich Classic of New Orleans	Seung-Yul Noh
Wells Fargo Championship	J.B. Holmes
The Players Championship	Martin Kaymer
HP Byron Nelson Championship	Brendon Todd
Crowne Plaza Invitational	Adam Scott
Memorial Tournament	Hideki Matsuyama
FedEx St. Jude Classic	Ben Crane
U.S. Open Championship	Martin Kaymer (2)
Travelers Championship	Kevin Streelman
Quicken Loans National	Justin Rose
Greenbrier Classic	Angel Cabrera
John Deere Classic	Brian Harman
RBC Canadian Open	Tim Clark
WGC - Bridgestone Invitational	Rory McIlroy (3)
Barracuda Championship	Geoff Ogilvy
PGA Championship	Rory McIlroy (4)
Wyndham Championship	Camilo Villegas

PGA TOUR PLAYOFFS FOR THE FEDEXCUP

The Barclays	Hunter Mahan
Deutsche Bank Championship	Chris Kirk
BMW Championship	Billy Horschel
Tour Championship	Billy Horschel (2)
Frys.com Open	Sang-Moon Bae
Shriners Hospitals for Children Open	Ben Martin
McGladrey Classic	Robert Streb
Sanderson Farms Championship	Nick Taylor
OHL Classic at Mayakoba	Charley Hoffman

SPECIAL EVENTS

CVS Caremark Charity Classic	Steve Stricker/Bo Van Pelt
PGA Grand Slam of Golf	Martin Kaymer (3)
Callaway Pebble Beach Invitational	Tommy Armour
Hero World Challenge	Jordan Spieth (2)

Franklin Templeton Shootout	Jason Day (2)/Cameron Tringale
PNC Father/Son Challenge	Bernhard Langer (6)/Jason Langer

WEB.COM TOUR

Pacific Rubiales Colombia Championship	Alex Cejka
Chile Classic	Adam Hadwin
Brasil Champions	Jon Curran
Panama Claro Championship	Carlos Ortiz
Chitimacha Louisiana Open	Kris Blanks
El Bosque Mexico Championship	Carlos Ortiz (2)
WNB Golf Classic	Andrew Putnam
South Georgia Classic	Blayne Barber
BMW Charity Pro-Am	Max Homa
Rex Hospital Open	Byron Smith
Cleveland Open	Steven Alker
Air Capital Classic	Sebastian Cappelen
United Leasing Championship	Greg Owen
Nova Scotia Open	Roger Sloan
Utah Championship	Andres Gonzales
Albertsons Boise Open	Steve Wheatcroft
Midwest Classic	Zack Sucher
Stonebrae Classic	Tony Finau
Price Cutter Charity Championship	Cameron Percy
News Sentinel Open	Martin Piller
WinCo Foods Portland Open	Carlos Ortiz (3)
Hotel Fitness Championship	Bud Cauley
Chiquita Classic	Adam Hadwin (2)
Nationwide Children's Hospital Championship	Justin Thomas
Web.com Tour Championship	Derek Fathauer

PGA TOUR CANADA

PC Financial Open	Joel Dahmen
Bayview Place Island Savings Open	Josh Persons
Syncrude Boreal Open	Joel Dahmen (2)
SIGA Dakota Dunes Open	Matt Harmon
PGA Tour Canada Players Cup	Timothy Madigan
Staal Foundation Open	Wes Homan
ATB Financial Classic	Brock Mackenzie
Forces and Families Open	Greg Machtaler
Great Waterway Classic	David Bradshaw
Wildfire Invitational	Nate McCoy
Cape Breton Celtic Classic	Mark Silvers
Tour Championship of Canada	Ryan Williams

PGA TOUR LATINOAMERICA

Arturo Calle Colombian Open	David Vanegas
TransAmerican Power Products CRV Open	Marcelo Rozo
Stella Artois Open	Armando Favela
Mundo Maya Open	Daniel Mazziotta
Abierto OSDE del Centro	William Kropp
Roberto de Vicenzo Invitational Copa NEC	Ty Capps
Dominican Republic Open	Michael Buttacavoli
Lexus Panama Classic	Julian Etulain
All You Need is Ecuador Open	Tyler McCumber
Arturo Calle Colombian Classic	Nicholas Lindheim
TransAmerican Power CRV Mazatlan Open	Tyler McCumber (2)
TransAmerican Power CRV Abierto Mexicano	Oscar David Alvarez
Bridgestone America's Golf Cup	Emilio Dominguez/Rafa Echenique
Lexus Peru Open	Julian Etulain (2)

Aberto do Brasil/Aberto do Atlantico	Rafael Becker
Hyundai - BBVA Abierto de Chile	Jorge Fernandez-Valdes
Personal Classic	Fabian Gomez
VISA Open de Argentina	Emiliano Grillo

EUROPEAN TOUR

Volvo Golf Champions	Louis Oosthuizen
Abu Dhabi HSBC Golf Championship	Pablo Larrazabal
Commercial Bank Qatar Masters	Sergio Garcia
Omega Dubai Desert Classic	Stephen Gallacher
Trophee Hassan II	Alejandro Canizares
NH Collection Open	Marco Crespi
Madeira Islands Open - Portugal - BPI	Daniel Brooks
Open de Espana	Miguel Angel Jimenez (2)
BMW PGA Championship	Rory McIlroy
Nordea Masters	Thongchai Jaidee
Lyoness Open	Mikael Lundberg
Irish Open	Mikko Ilonen
BMW International Open	Fabrizio Zanotti
Alstom Open de France	Graeme McDowell
Aberdeen Asset Management Scottish Open	Justin Rose (2)
The Open Championship	Rory McIlroy (2)
M2M Russian Open	David Horsey
Made in Denmark	Marc Warren
D+D Real Czech Masters	Jamie Donaldson
Open D'Italia	Hennie Otto
Omega European Masters	David Lipsky
KLM Open	Paul Casey
ISPS Handa Wales Open	Joost Luiten
The Ryder Cup	Europe
Alfred Dunhill Links Championship	Oliver Wilson
Portugal Masters	Alexander Levy (2)
Volvo World Match Play Championship	Mikko Ilonen (2)

THE FINAL SERIES

BMW Masters	Marcel Siem
WGC - HSBC Champions	Bubba Watson (3)
Turkish Airlines Open	Brooks Koepka
DP World Tour Championship	Henrik Stenson

CHALLENGE TOUR

Barclays Kenya Open	Jake Roos
Challenge de Catalunya	Antonio Hortal
Turkish Airlines Challenge	Oliver Farr
Karnten Golf Open	Moritz Lampert
D+D Real Czech Challenge	Thomas Linard
Fred Olsen Challenge de Espana	Moritz Lampert (2)
Najeti Hotels et Golfs Open	Jordi Garcia Pinto
Belgian Challenge Open	William Harrold
Scottish Hydro Challenge	Andrew Johnston
Aegean Airlines Challenge Tour	Jake Roos (2)
D+D Real Slovakia Challenge	Andrew McArthur
Swiss Challenge	Pierre Relecom
Le Vaudreuil Golf Challenge	Andrew Johnston (2)
Azerbaijan Golf Challenge Open	Moritz Lampert (3)
Norwegian Challenge	Benjamin Hebert
Vacon Open	Mark Tullo
Rolex Trophy	Byeong-Hun An
Northern Ireland Open Challenge	Joakim Lagergren

Open Blue Green Cotes d'Armor Bretagne	Benjamin Hebert (2)
Kazakhstan Open	Sam Hutsby
EMC Golf Challenge Open	Ricardo Gouveia
Shankai Classic	Johan Edfors
Foshan Open	Jason Palmer
National Bank of Oman Golf Classic	Max Orrin
Dubai Festival City Challenge Tour Grand Final	Benjamin Hebert (3)

ASIAN TOUR

King's Cup	Prayad Marksaeng
SAIL-SBI Open	Rashid Khan
Solaire Open	Richard T. Lee
EurAsia Cup	Tied
Maybank Malaysian Open	Lee Westwood
CIMB Niaga Indonesian Masters	Anirban Lahiri
The Championship	Felipe Aguilar
ICTSI Philippine Open	Marcus Both
Queen's Cup	Thaworn Wiratchant
Yeangder Tournament Players Championship	Prom Meesawat
Worldwide Holdings Selangor Masters	Chapchai Nirat
Mercuries Taiwan Masters	Steve Lewton
Hong Kong Open	Scott Hend
Venetian Macau Open	Anirban Lahiri (2)
CIMB Classic	Ryan Moore
WGC - HSBC Champions	Bubba Watson (3)
Panasonic Open India	S.S.P. Chowrasia
Chiangmai Golf Classic	Rashid Khan (2)
Resorts World Manila Masters	Mardan Mamat
King's Cup	Thaworn Wiratchant (2)
Bank BRI Indonesia Open	Padraig Harrington
Thailand Golf Championship	Lee Westwood (2)
Dubai Open	Arjun Atwal

ONEASIA TOUR

Enjoy Jakarta Indonesia PGA Championship	Michio Matsumura
Volvo China Open	Alexander Levy
GS Caltex Maekyung Open	Jun-Won Park
SK Telecom Open	Seung-Hyuk Kim
Fiji International	Steve Jeffress
Nanshan China Masters	Hao-Tong Li (2)
Kolon Korea Open	Seung-Hyuk Kim (3)
Dongfeng Nissan Cup	Asia Pacific

PGA TOUR CHINA

Mission Hills Haikou Open	Jeung-Hun Wang
Buick Open	Sam Chien
United Investment Real Estate Wuhan Open	Brett Drewitt
Lanhai Open	David McKenzie
Earls Beijing Open	Xin-Jun Zhang
Yulongwan Yunnan Open	Gunn Charoenkul
Chateau Junding Penglai Open	Todd Baek
Cadillac Championship	David McKenzie (2)
Jianye Tianzhu Henan Open	Hao-Tong Li
Nine Dragons Open	*Cheng Jin
Hainan Open	Hao-Tong Li (3)
CTS Tycoon Championship	Hao-Tong Li (4)

JAPAN TOUR

Token Homemate Cup	Yusaku Miyazato
Tsuruya Open	Hiroyuki Fujita
The Crowns	Hyung-Sung Kim
Kansai Open	Koumei Oda
Gateway to the Open Mizuno Open	Dong-Kyu Jang
Japan PGA Championship	Taichi Teshima
Japan Golf Tour Championship	Yoshitaka Takeya
Nagashima Shigeo Invitational	Ryo Ishikawa
Dunlop Srixon Fukushima Open	Satoshi Kodaira
RZ Everlasting KBC Augusta	Hiroyuki Fujita (2)
Fujisankei Classic	Hiroshi Iwata
ANA Open	Katsumasa Miyamoto
Asia-Pacific Diamond Cup	Hiroyuki Fujita (3)
Top Cup Tokai Classic	Seung-Hyuk Kim (2)
Toshin Golf Tournament	In-Hoi Hur
Japan Open Championship	Yuta Ikeda
Bridgestone Open	Koumei Oda (2)
Mynavi ABC Championship	Ryuichi Oda
Heiwa PGM Championship	Tomohiro Kondo
Mitsui Sumitomo VISA Taiheiyo Masters	David Oh
Dunlop Phoenix	Hideki Matsuyama (2)
Casio World Open	Shingo Katayama
Golf Nippon Series JT Cup	Katsumasa Miyamoto (2)

AUSTRALASIAN TOUR

Lexis of Blackburn Victorian PGA Champ.	Gareth Paddison
Coca-Cola Queensland PGA Championship	Anthony Summers
Oates Victorian Open	Matthew Griffin
New Zealand Open	Dimitrios Papadatos
Isuzu Queensland Open	Andrew Dodt
South Pacific Open Championship	Adam Stephens
John Hughes/Nexus Risk Services WA Open	Ryan Fox
ISPS Handa Perth International	Thorbjorn Olesen
WA Goldfields PGA Championship	Ryan Lynch
Mazda NSW Open	Anthony Brown
BetEasy Masters	Nick Cullen
Emirates Australian Open	Jordan Spieth
Nanshan NSW PGA Championship	Lincoln Tighe
Australian PGA Championship	Greg Chalmers

AFRICAN TOURS

Joburg Open	George Coetzee
Africa Open	Thomas Aiken
Dimension Data Pro-Am	Estanislao Goya
Tshwane Open	Ross Fisher
Investec Cup	Trevor Fisher, Jr.
Telkom Business PGA Championship	Titch Moore
Golden Pilsener Zimbabwe Open	Jbe' Kruger
Investec Royal Swazi Open	Danie van Tonder
Mopani Copper Mines Zambia Open	Wallie Coetsee
Lombard Insurance Classic	Christiaan Basson
Zambia Sugar Open	Lyle Rowe
Vodacom Origins of Golf - Euphoria	Danie van Tonder (2)
Sun City Challenge	Dean Burmester
Vodacom Origins of Golf - Arabella	Jean Hugo
Vodacom Origins of Golf - St. Francis	Keith Horne
Wild Waves Golf Challenge	Colin Nel

Vodacom Origins of Golf - Wild Coast Sun	Louis de Jager
Vodacom Origins of Golf - Vaal de Grace	P.H. McIntyre
Sun Boardwalk Golf Challenge	Titch Moore (2)
BMG Classic	Merrick Bremner
Vodacom Origins of Golf Final	Keith Horne (2)
Nedbank Affinity Cup	Louis de Jager (2)
Lion of Africa Cape Town Open	Jaco Ahlers
Nedbank Golf Challenge	Danny Willett
Alfred Dunhill Championship	Branden Grace

U.S. LPGA TOUR

Pure Silk Bahamas LPGA Classic	Jessica Korda
Honda LPGA Thailand	Anna Nordqvist
HSBC Women's Champions	Paula Creamer
JTBC Founders Cup	Karrie Webb (2)
Kia Classic	Anna Nordqvist (2)
Kraft Nabisco Championship	Lexi Thompson
LPGA LOTTE Championship	Michelle Wie
Swinging Skirts LPGA Classic	Lydia Ko
North Texas LPGA Shootout	Stacy Lewis
Kingsmill Championship	Lizette Salas
Airbus LPGA Classic	Jessica Korda (2)
ShopRite LPGA Classic	Stacy Lewis (2)
Manulife Financial LPGA Classic	Inbee Park (2)
U.S. Women's Open	Michelle Wie (2)
Walmart NW Arkansas Championship	Stacy Lewis (3)
Marathon Classic	Lydia Ko (2)
International Crown	Spain
Meijer LPGA Classic	Mirim Lee
Wegmans LPGA Championship	Inbee Park (3)
Canadian Pacific Women's Open	So Yeon Ryu
Portland Classic	Austin Ernst
Yokohama Tire LPGA Classic	Mi Jung Hur
Reignwood LPGA Classic	Mirim Lee (2)
Sime Darby LPGA Malaysia	Shanshan Feng
LPGA KEB - HanaBank Championship	Kyu Jung Baek
Blue Bay LPGA	Lee-Anne Pace (2)
Fubon LPGA Taiwan Championship	Inbee Park (4)
Lorena Ochoa Invitational	Christina Kim
CME Group Tour Championship	Lydia Ko (3)

LADIES EUROPEAN TOUR

Mission Hills World Ladies Championship	Inbee Park
Lalla Meryem Cup	Charley Hull
Turkish Airlines Ladies Open	Valentine Derrey
Deloitte Ladies Open	Kylie Walker
Allianz Ladies Slovak Open	Camilla Lennarth
Ladies Italian Open	Florentyna Parker
ISPS Handa Ladies European Masters	I.K. Kim
Ricoh Women's British Open	Mo Martin
Ladies German Open	Kylie Walker (2)
Sberbank Golf Masters	Julie Greciet
Aberdeen Asset Mgmt Ladies Scottish Open	Trish Johnson
Helsingborg Open	Dewi Claire Schreefel
Evian Championship	Hyo-Joo Kim
Tenerife Open de Espana Femenino	Connie Chen
Lacoste Ladies Open de France	Azahara Munoz
Cell C South African Women's Open	Lee-Anne Pace

Sanya Ladies Open	Xi Yu Lin
Xiamen Open	*Ssu-Chia Cheng
Hero Women's Indian Open	Gwladys Nocera
Omega Dubai Ladies Masters	Shanshan Feng (2)

JAPAN LPGA TOUR

Daikin Orchid Ladies	O. Sattaya
Yokohama Tire PRGR Ladies Cup	Yuki Ichinose
T-Point Ladies	Rikako Morita
AXA Ladies	Ayaka Watanabe
Yamaha Ladies Open	Sun-Ju Ahn
Studio Alice Ladies Open	Esther Lee
Vantelin Ladies Open KKT Cup	*Minami Katsu
Fujisankei Ladies Classic	Phoebe Yao
Cyber Agent Ladies	Yuki Ichinose (2)
World Ladies Championship Salonpas Cup	Misuzu Narita
Hokken no Madoguchi Ladies	Bo-Mee Lee
Chukyo TV Bridgestone Ladies Open	Sun-Ju Ahn (2)
Resort Trust Ladies	Teresa Lu
Yonex Ladies	Misuzu Narita (2)
Suntory Ladies Open	Sun-Ju Ahn (3)
Nichirei Ladies	Jiyai Shin
Earth Mondahmin Cup	Miki Sakai
Nichi-Iko Ladies Open	Yeon-Ju Jung
Samantha Thavasa Girls Collection Ladies	Misuzu Narita (3)
Century 21 Ladies	Bo-Mee Lee (2)
Meiji Cup	Jiyai Shin (2)
NEC Karuzawa 72	Bo-Mee Lee (3)
CAT Ladies	Momoko Ueda
Nitori Ladies	Jiyai Shin (3)
Golf 5 Ladies	Shiho Oyama
Japan LPGA Championship	Ai Suzuki
Munsingwear Ladies Tokai Classic	Jiyai Shin (4)
Miyagi TV Cup Dunlop Ladies Open	Miki Sakai (2)
Japan Women's Open Championship	Teresa Lu (2)
Stanley Ladies	Sun-Ju Ahn (4)
Fujitsu Ladies	Sun-Ju Ahn (5)
Nobuta Group Masters Golf Club Ladies	Shiho Oyama (2)
Hisako Higuchi Morinaga Ladies	Momoko Ueda (2)
Mizuno Classic	Mi Hyang Lee (2)
Itoen Ladies	Yoko Maeda
Elleair Ladies Open	Sakura Yokomine
Japan LPGA Tour Championship Ricoh Cup	Teresa Lu (3)

AUSTRALIAN LADIES TOUR

Moss Vale Classic	Bree Arthur
Mount Boughton Classic	Daniela Holmqvist
Bing Lee Fujitsu General Women's NSW Open	Joanna Klatten
ISPS Handa New Zealand Women's Open	Mi Hyang Lee
Volvik RACV Ladies Masters	Cheyenne Woods
ISPS Handa Women's Australian Open	Karrie Webb
Oates Victorian Open	*Minjee Lee

CHAMPIONS TOUR

Mitsubishi Electric Championship	Bernhard Langer
Allianz Championship	Michael Allen
ACE Group Classic	Kirk Triplett
Toshiba Classic	Fred Couples
Mississippi Gulf Resort Classic	Jeff Maggert
Greater Gwinnett Championship	Miguel Angel Jimenez
Insperity Invitational	Bernhard Langer (2)
Regions Tradition	Kenny Perry
Senior PGA Championship	Colin Montgomerie
Principal Charity Classic	Tom Pernice, Jr.
Big Cedar Lodge Legends of Golf	Fred Funk/Jeff Sluman
Encompass Championship	Tom Lehman
Constellation Senior Players Championship	Bernhard Langer (3)
U.S. Senior Open	Colin Montgomerie (2)
3M Championship	Kenny Perry (2)
Dick's Sporting Goods Open	Bernhard Langer (5)
Boeing Classic	Scott Dunlap
Shaw Charity Classic	Fred Couples (2)
Quebec Championship	Wes Short, Jr.
Pacific Links Hawai'i Championship	Paul Goydos
Nature Valley First Tee Open	John Cook
SAS Championship	Kirk Triplett (2)
Greater Hickory Kia Classic	Jay Haas
AT&T Championship	Michael Allen (2)
Charles Schwab Cup Championship	Tom Pernice, Jr. (2)

EUROPEAN SENIOR TOUR

ISPS Handa PGA Seniors Championship	Santiago Luna
Bad Ragaz PGA Seniors Open	Rick Gibson
The Senior Open Championship	Bernhard Langer (4)
SSE Scottish Senior Open	Mark Davis
English Senior Open	Cesar Monasterio
Travis Perkins Masters	Colin Montgomerie (3)
Russian Open	Colin Montgomerie (4)
Senior Open de Portugal	Tim Thelen
WINSTONgolf Senior Open	Paul Wesselingh
French Riviera Masters	Philip Golding
Dutch Senior Open	Ian Woosnam
Coca-Cola Australian PGA Seniors Champ.	Simon Owen
MCB Tour Championship	Paul Wesselingh (2)

JAPAN PGA SENIOR TOUR

Kanehide Senior Okinawa Open	Hatsuo Nakane
Kyoraku More Surprise Cup	Seiki Okuda
Starts Senior	Shinji Ikeuchi
ISPS Handa Cup Philanthropy Senior	Hideki Kase
Maruhan Cup Taiheiyo Club Senior	Gregory Meyer
Fancl Classic	Yutaka Hagawa
Komatsu Open	Tateo Ozaki
Japan PGA Senior Championship	Naomichi Ozaki
Japan Senior Open Championship	Masahiro Kuramoto
Fuji Film Senior Championship	Kiyoshi Murota
Iwasaki Shiratsuyu Senior	Masahiro Kuramoto (2)

Multiple Winners of 2014

PLAYER	WINS
Bernhard Langer	6
Sun-Ju Ahn	5
Hao-Tong Li	4
Rory McIlroy	4
Colin Montgomerie	4
Inbee Park	4
Jiyai Shin	4
Hiroyuki Fujita	3
Benjamin Hebert	3
Martin Kaymer	3
Seung-Hyuk Kim	3
Lydia Ko	3
Moritz Lampert	3
Bo-Mee Lee	3
Stacy Lewis	3
Teresa Lu	3
Misuzu Narita	3
Carlos Ortiz	3
Bubba Watson	3
Michael Allen	2
Fred Couples	2
Joel Dahmen	2
Jason Day	2
Louis de Jager	2
Julian Etulain	2
Shanshan Feng	2
Adam Hadwin	2
Keith Horne	2
Billy Horschel	2
Yuki Ichinose	2
Mikko Ilonen	2
Miguel Angel Jimenez	2

PLAYER	WINS
Andrew Johnston	2
Rashid Khan	2
Jessica Korda	2
Masahiro Kuramoto	2
Anirban Lahiri	2
Mi Hyang Lee	2
Mirim Lee	2
Alexander Levy	2
Hideki Matsuyama	2
Tyler McCumber	2
David McKenzie	2
Katsumasa Miyamoto	2
Titch Moore	2
Anna Nordqvist	2
Koumei Oda	2
Shiho Oyama	2
Lee-Anne Pace	2
Tom Pernice, Jr.	2
Kenny Perry	2
Patrick Reed	2
Jake Roos	2
Justin Rose	2
Miki Sakai	2
Jordan Spieth	2
Kirk Triplett	2
Momoko Ueda	2
Danie van Tonder	2
Jimmy Walker	2
Kylie Walker	2
Karrie Webb	2
Paul Wesselingh	2
Lee Westwood	2
Michelle Wie	2
Thaworn Wiratchant	2

World Money List

This list of the 350 leading money winners in the world of professional golf in 2014 was compiled from the results of men's (excluding seniors) tournaments carried in the Appendixes of this edition. This list includes tournaments with a minimum of 36 holes and four contestants and does not include such competitions as pro-ams and skins or skills contests. It does not include annual performance bonuses such as for the FedExCup (U.S.) and the Race to Dubai (Europe).

In the 49 years during which World Money Lists have been compiled, the earnings of the player in the 200th position have risen from a total of $3,326 in 1966 to $690,258 in 2014. The top 200 players in 1966 earned a total of $4,680,287. In 2014, the comparable total was $381,220,961.

The World Money List includes the official money lists of the U.S. PGA Tour, PGA European Tour, PGA Tour of Japan, Asian Tour, OneAsia Tour, Sunshine Tour, PGA Tour of Australasia, PGA Tour Latinoamerica and PGA Tour Canada, along with winnings in established unofficial tournaments when reliable figures could be obtained. The conversion rates used for 2014 were: Euro = US$1.30; Japanese yen = US$0.009; South African rand = US$0.09; Australian dollar = US$0.865; Canadian dollar = US$0.91.

POS.	PLAYER, COUNTRY	TOTAL MONEY
1	Rory McIlroy, N. Ireland	$10,526,012
2	Bubba Watson, USA	7,963,951
3	Jim Furyk, USA	6,187,395
4	Sergio Garcia, Spain	5,667,296
5	Justin Rose, England	5,641,004
6	Jordan Spieth, USA	5,613,273
7	Martin Kaymer, Germany	5,584,025
8	Rickie Fowler, USA	5,312,013
9	Henrik Stenson, Sweden	5,135,276
10	Jimmy Walker, USA	5,102,489
11	Matt Kuchar, USA	5,054,925
12	Billy Horschel, USA	4,975,554
13	Patrick Reed, USA	4,551,776
14	Adam Scott, Australia	4,396,209
15	Jason Day, USA	4,324,575
16	Chris Kirk, USA	4,198,802
17	Hunter Mahan, USA	3,600,416
18	Kevin Na, USA	3,596,691
19	Hideki Matsuyama, Japan	3,574,807
20	Zach Johnson, USA	3,422,734
21	Victor Dubuisson, France	3,372,263
22	Brendon Todd, USA	3,341,287
23	Graeme McDowell, N. Ireland	3,340,683
24	Ryan Palmer, USA	3,313,085
25	Brooks Koepka, USA	3,087,763
26	John Senden, Australia	2,967,056
27	Russell Henley, USA	2,925,918
28	Keegan Bradley, USA	2,907,971
29	Ryan Moore, USA	2,906,413
30	Jamie Donaldson, Wales	2,874,514

POS.	PLAYER, COUNTRY	TOTAL MONEY
31	Dustin Johnson, USA	2,849,180
32	Bill Haas, USA	2,811,314
33	Kevin Streelman, USA	2,792,637
34	Marc Leishman, Australia	2,755,068
35	Joost Luiten, Netherlands	2,737,169
36	Charley Hoffman, USA	2,701,484
37	Danny Willett, England	2,682,250
38	Gary Woodland, USA	2,641,070
39	Mikko Ilonen, Finland	2,636,002
40	Robert Streb, USA	2,620,146
41	Ben Martin, USA	2,592,089
42	Tim Clark, South Africa	2,583,921
43	Cameron Tringale, USA	2,573,453
44	Stephen Gallacher, Scotland	2,569,593
45	Webb Simpson, USA	2,568,371
46	Louis Oosthuizen, South Africa	2,568,244
47	Marcel Siem, Germany	2,512,655
48	Lee Westwood, England	2,489,415
49	Shane Lowry, Ireland	2,487,672
50	J.B. Holmes, USA	2,451,391
51	Luke Donald, England	2,448,922
52	Steven Bowditch, Australia	2,424,203
53	Charl Schwartzel, South Africa	2,412,098
54	Alexander Levy, France	2,392,859
55	Matt Every, USA	2,387,834
56	Phil Mickelson, USA	2,283,140
57	Ian Poulter, England	2,208,962
58	Thongchai Jaidee, Thailand	2,202,808
59	Seung-Yul Noh, Korea	2,198,483
60	Graham DeLaet, Canada	2,190,251
61	Will MacKenzie, USA	2,156,058
62	Brian Harman, USA	2,135,503
63	Ross Fisher, England	2,110,958
64	Shawn Stefani, USA	2,098,415
65	Sang-Moon Bae, Korea	2,064,269
66	Tommy Fleetwood, England	2,054,061
67	Harris English, USA	2,036,535
68	Jonas Blixt, Sweden	2,013,879
69	Kevin Stadler, USA	1,976,200
70	Brandt Snedeker, USA	1,969,823
71	Ernie Els, South Africa	1,949,122
72	Matt Jones, USA	1,935,302
73	Erik Compton, USA	1,903,359
74	Russell Knox, Scotland	1,895,487
75	Angel Cabrera, Argentina	1,884,759
76	Francesco Molinari, Italy	1,881,756
77	Jason Dufner, USA	1,881,333
78	Brendon de Jonge, Zimbabwe	1,854,072
79	George McNeill, USA	1,818,191
80	Thomas Bjorn, Denmark	1,805,621
81	Geoff Ogilvy, Australia	1,797,159
82	Pablo Larrazabal, Spain	1,779,946
83	Jerry Kelly, USA	1,773,731
84	George Coetzee, South Africa	1,724,665

POS.	PLAYER, COUNTRY	TOTAL MONEY
85	Camilo Villegas, Colombia	1,692,463
86	Freddie Jacobson, Sweden	1,626,843
87	Marc Warren, Scotland	1,625,256
88	Thorbjorn Olesen, Denmark	1,615,029
89	Scott Stallings, USA	1,605,966
90	K.J. Choi, Korea	1,601,162
91	Paul Casey, England	1,576,986
92	Morgan Hoffmann, USA	1,562,792
93	Branden Grace, South Africa	1,551,889
94	Charles Howell, USA	1,549,026
95	Chesson Hadley, USA	1,539,704
96	Kevin Chappell, USA	1,524,754
97	Ben Crane, USA	1,511,294
98	Steve Stricker, USA	1,507,747
99	Stuart Appleby, Australia	1,468,626
100	Koumei Oda, Japan	1,442,338
101	Daniel Summerhays, USA	1,421,312
102	David Hearn, Canada	1,409,382
103	William McGirt, USA	1,407,960
104	Ryo Ishikawa, Japan	1,406,273
105	Jason Bohn, USA	1,355,472
106	Brendan Steele, USA	1,336,879
107	Carl Pettersson, Sweden	1,331,588
108	Robert Karlsson, Sweden	1,310,750
109	Andrew Svoboda, USA	1,309,431
110	Justin Hicks, USA	1,263,571
111	Hiroshi Iwata, Japan	1,261,815
112	Pat Perez, USA	1,257,123
113	Gonzalo Fernandez-Castano, Spain	1,254,075
114	Chris Stroud, USA	1,243,364
115	Brian Stuard, USA	1,242,015
116	Danny Lee, New Zealand	1,238,510
117	Billy Hurley, USA	1,224,380
118	Bernd Wiesberger, Austria	1,202,245
119	Scott Langley, USA	1,197,573
120	Retief Goosen, South Africa	1,190,867
121	Edoardo Molinari, Italy	1,178,945
122	Andy Sullivan, England	1,163,241
123	Fabrizio Zanotti, Paraguay	1,162,602
124	Rafa Cabrera-Bello, Spain	1,159,011
125	Scott Brown, USA	1,144,587
126	Kevin Kisner, USA	1,143,594
127	Tyrrell Hatton, England	1,141,641
128	Jason Kokrak, USA	1,140,370
129	Romain Wattel, France	1,135,009
130	Kristoffer Broberg, Sweden	1,085,819
131	Richard Sterne, South Africa	1,077,806
132	Richie Ramsay, Scotland	1,071,884
133	Simon Dyson, England	1,071,243
134	Nicolas Colsaerts, Belgium	1,046,601
135	Hiroyuki Fujita, Japan	1,046,476
136	Bo Van Pelt, USA	1,033,362
137	Boo Weekley, USA	1,033,174
138	Martin Flores, USA	1,025,882

POS.	PLAYER, COUNTRY	TOTAL MONEY
139	Rory Sabbatini, South Africa	1,018,997
140	Hideto Tanihara, Japan	1,016,429
141	Kiradech Aphibarnrat, Thailand	1,001,773
142	Hyung-Sung Kim, Korea	999,502
143	John Huh, USA	987,604
144	Seung-Hyuk Kim, Korea	983,370
145	David Lingmerth, Sweden	982,499
146	Emiliano Grillo, Argentina	976,949
147	David Lipsky, USA	976,621
148	Bryce Molder, USA	976,050
149	Oliver Wilson, England	968,205
150	Mike Weir, Canada	965,553
151	Nicholas Thompson, USA	964,583
152	Tomohiro Kondo, Japan	963,802
153	Martin Laird, Scotland	946,429
154	Hennie Otto, South Africa	934,773
155	David Toms, USA	934,230
156	Tony Finau, USA	930,614
157	Matteo Manassero, Italy	923,718
158	Anirban Lahiri, India	922,666
159	Troy Merritt, USA	917,248
160	Prayad Marksaeng, Thailand	914,278
161	Nick Watney, USA	907,444
162	Robert Garrigus, USA	903,640
163	Hudson Swafford, USA	895,264
164	Thomas Aiken, South Africa	885,513
165	Stewart Cink, USA	879,544
166	Justin Thomas, USA	873,193
167	Nick Taylor, Canada	871,387
168	Michael Thompson, USA	868,566
169	Eddie Pepperell, England	856,544
170	David Howell, England	845,579
171	Brice Garnett, USA	840,560
172	Jeff Overton, USA	840,300
173	Michael Putnam, USA	839,189
174	Bud Cauley, USA	822,446
175	Katsumasa Miyamoto, Japan	819,433
176	Wade Ormsby, Australia	819,108
177	James Hahn, USA	817,618
178	Michael Hoey, N. Ireland	811,126
179	Jim Renner, USA	782,338
180	Shingo Katayama, Japan	777,542
181	Jhonattan Vegas, Venezuela	772,406
182	Andres Romero, Argentina	771,074
183	Carlos Ortiz, Mexico	765,102
184	Brian Davis, England	762,104
185	Darren Fichardt, South Africa	761,850
186	Cameron Smith, Australia	754,441
187	Aaron Baddeley, Australia	747,088
188	Oliver Fisher, England	746,625
189	Charlie Beljan, USA	745,392
190	Jonathan Byrd, USA	742,163
191	Tim Wilkinson, New Zealand	734,208
192	Adam Hadwin, Canada	714,504

POS.	PLAYER, COUNTRY	TOTAL MONEY
193	Will Wilcox, USA	706,044
194	Greg Chalmers, Australia	704,530
195	Yuta Ikeda, Japan	697,976
196	Scott Piercy, USA	695,778
197	Felipe Aguilar, Chile	695,423
198	Ricky Barnes, USA	693,842
199	Robert Allenby, Australia	691,158
200	Ken Duke, USA	690,258
201	Justin Leonard, USA	688,500
202	Chris Wood, England	684,912
203	Andres Gonzales, USA	681,978
204	Padraig Harrington, Ireland	666,182
205	Yoshitaka Takeya, Japan	663,970
206	Jason Allred, USA	662,981
207	Roberto Castro, USA	653,029
208	Luke Guthrie, USA	651,322
209	Peter Uihlein, USA	626,421
210	Derek Fathauer, USA	624,600
211	Prom Meesawat, Thailand	618,732
212	Richard Lee, New Zealand	617,056
213	Ben Curtis, USA	612,579
214	Matthew Baldwin, England	610,021
215	Andrew Loupe, USA	608,921
216	Brad Fritsch, Canada	602,906
217	Richard Bland, England	602,880
218	Jason Gore, USA	601,505
219	Heath Slocum, USA	600,730
220	Angelo Que,Philippines	598,830
221	David Horsey, England	597,467
222	Dong-Kyu Jang, Korea	583,027
223	Alejandro Canizares, Spain	581,489
224	Yusaku Miyazato, Japan	578,698
225	Blayne Barber, USA	576,022
226	Scott Hend, Australia	565,354
227	In-Hoi Hur, Korea	556,885
228	Yoshinori Fujimoto, Japan	551,568
229	Alex Cejka, Germany	545,330
230	Graeme Storm, England	540,593
231	Magnus A. Carlsson, Sweden	538,570
232	Dawie van der Walt, South Africa	533,092
233	Andrew Putnam, USA	530,446
234	Taichi Teshima, Japan	528,334
235	Gregory Bourdy, France	526,809
236	Richard Green, Australia	522,988
237	Sean O'Hair, USA	519,185
238	David Oh, USA	513,973
239	Chris Doak Scotland	507,879
240	Fabian Gomez, Argentina	502,703
241	John Peterson, USA	496,330
242	Mark Foster, England	495,580
243	Tommy Gainey, USA	493,968
244	Raphael Jacquelin, France	490,213
245	Johnson Wagner, USA	488,623
246	Tyrone van Aswegen, South Africa	481,996

POS.	PLAYER, COUNTRY	TOTAL MONEY
247	Hao-Tong Li, China	479,063
248	Scott Jamieson, Scotland	478,070
249	Alvaro Quiros, Spain	477,782
250	John Merrick, USA	477,668
251	Chad Campbell, USA	476,784
252	Thomas Pieters, Belgium	475,657
253	Zachary Blair, USA	475,006
254	Julien Quesne, France	463,802
255	John Rollins, USA	459,360
256	Sang-Hyun Park, Korea	453,689
257	Jon Curran, USA	450,350
258	Chad Collins, USA	450,046
259	Danie van Tonder, South Africa	446,827
260	Bradley Dredge, Wales	445,735
261	Toshinori Muto, Japan	444,320
262	Robert-Jan Derksen, Netherlands	437,562
263	Wes Roach, USA	435,843
264	Satoshi Kodaira, Japan	431,232
265	Kyoung-Hoon Lee, Korea	425,456
266	Shiv Kapur, India	421,262
267	J.J. Henry, USA	418,086
268	I.J. Jang, Korea	417,493
269	Ryuichi Oda, Japan	414,757
270	Gregory Havret, France	413,106
271	Seve Benson, England	407,888
272	Rikard Karlberg, Sweden	404,842
273	Colt Knost, USA	399,104
274	Mark Wilson, USA	398,442
275	Rod Pampling, Australia	393,526
276	Michio Matsumura, Japan	393,267
277	Andrew Johnston, England	393,257
278	Brad Kennedy, Australia	392,196
279	Kyle Stanley, USA	391,579
280	K.T. Kim, Korea	382,567
281	Gaganjeet Bhullar, India	382,010
282	Tadahiro Takayama, Japan	380,088
283	D.A. Points, USA	379,189
284	Spencer Levin, USA	376,126
285	Gary Stal, France	375,072
286	Morten Orum Madsen, Denmark	374,392
287	Brett Rumford, Australia	373,714
288	James Morrison, England	372,930
289	Anders Hansen, Denmark	372,687
290	Paul Waring, England	370,838
291	Jim Herman, USA	370,381
292	Sang-Hee Lee, Korea	365,485
293	Jason Knutzon, USA	365,295
294	Lucas Bjerregaard, Denmark	364,347
295	Trevor Immelman, South Africa	362,998
296	Wen-Chong Liang, China	362,466
297	Robert Rock, England	357,558
298	Daniel Berger, USA	355,669
299	Greg Owen, England	354,875

POS.	PLAYER, COUNTRY	TOTAL MONEY
300	David Drysdale, Scotland	353,494
301	Charlie Wi, Korea	351,031
302	Damien McGrane, Ireland	350,795
303	Mikael Lundberg, Sweden	350,597
304	Jbe' Kruger, South Africa	348,158
305	Ted Potter, Jr., USA	346,552
306	Ashun Wu, China	345,225
307	Kyle Reifers, USA	344,983
308	Peter Hanson, Sweden	340,431
309	Craig Lee, Scotland	327,893
310	Jamie Lovemark, USA	325,657
311	Kazuhiro Yamashita, Japan	325,569
312	Thanyakon Khrongpha, Thailand	324,164
313	Maximilian Kieffer, Germany	321,055
314	Adam Bland, Australia	319,921
315	Hyun-Woo Ryu, Korea	319,450
316	Thaworn Wiratchant, Thailand	318,612
317	Soren Kjeldsen, Denmark	318,321
318	Rahman Siddikur, Bangladesh	318,009
319	Zack Sucher, USA	313,466
320	Max Homa, USA	308,765
321	Jin Jeong, Korea	305,632
322	Steven Alker, New Zealand	304,723
323	Tom Lewis, England	303,183
324	Steve Marino, USA	303,130
325	David Lynn, England	302,604
326	Michael Hendry, New Zealand	300,259
327	Josh Teater, USA	298,742
328	Johan Carlsson, Sweden	297,360
329	Antonio Lascuna, Philippines	295,588
330	Nicholas Fung, Malaysia	294,159
331	Lee Slattery, England	293,989
332	Eduardo de la Riva, Spain	293,651
333	S.S.P. Chowrasia, India	293,062
334	Cameron Percy, Australia	292,597
335	Byeong-Hun An, Korea	291,650
336	Juvic Pagunsan Philippines	289,727
337	Brian Gay, USA	289,251
338	Derek Ernst, USA	288,290
339	Jung-Gon Hwang, Korea	283,085
340	Steve Webster, England	278,750
341	Matthew Nixon, England	277,601
342	Dicky Pride, USA	277,267
343	Anthony Wall, England	275,067
344	Byron Smith, USA	273,564
345	Seuk-Hyun Baek, Korea	273,402
346	Paul Lawrie, Scotland	272,384
347	Satoshi Tomiyama, Japan	272,274
348	Carlos Del Moral, Spain	271,936
349	Brendan Jones, Australia	271,293
350	Alex Prugh, USA	271,053

World Money List Leaders

YEAR	PLAYER, COUNTRY	TOTAL MONEY
1966	Jack Nicklaus, USA	$168,088
1967	Jack Nicklaus, USA	276,166
1968	Billy Casper, USA	222,436
1969	Frank Beard, USA	186,993
1970	Jack Nicklaus, USA	222,583
1971	Jack Nicklaus, USA	285,897
1972	Jack Nicklaus, USA	341,792
1973	Tom Weiskopf, USA	349,645
1974	Johnny Miller, USA	400,255
1975	Jack Nicklaus, USA	332,610
1976	Jack Nicklaus, USA	316,086
1977	Tom Watson, USA	358,034
1978	Tom Watson, USA	384,388
1979	Tom Watson, USA	506,912
1980	Tom Watson, USA	651,921
1981	Johnny Miller, USA	704,204
1982	Raymond Floyd, USA	738,699
1983	Seve Ballesteros, Spain	686,088
1984	Seve Ballesteros, Spain	688,047
1985	Bernhard Langer, Germany	860,262
1986	Greg Norman, Australia	1,146,584
1987	Ian Woosnam, Wales	1,793,268
1988	Seve Ballesteros, Spain	1,261,275
1989	David Frost, South Africa	1,650,230
1990	Jose Maria Olazabal, Spain	1,633,640
1991	Bernhard Langer, Germany	2,186,700
1992	Nick Faldo, England	2,748,248
1993	Nick Faldo, England	2,825,280
1994	Ernie Els, South Africa	2,862,854
1995	Corey Pavin, USA	2,746,340
1996	Colin Montgomerie, Scotland	3,071,442
1997	Colin Montgomerie, Scotland	3,366,900
1998	Tiger Woods, USA	2,927,946
1999	Tiger Woods, USA	7,681,625
2000	Tiger Woods, USA	11,034,530
2001	Tiger Woods, USA	7,771,562
2002	Tiger Woods, USA	8,292,188
2003	Vijay Singh, Fiji	8,499,611
2004	Vijay Singh, Fiji	11,638,699
2005	Tiger Woods, USA	12,280,404
2006	Tiger Woods, USA	13,325,949
2007	Tiger Woods, USA	12,902,706
2008	Vijay Singh, Fiji	8,025,128
2009	Tiger Woods, USA	10,998,054
2010	Graeme McDowell, N. Ireland	7,371,586
2011	Luke Donald, England	9,730,870
2012	Rory McIlroy, N. Ireland	11,301,228
2013	Tiger Woods, USA	9,490,217
2014	Rory McIlroy, N. Ireland	10,526,012

Career World Money List

Here is a list of the 50 leading money winners for their careers through the 2014 season. It includes players active on both the regular and senior tours of the world. The World Money List from this and the 48 previous editions of the annual and a table prepared for a companion book, *The Wonderful World of Professional Golf* (Atheneum, 1973) form the basis for this compilation. Additional figures were taken from official records of major golf associations. Conversion of foreign currency figures to U.S. dollars is based on average values during the particular years involved.

POS.	PLAYER, COUNTRY	TOTAL MONEY
1	Tiger Woods, USA	$133,318,377
2	Ernie Els, South Africa	87,269,152
3	Phil Mickelson, USA	83,026,796
4	Vijay Singh, Fiji	82,913,648
5	Jim Furyk, USA	73,672,941
6	Sergio Garcia, Spain	57,934,248
7	Lee Westwood, England	54,662,744
8	Davis Love, USA	52,829,188
9	Retief Goosen, South Africa	51,351,213
10	Padraig Harrington, Ireland	51,156,966
11	Luke Donald, England	50,465,292
12	Adam Scott, Australia	50,414,608
13	Bernhard Langer, Germany	47,450,272
14	Justin Rose, England	46,624,446
15	Steve Stricker, USA	45,143,213
16	Colin Montgomerie, Scotland	44,486,730
17	David Toms, USA	43,373,927
18	Kenny Perry, USA	42,519,368
19	Rory McIlroy, Northern Ireland	42,325,884
20	Fred Couples, USA	40,895,860
21	Ian Poulter, England	39,243,715
22	Zach Johnson, USA	38,599,655
23	Nick Price, Zimbabwe	37,767,234
24	Hale Irwin, USA	37,478,499
25	Justin Leonard, USA	36,984,788
26	Stewart Cink, USA	36,918,151
27	Robert Allenby, Australia	36,685,376
28	Matt Kuchar, USA	36,498,382
29	Graeme McDowell, Northern Ireland	36,343,744
30	Mark Calcavecchia, USA	35,661,828
31	K.J. Choi, South Korea	35,478,939
32	Tom Lehman, USA	35,048,992
33	Fred Funk, USA	34,100,569
34	Jay Haas, USA	34,007,115
35	Miguel Angel Jimenez, Spain	33,493,175
36	Darren Clarke, Northern Ireland	33,436,447
37	Stuart Appleby, Australia	33,102,927
38	Geoff Ogilvy, Australia	32,961,977
39	Rory Sabbatini, South Africa	31,494,667
40	Tom Kite, USA	31,144,293

POS.	PLAYER, COUNTRY	TOTAL MONEY
41	Mike Weir, Canada	30,941,517
42	Paul Casey, England	30,929,132
43	Jeff Sluman, USA	30,417,034
44	Charles Howell, USA	29,526,731
45	Tim Clark, South Africa	29,343,685
46	Scott Verplank, USA	28,881,073
47	Jerry Kelly, USA	28,844,321
48	Loren Roberts, USA	28,819,937
49	Thomas Bjorn, Denmark	28,680,000
50	Tom Watson, USA	28,678,242

These 50 players have won $2,183,347,018 in their careers.

Women's World Money List

This list includes official earnings on the U.S. LPGA Tour, Ladies European Tour, Japan LPGA Tour and Australian Ladies Tour, along with other winnings in established unofficial events when reliable figures could be obtained.

POS.	PLAYER, COUNTRY	TOTAL MONEY
1	Stacy Lewis, USA	$2,574,039
2	Inbee Park, Korea	2,347,452
3	Lydia Ko, New Zealand	2,107,303
4	Michelle Wie, USA	1,924,796
5	Shanshan Feng, China	1,690,854
6	So Yeon Ryu, Korea	1,551,849
7	Sun-Ju Ahn, Korea	1,452,567
8	Anna Nordqvist, Sweden	1,250,253
9	Azahara Munoz, Spain	1,207,317
10	Teresa Lu, Taipei	1,172,156
11	Suzann Pettersen, Norway	1,129,843
12	Karrie Webb, Australia	1,107,990
13	Bo-Mee Lee, Korea	1,078,053
14	Chella Choi, Korea	1,048,932
15	Lexi Thompson, USA	1,036,764
16	Jiyai Shin, Korea	999,204
17	Na Yeon Choi, Korea	995,813
18	Cristie Kerr, USA	946,883
19	Mirim Lee, Korea	933,849
20	Misuzu Narita, Japan	901,049
21	Miki Sakai, Japan	832,906
22	Jessica Korda, USA	817,885
23	Shiho Oyama, Japan	794,625
24	Brittany Lincicome, USA	790,661
25	Pornanong Phatlum, Thailand	788,435
26	Paula Creamer, USA	784,941

POS.	PLAYER, COUNTRY	TOTAL MONEY
27	Julieta Granada, Paraguay	762,803
28	Angela Stanford, USA	754,728
29	Erina Hara, Japan	722,103
30	Jenny Shin, Korea	720,046
31	Sakura Yokomine, Japan	718,701
32	Na-Ri Lee, Korea	707,850
33	Hyo-Joo Kim, Korea	699,901
34	Mo Martin, USA	680,624
35	Ayaka Watanabe, Japan	674,907
36	Lizette Salas, USA	669,106
37	Momoko Ueda, Japan	668,840
38	Caroline Masson, Germany	651,469
39	Lee-Anne Pace, South Africa	646,414
40	Carlota Ciganda, Spain	618,405
41	Amy Yang, Korea	618,180
42	Lala Anai, Japan	592,095
43	Meena Lee, Korea	589,337
44	Mi Hyang Lee, Korea	573,602
45	Christina Kim, USA	570,374
46	Rikako Morita, Japan	564,506
47	Morgan Pressel, USA	558,534
48	Brittany Lang, USA	551,703
49	Mi Jung Hur, Korea	547,646
50	Catriona Matthew, Scotland	547,018
51	Ai Suzuki, Japan	543,820
52	O. Sattaya, Thailand	540,358
53	Esther Lee, Korea	535,236
54	Karine Icher, France	532,365
55	Eun-Hee Ji, Korea	522,829
56	Sandra Gal, Germany	517,631
57	Ilhee Lee, Korea	501,146
58	I.K. Kim, Korea	497,265
59	Pernilla Lindberg, Sweden	471,232
60	Gerina Piller, USA	466,497
61	Caroline Hedwall, Sweden	447,826
62	Hee Young Park, Korea	447,658
63	Austin Ernst, USA	439,089
64	Ritsuko Ryu, Japan	434,361
65	Kotono Kozuma, Japan	427,678
66	Yumiko Yoshida, Japan	427,169
67	Beatriz Recari, Spain	409,058
68	Belen Mozo, Spain	401,675
69	Ji-Hee Lee, Korea	394,807
70	Mariajo Uribe, Colombia	385,313
71	Line Vedel, Denmark	377,197
72	Junko Omote, Japan	368,504
73	Erika Kikuchi, Japan	367,039
74	Mi-Jeong Jeon, Korea	361,733
75	Saiki Fujita, Japan	361,258
76	Haru Nomura, Japan	353,892
77	Charley Hull, England	342,026
78	Yani Tseng, Taipei	340,681
79	Moriya Jutanugarn, Thailand	337,973

POS.	PLAYER, COUNTRY	TOTAL MONEY
80	Yeon-Ju Jung, Korea	336,877
81	Mami Fukuda, Japan	333,546
82	Haeji Kang, Korea	333,072
83	Mina Harigae, USA	326,339
84	Kaori Ohe, Japan	322,032
85	Stephanie Meadow, N. Ireland	321,155
86	Phoebe Yao, Taipei	318,907
87	Danielle Kang, USA	316,239
88	Jodi Ewart Shadoff, England	312,060
89	Gwladys Nocera, France	303,275
90	Katherine Kirk, Australia	295,743
91	Asako Fujimoto, Japan	292,052
92	Jennifer Johnson, USA	286,084
93	Yuki Ichinose, Japan	284,463
94	Mika Miyazato, Japan	275,772
95	Kim Kaufman, USA	275,273
96	Mayu Hattori, Japan	272,881
97	Se Ri Pak, Korea	271,888
98	Yoko Maeda, Japan	266,856
99	Soo-Yun Kang, Korea	265,813
100	Rui Kitada, Japan	264,467
101	Sun Young Yoo, Korea	261,351
102	Dewi Claire Schreefel, Netherlands	258,444
103	Na-Ri Kim, Korea	253,931
104	Laura Davies, England	253,301
105	Sarah Jane Smith, Australia	253,150
106	Thidapa Suwannapura, Thailand	252,436
107	Mamiko Higa, Japan	251,966
108	Megumi Kido, Japan	250,995
109	Ayako Uehara, Japan	245,445
110	Hikari Fujita, Japan	244,272
111	Amelia Lewis, USA	240,816
112	Yukari Baba, Japan	237,988
113	Nikki Campbell, Australia	236,519
114	Rumi Yoshiba, Japan	231,653
115	Marina Alex, USA	224,330
116	Candie Kung, Taipei	224,164
117	Xi Yu Lin, China	218,460
118	Akane Iijima, Japan	209,850
119	Da-Ye Na, Korea	207,547
120	Yukari Nishiyama, Japan	207,227
121	Natsuka Hori, Japan	203,369
122	Tiffany Joh, USA	200,607
123	Dori Carter, USA	194,011
124	Ai Miyazato, Japan	192,370
125	Kris Tamulis, USA	190,568
126	In Gee Chun, Korea	181,109
127	Megumi Shimokawa, Japan	177,666
128	Juli Inkster, USA	175,505
129	Miki Saiki, Japan	174,653
130	Ji Young Oh, Korea	173,090
131	Sydnee Michaels, USA	170,987
132	Laura Diaz, USA	167,595

POS.	PLAYER, COUNTRY	TOTAL MONEY
133	Giulia Sergas, Italy	167,327
134	Holly Clyburn, England	164,415
135	Eun-Bi Jang, Korea	163,241
136	Sarah Kemp, Australia	160,063
137	Ji-Woo Lee, Korea	158,445
138	Valentine Derrey, France	158,408
139	Paula Reto, South Africa	154,880
140	Yuri Fudoh, Japan	154,717
141	Haruka Kudo, Japan	151,311
142	Nana Yamashiro, Japan	150,601
143	Katie Burnett, USA	149,364
144	Mihoko Iseri, Japan	144,476
145	Beth Allen, USA	143,206
146	Maiko Wakabayashi, Japan	141,635
147	P.K. Kongkraphan, Thailand	140,304
148	Joanna Klatten, France	140,048
149	Florentyna Parker, England	139,531
150	Stacy Lee Bregman, South Africa	138,360
151	Christel Boeljon, Netherlands	138,069
152	Jane Park, USA	136,521
153	Kylie Walker, Scotland	134,982
154	Kaori Nakamura, Japan	131,711
155	Kumiko Kaneda, Japan	129,990
156	Amy Anderson, USA	129,742
157	Sophie Giquel-Bettan, France	129,178
158	Ji-Min Lee, Korea	125,999
159	Satsuki Oshiro, Japan	124,504
160	Jennifer Song, USA	124,446
161	Camilla Lennarth, Sweden	123,375
162	Trish Johnson, England	123,315
163	Airi Saitoh, Japan	123,234
164	Malene Jorgensen, Denmark	123,029
165	Alison Walshe, USA	119,992
166	Brooke Pancake, USA	117,051
167	Kelly Tan, Malaysia	116,294
168	Jennifer Rosales, Philippines	115,487
169	Kaori Yamamoto, Japan	115,019
170	Lindsey Wright, Australia	114,718
171	Hannah Burke, England	112,042
172	Hiroko Azuma, Japan	111,723
173	Shiho Toyonaga, Japan	111,255
174	Young Kim, Korea	110,939
175	Ariya Jutanugarn, Thailand	110,490

Senior World Money List

This list includes official earnings from the U.S. Champions Tour, European Senior Tour and Japan Senior Tour, along with other winnings in established official and unofficial tournaments when reliable figures could be obtained.

POS.	PLAYER, COUNTRY	TOTAL MONEY
1	Bernhard Langer, Germany	$3,508,189
2	Colin Montgomerie, Scotland	2,380,780
3	Miguel Angel Jimenez, Spain	2,361,129
4	Jay Haas, USA	1,939,974
5	Kenny Perry, USA	1,772,446
6	Tom Pernice, Jr., USA	1,580,313
7	Kirk Triplett, USA	1,455,418
8	Michael Allen, USA	1,421,098
9	Fred Couples, USA	1,407,596
10	Fred Funk, USA	1,273,317
11	Jeff Sluman, USA	1,248,105
12	Woody Austin, USA	1,106,639
13	Scott Dunlap, USA	1,102,426
14	Tom Lehman, USA	1,101,812
15	David Frost, South Africa	1,052,723
16	Jeff Maggert, USA	1,032,676
17	Joe Durant, USA	1,021,945
18	Gene Sauers, USA	991,799
19	Marco Dawson, USA	960,059
20	Wes Short, Jr., USA	916,684
21	Russ Cochran, USA	877,676
22	John Cook, USA	826,795
23	Olin Browne, USA	825,906
24	Billy Andrade, USA	811,143
25	Mark O'Meara, USA	775,695
26	Bart Bryant, USA	762,415
27	Duffy Waldorf, USA	750,448
28	Paul Goydos, USA	726,634
29	Vijay Singh, Fiji	716,743
30	Doug Garwood, USA	708,066
31	Esteban Toledo, Mexico	694,180
32	Mark Calcavecchia, USA	676,942
33	Mark Brooks, USA	653,779
34	Rocco Mediate, USA	622,173
35	Steve Pate, USA	599,265
36	Roger Chapman, England	576,709
37	Davis Love, USA	543,240
38	Kiyoshi Murota, Japan	502,136
39	Bill Glasson, USA	500,725
40	Mark McNulty, Zimbabwe	489,417
41	Steve Lowery, USA	488,087
42	Tom Watson, USA	471,690
43	Mike Goodes, USA	456,108
44	Tom Byrum, USA	452,801
45	Corey Pavin, USA	435,402
46	Jeff Hart, USA	417,513

POS.	PLAYER, COUNTRY	TOTAL MONEY
47	Chien Soon Lu, Taipei	408,275
48	Tommy Armour, USA	407,453
49	Barry Lane, England	394,788
50	Peter Senior, Australia	383,551
51	John Riegger, USA	368,997
52	Kevin Sutherland, USA	368,973
53	Masahiro Kuramoto, Japan	353,632
54	Steve Elkington, Australia	352,238
55	Loren Roberts, USA	347,083
56	Rod Spittle, Canada	316,384
57	Paul Wesselingh, England	314,903
58	Willie Wood, USA	314,315
59	Brad Faxon, USA	310,746
60	Rick Gibson, Canada	310,721
61	Bob Tway, USA	309,158
62	Joe Daley, USA	300,903
63	Joey Sindelar, USA	288,016
64	Lee Janzen, USA	281,352
65	Scott Hoch, USA	273,251
66	Peter Jacobsen, USA	266,310
67	Gary Hallberg, USA	262,310
68	Yutaka Hagawa, Japan	256,443
69	Dan Forsman, USA	255,646
70	Philip Golding, England	254,422
71	Naomichi Ozaki, Japan	242,686
72	Larry Mize, USA	242,280
73	John Inman, USA	239,373
74	Stephen Ames, Canada	232,140
75	Skip Kendall, USA	225,930
76	Cesar Monasterio, Argentina	225,224
77	Seiki Okuda, Japan	223,043
78	Kohki Idoki, Japan	218,955
79	Mark Mouland, Wales	204,611
80	Hale Irwin, USA	202,380
81	Miguel Angel Martin, Spain	194,815
82	Bob Gilder, USA	190,014
83	Tsukasa Watanabe, Japan	189,558
84	Hideki Kase, Japan	177,918
85	Brad Bryant, USA	173,767
86	Scott Simpson, USA	173,544
87	Sandy Lyle, England	172,990
88	Tom Kite, USA	170,573
89	Boonchu Ruangkit, Thailand	168,781
90	Tim Thelen, USA	168,090
91	Bobby Clampett, USA	164,808
92	Shinji Ikeuchi, Japan	162,456
93	Mike Reid, USA	162,401
94	Craig Stadler, USA	156,137
95	Jim Rutledge, Canada	155,162
96	Steen Tinning, Denmark	150,272
97	Takeshi Sakiyama, Japan	149,043
98	Wayne Levi, USA	148,943
99	Jim Carter, USA	146,703
100	Peter Fowler, Australia	146,429

1. The Year in Retrospect

The Mark H. McCormack Award was created in 1998 to honor the professional golfer who was No. 1 in the Official World Golf Ranking for the most weeks in a calendar year. It was McCormack, of course, who originated the idea of a world ranking 30 years earlier for this very publication. And it was Tiger Woods who effectively made so many people forget about the award by winning it the first 13 times. Rory McIlroy won the award for 2014 in a race that only looked close in chronological terms. Woods was No. 1 for the first 19 weeks of the year. Adam Scott took over for 11 weeks. And then McIlroy was No. 1 for the last 22 weeks.

McIlroy winning the award didn't generate headlines, though it should be remembered for the timeline and the characters — from Woods, the best of his generation, and then briefly to Scott, once looked upon as a suitable heir, and finally to McIlroy, whose back-to-back majors earned him the label as golf's next big thing.

This should not be remembered as the year that McIlroy dominated the world of golf, because the 25-year-old from Northern Ireland had done this before. Only two years ago, he painted a masterpiece at the end of the season with a record-setting margin of victory (eight shots) in the PGA Championship at Kiawah Island, successive victories in the FedExCup Playoffs and then the DP World Tour Championship in Dubai on the European Tour.

McIlroy might have been even better this time in the face of so many distractions. He started the year by getting engaged and then sliding into one of his mini-slumps highlighted by a press-generated phenomena known as either "Freaky Friday" or "Black Friday" — terrible rounds, or at least a terrible nine-hole stretch — on Friday that took him out of the tournament. He ceremoniously broke off his engagement to tennis star Caroline Wozniacki with a telephone call and then won his first tournament of the year that same week with a magnificent comeback at Wentworth in the BMW PGA Championship. He won the Open Championship, the World Golf Championship - Bridgestone Invitational and the PGA Championship in consecutive starts. He became the face of golf. Only what makes 2014 stand out even more is that McIlroy became the face of change.

We might look back on 2014 as the definitive generational shift in golf. Out with the old, in with the new. The old in this case was Woods, who showed obvious signs of age, not to mention wear-and-tear. And while McIlroy led the charge, he had a supporting cast that pumped new blood into the royal and ancient game. Martin Kaymer, in his final year in his 20s, won The Players Championship and U.S. Open as the German asserted himself as a force with a greater variety of shots and that reliable discipline. Patrick Reed didn't quite live up to his boast of being top five in the world, though his two victories and assertiveness in the Ryder Cup made people pay attention. Jordan Spieth, who celebrated his 21st birthday with a Las Vegas bash in July, ended the year with two wins that left the field wondering how good he could be. Rickie Fowler was mentioned as a potential rival for McIlroy after joining Woods and Jack Nicklaus as the only players to finish in the top five in all the majors. And not to be overlooked, though it was easy to do because of the language barrier, Hideki Matsuyama won the Memorial for his first PGA Tour victory, and then went all four rounds with Spieth and finished one shot ahead in the Dunlop Phoenix and won in a playoff. In the final World Ranking of 2014, half of the top 20 players had yet to turn 30 until the season was over. Woods, who has carried professional golf like no other player in his generation, not only had another rival to beat. He had a slew of them.

Of course, it wasn't a fair fight. That's the phrase NBC Sports analyst Roger Maltbie used in the 2000 U.S. Open at Pebble Beach not so much to describe Woods as to defend the poor souls trying to beat him. Now, it is more of an explanation why Woods wasn't part of the conversation in 2014. His season was filled with more acronyms than trophies. There was the MDF (made the cut, did not finish 72 holes) at Torrey Pines, the WD (withdraw) from the Honda Classic and Bridgestone Invitational, the MC (missed cut) at the Quicken Loans National and the PGA Championship and the DNS (did not start) from missing four tournaments following March 31 back surgery, and four more tournaments when he failed to even qualify for the FedExCup Playoffs. He played only nine tournaments, his fewest since Woods managed only seven starts in 2008 because of reconstructive surgery on his left knee following his 2008 U.S. Open victory at Torrey Pines, which remains the last major he won. Ultimately, his year was best summed up by another acronym — MIA.

This youth movement not only proved to be more than capable in 2014, the collection of players also had something else in their favor. None ever had to deal with Woods at the peak of his game. Sure, it was only a year ago that Woods won five times on the PGA Tour and made a lot of those wins look easy. But there remained some missing links. Woods still had not won a major, and every year since then the competition was getting stronger, younger, deeper. The kids that Woods now had to beat grew up watching the way he worked, they way he trained, the way he thought on the golf course, and they tried to emulate that. That's a vast difference from when Woods first turned pro at the end of 1996, and his fellow competitors didn't know what hit them.

Charles Howell was part of that early tidal wave that was Tiger Woods. He remembers seeing shots from Woods during their play time at Isleworth that no one on the planet could hit. And he saw the change with the new wave of players. "They've studied the guy. They've learned from the guy," Howell said. "Tiger ruined a lot of guys' lives. He caused a lot of people some sleepless Sunday nights. But he also motivated an entire generation behind him."

Graeme McDowell was asked about this going into the Masters, where Woods again was considered the favorite. (This was two weeks before Woods disclosed he had a surgery to alleviate a pinched nerve that would keep him away from Augusta National for the first time in his career.) Is the aura different? Do the kids in this generation fear Tiger? Is it easier to face him without having endured so many thrashings from Woods that the likes of Ernie Els and Davis Love and so many others experienced? Was the presence as strong? Go back to 2000 at St. Andrews for the Open. Els had opened with a 66 and the second question from the press is whether he noticed that Woods had a 67 in the morning. There was no escaping.

And then there was television. McDowell pointed out that Woods appeared unbeatable when he was around the lead except against Europeans. Thomas Bjorn beat him in Dubai while playing all 72 holes with him. Lee Westwood overcame a 54-hole deficit to Woods in Germany. Darren Clarke beat him in the 36-hole final of the Accenture Match Play Championship at La Costa. Michael Campbell didn't flinch when Woods was charging at Pinehurst No. 2 in the 2005 U.S. Open. "But the Americans didn't do it," McDowell said. "I felt they were being force-fed this stuff week in and week out. You turn on Golf Channel and it was 'Tiger's 10 greatest shots' or 'Tiger's 10 greatest comebacks.' So it was where they actually started to believe it when they were standing side-by-side with him on Sunday afternoon. That was my theory, whether right or wrong. We still have Tiger's 10 greatest comebacks. But you have two sides of the media — one that builds him up, one that cuts him down. But that negativity now exists. Guys are not being force-fed the invincibility aura anymore." Throw in a deeper talent pool of young players, and the aura loses another layer. "It's not what Tiger did. It's what everyone is capable of doing," McDowell said.

If there was a tournament that summed that up, it might have been Sunday at the WGC - Cadillac Championship at Doral. Reed had a two-shot lead going into the final round, with Woods only three shots back after a 66 in the third round. Woods was in the penultimate pairing with Hunter Mahan, and that bright red shirt would be clearly visible to Reed. Except that Reed had on a red shirt of his own. He idolized Woods growing up and decided when he turned pro to wear the black trousers and red shirt ensemble. Anyone wearing a red shirt on Sunday once was said to be brave. Luke Donald had white pants and a red shirt — England colors — in the final round of the 2006 PGA Championship at Medinah, which Woods won by five shots (Woods shot 68, Donald 74). A week later, Paul Casey had a red shirt picked out for Sunday when the tee times were changed because of rain in the forecast. The final round featured threesomes, putting Casey in the last group with Woods. He changed shirts to green. And now there was some kid in his second full year on the PGA Tour dressed up like Woods who embraced the occasion. Woods walked onto the practice range with much fanfare. Reed didn't blink. A few hours later, Woods was wincing with back pain, and Reed was bulldozing his way to a World Golf Championship title.

Reed made news that week for proclaiming in a television interview, and later with the press, that he felt he was one of the top five players in the world. He had won three times in the last seven months, though the Cadillac Championship was his first win against a world-class field. He had yet to even play in a major. Reed was scorned in some corners for his audacity, praised in other corners for his bravado.

Perhaps most telling was when Reed was asked in his press conference to name the "other four players" he considered to be among the top five in the world. He mentioned Woods and Phil Mickelson. And there was Adam Scott, the reigning Masters champion. He also mentioned McDowell, mainly because he was surprised how much McDowell got out of his game, which was a backhanded compliment. He was running out of space, and he smiled when he realized it. Even so, this little exercise ended without Reed mentioning McIlroy, U.S. Open champion Justin Rose, Sergio Garcia, Henrik Stenson or even a pair of recent winners — Jason Day (Accenture Match Play) and Bubba Watson, who won at the Northern Trust Open and was soon to be a two-time Masters champion. It was clear, in the most innocuous fashion, that golf was loaded with good players, perhaps deeper than ever. McIlroy wound up at the top, and on that there was no argument. At that point, no one knew the severity of Woods' injury and how little he would play during the year. But even then, the first full week in March, Woods was seen as part of the crowd.

There was a large crowd on the LPGA Tour, without any one player standing out. Inbee Park and Stacy Lewis shared time at No. 1 in the Women's World Rolex Rankings, although Lewis took more of the honors at the end of what arguably was one of the best LPGA Tour seasons in more than a decade. Lewis won the LPGA Tour money title over Park, and she captured the points-based Rolex Player of the Year award for the second time in three years. Lewis also won the Vare Trophy for the lowest scoring average. Park finished the year at No. 1, and she added to her major total by winning the Wegmans LPGA Championship, held for the final time at Locust Grove outside Rochester, New York.

Throw in 17-year-old Lydia Ko, and three became quite a crowd. The South Korean-born, New Zealand-bred teenager already had won twice on the LPGA Tour as an amateur. In her first year as a pro, she won the Swinging Skirts LPGA Classic at Lake Merced in San Francisco with a dramatic finish that featured Lewis in the hunt, and then Ko won again at the Marathon Classic in Ohio. She capped off the year by claiming the richest payoff in the history of women's golf — the CME Group Tour Championship worth $500,000 and the $1 million bonus for claiming the inaugural "Race to the CME Globe."

Except there was more to this crowd. Michelle Wie produced the defining moment for herself and the tour when she won the U.S. Women's Open at Pinehurst No. 2 for her first major, and it was the appropriate stage for her star power. Already the biggest event in women's golf, the U.S. Women's Open received even more attention because it was on the same course as the men, one week later. Lexi Thompson won the Kraft Nabisco Championship in a duel with Wie, and she challenged Wie at Pinehurst No. 2 before her season faded. Still, it was a banner year.

But there was no doubting the biggest star in 2014, and that was McIlroy.

Go back to the end of 2013 to see the starting point for McIlroy's resurgence. Coming off a year in which he had an acrimonious split with his Irish-based management company and was scrutinized for his wholesale switch to Nike golf clubs, McIlroy won the Australian Open when he was trailing by one shot and made birdie on the last hole as Adam Scott went long and made bogey. It wasn't a world-class field, but it was a win. And after a year of not winning, it mattered.

And it appeared to carry over into the start of 2014 when he tied for second in the Abu Dhabi HSBC Golf Championship — in which he received a two-shot penalty in the third round for an incorrect drop. His turnaround looked as though it would start much earlier when he showed off his world-class form in the first big event of the year at the Honda Classic, which featured seven of the top 10 players from the World Ranking. Playing alongside Scott, it was a mesmerizing display of driving at PGA National, and a brilliant display by McIlroy, who opened with rounds of 63 and 66 for his first 36-hole lead on the PGA Tour in 18 months. But he couldn't finish, much as he tried. Staked to a two-shot lead, he fell apart on the back nine and was one shot behind until he hit a five wood to a peninsula green on the par-five closing hole and watched it settle 10 feet from the hole for a chance to win. He missed, and then chopped up the 18th in a four-man playoff as Russell Henley emerged the winner. Call it progress for McIlroy, but it was coming slowly. And for the next few months, he would not be someone inclined to say, "Thank God It's Friday."

It started the following week at the WGC - Cadillac Championship at Doral when McIlroy played the front nine in 40. No one noticed because the Blue Monster was a beast that day. After a short break, McIlroy ran off a string of top-10s in the Shell Houston Open, the Masters, the Wells Fargo Championship at Quail Hollow and The Players Championship. On paper, the results were solid. Closer inspection, however, revealed a troubling trend. McIlroy took himself out of the hunt on Friday at Augusta National when he shot 40 on the back nine on his way to a 77. He got off to a great start in the Wells Fargo Championship until he made back-to-back double bogeys on the front nine at Quail Hollow and shot 40 to fall out of contention with a 76. McIlroy had only made the cut once at The Players Championship before, and he made it this time with no shortage of drama. Again on Friday, he shot a 42 on the front nine and made a birdie on the 18th to narrowly get to the weekend. His episode with "Freaky Friday" was not quite finished, but when McIlroy headed back to Europe for the BMW Championship, the most significant day of the week turned out to be a Wednesday.

McIlroy began 2014 with a stunning announcement on Twitter: She said yes. That would be Wozniacki, his girlfriend of more than two years. They were engaged in Sydney ahead of Wozniacki's first Grand Slam event of the tennis season at the Australian Open. McIlroy considered it his "first victory" of 2014. But it ended in a fashion that was no less shocking. Just a few days after the couple sent out wedding invitations, McIlroy called off the engagement with a phone call to Wozniacki and a statement to the press early in the week of the flagship event on the European Tour. He blamed himself for not realizing until the invitations went out that he was not ready for marriage. In a subdued press conference at Wentworth, he said he would be concentrating on his golf and would only answer questions about his game. Coming off a year in which he split with his management company and was criticized in some circles — Nick Faldo was one — for changing all his equipment at once, this appeared to be another off-course setback.

Except that it turned out to be just the beginning. McIlroy was seven shots behind going into the final round when he closed with a six-under 66 for a one-shot victory. "I guess when I got inside the ropes this week, it was a little bit of a release, and I was on my own and doing what I do best, which is playing golf," he said. "It's obviously been a week of very mixed emotions, but I'm sitting here looking at this trophy going, 'How the hell, how did it happen this week?' But it did."

Equipped with his most significant win since the DP World Tour Championship in Dubai to close out the 2012 season, McIlroy got back into his Friday mode. After opening with a 63 at the Memorial, McIlroy came unglued in the second round. He hit into the trees twice and made double bogey. He went into the water and made double bogey. And then he made his third straight double bogey by double-hitting a wedge. He shot 43 on the back nine (he began on No. 10) and shot 78 to give up a lead he never got back. It was his fourth straight PGA Tour event where he had at least 40 over nine holes, all of them on Friday.

"These little runs I'm getting on where it gets away from me, I was able to avoid that last week (at Wentworth). Not so much this week," he said.

He had one more episode. After missing the cut at the Irish Open, McIlroy tuned up for the Open Championship by going to the Aberdeen Asset Management Scottish Open. He was on fine form with a 64 in the opening round at Royal Aberdeen. And then the clock turned to Friday. McIlroy shot a 78 and narrowly made the cut. It was the sixth time in his last eight events that he had a nine-hole score of 40 or higher. It was so bizarre that when McIlroy began the Open with a 66 at Royal Liverpool to take the lead, the talk was more about what would happen on Friday than the prospect of his name on the claret jug.

But it was on that Friday that his year, and his dominance, took shape. McIlroy began Friday with a bogey, and you could almost hear the whispers in the gallery of "Here we go again." Not so fast. He made four birdies in a six-hole stretch around the turn. He made three more birdies over the final four holes. He had another 66 to build a four-shot lead over Dustin Johnson. And he was on his way. He stretched that lead to six shots after Saturday, and no one got within two shots of him in the final round.

If there was a moment that defined the year of McIlroy, it was late Saturday afternoon at Hoylake. Right when Fowler was starting to get close, McIlroy took off like a rocket with a pair of eagles on the 16th and 18th holes. The final eagle was pure class. He hit a five iron and held his pose, knowing it had no imperfections. He crouched as it descended and lightly pumped his fist when it settled 10 feet away. And when he holed the putt, instead of a wild celebration or roundhouse fist pump, he stiffened his back and looked out defiantly at the grandstands packed with fans who clearly appreciated this performance. No smile. Just a look.

Jim Furyk was 10 shots behind and had seen that look — and that game — before. "He's just so explosive. He won the U.S. Open by eight shots. He obviously doesn't have any issue as the front-runner, and has no issue trying to extend that lead, much like Tiger used to."

That began a stretch of golf not seen since Woods at his peak. In three successive tournaments, McIlroy won two majors and a World Golf Championship, and he won them in three different manners. The Open was a wire-to-wire coronation. The WGC - Bridgestone Invitational was a stirring comeback. The PGA Championship was a free-for-all in which McIlroy had control, lost it, and regained it with a three wood into the 10th green at Valhalla for an eagle and a nine iron from a fairway bunker on the 17th hole to 10 feet for a birdie that put the final major of the year back into his grasp. Most significant about Firestone was that it gave McIlroy his first World Golf Championship, allowing him to join a group of 12 other players who have won majors and a WGC event. It also put him back to No. 1 in the world for the first time since March of 2013.

Much like Woods used to reduce Ernie Els to runner-up status in big events, Sergio Garcia was second fiddle to McIlroy. The Spaniard was the only one to seriously challenge him at Hoylake, and Garcia had a three-shot lead going into the final day at Firestone. Such was the explosiveness of McIlroy that the lead was gone in three holes. McIlroy punched an eight iron out of the trees and up the slope to three feet on the first hole. He smashed a four iron onto the green at the par-five second for a two-putt birdie, and then he holed an eight-foot birdie on the third. Garcia couldn't stop him. "Everybody saw it. He played very, very well. He drove the ball miles and very, very straight for the most part," Garcia said.

McIlroy led the World Money List for the second time in three years with $10,526,012.

Comparisons are inevitable in golf, and with McIlroy, there was only one — Woods. When he won the PGA Championship, McIlroy joined an awesome triumvirate in golf by capturing his fourth career major at 25 or younger. The others were Woods, Jack Nicklaus and Bobby Jones, three of the greatest in the game. His record after 2014 still paled compared with Woods. At age 25, McIlroy had 14 victories around the world, four majors and one World Golf Championship. When Woods was 25, he had 34 wins around the world and seven majors, including the career Grand Slam. Even so, the kid had the well-rounded game, and he was living up to the hype, minus a few mini-slumps here and there. Most impressive was his driving, as Garcia witnessed at Firestone. Geoff Ogilvy was asked at Valhalla if he thought McIlroy had the greatest combination of power and accuracy off the tee since Greg Norman. Ogilvy said it was the best since Woods. "Tiger did everything so well in 2000 that his driving never got any attention," he said.

For Woods, the conversation shifted from what he once did instead of what he was capable of doing. Coming off a five-win season, there were small indications in retrospect what the immediate future held for the greatest player of his generation when he had back pain at The Barclays. And there was immediate feedback what kind of year was in store at the Farmers Insurance Open. As the defending champion at Torrey Pines, on a course he had won eight times, Woods never broke 70 in three rounds — that's right, three rounds — and missed the 54-hole cut for the first time in his career. Then, it was on to the Omega Dubai Desert Classic, where he had won twice and only once had finished out of the top five. He tied for 41st.

That looked to be nothing more than a slow start, especially when he arrived in south Florida for the Honda Classic and fired off a 65 in the third round that at least got him within shouting range of McIlroy. But if there was one day that epitomized his season, it was Sunday at PGA National. Woods was five over through his round when Luke Guthrie noticed Woods bending over gingerly to get his tee from the ground or his ball from the cup. After 13 holes, Woods walked over to Guthrie and told him he was done. He rode out to the parking lot, switched out of his shoes and was gone. The last time Woods withdrew from a tournament in the middle of a round because of injury was at Doral in 2012. He won at Bay Hill in his next start and was on his way back to No. 1. Not this time.

Woods played the following week at Doral and was a factor for the first time all year. He made eight birdies on a tough course for a 66 in the third round to get within three shots of the lead, and in the penultimate group. But his back injury flared up after an awkward stance for a shot out of the bunker on No. 6, and Woods grimaced his way around the rest of the way. He didn't make a birdie in the final round for the first time in his PGA Tour career, and his 78 was his worst Sunday score ever. By the end of the year, the tie for 25th in the Cadillac Championship would be his second-best result of 2014. The best finish was the Hero World Challenge. He tied for 17th in an 18-man field.

The road to the Masters suddenly got very bumpy for Woods, and then it came to a dead end. Even as pundits were debating his fitness for the first major of the year, Woods surprised everyone with an announcement that he had back surgery on March 31 in Utah to relieve a pinched nerve. The process was referred to as a "microdiscectomy," and it kept Woods from Augusta National for the first time since 1994, when he was still in high school.

He wound up missing the U.S. Open, too, and then came another surprise. Right when the debates were stirring about whether he would take the rest of the year off, Woods decided to play the Quicken Loans National at Congressional, a tournament that his foundation runs and one that had a new sponsor. The idea was to test his health and shake off some rust. In his eyes, he accomplished both. He had rounds of 74-75 to miss the cut, though he was excited to be pain-free and said he was able to swing the driver at full speed without worry. Those silly mistakes that cost him so many strokes could easily be corrected before the Open, he said, and when he opened with a 69 at Hoylake, it looked like the recovery was right on schedule.

He never broke par the rest of the week. He finished at six-over 294, matching his highest score in the Open. He finished in 69th place, his lowest position after 72 holes in any major. And he wound up 23 shots behind McIlroy, by six shots his largest deficit in the majors. Woods didn't sound overly concerned. Neither did Ryder Cup captain Tom Watson, who had been saying all along that he wanted Woods on the American team provided he was playing well and was healthy. At the time, only one of those appeared to be true. And even that didn't last.

Two weeks later, on another course (Firestone) where Woods had won eight times, he again was teeing off in the final round at the Bridgestone Invitational before the leaders had even arrived for lunch. On the second hole, Woods faced a shot from the top bank of a bunker, and then he hopped down into the sand after the strike. Something jarred his lower back, and that familiar image was back — Woods walking with discomfort, the occasional grimace and the early departure. This time, he could barely tie his shoes at his car as he prepared to leave. And this time, there was serious concerns he could even make it to the PGA Championship, much less be a viable pick for the Ryder Cup.

In one of the more bizarre scenes of the golfing year, the center of attention at Valhalla was an empty parking space reserved for Tiger Woods. He finally showed up Wednesday afternoon, in time to get in nine holes of practice on a course where he won the PGA Championship 14 years earlier. He had never prepared so little for a major. Expectations were never so low, and Woods lived up to them. He opened with a 74, his lone birdie coming on a chip-in. Woods looked so fragile that he even got sympathy from Phil Mickelson, who said he thought his longtime rival played with heart. The next day, Woods rallied for a 74 and missed the cut by five shots. And a week later, he removed any suspense by announcing he was removing his name from consideration as a Ryder Cup captain's pick.

Because he had started only seven PGA Tour events and finished 72 holes in two of them, he was not remotely close to making the FedExCup Playoffs. That was the end of his season, and it was forgettable due to the injuries. He played only six rounds in the majors and broke par one time. He failed to qualify for the Ryder Cup team for only the second time in his career. His official earnings on the PGA Tour were $108,275 — Woods made more than that his first four PGA Tour events as a pro in 1996. And he announced another long layoff, this time to make sure his body (and his back) were strong enough to be like the Tiger of old instead of an old Tiger Woods. A new vocabulary entered his vernacular, words like "speed" and "explosiveness." The Playoffs went on without him, as did the Ryder Cup and the start to another PGA Tour season.

Woods targeted his return to the Hero World Challenge, his holiday event with a new title sponsor and a new golf course. It moved to Isleworth, where Woods lived for the first 16 years of his PGA Tour career. He has played Isleworth more than any other course. He once shot 59 before it was lengthened and toughened. In this return, his tee shot went left into a neighbor's yard and out-of-bounds. He ended his year in a tie for last place. At least he had his health. "I made some progress. I hadn't played in four months and I'm in absolutely no pain, which is nice," Woods said. "To be able to go all out on some of these drives like I did this week really reinforces what I'm doing is the right thing for my body."

A struggle back for Woods was in sharp contrast to what was a breakthrough for Bubba Watson that went beyond his second victory in the Masters. A decade ago, Watson was lucky to even get his PGA Tour card despite his awesome length off the tee and creative shot-making skills. He was 21st on the Nationwide Tour money list at a time when only the top 20 received PGA Tour cards. But because the leader that year was Jason Gore, who had won three times to earn an instant promotion, the tour decided to count the 21st player on the list. That was Watson, and there has been steady progress since then, including his Ryder Cup debut in 2010 and his Masters victory in 2012. But this year was different. He lost the Waste Management Phoenix Open with careless mistakes over the last few holes, and then bounced back to win the Northern Trust Open at Riviera by going the final 39 holes without a bogey and closing with a 64 for a two-shot victory. It was his first win in 22 months dating to the Masters. More was to follow.

Watson won his second green jacket at Augusta National and was determined to finish the year strong, unlike his previous Masters victory. And while he didn't win again until late in the year, he contended at the Memorial and finished third, and he had a chance in the BMW Championship at Cherry Hills until finishing runner-up. And then he showed that his game could travel when he won the WGC - HSBC Champions in Shanghai in a manner that fits his unpredictable nature. He blew a late lead by making a bogey on the reachable par-four 16th at Sheshan International, and then taking two shots to get out of a bunker and making double bogey on the par-three 17th. From a greenside bunker on the par-five closing hole, he knocked in his sand shot for an eagle to get into a playoff, and then made a birdie to win. It was his third win of the year, all against strong fields, and he wound up No. 2 on the World Money List behind McIlroy with $7,963,951. Not bad for a guy named Bubba from Bagdad (Florida). And he finally had a worldwide win on his résumé, which was important to him.

"It's a global game. I was watching when I was growing up the greats of the game win outside the U.S. Being able to win outside the U.S., I just wanted to be able to travel and get through the jet lag, get through all the things and still perform at a high level," Watson said. "So for me to win out here, this is very big. This is very special for me."

For Kaymer, this wasn't a breakthrough to a new level as much as it was a resurrection. The 29-year-old German reached No. 1 in the world back in February 2011 and stayed there for eight weeks. In nearly 30 years of the Official World Golf Ranking, the only players who have spent less time at the top were Bernhard Langer (three weeks when the OWGR began in 1986) and Tom Lehman (one week). This could be construed as a case of a player reaching the pinnacle — either the No. 1 ranking or winning a major — and believing he needed a game to match that status.

Kaymer had a long-term view. He was known mainly for his fade, and Kaymer felt like he needed a well-rounded game if he wanted to remain among the elite for the length of his career. He spent nearly two years trying to develop the right shot for every occasion, and the results showed the struggle. He won only one tournament in 52 worldwide starts over two years, and that was the Nedbank Challenge at the end of 2012 against a limited field. There were long hours on the practice range. There was frustration. There were drills, such as placing a tennis ball between his forearms to keep them in place, and then figuring out that if he ran a rope through the ball and wore it like a necklace he wouldn't have to fetch the ball after each swing. But it paid off in a big way. Preceding his remarkable run through Pinehurst No. 2 in his wire-to-wire U.S. Open victory was a display equally impressive against the strongest and deepest field of the year at The Players Championship.

He tied the course record on The Players Stadium Course at TPC Sawgrass with a 63 in the opening round. He never lost the lead, though he faced a stern test from Jordan Spieth when they went into the final round tied for the lead. One of the best putts of the year came on one of golf's most notorious holes. Kaymer found the island green on the par-three 17th, though the ball took a curious hop and spun down the slope and nearly into the water. His chip was weak, leaving him 30 feet for par on a putt that went up the ridge and then picked up speed as it broke sharply to the right. He had a one-shot lead. A two-putt bogey would have required a strong effort. Kaymer remarkably holed the par putt and went on to a one-shot victory. It was his biggest win since the 2010 PGA Championship in a playoff over Watson at Whistling Straits.

And it was confirmation that he was on the right track. The technical-minded German was swinging freely. "I stopped thinking," he said. Further confirmation of his game was at the U.S. Open on one shot that hardly anyone would have noticed in his 65-65 start at Pinehurst. He was between clubs on the par-four fourth hole, and he felt as though the shot called for a draw. So he took one less club and tried to hit a hard draw to gain a little extra yardage. It wound up 10 feet short of the hole, and Kaymer never smiled so wide as when he looked at caddie Craig Connelly. "I pulled off the shot and said to Craig, 'How good was that golf shot?' The rhythm was good. It was a crisp hit. The flight was good. For me, it was the best shot I hit all week." And he was back among the elite.

Watson and Kaymer shared one thing in common beyond a major title. They denied signature victories to Spieth, the fast-rising Texan who was still only 20 when he nearly won the Masters and The Players Championship. Spieth had a two-shot lead with 11 holes to play at Augusta National when Watson seized control with a two birdies and just enough mistakes from Spieth. A month later, Spieth went 58 holes at Sawgrass without making a bogey until it slipped away from him and he closed with a 74. "It's not fun being that close and having opportunities and being in the lead on Sunday and not pulling it off," Spieth said. He would find a way by the end of the year.

As much as the year was defined by the greatness of McIlroy and the incomplete grade assigned to Woods, Spieth was among several youngsters who at least showed they are on the cusp of challenging for big titles. Spieth worked his way into the conversation late in the year. He played what he considered the finest golf of his young career with a 63 in the final round at the Emirates Australian Open for a six-shot victory. Four days later and on the other side of the world, he finished his year at the Hero World Challenge in Florida. And while much of the attention was on the return of Woods, Spieth stole the show with the kind of runaway victory that Woods once produced with regularity. He had rounds of 66-67-63-66 to finish at 26-under 262 and win by 10 shots.

Adding to that impressive display was his itinerary. In this global game, Spieth played in Japan, Australia and the United States in successive weeks. He finished one shot out of a playoff at the Dunlop Phoenix and won the next two tournaments by a combined 16 shots. This was three months after Spieth was asked who would be a natural rival for McIlroy in the years to come. He mentioned the need to win majors, and then he paused to state the obvious. "We need to win another tournament," he said, placing emphasis on the final word. The end of the year doesn't get as much attention, but he got the job done.

That wasn't the case for the 25-year-old Fowler, though he sure got everyone's attention during the four biggest weeks of the year. Fowler started the final round of the Masters two shots out of the lead and stumbled early, never making up ground. Still, he tied for fifth to match his best finish in a major. He was leading the "B Flight" at Pinehurst No. 2 and at least got into the final group at a major for the first time, although he trailed Kaymer by five shots and never seriously challenged him. At least he shared the silver medal with Erik Compton. Fowler was in the final group for the second straight major at Royal Liverpool, this time facing a six-shot deficit to McIlroy. He never put any pressure on McIlroy — Garcia was the one who did that — but Fowler settled for another runner-up finish in a major. The final major was Fowler's best chance. He was among four players who had a share of the lead on the back nine at Valhalla, but a loose tee shot that led to bogey on the par-three 14th hole was a mistake he never got back. Fowler had a long eagle putt in the darkness on the final hole to force a playoff. He three-putted for par and finished third.

Instead of winning a major, Fowler settled for a footnote in history by joining Nicklaus and Woods as the only players to finish among the top five in all four majors in a year. That was good company, except that Nicklaus and Woods at least won majors in those years. Fowler didn't win anywhere, and while his work with Butch Harmon showed great strides, there was a growing chorus of skeptics that felt like Fowler needed to start winning. His only victories in five years as a professional were at the Wells Fargo Championship and the Korea Open. McIlroy was runner-up both times.

Two other players in their 20s were part of that group — Reed and Jason Day of Australia. Even though Reed said he felt like he was among the top five in the world when he won the Cadillac Championship at Doral, he never got higher than No. 20 all year. But he showed plenty of game when he started 63-63-63 at the Humana Challenge and held on to win, and then beat back a world-class field at Doral. He showed even more moxie at the Ryder Cup when Reed partnered with Spieth to go 2-0-1 in their matches, and then Reed rallied to beat Henrik Stenson in singles to cap off a 3-0-1 week, highlighted by a Sunday match when he pressed his finger to his lips to silence the Scottish gallery. It showed his bravado, and he is not lacking in that department.

Day might be the most explosive in that group, though also the most injury prone. He has been slowed by nagging injuries ever since he reached the PGA Tour, and this year was no different. After blitzing his way to victory in the WGC - Accenture Match Play Championship, Day revealed that his thumb was injured over the weekend. He didn't play again for two months until the Masters. He didn't play for nearly two months after that until the Memorial. And then he tied for fourth in the U.S. Open. He finished in the top 10 at three FedExCup Playoff events. The exception was the BMW Championship, where he withdrew with a sore back. Day was in dire need of good health, and more wins. The Match Play was only the second win of his PGA Tour career.

Mickelson and Jim Furyk would have settled for any win at all. Mickelson is the most prolific winner next to Woods in his generation. Furyk has been rock solid his entire career. A swing only a mother could love has produced over $60 million in worldwide earnings. All of them came up empty this year.

Mickelson will get the most attention because of his stature and skill in the game, though the year wasn't a total loss. It wasn't as bad as 2003, when he failed to win or even record a runner-up finish during a year marked by the near-death of his wife and newborn son during childbirth. He started the year with a runner-up finish in the Abu Dhabi HSBC Golf Championship, and with so much attention on the U.S. Open at Pinehurst No. 2 and Mickelson's first shot at the career Grand Slam, he appeared to be off on the right foot. It changed quickly. He narrowly made the cut at the Farmers Insurance Open at Torrey Pines, only to withdraw with a bad back. He withdrew from the Valero Texas Open with another injury. And the real sign of trouble was two weeks later when he missed the cut at the Masters for the first time since 1997. He was never a factor at Pinehurst or Royal Liverpool. Unpredictable as ever, Mickelson showed up at Valhalla for the final major and nearly won it. He was in the four-man chase for the PGA Championship. Needing an eagle to force a playoff, he nearly chipped in from short of the green. Always a thrill for Phil. The consolation prize for his strong play at Valhalla should not be taken lightly. Mickelson qualified for the Ryder Cup team for the 10th straight time — two decades of never needing to be a captain's pick, and an American record for most teams. He qualified for his first team when Greg Norman was No. 1 in the world and Woods was still an amateur. That figures to be a standard that will be tough to match.

Furyk qualified for the Ryder Cup team at No. 3, which in a way speaks to the aggravation of his year. Amid whispers that the game was passing him by because of his lack of modern power, he turned in one of his finest seasons at age 44 except that he didn't have a trophy to show for it. He was runner-up at the Wells Fargo Championship and The Players Championship in successive weeks. He had the lead in the RBC Canadian Open until Tim Clark closed with a 65 to beat him by one at Royal Montreal. He was tied for the lead with Jason Day at The Barclays and closed with a 70 to finish eighth. During his four-year drought on the PGA Tour, it was the eighth time that Furyk had at least a share of the 54-hole lead and failed to convert. He could accept failure, though the questions nagged at him.

"I feel like every time I go to the press room, I understand the questions coming and I feel like we're in a morgue. Everyone is looking at me with this blank stare and they ask me depressing questions. And they bring up the Ryder Cup the last time (a singles loss to Sergio Garcia), and we go through Akron (a double bogey on the 18th hole) ... and I leave there like I lost my dog," Furyk said. "It's golf. I didn't die out there today. I don't expect anyone to feel sorry for me."

His lone victory might have been setting an example in today's game on how to face losing with honesty and dignity. He ended his year in September at the Tour Championship, closing with two straight bogeys for another runner-up finish. Feel sorry for Furyk? He finished the year at No. 3 in the World Money List at $6,187,395, making him the first $6 million man in golf without a victory. He ended 2014 at No. 7 in the World Ranking, and until Watson won in Shanghai, Furyk was the highest-ranked American. All in all, it was an impressive performance for a 44-year-old.

But when it comes to ageless wonders, no one can match Bernhard Langer. The 57-year-old German won the opening event in Hawaii on the Champions Tour, and he kept right on going until he captured another Charles Schwab Cup as the best in the 50-and-older division. If that wasn't enough, the two-time Masters champion was on the fringe of contention at Augusta National this year until he tied for eighth — with McIlroy, among others. Against players his own age, Langer had no peer. He won five times, adding a pair of Champions Tour majors at the Constellation Senior Players Championship and the Senior Open Championship.

No one in the world of professional golf won more than Langer's six titles, which includes the PNC Father-Son Challenge to end the year. In official events, his five wins pushed his career total on the Champions Tour to 23 since he arrived in 2007. He also broke Hale Irwin's single-season money record with $3,074,189, topping Irwin's record of $3,028,304 set in 2002. Langer was the leading money winner for the sixth time in seven years. He is relentless. "It's still mind-boggling to reflect on my year," he said.

He wasn't the only star among the seniors. Colin Montgomerie finally won a major, and then he won another. The Scot known for years as the best to never win a major on the regular tours won the Senior PGA Championship for his first major title on any tour, and then added the U.S. Senior Open.

In a year in which no female distinguished herself over another, 2014 still goes down as one of the best years for women in general — on and off the golf course. On a chilly afternoon in September, Royal & Ancient Secretary Peter Dawson emerged from the stately clubhouse at St. Andrews and announced that the R&A had voted overwhelming to allow women to join the club for the first time in its 260-year history. "I can confirm that The Royal & Ancient Golf Club of St. Andrews is now a mixed membership club," Dawson said before taking a few questions and stepping back inside without fanfare. He said that would not affect the decisions of single-gender clubs that host the Open Championship, such as Muirfield, Royal St. George's or Royal Troon. But it was a big day for women, and a month later it was revealed that Augusta National had added to its female membership roll at the home of the Masters. Aside from those moments, there was plenty of action on the golf course.

One player who received plenty of attention ended her round with an ice cream cone. Go back to a Sunday at Augusta National for the inaugural "Drive, Chip and Putt Championship" meant to attract more kids. One of the winners from her age group was 11-year-old Lucy Li from California. Masters chairman Billy Payne gathered the winners together in the press center and announced, "We're going to be hearing from some of these kids again." It didn't take long. A month later, Li made history as the youngest player to qualify for the U.S. Women's Open. She won her sectional qualifier at Half Moon Bay. She finished her opening round of 78 at Pinehurst No. 2 by speaking to reporters with an ice cream cone in her hand. She followed with another 78 and then hung around for the weekend to watch the stars after she missed the cut.

Then, another teen prodigy stole the show. Michelle Wie was 10 when she qualified for the U.S. Women's Amateur Public Links, and she won the USGA title at 13. She was 14 when she shot a 68 at the Sony Open on the PGA Tour, and as a 16-year-old she had a chance to win three LPGA Tour majors in the final hour. But injuries and extreme scrutiny slowed her path, although the Hawaii native never lost her way. She stuck to her plan of going to college and earned a degree from Stanford while playing part-time on the LPGA Tour.

Victories came slowly until she developed her own putting stroke — her back bent perpendicular so that it was parallel to the ground, eyes over the ball. Given her six-foot figure, she at times resembled a giraffe stooped over to get a drink of water. But she was in the final group of the Kraft Nabisco Championship, won by 19-year-old Lexi Thompson, and then Wie won in Hawaii before the home crowd.

But the 24-year-old came into her own at Pinehurst. With a combination of power and putting, she held on to win the biggest title in women's golf at the U.S. Women's Open and her first major championship. Much like her journey, there were unexpected turns. Right when the tournament was in hand, Wie tried to hit a hybrid from a fairway bunker on the 16th and narrowly escaped with double bogey to keep a one-shot lead. Then, she holed a fast, bending birdie putt from 25 feet that sewed up the championship. She missed the cut at the Ricoh Women's British Open and injured her hand, having to take time off at the end of the year.

Even so, it was a signature win for women's golf. Lewis has emerged as the steadiest American. Park is the player accumulating the most majors. Lydia Ko could be the next big star in women's golf. Wie, however, has been celebrated for her youth, for her power, for playing against the men, for her failures ... for just about everything she does. And she finally had a win that matched the hype — at Pinehurst, one week after the men's U.S. Open.

"I think that scene on 18, being on network TV, as many people as we had around there at Pinehurst No. 2 and Michelle Wie winning the golf tournament, I don't think you can script it any better," Lewis said. "I think it's great for the game of golf. I think it's even better for women's golf. I'm so happy for Michelle Wie. I mean this has been such a long time coming for her."

There were other big moments as LPGA commissioner Mike Whan continued to expand playing opportunities. During the first Asian swing, Paula Creamer produced a putt and a reaction that made the HSBC Women's Champions in Singapore memorable. In a sudden-death playoff on the par-five 18th hole, Creamer had some 75 feet for eagle and a roller-coaster putt that most would be happy to get down in two. She sent it on its way and high-stepped across the green when it dropped for eagle and the victory, falling to her knees and buried her head in the ground in disbelief. Creamer has been slowed by injuries, but she still moves the needle.

Whan also introduced the International Crown, an eight-team event that felt like the Olympics had arrived to golf two years early. It was big news in the Far East when the United States faced South Korea in a semi-final, and the Koreans advanced. The winner was Spain, and the flag-waving enthusiasm of the players made the most global tour feel that way.

Lost in the battle of Park and Lewis for the season awards, and the emergence of Ko, was the most endearing of the major championships. Mo Martin, who had never won on the LPGA Tour, grinded her way across Royal Birkdale in the Ricoh Women's British Open. This was a great chance for Park to capture the career Grand Slam, but that was until Martin stepped up and hit what could also be considered for the shot of the year. Her three wood rolled onto the green at the par-five 18th and struck the pin solidly, settling six feet away for an eagle in a one-shot victory. "When it was in the air, I said, 'Sit.' And then I said, 'Stop.' And then when it was going toward the hole, I said, 'OK, I don't have anything more to say to that ball.' I actually heard it hit the pin. It's definitely one to remember," Martin said.

In a roundabout way, gender also was an issue in one of the few controversies of the year. Ted Bishop was finishing up his two-year term as president of the PGA of America and was still smarting over another American loss in the Ryder Cup. It was Bishop who decided to make Tom Watson, 65, the oldest Ryder Cup captain in history. The move backfired when Watson was criticized for benching Mickelson in both Saturday matches. Ian Poulter mentioned as much in the book he wrote, and Poulter also took issue with Nick Faldo criticizing the play of Sergio Garcia when Faldo was the European captain in 2008. Bishop was perturbed that Poulter would have audacity to treat two Hall of Fame players like that, and referred to his complaining as a "lil girl" on Twitter and on Facebook. It was seen as disparaging to females, and the uproar was so great that the PGA of America ousted Bishop as president in his final month, and stripped him of all privileges and access typically afforded past presidents.

Another messy moment for golf was when Dustin Johnson decided to take a break from the game to seek professional help for what he described as "personal challenges." Golf.com reported he had been suspended for six months for failing a drug test for the third time. Either way, one of the best Americans was out of action the rest of the year. He was No. 4 in the FedExCup standings and a lock to make the Ryder Cup team. With so much attention on the captains — questions over Watson's decision, praise of Paul McGinley pushing all the right buttons for Europe — rarely discussed that week in Gleneagles is that the Americans did not have Tiger Woods or Dustin Johnson. Who would have guessed that at the start of 2014?

The names change but never the surprises. Go back to the start of the year. Woods was No. 1 in the world coming off a five-win season. He finished the year at No. 390 on the World Money List after only completing 72 holes in four tournaments. The major champions were all familiar, though it is worth noting that this was the first time since 2000 that there were no first-time winners in the Grand Slam events. That year, Vijay Singh won his second major at the Masters, and then Woods won the next three on his way to an unprecedented sweep of the majors.

Was McIlroy headed down the same path? The characters have changed. The competition was never stronger.

2. Masters Tournament

It's not hard to imagine that for people who chart history, the 2014 Masters was barely over and they could hardly wait for the 2015 edition. Question: Was the 2014 Masters merely a case of Bubba Watson winning his second green jacket in a three-year span, or would it have far greater significance some day?

That is, was it the start of the Bubba Watson Era?

It can be argued there are three Masters eras — distinct periods in which a given golfer dominated: the Arnold Palmer (his four wins from 1958 through 1964); the Jack Nicklaus (six wins, five from 1963 through 1975 plus the historic sixth in 1986 at age 46), and the Tiger Woods (four, 1997 through 2005, and holding, depending on health).

It's foolish to predict in the Masters, but speculation is permissible, and in this case, Bubba Watson seems so in harmony with the demands and temptations of the pristine course that it's reasonable to expect him to win more. He has prodigious length, he has a short game that brushes off the modest rough, he can shape shots despite the grudging technology of the modern golf ball, and he can putt the treacherous Augusta National greens. That sounds like a formula for success.

In 2015, he will be shooting to join the five who won three times, including Phil Mickelson, who of course will be trying to join the four-time winners. Or could Watson end up with the eight who now are forever stuck on two?

"A small-town guy named Bubba now has two green jackets," Watson said, that Sunday evening of April 13, 2014, and it was clear from the tone of his statement that he wasn't willing to settle for just two. He has reached a point in golf history.

There were other historical moments in the 2014 Masters:

• Tiger Woods, 38, after surgery for a pinched back nerve, missed his first Masters since he began playing in 1995. This stalled his quest for his fifth Masters and his 15th major in pursuit of Jack Nicklaus' record of 18.

• Augusta National's efforts to boost golf entered the kid stage in a big way with the first Drive, Chip and Putt National Championship, with the final conducted the Sunday of Masters week at the club. The program is a collaborative effort of the Masters, the U.S. Golf Association and the PGA of America to attract young people to golf. Masters Chairman Billy Payne said the plan was to expand the qualifying system to all 50 states for 2015, hoping to attract some 50,000 entrants.

• Ike, nearly 50 years after his death, finally got his wish. The "Eisenhower Tree" was gone. The 65-foot tall Loblolly Pine some 210 yards down the fairway at the par-four 17th had to be removed after being severely damaged in a February ice storm. The tree so tormented President Dwight Eisenhower that he proposed it be removed. Cliff Roberts, then chairman of Augusta National, said no. Seems it was more of an irritant than a hazard. Since 1980, the toughest the hole played with the tree was at an average of 4.306 in 1999. In 2014, without the tree, it played at 4.24.

• A record 24 first-time players were in the starting field of 97, topping the previous high of 22 in 1935, the second Masters. What chance did a first-timer have of winning? History says practically none. Apart from Horton Smith in the first Masters in 1934, only two did it — Gene Sarazen in 1935 and Fuzzy Zoeller in 1979.

First Round

Phil Mickelson lost a dollar bet in practice to a taunting fan because he couldn't get up and down at a hole. That's all he was going to lose in this Masters, Mickelson insisted. He was in great shape, thanks to a workout regimen. "I'm able to swing as hard as I want and hit the shots I need to hit," he said. And so he set out firmly resolved in the first round, but by No. 7, where he triggered a triple-bogey-seven by chipping all the way off the green from the back, his chances for a fourth Masters title were iffy. By the par-five 15th, after another seven, the halfway cut was his goal. "I've got a lot of work to do," Mickelson said.

So this Masters was back to square one looking for a favorite, and the role fell not to Bill Haas, who took the first-round lead with his four-under-par 68, but to Adam Scott and Bubba Watson, who had been there and done that. Scott was the defending champion and Watson won the year before, in 2012, and both spoke of a certain comfort that comes with winning a Masters. As Watson put it: "The comfort level is knowing you have a green jacket already." They tied for second at 69, along with Louis Oosthuizen, playoff runner-up to Watson in 2012. Augusta National was playing so firm and fast that these were the only four scores in the 60s in the first round.

Watson, who prided himself on being a small-town guy from Bagdad, Florida (pop., about 1,500), was pleased that the spotlight had shifted and the attention had eased. "I haven't had any media this week, because nobody cares about the guy [who won] a couple years ago," Watson said. "So it's been good." Watson logged three easy birdies, first at the third, then playing to his strength — power — at both back-nine par-fives, the 13th and 15th. Scott was four under through the 11th, then double-bogeyed the vexing little 12th after watering his tee shot. Fans had given him a standing ovation as he approached the 12th tee. "But then I went and hit it in the water," he said.

Haas, 31, whose best in four previous Masters was a tie for 20th, brushed off an opening bogey, birdied five of the next 15 holes, bogeyed the 17th, then birdied the 18th for his all-time Masters low, a 68. Three of his birdies were longer than 20 feet, and the last, a four-footer, was one of only four at the 18th all day. Haas, a five-time winner on the PGA Tour, wasn't celebrating anything yet. "I know that I can't expect too much," he said. He had one thought: Hitting the fairway at No. 1 tomorrow.

That first Masters comes as quite a shock, or at least a revelation. There were a record 24 first-timers this year, and three of them found the debut exhilarating, joining a seven-way tie for fifth at 70. Kevin Stadler was a toddler when his dad, Craig, won the Masters in 1982. Now Kevin, 34, and Craig, 60, were the first father-son combination in the same Masters. Craig, playing four groups later, shot 82. And now in the field on his winner's lifetime exemption, Craig allowed as how these days, the Masters is more fun outside the ropes.

Kevin bunched four birdies and two bogeys in the middle nine holes.

Jimmy Walker, a three-time winner on the tour this season, admitted his first Masters might have gone totally sour after he hit a tree and bogeyed the 13th to go two over. "But you can't do that to yourself," he said. He birdied the next four. Jonas Blixt made six birdies and needed just 27 putts — amazing for a rookie — but the 26th cost him a share of the lead. It was a 15-foot par putt that rimmed the cup and left him a tap-in for his fourth bogey and a 70. "That was a little heart-breaker," Blixt said, "but I made a lot of putts on the front, so I can't really complain."

If some first-timers found Augusta National hospitable, some veterans surely did not. Luke Donald, former No. 1 in the world, accidentally grounded his club in a bunker and made eight on the par-four No. 9 and shot 79. Jason Dufner was out in par 36, but got crushed coming in. He double-bogeyed the 10th, then at the par-five 13th crashed to a nine, the highest score of the day, after reaching the greenside rough in two. Simple and cruel: His chip ran across the front of the green and down the bank and into the stream, and his splash-out from shallow water came back down to him. He shot 80.

Rory McIlroy — was he emerging from his slump? — hit 15 greens in his 71, but needed 34 putts. He three-putted three times, bogeying each time, at Nos. 8, 12 and 18. "It's about putting your ball in the right place," he said. "That hasn't been my forte, but I'll learn to love it this week."

The senior contingent was looking good. Spain's Miguel Angel Jimenez, 50, rushed off to a four-birdie 32 going out, but a bogey at the 11th and a double bogey at the 12th brought him in at 71, three off the lead. "I played beautiful golf today," he said. "Only two holes, I made bad mistakes." Bernhard Langer, 56, owner of two green jackets, also double-bogeyed the 12th, but wasn't crying. "A 72 is not that shabby," he said. And Fred Couples, 54, the 1992 champ, had a three-birdie 71. "Can a 50-year-old win here?" Couples said, answering a question. "I think so. I'm one of them."

First-Round Leaders: Bill Haas 68, Adam Scott 69, Bubba Watson 69, Louis Oosthuizen 69, Kevin Stadler 70, Jonas Blixt 70, Gary Woodland 70, Jimmy Walker 70, K.J. Choi 70, Brandt Snedeker 70, Marc Leishman 70.

Second Round

Years ago, the world wouldn't have known how Canadian Graham DeLaet felt about his first and failed appearance in the Masters. But this is the age of social media. So through Twitter, the world knew immediately after he shot 80-72 and missed the cut badly. "Still the best week of my life," DeLaet wrote.

The second round was a day of impressive bursts, such as Bubba Watson sprinting to five straight birdies for a 68 and the second-round lead; Australia's John Senden, having his best Masters round and taking second; defending champion Adam Scott, lifting himself out of a slide, and Jim Furyk moving into contention. And think of the tales Thongchai Jaidee could take back to Thailand, reaching the weekend for the first time in his three Masters. And the reverse was painfully true for others, among them, Gary Woodland, staggering down the homestretch to four straight bogeys to a 77; Rory McIlroy, with two double bogeys, shooting 77 and making the cut by the skin of his teeth; Bill Haas, the first-round leader, with a train-wreck of a back nine, and the awesome plunge of Marc Leishman.

After his opening 68, Haas soared to a 78. The crash came without warning. One moment he was still four under for the tournament. Next, a fat uphill approach at No. 9 send him spiraling into a bogey-bogey-double bogey-bogey-bogey dive. He made the cut by two, but he'd dug himself a hole he couldn't climb out of. "At least I'll be around for the weekend," Haas said

But others couldn't say as much when the halfway cut struck Friday afternoon. The unkindest cut of all — a candidate for "Worst Ever" — felled Leishman, an Aussie in his third Masters. After an opening 70, he blazed into the second round with a birdie-birdie-birdie start and a share of the lead. From there, it was out the door. He went 10 over par on the last 14 holes. Starting at No. 4, Leishman took six bogeys and two double bogeys for a 79 and a 149 total, missing the cut by one. "It started good," a stunned Leishman said, "and just went from bad to worse."

Phil Mickelson, after his 76 start, was battling just to make the cut. Then he crashed to a nightmarish triple bogey at the par-three 12th. He blasted out of the front bunker, across the green into a back bunker, then blasted back into the front bunker, where he'd started. He made six, his second triple bogey of the tournament, shot 73 and missed by one — his second miss in 22 Masters. Luke Donald came back from a 79 but fell short with a bogey at the 18th, and Sergio Garcia bogeyed the last two and was gone. The cut, at four-over 148, left 51 players for the final two rounds.

Watson parred the first six holes, birdied the seventh, then made his first bogey of the tournament at the ninth. He caught fire coming in, racing to five straight birdies. The streak started at the par-three 12th, off a lofty nine iron to four feet. He got up and down at both par-fives, the 13th and 15th. The lifesaver came in between, at the par-four 14th. Watson had put his second shot on the undulating green some 40 feet from the hole. Fortunately, he could go to school on Sergio Garcia's chip shot from just off the green. Watson was amazed by the huge break. "Without Sergio's chip, I probably would have three-putted," Watson said. He sent his ball wide to the right and watched it take a huge swing to the left and roll right into the cup for a birdie. Then he birdied the par-three, 170-yard 16th after nearly acing it. "I hit a great nine iron downwind," Watson said. The ball landed softly to the right and trickled down to within four feet of the flag. Then the 18th got away from him. He missed the green, then missed his four-footer for par and finished with his second bogey of the day and only the second of the first two rounds.

Watson's 68 gave him his first 36-hole lead in six Masters, leaving a United Nations pileup behind him. Senden, an Australian, was three behind after his 68 and 140, both his Masters best. Four tied for third behind him: Denmark's Thomas Bjorn (68) played the last five holes in four birdies and a bogey; Sweden's Jonas Blixt (71), a first-timer, stumbled to a double-bogey-six at the 11th; defending champion Adam Scott (72) righted himself with three birdies coming in after making three bogeys going out, and Jordan Spieth.

Spieth, a rapidly maturing 20-year-old, already ranked 13th in the world and was very much part of the chase. First-timers, if they've had a good first round, generally start to show nerves in the second. But Spieth shot 71-70. Of his three bogeys, the first at No. 1, suggested nerves. That kind of start generally would set a rookie's nerves jangling. Not Spieth. He went on to birdie twice on the front, and got his first Masters eagle at the par-five 15th. His biggest concern? Ben Crenshaw, a two-time champion, told him the problem would be emotions.

"Mr. Crenshaw [did Ben ever foresee the day when a fellow pro would be calling him 'Mr.'?] says ... the Masters brings out emotion in guys that aren't emotional," Spieth said. "I'm already emotional, and I have to keep it on the down-low."

The third round should be an interesting test.

Watson reduces the game to its ideal basics: fairways and greens. "It's not science here," Watson said. "It's — try to hit the greens, and if you're hitting the greens, that means you're obviously hitting your tee shots well. So that's really all I was doing and that's what I've done the last two days, and it's worked out so far."

In fact, it worked so well, Watson was 20-for-28 in fairways hit and 28-for-36 in greens. (Of course, it helped that after he had 32 putts in the first round, he needed just 26 in the second.) He'd made only two bogeys, both in the second round, when he missed the greens at Nos. 9 and 18, and missed four-footers for par each time. A couple more days of this and that spotlight would be back.

Second-Round Leaders: Bubba Watson 68–137, John Senden 68–140, Thomas Bjorn 68–141, Jonas Blixt 71–141, Adam Scott 72–141, Jordan Spieth 70–141, Fred Couples 71–142, Jimmy Walker 72–142, Jim Furyk 68–142.

Third Round

When the leader — the champion just two years ago — starts bogey-eagle; when a rookie of 20 whose nerves should be frazzled is playing like a crusty vet; when a 50-year-old hurls himself onto the threshold of history, and when the round ends with 13 golfers within four strokes of the lead — all of them within reach on a firmer, faster, more demanding Augusta National, what do we call all that?

The word "chaos" comes to mind, and that was the word stamped on the third round of this 2014 Masters.

Said Bubba Watson, who led by three going into the third round and was tied coming out: "It was a difficult round. The greens have really firmed up a lot. They're faster and harder than the day before. They're the firmest I've seen them in years."

Jim Furyk, who jumped into contention, put something of a number on it. "I found maybe six ball marks, at most, today," he said.

Miguel Angel Jimenez, however, found the course most welcoming in the morning, even to a 50-year-old. And he was bidding to make history — the oldest to win the Masters, replacing Jack Nicklaus, who did it at 46. And also the oldest ever to win a major. Jimenez was in the Masters as a kind of stop-off on his way to making his debut in the Champions Tour (over 50) in the nearby Greater Gwinnett Championship. He birdied twice on the front nine, then got cracking on the back. He birdied the 10th and 11th, tripped over the par-three 12th, and brushed off that bogey and nearly eagled the par-five 13th, getting a birdie after his bunker shot hit the flagstick. He birdied the 14th and 16th as well for a 66 (which would hold up as the tournament-low) and a tie for fifth, two off the lead. "Sometimes you feel that good," he said, "that you want to see the birdies coming before you hit the shot."

Rory McIlroy, first off alone in the morning (with a non-scoring marker), was asked about the chances of someone catching up with Watson. "I think," said McIlroy, noting that the course was getting firmer and faster, "it will be more about if Bubba comes back to the field." And Bubba would come back, and throw this Masters into a tizzy.

But first, the field was busy sorting itself out. For Adam Scott, chances for a repeat title were all but dead. He was four behind Watson starting out, then bogeyed No. 1 and double-bogeyed No. 4 after missing the green. Scott shot 76 and finished six behind, but refused to give up. "There are a lot of people between me and the leader," Scott said. "It would be fun to post a number and sit in the clubhouse and watch." Gary Woodland found plenty of touch to go with his power and roared off, tying the Masters front-nine record with a 30 that included four birdies and an eagle at the par-five No. 2, off a seven iron to two feet. Still hot, he birdied the 10th, then took a chill and shot 39 coming home for a 69. "I was trying to birdie every hole," said Woodland, five off the lead and swallowing the frustration. "I just have to say I shot three under and move on."

While Jimenez was trying to become the oldest winner, Jordan Spieth, at 20, was trying to become the youngest. He was also trying to become the first first-timer to win in 35 years, since Fuzzy Zoeller in 1979. So was Sweden's Jonas Blixt, older at 29 but just as determined as Spieth. Blixt scattered four birdies but bunched three bogeys on the back nine for a 71 and would tie for third with the Matt Kuchar, a Masters fixture, one off the lead. Blixt averaged some 27 putts per round and had yet to three-putt. "I'm putting really well right now," Blixt said. "I feel like almost everything in my bag is working well. If I can put the ball in the fairway tomorrow, I think I'll be dangerous."

Watson seemed to take control after a bogey at No. 1. At the par-five No. 2, he fired a downhill seven-iron second to six feet and made the eagle. Then his putting touch turned iffy. He three-putted twice and needed 33 putts all told. And his iron play turned erratic. He hit only 12 greens. It could have been an alarming sign, but wasn't. "A lot of my bogeys were long or short," Watson said. "It wasn't left or right, so I'm not too worried." His two-over 74 tied him at five-under 211 with Spieth, who had finished about a half hour earlier. Watson wasn't concerned about his day's work. "If somebody told me on Monday I'd have a 74 and still be tied for the lead, I'd have taken it all day long," Watson said.

Spieth, on the other hand, had a smoother time of it, with two widely scattered bogeys and four birdies, including back-to-backs from the 13th. He clinched his 70 with a strong par from a fairway bunker at the 18th. So Watson and Spieth, sharing a one-stroke lead, would be in the final pairing in the last round.

Third-Round Leaders: Bubba Watson 74–211, Jordan Spieth 70–211, Jonas Blixt 71–212, Matt Kuchar 68–212, Miguel Angel Jimenez 66–213, Rickie Fowler 67–213, Lee Westwood 70–214, Jim Furyk 72–214, Thomas Bjorn 73–214.

Fourth Round

Bubba Watson did not have to invent a wild, exhilarating, impossible hook wedge out of the trees this time, they way he did when he won his first Masters, in 2012. No, this time he had such riches that he could afford a little banter with his caddie on the final green. Watson came to Augusta's 18th on in two, leading by three, and looking at a 15-footer for birdie.

"I went over to him," Watson said with a chuckle, "and I said to him, 'I'm not very good at math, but we've got four putts, right?'"

Watson used just two, parring the final hole for a three-under 69 and a three-stroke win over Jordan Spieth, who had come so close to winning his first major and becoming the youngest to win the Masters.

Most Masters begin on the back nine on Sunday, but this one was pretty much over on the front.

History flitted from Spieth's eager fingertips on two weak shots, at the eighth and ninth, both costing him bogeys and abruptly reversing him from leading to trailing when Watson birdied both and would be too tough to catch.

If there were any surprises in the final round, it was the succession of clubhouse leaders. Two-time champion Bernhard Langer, 56, now a Champions Tour star, closed with a 69 and a par 288 total. England's Lee Westwood followed with 73–287, then Rickie Fowler at 73–286, then the amazing Miguel Angel Jimenez. His bid to make history at the age of 50 ended with three early bogeys. "It's not enough putter," Jimenez said, after his 71 and four-under 284. He finished fourth.

A free-for-all was set for the final round, with nine players separated by only three strokes. Matt Kuchar tied for the lead with two quick birdies, then fizzled with a four-putt double bogey at No. 4. Fowler's try ended with bogeys at the 10th and 11th. Jonas Blixt opened one shot out of the lead but never really challenged, shot 71 and tied for second with Spieth.

But the round developed into a Bubba Watson-Jordan Spieth show. And Spieth was on his way to those landmarks. He broke the tie with a birdie at No. 2 and went two up on Watson's bogey at No. 3. At the par-three fourth, playing 222 yards, Watson stuck his five-iron tee shot to six feet. He made the putt, and had to because Spieth beat him to the birdie by holing out from a bunker. Spieth's lead slipped to one on a bogey at No. 5, and after both birdied No. 6, Spieth birdied the seventh and was two ahead coming to the pivotal point of this Masters.

At the uphill, par-five No. 8, Spieth missed the green with his second shot, and from a short distance, hit what he thought was a good pitch. He was stunned when the ball stopped rolling 30 feet short of the flag. He three-putted and bogeyed, and Watson birdied. They were tied on the two-shot swing. Worse for Spieth, at the par-four No. 9, his uphill nine-iron approach didn't clear the false front and the ball came rolling back down into the fairway. Watson birdied again and led by two. Then he bogeyed the 10th.

Spieth hurt himself again with yet another weak shot, this at the par-three 12th. His tee shot came down short on the bank and trickled into the water. A bogey put him two behind.

Watson all but clinched it at the par-five 13th with a stunning tee shot that was both thunderous and lucky as he cut around the trees at the dogleg-left.

"It was cutting a little too much," Watson said. "I hit it really hard. When you get a roar on your tee shot, you know it's pretty good." It was more than just pretty good. It nicked a tree, but instead of caroming left into the trees, it kicked right, back into the fairway. It was a drive of some 360 yards, leaving him just a sand wedge to the green. He birdied and was up by three. Spieth parred in for a 72–283, tying Blixt for second.

Watson then would have his little fun at the 18th, use two of the four putts he joked about, post his 69–280 and win by three, and be greeted by his wife Angie and their son Caleb, 2. Then it really hit him.

"Small-town guy named Bubba now has two green jackets," Watson said. "It's pretty wild."

The Final Leaders: Bubba Watson 69–280, Jordan Spieth 72–283, Jonas Blixt 71–283, Miguel Angel Jimenez 71–284, Rickie Fowler 73–286, Matt Kuchar 74–286.

3. U.S. Open Championship

One wonders — if Donald Ross were still alive, would Pinehurst No. 2 be done yet? History tells us that Ross was forever changing and fidgeting and tweaking his magnum opus, almost until his death in 1948. It was as though da Vinci had never quit taking the brush to the *Mona Lisa*. Ross is said to have done some 400 courses, and of them all, No. 2 was his favorite. "The fairest test of golf I have ever designed," he called it.

Given all of Ross' changes, he might be the only one who would recognize No. 2 when the U.S. Open and U.S. Women's Open came to the course in 2014. Most if not all courses that have hosted the U.S. Open for decades have gone through changes, but probably none went through the upheaval that returned No. 2 to the days of Donald Ross.

It's said that when course architects Bill Coore and Ben Crenshaw were through with their "restoration," No. 2 looked like the course Ross would remember and not the one that hosted the 1999 and 2005 U.S. Opens. First off — it was no longer a classic U.S. Open course with demanding rough and narrow fairways. Coore and Crenshaw ripped out some 35 acres of Bermuda rough and replaced it with sandy waste areas and various native vegetation. "It's what they want to call undergrowth," said two-time U.S. Open champion Curtis Strange. "I call it weeds." The fairways were not the standard USGA-issue 25-or-so yards wide, but 40. But golfers, Strange allowed, still had better hit the fairways. Hitting out of what had replaced rough would not be inviting.

No. 2's principal problem remained the turtleback greens, which Ross installed in the 1930s, a far cry from the original flat sand greens. The turtlebacks made approach shots chancy, chipping problematic and putting frustrating. Ross put it this way: "This mounding makes possible an infinite variety of nasty short shots that no other form of hazard can call for. Competitors whose second shots have wandered a bit will be disturbed by these innocent appearing slopes and by the shot they will have to invent to recover."

Some in the field had played No. 2 before, but not this No. 2. It would be pretty much a new experience for everyone.

"I love the waste areas to the side," said Jordan Spieth, in his third U.S. Open. "I've never played anything like it. And it's already — with the pins in the middle of the greens — hard enough for even par to win."

Phil Mickelson, runner-up to Payne Stewart at No. 2 in 1999, admired No. 2 for its flexibility. "The golf course here gives you a variety of options off the tee," he said. "There's really two or three clubs every single hole that you could choose to hit. ... The greens are so repellant that you need to get as close to them as possible. So if you can get the ball closer to the green off the tee, and hit driver, I think it's worth it."

Mike Davis, executive director of the USGA and instrumental in getting the U.S. Open to No. 2, praised Coore and Crenshaw. "The accolades they are receiving are so deserved," Davis said. "Their vision, the fact that they respected Donald Ross and the original architecture and went back to the

1930s, 1940s and just said, let's restore it to that, I don't think anybody — in fact, if you're a golf course architectural aficionado, you couldn't have imagined that it would have come out this great."

First Round

The 2014 U.S. Open got under way with one dream on hold and another beckoning like a paradise island on the distant horizon.

On hold: Tiger Woods' hopes for a fourth U.S. Open and a 15th major. "Unfortunately, I won't be there because I'm not yet physically able to play competitive golf," Woods announced. He was still recovering from the March 31 surgery for a pinched nerve.

The dream beckoning: Phil Mickelson was by far the sympathetic favorite. The U.S. Open had been taunting him for years. He finished second an amazing six times — three solos, three ties.

It was at Pinehurst in 1999 that he came close and lost for the first time. He was anxious that week, playing with a pager in his bag, ready to quit instantly and head home for the birth of his first child (Amanda arrived on Monday). On the last hole, Payne Stewart beat him on a 15-foot par putt. Four months later, Stewart died in an eerie plane accident.

Mickelson, who would turn 44 in a few days, needed the U.S. Open to complete his career Grand Slam. "I feel like the five players that have done that, have separated themselves from the other players throughout all time," he said. "If I'm able to do that, I feel that I would look upon my own career differently." But he would have to wait another year. He got off to a good start, a three-birdie, three-bogey par 70. He would tail off from there and tie for 28th.

With Woods absent, Mickelson playing so-so and Rory McIlroy still slumping, who might step into the power vacuum?

The single-round scoring record for the U.S. Open was 63, shot by Johnny Miller in the final round as he raced to the 1973 championship. It's also the record in the other three majors. As the 2014 Open got under way, it seemed another 63 might be in the making.

The personable Martin Kaymer, 29, was the best German golfer to come along since the world-class Bernhard Langer, who was now all but ruling the over-50s on the Champions Tour. Up to this point, in mid-June 2014, Kaymer had some quick flashes of fame.

First, as an almost unknown, he won the 2010 PGA Championship. Second, he was World No. 1 briefly and, he said, most uncomfortably. He fell into a mysterious slump. Later, he sank the putt that won for Europe in the 2012 Ryder Cup.

It turned out there was no real mystery to the slump. Kaymer was trying to change his swing, to improve his game, with predictable early results: frustration.

Kaymer resurfaced in 2014, winning The Players Championship in May. A month later, he was handling Pinehurst No. 2, a retooled classic, like the town muni.

Kaymer posted six birdies against just one bogey for a five-under-par 65, a U.S. Open record for Pinehurst, and a three-stroke lead on a well-mixed group of four — Graeme McDowell, who won the 2010 U.S. Open at Pebble

Beach; Korean-born American Kevin Na; beefy Zimbabwean Brendon de Jonge, who can make birdies in bunches, and most unlikely of all, Fran Quinn, 46, of Worcester, Massachusetts, a little-known pro who had to come through both local and sectional qualifiers to get into the field.

A 65 was the last thing Kaymer expected. He told a writer, after a practice round, that he'd take eight over for the championship, that's how tough the course was playing.

Opening day caught him by surprise. "It was more playable than I thought," Kaymer said. "I think that you feel like there are actually some birdies out there, not only bogeys. Obviously, they softened the conditions a little bit..."

His record 65 began with a birdie at the par-four No. 1, on a wedge to three feet. At the 576-yard No. 5, one of only two par-fives, he cut a three wood to 20 feet and two putted. No. 10, the other par-five, fell to an 85-yard wedge to two feet. He rushed in with three tightly packed birdies — a three-foot putt at the 14th, a six iron to 10 feet at the 16th, and at the par-three 17th, a six-iron tee shot to 10 feet. His lone bogey came at the seventh. He should have chipped, he figured, rather than try to negotiate the turtleback green with a putter.

Bubba Watson, just two months after winning his second Masters, couldn't find the secret to No. 2. "This course," he said, after a 76, "is better than me right now." Some others might say the same thing: Lee Westwood shot 75, Luke Donald 77 and 2009 U.S. Open champion Lucaș Glover 79.

Adam Scott, the World No. 1, was barely fazed by his 73. "You know how it's going to be at the end of the week," he said. "We're going to be looking at even par, or something around that."

There was one other star in the first round: the improbable Fran Quinn, age 49, a Web.com Tour player, who had to qualify to get into the field. In other words, the spirit of the U.S. Open. With some crisp iron play, Quinn had a four-birdie, two-bogey 68, and conceded it was only one round. "But ... it was a dream start," he said. "It was everything I could want and more."

For Kaymer, tomorrow would be another day, another set of golf problems. "So no one really should expect me to shoot another five under par the next three rounds," he said. "I don't."

First-Round Leaders: Martin Kaymer 65, Brendon de Jonge 68, Graeme McDowell 68, Kevin Na 68, Fran Quinn 68.

Second Round

Martin Kaymer left the first round cautioning people not to expect another 65 from him. "I don't," he had offered. Then to everyone's amazement, including his own, he did it again, and led Brendon Todd by six strokes. Kaymer had just one bogey in the first 36 holes, and that was in the first round.

"I heard he played the No. 3 course — is that true?" Kevin Na cracked. Na himself followed his opening 68 with a 69, and he stood at three-under 137, a good number in a U.S. Open. But he found himself seven shots behind Kaymer. "It's unbelievable what he's doing," Na said. "Is four or five out there? Yes. Ten under out there? No, I don't think so."

Said World No. 1 Adam Scott: "If he does it for two more days, we're all playing for second spot." Two more 65s? That would be off the charts for a U.S. Open.

Kaymer started at the par-five 10th, flipping a wedge to five feet for his first birdie. He followed with long putts at the 13th and 16th, from 20 and 25 feet. Coming in, he plucked a birdie at the risk-reward par-four No. 3, playing at 315 yards. He threaded his tee shot between the front bunkers and onto the green, and two-putted. Then two putts from the front at the par-five fifth brought him his second 65. But it wasn't as easy as it looked. He made three straight tough par saves, out of bunkers at the difficult par-three sixth and the seventh, and two putts from the front at the eighth. Two 65s in a U.S. Open?

"Somebody has to do it at one stage," Kaymer said. "I think that you need to play very solid and you need a little bit of luck here and there, and that was on my side so far. It's quite nice. I'm enjoying it."

Todd, who scored his first win in the Byron Nelson Classic just weeks earlier — and playing in his first major — cut Kaymer's lead to six with a bogey-free 67. "He's playing a brand of golf we haven't seen in a long time," Todd said.

Kaymer's 130 tied the U.S. Open record for the biggest halfway lead set by Tiger Woods in 2000 at Pebble Beach (he won by 15) and tied by Rory McIlroy at Congressional in 2011 (he won by eight).

Said Kaymer: "I played Congressional and I thought, 'How can you shoot that low?' And that's probably what a lot of people think about me right now."

McIlroy, no stranger to low scoring, was pleased with a 68 and a one-under 139. For a U.S. Open. "But what Martin has done over the first couple of days has made a one-under look pretty average," McIlroy said. Dustin Johnson was one better at 69–138 and noted: "I wouldn't have thought it would be eight shots behind."

The Grand Slam was safe for another year. Bubba Watson, who won the Masters with such ease in April, shot 70 and fell one stroke short of making the cut. And the strange story of Luke Donald went grinding on. Donald, ranked No. 1 in the world as late as 2012, shot 77-69 and missed the cut for the fourth consecutive major. He had company from golf's elite: Jason Dufner, former PGA Champion; Angel Cabrera, who won both the U.S. Open and the Masters, and the ever-threatening Lee Westwood. The cut left 67 players who scored 145 or better.

At day's end, Kaymer's closest pursuit was strung out comfortably behind him — Todd six behind, Na and Brandt Snedeker seven, five others eight. He quickly formulated a game plan for the third round — for everyone else.

"I would like to see it as tough as possible," he said. "I was always a fan of a golf course where you need to hit good golf shots and not really have a putting competition."

Second-Round Leaders: Martin Kaymer 65–130, Brendon Todd 67–136, Kevin Na 69–137, Brandt Snedeker 68–137, Keegan Bradley 69–138, Brendon de Jonge 70–138, Dustin Johnson 69–138, Brooks Koepka 68–138, Henrik Stenson 69–138.

Third Round

Not that they'd given up, but golfers tend to be realists, and so it was becoming pretty clear that this U.S. Open was over, all but the battle for second place. Martin Kaymer had taken the best No. 2 could throw at him — the scruffy growth, the sand, the turtleback greens — taken them all and shrugged them off. Granted, it took a bigger shrug on Saturday.

With Pinehurst No. 2 under high heat and with pins riding the shoulders of the turtleback greens, Kaymer shot a two-over 72 — his first round over par — and if anyone was playing a different course, as the joke goes, it was Rickie Fowler and Erik Compton. They shot three-under 67s, the only two rounds under par for the day.

"They've set it up so that no one can go low," said Retief Goosen, a two-time U.S. Open champion, after a 71. "Some of the pins look like they're about to fall off the green."

Erik Compton, the man with his second heart transplant, had an eagle, five birdies and four bogeys for his 67. He got the eagle at the 576-yard, par-five fifth, on a drive and a four iron from 237 yards and one putt, and figured it was more than just a three. He dreaded the score he might have made if he'd missed that approach. "If it gets down there on that left side, you could spend all day there chipping," Compton said.

There was still a considerable distance between him and Kaymer — five strokes — but Compton could at least think of what winning the U.S. Open would mean.

"It would mean the absolute world to me," said Compton, a heroic figure wherever golf is played. "It would be something extremely special, not only for me, but for my family and for those who have been around me, and I think also for the community and those who have been through some tough times. I might," he added, laughing, "just sail off and never play golf again."

Fowler, who's almost as much teen idol as golfer, solved the tricky pins for five birdies, none more elegant that the one at the par-three 17th, playing 180 yards. "Some of the pins were tucked more close to the edges," he said. "If you got it two paces in the wrong direction, you were off the green and quite a ways away." After seeing Steve Stricker's six-iron tee shot go long, he took his seven iron to attack a pin on the right. "Probably hit about a 10- to 15-yard cut," he said. It came down perfectly, pin high and about 15 feet from the cup.

For all of the beauty of their 67s, Compton and Fowler, tied for second at 207, were five big strokes behind.

"If you're four shots, five shots, six shots [ahead], if you play a golf course like this, it can be gone very quickly," Kaymer said. "You could see it today. So the challenge tomorrow is to keep going."

Kaymer made two bogeys in a hurry. He was short of the green at the par-four second and didn't get up and down, and thus ended a streak of 30 holes without a bogey. Then his bogey at the par-four No. 4 was of museum quality. He hooked his drive, and his ball ended up in a washed-out sandy area and against a thick stack of pine straw, a predicament that left him without an out but didn't dent his sense of humor. He turned to the rules official, who happened to be Tom O'Toole, president of the U.S. Golf Association. "If you have a way to play it," Kaymer said, "I'll follow you." Kaymer took a penalty drop for the unplayable lie, punched out to the fairway, and from 165 yards stuck his approach to 15 feet and dropped the putt for a bogey that could have been much worse. He came back with at eagle at No. 5, and after scattering three bogeys through the 15th, he birdied the 18th for a 72. For all of his struggles, he had dropped just a shot of his lead. He was five ahead going into the final round.

The time came for any and all challengers, such as they were, to get a read on the final round.

• Compton, five strokes back: "I have nothing to lose. Nobody expects me to do anything. So … if I shoot 90, I don't think anybody will be surprised. But if I shoot 67 again, you may be surprised."

• Fowler, five behind: "I look at it as similar to what Bubba [Watson] was doing at the Masters. He was so far out in front that you can't focus on him."

• Dustin Johnson, who hit a nine iron left-handed, upside-down to escape from under a bush and still parred No. 7, six behind: "I've yet to feel like I've played a great round of golf. It's in there. Anything can happen. It's a U.S. Open."

• Brooks Koepka, eight behind: "I just got to take care of business. You never know what can happen. … you are never too far out of it … in a U.S. Open."

For all of their good spirits and resolve, Kaymer didn't leave them much to grasp at. For anyone thinking he would protect his lead in the final round, he had this statement of intent: "If you think of defending anything, then you're pulling back, and that's never really a good thing. You just want to keep going."

Third-Round Leaders: Martin Kaymer 72–202, Erik Compton 67–207, Rickie Fowler 67–207, Dustin Johnson 70–208, Henrik Stenson 70–208, Brandt Snedeker 72–209.

Fourth Round

There was something fair about golf after all.

It was only fair that the battle for second place in this 2014 U.S. Open was fought to a draw. Rickie Fowler and Erik Compton had started the fourth round tied for second, and because they were the closest in the hunt for Martin Kaymer, they had to endure the greatest sense of futility. So it was only fair that they share in the greatest success — after Kaymer, of course. Both shot two-over 72 and tied for second at one-under 279, the best finish ever in a U.S. Open for both. Without Kaymer, this would have been a crackling U.S. Open finish. Eight players were within three strokes of Fowler and Compton. But 10 from Kaymer.

This U.S. Open had been over for some time, perhaps since the second round. It just needed the formal completion of 72 holes. Kaymer did it with a 69 in the fourth round and a nine-under total of 271 to win by eight, achieving these distinctions:

• He was the seventh winner to lead wire-to-wire in the championship's 114 years.

• He was the first player from continental Europe to win a U.S. Open.

• He extended European domination of the American national championship, becoming the fourth European in five years to win the U.S. Open, following Graeme McDowell, Northern Ireland (2010); Rory McIlroy, Northern Ireland (2011), and Justin Rose, England (2013). American Webb Simpson interrupted this reign in 2012.

"I would say it was probably the toughest day that I played golf, today," Kaymer said. "If you lead by five shots, it's not easy. A lot of people think, well you have a little bit of a cushion, but if you approach that day ... with that attitude, it can be gone so quickly. ... I overcame that feeling, I stayed aggressive ... So I'm very proud of that."

Compton came the closest to putting pressure on Kaymer. A birdie at the eighth pulled him within four strokes, but he bogeyed the par-three ninth. Kaymer came along in the following group, the last, and turned that into a two-stroke swing, firing an eight iron to four feet and birdieing the ninth for the first time in the tournament.

"It's a dream come true," said Compton, who had to qualify to get to Pinehurst, and better, he not only had to go through a 36-hole qualifier, he had to go 38 holes, making it through a 5-for-3 playoff. "And to finish second and I'm in contention with guys like Rickie Fowler and Justin Rose," he added, "and I mean my name is in there, it is pretty neat. I won't really know the significance of what I've accomplished until I sit back and maybe watch the tapes and enjoy it."

Fowler was paired with Kaymer and said he knew it would take a small miracle to catch him. "I figured I would have to ... shoot a couple under on the front nine and at least put a little bit of heat on him," Fowler said. "That was stopped quickly when I made a quick double [bogey] there on No. 4 and [fell eight strokes behind]. Unfortunately, I wasn't able to get close enough to put any pressure on Martin."

Kaymer wasted no time putting more distance between himself and the field. He birdied the third hole to get to nine under, but bogeyed the seventh, then birdied the par-three No. 9 for the first time all week to make the turn at 34, nine under and six ahead of Compton and eight on Fowler. Then came the tightest moment of the round. Compton birdied the par-five 10th, and Kaymer bogeyed it for the first time. The two-shot swing cut Kaymer's lead to four. Then it was over quickly. Compton bogeyed the 11th and 12th, and Kaymer birdied the 13th and 14th. He was up by eight again. Compton bogeyed the 15th and parred in for his 72, and Kaymer bogeyed the 16th and parred in for his 69 and the eight-stroke win.

Despite his luxurious lead, Kaymer refused to let up, as everyone could tell at the drivable par-four 13th. He went for it, caught a greenside bunker, and got up and down for a birdie. "That was a big relief," he said. "Because then I looked at the scoreboard and I was, I think I was seven ahead. I thought, okay, seven ahead, six to go, that's fine."

The U.S. Open ended as usual, on Father's Day. But Germany's Father's Day had been celebrated a few weeks earlier. No matter. Kaymer could make the best of it. "I didn't get anything for my father that day," Kaymer said. "So maybe this will work."

Final-Round Leaders: Martin Kaymer 69–271, Erik Compton 72–279, Rickie Fowler 72–279, Keegan Bradley 67–281, Jason Day 68–281, Dustin Johnson 73–281, Brooks Koepka 71–281, Henrik Stenson 73–281.

4. The Open Championship

Visually, at least, there was little in common between the Open Championships played on the links of Royal Liverpool at Hoylake in 2006 and 2014. On the first of those occasions, when Hoylake returned to the Open rota for the first time in 39 years, a summer heatwave left the course parched. It was not just brown but a yellowy-white in places and became a prized exhibit in the movement away from the excessive watering of golf courses. Famously, Tiger Woods hit his driver only once all week and instead produced a series of stunning long- and mid-iron shots, all the better to control the ball on the rock-hard surfaces.

In 2014, the weather gods were playing a very different game. A long, wet winter left the links a vivid green color, while recent summer warmth proved ideal for thickening up the rough, which eight years earlier had been of the sparse and wispy variety. Perhaps the dramatic change in appearance prompted it, but there was some pre-tournament speculation that the course was not quite up to the mark for a major championship, that its architecture no longer tests the very best of modern players. Bernard Darwin would be dismayed at this talk for long ago he wrote that at Hoylake, "the golfing pilgrim is emphatically on classic ground."

Scenically, snuggled between the red-bricked houses of this corner of the Wirral peninsula, it may lack something compared to other venues, except when the course finds the dramatic sand dunes along the Dee Estuary and views emerge of the sun dancing on the hills of North Wales across the water. When the sun shines. This is not guaranteed and those who only know the links from its two modern Open stagings cannot have an appreciation for the ferocity of the elements that often blow in from the Irish Sea. It snowed once during Open week — in July! — and commentator Henry Longhurst's notes were reduced to an unreadable soggy mess within minutes of one stint up an early, primitive television commentary tower. Competitors at the Ricoh Women's British Open in 2012 know this all too well: One day's play was cancelled due to gales and the 36-hole marathon on the final day was a survival battle against cold, wind and rain. The threat of a thunderstorm that did not materialize on the third day of the 2014 men's Open was small beer in comparison.

Interestingly, the lowest score achieved in an Open at Hoylake is higher than for any other current venue for the championship. Five of the courses have seen 63s, the other three 64s. Woods set the record of 65 in the second round in 2006, later matched by Ernie Els, Chris DiMarco and Sergio Garcia. That score was not bettered this time. Dustin Johnson matched it in the second round and the quartet of Chris Wood, Shane Lowry, Marc Leishman and Jim Furyk did so in the final round, although none of them started closer than 10 strokes behind the leader, so they were charging from too deep.

While Woods praised the "amazing creativity" required in 2006, Rory McIlroy said eight years later on his first appearance at the venue: "It's a great course, a very fair course. We didn't play it in its hardest conditions this week and that's why the scores were quite low." Easy for him to say, perhaps, but despite the look of the links, the ground could in no way be confused with soft, so as well as his relentless, pounding driving, it was McIlroy's ability to hit towering iron shots that landed with a delicate, precise touch that brought him victory.

What links the wins of Woods and McIlroy, of course, is that each triumphed as the undisputed World No. 1. Hoylake has always brought out the best in the best. Past Open winners on the links include J.H. Taylor, Walter Hagen, Bobby Jones (in his Grand Slam year of 1930) and Peter Thomson, who claimed a hat-trick of victories here in 1956. Among the runner-ups have been the other two members of the Great Triumvirate, James Braid and Harry Vardon, Ted Ray and, in his only Open at Hoylake before its retreat from the rota, Jack Nicklaus in 1967.

As Woods did in 2006, McIlroy won by two strokes, over Sergio Garcia and Rickie Fowler, although it felt a more emphatic win than that as the Northern Irishman was in control throughout. While Woods took the lead on the second day eight years earlier, McIlroy led from start to finish, seeing his lead increase from one after the first round to four on day two and six after 54 holes. He joined Ray, Jones, Gene Sarazen, Henry Cotton, Tom Weiskopf and Woods from 2005 at St. Andrews in being the seventh player to lead outright after every round since the championship was extended to 72 holes in 1892. This was also the first time in major championship history that two consecutive majors had been won wire-to-wire, following Martin Kaymer's dominant U.S. Open performance.

Kaymer won by eight strokes at Pinehurst, which was the margin of victory for McIlroy in his first two major victories, the 2011 U.S. Open, which he also won wire-to-wire, and the 2012 PGA Championship. That was back in his "Boy Wonder" days. At Hoylake the 25-year-old appeared to enter a new phase of his career. It was a thoroughly mature performance which again saw him linked with the very greatest in the game's history, becoming the third youngest player to win three different majors after Nicklaus (23) and Woods (24). Both of those titans had won the Masters first and completed Grand Slams at the Open. McIlroy just needs a victory at Augusta to join those two, plus Sarazen, Ben Hogan and Gary Player, with a career slam.

"I'm immensely proud of myself," McIlroy said. "To sit here, 25 years of age, and win my third major championship and be three-quarters of the way to the career Grand Slam, yeah, I never dreamed of being at this point of my career so quickly."

Although McIlroy is the course record holder at Royal Portrush, he grew up playing an inland, parkland course at Holywood and links golf has not always come naturally to him. He won the silver medal in his only appearance as an amateur at Carnoustie in 2007, but it took him six more attempts to upgrade to the gold medal (plus the claret jug). He was third in 2010 at St. Andrews, but that was after wasting an opening 63 by following it with a second-round 80. Otherwise his best finish was a tie for 25th in 2011 at Sandwich, where in contrast to the champion Darren Clarke, his fellow Ulsterman who needs only the odd Guinness to fortify himself against all elements, McIlroy moaned that he was not a fan of tournaments "where the outcome is predicated so much by the weather."

He was 60th in 2012 and missed the cut at Muirfield in 2013. "That was a low point," he said. "I had never missed a cut in the Open before and I really missed playing on the weekend. I said to myself, I'll never make that happen again. It's been huge what a difference a year makes."

His remedy was to play more links golf prior to the championship, making an early private visit to Hoylake and then playing in the Aberdeen Asset Management Scottish Open at Royal Aberdeen. In truth, to say McIlroy arrived at Hoylake as the undisputed World No. 1 would be false since Adam Scott still topped the Official World Golf Ranking at that point. It was his triumph, and subsequent victories at the WGC - Bridgestone Invitational and the PGA Championship, that re-established his status as the game's current best of the best.

It had been a rollercoaster time both on and off the course for McIlroy since he last dominated the scene at the end of 2012. After changing his club contract in 2013, he did not win until the Australian Open at the end of the year, while his sole victory in 2014 came at the BMW PGA Championship. It was a stunning comeback from seven strokes behind on the final day but also a subdued celebration as he had publicly broken off his engagement to tennis star Caroline Wozniacki on the eve of the tournament.

His victory at Hoylake made him the first player to do the double of Britain's two premier championships, the Open and the PGA, in the 60-year history of the latter. McIlroy said the win at Wentworth in May had been a huge part of his later success. "You can't doubt your own ability," he said. "The ability was still there, I was just trying to find a way to make it come out again."

McIlroy added: "I've really found my passion again for golf. Not that it ever dwindled, but it's what I think about when I get up in the morning, it's what I think about when I go to bed. I just want to be the best golfer I can be."

First Round

Rory McIlroy meant business from the moment he teed off on a sunny, calm Thursday morning. His first three approach shots finished no more than five feet away and at the second he hit a six iron from 191 yards to four inches for the first of six birdies. He birdied three of the par-fives, the fifth, 10th and 16th, as well as the sixth and 12th holes. "We had perfect scoring conditions out there this morning, there wasn't much wind early on," he said. "There are quite a few holes on the back nine that are right-to-left doglegs, which suits my natural shot shape. And I don't feel like you're too restricted in your approach shots. The greens are quite generous, quite flat, and you can be quite aggressive with your second shots."

McIlroy could not get up and down from a bunker for a birdie at the 18th, as he had at the 16th, but a 66 still put him one ahead of Matteo Manassero and two in front of Sergio Garcia, Adam Scott, Jim Furyk, Shane Lowry, Brooks Koepka and, on a good day for Italy, the Molinari brothers, Edoardo and Francesco. Matteo Manassero, having driven into a bunker at the first, holed a nine iron for his third shot, while Garcia hit the flagstick on the first and had a tap-in for his birdie.

Much of the attention on the first day naturally focused on Tiger Woods, who had missed both the Masters and the U.S. Open following microdiscectomy surgery for a pinched nerve in his back in March. He had missed the cut in his only tournament since his return, and the 38-year-old bogeyed the first two holes. He had bogeyed his opening hole in 2006, but it would take a remarkable putting display to bring him back into contention here. Five birdies in six holes on the back nine gave Woods a 69 alongside those of Fowler, Leishman, Robert Karlsson and Jimmy Walker, among others. "It felt good to be back out there competing," Woods said. "It wasn't exactly the greatest of starts but then I turned it around."

Others had a mixed time. Henrik Stenson snapped a wedge over his knee at the 17th during a 72, while Justin Rose was on the same mark after teeing off without a driver. His favored beast had got mixed up with two similar models and ended up 190 miles away with a friend of his caddie on Wednesday evening. It was driven back after Rose, who was fortunately playing in the afternoon, discovered the error the next morning and it arrived with him on the third hole. He had not been planning to use it before the par-five fifth.

Phil Mickelson, the defending champion, opened with a 74 and said: "Certainly, the score sucks but my game is as good as it's been in a long time." His playing partner, Ernie Els, hit a spectator on the chin with an off-line drive at the first. While the spectator was fine after receiving stitches for the wound, Els never recovered and scored 79. "It wasn't nice, there was blood everywhere," Els said. "Hurting the guy the way I did, I felt pretty bad. I was quite rattled."

Although the breeze got up in the afternoon, with all but three of 18 sub-70 scores posted early, the day's best nines both came later on, with Scott going out in 31 with an eagle at the fifth and Lowry coming home in 32. As Scott said: "It was important to keep pace with Rory. He has the potential to really put his foot down. We've seen him win majors by eight and there is nothing stopping him from shooting a low round again tomorrow."

Apart from maybe himself.

First-Round Leaders: Rory McIlroy 66, Matteo Manassero 67, Brooks Koepka 68, Edoardo Molinari 68, Francesco Molinari 68, Jim Furyk 68, Sergio Garcia 68, Adam Scott 68, Shane Lowry 68.

Second Round

Rory McIlroy appeared to be having a "Freaky Friday" problem in 2014 — although no one had forgotten the Friday afternoon 80 at St. Andrews in 2010. It started in Dubai when he opened 63-70 and in only three of 13 stroke-play tournaments had he scored lower in the second round than in the first. He almost missed the cut at the Masters with a 77 on second day, while at the Memorial Tournament he opened 63-78 — "How the hell do you do that?" asked Jack Nicklaus — and at the Scottish Open the previous week he had gone 64-78. "Maybe I'm just going out with higher expectations on a Friday after shooting a low round," McIlroy said. "I've just got to try and put those expectations aside and take it one hole at a time."

Easier said than done, but McIlroy managed it nonetheless. Not even a bogey at the first hole, his first of the championship, could distract him, nor a pheasant wandering across the eighth green. Birdies at the fifth, sixth and eighth, where he holed from seven feet once the wildlife had played through, put him out in 33, and after a four at the 10th, he birdied three of the last four holes. "Even though I started a little shaky with that bogey, I was still confident that I had some chances coming up," he said. "I am very comfortable in what I am doing right now. It is hard to describe and I wish I could get into it more often. My second rounds this year have been terrible and there isn't really an explanation. But hopefully I put it to bed today."

McIlroy holed from five feet for a four at the 18th for his second successive 66, which established a four-stroke lead over Dustin Johnson, whose 65 matched the course record and was the only round of the day not to contain a bogey. Rickie Fowler and Sergio Garcia were among those two further back and George Coetzee, who celebrated his 28th birthday with three birdies in a row to briefly share the lead at six under. That was before he bogeyed the next two holes — "I think it is obviously I looked at the board as soon as I was at the top," he admitted — and before McIlroy had even teed off.

Starting out at one under par, Johnson birdied the first from 10 feet, the third from five feet and got up and down from a greenside bunker for a four at the fifth. He was out in 32 and then he birdied the 10th and 11th, then the 17th, where his huge drive at the 458-yard hole left only a short pitch to four feet, and the 18th. "I couldn't be happier with the position I'm in," Johnson said. "I thought it was really tough out there today, so to shoot seven under was a very good score this afternoon."

While Garcia almost holed a full shot at the opening hole on the first day, the Spaniard claimed an eagle-two at the second hole on the second day. He had done exactly the same at the same hole in 2006, using a nine iron in the third round. In the second round here he needed a six iron from 162 yards into a stiff breeze. "It's another great memory to have on that hole," he said.

This was the day it became apparent Tiger Woods would not feature in contention this time around. He started with a double bogey and then drove out of bounds at the 17th and had a triple. He birdied the 18th to make the cut, while Tom Watson, at the age of 64, also survived with two scores of 73 to extend his record from two years previously as the oldest known player to complete four rounds. Among those missing the 146 qualifying mark were Lee Westwood (71-76), Ian Poulter (73-74) and Masters champion Bubba Watson (76-72).

Second-Round Leaders: Rory McIlroy 66–132, Dustin Johnson 65–136, Francesco Molinari 70–138, Ryan Moore 68–138, Rickie Fowler 69–138, Sergio Garcia 70–138, Charl Schwartzel 67–138, Louis Oosthuizen 68–138.

Third Round

For the first time in the history of the Open, there was a two-tee start on the Saturday morning due to the threat of a severe thunderstorm. Gregory Bourdy struck the first shot from the 10th tee, under the supervision of European Tour official Mike Stewart, who undertook starting duties while Ivor Robson, in his 40th appearance at the Open, remained on the first tee. As it turned out, the day's best scores both came from playing the course the "wrong way round" with 67s for Darren Clarke and Jordan Spieth.

While there was heavy rain for the first starters, much of the day was dry and eerily still. Rory McIlroy could not take advantage, and a bogey at the 12th left him even par for the round. Rickie Fowler and Sergio Garcia, however, were both out in 32. Fowler birdied four of the first six holes and then the first three on the inward half. He and McIlroy were now tied for the lead. But not for long. Fowler made three bogeys in four holes from the 14th and had to birdie the 18th to remain only six behind. A 68 had given him second place, one ahead of Garcia, who had a 69, and Dustin Johnson, who scored 71.

McIlroy finished his round with a burst that ultimately won him the title. He holed a putt from over 30 feet at the 14th and then had two eagles in the last three holes. At the 16th he hit a four iron to 20 feet, and then, after dropping a shot at the 17th, he hit a drive and a five iron from 237 yards to 11 feet at the last. They were two wondrous shots and the putt was like a dagger to the rest of the field. "I felt like those two shots into 18 deserved an eagle," he explained. "I wanted to finish it off the right way." McIlroy received a huge ovation at the last that gave him goosebumps and it was hard not to think of Roberto de Vicenzo's famous shot across the corner of the practice ground — now the tented village — at the same hole in 1967. The differences then were that it was the 16th hole, it was the last day and he made a birdie to stay ahead of Nicklaus.

McIlroy was now 16 under par and six ahead of the rest. No one had lost such a lead with a round to go, though Macdonald Smith and Jean Van de Velde had both lost from five ahead after 54 holes. "The way I look at it, six shots is better than five," McIlroy said. "I just wanted to try and be as many ahead as I possibly could. That's why I was grinding over that putt at the last. I was conscious of Rickie getting a little closer, so it was nice to be able to come up with the goods when I needed them over the last few holes and restore that lead."

As for the decision to play early, McIlroy's comments on the subject were virtually drowned out in his post-round interview by a prolonged rainstorm that would have suspended play. "It is the second-best decision the R&A have made this year," he said, referring to the announcement that the Open would return to Royal Portrush, host of the 1951 championship, at a future date.

Garcia said: "It looked like Rory might have a one- or two-shot lead, and now all of a sudden he's got a six-shot lead. Rickie and I helped him a bit with that, but more than anything, Rory helped himself with the way he finished. He hit a great shot on 18. Something like that, the only thing you can do is say 'well done.' It's difficult to see anyone catching him when he's playing like that, but the only thing I can do is play well and try to put a little pressure on him and see how he reacts."

Third-Round Leaders: Rory McIlroy 68–200, Rickie Fowler 68–206, Sergio Garcia 69–207, Dustin Johnson 71–207, Victor Dubuisson 68–208, Edoardo Molinari 68–209.

Fourth Round

Sergio Garcia was true to his words, actually exerting a great deal of pressure, so Rory McIlroy was thankful for the cushion those two eagles on Saturday had given him for the final round. With scoring impressively low, McIlroy was the only one of the leading finishers not to break 70. He did not need to. A 71 gave him a total of 17 under par, one outside Woods' score from 2006 and two off Tiger's record from 2000 at St. Andrews. He won by two over Garcia's 66 and Rickie Fowler's 67, while Jim Furyk had a 65 to be fourth, Marc Leishman the same to be fifth with Adam Scott, who had a 66. Dustin Johnson had an erratic closing 72 to drop to joint 12th in what was his last tournament before taking a leave of absence from the tour for personal reasons.

There was little anticipation of any drama after McIlroy birdied the first hole from 18 feet to extend his lead. But at the fifth, a routine birdie hole, his second shot found the stand on the right and his chip from the drop zone ran over the green. He took a six and then missed the green at the short sixth for another bogey. Only two shots dropped, but Garcia was making a charge. He birdied the first from 10 feet, the third from 20 feet, got a four at the fifth and then eagled the 10th with a six iron to 15 feet.

The Spaniard was excited now, as was the huge gallery, and McIlroy realized there was work still to be done. He made a fine up-and-down from a bunker at the seventh, then hit an eight iron to 15 feet at the ninth for a two and got his four at the 10th. He had stuck with his two key words: "process" and "spot". He explained: "With my long shots, I just wanted to stick to my process and stick to making good decisions and good swings. The process of making good swings, rather than thinking about the end result.

"And spot was for my putting. I was just picking a spot in the green and trying to roll it over my spot every time. I wasn't thinking about holing it, or what it would mean, or how many further clear it would get me. I just wanted to roll it over my spot and if it went in, great. If it didn't, then I'd try it the next hole."

Garcia was having some luck up ahead, rebounding off a grandstand safely into play at the 12th and just missing a pot bunker at the short 13th. When McIlroy bogeyed the 13th, Garcia was within two strokes again, but with the leader watching from the tee, the crucial moment arrived on the par-three 15th. Garcia was in a bunker and left his first recovery attempt in the trap. "I just got too cute," he said. "When you know you can't make any mistakes, it's hard." A bogey-four halted his moment, though he did finish with two birdies in the last three holes.

Fowler had been quiet all day, other than a birdie at the second and another at the 10th. The 25-year-old finished strongly with three birdies in the last four holes but had to settle for a joint runner-up finish for the second major running. He did achieve four rounds in the 60s, the seventh time it has been done in the Open and the fourth time by a non-winner, Els having done it twice and Jesper Parnevik once. Fowler accompanied McIlroy up the 18th fairway and the new champion received a tumultuous reception which the American appreciated. "It's definitely up there as the best walk in golf, especially Sunday when you're in the final group," he said.

"To be there with Rory when he was about to win, that was fun."

McIlroy almost holed a bunker shot at the last but settled for a par. He said: "Especially being someone from around here, the Open Championship was the one you really wanted growing up, the one you holed so many putts on the putting green. Didn't quite need to hole a putt today to do it, just a little tap in, which was nice."

With which he sought out his mother, Rose, who was at the back of the green and rushed on for a congratulatory hug. His father Gerry had been present for McIlroy's first two major wins but not his mother. "This one's for you, mum," he said.

The Final Leaders: Rory McIlroy 71–271, Sergio Garcia 66–273, Rickie Fowler 67–273, Jim Furyk 65–275, Marc Leishman 65–276, Adam Scott 66–276.

5. PGA Championship

Was the 2014 PGA Championship a pivotal point in golf history? Was this the time and place that the Era of Rory McIlroy dawned and the Era of Tiger Woods flickered out?

If so, let history note that it happened at the 96th PGA Championship at Valhalla Golf Club at Louisville, Kentucky, August 7-10, 2014. Or in Woods' case, August 7-8. If golf were grand opera, the audience would have been spellbound in Act IV, awaiting the entrance of the young prince. But this prince was no longer young at 38, and he was hurting in body and game. While McIlroy went on to win with solid play highlighted by flashes of brilliance, the PGA ended quietly for Woods. He missed the halfway cut by five strokes, shooting 74-74–148. Woods covets the majors above all, and this was the fourth and final of the year, leaving him stalled at 14 wins in his pursuit of Jack Nicklaus' record 18. He hadn't won a major since the 2008 U.S. Open.

It was one of the most un-Tiger-like performances of his career. In the two rounds, he had a total of three birdies, seven bogeys, one double bogey, and was never under par. There was nothing encouraging about his return from the back surgery of March 31. Even for a talent of his wattage, it was probably too much to expect anything approaching full recovery and peak performance. He had returned the week before, in the WGC - Bridgestone Invitational, and withdrew with back pain in the fourth round, after he jumped into a bunker, the latest in a catalog of injuries and ailments dating, it seems, to the mid-2000s.

"It's not the site of the surgery," Woods said, before the PGA. "This is something totally different. As I was explaining to you guys [media] last week, I haven't been able to do my agility stuff because I'm still building my back up, still playing. I can't do both at the same time. So when the season is over, in the off season, getting back to my agility work, my explosiveness, my power, all that stuff, back up to where I used to be."

He talked about his game after missing the cut. "I couldn't make a back swing," he said. "I can't get the club back. Coming through is fine. I can't get the club back."

Woods finished 2014 with seven starts, missing two cuts and withdrawing twice. His best finish was a tie for 25th.

It was a harsh juxtaposition: McIlroy's star was rising. Coming into the PGA, he'd made 13 starts on the PGA Tour and had six top-eight finishes before the two victories. History buffs spoke of the McIlroy Era.

"Yeah, of course, I've heard it and I've read it," he said. "Sometimes I feel that people are too quick to jump to conclusions ... Look, I said at the start of the year that golf was looking for someone to put their hand up and sort of become one of the dominant players in the game. I felt like I had the ability to do that ... I'm not necessarily sure you can call that an era or the start of an era."

Romantics said the torch was being passed.

"I don't think any torch has been passed and I don't think any torch will ever be passed because I never think of myself in that way," McIlroy said. "I never see myself like that. I don't see the need for me to carry any sort of torch. I just want to win golf tournaments."

First Round

As usual, Tiger Woods had the stage pretty much to himself. The theater was compelling. Discounting the abortive appearance in the Bridgestone Invitational a week earlier, Woods was making his comeback and this time was in his element, a major. He was seeking his fifth PGA Championship and 15th major in pursuit of the Jack Nicklaus' record. He was playing in the morning, and Rory McIlroy wouldn't be teeing off for five hours. Woods was paired with two other former PGA winners — Phil Mickelson, who had something of a following of his own, and Padraig Harrington, whose game had gone sour. Woods' faithful turned out in droves. He pained them from the start. He bogeyed both par-threes on his first nine (the back), got his only birdie on a long chip shot, and showed his wildness at his 16th (the par-five seventh), where he fired a tee shot wide right, over the gallery and near a drink cart. He shot a three-over 74.

"It wasn't very good," Woods said.

Mickelson scared himself with his start. He stepped up for his opening tee shot at the par-five 10th full of confidence. "I stood on the first tee ... I thought I was going to light it up," he said. "I hit the ugliest shot. I mean, it was so far left ... Horrific." He scratched out a par, but was wild at the next and bogeyed. But he recovered and played the last 10 holes in four under for a 69, his best start in eight PGAs. As for the second round? "I expect to play with a little bit more assertiveness and confidence from the first hole on," Mickelson said.

England's Lee Westwood, playing ahead, was giving the Woods grouping something to look at. Westwood, 41, in the running for the "best never to win a major" tag, got off to his best start ever in 17 PGAs, a six-under-par 65 to tie for the first-round lead with Kevin Chappell and Ryan Palmer. Westwood was out in four birdies and a bogey, but double-bogeyed his 10th, the par-four first. Then he birdied five of his last six holes, capping the outburst with a 40-foot putt at the par-four No. 9.

Westwood was a former World No. 1 in 2010, who had 17 top-10 finishes and seven top-three finishes in the majors. "I've played better rounds, but I was really pleased with today," he said.

Chappell, 28, the 2008 NCAA champion out of UCLA, had one professional win, that on the Web.com Tour, so he wasn't about to be misled by his bogey-free 65. "You're in the lead, you're in 20th place — it's not that big of a difference to the 72 holes we have to play," he said. He made three birdies on each side, including a hole-out from a bunker at the 10th.

Ryan Palmer, with a tie for 19th his best in seven PGAs, enjoyed his best round, the 65, but let himself be lured by the thought of breaking the majors record of 63. Starting on the 10th, Ryan raced off with five birdies for a 31, then birdied his 14th and 16th. That put him seven under and with his first lead in any major. He needed two more birdies. "The one thing I thought about on eight and nine was to birdie and shoot 62," Palmer said. "I knew where I stood. I wanted to get eight [under] so bad, and it kept driving me." But he was long with his tee shot to the par-three No. 8, and his par putt horseshoed out, costing him his only bogey. "I don't believe the seven iron went that far," he said.

McIlroy, who won the 2012 PGA by a record eight shots, now was fresh from winning the British Open and the Bridgestone Invitational and won the battle of the major winners. He was in a group at 66, tied for fourth. Masters winner Bubba Watson had a ragged 70 that included an eagle at No. 7 and two late bogeys. U.S. Open champion Martin Kaymer also shot 70, but quietly, with two birdies and a bogey. McIlroy got to three under on the front with birdies at Nos. 4, 7 and 9, then had to start over. At the 10th, he pulled his second shot out of bounds and double-bogeyed. He got, as he said, "Very, very hot ... because it's one of the only bad shots I've hit in a few weeks." He followed it with a bogey at the 11th and was back at even par again. "Walking onto 12th tee, I was muttering a few things to myself," he said. It must have been a form of inspiration. He birdied the next four holes, then added another at the 18th after just missing an eagle then tapping in for birdie with his 27th putt.

"Just where I am with my golf game right now," McIlroy said. "I'm hitting the ball great, seeing good shots out there, holing putts. It's easier to get back in the right frame of mind after what happened on 10 and 11."

First-Round Leaders: Lee Westwood 65, Kevin Chappell 65, Ryan Palmer 65, Jim Furyk 66, Edoardo Molinari 66, Henrik Stenson 66, Rory McIlroy 66, Chris Wood 66.

Second Round

Tiger Woods' optimism, always bright, flickered out in the second round. It was pretty much gone before he reached the turn. From No. 4, he went bogey-par-double bogey-bogey, and went on to his second 74, and at six-over 148, he missed the cut by five shots. It was his second miss in 17 PGAs, his fourth miss in a major as a pro. It was two days of erratic driving and errant putts. And he admitted that his back was hurting. "[It] was telling me on the range, probably wasn't a good idea [to play]," Woods said. And with that, he was into a car and gone.

And this on a day when the field jumped on a Valhalla softened by rains that delayed play and closed parking lots.

"I wasn't quite sure we should have teed off," said Ryan Palmer, after a 70 that would leave him two off Rory McIlroy's lead going into the third round. "We were hitting into puddles ... They said that's just golf. Tell the guy sitting indoors making the decision to come and check it out. It's wet."

Rory McIlroy agreed — the course was wet. It was especially tough trying to blast out of bunkers, with the sand so compacted. Bunkers cost him two bogeys. But he wasn't complaining. Not after a 67 for a 133 and a one-stroke lead. His secret: He'd hit 20 of 28 fairways through the two rounds and needed just 27 putts for the second day. His lead was only one, but it was a lead — not always his favorite spot.

"I maybe wasn't quite comfortable in that position at the start of my career," McIlroy admitted, thinking principally of squandering a four-stroke lead in the final round of the 2011 Masters. He'd gotten more than comfortable with the aggressive approach. Said McIlroy: "If I'm two ahead going into the weekend, I'm going to try to get three ahead; and if I'm three ahead, I'm going to try to get four ahead; and if I'm four ahead, I'm going to try to get five ahead. I'm just going to try to keep the pedal down and get as many ahead as possible."

He started on the back nine and bogeyed No. 12 out of a bunker, and bounced back to go four under through the turn — a wedge to 12 feet at the 13th for one birdie, an eight iron to 20 feet at the 15th for another, and then an eagle at the par-five 18th, off a four iron to 25 feet. That got him his first lead. He bogeyed the second coming home, birdied the par-five No. 7 after just missing an eagle from eight feet, and finally dropped a 20-footer for birdie at No. 9, his last hole. His 67–133 put him one ahead of Jim Furyk and Jason Day going into the third round.

Furyk, runner-up at the 2013 PGA, birdied the 18th with a strong up-and-down for a 68, but felt at a disadvantage on the wet course. "The guy that hits it my length, there aren't that many holes [when] I've got eight iron in my hand where I feel like I can be aggressive," he said. Day torched the front nine. "That's the last thing that I expected, to shoot 30 on the front," Day said. An eagle at No. 7 was the jewel — a superb drive and a one iron from 250 yards to 10 feet. And he was a strong closer: A wedge to six feet at the 17th and an up-and-down over a bunker at the 18th, both for birdies. "Being able to play with Rory in the last group tomorrow would be fun," Day said. "But I've still got a lot of golf to play and I just have to go out there and play my own game."

The picture changed dramatically in the second round. The three co-leaders of the first round drifted back. After Palmer's 70 for 135, two behind, Lee Westwood reached eight under but double-bogeyed the 13th and bogeyed the 15th and 16th for a 72–137. Kevin Chappell struggled to a 74–139. It was even tougher for former PGA champion Keegan Bradley, U.S. Open champion Martin Kaymer, and young lions Jordan Spieth and Kevin Na. They all missed the cut, which came in at one-over 143.

Rickie Fowler was two behind with 66–135 but wasn't encouraged by what he saw from McIlroy. "He's the best player in the world right now," Fowler said. "And ... a lot of that is his confidence with the way he's driving the ball."

Phil Mickelson eagled the 18th for a 67 and was three off. "It's fun to be back in it," he said, "to feel like my game is there and to not show up at the golf course hoping that I find something to work with."

Heading into the third round, McIlroy didn't leave much room for optimism for the rest of the field. He wasn't figuring on letting up. "Look," he said, "I went protection mode once in my career, and it was the 2011 Masters. That didn't work out very well. So I said to myself, I'll never do that again."

Second-Round Leaders: Rory McIlroy 67–133, Jason Day 65–134, Jim Furyk 68–134, Ryan Palmer 70–135, Rickie Fowler 66–135, Mikko Ilonen 68–135, Phil Mickelson 67–136, Bernd Wiesberger 68–136.

Third Round

Rory McIlroy won his three majors with the luxury of plump leads coming out of the third round. In the 2011 U.S. Open, he was leading by eight shots, the 2012 PGA Championship by three and the 2014 British Open by six. Now, in the PGA just a few weeks later, McIlroy would have to work without a safety net. This time, not only was he leading by a mere shot, but there were eight golfers within four strokes of him.

McIlroy didn't get the lead until the final green of a wild third round, after he birdied three of the last four holes for a 67 and a 13-under 200. Six players held the lead at some point in the attack on the rain-softened Valhalla. McIlroy had two birdies and a bogey into the turn and started home with a birdie at the par-five 10th. But on a bogey at the 12th, he sensed trouble closing in. "I wanted to just get back in the lead," McIlroy said. "I didn't really look — I knew Phil was making a run. I knew Rickie was making a run. And Bernd Wiesberger. I knew I needed to do something in the last few holes...."

He put on a finishing kick of Olympic caliber: At the par-four 15th, a nine iron from 140 yards to 20 feet — birdie. At the par-four 16th, a nine iron from 172 yards to tap-in range — birdie. And at the par-five 18th, a five iron into a greenside bunker and an up-and-down on an eight-foot putt — birdie.

This PGA would finish like a United Nations Open. There was McIlroy from Northern Ireland followed by Austria's Bernd Wiesberger, mostly unknown outside Europe; Americans Rickie Fowler and Phil Mickelson, Australia's Jason Day, South Africa's Louis Oosthuizen, Sweden's Henrik Stenson, Finland's Mikko Ilonen and American Ryan Palmer.

"Tomorrow," McIlroy said, "standing on the first tee is going to feel different than how it felt a month ago at Hoylake. It is going to be a shootout."

Ryan Palmer, first-round co-leader, came in with a two-under 69 and a nine-under 204 that included a bogey at the 17th that dimmed a three-birdie round but not his outlook. "I'm excited," he said. "Never been in this position in a major event."

Mikko Ilonen, 35, a five-time winner on the European Tour, shook off a double bogey at No. 2 and birdied Nos. 3, 4, 9 and 10 for a 69–204. He credited his putting. "But I've got to hit more fairways," he said.

Henrik Stenson, also four back, had a symmetrical 67. He bogeyed Nos. 5 and 15, but had two birdies before, two between and two after, the last at the 17th and 18th.

Former British Open champion Louis Oosthuizen bogeyed No. 4 then spread five birdies the rest of the way for a 67–204. "The way the golf course is now, you can attack quite a bit," he said. "I think it should be very interesting tomorrow to see the guys probably go at a lot of pins."

Jason Day, with a four-birdie 69–203, won the Par of the Day award. At the par-four No. 2, he drove wildly to the right, over a little stream and into a shaggy area. He took off his shoes and socks, waded over, hit out bare-footed and made his par. "It was a great four there," Day said. "A lucky four."

Phil Mickelson closed with a rush, birdieing Nos. 14, 15, 16 and 18 for a 67 and was tied with Day, three behind. Someone noted that many of the challengers had never won a major. What would they feel like? "Hopefully ... a little tight around the collar," he said.

Rickie Fowler was two behind after a bogey-free 67. "Very clean round of golf," he said. His four birdies came at No. 3 and all three par-fives — Nos. 7, 10 and 18. "I'm excited for tomorrow," he said.

Bernd Wiesberger figured there were 100,000 golfers back home in Austria and that 90,000 would be watching on TV. He birdied the last three holes for a bogey-free 65 to close to within a stroke of McIlroy. "I've not been in contention in a major championship," he said. "I'm just trying to enjoy it as I did today."

McIlroy closed the day with something of a challenge. "It's not the biggest lead I've ever had," he said, "but I'm still in control of this golf tournament."

Third-Round Leaders: Rory McIlroy 67–200, Bernd Wiesberger 65–201, Rickie Fowler 67–202, Phil Mickelson 67–203, Jason Day 69–203, Louis Oosthuizen 67–204, Henrik Stenson 67–204, Mikko Ilonen 69–204, Ryan Palmer 69–204.

Fourth Round

Rory McIlroy, now 25, winner of three majors off luxurious leads, entered the final round of the 2014 PGA and, significantly, leading by just one. It was as though the gods of golf were saying, "Okay, kid, you did great with nice cushions. Now let's see what you can do under the heat."

It was possibly McIlroy's toughest test. He would pass it by that one shot, but not before this PGA had put on one of the greatest shows in the majors. It turned into a Hitchcock suspense tale in a Wild West shootout, and would end in darkness and controversy. Along the way Henrik Stenson, Phil Mickelson and Rickie Fowler all had a share of the lead down the final nine, leaving McIlroy having to do desperate, heroic things to prove himself.

The triggering episode: A tournament that was nagged by rain got one final heavy dose on Sunday, forcing a delay of almost two hours. Play resumed at 2:40, and the last pairing, McIlroy and Bernd Wiesberger, teed off at 4:19. There was little room for error. Officials were hoping they could finish before dark. The tension was thick. They almost didn't.

The surprising Wiesberger faded fast and ended up tied for 15th, as did Jason Day, after a double bogey at the 16th. It became a four-man chase, with a dramatic twist.

For Fowler, it seemed that first major win was about to materialize. After a bogey at the second, he birdied four of the next five holes, including a chip-in at No. 5, to take the lead at 13 under. It didn't last long. Stenson started four shots off and made up ground with a blistering run — five birdies for an outward 30, then reached 15 under with another at the 13th. Mickelson rushed up from his three-shot deficit with a four-birdie 31 on the front, and reached 15 under with a birdie at the 11th. The pressure was building. Of McIlroy's three challengers, there was only one bogey on the front nine. McIlroy was flunking his big test on the front. He bogeyed the third and sixth, and made just one birdie, at the seventh. He started ahead by one, but was three behind at the turn.

"I didn't get off to the best of starts, and the guys came at me pretty quickly, and I just couldn't really get anything going. So I needed to stay patient and just ... wait for something to click."

Something did click. At the par-five 10th, he hit a good drive, then authored a Hall of Fame second shot, a three wood from 284 yards.

"The ball flight was probably around 30 feet lower than I intended, and the line was probably around 15 yards left of where I intended," McIlroy said. "It was lucky..."

The ball stopped seven feet from the flag. He made the eagle, devouring two shots of his three-shot deficit.

Up ahead, Stenson missed a three-foot par putt at the 14th, bogeyed, and stalled out.

Mickelson caught Fowler with a birdie from 10 feet at the 11th, then saved par at the 12th, holing a 30-footer.

McIlroy tied them at 15 under with a birdie at the 13th.

Just ahead, Fowler bogeyed the 14th. It was fatal.

As McIlroy was parring along, Mickelson bogeyed the 16th. McIlroy was back in the lead — by a shot — and daylight was failing.

With the first of two late, great shots, McIlroy added to his lead. At the par-four 17th, he slashed a nine iron out of a fairway bunker to 10 feet and made the birdie that gave him a two-stroke lead. It would prove to be the winner.

The PGA then closed with an operatic finale at the par-five 18th. Darkness was falling and officials weren't sure that McIlroy, in the final group, would be able to finish. Mickelson and Fowler, both two behind, had already hit their tee shots. They hadn't reached them when officials allowed McIlroy to hit his. Then they had to stand aside at the green when officials interrupted them to let McIlroy hit his second. Were they giving McIlroy special treatment? Were they upsetting Fowler and Mickelson?

"We were cool with hitting the tee shot," Fowler said. "We weren't expecting the approach shots."

Mickelson was visibly unhappy with the situation, but said later: "It didn't affect the outcome of the championship at all, I don't think. It's not what we normally do. It's not a big deal either way."

It was an awkward situation. Without letting McIlroy play, it's possible everything would be put on hold till Monday morning. This would include a three-hole playoff if they'd ended up tied.

At all events, Fowler was on in two and needed an eagle from 50 feet to tie for the lead. He missed that and missed his short birdie try as well, and it cost him his third straight runner-up finish in a major. Mickelson, short with his approach, nearly holed his chip shot for a tying eagle. But he birdied for a 66 and a 269.

McIlroy had hit his second into a bunker, blasted out and was 35 feet from the cup. His birdie try ended up 10 feet away. Then, in the deepening gloom, he tapped in for his par, a 68, a 16-under 268 and a one-stroke win. It was his second straight major, his third straight win. He had passed the test.

"I think I showed a lot of guts out there to get the job done," McIlroy said.

Said Mickelson, runner-up in a major for the ninth time: "He's better than everyone else right now."

Final-Round Leaders: Rory McIlroy 68–268, Phil Mickelson 66–269, Rickie Fowler 68–270, Henrik Stenson 66–270, Jim Furyk 66–272, Ryan Palmer 68–272.

6. The Ryder Cup

Ever since the first time groups of professional golfers from Britain and America met at the newly created Gleneagles in 1921 — the first official Ryder Cup took place six years later — the question has been posed about how much influence the captains have on the result. Well, perhaps it is a more modern phenomenon, in these days of non-playing captains and the meetings of the USA and Europe becoming golf's most intense three days every two years. Certainly, the debate raged in the wake of Europe's 16½-11½ victory back at Gleneagles in 2014.

At least, in the American team room. And not just there. One of the lasting memories of the 40th Ryder Cup came afterwards, in the interview room. Tom Watson, the U.S. captain, was magnanimous in defeat. "They played better golf than we did," he said of the Europeans. "The bottom line is that results spoke of that. The disappointment is going to sit for a long time."

But soon his senior player, Phil Mickelson, was indirectly criticizing the captain by eulogizing about a predecessor, Paul Azinger, the leader of the only winning American team this century when he split his 12 players up into "pods" of four. "We have strayed from a winning formula we had in 2008 for the last three Ryder Cups," Mickelson said. "Paul got everyone invested in the process and he had a great plan for us. Those are the two things that allow us to play our best. We use the same process at the Presidents Cup and we do really well." Mickelson, who did not play at all on the Saturday, emphasized that none of the players contributed to the decision-making. "No, nobody here was in on any decision."

Asked how he responded, Watson said: "He has a difference of opinion. That's okay. My management philosophy is different than his."

Watson had been invited to return to the role he had first served 21 years earlier by Ted Bishop, president of the PGA of America. He remained the last American captain to win in Europe. If he was appointed for his success in Scotland, winning four Open Championships, it was a flawed strategy. If he was appointed to take tough decisions about who played when and with whom, then that is exactly what he did. It was just that he did not always get those decisions right and in the process lost the support of the players. Within days there were stories of Watson telling the players that "they stink" after losing the foursomes 7-1 and of Mickelson giving a team talk on the Saturday night with his back to Watson. A week later Watson was forced into issuing a written statement, which said in part: "I take complete and full responsibility for my communication, and I regret that my words may have made the players feel that I didn't appreciate their contribution and dedication in winning the Ryder Cup. My intentions throughout my terms as captain were both to inspire and to be honest."

Watson arrived in Scotland without the services of Tiger Woods and Jason Dufner, both injured, and Dustin Johnson, on a "personal leave of absence" from the game. Europe had the advantage of having four of the top six players in the world and, as Watson had indicated, played better golf. They did not lose a foursomes match, made 19 birdies on Friday afternoon in the worst conditions while playing alternate shot, to the Americans' 13, and in the Sunday singles their four major champions won 3½ points, while America's six won two points.

For Europe, however, it was no accident that their players performed their best. In Paul McGinley they had a captain that contrasted in every way with Watson. No major champion, a journeyman tour pro who first dreamed of a Gaelic football career in his native Dublin, McGinley had been the first choice of the players themselves to lead the team. He had played on three Ryder Cup teams, been a vice captain twice and captained two Seve Trophy teams — and won on every occasion.

McGinley talked of taking the European "template" from past matches and merely refining it. He thought of virtually everything, having a consistent theme to the videos he showed the players and the imagery around the team room. He brought in former Manchester United manager Sir Alex Ferguson to talk to his players about embracing the tag of favorites, winning when you are expected to win, not letting complacency creep in. He had a fifth vice captain to shepherd the players who were not playing. And while Watson repeated a line of many past American captains that one of the highlights of the week was "getting to know the players during the week," McGinley knew them inside out before they arrived, including Victor Dubuisson, the French rookie who usually keeps himself to himself.

Rory McIlroy, the World No. 1, spoke for the rest of the team when he said: "He has been the most wonderful captain and I can't speak highly enough of him. He was meticulous in his planning. He left no stone unturned, everything tied in together, part of the plan of trying to win this Ryder Cup."

First Day

One thing out of McGinley's control was the weather. A warm September had meant the rough on the PGA Centenary course, designed and then tweaked further ahead of the match by Jack Nicklaus, was thicker than the home captain had ideally intended. The cool conditions, and with some teasing cross-breezes, made scoring particularly tricky on the first day. Even at 7:35 in the morning a huge gallery was in position in the huge horseshoe grandstand around the first tee, lining the fairway or on the hill behind the green. "I have never seen so many people on one hole in my life," said Justin Rose, who led off for Europe with Henrik Stenson against an out of sorts Bubba Watson and Webb Simpson.

Stenson birdied the par-five second, Rose the short fourth and then Stenson got another four at the par-five ninth. On the same hole Rose was stung by a wasp, but it did not stop him holing a long putt for another two at the 10th. The Europeans closed out a 5-and-4 victory in which the Americans had not won a hole or made a birdie. Simpson had pleaded for his place in the team in an early morning call to Watson on the day the wild cards were announced. Watson changed his mind and left Bill Haas off the team. As it was, Simpson did not appear again until the singles.

Martin Kaymer and Thomas Bjorn won three of the first four holes against Rickie Fowler and Jimmy Walker, but this match went all the way. Walker, on his debut, holed a bunker shot at the ninth to get back to one down and then, after Bjorn chipped in at the 13th, chipped in himself at the 16th.

Kaymer missed a chance to win the match at the short 17th, while both the Europeans had putts on the last green to win, only for Walker to get up and down to claim a half.

A disappointment for the Scottish gallery was the performance of Stephen Gallacher, the nephew of former captain Bernard and the only home rookie selected for the fourballs, and his out-of-sorts partner, Ian Poulter. Europe's Ryder Cup talisman missed a three-footer on the first green for a half and that set the tone. The all-rookie combination of Jordan Spieth and Patrick Reed took no time at all to get into the contest. They proved a potent combination with Spieth's calmness and Reed's fieriness. When Poulter left a putt short at the 14th, the Americans had won 5 and 4. It ended Poulter's European record of seven Ryder Cup wins in a row and was the worst of his four defeats. Not since 2004 had he lost prior to the 18th green. He was one of two players the Americans were attempting to "target". "Everybody on our teams wants Poulter and we were able to have him first," said Spieth.

The other, of course, was McIlroy, winner of the last two majors, who was out with Sergio Garcia against Mickelson and Keegan Bradley. On one of the practice days, Mickelson took a pop at McIlroy's involvement in a lawsuit against his former management company, Horizon, which at the time also represented Graeme McDowell. Mickelson joked: "Well, not only are we able to play together, we also don't litigate against each other and that's a real plus, I feel, heading into this week."

Although McIlroy halved the first with a long birdie putt and Garcia holed a bunker shot at the fourth, the match was of variable quality. The Americans went two up at the 10th but lost three holes to pars coming home. Yet Bradley eagled the 16th and Mickelson got up and down at the last to win by one hole. Mickelson and Bradley now matched Watson and Jack Nicklaus in having a 4-0 record, behind only Arnold Palmer and Gardner Dickinson on 5-0, and America had pinched the session 2½-1½. Europe had won only one of the last nine sessions of fourballs or foursomes.

Yet the final match had taken five and a half hours, and with neither Mickelson nor Bradley in the best of form, it was a gamble to send them out again for the foursomes. At the time that Watson had to hand in his pairings for the afternoon, they were a long way from being guaranteed a victory. But Watson had decided not to play his namesake, Bubba, nor to send out his rookies, Spieth and Reed, despite their obvious desire to return to the fray. "It would have been great to get back out there with the momentum of what we had just done," Reed said. Watson said Reed had accepted the decision but then added: "Well, really captain, I'm not all right with it." "That's the way I want you to be," Watson told him.

Mickelson and Bradley found themselves in the anchor match against McDowell and Dubuisson. McGinley had entrusted McDowell with looking after the enigmatic Frenchman and wanted the pair fresh for the afternoon. Dubuisson's approach at the second set up McDowell for a birdie to take the lead and three holes later they were three up. But with the Americans missing a number of short putts, the next time the home pair needed a birdie to win a hole was on the 16th, where McDowell again holed to seal a 3-and-2 victory.

Europe's other new pairing was another that featured a rookie and a veteran. Jamie Donaldson and Lee Westwood were in the top match to face Jim Furyk and Matt Kuchar. It was a terrific match, with Donaldson showing he felt quite at home in the rarified atmosphere. After losing the third hole, the Europeans won the sixth, seventh and 11th, and though Furyk hit close at the 14th, Donaldson holed from long range for the half. The Americans won the 16th, but Donaldson and Westwood secured a 2-up victory at the last.

Rose and Stenson picked up where they left off in the morning with Rose holing from 20 feet on the first green. They never trailed against Hunter Mahan and Zach Johnson and it ended in a 2-and-1 win at the 17th when Mahan raced his first putt five feet past and Johnson missed the one back.

Europe could not sweep the session as McIlroy and Garcia, who had hooked a tee shot out of bounds at the fifth, found themselves two down with two to play against Fowler and Walker. The Americans had again shown themselves to be a gritty combination, but Walker missed a 15-footer to win the match on the 16th, which was all the encouragement the home pair required. At the 17th McIlroy holed from 40 feet for a two, the ball hitting the back of the cup at pace but jumping into the hole. At the last, however, he drove off line to the right and Garcia was faced with a difficult shot from the rough with the ball above his feet. Yet the Spaniard struck the shot of the day from over 220 yards and the ball found the back of the green. When Fowler missed from 15 feet to halve the hole, Europe had squeezed out another half point and had taken the session 3½-½. "It felt better than a half," McIlroy said. "It was a long day, and if we had not got anything to show from it that would have been tough. A half feels like a mini victory."

First Morning Fourballs: Justin Rose and Henrik Stenson (Europe) won 5 and 4 over Bubba Watson and Webb Simpson; Thomas Bjorn and Martin Kaymer (Europe) halved with Rickie Fowler and Jimmy Walker; Jordan Spieth and Patrick Reed (USA) won 5 and 4 over Stephen Gallacher and Ian Poulter; Keegan Bradley and Phil Mickelson (USA) won 1 up over Sergio Garcia and Rory McIlroy.

First Afternoon Foursomes: Jamie Donaldson and Lee Westwood (Europe) won 2 up over Jim Furyk and Matt Kuchar; Justin Rose and Henrik Stenson (Europe) won 2 and 1 over Hunter Mahan and Zach Johnson; Rory McIlroy and Sergio Garcia (Europe) halved with Jimmy Walker and Rickie Fowler; Victor Dubuisson and Graeme McDowell (Europe) won 3 and 2 over Mickelson and Bradley.

Second Day

Watson's response to Europe taking an opening day lead for the first time since 2006 was to drop Mickelson and Bradley from the morning fourballs on Saturday. Furyk and Mahan came in for them and Kuchar replaced Simpson alongside Bubba Watson in the top match. The change did the Masters champion good and the pair were involved in one of the finest matches in Ryder Cup history. Each had two birdies in the first six holes to go two up on Rose and Stenson. Only one hole was halved in pars, the par-three fourth, while six were halved in birdies. From the seventh, Rose and Stenson birdied 10 holes in a row. They were level by the eighth, won the 12th and 13th holes, but the Americans extended them to the 16th. The home pair were 12 under for those 16 holes, the Americans nine under.

The pair of Rose and Stenson had been another of McGinley's hunches and was based not just on their golf but "my understanding of them as people." They had practiced together at Lake Nona the week before, as they do on any week off the tour, and had their third point in a row. Stenson, with a tender back, was rested for the afternoon, while Rose joined McIlroy in playing all five sessions for the second Cup in a row. "It was one of those days with the putter," Rose said. "I felt I was reading the greens so well."

Europe needed their contribution since elsewhere America were surging back into contention. Furyk and Mahan were too good for Westwood and Donaldson in the second match. The Americans won the first, the third and the seventh, and Mahan drove the green at the 14th and holed from 12 feet for an eagle to go dormie-up. They completed a 4-and-3 victory and were nine under par for their 15 holes after going out in a better-ball of 30.

In the third match, the youngsters Spieth and Reed, with a combined age of only 45, were channeling their disappointment from missing out the previous afternoon in the right way. They recovered from losing two of the first three holes to record another thumping victory, this time 5 and 3 over the experienced duo of Bjorn and Kaymer.

The morning's only action at the 18th came in the anchor match. With Garcia rested, McIlroy was out with Poulter. The Englishman birdied the first two holes but otherwise was as out of form as the previous morning. McIlroy carried him with three birdies in four holes to go two up at the turn, but yet again Fowler and Walker showed they would not give up. The Americans birdied five of the next six holes and, after Fowler's fine approach at the 15th, would have gone two up had not Poulter woken up and chipped in for a half. The self-described "postman" had finally delivered. "Rory was saying the mail's late but better late than never," he said.

Poulter also birdied the 16th to get back to even and the match ended all square at the last. It was the difference between the teams being back on level terms, as the Americans had hoped at one point, and Europe retaining a one-point lead despite losing the session 2½-1½ as the previous morning.

Saturday's foursomes also ended in an identical score line to the previous afternoon. Another 3½-½ victory for Europe proved the decisive session. Mickelson and Bradley, despite pleading with their captain Watson by text, were again benched, the first time Mickelson had missed a whole day of Ryder Cup action. Instead Fowler and Walker went for a fourth session in a row after going the 18 holes on each previous occasion. They had little left in the tank but were also facing the inspired, and rested, pairing of McDowell and Dubuisson in the anchor match. The Frenchman produced some superb shots and the Northern Irishman only had to point him in the right direction. They birdied three of the first six holes, and then when the Americans had a double bogey at the eighth, the home pair were five up. At the short 10th Dubuisson hit his tee shot to a foot, only for Walker to summon up the energy to reply with an equally fine blow to the same distance on the other side of the hole.

"He's ridiculously talented, it was a pleasure to play alongside him," McDowell said of his partner. They went on to record a 5-and-4 win, the second point of the session for Europe after the top match went to Westwood and

Donaldson 2 and 1 over Johnson and Kuchar. It was a tight match, with the Europeans going two up at the 10th only for the Americans to eagle the short par-four 14th. A birdie at the 16th followed by Donaldson's fine chip at the 17th sealed a 2-and-1 win. With his second win of the contest, Westwood moved to 23 points and past Seve Ballesteros in the all-time European ranking, behind only Sir Nick Faldo, Bernhard Langer and Colin Montgomerie. "To go past Seve, that means a lot," Westwood said. Donaldson said: "We seemed to gel much better in the foursomes, which is the harder format, than in the fourballs."

McIlroy and Garcia, back together again, won the first two holes against Furyk and Mahan, and despite losing the third hole, they stayed in front to win 3 and 2. With one match left on the course, America still had hope in the form of Spieth and Reed. They had led Rose and Kaymer two up after 10 holes but then bogeyed four of the next five holes. Having gone level at the 15th, they should have won the par-five 16th, but Reed's tap-in, from little more than six inches, lipped out. They did go ahead at the short 17th, but Spieth's putt for victory at the last missed on the right. After Kaymer's bunker shot, Rose was left with a five-footer to grab a half and he holed it. "All the way up the 18th Martin was saying we really deserve to get a half out of the game," Rose said. "That gave me a lift, made the task simple, everything else was forgotten, all the mistakes we made prior."

"That half-point was absolutely huge," McGinley said. "If we go on to win this Ryder Cup, that to me was a very pivotal moment. A four-point lead going into the last day is great but, obviously, the big word is complacency." It played into his theme for the week of being strong enough to play as favorites but not take anything for granted. No one in the European team room needed reminding that a 10-6 lead was not insurmountable, having overturned that deficit at Medinah, but it was Westwood, the sole survivor from Brookline in 1999, when Europe lost such a lead, that McGinley turned to at the team talk that evening.

The American team room was talking about the exact same subject. "As I recall, there's been a little bit of history with 10-6 comebacks," Watson said. Having said his team had got "shellacked" in the afternoon, he added: "I have trust in my players that they can get it done."

Second Morning Fourballs: Justin Rose and Henrik Stenson (Europe) won 3 and 2 over Bubba Watson and Matt Kuchar; Jim Furyk and Hunter Mahan (USA) won 4 and 3 over Jamie Donaldson and Lee Westwood; Patrick Reed and Jordan Spieth (USA) won 5 and 3 over Thomas Bjorn and Martin Kaymer; Rory McIlroy and Ian Poulter (Europe) halved with Jimmy Walker and Rickie Fowler.

Second Afternoon Foursomes: Jamie Donaldson and Lee Westwood (Europe) won 2 and 1 over Zach Johnson and Matt Kuchar; Sergio Garcia and Rory McIlroy (Europe) won 3 and 2 over Jim Furyk and Hunter Mahan; Martin Kaymer and Justin Rose (Europe) halved with Jordan Spieth and Patrick Reed; Victor Dubuisson and Graeme McDowell (Europe) won 5 and 4 over Jimmy Walker and Rickie Fowler.

Third Day

The players in red, white and blue certainly gave it their all early in the Sunday singles. There was just a moment when there was enough red on the scoreboard to get America a tie, though that would have been enough for Europe to retain, but it was a fleeting moment with most of the matches having too far to go. In the first five matches, Americans led in four of them at some point on the front nine and in two of them had significant leads. After McDowell, in the top match, lipped out at the first when he thought he had won the hole, Spieth was three up after five holes, while Mahan went four up after six holes on Rose. Turning those two matches around ultimately showed there would not be a "Glory at Gleneagles" comeback to go with the "Miracle at Medinah."

But first McIlroy was showing no mercy to one of his nearest pursuers from the Open and the PGA Championship. McIlroy had an eagle and four birdies in the first six holes to go five up on not just anybody, but Fowler, a fellow 25-year-old who turned himself into a major contender in 2014. McIlroy gave a hole back at the seventh but was eight under when he won 5 and 4 to deliver Europe's first point. "I was more up for it today than for my two major wins," McIlroy declared.

McDowell had been put in the top match by design by McGinley. It had been his plan all along to give the former U.S. Open champion a big role for the week — firstly to guide rookie Dubuisson through two foursomes and then, still fresh, to lead off the singles and set the right tone at the top of the order. It almost backfired. "Yes, I was fresh, but I nearly didn't have enough tournament play under my belt this weekend," McDowell said.

Ultimately McGinley was correct, because his number one simply willed himself back to form and to victory. A crucial moment came at the seventh when Spieth missed a chance to go four up. The next two holes were halved in birdies. At the short 10th, Spieth missed a short par putt and McDowell had an opening. He birdied three of the next five holes as Spieth, as he had on the back nine of the final rounds of the Masters and the Players, began to fade. McDowell won four holes in a row and five out of six to win 2 and 1.

In the second match Spieth's partner Reed was having the time of his life against Stenson. Reed was heckled on the first tee about the tiny putt he missed the day before but took it in his stride. He hit close at the par-three sixth to level the match, and when he birdied the seventh for a half, he put his finger to his mouth to hush the crowd. It had the opposite effect. "What in the world is he doing?" gasped Nicklaus on Sky television. He went two up at the 12th, but the Swede fought back and they went up the last only for Reed to birdie and win 1 up. The rookie was America's leading point scorer with 3½ out of four and their only unbeaten player.

It was only a minor blip for Europe. In a battle of the U.S. Open and Masters champions, Kaymer went four up after six on Bubba Watson and chipped in for an eagle at the 16th for a 4-and-2 victory. Kuchar beat Bjorn 4 and 3, never having trailed, and Mickelson defeated Gallacher 3 and 1. The Scot had finally got into his home Ryder Cup when he birdied the second hole to go ahead, but the left-handed American had too much experience. It was only then that the fourth match concluded, having gone to the final green. From four down after six, Rose had produced eight birdies in the last

12 holes, including at the last to grab another important half point against Mahan. At the 13th, Rose hit a remarkable shot from under a bush and grinned at a television camera: "A bit of Seve for you."

Europe were close to victory now, and in the 10th match Donaldson was in control against Bradley. The 38-year-old Welshman led from the fifth hole onwards, going two up at the ninth, then winning the 11th and 12th holes. He had a chance to win the Ryder Cup at the 14th but it slipped by. At the next, he hit a fine drive and then had 140 yards to the flag. "The perfect number for a wedge for me," Donaldson said. He struck it perfectly and it finished a foot away. "It was the wedge shot of my life," he said. "In the air, you're just hoping it is going to be good and it turned out spot on." He raised an arm in the air, and although McGinley and Tom Watson congratulated him, Donaldson marched to the green and only after Bradley took his hat off and offered a handshake in concession of a 4-and-3 win did the player celebrate with his teammates.

Europe eventually won the singles 6½-5½ to claim a third successive victory and an eighth in 10 matches. McGinley, who had talked during the match about orchestrating "wave after wave of attacks," said afterwards: "I didn't execute the plan, the players did that. I did the easy bit, they did the hard bit."

For America, the hard bit was still to come. Within weeks a "Task Force" was announced by the PGA of America to look into how to organize their Ryder Cup efforts better, a panel that included Mickelson and Tiger Woods but not Watson. Then Ted Bishop, the organization's president, was removed from office a month before he was due to stand down following inappropriate comments on social media in response to criticisms of 2008 European captain Nick Faldo in a book published right after this match by Ian Poulter. Long after the Glens fell silent, the fallout across the Atlantic was ongoing.

Third Day Singles: Graeme McDowell (Europe) won 2 and 1 over Jordan Spieth; Patrick Reed (USA) won 1 up over Henrik Stenson; Rory McIlroy (Europe) won 5 and 4 over Rickie Fowler; Justin Rose (Europe) halved with Hunter Mahan; Phil Mickelson (USA) won 3 and 1 over Stephen Gallacher; Martin Kaymer (Europe) won 4 and 2 over Bubba Watson; Matt Kuchar (USA) won 4 and 3 over Thomas Bjorn; Sergio Garcia (Europe) won 1 up over Jim Furyk; Ian Poulter (Europe) halved with Webb Simpson; Jamie Donaldson (Europe) won 4 and 3 over Keegan Bradley; Jimmy Walker (USA) won 3 and 2 over Lee Westwood; Victor Dubuisson (Europe) halved with Zach Johnson.

7. Women's Major Championships

Kraft Nabisco Championship

Lexi Thompson was still a kid in golf terms — just over 19 — but she had been around for so long and had done so much that she seemed to be a fixture on the LPGA Tour. It was easy to forget that if she wasn't playing in the Kraft Nabisco Championship, the first of the tour's five designated major events, she probably would be fussing over which sorority to pledge, which classes to take and which boys to date. It's easy to forget that she turned professional at age 15 and won her first LPGA event at 16 — the first of four. Michelle Wie was already practically a child prodigy when she turned pro at age 16. Wie had played in men's professional tournaments, though she had not yet fulfilled what seemed to be her huge promise. So when the two hooked up in a shootout — with Thompson winning — it was the future of the tour in progress. They were the young leaders taking their place in the game.

A little episode underlined this reality. Angel Yin, 15, and one of 10 amateur invitees to the tournament, was asked which player she'd like to meet. "Michelle Wie," she said. "If she sat next to me and said 'Hi,' I'd probably run."

Wie, 24, laughed. "These girls are starting to make me feel old," she said.

This Kraft Nabisco had a somber undertone. It was the last. The Kraft Nabisco contract was expiring, ending a run that began in 1972 when entertainer Dinah Shore founded the event with Colgate as the sponsor. Then came Nabisco in 1982, and Kraft Nabisco in 2002. LPGA Tour Commissioner Michael Whan announced that he was in talks with potential sponsors and that the tournament would return to Mission Hills in 2015.

But it was business as usual on the tour coming into that first week in April. Karrie Webb, 39, had already added to her Hall of Fame résumé, winning two of the first six events — the Women's Australian Open and the LPGA Founders Cup. She also owned two Kraft trophies, from 2000 and 2006, but there would be no third this time. She had bookend 73s at the par-72 Mission Hills and would tie for 11th, 12 shots behind Thompson. Paula Creamer, who won the HSBC Women's Champions a month earlier, also didn't fare well, tying for 34th. But she preserved her record of never missing a cut in a major, making the Kraft her 37th. In 211 pro starts, she missed only six.

Thompson and Wie, on a collision course, started out on different roads. Thompson managed only a one-over 73 in the first round, with one birdie, at No. 13, but bogeys at the fifth and 17th, ending up seven shots behind the 66 posted by China's Shanshan Feng on a perfect morning. "It was playing easier because there was no wind," said Feng, who was encouraged after her erratic start to the season. "I was a little lost because I lost a little weight and ... I wasn't swinging very comfortably," Feng said.

Wie was making her 12th start in the tournament and had a name to live up to. She finished ninth in 2003, at age 13, was fourth in 2004, and tied for third in 2006. "I think when you're younger, you're kind of fearless," Wie said. "You don't know what failure is." She gave a demonstration, shooting a four-hole stretch from No. 9 in birdie-birdie-eagle-birdie. The eagle was on a 25-foot putt at the par-five 11th, and the birdie at the 12th, on a 15-footer, tied her for the lead. A bogey at the 17th gave her a 67, a stroke behind Feng.

Wie was joined at 67 by Hall-of-Famer Se Ri Pak, 36, winner of five majors but not a Kraft. "Just a solid round," said Pak, who led the Korean surge in women's golf. Lydia Ko, 16, newest in a string of prodigies, was in a group at 73, and defending champion and Rolex Rankings No. 1 Inbee Park, battling her putter, shot 74. Third-ranked Stacy Lewis, battling her tee shots, shot 71. "If I can straighten out my driver," she said, "I'll be right there."

By the second round, Lexi Thompson found a putting touch to go with her booming drives and rocketed to the top of the leaderboard, where she would stay for the next three rounds. She'd needed 35 putts in her opening 73, but only 25 in the second round, shooting a flawless 64 for a seven-under 137 total, tying Se Ri Pak (70) for the lead. "I just had a little bit of speed issues yesterday," Thompson said. "I didn't really commit to my lines, and I came up short a lot. I just went out today and picked my line and sped up my tempo a little bit, and went up to it and said, 'I'm going to knock it in.'" And so she did. Thompson started on the back nine and parred the first five holes, meaning she played the last 13 in eight under. Her run was highlighted by a 20-footer at the 17th (her eighth), a 30-footer at No. 1, a 20-footer at No. 4, and a 10-footer at the ninth, her final hole.

"I had the same confidence over every shot, just committing to my line and just being confident," Thompson, and then she revealed the strategy that would win her this Kraft. "I'm really comfortable with the golf course," she said. "I get to hit a lot of drivers, so I just aim up the right side and hit my little draw." With her putter behaving, it would be her raw power that would conquer Mission Hills.

Se Ri Pak, playing some of her finest golf in years, birdied the last hole for a two-birdie, no-bogey 70 to tie Thompson at 137. There was nothing spectacular, Pak said. "Everything has just been solid," she said. "I kept it fairways, greens — always the goal, every hole."

Michelle Wie, starting on the back nine, dropped a 10-footer for birdie on her first hole. A stray drive cost her a bogey at No. 13 (her fourth), and she three-putted the par-five 18th — missing a three-footer for birdie. She birdied her 10th (No. 1), and that was it. Said Wie: "It felt good to start off with a birdie. After that, really just couldn't get anything going."

Much the same could be said for others trying to negotiate the tricky Mission Hills. Shanshan Feng, the first-round leader, bogeyed her last two holes and shot a four-bogey 73. Paula Creamer lost ground with a bogey and double bogey against only one birdie for a 74. Angel Yin, the young amateur too shy to meet Creamer, shot 79 and just ducked in under the cut at 150.

It could be said that this Kraft Nabisco began with the third round. It set up the Thompson-Wie shootout. When the day ended, Thompson had a one-bogey 69, and Wie shot a flawless 68 to tie at 10-under 206, sharing a two-stroke lead, setting a perfect stage for great finish to the last Kraft Nabisco.

Wie, playing in the next-to-last pairing ahead of Thompson, made hay over the first 11 holes. She birdied No. 1 for the second straight day by holing a 20-footer, lofted a nine iron to 12 feet at No. 6, wedged to five feet at the par-five ninth, and then holed a three-footer at the 11th for her 68. It was the first time since 2006 that she would be in the lead in a major going into the final round, and she felt ready this time. "I think I definitely am not as wide-eyed as I used to be," she said.

Said Thompson of her 69: "I would say I had a few mis-reads." She two-putted for a birdie at the par-five second, and then her putter, so cooperative the day before, turned cranky. She missed two ripe birdie chances — a 30-incher at the fourth and a four-footer at the seventh. She cashed in three coming home, chipping to 18 inches at the 11th, wedging to four feet at 12, then making a five-footer at 15 to take the lead. At various points, Thompson, Pak and Wie held the outright lead. It was Thompson's until the scrambled 18th — a scary recovery from a fairway bunker, an 80-footer, then a three-footer for par. Which she missed. "Not the ending I wanted," Thompson said. The bogey dropped her into the tie with Wie. Not that she knew it at first. "Every time I passed the leaderboard I looked the other way," she said.

Only Se Ri Pak and England's Charley Hull, tied two strokes behind, had any real chance of catching them. Pak shot 71, bogeying three of her last six holes. "There's nothing to complain about," she said. Hull birdied six of the last 12 holes for a 66 and, newly 18, she could become the youngest major champion in LPGA history. "It would be the best feeling ever," she said. (Pak would close with a 74 and tie for fourth, and Hull with a 76 and tie for seventh.)

So Thompson and Wie headed for the last round, tied for the lead, an almost scripted finish for the final Kraft Nabisco. It would be a test of both nerves and strategy. "I probably won't sleep that well," Wie said. "You want something so badly." Said Thompson: "I think if you're not nervous, you don't care. But it's a good nervous."

All other things being equal — they never are in golf — the final round would be a test of strategies. Thompson and Wie are both big hitters. Thompson would take on Mission Hills with her power. "My driver won't get me in any trouble on a lot of the holes here," she said. "So laying up wouldn't really make sense." For Wie, finesse was the key. Opting for accuracy over distance, she was using fairway woods for the low "stinger" tee shot. Getting to the green was the first task, putting the second, and that's when the magic touch of the second round returned to Thompson and put the strain on Wie.

In the final round, Thompson needed just 13 putts on the front nine. She birdied Nos. 1, 4, 5 and 9, and made the turn with a luxurious five-shot lead after Wie sputtered to just one birdie but two bogeys. Thompson parred her way home while Wie, struggling to catch up, did manage three birdies, but also a bogey for a par 71. Thompson, with a four-under 68 and a 14-under 274, won her first major by three.

Should Wie have changed and gone to her driver? "I stuck with my game plan, and I think it was the right play," Wie said. "I gave myself a lot of chances, but just couldn't get the speed right ... I needed to come back with a lot of birdies, and ... I tried to force it."

And Thompson's power strategy? "Well, I would say the greens were a little firmer this week," Thompson said, "so even with a wedge in your hand you had to play for quite a bit of bounce-out. I figured … even if I was in the rough, I could get it pretty close to the hole."

It was five years since Thompson first played the Kraft Nabisco as an amateur, just 14. At 19 years, 1 month and 27 days, she became — after Morgan Pressel in the 2007 Kraft Nabisco — the second-youngest winner of a major.

Said Thompson: "It has been an honor to play at this tournament so many years. Only being 19, and to win, is even the biggest honor ever."

And that raised the next question as the final curtain rang down on the Kraft Nabisco Championship: Whatever the name, would there be a title for Lexi Thompson to defend in 2015?

U.S. Women's Open

It was as though the fates had to torment Michelle Wie one last time.

There were all those high expectations over the years, brought on by her talent as a kid, and all those years of promise, and the falling short, time after time. And then came the 2014 U.S. Women's Open, at historic Pinehurst No. 2, with the unprecedented double, coming the week after the U.S. Open. Then, on the tough, crusty classic course that was Pinehurst No. 2, Wie was leading or sharing the lead much of the way. At last, she was about to win her first major. She was leading by three shots with just three holes left to play. And there came another jolt, a double bogey that all but ended her chances. It looked like failure again.

But this time, Wie pulled herself together, and there it was — the U.S. Women's Open, her fourth win as a professional, but infinitely more important, it was the accomplishment that was forecast since she was 13. She had won a major. She had been through a lot, and even had challenged twice in the Women's Open, in 2005 at Cherry Hills, when she was a 15-year-old amateur, and in 2006 at Newport Country Club, at 16 and a professional. A lot of disappointment followed, and now she was 24.

"I think it just means so much more to me," Wie said. "I think life is just so ironic. I think that without your downs, without the hardships, I don't think you appreciate the ups as much as you do. I think the fact that I struggled so much, the fact that I kind of went through a hard period of my life, the fact that this trophy is right next to me, it means so much more to me than it ever would have when I was 15. I am just so grateful … just because of everything I've been through. I feel extremely lucky."

In raw figures, Wie shot 68-68-72-70 on the par-70 No. 2, and with the two-under 278 total, she was the only player under par, winning by two over fast-closing Stacy Lewis, No. 1 in the Rolex Rankings. Lewis was part of Wie's final test, a real fright. Lewis finished at even-par 280 with a four-under 66, tying the tournament low shot by Juli Inkster and Catriona Matthews.

"I don't think you can script it any better," Lewis said, summing up Wie's finally breaking through, at such a historic setting. "I think it's great for the game of golf. I think it's even better for women's golf. I'm so happy for Michelle Wie. ... this has been such a long time coming for her."

Wie, a Stanford University graduate, knew how to study. She crammed for this big exam at Pinehurst. She borrowed the yardage books from two friends who played the U.S. Open the week before, Rickie Fowler and Keegan Bradley. "I did a lot of homework," said Wie , allowing for the course's playing about 1,000 yards shorter for the women. "I definitely learned a thing or two."

Perhaps it showed how badly she wanted a Women's Open that in four of the last six, she started with 80 or higher, but this time she opened with a 68, her lowest start ever in the Women's Open. Was that a sign? She was one over through the turn in the first round, then birdied the 10th, 12th and 14th (the latter two on long putts), but bogeyed the 16th, an omen of future trouble. She saved par at the 17th after a bunkered tee shot, and fired her approach to five feet at the 18th, setting up a closing birdie. She was a stroke behind Lewis, a pre-tournament favorite who had already won twice in 2014. "I played really, really solid," said Lewis, after her 67. "I didn't put myself in too bad of a spot. It was such an easy day." (That was about to change.)

Only five players broke par in the first round, tied at 69, among them Australian Minjee Lee, 18, one of 25 amateurs in the field.

Defending champion Inbee Park was aiming for her third Women's Open and to become the first to win two straight since Karrie Webb in 2000-2001. But she hurt her chances with an uncharacteristic blow-up, making two double bogeys and four bogeys for a 76. "I didn't feel like I played horrible," said Park, who won the Manulife Financial Classic, the previous stop on the LPGA Tour. "It was just so quick, and I just don't know what happened." Park contemplated her situation. She was almost resigned. "Not so much about the trophy now anymore," she said. "Just trying to keep it in play." Her big problem would be making the cut.

No matter what the scores, this U.S. Women's Open — the first two rounds, at least — belonged to Lucy Li, an amateur from California's Bay Area. And she made it into the U.S. Golf Association Museum before she had won anything. The reason: Lucy was 11, the youngest ever to qualify for the championship. And all spiffy in braces and sparkly skirts, she charmed everyone. She shook off her opening 78. "It was a lot of fun," she said. "I kind of struggled today, but it was great." Said Catherine O'Donnell, a second-year pro: "She looks 11, she doesn't talk 11, and she doesn't hit the ball like she's 11."

Li shot another 78 in the second round for a 16-over 156, and at that, she tied the great Laura Davies, tied Natalie Gulbis, finished better than 30 others, including Japan's Mike Miyazato, a former winner on the LPGA

Tour and co-runner-up in the 2012 LPGA Championship. Li made two triple bogeys, three doubles and eight singles, and four birdies — at Nos. 1 and 5 in the first round, and 3 and 14 in the second. And she had her bright memories. "I got birdies after I got doubles and triples, so that's what I'm really happy about," she said. She donated the American flag shirt she wore in the first round and the ball she used in the second to the USGA Museum.

In retrospect, the sign this was Michelle Wie's Women's Open came in the second round, on a course that was hard and dry despite a brief afternoon shower. Only two players finished the day under par at the halfway point, Wie and teen star Lexi Thompson. Both shot 68s, leaving Wie at four-under 136 and three ahead of Thompson. Wie was in control of her game. She bogeyed only once, but made two clutch par saves and three birdies, two of them on her closing holes (she started on the back), a six iron to 12 feet at the par-three eighth (her 17th) and a 15-footer at the par-five ninth. "It's a grind out there," she said. "Really grateful ... I can't complain."

Thompson also started on the back and bogeyed her ninth, then birdied three straight from No. 3 (her 12th) for the 68. Thompson won her first major in the Kraft Nabisco Championship in April and beat Wie by three, head-to-head. Was a rematch in the making here?

"Definitely too early," Thompson said, laughing. "Thirty-six holes in a major — that's a lot of golf to be played. Especially at a U.S. Women's Open." Thompson may have been a teenager, but she knew her golf.

Wie's three-stroke lead disappeared in a back-nine stumble in the third round. It had all the signs of the collapses that ruined her so many times in the past. But she managed to hold on to a share of the lead. Wie had birdied back-to-back through the turn, on an eight-foot putt at the ninth and two putts from 80 feet at the par-five 10th, and she was six under. But at the 11th, 444 yards from the back tee, she hooked her tee shot into the stately pines and double-bogeyed. Then she bogeyed the 12th and 14th. She settled down and parred in for a 72, tying for the lead with Amy Yang (68) at two-under 208.

Hall-of-Famer Karrie Webb, a two-time champion, was encouraged. "Michelle Wie has put a few of us back into the tournament," she said. "Two hours ago, I didn't think I had a shot. I'm pretty happy about that." (A 70 left Webb five shots back. But that elusive third Open title slipped out of reach with a 77 in the final round.)

Among the players very much in the running, just four behind, were the rookie Stephanie Meadow (69) and Hall-of-Famer Juli Inkster, 53, who shot the tournament-low 66 (it would be tied later). Inkster, a two-time champion, had said that this, her 35th, would be her last U.S. Women's Open. Did the 66 change anything? "You can think and you can dream all you want," Inkster said. "But the bottom line is you've got to come out and make the shots. And if I'm tied for the lead coming up 18 [tomorrow], then maybe I'll think about it."

Wie also knew not to be tempted by low scores. "U.S. Opens are tough," she said. "I'm just grateful for another opportunity. Tomorrow, I'm going to play as hard as I can and hope for the best."

But it was a tough start to the final round. Wie bogeyed No. 1 for the third straight day and ground out pars into the turn. Stacy Lewis, meanwhile, was in hot pursuit. She had started six off the lead, and after a birdie and two bogeys, she picked up steam with five birdies in eight holes from No. 6. Wie held her off at the shortened par-five 10th, hitting an eight-iron second to 10 feet and getting the eagle for a four-stroke lead. Her moment of truth lurked just on the horizon.

Lewis' hot streak ended with bogeys at the 14th and 16th, but then she would birdie the 17th and 18th, closing with a 66 and a par-280 total. Before long, she would be warming up for a playoff.

Wie nearly threw it all away. She led by three coming to the par-four 16th. She drove into a fairway bunker, then, despite her comfortable lead, tried to hit a hybrid to the green. "I was kind of a dummy for not laying up," she said. "And it kind of bit me in the butt. But I laughed it off. Stuff like that does happen."

But she wasn't laughing at first. No one could find her ball. Anxiety set in. Then finally, after a three-minute search, it was found in a bush. Prudently, she took a penalty drop, chipped to about 35 feet, and ran her bogey putt five feet past. Her lead was already down to one. If she missed the testy comeback, she would be tied. But she made it, and then, seemingly without nerve, birdied the par-three 17th, hitting an eight-iron tee shot to 25 feet and rolling in the dangerous putt.

Lewis got the word and quit warming up.

"That kind of emotion, that kind of pressure," Wie said. "I'll think of that putt as one of the best putts I've ever hit in my life."

For all of the success by so many others who passed her by, Wie, since her early teens, remained the biggest name in women's golf, and was famed — or notorious, depending on one's viewpoint — for playing against the men on the PGA Tour. In 11 starts in the Women's Open, she contended at age 15, but shot 82 in the final round. A year later she missed a playoff by two strokes and tied for third. And now it was all behind her.

"Oh, my God," Wie said. "I can't even think straight."

Ricoh Women's British Open

Arriving at Royal Birkdale for the Ricoh Women's British Open, there was quite a buzz about the women's game. Michelle Wie, the name perhaps most widely known, had just won the U.S. Women's Open. Lexi Thompson, one of an exciting group of teenagers, had won the first major of the year, the Kraft Nabisco Championship. Stacy Lewis was the World No. 1 and the defending champion. Inbee Park, who won three majors in a row in 2013, was seeking the title that had eluded her the previous year. Suzann Pettersen had won the inaugural Evian Championship less than a year earlier, pipping Lydia Ko, then an amateur, now the most sensational new talent in either the men's or the women's professional games. And don't forget Charley Hull, a young English star whose first LET victory had come earlier in the year, and Laura Davies, playing in the Championship for the 30th time, a winner at Birkdale in 1986 and now, courtesy of Her Majesty The Queen, Dame Laura.

Where, exactly, did Mo Martin fit in with that lot?

It turned out "Mighty Mo" was a diminutive 5-foot-2 Californian with a big heart who produced a most surprising but deserved victory. The 31-year-old started the week ranked as the 99th best player in the world, not having won before, nor finished better than 29th in a major. If anything was known about her, and then only by the LPGA regulars, Martin was one of the most accurate players on tour — topping the fairways hit category in only her second season on the LPGA in 2013 — and she was one of the most popular. Both those facts were confirmed at the climax of her triumph.

A surprising halfway leader who understandably wilted in the spotlight during the third round, Martin was still in contention on a windy final day when she came to Birkdale's par-five finishing hole. Just when she needed it most, her drive landed in the middle of the fairway. She had 240 yards to the hole with a strong wind across.

"I aimed very far left and hit a full three wood," Martin said. "When it rolled on the ground I said, 'Sit'. Then I said, 'Go'. But then it looked perfect so I didn't have to say anything. It was the best shot of my life."

Martin's ball hit the flagstick and almost went in for an albatross but rebounded only a short distance away. She holed the putt from six feet for an eagle as if it was the winning moment. About an hour later, it was. Her closing 72 matched Anna Nordqvist for the lowest round of the day and she was the only player to end the week in red figures, at one under par with a total of 287.

Among those still to finish were some far more illustrious figures, yet the wind and a fickle links had worn down even the best players. Park and Shanshan Feng, winner of the 2012 LPGA Championship, both needed a birdie at the last to tie, but Feng missed her putt and Park drove into the rough and took a six. Pettersen birdied the last two holes but was left one adrift alongside Feng.

Martin had been on the practice range, preparing for a possible playoff, but on being driven back to the 18th green, she was sprayed with champagne and mobbed by a huge group of fellow players who were all genuinely delighted by her success. "Everyone wanted her to win, she is so nice," Feng said. Pettersen added: "I am disappointed to be one short but very happy for her. Mo is one of the most popular players on tour."

"Is this real life?" Martin gasped during the celebrations. Later she reflected: "It's definitely a Cinderella story." She was introduced to the game at the age of four. Her father built a cage in their backyard and taught her and her brother from Hogan's *Five Fundamentals* instruction book. Family and friends helped to get her to junior events and to play at UCLA even though she did not get a golf scholarship. She spent six years on the Symetra Tour, the feeder circuit, winning three times before making it to the LPGA.

When Martin was 19 her father passed away. Up until then she had had little contact with her paternal grandfather, Lincoln Martin, a former geophysicist and aeronautical engineer. "I knew my grandpa was somebody I really wanted to get to know." She drove up to his ranch in Porterville, California, and discovered he had been following her career all along. "I walked into his office and there were these newspaper articles and pictures. I started crying, I was overwhelmed, because I didn't know he was that involved in my life. Like he was like a silent follower, but he was caring and loving me all the time."

Lincoln Martin was present for all her Symetra wins and at many of her early LPGA events, handing out "Go Mo" badges. In March 2014, Martin took another trip back to his ranch just in time to say goodbye before he passed away. He was 102. "He changed my life," Martin said. "He made everything so much brighter and better. I miss him, but I'm so grateful that I had the time I had with him. I'm incredibly blessed."

A recent convert back to the short putter, having used a broom handle all her career, Martin could not have been happier when she arrived at Royal Birkdale. "I fell in love with the course the moment I saw it," she said. "My caddie, Kyle Morrison, and I came up with a great plan and I executed it well. I think the layout is absolutely phenomenal and the officials set it up perfectly. Every hole, every shot is its own test. It really keeps you in the moment. It's a fun challenge. It's the epitome of creativity. We only get to do this once again at the British Open."

With the rough severe in places following a wet winter and recent hot spell, Martin's accuracy was a prized asset. Determined to keep the ball in play at all times, she often took her three wood despite being one of the shortest hitters on tour. She opened with a 69, three under par, to be one behind Japan's Ayako Uehara.

Morgan Pressel, Mina Harigae and Sarah Kemp all had 70s, while Lewis and So Yeon Ryu were among those on 71. Only nine players broke par. Park, Pettersen, Thompson, Ko and Emma Talley, who went on to win the Smyth Salver as the leading amateur, were among those on 72. The 18-year-old Hull recovered well from a double bogey–bogey start but went out of bounds at the last for a six to fall back to a 73.

Michelle Wie opened with a 75 but then had a 78 to miss the cut by three strokes. The U.S. Open champion never felt comfortable on a course where she was third as a 15-year-old in 2005. At the 16th she hit into a bush and hoped to get a free drop from the plaque that commemorates a thrilling escape by Arnold Palmer from the 1961 Open Championship. "But it was not close enough," she said. She took a double bogey, bogeyed the par-five 17th and three-putted the 18th for a par. "It really sucks," she said. "I didn't hit the shots I needed to hit."

Karrie Webb (72-79), Yani Tseng, the 2010 champion at Birkdale (82-72), and the last two home champions, Catriona Matthew (74-83) and Karen Stupples (77-81), also missed the cut. For Stupples, the 2004 champion at Sunningdale, it was a last regular appearance as a player as she took up television commentary full-time.

Martin had a second successive 69 and, at six under, found herself three ahead of Ryu and Spain's Beatriz Recari, who had a 67 with birdies at the last three holes. Sun Ju Ahn also had a 67, with four birdies in the last five holes, to be four behind with Julieta Granada. Park had another 72, while Lewis returned a 74 and Hull slumped to a 76, with a seven at the 18th after again driving out of bounds on the right and finding her second drive only inches in play.

In order to try and hit the 18th fairway on Saturday, Hull imagined herself playing through a tree-lined funnel as at her home club of Woburn. It worked and she ended up with a birdie and a 66, the lowest score of the week. She bogeyed the first two holes then had nine birdies in the last 16 holes, including four twos at the par-threes. "I feel I stepped up there today and really proved myself," Hull said. "I felt like I had a bit of pressure on me coming into this week, especially with Ricoh as my sponsor and people expecting a lot of me."

Hull jumped from 51st into a tie for seventh and from 11 strokes off the lead to only three behind Park. That was after the presumed third-round leader Ahn was penalized two strokes at the 18th for stamping down too enthusiastically in the sand to level out her stance at the side of a bunker where it was anything but. "I didn't know about the rule," Ahn said, "I was just trying to make a stance."

A 71 left the Korean on three under alongside Pettersen, 68, and Feng, 69, and one behind Park, who had a 68 after a fine outward 32. She birdied four of the first six holes and her only two bogeys were from three-putts — not a great endorsement for the latest replacement for the magical wand she had used to win three majors the previous year. According to a statement from the LPGA, although there are now five majors, winning a fourth different one, as Park was trying to do, would still count as a career grand slam. Winning all five would be a "career super slam" — don't mention that Park also won the Evian Masters prior to it becoming a major.

Martin knew she would be nervous playing in the last group of the day and never quite recovered from bogeying the first two holes. A 77 left her on one under and in a tie for seventh place. Out early on the final day, she was away from the attention. Two bogeys and a birdie going out were followed by a bogey at the 13th, but she was avoiding the disasters going on around her. With the strongest wind of the week, Pettersen had two double bogeys, at the first and 13th holes, while Park had a double at the 10th and a bogey at the 11th when she had looked in command. Feng and Pettersen had 75s, Park and Granada 77s, Ahn a 79. Davies returned a 73 to finish tied for ninth, but Hull closed with a 78 to share 12th place with Lewis, who had a 78.

Martin, however, was in her element. "I love the wind," she said. "I love working the ball against the wind and having fun with it." It was the first time since 1999 that Americans had won the first three majors of the season. Part of the spoils will go towards securing her grandpa's ranch. "We're going to be able to keep the ranch, which is what I wanted. It is kind of my sanctuary, I have all these memories of being with my grandpa. My aunt Mary made the big effort and it's almost finalized to keep it in the family, but now I can help keep it up, we need a new roof, things like that."

Martin added: "I just want to say there are so many amazing people in this world and not enough is said about the good deeds people do, things unspoken, unspoken kindness. So many people have helped me when I've needed it. I've definitely had a few angels in my life. I'm just grateful for having the career I have. I'm living the dream every day."

Wegmans LPGA Championship

The LPGA Championship, the flagship of women's professional golf, was first played in 1955 at Orchard Ridge Country Club at Fort Wayne, Indiana, and was won by Beverly Hanson.

The last Wegmans LPGA Championship was played in 2014 at Monroe Country Club, near Rochester, New York, and was won by Inbee Park.

It seems odd to think of the venerable event that way, but on that Sunday evening, August 17, when the final putt dropped and the closing ceremonies had ended, the Wegmans LPGA Championship ceased to exist, a victim of the various ills of modern golf — sponsorships, TV ratings and all the rest of the commercial and economic aspects. The tournament was being played in the Rochester area for the 38th year, and when the latest title sponsor, Wegmans supermarket chain, declined to renew, the championship had to be rescued in a historic move. It will reemerge in 2015 as the KPMG PGA Women's Championship, sponsored by an accounting firm and operated by the PGA of America, and will make its debut at Westchester Country Club.

It all meant that Korea's Inbee Park, who won the 2013 LPGA in a playoff, was in position not only to win a rare back-to-back championship but also would be the last winner. "I think it'll be such an honor because being the first or being the last is always very memorable," Park said.

Park, meanwhile, had been having a decidedly un-Inbee Park kind of year on the LPGA Tour. Despite her victory in the Mission Hills World Ladies Championship on the Ladies European Tour, this was not the Inbee Park who dominated the LPGA Tour in 2013, winning six tournaments, three of them majors. She did break out of the doldrums in her 11th start, winning the Manulife Financial LPGA Classic in June, where she closed with a 61, but then she tied for 43rd in the U.S. Women's Open in the following start.

"I think it's not a bad season at all for me because I had a win," she said, "and I've played very consistently this year, and I feel like my game is actually improving, just except for the putter. I mean, that's because last year I just holed so many putts, and this year — my game, my ball-striking, my greenside chipping, and everything has really improved. But just not many putts. But it's so hard to beat whatever I did last year."

Still, this was Inbee Park, Rolex Rankings No. 3, and she was among the pre-tournament favorites for the LPGA. Park opened quietly, with a pedestrian par 72, with birdies at the eighth and 14th and bogeys at the fourth and 12th.

The first-round stage belonged to Meena Lee, 32, a two-time winner on the tour, and teenage prodigy Lexi Thompson, 19, who won her first major at the Kraft Nabisco Championship in April, each making eight birdies and two bogeys and tying for the lead at six-under-par 66. "It's very exciting," the restrained Lee said, "and then, well, it's just the first day."

The power-hitting Thompson was delighted to see the beckoning wide fairways. The championship had been played at Locust Hill, in the Rochester area, for 37 consecutive years. The tournament this time was switched from June to August, and also to Monroe Country Club, about 300 yards longer at some 6,700 yards.

Thompson, who was averaging 271 yards off the tee, figured to have the edge with her driving.

"Coming into the week, I knew this golf course was going to be set up good for me," Thompson said. "After I played Monday, I knew I could take driver on every hole, which I definitely feel comfortable with." She hit 10 of the 14 fairways and 16 greens in regulation, and birdied the four par-fives.

Thompson and Meena Lee led by a stroke over Canadian rookie Jennifer Kirby, Colombia's Lisa McCloskey and Brittany Lincicome, another big hitter (nicknamed "Bam Bam") who would find the generous fairways inviting. But the course was hardly out of reach of the shorter hitters. "I'm nowhere near a long hitter, and I still think the course is pretty fair," said McCloskey. "On holes that are longer, they still have that kind of big run-up area right before the green, so you can run a wood up there."

So there was the strategy for Monroe — the big hitters could fly it to the greens, the shorter hitters could run it up. In either case, though, first hit the fairways.

McCloskey closed strong for her 67, birdieing six of her last eight holes and the last four in succession. Lincicome enjoyed the best of both worlds, power and finesse, in her 67. She noted that rain a few days before had softened the course a bit. "So the farther you hit it, the better," said Lincicome, who had eight birdies and three bogeys. "Each of the par-fives is reachable, so that fits into my game." But her short game helped immensely. "I was hitting things to a foot and just tapping them in," she said. "It was stress-free."

The second round was an interesting mix of leaders finding confidence, coming from different directions: Lincicome, troubled by doubt but holding steady and taking the lead; Park, relieved and rocketing up the leaderboard, and Thompson, slipping but encouraged anyway.

Thompson struggled to shoot par. Starting on the back nine, she made two early birdies, then bogeyed her eighth and ninth, then ground out pars to finish. "Just didn't hit it as well," Thompson said, "but I did make a lot of good putts, so I'm going to take a positive out of it." She tied Park for second at 138, three off Lincicome's lead.

If body language is any real indicator, Lincicome was dejected after three-putting No. 1 for a bogey. After a strong start to her career, her confidence had become somewhat fragile. She said she'd been doing good things all year, but ... "Hitting well, putting well, chipping well," she said. "They just don't seem to all come together on the same day." But they did this day. After that opening bogey, she birdied Nos. 5, 9 and 12, and pitched in from the rough for an eagle at the par-five 14th for a 68, nine-under 135 and a three-stroke lead. "It doesn't matter how big lead you have with her ... behind you," Lincicome said.

She meant Inbee Park, who exploded from her benign start with birdies at Nos. 1, 3, 4, 11 and 15 — and an eagle at the 14th — a streak cooled a bit by a bogey at the 17th for a 66–138. "It was a great day —quite different from yesterday," said Park, who chipped in for one birdie and holed a bunker shot for the eagle. "Yesterday, nothing really wanted to drop for me, and today it was just falling from outside the greens."

Brittany Lincicome, who hadn't held a second-round lead since 2009, was nervous in the third round. "Nervous is probably an understatement," she said. "My stomach was in knots. I haven't been in this position in a while. Hopefully, going into tomorrow, it's out of my system."

Lincicome had won five times — including one major, the 2009 Kraft Nabisco — but was winless since 2011. But she braced herself and shot a one-under 71 and finished the third round at 10-under 206. That gave her a one-stroke lead on Suzann Pettersen (67) and Inbee Park (69). Lincicome didn't forget that she lost two strokes of the lead she'd started with, and that she owed her position atop the leaderboard pretty much to her length. She was 11 under on the par-fives through the third round. She had birdied all four of them in the first round, got two birdies and an eagle in the second, then birdied three more in the third, Nos. 9, 12 and 14. Clearly, power was her big edge.

"I hate talking about it — I feel like I'm going to jinx myself," Lincicome said. "If I can hit it on the fairway, get it on the green and two-putt, it's stress-free."

Park couldn't come close to matching Lincicome's power. "This golf course is not exactly for short hitters," said Park, who would play the par-fives in five under — four birdies, an eagle and a bogey. "She was probably 50 yards ahead of me. It's an easy birdie for her." Park shot 69 with four birdies — one at the par-five 14th — and a bogey.

Suzann Pettersen, who won the 2013 Evian Championship and had four other top-five finishes in her last eight majors, made her move in the third round. After a bogey at No. 1, she rang up six birdies over the next 14 holes for a 67, tying Park for second at 207, a stroke behind Lincicome.

Pettersen, playing with Lincicome in the final pairing of the last round, was out of the chase in a hurry. A double bogey at No. 1 sent her on to a ragged 76. She ended up in a tie at 283 along with Rolex No. 1 Stacy Lewis

(68), whose chances died when she couldn't solve Monroe's three closing holes. In the first three rounds, she played them in seven over and without a birdie.

The big question, then, was whether Lincicome's power would be enough to offset the case of nerves that was building in her.

With Pettersen gone, and with Lydia Ko and Azahara Munoz challenging only briefly, the tournament settled into a struggle between Lincicome and Park. Lincicome dealt with the nerves most of the way. She saved par from 12 feet at the first, birdied the par-five third, three-putted the sixth for a bogey, but got that stroke back with a birdie at the eighth, and went three ahead of Park with a birdie at the 11th.

Park, playing with Mirim Lee in the pairing just ahead, was even par on the front with a birdie at No. 4 on a 20-foot putt and a three-putt bogey at No. 7. Ironically, it was a par-five that hurt Lincicome badly. Park birdied the 12th, and Lincicome followed and bogeyed it — her only bogey at a par-five all week — after needing two chip shots to get on the green. The two-shot swing cut her lead to one. She got the stroke back at the next par-five, the 14th, but she was going to need the stroke she no longer had.

Park crept back to within one when she dropped a 20-foot putt at the 17th. Lincicome then almost matched her, but her birdie try from 25 feet stopped agonizingly close. Even so, when Park could only par the 18th — for the fourth time, and a 70 — Lincicome still had a shot in hand playing the final hole. Then the nerves really set in. Lincicome, who had parred it the first three visits, hit her second to the left fringe, about 30 feet from the flag. She left her first putt eight feet short, missed that for a winning par, and bogeyed for a one-under 71 to tie Park at 11-under 277 and force a playoff.

They returned to the 18th. Both drove into the fairway, Lincicome about 50 yards ahead of Park. Both missed the green. Lincicome chipped six feet past, Park chipped to within two. Lincicome missed her putt, and Park made her par for the win, her second consecutive LPGA Championship and second in a playoff. It was her fifth major and 11th tour win.

"I was really nervous coming down the stretch," Lincicome said. "I was shaking like a leaf. It's hard to do anything when you're shaking."

Said Park: "Being able to become a winner, there has to be some luck on your side."

And then noting she had just won the final LPGA Championship, she added: "Just very happy to be part of history."

Evian Championship

With her victory at the Evian Championship, Hyo-Joo Kim both created history herself and denied Karrie Webb adding to her illustrious career. In the first round Kim became the first player, male or female, to score 61 in a major championship. She led by four strokes over Webb at that stage, but there was a long way to go: One record round does not necessarily win a championship. She was not even leading by the following evening.

But Kim was back in front after 54 holes, and for much of the final round, going in front by three after 12 holes. A four-shot swing to Webb in three holes from the 14th, however, changed the picture entirely and made for a dramatic finale. Webb's 25-foot birdie putt at the 17th, from the lower tier of the green, never had enough speed and pulled up seven feet short. Suddenly ahead for the first time, was the veteran about to falter? No, she was not. Webb holed the par putt and walked to the final tee with her one-stroke lead intact.

The 39-year-old Australian, giving away two decades to her South Korean opponent, was within touching distance of an eighth major championship, her first in over eight years since winning the Kraft Nabisco Championship in 2006, and her sixth different major. She won the Kraft Nabisco and the U.S. Women's Open twice each, as well as the Women's British Open in 2002 — her two earlier victories in the British Open were before it was recognized as a major on the LPGA tour — but her first official LPGA major title was the old du Maurier Classic in 1999. She had already been credited with a super career grand slam, but adding the latest women's major, the Evian Championship, would make for an unrepeatable feat.

Webb won the old Evian Masters in 2006, but the course changes that preceded the first Evian Championship in 2013 had made the 18th a tough finishing hole. Webb's second shot with a four iron finished on the fringe on the left side of the green. Kim, whose nerves were apparent when she all but duffed her second shot at the previous hole, now responded with the stroke of a champion. From a similar distance to Webb, around 175 yards, Kim hit her approach to 12 feet.

Webb faced a delicate shot from the fringe that was downhill and, using a belly wedge, could not get the ball to stop. It almost went in but rolled on 10 feet past the hole. Webb could only watch as Kim holed in her birdie putt which left the Australian needing to make her par effort to force a playoff. It did not come close to going in. "It was a very poor putt," Webb admitted. "The first one was a lot faster than I thought, and it was a rush of adrenaline with the belly wedge.

"I don't know what hit me, actually," Webb added. "Two pretty good swings, just didn't get that four iron to cut in there. But her shot at the last was really impressive. I let the foot off the pedal a little bit, which probably let her have a little bit more of a free putt at it. But she still had to make it and she did."

Webb concluded: "Impressive for a 19-year-old. The putt's probably 19-year-old nerves, but the shot in was definitely very mature. She played great today."

Kim, who spoke through an interpreter, had looked composed throughout but said she was "flying like a bird" after realizing she had won, which only came with confirmation from her Scottish caddie, Gordon Rowan. The pair mainly communicated by hand and facial gestures, but it worked. The only previous time they had worked together was at the Evian Masters in 2012 when Kim had finished fourth as an amateur. In the meantime Rowan had given up caddieing full-time and taken a job working for a company in China that makes women's lingerie.

In two years as a professional, Kim had won four times on the Korean LPGA circuit, including three times already in 2014, while in her first year of a physical education degree at Seoul University. Not yet a member of the LPGA, this was her first appearance in a major championship but she was ranked 20th in the world at the start of the week and ended it as the third youngest winner of a major, behind 18-year-old Morgan Pressel and 19-year-old Lexi Thompson from earlier in the season. Ironic that two teenagers should win majors in 2014 and neither of them was rookie professional Lydia Ko. At 17 years and four months, this was the World No. 3's last opportunity to became the youngest-ever major winner, but Young Tom Morris' record from 1868 will be safe for a while yet as Ko finished tied for eighth at the same venue where she was runner-up to Suzann Pettersen as an amateur the year before.

The inaugural Evian Championship got off to an inauspicious start as a major in 2013 with the substantial course changes not having had long enough to mature and torrential rain forcing the event to be cut to 54 holes. For 2014, everything was in place and Kim got off to a stunning start with a 10-under-par 61. She breezed past Webb's 65, the best of the morning starters, and kept going. She was out in 30 and added another five birdies on the back nine, including at the 18th. She needed only 23 putts, one of them from over 50 feet at the 14th. She had realized the course would play far harder than on her previous visit in 2012 but kept a bogey off her card. "I like hard courses, so I like it," said Kim. "I feel very comfortable today."

Rowan, her caddie, observed: "She has a very good all-round game. She's not a massive hitter but has a very decent length and keeps up with the girls, but she's so straight, and this is a course where you need to hit fairways because the rough is very thick. Her accuracy into the greens means that she's never far away. She also has a very good temperament."

Kim's score was one better than the previous women's major record of 62 set by Minea Blomqvist at Sunningdale in 2004 and equaled by Lorena Ochoa at Mission Hills during the Kraft Nabisco Championship in 2008. In men's majors, no one has gone lower than 63.

Behind Webb, who only had 25 putts after turning to a putter she had last used 12 years earlier, was Mi Jung Hur on 66, with Brittany Lincicome and Pettersen on 67. Lincicome birdied three of the last four holes, but the defending champion, having been one over par after 13 holes, birdied the last five holes. "I was patient enough to wait for something to happen and not flip out that I didn't kind of play good," said Petersen.

Michelle Wie's return from injury ended prematurely when she withdrew on the 13th hole as she suffered a stress reaction in her right index finger. The finger had started to hurt again after a shot on the fourth hole and the U.S. Women's Open champion eventually decided to seek help. "It was probably a week or two too soon to play," said Wie, who missed the LPGA Championship after suffering the injury in August. "I just wanted to see if I could play. The doctors did tell me if it did hurt to stop right away just because it could get worse. I was having so much fun out there I wanted to keep playing. But it got to the point where it was too painful."

Wie stayed at Evian until the Sunday presentation of the Rolex Annika Major Award, when the Hawaiian was confirmed as the inaugural winner. The award offers points to top-10 finishes in the majors, with the winner having to be one of the major champions. Wie topped the table thanks to her second place at the Kraft Nabisco as well as the U.S. Open victory. Inbee Park was second and Thompson was third, after both finished tied for 10th in the Evian, with Kim and Mo Martin sharing fourth place and Stacy Lewis finishing as the leading non-major winner. "It's awesome just to be a part of history to win the first one," said Wie. "I remember hearing that we were going to have this award last year, and I set that goal for this year. I really wanted to win it. I tried really hard at all the majors."

With more wind and tougher pin positions on the severely undulating greens, there was no repeat of Kim's record scoring during the rest of the week. Not least from Kim herself on the second day when she returned a 72, 11 strokes higher than the day before. Instead it was Lincicome with a 65 who took over the lead at 10 under par. The American also led after 36 holes at the Wegmans LPGA Championship the previous month, as well as after 54 holes before losing a playoff to Park.

Lincicome said practicing barefoot had helped her tempo, which led to her regaining her confidence in the biggest tournaments. "It makes me swing a lot slower, which is really good for me," she said. "Especially with a driver I tend to want to hit it really hard, and with no shoes on I can't do that."

The American led by one over Kim, with Hur two strokes further back and Webb and Pettersen on six under par after rounds of 71 and 69 respectively. So Yeon Ryu was disqualified after an incident on the fourth green. Frustrated with missing a putt, she hit her putter against her shoe and bent the shaft. However, she then tapped in before notifying an official on the following hole that she had played with a club that had been damaged not in the normal cause of play.

Frustrations ran higher on Saturday when conditions were at their most tricky. Only seven players broke 70, the best of them 67s by Na Yeon Choi and Jane Park, while Lincicome fell back into the pack with a 77. Hur took the lead only to have a triple-bogey-six at the short 6th. Chipping from behind the green, downhill to an particularly difficult hole location, Hur topped the ball across the green into the water hazard on the other side. Kim was watching from the tee and understandably played safe, taking a bogey. Earlier birdies at the 12th and 13th holes, however, helped Kim to a second successive 72 with which she re-took the lead. At eight under par, she was one ahead of Webb, who was steady for a 70, two in front of Hur and three ahead of Anna Nordqvist and Mariajo Uribe.

Webb birdied the first hole of the final round but then had a double bogey at the next, while Kim got a two for a three-shot swing. Others made good starts with Choi birdieing four of the first five holes and Ha-Na Jang four of the first seven. Jang would bogey the last and Hur the 17th to tie for third place, two behind the winner, with Choi bogeying two of the last three to be fifth, with Pettersen sixth and Paula Creamer seventh.

After the final pairing were quiet for much of the front nine, Webb birdied three holes in a row from the ninth, while Kim birdied three out of four. However, there was a two-shot swing to the Australian at the short 14th, then Webb birdied the 15th and Kim bogeyed the 16th. Suddenly, it was Webb's to lose, though in truth Kim produced a stunning final hole to steal the victory.

"I believe in fate and obviously it wasn't meant to be today," Webb said. "But I hit shots today that I don't think I've ever been able to hit, so I'm really excited about that."

8. American Tours

If one can grade golf seasons by the number and quality of 19th hole topics produced, then 2014 was a vintage year. And of the topics, three were, by observable attention, purely top-shelf. (The ranking is left to individual taste.)

- The return of Rory McIlroy
- The disappearance of Dustin Johnson
- The absence of Tiger Woods

After a long slump, McIlroy rocketed back to the top with three huge wins. It's left to students of psychology and the arcane to decide whether it was cause-and-effect or sheer coincidence that his game returned shortly after he broke his engagement to Danish pro tennis star Caroline Wozniacki. He proposed on New Year's Eve, 2013, and they had sent out wedding invitations. Then he broke off the engagement on May 21, saying: "The wedding invitations ... made me realize that I wasn't ready for all that marriage entails."

Just four days later, he came from seven shots behind in the final round to win the European Tour's BMW PGA Championship — his first win on either the European or PGA Tour in 18 months. Then in the summer, he scored three big wins, in the Open Championship, the WGC - Bridgestone Invitational and the PGA Championship.

Perhaps he'd finally gotten used to his new equipment. The prevailing opinion among experts was that the change had thrown him off his game, a notion he rejected. Whichever was the case, McIlroy made his argument by topping the PGA Tour money list with over $8.2 million and winning the Player of the Year Award and just about every other honor in golf.

The Dustin Johnson episode would be among the strangest in the game's history. Johnson seemed to be on his game. He'd tied for fourth in the U.S. Open and tied for 12th in the Open Championship, and had won some $4 million. He was also No. 5 in the Ryder Cup standings and virtually sure to earn an automatic spot. Then on July 31, he announced he was taking a leave of absence, and with no date of return. "I will use this time to seek professional help for personal challenges I have faced," Johnson said. The media rumor mill immediately speculated that it was a PGA Tour suspension for failing a drug test. The tour denied it. At all events, the rest of 2014 passed without Johnson reappearing.

Woods' spotty career of recent years continued in 2014. He missed his first Masters since 1994 after having back surgery, and he made seven scattered starts. He missed two cuts, withdrew twice, and finished tied for 80th in the Farmers Insurance Open, tied for 25th in the Cadillac Championship and solo 69th in the Open Championship (his worst finish in a major in which he'd played 72 holes). He did play in his Hero World Challenge, where he tied for 17th and last, 26 strokes behind the winner, Jordan Spieth.

Spieth, playing in his first Masters and at age 20, was threatening to become the youngest winner until the final nine. He tied for second.

In the majors:

- McIlroy led wire-to-wire in his first Open Championship win, beating

Rickie Fowler and Sergio Garcia by two. After taking the WGC - Bridgestone, he won his second PGA Championship (and fourth major) in the near darkness, beating Phil Mickelson by one. McIlroy, a three-time winner on the tour in 2014, scored all three wins in a span of four weeks.

• Bubba Watson took his second Masters, rallying from behind from No. 8 in the final round to win by three over Spieth and Jonas Blixt. With victories in the Northern Trust Open and WGC - HSBC Champions, Watson was also a three-time winner.

• Germany's Martin Kaymer became the first from Continental Europe to win the U.S. Open. He started 65-65 and rolled to an eight-shot win over Fowler and Erik Compton. Emerging from a long slump, he'd started his run by winning The Players Championship in May, a one-stroke decision over Jim Furyk.

There were three other double-winners in 2014: Jimmy Walker, Sony Open and AT&T Pebble Beach National Pro-Am; Patrick Reed, Humana Challenge and WGC - Cadillac Championship, and Billy Horschel, the BMW Championship and the Tour Championship, along with the FedExCup Playoffs for the $10 million bonus.

Elsewhere, the year was illuminated by some interesting observations:

• Patrick Reed, on winning the Cadillac Championship: "Now I have three wins [in a year] ... I just don't see a lot of guys that have done that, besides Tiger Woods ... I'm one of the top five players in the world."

• Steven Bowditch, ranked 339th in the world, on daydreaming down the stretch of the Valero Texas Open, his first win: "...looking ahead to the Masters and winning golf events and making my speeches before I was finished — I had to pull myself in every time. And it happened a lot today."

• Charley Hoffman, OHL Classic winner, on not playing it safe: "I wasn't going to shoot for middle of the greens and let someone else beat me."

• Jordan Spieth, 20, after wind and rain cost him a chance to win the AT&T Pebble Beach National Pro-Am: "You want to play Pebble Beach in that weather once in your life. You just don't want it to be Saturday when you're in the lead."

• France's Victor Dubuisson, Accenture Match Play runner-up, on his incredible saves from cactus and bushes in the final against Jason Day: "I just play my shot 100 percent like it was a playable shot, like I have nothing to lose."

• Billy Horschel, after beating Bubba Watson in the BMW Championship, on who might be the favorite in the Tour Championship the following week: "If I were a betting man, I'd put some money on me."

• Billy Horschel, on winning the Tour Championship the next week, along with the FedExCup, total take $11.44 million: "I'm not sure life can be better than this."

U.S. PGA Tour

Hyundai Tournament of Champions

Maui, Hawaii
Winner: Zach Johnson

The PGA Tour's 2014 schedule got under way the first week of January with the Hyundai Tournament of Champions, and it proceeded to become a curiosity piece. The tournament, with an exclusive field of 30 winners from 2013, figured to be the domain of the big hitters such as Dustin Johnson, the defending champion. This was because the Plantation course, a par-73, stretched 7,411 yards and had generous fairways, especially at the par-fives — a welcome mat for the big hitters. But it was the other Johnson — Zach — who won. And he is not to be confused with a big hitter. How did this happen?

"I picked it apart," Zach Johnson said.

The final scorecards told the power story. Dustin Johnson played the par-fives in 12 under, Zach in six under. It didn't matter.

Leading in the second and fourth rounds, Zach shot the Plantation course in 67-66-74-66, a 19-under-par total of 273, nipping young sensation Jordan Spieth by a stroke.

Spieth, 20, took the spotlight immediately, tying for the first-round lead on seven-under 66 with Michael Thompson, Chris Kirk and former U.S. Open champion Webb Simpson. "I did a lot of hard work the last two or three weeks getting ready for today," Spieth said. Johnson, despite his lack of length, got his 67 with the help of the par-fives — a birdie at the fifth and an eagle at the ninth, that on a downhill eight-foot putt.

The tournament came down to a chase down the stretch with Dustin Johnson and Spieth. Dustin liked his chances because of his power, noting that he could reach the par-fives in two and get close on some of the par-fours. "So if I chip and putt well, I'm going to shoot a good score," he said. His thinking was spot-on, but his execution let him down. He was tied for the lead with Spieth and Webb Simpson going into the final round, then three early bogeys sidetracked him. Simpson bogeyed the third and fourth and couldn't catch up, tying for third.

For Spieth, calming the impatience of youth was the key. In the duel with Zach Johnson down the stretch, it wasn't bogeys that hurt him but failing to get birdies at the softer 14th, 15th and 16th. But he resisted getting ahead of himself. "I was very pleased with the finish, being able to birdie the last two holes and at least have somewhat of a chance on 18." He needed an eagle at the 18th to catch Johnson, but that meant holing a 100-foot putt. He did birdie for a 69 to finish a stroke back.

Accuracy was the key for Zach Johnson. "Getting the ball in the fairway and giving my wedges a chance was crucial," he said. As he showed on the final nine, where five players had a chance to win. His wedges set up birdies at Nos. 12, 14, 15 and 16 for a 66. He had picked the course apart to put together a one-shot win.

Sony Open in Hawaii

Honolulu, Hawaii

Winner: Jimmy Walker

The romantics would say the stars had aligned for Jimmy Walker, golf's preeminent astronomy student. Others would say that he was lining up putts better. Whichever the case, with the Sony Open in Hawaii safely in his bag in mid-January, Walker — who had gone seven years and 187 PGA Tour tournaments without a win — suddenly had his second in six starts. It was also a great birthday gift. Walker, who had taken up photographing the heavens, turned 35 just a few days after the tournament.

"I always felt like I belonged, and you always need affirmation every now and then," said Walker, who had finally broken through in the Frys.com Open in October. "It's nice to get it done and do it again today."

If Walker wasn't a surprise winner in the Sony, he was at least unexpected. He trailed through the first three rounds and entered the fourth among a dozen players within three strokes of the lead. Chris Kirk, who hadn't played since winning the McGladrey Classic back in November, edged into the third-round lead with an up-and-down birdie out of a bunker at the par-five 18th. Harris English (67) and Will Wilcox (64), making his tour debut, were tied for second, one back. Said Wilcox, surprised at his start: "Making the cut was a dream come true. Playing well on Saturday was a dream come true. Getting to have a decent shot tomorrow is ridiculous. We'll see." (He would tie for eighth and win $119,000.)

Walker, starting 66-67-67, entered the final round two off the lead and attracted a little attention when birdies at the second and ninth got him into the chase at 12 under. Then he caught fire, posting five birdies down the back nine at Nos. 10, 13, 15, 16 and 17 for a bogey-free 63 and a 17-under 263, beating Kirk by a stroke.

Walker started his run with the birdie at the 10th which dropped him to 13 under. After a birdie at the 13th, he saved par at No. 14 with a 12-foot putt. He gave Harris English something to think about when he rolled in a 15-foot putt for birdie at the 15th, which held up for the lead when English, playing behind him in the final group, came along and bogeyed it out of a bunker. "Just started hitting it better, but putting a little worse," English said.

Walker wrapped up his round with a birdie at the 16th, on a seven-foot putt, and another at the par-three 17th, on a seven-iron tee shot to six feet. He parred the 18th for his 63. Kirk, in the last group, had to eagle the 18th to tie Walker, but his 30-foot chip shot missed. He made the birdie for a 66 and took second by a stroke.

Humana Challenge

La Quinta, California

Winner: Patrick Reed

If the PGA Tour offered an Understatement of the Year Award, Patrick Reed would have had it pretty well wrapped up by mid-January at the Humana Challenge.

His award-winner: "It's great to have that feeling that you can go out and shoot 63," Reed said. This was after the second round. He'd already shot one in the first. And he would shoot a third straight in the third. "Almost seems like I'm in a putting coma," Reed said.

He got a 63 at each of La Quinta's three tournament courses — in order, the Palmer, the La Quinta and the Nicklaus, all par-72s. He led by as many as seven shots, that through the third round, then cooled to a 71 in the fourth on the Palmer course for a 28-under 260 and a two-stroke win over Ryan Palmer. It was, of course, a wire-to-wire win.

"It was tough out there," said Reed, after racing through the first 54 holes in 27 under, breaking a tour record that had stood since 1967. It was also the first time a player shot the first three rounds in 63 or better. All told, he had two eagles, 30 birdies and six bogeys, four of them in the final round. Reed, 23, a Texan, was a Rolex junior All-American for three years, played college golf at the University of Georgia and Augusta State, turned pro in 2011 and joined the tour in 2012.

Reed started his spree with a bogey-free first round that told the story for the field. "The rough isn't very high, the fairways are perfect and the greens are rolling very true," he said, taking a one-stroke lead that was the start of a scoring feast for the entire field. Of the 84 finishers, Jhonattan Vegas finished dead last at five-under 283.

While Reed was making his second 63 on the La Quinta course, Brendon Todd was shooting one on the Palmer, completing two rounds without a bogey to sit two behind. "Feeling like I should birdie every hole," said Todd, who then went the first 58 holes without a bogey, made only two in the tournament and tied for sixth.

Reed's 63 put him two ahead, and then with his third round, he rocketed to a seven-shot lead over Todd and Charley Hoffman. Starting on the back, he birdied three of his first five holes and eagled his seventh, the par-five 16th. Birdies at his 10th and 13th put him seven under, and a bogey at his 14th, No. 5, was a bump. He snapped back with birdies at his 15th, 16th and 18th. Could he make it four straight 63s?

"I'm just going to treat tomorrow as if it's a Monday qualifier, 18-hole shootout," Reed said. "Everybody's tied at even par."

There was no 63, but the five-birdie, four-bogey 71 had its compensations. "To not have my full game, and to have that much of a cushion to be able to just coast in," Reed said, "that's a good feeling."

Farmers Insurance Open

La Jolla, California

Winner: Scott Stallings

Golfers being the competitive animals they are, they will always welcome a challenge. But from the caddie? So starts the story of Scott Stallings in the Farmers Insurance Open.

The 18th at Torrey Pines South, one of two courses used for the Farmers and the site of much drama in the past, is a robust par-five of 570 yards. Stallings had trailed all the way and was three behind starting the final round, then came to the 18th tee needing a birdie for a chance to win. But he had to hit the fairway to have any real chance at one.

Said his caddie: "Let's see what you've got."

One thing Stallings didn't need was more pressure. "We're at the last hole," Stallings recalled telling himself, "and you're going to tell me that now?"

At all events, he responded with a long drive into the fairway, but when he got to his ball he found a golf problem and a bad memory. His ball was on a hanging lie, a slight slope above his feet. The ball sweeps to the left from one of these unless the golfer adjusts his swing. A year earlier, at the final hole of the Humana Challenge, Stallings failed to adjust and it cost him a triple bogey and the win. He adjusted this time, and fired a four-iron from 222 yards over the front pond and onto the green, and two-putted for a birdie and his third tour victory.

"I actually thought about 18 at Humana the whole time on 18 today," Stallings said. "Not that I was [saying], 'Oh, don't hit it in the water.' But it was, 'Just make sure you pay attention to everything that's going on.'"

Before Stallings could become the surprise winner, Tiger Woods, making his 2014 debut, was a surprise of another kind in the third round. Remarkably, he made back-to-back double bogeys, then five straight bogeys, shot 79 and missed the cut, this on a course where he had won eight times.

Stallings, playing the second round on Torrey North and the others on the harder and famous South course, shot 72-67-72-68–279, nine under, to win by one over five others — K.J. Choi, 66; Graham DeLaet, 68; Jason Day, 68; Pat Perez, 70, and Mark Leishman, 71. The most disappointed, however, had to be big-hitting Gary Woodland, who led by a stroke going into the final round and was a stroke behind and well within reach of the 18th in two. But he double-bogeyed the 17th off a hooked tee shot into the canyon and missed a birdie try at the 18th and finished three behind. "I felt like I gave one away today," Woodland said.

Stallings started eight behind Stewart Cink's lead of 64, climbed to four behind Jordan Spieth in the second round, and three behind Woodland through the third. In the fourth round, Stallings made six birdies and three bogeys through the 16th and came to the 18th under the weight of a needed birdie and a caddie's challenge.

Waste Management Phoenix Open

Scottsdale, Arizona

Winner: Kevin Stadler

A new name entered the world of golf early in February — the "Smallrus." It rhymes perfectly with "Walrus," as in Craig Stadler, the 1982 Masters champion, and it's no coincidence. Smallrus also is a Stadler — his son, Kevin, 33.

Until the Waste Management Phoenix Open, at TPC Scottsdale, Kevin was best known for his Stadleresque bulk and for having gone 238 PGA Tour starts without a victory. It seemed he would come up empty for the 239th time early in the final round.

Stadler stayed close to the lead through the first three rounds, and was two behind Bubba Watson through the third. He burst into the fourth with three straight birdies, then edged ahead with another at the ninth. Was he ever sitting prettier? Then came the par-four 11th — a tee shot into the cactus, a penalty drop and two putts for a double bogey. "Eleven has had my number for years," Stadler said. "I butcher that hole every year."

It was a shootout down the final stretch. Stadler and Watson both hit into the water at the par-five 15th and scratched out pars. Stadler caught Watson at the par-three 16th with a par against a bogey out of the bunker. Both made remarkable birdies at the 374-yard 17th, driving the green and two-putting from 90 feet to stay tied.

A playoff seemed to be in the offing, and this concerned Stadler. He wanted to watch the Super Bowl game between his beloved Denver Broncos and the San Francisco 49ers.

At the final hole, the par-four 18th, Stadler put his 110-yard approach 10 feet from the back-right pin. Watson made a fatal error. He drove into the right rough and, from 120 yards, put his approach over the green. He bladed his next from trampled-down rough into the bank of the green, then chipped five feet past the hole. Stadler, putting first, missed his 10-foot birdie try and tapped in for par. What was going through Stadler's mind with his first victory in sight?

Said Stadler: "How long the playoff was going to take and how long until I can watch the football game?"

Watson answered both questions when he missed his short par putt. "Obviously, I misread that, too," said Watson, who finished with a par 71 and tied fast-closing Graham DeLaet (65) at 269. Stadler scored his first victory on his 239th start on a card of 65-68-67-68–268, 16 under.

"I fully expected him to make the putt," Stadler said. "I would have rather made mine to win it."

If there was a huge distinction, it didn't matter to Craig Stadler. The win made them the first father-son combination in the Masters.

"It's going to be great for me," Craig said. "I kept saying, 'When he gets in, that's my last one.' I'm proud of him. It's awesome."

The tournament, by the way, famous for its crowds, drew an estimated 563,008 fans for the week, said to be a record for golf.

AT&T Pebble Beach National Pro-Am

Pebble Beach, California

Winner: Jimmy Walker

Jimmy Walker's 66 didn't lead the first round of the AT&T Pebble Beach National Pro-Am, but it was the low score at Pebble Beach. In his return to Pebble for the final round, he shot 74, and one had to search some 30 players deep to find a worse score. It was a tough finish for a winner.

"It's drama, man — it was too much for me," said Walker, who led by six starting the final round, then won by only one. Walker, 35, winless before the 2013-14 season, had now chalked up his third victory. But barely. Over the first three rounds, he shot 66-69-67, at Pebble, Spyglass Hill and Monterey Peninsula, respectively. The finale had everyone back at Pebble, where he used nearly all of that six-shot cushion. It was the stumble down the back nine that got him, and it couldn't have come at a worse time — just as Dustin Johnson and the hopeful Jim Renner were revving up.

"I've never had whatever big lead this is going into the last round," said Walker, who got it in the teeth of heavy weather. For the final round? "Play good golf and see what happens."

Walker made the turn in one under for the day, then came the near-fatal back nine. He bogeyed the 10th, but answered with a birdie at the 11th on a 10-foot putt. Then came three bogeys — a poor chip at the 12th, a three-putt at the 13th, and another at the par-three 17th, after missing his par putt from three and a half feet. He had one last scare. Trying to play safe, he took an iron off the 18th tee, and still caught the rough. But he steadied himself, finally two-putting from 25 feet for a par and the 74 for the one-stroke win over Johnson and Renner, closing strong about an hour ahead of him.

Johnson eagled the par-five second and rang up seven birdies, but could only groan over what might have been. "I'd like to have the par-threes over," he said. He bogeyed three of the four and shot 66, tying for second with Renner, who shot 67 and still felt like a winner. Renner, a Web.com Tour graduate, was scrambling to gain a foothold on the big tour. This was his first made cut after four misses, and the finish was worth $580,000. "My back was up against the wall," Renner said. "I'm happy that I freed myself up a little bit for the rest of the year."

Young whiz Jordan Spieth, 20, who tied for fourth, showed a sense of humor to go with his lofty game. The notorious Pebble Beach wind and rain hit in the third round, knocking him into a 78 and out of a chance for his second win. "You want to play Pebble Beach in that weather once in your life," Spieth said. "You just don't want it to be Saturday when you're in the lead."

Northern Trust Open

Pacific Palisades, California

Winner: Bubba Watson

It took nearly two years, but Bubba Watson finally emerged from the trees at Augusta National.

Much was expected from the talented Watson when he won his first major, the 2012 Masters, with that spectacular hooked wedge from the trees. But then, oddly enough, he fell silent. In 2013, he posted only three top-10s, but he couldn't crack the top three. Then once 2014 got under way, he showed signs of the other Bubba Watson. He was threatening in only his second start, the Phoenix Open, but he missed a short par putt at the final hole and tied for second behind Kevin Stadler. Two weeks later, in mid-February, he didn't let the Northern Trust Open get away.

"It doesn't feel like two years, no," Watson said, gauging time by his favorite subject, Caleb, the baby boy he and his wife adopted at the time of the 2012 Masters. "I can't believe he's about to be two."

Watson started the year with a tie for 23rd at the Farmers Insurance Open late in January. Next came the tie for second at Phoenix. His start in the Northern Trust could be called recovery golf. His opening one-under 70 included double bogeys at his first and third holes (10 and 12). He was out in 38, back in 32. He also double-bogeyed No. 9 in the second round, and shot 71, for a one-under 141, to make the cut by three. That left him eight behind at the halfway point — comfortably out of it again, by most accounts.

"So I went into the weekend just trying to play solid golf," Watson said. He did better than that. He played the final 39 holes without a bogey and closed with 64-64 for a 15-under 269, two ahead of Johnson. It was his fifth tour victory but the first in 22 months and 41 starts, and sidetracked some dreamers, including two looking for that first win.

William McGirt, 34, a mini-tour veteran, was leading by two going into the final round and shot 73, slipping to joint sixth. Jason Allred, in his first tour event since 2010, shot 68 and tied for third, his career-best. Johnson, opening and closing with 66s, was the most frustrated. "I had a chance on the back nine," said Johnson. "That's all you can ask for."

Watson wiped out a four-stroke deficit in a hurry, with five birdies on the front nine. The keys were a 15-foot putt at No. 4, holing out of a bunker at No. 6, then taking the lead with a 15-footer at No. 8. After another birdie at No. 11, he saved par at the next two on seven-footers, then closed spectacularly. At the uphill par-four 18th, he hit a wedge from 164 yards to 15 feet and holed the birdie putt for the 64. He was ready for the media, with a big grin.

"I know y'all are going to ask," said Watson. "My first win since the Masters..."

WGC - Accenture Match Play Championship

Marana, Arizona

Winner: Jason Day

Jason Day, long seeking a World Golf Championship, finally found one in the thin air of Arizona's high desert, the WGC - Accenture Match Play. At the same time, golf found a new folk hero: Scratch a Frenchman, find a Spaniard.

Day, the 26-year-old Australian, was hardly a surprise winner. The talented Aussie was seeded No. 2 in his bracket in the 64-man field off the top of the Official World Golf Ranking. But France's Victor Dubuisson, 23 — seventh in his bracket and known in European golf if at all — was practically Seve Ballesteros reincarnated, getting into awful messes then escaping by magic. First, it was amazing that Dubuisson even made it to the final, beating such big names along the way. Then given little chance against Day, he forced the final to the 23rd hole, and by then was practically a household name.

"I felt like I had a heart attack out there a couple of times," an admiring Day said.

The unlikely Dubuisson beat Kevin Streelman and Peter Hanson without too much trouble, then ran the gantlet against some real heavyweights — Bubba Watson, Graeme McDowell and Ernie Els — all in 1-up matches. Day faced something of a lighter chore, ousting Thorbjorn Olesen, Billy Horschel (going 22 holes), George Coetzee, Louis Oosthuizen and Rickie Fowler.

Day was a clear favorite to make short work of Dubuisson in the final. There were some heady moments. Day, for example, matched Dubuisson's birdie at the par-five 11th on a three iron from 269 yards to five feet. At the 17th, Dubuisson was 2 down with two to play and in a fairway bunker 174 yards away. He slashed the shot to 15 feet and made the birdie. At the 18th, Day bogeyed and they were tied.

At the first extra hole, enter the spirit of Ballesteros. Dubuisson hit over the green and against the base of a cholla cactus in the desert. It looked unplayable, but he slashed his nine iron through the cactus, sending the ball up the grassy slope and to four feet from the hole. He made the par. At the next, he missed the green well left and ended up in a desert bush, unplayable again. But he escaped again. Finally, at the fifth extra hole, Day pitched to four feet and birdied to win.

Dubuisson explained his escapes: "I just play my shot 100 percent like it was a playable shot, like I have nothing to lose."

Said Day: "Vic coming down the stretch was just unbelievable. I kept shaking my head because ... I thought he was absolutely dead. But I'm just so thankful to be here."

This was last WGC match play under the traditional single-elimination format. Hoping to keep the top seeds in the event longer, for the TV audience, organizers have changed the 2015 tournament to a round-robin format for the first two rounds, with the 16 survivors advancing to the elimination bracket for the weekend.

Honda Classic

Palm Beach Gardens, Florida

Winner: Russell Henley

Russell Henley deserved better from history. He was already in the books for winning his PGA Tour debut, the 2013 Sony Open. Now, more than a year later, he took his second title, but it is surely to be known more for the wild four-man finish and, even more, as another chapter in the Strange and Painful Tale of Rory McIlroy.

McIlroy remained a puzzle: To lead for the first three rounds, then fold in the fourth and lose in the playoff? Was he slowly making his way back from his slump, or was he mired in it for good? "When you have a two-shot lead, you have to go out and play well," McIlroy said. He was showing great promise. This was his seventh top-10 finish in his last 10 (including a win in the Australian Open, but he hadn't won on the PGA Tour for 18 months).

The Honda was up for grabs then, when McIlroy faltered. After leading on rounds of 63-66-69, McIlroy came undone, playing the last 12 holes in five over, with four bogeys and a double bogey at the 16th, but a birdie at the 18th for a four-over 74 that got him into the playoff at eight-under 272. He tied with Ryan Palmer (69), Russell Knox (71) and Henley, who shot a two-over 72. There followed a playoff with one of the shortest discussions known.

Said Henley: "I told Ace [caddie Adam Hayes] no matter what, I'm going to hang in there the best I can, make good golf swings, and I've got nothing to lose playing against these guys."

The playoff was over quickly, on Hayes' instructions. "Let's end this fast," the caddie told Henley. Appropriately, Henley drove it into the fairway.

"Let's put it on the green first," Hayes said.

Henley was the only one to reach the 549-yard par-five in two, smacking a five wood 241 yards to 40 feet. He two-putted for a birdie for the victory, the winner from three feet.

This Honda would also be known as the one Tiger Woods left in the final round because of lower back spasms. He'd shot 71-69-65 and was five under and seven off McIlroy's lead going into the final round. He was five over when he quit after the 13th.

McIlroy stirred his fans with his rocketing start, a bogey-free 63 for a one-stroke lead over Henley. He led by one through the second round and by two over Henley through the third. "I've been building and building toward getting my game to a level where I feel it should be," McIlroy said. And then there was the fourth round.

Henley had a so-so record since winning his rookie debut in 2013. He'd had only two top-10 finishes since then, and he had missed four cuts in his previous nine starts.

"So this is kind of out of nowhere," Henley said. "This doesn't feel real. This is not exactly what I was expecting at the start of the week."

WGC - Cadillac Championship

Miami, Florida

Winner: Patrick Reed

Golfers are noted for their cautious talk, as if fearing to bring down a curse from the jealous fates with bold statements, but on occasion along will come one who lets it fly. Introducing Patrick Reed, 23, a second-year man on the PGA Tour. Put him at the head of the class.

On going wire-to-wire in the WGC - Cadillac Championship for his third victory in 14 months, Reed noted:

"I've worked so hard ... did great things in [my] amateur career ... and now I have three wins ... I just don't see a lot of guys that have done that, besides Tiger Woods ... I'm one of the top five players in the world."

He'd also worn a red shirt and black slacks for the final round. Explained the unabashed Reed: "The best player ever to live ... wore black pants and a red shirt."

(Tiger Woods, also in uniform, didn't fare too well. He had broken par in 34 of his 39 rounds on Doral's par-72 Blue Monster, but this time managed only 76-73-66-78, a five-over 293, tied for 25th in the 67-man field.)

Whether listeners would agree with Reed and his self-assessment or not, he offered skeptics his case. He scored his first victory in the Wyndham Championship the previous August, then won the Humana Challenge in January and now the Cadillac in March, in which he shot the toughened Blue Monster in 68-75-69-72 for the four-under 284 and a one-stroke win over Jamie Donaldson and Bubba Watson.

Reed took a grip on the storm-battered tournament in a four-hole stretch in the third round. He dropped a 40-foot putt for eagle at the eighth and birdied the 10th and 11th. He took the outright lead at the par-four 16th, driving the green and getting a two-putt birdie on his way to a 69, a four-under 212 and a two-stroke lead on Jason Dufner (68) and Hunter Mahan (71).

"The tournament will not be over until the last putt drops on 18," Mahan said, in a kind of statement of intent. Reed agreed.

"We've played great," Reed said. "And if I continue doing what I'm supposed to be doing, come Sunday afternoon, hopefully we're holding the trophy."

And he got help. Mahan and Dufner both shot 76. Donaldson (70) made three birdies coming home and got to within a stroke, then bogeyed the 18th. Watson, bogey-free for the last 27 holes, saved par at the 18th for a 68.

Reed cobbled together a conservative, erratic but effective final round. He birdied No. 1, but a bogey out of a bunker at No. 2 cut his lead to one. He holed a 25-footer for birdie at No. 3, dropped an 18-footer for another at the fourth, then saved par from bunkers at 11, 13 and 15. Bogeys at 14 and 18 got him back to par 72, his third win and his proclamation.

Puerto Rico Open

Rio Grande, Puerto Rico

Winner: Chesson Hadley

At the very least, winning the Puerto Rico Open meant that Chesson Hadley could eat again. No, it wasn't a matter of being broke. It was a matter of keeping food down.

"I was so nervous," said Hadley, 26, a PGA Tour rookie from Raleigh, North Carolina. "I didn't eat well last night. I didn't eat well this morning. I wasn't vomiting or anything, but there were a couple of times where I felt nauseated out on the course." Finishing without incident, he shot Trump International–Puerto Rico in 21-under-par 267 for a two-stroke win over old friend and fellow Web.com Tour graduate Danny Lee, back for his second PGA Tour stint.

The tournament, played opposite the WGC - Cadillac Championship, was Hadley's 13th tour start in the new wraparound season. He'd had two top-10 finishes, his previous best a tie for fifth.

Hadley's nerves didn't start to tighten until he moved closer to the top in the second round. He had opened with a four-under-par 68, which was encouraging, because he was high on the leaderboard, but comfortable because he was two strokes off Brian Stuard's lead and not under the harsh spotlight. In the second round, James Driscoll racked up seven birdies and an eagle, tying the course record with a 63 despite the rain and the gusting March winds. Hadley climbed to within one with a 65, and that was a huge relief. "I've been struggling, just finding the planet," he said.

Hadley took the lead with an amazing third round. Amazing because he hit 17 greens in regulation, made no bogeys, but managed just one birdie over his last 11 holes, shooting 67 for a one-stroke edge on Lee. "It was frustrating," Hadley said. "But I'm leading, and that's great."

Great, that is, except for trying to sleep on a one-shot lead and getting something to eat.

The final round would be a rematch for Hadley and Lee. The previous May, they fought it out in the last round of the Web.com's Rex Hospital Open. Hadley won that battle with a 64. Now they both were looking for that first PGA Tour win.

Hadley started this shootout with three birdies over the first five holes, including the pivotal moment of his win. "Probably the shot that won me the tournament was the chip-in on No. 5," Hadley said. "I mean, I was dead over there, and I hit the nastiest little nipper, and it sneaked in the back door." Lee responded with a hot finish, birdieing three of the last four holes, but he came up two shots short with a 68.

"I gave it my best, but Chesson was just playing rock-solid," Lee said. "He didn't make any silly mistakes at all."

Said Hadley, with that precious first win in his bag: "It'll be nice to sleep on it and wake up in the morning knowing I'm a PGA Tour champion." Nobody thought to ask what he was having for dinner.

Valspar Championship

Palm Harbor, Florida

Winner: John Senden

They came away from the Valspar Championship at the Innisbrook Copperhead course with a variety of resolutions. For John Senden, it was to stay in the moment, as the golfers like to put it. For the notoriously slow Kevin Na, it was to get the clock off his back. Scott Langley just wanted to hit a few more greens. As for Robert Garrigus — he would put down the fishing pole and take up the chain saw.

The big-hitting Garrigus, looking for that second PGA Tour win, decided to try the strategy that won him the Children's Miracle Network Classic in 2010. Namely, that he went fishing instead of playing practice rounds. The magic worked again — until the fourth round. Next year, no fishing, Garrigus vowed. "I'm going to bring a big, damn chain saw and cut down a few trees," he said. A closing 75 dropped him to a tie for fourth. Langley finished third even though he didn't hit a green down the final four holes. Kevin Na finished second by a stroke despite the pressure of being timed.

Senden had said he could win, "If I could just stay in the moment." Well, he could and he did, scoring his second PGA Tour win, more than seven years after the 2006 John Deere Classic. "Now it makes me feel [validated after] the John Deere," he said.

But early on in the Valspar, the end of his long drought was nowhere in sight. He made the cut with his 71-72 start. But he trailed through the first three rounds and was eight behind Garrigus after 36 holes. Senden built his win with some long-range successes. In the third round, a 30-foot birdie putt at the 18th gave him a 64 and lifted him 32 spots up the leaderboard, two off Garrigus' lead. Then thoughts of a win, and the Masters invitation that went with it, began to creep in. But he had to stay in the moment, he told himself.

The final chase was a coin toss, what with a three-way tie coming down the "Snake Pit," Copperhead's tough final three holes. Langley got to six under, then bogeyed the 16th when he missed the green long. He finished third, two behind. Senden leaped to the advantage by chipping in from 70 feet for one of only two birdies at the 16th in the final round. He went up by two with a 20-foot birdie putt at the 17th, then nearly holed a 40-foot birdie putt at the 18th, and tapped in for a 70 and a seven-under 277. Na, playing behind Senden, got to within one on a 15-foot birdie putt at the 17th, but a too-long wedge held him to a par at the 18th and a 72, second by a shot. Senden had his first win in some seven years. And he took an important precaution after lifting that trophy.

"I didn't turn my phone on," he said. "because I know there's going to be 4,000 messages."

Arnold Palmer Invitational

Orlando, Florida

Winner: Matt Every

Among those who were surprised to see Matt Every win the Arnold Palmer Invitational, no one was more surprised than Matt Every himself.

How to measure surprise? Well, on being congratulated by Arnie himself, the best Every could do in response was to say: "I ... I ... I can't believe I won — I just ... I really can't."

But it was true. Every, 30, had finally won on the PGA Tour, in his 92nd start. Still, his prospects were dim this time. Shooting Palmer's par-72 Bay Hill in 69-70-66 over the first three rounds, he was a mere tag-along and trailed by as much as nine strokes. But he closed with a 70 and was the clubhouse leader facing a short, agonizing wait. Would his 13-under 275 hold up? In the final pairing just behind him, Adam Scott was out of it but Keegan Bradley still had a chance.

Ultimately, the question was, which was greater — Every's joy or Scott's pain?

Scott, who nearly withdrew because he felt ill, had the title all but in his hands. He'd opened with a sizzling, two-eagle 62 ("...the hole was a bit like a bucket," he said) and led through the first three rounds, by three, seven and three strokes. Then came a letdown in the final round, a five-bogey 76. For the second time in six tournaments, he'd squandered a big lead on the last day. "Today was a bit shaky," said Scott. "My short game just wasn't there." So Scott, just three weeks from defending his Masters championship, slipped to third place, two strokes back, leaving the door open for Bradley to challenge Every.

But a double bogey and three bogeys through the first 11 holes left Bradley with too much to do. He birdied the 12th, 16th and 17th, but just missed a tying 30-foot birdie try at the 18th, and shot 72, finishing second by a stroke. "I thought I made that putt," Bradley said. "It was breaking in perfect and it just stopped breaking."

Every started the final round four shots out of Scott's lead and one behind Bradley, and started off tentatively, with a birdie at the fourth and a bogey at the eighth. But with the shaky starts by Scott and Bradley, he was smack in the hunt. He bolted into the lead in a burst of four birdies across five holes, starting with a big break at No. 9. He thought his tee shot had veered out of bounds, but somehow it bounced down a cart path and ended up a birdie. He needed it, the way he played the par-five 16th. He drove into the woods, hit a tree trying to escape, and bogeyed. He also bogeyed the 18th, missing a four-footer for par, then waited. And won.

"It's tough," Every said. "You just never know if it's going to happen. You get there so many times. It's nice to get it done."

Valero Texas Open

San Antonio, Texas

Winner: Steven Bowditch

Between the stiff March winds and the daydreams, Steven Bowditch had trouble keeping rubber on the road in the Valero Texas Open. The mere thought of finally winning would, of course, be unsettling to a 30-year-old ranked 339th in the world, whose career highlights were two top-10 finishes in eight years on the PGA Tour, and who was looking at a $1.1 million prize and an invitation to the Masters in two weeks.

He did it, but it doesn't seem fair — golf never is — that Bowditch, who endured so much and then finally succeeded, was overshadowed by a player who couldn't even finish the tournament.

Well, that player happened to be Phil Mickelson, and what befell him at TPC San Antonio might well have stamped his entire year. First, he opened with a five-over-par 77. "I've been playing real well at home," Mickelson said. "So to come out and play like this is disappointing." But he perked up with a 70 in the second round, just made the cut, and pronounced himself fit to proceed. "My back feels great, my body feels great and I'm able to hit the ball hard again," Mickelson said. Actually, too hard. He withdrew after 10 holes in the third round. "I pulled a muscle ... trying to hit it hard," he said. A bad back had knocked him out of the Farmer's Insurance Open in January. His prospects for playing in the Masters were looking dim.

While the Mickelson drama swirled, Bowditch, the obscure Australian, was climbing the leaderboard — an exercise unfamiliar to him. Then, oddly enough, his winning finish was even more surprising than his climb.

Bowditch took the lead for the first time ever on the tour in the second round, after a hole-out eagle from 83 yards at the par-four 12th sparked a 67 for a one-stroke edge. He went three ahead with a 68 in the third round on an amazing short game. He chipped in twice — a birdie at No. 1, an eagle at No. 2, and to set up a four-foot birdie at No. 5. Next came two big questions.

His three-shot lead? "I didn't feel ... I had a big enough cushion to take it all at the last [hole]," he said.

And his nerve? "I've never slept on a lead," he said, "so we'll see how we go."

It didn't go well in the final round. After posting 69-67-68–204, for a three-stroke lead through 54 holes, he closed with a thumping 76. He double-bogeyed the par-four fourth, bogeyed the 13th, birdied the 14th, then bogeyed the 18th, two-putting from three feet. But at eight-under 280, he had enough to get home a stroke ahead of Daniel Summerhays (71) and Will Mackenzie (70). And he survived the daydreaming.

"Looking ahead to the Masters and winning golf events and making my speeches before I was finished — I had to pull myself in every time," Bowditch said. "And it happened a lot today."

Shell Houston Open

Humble, Texas

Winner: Matt Jones

Not to paraphrase a cliché, but on a scale of 1 to 10, Matt Jones was an 11 at Redstone's 18th. First, Jones, who trailed by six strokes starting the final round, birdied the 18th with a 46-foot putt to tie Matt Kuchar in regulation. Then he birdied it again as the first playoff hole, chipping in from 42 feet to take the Shell Houston Open, his first PGA Tour win and a berth in the Masters the next week, his first.

And with the big guns on his heels. Rory McIlroy tied for seventh, Phil Mickelson for 12th.

Said a stunned Kuchar: "Certainly fantastic stuff to birdie 18 twice. That's probably the hardest hole on the golf course."

Jones, a 33-year-old Australian who played his college golf at Arizona State University, was no threat to Kuchar or anybody else as the lead changed hands through the first three rounds. Shooting 68-68-71, he trailed Bill Haas and Charley Hoffman by three in the first, Sergio Garcia by four in the second and Kuchar by six going into the fourth. His chances didn't look especially good — in fact, he was trailing by three on the back nine — so he ignored his predicament.

"I didn't look at the scoreboard too much because I knew I just had to make birdies," Jones said. "I actually told myself before I teed off, 'This is just like playing a practice round ... be aggressive and try to make as many birdies as you can.'"

Playing ahead of Kuchar, Jones bogeyed No. 1, then birdied seven out of 14 holes from No. 3. Kuchar, meanwhile, was having an erratic spell. He also bogeyed the first. He birdied the second, then bogeyed the sixth. Birdies at Nos. 10, 13 and 15 put him back in command, but he bogeyed the 16th, and then the 18th, knocking his fairway wood approach into the water. Earlier, Jones' birdie spree had ended at the par-four 17th, where a bogey left him two strokes behind.

At the 18th, with Kuchar watching from the tee, Jones rolled in the 46-footer for a 66. "That was a little double break," he said. "As soon as it got on top of the ridge and started going down, I thought it was in."

When Kuchar bogeyed the last for a par 72, they were tied at 15-under 273. In the playoff, at the 18th, Jones bunkered his tee shot and put his second just short of the greenside bunker. Kuchar drove into the fairway, and bunkered his second. Then Jones called his next shot.

"I walked up there and told my caddie I was going to chip it in," Jones said, and using his 54-degree wedge, he gently sent the 42-foot shot home. It was as bold a move as his 45-foot tie-clinching putt.

"I was going to three-putt before I left it short," Jones said. "I didn't care about finishing second or third or fourth."

Masters Tournament

Augusta, Georgia
Winner: Bubba Watson

See Chapter 2.

RBC Heritage

Hilton Head Island, South Carolina
Winner: Matt Kuchar

"It's awfully sweet to have another chance," lanky Matt Kuchar was saying, and he could have been talking about any of four straight springtime tournaments. This one happened to be the RBC Heritage, the one he won in mid-April. But it was merely the sign-off of a remarkable streak. It's unusual for a golfer of his stature to play for four straight weeks, and even more unusual to finish so consistently high. He tied for fourth in the Valero Texas Open, was a playoff second to Matt Jones in the Shell Houston Open, and tied for fifth in the Masters after a four-putt double bogey at the par-three fourth knocked him out of contention. And then he won the Heritage on the last hole, blasting in from a bunker against Luke Donald at Harbourtown Links' "lighthouse" 18th.

His final-round scores offered a key to his finishes. Starting with the Texas Open, his final rounds were 75, 72, 74. This time, apart from some errant shots, he calmed the Sunday gremlins for a 64 for his seventh PGA Tour win but his first in about 10 months, since the 2013 Memorial.

Kuchar started strong in this Heritage, with a five-under-par 66, tying with Scott Langley and William McGirt. Trouble loomed in the second round. Kuchar double-bogeyed the fourth and the sixth and shot 73. But he closed with 70-64 for an 11-under 273, edging Donald by one.

Kuchar actually seemed out of the running after the third round, when Donald, former World No. 1, started with an eagle at No. 2 and birdied four of the first six and shot 66. He led by two but was four ahead of Kuchar. Kuchar then went on a tear in the fourth round, with seven birdies over the first 10 holes. He stung himself at the par-three 17th, three-putting from four feet for a bogey, missing a 30-incher for par. "A little shocked that that missed," Kuchar said. "But I think I did a great job of shaking it off on 18."

Kuchar, playing ahead of Donald but tied with him, came up short in a front bunker with his five-iron approach at the 18th. "There are a lot worse places on 18 to be than the front bunker," Kuchar was to say. "I knew it was at least an easy par. Bunker game is good. No problem."

It was even less of a problem when Kuchar hit that bunker shot. "I heard the crowd go crazy," he said. "Then I went crazy."

Donald had an erratic finish. He had five birdies, but a bogey and a double bogey, and finished with six straight pars for a 69, one behind Kuchar. "Usually, a solid 69 on a windy day with a two-shot lead is enough to get it done on Sundays," Donald said.

Said Kuchar: "And amazing to have four straight weeks of chances on four completely different golf courses."

Zurich Classic of New Orleans

Avondale, Louisiana

Winner: Seung-Yul Noh

Seung-Yul Noh was a young man walking a high wire in high winds in the Zurich Classic of New Orleans. He was 22, in his third year on the PGA Tour, and not only was he inching his way to his first win, he was doing it without a bogey.

But that magic ended at the start of the final round. After a tournament-record 54 holes without a bogey, he made his first at No. 1 in the final round, and then held himself together the rest of the way against a variety of challengers and buffeting April winds that reached 30 mph for his first win in 78 tour starts. He became the fifth Korean-born player to win on the tour. But it was national sorrow more than pride that he carried. Some 300 people were dead or missing after a Korean ferry had capsized. Noh wore black and yellow ribbons on his golf hat, hoping that he brought some relief to a grieving country.

"Hopefully, I'll make all the Korean people happy," said Noh. He did it with a strong finish in his card of 65-68-65-71–269, 19 under at TPC Louisiana. It included a tournament-record 198 for the first 54 holes.

First, Noh was looking at a double record start by Web.com Tour graduate Ben Martin, who opened with a course-record, 10-under-par 62. "It was one of those days, just like you draw it up," said Martin, 27, out of South Carolina. He added a 67 for a two-round record, 15-under 129.

Noh took the lead in the third round on a 65 fuelled by three straight birdies — putts of 13 and 10 feet at the 14th and 15th, then a 112-yard approach to a foot at the 16th that brought him to 18 under and two ahead of Keegan Bradley (65) going into the final round.

The toughest was yet to come for Noh in the windy final round. First, his no-bogey string ended on the first hole — he would make two others — and he would have to weather the threats of others while saving his own game with some clutch shots. At the 13th, facing a tricky downhill chip shot, he hit the flagstick and was left with an easy birdie. Hitting into the wind at the 16th, he put his approach to three feet for his last birdie, and at the 17th, saved par with a 14-foot putt, preserving his two-shot margin.

And Noh's threats down the stretch? Bradley self-destructed on the front nine. After a birdie at the second hole, he bogeyed the fifth, missing a par putt of two feet, then double-bogeyed the par-four sixth after a watered drive, shot 75 and dropped to a tie for eighth. Robert Streb eagled the par-five second, but double-bogeyed the ninth and bogeyed the 10th, shot 70

and tied for second with Andrew Svoboda (69), two behind.
Said Noh: "Dreams come true."

Wells Fargo Championship

Charlotte, North Carolina
Winner: J.B. Holmes

The challengers were falling away, one by one. For J.B. Holmes, that was a gift. But that he was playing golf at all was a miracle. He could prove it. There was a piece of his skull sitting in the closet back home.

"It's been a long journey for me," said Holmes, after winning the Wells Fargo Championship, the third win of his career, his first in six years. "I've had some ups and downs. It's a great feeling to be out there and to get one done."

It was a tough journey, too. Holmes, known for immense power, had won twice, the FBR Open in 2006 and 2008, and starred on the 2008 Ryder Cup team, but in 2011 began suffering dizzy spells. The diagnosis was a malformation of his skull. He underwent brain surgery twice — hence the "souvenir" — then hurt his elbow practicing too much, requiring surgery there, then broke his ankle in aggressive exercise. It was indeed great just to be playing golf, doubly so to be able to hold up against Phil Mickelson, Jim Furyk and others at tough Quail Hollow.

Holmes stayed close to Angel Cabrera with his 70-67 start. (Amazing footnote: Martin Kaymer, in a first-round 69, played his final four holes in two under without a birdie or a par. The answer: bogey-eagle-eagle-bogey.) Holmes' power carried him into the lead in the third round. At the 490-yard 18th, he had only a nine iron left and fired it to within 20 feet of the flag. The birdie gave him a six-under-par 66 and a one-stroke lead on Martin Flores, 32, a third-year man seeking his first win.

In the last round, Flores remained a serious threat until a three-putt bogey at the 13th. Phil Mickelson, going through one of the most erratic tournaments of his career, started just two shots out of the lead, then short putts did him in. At the eighth, he three-putted from 15 feet, missed a three-footer for par at the 11th, a four-footer for birdie at the 14th, and then he four-putted the 16th from 30 feet. Said Mickelson, after shooting 67-75-63-76: "I had two great rounds and two pathetic rounds this week." Jason Bohn had a chance, but watered his tee shot at the 17th and double-bogeyed. That left Furyk the leader in the clubhouse at 65–275 and watching to learn his fate.

Holmes bogeyed No. 2, then racked up three birdies through the turn from No. 8, including dropping a 30-foot putt at the 11th for a two-shot lead. He went three ahead at the 15th, smashing a fairway wood out of the rough to three feet for another birdie — the one that saved him when he bogeyed the 16th and 18th — and closed with a 71 and a 14-under 274 total, edging Furyk by a stroke.

"Just enjoying the moment...," Holmes said. "Thanking God for letting me have the opportunity to do it."

The Players Championship

Ponte Vedra Beach, Florida

Winner: Martin Kaymer

Martin Kaymer's star rose with his victory in the 2010 PGA Championship. Then, except for a flash in the 2012 Ryder Cup, he pretty much faded from view. Next came his surprising return in the 2014 Players Championship, starting with a record 29 for nine holes on his back nine and a record-tying 63 at TPC Sawgrass for the first-round lead. Something was different. Kaymer revealed his secret.

"Well, I stopped thinking," Kaymer said, drawing laughter from the media corps. "That's pretty much the bottom line," he added. "I thought a lot the last two years about swing changes — that every shot I made I reflect on it, what I did wrong, what I did right ... I just trust myself a lot more, and ... the bottom line is, I think less."

Thus armed, Kaymer added rounds of 69-72-71, survived a shaky finish and posted a 13-under 275 for a wire-to-wire victory over Jim Furyk, who closed to within a stroke with a 66. It was Kaymer's first win in nearly 18 months, and it almost didn't happen.

The tournament became a classic duel — the veteran making a comeback vs. The Kid — Jordan Spieth, age 20, rising fast in his young career. Spieth opened with a 67 and trailed Kaymer by four, but closed the gap to one with a 66 in the second round. It wasn't as simple for others. Rory McIlroy shot 42 on the front nine but recovered for a 74 and made the cut. Phil Mickelson was a different story. He missed with 75-70–145. "Mentally, I'm just really soft right now," Mickelson said.

Spieth caught Kaymer in the third round, a 71 to a 72, and the final round figured to be a shootout. It was, but not with Spieth. After two early birdies, Spieth, who had gone bogey-free for his first 58 holes, bogeyed five of 11 holes from No. 5. He dropped to a tie for fourth with a closing 74. "I'm stinging right now," Spieth said.

Furyk, playing five holes ahead of Kaymer, had to sit and wait with the clubhouse lead at 276. "I did what I could," he said.

Kaymer had birdied Nos. 2, 9 and 11, then developed problems. The most serious was at the par-four 15th, after a rain delay, where he got behind a pine tree and double-bogeyed. He only parred the par-five 16th when he tried to putt instead of chipping from 94 feet. Then came the par-three island 17th, about 135 yards. His wedge tee shot stopped just short of spinning back into the water, and he left his pitch from 65 feet 29 feet short. And he holed the putt for his par. "It was a very strange way to make three," he said. At the 18th, he two-putted from 42 feet for a par, a 71, a 275 total and the one-stroke win.

"The belief is always there," Kaymer said. "I knew that I could win again."

HP Byron Nelson Championship

Irving, Texas

Winner: Brendon Todd

Brendon Todd, one of the many promising young golfers trying to get their feet under them, never saw a predicament he didn't like, such was the caliber of his short game. But even his imagination was strained by the fix he found himself in, in the final round of the HP Byron Nelson Championship.

Todd was four under for the round and leading when he came to the 185-yard, par-three 13th. There, he knocked his tee shot wide of the green and found his ball sitting 65 feet from the green, but a foot from a tree, leaving him no shot. Until he remembered his brother-in-law's putter. Todd, a right-hander, took his four iron, then setting up "wrong way," swung left-handed and hit the ball with the back of the club. He knocked it to seven feet, then sank the putt, saving his par and, as it turned out, his first victory.

"My brother-in-law is left-handed," Todd explained. "I putted with his left-handed putter before and I'm pretty good at it. So I tried to use that stroke."

Then putting his own way at the 17th, he dropped a 17-footer, saving another par and adding a little cushion to his lead. A par at the 18th wrapped up his card of 68-64-68-66, a 14-under 266 total at TPC Four Seasons, and a two-stroke win over former Masters champion Mike Weir, struggling to regain his game. Weir, now 44 and nagged by injuries for years, had his best tournament since a second at Pebble Beach in 2009, and he hadn't had a top-25 finish since 2010. "I was definitely determined to try and win today," Weir said, "but I can feel good about the way I handled things."

Todd, who had to go back to the Web.com Tour twice in the past five years to regain his tour playing card, nearly squandered all of a good start. He was out in 31 in the first round, but took a double bogey and a single coming in and settled for a two-under 68. He took the lead in the second round with a 64–132 that put him two ahead of a pack of eight. The traffic jam included Weir, Martin Kaymer, who won The Players Championship the week before, and England's long-quiet Paul Casey, who was just hoping to make the cut but turned in a 63 that included a tour-record eight-under 27.

The recovering injured included former Open Championship winner David Duval, 42 — briefly. Duval, who had fallen from World No. 1 to 890th, opened with a 66, one off Peter Hanson's lead, then came back with a 76 and missed the cut.

Todd was tied in the third round by another ailing golfer, former British Open champion Louis Oosthuizen. Oosthuizen couldn't keep pace in the fourth round, leaving the chase to Todd and Weir, which finally came down to Todd's short game.

"I have a great short game," Todd said, "and even I will say it was special this week."

Crowne Plaza Invitational

Fort Worth, Texas

Winner: Adam Scott

Getting to be No. 1 in the world is one thing, staying there quite another, as Adam Scott discovered in a hurry. In fact, just days after he took the lofty perch. Scott got there when the mechanics of the point system lifted him above the idle Tiger Woods, recuperating from back surgery. Now Scott had to finish higher in the Crowne Plaza Invitational than the ambitious Henrik Stenson would in the European PGA Championship that week.

Things didn't look promising. The Crowne, at the par-70 Colonial Country Club, turned into duel between Scott and Jason Dufner, but not until the final round and into a playoff. Scott shot 71-68-66-66, and Dufner 67-69-69-66, tying at nine-under 271. Dufner was two behind, then three in the first two rounds, and Scott by six through each of them. Then came the hectic third, and when it ended, David Toms, Hideki Matsuyama, Chad Campbell and Chris Stroud were tied for the lead at seven-under 203, and 21 others were within three strokes, including Scott and Dufner, locked in a seven-way tie for 11th, two off the lead. They came through the free-for-all with 66s and, with the others fading, they topped the leaderboard a stroke ahead of the field. But it was scary for Scott.

Scott had four birdies on the front nine but nearly sank himself with some shaky putting. He bogeyed No. 3, three-putting from 24 feet, and double-bogeyed No. 9, three-putting from 17. Scott got a reprieve when Toms, leading through the turn, took three bogeys coming home. Scott did his part, birdieing Nos. 11, 12 and 14 on putts of nine, four and 39 feet. Dufner holed a 25-footer at the 18th for his 66, getting to nine under, and about a half hour later, Scott narrowly missed a winning birdie from 31 feet. He got the par for his 66 to force the playoff.

They parred the first extra hole, No. 18, and at the second, the 17th, Dufner hit his approach to inside five feet and had to make the birdie after Scott preceded him from 14 feet. "I thought I could sneak one in there, but he topped me," Dufner said. Back to No. 18, where Dufner's approach ended up 40 feet from the hole. He missed his birdie try, but Scott, with a seven-footer, didn't. Scott, of course, held on to his No. 1 ranking. Stenson tied for seventh in England.

"I didn't want to let this one slip," Scott said. "As always, a bit of luck involved. Maybe added a little pressure for myself, trying to play like a No. 1. But the way you come back and get it done — and I felt like I certainly played like one of the best players in the world out there on the back nine."

Memorial Tournament

Dublin, Ohio

Winner: Hideki Matsuyama

If ever a golfer would adopt a hole, it would be Hideki Matsuyama, taking home the 18th at Muirfield Village. The 18th is a fitting finish to a demanding Jack Nicklaus masterpiece — a 484-yard, par-four, dogleg-right, uphill to an elevated amphitheater green. Muirfield Village is Nicklaus' course, but the 18th is Matsuyama's hole.

Matsuyama met Muirfield Village in the 2013 Presidents Cup as a 21-year-old rookie pro. He was partnering Australia's Adam Scott in a four-ball match, and saved the team a half when he fired a stunning approach from the right rough to 20 inches, setting up a birdie. Fast-forward seven months to the spring of 2014, and Matsuyama essentially won the Memorial Tournament, his first PGA Tour victory, at the 18th. He led a charmed life on the course's toughest hole. He birdied it in all four rounds, and nobody had ever done that in the Memorial's 38 years.

Matsuyama shot 70-67-69-69 and tied with fast-closing Kevin Na (72-69-70-64) at 13-under 275, and the way before them was cleared when early leaders faded dramatically. Rory McIlroy zoomed from an opening 63 to a 78, and second-round leader Paul Casey from 66 to 76. Then Bubba Watson took the third-round lead with a 69 and led Scott Langley by one, but was five up on Matsuyama, six on Adam Scott, and 10 on Na. Then the finish was unreal.

Coming down the stretch, Scott double-bogeyed the 12th out of the water, birdied the 13th, and bogeyed three straight, shot 71 and tied for fourth. Watson hit two punishing hooks, bogeying the 14th and double-bogeying the 15th, shot 72 and finished third, a stroke out of the playoff.

Kevin Na had finished about two hours earlier with the clubhouse lead at 13 under. Matsuyama, after seven birdies and two bogeys, double-bogeyed the par-three 16th out of water, then bogeyed 17 after missing the green. So he needed a birdie at the 18th. But his tee shot looked doomed, zipping off to the right. But his ball hit a tree and caromed back into the fairway. "That's when I was able to think I still have a chance," Matsuyama said. Indeed: He hit a seven iron to five feet, made the birdie — his fourth there — for a 69 to tie Na at 13 under.

The playoff lasted one hole — the 18th — and Matsuyama didn't birdie. He won with a miracle par, instead. He drove into a bunker, then his five-iron approach hit a spectator at the green. He hit a flop shot to 10 feet and made the par putt before Na, who had driven into the creek, could address his bogey putt.

Matsuyama's secret at the 18th? Simple, he said. Hit the fairway, have the right yardage to the green, get it close, make the putt. "And therein lies maybe the success I had at 18," he said.

Maybe Matsuyama didn't need to adopt the 18th. Maybe the 18th adopted him.

FedEx St. Jude Classic

Memphis, Tennessee

Winner: Ben Crane

At the end of the second round of the FedEx St. Jude Classic, Ben Crane, struggling these many years, found himself still in the lead. Said Crane, pleased but surprised, "I certainly didn't see this coming." The statement would still fit when the tournament ended and he found himself with his fifth career victory and, finally, his first since 2011. He'd wondered whether he'd ever win again. He would wobble a bit at the end, but he shot the par-70 TPC Southwind in 63-65-69-73–270, for a wire-to-wire run, edging winless Troy Merritt by a stroke.

For another context, consider what he said after the tournament, on where he feared his career might be heading. "I had to finally become okay with golf not being in the picture," he said. Did that mean quitting? He didn't elaborate, but back problems left him wondering whether he could compete. The season was looking sour. He'd missed six cuts, four straight in recent starts, and he had a host of high double-digit finishes. He'd spent six months changing his swing to protect his back. At last, the changes seemed to be working.

Then came the weather-battered St. Jude. Crane posted a bogey-free 63 first round. "I didn't expect the hole to open up like that, and just started making putts from everywhere," Crane marveled. Meanwhile, attention was focused on Phil Mickelson, trying to get his troubled game in shape for the U.S. Open the following week. Mickelson birdied three of his last four holes for a 67, his first round in the 60s since the Wells Fargo five weeks earlier. "Tomorrow's round, same thing," he said. But he would finish in a tie for 11th. Crane was riding a hot putter, and once he completed the interrupted second round Saturday morning with a 65, he had a four-stroke edge he couldn't believe.

Backups from the storms left Crane to play 30 holes on Sunday. He resumed his third round, then leading by four with 12 holes to play. He made just his second bogey of the tournament at No. 10, and shot a two-birdie, one-bogey 69 to hold the lead. Then he moved into the final round and closed with an undistinguished no-birdie, three-over 73, for the one-stroke win.

A number of golfers turned in some strong performances, led by free-spirited Englishman Ian Poulter. Still seeking that first PGA Tour win, he tied for sixth, his 31st top-10 finish in 175 starts. Rookie Peter Malnati, who missed the cut in eight of his 12 starts and the last four in succession, tied for 19th, his third top-25 finish. The veteran Carl Pettersson tied for third, cracking the top 10 in a full-field event for the first time in nearly two years. As for Crane, he was left to marvel at the cell phone's capacity for congratulatory messages.

"Oh, my gosh," Crane said. "How many can a phone hold?"

U.S. Open Championship

Village of Pinehurst, North Carolina

Winner: Martin Kaymer

See Chapter 3.

Travelers Championship

Cromwell, Connecticut
Winner: Kevin Streelman

What do golfers think about when they're on a hot streak and don't want to think about it?

Kevin Streelman was on such a streak and approaching his second PGA Tour victory when he wanted to get his mind off what he was doing. "I was thinking about her on those last couple of putts," he said, meaning his infant daughter Sophie. "I was thinking, 'You know what? If these go in, great. If not, great. She's going to love me either way...'"

The day would come that he would tell Sophie the putts did go in, that he set a PGA Tour record for closing out a round by the winner with seven straight birdies, and in the process won the Travelers Championship. He broke Mike Souchak's record of six, set in the 1956 St. Paul Open. Streelman, not leading along the way, closed with a second straight six-under-par 64 to edge Sergio Garcia and K.J. Choi by a stroke at 15-under 265 at TPC River Highlands.

What started him thinking was the way the putts were dropping. "I had 10 one-putts in a row," Streelman said. "That's something I've definitely never done before." If the putting was a surprise, so was the victory. "I didn't have too many expectations coming here," Streelman admitted. Streelman, 35, won once before, in the 2013 Tampa Bay Championship, but 2014 was not going encouragingly at all, and he'd missed the cut in his last four starts.

He probably had few expectations from the start, opening with 69-68-64 at TPC River Highlands. He trailed by seven through the first two rounds and by four going into the fourth as the rain-softened course took a beating.

Brendan Steele led it off with a hole-out eagle from 129 yards at his first hole and shot 62. "On 14, I started to think 59, which is probably why I slowed down a little bit," Steele said. Scott Langley, a second-year player looking for his first win, took the halfway lead with a 65 that included eight birdies. Next up was Ryan Moore, a three-time winner, taking the third-round lead with 66–197, 13 under. Streelman's 64 left him four behind.

"I felt like I was in contention on the first tee," Streelman said. But he was even worse off, bogeying the second and seventh. "The ninth tee — I knew I had some work to do," he said, and a birdie kept his head above the water. Par saves at the next two had a calming effect. And the streak started at the par-four 12th. He holed an improbable 37-foot putt at the 16th for his fifth in a row, and finished with a wedge to nine feet at the 18th.

"I am a little shocked," Streelman said. "You know, to birdie the last seven. To even say it is crazy."

Quicken Loans National

Bethesda, Maryland
Winner: Justin Rose

It seems Justin Rose collects golf courses the way fans collect celebrity autographs — Muirfield Village (Memorial Tournament), Cog Hill (BMW), Doral (Cadillac), Merion (U.S. Open) and Arnonimink (in 2010 when the tournament was named the AT&T National). When the opportunity arose in June, he also nailed Congressional Country Club to his wall, in the form of the Quicken Loans National. Thanks to firmer fairways and greens, Congressional was considerably tougher than it was when Rory McIlroy ran away with the soggy 2011 U.S. Open, but the strategic problems were pretty much the same. This time, Rose and second-year PGA Tour player Shawn Stefani tied at a grudging four-under-par 280. Rose won the playoff with a par at the first extra hole.

Why so good on tough courses? "You're going to be challenged, you're going to have to grind and you're going to have to do everything at some point," Rose said. "And that's the type of golf I like, that tests all your skill-sets. I think it's great to win on a golf course like this because you can't sort of luck into it. You've got to play good golf, and through spells this week, I had to rely on different parts of my game." For example, the bold three wood out of heavy rough at the 14th in the final round, which set up a saving par.

Rose had to rely on his resolve at the watery, par-four 18th. Playing it in regulation, he tried to hit a four iron from 209 yards through a gap in the trees and caught water instead. He saved a bogey with a 15-foot putt, completing a card of 74-65-71-70, tying with Stefani (74-68-68-70), who parred it after just missing a 20-foot birdie putt for the win. And then Stefani fell victim to the 18th in the playoff. He found the water and Rose won with a routine par four.

The loss didn't hurt Stefani as much as it might have. He had come close in only his second year. "It was great to put myself in position … to win a tournament," he said. "This is the first time I've been in that position, coming in on Sunday late, and really happy about it. It definitely gives me the belief that I can win on the tour."

If Stefani was disappointed, Patrick Reed, already a three-time winner, was upset. Reed tied for the lead in the second round, then held it alone by two strokes going into the final round. He was still two ahead going into the final nine, but stumbled to two back-to-back double bogeys and shot 77, tying for 11th. "This definitely burns," Reed said.

And in an odd twist, host Tiger Woods (the event benefits his foundation), playing for the first time in nearly three months, since back surgery in March, had the shortest tournament résumé: Played lousy, felt great. He shot 74-75, missed the cut by four shots, had no setbacks and noted: "I'm really encouraged."

Greenbrier Classic

White Sulphur Springs, West Virginia
Winner: Angel Cabrera

Angel Cabrera, beefy Argentinean, now 44, was beginning to wonder whether he could win anything but a major. And he had the credentials to prove it — the 2007 U.S. Open and the 2009 Masters, and nothing else but a number of top-10 finishes to show for his 17 years on the PGA Tour. Then came his visit to the forested, round-topped mountains of West Virginia.

Whatever it was that allowed Cabrera to rise to the occasion in those majors — and nearly again in the 2013 Masters, where he lost in a playoff to Adam Scott — emerged at the Greenbrier Classic on the Fourth of July weekend. But he would need some help. First, the Curse of the Third Round at the Old White TPC would have to strike again.

Billy Hurley, a former U.S. Navy officer, took the halfway lead with a seven-under-par 63 in the second round, and held it with a 67 in the third, two up on Cabrera, who opened with 68-68-64. "I figure if I shoot the lowest score tomorrow, I can't lose," Hurley said. His reasoning was sound, but he didn't factor in the curse: No third-round leader had held on to win in the tournament's five-year history. Hurley opened the final round with a birdie, then bogeyed four of the next five holes, and while he was sinking, a new obstacle was rising to confront Cabrera.

George McNeill came from nowhere, birdied four straight from the fourth, eagled the eighth and went on to a 61 and was sitting with the clubhouse lead at 14 under while Cabrera still had to play the back nine. Cabrera himself was running hot. He went seven under through an 11-hole stretch from No. 3, with five birdies, then an eagle at the par-four 13th, where he holed an uphill eight iron from 176 yards. The spurt carried him three ahead of McNeill. Then Cabrera made things iffy with two quick bogeys, missing the green at the 14th and 15th. He restored order with his power. At the 16th, he bashed a drive 330 yards over the lake, setting up a par, then reached the 616-yard 17th in two and two-putted for a birdie. A par at the par-three 18th gave him another 64 and a two-shot win over McNeill at 16-under 264.

"The big thing was the drive today," Cabrera said, when asked for the key to his round. "It made the course play a little shorter ... but it was definitely my driver."

And was it intimidating, with McNeill already in with a 61? "I just knew it was up to myself," he said. "I knew I had to play, so the fact of the matter was I just had to keep focused and play."

And finally winning something other than a major? It didn't leave much of an impression. "After the 2009 Masters victory, I haven't been too consistent," he said, "but I've been working very hard of late to get back to where I think I should be."

John Deere Classic

Silvis, Illinois

Winner: Brian Harman

The John Deere Classic was Zach Johnson and Steve Stricker country. Not much room for a Brian Harman there.

Johnson is a native son of the area and a huge local favorite. He won the tournament in 2012, and rare is the Deere when he's not in the chase. Stricker, son of Wisconsin, won three straight from 2009. They were both in the hunt down the stretch, as was Brian Harman, 27, a third-year veteran of the PGA Tour, a native of Georgia known but to University of Georgia fans, and who would be enshrined in golf history for his response to cheering fans upon scoring his first victory. "Don't give me a cheer," he yelled. "Give me a beer."

A beer, $846,000 and a charter flight to his first Open Championship, leaving that evening, once he'd collected his prizes and his wits.

Fittingly, what ended in a head-to-head battle also began as one with Harman, Johnson and Rory Sabbatini tied for the first-round lead at eight-under 63. It was another assault on golfer-friendly TPC Deere Run, and it was practically a free-for-all from there.

Harman, on his way to a 63-68-65-66–262 card, 22 under par, was out of the lead only in the second round. It would be a shootout the rest of the way, with Harman taking the lead in the third on a 65 and a 196 total, one ahead of Stricker (64) and three up on Johnson (69).

"It was definitely stressful out there, with Zach playing so well," said Harman, whose best previous finishes were ties for third. "I knew if I stuck to my game plan ... if I could just get a couple putts to drop, I'd be in good shape."

That definitely was an oversimplification. Stricker would get sidetracked in the final round, taking a double bogey at the par-three 12th off a tee shot beyond the green. Johnson would post a flawless, seven-birdie 64 and come up a stroke short of Harman, who proved a durability beyond his experience. Witness his performance at the drivable par-four 14th, when he bunkered his attempt but got up and down for birdie with a 14-foot putt. Harman set out by posting his third eagle of the tournament, firing his approach 223 yards to four feet at No. 2. He bogeyed the fifth, then rang up five birdies from the ninth through the 16th for a two-stroke cushion, which absorbed the bogey at the 18th, leaving him with 66 and a one-stroke win at 22-under 262.

"To me," said Johnson, praising Harman, "it was just a matter of time. I think what we saw today is totally indicative of a lot of hard work and perseverance."

"Today it was very nerve-racking," Harmon said. "It was very hard ... Just trying to not let your mind run wild is the hardest part out there. I knew that my golf game was good enough, and I just kept having to go back to that and just trust it."

The Open Championship

Hoylake, England

Winner: Rory McIlroy

See Chapter 4.

RBC Canadian Open

Ile Bizard, Quebec, Canada

Winner: Tim Clark

If ever a golfer could be called star-crossed, it would be Jim Furyk. The 54-hole lead had become a curse. It struck again at the RBC Canadian Open at Royal Montreal. This time, the villain — if he can be called a villain —

was South Africa's Tim Clark, known for his diminutive stature, 5-foot-7, his good nature and mastery of the long putter.

It was the seventh straight tournament that Furyk lost after holding the 54-hole lead.

Furyk tied for the lead in the second round, took the solo lead in the third, by three over Clark, who immediately fell four behind with a bogey to start the fourth. Then the chase was on. While Furyk couldn't get his game out of neutral, Clark passed him at the 15th and went on to his second PGA Tour victory.

"Going into the back nine, I suddenly had nothing to lose," Clark said. "I think ... I'm going to have to go make some birdies."

Which Clark did, shooting 30 on the back nine for a 65 against Furyk's struggling 69 for the one-stroke win. Clark played the par-70 Royal Montreal in 67-67-64-65–263 to Furyk's 67-63-65-69–264. Justin Hicks finished third, four off the lead.

Once again, Furyk was baffled. "I felt like I hit the ball well today," he said. "I played definitely good enough to win the golf tournament, but I only made two birdies and I've got to make more putts." He made only two bogeys in the tournament, both at No. 4, in the first round and the fourth. He made 16 birdies over the 53 holes in between. It was the uninspired final-round 69 that did him in — the bogey and just two birdies. "I didn't play a bad round of golf," he said, "but ... I didn't score, didn't get the ball in the hole. I feel like my short game, my putting was not very good, and on a day when the greens were this soft, the wind wasn't blowing that much, I only went out and made two birdies."

Clark had an indifferent front nine — the bogey at No. 1 and a birdie at No. 6. He won the tournament on the back nine. He was three behind Furyk through the turn, and credited his up-and-down for par at the 10th as the spark for the back nine. "I could easily have made bogey, and that would put me four back," Clark said. He followed that up with birdies at 11, 12 and 14 to tie Furyk, then after a short rain delay, took the lead at the 15th, on a 12-foot birdie putt. After both birdied the 17th, Clark locked up the win at the par-four 18th. He had a 44-footer for birdie, but left it six feet short. Furyk had a 12-footer for a tying birdie, but missed. Then Clark holed the six-footer that hurt Furyk yet again.

"It stings," Furyk said. "I've got no one to blame but myself."

WGC - Bridgestone Invitational

Akron, Ohio

Winner: Rory McIlroy

Golfers talk about the "zone." It's a psychological place where the swing is automatic, the line is engraved and the hole is two feet in diameter. For Rory McIlroy, it was someplace a little different. It was where golf is just the shot at hand.

"It's the most comfortable I've ever felt trying to close out a golf tournament out there today," McIlroy said, and he did close it out — the World Golf Championships - Bridgestone Invitational, for his second straight victory, after the Open Championship. Trailing through the first three rounds, he shot Firestone Country Club, a grinding par-70 of 7,400 yards, in 69-64-66-66–265, 15 under par, beating Sergio Garcia by two, and in comfort. "I felt like it was the first round or the second round," McIlroy said.

To others, it felt like his win in the Open Championship was no fluke and that he finally had broken that 18-month slump. Curiously enough, it was the reverse of the Open Championship. There, Garcia chased McIlroy. This time, McIlroy had to chase Garcia, and without the threat of Tiger Woods, who won eight times at Firestone. He withdrew after eight holes in the final round, citing a back injury.

Garcia trailed Marc Leishman by four with his first-round 68, then reduced long and demanding Firestone to a playground in the second, tying the course record with a nine-under-par 61. It was the third 61 at Firestone but the strangest. Garcia started his stunning run with only one birdie on the front nine, that at the par-five No. 2. Then he caught fire. He birdied the 10th, parred the 11th, then ran off seven straight birdies for a course-record 27. He one-putted the last 11 holes, and his birdies ranged from two and three feet, to 15, 20 and 25.

"Just one of those moments that you love and enjoy," Garcia said, "and you wish there were no end." The 61 gave Garcia a two-shot lead on Justin Rose (67), who missed only two greens, and he was four up on McIlroy. Through the third round, Garcia (67) was three up on McIlroy. And McIlroy erased that deficit in a hurry in the final round. He birdied the first hole from three feet, the second on two putts and the third from 10 feet. Garcia played them in par-par-bogey and trailed by one.

McIlroy moved two ahead with a seven-foot birdie putt at the fifth. But he bogeyed the eighth out of a bunker, and Garcia tied him with a birdie at the ninth on a 15-footer. Then came the decisive break. McIlroy regained the lead at the 11th, holing an eight-foot birdie putt, then Garcia bogeyed the 15th after missing the green to fall two behind, and that's where the tournament finished, McIlroy shooting 66 to Garcia's 71.

Said McIlroy: "What I'm really proud of was following up the Open Championship with a performance like this."

Barracuda Championship

Reno, Nevada

Winner: Geoff Ogilvy

It was a long way from the Canadian Open at Montreal to the Barracuda Championship at Reno, Nevada. But for Geoff Ogilvy, it was a lot farther from Winged Foot in New York, where he won the 2006 U.S. Open. Ogilvy, 37, arrived at Reno on the verge of losing his PGA Tour playing card. He had become so discouraged, in fact, that he had to be talked into entering the tournament. This after another depressing outing, a tie for 34th at the RBC Canadian Open. In 27 starts, he had missed nine cuts, and apart from a tie for 10th, most of his finishes were in the high double-digits. Hence, the Barracuda, played opposite the Bridgestone Invitational, which he had not qualified for, was looking like a waste of time.

"I was 50-50, coming here this week," Ogilvy said. "I was tired and frustrated." In his 14 years, the last of his seven victories came in 2010. But friends prevailed upon him, and so off he went to Reno. The Barracuda was the latest incarnation of the old International, played under a modified-Stableford system, which meant scoring in points instead of strokes — two points for a birdie, five for eagle, eight for double eagle, and costing one for bogey and three for double bogey or worse. But no matter how it was scored, it added up to a win and a rebirth for Ogilvy at Montreux Golf and Country Club.

Nick Watney boomed into the first-round lead with 18 points on nine birdies and no bogeys. In stroke play, that would translate to a 63. He credited his driver. "I missed a few greens early and chipped to within tap-ins, and hit some really nice wedges," Watney said. "But that was the result of good driving." Ogilvy, also bogey-free, tied for second with 16 points, putting himself into the chase for his first win in four years. Ogilvy had a wry explanation for his long slump. "I've been hitting it well every week, I just haven't made any putts. It's the normal story when you ask most of us out here what's working and what's not."

Ogilvy got up and down for a birdie at the 18th to take the lead in the third round with 12 points on a hot, windy day, and locked up his eighth win with a 14-point final day, highlighted by a eagle at the par-five 13th on a 25-foot putt for a five-point margin over Justin Hicks. He left Reno with his playing card for the coming season, berths in some big tournaments and a new outlook on life.

"It's been a long time coming," Ogilvy said. "It's been a bit rough the past few years. Got off to a really good start. Holed a couple nice putts on the front nine on Thursday. From then on, I barely missed a shot ... But for 72 holes, it was one of the better bodies of work I've put together."

PGA Championship

Louisville, Kentucky

Winner: Rory McIlroy

See Chapter 5.

Wyndham Championship

Greensboro, North Carolina

Winner: Camilo Villegas

The good news for the long-slumping Camilo Villegas at the Wyndham Championship was that he had the first-round lead. That was, for two reasons, also the bad news. For one, the first-round lead has been a jinx since the tournament returned to Sedgefield Country Club in 2008. Only Arjun Atwal, in 2010, went on to win. And then Villegas himself hasn't exactly flourished from the front. He held the first-round lead twice in 2013. He missed the cut in one, finished 71st in the other. But then, the Colombian's game had long been sour. He hadn't won in over four years and he'd plunged from

No. 7 in the world to No. 254. So the knowledgeable just nodded when he slipped out of the lead in the second round.

Then, amazingly, the final round found him with the clubhouse lead, sweating out 40 minutes while one challenger after another threatened to overrun him.

"I was hoping for a playoff," Villegas said. "I thought I needed one more." But he didn't need that extra stroke. His 17-under-par 263 held up for a one-stroke win over Bill Haas and Freddie Jacobson, two of a bunch of challengers who fell short. Villegas, after that opening 63, slipped a bit with 69-68 middle rounds, then charged back for another 63 to close. Both were bogey-free, and ironically, in both, he went birdie-eagle at Nos. 4 and 5. He made only four bogeys for the tournament. His 17-under finish was, significantly, not only his best of the season but also only his second in double-digits under par. He had only two top-10 finishes in the past three years, and he was so discouraged, just a week earlier, he withdrew after the first round of the RBC Canadian Open and headed home to Colombia, leaving his golf clubs behind. "I just thought it was appropriate," he said, "to hop on a plane and see mom and dad and recharge a little bit." But he was all nerves as the challengers came into view.

Haas was running bogey-free and needed just one more birdie to tie, but could only par the last three holes for a 64.

Jacobson needed a par at the 18th to force a playoff, but missed the green short and bogeyed for a 66, tying Haas for second.

Heath Slocum was tied for the lead with two holes to play, but bogeyed both, flubbing a chip at the 17th and missing a six-foot par putt at the 18th. He shot 67 and finished fourth.

Nick Watney was the biggest threat. He was already 17 under — Villegas' finish — through No. 13. Then he three-putted the 14th for a bogey, and needing a birdie at the 18th to tie, he drove out of bounds and double-bogeyed for a 70 and tied for fifth.

Said Villegas, when it was all over: "There's times you go, like 'Man, I hate this game.'"

But this, he agreed, wasn't one of them.

PGA Tour Playoffs for the FedExCup

The Barclays

Paramus, New Jersey
Winner: Hunter Mahan

Hunter Mahan had four good reasons for wanting to win The Barclays, the start of the FedExCup Playoffs: First, he hadn't won in 48 starts and almost two and a half years; second, he had reached the Tour Championship, the final event, every year since the Playoffs began in 2007 and wanted to keep that streak alive; third, he wanted to make a strong pitch to U.S. captain

Tom Watson to make him a captain's pick for the Ryder Cup team, and fourth, last but not least, the $1.44 million first prize.

"This game," Mahan said, upon accomplishing all four goals, "is all about winning. You can have a great year, and if you don't win, it just feels like you missed out on something. So to get a win, and do it in a tournament like this in this kind of fashion with a 65 on Sunday, feels great."

This "fashion" included staying close for three rounds, on 66-71-68, breaking from behind with a burst of three straight birdies down the final stretch for a six-under-par 65 to win by two at 14-under 270. The win over Stuart Appleby (65), Jason Day (68) and Cameron Tringale (66), who tied for second, looked comfortable enough, but in fact, six players had at least a share of the lead in the final round. That included Jim Furyk, who stretched to eight the number of times he didn't win after holding the 54-hole lead. He finished with a four-bogey 70 and tied for eighth. World No. 1 Rory McIlroy, who was going for his fourth straight win — after the Open Championship, Bridgestone Invitational and PGA Championship — finally cooled off. He tied for 22nd.

Phil Mickelson didn't make the third-round cut but did provide two talking points. In the second round, he tried to drive the short par-four fifth and ended up on the deck in the hospitality area. He opted to play off the carpet and bogeyed. He tried to drive it again in the third round, ended up on the deck, played from there again, and parred.

The tournament had started like a stampede. Bo Van Pelt took the lead with a 65, and fully eight others tied for second at 66, including Mahan, who set the tone for himself: "I have nothing to be nervous about ... because everything I'm doing is good."

Mahan started the final round a shot off the lead and soon was in the thick of it with birdies at Nos. 1, 5, 11 and 13. Then came the three-birdie sprint: A 10-foot putt at the 15th gave him the lead. He wedged to three feet at the 16th and dropped a 20-footer at the par-five 17th to go up by three. A bogey out of the trees at the 18th merely dented his margin. When the trophy broke as he was picking it up, he was left with a big wreath of roses.

Said Mahan, grinning: "Am I supposed to put this on, Kentucky Derby-style?"

Deutsche Bank Championship

Norton, Massachusetts

Winner: Chris Kirk

The Deutsche Bank Championship, second stop on the FedExCup Playoffs, began as a tale of two golfers on the same golf course. Ryan Palmer breezed through TPC Boston in an eight-under-par 63. He needed only 21 putts and birdied half of the holes, taking a two-stroke lead. Then there was Chris Kirk, 29, a two-time winner since going full-time on the PGA Tour in 2011. Kirk probably was wishing for mulligans. He double-bogeyed his third hole (No. 12), bogeyed his fifth, and finished with a two-over 73 that was worse than it looked. In a field of 93 starters, there were only 17 scores higher.

"Usually, after playing a poor round, I would have gone to hit some balls," Kirk said. "But I just told my caddie, I don't feel like going to hit balls. I'll see you tomorrow."

Something clicked. The next day, he made only two bogeys and also made two eagles, shot 66, and went on to play the last 37 holes not only without a bogey but in 14 under, closing with 64-66 for a 15-under 269 total and a two-stroke win over Billy Horschel, Geoff Ogilvy and Russell Henley. And he did it with the added pressure of playing the last two rounds with World No. 1 Rory McIlroy, winner of the recent Open Championship, Bridgestone Invitational and PGA Championship.

"So this is definitely the biggest win of my career against the strongest field under the biggest spotlight," Kirk said. "So I'm very proud of that."

The threat of McIlroy was ever-present, as seen in his third-round 64. "It feels normal," McIlroy said. "It feels like it's what I'm supposed to do." He was tied with Kirk at 10-under 203, behind Russell Henley (65–201). McIlroy would fade, but a heated third round ended with 10 players separated by four strokes.

In his flawless final round, Kirk took command with three key putts down the final stretch. He dropped a 25-footer for birdie at the 13th, taking the outright lead for the first time. He saved par out of a bunker with a 15-footer at the 15th, and then took a two-stroke lead on a 12-footer for birdie at the 16th and parred in for the 66.

Horschel, standing in the fairway of the par-five 18th, had a chance to beat Kirk or at least tie him. But he chunked his six iron badly and bogeyed. "I thought I was going to hit it on the green, I thought I was going to make the putt and make the eagle and win it outright," Horschel said. "Worst swing I've made all week."

The big question this Labor Day weekend: U.S. captain Tom Watson would announce his three captain's picks for the coming Ryder Cup the next day. Would Kirk be one of them?

Said Kirk: "Winning the Deutsche Bank and going to No. 1 in the FedExCup, and $1.4 million — that's plenty for me for one day."

BMW Championship

Cherry Hills Village, Colorado

Winner: Billy Horschel

Billy Horschel, still simmering over barbs on social media, took the opportunity to set the record straight, and with obvious satisfaction.

"After last week," said Horschel, irked at what golfers consider an insult, "a lot of people on Twitter were calling me a choker. I didn't choke. I made one bad swing at a bad time." He was referring to the six-iron approach he chunked at the final hole of the Deutsche Bank Championship, second leg of the FedExCup Playoffs. He tied for second, his best finish of the year to that point, but the bad shot cost him a chance to win. And this the week after he'd missed the halfway cut in the playoff opener, the Barclays.

Now, in the BMW Championship, the third leg of the Playoffs, he was facing another critical shot on the final hole. This time he lofted an effortless nine iron to the green and two-putted for a par and a two-stroke victory over Bubba Watson, for the second win of his career, and it carried him to the grand finale, the Tour Championship the following week. It also carried a $1.44 million first prize. And more.

"I guess you'd say it's redemption," Horschel said. "I think what I'm more proud about is the way people on Twitter ... say that I choked. But I just like to stick it to them ... and it was nice to get that victory and stick it to some of those people..."

Horschel accomplished all this in the thin air near Denver, shooting Cherry Hills 68-66-63-69–266, 14 under par. Horschel started off a stroke behind the three-way tie of Rory McIlroy, Jordan Spieth and Gary Woodland. Sergio Garcia fired off three great shots to take the second-round lead with a 64 — a hole-out from a bunker for a birdie at the second, a holed-out fairway wedge for an eagle at the seventh, and a wedge to a foot to save par at the 17th. Horschel capped a bogey-free day with a 32-foot birdie putt at the 18th for a 63 and a three-shot lead over Ryan Palmer in the third round.

Then, ironically, after a chunked shot had cost Horschel a chance to win the Deutsche Bank, it was another chunked shot that helped him win the BMW. Palmer had caught him twice in the final round and was just a stroke behind playing the 13th. Both had driven into the rough. Horschel hit his second onto the green. Palmer shanked his into the fronting creek. He double-bogeyed and fell three back. A bad shot sidelined Garcia, too. A watered chip cost him a triple bogey at the par-five 17th. Horschel, meanwhile, parred his way home after a birdie at the seventh for a 69, the win and the ticket to the Tour Championship. And the $1.44 million first prize and the $10 million bonus.

"If I were a betting man," said Horschel, "I'd put some money on me."

Tour Championship

Atlanta, Georgia

Winner: Billy Horschel

Billy Horschel remembered throwing up his arms and heading home to talk with his wife. Golf had come to that. It was a bleak season. He'd had just two top-10 finishes, and now he'd missed the cut in the Barclays, the FedExCup Playoff opener. "She said, 'You're probably just waiting for the season to be over and start a new season,'" Horschel said. "I sort of was." But something told him to hang in there. Three weeks later he was wrapping up an astonishing run in the FedExCup Playoffs, taking the season-ending Tour Championship and its $1.44 first prize and the $10 million FedExCup bonus. The week before, he won the BMW Championship and $1.44 million, and before that he tied for second in the Deutsche Bank Championship, all told taking nearly $13.5 million from the FedExCup Playoffs.

Said Horschel: "I'm not sure life can be better than this."

At the Tour Championship at East Lake Golf Club, Horschel led or shared the lead wire-to-wire, shooting 66-66-69-68 for an 11-under-par 269 total and beating top-ranked Rory McIlroy and Jim Furyk by three strokes. His secret? "I just needed to get out of my own way," he said.

With his 66-66 start, Horschel tied Chris Kirk for the first-round lead, then led McIlroy by two in the second. McIlroy caught him in the third with an excellent 67. McIlroy shook off a pair of three-putt bogeys, rebounding with an eagle at the 15th on a 25-foot putt and a tough par save from the rough behind the 18th. Horschel had led by three, but bogeys at the 10th and 13th dragged him back into a tie with McIlroy at 201. Furyk was two behind with a 67.

McIlroy's season had turned stunning. He'd won the Open Championship, the WGC - Bridgestone Invitational and the PGA Championship in a four-week span. Adding the Tour Championship, he offered, would be "poetic justice." Furyk last won in 2010, taking the Tour Championship and the FedExCup and didn't care to think about the final round. Said Horschel: "It's going to be an exciting day."

McIlroy's poetic justice would have to wait. In the last round, he double-bogeyed the par-three sixth out of water, then bogeyed three straight from No. 9. But a streak of three straight birdies coming home got him a 71 and a 272 total. Furyk ran aground again, bogeying Nos. 17 and 18 for a 69 to tie McIlroy.

Horschel edged ahead with birdies at Nos. 4 and 5, bogeyed the 10th, but saved par at the 13th on an eight-foot second putt. He all but wrapped things up with an improbable birdie at the par-five 15th, where he drove into the trees, pitched out, and his approach left him facing a 30-foot putt over a ridge for birdie. When the ball cleared the ridge, "...I said, this looks good," Horschel said.

It was good. And thus did Billy Horschel ring down the curtain on a season that almost wasn't.

The Ryder Cup

Auchterarder, Perthshire, Scotland

Winner: Europe

See Chapter 6.

Frys.com Open

Napa, California

Winner: Sang-Moon Bae

Golf has a lot of quaint sayings, none truer than the one that says, "You can't win the tournament in the first round, but you can lose it."

South Korea's Sang-Moon Bae put something of a new twist on it in the Frys.com Open at Silverado, namely, that you can pretty well win it in the third round. Of course, he didn't actually wrap up the title in the third round, but he built himself a commanding four-shot lead, and only a golf catastrophe would keep him from his second win on the PGA Tour.

First off, with his start in the third, he seemed bent on running away with the tournament — a run of five straight birdies, beginning at the par-three No. 2, where he fired his tee shot to three feet. The spurt carried him to a three-stroke lead. "Five birdies in a row was a lot of fun," Bae said. "I read every break on the green. It was a really easy game." The game got a little tougher at the seventh, where he three-putted for a bogey. A bogey at the 13th hurt him further. Then he gathered himself and sprinted home.

First came the birdie at the par-four 15th. But he started to stumble at the par-five 16th. His second shot got away and ended up in a ditch. He played out, and then got his fourth only as far as the fringe, 15 feet from the cup. He was looking at a bogey. But he got the putt down, saving both his par and his finish. The 17th was a risk-reward par-four, playing at 292 yards. He drove the green and was inside six feet and holed the putt for an eagle. And then he birdied the par-five 18th, dropping a 15-footer, adding a seven-under-par 65 to his 66-69 start, and led by four going into the last round.

"It's a good score," Bae said. "Four-shot lead makes me a little comfortable, but I don't think about a win."

The cushion turned out to be a lifesaver. Bae boosted his lead to six shots through the 10th, then had a nervous and rough ride coming home. A birdie at the 12th slowed his fall while he was in the process of bogeying 11, 13 and 14, all on three putts, with Steven Bowditch, up ahead, giving him something to worry about. Bowditch finished with a 67 and a 13-under 275. "There's always pressure on Sunday," Bae said. Bae figured he saved himself at the 16th with a clutch chip from behind the green for a tap-in par. "If I made bogey on that hole," he said, "I think I lose focus next hole."

But Bae kept his grip and parred in for a one-over 73, a 15-under 273 and a two-shot win, adding the Frys.com to his 2013 Byron Nelson Championship. The first two wins, Bae said, were the toughest. "I think third and fourth will come easy," he added, "since I have the confidence."

Shriners Hospitals for Children Open

Las Vegas, Nevada

Winner: Ben Martin

Kevin Streelman had made it a point not to look at scoreboards. But he couldn't avoid the one at the final hole. He had hopes of a championship in his mind as he approached it, and then he saw the tournament pass before his eyes.

"I saw I was up one on the 18th green," he said, "...and then I saw I was one down."

Streelman, who finally battled his way into the lead, had suddenly been knocked out of it, and probably out of a chance to win, by Ben Martin. That's what the roar back out on the course was all about. The scoreboard showed that Martin had eagled the 16th, leapfrogging back into the lead. His breakthrough was in sight. Martin, 27 and in his 56th start, would have his first PGA Tour win if he could hold on for two more holes. He could and he did.

"It was an awesome way to finish," said Martin. "I didn't feel like I had much going all day. Four under on my last four to cap my first win was just awesome."

Martin trailed by four after the first round and by two through the second with his 68-66 start, then blistered TPC Summerlin with a nine-under-par 62 in the third. He started modestly enough, with a birdie at No. 1 and a bogey at No. 3. Then he played the remaining 15 with nine birdies, including five straight from the 13th. "I felt it from the first hole — I made a 20-footer for birdie," Martin said. "I did [the] job staying in each shot and taking them one at a time." The 62 gave him a two-stroke lead on Scotland's Russell Knox. He was five up on Streelman, who raced to a 63 with eight birdies over a nine-hole stretch from No. 8.

Martin also refused to look at scoreboards. "I was nervous enough," he said. And the finish was a tad more exciting than he wanted, and actually built to a climax after Knox left the hunt with a double bogey at the ninth. Martin led by four through the 10th, then bogeyed the 11th after driving behind a tree. Streelman began a birdie march, notching five over six holes from No. 12, and taking the lead in the process. Then Martin woke up. He drove the green at the short, par-four 15th and two-putted for a birdie, closing to within a stroke of Streelman. Then came his pièce de résistance.

At the par-five 16th, Martin hit a six-iron approach that finished up 45 feet beyond the flag. His putt coasted lazily toward the cup, then bent toward the left over the last few feet and dived in for an eagle, lifting Martin from one behind to one ahead. He parred the 17th, then birdied the 18th for a 68 and the two-stroke win.

"This," said Martin, "is just a great feeling."

McGladrey Classic

St. Simons Island, Georgia

Winner: Robert Streb

All the signs for Robert Streb in the McGladrey Classic were unmistakable. Which is to say, he was doomed.

Streb had opened the tournament with a wild duck hook into a bush and double-bogeyed. With the scores running low, he spent the first two rounds wondering whether he could even make the cut. He made it okay, but he was five behind starting the final round. Then he bogeyed the first hole out of a fairway bunker. Next, just as he was picking up steam, he three-putted the 13th for a bogey, falling four behind with only five to play. If ever there was a recipe for failure, Streb was whipping up a pièce de résistance.

Streb, 27, had one win on the Web.com Tour, in 2012, and was in his second season on the PGA Tour and still looking for that precious first win as October was winding down. After all the signs pointed to failure, how on Earth did Streb win the McGladrey?

The simple answer is that after barely staying in the hunt, shooting 69-66-68 through the first three rounds, he swept to a seven-under-par 63 in the fourth, then beat Will MacKenzie and Brendon de Jonge in a playoff. However, a few other elements are needed to complete this picture. First, Streb's near-hopeless four-stroke deficit with five holes to play. Then, after he posted his 266 total, 14 under at Sea Island, an agonizing wait for an hour and a half to see whether it was any good.

"I honestly thought somebody would probably get to 15 [under]," Streb said. Well, his 266 was good for a tie with MacKenzie, who closed with a 68, and de Jonge (65). Streb was facing his first playoff on either tour.

Streb had been making birdies in bunches — three over the last four holes in the first round, four out of six from the 10th in the second. "I was just doing everything I could to try to give myself a decent chance to play on the weekend," he said. In the third, he birdied the 11th, then eagled the par-five 15th and was five behind MacKenzie. He bogeyed to start the fourth round, falling six behind Then came the fireworks. He made five birdies from No. 3 for a 31 on the front, bogeyed the 13th, and ran off four straight birdies from the 14th for the 63. Then came the long wait.

De Jonge, bogey-free in his final-round 65, missed birdie chances over the last six holes. MacKenzie bogeyed 16, birdied 17 from five feet, and two-putted from 80 feet for par at the par-four 18th for his 68. In the playoff, at the 18th, MacKenzie bogeyed and was out. At the next, the par-three 17th, Streb lofted an eight iron to four feet and made the birdie to win. His celebration plans were simple.

"Probably just hang out with the family — that would be my guess," Streb said.

CIMB Classic

Kuala Lumpur, Malaysia

Winner: Ryan Moore

See Asia/Japan Tours chapter.

WGC - HSBC Champions

Shanghai, China

Winner: Bubba Watson

See Asia/Japan Tours chapter.

Sanderson Farms Championship

Jackson, Mississippi

Winner: Nick Taylor

Nothing like a hot putter to cure what ails a game.

And so on that November Sunday, rookie Nick Taylor, fresh up from the Web.com Tour, found himself hoisting the rooster — the rooster trophy — at the Sanderson Farms Championship. Taylor started at the top. He hadn't won on either the PGA Tour Canada or the Web.com Tour. But he scored his first victory on the PGA Tour.

"Going into today, I was feeling good about my game," said Taylor, a 26-year-old Canadian, in his fourth start on the PGA Tour. "But until it really happens, you never really expect it. It's very surreal."

Taylor earned his PGA Tour card some weeks earlier with a final-round charge to a 63 that tied him for 21st in the Web.com Tour Championship. He showed the same closing punch at the Country Club of Jackson in the Sanderson. He trailed by two shots each day in his 67-69 start, and a 70 in the third round left him four behind heading into the final round, seemingly too much of a load for a newcomer under that kind of pressure. But then came the magic of his putter.

John Rollins, the third-round leader, got stuck in neutral in the fourth, and Taylor jumped in with his charge. He made five birdies and a bogey on the front nine, getting to 14 under and tying for the lead, and then took control with three straight birdies from the 13th. A bogey threatened at the 16th, but he rolled in an eight-footer for par to keep his three-shot lead. He parred the 17th and had the luxury of a three-putt bogey at the 18th for a 66, a 16-under 272 and a two-stroke win over Boo Weekley (66) and Jason Bohn (69). Weekley had the fewest bogeys in the tournament, only three, and none over the last 28 holes. Bohn had only one in the final round.

So ended the amazing ride of Nick Taylor. He used just 24 putts through the first 17 holes, and one-putted 10 of the first 16 greens.

"The highest ever," he said, rating his putting day. "All my birdie putts were scarring the hole or going in, and that par putt on 16 was huge. This reminded me a lot of my last round at the Web.com finals at Sawgrass. I putted the lights out there and it was similar today. My speed was good and they all just seemed to go in."

But he was just another name for three rounds. Denmark's Sebastian Cappelen, a fellow Web.com graduate, opened with a 65, then faded. Former PGA Championship winner David Toms ran a bogey-free streak for 39 holes that got him a share of the halfway lead with Rollins, a three-time career winner. Rollins dropped to a tie for fourth, bogeying three of the last seven for a 73, paving the way for Taylor to hoist the rooster trophy.

"I like roosters now," Taylor said, grinning. "It's my favorite animal."

OHL Classic at Mayakoba

Playa del Carmen, Mexico

Winner: Charley Hoffman

The PGA Tour came down to its final tournament of 2014 at the OHL Classic at Mayakoba in mid-November, and fittingly, the hopefuls gave it a rousing start — a six-way gridlock tie at 65 for the first-round lead. Unfortunately, the course did not reward their enthusiasm. The closest any of them got to winning was a tie for seventh by big-hitting Tony Finau, of Salt Lake City, the first person of Tongan and American Samoan ancestry to play on the PGA Tour.

The OHL finally went to Charley Hoffman, his third career victory but the first after 105 starts and some four years. He edged Shawn Stefani by a stroke, shooting El Camaleon in 66-68-67-66–267, 17 under par.

"It's been awhile," said a relieved Hoffman, who won the 2010 Deutsche Bank Championship and before that the 2007 Bob Hope Chrysler Classic. "You sometimes wonder if you're ever going to win again. I'm about to turn 38. Expectations were probably a little bigger after the win four years ago."

And Hoffman won it only after contenders did some remarkable scrambling to open the door.

Michael Putnam, for example, took the halfway lead with a bogey-free 66-64–130, then blew to a 77 in the third round. Danny Lee, 24, with one win on the Web.com Tour and one on the European Tour, was racing off with the OHL in the fourth round, sprinting to seven straight birdies from No. 3. Then he turned cold and bogeyed three times coming in for a 67. "I think I was a little bit nervous and I was rushing myself," Lee said. "I should have taken a little bit more time. But there's always next week and next year." Lee finished two strokes back, tying for third at 269 with Andres Gonzales, who finished with a bogey-free 67. Jason Bohn, the third-round leader, fell away with a 40 on the front nine.

The finish was practically match play between Shawn Stefani, who started one behind Bohn, and Hoffman, three behind. Stefani birdied three straight from No. 5, and Hoffman birdied Nos. 4, 5, 6 and 9. Stefani was leading by a shot. Then came the 13th.

"I had about 61 yards to the flag and was able to hit it close," Hoffman said. "And Shawn was in the middle of the fairway and thinking he was in sort of control, and he ended up hitting it into the hazard and ... making bogey, and I made a birdie." Hoffman was ahead by one. He birdied the 16th, Stefani birdied the 17th, and both bogeyed the 18th, Hoffman for a 66, Stefani a 67.

Hoffman won it with bold iron play, firing at the flags all down the back nine. "I wasn't going to shoot for middle of the greens and let someone else beat me," Hoffman said. "I wanted to win the golf tournament."

It was a fitting goodbye to 2014.

Special Events

CVS Caremark Charity Classic

Barrington, Rhode Island
Winners: Steve Stricker and Bo Van Pelt

Just about the time Peter Jacobsen and Jimmy Walker thought they had their edge — Jacobson having stiffed his approach at the par-four 15th — Steve Stricker got inside him, and in the exchange of birdie putts, Stricker and Bo Van Pelt kept the lead and went on to win their second straight CVS Caremark Charity Classic at Rhode Island Country Club.

The CVS is a stroke-play better-ball event, but in the best traditions of a Ryder Cup shootout, the two teams battled in birdies down the stretch, and the duel wasn't settled till the final hole. They had tied at nine-under-par 62 in the first round, topping the 10-team field by a shot. In the second round, after ties in birdies on the first two holes, Stricker and Van Pelt edged ahead with another at the third, and went two up with another at the sixth. Jacobsen and Walker ran off three straight birdies from the 11th, tying at eight under with the third at the 13th.

Stricker and Van Pelt took the lead for good with a birdie at the 14th. After the birdie exchange at the 15th, Walker faced a 10-footer for birdie at the par-three 17th, but Jacobsen saved him the trouble by holing out from a bunker. Stricker matched him, holing a 10-foot putt. The challengers had one last chance, Jacobsen's 12-foot birdie try at the 18th. But he just missed. Stricker and Van Pelt took the title by a stroke with 62-60–122, 20 under. Jacobsen and Walker shot 62-61. Russell Henley and Harris English (63) and Jonas Blixt and Suzann Pettersen (61) tied for third at 127.

PGA Grand Slam of Golf

Southampton Parish, Bermuda
Winner: Martin Kaymer

The PGA Grand Slam of Golf is staged as a showdown of the winners of the four majors, but the 2014 edition turned into another Martin Kaymer-Bubba Watson head-butting. Make it Kaymer, 3-0.

Just a few weeks earlier, Kaymer beat Watson in the Ryder Cup, chipping in for an eagle at the 16th, and won the 2010 PGA Championship on the last hole after Watson watered a shot. This time at Port Royal, a wild final round ended on the first hole of a playoff. Kaymer dropped his 10-footer for a birdie, and Watson missed his four-footer.

"It's just one of those things," Watson said. "It was Martin's time and not mine."

Kaymer, the U.S. Open champion, had shot 65-71, and Watson, the Masters champion, 67-69, tying at six-under-par 136. Rory McIlroy, winner of both the Open Championship in Britain and the PGA, was third with 69-75–144, and Jim Furyk, invited to make it a foursome, shot 72-73–145.

In the wild second round, Kaymer led by three through No. 7. The lead was gone by the 10th. He was leading by three through the 12th, only to have Watson catch him. At the 16th, Watson went up by two on a birdie-bogey exchange, then Kaymer tied him the same way at the 17th. They parred the 18th, and then Watson missed the short putt in the playoff.

"You don't want to win a golf tournament that way," Kaymer said, "but I'll take it."

Callaway Pebble Beach Invitational

Pebble Beach, California

Winner: Tommy Armour

In terms of diversity, the Callaway Pebble Beach Invitational has to be the most ambitious, most scrambled event on the golf scene, what with golfers from the PGA Tour, the Champions, the LPGA, the Web.com and even a scattering of club pros. And it's the most far-flung, played over three courses — Del Monte, Spyglass Hill and host Pebble Beach. From this rich mélange emerged a familiar face — Tommy Armour, winning it for the third time in its 43-year history. But this one had to be the crown jewel of the three.

First, he had to escape from the beach at the final hole, and then he had to beat Lee Janzen in a playoff, which he did with a four-foot putt on the first extra hole. They had tied at 14-under-par 274, Armour shooting 72-69-66-67 and Janzen 65-68-72-69.

Armour hit his drive onto the beach at No. 18 in the final round and realized his prospects had just dimmed considerably. Janzen had just dropped a 30-foot birdie putt from the fringe. But about the predicament on the beach: "I've had that shot before," Armour said, "but I've never made it." He did this time, and holed a 17-foot putt birdie to tie Janzen. Both hit behind trees to start the playoff. Both were on in three and putting for birdies. Janzen missed from 15 feet, and Armour holed his four-footer for the win.

Hero World Challenge

Windermere, Florida

Winner: Jordan Spieth

If they gave an award for who traveled the farthest to play in the Hero World Challenge, like in a class reunion, Jordan Spieth would have won hands down. He came 9,000 miles from Down Under, right after winning the Emirates Australian Open, and by six shots. As it is, he won the World Challenge hands down, by 10.

"He's playing some pretty special golf right now," said Tiger Woods, host of the tournament, playing his first golf in some four months and still recovering from back surgery in March.

Spieth, 21 and ending his second season as a professional, had to be careful not to let complacency or boredom set in. So as he headed into the final round with a seven-stroke lead, he set a target of boosting his lead to 10 shots. This he did at Isleworth's par-five No. 7, where he reached the green in two with a hybrid club and made his putt for an eagle. He got his lead up to 11 shots through the ninth, at which point he was content to get home without trouble.

Spieth moved easily through Isleworth, shooting 66-67-63-66–262, 26 under par, breaking the tournament record of 266. Henrik Stenson, with four rounds in the 60s, could just marvel — shoot 16 under par and finish second by 10 strokes.

Woods shot 77-70-69-72–288, 26 shots behind Spieth and tied with Hunter Mahan for last in the 18-man field.

Franklin Templeton Shootout

Naples, Florida

Winners: Jason Day and Cameron Tringale

Cameron Tringale had a nice, short explanation for the success he and partner Jason Day had in the Franklin Templeton Shootout. Said Tringale: "The abridged version is, I hit first, and then let Jason loose." He was speaking about how they tore through the field for the first-round lead, but he could well have been talking about how well they teamed for all three rounds. The bottom line: a one-stroke victory in the 12-team field at Tiburon Golf Club.

Tringale and Day set the tone in the first round, tying the tournament scramble record with a 17-under 55 for a two-stroke lead over defending champions Matt Kuchar and Harris English.

"To go 15 under is great," said Kuchar, which he and Harris did. "To go 17 is quite amazing."

"Scramble," said Day, "is one of those formats where you have to go at it and shoot lights out. It definitely helps when you have a partner who hits it down the middle all the time and putts great." They went 12 under on their last 12 holes in a stunning streak. They were hoping to get to 25 under in the second round. "Pretty good scoring," Day said, and they did, with an eight-under 64, increasing their lead to three strokes. They wrapped it up with a 65 in the better-ball third round for a 32-under total and a one-stroke win over Kuchar and English.

PNC Father/Son Challenge

Orlando, Florida

Winners: Bernhard and Jason Langer

The Langers were going to defend the family title once again in the PNC Father/Son Challenge in December. Bernhard and son Stefan had won in 2005 and 2006, and for 2014 he planned to win with daughter Cristina. But when she hurt her back, he drafted son Jason, a mere 14. Now things were getting iffy.

"When I saw him tee off on the first tee, when they announced his name and there are hundreds of people around, he just nailed it down the middle," Langer said. "I knew we were going to be okay." The Langers were on their way to a third Father/Son title, and Jason on his way to becoming the youngest champion.

The Langers and Team Strange — Curtis and son Tom — tied in the better-ball event at 62 in the first round in the 20-team field at the Ritz-Carlton Golf Club. In the second, an 85-foot eagle putt at No. 3 gave the Langers a 59 and the win at 23 under, two better than Davis and Dru Love.

Vijay Singh and son Qass, and Curtis and Tom Strange tied for third at 20 under.

"It was an unbelievable, magical week, just like the whole year," Bernhard Langer said. "Jason ... played better the last two days than he has ever played in his whole life, under this kind of pressure. It's unbelievable. ... I am so proud of him."

Said Jason: "Just to be out here, I was hoping for maybe a top-10, even a top-five if I played really well, but nothing near like this."

Web.com Tour

The 2014 Web.com Tour went triumphantly into the books, sending 50 players on to the PGA Tour, and also spinning out three of the more fascinating storylines seen in years. It's the stuff of legend if they ever make it big.

• Carlos Ortiz might well be the best-ever Mexican male golfer, and will be a happy man if he can even approach what Lorena Ochoa did for Mexico in women's golf. Ortiz had a solid but hardly sparkling collegiate career at the University of North Texas, but he was a fast-track golfer after that. He turned professional in 2013, went through the qualifying school and won three times on the Web.com Tour in 2014, earning his PGA Tour card. Ortiz, a reedy six-footer, was still 22 when he won the Panama Claro Championship and the Bosque Mexico Championship, and took the WinCo Foods Portland Open after turning 23. He totaled $515,403 on the Web.com, then made four cuts in four starts on the PGA Tour in the fall. Ortiz said he hopes to follow his heroine, Lorena Ochoa. "I really would like ... to help put the name of golf out there in Mexico, how Lorena did," he said.

(Ortiz was second to Canada's Adam Hadwin, who led the money list with $529,792 and had two victories, the Chile Classic and the Chiquita Classic.)

• Tony Finau, a power-hitter from Salt Lake City, is the only player of Tongan and Samoan-American descent on the tours. Finau turned down college basketball scholarship offers to stay with golf, turned professional at 17 and played the mini-tours. He joined the Web.com in 2014, won the Stonebrae Classic in August, shortly before turning 26, posted 13 other top-25 finishes in 23 events and finished seventh with $319,756, easily securing his PGA Tour card. He started easing back on the power, aiming for precision. "I know I'm not going to lead the tour in driving accuracy if I'm leading the tour in driving distance," he said. "It doesn't work out that way."

• Nick Taylor, a Canadian who played at the University of Washington, finished with $114,724 and didn't win on the Web.com Tour. But come November, he did win on the PGA Tour — the Sanderson Farms Championship — coming from four shots back with a closing six-under 66 for a two-stroke win. Taylor, who turned 26 in April, was the first Canadian-born player to win on the PGA Tour since Mike Weir in 2007. He won not only $720,000 but a two-year exemption on the tour as well. Said Taylor: "Six months ago I was struggling ... it's pretty surreal. I'm in shock, but I'm certainly happy about it."

Other interesting stops on the Web.com Tour in 2014:

• Derek Fathauer, a former PGA Tour player, won a return ticket with a victory in the Web.com Tour Championship in September. Fathauer closed with a two-under 68 for a 266 total and a one-stroke win over Zac Blair. Fathauer averaged 24.5 putts for the tournament.

• Kris Blanks started the final round of the Chitimacha Louisiana Open with practically no hope — seven shots off the lead. Then he shot 62, finished tied for the lead with Brett Stegmaier at 14-under 270, and won on the third playoff hole with a 10-foot birdie putt. Blanks, 41, found a new meaning to the word "patience" in golf. He was in the 14th of 34 groups and had a long wait to see whether anyone could catch him. "I thought if my number could stay solid until the guys made it to the back nine that I'd have a chance," said Blanks. "I didn't think it was going to hold up. The longer we stood around the better my chances got."

• The tournament that wouldn't end: In the Cleveland Open, New Zealand's Steve Alker, 42, holed a three-foot birdie to beat Dawie van der Walt in a playoff on the tour-record 11th extra hole. "I got a little bit dizzy out there," Alker said. "At one point, and I can't recall when, Dawie and I looked at each other and I said 'is anybody going to win?'"

• Patience was the order of the day for England's Greg Owen at the United Leasing Championship in June. At that, Owen was the unlikeliest winner. Owen, 42, never led in the tournament and started the final round seven strokes behind, then triple-bogeyed No. 1 to fall 10 behind with 17 holes to play. He shot a day's-low 67, then had to sit and fret for almost an hour and a half as five challengers stumbled down the stretch and left him a winner by one. Said Owen: "It's just a crazy game."

• Long-range homecookin': Roger Sloan is from Alberta, in Western Canada, and Nova Scotia is on the Eastern seaboard, but it was "Oh, Canada" from the fans when he birdied the first playoff hole to beat Derek Fathauer in the Nova Scotia Open. "I love being a Canadian," said Sloan, who added, "I don't know which feels better — to win or to be done today. It was a long day." The field had to play 36 holes on Sunday after heavy winds forced the cancellation of the third round Saturday.

• Not that Andrew Putnam was going to give it back, but he would have preferred winning the WNB Golf Classic over all 72 holes. But thanks to high West Texas winds, the final round had to be canceled. That left Putnam with his first professional win — by eight shots. Putnam outran the field with a 64 in the third round, led by seven, and was up by eight when play was stopped in the fourth round. "It's a bummer that we couldn't play it all the way out," Putnam said. "I'm sure it would have been a different feeling walking up 18 with a big lead. I can't remember the last time I won."

PGA Tour Canada

How was life in Year Two of the PGA Tour Canada? (This being the second year of the new version of the old, storied and troubled Canadian Tour, now under the umbrella of the PGA Tour.)

One could draw the conclusions from these three numbers: The Five, 12 and nearly 100.

First, "The Five" is more than just a number. It's a designation that has taken on an identity of its own and that the entire tour is chasing. The top five players on the money list at the end of the year graduate into full status on the Web.com Tour, which is the gateway to the big time, the PGA Tour.

Second, 12. The schedule took an immediate jump, from nine tournaments in 2013, to 12 in 2014, each with a purse of C$150,000.

Third: The PGA Tour Canada's qualifying tournament, held at three sites in the spring, drew so many applicants (with an entry fee of $2,750) that nearly 100 of them had to be relegated to alternate status.

Next, The Five:

No. 1. Joel Dahmen, of Clarkston, Washington, C$80,992, topped the money list from start to finish. Dahmen was the only two-time winner, taking two of the first three events, the PC Financial Open and, two stops later, the Syncrude Boreal Open. Dahmen also had two other top-10 finishes, was second in scoring average at 69.09 and first in birdies per round with 4.64. Dahmen won the PC Financial with an amazing finish. He caught up when Brad Clapp bogeyed the 17th and won with a two-putt birdie at the 18th. Then he ran away with the Syncrude by five. "I didn't make many putts, but I didn't really have to," he said. "I made a birdie on nine ... and after that nobody really made a push on me." It all added up to the tour's Player of the Year Award.

No. 2. Matt Harmon, of Grand Rapids, Michigan, C$60,119. He won the SIGA Dakota Dunes Open and was a playoff runner-up to Mark Silvers in the Cape Breton Celtic Classic. All told, Harmon finished in the top 25 eight times in 12 starts and tied the tour lead with four top-10 finishes. Harmon started the final round of the Dakota Dunes with a five-stroke lead, made seven birdies in a 66 and won by three. "I knew I was playing well and that good results were coming," Harmon said. "This feels incredible."

No. 3. Tim Madigan, of Rio Rancho, New Mexico, C$59,436. A rookie, Madigan, 25, crashed the party with a win in the Players Cup and two other top-three finishes in his first five starts. He was one of four who made the cut 11 times in 12 starts for the season. Madigan locked up the Players win with a late chip-in birdie and holing a clutch three-foot putt for par at the last hole. "Making that three-footer — that's why I practice," Madigan said, "...to be in that moment, to have that chance to get a win."

No. 4. Brock Mackenzie, of Yakima, Washington, C$56,222. He shot a record 27 under par in taking the ATB Financial Classic and won by four over Dahmen and Stephen Carney. It was the second-lowest score, in relation to par, in tour history. He missed one cut in 11 starts and finished fourth in scoring average at 69.26. "I honestly didn't expect to shoot 27 under at the beginning of the week," Mackenzie said. "I just kept the pedal to the metal ... and it went my way."

No. 5. Greg Eason, of Leicester, England, C$43,367. He was the first to crack The Five without winning a tournament. He finished second by a stroke to Wes Homan at the Staal Foundation Open and posted eight top-25 finishes. He was one of only four players to make 11 cuts. Like many foreign golfers, Eason played college golf in the U.S., the University of South Florida in this case. The fans took to him at the Staal, and tagged him with a nickname. "I've never been called the 'Big E' before," Eason said, chuckling. "I guess I'll take it."

In addition to The Five, five others, Nos. 6 through 10, earned exemptions into the final stage of Web.com Tour qualifying school: No. 6 Ryan Williams, of Vancouver, British Columbia; No. 7 Nate McCoy, Des Moines, Iowa; No. 8 Josh Persons, Fargo, North Dakota; No. 9 Wes Homan, Cincinnati, Ohio, and No. 10 Mark Silvers, Savannah, Georgia.

Highlights elsewhere on the tour for 2014:

• Brady Schnell shot a 13-under 59 in the second round of the ATB Financial Classic. He topped off his 11 birdies with a hole-out eagle from 122 yards at his last hole, the par-four No. 9. "I was just trying to make another birdie and ... shoot 60 and just move up the leaderboard," he said. He tied for fourth.

• Greg Machtaler won the Forces and Families Open with a burst in the final round, playing the last 11 holes in nine under, including two eagles and a 70-foot birdie putt at the 18th for a 62 and a one-shot win.

• Nate McCoy got his first tour win in the Wildfire Invitational, but had to go four extra holes to do it. McCoy closed with a 65 and Matt Gligic tied him with a 66. McCoy won with a par after Gligic missed the green and bogeyed. "Going in, I was just trying to keep my card," McCoy said. "Now we'll see how far I can go."

• Mark Silvers scored his first tour win just in time, in the Cape Breton Celtic Classic, the next-to-last tournament of the season. "Coming into the end of the year, I wasn't going to have Web.com Tour status for next year, and had I not played well, I wouldn't have had PGA Tour Canada status for next year," Silvers said. He came from behind for a closing 66, tying with Matt Harmon, and won with a par on the first extra hole.

PGA Tour Latinoamerica

The scorecard for 2014 told the tale of the NEC Series-PGA Tour Latinoamerica: The schedule was up by three new tournaments over the year before, to 17. (The 18th, the inaugural Bridgestone America's Golf Cup, is an unofficial, two-man team event.) The tour also played in more countries than before, growing from seven in the first year, 2012, to nine in 2013, to 11 in 2014 — Argentina, Brazil, Chile, Colombia, Dominican Republic, Ecuador, Guatemala, Mexico, Panama, Peru and Uruguay.

That's a thumbnail description of vigor and growth. But another number remained the same. No matter what the language, it's the magic number — Five. Or in Spanish, "Los Cinco." These are the top five players on the final money-winning list. As with the PGA Tour Canada and the PGA Tour China, the top five from the PGA Tour Latinoamerica advance to playing privileges on the Web.com Tour, the path to the PGA Tour, as Commissioner Tim Finchem described it.

The Latinoamerica top five for 2014, in order:

No. 1: Julian Etulain, 26, Argentina; $92,394. Etulain was the first two-time winner in 2014. He won the Lexus Panama Classic in May, taking the lead in the third round with a 66, then winning by two with a closing 69 for a 17-under-par 271 at Buenaventura Golf Club. "I felt very comfortable with my swing," he said. It wasn't that way at the Lexus Peru Open in November, where he successfully defended his title. He led by three through the third round, then had a shaky fourth round, but birdied the last hole for a 72 and a three-stroke win on a 14-under 274 total at Los Inkas Golf Club. "I'm truly happy because I pulled this one off on a day I didn't play well," Etulain said.

No. 2: Marcelo Rozo, 24, Colombia; $89,117. A seven-way playoff? Much to Rozo's regret, it was just about like starting all over again in the TransAmerican Power Products CRV Open at Guadalajara, Mexico.

"Yesterday, I said it was going to be a battle because there were seven or eight guys within one or two shots of the lead," said Rozo. He led by one going into the final round, but missed a winning nine-foot birdie putt on the par-five 18th. He finished with a two-under 69 and 267 total, 17 under at Las Lomas Golf Club. That made it a seven-way tie.

Mexico's Roberto Diaz and Matt Ryan of the United States bowed out on the first playoff hole. On the second, again at the 18th, Rozo reached in two and holed a 13-foot putt for eagle, beating the remaining four — Argentina's Julian Etulain and Luciano Dodda, Mexico's Mauricio Azcue, and Rick Cochran of the United States.

No. 3: Tyler McCumber, 23, United States; $86,164. McCumber, son of former PGA Tour player Mark McCumber, was the tour's other two-time winner. He got his first in the Ecuador Open late in September, when three birdies over four late holes boosted him to a five-stroke win at the Quito Golf and Tennis Club. Tyler got his second win two weeks later in a playoff with Jorge Fernandez-Valdes in the TransAmerican Power Products CRV

Mazatlan Open at Estrella del Mar. He double-bogeyed the 17th — "I made three mistakes there, definitely not at a good time," he said — but he birdied the 18th on a 12-foot putt for a 70 to tie Fernandez-Valdes at 10-under 278, then won with a par on the first extra hole.

No. 4: Brad Hopfinger, 25, United States; $68,719. He was the only one to crack the top five without winning. Hopfinger, 25, an American from Mission Viejo, California, and a graduate of the University of Iowa, did it on the strength of a wealth of high finishes. He was a solo second in the Argentina Open and tied for second in both the Mundo Maya Open and the Arturo Calle Colombian Classic. He also had five other top-10 finishes in his 16 starts.

No. 5: Jorge Fernandez-Valdes, 22, Argentina; $67,523. The baby of the five, Valdes scored his win in the Hyundai Chile Open at Los Leones Golf Club. He took the lead with a 62 in the second round and looked like a runaway winner after a five-birdie front nine put him up by five at the final turn. But he dropped four shots turning for home and saw his lead shrink to one. "I was a bit nervous," he said. But he pulled himself together and closed with a 70 and a 17-under 271 to win by two.

These other developments also marked the 2014 Latinoamerica tour:

• Of the 17 winners, 14 were in their 20s, and nine of them were 25 or younger. The average age of the winners was 26.

• U.S. golfers won seven events, Argentina six, Colombia three, and Mexico and Brazil, one each.

• Fernandez-Valdes had the lowest stroke average, 69.19, and also the lowest final-round average, 67.13.

• Rafael Becker, who eagled three of the last eight holes to win the Brazil Open, was the first Brazilian to win on the tour.

• The inaugural Bridgestone America's Cup, a better-ball event with two-man teams of Latinoamerica and PGA Tour players, was won by Argentina's Emilio Dominguez and Rafael Echenique at Olivos Golf Club, Buenos Aires, in October.

Elsewhere, the tour was showing signs of growing up.

American Zac Blair was the first Latinoamerica player reach the PGA Tour in the same season. In the first half of the season, he finished in the top six three times and had three other top-25 finishes. Next, on the Web.com Tour, he was runner-up twice and had six top-25 finishes. Then on the PGA Tour, he tied for 12th in the Frys.com Open.

Mexico's Oscar Fraustro became the first "Los Cinco" (2012 class) from the Latinoamerica Tour to win his PGA Tour card, making it through the Web.com Tour finals.

9. European Tours

Even by the recent high standard of achievement by European golfers, the season of 2013 was remarkable. Indeed, in terms of major championships won, it was unique. Never before had three of them been annexed by players from Europe.

And they were dominating performances, too. For the first time ever, two consecutive majors were won from wire-to-wire, Martin Kaymer winning the U.S. Open at Pinehurst No. 2 by eight strokes and Rory McIlroy claiming the claret jug at Hoylake, where the Northern Irishman was always in control even if the ultimate winning margin was narrowed to two shots by Rickie Fowler and Sergio Garcia. McIlroy then won the PGA Championship after a thrilling comeback on the last nine holes in the dark at Valhalla. He joined Sir Nick Faldo and Padraig Harrington as the only Europeans to win two majors in the same year.

Almost as an afterthought the Ryder Cup was won at Gleneagles, though it was achieved with extensive forethought by Europe's meticulously prepared captain, Paul McGinley. Ryder Cup victories have become commonplace, this was Europe's eighth in 10 matches, but for two decades they appeared the pinnacle of success. Team victories in 1995 and 1997, and again through a hat-trick of victories in 2002, 2004 and 2006, were not accompanied by any major victories in the same season.

All that changed in 2010, when Kaymer and Graeme McDowell claimed majors and were part of a Ryder Cup victory at Celtic Manor. Europeans have won at least one major each year since and at Gleneagles posted another hat-trick of victories over the Americans. McGinley's unbeaten run continued after winning three times as a player and twice as a vice captain. This mission was to ensure his players performed at their best and was rewarded with a 16½-to-11½ triumph. McGinley had the better players, with four of the top six in the world, and it showed in the foursomes, which Europe won 7-1 over two sessions, and in the singles where his four major champions — Kaymer, McDowell, McIlroy and Justin Rose — delivered three and a half points.

What came across throughout the week, however, was that while the Europeans worked beautifully as a team, each player's own individuality came shining through, from veterans such as Lee Westwood and Sergio Garcia to the rookies. Only Stephen Gallacher, the lone Scot on home soil, struggled to make an impact, but France's Victor Dubuisson blossomed on the grand stage and Jamie Donaldson, after years of climbing up the ranks, had the glory of delivering the winning shot.

But, rightly, the focus should return to the year's history makers. Perhaps nothing sums up the season better than the fact that McIlroy was the unanimous choice as the European Tour's Golfer of the Year and winner of the Golf Writers' Trophy, hardly surprising after re-establishing himself as the undisputed World No. 1. However, back in June it would have been unthinkable that such awards would not be heading to Kaymer. Within a month he won both The Players Championship and the U.S. Open. At Sawgrass the German also won wire-to-wire, although not without overcoming a late wobble as play was concluded late in the evening after an earlier delay. His long, curvaceous putt at the 17th for a vital par will live long in the memory.

Two 65s at Pinehurst put him six ahead at the halfway stage, and there was no wobble this time as he remorselessly went on his way to a second major title. A former World No. 1, this was a stunning return to form after a period when he had struggled to live up to high status and tinkered with his technique. In his typically understated fashion, but with Germanic regard for precision, he said at Pinehurst: "That was a job extremely well done." His other notable comment came when he was nonplussed by the fuss that followed a picture on social media showing him sitting on the floor at Jacksonville airport charging his phone while his flight was delayed. "I don't really know what the problem is with sitting on the floor," he said. "I'm not a king or anything."

McIlroy became the game's reigning monarch when he won, in succession, the Open Championship, the WGC - Bridgestone Invitational at Firestone and then the U.S. PGA at Valhalla. He had earlier won the BMW PGA Championship at Wentworth in unlikely circumstances. On the eve of the event he publicly broke his engagement to tennis player Caroline Wozniacki and then he rallied from seven strokes behind in the final round. The celebrations were muted, but it was a vital boost to McIlroy's confidence, following his struggles in 2013 which brought only one win in Australia. In the 60-year history of the PGA, McIlroy went on to become the first player to do the double of Britain's premier championships by claiming The Open.

It was at Hoylake that he showed he had fully matured as a championship winner. He moved smoothly from one gear to another whenever required, memorably establishing a six-shot lead after 54 holes, after he had briefly been caught by Fowler during the back nine, with two eagles in the last three holes. At the 18th he hit a towering five iron that landed delicately only 11 feet from the hole. At the age of 25 he had become the third youngest player to win a third different major, after Jack Nicklaus and Tiger Woods. A fourth major title followed at Valhalla, and at Augusta in April 2015 he will attempt to become the sixth player to claim a career Grand Slam.

"I've found my passion again for golf," he said. "Not that it ever dwindled. I just want to be the best golfer I can be."

McIlroy topped the Race to Dubai points table for the second time, while the 2013 winner, Henrik Stenson, clinched second place with victory in the season-ending DP World Tour Championship. There were two victories each for young Frenchman Alexander Levy and Finland's Mikko Ilonen, who claimed the Irish Open and the Volvo World Match Play on its 50th anniversary. There were wins for Rose, Westwood, McDowell and Paul Casey, as well as the Rookie of the Year, Brooks Koepka, who overcame a strong field at the Turkish Airlines Open, one of four Final Series events.

Miguel Angel Jimenez, after turning 50 at the start of the year and winning on his debut on the Champions Tour in America, won the Spanish Open on his 27th appearance in his national championship, in the process extending his own record as the oldest winner on the European Tour. There was a first victory for former Ryder Cup player Oliver Wilson at the Alfred

Dunhill Links Championship, after nine runner-up finishes and following a loss of form that saw him struggling on the Challenge Tour prior to beating McIlroy, among others, at the Home of Golf. His triumph sparked an outpouring of congratulations from his fellow players.

With challenging financial times still affecting the strength of the European Tour within Europe itself, the loss of long-term partners such as Volvo, who will now only concentrate on the China Open, was offset by the likes of McIlroy stepping forward to host the Irish Open in 2015, and Ian Poulter and others helping to revive the British Masters. It was announced that George O'Grady will be standing down as chief executive of the European Tour in 2015 following a 40-year career with the tour as everything from a referee and tournament director to commercial manager and deputy to Ken Schofield before taking over the top job. His contribution behind the scenes has been a vital component in the rise of European golf in modern times.

Volvo Golf Champions

Durban, KwaZulu-Natal, South Africa

Winner: Louis Oosthuizen

Louis Oosthuizen started 2014 exactly the same way he began 2013, with a one-stroke victory in the Volvo Golf Champions at Durban Country Club. In fact, given he won the Africa Open in 2011 and 2012, it marked the fourth year in a row he had won his first event of the year. This time Oosthuizen arrived in Durban following a trip to the Namibian bush with friends and family. "It's great to start the year with a win again," he said, "and this is a special event to defend at. It looks like proper rest, with no golf, is the key for me. It doesn't work all of the time, but it has for the last few years."

Oosthuizen was plagued by a bad back in 2013 and the rest had done it good, although he admitted he had not been required to hit many drivers on the fast-running but tight seaside course, which also helped. It was the 31-year-old South African's seventh European Tour title, the fourth of them in his home country, where he has now won nine times in all. He recorded rounds of 68, 69, 71 and 68 for a 12-under-par total of 276, the same tally as a year previously. Branden Grace, winner of the tournament of champions–style event in 2012, finished second after following an opening 74 with rounds of 67, 68 and 68. Grace took the lead with three birdies in a row from the sixth, while Oosthuizen parred the first seven until he eagled the eighth from 12 feet.

He bogeyed the 10th but birdied four of the last six holes, starting at the 13th and 14th holes before taking a bogey at the 16th, where he had suffered a triple-bogey-seven the previous day after hitting his tee shot into a bush. Grace bogeyed the 15th but birdied the 16th and 18th holes to set the target at 11 under. Oosthuizen pipped him with birdies at the last two holes, hitting a wedge to two feet at the 17th and driving just off the green at the last and chipping to tap-in range.

Third-round leader Tommy Fleetwood, on 10 under after a 72, shared third place with Joost Luiten, who closed with a 71. The pair had been tied at the top after day two, when Luiten made an albatross at the par-five 10th, holing a four-iron shot from 248 yards. The shot helped the Dutchman, along with fellow pro Dawie Van der Walt and amateur Enrique Vilchis Calderon, win Friday's "Playing with the Pros" team event.

Abu Dhabi HSBC Golf Championship

Abu Dhabi, United Arab Emirates

Winner: Pablo Larrazabal

In a tournament of bewildering twists and turns, Pablo Larrazabal made sure the decisive moment was the 30-year-old Spaniard holing from five feet on the final green to win the Abu Dhabi HSBC Golf Championship. In winning his third title on the European Tour, and the first since the 2012 BMW International, Larrazabal claimed the biggest win of his career by beating Rory McIlroy and Phil Mickelson by a stroke. He closed with a 67, after scores of 69, 70 and 68, to finish on a 14-under-par total of 274. A fine mid-iron approach from thick rough to two feet at the 13th put him at the top of the leaderboard, and a five wood at the par-five last, one of the best shots of his career, he reckoned, gave him a good eagle chance. His first putt came up well short, but he held his nerve to sink the birdie putt. "I beat two of the three most talented guys of my era," Larrazabal said.

Both McIlroy and Mickelson could only birdie the last hole, closing with rounds of 68 and 69 respectively, and had differing regrets about the week. Mickelson only qualified for the last 36 holes on the cut-line but then added a 63 on Saturday to zoom into contention. He was leading on Sunday until a triple bogey at the 13th hole, where he tried to play a right-handed escape from under a bush and suffered a double hit and a one-shot penalty. The left-hander birdied three of the last five holes but came up just short. "I don't remember doing it before but I'm sure I have," he said about the double hit, "because I've done a lot of crazy shit."

McIlroy was given a two-shot penalty at the conclusion of his third round due to an incorrect drop at the second hole. He took relief from a spectator crosswalk but had not noticed that his left foot was still inside the marked off area. The infraction was noticed by Dave Renwick, the caddie for his playing partner. Renwick did not have time to shout and stop McIlroy from playing the shot, so informed the Northern Irishman as they left the 18th green since he did not want to disrupt the rest of his round. McIlroy went back to the scene with a rules official and accepted the penalty but was frustrated at seeing a 68 turn into a 70. "There are some stupid rules in golf and this is one of them," he said. "I played the least amount of shots of anyone so I can count that as a moral victory."

Commercial Bank Qatar Masters

Doha, Qatar

Winner: Sergio Garcia

A year after being pipped by Chris Wood's eagle at the final hole, Sergio Garcia returned to the Commercial Bank Qatar Masters and took the title after a three-hole playoff against Mikko Ilonen. Just as the year before, Garcia put in a strong final-round charge, but when his birdie putt at the last lipped out there was still the chance he could be caught. Ilonen did just that after holing from 20 feet for a birdie.

They played the par-five 18th three more times, the first two being halved in birdies. Garcia had another chance to win on the first extra hole, while on the second hole he played an exquisite bunker shot to ensure a four while Ilonen just missed with his eagle chance. At the third time of asking the Finn could not get up and down from a bunker, while Garcia carefully two-putted for a winning four. Victory in his second outing of the new season followed a win in his last start of 2013 in Thailand, while his 11th European Tour win came two and a quarter years after his last at the Andalusia Masters in 2011.

"It's been a bit of a wait for my 11th win, I came close a few times last season, including here in Qatar, but didn't quite manage to get the job done," Garcia said.

Garcia had struggled with his form on a first day and was pleased to post a 71, but he then added scores of 67, 69 and 65 for a 16-under-par total of 272. Starting the last day three behind overnight leaders Rafa Cabrera-Bello and Steve Webster, the 34-year-old Spaniard sprinted into contention on the last day with four birdies in five holes around the turn and then added two more at the 14th and 16th holes, also making crucial par putts at the 15th and 17th. Ilonen bogeyed the 13th hole after going out in 32 but rallied with three birdies in the last five holes for his 66. Thorbjorn Olesen missed a 15-footer for eagle on the final green to make the playoff and instead shared third place with Cabrera-Bello.

Webster finished in a tie for fifth place after becoming the first player to start a European Tour event with an albatross. Teeing off at the par-five 10th in the first round, Webster holed a five wood from 254 yards to be three under after only two strokes. It was his second albatross on tour, having made one during the 2011 Italian Open.

Omega Dubai Desert Classic

Dubai, United Arab Emirates

Winner: Stephen Gallacher

Stephen Gallacher was delighted to appear in the past champions celebration event on the Tuesday before the Omega Dubai Desert Classic as the tournament celebrated its 25th anniversary after being founded in 1989 — but not played in 1991. Gallacher, finishing fifth behind joint Henrik Stenson and Rafa Cabrera-Bello, was among the 20 surviving champions who teed up in the special event, which also included Javier Ballesteros, the son of Severiano, who won the tournament in 1992. But the 39-year-old Scot was even more pleased at the end of the week to join Ernie Els and Tiger Woods as the only multiple winners of the tournament proper and the first to successfully defend the title.

Gallacher extended his streak on the Emirates course to second-first-first as he beat Emiliano Grillo by a stroke, with Romain Wattel and Brooks Koepka a further shot back. Gallacher played in the first two rounds with Woods, who finished tied for 41st, and Rory McIlroy, who opened with a flawless 63, containing an eagle and seven birdies. McIlroy, the 2009 winner, led for the first two days, but then Gallacher returned his own 63 on Saturday. It was a remarkable round. He parred the first seven holes and then bogeyed the eighth. He then played the last 10 holes in 10 under par, making eight birdies, plus an eagle at the 13th. Only at the 14th hole did he so much as make a par.

The Scot now led McIlroy by two strokes but made four bogeys on the outward half in the final round. McIlroy could not take advantage as he struggled with his driving and, on the greens that were now firm and shiny, his putting. He closed with a 74 to fall to ninth place. Koepka led for much of the day, but it was Grillo who posted the clubhouse target when he eagled the last hole, his second shot rebounding off the hospitality unit behind the green onto the putting surface. He then holed from 40 feet for a 66 and 15 under par.

Gallacher rallied at the short 11th by holing a long birdie putt and then claimed a four at the par-five 15th. A six-footer at the 16th put him level with Grillo and then he drove just short of the green at the 17th, which on the weekend was shortened to 325 yards with a prize of $2.5 million for a hole-in-one which went unclaimed. Gallacher got up and down for his fourth birdie of the back nine and then parred the last despite his third shot almost spinning off the green into the water. He closed with a 72 for a 16-under-par total of 272. "I never do anything easy, I'm afraid," Gallacher said.

Joburg Open

Johannesburg, South Africa

Winner: George Coetzee

See African Tours chapter.

Africa Open

East London, Eastern Cape, South Africa

Winner: Thomas Aiken

See African Tours chapter.

Tshwane Open

Centurion, South Africa

Winner: Ross Fisher

See African Tours chapter.

Trophee Hassan II

Agadir, Morocco
Winner: Alejandro Canizares

Patience was finally rewarded for Alejandro Canizares as he won for the second time on the European Tour at the Trophee Hassan II. The 31-year-old Spaniard won only his third start as an affiliate member at the 2006 Russian Open and had to wait another 199 events for his second victory. When it came, at Golf du Palais Royal in Agadir, Canizares excelled with a wire-to-wire five-stroke victory.

If you are going to get unlucky, it might as well come on the 72nd hole with a seven-stroke lead. His approach rolled off the green and rested against a piece of turf that had not been replaced in its divot hole. Hampered by this, his chip rolled back to his feet, but he eventually holed out for a double bogey, a closing 70 and a total of 269, 19 under par. The first 71 holes were superb, however. He opened with a 10-under 62, before adding rounds of 68 and 69 to lead by six with a round to play. On the Sunday he calmly went about his business, adding six birdies and two bogeys over the first 17 holes.

"It's been long time since my last win," he said. "I felt like it was never coming, but this week I played some of the best golf of my career. It was a pity to end like that, but who cares? I won the tournament..." The son of former Ryder Cup player Jose Maria Canizares had not missed a cut for 16 tournaments over six months, but his consistency was sparked into something more spectacular by some brilliant putting on the opening day. "Hopefully, this is the first step for a little bit of improvement in my career," he added, "and I can get to the point where I play as naturally as I did this week."

England's Seve Benson chased Canizares all week after an opening 63 put him just one behind after the first round. He was still one back at halfway and remained the Spaniard's closest pursuer after 54 holes despite a 74 in the third round. A closing 71 left him tied for third place with Magnus Carlsson, as Andy Sullivan came home in 29 — three birdies to start the back nine, four in a row to finish off the tournament — and took second place with a 63 to be 14 under par.

EurAsia Cup

Kuala Lumpur, Malaysia
Winner: Team Europe and Team Asia tied

See Asia/Japan Tours chapter.

NH Collection Open

Cadiz, Spain
Winner: Marco Crespi

Italy's Marco Crespi claimed his maiden victory on the European Tour at the age of 35 at the NH Collection Open at La Reserva de Sotogrande. Crespi won the event co-sanctioned between the main circuit and the Challenge Tour by two strokes over Spain's Jordi Garcia Pinto and Scotland's Richie Ramsay.

Crespi started the final round a stroke behind Matthew Nixon but produced four birdies on the front nine to top the leaderboard. He recovered from a couple of bogeys at the 12th and 13th holes to birdie the 14th, and that was good enough for a 69 which saw him finish on 278, 10 under par. Garcia Pinto had made a great charge when he birdied five of the first seven holes before cooling off and posting a 66, while Ramsay birdied four of the last five to finish with a 68. Felipe Aguilar was also in contention before settling for a 71 and a share of fourth place with Nixon, who closed with a 73.

"I started very well today," Crespi said. "I birdied the first and that gave me the confidence to go low and that's it. I just had to manage my pressure on the back nine. Felipe was very close but he made a couple of mistakes so he made it easier for me.

"Putting has been the key this week," added Crespi, a longtime Challenge Tour player who earned his way onto the European Tour from the 2013 qualifying school. "The greens were perfect, I felt very confident and the ball rolled beautifully. I have been waiting a long time for this moment and I would like to dedicate my win to my wife Elena and to Carlotta, our two-year-old daughter."

Maybank Malaysian Open

Kuala Lumpur, Malaysia

Winner: Lee Westwood

See Asia/Japan Tours chapter.

Volvo China Open

Shenzen, China

Winner: Alexander Levy

See Asia/Japan Tours chapter.

The Championship

Singapore

Winner: Felipe Aguilar

See Asia/Japan Tours chapter.

Madeira Islands Open - Portugal - BPI

Madeira, Portugal

Winner: Daniel Brooks

There was a tragic ending to the Madeira Islands Open - Portugal - BPI, the 1,500th event played on the European Tour, when Iain McGregor, caddie for Alistair Forsyth, collapsed and died on the ninth fairway at Santo da Serra during the final round. The tournament was halted for an hour but, after a minute's silence conducted outside the clubhouse, play was resumed. Many were upset at the decision, with some players withdrawing, but a statement from the European Tour said: "The circuit extends out deepest sympathies to the friends and family of Iain at this time. Following consultation with the players and caddies involved, however, it has been decided that play should finish."

Forsyth, who was playing his last hole when the tragedy occurred, was among those consulted but admitted he was in shock. "To see that happen to someone in front of your eyes — I don't know how or when you get over that." A week later, at the Spanish Open, chief executive George O'Grady met a delegation of the caddies and afterwards issued a public apology for the distress caused. McGregor's funeral took place in Madeira a week later when there was a "Wear black for Mac" day at the BMW PGA Championship.

The tournament was plagued by the weather, as fog meant there was no play on the first day, while the first round continued from Friday into Saturday. The event was reduced to a 36-hole event in which Daniel Brooks, with rounds of 68 and 67, and Scott Henry, after a 67 and a 68, tied at 135, nine under par. They finished three ahead of Jordi Garcia Pinto, Antonio Hourtel, Julien Guerrier and Fabrizio Zanotti.

Brooks won the playoff at the first extra hole with a par-four at the 18th, two-putting from 12 feet after Henry three-putted from 25 feet. It was a maiden victory for the 27-year-old from Essex.

"It's great to get a win, but it's not nice to do it in these circumstances," Brooks said. "It's horrible what happened out there, so my condolences go out to all of his family."

Open de Espana

Girona, Spain

Winner: Miguel Angel Jimenez

Within the last year, Miguel Angel Jimenez had returned from breaking his leg in a skiing accident, played his 600th event on the European Tour, extended his record as the oldest winner on the circuit by claiming the Hong Kong Open, turned 50 in January 2014, won on his debut on the Champions Tour in America in April (a week after finishing fourth at the Masters) and then got married. How could life get any better? By winning his national championship for the first time, it turned out, as Jimenez won the Open de Espana at the 27th time of asking at the PGA Catalunya Resort in Girona.

Jimenez was a runner-up in the tournament in 1999, but this time survived a playoff by getting up and down from beside the green for a winning par. Neither Richard Green nor Thomas Pieters could match him, though Pieters came closest only to see his par putt horseshoe back at him. Jimenez became the first 50-year-old to win on the European Tour, extending his record as the oldest winner for the second time. Previously, the oldest-ever winner of the Spanish Open had been a 45-year-old Arnold Palmer in 1975.

"There is no secret," he said when asked how he kept going so successfully.

"Good food, good wine, good cigars and some exercise!" This was Jimenez's 21st victory on the European Tour and his 14th since the age of 40. "There's no words to describe what it means to me, you need to be into my skin, but I'm not going to let you!" he added. "All the victories are special, all are unique, some of them give you more money, some less, but all of them are important. You play to win and when you make it you have to appreciate it."

Pieters, a 22-year-old Belgian in his first full season on the European Tour who won the NCAA title while at college in America, showed his impressive potential as he led after the second and third rounds. Three early bogeys on the final day opened up the contest, but everyone was struggling on a demanding course with some severe day-four pin placements. Australia's Green led until a triple bogey at the 14th, but he birdied the next and set the clubhouse target at four under par. Pieters eagled the 15th but bogeyed the 17th, as did Jimenez, so they, too, ended on 284, the Spaniard after a closing 73, Pieters with a 75 and Green with a 72.

BMW PGA Championship

Virginia Water, Surrey, England

Winner: Rory McIlroy

A week that started with a terse statement of heartbreak ended with a winner's speech for Rory McIlroy. The 25-year-old Northern Irishman split from his fiancée, tennis star Caroline Wozniacki, on the eve of the BMW PGA Championship. "The problem is mine," McIlroy said. "The wedding invitations issued at the weekend made me realize that I wasn't ready for all that marriage entails. I wish Caroline all the happiness she deserves and thank her for the great times we've had."

Early in the tournament, McIlroy struggled with his concentration, although admitting it was a "release" from his woes to be on the fairways. He had given away his laptop and not turned on his phone for days. After rounds of 68, 71 and 69, McIlroy was seven behind leader Thomas Bjorn. On 15 under, the great Dane was five ahead of Luke Donald, a two-time winner, after a remarkable first three rounds. He opened with a 10-under 62, equaling Robert Karlsson's course record, and on the back nine on Saturday made six birdies in a row from the 11th and added another at the 18th to give himself a handsome cushion going into the final round.

But Bjorn suffered a triple bogey at the sixth hole, after leaving his second shot in a fairway bunker, as did Donald. Shane Lowry took over the lead, helped by three birdies in a row from the 10th, but then had a double bogey at the 13th after taking an unplayable in the trees.

McIlroy avoided any big numbers. He eagled the fourth but was only one under for the day at the turn, still short of the target of 15 under set by his caddie J.P. Fitzgerald. But he chipped in for a birdie on the 10th, birdied the 12th, which he played in six under for the week, and the 13th before getting up and down at each of the last three holes, claiming birdies at the two par-five finishing holes. He closed with a 66 to finish on 264, 14 under par, and won by one over Lowry, who sank a long birdie putt from the front of the final green for a 68. Donald, who came home in four under and saved par at the 18th despite finding the water, had a 70 and Bjorn a 75, to share third place on 12 under par.

It was McIlroy's sixth European Tour win and his first for 18 months, and followed a run of seven top-10 finishes so far in the season. Yet his subdued reaction was understandable. "Partly it was that I didn't know I had won when I finished, but partly it's been a weird week of mixed emotions," he said. "I was looking at the trophy and thinking how the hell did this happen."

Nordea Masters

Malmo, Sweden

Winner: Thongchai Jaidee

With a par-five finishing hole at PGA Sweden National, the new venue for the Nordea Masters in Malmo, Thongchai Jaidee did not think his 16-under-par score would earn him victory. "I thought it would be second or third," admitted the 44-year-old Thai. Jaidee had not managed to birdie the 18th in his closing round of 65 and, as it turned out, few others did either. Victor Dubuisson three-putted from just off the green for a five and finished with a 67 to match Jaidee's total of 272. Stephen Gallacher did get a four, holing from just outside 20 feet, to make up for a bogey from sand at the 17th and the Scot joined the other two on 16 under.

But still to come was Henrik Stenson, the World No. 2 and bidding for his home title for the first time. Stenson was the joint third-round leader with England's Eddie Pepperell and came to the 18th needing an eagle to win. He had the power to get home in two but put his approach well right of the green. It was an awkward pitch and his shot came up short of the green, ending up in a bunker. Now he needed to hole from the sand to tie but ended up with a bogey.

Stenson, who had roared into contention with a 64 in the third round, closed with a 71 and finished in fifth place, one behind Robert-Jan Derksen, who missed the playoff by one after a 65. Pepperell, who claimed a share of the lead on each of the first three days, had a 72 to tie for sixth with Robert Karlsson, who closed with a 63, and Alvaro Quiros.

Jaidee had started four strokes behind on the final day but birdied each of the first three holes and added another at the sixth. His only dropped shot came at the seventh, but he eagled the 11th and added two more birdies at the 14th and 15th holes.

In the playoff at the 18th, with none of the three contestants reaching the green in two, Jaidee's 94-yard pitch to three feet proved decisive. Neither Dubuisson nor Gallacher could match his birdie as Jaidee tapped in for his sixth victory on the European Tour and his first since the Wales Open in 2012.

"My goal was to get in the top 10, so to get into a playoff and win was very special," he said. "To win outside Asia for the second time makes it a special week for me."

Lyoness Open

Atzenbrugg, Austria

Winner: Mikael Lundberg

Getting your putt in first is a golfing truism going back to the days of Mary Queen of Scots and is just as relevant today as Mikael Lundberg proved again in winning the Lyoness Open. At the first hole of their playoff, on the par-three 18th, Lundberg holed a 40-foot putt for a birdie and then saw home favorite Bernd Wiesberger miss from 18 feet to keep alive his hopes of regaining the title he won in 2012 at the Diamond Club in Atzenbrugg, in Austria.

"It was great to see that putt drop in the playoff," Lundberg said. "I think if I hadn't holed mine then Bernd might have holed his, so it was crucial to put the pressure on."

It was Lundberg's third win on the European Tour, the previous two both coming at the Russian Open, in 2005 and 2008. The 40-year-old led for the first two days after rounds of 67 and 68 but then crashed to a 76 in the third round.

Holland's Joost Luiten took over the lead by two over Austrian Wiesberger after both returned 66s. Luiten closed with a 72 to take third place but was pipped by one shot on 276, 12 under par, by Wiesberger, who had a 69, and Lundberg, who charged back into contention from six behind with a 65 which included four birdies in five holes early on the back nine. Lee Slattery took fourth place and new Vienna resident Miguel Angel Jimenez, who moved to the city following his recent marriage, tied for fifth place with Fabrizio Zanotti.

"I was a long way back at the start of the day, so I didn't really think I would be sitting here with this trophy," admitted Lundberg. "I was just hoping to play well and finish strongly. But I knew I had a chance when I finished on 12 under. I felt under pressure going into yesterday's round, and nothing really went right for me. My swing wasn't quite there, but today it felt better. My short game today was very good — that made all the difference in the end."

There was consolation for Wiesberger in that he moved up to 60th place on the World Ranking and in so doing claimed a place in the following week's U.S. Open at Pinehurst.

Irish Open

Co. Cork, Ireland

Winner: Mikko Ilonen

Mikko Ilonen celebrated his 330th appearance on the European Tour by wining the Irish Open at Fota Island. Like Martin Kaymer the previous week at the U.S. Open, Ilonen won wire-to-wire, eventually finishing one ahead of Edoardo Molinari. Kaymer's performance at Pinehurst was the inspiration behind Ilonen's fourth victory.

"Wire to wire, it was very much a Martin Kaymer inspired win," said the 34-year-old Finn. "I sent a message to him last week that I really enjoyed watching his golf. I very rarely enjoy watching golf — I would rather play golf — but Martin's win definitely inspired me."

Ilonen birdied five of his last seven holes on the opening day to set a new course record of seven-under 64 and lead by two shots. After further rounds of 68 and 69 he was only one ahead of Danny Willett, who lowered the record to 63 during a third round in which he holed his eight-iron tee shot at the 165-yard seventh hole.

Ilonen birdied two of his first four holes on the last day and then cruised to victory. Willett closed with a 71 to tie for third place with Matthew Baldwin and Kristoffer Broberg, while Molinari birdied three of the last six holes for a 67 to sneak into second place. Molinari, Baldwin and Willett took the three qualifying places for the Open Championship at Hoylake, where Ilonen will return as the British Amateur champion from the course in 2000.

Huge galleries at the Cork venue, hosting the Irish Open for the first time in 12 years, tried to help Graeme McDowell to victory but he made only one birdie and admitted to "one of the worst putting weekends of my career when in contention." He missed chance after chance and finished tied for sixth place.

Ilonen added: "I've won four times on the European Tour now, but this would have to be the biggest win of my career. When I looked back from the 18th green, I couldn't believe how many people there were. It was great to see. It was a very humbling moment."

BMW International Open

Koln, Germany

Winner: Fabrizio Zanotti

Fabrizio Zanotti made history by becoming the first player from Paraguay to win on the European Tour at the BMW International Open at Gut Larchenhof in Cologne. But the 31-year-old had to do it the hard way as not even twin weekend rounds of 65 were enough as 19 players were at one point within three of the lead on the final day. Zanotti eventually had to outlast three other players, including World No. 2 and 2013 Race to Dubai winner Henrik Stenson, over five holes of an enthralling playoff.

Zanotti set the target at 269, 19 under par, before he was joined by Gregory Havret, after a closing 66, Stenson and Rafa Cabrera-Bello, who both scored 67s. Cabrera-Bello finished birdie-eagle-birdie to make the playoff, while Stenson produced four birdies on the back nine and an eagle at the 13th but saw his birdie putt at the last finish an inch short of the hole.

After all four parred the 18th on the first playoff hole, all but Havret birdied it next time around to send the Frenchman out. The three remaining players all birdied the short par-four 17th before Cabrera-Bello departed when his second found the water at the 18th. On the fifth extra hole, Stenson drove into the water by the green at the 17th and then found sand to hand victory to Zanotti.

Zanotti said: "To be the first player from Paraguay to win on the European Tour is pretty huge. Everybody was expecting a lot from me in Paraguay, so I think it's going to be a great day. Everybody is going to be very happy with me. I feel very happy. This is a moment I've been waiting for a long time.

"The playoff, I think it was great, and in the first hole, I made a great putt and on the second again. When Henrik hit into the water on the fifth extra hole I changed club. I was going to hit driver, but when I saw the ball go to the water, I changed it and just aimed to that left bunker on the green. Thankfully, it worked out perfectly."

Alstom Open de France

Paris, France

Winner: Graeme McDowell

A tournament that began in stunning Parisian weather deteriorated over the weekend to a wet and miserable finale, except for Graeme McDowell. The man from Northern Ireland successfully defended his title at the Alstom Open de France for his first win since lifting the same trophy at Le Golf National a year earlier. McDowell began the final day eight strokes behind Kevin Stadler, who had led ever since an opening seven-under 64.

Stadler produced an unwelcome progression of scores with subsequent rounds of 68, 72 and 76. His three-shot lead after 36 holes would have been higher but for a double bogey at the 18th, while he was four ahead after 54 holes. But he was hampered by a back complaint for the last 27 holes and it showed on the front nine on the last day when went out in 41.

McDowell, meanwhile, birdied the second and ninth, then the 13th, 14th and 16th holes, the last of which came thanks to a 25-foot putt at the par-three. He drove into thick rough at the last and had to lay up, settling for a bogey, a 67 and a five-under-par total of 279. Stadler rallied with birdies at the 14th and 16th holes to reach five under and put his approach on the green at the dangerous 18th before putting up to two and a half feet. But to his shock and McDowell's surprise, he missed and fell into a tie for second place with Thongchai Jaidee, who recovered from dropped five shots in the first four holes for a 72.

"It was so miserable on the front nine today. It was tough and I drove it terrible," Stadler said. "It was unfortunate on the last, I played a little safe with the second shot and I felt good over the putt, but just whiffed it."

"I'm very surprised," McDowell said after claiming his 10th European Tour title. "Midway through my second glass of red wine last night, when I was very disappointed with my back-nine performance on Saturday, I really didn't think I'd be standing here with an opportunity to be in a playoff, and now with a trophy in my hands.

"I feel very fortunate. Kevin Stadler is a great player. I didn't expect him to miss that. It's not really the way you like to win but I'll take it and run. I really needed this victory. I'm very proud to defend my first title ever."

Aberdeen Asset Management Scottish Open
Aderdeen, Scotland
Winner: Justin Rose

Having waited a year to win his first tournament since the U.S. Open in 2013 when he claimed the Quicken Loans National on the PGA Tour, Justin Rose crossed the Atlantic and won in his very next event a fortnight later at the Aberdeen Asset Management Scottish Open. The 33-year-old admitted he felt "absolutely horrendous" on the day before the event and worried he had lost his game in the journey over from the States. But after an opening 69, Rose added scores of 68, 66 and 65 for a 16-under-par total of 268 at Royal Aberdeen. He won by two strokes over Sweden's Kristoffer Broberg and by five over Scotland's Marc Warren.

Rose and Warren were tied at the start of the final round, when scoring was at its lowest following heavy rain and with no wind. Rose made the perfect start, birdieing four of the first six holes and making long putts at the second, third and sixth holes. In contrast, Warren never got going and finished with a 70 in third place, while Broberg's 66 included birdies at the 12th, 14th and the 17th, where he nearly holed in one, to keep the pressure on the leader. Rose had birdied the ninth to be out in 31, and then the 12th, but still needed a fine up-and-down at the 16th to seal the victory.

Rose had never won twice in a row before but was looking to make it three out of three with the Open Championship following the next week. In 2013 Phil Mickelson had won both the Scottish Open and the Open. "I thought I'd try and do a Phil, so I put this event on my schedule," Rose said. "So far, so good. It's uncharted territory for me, I've never won two in a row before, never mind three. It's unbelievable to be back in the winner's circle so quickly, but right now I am feeling great. I don't feel the two wins have taken a lot out of me."

Broberg earned a place in the Open alongside Tyrell Hatton, who was fourth with Stephen Gallacher, Shane Lowry and Matteo Manassero, and Scott Jamieson joint fifth. Gallacher and Felipe Aguilar both had 63s in the last round to break the course record set by Rory McIlroy on the first day with a 64. He drove the green at the 456-yard 13th, though it was playing downwind. However, in line with other events in 2014, McIlroy struggled on the second day with a 78 and eventually finished tied for 14th, one shot behind defending champion Mickelson.

The Open Championship
Hoylake, England
Winner: Rory McIlroy

See Chapter 4.

M2M Russian Open

Moscow, Russia

Winner: David Horsey

After spending most of the M2M Russian Open at the top of the leaderboard, David Horsey suddenly found himself three behind with two holes left. The 29-year-old Englishman then found a bit of magic to chip in from the back of the 17th green for an eagle, and although it took an extra hole, he claimed a third European Tour title.

Horsey won the BMW International in 2010 and the Hassan Trophy the following year but had to wait until this week at the Tseleevo Club in Moscow to add to his tally. He opened with a seven-under 65, with three birdies in the last four holes, to lead by one stroke and doubled his advantage with a 68 on the second day. A 70 in the third round meant he was caught by Scotland's Peter Whiteford, who had a 66 in which he holed a bunker shot at the first and chipped in at the third.

But a 75 on the last day left Whiteford in fifth place. Horsey had a 72 to finish with a 13-under-par total of 275 and looked to be heading for a comfortable victory until a double bogey at the 12th. He almost dropped a shot at the 14th before he recovered a shot at the 15th. Scott Jamieson briefly went past him but had to settle for a 69 to be third, one ahead of Sam Hutsby.

It was Ireland's Damien McGrane who swept into the lead with three birdies in a row from the 15th. But as Horsey was chipping in at the 17th, McGrane was dropping a shot at the last, so his 66 left him on a total that Horsey could match by parring the 18th. At the same hole in the playoff, Horsey again got his four, while McGrane found a greenside bunker and bogeyed the hole for the second time in a matter of minutes.

"I'm relieved really — that's the word that sums it up," Horsey said. "I didn't know where I was in the tournament until the 17th. I hit it through the back of the green there and then realized I was three behind and needed to do something drastic quite quickly."

Made in Denmark

Aalborg, Denmark

Winner: Marc Warren

Marc Warren capitalized on a good run of form that had seen him finish third at the Scottish Open and 15th in the previous week's U.S. PGA Championship at Valhalla to win the inaugural Made in Denmark tournament at Himmerland. The 33-year-old Scot had waited since the 2007 Johnnie Walker Championship for his next win, his third in all. He was the Rookie of the Year in 2006, when he won the Scandinavian Masters, but lost his card in 2010 and had to reclaim it via the qualifying school.

Ironically, his victory came at the expense of Bradley Dredge, who won the second of his two European Tour titles back in 2006. Dredge was four strokes clear of the field after rounds of 66 and 68, but in winds gusting up to 30 mph on Saturday the Welshman slumped to a 73 and was caught by Warren, who after earlier scores of 71 and 70, returned a fine 66. With Dredge bogeying three times in the first six holes of the final round, there was an early four-shot swing to Warren, who was out in 33 before birdieing the 12th and holing a monster putt at the 14th to match Dredge's own three.

"I felt the last couple of years I've been close to winning a couple of times, but for whatever reason it hasn't quite happened for me," Warren said. "This summer I feel more confident than I've ever done. Today I kept telling myself I was swinging the club really well and I was confident in what I was doing."

Warren closed with a 68 for a nine-under-par total of 275 and finished two ahead of Dredge, who had a 70, and five clear of Phillip Archer. Thomas Bjorn, who shared the first-round lead on 66 with Dredge and Felipe Aguilar, finished in a tie for fourth place and virtually secured a berth on the European Ryder Cup team.

Bjorn was one of the prime movers behind the event, the first on the European Tour in Denmark for 11 years. Over 80,000 spectators attended and the 128-yard 16th hole had a terrific atmosphere with over 3,000 people packing the hill that horseshoed behind the green. Said home favorite Soren Kjeldsen: "Walking up to the green, it was like the ground was shaking with the noise and I could feel the goosebumps all over me. It was a career highlight, certainly."

D+D Real Czech Masters

Prague, Czech Republic

Winner: Jamie Donaldson

Victory for Jamie Donaldson at the D+D Real Czech Masters secured the 38-year-old Welshman a place on the European Ryder Cup team at Gleneagles. Donaldson had slipped down the rankings after a good start to the qualifying campaign and could not quite get over the line. He needed a seventh-place finish at the Albatross Resort near Prague and won by two strokes over Bradley Dredge.

Donaldson led after the first two days with scores of 66 and 69, but Dredge had gone ahead by two on the third day when he had a 66 to Donaldson's 71. Three birdies in the first three holes was the perfect start for Donaldson in the final round, and a 68 gave him a 14-under-par total of 274. Dredge closed with a 72, chipping in for one of two birdies at the 14th, while Soren Kjeldsen also challenged during the day but finished with a 71 to tie Merrick Bremner for third place. It was Dredge's second runner-up finish in a row, and his consolation was knowing the money earned in his last two tournaments would regain the tour card that he lost in 2012.

Stephen Gallacher, who started the week just outside the automatic qualifying positions for the Ryder Cup, was the other player focused on Gleneagles, and the Scot finished in a tie for seventh place. He needed to go to the Italian Open the following week, the last qualifying tournament, to try to earn a place on the team.

Donaldson struggled with back problems for years but has blossomed in recent years with three wins coming in three successive seasons. "It's been an amazing week," said Donaldson. "I didn't get here until late. I needed to play well either this week or next week, or both, to guarantee my place in the Ryder Cup team, so there was a lot on the line and this week I played really well, so that's great.

"It's so difficult to get into the team, the lads are playing so well. You know that you have to play well to secure your place and it did come down to the wire. But that's how it is to get into the team — I played as well as I can play for 18 months, and then a couple of slow events and you rocket down the list, so it's great to come here and play so well and do enough to get into the team."

Open D'Italia

Fiano, Torino, Italy

Winner: Hennie Otto

Another time Hennie Otto's second victory in the Open D'Italia, and in only his second tournament since undergoing back surgery in June, would have claimed more of the attention. Instead, the focus at Circolo Golf Torino was on the final stages of qualifying for the European Ryder Cup team — and specifically whether Stephen Gallacher could force his way into the team. He needed to finish no worse than a two-way tie for second place to overtake Graeme McDowell, and at lunchtime on Friday, it was not looking good. With Otto scoring a 62 in the second round to take a three-stroke lead over Bernd Wiesberger, Gallacher, after an opening 72, was 15 strokes behind the leader and 12 behind second place.

The 39-year-old Scot proceeded to score a 65, including an eagle, seven birdies and a double bogey, and after flirting with missing the cut, he came home in 30 to keep his hopes alive. "I don't think I can say on air what I was thinking at lunchtime," Gallacher said on television after his round.

Otto still led by two strokes after a 71 in the third round, while Gallacher closed the gap slightly with a 69. The Scot started the final round brilliantly, with six birdies in the first eight holes. He was out in 30 and alone in second place, but then David Howell went mad. The Englishman had an eagle at the first, then made seven birdies in nine holes from the seventh. Howell's 63 left him at 18 under par. Gallacher birdied the 12th but otherwise parred in. At the last he had to hole a bunker shot to match Howell but came up short. A 65 left him on 16 under in third place and missing out on qualifying by 1.61 points. "It was a tall order, but I am proud of the way I have played," Gallacher said.

Howell, genuinely upset at the thought of denying Gallacher his dream, said: "It was a supreme effort, and if a captain needs an example of a player in form who can play under pressure, he has had it this weekend." Paul McGinley, Europe's captain, agreed and two days later selected Gallacher as a wild card alongside Lee Westwood and Ian Poulter. "That's brilliant, wee man," Gallacher told the captain when informed of his selection.

Without the pressure of Ryder Cup selection, South African Otto scored a bogey-free 68 to win by two over Howell on 268, 20 under par. He also won the event in 2008 in Milan and it was his third European Tour win. "To come back after two operations and win in my second week, I will take that any day," Otto said. "It wasn't easy because the guys played so well with some of them trying to get the Ryder Cup spots."

Omega European Masters

Crans Montana, Switzerland

Winner: David Lipsky

David Lipsky became the first member of the Asian Tour to win the Omega European Masters since the event became co-sanctioned between the European and Asian Tours in 2008. Lipsky won in a playoff against Graeme Storm, who bogeyed the 18th hole in extra time. The Englishman drove off-line and could only chip back to the fairway. That made Lipsky's decision easier after he had driven into a bunker.

Although less than 100 yards from the green, Lipsky elected to lay up and avoid flirting with the water in front of the green. He then chipped close and tapped in for his four. "I was nervous in the playoff," said the 26-year-old from Los Angeles. "It's a tough tee shot anyway, but when there's the title on the line, it's very tough. You have to draw your tee shot from right to left to hold it against the hill, and I thought I'd hit a great shot, but it ended up going in the bunker. It was a tough shot out of the bunker and, with Graeme only going to make par at best, I decided not to risk going in the water. In the end it was the right play, and I'm so pleased to get the job done."

Lipsky became the first American to win the title since Craig Stadler in 1985. Earlier, he had hit his second shot to within inches of the hole for a closing birdie. Starting the final day three behind Storm, Lipsky birdied the third, fourth and fifth holes before driving the green at the par-four seventh, tapping in for an eagle after just missing an albatross. His closing 65 set a total of 262, 18 under par, which Storm matched after a par at the last and a 68. Brooks Koepka was sharing the lead before a bogey at the 17th, and the American finished tied for third with Tyrell Hatton, who had matching 65s over the weekend.

Storm had the consolation of winning a £100,000 BMW sports car after a hole-in-one at the 217-yard 11th in the third round. "I had a hole-in-one earlier in the season in Morocco and won a lamp, so I think this prize just about tops that one," he said. "I got a member's bounce off the bank, but I've been here a few times, so I've probably just about earned it." Romain Wattel also aced the 11th on the final day, and although Storm had already claimed the main prize, the Frenchman was allowed to choose an alternative from the range on display in the tented village.

KLM Open

Zandvoort, The Netherlands
Winner: Paul Casey

Paul Casey made up eight strokes over the weekend to win for the first time as a new father just a fortnight after the arrival of a baby boy. "My first tournament as a dad, my first win a dad," said the 37-year-old Englishman after his 13th European Tour victory. On Saturday, Casey equaled Pablo Larrazabal's course record of 62 from the previous day. Casey's approach at his last hole, the par-four ninth, almost went in for an eagle, which would have given the first 59 on the European Tour. But the ball spun back past the hole and off the green and he took three to get down for his only bogey of the day.

Casey started the last round four behind Romain Wattel, who was three in front of the field. But with the Frenchman scoring over 70 for the first time in 11 rounds, a 74 leaving him tied for fifth, the door was ajar for the rest. Casey went out in 32, birdied the 14th, and although he dropped a shot at the next, his closing 66 gave him a 14-under-par total of 266. He won by one stroke over Simon Dyson, who came home in 30 for a 65 with a birdie at the last, while Andy Sullivan was third after a hole-in-one with a nine iron at the 15th hole. The prize was a trip into space, which Sullivan was debating whether to accept. "I'm not great with heights or flying! I might have to pluck up some coverage. But my daughter will think I'm the best dad in the world — a professional golfer and an astronaut."

"I'm a bit emotional to be honest," said Casey. "It was very carefree for three and a half days, because if I played well or poorly I was going to go home to see my baby, and then I got to the last three holes and I thought, I really want this. Just having my first child was a great distraction. I had no expectations coming into the week and I did very little practice. I couldn't have dreamed it would turn out this way."

In the first round Fabrizio Zanotti was taken to the hospital after being hit on the head by a stray ball. Zanotti was on the 16th fairway when he was struck by the tee shot at the 14th hole of Alexandre Kaleka. Zanotti did not lose consciousness, but after treatment on the course he was taken to hospital where neurological tests proved negative and he was later released. Fellow players Felipe Aguilar and Ricardo Gonzalez accompanied Zanotti to the hospital and withdrew from the tournament.

ISPS Handa Wales Open

City of Newport, Wales
Winner: Joost Luiten

A week after finishing fifth in defense of his KLM Open title from the previous year, Joost Luiten claimed his fourth European Tour victory at the ISPS Handa Wales Open. Luiten showed all the patience and determination required to win the hard way and demonstrate that in two more years he could be featuring in the European Ryder Cup team rather than being on the fringes of selection as in 2014.

Luiten led after an opening 65, fell one behind Shane Lowry on day two, but went two clear of the Irishman after another 65 on the third day. However, bogeys at the first two holes saw the 28-year-old Dutchman's advantage disappear. A battle of attrition unfolded at Celtic Manor, with Luiten reasserting his presence on the back nine, which he played in 13 under par for the week, as opposed to be one under on the outward half. Birdies at the 11th and 12th were followed by a bogey at the 14th, a shot which he reclaimed at the 15th.

With Lowry never quite keeping pace with the leader, Tommy Fleetwood put the pressure on despite a double bogey at the 13th. He chipped in for a birdie at the 14th, eagled the 15th from five feet, and birdied the last three holes for a 67 and 13 under par. Luiten needed to par the last three and got up and down at the 17th before driving wildly at the last. It took awhile to find his ball in the rough, from where he could only find the rough on the other side of the fairway. But his third cleared the water and found the green and he made his par with a 71 giving him a total of 270. Lowry birdied the last to tie Fleetwood for second place, while Ryder Cup debutant Jamie Donaldson finished in a tie for fourth.

"It was hard work down the last," Luiten admitted. "I didn't have the start I wanted with two bogeys and I just tried to hang in there and wait for my chances. You just try to settle down and I got my game back and made some nice birdies at the end, and a par down the last luckily enough."

The Ryder Cup

Auchterarder, Perthshire, Scotland
Winner: Europe

See Chapter 6.

Alfred Dunhill Links Championship

St. Andrews & Fife, Scotland
Winner: Oliver Wilson

Rarely has a victory elicited such genuine affection on social media from fellow players, but Ian Poulter's tweet summed up the mood: "I can't tell you how happy every player on Tour will be for Oliver Wilson winning the Dunhill Links. It's been a long road back. Congrats."

In an emotional finale, Wilson parred the last to beat by one stroke World No. 1 Rory McIlroy, longtime leader Richie Ramsay and Tommy Fleetwood, whose birdie putt at the 18th only just missed. It was a maiden victory in his 228th start on the European Tour and after finishing second no less than nine times. The last of them came in 2009, the year after he had represented Europe in the Ryder Cup.

But loss of form meant he lost his tour card in 2012, and although two more runner-up finishes arrived on the Challenge Tour, and despite a course-record 63 in Kazakhstan the previous month, Wilson was lying outside the top 100 on the Challenge Tour Rankings and 792nd in the world when he received an invitation to play in the Links Championship.

Wilson opened with a 64 at Carnoustie, had a 72 at Kingsbarns and then a 65 at St. Andrews to lead by three strokes. He bogeyed the fourth hole to be out in one over on the Old Course in the last round and only got going again when he birdied the 10th and 11th. Ramsay had eight birdies, but bogeys at the 16th and 17th holes were crucial. Fleetwood had four birdies in the first eight holes but then no more. McIlroy hit into the Swilken Burn for a double bogey at the first and, short of the green in two at the 17th, putted into the Road Hole bunker for a bogey, but also made seven birdies.

It was Wilson's stunning approach from 220 yards for a short birdie putt that put him in front again. "That was the shot of my life," he said. He pitched close to save par at the 17th and held on at the last. "I don't have words for it," Wilson said. "It's been 10, 11 years. There were nine runners-up and I hadn't done a whole lot to lose those, but nothing had really gone my way. To be given a big opportunity by Dunhill to play, I can't thank them enough.

"Before I went out today I thought about how I've never gone out and won a tournament. I've played all right coming down the stretch and not lost it and other guys have just got over the line ahead of me, and today I was just trying to be patient. I could be drunk for a while — I've had a lot of champagne on ice over the years!"

Portugal Masters

Vilamoura, Portugal

Winner: Alexander Levy

Torrential rain at the Oceanico Victoria Golf Club in Vilamoura left the Portugal Masters cut to 36 holes and Alexander Levy the winner by three strokes over Nicolas Colsaerts. At 24, Levy became the youngest multiple winner on the European Tour from France, his maiden victory having come five months earlier at the Volvo China Open. Levy also joined Jesper Parnevik, at the 1995 Scandinavian Masters, and D.J. Russell, at the 1992 Open de Lyon, in winning European Tour events without having a bogey, although both Parnevik and Russell managed the feat over 72 holes.

Colsaerts came agonizingly close to scoring the first 59 in European Tour history in the first round. He had seven birdies in the first 12 holes and then eagled the 15th and 17th. At the 18th he had an 18-foot birdie putt and it just missed on the left lip. It was the 19th time a player has scored 60, one of the previous efforts coming from his playing partner Branden Grace. "Too bad, I thought it was a pretty good effort," Colsaerts said of his putt at the last.

Levy opened with a 63 and then added a 10-under-par 61 in the second round with five birdies on each half. He was one of the few players to finish on Friday after play was suspended due to a waterlogged course, having posted an 18-under-par total of 124. Colsaerts finished off a 67 on Saturday, to be three behind, with Felipe Aguilar two further back after rounds of 65 and 64.

With the tournament reduced to 54 holes, the third round began on Sunday, but after the leaders had played just one hole, with pars for both Levy and Colsaerts, another rainstorm swept in and play had to be abandoned. Close to three inches of rain fell during the week.

"I played only four shots at the weekend and I won the tournament, but the most important thing is I have the trophy in my hand," said Levy. "If at the start of the year you had said I would win two tournaments, I would say 'never!' to you. It's a very nice feeling and I'm very happy. I work hard on this game and I think I played a good game this week."

Volvo World Match Play Championship

Ash, Kent, England

Winner: Mikko Ilonen

Mikko Ilonen claimed the biggest victory of his career when he won the Volvo World Match Play Championship on the International course at The London Club. The 34-year-old became the first Finn and only the third continental European golfer after Seve Ballesteros and Nicolas Colsaerts to win the event which was celebrating its 50th anniversary after starting at Wentworth in 1964.

Ilonen, the 10th seed, defeated top-seeded Henrik Stenson 3 and 1 in the final for his fifth European Tour victory and his second of the season after claiming the Irish Open in June. Ilonen won three holes out of five from the eighth, and although a tired Stenson twice got back to two down, a birdie at the 17th sealed the victory for Ilonen.

"I see Henrik as one of the world's top players, obviously, but I see him as my friend," Ilonen said. "He didn't intimidate me at all. We've played so much golf together over the years, so I felt quite comfortable playing with him. It could have gone either way really. I had a better afternoon than he did. If tomorrow morning we play, it might go the other way. But we were obviously playing for the trophy as hard as we could, and I came out on top."

Ilonen beat Joost Luiten 2 and 1 in the semi-finals after Luiten had been the only undefeated player in the group stage, beating Ilonen in their first match, then Alexander Levy and defending champion Graeme McDowell, who was also defeated by Ilonen and failed to make it out of the group. Luiten beat Pablo Larrazabal 6 and 5 in the quarter-finals before running out of steam against Ilonen, who beat Victor Dubuisson by two holes in their quarter-final with eight birdies against the Frenchman's two eagles, five birdies and three bogeys.

Patrick Reed, the lone American in the 16-man field, put out Ryder Cup hero Jamie Donaldson in the last round of group matches but then lost 2 and 1 to South African George Coetzee, who was a last-minute replacement after Thomas Bjorn withdrew due to injury. Stenson beat Jonas Blixt at the 18th in the quarter-finals and only squeezed past Coetzee in the semi-finals with a birdie at the last. The Swede had not led until that moment. Luiten defeated Coetzee at the 19th hole in the third-fourth-place playoff.

Hong Kong Open
Fanling, Hong Kong
Winner: Scott Hend

See Asia/Japan Tours chapter.

ISPS Handa Perth International
Perth, Western Australia
Winner: Thorbjorn Olesen

See Australasian Tour chapter.

The Final Series

BMW Masters
Shanghai, China
Winner: Marcel Siem

Marcel Siem had planned to go on holiday to Thailand the week after the BMW Masters in Shanghai, but after chipping in to win a playoff at Lake Malaren he got to stay in the city to play in the WGC - HSBC Champions, the second leg of the European Tour's Final Series. The 34-year-old German collected his fourth European Tour victory when he defeated Alexander Levy and Ross Fisher at the first extra hole after the trio tied on 272, 16 under par.

It was quite a turnaround in emotions for Siem who had bogeyed the last two holes, missing from six feet on the 18th green, and four of the last seven, to fall into the playoff. With the wind up, scoring conditions were much more difficult than on the previous three days. Levy held the 54-hole lead on 22 under par by four strokes over Jamie Donaldson, by five over Siem — and by 11 over Fisher.

But Fisher posted a 67 early in the day and then waited as the leaders struggled. Levy had the worst of it, slumping to a 78, 15 strokes higher than his third-round 63. Like Siem, Levy bogeyed the 18th, as did Justin Rose, who tied for fourth place with Donaldson, whose birdie putt at the last stopped just short. Rose closed with 72, Siem 73 and Donaldson 75.

In the playoff both Fisher and Levy had birdie putts, but Siem chipped in from just off the green, and then neither of them could hole out to stay alive. "In the playoff, I thought I actually have to hole it just to stay in," Siem said. "I was expecting one of the guys to hole their putt actually. It's just fantastic. A chip-in is always cool, but to have it in a playoff is even cooler.

"I have never been in a position like this, to be honest, in such a big tournament. You try not to think about the prize money, but it's crazy prize money here. I think the key today was not to have a double bogey or triple bogey somewhere and I managed to do that. People who know me know that finishing bogey, bogey, I don't like that and my emotions could go a little crazy sometimes. But I stayed really, really calm and I'm proud of that. I'm getting older, two kids now, so maybe that's the reason why."

WGC - HSBC Champions

Shanghai, China
Winner: Bubba Watson

See Asia/Japan Tours chapter.

Turkish Airlines Open

Antalya, Turkey
Winner: Brooks Koepka

Brooks Koepka won the Turkish Airlines Open at the Montgomerie Maxx Royal for his maiden victory on the European Tour. It was the second year running a player had won the third leg of the Final Series for his maiden victory after Victor Dubuisson achieved the feat in 2013. Koepka's win, by one stroke over Ian Poulter and by three over Henrik Stenson, secured him the Rookie of the Year award in succession to his friend and compatriot Peter Uihlein. The 24-year-old American had won his promotion to the European Tour by winning three times on the Challenge Tour in 2013.

After rounds of 69, 67 and 70 to lie a stroke behind 54-hole leader Wade Ormsby, Koepka produced a bogey-free 65 in the final round. He was out in 31 and then holed a 40-footer at the 10th for a birdie, and a brilliant approach at the 13th set up an eagle putt from eight feet. Poulter was also out in 31 but was only able to birdie the 13th and otherwise parred home. He had a six-footer on the final green to tie but saw it swing in front of the hole.

"It's a special week obviously, these four events and the Race to Dubai are ones you prepare for all year, and to win one of them is very special," said Koepka. "I feel like I've been playing really well. I've been knocking on the door these last few months. To look where I was a year and a half ago on the Challenge Tour and now to be a winner on the European Tour is incredible."

Poulter, whose opening 64 had left him one behind Miguel Angel Jimenez, led by no less than six strokes after a 66 in the second round. However, the Englishman was left ruing a 75 in the third round. Stenson finished with a 64 as he headed to Dubai for the defense of his DP World Tour Championship title the following week.

Rory McIlroy was crowned winner of the Race to Dubai even before arriving at the final event and having missed the preceding tournaments as he prepared for his court case with former management company Horizon. One of Marcel Siem, Jamie Donaldson or Sergio Garcia had to win in Turkey to keep the season-long contest alive, but the best of them was Siem who tied for eighth place despite pulling a rib muscle in the gym on Sunday morning.

DP World Tour Championship

Dubai, United Arab Emirates
Winner: Henrik Stenson

Having not won since claiming the DP World Tour Championship in 2013, where he wrapped up the double of Race to Dubai winner as well as FedEx-Cup champion, Henrik Stenson chose a fine time to defend a title successfully for the first time in his career. Victory could not dethrone Rory McIlroy as the European No. 1 for 2014, but it did secure Stenson second place on the Race to Dubai as well as the World No. 2 spot.

In a tight finish Stenson, the leader after 36 and 54 holes, rallied from a double bogey early on the back nine of the final round to birdie the last two holes and win by two strokes over McIlroy, Justin Rose and Victor Dubuisson, with Shane Lowry a stroke further back.

Stenson had rounds of 68, 66, 68 and 70 for a 16-under-par total of 272. He looked comfortable after three birdies in the first seven holes, but then he bogeyed the seventh and had a double at the 11th after hitting a two iron out of bounds. "I walked up to the tee with too much club in my hand, and instead of changing, I tried to cut a two iron but hit a push, slice, shank straight into the buildings," Stenson explained. "That knocked me back, but I did not give up. I just had to dig in there and wait for something to happen."

What happened was that Rafa Cabrera-Bella, who had inherited a two-stroke lead, bogeyed the 12th and then had back-to-back double bogeys at the 16th and 17th holes. At the par-three 17th, Stenson hit a glorious five iron to a foot for a two and then made a four at the last where both McIlroy and Rose, after missing the green with their second, had only claimed pars. McIlroy, the first-round leader alongside Lowry with an opening 66 after six weeks off the tour, had reason to rue back-to-back double bogeys of his own at the 12th and 13th holes in the third round.

This was Stenson's ninth European Tour victory and his fourth in the Middle East. "I'm exhausted to say the least," said the Swede. "It was hot out there and tricky on the back nine. I had a couple of close calls this year to get my win and it was not to be. It's been close, but eventually you get something if you stick around and I surely did that."

Nedbank Golf Challenge

Sun City, South Africa
Winner: Danny Willett

See African Tours chapter.

Alfred Dunhill Championship

Malelane, South Africa
Winner: Branden Grace

See African Tours chapter.

Challenge Tour

Two players won three times on the Challenge Tour in 2014 to secure their cards on the European Tour. Moritz Lampert, a 22-year-old German, managed the feat by August, winning three times in seven events and 10 weeks to earn an instant promotion to the main circuit. His victories came at the Karten Golf Open, the Fred Olsen Challenge de Espana and the Azerbaijan Golf Challenge Open. At the last of them, Lampert was three over after nine holes on the first day but then produced 16 birdies and four eagles in the remaining 63 holes.

"It all feels a bit surreal at the moment," Lampert said. "Everything's happened so fast. My first win in Austria seems like only last week, and since then I've just been riding a wave. This win has definitely been the most unexpected. After nine holes on Thursday I would've been surprised to make the cut, let alone win the tournament. But I found something on my back nine. I'm so happy and I can't wait to get onto the European Tour."

Benjamin Hebert's third win came in the season-ending Dubai Festival City Challenge Tour Grand Final. He had earlier won the Norwegian Challenge and the Open Blue Green. A five-stroke victory at Al Badia to finish the season meant he became the first player to win three times in a season on two occasions. He had previously achieved the feat in 2011 but did not retain his European Tour card at the end of the 2012 season.

"It is a perfect end to the season for sure," said the 27-year-old Frenchman. "My game is much better than the last time I graduated. My goal will be to keep my card next year. Winning three times in two different seasons has never been done before, which is a great achievement, but I would exchange all of those for one win on the European Tour."

Also returning to the European Tour stronger than before is Andrew Johnston, who pipped Hebert to become the No. 1 on the Challenge Rankings. The Englishman got the 15th card in 2011 but lost his status in 2012 and missed six months the following year due to a wrist injury. A winter full of rehabilitation and fitness work led to a season of eight top-10s, including victories at the Scottish Hydro Challenge and Le Vaudreuil Golf Challenge and second place in the lucrative Kazakhstan Open, behind compatriot Sam Hutsby.

"It feels awesome to be Number One," said Johnston. "It's been a great finish to the year. I'm looking forward to everything about the European Tour. I think I'm more assured and trust my game a bit more. I've learned so much over the last couple of years and that experience really helps. I'm a lot calmer out there now and don't panic as much."

Among the graduates in 2014 were Germany's Florian Fritsch, who finished as runner-up three times and took the 12th card despite only playing in Europe where he could drive to events. Since 2006 he has had a fear of flying and he has avoided doing so since 2010. "Now I am at a point where I have accepted my fear and I am happy with my life," he said. "To be honest, the fear was one of the best things that ever happened to me."

His knowledge of the ferry routes around Europe is second to none.

Another graduate, England's Jason Palmer, who took the eighth card, chips one-handed — only using his right hand on the club for shots within 40 yards of the green and even from some bunkers.

The remaining graduates were: Byeong-Hun An, Mark Tullo, Hutsby, Jordi Garcia Pinto, Michael Lorenzo-Vera, Oliver Farr, Edouard Espana, Jerome Lando Casanova, Jake Roos and Jason Barnes. Lando Casanova jumped 25 places to 13th by finishing second at the Grand Final, despite an opening 78. His card was only secured when he birdied the last hole and Farr drove into the water to take a bogey and finish in third place.

10. Asia/Japan Tours

Chances are that anyone asking Thaworn Wiratchant for golf tips won't be talking about grip, stance, short game, putting or any of that. Wiratchant has a deeper secret. The real question will be, "How do you keep winning in your 40s?" The Thai wizard's play in 2014 would have been superb for anyone, but for a golfer of 47, it was remarkable.

Wiratchant won twice, topping a small and diverse group of two-time winners: England's Lee Westwood, 41, a PGA Tour standout; India's Anirban Lahiri, 27, and the baby of the group, India's Rashid Khan, 23.

Oddly enough, it was a one-time winner who topped the Order of Merit. American David Lipsky won the rich Omega European Masters, co-sanctioned by the European and Asian Tours, and took the money title with $713,901 in his 13 events.

Wiratchant came out of 2014 with a matched set of trophies. "It feels good to have the complete Royal collection," he said. Wiratchant won the Queen's Cup in June through a great display of veteran calm and skill. He birdied five holes in a nine-hole stretch, then birdied the 18th for a one-stroke win. Then came the King's Cup in November, when he badly wanted a birdie at the 18th. "I was confident of winning in regulation play," he said, "but not in a playoff." He got his birdie and the win, raising his Asian Tour record to 18 victories.

(There was also a King's Cup in January, the one postponed from 2013. That one was won by Thailand's Prayad Marksaeng, making him the first to win both royal cups. Wiratchant would follow with his double later in the year.)

Khan burst into the SAIL-SBI Open lead with an 11-under 61 in the first round, then got his first Asian Tour victory with a superb three wood that set up a birdie for a playoff win over Siddikur Rahman. Then he posted his second victory in a tight finish to the Chiangmai Golf Classic. Khan made 21 birdies but a saved par out of a bunker at the 15th in the final round was the key. "I needed to maintain my lead," he said. It boosted him to a one-shot win over Thanyakon Khrongpha, 24, seeking his first win, and Indian veteran Jyoti Randhawa, 42, chasing his ninth.

Lahiri had three victories in his homeland, India, but he felt he needed to prove himself by winning on the Asian Tour. This he did in the CIMB Niaga Indonesian Masters in April, with a late birdie and an eagle. Then he got his second in the Venetian Macau Open, celebrating the Indian holiday of Diwali with fireworks of his own. He opened with a 61, then won by a stroke, ending a shootout with Scott Hend with a par at the final hole.

Westwood, taking his first win in two years, ran away with the Maybank Malaysian Open by seven strokes in April, and summed it up simply: "I played well, I putted well, and the short game is good." His second victory was of the other variety, a battle all the way in the Thailand Golf Championship in December, his final outing of the year. "It's been a good last day at school," he said.

The season-ending Dubai Open was a late addition to the Asian Tour schedule but came along just in time for Arjun Atwal. "I almost wanted to quit," said Atwal, 41, who slumped badly after winning on the PGA Tour in 2010. He started sluggishly in the Dubai, then won with a closing 66. As he'd said earlier, "Felt like the old days."

On the OneAsia Tour, Korea's Seung-Hyuk Kim stormed to the Order of Merit title with two victories in the nine events for a total of $501,990, far ahead of the $219,982 won by Hao-Tong Li, 19, star of the inaugural PGA Tour China.

Kim survived a triple bogey in the first round and a double bogey in the fourth for a one-stroke victory in the SK Telecom Open, his first win since turning pro in 2005. In the Kolon Korea Open, he patiently parred the last five holes to win by two. "My game plan was just to make pars," Kim said.

Li, who won three times on the China Tour by eight, six and five strokes, took the Nanshan China Masters by four. His secret: "Don't think about winning," he said.

Elsewhere, the OneAsia had a good international mix of winners. Japan's Michio Matsumura took the Indonesian PGA Championship, France's Alexander Levy the Volvo China Open, and Australia's Steve Jeffress the Fiji International.

Both Asian tours had cup competitions. In the Asian Tour's inaugural EurAsia Cup, Thongchai Jaidee captained Asia out of a 7-3 deficit to a rally in singles for a 10-10 tie. In the OneAsia Tour's Dongfeng Cup, Team Asia Pacific, under captain Peter Thomson, rallied to beat Team China, 15-9.

It was a big year for the native-born veterans on the Japan Tour.

Japanese pros, led by Koumei Oda, populated the first eight positions on the final money list, as, other than Japanese, only four South Koreans and U.S.-born David Oh scored victories during the 24-tournament season. And the youngest of the top six was 33 years old. Oda was 35 and three were in their 40s — Shingo Katayama, 41; Katsumasa Miyamoto, 42, and runner-up Hiroyuki Fujita, 45.

Oda landed just two victories — Kansai and Bridgestone Opens — but had three second-place finishes, including a playoff loss to Ryo Ishikawa in the Nagashima Shigeo Invitational, and four other top-10s. His ¥137,318,693 was the lowest No. 1 total in a decade.

Only two other players posted multiple victories. Fujita had three — Tsuruya, KBC Augusta and Asia-Pacific — and Miyamoto had two with his season-ending Japan Series JT Cup triumph and earlier ANA Open victory. Oh, when he won the late-year Taiheiyo Masters, became the sixth and last first-time winner of the season.

Asian Tour

King's Cup
Hua Hin, Thailand
Winner: Prayad Marksaeng

Prayad Marksaeng, nearing 48, was too young to qualify as the Grand Old Man of Thai golf. That spot is held by Boonchu Ruangkit. But he started 2014 by establishing a different distinction for himself on the Asian Tour — the first to win both the King's and Queen's Cup.

Marksaeng, who took the Queen's Cup the previous June, completed the double in January, bolting down the homestretch to nip Sweden's Rikard Karlberg by a nose at Black Mountain Golf Club.

"I feel proud because both trophies are in Thailand," Marksaeng said. "It makes me especially happy and proud because I'm the first Thai to win two of these very important trophies." Proud? When his winning par putt dropped at the last hole, he jumped into the nearby lake.

Karlberg felt the opposite. Co-leader through the first two rounds, Karlberg was tied with Marksaeng, three behind going into the final. They matched birdies at the first, second and fourth. Then Karlberg birdied the eighth and ninth and was 11 under par going into the turn. Marksaeng fell three behind, going bogey-birdie-bogey from No. 5. Marksaeng sprinted from there — a birdie at the 10th, an eagle at the 13th on a 20-foot putt that brought a roar from the homefolks, and a birdie at the 17th. Karlberg bogeyed the 13th and 14th, and two closing birdies for a 67 left him one short. Marksaeng shot Black Mountain in 68-71-71-66–276, 12 under, for his eighth Asian Tour win.

"I made par on 12 and I saw that I was trailing by a few strokes," Marksaeng said. "I told myself that it is fine because I can still chase the leader. Then I eagled the 13th hole and Rikard bogeyed the same hole. That was the turning point in the round."

SAIL-SBI Open
New Delhi, India
Winner: Rashid Khan

India's Rashid Khan got his foot in the door for his first Asian Tour victory with a sizzling 61 in the first round, but it was a bad shot that turned out really good in the final round that saved him in the Asian Tour's season-opening SAIL-SBI Open.

Khan, a reedy 23-year-old, opened with that 11-under-par 61 on nine birdies and an eagle, and he rode the lead in relative comfort, but then as the final round ground down, he needed a birdie at Delhi Golf Club's tricky par-three 17th to catch Bangladesh's Siddikur Rahman. Of all the times to misfire.

"I actually hit a bad shot, hit it right," Khan said. "I don't know how my ball pitched over the bunker and rolled to one and a half feet to the flag. I was shocked. I was really lucky." He accepted Lady Luck's gift and dropped the 18-incher for a birdie to tie Siddikur, who had jumped into the battle with an eagle at No. 1. Both then birdied the par-five 18th on short putts. Khan shot 61-69-69-71, Siddikur 67-67-67-69, tying at 18-under 270. The playoff went back to the 18th. Siddikur was on in three, 10 feet from the cup. Khan went after it boldly — a good drive and a three wood from 269 yards to the apron, 20 feet from the pin. Khan missed the eagle try, Siddikur missed his birdie, and Khan holed the birdie try for the win.

"I had to be aggressive, I had to go for it," said Khan, recalling that he lost the SAIL a year ago in a playoff with countryman Anirban Lahiri. "I don't like playoffs. I played in seven in the last 14 months and I won only three." But he won the one that really counted.

Solaire Open

Laguna, Philippines

Winner: Richard T. Lee

Cliché or not, that first win is always a dream come true. And so it was for Canada's Richard T. Lee at the Solaire Open. But he couldn't have realized that his dream would come from someone else's nightmare.

That was Filipino veteran Angelo Que. Leading since the second round, he was hot on the trail of his fourth Asian Tour victory. Then fate dictated otherwise in the fourth. At The Country Club's par-five No. 2, he knocked three balls out of bounds, made a 12 and shot 82. Ironically, just a stroke behind him, Miguel Tabuena, 19 — his playing partner and his admirer — shot 76. Lee, 23, in his second year on the tour, had hung close on rounds of 68-70-70 and trailed by four entering the last round. He saw the door open.

"When I made birdie on 12, I told myself if I can make one more birdie, I can make it happen," said Lee, and he got it at the 15th on an unlikely 25-foot putt. "I think that birdie made me win the tournament." It carried him to a closing 69 and a seven-under 277 for a one-stroke victory over Thailand's Chawalit Plaphol.

Lee had a bright amateur career, played in the U.S. Open as a teenager, and later was on the Nationwide Tour (now the Web.com Tour). He failed to keep his playing card, and in 2013 was runner-up at the qualifying school for both the Asian and OneAsia Tours.

There was a somber note to Lee's victory. "I wished Angelo luck yesterday," Lee said. "It was unfortunate to see what happened to him."

Que shrugged off his crash. "I can't take my round back," he said. "I had a chance to win, but blew it on one hole. That's golf, and life."

Major Champions

Back-to-back champion: After claiming a first Open title, Rory McIlroy won a second PGA Championship.

A second major for Martin Kaymer at the U.S. Open.

A second Masters green jacket for Bubba Watson.

Masters Tournament

Harry How/Getty Images

A closing 69 for a three-stroke win gave Bubba Watson a second Masters title in three years.

Andrew Redington/Getty Images

Sweden's Jonas Blixt tied for second place.

Harry How/Getty Images

A best-ever finish of fourth for 50-year-old Miguel Angel Jimenez.

Andrew Redington/Getty Images

Rickie Fowler tied for fifth with Matt Kuchar.

David Cannon/Getty Images

Joint runner-up Jordan Spieth led early on Sunday.

U.S. Open

Streeter Lecka/Getty Images

Martin Kaymer dominated at Pinehurst No. 2 winning wire-to-wire by eight strokes.

David Cannon/Getty Images

Eric Compton, after two heart transplants, tied for second place.

Streeter Lecka/Getty Images

Rickie Fowler tied with Compton for second.

David Cannon/Getty Images

Keegan Bradley closed with a 67 to tie for fourth.

Andrew Redington/Getty Images

Injury-plagued Jason Day tied for fourth place.

Andrew Redington/Getty Images

Brooks Koepka tied fourth, his best major result.

The Open Championship

Stuart Franklin/Getty Images

Rory McIlroy claimed the claret jug for the first time with a two-stroke, wire-to-wire win at Hoylake.

David Cannon/R&A

Sergio Garcia, 66, put pressure on McIlroy but ended as joint runner-up with Rickie Fowler, 67.

Warren Little/R&A

Adam Scott tied for fifth place.

Ian Walton/R&A

Jim Furyk closed with a 65 to be fourth.

PGA Championship

Sam Greenwood/Getty Images

Rory McIlroy won his second major in a row after a late charge in the gloaming at Valhalla.

Jeff Gross/Getty Images

Phil Mickelson's challenge fell one short after a brilliant closing 66.

Andy Lyons/Getty Images

Ryan Palmer shared fifth place.

Jeff Gross/Getty Images

Rickie Fowler led before finishing third.

Sam Greenwood/Getty Images

Henrik Stenson joined Fowler in third.

Ryder Cup

Jamie Squire/Getty Images

Led by a meticulous and inspirational captain in Paul McGinley, Europe won 16½-11½ at Gleneagles.

Harry How/Getty Images

Graeme McDowell won three points.

Harry How/Getty Images

Ian Poulter collected two half points.

Andrew Redington/Getty Images

Jamie Donaldson, of Wales, claimed the winning point.

David Cannon/Getty Images

Successful U.S. rookies Jordan Spieth and Patrick Reed.

Mike Ehrmann/Getty Image

Phil Mickelson did not play at all on Saturday.

Harry How/Getty Images

Justin Rose claimed the most points with four.

Andrew Redington/Getty Images

Captain McGinley left nothing to chance.

Ross Kinnaird/Getty Images

Europe's stars get the celebrations underway.

Around The World

Victory at the BMW PGA Championship was the first of four for Rory McIlroy.

Richard Heathcote/Getty Images

Henrik Stenson retained his title at the DP World Tour Championship in Dubai.

Ross Kinnaird/Getty Images

Kevin C. Cox/Getty Images

Billy Horschel was the FedExCup champion.

Andrew Redington/Getty Images

Bubba Watson won his first WGC in Shanghai.

Kevin C. Cox/Getty Images

Martin Kaymer was The Players champion.

Jim Rogash/Getty Images

Chris Kirk triumphed at the Deutsche Bank.

Streeter Lecka/Getty Images

Matt Kuchar won the RBC Heritage.

Tom Pennington/Getty Images

Adam Scott won the Crowne Plaza Invitational as the World No. 1.

Darren Carroll/Getty Images

Hunter Mahan picked up The Barclays.

Sam Greenwood/Getty Images

Jim Furyk, 44, had numerous near-misses.

Getty Images

Justin Rose with the Scottish Open trophy.

Stuart Franklin/Getty Images

Jason Day won the WGC Accenture Match Play.

Sam Greenwood/Getty Images

Jordan Spieth won twice late in the year.

Tony Marshall/Getty Images

Jamie Donaldson claimed the Czech Masters.

Ross Kinnaird/Getty Images

Sergio Garcia survived a playoff in Qatar.

Jimmy Walker at the Sony Open, one of two wins.

Tom Pennington/Getty Images

Bill Haas, a runner-up at the Wyndham.

Jared Wickerham/Getty Images

Phil Mickelson had a winless season for the first time in a decade.

Ross Kinnaird/Getty Images

After Patrick Reed's antics with the crowd at Gleneagles, European Ryder Cup stars (L-R) Henrik Stenson, Graeme McDowell, Jamie Donaldson, Victor Dubuisson and Stephen Gallacher jokingly tell the American to be quiet at the Volvo World Match Play Championship.

Richard Heathcote/Getty Images

EurAsia Cup

Kuala Lumpur, Malaysia

Winners: Tied

There's a chapter in the Ryder Cup primer titled, "How to Escape by the Skin of Your Teeth." It must have been required reading for Team Asia. That would explain how they rallied to throw off a huge four-point deficit, win seven of the 10 points in singles, and wrestle to a 10-10 tie with Europe in the inaugural EurAsia Cup.

"The team played fantastic," said Thai star and Asia captain Thongchai Jaidee. "I told the boys to push to the limit, try everything they could, and stay positive."

That's easier said than done, but the Asia golfers got it done in a wild finish at Malaysia's Glenmarie Golf and Country Club. Their desperate charge in the singles raised memories of great Ryder Cup rallies from 10-6 deficits.

Asia had to reach deep in this one. First, they got swept in the opening four balls (better-ball), 5-0. Europe captain Miguel Angel Jimenez, paired with fellow Spaniard Pablo Larrazabal, posted two eagles and three birdies in a 2-and-1 win over Jaidee and Kiradech Aphibarnrat. Jaidee was displeased. "We are breaking all the pairings, except myself [with Kiradech]," he said. It proved to be a good move. In Friday's foursomes (alternate shot), Prayad Marksaeng and Hyung-Sung Kim's 4-and-3 rout of Thomas Bjorn and Thorbjorn Olesen led Asia to two wins and two halves. Europe still had a big lead, 7-3, going into the singles. Then victories by Jaidee, Aphibarnrat, Kim, Gaganjeet Bhullar, Anirban Lahiri and Siddikur Rahman, plus two halves, capped the Asian surge to the tie.

Said Jimenez: "It was an amazing day of golf. Asia, Europe — they both win. Nobody loses."

Maybank Malaysian Open

Kuala Lumpur, Malaysia

Winner: Lee Westwood

For those inclined to think Lee Westwood's seven-shot victory in the Maybank Malaysian Open must have been flawless, a short review is in order. He bogeyed his first hole, the 10th. In the second round, he watered his tee shot and double-bogeyed the par-three 11th. And in the third, he bogeyed both the par-four second and the par-five 18th.

Offsetting those five dropped shots, Westwood battered Kuala Lumpur Country Club for 23 birdies, and that worked out to a card of 65-66-71-68 and an 18-under-par 270 total. The wire-to-wire victory ended a long, strange time for Westwood. He once was ranked No. 1 in the world. But now, nearing 41, he had gone two years without winning, and he slipped to 36th, the highest ranking player in the field for this co-sanctioned Asian-European Tour event. He'd known little more than frustration till recently. He finished seventh in the Masters the previous week. He attributed the spark to a new coach and an old caddie. "So I was going back to what I had done before, because it had worked," Westwood said.

Oddly enough, Westwood's seven-shot win wasn't the romp it seemed. He led by one after the first round and four after the second. Then England's Andy Sullivan, seeking his first win, closed the gap to one with a 66 in the third. But Sullivan's dream blew up in the fourth round when he triple-bogeyed the par-three second out of the water on his way to a 78. And while Westwood was working on a bogey-free 68, nobody took a good run at him.

"I played well, I putted well, and the short game is good," Westwood said. "It makes a hell of a difference if you can get up and down if you miss a few greens...."

CIMB Niaga Indonesian Masters

Jakarta, Indonesia

Winner: Anirban Lahiri

Not to contradict a hallowed sports adage, but sometimes winning isn't everything. Sometimes it's where you win. That was the point India's Anirban Lahiri made after his spectacular eagle at the final hole locked up the CIMB Niaga Indonesian Masters in April — his fourth Asian Tour victory, but the first away from his homeland.

"It's really great to get my first win outside of India," said Lahiri, but it was more pragmatism than ego speaking. "I need the world ranking points." The idea was to get on the world stage, and Lahiri took that first step at the Royale Jakarta Golf Club, shooting 70-69-64-68–271, winning by a stroke over Australian rookie Cameron Smith and South Korea's little known Seuk-Hyun Baek, both seeking that first win.

The question was who would handle the final-round pressure. Baek, coming from the pack, applied the pressure with a one-bogey 65 and the clubhouse lead at 16 under. Smith, leading by one, stumbled early to a double bogey and two singles. Lahiri, playing with him in the final group, zipped right by and got to 16 under with three birdies from No. 2. A bogey and a birdie later, he double-bogeyed the par-four 13th, triggering a free-for-all. Lahiri, who raced into contention with a flawless 64 in the third round, needed a rousing finish, and he delivered. He birdied the 14th, getting to 15 under, then eagled the par-five 18th after firing a bold approach to 20 feet.

"My mind was blank," Lahiri said. "All I told myself was I had to get it into the hole." And he did, for a 68 and a 17-under 271 to win by a shot. That first win away from home was worth it — a rocket ride from 102nd to 67th in the world.

The Championship

Singapore

Winner: Felipe Aguilar

The conversations are generally mundane, and usually begin, "I told my caddie..." But Felipe Aguilar's chat with his caddie in the final round of the Championship at Laguna National was one for the archives.

Said Aguilar: "I told my caddie on [No.] nine, if I can get going on the back nine, I could do some damage..."

Then: "On the 17th green, I told my caddie, if I make a birdie on 18, I might put some pressure on the leader..."

Then caddie to Aguilar: "The way you're hitting the ball, you might make two."

Considering that the 18th at Laguna National is a par-four, that would take some doing. But Aguilar, 39-year-old Chilean, did it. In fact, he did all three, closing with a flawless 10-under-par 62 for his second Asian-European Tour co-sanctioned win. Ironically, the first was in the 2008 Indonesian Open, with a birdie on the last hole.

Aguilar started the final round four strokes behind the co-leaders, Thailand's Panuphol Pittayarat and Denmark's Anders Hansen. When an outward two-under 34 didn't do much good, he felt his chances were gone. Pittayarat led from the start but was slipping. But Hansen was working on his third 67 (the second round was a 66) and seemed beyond reach. Then Aguilar caught fire. He birdied Nos. 10, 11, 12 and 13, then 15. At the par-three 17th, he stuck his tee shot 10 feet from the cup and made it. That's when he began talking to his caddie about a birdie at the 18th — and his caddie to him about an eagle.

And Aguilar holed his approach at the 386-yard 18th, wrapping up a 65-67-72-62–266, 22-under card and ducking into a one-stroke win over Hansen and American David Lipsky.

ICTSI Philippine Open

Manila, Philippines

Winner: Marcus Both

Marcus Both, the tall Australian, had lost his playing card in 2013, then missed the qualifying school cut by a stroke. Both, 34, was thinking of throwing in the towel. Then came the sponsor's invitation to the ICTSI Philippine Open. What did he have to lose?

As Both would say: "Words can't describe how it feels to go from being an invite to a winner this week." But he had to survive a scary finish. Both led by two strokes after a 70-66 start, then stumbled in the third round, bogeying three of the last four holes for a 76, and trailed American Chan Kim by one going into the last. To Both's relative comfort, nobody put any great pressure on him in the final round.

Kim took himself out of the hunt with four bogeys and three birdies, then triple-bogeyed the 18th and dropped with a 76. Siddikur Rahman, Nathan Holman, Antonio Lacuna, Armond Vongvanij and Jay Bayron all had a shot at Both but fell short and tied for second, two behind. Both was his own greatest threat. At first, he was putting on a career performance. Three birdies and a bogey on the front nine got him to six under. He birdied the 15th with a 20-foot putt and dropped a short putt for a birdie at the 16th for a three-stoke lead. Then Both tripped over the last two holes for bogeys and closed with a 70 for a two-stroke victory at six-under 282. It was his third Asian Tour win, but first in five years.

"It was an emotional year on and off the golf course," Both said, near tears. "To come away with a trophy is amazing. I'm a bit lost for words."

Queen's Cup
Samui, Thailand
Winner: Thaworn Wiratchant

Youth must be served, the saying goes. And so it must, unless it runs into age and experience in the person of Thailand's Thaworn Wiratchant, 47, who brushed youth aside and plucked the Queen's Cup out of the eager grasp of Thai rookie Poom Saksansin on the last hole.

"I knew I had to play well on 18," said Wiratchant, recapping Samui Country Club's tough par-five finishing hole. "I aimed for the green, and if it didn't get on the green, I knew it would be around the green, which would give me a birdie chance." Wiratchant capitalized on the chance, wrapped up a card of 71-68-67-66–272, 12 under par, and brought his Asian Tour record for wins to 17.

The 18th became the key to the tournament when Wiratchant, Saksansin and Bangladesh's Siddikur Rahman came to it tied for the lead in the final round. Whoever won the hole would win the tournament. Siddikur got hurt the worst. He bogeyed, shot 72 and tied for third.

Saksansin led through the first three rounds, then the tension became too great in the last. He bogeyed three times on the front nine. "There was pressure," he said. His ball, he said, "was like a bird — it was going everywhere." He regrouped and birdied the 16th and 17th but parred the 18th. Wiratchant had trailed all the way, then in the final round birdied five of nine holes from No. 6 and took the lead. A bogey at the 17th put him into the tie. His strategy for the 18th was solid, and he ended up facing a five-foot birdie putt to win.

"The putt for birdie, felt I could make it," Wiratchant said. And he did.

Omega European Masters
Crans Montana, Switzerland
Winner: David Lipsky

See European Tours chapter.

Yeangder Tournament Players Championship
Chinese Taipei
Winner: Prom Meesawat

Patience is the byword of golf, but eight years is a bit more of it than Thailand's Prom Meesawat had in mind. Thus some rejoicing was in order when he came from behind in the final round to tie the Philippines' entry in golf's youth derby, Miguel Tabuena, 19, and beat him in a playoff in the Yeangder Tournament Players Championship.

"I've been waiting for this win for a long time," Meesawat said. "Hopefully, I won't have to wait another eight years to win again."

Meesawat, 30, knew patience. He turned professional in 2004, showed big promise in a flurry of top-10 finishes and broke through in the 2006 SK Telecom. And that was it, until the 2014 Yeangder, and even that didn't look good till the final round. Meesawat, coming from the coolness of Switzerland, was hit by the heat and humidity of Linkou International in Chinese Taipei, and didn't get in a practice round. "I'm struggling with the temperature change," he said. Shooting 67-73-68, he trailed through the first three rounds, by three in the second, and was two behind Tabuena entering the fourth. He finished with a one-bogey, four-birdie 69, the last on a clutch 15-foot putt at the final hole. Tabuena took two early bogeys, bounced back for four birdies, then bogeyed the 17th for a 71 and a tie at 11-under 277.

Meesawat two-putted for a par at the second extra hole, the par-five 18th, for his first playoff win in three tries and his first win in eight years.

"Things just didn't turn out the way I wanted it to be," said Tabuena.

Meesawat didn't wish a wait on Tabuena. "He has a bright future," he said. "I hope he gets his win soon."

Worldwide Holdings Selangor Masters

Petaling Jaya, Selangor, Malaysia

Winner: Chapchai Nirat

Thailand's Chapchai Nirat took the 2009 SAIL Open by 11 strokes and with the remarkable score of 32-under-par 256. A performance of that magnitude suggests it would be followed by other wins. But it wasn't, to the surprise of everyone, especially Nirat himself. Five years later, Nirat was still wondering.

"I don't know why I haven't won in such a long time," Nirat was saying, at the 2014 Worldwide Holdings Selangor Masters. "I might need a bit of luck to win again." And that's what he got.

India's Anirban Lahiri comes under the heading of "Tough Luck." Lahiri was running smoothly from the start, shooting 64-68, and leading by two each day. In the third round, he was seen with a grimace on his face and a severe abdominal illness. He lurched to a 76.

Nirat closed with 69-68 and tempted fate. He was up by two with two holes to play, but he erased his lead by bogeying both after missing the fairway. He tied at 274 with the Philippines' Antonio Lascuna, who finished with 71-63. Nirat needed one more bit of luck, and he got it at the first playoff hole. Both were on the green, facing par putts. Lascuna's was from five feet. The ball was headed home, but veered away at the last moment. "I saw it as a straight putt," Lascuna was to say. "But the ball turned away at the end." Said Nirat: "It took the pressure off me a bit." Nirat then dropped his four-footer for his fourth Asian win, but first in five years. He enjoyed a moment of quiet jubilation.

"I didn't think this day would happen," Nirat said. "I didn't think I'd have a chance to win."

Asia-Pacific Diamond Cup

Ibaraki

Winner: Hiroyuki Fujita

See Japan Tour section.

Mercuries Taiwan Masters

Chinese Taipei

Winner: Steve Lewton

It's one of golf's great mysteries: What is it that turns on a golfer's game? For England's Steve Lewton, for example, in getting his first Asian Tour win in the Mercuries Taiwan Masters, it was the scoreboards in the final round — not seeing them, that is.

"It's strange that I didn't feel any pressure during the round," Lewton said. No pressure? Not even going into the final round with the narrowest of leads, for that first victory? "Maybe," Lewton ventured, "because I didn't get to see a lot of scoreboards out there."

So Lewton didn't have the pleasure — or pressure — of seeing his name up on the board after missing the cut in the tournament in his first two visits. This time it was consistently good golf — 70-72-70-71 — that kept him up there. In the first round, he tied for second, two behind France's Lionel Weber, who wielded a magic putter. Weber needed just nine putts on his back nine for his four-under-par 68. But he couldn't solve the winds that hit Taiwan Golf and Country Club the next day and kited to an 80.

Lewton, 31, was one behind Brazil's Adilson Da Silva at the halfway point, then rode three straight birdies from No. 5 to a one-stroke lead through the third round. He had to battle through the fourth, posting five birdies against four bogeys for his closing 71 and a five-under 283 total, winning by two over Da Silva and the Philippines' Antonio Lascuna. He dedicated the victory to his father, who passed away in January.

"He kept me going in golf when I was struggling the past few years," Lewton said. "It's a shame he's not here to witness this, but I'm sure he will be happy for me wherever he is."

Hong Kong Open

Fanling, Hong Kong

Winner: Scott Hend

"This victory is to be treasured," Scott Hend said, and for more reasons than most people knew when he hoisted the Hong Kong Open trophy.

The victory was not only his sixth on the Asian Tour, it was the biggest. It put him on a historic trophy, along with Tom Watson, Greg Norman, Bernhard Langer and others. And since the tournament was a co-sponsored event, the victory gave Hend a berth on the European Tour.

But it came the hard way. He had to beat the Philippines' Angelo Que in a playoff after a duel in which neither one led until the end. Hend shot the par-70 Hong Kong Golf Club in 67-66-67-67, Que in 65-69-67-66, to tie at 13-under 267. In the final round, Que had an erratic mix of three birdies and three bogeys through the 10th, then sprinted into the lead with birdies at Nos. 12, 13 and 14. Hend, after two birdies and two bogeys on the front nine, took the lead with birdies at Nos. 10, 12 and 14. Que responded at the 18th with a spectacular approach from the edge of the woods to a foot — "the shot of my career," he said — and birdied for the tie. On the first playoff hole, Que missed the green, and Hend, safely on, holed a five-foot putt for a par and the win.

Que was far from crushed. "My goal today was to just go under par," he said, "but this is even better."

Two prominent names fell short. Spain's Miguel Angel Jimenez, going after his fifth Hong Kong Open and third in succession, missed the cut, knocked out by abdominal cramps. Ernie Els, turning 45, took the second-round lead, then suffered a cool putter and a sore right hip.

Venetian Macau Open

Macau

Winner: Anirban Lahiri

Anirban Lahiri's timing couldn't have been better. Back home in India, they were marking Diwali, a holiday celebrated with fireworks. Lahiri got off some fireworks of his own to start the Venetian Macau Open, torching Macau Golf and Country Club for a 10-under-par 61 on his way to his second win of the year.

"Happy Diwali to everyone back home," Lahiri said with a grin, after needing just 22 putts on a day when the rain-softened course took a beating under the preferred lies rule, with 33 players in the 60s. Scott Hend, who won the Hong Kong Open the week before, shot 62, setting the stage for a Lahiri-Hend battle the rest of the way.

With the winds up in the second round, Hend (70) tied with Adam Groom (67) at 10 under, while Lahiri tripped to a 73 and was two back. Hend ran hot-cold-hot in the third round. He birdied four straight from No. 2, made three bogeys in mid-round, then birdied three down the stretch for a 67–199. Lahiri was steadier with a bogey-free, four-birdie 67 to close within two.

Hend closed with a strange 69. He eagled No. 2, then alternated erratically between birdies and bogeys much of the way until a fatal lip-out par putt from four feet at the 18th. "I thought I made that putt," Hend said. Lahiri, after four birdies and a bogey, was two behind at the final turn, then negotiated the critical stretch. He birdied the par-three 14th off a high, hard seven iron and took the lead with a birdie at the 15th. Hend squared it with his birdie at 16. It came down to the 18th. Lahiri made his par, Hend lipped out the putt. Then the holiday really began.

CIMB Classic

Kuala Lumpur, Malaysia
Winner: Ryan Moore

Autumn can mean different things to different people — leaves changing color, the harvest, football, etc. For Ryan Moore, it means it's time to win again. Accordingly, Moore came from behind in the last two rounds to take his second straight CIMB Classic, but a bit more comfortably this time. It was his career-fourth victory, but the third in the fall, following the Shriners Hospitals for Children Open in October 2012, and the CIMB in October 2013, and this one, in early November. Was it autumn magic?

"I've been ... trying to figure out why," Moore said. "Maybe it's because ... it's kind of the home stretch ... just play some good golf and finish off the year."

That's what Moore had — a strong finish for a 17-under-par 271 total and a three-shot win at Kuala Lumpur Golf and Country Club. He trailed with a 68-69 start, then closed with a pair of 67s, tying for the lead with Kevin Na at 12 under through the third round, then winning by three, but only after some uncertain moments.

Moore posted eight birdies in the final round, but two of his three bogeys came at the 12th and 16th, with contenders in hot pursuit. A birdie at the 17th and fate bailed him out. Sergio Garcia (69) lost steam when a palm tree cost him a double bogey at the 10th. Then Na (70) lost his tee shot in the top of a palm at the 17th and double-bogeyed. Big-hitting Gary Woodland (67), who lost to Moore in a playoff in 2013, had a different problem. "The par-fives cost me all week," he said, meaning he managed only seven birdies on them, but also bogeyed twice.

How could three different contenders all fade together? Maybe because it was autumn — it was Moore's time.

WGC - HSBC Champions

Shanghai, China
Winner: Bubba Watson

Bubba Watson had just blown a sure thing, and now was standing in a bunker at the par-five 18th, the final hole of the World Golf Championships - HSBC Champions. "It's been a miserable couple holes here, but this will change everything if it goes in," Watson said to his caddie. Watson had made that great wedge shot from the trees to set up his 2012 Masters victory, but this time, he lay two in a bunker 60 yards from the green.

Then Watson blasted out and watched the ball land on the distant green and roll in for an eagle. "You always joke about holing it," said Watson.

The miraculous eagle added a two-under-par 70 to Watson's 71-67-69 for an 11-under 277 at Sheshan International. But the eagle didn't win for him. South Africa's Tim Clark came along and holed a five-footer for birdie at the 18th to tie.

On the first extra hole, Clark's 25-foot birdie try pulled up just short. Watson, back in the same bunker, this time blasted to 20 feet and holed the birdie putt for his third win of the year and his first victory outside the United States.

The Chinese were fast becoming accustomed to golf, but must have thought Watson's final-round 70 was of the Wild West variety. Watson scattered six birdies (three in succession from No. 6), three bogeys, a double bogey and, finally, the eagle at the last hole. He had come to No. 16 leading by two. He left the par-three 17th trailing by one. At the par-four 16th, he missed the green and bogeyed. At the 17th, he bunkered his tee shot and double-bogeyed. As he told his caddie from the bunker at the 18th, holing that shot would change everything.

Panasonic Open India

New Delhi, India

Winner: S.S.P. Chowrasia

Rahil Gangjee, after an opening 66, likened his golf to a game of chess. "You go from Point A to Point B and you make a putt," he was saying. That elegant strategy worked beautifully for three and a half rounds. He was on the verge of winning the Panasonic Open India when S.S.P. Chowrasia came out of nowhere and jumped on his square.

Chowrasia, 36, turned the tournament into a psychology lab. He explained that he didn't win because he was confident, but rather because he was trying to become confident. The distinction was lost on Gangjee and Mithun Perera. Chowrasia trailed through first three rounds, then zoomed up the leaderboard to tie them at 12-under-par 276, then beat them with a birdie on the first extra hole for his third Asian Tour win and first since early in 2011.

"I worked very hard for this win because I wanted to boost my confidence," Chowrasia said.

Gangjee, 36, led through the first three rounds, shooting Delhi Golf Club in 66-68-71, and Perera closed in with 70-67-69. Chowrasia, on the other hand, shooting 70-71-69, trailed by four, seven, and then by five entering the final round.

"At the start of the day, I was thinking that if I could shoot four or five under, I will have a chance to win," Chowrasia said.

Chowrasia, looking at a five-stroke deficit starting the final round, was out in one under, and after birdies at the 10th and 12th, birdied three straight from the 15th. He closed with a 66 to tie Gangjee (71) and Perera (70). He holed a 15-footer for birdie on the first playoff hole for the win.

"I always had the belief I could win on the Asian Tour again, and I did," Chowrasia said.

Chiangmai Golf Classic

Chiangmai, Thailand

Winner: Rashid Khan

For all of the 21 birdies Rashid Khan harvested in the Chiangmai Golf Classic, it was a clutch par that pretty much saved his win.

"I found the bunker on the 15th hole," said Khan, who had just taken the lead for the first time on the previous hole. "I had a shot, but it was a tight line. It was very important because I only had a one-shot lead going into the 18th. That par gave me a bit of a boost because I needed to maintain my lead. The last three holes were very exciting."

Khan, 23, who got his first win in the SAIL-SBI Open in March, calmed himself and stayed ahead of the pack with a card of 68-69-66-68 for a 17-under-par 271 total at the Alpine Golf Resort in Chiangmai. That left him that precious one stroke ahead of the Thanyakon Khrongpha, a lanky 24-year-old Thai seeking his first win, and Indian veteran Jyoti Randhawa, 42, chasing his ninth.

Khan stuck to their heels while Randhawa (65-70) and Khrongpha (65-67) exchanged the lead through the middle rounds. Khrongpha admitted to a build-up of nerves. "But I think there is more excitement than pressure," he said. Randhawa saw it as a battle of ages: "It's a young man's game now ... hopefully my experience will count."

Randhawa bogeyed twice in the final round, but two late birdies gave him a 69. Khrongpha birdied the 13th and 14th but three-putted the 16th for his third bogey. A birdie at the 18th gave him a 71 and a tie for second with Randhawa. Khan moved in with birdies at Nos. 9, 10, 12 and 14 — plus the great par save at the 15th — for his winning 68.

"Heading into the last few holes," Khan said, "I was very confident I could win."

Resorts World Manila Masters

Manila, Philippines

Winner: Mardan Mamat

Singapore's Mardan Mamat showed them a new way to celebrate. Not the ever-popular fist pump, not the two-handed heavenward thrust, not clutching the head. Mamat, on tapping in his final putt at the Resorts World Manila Masters, simply sank to his knees, bent down and kissed the ground.

A six-shot, start-to-finish victory will do that to a 47-year-old veteran whose career was hanging by a thread.

"Three weeks ago, I was thinking about quitting," said Mamat, a four-time winner who last won in 2012. "This was my last year of exemption. I needed to play well to keep my card."

The tournament was in doubt for only the first two rounds, when Mamat shot 65-68, tying Japan's Daisuke Kataoka for the first-round lead and Korean Jeung-Hun Wang, 19, at the halfway point. Then Mamat was on his way. A 66 in the third round put him four ahead of Thai star Kiradech Aphibarnrat, and a closing 69 gave him the six-stroke margin over France's

Lionel Weber, on 268, 20 under par at Manila Southwoods.

Said Weber, who closed with a 70: "I did think I had a chance to catch Mamat when I birdied the first hole." Thailand's Prom Meesawat, after barely making the cut, shot 63-68 and finished third, eight back. "It's still a good week for me," Meesawat said.

Mamat put on an amazing birdie show. In his opening 65, he birdied seven of 13 holes from No. 2. Then came the blistering eight straight birdies over two rounds — the last four in the second round (he finished on the front nine), and the first four of the third. It was a runaway.

Said Mamat: "I wanted to win again. I needed to keep to my own pace, keep to my own strength, and it worked out."

King's Cup

Khon Kaen, Thailand

Winner: Thaworn Wiratchant

Now Thaworn Wiratchant, esteemed veteran of the Asian Tour, was pleased. He had the full set.

"It feels good to have the complete Royal collection," he said. "I won the Queen's Cup twice, and now I can add the King's Cup to my trophy cabinet."

It was already bulging. This King's Cup gave Wiratchant an unprecedented 18th Asian Tour victory. (The King's Cup played in January, won by Prayad Marksaeng, had been postponed from the 2013 schedule.)

True, it's a wise golfer who knows his own game, but Wiratchant, 47, also seemed to have developed an uncanny notion of the elastic properties of confidence. How far would that treasured commodity spread? Wiratchant was convinced he knew.

"I really wanted to birdie 18, as I did not want to go into a playoff," he said. "I was confident of winning in regulation play, but not in a playoff."

And so after trailing through the first three rounds, Wiratchant treated his 15-foot birdie putt at the final hole like a tap-in. He rolled it home for a two-stroke victory, posting a card of 68-67-66-67–268, 20 under par at Singha Park. The birdie gave him a cushion against India's Anirban Lahiri (70), who led for the first three rounds, and Australia's Andrew Dodt (67), who charged to birdies over the last three holes.

It seemed Wiratchant took awhile to get warmed up. After his 68-67 start, he birdied five straight from No. 2 in the third round and posted a flawless 66, and took control in the fourth round, birdieing Nos. 3, 4, 6 and 8 for 32 going out, added another birdie at the 10th, then bogeyed the 12th (one of only three overall, plus a double bogey). "I got a little shaky on 12 when I bogeyed," Wiratchant said. "But I maintained my composure and managed to see it through."

That's confidence for you.

Bank BRI Indonesia Open

Jakarta, Indonesia

Winner: Padraig Harrington

Padraig Harrington had come too far to let this one get away. He had come four years and 63 holes, to be approximate.

The personable Irishman, owner of two British Open Championships and a PGA Championship, last won in the Asian Tour's 2010 Iskandar Johor Open. Here he was back on the Asian Tour in the 2014 Bank BRI Indonesian Open, and well into the final round. He led by four shots starting the round, but soon found himself an alarming two behind. He bogeyed the first hole and double-bogeyed the par-three seventh, while Thailand's up-and-coming Thanyakon Khrongpha, 24, birdied three of the first five. Harrington was looking for help.

"I was really praying for a rain delay," Harrington said. "My momentum was gone but Thanyakon was flying and he didn't miss a shot."

Harrington's prayers were answered. The rains did hit Damai Indah and play was suspended.

"The rain delay stopped my momentum," said Khrongpha. "The pressure made me scared."

The tournament they had made their own private battle turned once again. Harrington got a stroke back with a birdie at No. 8. He got to 16 under on birdies at the 13th and 17th. Thanyakon bogeyed the 12th, but rebounded with birdies at 13 and 17 and was tied with Harrington. Then experience proved out over youth.

Khrongpha hit his approach into the water at the par-four 18th, letting Harrington, who had hit his tee shot to the edge of a hazard, change his strategy.

"When Thanyakon hit it into the water, there was no point to taking a chance," he said. "So I went back to the fairway and hit my six iron for my best shot of the week."

Two putts later, Harrington had his first win in four years.

Thailand Golf Championship

Chonburi, Thailand

Winner: Lee Westwood

Back in 2011, England's Lee Westwood launched the brand-new Thailand Golf Championship with uncommon gusto, opening with a 60, leading by 11 shots at one point, and winning by seven.

The 2014 edition was quite the opposite. Westwood didn't lead until the final round, and he had to stage a furious rally to edge Germany's Martin Kaymer, the reigning U.S. Open champion, and Australia's Marcus Fraser, rebounding from an eight-week layoff after wrist surgery.

"I don't think anyone will be running away with the title," Westwood said, on falling two behind after the third round. "I just need to fine-tune my game."

If it was sweet music he was looking for, those were sure a couple of clunkers he hit to open the final round. The pair of bogeys knocked him four behind. Then he regained his touch. He made four straight birdies from No. 6, and added birdies at the 11th, 14th and 15th, and parred the last three for a 67 and an eight-under 280 for a one-stroke win over Kaymer (68), who bogeyed the 17th, and Fraser (70), who bogeyed the 18th.

Getting to that point, however, was a different story. Westwood trailed with his 70-71-72 at the par-72 Amata Spring Country Club. He was one behind Fraser and a traffic-jam at 69 in the first round. He was still one back when England's little known Tommy Fleetwood, one of only 12 to break par on the windy day, took the halfway lead at 69–140. Westwood slipped two behind in the third round, and Fraser, with a 70, took a one-shot lead that, he noted, "is almost irrelevant with the caliber of players on the leaderboard."

Westwood noted that the mid-December tournament was his final outing of the year. "It's been a good last day at school," he said.

Dubai Open

Dubai, United Arab Emirates

Winner: Arjun Atwal

Arjun Atwal suddenly was talking about the good old days. They were quite good but not all that old, and sorely missed. One minute Atwal was in the international spotlight, leaping from Asian Tour No. 1 to becoming the first Indian to win on the PGA Tour. That was only four years ago, in 2010. And then it was gone. Now he was getting a taste of it again, in the inaugural Dubai Open at the Els Club Dubai. He'd started with a dreary 73, seven shots off the lead. But he followed that with a flawless 65 that lifted him within a shot of the halfway lead. Atwal, 41, hadn't been in that neighborhood in a while.

"It really felt good, actually," he said, smiling. "Felt like the old days. No mistakes, no bogeys, just solid."

The third round felt even better. The tournament turned into a horse race. Atwal, with a 68, was tied for the lead at 10 under with Shiv Kapur (69), Jbe' Kruger (64) and Korea's Jeung-Hun Wang (68). Six others were a stroke behind, and all told, 21 players were within three strokes of the lead going into the final round.

Atwal closed strong, with an eight-birdie, two-bogey 66, but he needed help. Wang, 19, seeking his first tour victory, provided it when he stumbled and bogeyed the last two holes. "I tried to play my game, but I cannot do that because of the pressure," he said.

And there was Atwal, with his first win in four years.

"I've gone through some really tough times the last few years, with injuries and losing my card on the PGA Tour," Atwal said. "I almost wanted to quit. Thanks to a few of my family and friends, I didn't, and here we are."

OneAsia Tour

Enjoy Jakarta Indonesia PGA Championship

Jakarta, Indonesia
Winner: Michio Matsumura

As a golf tournament, the Enjoy Jakarta Indonesia PGA Championship took an interesting twist and became the occasion for self-deprecation, pithy observations and a reach for self-esteem, among other things.

First in the tournament, co-sanctioned by the OneAsia and Japan Tours, came New Zealand's Gareth Paddison, not fully convinced he was capable of the eight-under-par 64 that just got him the first-round lead. "It was out of left field," Paddison said. "I didn't expect that of myself."

Australia's Rhein Gibson slipped well behind with a 72 in the third round, then hurtled back into the clubhouse lead in the fourth with a 10-under 62. Said Gibson: "I had some really cheap birdies."

The Philippines' Juvic Pagunsan bounced his way through an erratic fourth round, birdied three of the last four holes for a 69, and fell just one short and tied Gibson for second. "It just wasn't going to be the day today," he lamented.

And Japan's Michio Matsumura, who won three times on the Japan Tour, badly needed to prove himself. "It has been my dream since I became a professional to win a tournament outside Japan," he said. And so he did, but it took a rousing finish.

Matsumura was in the hunt with 65-67-67 at the par-72 Damai Indah — excellent golf, but just a stroke short all the way. Then in the fourth round, he all but killed his chances with a bogey at No. 1 and a double bogey at No. 6, and this with Gibson burning up the course in front of him. Then Matsumura did some torching of his own. He birdied six holes coming home, including the last three, for a 68, a 21-under 267 and a one-stroke win over Gibson and Pagunsan. Matsumura had made his dream come true.

Volvo China Open

Shenzhen, China
Winner: Alexander Levy

The practice is prevalent on the LPGA Tour: A first-time winner being sprayed by friends with beer or soda pop. The ceremony reached the Volvo China Open in April, and with the French, it had to be champagne. When little-known Alexander Levy, 23, broke through at the OneAsia-European Tour co-sanctioned tournament, he was greeted by countrymen wielding bottles of bubbly (label and vintage unknown).

Levy, in his second year on the European Tour, stamped the event as his with a dazzling second round. He opened with a 68, then torched Genzon

Golf Club for a 10-under-par 62, and was nearly breathless. "I played unbelievably," Levy said. "I shot 63 at Kingsbarns during the Dunhill Links in Scotland last year, but this course is a lot tougher and I am only starting to realize how good that score is." He made the turn in 30, capping four birdies with an eagle on a 25-foot putt at No. 9. He came home with birdies at Nos. 10, 12, 14 and 17 for a four-stroke lead.

Some pressure was off when the always threatening Ian Poulter was penalized for an incorrect drop at the 13th. "...Turned a bad six into a really bad eight," Poulter said. A 74 knocked him out of the hunt.

Levy closed with 70-69 for 19-under 269, and weathered threats by Spain's Alvaro Quiros, who closed with a 72 and finished third, and England's Tommy Fleetwood, the runner-up with a 68. Levy shook off a double bogey at the 15th and birdied the 17th and 18th for his 69.

Said Levy, after the champagne shower: "I woke up very early this morning, thinking about too much. On the golf course, I was only thinking about my job, and that's why I've got the trophy in my hands."

GS Caltex Maekyung Open

Seoul, South Korea

Winner: Jun-Won Park

When it comes to being the new kid on the block, they don't come any newer than South Korea's Jun-Won Park. He joins the OneAsia Tour on Wednesday and he's hoisting a trophy on Sunday. If he should someday end up in the World Golf Hall of Fame, history will note that his trip began with the GS Caltex Maekyung Open.

Park, 27, was not only the newest, he was one of the most obscure. He arrived at Namseoul Golf and Country Club ranked 724th in the world. The victory, his first, lifted him to 416th.

"My putting was really great all week, and that was the key," Park said.

Park trailed by four after an opening 72, then joined the hunt in the second round with a tournament-low 64 built around a hole-out eagle from 80 yards at the par-five ninth and five birdies coming home. That got him to within two of Kyoung-Hoon Lee at the halfway point. It was new territory. "This could be my big chance," Park said. "I really haven't been in this position before. I do know this course very well. It is short and tight, but it suits my game."

And suited his game to a tee (no pun intended). He tied Sang-Hyung Park with a 70 in the third round, then won by three on a flawless 67 for a 15-under 273. The win capped a frustrating young career. Jun-Won took up golf as a kid, turned pro in 2006, and after his mandatory two years of military service, he returned to golf. But he showed little of the talent that was to blossom in the Maekyung.

"Although I hadn't won before," said Park, "I never gave up hoping that this day would come. This year, I was determined to make it happen."

SK Telecom Open

Incheon, South Korea

Winner: Seung-Hyuk Kim

For those collecting improbable winners, South Korea's Seung-Hyuk Kim proved himself worthy of consideration in the OneAsia Tour's SK Telecom Open. His case starts with a triple bogey in the first round, which should have cost him the lead but didn't, to a double bogey in the last round, which should have cost him the victory — but didn't. Kim patched together a card of 66-74-67-70–277, 11 under par at the Sky 72 Golf Club for his first win since turning pro in 2005, a one-stroke win over countrymen Tae-Hee Lee and K.T. Kim.

Seung-Hyuk Kim was sizzling for much of the first round. Starting on the back nine, he birdied his second hole, and then his seventh, eighth and ninth to turn in 32. Then he birdied four of his first five coming in and was thinking of the course record of 63. Then on his sixth hole (No. 15), he hit his tee shot out of bounds and three-putted for a triple-bogey-seven. "I thought I could hit anything," Kim said, "but I sliced my iron off the tee and that was the end." Then at his 18th, he holed a 50-foot putt from the fringe for a birdie and the 66 and a two-shot lead.

The fourth round was a scramble that saw four men tied for the lead at one point. Kim nearly knocked himself out of the race with a double bogey at No. 4. "I didn't panic," he said. "There were a lot of holes left." It finally came down to the 18th and the battle of the Kims, both needing birdies to win.

K.T. Kim's 20-foot putt just slipped by, but Seung-Hyuk's nine-footer dropped. "It was a fantastic feeling when it went in," Seung-Hyuk said. "Now I know I can win a golf tournament."

Fiji International

Nadi, Fiji

Winner: Steve Jeffress

A camera clicks, someone coughs, a bird calls — golfers have been distracted at critical times by all kinds of things. How about a party on a beach?

In an Aussie-vs.-Aussie finish in the inaugural Fiji International, Jake Higginbottom, 20, and Steve Jeffress, 38, a 15-year veteran of the Australasian Tour, had arrived at the par-three 15th tied for the lead. Out of sight on a nearby beach, someone yelled just as Higginbottom was hitting his tee shot. He flinched and dumped the ball into the hazard short of the green. An excellent chip shot held the damage to a bogey, but it was his third in six holes, and suddenly he was two behind when Jeffress birdied. Higginbottom also bogeyed the 16th and Jeffress birdied the 18th, filling out a card of 69-70-69-70 for a 10-under 278 at Natadola Bay and a four-stroke win in the co-sanctioned event, his first on the OneAsia Tour.

"I am over the moon and a bit surprised," said Jeffress, whose only other significant win was in the 2006 Victorian PGA on the Australasian Tour. "It has been year of hard work, so it feels very special."

Said Higginbottom, who won the 2012 New Zealand Open as a teenage amateur: "If you'd have said I would finish second at the start of the week, I would have taken it. It was a little disappointing as I was in control there for a while."

Higginbottom was in a seven-way tie for the lead at 68 in the first round, led by two through the second, and he and Jeffress were tied going into the fourth. Higginbottom's game began to slip from there. He finished with a four-birdie, six-bogey 74, while Jeffress, after a bogey at No. 1, birdied three of the last four holes.

Nanshan China Masters

Nanshan, China

Winner: Hao-Tong Li

At the Nanshan China Masters, they were announcing Hao-Tong Li as winner of the recent Henan Open — by eight shots. That was on the developmental PGA Tour China Series. Two weeks later, they were announcing Li as winner of the OneAsia Tour's Nanshan China Masters, by four shots, and at age 19 — the youngest-ever OneAsia winner.

Was Li another young phenom out of China, or was the excitement premature? Time, of course, would tell. Meanwhile, there was the secret to Li's success: Don't think about winning. Because, he said, "every time I do, I get thirsty to win, and then I don't win." So keeping his mind on what he was doing, he shot the par-71 Nanshan International in 68-65-72-70–275, nine under par, for the comfortable margin over Australia's Jun-Seok Lee.

In one of his few errors, Li bogeyed the 18th in the first round, costing himself a share of the lead at 67. Then he was off and winging. He shot the course-record 65 in the second round in freshening winds. Starting on the back nine, Li birdied Nos. 12, 15, 16 and 18, then birdied Nos. 3 and 5 coming in for a three-stroke lead. He barely held on in the third round as some shaky putting cost him three inward bogeys for the one-over 72. "I think I just lost my luck on the back nine," he said. The big test came in the heavier winds of the final round. "I could not stand sometimes when I was putting," Li said. He bogeyed the 11th and double-bogeyed the 12th, but pulled himself together and birdied three of the last four for the 70 — a champion at 19.

Li grinned at the thought. "I think I am too young to win a Masters event," he cracked.

Kolon Korea Open

Cheonan, South Korea

Winner: Seung-Hyuk Kim

Seung-Hyuk Kim did the math.

He was two under par for the tournament with five holes to play — the leader on the course, for what that was worth. Behind him, Jeong-Woo Ham, the amateur and third-round leader, was showing a heavy case of nerves and was now trailing him by a stroke. And Seung-Yul Noh was the leader in the clubhouse at even-par 284.

Conclusion: All things being equal, if Kim could par the last five holes of the demanding Woo Keong Hills course, the Kolon Korea Championship would be his. He had to trust his patience and his game.

"My game plan was just to make pars," said Kim, posting his second OneAsia Tour victory of the year, after the SK Telecom Open in May. "It's a difficult course, and you really have to manage your game if you expect to win here."

Kim did control his game, parring in to complete a card of 73-68-71-70, a two-under 282 for a two-shot win over Noh, a one-time winner on the PGA Tour. Kim had read Ham correctly. The unfortunate amateur had already spun out of the lead with a bogey and a double bogey on a fog-delayed Sunday, before darkness halted play. He wrapped up his round with bogeys at the 15th and 17th, finishing with a 75, three strokes back.

Patience was Kim's name from the start. He was all of six off the lead to start, with Yun-Cheol Jeon opening with a 67, and still back in the pack at the halfway point, as morning fogs continued to bump rounds into the next day. He was still chasing the lead into Monday morning, then did what he had to do. And it all added up for him.

Emirates Australian Open

Sydney, New South Wales

Winner: Jordan Spieth

See Australasian Tour chapter.

Dongfeng Nissan Cup

Guangzhou, China

Winner: Asia Pacific

All it took, it seems, was a little inspiration.

"The players reacted after my plea for them to get serious and play hard after the first round," said Peter Thomson, captain of the Asia Pacific Team in the Dongfeng Nissan Cup at Foison Golf Club. Team China had put on a good show the first day, taking a 4-2 lead in the four-ball matches. Something seemed to click for Asia Pacific.

"The second and third days were a surprise to us to outscore the China team," said Thomson, the legendary Aussie who won five Open Championships. “It was beyond our wildest dreams we should win by such a margin.”

If falling behind 4-2 in the opening matches wasn’t upsetting enough, what alarmed Thomson was that his team lost the first three matches. Asia Pacific reversed the process in the alternate-shot foursomes, 4½-1½, and took a one-point lead into the Sunday singles. Asia Pacific then stormed to eight wins in the 12 singles for a 15-9 margin and its third victory in the four Dongfeng events.

“We played some good golf in some pretty funny conditions today, and it was a good effort,” said Thompson, now 3-1 as the Asia Pacific captain. China got its lone win in 2013.

“We lost, but it’s a good experience for our young players,” said China vice-captain Jun Wang. Among them were Zihao Chen, 18, and Cheng Jin, a 16-year-old amateur. “This format is very good for the young Chinese players, who can get a lot of experience through this tournament,” Wang Jun added. “It’s good for the young Chinese players and good for Chinese golf fans to see what progress China has made.”

Australian PGA Championship

Gold Coast, Queensland

Winner: Greg Chalmers

See Australasian Tour chapter.

PGA Tour China

The PGA Tour China made its historic debut in 2014, and the opening act was a show-stopper. It came in the season-opening Mission Hills Haikou Open — a South Korean kid winning a Chinese tournament, then thrusting both arms into the air and yelling "Yes!" — pure American slang for success in sports. And winning by 10 shots.

This was Jeung-Han Wang, only 18, a native of Seoul, after dropping his last birdie putt at the final hole of the Haikou. The arm thrust and the "Yes!" — actually, it's stretched out to "Yessss!" — came from an American broadcaster in pro basketball, who used it on exciting shots that clicked. It might have been lost on Chinese fans that the arm thrust is the referee's signal for a three-point basket in basketball and a touchdown or field goal in football. Even so, the broader message was that golf has no borders.

The PGA Tour China is a developmental tour, an effort to establish professional golf conducted by a partnership of the PGA Tour, the China Golf Association and the event promoter, the China Olympic Sports Industry. The 2014 season consisted of 12 tournaments, with golfers from all over the world getting their playing privileges through a qualifying tournament.

It had nine different winners from five countries — China (5), Australia (3), South Korea (2), Thailand and the United States, one each.

As with the PGA Tour Canada and the PGA Tour Latinoamerica, the China Tour would send the top five money-winners to the Web.com Tour, the pathway to the PGA Tour. And if one characteristic stamped this debut year, it was "Youth must be served."

That was clear enough when two 19-year-old Chinese golfers finished 1-2 atop the big five — Hao-Tong Li, who exploded for three wins in the last four tournaments, with $156,101, and Xin-Jun Zhang, with $104,844. They were followed by Australia's Brett Drewitt, $94,391; the United States' Sam Chien, $92,578, and South Korea's Todd Baek, $86,443.

"This is very exciting to me to know that I will play on the Web.com Tour next year," said Li. "And I know that [the tour] has really helped me in my preparation for playing on the Web.com Tour."

Li, playing in all 12 events, ran away with the tour once he got warmed up. Early in the season, he fell just short in the United Investment Real Estate Wuhan Open, losing to Drewitt in a playoff. Come the fall, the tour was his. He won the Jianye Tianzhu Henan Open by eight shots, then won the next-to-last Hainan Open by six and the season-ending CTS Tycoon Championship by five. That's three wins by an average of 6.3 strokes.

The Henan Open win was his first as a professional, and it was a tough test for the youngster, coming in the rain, cold and wind. "I knew I had a three-shot lead after the turn, and on the back nine I was so focused on my game I didn't pay too much attention to the leaderboard," Li said. "It was not until the final hole where … I saw I had built such a big lead." Indeed — he won by eight.

Li had been working towards this time since winning the 2010 China Open

Junior Match Play Championship when he was 14. He played in the China Open at 15, tied for 21st in the 2011 Nanshan Masters on the OneAsia Tour, and turned professional at age 16.

Zhang got a lot out of eight starts — a win in the Earls Beijing Open and three seconds to finish second on the money list. Drewitt won the third tournament, the Wuhan Open, then had six other top-10 finishes, playing all 12 events and not missing a cut. Drewitt was third in birdies, with 170, and was tops on the par-fives, playing them in an aggregate of 92 under par.

Sam Chien set a hot pace, beginning the season with 10 straight rounds under par. His win came in the midst of that streak, the Buick Open, the second tournament. Then he got an odd and big boost from the Nine Dragons Open late in the season, getting first-place money without winning. That was because another bright young Chinese talent flashed. Cheng Jin, only 16, hung on to win. But he was an amateur, so first-place money went to the highest-finishing pro — Chien, who finished second by a shot.

("I didn't really think about winning before the week," said Jin. "This really gave me a lot of confidence and is a turning point for myself and for my future in golf.")

Todd Baek, 23, locked up the fifth and final ticket to the Web.com Tour with his first win as a professional in the Chateau Junding Penglai Open. He played in all 12 events, made every cut and had six other top-10 finishes. Baek wouldn't be a totally raw rookie when he got to the Web.com Tour. He had played in one Web.com tournament and had third-place finishes on the PGA Tour of Australasia and the OneAsia Tour.

Tour officials were pleased with the debut year. "It didn't take long for players to make the decision that they wanted to play in China," said Greg Carlson, executive director. "We ended up with players from 20 different countries at our two qualifying tournaments, with 14 represented in our final 2014 membership."

The diversity was marked. "We had post-round press conferences with players speaking Mandarin, English, Korean, Thai, Japanese," Carlson said. "And one player, Lucas Lee [Brazilian], could have done his interviews in Portuguese, Korean or English."

Said Paul Johnson, a member of the PGA Tour's executive committee: "We learned a lot in this first season. We know all the things that went well, and like with any new enterprise, there is room for improvement. We are working on them already for 2015 while losing none of the momentum we have from 2014."

Japan Tour

Enjoy Jakarta Indonesia PGA Championship

Jakarta, Indonesia
Winner: Michio Matsumura

See OneAsia Tour section.

Token Homemate Cup

Nagoya, Mie
Winner: Yusaku Miyazato

At least for a few months Yusaku Miyazato stole the stage from his more celebrated and successful younger sister Ai. After bagging his first victory in more than a decade on the Japan Tour in the 2013 Nippon Series finale in December, Miyazato followed up with another win in the circuit's second tournament of 2014. Saddled in 55th place after a first-round 71, Miyazato burned up the Token Tado Country Club course the next three days to score a two-stroke victory with a 14-under-par 270.

The move began Friday when his 66–137 advanced him into a tie for 11th place, still four behind co-leaders Yujiro Ohori (66-67) and Toshinori Muto (67-66). In tougher conditions Saturday, scoring rose noticeably and Miyazato's 68–205 jumped him into a five-way, second-place tie with Hiroshi Iwata, Tadahiro Takayama, Tomohiro Kondo and Australian rookie Adam Bland. Daisuke Maruyama, a two-time tour winner, led by a stroke after rounds of 67-68-69–204.

Miyazato came out firing Sunday. He birdied the first five holes, gave a shot back at the 10th, but birdied three of the next four holes to solidify his hold on the lead. He finished bogey-par-par for 65–270, two strokes in front of runner-up Iwata (67) and three ahead of Koumei Oda (65). Maruyama plummeted into a 14th-place tie with a 74.

Tsuruya Open

Kawanishi, Hyogo
Winner: Hiroyuki Fujita

What more likely place for Hiroyuki Fujita, one of Japan's most consistent winners, to bounce back from his slim, injury-plagued 2013 season than at Yamanohara Golf Club in the Tsuruya Open. After all, the 44-year-old Fujita had won two of his 15 Japan Tour titles there (in 2010 and 2012). But, he had to win a playoff against South Korea's Sang-Hyun Park, who shot a seven-under-par 64 in the final round to force the overtime.

The tournament got off to a marquee start as Fujita, the 2012 leading money winner, and Shingo Katayama, the five-time No. 1, led with 66s. Katayama, winner of 27 titles but with only a single victory since 2008, remained on top Friday with 68-134 as Fujita slipped with 72-138. Katayama was tied for first place with lightly regarded Atomu Shigenaga, who followed his 66-134 with a 68 Saturday to lead New Zealand's Michael Hendry (66) by one and Fujita (66) and Katayama (70) by two after 54 holes.

The finish Sunday was dramatic. Park, off well ahead of Fujita in a tie for 11th place, capped a five-under round with an eagle at the 17th hole for the 64 that he posted 45 minutes before Fujita finished ... and it was quite a finish. A double bogey at the 11th hole put him in serious jeopardy, but he recovered in veteran fashion with three birdies for 67 and the tying 271. He denied Park his first win in Japan when he parred the playoff 18th hole for his 16th victory. Until his winless 2013, Fujita had scored at least one victory every season since 2007.

The Crowns

Togo, Aichi

Winner: Hyung-Sung Kim

Hyung-Sung Kim turned around what at first appeared likely to be an encore performance by Michio Matsumura and walked off with a four-stroke victory in the venerable The Crowns tournament.

Matsumura came to the Nagoya Golf Club as the defending champion and winner of the Japan Tour season-opening Indonesia PGA Championship in March and promptly produced a mind-boggling 10-under-par 60 in the first round on the Wago course, taking a four-stroke lead. But, from that point on, Kim took charge. The South Korean, with a win in each of the previous two seasons, overtook him the second day, as Matsumura slipped to 71 and Kim added a 67 to his opening 64 for the tie at 131.

Though shooting just a par-70 round, the 33-year-old Kim moved two shots ahead of Tomohiro Kondo (69-203) on the Saturday. That day Matsumura shot 74 to drop from contention, and international star Ryo Ishikawa, home from the United States, moved into contention at 204. But Kim shed the opposition Sunday with a solid 68-269. He followed six opening pars with birdies at the seventh, 12th and 18th against a lone bogey to establish the four-stroke margin over countryman I.J. Jang (69).

Ishikawa finished with a 72 to tie for fifth and Matsumura sank to 19th with a 76.

Kansai Open

Nishinomiya, Hyogo

Winner: Koumei Oda

Of his seven victories on the Japan Tour, Koumei Oda never won in such spectacular fashion as he did in the Kansai Open. Tied with third-round leader and playing partner Yoshinori Fujimoto after 71 holes, Oda eagled the par-five 18th to pick off the victory with 67–273, 15 under par at Rokko Country Club.

The 35-year-old Oda gained ground steadily through the early rounds, but still trailed Fujimoto by four strokes entering the final 18 holes. He began the tournament with a 71, five strokes off the 66 shot by Yoshikazu Haku, who subsequently plunged to 61st position. Oda jumped into a tie for sixth when he shot 66 Friday, then trailing second-round leaders Dong-Kyu Jang, Tetsuji Hiratsuka and Michael Hendry (135) by two shots.

Fujimoto made his move Saturday, firing a 66 for 202 and a two-stroke lead over Hiratsuka (69) and four over Oda (69) and Daisuke Kataoka (70). Oda then made up the four-shot deficit Sunday before the winning eagle. Fujimoto shot 73 and finished a stroke ahead of defending champion Brad Kennedy, Hiroo Kawai and Jang. Hiratsuka, a six-time winner without a victory since 2011, slipped to sixth place with a 73 for 277.

Gateway to the Open Mizuno Open

Kasaoka, Okayama

Winner: Dong-Kyu Jang

The Japan Tour crowned its initial first-time winner of the season when Dong-Kyu Jang scored a three-stroke victory in the Gateway to the Open Mizuno Open. The 25-year-old South Korean shot a final-round 69 to wrap up the title and the tournament's bonus — an invitation to The Open Championship in England — with his 15-under-par 273.

Jang took the lead in Saturday's third round after Yui Ueda and Hiroshi Iwata shared the opening-day lead with 66s and Iwata remained in front Friday when he followed with 69, tied for the lead then with Taichi Teshima (67-68–135). Jang, then two back after rounds of 70 and 67, jumped in front the next day with another 67, his 204 putting him two strokes in front of Juvic Pagunsan of the Philippines, who fired 65, the week's low round.

A fast start Sunday eased Jang's path to victory. He birdied three of the first seven holes to reach 15 under, then faltered with bogeys at the 11th and 13th holes to tighten the race with Pagunsan. However, Jang finished with a flourish with birdies on the last two holes to establish the three-shot margin on the Filipino, who closed with 70–276. Hyung-Tae Kim (66) and Tomohiro Kondo (67) tied for third at 277, they along with Pagunsan also earning berths at Royal Liverpool in July.

Japan PGA Championship

Hyogo

Winner: Taichi Teshima

Taichi Teshima scored one for the old-timers at the Japan PGA Championship. That gave the 45-year-old seven victories sprinkled over his 22 years on the Japan Tour, the highlight his other major title — the Japan Open in 2001. It had been seven years, though, since he posted win No. 6 in the 2007 Casio World Open.

Teshima was solid all week at Hyogo's Golden Valley Golf Club. His opening 71 set him three behind another veteran, the highly successful Toru Taniguchi, but in a tie for fifth place. Teshima's following 68 moved him into a tie for third with Taniguchi (71), as Hyung-Tae Kim (69-69) and unknown Keisuke Otawa (71-67) took over the lead by a stroke.

Teshima completed the climb into the lead Saturday, shooting 69 for 208, edging a shot ahead of Kyoung-Hoon Lee (68) and Koumei Oda (67), winner of the Kansai Open two weeks earlier. Kim slipped to fourth place with 72, but Otawa self-destructed with 82. As things turned out Sunday, the top three players finished in the same position in the standings as all three wound up with 71s, Teshima for the winning, nine-under-par 279, Lee and Oda for 280s. Dong-Kyu Jang, who won the previous week's Mizuno Open, was three strokes further back after a closing 68. Second-place money of ¥12.6 million elevated Oda into first place on the Japan Tour money list.

Japan Golf Tour Championship

Kasama, Ibaraki

Winner: Yoshitaka Takeya

A remarkable chain of circumstances led little-known Yoshitaka Takeya to the important Japan Golf Tour Championship and a berth in World Golf Championship - Bridgestone Invitational in the United States.

Consider that Takeya, now 34, had been struggling in his limited action over eight years on the Japan Tour, never managing a top-10, and was out of sight in the 996th spot in the Official World Golf Rankings when he teed off at Shishido Hills Country Club in the year's second major championship. After an opening 69, he advanced into a first-place tie with South Korea's Dong-Kyu Jang, the Mizuno Open winner three weeks earlier, with a second-round 65. The two men matched 69s Saturday, then Takeya took a commanding lead with five straight mid-round birdies in the final round before faltering with two closing bogeys for 68–271.

Then came the next unexpected twist. In hot pursuit, South Korea's Sang-Hee Lee closed fast with eight birdies and, with a par at the final hole for an apparent 65 and a tying 271, seemed to have forced a playoff for the title. But wait. Before he signed for the 65, tournament officials assessed him a two-stroke penalty, determining that he had improved his line of play at the 11th hole by pressing down on it while removing debris.

Ergo. Takeya was a two-stroke victor, had a major title on the Japan Tour, his first win after years of obscurity, and earned a trip to America later in the season to play with the world's top players at famed Firestone Country Club in Akron, Ohio.

Nagashima Shigeo Invitational

Chitose, Hokkaido

Winner: Ryo Ishikawa

Hideki Matsuyama beat Ryo Ishikawa, his rival young Japanese superstar, to the punch earlier in 2014 when he won a tournament on the U.S. PGA Tour, a feat Ishikawa had yet to accomplish as the two young players campaigned in America. So, Ishikawa felt a measure of revenge when he captured the Nagashima Shigeo Invitational Sega Sammy Cup when the two returned home to play in the tournament in Hokkaido. Matsuyama never contended and finished in a tie for 17th place.

It took a rally and a playoff, though, for the 22-year-old Ishikawa to score his first win in Japan since the 2012 Taiheiyo Masters and boost his total to 11. After 36 holes, Ishikawa trailed leaders Koumei Oda, Kazuhiro Yamashita and Jung-Gon Hwang by four after rounds of 69 and 71. Ishikawa's third-round 67 lifted him into third place, two behind Oda, who edged a shot into the lead over Yamashita with 69–205.

Oda repeated his 69 Sunday for 10-under-par 274 and Ishikawa added another 67, preserving his chances when he saved par at the final hole and forced a playoff. He defeated Oda, the Kansai Open winner in May, on the third extra hole.

The outcome shuffled the top of the tour money list. Oda climbed a spot into first place and Ishikawa, with only two previous 2014 starts, moved into second place.

Dunlop Srixon Fukushima Open

Nishigo, Fukushima

Winner: Satoshi Kodaira

The arrival of the Dunlop Srixon Fukushima Open as a newcomer on the Japan Tour schedule was a welcome sight for Satoshi Kodaira, who needed something to turn around what up until then had been a dismal season. He had missed cuts in six of his previous seven starts and finished 59th in the other.

Things didn't look any brighter when he shot 72 and sat in a 51st-place tie after the opening round at Grandee Nasushirakawa Golf Club. But the 24-year-old, winner of the 2013 Japan Tour Championship, perked up Friday with a 68–140 to easily make the cut. He then followed with a blazing, eight-under-par 64 and a closing 68 to secure a two-stroke victory with his 272.

Kodaira's opening 72 left him eight strokes behind 45-year-old Taichi Teshima, a former Japan Open champion who added the Japan PGA Championship earlier in the season for the seventh victory of his 22-season career. Teshima's 71 in the rain-interrupted second round dropped him a stroke out of the lead, then shared by Hiroshi Iwata (70-64), Thanyakon Khrongpha of Thailand (69-65) and Ruytaro Nagano (68-66). Kodaira was still six shots off the lead, but his 64 Saturday pulled him into a four-way tie for third place, three behind Nagano and Khrongpha.

Kodaira was solid Sunday, shooting a bogey-free 68 to claim the title, two shots better than Kazuhiro Yamashita, Yuki Inamori, Ryosuke Kinoshita, Iwata and Nagano, who shot 73. Khrongpha dropped to 11th place with a 75.

RZ Everlasting KBC Augusta

Shima, Fukuoka

Winner: Hiroyuki Fujita

Age certainly doesn't seem to slow down Hiroyuki Fujita. Nor do extra holes or big deficits.

Earlier in the 2014 season, the 44-year-old Fujita came from two off the pace to win his 16th tournament on the Japan Tour in a one-hole playoff. He was even more impressive in August at the RZ Everlasting KBC Augusta, overcoming a six-shot deficit and going five holes into overtime to land his 17th title, 17 years after the first victory of his 23-year career.

Fujita's win came at the expense of South Korea's Hyung-Sung Kim, who was also seeking his second victory of the season. Kim led for three days in the rain-plagued tournament at Keya Golf Club in Fukuoka Prefecture. His opening 65 started him off with a one-stroke lead and, after an overnight rain interruption of his second round, he remained a shot in front with his follow-up 69–134. He was still just one ahead after his third-round 71 with Shigeru Nonaka in second place, Wen-Chong Liang (67) and Yoshitaka Takeya (68) two back, and Fujita sitting six off the pace after rounds of 71, 66 and 74.

As Kim faltered with a 72 Sunday, Fujita reeled off an eight-birdie 65 and was joined at 276 by Liang, who closed with 69 and forced the lengthy playoff. With the loss, the Chinese pro, a four-time winner and former No. 1 on the OneAsia Tour, had to settle for his fifth runner-up finish without a victory in Japan.

Fujisankei Classic

Fujikawaguchiko, Yamanashi

Winner: Hiroshi Iwata

His first Japan Tour victory was a long time in coming for 33-year-old Hiroshi Iwata, but his earlier performances during the 2014 season hinted that it was getting close. He mustered top-10 finishes in seven of his 12 starts, twice finishing in second place. Iwata eventually needed a final-hole birdie, though, to gain that initial win in the Fujisankei Classic, his closing 66 for 10-under-par 274 giving him a one-stroke triumph.

Even without a victory, Iwata stood sixth on the circuit's money list and he jumped to second place with the ¥10 million first prize with the win at Fujizakura Country Club in Yamanashi.

Iwata climbed steadily up the standings, starting with a 69, three strokes behind the heralded Toru Taniguchi and veteran Daisuke Maruyama. At the tournament's midpoint, with another 69, he was tied for fifth place but four behind Seung-Hyuk Kim, who shot 64 for 134. Iwata's third-round 70 moved him into a third-place tie with Hyung-Sung Kim, the Crowns winner in May, and Yoshinobu Tsukada at 208, as Yuta Ikeda went in front with 69–206, a stroke ahead of In-Hoi Hur (72).

Hur gave Iwata a run for this money, but Iwata's five-under 66 gave him the one-shot win as the South Korean closed with 68–275. Australian Brendan Jones, a 13-time winner in Japan who had been hampered by a wrist injury and complications for nearly a year, also challenged, a bogey at the last hole and 67–276 placing him in third place.

ANA Open

Kitahiroshima, Hokkaido

Winner: Katsumasa Miyamoto

It had been a peculiar season for Katsumasa Miyamoto when he teed off in the ANA Open. For most of the year, the 41-year-old Miyamoto was either finishing in a seventh-place tie — four times — or missing the cut. He pulled it all together on the Wattsu course at Sapporo Golf Club and scored a playoff victory against Hideto Tanihara, the ninth of his long career and first since 2010.

Contenders all week, Miyamoto and Tanihara, a 10-time winner himself, went into the final round tied for the lead with 13-under-par 203s but with 11 other players within three shots of them. Tanihara had gone in front in the second round with his 66-68 cards and shot 69 Saturday, while Miyamoto was holing a 72-yard pitch for an eagle at the 17th hole and a 68 to overtake him.

Nobody could catch them Sunday as they both shot 67s for 280s, Miyamoto again gaining the necessary ground at the par-five 17th, where he made his final birdie. They both parred the final hole to force the season's fourth playoff. It ended quickly when Katsumasa birdied the 18th, the first extra hole.

Asia-Pacific Diamond Cup

Ibaraki

Winner: Hiroyuki Fujita

Hiroyuki Fujita got an extra kick out of his victory in the Asia-Pacific Diamond Cup, his third of the season.

"This win (his career 18th) is particularly rewarding," proclaimed the 45-year-old Fujita. "The fact that I was able to play among Asia's leading players and win the tournament gives me a lot of confidence."

Just as was the case in his two earlier 2014 victories, the win at Otone Country Club did not come easily. The first two came in playoffs, and here Fujita had to make up a four-stroke deficit with a final-round, five-under-par 66 to land a two-shot victory and the Diamond Cup with his six-under-par 278.

He was in the thick of things the first two days with 68-71 cards as Cameron Smith led after the opening round with 66 and Adam Bland at the midpoint with 69-68–137. But Fujita fell back into a 14th-place tie, four back of leader Wen-Chong Liang, when he shot 73 on Saturday. Fujita then ran off six birdies against a single bogey in his solid final round. Thailand star Kiradech Aphibarnrat, back in action after being shelved by an injury for six weeks, fired a 67 Sunday to join Jason Knutzon (68) and S.K. Ho (69) in second place at 280. Liang shot 74, dropping into a tie for ninth place.

The two-stroke victory strengthened Fujita's hold on the No. 1 spot on the Japan Tour money list in his bid to cop the season-end title for the second time in three years.

Top Cup Tokai Classic

Miyoshi, Aichi

Winner: Seung-Hyuk Kim

South Koreans took charge of the Japan Tour when it reached its usual stop at Miyoshi Country Club for the Top Cup Tokai Classic. Other than after the second round, the visitors from the west controlled first place every day and occupied the top four places at tournament's end. Seung-Hyuk Kim, in his second season in Japan, claimed his first victory, one stroke ahead of compatriots Hyung-Sung Kim and Jung-Gon Hwang and two in front of In-Hoi Hur.

Only Japan's Yoshinori Fujimoto interfered with the South Korean monopoly all week. He snared the lead the second day from the ultimate winner and Sung-Yoon Kim (66s) with his 69-68, one ahead of Koumei Oda, the second-leading money winner. But the weekend belonged to foreign neighbors.

Hyung-Sung Kim, who won his third Japan Tour title earlier in the season at The Crowns tournament, swung into the lead Saturday with 69–208, two in front of Hur (72-71-67) and three ahead of Seung-Hyuk Kim and Tomohiro Kondo. He seemed well on his way to another win Sunday when he fattened his lead with three birdies on his first seven holes, but the 33-year-old came unglued after that, dropping six shots on the next seven holes. Seung-Hyuk took the lead with birdies at the 14th and 16th holes, cushion enough for his lone bogey at the 18th for 70–281, seven under par. Hyung-Sung Kim shot 74 and Hwang 70 for their 282s and Hur 73 for his 283.

Toshin Golf Tournament

Tomika, Gifu

Winner: In-Hoi Hur

A strong showing in the Tokai Classic whetted In-Hoi Hur's appetite and spurred him to an impressive initial victory the next week in the Toshin Golf Tournament. Hur, who finished a solid fourth in the Tokai, never trailed on Toshin Golf Club's Central course and rolled to a four-stroke win, the second straight triumph by a South Korean on the Japan Tour. He was 28 under par with his 260, by seven strokes the lowest total at that point of the season.

Hur got away fast with an eight-under-par 64, matched by Yoshinori Fujimoto, who finished right behind him the previous week. The South Korean went one stroke better Friday with a 63–127 and opened a three-shot lead over Kunihiro Kamii, who also posted a nine-under-par round. Hur stretched it to four strokes Saturday with 66 for 193, then with only one bogey to show for 54 holes. The lead would have been even wider except that his fellow countryman Seung-Hyuk Kim, coming off his Tokai win, produced a 61 with an eagle and 10 birdies for 197.

The winner created more comfort with two birdies on the first three holes the last day. Despite two bogeys, he went on to a 67 for the remarkable 260 and became the season's fifth first-time winner. Kim, with 67, took second place with 67–264, and Tomohiro Kondo shot 65–266 to finish third.

Japan Open Championship

Noda, Chiba

Winner: Yuta Ikeda

Yuta Ikeda made his annual visit (or visits) to the winner's circle of the Japan Tour at a most propitious time — the Japan Open Championship. The 28-year-old Ikeda, who had won at least one tournament every season since 2009, struggled at the end but held on for a one-stroke victory to keep the string intact. He managed a final, two-over-par 72 for a 10-under-par 270 total, edging Satoshi Kodaira and 27-time-winner Shingo Katayama.

Ikeda, who ran off consecutive four-victory seasons in 2009 and 2010 and won the 2009 Japan PGA Championship, put together three solid rounds on the Umesato course of Chiba Country Club and built a three-shot lead after 54 holes.

Ikeda was on the heels of Thailand's Prayad Marksaeng for two rounds. He put up a 64 to the opening 63 of the 48-year-old Marksaeng, a four-time winner in Japan, and matched his two-under-par 68 Friday before taking over the lead in the third round with 66–208. Katayama, the Japan Open champion in 2003 and 2008, shot 67 as the long-time star sought just his second victory in six years. He was tied for second at 211 with Marksaeng, who posted a 70.

Ikeda's lead nearly slipped away as he lost three strokes early on the back nine, but his 72 was just enough to hold off Katayama, who shot 70–271, and the 24-year-old Kodaira, who charged home with 66 for his 271. The ¥40 million purse jumped Ikeda into fourth place on the tour's money list, on which he finished second to Ryo Ishikawa in 2009.

Bridgestone Open

Chiba

Winner: Koumei Oda

Koumei Oda and Hiroyuki Fujita exchanged positions atop the Japan Tour money list as the two men dominated the final round of the Bridgestone Open. No. 1 Fujita, in peril of missing the cut after his 73 the first day put him in 66th place, nearly pulled out a victory when he stormed home Sunday with a seven-under-par 64. It wasn't quite enough to catch No. 2 Oda, who capped an up-and-down final round with his fifth birdie on the 18th hole for 68–269 and a one-stroke victory. The ¥30 million prize jumped him ¥6 million past Fujita into the top money spot, a position he held briefly after his earlier seventh career victory in May.

Oda, who hadn't carded a top-10 finish since July, didn't show any problems at Sodegaura Country Club. He took a one-shot lead the second day with his 67-65–132, a stroke ahead of Azuma Yano, the first-round leader (65) whose last win was in 2008. Oda followed with 69, which expanded his margin to three strokes over Yano and his one-over-par 72. Fujita was tied for 11th place after middle rounds of 68-65, five behind the leader.

On Sunday, while Fujita was racking up birdies and closing the gap, Oda was just one under for the round when he reached the 15th hole. Then he finished with three birdies and a bogey on the final four holes for the win.

Mynavi ABC Championship

Kato, Hyogo

Winner: Ryuichi Oda

The other Oda stepped up at the Mynavi ABC Championship. A week after Koumei Oda won the Bridgestone Open, his lesser-known namesake, Ryuichi Oda, emerged from the pack and snatched his first victory since his only other career win — a significant one, the Japan Open in 2009.

Until then, Oda's 2014 season had been a mixture of middle-of-the-field finishes and missed cuts. No top-10s. A tie for 15th at the Bridgestone his best showing. Then, the 37-year-old journeyman came alive at the ABC Golf Club with four rounds in the 60s, capped by a final-day, nine-under-par 62 that propelled him to a five-stroke victory over Hideto Tanihara and, ironically, Koumei Oda, the tour's leading money winner.

All three were well-positioned at the halfway point after South Korea's Kyoung-Hoon Lee broke from a six-player cluster of first-round leaders (66) to take a one-stroke lead over Koumei with a 66-67–133. Bunched with Tanihara (69-66) and two others two off the lead, Ryuichi (68-67) followed with 66 Saturday that carried him into a share of first place with S.K. Ho (also 66) at 201. Tanihara (68) was then two behind and Koumei Oda (70) three back.

Ryuichi Oda saved his best for last. Koumei came out firing Sunday and produced a 64. To no avail. Ryuichi blazed to a 62, going five under on the last five holes for the winning 263. The runner-up finish strengthened Koumei Oda's grip on the money lead.

Heiwa PGM Championship

Kasumigaura, Ibaraki

Winner: Tomohiro Kondo

Tomohiro Kondo ended a three-year victory drought at a lucrative time — the start of the Japan Tour's rich finishing run of healthy-pursed tournaments at the Heiwa PGM Championship. And he gave fair warning that the long dry spell was about to come to a halt.

The 37-year-old veteran, whose long record sported five victories, had three top-five finishes in his previous four starts coming into the ¥200 million tournament at Miho Golf Club in Ibaraki.

The first two days, though, belonged to another experienced winner. Hideto Tanihara, coming off a second-place finish in the ABC Championship and an earlier second and two thirds during the season, jumped off in front Thursday with a seven-under-par 64, sharing the lead with Australia's Brad Kennedy. He stayed on top Friday with 68–132, tied then with South Korean Hyun-Woo Ryu (67-65).

Kondo, two back after rounds of 68 and 66, seized the lead with a 64 of his own Saturday, his 15-under-par 198 giving him a two-stroke edge on Tanihara (68) and Kennedy and Yoshinori Fujimoto, who both also fired 64s. Even par after two birdies and two bogeys on the first seven holes Sunday, Kondo played flawlessly the rest of the way, five birdies leading him to a closing 66 and the winning, 20-under-par 264. Left four back in a tie for second were Tanihara and Fujimoto (68s) and Ryu (67).

Mitsui Sumitomo VISA Taiheiyo Masters

Gotemba, Shizuoka

Winner: David Oh

A potential headliner finish to the Mitsui Sumitomo VISA Taiheiyo Masters fizzled over the weekend and David Oh stepped into the breach to win for the first time on the Japan Tour.

At the 36-hole mark, Hiroyuki Fujita (67-69–136), the circuit season's No. 2 money winner, and two-time Masters champion Bubba Watson (67-70–137) stood one-two on the leaderboard, promising an exciting race to the wire on the Taiheiyo Club's Gotemba course. Both players unexpectedly stumbled out of contention Saturday, though, Fujita with a 73 and Watson with a shocking 77. American-born David Oh, a 10-year professional in his third season in Japan, took over the lead and held on for a one-stroke victory Sunday with a 12-under-par 276.

The 33-year-old Oh shot 68–206 Saturday to lead Han Lee and Wen-Chong Liang by a shot and Toshinori Muto and Ashun Wu by two, but didn't sew up the win Sunday until he birdied the final hole for an up-and-down 70 that included five birdies and three bogeys. Muto shot 69–277 to finish alone in second place. Watson placed 24th with a closing 71, and Fujita dropped into a tie for 30th with his final-round 77, blowing an opportunity to drastically narrow the money race gap behind Koumei Oda, who missed the cut.

Oh's prosperous week came out of the blue. He hadn't finished any higher than 18th place in his last nine starts since finishing fifth in the Nagashima Shigeo Invitational in early July. He was the sixth first-time winner of the season.

Dunlop Phoenix

Miyazaki

Winner: Hideki Matsuyama

Japanese golf fans got a good look at what they had been missing all year when Hideki Matsuyama played in his homeland for just the second time in 2014 in the venerable Dunlop Phoenix tournament. Matsuyama, who went international after his huge rookie season on the 2013 Japan Tour, rode a second-round 64 to a playoff victory over Hiroshi Iwata on an exciting final day at Phoenix Country Club when he barely held off the challenge of talented American star Jordan Spieth.

The 22-year-old Matsuyama soared to fame with his four victories and the money title in 2013 after winning the highly regarded 2012 Taiheiyo Masters as an amateur. He returned home after a successful 2014 season in the United States, where he won the prestigious Memorial Tournament.

Young players dominated the Dunlop Phoenix from the start as 20-year-old Yuki Inamori led the first day with a seven-under-par 64 before Matsuyama took charge. With his own 64 Friday for 132, Matsuyama went a stroke atop Spieth (69-64) and In-Hoi Hur (67-66), the Toshin winner in September.

Matsuyama (67) and Spieth (68) remained one-two in the standings after 54 holes and battled for the lead all day Sunday, when Iwata torridly entered the fray. Iwata, whose Fujisankei win was among nine top-10s during the season, raced to the top of the leaderboard with a 63. Matsuyama, after bogeys at the 15th and 16th holes, had to birdie the last two holes for 70 to match him at 269 and nip Spieth and Australian veteran Brendan Jones by a stroke.

Matsuyama needed only a par on the first playoff hole to score his sixth Japan Tour triumph.

Casio World Open

Geisei, Kochi

Winner: Shingo Katayama

Shingo Katayama is not ready to turn center stage over to the young stars on the Japan Tour just yet. Pickings had been slim for the colorful, 41-year-old pro since his dominant days in the early 2000s with only a single victory being added to his gaudy record since 2008. Things perked up in 2014. He mustered five top-10 finishes, including a runner-up showing in the Japan Open, before breaking through with his 28th victory in the Casio World Open at the end of November. Katayama finished with a flourish, firing a final-round, seven-under-par 65 at Kochi Kurashio Country Club to win by three strokes with his 271 total.

It capped an up-and-down week for Katayama. He started moderately with 70, four strokes behind tri-leaders Shinichi Yokota, Sang-Hyun Park and Shugo Imahira, then roared into a one-shot lead the second day with a 64. He was a stroke in front of Kyoung-Hoon Lee and two ahead of Yokota and Koumei Oda, the money leader and two-time Casio champion.

Stung by a double bogey, Katayama managed only a par 72 Saturday and slipped a stroke behind tri-leaders Satoshi Kodaira, Yasuki Hiramoto and

Imahira at 205. Kodaira, the Fukushima winner and co-runner-up with Katayama in the Japan Open, shot 67, Hiramoto and Imahira 68s.

It was almost no contest Sunday. Only runner-up Satoshi Tomiyama, three back at 274, finished within six strokes of Katayama. The win tied Katayama with Teruo Sugihara for sixth place on the tour's all-time career victory list.

Golf Nippon Series JT Cup

Inagi, Tokyo

Winner: Katsumasa Miyamoto

The long history of the Golf Nippon Series is splattered with the names of players who have won the season-ending tournament three or more times, including most of the country's biggest stars of the past. Katsumasa Miyamoto joined that august group in 2014, squeezing out a one-stroke victory the first week of December to go with his Series triumphs in 1998 and 2001. The 42-year-old Miyamoto cranked out a five-under-par 65 at Tokyo Yomiuri Country Club, the final day's best round, as he overcame a three-stroke deficit and posted his 10th career victory on the Japan Tour.

Koumci Oda, who eventually tied for third and wrapped up the money-winning title, made an early bid for his third win of the season with his opening 64. But he slipped a stroke behind Miyamoto and Sang-Hee Lee (68-67s) and Yusaku Miyazato, the defending champion (67-68), the second day.

Lee, winless on the tour and a marginal qualifier for the Series off the money list, shot 68–203 Saturday and edged a stroke in front of Miyazato (69) and Toshinori Muto (65). Miyamoto made his move quickly the last day, ringing up three birdies on the first six holes as the leaders faltered. He bounced back from his lone bogey at the 11th hole with his final three birdies over the last six holes for the winning 65, his par at the 18th preserving his one-stroke margin over Thailand's Prayad Marksaeng, who was in the clubhouse with 67–272.

Both standouts Hideki Matsuyama and Shingo Katayama, the winners of the previous two tournaments, skipped the 30-player finale.

Oda won his first money title with ¥137,318,693, more than ¥20 million ahead of runner-up Hiroyuki Fujita, the 2012 titlist.

11. Australasian Tour

Adam Scott's return to his homeland for the big end-of-season events on the PGA Tour of Australasia was not quite as successful as his trip Down Under in 2013 when he won twice and was only pipped for the Australian Open by Rory McIlroy on the very last hole. Scott finished runner-up to Nick Cullen at the BetEasy Masters, which he was attempting to win for a third year in a row, and was then fifth at the Emirates Australian Open as young American Jordan Spieth produced a scintillating performance to win by six strokes. At the Australian PGA Championship, Scott almost defended his title but succumbed to a three-putt at the seventh extra hole against Greg Chalmers.

Although Scott did not add to his Masters title at the majors in 2014, with a tie for fifth in the Open Championship his best result, he did become the 17th player to top the Official World Golf Ranking. He took over from Tiger Woods on a week in May when he was not playing, but on his first appearance as the World No. 1 the following week he won the Crowne Plaza Invitational at Colonial in a playoff over Justin Dufner. The victory made Scott the first player to achieve the Texas Slam, winning the Texas Open, the Houston Open, and the Byron Nelson Championship as well as at Colonial. His run at the top of the World Ranking lasted until McIlroy regained his former status after winning the WGC - Bridgestone Invitational. Scott ended the year as the world No. 3, as well as a married man, his wedding a low-key affair that only became public a month after it took place, and expecting to become a father early in 2015.

Jason Day moved into the world's top 10 by winning the WGC - Accenture Match Play for his second victory on the PGA Tour. During the week Day defeated Billy Horschel at the 22nd hole, Louis Oosthuizen in the quarter-finals, Rickie Fowler in the semi-finals and then had an epic match with Victor Dubuisson in the final. The Frenchman showed off some outrageous recovery skills to extend the match to the 23rd hole. Frustratingly, much of Day's season was plagued by a wrist injury.

On the PGA Tour of Australasia there were a number of first-time winners, including Ryan Lynch, son of the renowned coach Dale, and Ryan Fox, son of All Black rugby legend Grant. Chalmers claimed the Order of Merit after his victory at the Australian PGA, when he rallied from seven behind before outlasting Scott in the long playoff for one of Australia's major events. It was a second PGA title to go with his two Australian Opens and came after the 41-year-old had lost his card on the PGA Tour. "I lost my status in the States this year, I don't have full status next year, so I think winning the Order of Merit in Australia helps me," said Chalmers. "I'm forever thankful to our tour here for those kinds of exemptions, it's very important for players and gives us a lot of chances."

Undoubtedly the performance of the year in Australia came from Spieth as the 21-year-old claimed the Australian Open with a closing 63 at The Australian Club. He spread-eagled a field that including Scott and McIlroy for his second win as a professional, and the 21-year-old left behind a fine impression both as a player and person.

Lexus of Blackburn Victorian PGA Championship

Melbourne, Victoria
Winner: Gareth Paddison

Gareth Paddison beat his compatriot Michael Hendry as the New Zealanders completed a one-two at the Lexus of Blackburn Victorian PGA Championship at Heritage. It was Paddison's fifth victory on the Australasian Tour and his second in the event after he claimed the title in 2011. A closing 71 on a windy final day left him on a 16-under-par total of 272 and one clear of Hendry, who returned a 69, with Australia's Jamie Arnold a further stroke behind.

Rounds of 67, 68 and 66 put Paddison two clear of the field and the Wellington professional was in control during the final round until an untimely bogey at the 17th. However, he responded strongly at the last to make a three-foot putt for a winning birdie.

"Golf is a real mental battle, to birdie the last when you have to, that is what all the practice is about," said Paddison, who was dressed all in black on the last day. "Mike played exceptionally well to draw level with me. To beat a compatriot, especially Mike Hendry, is great. He has beaten me enough over the years. But it's nice to see him playing well, first and second on the leaderboard is great for New Zealand golf."

Coca-Cola Queensland PGA Championship

Toowoomba, Queensland
Winner: Anthony Summers

Anthony Summers turned professional in 1991 and has a degenerative neck condition that required treatment on the third evening and prior to the final round, but the 44-year-old finally claimed his maiden victory at the Coca-Cola Queensland PGA Championship. It took a miracle shot at the 16th hole at the City Golf Club in Toowoomba to get him over the line. In the trees off the tee, he then holed his second shot at the par-four. "It was just ridiculous. It was a blind under-a-branch, over-a-tree shot that could have gone anywhere and I've holed it," Summers said.

Summers won by three strokes over Ryan Fox, with David Bransdon taking third place. All three men scored 61s on the first day to tie for the lead, but Summers added a 62 the next day to go in front by five. A 70 in the third round allowed Fox, with a 64, to go one shot ahead, but a 63 in the final round to Fox's 67 gave Summers victory on a 24-under-par total of 256. He had 25 birdies and the eagle over the four days. Bransdon roared back into the top three with a closing 62.

"There have been moments I've thought I'd never get a win because time was running out on my career," Summers said. "But we are some of the luckiest guys on the planet to do what we do and there has always been something to light the feeling that I want to keep going."

Oates Victorian Open

Barwon Heads, Victoria
Winner: Matthew Griffin

Matthew Griffin won for the first time as a professional on home soil and got his name on a trophy alongside some of the greats of Australian golf. Griffin beat Matthew Stieger after a three-hole playoff to win the Oates Victorian Open at 13th Beach Links and claim his state championship. The 30-year-old Victorian had won before in New Caledonia on the Australasian PGA Tour and twice outside Australia on the OneAsia circuit, but this was a first win in front of a home gallery.

"To win your state Open is huge, aside from that, the Australian Open is next," Griffin said. "It's just great to win at home. My childhood hero's Greg Norman, so it's nice to put your name on the same trophy as a great and other amazing players, Peter Thompson is incredible."

Griffin recorded rounds of 74, 71, 68 and 68 for a seven-under-par total of 281. He started the final day two behind Brett Drewitt but holed a 30-footer at the 17th and then saw Stieger birdie the last to tie and Drewitt just miss an eagle putt, leaving the overnight leader back in third place. Griffin and Stieger birdied the 18th hole twice in a row — making three times in a row for Stieger — but at the third extra hole Stieger three-putted from the fringe while Griffin got up and down from a bunker, holing from six feet for the victory.

New Zealand Open

Queenstown, New Zealand
Winner: Dimitrios Papadatos

Dimitrios Papadatos only turned professional at the end of 2012, just around the same time as his friend Jake Higginbottom won the New Zealand Open as an amateur. With the tournament rescheduled for a late summer date, there was no staging of the event in 2013 and Papadatos claimed the title in 2014 for his maiden victory as a professional. His best result previously was finishing third at the 2013 Perth International. The 22-year-old Australian confidently extended his 54-hole lead into an accomplished victory by four strokes over New Zealander Mark Brown, with David Klein in third place a further shot back.

Papadatos, the son of a professional wrestler, had two birdies and a bogey going out, but on the way home he excelled over The Hills course with five birdies for an inward 31. He closed with a 66 for an 18-under-par total of 270, while the 39-year-old Brown had a 69 with birdies at the 13th, 15th and 17th holes coming home. "I wouldn't have told you at the start of the week I was capable of this," Papadatos said. "I just wanted to not get too overwhelmed with what was happening."

The pro-am style event was played over The Hills and Millbrook courses in Queenstown for the first two days, with the headlines taken on the first day by former Australia cricket captain Ricky Ponting, who grabbed six birdies for his team at Millbrook.

Fiji International

Nada, Fiji

Winner: Steve Jeffress

See Asia/Japan Tours chapter.

Isuzu Queensland Open

Brisbane, Queensland

Winner: Andrew Dodt

Andrew Dodt made up six strokes in the final round to win the Isuzu Queensland Open at Brookwater by two shots. It was his first victory in Australia, his only previous win coming in the 2010 Avantha Masters on the European and Asian tours. Dodt knew the course well from practicing there in his amateur days, but the 28-year-old was a low-key contender until he birdied four of the last six holes. A closing 67, after rounds of 72, 70 and 72, gave Dodt a seven-under-par total of 281.

Tom Bond, the third-round leader, made three bogeys early on the back nine but birdied the 17th to draw within one. He needed a birdie at the last to force a playoff but took a bogey for a closing 75. He finished two strokes ahead of a five-way tie for third place that included Anthony Brown, who led on the first day with a course-record 65, and Jake Higginbottom. Amateur Kade McBride, who shared the lead with Brown after two rounds, finished in a tie for eighth place.

"This is my second win as a professional, so I am pretty pumped right now. To win your state Open means a lot," said Dodt. "I knew I was playing well and I know the course well. I had a good game plan and I stuck to that all week. Patience was the key. I stayed patient all week, hung in there when I needed to, holed the putts when I needed to and came out on top."

South Pacific Open Championship

Noumea, New Caledonia

Winner: Adam Stephens

Adam Stephens claimed his maiden victory at the South Pacific Open Championship by five strokes at the Tina Club in Noumea, New Caledonia. The 26-year-old from New South Wales earned a two-year exemption on the Australasian Tour and places in the main summer tournaments at the end of the year.

Rounds of 67 and 64 put Stephens in the lead at the halfway stage, and a 68 in the third round extended his advantage to four strokes. He three-putted the first for a bogey, but birdies at the 10th, 13th and 14th holes put the result beyond doubt. A bogey at the 16th left Stephens with a closing 70 for a 15-under-par total of 269. Sharing second place were Kota Karachi, who finished with a 70, Andrew Kelly, 68, and New Zealand amateur Luke Toomey, who also closed with 68. Michael Wright, who shared second place after 54 holes, closed with a 74 to drop out of the top 10.

"I didn't have any expectations this week. I was just going out there to play golf," said Stephens. "The three-putt at the first really woke me up and focused me. I played my C-grade game today but managed some A-grade scoring, I hit a couple of loose shots out there but managed my misses really well."

John Hughes/Nexus Risk Services WA Open

Perth, Western Australia
Winner: Ryan Fox

With a rugby legend for a father in Grant Fox of All Blacks fame, New Zealand's Ryan Fox started to make a name for himself in his chosen sport by winning his maiden title at the John Hughes/Nexus Risk Services WA Open. Fox won by no less than six strokes over West Australian Stephen Dartnall after watching New Zealand beat Australia at rugby union the previous evening. "It was actually good to see the national team do so well and see what they did to win, I definitely drew some inspiration out of that," Fox said. "The Aussies probably should have won, but that New Zealand team just know how to win and they got the job done."

The big-hitting Fox found the Cottesloe course in Perth to his liking and opened with a 64 to be one behind Steve Jones' new course record. He took the lead with a 66 on day two, but after a 68 on Saturday was caught by Paul Spargo. But while Spargo followed three successive 66s with a 74, Fox kept going on the final day with six birdies in his first 10 holes. A closing 67 left him on a 23-under-par total of 265. Dartnall birdied the last for a 69 to nick second place from Rhein Gibson, Daniel Nisbet and Spargo.

"It's great to win my first tour event. I have been in this position a couple of times but hadn't quite got it done" said the 27-year-old Fox. "It's nice to turn all that practice into a winning result. It was great to get off to a good start, get a decent lead and be able to enjoy the last few holes."

ISPS Handa Perth International

Perth, Western Australia
Winner: Thorbjorn Olesen

Thorbjorn Olesen became the first European to win the ISPS Handa Perth International in its third edition as a co-sanctioned event on both the Australasian and European tours. The 24-year-old Dane claimed his second victory after winning in Sicily in 2012 and after recovering from pulling a muscle when falling off a camel on a visit to the desert in the Middle East at the start of the year. He won by three strokes at Lake Karrinyup over Ryder Cup star Victor Dubuisson and by five over Mark Foster.

Olesen set a new course record of 64 alongside John Wade in the first round. Wade had birdied the last three holes in the Monday qualifier to get the chance to tee up, but it was the Dane who kept up the challenge throughout the tournament. Olesen fell a stroke behind Peter Whitehead who took the halfway lead but then fell away over the weekend as his hopes of retaining his European Tour card were dashed.

After a second round of 69, Olesen added a 67 to lead by three strokes, but none of his nearest challengers were able to put on any pressure. Four birdies and three bogeys for a 71 left Olesen on a 17-under-par total of 271. It was Dubuisson who made a charge with a bogey-free 66 including four birdies in five holes on the back nine. Foster closed with a 69. "It was a tough day, but it was worth it — that walk down 18 was beautiful," Olesen said.

"I missed a few short putts today in the middle of the round and I think that the lead got down to one shot, but I was just thinking about getting my round back to under par, keeping focused, and seeing if I could make a few birdies coming in. It's been a couple of years since I won last time, so this gives me a lot of confidence and belief for the last bit of the season; this has been a great week and I've really enjoyed being here."

David Drysdale made a 30-footer for a birdie on the 18th green to finish in a tie for fourth place and keep his European Tour card after jumping from 116th to 103rd on the Race to Dubai. The top 111 kept their cards, but Italy's Andrea Pavan, winner of the Challenge Tour in 2013, had a double bogey at the last to lose his card.

WA Goldfields PGA Championship

Kalgoorlie, Western Australia

Winner: Ryan Lynch

Ryan Lynch, the son of the renowned golf coach Dale Lynch, whose clients have included Geoff Ogilvy and Aaron Baddeley, claimed his maiden victory at the WA Goldfields PGA Championship at Kalgoorlie. Lynch came from six strokes behind in the final round to win by one over Chris Gaunt and Peter Cooke.

Lynch had scores of 68, 69, 72 and 67 for a 12-under-par total of 276. Six birdies in eight holes around the turn put him in contention, but a bogey at the 17th, the hardest hole on the day, made for a nervous wait after overtaking Cooke as the clubhouse leader. Gaunt had led after the second and third rounds, but three bogeys in the last four holes were his undoing. Like Lynch he bogeyed the 17th, but he also dropped a shot at the 18th to hand victory to Lynch, who was on the practice range warming up for a playoff.

"I thought I might have needed one or two more birdies coming in with three to play, so the three-putt on 17 hurt, but it didn't dull the confidence," said the 25-year-old Lynch, in his third year as a professional. "I am on top of the moon. I am really happy to get the monkey off the back and get my first win. My mindset today was to stay patient. I knew that I was playing well enough, if I could make a few birdies, I could climb the leaderboard."

Mazda NSW Open

Sydney, New South Wales

Winner: Anthony Brown

It took three birdies in a row at the 18th hole at the Greg Norman-designed Stonecutters Ridge for Anthony Brown to win for the first time at the Mazda NSW Open. With the wind gusting up to 45 mph on the final day, Brown made up three strokes on overnight leaders Josh Geary and James Nitties before beating Geary at the second extra hole.

After scores of 71, which included a hole-in-one at the sixth hole, a 65 and 69, Brown closed with another 69 to set the target at 14 under par with a total of 274. After three birdies on the way home, a bogey at the 16th dropped Brown out of a share of the lead, but he rallied with a birdie at the last. Nitties bogeyed the 16th and Geary the 17th, but the latter also birdied the last for a 72 to force a playoff. Nitties had a 73 to finish third, while U.S. Amateur champion Gunn Yang was fourth.

Both Brown and Geary birdied the 18th in the playoff, but when they played the hole again, only Brown made it three in a row. The 32-year-old from Victoria said: "It was a pretty tough week, it was stinking hot Friday, then today with this wind I am just relieved to be done. I came second in the Australian PGA Championship a few years ago, it's about time I stood up and had a win, it feels great."

BetEasy Masters

Oakleigh, Victoria

Winner: Nick Cullen

Adam Scott's quest to win the BetEasy Masters for the third year running was halted by South Australian Nick Cullen's one-stroke victory at Metropolitan Golf Club. Scott won the gold jacket in 2012 before going on to claim the green jacket at Augusta the following year and successfully defending his Australian Masters crown. But an opening 73 left him with too much ground to make up. He added scores of 68, 71 and 68, but his putt at the last for birdie just missed.

Cullen also opened with a 73 and then had a 71, but a 66 in the third round left him only two behind 54-hole leader Paul Spargo. With Spargo closing with a 73 to fall into a tie for fifth place, Cullen hit the front with an eagle at the fourth and birdies at the sixth, eighth, 11th and 12th holes. His third bogey of the day at the 15th meant he came to the 18th one shot clear, but he still needed to play a fine bunker shot, which only required a tap-in for the victory. A 69 left him with a nine-under-par total of 279 and just ahead of Scott, John Younger and James Nitties.

"You always think about winning and you want to win," Cullen, 30, said. "I wanted to play better, to contend a little bit, be close, but to win the event with guys like Adam Scott and Geoff Ogilvy playing is unreal."

Scott said: "It's hard to win a tournament, let alone three years in a row. Defending was a big thrill for me, but it is very difficult to show up and win every year, it doesn't happen very much."

Emirates Australian Open

Sydney, New South Wales
Winner: Jordan Spieth

Jordan Spieth produced one of the best final rounds ever seen at the Emirates Australian Open to claim a six-stroke victory at The Australian Club. Tied for the lead after 54 holes with Greg Chalmers and Brett Rumford, Spieth scored an eight-under 63 which counted as a new course record after Jack Nicklaus recently renovated his earlier re-design of the historic Sydney course. It was a first international victory for the 21-year-old from Texas, who won the John Deere Classic on the PGA Tour as a rookie in 2013.

Spieth birdied four of the first seven holes to take a two-shot lead but then added six crucial pars to go four ahead after 13 holes. Four birdies in the last five holes was a stylish way to finish the tournament and left the young American with a myriad of admirers Down Under.

"What an incredible honor to put my name on here," said Spieth after being presented with the Stonehaven Cup. "It's definitely the best round I have ever played and the best win I have ever had. Being able to spread out from the field was a pretty awesome experience.

"I didn't think the round was out there, but the putts just kept going in. It's been an incredible week. I love Australia, the fans were fantastic and the golf course was in top shape."

Spieth had earlier rounds of 67, 72 and 69 to give him a 13-under-par total of 271. Rod Pampling, despite three bogeys in the first four holes, closed with five birdies in the last six holes for a 68 to take second place as he, Rumford and Chalmers earned exemptions for the 2015 Open Championship at St. Andrews. Adam Scott's challenge ended with a double-bogey-seven at the fifth, while defending champion Rory McIlroy was derailed by a triple bogey at the ninth followed by a double at the 10th on the third day. He finished tied for 15th.

Nanshan NSW PGA Championship

Cattai, New South Wales
Winner: Lincoln Tighe

An opening 63 and a closing 64 helped Lincoln Tighe win his maiden title on the PGA Tour of Australasia at the Nanshan New South Wales PGA Championship at Riverside Oaks. Tighe started the final round five strokes behind Scott Arnold but got his charge going by birdieing four of the first five holes. "I was hitting it unreal, stumping everything to inside 10 feet," he said. But after Arnold bogeyed the 16th, it was Tighe's eighth birdie of the day at the 17th that finally put him in front. The victory was not secured until Arnold had missed from six feet for a playoff at the last.

Arnold, whose brother Jamie finished tied for ninth place, had scored a 62 in the third round to top the leaderboard by four shots but closed with a 70, in behind Tighe's 19-under-par total of 265. Amateur Troy Moses, who scored his own 62 in the second round to lead at the halfway stage, shared third place with Kristopher Mueck, four behind Arnold.

"This is huge for me, I was actually going back to first stage Tour School," said the 25-year-old Tighe. "I didn't want to go back for the fourth year in a row, it's heart attack central out there. It's just good that I can have a Christmas at home and not have any worries the next two years."

Australian PGA Championship
Gold Coast, Queensland
Winner: Greg Chalmers

It took seven extra holes, the longest playoff in a top-level Australian event, before Adam Scott relinquished his crown and Greg Chalmers won the Australian PGA Championship for the second time. Playing the tough par-four 18th hole at RACV Royal Pines on the Gold Coast time after time, pars were the order of the day apart from on two occasions. On the third extra hole both Chalmers and Scott made birdies, while Wade Ormsby, the third member of the playoff, missed the green and went out with a bogey. Then on the seventh occasion, Scott, who had missed several chances for victory, three-putted to hand victory to Chalmers, who had previously won the title in 2011. The victory clinched the Order of Merit title for the 41-year-old left-hander.

Chalmers rallied from seven behind with a closing 64, following three 71s, to set the clubhouse target at 11-under-par 277. He holed from over 50 feet at the second and birdied three of the first four holes. He kept making putts, including from 12 feet on the last green. Ormsby made a long putt at the last to join the playoff as he and Scott, who shared the 54-hole lead with Scott Strange, closed with 71s.

Scott had hardly got a significant putt to drop all day and his luck did not change in extra time. Though he continually split the fairway, Chalmers found a bunker four times and the trees once but scrambled brilliantly.

"It was an epic day," Chalmers said. "I just wasn't sure Scotty was ever going to hit a loose shot. I was trying to drive it in the fairway; I kept driving it in every bunker. I thought, just keep making someone win it, and today it turns out that a mistake was made and I'm on the trophy."

12. African Tours

For the fourth year in a row Louis Oosthuizen won his first tournament of the year. The former Open champion successfully defended his title at the Volvo Champions at Durban Country Club, a tournament sanctioned only on the European Tour. But it proved a year when South Africa's best faltered to deceive. Only by finishing second at the last event of the year, the Alfred Dunhill Championship, did Oosthuizen retain his place in the world's top 50 alongside his friend Charl Schwartzel.

It was a year without a win for Schwartzel, and neither of the pair made an impact at the major championships in 2014. Oosthuizen was never out of the top 40, but his best result was a tie for 15th at the PGA Championship, while Schwartzel missed the cut at the Masters and the U.S. Open before rallying with a tie for seventh at the Open Championship and finishing 15th at Valhalla. Tim Clark claimed South Africa's only victory on the PGA Tour at the RBC Canadian Open, following up from his Players Championship win in 2010.

The Sunshine circuit's big co-sanctioned events with the European Tour at the start of the year went to George Coetzee, Thomas Aiken and Ross Fisher, and at the end of the year to Danny Willett and Branden Grace. Willett became the third Englishman to win the Nedbank Golf Challenge after Nick Faldo and Lee Westwood with a wonderful weekend display at the Gary Player Country Club. Scores of 65 and 66 put him four ahead of Fisher and six in front of 54-hole leader Luke Donald. It was a fine victory for the Yorkshireman, following on from his maiden victory at the 2012 BMW International.

Grace also produced a marvelous performance after a lull for a couple of years. In 2012 he won four times on the European Tour and five times in all. His last victory was a wire-to-wire win at the Alfred Dunhill Links Championship and he repeated the feat at Leopard Creek to become the first player to win both titles sponsored by Alfred Dunhill. "This is one that any South African wants to tick off the list," said Grace. "It's extra special to be the first guy to win both Dunhills, so that's something for the record books." An opening 62 set up what would become a seven-stroke victory over Oosthuizen. It was a reminder that the 26-year-old graduate of the Els Foundation at Fancourt can produce world-class golf on any given week.

There were two wins during the year for Danie van Tonder, including the Swazi Open, Telkom PGA champion Titch Moore, Keith Horne, who claimed the Vodacom Origins of Golf Final, and Louis de Jager, who triumphed in two three-way playoffs, including at the Nedbank Affinity Cup. Van Tonder, who was the rookie of the year in 2012 and was a runner-up twice to go along with his first two Sunshine Tour titles, was leading the money list ahead of Fisher, Aiken and Grace at the end of the year with one event remaining, the South African Open which was moved to early January 2015.

Joburg Open

Johannesburg, South Africa

Winner: George Coetzee

Timing was everything for George Coetzee as he secured his maiden victory on the European Tour after posting 24 top-10 finishes. Coetzee won the Joburg Open by three strokes over Justin Walters, Jin Jeong and Tyrell Hatton at Royal Johannesburg and Kensington. The 27-year-old from Pretoria also won for the fifth time on the Sunshine Tour, but after all his near-misses on the European circuit, he was delighted to win a co-sanctioned event.

"I bought a new house a new weeks ago, so this should help pay for it," he said, before adding that it was his mother's birthday on the Saturday so "this is for her, since I forgot to get her a present."

By jumping up to 59th on the World Ranking, Coetzee secured a place in the WGC - Accenture World Match Play, while his victory also booked him a spot in the Open Championship for the fourth successive year. There were qualifying places for Hoylake available to the top three non-exempt players and compatriot Walters and former British Amateur champion Jeong took the other spots. Hatton missed out because ties were decided by the World Ranking and the young Englishman was ranked only 276th.

It was an impressive final round of 66 from Hatton as he birdied the last two holes, and he was joined on 16 under by Jeong, after a 71, while Walters bogeyed the last for a 73. Walters had shared the third-round lead with Thomas Aiken, who closed with a 74 to tie for fifth place.

But Coetzee produced a bogey-free 66 to top the leaderboard, making three of his four birdies on the outward half. Three of them came at par-fives and he holed from 10 feet at the fourth before he converted from six feet at the 10th to take the lead for the first time. He saved par from rough at the 11th and a bunker at the 12th, while his drive at the 15th appeared to be hooking into water before it hit a tree and rebounded to safety. He hit his approach to 20 feet and holed the putt for his sixth birdie. He finished on a 19-under-par total of 268.

"I've been waiting awhile for this and I started doubting, so I'm very happy," Coetzee said. "This was the next step for me, winning a co-sanctioned event."

Africa Open

East London, Eastern Cape, South Africa

Winner: Thomas Aiken

Thomas Aiken had waited for over five and a half years to win on home soil, but when he did so, it was in some style. He holed a birdie putt from 40 feet at the first extra hole to defeat England's Oliver Fisher in a playoff at the Africa Open. His eighth Sunshine Tour victory was the biggest to date and came at the historic East London Golf Club. It was also the 30-year-old's third European Tour title after victories in Spain in 2011 and India in 2013.

"I've been waiting for this for quite some time," Aiken said. "I've won a couple of times overseas, but there is nothing like winning in front of a home crowd. The South African fans have been unbelievable throughout my whole career, so it's nice to finally get one for you guys."

Aiken was helped by having his wife Kate caddie for him for the first time, after his regular bagman needed a week off to attend to duties at home. He had not asked her advice all week until the playoff hole at the 18th, when he was between clubs with the approach shot. He was either going to try a soft shot with a longer club to get the ball to the flag or hit harder with a shorter club and find the middle of the green. "She said just go for the middle of the green and then I holed that massive putt," he said. "It was the best advice I got all week. We might have to do this again."

Aiken returned rounds of 66, 65, 66 and 67 for 20-under-par total of 264. He eagled the third hole in the final round and posted the target score after birdieing the 15th and 16th holes. Fisher, who had a 63 in the second round, closed with a 69, just missing from 12 feet for a winning birdie at the last. In the playoff, he missed the fairway and the green before chipping down to eight feet but never got a chance to make his par.

The pair finished one ahead of American John Hahn and England's David Horsey, while overnight leader Emiliano Grillo tied for fifth place after a 73. The Argentinean scored a 63 and a 62 in the second and third rounds but opened the last round with a quintuple-bogey-nine. He went out in 43 but made an impressive rally by birdieing the last five holes.

Dimension Data Pro-Am

Fancourt, George, South Africa

Winner: Estanislao Goya

Estanislao Goya made the right decision to stay on in South Africa after missing the cut in the Joburg and Africa Opens. A brilliant inward half of his final round gave the 25-year-old Argentinean a one-stroke victory at the Dimension Data Pro-Am on the Montagu course at Fancourt. Four behind going into the final round and then going out in one over par left Goya with much work to do, but he responded with five birdies while coming home in 31, holing from 10 feet at the last for the victory. He just pipped Lucas Bjerregaard, Keith Horne, Jean Hugo and Adilson Da Silva, who had led after the second and third rounds and saw his birdie effort at the last to tie from 22 feet just miss.

Goya won the Madeira Islands Open in 2009 but twice had to go back to the qualifying school to retain his European Tour privileges for 2013 and again for 2014. With a lowly card, he had to take every opportunity going, and although this event was not a co-sanctioned tournament, it got him into the Tshwane Open, which is, as well as the WGC - Bridgestone Invitational later in the season.

"It's nice to win again," Goya said. "I decided to give it everything on the back nine, and when I saw the leaderboard at the 18th, I was just happy to have a chance, and happy to take it."

Tshwane Open

Centurion, South Africa

Winner: Ross Fisher

On the longest course in the history of the European Tour, it was Ross Fisher's putting which helped him to victory at the Tshwane Open. The Els course at Copperleaf, hosting the event for a second year running, measures 7,964 yards, so a big hitter such as Fisher could be expected to revel at the venue, but it was on the greens that the 33-year-old Englishman really clicked. Ironically, he missed a par putt on the last green but had still done enough to secure a three-stroke victory over Michael Hoey and Danie van Tonder. After rounds of 66, 65 and 67, it only meant a closing 70, rather than a fourth successive score in the 60s, for a 20-under-par total of 268.

This was Fisher's first win in South Africa and his fifth on the European Tour, the last having come back in 2010, the year he played in the Ryder Cup at Celtic Manor. It was also the fourth time in stroke play events where Fisher successfully converted a 54-hole lead. He was five clear starting a rainy final round and immediately put his approach at the first hole close for a tap-in birdie. While South African van Tonder produced a bogey-free 66 to set the clubhouse target at 17 under, Hoey played alongside Fisher and, after matching birdies at the first, started to haul in the leader with an eagle at the 685-yard fourth hole. The Northern Irishman added birdies at the eighth and the 11th, where he holed from 30 feet, to get within one of Fisher before he found water with his approach at the 12th and took a double bogey.

Hoey birdied the 15th, on the way to a 68, but it was at the same hole that Fisher stamped his authority once more by holing from 25 feet for his second eagle of the week at the par-five. "That was a big putt for me," Fisher said. "That hole has been good to me." Now four clear with three to play, Fisher went on to hole good par-savers at the next two holes.

"I'm thrilled to get over the line," he added. "It was a testing day with the weather conditions and playing with Mike, he put up a great challenge for me. My form has been coming back for some time, but the putting has just let me down. This week I holed more putts than I have for a very long time. I'm excited for the rest of the year."

Investec Cup

Sun City, South Africa

Winner: Trevor Fisher, Jr.

Trevor Fisher got his timing spot on when he claimed the biggest title of his career at the Investec Cup and with a double victory. The 34-year-old also topped the Chase to the Investec Cup points race for a bonus of R3.5 million on top of first prize of R163,400 for his one-shot victory at the Lost City course at Sun City. Fisher was unaware of Jacques Blaauw eagling the final hole from 10 feet in the group ahead of him to get within one, but a chip and two putts for a par were good enough for an eighth victory on the Sunshine Tour.

Fisher closed with a 66, after rounds of 69, 70 and 67, to finish on a 16-under-par total of 272. There were also 66s for Blaauw and defending champion Jaco Van Zyl, who shared third place with Keith Horne, who was pressing Fisher until a bogey at the 17th when he drove into thick rough. George Coetzee finished fifth after starting the day with the lead, one ahead of Fisher. But two double bogeys undermined his challenge and the second of them at the 12th hole gave Fisher the lead as he birdied the same hole. An earlier eagle at the fourth had been a good start to the round, and after birdieing the 15th, he parred home despite being unaware of Blaauw's late charge.

"I thought I just had to make par for a two-stroke win," Fisher said. "Because of that, I was quite calm coming up the fairway to the 18th, but I'm glad I was able to get the job done. It was always going to be tough to win this. It's another notch on the belt and it gives you confidence. But this is really life-changing, no question about it."

Telkom Business PGA Championship

Johannesburg, South Africa

Winner: Titch Moore

After waiting six years and four months for his seventh Sunshine Tour victory, Titch Moore was ultimately happy that he had to wait an extra five holes to seal the win. Moore eventually defeated Ulrich van den Berg with a birdie at the fifth extra time of playing the 18th hole at the Country Club of Johannesburg. Van den Berg had two opportunities to make a birdie and end the playoff earlier, but it was Moore who was able to put the trophy in the hands of his six-year-old son who had been waiting for the moment his whole life. "It was also my younger son's third birthday today, so there's real cause to celebrate," Moore said.

Moore closed with a 67 to post a total of 273, 15 under par, and saw his birdie at the 18th hole in regulation matched by van den Berg as he closed with a 68 to tie. J.J. Senekel was third, just one stroke outside the playoff, while overnight leader Oliver Bekker closed with a 73 to share fourth place.

"I had a lot of seconds last year, and to finally win a summer tournament on the Sunshine Tour is fantastic," Moore said. "I feel really bad for Ulrich. He's a good player and he's been playing nicely for a while, but I've also been knocking on the door for the last year."

Golden Pilsner Zimbabwe Open

Harare, Zimbabwe

Winner: Jbe' Kruger

Returning to the Golden Pilsner Zimbabwe Open was just what Jbe' Kruger needed to get back in the winner's circle. Kruger won the event in 2010 and had not won on the Sunshine Tour since. The 27-year-old claimed victory at Royal Harare by one stroke over Jacques Blaauw, by two over overnight leader Haydn Porteous and by three over Jaco Ahlers.

Kruger produced a final round of 66, only beaten by Ahlers' 65, to post a total of 18-under-par 270. He came from five behind rookie Porteous, who struggled to a 73 after dropping four shots in three holes around the turn. Kruger started brilliantly with five birdies in an outward 31 and also birdied the 12th before bogeying the next two holes. He rallied with birdies at the 16th and 17th holes, the latter a crucial blow after playing the hole in two over par for the first three rounds. "I didn't like that 17th hole the whole week," said Kruger, "so I knew it was the hole that was going to make or break the tournament for me. I hit an absolutely perfect shot and made the putt."

Blaauw, who scored a 68, eagled the 16th hole but could not birdie either of the final two to tie. Kruger won the Avantha Masters on the European Tour in 2012.

Investec Royal Swazi Open

Mbabane, Swaziland

Winner: Danie van Tonder

Danie van Tonder claimed his maiden victory in the grand manner with four birdies in a row to win the Investec Royal Swazi Open in a playoff. Three of those birdies came on the last three holes of regulation as the 23-year-old posted a closing round of 18 points under the modified-Stableford format of five for an eagle, two for a birdie, none for par, minus one for a bogey and minus three for a double bogey or worse. He tied at 48 points for the tournament with Jared Harvey, who scored 16 on the final day, and Jacques Blaauw, who scored 12. At the par-three 18th for the playoff, van Tonder put his tee shot to eight feet and holed the putt for the winning birdie.

"Playing 16 I saw that I was a bit behind and had to make three birdies in a row, which I managed to do," said van Tonder, who was runner-up in the event in 2012, the year he earned Rookie of the Year honors on the Sunshine Tour. "There are always nerves, that's not the question, it's about how you cope with it. I like pressure, so I just got over the putts and hit them in the hole."

Mopani Copper Mines Zambia Open

Kitwe, Zambia

Winner: Wallie Coetsee

After waiting 17 years after winning the Namibia Open in 1997, Wallie Coetsee finally got to celebrate another victory as he claimed the Mopani Copper Mines Zambia Open at Nkana Golf Club. The 41-year-old from Jeffrey's Bay survived an emotional afternoon to win by one stroke over Justin Harding and Danie van Tonder. Rounds of 65, 69 and 68 had put him in the lead after the second and third rounds and a closing 71 left him on a 15-under-par total of 273. Harding closed with a 68 and Van Tonder a 71 as both kept the pressure up with birdies at the 16th and 17th holes.

Coetsee was out in two under and made a crucial par at the 12th after finding thick rough where he could only advance the ball 10 yards before playing an exquisite chip to three feet. He did drop a shot at the 16th but rallied with a birdie at the next, which meant another drop at the last did not matter.

"There are no words to describe how this feels, it's just so special," Coetsee said. "I knew that victory was close and today it came down to having 22 years of experience. I hit the shots like I practice them every day. We live to play tournament golf, to be in contention, and to feel that adrenaline. There's no better feeling than making those big shots and to walk down the last like I did today."

Lombard Insurance Classic

Mbabane, Swaziland

Winner: Christiaan Basson

Christiaan Basson started the final round of the Lombard Insurance Classic two off the lead in fifth place. The little matter of a closing score of 62, 10 under par, gave the 32-year-old a five-stroke victory. With opening rounds of 69 and 66, Basson finished the 54-hole event on a total of 197, 19 under par, and without dropping a stroke to par throughout the tournament. Jake Redman, the overnight leader, closed with a 69 to finish on 14 under par alongside Ruan de Smidt (64), Adilson Da Silva (65) and Neil Schietekat (68), who all shared second place.

It was Basson's third victory on the Sunshine Tour and his second at Royal Swazi Spa, where he won the Royal Swazi Open in 2012. He found water on the 17th hole in the second round but escaped with a par and required only 23 putts for the final round. It was his charge on the back nine that sealed his runaway victory as he came home in 29 strokes. He birdied the 10th, then eagled the 12th, birdied the 13th and finished with three birdies at the last three holes.

"Initially when you start any tournament, the plan is to go bogey-free, but it doesn't always work out that way," said Basson. "Luckily I played really solid this week. I must say this was one of the best performances I've ever carded."

Zambia Sugar Open

Lusaka, Zambia

Winner: Lyle Rowe

Lyle Rowe opened the Zambia Sugar Open with a 76 to be 10 strokes off the lead, but he responded with rounds of 69, 66 and 68 to post his maiden victory by four shots at Lusaka Golf Club. A tip from his friend Jake Redman transformed his fortunes at the halfway stage, and some outstanding putting on tricky greens helped him ease away from the field.

With a cold wind causing havoc during the final round, Rowe's five-under 68 was the best score of the day by three strokes. He made seven birdies, including three in a row from the 12th, and dropped only two shots to finish on a 13-under-par total of 279. Neil Schietekat took second place on nine under, two ahead of P.H. McIntyre and Ulrich van den Berg, who was the 54-hole leader but closed with a 75.

"It's nice to get a win under the belt," said Rowe, who turned professional in 2009. "Obviously you wonder when it's going to come, so to get it done and to get it done on a nice course like this is awesome."

Vodacom Origins of Golf - Euphoria

Naboomspruit, Limpopo, South Africa

Winner: Danie van Tonder

Danie van Tonder targeted winning the Sunshine Tour Order of Merit after claiming his second win in five starts at the opening leg of the Vodacom Origins of Golf series. He moved into second position on the money list behind Ross Fisher after a consistent season when patience allowed the 23-year-old to produce his best golf at the right time. Van Tonder did just that on the back nine on the Annika Sorenstam-designed Euphoria course when birdies at the 12th, 13th and 15th holes brought him home in 33. A closing 70, after a pair of 67s, gave him a 12-under-par total of 204 and a one-stroke win over Tyrone Ferreira, who scored a 68. It was Ferreira who showed it was possible to attack the course as he chalked up six birdies in a row from the seventh. Ulrich van den Berg finished a shot further back after a 70.

"Sometimes I want to look at leaderboards to see if I need to make more birdies and on a course like this you need to know whether to go for it or not. My first nine was a bit dodgy, but I came through with a few birdies and managed to win it," van Tonder said. "I've learnt this year you have to be patient and wait for it, otherwise you'll mess up. The goal I've got now is to win the Order of Merit and get into the Nedbank Golf Challenge."

Sun City Challenge

Sun City, South Africa

Winner: Dean Burmester

Dean Burmester hung on to win for the second time on the Sunshine Tour at the Sun City Challenge. The 25-year-old from Bloemfontein led by three with a round to play, but when Haydn Porteous made his fifth birdie of the day at the 16th hole, Burmester was one behind. Porteous then took four to get down from the left edge of the 17th green for a double bogey to put Burmester one ahead again, only for the leader to bogey the same hole.

With Porteous in the clubhouse after a 69, Burmester needed a birdie at the par-five 18th and achieved it by chipping from behind the green to a foot and tapping in. He had rounds of 68, 67 and 71 for a 10-under-par total of 206 to win by one stroke over Porteous, with Merrick Bremner taking third place after a 66.

"Any time you do what you have to do under pressure is sweet, and it gets sweeter every time," said Burmester, who won for the first time at the

Polokwane Classic in 2013. "The first win can come out of nowhere and it is always nice to do it a second time."

Vodacom Origins of Golf - Arabella

Western Cape, South Africa
Winner: Jean Hugo

Jean Hugo overcame some tough conditions to win the Vodacom Origins of Golf event at Arabella. The tournament was cut to 36 holes after a gale on the second day led to the second round being suspended mid-morning. It was then concluded the following day when freezing, heavy rain fell throughout. Hugo, who was one behind four players after an opening 68, produced the best score of the second round with a 69 to finish on a seven-under-par total of 137.

A birdie at the waterlogged 18th hole took the 38-year-old one clear of Rhys West, who returned a 71. After Hugo had bogeyed the 10th, he made a 40-footer for birdie at the next and also birdied the 13th to tie West before claiming his 15th Sunshine Tour victory at the last. It was also his ninth win in the Origins of Golf series, the most of anyone, and his first since the corresponding event in the Western Cape in 2013.

"It's not that I've been stuck for a long time," said Hugo, "but it felt like a long time that I've been on 14 wins, and I've had a few chances to extend that number, so it's nice to get off that 14. Out there it felt like a marathon, but you have to just refocus. To have knuckled down and be three under for the last eight holes to win a tournament is good stuff in my book."

Chris Swanepoel shared third place with Trevor Fisher Jr., Ulrich van den Berg and Adilson Da Silva on four-under-par 139.

Vodacom Origins of Golf - St. Francis

Eastern Cape, South Africa
Winner: Keith Horne

Cool, breezy, rainy conditions at St. Francis Links favored experience in the final round of the Vodacom Origins of Golf tournament and 43-year-old Keith Horne, in his 18th season on tour, took advantage to win by three strokes. Horne had set a course record with a 65 in the first round, but a 71 on day two had allowed Erik van Rooyen to tie after 36 holes.

Horne made the better start to the final round with birdies at the first three holes and another at the fifth to go four clear. With the wind picking up on the inward half, both men struggled, with Horne having three bogeys and only one birdie while van Rooyen came home in two over for a 74. Horne's second successive 71 gave him a nine-under-par total of 207. The pair had long since separated themselves from the field, with Ulrich van den Berg and Wallie Coetsee sharing third place, five strokes behind the runner-up.

"I made sure I didn't go out in a tentative frame of mind on the final day," said Horne. "I really took dead-aim at a lot of the flags early on and it paid off." His sixth Sunshine Tour victory was not totally unexpected as he explained: "I felt that I could win this week — in fact, I told my daughter I'd win it."

Wild Waves Golf Challenge

KwaZulu-Natal, South Africa

Winner: Colin Nel

Colin Nel only got to play two holes of the final round of the Wild Waves Golf Challenge but still recorded his maiden victory. Play was suspended at Wild Coast Sun due to high winds which were gusting up to 40 mph, but having to wait around for three hours to find out what would happen may have made Nel more nervous than actually having to play. Eventually, play was abandoned, the tournament decided over 36 holes. Nel had scored back-to-back 65s for a 10-under-par total of 130 to win by three strokes over Ulrich van den Berg and Jared Harvey.

"It's a great feeling that hasn't quite set in yet," Nel said. "After coming off and waiting for three hours, it got a bit nerve-wracking, so I'm very pleased with the victory. Everyone is going for their first win, and often once the ice is broken then more wins follow.

"I went to university at Oklahoma City and it blows a bit there, but I've never played in conditions quite like this. Today I got to the third tee when they pulled us off and the first few holes were treacherous. The wind was very strong and I think it was the right call, because the balls were moving and flags were being blown off the greens."

Vodacom Origins of Golf - Wild Coast Sun

KwaZulu-Natal, South Africa

Winner: Louis de Jager

A par at the first extra hole gave Louis de Jager a playoff victory over Haydn Porteous and Jaco Ahlers at the Vodacom Origins of Golf event at Wild Coast Sun. But it was a roller-coaster ride for the 27-year-old who scored 14 strokes higher in his last round than in his first.

De Jager opened with a 63 for a four-stroke lead and then added a 68 to move five clear of the field with a round to play. But he started with a triple bogey at the first hole on a breezy final day and also had a double bogey at the fifth. There were two birdies going out and another at the 13th, so he still had enough of a cushion to bogey the last five holes and still make it into the playoff. He closed with a 77 for a two-under-par total of 208 which had earlier been posted by Porteous with a 67 and Ahlers with a 72.

"On the first I hit probably the worst shot of my tournament for my second, and it went into the hazard," said de Jager, whose second Sunshine Tour win came five years after his first. "It was very tough out there and I'm just glad I could pull it through. I just kept my head and stuck to my gameplan, and it worked out in the end. That was the first playoff of my career, so I didn't know what to expect, but I think that helped me in the end."

Vodacom Origins of Golf - Vaal de Grace

Parys, South Africa
Winner: P.H. McIntyre

A fierce battle in the Vodacom Origins of Golf event at Vaal de Grace between P.H. McIntyre and Jake Roos went all the way to a third extra hole. McIntyre finally clinched his maiden title with an eight-foot birdie putt, after Roos has seen his effort for a three at the 18th from 10 feet stop on the right lip.

McIntyre's 64 in the first round put him one in front of Roos, but a 67 to a 68 the next day saw Roos draw even. Both men birdied three of the first seven holes in the final round, and then twice McIntyre went ahead only to bogey. But his birdie at the 14th was not matched by Roos until the 17th as the pair returned 68s to tie on a 16-under-par total of 200. Playing the 18th in the playoff, Roos was out of position on the first extra hole but survived, while both men had lengthy birdie chance on the second extra hole before McIntyre got his three next time around. Roos had won all five of his previous playoffs on the Sunshine Tour.

It was an emotional victory for the 28-year-old McIntyre, who explained: "My Dad has been very ill. He's been in intensive care for about a month, and it was a very difficult time — flying to visit him in the Cape. So this win's for him."

Sun Boardwalk Golf Challenge

Port Elizabeth, South Africa
Winner: Titch Moore

Titch Moore, a local from Port Elizabeth, won the inaugural Sun Boardwalk Golf Challenge at Humewood after eight pars on the way home and a birdie at the last. With the second day's play cancelled due to high winds, the event was cut to 36 holes with Moore's back-to-back 70s for a four-under-par total of 140 giving him a one-stroke victory over Roberto Lupini and Steve Surry.

Lupini had led on the first day with a 68 but scored a 73 in the second round, although a birdie at the 17th had given him a chance of tying with another at the 18th. Surry matched Moore's 70 with three birdies in the last six holes following a double bogey at the eighth. Peter Karmis and Heinrich Bruiners both shot 69 to tie for fourth, while Ryan Tipping, Doug McGuigan and Ulrich van den Berg shared sixth place on one-under-par 143.

It was a ninth Sunshine Tour victory for the 38-year-old Moore and a second of the year. "I've been playing nicely for a while now and the win at the Telkom Business PGA Championship in April was big. We're starved of decent sport here in Port Elizabeth and to win in front of the home fans is a treat," he said.

BMG Classic

Johannesburg, South Africa
Winner: Merrick Bremner

Merrick Bremner produced a moment of magic by holing out from a bunker to win the BMG Classic at Glendower. Bremner's fourth win on the Sunshine Tour came after he made up four strokes on overnight leader Darren Fichardt with a brilliant inward half of 31 that included birdies at three of the last four holes.

Bremner had rounds of 66, 71 and 67 for a 12-under-par total of 204, while Fichardt closed with a 72. Out in 39 with a double bogey at the eighth when he left a shot in a bunker, Fichardt made three birdies coming home but could not force a tying birdie at the last hole. Haydn Porteous matched the low round of the final day with another 67 to take third place, one behind Fichardt after coming home in 32.

"It took more than one good shot to win the tournament," said Bremner, "but that bunker shot on the last was something special. It was a very difficult shot, I think about 20 meters, and a little bit of turn from left to right. I just caught it perfectly, watched it bounce and trickle in. I had been in about 20 bunkers this week and not come close to holing out. So I said to my caddie that we were due for a change in fortunes and I was going to hole it."

Vodacom Origins of Golf Final

Western Cape, South Africa
Winner: Keith Horne

Keith Horne was less than complimentary about his putting but only needed to hole out from two feet for a birdie at the last to win the Vodacom Origins of Golf Final at Pezula. Horne won his second tournament of the series, after taking the St. Francis event in August, by one stroke over Ulrich van den Berg, who was a runner-up for the third time in the season.

Horne had rounds of 65, 71 and 67 for a 13-under-par total of 203. His only dropped shot of the final round came at the second hole, and then he made two birdies going out and four coming home. Van den Berg made a great charge with a 65, and four birdies in five holes to start the back nine put him in command. But he bogeyed the 15th before birdieing the last to force Horne to do the same. Dylan Frittelli was third after a 69.

"That was probably as badly as I have putted for a long time," said Horne, who had 34 putts in his closing 67. "It was a good thing that I was hitting it close all day. I kept finishing inside 10 or 12 feet, and that made things a little easier for me.

"My ball-striking was excellent this week, especially the last 27 holes. I hit the ball so well that I put myself under no pressure. I missed one fairway in two days and two greens in two days. Thank goodness for that, because the putter was diabolical."

Nedbank Affinity Cup

Sun City, South Africa

Winner: Louis de Jager

Louis de Jager won for the second time in two months as he took the Nedbank Affinity Cup in a playoff over Danie van Tonder and Vaughn Groenewald at Lost City. Groenewald and van Tonder both scored 66s in the final round to set the target at 12-under-par 204 and de Jager birdied the last two holes for his third successive 68 to also join the playoff. Van Tonder dropped out when the other two both birdied the 18th on the first extra hole, and then de Jager managed it for a third time in a row with a chip to eight feet to win at the second extra hole. Jake Redman took fourth place, just one shot outside the playoff, while overnight leader Ruan de Smidt tied for fifth place after a closing 74.

"It's always a great feeling to win, especially when you do it in a playoff. There's extra pressure and I'm really happy that I could play some good shots and make it count," de Jager, 27, said. "It still hasn't sunk in completely, but to win twice this year has made it a special season for me. Two playoff wins is an achievement, but I'm also really happy with the way I played throughout this week."

Lion of Africa Cape Town Open

Cape Town, South Africa

Winner: Jaco Ahlers

Jaco Ahlers timed his first win in five years perfectly as victory at the Lion of Africa Cape Town Open got him the final spot in the Nedbank Golf Challenge the following week. Ahlers won in a playoff that lasted four holes before Ross McGowan missed from three feet on the 18th green at Royal Cape. Hennie Otto, the leader for the first three rounds, had departed with a bogey at the first extra hole.

Ahlers had rounds of 71, 69, 68 and 68 for a 12-under-par total of 276. McGowan also closed with a 68 to match Ahlers, while Otto struggled as the wind got up and had to birdie the 18th to join the playoff after a closing 72. Jbe' Kruger had a 65 early in the day to tie for fourth place with Thomas Aiken.

"I can't describe how happy I am right now," said Ahlers. "I aged years during that playoff. I turned 32 last week, but right now I feel about 40 years old. But it's a happy 40."

Ahlers added: "This is life-changing for me. Now I'm going to Sun City. That is a lifelong dream come true. I have to give Ross and Hennie credit though. We all got into the playoff because we played great golf, but I'm sorry boys — I'm going to enjoy this one!"

Nedbank Golf Challenge

Sun City, South Africa

Winner: Danny Willett

Luke Donald was set up for a special way to celebrate his 37th birthday when he led by one stroke going into the final day of the Nedbank Golf Challenge on the Gary Player course at Sun City. But Donald slipped to third place as a man 10 years his junior, Danny Willett, claimed a four-stroke victory over Ross Fisher, Englishmen filling the top three spots on the leaderboard.

Willett had a superb weekend with scores of 65 and 66 as the Yorkshire man finished on an 18-under-par total of 270 on his debut on the Gary Player course. On Saturday it was only a birdie at the final hole that kept Donald in front, but on Sunday Willett quickly established a comfortable lead as he birdied the second and then benefitted from two two-shot swings against Donald at the third and fifth holes.

After Fisher, winner of the Tshwane Open earlier in the year, led with a first round of 66, Donald responded with a 63 on the second day. A mark of the quality of the round was that while Donald was nine under par, the other 28 players were a collective eight under par. Having returned to his old coach, Pat Goss, in recent months, Donald was pleased with an upturn in form, but his weekend rounds of 69 and 73 left him six behind Willett. "There were a lot of positives and it's nice to put myself back in position," he said. "Danny played really focused golf today and hats off, he's a deserved winner."

Fisher clinched second place with a closing 68, while Willett had matching halves of 33 and recorded only three bogeys during the week.

With the event counting as the opening tournament on the 2015 European Tour, Willett claimed a second title following the BMW International in 2012. He also became the third Englishman to win the tournament, an unofficial event for most of its history, after Nick Faldo and Lee Westwood. "They are some good names to be next to," Willett said. "It's always nice walking up the ninth, obviously with the names engraved on the pathway up the left, you kind of realize how many great players have been here and walked over the same bridge as you have and had a great week.

"South Africa is a place that's suited me in the past. I've played good golf down here, love the place, love the people, everything about it is great. It's been a truly fun test of golf."

Alfred Dunhill Championship

Malelane, South Africa

Winner: Branden Grace

Two years after winning the Alfred Dunhill Links Championship at St. Andrews, Branden Grace ended his wait for a next title by claiming the Alfred Dunhill Championship at Leopard Creek. The 26-year-old South African became the first player to win both titles. Just as at the Links Championship, Grace led from wire-to-wire as he romped to a seven-stroke victory over Louis Oosthuizen. It was his fifth European Tour victory, three of them coming in his homeland, and a fourth Sunshine Tour title for Grace.

He opened with a 62 thanks to hitting all 18 greens in regulation and making the birdies. His score was one outside Charl Schwartzel's course record and gave him a three-stroke lead which he extended to five strokes the next day with a 66. A 72 in the third round allowed Lucas Bjerregaard to get within one stroke and Danny Willett, winner of the Nedbank Challenge the previous week, within two. But while Grace compiled a 68 with six birdies and only two dropped shots, his nearest pursuers struggled. Denmark's Bjerregaard had a triple bogey at the seventh and then collapsed completely, coming home in 50 for an 89 to fall to a tie for 49th place. Willett ran out of stream when he finished with a double bogey, a bogey and a triple bogey to drop to joint fourth place.

Grace posted a 20-under-par total of 268, while Oosthuizen had steady rounds of 69, 69, 68 and 69 to finish two ahead of Andrew Johnston, an Englishman in his first event of the 2015 season after topping the 2014 Challenge Tour.

"It's been a phenomenal week," Grace said. "It's special to win it wire-to-wire, more so because it's in front of a local crowd. It was a pretty flawless round today and the perfect way to finish off an incredible tournament, a great week in the office.

"It's been a long year, a hard year, but now it's a fairytale ending just before Christmas. One of the main things this week has been the driving. I just put a new driver in the bag in Dubai and that's been the key this week."

13. Women's Tours

As 2014 rolled to a close, it surprised no one that Stacy Lewis, Inbee Park and wonder kid Lydia Ko, 17, emerged as the Big Three of the LPGA Tour. But something else emerged that might come as a surprise to many — a bigger LPGA Tour and, by all indications, a stronger one.

The tour announced a 2015 schedule of 33 events — 34 counting the Solheim Cup — with a record $61.6 million in prize money. That's one more tournament and $4 million more than in 2014.

The schedule itself contains major overhauls in two of the tour's five majors:

• In a landmark move, the LPGA Championship, the tour's flagship event, disappeared and was replaced by the KMPG PGA Women's Championship, to be run by the PGA of America. It is scheduled for June 8-14 at Westchester Country Club. "We're going to evolve the LPGA Championship, a women's major that's been with us for more than 60 years, into a new era if you will," LPGA Commissioner Mike Whan said.

• In a sponsorship change, the ANA Inspiration, sponsored by All Nippon Airways, replaced the Kraft Nabisco Championship. It remains at Mission Hills, Rancho Mirage, California, and will be played March 30-April 5.

These developments capped a year dominated by Lewis, Park and Ko. Among them, they won nine tournaments, had 33 top-five finishes and 50 top-10s.

Lewis won the Rolex Player of the Year Award with a remarkable record. Lewis scored three wins, including the North Texas LPGA Shootout and the ShopRite LPGA Classic by six shots each. In 28 events, she also had five solo seconds, one tie for second, 11 top-five finishes and 18 top-10s. And she made every cut.

Park retook the Rolex No. 1 ranking from Lewis, winning three times, including the LPGA Championship, and had two seconds, four third places, and 17 top-10s in 23 starts. She missed just one cut. Lewis finished No. 2 in the Rolex Rankings, and Ko No. 3.

Ko won the Rolex Rookie of the Year Award going away. With her powerful amateur record, she was granted the special exemption that enabled her to join the tour in 2014 at age 17. She won three times, had two seconds and three thirds, and was in the top five 10 times. And she made every cut in her 26 events.

She also enjoyed the biggest payday in tour history — $1.5 million — when she won both the season-ending CME Group Tour Championship, with its $500,000 first prize, plus the $1 million bonus for also winning the season-long points competition, the inaugural Race to the CME Globe.

Ko also was named to *Time Magazine*'s 100 Most Influential people for 2014, for sparking interest in golf.

"This year has been awesome," Ko said. "I'm looking forward to what's coming up next year."

Lewis also won the Vare Trophy, for the lowest scoring average, 69.53 strokes per round, and also the money-winning title, with $2,539,039, followed by Park, $2,226,641, and Ko, $2,089,033. In all, 11 players topped the $1 million mark.

The five majors gave a glimpse into the future of the LPGA. Two golfers scored their first victories, two others won their first majors, and two teenagers were among them.

• Kraft Nabisco Championship: Lexi Thompson, at 19, became the second-youngest to win a major when she took the final Kraft Nabisco by three for her first her first major. Thompson didn't spare her driver. "Laying back wouldn't really make sense," she said.

• U.S. Women's Open: After years of expectations, Michelle Wie, now 24, won her first major and her second title of the season. She came through a shaky final round for a two-shot win over Stacy Lewis.

Wie also won the inaugural Rolex Annika Major Award, named after the retired Annika Sorenstam and honoring the player with the best overall record in the five majors.

• Ricoh Women's British Open: Diminutive Melissa "Mo" Martin got her first win and her first major with a spectacular eagle on the final hole, a three-wood approach that hit the pin and left her a six-foot putt.

• Wegmans LPGA Championship: In the final edition of the venerable tournament, Inbee Park beat Brittany Lincicome in a playoff for her fifth major title and fourth in the last two seasons.

• Evian Championship: Korea's Hyo-Joo Kim, 19, dropped a 12-foot birdie putt for a one-stroke win over Hall-of-Famer Karrie Webb. Said Kim, through an interpreter: "I feel very happy, like a bird. I want to fly in the sky."

On the Japan LPGA Tour, Sun-Ju Ahn led a parade of multiple winners as she clamped onto her third money-winning title in decisive fashion. The 26-year-old South Korean, also No. 1 in 2010 and 2011, piled up five victories and ¥153,075,741 in prize money in a year in which she and eight other players captured 26 of the season's 37 tournaments. Ahn, whose record sports 18 wins, took the title by ¥30 million despite nursing a sore wrist through the final month.

Taiwan's Teresa Lu, also 26, put on a late-season surge to grab second place in the standings. With the Japan Women's Open and Resort Trust titles already in the bag, she won the Japan Tour Championship finale following a second-place finish the previous Sunday. The other majors went to two of the tour's youngest players — Ai Suzuki, 20, the PGA Championship, and Misuzu Narita, 21, the Salonpas World Championship.

Nine ladies won for the first time, the most remarkable of whom was 15-year-old schoolgirl Minami Katsu, who, with her victory in the Vantelin Open, became the youngest winner in Japan LPGA Tour history.

On the other side of the coin, Sakura Yokomine scored her 23rd title in the Elleair Open before heading to America and qualifying for the 2015 U.S. LPGA Tour. The Elleair prize money made Yokomine just the second player to surpass the ¥1 billion mark, joining 50-tournament-winner Yuri Fudoh, who last won in 2011.

U.S. LPGA Tour

Pure Silk Bahamas LPGA Classic

Paradise Island, Bahamas
Winner: Jessica Korda

Jessica Korda didn't have that shot before. Indeed, who did — putting from off the green and from under TV cables? But she had it when she needed it, at the final hole, and it boosted her to the Pure Silk Bahamas LPGA Classic to open the tour's 2014 season late in January.

"It wasn't a hard decision at all," said Korda, 20, posting her second tour win. At the Ocean course's par-five 18th, which she'd already played in birdie-birdie-eagle, she had run her 200-yard four-iron approach over the green and to the fringe near the grandstand, in a cluster of TV cables. She decided that a free drop would just leave her worse off, so she asked some nearby people to hold up the cables — "It was like jump rope" — and faced a choice. The situation called for a chip shot, but she opted for her putter, instead. By most accounts, it was a needlessly risky choice, but she stuck with it and ran the shot up onto the green and down to within six feet of the flag. She had already birdied the 15th and 17th, and now she needed one more for the win. Her nerves responded accordingly.

"I could barely put the ball down and line up," Korda said. But she rolled it in, wrapping up a 19-under card of 69-66-72-66–273 to beat World No. 3 Stacy Lewis by a stroke. It had been a productive day on the greens — eight birdies, only one bogey. Where did the putting come from?

"I honestly have no idea," she said. "I was rolling the ball same as I was yesterday, and I was actually making putts today."

The Pure Silk opened with fanfare. Lydia Ko, who won twice on the LPGA Tour as a kid amateur sensation, was 16 now and making her professional debut. History will show she shared the first-round lead, shot 68-70-71-68–277, 15 under, and tied for seventh and won $31,543. "I just tried to play my own game and be relaxed," she said. Was this the start of something big? History would tell.

ISPS Handa Women's Australian Open

Victoria, Australia
Winner: Karrie Webb

See Australian Ladies Tour section.

Honda LPGA Thailand

Chonburi, Thailand

Winner: Anna Nordqvist

The future looked incredibly bright for Anna Nordqvist that week in 2009, when as a rookie in just her fifth start she came out of nowhere and won the LPGA Championship. "It was my time," she said then. It surely looked like her time that November, when she outran Lorena Ochoa, No. 1 in the world, to take the LPGA Tour Championship. The Swede, then just 22, so recently a star at Arizona State, now looked like the next coming of Annika Sorenstam. But then everything went dim.

"I kind of lost the reason why I play golf — the fun of it," Nordqvist was to say.

Five years and 95 starts later, things brightened again for her at the Honda LPGA Thailand. She broke the long drought, and it was an encouraging comeback because she didn't have cushy leads to comfort her. Shooting 66-72-67-68, she had to hold up under the pressure of one-stroke leads, then strong challenges from Michelle Wie and Rolex World No. 1 Inbee Park, the defending champion, before winning by two strokes.

Nordqvist led wire-to-wire, and by one through the first two rounds. "I'm excited," Nordqvist said at the halfway point. "This is a position I've been practicing to be in." In the third round, her 67, off four birdies and an eagle, put her 11 under and widened the gap, but just behind her were Wie (69) and Park (67), four back but gathering steam. "I think I still left four birdies out there," Park said.

Nordqvist started the final round up by four but saw it slip quickly to one with a double bogey at No. 5 and Wie's birdie there. Then she locked up in a duel with Park. Nordqvist birdied No. 7 from 12 feet, and Park birdied Nos. 7 and 8. But Nordqvist notched five of her seven birdies coming home, including a run of three starting with a 20-foot putt at the 10th. Her closing 68 gave her a 15-under 273 and a two-stroke win over Park.

Said Nordqvist: "Just unbelievable to get that win again."

HSBC Women's Champions

Singapore

Winner: Paula Creamer

There are various ways to celebrate a victory — the fist pump, two-handed up-thrust, gripping the head and others. Paula Creamer demonstrated a new one at the HSBC Women's Champions. At the second hole of a playoff at the Sentosa Golf Club's par-five 18th, Spain's Azahara Munoz had laid up, and Creamer reached the green in two but was sitting 75 feet beyond the flag. A three-putt was in the books.

Creamer, playing the ball well outside-right, gave it a good rap, and it rolled down the slope, up over a ridge, and then took the sweeping left turn and dropped — an eagle. Creamer went racing, then dropped to her knees, bent her head nearly to the ground, and slapped the turf, laughing, clearly in disbelief.

"I was just hoping it would slow down, and then it disappeared," Creamer said. "I seriously cannot tell you the way I felt. It was like somebody just knocked the wind out of me."

Creamer shot 67-73-69-69 for a 10-under 278 to tie Munoz, who closed with a 70 after bogeying the first two holes. It was Creamer's 10th tour victory, coming after 79 winless starts since she took the 2010 U.S. Women's Open. Munoz, seeking her second victory, could only shrug. "Nothing you can do about it," she said. "Just congratulate her."

Karrie Webb, who won her 40th tour title two weeks earlier in the Women's Australian Open, was even more disappointed. She had led through the first three rounds and went into the final round up by one over Angela Stanford, three over Munoz and four over Creamer. But she bogeyed the 13th, 15th and 18th for a 74 to finish third, a stroke out of the playoff. "Just not a lot of good decisions," Webb said. "Doesn't feel great at the moment."

For Creamer, it was a huge relief. "I definitely tested myself coming down the stretch," she said. "I had to make a bunch of six-, seven-footers, but I just kept grinding. I'm shaking. Oh, my gosh, this has been such a long time coming."

JTBC Founders Cup

Phoenix, Arizona

Winner: Karrie Webb

What with young pro Morgan Pressel flirting with a 59, and rookie Mirim Lee making a rush, and teen prodigy Lydia Ko taking the lead, it's no wonder that Hall-of-Famer Karrie Webb was barely noticed at the JTBC Founders Cup.

It's a fanciful notion, but it almost seemed that Webb, 39, let the kids have their fun for three rounds, then rolled up her sleeves and showed them how it's done. There's a certain instructive value in overcoming a six-shot deficit and closing with the course record.

"It's a very special event," Webb was to say, when the drama had ended. The tournament, in its fourth year, honors the 13 women who founded the LPGA in 1950. Webb, shooting 66-71-69-63 — the last tying the course record — trailed all the way to the birdie on the last hole for a 19-under 269 to win by one. But it was an uphill battle.

Webb was two behind when Lee, 23, in her third start, took the first-round lead with a 64. Pressel, 25, set Wildfire humming with thoughts of a 59 when she got to nine under through 11 holes. "Then I came back to earth," she said. She shot 65.

Webb fell six behind at the halfway point after Lee went five under on her final eight holes for a 67. Lee led by two over Ko, who turned pro late in 2013 and was all of 16 now and playing like a veteran. Ko went six under for her last seven holes for a 66. Ko took the third-round lead with a 67, a stroke up on Lee (70) and another youth, Jessica Korda (66).

Then Webb, six behind starting the final round, shook off a lone bogey and birdied five of the last six holes — including the 18th, on a 20-foot putt — for the 63. Then she had a nervous 90-minute wait to see if anyone could catch her. And then she had a one-shot victory. Ironically, she came from six behind to win the first Founders Cup in 2011.

"I just love the feeling of this event," said Webb. Clearly.

Kia Classic

Carlsbad, California

Winner: Anna Nordqvist

Life had been a little easier for front-runners on the LPGA Tour. Now add Anna Nordqvist to those who keep them looking over their shoulder.

"I still can't believe it," Nordqvist was saying. "I was a couple of shots back going into today, but this morning I told myself to give it a shot, and I ended up making quite a bit of birdies out there."

Six of them, to be precise, in the final round of the Kia Classic, and they carried her past Lizette Salas and Cristie Kerr to her second win in four starts. Golf had become fun again. This was the young lady who was a rookie sensation in 2009, winning the LPGA Championship and the Tour Championship. Then she fell silent. Golf was no longer fun, she said.

Nordqvist, now 26, got the spirit back at the Honda LPGA Thailand in February, and if winning there wire-to-wire was fun, how about coming from seven strokes behind at the halfway point of the Kia? Nordqvist shot the par-72 Aviara in 73-68-67-67, trailing Paula Creamer and Mariajo Uribe by six in the first round, and little known Dori Carter by seven through the second. (Carter shot her career-low 64 and said, "No matter what happens this weekend, I can't believe I'm here.") In the third round, Nordqvist closed to within two of Kerr (70) and Salas (69). Then Nordqvist went on a tear in the final round, with birdies at Nos. 1, 8, 9, 13, 14 and 16. She bogeyed the 17th for another 67 and a 13-under 275 total. Kerr slipped (73), and Salas (70) fell short with her rally on the back nine and finished second by a stroke. Lexi Thompson birdied four of the last nine for a 68 and third place.

For Nordqvist, who revealed she was close to quitting the tour in the off season, the Kia came down to a two-foot putt for par on the last hole, with Salas still a threat. "Yeah," she said, "my hands were definitely shaking."

Kraft Nabisco Championship

Rancho Mirage, California

Winner: Lexi Thompson

See Chapter 7.

LPGA LOTTE Championship

Kapolei, Oahu, Hawaii
Winner: Michelle Wie

It was homecookin', Hawaiian-style, for Michelle Wie at the LPGA LOTTE Championship.

"The highlight of this week was to come back home," Wie said. "There wasn't just one moment. From the first tee shot that I made, to the last putt, the aloha that I felt from everyone was unbelievable."

And so, almost, was the finish she put on to take the title, notching her third tour victory and ending a winless drought of 79 tournaments, dating back to the 2010 CN Canadian Women's Open.

The first order of business for the entire field of 144 was to deal with the capricious mid-April trade winds, gusting to 20 mph across Ko Olina Golf Club. Wie had an edge there, having grown up in Honolulu. At that, she didn't become a real threat until the final round, chasing the veteran Angela Stanford across the first three rounds. Stanford took the lead with an eight-under-par 64 in the second round, and added a 67 in the third. Wie, who opened with 70-67-70, trailed by four.

Then the aloha — if that's what it was — kicked in for Wie out of the starting gate in the final round. She birdied Nos. 1, 5 and 6, closing to within a stroke when Stanford birdied the third and bogeyed the sixth. Then a pile-up at 12 under followed at the par-three eighth, when Stanford bogeyed and Wie and South Korea's Hyo Joo Kim parred. Wie took command on the back nine, with birdies at the 12th, from 12 feet, and 13th, from 15, going up by two. Stanford birdied the 14th, getting a stroke back, but Wie dropped another 15-footer at the 16th. And when Stanford bogeyed the 17th, Wie was up by three, and a bogey at the 18th barely dented her. She finished with a 67 and won by two at 14-under 274, and tipped her hat again to the homefolks.

"I really think a lot of times, they willed the ball in," she said. "I give a lot of credit to them this week."

Swinging Skirts LPGA Classic

San Francisco, California
Winner: Lydia Ko

It would make a great Hollywood script: One day, the kids ask Lydia Ko, "Hey, mom, what did you do for your 17th birthday?" And she would smile. They'd never believe her.

The record would show that on Thursday, April 24, 2014, Ko turned 17; shot a 68, two off the lead, in the first round of the Swinging Skirts LPGA Classic, and also was named to *Time Magazine*'s "100 Most Influential People in the World." And for icing on this considerable birthday cake, three days later Ko came from behind and won on the final hole.

It was a landmark moment in what promises to be an outstanding career. Ko won six professional tournaments, four as a kid amateur. She took the Swinging Skirts World Ladies Masters in Thailand in December in her second start as a pro, at 16. This Swinging Skirts, at Lake Merced, was her first win on the LPGA Tour as a pro, at 17.

Said Ko: "Normally, they would say 'Sweet 16,' but I would say it's 'Sweet 17.'"

The tournament was a running battle between Ko, Rolex World No. 4, and Stacy Lewis, No. 3. Chasing Karine Icher in the first round, Ko shot 68, Lewis 69. Lewis moved in front with middle rounds of 69-68, and Ko was one behind with 71-68. Then came the duel in the final round. Ko caught Lewis with a birdie at the ninth and took a two-shot lead with a birdie to Lewis' bogey at the 13th. They matched birdies at the 14th, and Lewis closed to within one at the 16th, birdie-to-par. Finally, at the par-five 18th, Ko was in the rough again and pitched to six feet, with Lewis threatening from four feet. Ko holed the birdie for a 69 and a 12-under 276. Lewis followed for a 71 and her sixth runner-up finish since winning the Women's British Open the preceding August.

And if the kids should ever wonder, Ko made *Time*'s 100 for her influence in junior golf, and the other 99 included President Barack Obama, Hilary Clinton and Pope Francis.

North Texas LPGA Shootout

Irving, Texas

Winner: Stacy Lewis

Out of the mouths of babes — well, sort of.

Stacy Lewis, relaxing after a highly frustrating third round, was cuddling her three-year-old nephew. Someone asked the tyke what it would take for Aunt Stacy to do better. Lewis whispered something into his ear. The little guy took the cue.

"Make some putts," he said. So in the fourth round, Lewis took her own advice and had a ripping good time of it, racing off with the North Texas LPGA Shootout by a whopping six shots. It was the tour's most lopsided win since Jiyai Shin took the 2012 Women's British Open by nine.

"I've been wanting to do this for a long time," Lewis said, "...taking a tournament and running away with it." She did just that, leaving Meena Lee, her co-leader entering the final round, a distant and maybe breathless second.

Lewis' runaway went into the books as 71-64-69-64–268, 16 under par at Los Colinas. It was a deeply satisfying win for Lewis. It not only was her ninth tour win and first since the previous August, it was a payback for so many frustrations — six runner-up finishes in her previous 16 tournaments. After an opening 71, Lewis made her big move with a bogey-free 64 to tie for second with Natalie Gulbis at 135 through the second round. But the third round got to her. "I hit the ball so well ... gave myself a lot of good looks at birdie, and I couldn't get a putt to go in," she said. She hit only seven of 13 fairways, but all 18 greens in regulation, and yet needed 34 putts.

It all changed in the fourth round. She birdied the third, then scorched her way into the turn — an eagle at the par-five seventh on a 25-foot putt and birdies at the eighth and ninth. She bogeyed the par-three 11th out of a bunker, then birdied 12, 17 and 18.

"Honestly, I didn't change anything, I didn't do anything different," Lewis said. "But once you see putts going in, it's kind of contagious."

Kingsmill Championship

Williamsburg, Virginia

Winner: Lizette Salas

It's hard enough for a golfer trying to break through to her first win, but running afoul of the first hole in the final round borders on overload. That was the case of Lizette Salas in the Kingsmill Championship in May, chasing that first win in her third full year on the LPGA Tour.

She entered the final round leading by three shots, and at No. 1 she babied her first putt, coming up some 10 feet short. She needed that tough downhill bender to save her par and perhaps her composure, as well. With the calm of a veteran, she dropped it.

"Yeah, that was a big putt just to start off the day," Salas said. "I knew how important that was for me, mentally, and [from] a confidence standpoint." From there, Yani Tseng, Lexi Thompson, et al., were chasing a front-runner who seemed to have found herself.

Salas was in control of her game. Shooting the par-71 River course in 67-68-65-71, she went from No. 3 in the second round for 30 holes without a bogey, playing the string 12 under. The stretch included the third-round 65 that put her three ahead going into the final round. Once successfully past the crisis of the first hole, she all but locked up the tournament with birdies at the third and fifth. The only threat was minor. Tseng, who hadn't won since 2012, made three quick birdies coming in but took a double bogey at the 18th for a 69 and a tie for second with Thompson (69) and Sara Jane Smith (66). Salas bogeyed the eighth and 17th, closed with a 71, a 13-under 271 and a four-stroke win.

Salas had flirted with victory several times, and came to the realization she had to change her approach.

"I felt like I wanted to be perfect all the time," Salas said. "I felt like I needed to play like a top-tier golfer every week. That's not it. It's about feeling confident. I just tried to have fun this week."

Airbus LPGA Classic

Mobile, Alabama

Winner: Jessica Korda

The tournament came down to a simple problem for Jessica Korda. "Charley was birdieing, Michelle was birdieing and everybody behind us was birdieing," Korda offered, "so I knew I had to keep making birdies."

And so she did. A bunch of them, in fact — six on the final nine holes to rocket to a one-shot victory in the Airbus LPGA Classic, becoming the third two-time winner of the year by mid-May. Korda, 21, blistered Magnolia

Grove's back nine with a 30 to close with a seven-under-par 65 that carried her past the rejuvenated Anna Nordqvist, who shot 69. She outran a trio of 67s by two shots — Catriona Matthew, a 44-year-old Scottish mother of two; English teen whiz Charley Hull, and Michelle Wie, winner of the LOTTE Championship a month earlier.

Korda, who took the season-opening Pure Silk Bahamas Classic, this time authored a finish that was one for the books. Shooting 67-67-69, she was three strokes off the lead in each of the three rounds and was still tagging along in the fourth, making only one birdie on the front nine. Then she exploded down the back nine with birdies at Nos. 10, 12, 14, 15, 16 and 18. The birdies at the 10th and 12th pulled her into a six-way tie for the lead, just a stroke ahead of three others. Conservative play wasn't going to work, Korda reasoned. This was a birdie battle. She broke free with a birdie at the 14th, dropping a bending downhill putt, then holed a 25-footer for the lead at the 15th. The other two kept her nose in front. The last, at the 18th, was a gift, a curling 15-foot lag putt that went all the way.

"I was just trying to get it down there close, and it went in," Korda said.

Interestingly enough, Korda had tied for second at 20-under 268 the previous year. She didn't think it would be enough this time. "After the first two days," she said, "I saw how low the scores were, I said, well, maybe 20 under will win." And it did.

ShopRite LPGA Classic

Galloway, New Jersey

Winner: Stacy Lewis

Stacy Lewis birdied twice early in the final round to go up by two strokes, and then went ahead by three with two more birdies through the turn. Even so, she said, she never felt comfortable in the round. But then, there must be something reassuring about a six-shot margin.

That was Lewis' closing number at the ShopRite LPGA Classic in June, her second win of the year, and if the figure seemed familiar, it's because just three weeks earlier she won the North Texas Shootout by six. Lewis posted another significant number with this victory. She jumped to No. 1 in the Rolex Rankings, breaking Inbee Park's 59-week reign.

"It feels great," said Lewis. "I feel like I've played a lot of good consistent golf and ... I deserve to be here." Lewis underlined her claim with a 16-under-par 197 performance, shooting the par-71 Stockton Bay course in 67-63-67 to breeze past a re-emerging Christina Kim. In the first round, Lewis and Michelle Wie were five behind with 67s. Lewis surged to the top in the second round with a bogey-free 63, tying the tournament record of 130 for two rounds. She was leading Kim by a stroke, and talk of her returning to No. 1 heated up.

"I'm tired hearing ... everybody talk about it," Lewis said. "I would like to take care of that here this week." And so she did, but not without some uneasy moments. She entered the final round with a one-stroke lead, then moved up on birdies at the third and fourth holes, then the 10th on a 25-foot putt and the 11th from 15 feet against Kim's three straight birdies from the ninth. Lewis closed with bogey-birdie and eased to the six-shot margin when Kim bogeyed the 15th and double-bogeyed the 18th.

"I haven't been in contention in a while, so I forgot what it was like, having nerves," Kim said.

For Lewis, the subject turned to being No. 1. "I'm definitely just not going to take it for granted, and really enjoy it this time," she said.

Manulife Financial LPGA Classic

Waterloo, Ontario, Canada

Winner: Inbee Park

Seems all it took to sharpen Inbee Park's appetite for golf, to say nothing of her putting touch, was getting evicted from that No. 1 perch in the Rolex Rankings a week ago. After all, sitting in that catbird seat for 59 weeks made it seem like home. Then along came Stacy Lewis, the current occupant.

Park dominated the LPGA Tour in 2013, winning six tournaments, three of them majors. The last of them was the U.S. Women's Open in June, and then she fell winless for almost a full year. Come the Manulife Financial LPGA Classic early in June, it all clicked again.

"It sure felt longer than a year," Park said, marking her return with three solid rounds that kept her in the hunt — 69-66-65 — then erupting for a 10-under-par 61 and a 23-under 261 total for a three-stroke victory over a baffled Cristie Kerr. Kerr checked the scoreboard coming off the 17th and was stunned to see she was three behind. "Because," she said, "I was seven under for the day." She closed with 63 and a 20-under 264, two better than Shanshan Feng. The field had romped over the Gray Silo course — 70 of the 79 finishers were below par, and the top 23 were double figures.

"You think I'm motivated now?" Park asked, laughing.

Park, who made only one bogey in the entire tournament — that in the first round — trailed by four in the first two rounds, and by two entering the fourth, and then her putter caught fire. She needed just 25 putts in her 61.

"I put my putter behind the ball and it just went in the hole," Park said.

The victory, however, did not restore her to her accustomed No. 1 position. Lewis closed with a 63, shot 15 under and tied for sixth to stay on top by a narrow margin, an encouraging thing with the U.S. Women's Open coming up the next week.

"I just wanted to play well," Lewis said. "Still, even left a few out there today."

U.S. Women's Open

Village of Pinehurst, North Carolina

Winner: Michelle Wie

See Chapter 7.

Walmart NW Arkansas Championship

Rogers, Arkansas
Winner: Stacy Lewis

It's probably just an academic point, but could there be a heavier kind of pressure than when you're trying to please the homefolks? Stacy Lewis — Ohio-born, daughter of Texas, adoptive Arkansan — played three of the toughest rounds of her career in winning the Walmart NW Arkansas Championship.

"It's almost harder for me to play here than it is to play at a major championship," said Lewis. So from the missed four-foot par putt at the second hole of the tournament to the winning seven-foot birdie putt at the last, it was a long struggle for the former All-American at the University of Arkansas.

Lewis, runner-up to Michelle Wie in the U.S. Women's Open the previous week, needed help in this one, and she got it from Wie herself in the final round. Lewis, shooting the par-71 Pinnacle course in 70-66-65, was chasing the leaders all the way. Her outlook was pretty dim when Wie opened with 66-66–132, leaving her four behind entering the final round. Then help arrived. Wie bogeyed three straight from No. 9 and was gone. From there, Lewis had a running battle with teen whiz Lydia Ko and veterans Cristie Kerr and Angela Stanford. Lewis, making her only bogey at the ninth, took the lead with her sixth birdie at the par-four 16th to get to 11 under, then faced a choice: With Ko already in at 11 under, how to play the par-five 18th? She made the wise choice: She laid up, pitched her third to seven feet and holed the downhill putt for a birdie, a 65, a 12-under 201 and a one-stroke win. It was her third win in her last seven starts, and career 11th. Said her pursers, feeling varying degrees of frustration:

Ko (bogey-free 65): 'I don't know how many behind I was at the start, five ... so I'm pretty surprised."

Stanford (two-bogey 67): "So 13 and 14 ... they got me again..."

Kerr (bogey-free 67): "It didn't go wrong, it just didn't go right enough, okay?"

Said Lewis: "It's just really, really special to win here."

Ricoh Women's British Open

Lancashire, England
Winner: Mo Martin

See Chapter 7.

Marathon Classic

Sylvania, Ohio
Winner: Lydia Ko

Lydia Ko won her first professional event at age 14 (as an amateur), became the youngest to win on the LPGA Tour at 15 (still an amateur), turned pro at 16, became a millionaire at 17 on winning the Marathon Classic. And she still couldn't buy a car or take a drink. To celebrate winning her first million?

"I may do one of those teenage things," she said, grinning. "Like getting something electronic."

She had already celebrated in a different way — coming from behind in the final round and firing a clutch wedge shot tight for a birdie on the final hole to edge So Yeon Ryu by a stroke. Playing Highland Meadows in 67-67-70-65, a 15-under 269 total, Ko posted her second win of the season and the fourth on the LPGA Tour (two of them as an amateur).

A 72-yard shot under that kind of pressure is not expected of a 17-year-old. Spectators blocked her view. "But I kind of could tell what happened by the crowd's reaction," she said. They erupted when Ko's wedge shot ended up four feet from the cup. Ryu missed her birdie try from six feet, and Ko made her four-footer for the birdie, a flawless 65 and the win. Kerr dueled Ko most of the day and tied her with a birdie at the 13th, but parred in while Ko birdied two of the last three. "I didn't play 17 and 18 well all week," Kerr said. "You have to take advantage of those holes." She played the two par-fives in one over, Ko and Ryu flawlessly in five under. But Ryu didn't make enough birdies elsewhere.

Ko didn't lead any round till the last. From the start, it looked like Laura Diaz's tournament. She led the first two rounds with 62-69 and shared the third-round lead with Lee-Anne Pace while Ko was climbing the leaderboard. What mattered after that was the allowance Ko's mom gives her from her winnings — $10 per shot under par.

"I guess finishing 15 under," Ko said wryly, "is $150 extra."

International Crown

Owings Mills, Maryland

Winners: Spain

Azahara Munoz put it neatly after Spain, not highly regarded before the matches, won the inaugural International Crown.

"We're so good as a team because we're used to — since we were younger — playing together," Munoz said. "I always played with Belen and Carlota. They were always my foursome partners. It just is so special to be on a team with them."

So Munoz, Belen Mozo, Carlota Ciganda and Beatriz Recari, while they didn't have the individual credentials of, say, the South Koreans or the Americans, put it all together in the complex team format for the first International, played at Caves Valley Golf Club.

Ciganda gave the Spaniards an immediate boost in singles with a surprising 8-and-6 runaway over South Korea's battle-tested Na Yeon Choi. Her win led Spain to a sweep of the four singles matches and the championship.

"Even though we were maybe the underdogs because of the seedings, I knew deep inside that what you need in a team championship is what we have," said Mozo, who clinched the title with a 3-and-2 win over Moriya Jutanugarn of Thailand. "We have always played together, we have always won together. Coming in, we knew we had that advantage over the other teams."

Spain piled up a 7-2-1 record for 15 points to win the tournament, which began on Thursday with 32 players from eight countries playing three days of four-ball competition, then the singles. Sweden was second with 11 points, followed by Korea and Japan, 10 each; Thailand 9, United States 6, Chinese Taipei 4 and Australia 3.

The top-seeded American team — Paula Creamer, Stacy Lewis, Cristie Kerr and Lexi Thompson — shocked their fans by failing to win a single point in the first round. The anticipated showdown between the Americans and the second-seeded Koreans actually took place not for the championship but on Saturday in the wild-card playoff for a berth in the singles. Korea's Inbee Park and So Yeon Ryu beat Americans Lexi Thompson and Cristie Kerr, eliminating the American team from the singles.

Meijer LPGA Classic

Grand Rapids, Michigan

Winner: Mirim Lee

Mirim Lee's English was a bit halting, but her message was clear.

"I nervous 100 percent," she said, able to laugh now. "Because first time playoff in LPGA, so I'm really nervous, but very fun."

What's left to say for a 23-year-old rookie from South Korea who not only scored her first win in the inaugural Meijer LPGA Classic, but did it in a playoff against the formidable Inbee Park, countrywoman and idol.

"Inbee Park is like hero in Korea, so I just long to be her," Lee said.

Idol aside, it was a duel to the finish line. Down the backstretch, Lee bogeyed the 14th and birdied the 15th; Park bogeyed the 14th, and Suzann Pettersen birdied the 15th for a three-way tie. But Pettersen fell out with a bogey at the 16th. Lee parred the last three, and Park the last four and ended up in a tie. Lee shot the par-71 Blythefield in 70-64-67-69, and Park in 66-66-68-70, tied at 14-under 270.

In the playoff, Park, who closed with a 61 to win the Manulife Classic six weeks earlier, found this just wasn't her day. On the first extra hole, the 18th, she nearly holed out her approach. The ball hit both the flagstick and the cup, but rolled 15 feet away. Lee had put her approach 35 feet from the cup. They two-putted for pars. On the second hole, the short, par-four 17th, the long-hitting Lee tried to drive the green but caught a greenside bunker instead. She blasted out to five feet. Park put her approach 15 feet from the cup. Her birdie try lipped out. It was, she said, her problem for the week. "The putter just wasn't there," Park said.

And Lee, whose best previous finish was a tie for second in the Founders Cup, coolly sank her five-footer for the win. The breakthrough victory meant more than status and money to her. It plotted her course. The question was, where would she now play.

"In here I'm very young, but in Korea I'm very old," Lee said, "so I want to play here."

Wegmans LPGA Championship
Pittsford, New York
Winner: Inbee Park

See Chapter 7.

Canadian Pacific Women's Open
London, Ontario, Canada
Winner: So Yeon Ryu

In a tournament that practically rained holes-in-one — there were four — Korea's So Yeon Ryu was enjoying a festival of birdies in the Canadian Pacific Women's Open. She plucked 26 of them, in fact, en route to a nearly unchallenged victory. But there was an aspect to the game that meant even more to her.

"A lot of birdies is still a good sign, but no bogeys is more great sign because it means I play really consistent, and when I was in trouble, I handled it pretty well," Ryu said. "That's my goal — I aim for the bogey-free round all four days."

Ryu nearly pulled it off. She had only three bogeys in the 72 holes at the London Hunt and Country Club — at No. 3 in the third round, and at the 10th and 15th in the fourth. This meant she went the first 38 holes without a bogey, and then 24 more to the second. She was, then, three holes shy of being perfect. And going wire-to-wire, shooting 63-66-67-69, she won in relative comfort with a 265, 23 under par, and did have one regret.

"I'm a bit disappointed I couldn't reach Annika's record," Ryu said. That was Annika Sorenstam's tour record of 27 under.

As blemishes go, that was it for Ryu, winning her third title after the 2011 U.S. Women's Open and the 2012 Jamie Farr Toledo Classic.

Ryu's march to the Canadian Open was not without it's uneasy moments, chief of which came in the final round. She'd started with a four-stroke lead and was up by six going into the final nine. But bogeys at the 10th and 15th cut her lead to one when Na Yeon Choi made the fifth of her five birdies at the 15th. Ryu recovered and birdied the par-five 16th and parred in for a 69 and a two-stroke win on 23-under 265. There was one thing left.

"I've been waiting so long for the champagne," Ryu said, and sure enough, the champagne shower came.

Portland Classic
Portland, Oregon
Winner: Austin Ernst

Mark Ernst's phone rang. It was his daughter, Austin. She wasn't shopping, she didn't have a flat tire. She needed some advice. She was about to score her first win on the LPGA Tour, the Portland Classic, but she had just bogeyed the last two holes and was facing a playoff. Now what?

Austin Ernst, 22, had been a star golfer in college, but this was her second year on the LPGA Tour. Her dad, a PGA professional, knew the situation was about more than just this tournament. This was about a young golfer's nerves and confidence, and perhaps about embarrassment, and could affect her future.

Ernst, who had trailed all the way on three 69s, was playing Columbia Edgewater brilliantly in the final round, with five birdies and a chip-in eagle at the fifth, and was seven under for the day and leading by two with two holes to play. But at the 17th she drove into the trees, and she three-putted the 18th from the fringe for a 67 and a 14-under 274. A playoff looked probable. Two closing bogeys could inflict serious self-doubt in a second-year player trying for her first win. She just had time to call her dad while I.K. Kim and So Yeon Ryu were finishing.

"When I talked to my dad, he said, if you had made those two bogeys anywhere else in the round, nobody would think anything different," Ernst said.

Ryu, who won the Canadian Women's Open the week before, double-bogeyed the 18th out of sand and water, missing the playoff. Kim salvaged par from off the green to tie Ernst.

Dad's reassurance worked. In the playoff, Ernst drove into the fairway, hit a seven-iron approach to 25 feet behind the hole and two-putted, tapping in for the winning par after Kim missed from eight feet, going 0-5 in playoffs.

"I was very confident coming in," Ernst said. "Coming down the stretch, I was very proud of how I handled everything."

A quick call to dad helped. And it completed the family theme when Ernst then hugged her caddie — her brother.

Evian Championship

Evians-les-Bains, France

Winner: Hyo-Joo Kim

See Chapter 7.

Yokohama Tire LPGA Classic

Prattville, Alabama

Winner: Mi Jung Hur

From where Mi Jung Hur stood, the Yokohama Tire LPGA Classic was starting to look a whole lot better. She had, after all, just birdied the 16th and was four shots up on Rolex No. 1 Stacy Lewis with two holes to play. "The last two holes," Hur said, "I really enjoyed the golf."

This was the Hur-Lewis shootout, a battle between a little-known South Korean, age 24, who won once, as a rookie in 2009, and a three-time winner already this season. For added dramatic flavor, throw in South African rookie Paula Reto, 24, who moved to the United States and took up golf when she couldn't find a good field hockey game. She had missed the cut in 11 of her 18 starts.

Fittingly, Lewis and Hur tied for the first-round lead with bogey-free 64s at the Capitol Hill-Senator course, Lewis birdieing five of her last six holes, and Hur making four birdies on each side. Reto jumped into the fight in the second round, birdieing five of six holes on her front nine, fueling a 66 and a three-stroke lead on Hur (70) and going four up on Lewis (71). "Just trying to stay patient and not think too much," said Reto. The third round ended with Hur (67) and Reto (70) tied for the lead, and Lewis (70) four behind.

The final round seemed almost scripted for Hur. Reto was sidetracked by a 73, but had her best finish yet, a solo third place. Lewis kept the pressure on Hur. She made four birdies in a six-hole stretch from No. 3 to close to within two. She added birdies at the 10th and 13th and shot 66. She'd hoped to make a few more. "To give her something to think about," Lewis said. Hur faltered only once, with a bogey at the seventh. But from the ninth, she raced off for five birdies across eight holes for her own 66 and the four-stroke win with a 21-under 267.

She had discovered the secret. "I just played my own game," Hur said.

Reignwood LPGA Classic

Nankou, Beijing, China

Winner: Mirim Lee

There were those who remember Mirim Lee's words on her first win, in the Meijer LPGA Classic in August. "I nervous 100 percent," she said. All she had to do was beat her formidable countrywoman, Inbee Park, in a playoff. And now at the Reignwood LPGA Classic in Beijing in October, Lee noted: "I was a lot more nervous this time." Little wonder. This time, trailing all the way, Lee not only had to hold off Park, No. 3 in the world, but also had to overhaul No. 1 Stacy Lewis and Caroline Hedwall. It was a pretty good week's work for a rookie.

Lee wasn't exactly stumbling around the par-73 Reignwood Pine Valley course. Lewis birdied five of her last seven holes for a 66 and led by one in the first round. Lee (70) was four behind. Lewis held the halfway lead with a 68, two up on Brittany Lang. Lee (68) was still four back. Then trouble popped up for Lewis. After making just one bogey in the first two rounds, Lewis started the third with three straight. "...But I was able to finish off the round really well," she said, rallying for a 72 and a tie with Hedwall (68) at 13 under, two ahead of Lee (70).

But Lewis couldn't get untracked in the windy final round. After a one-under front nine, she bogeyed the 10th, 14th and 17th and shot 75, tying for sixth. Park, three back to start, was erratic until the final nine, then birdied the 13th, 16th and 18th, falling short with a 71, tying for third. Hedwall also labored. She logged two birdies and two bogeys through the 10th, then parred in for a 73–279, finishing second by two.

Lee made up her two-stroke deficit in a hurry, with three birdies through No. 8. A bogey at the 12th slowed her, then birdies at Nos. 16 and 18 gave her a 69, a 15-under 277 and a two-stroke win, just two months after her first.

Said Lee, once her nerves had settled: "I really didn't think I would get my second win this quickly."

Sime Darby LPGA Malaysia

Kuala Lumpur, Malaysia

Winner: Shanshan Feng

In the peculiar way golf so often works, failure produced success for China's Shanshan Feng. A week earlier, in the Reignwood LPGA Classic at Beijing, Feng was both the defending champion and a huge local favorite. But she tied for 49th. Next, in the Sime Darby LPGA Malaysia, she didn't expect much of herself.

"I think that's what I actually do very often," Feng said. "Like, when I win, I'm usually not leading after the first and second rounds. I like to come from behind. I had no pressure at all today."

This was not to suggest that she hung back for the first three rounds. Posting rounds of 67-67-69, Feng trailed successively by two, three and then by four shots going into the final round. At this point, the prime challengers were out of the way. Rolex No. 1 Stacy Lewis was not a factor. She took the first-round lead with at 65, six under par at the par-71 Kuala Lumpur Golf and Country Club, then slipped back into the field, where she would eventually tie for 21st. South Korea's So Yeon Ryu led at the halfway point with 65 and 11-under 131. But she closed with a pair of double bogeys in the third round and shot 72, and finished tied for third. And Thailand's Pornanong Phatlum birdied six of her first nine holes, shot 65–199 and led Japan's Ayako Uehara by three going into the finale. Phatlum couldn't keep pace, doubled-bogeyed the par-three 15th, and would finish 15-inder 269 — finding herself second behind Feng, who had already posted a 63 for an 18-under 266 and a three-stroke win.

It was Feng's fourth tour victory, but the first since the CME Group late in 2013. Feng birdied the fourth and seventh, exploded on the back nine for four straight birdies from the 11th, then eagled the par-five 16th for a bogey-free 63.

"What I was doing was just to focus on every shot," Feng said. "And just try to do my best. And hope that putts can fall. That's all I did."

LPGA KEB - HanaBank Championship

Incheon, South Korea

Winner: Kyu Jung Baek

It turned out Kyu Jung Baek was aiming a bit low.

"Going into the final nine, my goal was to come into the top five," she was saying. It was an understandably prudent ambition. Baek was only 19 and making her first start in an LPGA tournament. And then she was hoisting her first trophy, taking the LPGA KEB - HanaBank Championship — co-sanctioned by the U.S. and Korean LPGA tours — with a birdie on the first hole of a three-way playoff.

Posting scores of 74-69-68, Baek came from behind to tie for the third-round lead. In the fourth, she was even par through the 10th and in danger of getting overrun by Brittany Lincicome and In Gee Chun.

"So I concentrated on every hole and I started to make some birdies," Baek said. Indeed: Baek rang up five straight from the 11th, parred out for a 67 for a 10-under 278 total at the Sky 72 Golf Club, tying with Lincicome and Chun, who closed with a 66s. Lincicome had no bogeys, Chun just one. In the playoff at the par-five 18th, Baek and Lincicome put their third shots about four feet from the cup, while Chun's chances disappeared into the water beside the green. Lincicome missed her birdie, but Baek made hers for the win. She'd seen the putt before, in the KLPGA Championship.

"I was in a similar situation for a similar shot with a similar break," Baek said. "I was focused and was aggressive."

Of the three, only Baek was among the leaders over the first three rounds, and then only in the third. Haeji Kang (67) led by two in the first round, and France's Karine Icher led by one after 36 holes.

Baek became the fourth teenager to win on the LPGA Tour this season, after Lexi Thompson, Lydia Ko and Hyo Joo Kim.

Rolex No. 2 Inbee Park could have regained the throne with a win in the absence of No. 1 Stacy Lewis, but finished fourth. No. 3 Lydia Ko finished 29th. Suzann Pettersen, who had won the tournament three times, tied for 12th.

Blue Bay LPGA

Hainan Island, China

Winner: Lee-Anne Pace

South Africa's Lee-Anne Pace, 33, was nervously playing the final hole, the par-five 18th. Edgy but controlled, she hit her third shot to the green and saw the ball come to rest. And then she finally allowed herself a big smile. Her ball was sitting five feet from a birdie, and all she needed was a par to win. The inaugural Blue Bay LPGA, on Hainan Island, China, was about to become her first LPGA Tour victory.

"When I hit the ball quite close," said Pace, "I thought, 'All right. It's good now. You can enjoy this.'"

Pace holed the birdie putt, completing a card of 67-66-67–200, 16 under par at Blue Bay Golf Course, winning by three over Germany's Caroline Masson. Winning itself was nothing new to Pace. She'd scored her ninth Ladies European Tour victory just a week earlier.

"I looked back at last week and how I actually played better towards the end," Pace said. "So I thought, just do the same thing." Even so, she had her uneasy moments, and none worse than Masson's closing rush.

The tournament was battered by heavy rains, forcing officials to reduce it from 72 to 54 holes and sending the finish into Monday morning. Pace shared the lead entering the final round and was up by four when darkness ended play Sunday. The pressure came Monday morning, when Masson birdied four of the last six holes and the last three in a row for a 67 and the clubhouse lead.

"I saw Caroline making a move, but I said to myself, 'You're far ahead — come on,'" Pace said.

"I tried everything I could," Masson said.

Pace, who played the last 32 holes without a bogey, birdied Nos. 4, 5, 7 and 12 and led by two coming to No. 18, and knew the comfort of sticking her approach in tight. The birdie gave her a three-stroke win.

Said Pace, the second South African, after Sally Little, to win on the LPGA Tour: "I can't actually believe it. Now I can relax."

Fubon LPGA Taiwan Championship

Chinese Taipei

Winner: Inbee Park

It was either married life or the return to Rolex No. 1, but something agreed with Inbee Park.

She tore through Miramar Golf Club, leading wire-to-wire, to take the Fubon LPGA Taiwan Championship, in which the closest calls she had were a tie for the lead in the first round and some pressure from Stacy Lewis in the fourth that cut her winning margin to two strokes. She logged 24 birdies and two eagles against six bogeys, posting her third win of the year and 12th on the tour.

"I think this will be my wedding gift for myself," said Park, beaming after touring Miramar in 64-62-69-71–266, 22 under par. "It's a good feeling, and maybe people who said, 'She's not going to play as well as when she was not married' — I think we can put that wrong."

Park regained the top spot in the Rolex Rankings on Monday, and on Thursday began celebrating with a first-round 64, tying for the lead with Shanshan Feng. Park began her surge with five birdies over her last seven holes. "I can't remember the last time I putted like this," she said.

Park thought the unthinkable during her second-round 62 — shooting 59. That was shortly after she played the first eight holes in six under, including a hole-out eagle from 82 yards at the par-four eighth. "Yeah, definitely thought it was possible going into 13," she said. She led by three through the second round, then four through the third, over Lewis and Feng. Feng blew to a 76 in the final round, leaving the last challenge to Lewis, whom Park had replaced at No. 1 just six days earlier.

Park cooled to a 71 in the light rain, and Lewis made up some ground with a 69. "I don't think this will be the last time we'll be battling at the end," Lewis said.

"If she had beat me it would have been really tough today," Park said. "But I think being able to play good and under pressure, that gives me a lot of confidence."

Mizuno Classic

Shima, Mie, Japan

Winner: Mi Hyang Lee

See Japan LPGA Tour section.

Lorena Ochoa Invitational

Mexico City, Mexico
Winner: Christina Kim

It seemed that the spirited Christina Kim, 30, was about to be denied again. She had come to the Lorena Ochoa Invitational in mid-November having gone nine years and 221 starts without winning. But then victory finally was right at her fingertips. She had led from the start and arrived to the final round with high hopes and the luxury of a five-stroke lead. And then it disappeared.

In the final round, Chinese star Shanshan Feng caught fire just as Kim slipped into some shaky play. Kim gave herself quite a lecture. "Lots of expletives," she said, laughing.

They tied at 15-under 273, then Kim went on to beat Feng with a tap-in par on the second playoff hole. "This," Kim said, "is the greatest win of my life."

For a golfer so unaccustomed to the heat of the chase — she had won twice, once each in 2004 and 2005 — Kim was nothing but strong against a star-packed field of 36 in the no-cut event at Club de Golf Mexico, leading wire-to-wire on 65-69-68-71. And with the cream of the tour chasing her — Inbee Park, Stacy Lewis, whiz-kid Lydia Ko and all the rest.

But the fates had one more test for Kim. In the final round, she was even-par on the front with two birdies and two bogeys, while Feng picked up two strokes on her with an eagle, a birdie and a bogey. Kim then turned erratic coming home. While Feng was scattering four birdies, Kim birdied the 10th and 13th, slipped into a tie with bogeys at the 14th and 15th, and followed them with two birdies to regain the lead. At the 18th, she had a three-foot par putt for the win, but missed.

"My brain just didn't work right," she said.

On the second playoff hole, Feng bogeyed after hitting her tee shot close to a tree. Kim two-putted from 20 feet. At last, she had her win.

"I can't put into words how I'm feeling right now," Kim said. "I can't explain. I'm so overwhelmed right now."

CME Group Tour Championship

Naples, Florida
Winner: Lydia Ko

The CME Group Tour Championship was a kind of graduation for the precocious Lydia Ko. She'd already had a great rookie year, but at age 17 she really came of age in the LPGA Tour's rousing season finale. And what kind of graduation presents did she receive? Well, first, she couldn't drink champagne but she got showered with it. Then she got two beautiful crystal trophies. And then she got $1.5 million. And she never saw it coming.

Early in the week, Ko posed for a picture with a glass case full of cash. "I was like 'Wow, I wonder who the winner of that will be?'" she said.

With a field of 69, this no-cut finale was actually two tournaments in one — the Tour Championship, with a $500,000 first prize, and the inaugural

Race to the CME Globe, a $1 million bonus based on points accumulated through the season. Ko won both for the richest single payday in tour history. Oddly enough, she won the bonus before she won the tournament.

Nine players came into the CME with a mathematical chance to win the bonus. Without realizing it, Ko locked it up when she finished tied for first on 71-71-68-68–278, 10 under at the par-72 Ritz-Carlton Tiburon Golf Club. Ko trailed through the first three rounds, then shot a flawless 68 to catch Carlota Ciganda (70) and Julieta Granada (71). In the playoff, at the tough par-four 18th, Granada went out on the second playing with a three-putt bogey. Ciganda missed a winning five-foot birdie putt on the third playing. On the fourth, Ciganda watered her approach and Ko two-putted for a par and her third win of the season, becoming the first rookie to top $2 million.

Then the matter of a kid being a millionaire golfer came up.

"The great thing about my friends is most of them don't play golf," Ko said. "We don't talk about golf. That's what I really love. I feel like I can get off the course … and just be that teenager."

Which, at 17, she was.

Ladies European Tour

ISPS Handa New Zealand Women's Open
Christchurch, New Zealand
Winner: Mi Hyang Lee

See Australian Ladies Tour section.

Volvik RACV Ladies Masters
Queensland, Australia
Winner: Cheyenne Woods

See Australian Ladies Tour section.

ISPS Handa Women's Australian Open
Victoria, Australia
Winner: Karrie Webb

See Australian Ladies Tour section.

Mission Hills World Ladies Championship
Haikou, Hainan, China
Winner: Inbee Park

Inbee Park claimed her first victory of 2014 and gained revenge for her defeat to Suzann Pettersen the previous year when the world No. 1 won the Mission Hills World Ladies Championship by five strokes on the Blackstone course at the Mission Hills Haikou resort in Hainan, China. A fascinating duel between the top two players in the women's game fizzled out with the weather on the last day as Park closed with a six-under-par 67 to Pettersen's 72.

The Norwegian, who won by a stroke over Park in 2013, led for the first two rounds after scores of 67 and 68. She then added a 66 in the third round but was caught by Park's course-record 62. The 11-under effort, which included six birdies in a row from the ninth hole, matched the record on the Ladies European Tour, as did her inward half of seven under. Birdies at the first two holes on a rainy final day put Park ahead, and though Pettersen's birdie at the ninth and Park's bogey at the 10th meant the gap was down to one shot, the Korean responded with birdies at the 11th, 12th, 15th and 18th holes. "I knew that I left something out there last year, so coming back this year I definitely wanted to win," Park said.

Park finished on a 24-under-par total of 268 and led Korea to the team prize along with So Yeon Ryu, who was third in the individual event. They finished on 40 under par, 28 strokes ahead of China. Australian 17-year-old Minjee Lee shared fifth place, alongside Thailand's Ariya Jutanugarn, to win the amateur prize.

Lalla Meryem Cup

Agadir, Morocco
Winner: Charley Hull

Four days before her 18th birthday, Charley Hull claimed her maiden victory on the Ladies European Tour after the English teenager defeated Gwladys Nocera in a playoff to win the Lalla Meryem Cup at Golf de l'Ocean in Agadir. Hull never led during regulation play, scoring a final round of 62 with seven birdies and an eagle to set the target at 269, 15 under par. Nocera, who took the 54-hole lead with a 65 in the third round, was in front for the entire final day until the Frenchwoman three-putted the final hole for a bogey, her first since the eighth hole on Saturday. It meant a 67 and a playoff, as the pair finished four shots ahead of Sophie Giquel-Bettan.

At the par-three 18th, Hull hit a four iron to four feet, and after Nocera missed her birdie attempt from 15 feet, Hull rolled in the winning putt. She had missed a chance from 10 feet at the 18th in regulation but made no mistake in the playoff. "I never backed down," she said. "I finished birdie, birdie, par, which was nearly a birdie at the last, but I got there, I got my first win while I was still 17. I'm 18 next week so I'm really happy."

Hull opened her LET career in 2013 with five runner-up finishes, the first coming in the same event in Morocco. She went on to win the Rookie of the Year award and become the youngest-ever player in the Solheim Cup. The trophy presentation was made at the Royal palace as Hull lined up alongside Alejandro Canizares, winner of the Trophee Hassan II.

Turkish Airlines Ladies Open

Belek, Antalya, Turkey
Winner: Valentine Derrey

After the second round of the Turkish Airlines Ladies Open, Klara Spilkova said: "I really don't feel pressure, so pressure: what does it mean?" The 18-year-old from Prague found out on the final day when her overnight lead, which she extended from one stroke to four with two birdies in her first three holes, disappeared with a closing 78 at the National Golf Club in Antalya.

It will have been an invaluable, if unhappy, experience for the Czech, and instead it was the 26-year-old Valentine Derrey who came from three strokes behind to win for the first time on the Ladies European Tour. A previous victory on the Symetra Tour in America held the Parisian in good stead as she closed with a 70 for a seven-under-par total of 212.

Conditions were tricky all week with the second day washed out and the tournament reduced to three rounds. Derrey collected four birdies and dropped only one shot on the par-73 layout and parred in from the 14th for a two-stroke victory over Malene Jorgensen, who recovered from a bogey and a double bogey in the first three holes for a 73. Charley Hull was pushing for a second successive win when she birdied the 14th and 15th holes but dropped at the 16th to end her challenge.

"I tried to do my best and keep believing I could win," Derrey said. "I just learned to keep patient and play my own game, and that's what I've been working on mentally.

Deloitte Ladies Open

Amsterdam, Netherlands

Winner: Kylie Walker

Kylie Walker led after each of the first two rounds of the Deloitte Ladies Open but needed a playoff to claim her maiden title. The 27-year-old Scot from Glasgow, in her fifth year on the Ladies European Tour, was two shots ahead of the field after each of her first two rounds of 69 and 72. She closed with another 72 after parring the last 11 holes and missing a 10-footer for a birdie on the last that would have given her victory. Malene Jorgensen produced a six-under-par 67 to set the clubhouse target at 213, six under par, and Nikki Campbell, who led for much of the final day after five birdies in her first eight holes, joined the mark after three-putting the 15th.

The trio all parred the first extra hole and then on the 18th again it was Walker who holed from 20 feet for a birdie and the victory. "Amazing, absolutely brilliant. I'm delighted," said Walker. "I've been in playoffs to get in the British Open and U.S. Open but not to win on the LET. I was just really trying to win and I kept giving myself chances and not quite making the putts, although I did putt quite well. A lot of them looked good and didn't go in, so I'm delighted to win in the end."

Allianz Ladies Slovak Open

Brezno, Tale, Slovakia

Winner: Camilla Lennarth

Camilla Lennarth's birthday wish was to see a bear at the Grey Bear club at Golf Resort Tale in the Low Tatras Mountains. The Swede from Stockholm turned 26 on the Monday of the Allianz Ladies Slovak Open and the nearest she got to a bear was when she was handed the trophy at the end of the week. Her first victory, in her third year as a professional, came by four strokes over England's Melissa Reid, with Hannah Ralph and Sally Watson four shots further back.

Watson had led at the halfway stage after rounds of 69 and 67, with Lennarth six behind, but on a windy third day Watson's 75 and Lennarth's 69 meant the pair were tied at the top of the leaderboard. There was then an eight-shot swing as the Scot opened the final round with a bogey and a double bogey on the way to a 74, while Lennarth closed with a 66 for an 11-under total of 277. She had four birdies, including at the first and then three on the back nine, and holed a brilliant chip for an eagle at the ninth.

Reid, who claimed her best finish since her win at the Pilsen Masters two years ago following the death of her mother in a car accident in Germany, got within two shots after three birdies in four holes from the 11th. She closed with a 67, but Lennarth birdied the 15th and 18th holes to pull away again.

"I really like this place and hopefully next time I'll see a bear because that's what I've been talking about all week," she said.

Ladies Italian Open

Perugia, Italy

Winner: Florentyna Parker

An extra bottle of champagne left over from her 25th birthday celebrations the week before came in handy when Florentyna Parker won the Ladies Italian Open in the most spectacular fashion. Parker, whose caddie is her mother Gina, found the perfect time to make her first ever albatross at the 14th hole at Perugia as she claimed a one-stroke victory over Holly Clyburn.

One under for the day after a birdie at the 12th, Parker thought she might need three more birdies, but they all came on the same hole, the 427-yard 14th where she holed her six-iron shot from 167 yards. "I had two pars there the first two days which felt like a bogey, because it's such a short hole. My mum said, 'You need to make a birdie,' and I holed the shot, so I said, 'Are you happy now?' I was three under for three days on that hole which is good. I have some champagne left over from my birthday last week and I kept saying, 'we need to drink it,' and so I will!"

Parker got up and down from behind the 18th green for a 68 and, after previous rounds of 69 and 72, a seven-under total of 209. Clyburn was second after a 70, one ahead of Rebecca Hudson, who shared the 36-hole lead with Clyburn. Local favorite Diana Luna took fourth place behind the English 1-2-3. It was Parker's second victory on the LET after she won the 2010 Deloitte Open.

"It's been too long," she said. "My grandpa is Italian, so it was actually the perfect week."

ISPS Handa Ladies European Masters

Denham, Buckinghamshire, England

Winner: I.K. Kim

I.K. Kim won for the first time in four years thanks to the inspiration of her caddie for the week at the ISPS Handa Ladies European Masters. Kim, who crossed the Atlantic after an uninspired season on the LPGA Tour, engaged the services of LET caddie Gerald Adams, who a year earlier had missed the tournament while undergoing treatment for prostrate cancer.

During the Wednesday pro-am, Adams had his nose broken by an errant shot but still turned up for duties the next morning. "It's amazing that he was caddying for me on Thursday, because he got hit by a golf ball on Wednesday and was bleeding everywhere. His attitude towards living and daily life is inspiring to me and many people on the tour," said Kim.

After rounds of 71 and 68, Kim did not drop a shot at The Buckinghamshire over the weekend. On Saturday she equaled the course record with a 63 to take a four-stroke lead. She birdied the first two holes in the final round, added two more by the eighth and then parred her way to a five-stroke victory. She closed with a 68 for an 18-under-par total of 270. "This is my first time playing the course, so I'm really honored to win the championship," Kim said.

Nikki Campbell, who had two eagles in her closing 67, finished as runner-up, while two shots further back were Caroline Masson, Lee-Anne Pace and Stephanie Meadow. The Northern Irishwoman was playing in only her second event as a professional and matched her third-place finish at the U.S. Women's Open at Pinehurst by matching the course record with her own nine-birdie 63 on Sunday.

Ricoh Women's British Open

Lancashire, England
Winner: Mo Martin

See Chapter 7.

Ladies German Open

Worthsee, Germany
Winner: Kylie Walker

After three days of record scoring with birdies aplenty, it was eventually a par on the first playoff hole that brought a second victory of the season for Kylie Walker in the Ladies German Open. The 27-year-old from Glasgow beat Charley Hull after the Englishwoman drove into the trees at the 18th hole and had to chip back to the fairway. While Walker found the green in two and two-putted, Hull missed her five-footer to extend the playoff. It was a putt of a similar length on the 17th in regulation that had finally brought Hull even with the Scot after making up a six-shot deficit after 54 holes.

Walker opened with three scores of eight-under 64, equaling the LET 36-hole scoring record on 128 and setting a new record for 54 holes of 24-under 192. Hull and Yu Yang Zhang also had 64s on the first round, while Hull added another on day three before closing with a 65. Birdies at each of the first three holes and a bogey from Walker at the third cut the deficit to two strokes, but it was only at the 17th that the pair were level. Walker closed with a 71 to tie on 25-under-par 263. Defending champion Carlota Ciganda finished third, two strokes outside the playoff.

"Charley played brilliantly today because it was slightly tougher conditions as well," said Walker, who won the Deloitte Open in May. "I wasn't quite playing as well as I have done the rest of the week, but I'm delighted to have hung in there today and get the win. I'm just living the dream at the moment."

Sberbank Golf Masters

Prague, Czech Republic

Winner: Julie Greciet

Three years after she finished runner-up in the same tournament, Julie Greciet won her maiden title at the Sberbank Golf Masters at Golf Park Plzen in Dysina in the Czech Republic. The 27-year-old from Biarritz won by two strokes over Lee-Anne Pace and by three over Amy Boulden, who improved on her best result of fourth from the previous week.

Greciet took the lead after 36 holes with scores of 66 and 64 before closing with another 66 for a 17-under-par total of 196. Boulden, the rookie from Wales, made five birdies in the first six holes to catch the leader briefly, but Greciet responded with five birdies in seven holes from the ninth. A thunderstorm interrupted play for an hour, and although Pace, who was playing with Boulden, birdied the last two holes, Greciet could afford a bogey at the last. Pace had eight birdies but a double bogey at the eighth, while Boulden's only bogey came at the 14th, but she stalled from then on as she matched Pace's 65. Anne-Lise Caudal closed with a 62 to grab a share of fourth place.

Greciet, who had been recovering from surgery to remove a cyst on her wrist in February, said: "It's crazy because I didn't think it was possible to win this year and I'm very, very happy. I want to thank my caddie, who is my father, and my family and my boyfriend for supporting me this year."

Aberdeen Asset Management Ladies Scottish Open

East Lothian, Scotland

Winner: Trish Johnson

Trish Johnson became the oldest-ever winner on the Ladies European Tour when she claimed the Aberdeen Asset Management Ladies Scottish Open. The 48-year-old finished two clear of former winner Gwladys Nocera to eclipse Laura Davies, who was 47 when she won the Indian Open in 2010. It was four years since Johnson's last win, but she notched up a 19th tour victory in her 28th season despite almost withdrawing before the start. She had not practiced for a week prior to the tournament due to a back injury and only teed up after intensive treatment from the tour osteopath and masseuse.

"I wasn't expecting this, I'm chuffed to bits," Johnson admitted. "I had very low expectations and I guess that worked for me. I didn't have a practice round and I didn't play until Friday morning and probably played one of the best rounds of my life on Friday."

In poor conditions on the opening day, Johnson birdied the first three holes on the way to a 66 on the Fidra course at Archerfield Links and a three-stroke lead. She led by six after a second-round 70, but despite the fine weather on the last day she struggled to a 73 for a seven-under-par total of 209. She pulled her drive into a gorse bush at the seventh and took a double-bogey-seven but still had plenty of shots in hand. Nocera birdied the last for a 69 to take second place by one over Rebecca Artis and Stephanie Na.

"I just didn't putt as well as the first two days, but I didn't have the same mentality," Johnson said. "I suppose that was because I was defending a little bit."

Helsingborg Open

Helsingborg, Skane, Sweden
Winner: Dewi Claire Schreefel

Dewi Claire Schreefel produced an impressive wire-to-wire performance in the Helsingborg Open to win her maiden title on the Ladies European Tour by seven strokes. The only previous professional victory for the 28-year-old from the Netherlands came on the U.S. Futures Tour in 2009. In Sweden she tied for the lead with an opening 67 and then stayed clear of the field with further scores of 70, 68 and 66 to finish on a total of 271, 17 under par.

Schreefel began the final round with a two-stroke advantage over defending champion Rebecca Artis, and three birdies in a row from the fifth extended her lead despite a couple of bogeys on the front nine. Artis never gave up, however, and produced four birdies in five holes at the start of the back nine. But Schreefel responded again and five birdies for an inward 31 produced a runaway victory. Artis closed with a 71 to finish one ahead of Dame Laura Davies with Valentine Derrey in fourth place.

"It's a good way to win," Schreefel said. "Rebecca had a good chase on and I was glad to be playing well to keep up with her and I can't find a better way to win that this. I've been a pro for five years and every year has got better, but I felt like this year it was going to come. All the elements came together."

Evian Championship

Evians-les-Bains, France
Winner: Hyo-Joo Kim

See Chapter 7.

Tenerife Open de Espana Femenino

Tenerife, Spain
Winner: Connie Chen

A week practicing on the Canary island prior to the tournament and a new attitude to working with her father as her caddie helped Connie Chen to her maiden victory at the Tenerife Open de Espana at Costa Adeja. The 21-year-old born in Pretoria, in South Africa, but based in China since early in 2014, won by two strokes over local favorite Carlota Ciganda, with Beth Allen and Charley Hull in third and fourth places.

Chen, in her fourth year on tour, had missed seven cuts in 12 events in 2014 but had her best finish of seventh at the Sberbank Masters. A new relaxed approach was the key. "We worked really well this week, a little different to our usual disagreements on the golf course," Chen said of her father, Hong. "We just discussed that there are some things that work, with him being my father and us being so close, and some things that we need to get a little bit of distance in the relationship and chill out. He wants me to do so well, but he was able to let go of that and let me play my own game this week."

Chen had scores of 68, 70, 69 and 69 for a 12-under-par total of 276. She started the final round tied with Welsh rookie Amy Boulden, who led briefly on a fine but breezy day before a double bogey at the seventh. Four more bogeys followed for Boulden as she slipped to 10th place with a 75. Chen holed a 30-footer for an eagle at the 13th to go four clear, a gap that only closed with Ciganda's birdie at the 17th in her 69, and Chen's bogey at the last.

Lacoste Ladies Open de France

Saint-Jean-de-Luz, Aquitaine, France

Winner: Azahara Munoz

Azahara Munoz emerged from a Spanish shootout for the Lacoste Ladies Open de France to retain the title she won at Chantaco in 2013. Munoz was playing in a final three-ball that also included Carlota Ciganda and Maria Hernandez, who had led for the first three days. Hernandez led by four at the start of the final round and was still in front by three at the turn, but bogeys at the 10th, 13th and 16th suddenly opened up the tournament.

Although Munoz also bogeyed the 10th, she then found her touch on the greens, making good par putts on the next four holes and then birdieing three of the last four holes. Munoz had scores of 67, 68, 67 and 67 for an 11-under-par total of 269 to win by one over Hernandez, who followed rounds of 65, 67 and 66 with a closing 72, and Amy Boulden.

Boulden, the Welsh rookie, had a double bogey at the third hole, as did Munoz, but bounced back with four birdies in a row from the fifth and two more on the back nine. Boulden's 66 set the target at 10 under, and Munoz gave herself the chance of a playoff by holing from eight feet at the 17th and then won with a 10-footer at the last.

"I just love this place," said the 26-year-old Munoz after her third win on the LET. "I've been playing well all week, but putts weren't dropping, and so I guess it was my time."

Cell C South African Women's Open

Hibiscus Coast, South Africa

Winner: Lee-Anne Pace

Lee-Anne Pace won her national title for the first time with a playoff victory at the Cell C South African Women's Open at San Lameer. Pace defeated Holly Clyburn at the second extra hole for her ninth LET victory and first of the season. The 33-year-old from Mossel Bay started the final round four strokes behind Leigh Whittaker, while Clyburn was one behind. A birdie at the first hole put the Englishwoman in front, while Whittaker, from Germany, fell away with a 75.

Clyburn also birdied the 13th but otherwise made 16 pars, allowing Pace to catch her on the back nine. Turning one under for the day, Pace hit a five wood to 20 feet on the 13th and made the putt for an eagle before birdie-ing the 16th and 18th holes. The pair tied on five-under-par 211 with Pace having scores of 71, 73 and 67, while Clyburn closed with a 70. Gwladys Nocera was third, two behind. In the playoff both missed chances from 10 feet at the 18th, but playing the same hole again Clyburn found the water with her second shot while Pace hit a wedge to three feet and made a birdie.

Play was suspended on the first afternoon with Charley Hull taking the first-round lead the next morning with a 68 before starting the second round which was then cancelled due to a waterlogged course. The second round was played on Saturday with the tournament reduced to 54 holes.

Sanya Ladies Open

Sanya, China

Winner: Xi Yu Lin

Xi Yu Lin finished ninth as a 14-year-old amateur in the Sanya Ladies Open in 2010 and a year later was fifth on her professional debut. In 2014, aged 18, Lin claimed her first victory in her second season as a member of the Ladies European Tour. It was also her fifth win on the China LPGA Tour and second in a row after winning the previous week's Sanya's Hills Classic.

Lin opened with a 68 and then had two rounds of 67 for a 14-under-par total of 202. She won by five strokes over Charley Hull, who closed with a 69, and by six over Huei Ju Shin and Nikki Campbell. Lin started the final round with a two-stroke lead but at the turn was tied with Yu Yang Zhang. It was her run of birdie-eagle-birdie from the 12th that sealed her victory. Lin holed from 10 feet at the 12th and hit a hybrid from 200 yards to six feet at the next to set up the eagle.

"I think this is the biggest win of my career because it's my first win on the Ladies European Tour," Lin said. "My mum was with me this week and she always brings me good luck, because in 2012 she came to watch me for the first time in two years when I won my first professional career win on the CLPGA. This time she came and I earned my first win on the Ladies European Tour, so I think she's kind of my lucky star."

Xiamen Open

Xiamen, China

Winner: Ssu-Chia Cheng

Ssu-Chia Cheng, a 17-year-old amateur from Taiwan, won the Xiamen Open at Orient in her debut on the Ladies European Tour. She was the sixth amateur to win on the circuit and had previously won three professional events on the Taiwan LPGA Tour. In 2014 she had already claimed silver medals at the Youth Olympics and the Asian Games. Cheng won by three strokes over France's Marion Ricordeau, with Beth Allen and Alexandra Vilatte tying for third place.

After scores of 70 and 68 Cheng was sharing the lead with Spanish Open winner Connie Chen and Chloe Leurquin. Three birdies in the first four holes put Cheng in command and she dropped only one shot in a 68 that left her on a 10-under-par total of 206. Both Chen and Leurquin closed with 76s to fall into a tie for 11th place. Instead, Ricordeau finished with a 69 to claim her best result and pick up the first prize of €37,500, while Cheng was presented with a cake on the 18th green.

"I was pretty nervous today. For the last part my heart was like 'boom, boom, boom,' so I tried to stay calm," Cheng said. "It's the first time I've played in a Ladies European Tour tournament, so I feel it was a challenge to myself and made me play well. I did not have high expectations, I thought it would be a great result if I finished in the top 10. My plan is to turn pro next year. At that time I will try to qualify for the U.S. LPGA Tour and follow Yani Tseng's footprint. She is my idol."

Hero Women's Indian Open

New Delhi, India

Winner: Gwladys Nocera

A course record of nine-under-par 64 at Delhi Golf Club in the first round proved the foundation of a wire-to-wire victory for Gwladys Nocera at the Hero Women's Indian Open. The 39-year-old Frenchwoman went on to a five-stroke victory over Hannah Burke, Fabienne In-Albon and Hyeon Seo Kang.

In warm and calm conditions but on a tight layout lined by trees and featuring peacocks and squirrels among the foliage, Nocera started at the 10th on the first day and had four birdies on the back nine and then five on the front side, including the last three holes. "I felt like I was playing chess, you place the ball and then when you have the opportunity to hit close to the pin, you try your best. You can be offensive on the shot, but not on the strategy."

Nocera led by three strokes and then was two ahead after a second round of 72. A final round of 72 gave Nocera an 11-under-par total of 208. Her margin of victory expanded as her nearest challenger, local Vaishavi Sinha, closed with a 76 to fall to fifth place. Swiss 18-year-old In-Albon made sure of retaining her card in her rookie season with a closing 69 for her best-ever result.

Nocera also won in India in 2008, the year she won the Order of Merit, but did not win again until two victories in 2013. "I've played on tour for 12 years, so experience always helps and it did today," she said. "My putting was not too good, but I stayed patient and it paid off."

Omega Dubai Ladies Masters

Dubai, United Arab Emirates

Winner: Shanshan Feng

Shanshan Feng won the Omega Dubai Ladies Masters for the second time in three years. It was a dominating performance from the 25-year-old Chinese player, who shared the lead on the opening day after a 66 but went five clear with scores of 67 and 66 before a closing 70 completed a five-stroke victory. Her 19-under-par total of 269 was two shy of her own record from 2012.

Feng had three birdies going out to reach 20 under and lead by seven, with 22 under par her target score. But two bogeys coming home scuppered that thought before she added a birdie at the 17th. In 12 rounds on the Majlis course at Emirates she had been over par only once, an opening 76 in 2013, and was 43 under par all together.

"It's my second time to win here, and the staff just told me I'm actually one of the two people that has won twice here, and the other one is Annika [Sorenstam]. So it makes me like feel really proud of myself," Feng said.

Carlota Ciganda birdied the last to pip Caroline Masson for second place, with Anna Nordqvist in fourth. Charley Hull finished tied for fifth and stayed in front of Gwladys Nocera, who was joint 11th, to become the youngest-ever winner of the Order of Merit. The 18-year-old Englishwoman, in her second season as a professional, usurped Laura Davies, who was 22 in 1985. Wales's Amy Boulden was confirmed as the Rookie of the Year ahead of Scotland's Sally Watson.

Japan LPGA Tour

Daikin Orchid Ladies

Nanjo, Okinawa
Winner: O. Sattaya

Onnarin Sattayabanphot, better known in Asian golf as O. Sattaya, validated her reputation on the Japan LPGA Tour when she scored an impressive two-stroke victory in the season-opening Daikin Orchid Ladies, demonstrating that her initial LPGA victory in 2013 was no fluke.

Sattaya, Thailand's first and only winner on the tour, came from two shots off the pace (69-72–141) in the final round at Okinawa's Ryukyu Golf Club with a strong, five-under-par 67, swishing past five others, including Rikako Morita, the defending champion, 2013 leading money winner and the second-round co-leader with Ritsuko Ryu at 139.

Morita looked like a repeat victor in the early going Sunday. She birdied three of the first seven holes, but that is where 30-year-old Sattaya caught fire. She birdied there and at three of the next four holes to surge ahead to stay, parring in after a final birdie at the 14th for the 67 and an eight-under-par 208. Morita finished with a 71 for 210, tying for second with Mamiko Higa, Jiyai Shin and Akaya Watanabe, all with closing 68s, and Airi Saitoh, with a final 69.

Yokohama Tire PRGR Ladies Cup

Kanan, Kochi
Winner: Yuki Ichinose

It took Yuki Ichinose more than five years to land her first title on the Japan LPGA Tour, but just one tournament shy of a single season to get No. 2. Ichinose made up two strokes in the final round and prevailed in a playoff to win the Yokohama Tire PRGR Ladies Cup at Tosa Country Club.

South Korea's Bo-Bae Song rode along in first place for the first two days, tied for the lead with Asako Fujimoto and Mami Fukuda with 69s after the first round and alone at the top at the 36-hole mark with 71–140. Fujimoto shot 72 for 141, and Ichinose (70-72) sat in a five-player group at 142 that also included Miki Sakai and Yun-Jye Wei, who fired 67s; Rumi Yoshiba and Sun-Ju Ahn, twice the tour's leading money winner.

Sunday's final round was quite a scramble well into the back nine. The 25-year-old Ichinose birdied the par-five 15th to take the lead at seven under, then parred in for 67–209. Sakai, a non-winner, matched it moments later to force the playoff as Song (70) and amateur Haruka Morita (67) missed it by a shot. Ichinose ended the overtime quickly when she birdied the first extra hole.

T-Point Ladies

Saga

Winner: Rikako Morita

In the early going of 2014, Rikako Morita made it clear that she had retained the momentum that carried her through her title-winning 2013 season on the JLPGA Tour. Two weeks after she just missed a successful defense of the first of her four 2013 wins in the season-opening Daikin Orchid tournament, Morita rolled to a four-stroke victory in the T-Point Ladies and jumped into second place on the money list.

The 24-year-old standout put together rounds of 69 and 68 the first two days at Wakagi Golf Club at Saga and carried a one-stroke lead into the final round. Erina Hara, an eight-year veteran whose only tour victory came in 2008, occupied the runner-up spot, but neither she nor the others close behind mounted any threat in Sunday's final round.

Even though she managed only a one-over-par 37 on the outgoing nine, Morita was two ahead of Hara at the turn. She was flawless on the back nine, matching Hara's birdies at the 13th and 14th after Hara bogeyed the 11th. Morita posted a 34 for 71 and a final eight-under-par 208, the margin going to four when Hara bogeyed again at the final hole for 74–212. She edged Mami Fukuda and O. Sattaya by a shot.

AXA Ladies

Miyazaki

Winner: Ayaka Watanabe

Who would have thought Ayaka Watanabe would stand as she did in the winner's circle in the AXA Ladies tournament at Miyazaki? After all, she arrived at Miyazaki's UMK Country Club after a blowout 75-79 missed cut the week before in the T-Point tournament. Watanabe's transition from rags to riches came at the expense of Saiki Fujita, who blew a five-stroke lead over the last five holes.

The 20-year-old Watanabe, who had bounced back from her T-Point debacle with a field-leading 66 in the opening round, stood two behind Fujita after Fujita paired 67s the first two days. Also in the picture were Bo-Mee Lee, one of South Korea's finest, and 18-year-old hometown amateur Asuka Kashiwabara at 138.

Things were rosy for quite a while Sunday for Fujita, 28, a 10-year veteran with five victories on her JLPGA Tour record. Then her five-shot lead began to disintegrate. She bogeyed the 14th and 15th; Watanabe birdied the 16th and 17th to close the gap to one and then finished with a spectacular flourish by eagling the par-five 18th for 67–203, winning her first title by two when the shaken Fujita bogeyed that last hole for 71–205. A late bogey put Lee in third place at 207, and the young amateur finished with a 70 for 208.

Yamaha Ladies Open

Fukuroi, Shizuoka

Winner: Sun-Ju Ahn

The contenders passed the lead around all week at the Yamaha Ladies Open, and Sun-Ju Ahn had possession of it when it counted most — at the end of the season's first 72-hole tournament. The veteran South Korean, the leading money winner in 2011 and 2012, got her one-stroke victory almost by default when Yumiko Yoshida bogeyed the final hole.

The 26-year-old Ahn had trailed Yoshida by a shot entering the final round on the Yamana course at Katsuragi Golf Club after Rikako Morita, the No. 1 player in 2013, held the lead the first day with a six-under-par 66. Morita handed it over Friday to Ritsuko Ryu, whose pair of 69s gave her a one-stroke lead on Ahn and Young Kim with 70-69s and Yoshida with 68-71.

On a rugged Saturday when nobody broke 70, Yoshida moved in front with 71–210 as Ahn posted 72–211. Ahn edged ahead Sunday when she birdied the seventh hole and Yoshida bogeyed the ninth, but dropped back into a tie for the lead when she bogeyed the 16th. Ahn's par at the par-five 18th gave her a 72–283 and put a 14th victory on her tour record when Yoshida absorbed the fatal bogey.

Studio Alice Ladies Open

Miki, Hyogo

Winner: Esther Lee

Esther Lee labored through seven winless seasons on the Japan LPGA Tour, but certainly not in obscurity. Ten times in 2013, for instance, Lee posted top-10 finishes and placed 23rd on the money list. The breakthrough finally came in the Studio Alice Ladies Open, where she prevailed in a final-round duel with Thailand's O. Sattaya, winning by a stroke with her final-round 70 and nine-under-par 207.

Sattaya commanded the field over the first two rounds at Hanayashiki Golf Club in Hyogo Prefecture as she went after her second victory of the young season. Winner of the opening Daikin Orchid tournament, Sattaya rang up 11 birdies the first two days of the Studio Alice as she shot 67-68–135 and established a two-stroke lead over Lee (70-67) and four over 19-year-old Hikari Fujita (70-69).

Lee eliminated Sattaya's margin on the front nine Sunday, but fell one back when the Thai player ended a string of nine pars with a birdie at the par-five 10th hole. A birdie-bogey combination swung the lead back to the South Korean after 14 holes. Lee dropped back into a tie when she bogeyed the 17th, but secured the triumph with a final birdie on the 18th green.

Vantelin Ladies Open KKT Cup

Kikuyo, Kumamoto

Winner: Minami Katsu

What is it about golf on the Pacific Rim and especially in Japan that produces such remarkable young players? Lydia Ko at 14, Ryo Ishikawa at 15, Hyo-Joo Kim at 16, Ai Miyazato at 18, Hideki Matsuyama at 19. All of them winners at those ages on prominent professional tours. How about Tianlang Guan, the 14-year-old Chinese amateur who played in the Masters as the Asia-Pacific Amateur champion? Welcome 15-year-old Minami Katsu to that group of phenomenal players.

Katsu, the high schooler who first attracted notice in 2013 with a tie-for-12th in the Studio Alice tournament at age 14 and who won the New Zealand Women's Stroke Play Championship a few weeks earlier, got everybody's full attention at the Vantelin Ladies Open KKT Cup over the weekend and all but went wire-to-wire for a one-stroke victory. With it she became the youngest winner ever on the Japan LPGA Tour, undercutting Kim, who was 16 when she won the Suntory Open in 2012.

Katsu rang up five consecutive birdies en route to a 66 and a tie for the lead with Thailand's O. Sattaya, the leading money winner with a win, second and third in her six 2014 starts. Mami Fukuda, 21, came up with a 66 Saturday and slipped a stroke in front of Katsu and Sattaya, who matched 71s for 137. Katsu took command early Sunday. She birdied five of her first 13 holes, establishing a three-stroke lead over Bo-Mee Lee. Katsu bogeyed the 14th and the experienced Lee made a run at her with birdies on the last two holes for 69–206, one short of the teenage whiz, who parred in for 68–205.

Fujisankei Ladies Classic

Ito, Shizuoka

Winner: Phoebe Yao

Though six years older than Minami Katsu, the previous week's winner, Phoebe Yao put another first-time title on the Japan LPGA Tour in the hands of the young brigade with the most decisive victory of the early season in the Fujisankei Ladies Classic. The 21-year-old Yao wound up with a five-stroke win as a bevy of contenders fired and fell back at different stages of the final round at the Kawana Hotel's Fuji course.

The young Taiwanese player broke from a three-way tie Sunday. With rounds of 72-67–139, she shared the 36-hole lead with Esther Lee (71-68), the Studio Alice victor, and veteran Shiho Oyama (67-72), the first-round leader who was gunning for her 14th title in Japan. While Yao was piecing together a solid, four-birdie 68 for the winning, nine-under-par 207, Oyama uncharacteristically stumbled to a 77 and Lee to a 76.

Yao's challenges instead came from earlier starters. Twenty-year-old Mamiko Higa, a two-time winner in 2013, ripped off seven straight birdies on the front nine and reached seven under before taking a triple bogey at the par-three 17th. Playing partner Misuzu Narita birdied that hole, matching

Higa's final 68 to tie for second place at 212. Yao was the third consecutive maiden winner on the tour.

Cyber Agent Ladies

Ichihara, Chiba
Winner: Yuki Ichinose

Two weeks after 15-year-old Minami Katsu shocked the golf world by winning the Vantelin Open and a week after 21-year-old Phoebe Yao landed the Fujisankei Classic title, a pair of teenage amateurs took a serious run in the Cyber Agent Ladies tournament as the female youth movement continued.

However, a storybook finish was not to be. Experienced pro Yuki Ichinose took care of that. Trailing the two youngsters — co-leaders Haruka Morita, 17, and Kotone Hori, 16 — by two strokes going into the final round, Ichinose, 25, shot a three-under-par 69 for 207 and a two-shot victory, her second of the season (Yokohama Tire) and third of her seven-year career. Still, Morita (73) finished second, Hori (76) tied for fourth and 16-year-old Kana Nagai (73) took sixth place, an unprecedented showing by amateurs on the Japan LPGA Tour.

Ichinose and high school senior Morita opened with 68s at Tsurumai Country Club, one stroke behind leader Ayaka Watanabe, only 20, the AXA Ladies winner in March. Hori shot 67 and Morita 68 Saturday to move in front with 136, but were threatened by international star Jiyai Shin, who fired a 65 for 137. Ichinose took a 70 for 138, then came up Sunday with one of two low-round 69s on a day when only six players broke par. Ichinose capped her round with an eagle-three on the 54th hole to clinch the victory. Shin shot 73 and finished third at 210.

World Ladies Championship Salonpas Cup

Tsukubamiral, Ibaraki
Winner: Misuzu Narita

With a break in the schedule of the LPGA Tour in America, several of its regulars from Asia returned to the Orient to play in the World Ladies Championship Salonpas Cup, the richest early-season tournament on the Japan LPGA Tour, and made their presence felt. In particular, China's Shanshan Feng and homelander Mika Miyazato. But, in the end, they yielded to Misuzu Narita, 21, another of Japan's horde of talented young players.

Feng, a five-time winner in relatively few starts in Japan in 2011 and 2012, made her decision look good as she took the lead Thursday on Ibaraki Golf Club's West course with her first of three consecutive two-under-par 70s and carried a two-stroke margin into the final round with her 210. Narita, with single victories in each of the previous two seasons, moved into the runner-up spot and the final-round pairing with Feng with a six-under 66, a score bettered all week only by the 65 Friday of Minami Katsu, the 15-year-old winner of the Vantelin Open in April.

Miyazato roared into contention Sunday when she birdied six of the first

11 holes and moved a stroke ahead of Feng and Narita. From there in, it was a tight, three-player battle. It came down to the par-four final hole, where Miyazato, then a shot behind, and Feng bogeyed and Narita parred for 67 and the winning, nine-under-par 279 to edge the Chinese star by a shot and Miyazato by two. The ¥24 million first prize vaulted Narita into the No. 1 position on the money list.

Hoken no Madoguchi Ladies

Asakura, Fukuoka

Winner: Bo-Mee Lee

Bo-Mee Lee has been a major player on the Japan LPGA Tour since her full-time arrival in 2012 after establishing her credentials in the immediately preceding seasons in South Korea. She finished second on the money list that inaugural year and seventh in 2013 while scoring five victories and she isn't slowing down.

Despite a shaky start with a 73, Lee raced to win No. 6 in the Hoken no Madoguchi Ladies in mid-May and regained the top spot on the money list that she had held for three weeks before young Misuzu Narita had picked it off with her rich victory the previous Sunday. But, Lee had to dispose of Asuka Kashiwabara, yet another of the talented, teenage Japanese amateurs who kept popping up in contention in the early months of the season.

Kashiwabara, just 18, came out of obscurity in Friday's opening round at Fukuoka Country Club with a three-under-par 69, tied for the lead with veteran Yumiko Yoshida. The youngster then went in front alone Saturday with 68–137, a shot in front of South Korean stars Mi-Jeong Jeon (70-68) and Lee, who shot a bogey-free 65 to set up her Sunday run to victory. Kashiwabara held onto the lead until Lee birdied the 11th hole and fell behind for the first time when she bogeyed the 13th. Two more birdies enabled Lee to establish her winning 69–207, four ahead of Soo-Yun Kang, Mayu Hattori, Shanshan Feng and Jeon. Kashiwabara tied for sixth with her 75–212.

Chukyo TV Bridgestone Ladies Open

Toyota, Aichi

Winner: Sun-Ju Ahn

Sun-Ju Ahn scored a landmark victory in late May in the Chukyo TV Bridgestone Ladies Open. Ahn's 15th triumph in just 108 tournaments on the Japan LPGA Tour fattened her career earnings over ¥500 million, the quickest that feat was achieved by any of the 19 players who have passed that mark in circuit history. Japan's Sakura Yokomine, the previous record-holder, required 149 starts to reach that goal.

The 27-year-old South Korean, who won her first title in her initial start in the Daikin Orchid season opener in 2010 when her goal was just "to get one win," went on to capture the money title that year and in 2011, then finished fourth the following two years.

The Chukyo TV Bridgestone victory, her second of the season, was a bit of a dicey one for Ahn. Just a shot off the pace with her opening 69, she inched a stroke in front of a quartet — Akane Iijima, Na-Ri Kim, Kotone Hori and Misuzu Narita, the 21-year-old winner of the Salonpas World Championship — with another 69 the second day. Ahn birdied three of the last eight holes Sunday for 70 and an eight-under-par 208, but she didn't shake off Phoebe Yao, her last challenger, until Yao double-bogeyed the 17th hole while Ahn was birdieing the 16th behind her. In the end, Ahn finished three strokes in front of Sakura Yokomine, Ji-Hee Lee, Miki Saiki, Miki Sakai, Ritsuko Ryu and Yao.

Resort Trust Ladies

Miki, Hyogo

Winner: Teresa Lu

The temptation had to be there. Teresa Lu had gone eight frustrating years without a victory, until 2010 competing on the American LPGA Tour, before she won the Mizuno Open in late 2013. Since that tournament is a joint venture of the U.S. and Japan LPGA Tours, the victory gave the 26-year-old Taiwanese player the opportunity to return to the more prestigious and lucrative circuit in America.

Lu upheld her decision to remain in Japan for the 2014 season when she won again at the end of May in the Resort Trust Ladies tournament. She did it decisively, leaving the field in the wake of her eight-under-par 64 in the final round that carried her to victory. Her 12-under 201 gave her a five-stroke final margin over Ji-Min Lee and six better than Junko Omote, Bo-Mee Lee and Na-Ri Lee.

Lu's performance at Kansai Country Club in Miki, Hyogo, came as a bit of a surprise. She had missed the cut in her two previous starts before opening the Resort Trust with a 67, tied for the lead with Ji-Min Lee and Miki Saiki. Omote, 40, a three-time winner over 18 seasons, shot her second 68 and slipped a stroke ahead of Lu, Ji-Min Lee, both with 70s, and Na-Ri Lee (73-64) Saturday. The issue was settled early Sunday when Lu racked up four birdies on the front nine and she coasted home bogey-free with four more on the back nine.

Yonex Ladies

Nagaoka, Niigata

Winner: Misuzu Narita

For a 21-year-old, Misuzu Narita handles tournament pressure well. A month after winning a three-way battle with two of the JLPGA's prominent players on the final hole in the World Ladies Championship, Narita shrugged off a 54th-hole bogey and picked up her second title of the season with a turnaround birdie on the first hole of a playoff in the Yonex Ladies tournament.

Narita, who moved up to second place on the tour's money list with the victory, carried a mere one-stroke lead into the final round at Niigata's Yonex

Country Club after a pair of 68s. She was pursued not only by 13-time-winner Shiho Oyama, the first-round co-leader (67-70), and Erina Yamato (69-68), but the likes of Sun-Ju Ahn, already a two-time 2014 winner, and Junko Omote, the defending champion.

Two late bogeys killed Omote's bid for a repeat, and Ahn lost her chances when she knocked one out of bounds at the 13th hole Sunday. Oyama and Yamato remained a shot behind Narita as the three matched pars from the 14th hole in until Narita took the surprising bogey at the 18th hole. But Narita ended the playoff quickly by dropping a 14-foot birdie putt when she, Oyama and Yamato took on the 18th hole in overtime. It was Narita's fourth win in her three seasons on tour.

Suntory Ladies Open

Kobe, Hyogo

Winner: Sun-Ju Ahn

Sun-Ju Ahn got better by the victory. Already a 13-time winner as she entered her fifth season on the Japan LPGA Tour, the 27-year-old South Korean squeezed out a one-stroke victory in the Yamaha Ladies in April, won by three a month later in the Chukyo TV Bridgestone and breezed to a five-shot triumph in the Suntory Open in mid-June that put her atop the money list where she finished in 2010 and 2011.

Ahn made her move in the third round at Rokko Kokusai Golf Club at Kobe, Hyogo. Four behind countrywoman Na-Ri Lee after rounds of 69-71–140, she climbed into a first-place tie with a four-under-par 68 Saturday, knotted with Haruka Kudo (71-67-70), who hadn't finished higher than a tie for 15th all year.

Ahn quickly established a foothold on the lead with birdies on three of her first five holes Sunday. At the turn, she had two strokes on Akane Iijima, whose most recent of five tour victories came in the 2010 Suntory. Then, Ahn, who counts the 2011 Suntory among her title collection, stepped on the gas, racking up four more birdies in a bogey-free 32 on the back nine for a 66, a 14-under-par 274 and the five-shot margin over Iijima, who shot 69.

Nichirei Ladies

Sodegaura, Chiba

Winner: Jiyai Shin

Things hadn't gone particularly well for former World No. 1 Jiyai Shin in her full-time return to the Japan LPGA Tour in 2014, certainly not after her second-place finish in the season-opening Daikin Orchid. She had two more top-10s, but a pair of missed cuts and otherwise pedestrian showings among her first 11 starts.

The frustration ended in June in the Nichirei Ladies as the 26-year-old South Korean rolled to her sixth victory in Japan. She never trailed en route to a four-stroke win with a 12-under-par 204 at Chiba Prefecture's Sodegaura Country Club.

Shin's opening 69 gave her a four-way share of first place with Rumi Yoshiba, Na-Ri Lee and Kaori Nakamura before taking charge of things the second day with a seven-under 65. She rang up 10 birdies as she bolted to a four-shot lead over Esther Lee (71-67) and Hikari Fujita (73-65). Sunday, though, wasn't all easy. Both youngsters Fujita and Yoshida made runs at Shin, but she put it away on the back nine with three birdies on the last four holes for 70 and the four-stroke margin over Fujita (70) and Yoshida (68).

Earth Mondahmin Cup

Sodegaura, Chiba
Winner: Miki Sakai

One would think that, if the leading money winner led for two days, made a hole-in-one and eagled the 72nd hole, she would add another victory to her record. All of that wasn't quite enough for Sun-Ju Ahn as she lost in a playoff in the Earth Mondahmin Cup tournament to 23-year-old Miki Sakai, who fulfilled recent promise with her first victory on the Japan LPGA Tour.

Sakai, who had posted two runner-up finishes and two other top-fives earlier in the season, entered the final round at Camellia Hills Country Club tied for the lead at 202 with Mi-Jeong Jeon, one of South Korea's top stars, after both shot eight-under 64s Saturday. That moved them a shot ahead of Taiwan's Teresa Lu, the Resort Trust winner, and two in front of Ahn, who led the first two days with rounds of 66 and 69, the latter score including her ace.

Sunday's competition quickly became a duel between Sakai and Ahn, and they reached the final hole with Sakai holding a two-shot lead. Ahn then eagled the 18th for 67–271, bringing about the playoff when Sakai missed her birdie putt and shot 69 for her 271. Sakai, who had lost in a playoff in the Yokohama Tire tournament in March, evened the record when she sank a winning three-footer on the second extra hole. Jeon, with 71, placed third at 273.

Nichi-Iko Ladies Open

Toyama
Winner: Yeon-Ju Jung

Much the same script. Different actors.

A week after winless Miki Sakai defeated South Korea's brilliant Sun-Ju Ahn, Yeon-Ju Jung, another young player without a Japan Tour victory, outplayed Japan's 22-tournament winner Sakura Yokomine and made off with the title in the Nichi-Iko Ladies Open in Toyama. She was the sixth first-time winner of the season.

Jung stayed close to the top all week at Yatsuo Country Club. Her opening 66 put her just a stroke behind co-leaders Yokomine and Maiko Wakabayashi and she trailed only Wakabayashi after her second-round 68. Wakabayashi, who has two wins on her JLPGA record, shot 67 for 132. Yokomine, bogey-free both days, was at 70–135.

Wakabayashi's game tailed off Sunday, particularly on the back nine, as she faded to 76 and a tie-for-11th finish as the race narrowed to Jung, who gained her experience on the Korean LPGA Tour, and Yokomine, still looking for her first 2014 win. Although Yokomine remained without a bogey Sunday, too, she never caught Jung, who rang up seven birdies and a 65 for her winning, 17-under-par 199, two ahead of Yokomine, who closed with 66–201.

Samantha Thavasa Girls Collection Ladies

Ami, Ibaraki
Winner: Misuzu Narita

Once again, Misuzu Narita did it the hard way. The 21-year-old won her fifth Japan LPGA Tour title at the Samantha Thavasa Girls Collection Ladies and each of the last four came in playoffs. In all five cases, Narita trailed going into the final rounds by as much as six strokes.

She was in contention throughout the Samantha Thavasa as she won her third tournament of the 2014 season, matching money leader Sun-Ju Ahn in that department. Her adversary in overtime at Eagle Point Golf Club in Ibaraki Prefecture was lightly regarded Kotono Kozuma, 22, who stoked up a 64 Sunday for a 16-under-par 200. Narita birdied two of her final five holes to forge the tie a short time later with a 67 and knocked off Kozuma with a birdie on the first extra hole.

Narita had opened the tournament in a five-way tie at 66 with Na-Ri Lee, Jiyai Shin, Yumiko Yoshida and Kaori Nakamura and followed with 67, slipping a stroke behind South Korean Lee, who produced another 66 Saturday. Winless Kozuma sat four strokes off the lead after rounds of 67-69–136. Lee, who won her first two JLPGA titles in 2013, shot 69 Sunday, missing the playoff by a stroke.

Century 21 Ladies

Shizuoka
Winner: Bo-Mee Lee

It was a rare situation. The season's three most successful players entered the final round of the inaugural Century 21 Ladies tournament hot on the heels of 36-hole-leader Yun-Jye Wei, the Taiwanese veteran trying to win for the first time since bagging her fourth JLPGA title in 2010.

Her game didn't hold up Sunday against that trio — Bo-Mee Lee, No. 2 on the money list who trailed by a stroke; Sun-Ju Ahn, No. 1 with three wins, and two-time-winner Misuzu Narita, No. 3 with two wins, both two shots off the pace. Lee prevailed in the marquee battle, her two-under-par 70 carrying her to a two-stroke victory at 11-under-par 205.

Wei, who had the lead after shooting a pair of 67s, fell back early Sunday, finishing with a 76 that dropped her into a tie for 13th place, and Narita's hopes ended abruptly when she triple-bogeyed the first hole at IzuOhito Country Club. Ahn made two early birdies, but was one over par over the remaining 14 holes. Lee rang up three birdies over the first 11 holes and withstood all challenges with six pars and a bogey over the final stretch for her second win of the season and seventh career victory in Japan.

Ahn shot 71 and tied for second at 207 with Asako Fujimoto (71) and Keiko Sasaki (69), easily retaining her top spot in the tour standings.

Meiji Cup

Kitahiroshima, Hokkaido

Winner: Jiyai Shin

Jiyai Shin established herself as a legitimate challenger for the season's money-winning championship when she posted her second 2014 victory in the Meiji Cup in Hokkaido in early August. With the other win and two top-10 finishes in her previous three starts, Shin climbed to fifth place on the money list as she continued to justify her somewhat-surprising decision to concentrate her 2014 golf on the Japanese circuit.

Shin, who sports 11 LPGA Tour titles, including two British Women's Open championships, and had a brief tenure in 2010 atop the Rolex Rankings, emerged from a bunched field of contenders at Sapporo International Country Club with a two-stroke victory, posting a 12-under-par 204.

En route to her seventh Japan LPGA title, the South Korean star moved from a 70 start into a one-stroke lead with a second-round 66. At 137 were three-time-winner Misuzu Narita, Erina Hara and Teresa Lu, the Resort Trust titlist, who gave Shin the toughest challenge in the final round.

Lu and Shin shot 33s on the outgoing nine Sunday to distance themselves from the pack. Shin went two ahead with a birdie at No. 10, then matched Lu's bogey and 18th-hole birdie to wrap up the triumph. Bo-Mee Lee (No. 2) tied for fifth and Narita (No. 3) for 10th to move closer to No. 1 Sun-Ju Ahn, who skipped the Meiji Cup.

NEC Karuizawa 72

Karuizawa, Nagano

Winner: Bo-Mee Lee

It took a playoff victory in the NEC Karuizawa 72 tournament to do it, but Bo-Mee Lee reclaimed the No. 1 spot on the Japan LPGA Tour money list in mid-August from Sun-Ju Ahn, who had taken it away from her in June and held it for two months.

Lee carried a two-stroke lead into the final round on the North course of Karuizawa 72 Golf Club, having seized it from Na-Ri Kim, the first-day front-runner with 65. Lee's 69-64 moved her in front of three players at 135 — Yumiko Yoshida (67-68), Kumiko Kaneda (69-66) and Shiho Oyama (68-67).

Ahn, resting six shots back entering the final round, put an early 66 on the board, but her 11-under-par 205 wasn't good enough. Erika Kikuchi birdied the 13th and 14th holes and parred in for 66–203. Oyama, who reached 13 under with a birdie at No. 13, also parred the rest of the way for 68 and her 203, and Lee joined the tie when she birdied the 15th hole and ran off three closing pars.

The South Korean then captured her third win of the season and eighth in Japan when she holed a 14-foot birdie putt on the first extra hole. It was Oyama's second playoff loss of the season as she sought her 14th career victory on the Japan LPGA Tour.

CAT Ladies

Hakone, Kanagawa

Winner: Momoko Ueda

When Momoko Ueda won the Mizuno Open in 2007, its joint status with the U.S. LPGA Tour gave her playing privileges on that circuit and, although she went on to become the leading money winner on the Japan LPGA Tour that season, she subsequently played most of her golf on the America-based circuit, but without notable success.

In fact, when she teed it up in the CAT Ladies in Hakone in late August, her only victory in the interim had been in the Mizuno Open again in 2011. The decision to play in Japan paid off, though, as she bested the talented Rikako Morita by a stroke in a stretch duel Sunday at Daihakone Country Club in Kanagawa Prefecture in a finish that left her in tears, exclaiming, "It's been a long time … a really, really long time."

Morita, 24, the reigning money queen with seven titles to her credit, led the tournament the first two days. She started with 67 and went three strokes in front of Ueda (70-71) with her 71–138. Bo-Mee Lee, No. 1 on the money list, was tied for third with Ayaka Watanabe and Kaori Yamamoto at 142.

The Sunday battle belonged to Ueda and Morita, particularly after Ueda birdied three of the first four holes to overtake Morita. Morita carried a one-shot lead to the back nine, but her two bogeys at the 10th and 13th holes and Ueda's birdie at the 12th gave back the lead to Ueda, who parred in to a 69 and nine-under-par 210, securing her 10th win in Japan. Morita fell a stroke short with 73–211, and Lee took third place with 71–213, adding to her money-leading earnings.

Nitori Ladies

Eniwa, Hokkaido

Winner: Jiyai Shin

With three victories in six starts over a two-month stretch, Jiyai Shin put herself clearly in the mix for the money title on the Japan LPGA Tour, the third a wire-to-wire win at the end of August in the Nitori Ladies tournament in Hokkaido.

Shin, who had dedicated her efforts in 2014 to Japan, moved into a contending fourth position on the money list behind compatriot South Koreans Bo-Mee Lee and Sun-Ju Ahn and Japan's Misuzu Narita, all also sporting three 2014 victories.

Shin began her run to the Nitori title with a five-under-par 67 at Eniwa

Country Club, staking herself to a two-stroke lead over Saiki Fujita, a five-time JLPGA winner. She maintained the two-shot margin with a 71 Saturday for 138 as Fujita matched her card and was joined in second place by Yukari Nishiyama (70).

Bo-Mee Lee and Fujita challenged Shin Sunday, overtaking her on the front nine, all three six under par at the turn. However, they both bogeyed twice early on the back nine, and when Shin birdied the 13th and 15th holes she was home free with 70 and the winning, eight-under-par 208, three ahead of Lee (69) and Fujita (71). Neither Ahn nor Narita played at Eniwa.

Golf 5 Ladies

Gifu

Winner: Shiho Oyama

Shiho Oyama, one of the Japan LPGA Tour's biggest winners, seems to have overcome a persistent elbow injury that, until victory in the final tournament of the 2013 season, had kept her winless since 2008. She had been on the verge of another victory since the middle of the 2014 season and No. 14 seemed to be in the bag when she got off to a 65-63–128 start in the Golf 5 tournament in early September.

She led by six strokes, but a mediocre 72 Sunday made things interesting. Misuzu Narita, a three-time winner earlier in the season, mounted a charge before a late bogey led to a 68 and left her two strokes behind Oyama's winning, 16-under-par 200 at Mizunami Country Club in Gifu.

The 37-year-old Oyama led by just a shot after the opening 65, but with Saturday's 63, the margin ballooned to six over Narita (68-66) and eight or more in front of the rest of the field. Then, on Sunday, as Oyama methodically clicked off 15 pars and a bogey after her lone birdie at No. 2, Narita ran off four birdies in the middle of the round before the fatal bogey at the 16th hole.

Japan LPGA Championship

Minagi, Hyogo

Winner: Ai Suzuki

Although she won twice on Japan's secondary women's tour, 20-year-old Ai Suzuki had never even produced a top-10 finish in her 19 starts on the Japan LPGA Tour. Then, the second-year pro caught lightning in a bottle in the Japan LPGA Championship, the season's second major tournament in mid-September.

Shooting 67, the lowest score the entire week, in the second round, Suzuki went in front to stay with her seven-under-par 137, held off a quartet of challengers Sunday and, by a single stroke, became the youngest winner of the championship and its symbolic Konica Minolta Cup. Her five-under-par 283 was one better than the totals of Lala Anai, Na-Ri Lee and three-time 2014 winners Jiyai Shin and Misuzu Narita, a runner-up a second straight week.

The 67 gave Suzuki a four-stroke lead over Anai and five over Lee, Shin and Narita, but she came back to the field Saturday with a 75, fueled by two early double-bogeys. With Momoko Ueda and Kaori Ohe (69s) just one back, and Shin, Narita and Ah-Reum Hwang two behind, there were 26 players within seven shots of Suzuki entering the final round.

But the young player was solid most of the way Sunday, getting off to a fast start with four birdies on the first seven holes. A second bogey at the 16th after six straight pars put Suzuki in jeopardy, but a birdie at the 17th cushioned a final bogey on the home hole for the winning 71-283.

Munsingwear Ladies Tokai Classic

Minami, Aichi

Winner: Jiyai Shin

The four-way race for the No. 1 position at season's end tightened at the Munsingwear Ladies Tokai Classic when Jiyai Shin, taking advantage of the absence of Bo-Mee Lee, the leader, and No. 2 Sun-Ju Ahn, pulled out her fourth victory of the year and climbed past Ahn and Misuzu Narita into second place on the money list, ¥12 million behind Lee.

Shin, continuing to flourish in her fulltime return to the Japan LPGA Tour, came from a stroke back with a final-round 67 and 14-under-par 202 for a one-shot win over Na-Ri Lee, a runner-up for the second week in a row.

Rui Kitada, a six-time winner and the first-round leader with 66, yielded the lead Saturday to 22-year-old Mami Fukuda, who shot a back-nine 29 for 64 and, with 134, led Shin (67), Na-Ri Kim (68) and O. Sattaya (63) by a stroke going into the Sunday finale.

Winless Fukuda faded from contention on the front nine and the race for the title turned into a three-way battle on the final holes among Shin, Lee and Kitada. Shin, winning her ninth title in Japan, prevailed with birdies at the 16th and 17th holes for her fourth victory in her last nine starts on the JLPGA Tour.

Miyagi TV Cup Dunlop Ladies Open

Rifu, Miyagi

Winner: Miki Sakai

Miki Sakai joined the sizeable ranks of multiple winners on the 2014 Japan LPGA Tour with her one-stroke victory in the Miyagi TV Cup Dunlop Ladies Open. With that second win of the season, Sakai became the sixth player with more than a single victory. Those six won 17 of the year's first 28 tournaments.

The 23-year-old Sakai, who defeated second-ranked money winner Sun-Ju Ahn in a playoff in the Earth Mondahmin Cup tournament in June, entered the final round of the Dunlop four strokes off the pace, put a 67-208 on the board early and wound up a shot ahead of 21-year-old Ayaka Watanabe, the co-leader with Teresa Lu after 36 holes at Rifu Golf Club.

Sakai had opened the tournament in a five-way tie for the lead at 69 with Ahn, Natsuka Hori, Erina Yamato and Miki Saiki, but fell back into a tie for sixth Saturday when she shot a par 72. Watanabe fired a 66 and Lu a

65 that day for their leading 137s, both picking up four strokes on their last five holes. Ahn, the two-time money-winning champion, was third, two behind after rounds of 69-70–139.

Sakai, who was four under on the front nine Sunday, finished with two birdies on the last three holes for the winning, eight-under-par score. A double bogey at the 15th hole ruined Lu's bid (73–210), and Watanabe, who slid well behind early on, came up short (72–209) despite three closing birdies. Ahn (71) and Junko Omote (68) matched Lu's 210.

Japan Women's Open Championship

Ritto, Shiga

Winner: Teresa Lu

Teresa Lu put an exclamation point on her decision to stay on the Japan LPGA Tour this season despite the chance to give the U.S. circuit another shot when she won the Japan Women's Open Championship, the circuit's most prestigious tournament, on top of her earlier victory in the Resort Trust event.

A brilliant final round and the collapse of the 54-hole leaders combined to give the 26-year-old Taiwanese pro a one-stroke victory with an eight-under-par 280, her first major title and her third win in Japan. Lu, five strokes behind co-leaders Ai Suzuki and compatriot Yun-Jye Wei (208) going into the final round, fashioned six birdies on her first 11 holes, produced a five-under-par 67, the day's low score, and waited anxiously as the contenders, playing behind her, fell by the wayside.

Suzuki, the 20-year-old winner of the Japan LPGA Championship, and veteran Wei, a four-time titlist, fell back early, Suzuki eventually shooting 76 and Wei 77. Jiyai Shin, only two back and with an opportunity to close in on Bo-Mee Lee and Sun-Ju Ahn in the money race with a fourth 2014 victory, stuttered to a 75.

As it turned out, South Korea's Na-Ri Lee had the best shot at Lu. A two-time winner who finished second twice and sixth in the previous three events, Lee took her only bogey of the day at the final hole and, with 69, came up a stroke short of a tie and playoff. Amateur Kana Nagai shot 70–282 to finish third.

Stanley Ladies

Susano, Shizuoka

Winner: Sun-Ju Ahn

Sun-Ju Ahn found herself in a familiar spot after she scored an exciting, come-from-behind win in the Stanley Ladies tournament. Twice before (2010 and 2011) the money titlist on the Japan LPGA Tour, Ahn moved into the No. 1 slot in the standings for the first time in 2014 with the Stanley victory, her 17th in Japan.

Oddly, it took her four wins to get there and that fourth one did not come easily. For two days at Tomei Country Club, it appeared that Ji-Hee

Lee was the one who would land her 18th Japan LPGA title. Lee, who hadn't won since early in the 2012 season, shot 65 in the opening round, tied for first place with Thailand's O. Sattaya, then went three shots into a solo lead Saturday with 67–132. Misuzu Narita, a three-time 2014 winner, was at 135, and Ahn took over third position with a pair of 68s.

Lee's game crumbled on the back nine Sunday. While Ahn was putting the finishing touches on a bogey-free 66 for her 14-under-par 202, Lee was giving back seven strokes on the final seven holes. She ended with a 72, the runner-up by two strokes.

Fujitsu Ladies

Chiba

Winner: Sun-Ju Ahn

Sun-Ju Ahn's steam-roller run on the Japan LPGA Tour crushed on in mid-October. Red hot in her four starts since sitting out a month's worth of events, Ahn tied for third, finished fourth, won, then won for the fifth time in 2014 in the Fujitsu Ladies tournament and assumed a commanding lead in her quest for a third money title in Japan.

Although in front from the beginning with her eight-under-par 64, the South Korean star, who also won the Fujitsu in 2010, had to defeat two other competitors in a three-way playoff to make it two in a row and sock away her 18th career win on the circuit. The top prize moved her nearly ¥26 million ahead of compatriot Bo-Mee Lee on the money list.

The opening 64 gave Ahn a one-stroke lead over winless Erika Kikuchi, and the picture remained the same after the second round as both players shot 69s, Ahn taking a bogey at the 18th hole for the second day in a row. Sakura Yokomine, the 22-time winner and 2009 money titlist, climbed within two shots with 65–135.

Ahn faltered badly with three bogeys on the front nine Sunday and appeared to have lost out even after a birdie at the 16th. She was even par for the day and 11 under par total, two behind Kikuchi and one back of Yokomine, but Kikuchi bogeyed the final two holes and Yokomine the 17th to force the playoff as all three posted 205s. They went back to the 18th tee and Ahn got even with the hole with a winning birdie.

Nobuta Group Masters Golf Club Ladies

Miki, Hyogo

Winner: Shiho Oyama

It had been seven years since anybody won three in a row on the Japan LPGA Tour. Sun-Ju Ahn, who had a shot at accomplishing that feat after back-to-back wins three times in the interim since Mi-Jeong Jeon did it in 2007, nearly did it on her fourth try in the Nobuta Group Masters Golf Club Ladies tournament. Her strong bid in the final round fell two strokes short and she had to settle for second place as Shiho Oyama completed an impressive wire-to-wire victory.

Not surprising, though. The 37-year-old veteran won the Masters Golf Club tournament twice before — 2008 and 2011 — among her previous 14 career victories on the Japan LPGA Tour, most recently the Golf 5 tournament in September.

Oyama started with a bang Thursday, taking a one-stroke lead over Ahn with a seven-under-par 65. Ayaka Watanabe, 20, who won her first title early in the season, surged into the picture the next day with a sizzling 63 for 133, inching her a shot ahead of Ahn (68–134) as Oyama maintained her one-stroke lead with a six-birdie 67 for 132.

Oyama widened her lead to three shots Saturday with 69–201, then over Yumiko Yoshida (66) and Taiwan's Teresa Lu (67). Ahn (71) and Watanabe (72) were another stroke back. Oyama completed the job when she closed with 68–269. Although her 66 wasn't good enough for a win, the second-place money of ¥12 million strengthened Ahn's grip on the money title, moving her nearly ¥36 million ahead of No. 2 Bo-Mee Lee.

Hisako Higuchi Morinaga Ladies

Ichihara, Chiba

Winner: Momoko Ueda

A peculiar chain of events continued at the Hisako Higuchi Morinaga Ladies tournament. When Momoko Ueda eked out a one-stroke victory on that Sunday, it marked the seventh consecutive tournament at which the player had already won at least once in the 2014 season.

The streak would have ended had Ji-Hee Lee held onto the lead she carried for two days at Morinaga Takataki Country Club. Although the veteran South Korean owns 18 Japanese titles, she was in pursuit of her first win in two years. Lee started with a six-under-par 66 and a two-stroke lead and, despite a back-nine 38 Saturday, still had a one-stroke margin with 70–136.

One back were Ueda (68-69) and Junko Omote (69-68), who went on to battle each other for the title Sunday as Lee self-destructed with a 78. Omote, with three wins on her 17-season record, got away to the three-stroke lead with a front-nine 32. However, she had run out of birdies and, when she bogeyed the 15th and 16th holes, she dropped into a tie for the lead at nine under with Ueda. Ueda then raked in the title with a 15-foot birdie putt on the final hole to salt away her 10th career victory with her 10-under 206. It assured her best season since 2007 when, as a 21-year-old, she won five tournaments and the money title.

Mizuno Classic

Shima, Mie

Winner: Mi Hyang Lee

It's probably safe to say that never have so many players come as close to winning a tournament as was the case on the final day of the Mizuno Classic, the event in which the Japan LPGA hosts the LPGA of America on its annual visit to the Land of the Rising Sun.

Emerging from among 17 players who finished within two strokes of the winning score and from a three-player, five-hole playoff was 21-year-old South Korean Mi Hyang Lee with her first victory on either tour.

The remarkable final round began with the sentimental favorite, 51-year-old World Golf Hall of Fame inductee-to-be Laura Davies, tied for the lead at 68-67–135 with 20-year-old Ai Suzuki (71-64) and South Korean Ilhee Lee (69-66). They were one stroke ahead of Mi Hyang Lee and Kotono Kozuma (69-67s) and Chella Choi (68-68).

As one after another of the contenders finished their rounds at Kintetsu Kashikojima Country Club, the playoff was fashioned from among the massive number of players from both tours. The 10-under-pars, including Morgan Pressel, the first-round leader with 67, and Karrie Webb, who bogeyed the 18th, piled up, eventually totaling nine players, all a stroke short. Five others finished another shot back. Mi Hyang Lee, a second-year player on the American tour, and Kozuma took over the clubhouse lead with 69s for 11-under-par 205 totals and were joined by Ilhee Lee (70).

Even the subsequent playoff was unusual. All three matched scores the first four times they replayed the 18th hole — pars, pars, birdies and pars — before Mi Hwang's second birdie of the playoff won it.

Itoen Ladies

Chonan, Chiba

Winner: Yoko Maeda

The Japan LPGA Tour crowned its ninth first-time winner at the Itoen Ladies tournament as Yoko Maeda pulled out a playoff victory over Satsuki Oshiro at Great Island Club in Chiba.

More than doubling her earnings for the year with the ¥18 million first-place check, Maeda closed with a final-round 70 to overtake Oshiro, also without a tour victory, who had already finished with a 67 and a nine-under-par 207.

Oshiro came from four strokes behind Erina Hara and Asako Fujimoto, the second-round co-leaders who posted matching 68-68–136 scores.

Maeda (68-69) was just one back in a three-way tie with Ritsuko Ryu and Yukari Nishiyama (69-68s) after Saturday's play. Ai Suzuki, the 20-year-old Japan LPGA champion, who led the first day with 67, finished in a six-way tie for fourth place.

The results had virtually no effect on the money race as neither leader Sun-Ju Ahn, near clinching, nor No. 2 Bo-Mee Lee cracked the top 10.

Elleair Ladies Open

Kagawa

Winner: Sakura Yokomine

It took virtually all of the long Japan LPGA Tour season and a number of missed chances before Sakura Yokomine scored her first victory of the year, but when it came in the Elleair Ladies Open at the end of November it marked a milestone in the outstanding career of the 28-year-old star.

With the ¥18 million prize, Yokomine became just the second billionaire in tour history. She joined Yuri Fudoh, who amassed her billion-plus yens over 50 victories. Yokomine did it with her 23rd win in the current era of richer purses.

Yokomine emerged the winner at Elleair Golf Club by a single stroke in a six-way battle that wasn't decided until she safely parred the 18th hole for a 68 and an 18-under-par 270. She edged Rikako Morita (66), Taiwan's Teresa Lu (65) and Ai Suzuki, the third-round leader, who birdied the last hole for 71. All were at 271.

The lead changed hands each day. Momoko Ueda, the leading money winner in 2007, opened with 65 and a two-stroke margin, then yielded the top spot to Rui Kitada (67-66–133) the second day. Yokomine, trailing by four at that point, fired a 65 Saturday, moving into second place, two behind 20-year-old Suzuki, the reigning LPGA champion, who rocked Elleair with a 64, the best round of the week. Six players had realistic shots at the title in the closing stretch Sunday, but birdies at the 15th and 16th holes enabled Yokomine to win with a par-par finish.

Sun-Ju Ahn, who played with an aching wrist through November, tied for eighth and clinched her third money title in five years. The five-time 2014 winner was far out of the reach of runner-up Bo-Mee Lee heading into the Tour Championship finale.

Japan LPGA Tour Championship Ricoh Cup

Miyazaki

Winner: Teresa Lu

With Yani Tseng's fortunes waning on the LPGA Tour, Taiwan golf fans turned their attention to the Japan LPGA Tour and the excellent season racked up by their Teresa Lu. The 26-year-old Lu capped her finest year on tour when she scored a playoff victory in the season-ending LPGA Tour Championship and climbed into second place on the circuit's final money list.

Particularly impressive, Lu had captured the Japan Women's Open Championship earlier in the season and her majors double was a feat that hadn't been achieved since Shinobu Morimizato won a pair in 2009. Lu also won the Resort Trust tournament and now has four victories on her record.

The season finale came down to a duel between Lu and Lala Anai, 27, winless in her career but with 10 top-10 finishes in 2014, including a second in the LPGA Championship. The Taiwanese pro led at the halfway mark with 69-67–136, two ahead of Anai (70-68), Ayaka Watanabe (66-72) and Kotono Kozuma (68-70). Lu and Anai changed places Saturday, Anai shooting 67 to Lu's 70 to take a one-stroke lead after 54 holes.

On a tough Sunday when Shiho Oyama's 70 was the best score, Lu shot 72 and Anai 73 for 278s to force the playoff, which Lu won with a birdie on the second extra hole. Oyama and Yeon-Ju Jung tied for third, four back at 282.

Australian Ladies Tour

Bing Lee Fujitsu General Women's NSW Open

Sydney, New South Wales
Winner: Joanna Klatten

France's Joanna Klatten claimed her second victory as a professional at the Bing Lee Fujitsu General Women's NSW Open to add to her maiden title, also in Australia, at the 2012 Victoria Open. The 28-year-old Parisian once scored a nine-under-par round to win an amateur tournament at St. Cloud, the club she now represents, and she did it again at Oatlands with a new course record of 63 in the final round. She did not drop a shot, made five birdies on the outward half and nine in all, including at the last two holes to win by three shots over Australian Nikki Campbell. After earlier rounds of 70 and 67, Klatten finished on a total of 200, 16 under par. Campbell closed with a 66 to finish a stroke ahead of Hannah Burke and Stephanie Na.

"I have to say it was one of my best rounds of golf, ever," Klatten said. "I felt like I was in perfect control of my game and my emotions, so I am extremely happy." She had warmed up for the tournament by winning two pro-ams on the Club Car Series earlier in the month and said she would treat herself with dinner at her favorite restaurant in Sydney.

ISPS Handa New Zealand Women's Open

Christchurch, New Zealand
Winner: Mi Hyang Lee

Lydia Ko returned to the ISPS Handa New Zealand Women's Open for the first time as a professional, but the 16-year-old could not defend her title at Clearwater. The marketing slogan of "Here we Ko again" almost worked as she finished as runner-up, missing a 25-footer on the final green to force a playoff. But she was unable to tie Mi Hyang Lee, who claimed her maiden title after setting a new course record of 63 in the final round. Lee had returned par scores of 72 on both the first two days and was eight strokes behind second-round leader Anya Alvarez, who finished in a tie for third place with Beth Allen and Seonwoo Bae.

Both Lee and Ko had suffered from upset stomachs during the week after traveling from the opening LPGA event of the season in the Bahamas. It did not stop Ko scoring two 69s, but she could only add a 70 in the final round to finish one short of Lee's 207 total, nine under par. Lee holed from 20 feet for an eagle at the second hole and made two birdies before the turn and five afterwards, including at the last two holes.

"It's my best score in my life," said the 20-year-old from South Korea. "The last two days I couldn't concentrate because I was sick, but I was better today and the putting was much better." She added that since her father had bought her a car for Christmas, the only thing she needed now was a new backpack.

Volvik RACV Ladies Masters

Ashmore, Queensland

Winner: Cheyenne Woods

Cheyenne Woods, niece of the most famous golfer of the last two decades, made a name for herself by winning for the first time on the Ladies European Tour at the Volvik RACV Ladies Masters. The 23-year-old from Phoenix, Arizona, beat Australian Amateur champion Minjee Lee by two strokes, with Stacy Lee Bregman and Camilla Lennarth two strokes further back, while Caroline Hedwall tied for fifth place.

"I've been pro for two years and I think for majority of it people just know me as Tiger Woods' niece, so now I have a win, which is exciting," Woods said. "I think it's nice now to prove to people that I can play awesome; I'm not just a name."

Woods had rounds of 69, 67, 71 and 69 for a 16-under-par total of 276. After sharing the halfway lead and then taking a one-shot lead with a round to play, Woods was caught by Lee's hat-trick of birdies from the sixth hole. But she responded with her own birdies at the ninth, 12th, 15th and the last, while Lee could only make two more herself.

"Growing up with the last name of Woods there are a lot of expectations and pressure and spotlight on you, but I always knew I was able to win," Woods added. "It's a weight off my shoulders. It feels good, most importantly, it's self-satisfying."

ISPS Handa Women's Australian Open

Victoria

Winner: Karrie Webb

A week after being disqualified for signing for a wrong score during the Volvik Masters, Karrie Webb responded by winning the ISPS Handa Women's Australian Open for the fifth time. Webb was reminded of compatriot Stacy Keating signing for an incorrect score at the 2012 Ricoh Women's British Open only to go on and win her next two events on the Ladies European Tour. Webb was five shots behind leaders Chella Choi and Minjee Lee after rounds of 71, 69, and 68, but the wind picked up throughout the last day, making conditions extremely difficult at Victoria Golf Club.

Webb birdied her first two holes, made a 40-footer at the 11th and, despite a second bogey of the day at the 16th, she birdied the 18th after her 35-footer for eagle only just missed. Another 68 left her on a 12-under-par total of 276. Choi birdied the first but went out of bounds at the second and took a double bogey. She dropped another shot at the third and then parred the rest of the course, missing from 12 feet for a birdie to tie at the last. She closed with a 74 to finish one behind Webb and one ahead of Paula Creamer, who also had a 68, Karine Icher and Lydia Ko. Lee, the 17-year-old Australian

Amateur champion who was runner-up at the Volvik Masters, closed with a 78 to tie for 11th place. World No. 2 Suzann Pettersen, who led on the first day, closed with an 80, and Caroline Hedwall, the halfway leader after a hole-in-one and an eagle in a second-round 65, finished off with a 75.

"I feel very fortunate to have won today," Webb said. "But I liked my chances at the start of the day because of the wind picking up. I played as good as I have in a very long time. For me, the tougher the conditions the better, because I have to get out of my head and not think technically."

In a tournament tri-sanctioned by the ALPG, the LET and the LPGA, the 39-year-old Webb claimed her 40th LPGA victory and the 52nd of her career. "It's amazing what happens, what a difference a week makes," Webb added. "Obviously this time last week I wouldn't be expecting to be sitting here, so I'm glad things changed around quickly for me. Stacy Keating texted me last week and said, remember what happened to me after I got DQ'ed. I actually thought about that when I was walking up 18, that that might come true for me as well."

Oates Victorian Open

Bellarine Peninsula, Victoria

Winner: Minjee Lee

After a superb run of form to start the year, amateur Minjee Lee claimed a six-stroke victory at the Oates Victorian Open, played alongside the men's version at 13th Beach Links. In January the 17-year-old defended her Australian Amateur title and then in February she was runner-up to Cheyenne Woods at the Volvik Masters. The following week she was the joint third-round leader at the Australian Open, and despite falling to 11th on the final day, she earned a ringing endorsement as a fine talent from champion Karrie Webb.

Lee backed that up at the Vic Open with rounds of 73, 70, 68 and 68 for a 17-under par total of 279. Again in front after three rounds, this time Lee started nervously on the final day with two bogeys in the first three holes, plus a birdie at the second, but she then settled down and added seven more birdies. Scotland's Vikki Laing took second place after a closing 66, while Sarah-Jane Smith, who led for the first two days, was third, while another amateur, Su-Hyun Oh, shared fourth place.

Lee, the world No. 3 amateur, indicated her plans would change in the immediate future but said: "It feels unbelievable, it hasn't really sunk in yet, I'm pretty happy and just stoked that I have won. I saw the leaderboard after 15, and I was like, I just have to finish nicely and I'll be okay."

14. Senior Tours

Bernhard Langer was discussing his play in 2014. And never was heard a discouraging word from anyone in the audience.

"It's still mind-boggling just to reflect on my year," Langer was saying. "When you think about it, you play golf from January until now, it's 10 months, and to have played as consistently well as I've done in [21] tournaments is hard to believe, really."

It really was hard to believe. Langer, who turned 57 in August, won six tournaments, two of them majors, including the unofficial PNC Father/Son Challenge. He took the fun out of the Charles Schwab Cup race, piling up enough points to win it before it even got to the finale, the Charles Schwab Cup Championship. Overall, he had 12 top-three finishes and 18 top-10s in 21 starts, and topped the money list for the sixth time in seven years, this time with a tour record $3,074,189.

Langer's first major win of the year, his third as a senior, was in the Constellation Senior Players Championship, where he led much of the way but had to come from behind to tie fast-closing Jeff Sluman, then left him 1-for-9 in playoffs. ("If I'm in another playoff," Sluman said, "bet on the other guy.") Langer's career-fifth major was in the Senior Open Championship at Royal Porthcawl, where he led by eight going into the final round, and instead of coasting home, kept firing and won by an incredible 13.

Langer also won the season-opening Mitsubishi Electric Championship by three, the Insperity Invitational by one and the Dick's Sporting Goods Open by one for his fifth win of the season and 23rd on the Champions Tour. Some thought he might be ready to hang 'em up by now

"I'm having fun," Langer said. "Why should I quit?"

The season was one of sweetness and light for Colin Montgomerie, too. He won only twice, but they were both majors — the first and second of his entire Hall of Fame career.

Montgomerie finally broke through in the Senior PGA Championship in May. He had to hold off two other Hall of Famers to win it — Tom Watson and Bernhard Langer. "It might well have a senior connotation to it," said Monty, "but it is a major championship and I'm thrilled to be part of history." It was a breakthrough in more ways than one. In addition to being his first major, it was his first win in seven years, his first in the United States, his first as a senior.

Add another thrill: Two months later, Montgomerie won his second major, the U.S. Senior Open, beating Gene Sauers in a playoff. With a bagpiper playing "Flower of Scotland," no less.

"I'm really on top of the world now," Monty said.

Other items of interest from the 2014 Champions Tour season:

• The tour got its first 59, shot by rookie Kevin Sutherland in the second round of the Dick's Sporting Goods Open. It included a bogey at the last hole. The thing he remembered most: "The ovation I got at 18 … everybody stood up…"

• Spain's Miguel Angel Jimenez, "The Most Interesting Man in Golf," made his Champions debut with a wire-to-wire win at the Greater Gwinnett Championship, one week after he challenged at the Masters before finishing fourth.

• Rookie Scott Dunlap beat Mark Brooks in a playoff at the Boeing Classic, his first win after 15 Champions starts and 204 starts on the PGA Tour without a win. What did it mean? Said Dunlap: "It meant the wait was worth it."

• Tom Lehman had got into a zone, but not the kind golfers covet. This was a zone of second-guessing himself — second-guessing his reads, his strokes, and missing so many putts. He finally broke out of it in the Encompass Championship, leading wire-to-wire and going the first 48 holes without a bogey for his first win since 2012.

• Paul Goydos, a rookie, notched his first tour win in the Pacific Links Hawai'i Championship, but only after shaking off a multi-dose of adversity. First there was Tom Pernice's 60 in the first round. Then in the final round, finding his four-birdie charge blunted by Fred Funk's hole-in-one. Then, finally, overshooting the final green and facing a six-foot putt for bogey to win. Said the soft-spoken Goydos: "You're a little nervy up there."

The number "60" became something of a magic number for Jay Haas. A tour powerhouse only a few years ago, Haas was 60 now, and coming into the 2014 Greater Hickory Kia Classic, he hadn't won since 2012, a span of 27 months and/or 49 events. He shot three rounds, all in the 60s, to win by two. Said Haas: "Sixty — I guess it's just a number."

Montgomerie secured the Order of Merit title on the European Senior Tour in landslide fashion, thanks to those two major victories in America, his runner-up finish to Langer in the Senior Open Championship in Wales and two other wins on the European circuit, one the Travis Perkins Masters by 10 strokes. Montgomerie banked almost three times as much money as runner-up Canadian Rick Gibson.

Fellow Englishman Paul Wesselingh, the 2013 Order of Merit champion, was the only other multiple winner on that circuit in 2014. Both of his victories came in playoffs, the second in the MCB Tour Championship going six holes, he and Barry Lane matching birdies on the first five.

Masahiro (Massy) Kuramoto, one of the major stars of yesteryear in Japan, won the Japan Senior Open and the Iwasaki Shiratsuyu tournament and edged Kiyoshi Murota in the race for the No. 1 spot on the Japan Senior Tour money list.

Murota picked up his 12th title on the circuit (Fuji Film Senior), tying him with Katsunari Takahashi atop that category in the record book. Murota lost to Naomichi (Joe) Ozaki in a playoff in the Japan PGA Senior Championship and had another second-place finish in the Starts Senior.

Champions Tour

Mitsubishi Electric Championship

Ka'upulehu-Kona, Hawaii
Winner: Bernhard Langer

Brand-new year, same old Bernhard Langer.

It was mid-January, and Langer, now 56, came to the opener of the 2014 Champions Tour fresh from a dazzling 2013 season — two victories, five seconds, 10 other top-10 finishes and his fifth money-winning title. In the Mitsubishi, in his own unassuming way, he picked up where he left off. Despite hurting his thumb on Thursday, he overwhelmed Hualalai Golf Course and an exclusive field of 40 others and won by three for his 19th tour victory. Even more to the point, it was a masterpiece. After an eagle at No. 4, he made his only bogey of the tournament at No. 9, then birdied half of the remaining holes. Well, nearly half — 21 of the 45.

"It's a new year, and my goal was to get over the hurdle and win as soon as possible," Langer said.

Langer, coming from behind Rocco Mediate in the first round and breaking out of a tie with Fred Couples in the second, sprinted away from the field in the third, shooting 66-64-64 for a 22-under 194 total, winning by three over Couples, who closed with a 67, and Jeff Sluman (65).

Mediate, fighting a sore hip, notched a chip-in eagle and four birdies over his first seven holes for a nine-under 63 and the first-round lead by one. "This came out of nowhere," Mediate said. He would go on to finish fifth.

Langer and Couples edged ahead in the second round with birdies at the 17th, and though Langer was pouring on a barrage of birdies, the final round was a battle down the stretch. Sluman, trailing by two to start the final round, took the lead at the turn with his fifth birdie, off a strong short game. Langer tore off for five straight birdies from the 13th, tying Sluman and Couples there, taking the lead with a two-putt at the 14th, and closing with three more, all from inside 12 feet.

"I'm very pleased and extremely blessed to play golf like this," Langer said. "To be 22 under doesn't happen very often."

Allianz Championship

Boca Raton, Florida
Winner: Michael Allen

Michael Allen was faced with an identity crisis — one he surely didn't want.

"I didn't want to be known as the guy," Allen was saying, after taking the Allianz Championship, "who shot the lowest round on the Champions Tour and didn't win."

But he did flirt with that ignominious distinction after shooting a 60 in the first round. He had to do some tall playing, but he hung on, tied Duffy Waldorf, then beat him in a playoff. Allen shot the Old Course at Broken Sound in 60-69-69 to tie with Waldorf (68-63-67) at a tournament-record 18-under 198, then two-putted for a birdie on the second extra hole, the par-five 18th, for his sixth tour victory.

Said the winless Waldorf, who had 12 top-10 finishes in his first tour season in 2013: "The good news is, that's as close as I've come to winning. I was so far behind after the first day [eight strokes], I was glad to finally catch up on the last hole."

Allen's 60 was the ninth on the tour but the first on a par-72 course. It might have been a 59, but Allen began thinking about it at his 15th hole — the par-five sixth — and missed his birdie putt. "The story of my career — 'Almost,'" said Allen, recalling his 369 starts without a win on the PGA Tour. "After I missed the birdie putt on No. 6, I kind of figured it [the 60] wasn't happening." But Allen, who already had eight birdies and an eagle, regrouped and birdied his 16th and 18th for the 60.

Battling a cranky swing in the second round, he had to birdie four of his last eight holes for a 69 for one-stroke lead over Scott Dunlap (67) and Chien Soon Lu (65). In the final round, Allen birdied three holes through No. 7, bogeyed the eighth, birdied the 14th, bogeyed the 16th, and finally birdied the 18th to tie Waldorf and set the stage for his win.

"You shoot 60," said Allen, "you think you're going to win a little easier."

ACE Group Classic

Naples, Florida

Winner: Kirk Triplett

Kirk Triplett beat Bernhard Langer down the stretch again, for the second time — this at the ACE Group Classic — and some suggested he had Langer's number. Not so, Triplett said gently. The number is way too small for that. Or, as Triplett put it, with the precision of an academic (he holds a degree in civil engineering), "We're just going to say the sample size is still very small." In short, there's not enough evidence.

At any rate, Triplett did have his second victory over a formidable resident force on the Champions Tour, outlasting both Langer and Duffy Waldorf in a real scramble down the stretch at TwinEagles' Talon course. Triplett was the only one to hit the green at the par-four 18th. Waldorf bunkered his drive and two-putted for a bogey. Langer also bogeyed, missing the green and two-putting. That left it to Triplett, and it wasn't a lock. He knocked his 25-foot birdie putt six feet past and had to make that coming back for a par and his third tour win. He won on a card of 67-67-66–200, 16 under.

"That last hole is really hard, especially where that pin is," said Triplett. "It still kind of surprises me how sudden it's over, because 18 holes of back and forth, back and forth, either tied for the lead or in the lead, and then boom, it's over."

Langer, who won the season-opening Mitsubishi Championship two starts previously, took the first-round lead, crediting his eight-under 64 to a new putting stance. "I'm standing farther away — that's really all that is," he said.

Triplett tied him in the second round, setting the stage for the scrambling finish. Waldorf had three birdies and an eagle on the front, and birdies at the 13th and 16th got him to 16 under. Langer got there with birdies at 13, 15 and 17. Triplett eagled No. 3, birdied the 12th and 13th and parred in. Finally, at the 18th, came Triplett's comebacker par putt against two bogeys.

"It wasn't the best I made all day," he said, "but it was good enough."

Toshiba Classic

Newport Beach, California

Winner: Fred Couples

The redoubtable Bernhard Langer had chalked up his 19th Champions Tour win in the Mitsubishi Electric Championship leading off the 2014 season, and three starts later, he was well on his way to No. 20 in the Toshiba Classic. Then suddenly, in the third and final round, he was feeling like the one on the wrong end of a fox hunt, and it was Fred Couples who came out the other end with the prize.

Langer led by two going into the finale, then one little bogey did the trick. He bogeyed No. 1, and Chien Soon Lu caught him with a birdie there, and before long, he was overrun in the chase. Couples dived in with three birdies over the first 10 holes. Steve Pate, Jeff Hart, Scott Dunlap and Mark O'Meara also rushed in. It was anyone's tournament, but that "anyone" looked to be Colin Montgomerie at first. Monty was eight strokes back starting the final round, but caught fire and raced through Newport Beach Country Club, finishing early with a flawless, nine-under 62 and the clubhouse lead. "I don't envision winning," said Monty, who joined the tour the previous summer and was still looking for that first win. To his surprise, he came within a whisker. But Couples was picking up momentum.

Three behind starting the last round, Couples climbed the crowded leaderboard and tied for the lead with birdies at the second and fourth holes. But he couldn't stick, given a bogey at the 11th and the birdies dropping all around him. He did move back into contention with birdies at the 15th and 17th, and took the lead, finally, with a scrambled birdie at the par-five 18th, chipping to six feet from in front of the grandstand. Langer needed a last-gasp birdie at the 18th to tie him, but a visit to the rough held him to a tie for second.

Couples, shooting 65-67-66 for a 15-under 198, reduced his victory to a simple formula. "If you're near the lead and you birdie a few holes," he said, "you're going to win — like today."

Mississippi Gulf Resort Classic

Biloxi, Mississippi

Winner: Jeff Maggert

It's called a "lag putt." It's either so long or so difficult, the golfer is just trying to get it close enough to set up an easy one for his next. And so it was for Jeff Maggert in the final round of the Mississippi Gulf Resort Classic. Maggert was at Fallen Oak's par-three 17th, facing a bending 50-footer — time for a lag putt if there ever was one. He gave it a good rap, to get it up over the ridge, then patiently watched it take the left-to-right break, and roll and roll, and then — drop. Said Maggert, with a self-conscious grin: "You can't count on those going in very often."

But this one did, and Maggert, a three-time winner on the PGA Tour, went on to become the 17th player to win his Champions Tour debut. He shot Fallen Oak in 68-69-68–205, 11 under par, and won by two.

Maggert trailed by a stroke through the first two rounds, first behind Fred Couples, then Billy Andrade and Fred Funk. With 11 players within three shots of the lead, it looked like a wide-open race. First, the anticipated Andrade-Funk duel faded when Funk bogged down. After making 10 birdies in his 69-67 start, he made none in the final round but took three bogeys for a 75. Fred Couples had to work for a 72, and Jay Haas could manage only a 71. Bernhard Langer made a move with a 68, but fell well short.

Andrade, erratic after having played little for four years, made five birdies, but four bogeys and shot 71. "I haven't been in this type of situation in a long time," he said.

Maggert was steadier, seven birdies against three bogeys for his 68. His last bogey, at the 16th, dropped him into a tie with Andrade, and his tee shot at the 17th didn't show much promise, not leaving him 50 feet from the cup. He'd be lucky to two-putt from there, and he knew it. That first putt would be critical. Said Maggert: "I was just trying to hit an easy lag putt."

Greater Gwinnett Championship

Duluth, Georgia

Winner: Miguel Angel Jimenez

Spain's Miguel Angel Jimenez, "Golf's Most Interesting Man" (a phrase borrowed from a TV beer commercial), figured that while he was going to be in Georgia anyway, for the Masters, he might just as well drop in at the Greater Gwinnett Championship. And thus did he add to his growing legend — becoming just the third to lead wire-to-wire in winning his Champions Tour debut.

It looked easy. "When you hit the ball straight and put the ball near to the hole, it looks easy — nothing is easy," said Jimenez, fresh from nearly stunning the world of golf. A week earlier, at age 50, he challenged at the Masters before finishing fourth, just four strokes behind Bubba Watson.

Jimenez began the Gwinnett on a chill, rainy day that Bernhard Langer termed "as cold and ugly as you can get." But Jimenez was warmed by a bogey-free 65, seven under par at the TPC Sugarloaf, and a three-stroke lead. "Now it's time," he said, "for a nice, warm shower, a nice, fat cigar and a glass of Rioja." A man of such simple needs figures to be hard to distract, and so he was. He held off Langer and Fred Couples, closing with 70-67 for a 14-under 202 and a two-stroke win over Langer.

But easy it wasn't. In the second round, Jimenez had to birdie the 18th against Langer's three-putt par to re-take the lead. Then Jimenez all but locked up the win at two holes in the final round. He broke out of a tie and into a two-stroke lead at the eighth with a birdie to Langer's bogey. At the 15th, his trouble-bound tee shot bounced off a tree and back into the fairway. Then he bunkered his next, but still managed to par, and came home untouched.

Jimenez's debut in senior golf was also his farewell, for the moment. He was returning to the European Tour with one thought in mind. "To me, it's not about money," he said. "It's about some different goals. ... it would feel nice to play on the Ryder Cup team once more."

Insperity Invitational

The Woodlands, Texas

Winner: Bernhard Langer

To no one's surprise, Bernhard Langer took the Insperity Invitational lead in the first round and stayed there. But he did eventually weaken — not that it did anybody much good. It was pretty much the same old thing. At one point, Colin Montgomerie threw up his hands, and he could have been speaking for everyone who ever tried to rein in Langer once he gets rolling. "I've been trying all bloody year and I've not done it yet," said Monty. "Not many people have, to be honest."

Not this time, either. It was touch-and-go with a late-charging Fred Couples, but Langer, 56, despite staggering home, posted his second win of the season, his third in the Insperity and his 20th on the Champions Tour.

"Freddie played very well there on the back side, made a bunch of birdies," Langer said. "He came on pretty strong until the last hole when he bogeyed and that made it a little bit easier for me to play 18 with a two-shot lead."

Langer birdied the last six holes to tie Bart Bryant for the first-round lead at 66, then led the rest of the way with 68-71 for an 11-under-par 205 at the par-72 Woodlands Country Club. He led Montgomerie by three after the second round. But he had a battle on his hands in the last. Langer birdied four of the first seven holes, bogeyed No. 8 and led by five. Couples had a wild front nine, posting a bogey, a double bogey, two birdies and an eagle, then caught fire coming in, birdieing the 10th and four straight from the 12th to pull within one. But he stumbled at the 18th, taking a bogey after missing the green. Langer, who didn't make a birdie over his last 11 holes, bogeyed the 16th and 18th, shot 71, and won by one, becoming just the 10th Champions Tour player with 20 wins.

"I hope I'm not done," Langer said. "It's been a great run and a wonderful achievement. I just feel like I'm playing some of my best golf in my career."

Regions Tradition

Shoal Creek, Alabama

Winner: Kenny Perry

A golfer and his clubs are much like a violinist and his violin, and so Kenny Perry found his game out of tune after an airline broke the driver that launched him to his first two over-50 majors in 2013. He searched for

10 months and seemed to finally find that just-right replacement in time to win his third, the 2014 Regions Tradition.

True, he won the 2013 AT&T and the Charles Schwab Cup. "But I didn't really play great ... so hopefully this driver's going to solve my problems," Perry said.

It did, and he posted his first Champions Tour win of 2014, his sixth overall, and with the 2013 Senior Players Championship and U.S. Senior Open, he became the second player since Gary Player in 1987-88 to win three consecutive starts in majors.

Shoal Creek, never an easy test, proved stubborn again in a windy, chilly start in mid-May. Jay Haas, capping a three-birdie run with a 50-foot birdie putt at the 12th, joined a quartet leading at 69. Perry, still fidgeting with his driver, shot 72. Without fanfare, Perry switched to yet another driver for the second round, and it seemed to be the one he was looking for. He shot 68 and was two behind Calcavecchia (69). "I need another one of these ... to get back into it for Sunday," Perry said. He got it, a 69, for a one-stroke lead through the third round. Calcavecchia stumbled to two bogeys and a double bogey for a 74. "Two wrong clubs and a chunk in the water," he explained.

Things broke perfectly for Perry in the final round. John Cook had surged into the lead but double-bogeyed the 14th on a double hit coming out of a bunker and shot 72. Calcavecchia also slipped, missing two short par putts, and shot 70.

Perry made it home with a choppy par 72 — three birdies, three bogeys — for a seven-under 281 total and a one-stroke win over Calcavecchia. "Nobody was really running, so I knew par was a good score," Perry said. "I guess patience was the key word today."

Senior PGA Championship

Benton Harbor, Michigan

Winner: Colin Montgomerie

Colin Montgomerie had precisely the right words for the occasion: "Bloody great."

Well, he was speaking of an especially good shot, but it fit perfectly the next day when he won the Senior PGA Championship, and what a personal landmark it was — his first win in seven years, first as a senior, first in the United States and, most fulfilling, his first major title, something he didn't get in 71 majors on the regular tours.

"I feel fantastic, really — superb," Montgomerie said. "I've had a couple of failures here in America, and it's great to finally win, never mind a Champions Tour event, but a Senior PGA Championship."

But Montgomerie, 51, had to outlast two legends to do it — Tom Watson, 64, and Bernhard Langer, 56. The battle began at the halfway point, when they were stuck in a six-way tie for the 36-hole lead at 138, four under par at Harbor Shores. Monty, in his first Senior PGA, started 69-69 and broke away with a 68 in the third round, pulling one ahead of Langer (69) and four ahead of Watson (72).

In the final round, Langer bowed out on a double bogey at the par-three 11th. Montgomerie and Watson went toe-to-toe, but Monty had that four-shot edge to start. He had an early birdie and his lone bogey, then came the decisive stretch. "The birdies at eight, nine, 10 were key," Monty said. He birdied the eighth off a five wood to 10 feet, and the back-to-back par-fives — coming out of a bunker to 10 feet at the ninth, and chipping to four feet at the 10th. Watson birdied Nos. 10, 11, 13 and 14 in a bogey-free 65 and pronounced it one of his best rounds in years, except, "the putter felt like a snake in my hands."

Montgomerie kept pace with birdies at Nos. 12, 14 and 15 for his own 65 for a four-stroke win on a 271 total. "It might well have a senior connotation to it, but it is a major championship and I'm thrilled to be part of this history."

Principal Charity Classic

Des Moines, Iowa

Winner: Tom Pernice, Jr.

Most golfers have a favorite hole somewhere. For Tom Pernice, Jr. it's looking like No. 17 — wherever he's playing. At the 2013 3M Championship at TPC Twin Cities, he got a grip on the title at the 17th in the last round by holing a 40-foot putt. This time, in the final round of the Principal Charity Classic, he birdied the Wakonda Club's par-three 17th, chipping in from 30 feet, then beat little known Doug Garwood in a playoff for his third Champions Tour victory.

Pernice shot Wakonda, the new venue for the Principal, in 68-67-69, and Garwood tied him at 12-under 204 with a card of 68-65-71. Pernice summarized his win in elemental terms. "I ... kept the ball in play ... and holed some key shots at key times," he said.

It was the worst sort of loss for the obscure Garwood. He had played just three tournaments on the Web.com Tour since 2005 and was making only his fourth Champions start of 2014. His previous best finish was a tie for 25th. He entered the final round leading Michael Allen by one and Pernice by two, then finished awkwardly. He expanded his lead with birdies at Nos. 1, 4 and 5 but squandered it with three straight bogeys from No. 6. Then Garwood birdied the last two holes, while Pernice birdied Nos. 12 and 13, bogeyed 14, then rolled in that long and precious birdie at the 17th.

Garwood still smarted from the tour qualifying school, where he three-putted the final hole to miss his full exemption. But he wasn't kicking himself this time. "Here, I didn't feel like I gave it away," he said, "because I earned it with the birdies on 17 and 18."

The Principal opened with a four-way tie for the lead at 69, including Dan Forsman, who authored the tour's Birdie of the Year (to date). At the par-five 13th, Forsman drove into the rough, hit a tree with his second shot, put his third over the green, then holed out from 70 feet coming back. "That's why," he cracked, "we hit all those pitch shots."

Big Cedar Lodge Legends of Golf

Ridgedale, Missouri

Winners: Fred Funk and Jeff Sluman

Jeff Sluman figured he'd found the secret to team golf. "Maybe I've got a good eye for partners," he said, after teaming with Fred Funk to win the Big Cedar Lodge Legends of Golf. He'd also won it in 2013, but with Brad Faxon.

Funk saw it the other way. "He's the common denominator," Funk said.

But this one wasn't your father's Legends, not the way the tournament started in 1978, spawning the Champions Tour. This Legends, held at the Big Cedar Lodge Resort, was a historic departure and a bookkeeper's feast. Marveled Tom Watson before the tournament: "We're going to be playing alternate shot or foursome or twosome play. We're going to be playing best ball, and we're going to play a scramble format." And on two different courses — the regulation Buffalo Ridge course and also, for the first time in a PGA Tour-sanctioned event, a par-three course, the Top of the Rock.

But one thing hadn't changed: Shotmaking. Sluman dropped a six-foot par putt on the final hole, giving himself and Funk a six-under 48 at the rainy par-three course to beat Jay Haas and Peter Jacobsen by a stroke.

Sluman and Funk finished at 20-under 159. They shot an 11-under 61 in better-ball on Buffalo Ridge and 50 on Saturday on the par-three layout.

Haas and Jacobsen, the second-round leaders, shot 50. Haas missed an eight-foot birdie putt on the 17th hole of the day. "I'm disappointed because ... it was as easy a putt as you can get," Haas said.

In the nine-hole Legends finale, Jim Colbert and Jim Thorpe shot a 4-under 23 in better-ball to beat Bruce Fleisher and Larry Nelson by three. Colbert and Thorpe finished 11 under for 45 holes.

"The tournament was a lot of fun," Funk said. "It ... turned out to be a real treat to play this par-three." It was also seen as something of a test run for those who believe nine-hole par-three courses might help to rejuvenate the sagging game.

Encompass Championship

Glenview, Illinois

Winner: Tom Lehman

If anyone wondered whatever became of Tom Lehman, it's that he was stuck in a zone, but not the kind where the game turns magical.

"I've been living in this zone of second-guessing my reads, second-guessing my stroke, because I misread so many putts," said Lehman, who took the last of his seven Champions Tour victories in 2012. "It's been a very frustrating last couple of years." Lehman noted this after the first round of the Encompass Championship at North Shore in June, and if going the first 48 holes without a bogey and if going wire-to-wire against a classy field for a one-stroke win were any indication, then the Lehman who won the 1996 Open Championship had resurfaced.

In fact, he appeared in the first round, closing with a rush for a seven-under-par 65. Finishing on the back nine, Lehman birdied four straight holes from his 13th (No. 4), tapping in at the par-five sixth, and holing a 15-foot putt at No. 7. He led by one over England's Roger Chapman, who won two majors in his debut year, 2012, and Doug Garwood, playoff runner-up at the recent Principal Classic. Lurking behind were Colin Montgomerie (69), winner of the Senior PGA a month earlier, and Bernhard Langer (71), a two-time winner already this year.

Lehman, who led by three through the second round, closed with 66-70 for a 15-under 201 and a one-stroke win over the hard-pressing Michael Allen and Kirk Triplett, who both almost tied him at the 18th. Allen (67) birdied three of the last four holes, including the 18th, where he tapped in after just missing a tying eagle. Triplett (68) just missed on a 20-foot birdie try from the fringe.

Lehman's touch had faded a bit, and he parred the first 11 holes. "I wasn't putting like I did the first two days," he said. He made his first bogey at the 13th, another at 14. Then he birdied 15, 16 and 18 for the 70 and the win.

"It wasn't my very best performance today," Lehman said, "but it was good enough."

Constellation Senior Players Championship

Pittsburgh, Pennsylvania

Winner: Bernhard Langer

The big noise at the Constellation Senior Players Championship was supposed to come from the Bernhard Langer-Kenny Perry collision. Hadn't Perry even said he was going into the "attack mode" to run down his good friend in the final round?

Langer knew the heat was coming. "I still have to shoot under par tomorrow," he said.

And said Perry, the defending champion, after hot middle rounds of 63-65: "If he kicks my butt, I'll shake his hand, give him a hug, whatever."

But beware the silent golfer. That was the understated and diminutive Jeff Sluman, five strokes behind starting the final round, quietly making his way up the leaderboard, one birdie at a time across Fox Chapel Golf Club. He took the lead with a birdie at the 14th, and added another at the 16th, and was in with a five-under 65 and a 15-under 265 total. He shot 69-67-64-65. Meanwhile, Langer, who shot 65-64-66-70, led from the second round. Perry took up the chase with a 63 in the second. They began laboring in the fourth. Perry, three behind to start, was out in 31 with five birdies and a bogey, and tied with Langer, but came home in 38, with three bogeys, for a 69. "I wanted to shoot 65 or better," Perry said. He finished fourth.

Langer was out in four birdies and two bogeys, then bogeyed the 10th and double-bogeyed the par-four 12th. "This was not Bernhard Langer," he was to say. He was trailing Sluman by a stroke coming to the par-three 17th. There, he holed a 35-foot putt for birdie, shot 70 and tied Sluman at 265. The playoff was at the par-five 18th. They tied in pars on the first try. On the second, Langer pitched brilliantly from the rough to five feet and holed the birdie putt for his third win of the year, his third major as a senior and 21st senior win.

"It comes in all shades, I guess," Langer said.

Said Sluman, now 1-for-9 in playoffs: "If I'm in another playoff, bet on the other guy."

U.S. Senior Open

Edmond, Oklahoma

Winner: Colin Montgomerie

A bagpiper? At the U.S. Senior Open in the flatlands of Oklahoma? Clad in a heavy kilt in the oppressive July heat and humidity, and skirling away alongside the fairway? If this wasn't a sign, what was it? And just in time.

"I'm 5,000 miles from my home," said Colin Montgomerie, native son of Scotland, "... a thrill."

Montgomerie was chasing Gene Sauers in the final round, and he was running out of holes. The piper appeared at the 12th. Whether he was a sign, an inspiration or just a pleasant interlude, Monty finally ended up tied with Sauers and beat him in a three-hole aggregate playoff. So the man who couldn't win a major in 71 tries across a Hall-of-Fame career suddenly had his second senior major in four starts, adding the Senior Open to the Senior PGA Championship.

Montgomerie, shooting Oak Tree in 65-71-74-69, led through the first two rounds, stumbled in the third when he hit only six greens in regulation and trailed Sauers by four. He finally caught up in the fourth when Sauers (69-69-68-73) bogeyed the 16th out of a bunker. When Sauers' 10-foot birdie putt at the 18th lipped out, they were tied at five-under 279 and off to a three-hole playoff.

Both bogeyed the par-four 16th out of bunkers. Montgomerie took the lead with a two-putt par at the par-three 17th to Sauers' bogey. And at the par-four 18th, with Sauers sitting four feet from a par, Monty holed his own par from 16 feet for the win.

Sauers was disappointed, but far from crushed. Just three years earlier, he had flirted with death from a rare and painful skin disorder. "I'm glad to be able to be here and play with my friends again," Sauers said.

Said Monty: "I've been close in these USGA championships ... I've lost in a playoff and been one shot behind, and had to wait till 50 to finally win one. I'm really on top of the world right now."

And he remembered what the piper was playing. "'Flower of Scotland,'" Monty said. "Amazing."

The Senior Open Championship presented by Rolex

Bridgend, Wales

Winner: Bernhard Langer

See European Senior Tour section.

3M Championship

Blaine, Minnesota

Winner: Kenny Perry

Two glances were all it took to turn the 3M Championship into a sprint to the finish line. The thing was, it was one glance by Bernhard Langer, the other by Kenny Perry, setting up a shootout between two of the dominant forces on the Champions Tour.

First came Langer, who started the final round three strokes off Perry's lead. "I looked at the leaderboard somewhere around the eighth hole and saw I was four behind or whatever," said Langer, already a four-time winner this season, including the Senior Open Championship the week before, "and I figured I got to go really low here if I want to have any hope."

Then the nearly complacent Perry: "I was just cruising … thinking if I par in, it's over. And then I look up on 17 and we're tied."

It was a birdie-fest from the start. The field was pummeling the par-72 TPC Twin Cities, led by Marco Dawson's opening 63. As Rocco Mediate put it after his first-round 64: "I love the feeling that this is a sprint. If you shot one or two under today, you're done."

Perry, who started 65-63, kept up the pressure to start the final round, with four birdies through No. 8. That's what caught Langer's attention. He'd made three birdies, then a bogey, and lost ground. Perry then birdied the 10th and 12th and started thinking about pars. He woke with a jolt when he discovered that Langer birdied the 17th to tie him, capping a run of seven birdies over nine holes. It would be settled at the par-five 18th.

Langer, in the next-to-last group, missed the green with his approach, chipped on and two-putted for his par and a 63. Perry knocked his approach into the grandstand behind the green, took a free drop, pitched on to 15 feet and holed the putt for a 65, a 23-under 193 total and the one-stroke decision, his second win of the year.

"It was an easy putt for me," Perry said. "I don't always make them, but I feel I should..."

Dick's Sporting Goods Open

Endicott, New York

Winner: Bernhard Langer

It would take some doing to upstage Bernhard Langer, the way he'd been playing. And that's exactly what Kevin Sutherland did. While Langer was busy putting together a flawless fifth victory of the season in the Dick's Sporting Goods Open at En-Joie Country Club, Sutherland was making history, posting the Champions Tour's first 59. And that included a bogey.

Sutherland, 50, making only his third tour start, opened with a one-under-par 71, then caught fire in the second round. He birdied the first four holes — two of the putts were over 30 feet — and eagled No. 5, then birdied the next three for an outward 28. Coming in, he birdied Nos. 10, 11, 15, 16 and 17. His chance for a 58 ended with a three-putt bogey from 40 feet at the 18th.

"The ovation I got on 18 ... everybody stood up and was clapping," Sutherland said. "I think that's what I'm going to remember most." He closed with a 74 and tied for seventh.

Meanwhile, Langer was methodically making his way around En-Joie in a bogey-free 67-67-66–200, 16 under par. He trailed all the way, first by two behind John Cook and Olin Browne, who shot 65s. The second round belonged to Sutherland and his spectacular 59 for a one-stroke lead. The final round, Langer nursed a one-shot lead past Woody Austin and Mark O'Meara for his third victory in five starts, his fifth win of the season and 23rd on the tour.

It was a scramble coming down the homestretch. A Langer-Steve Lowery duel fizzled out when Lowery watered his five iron and double-bogeyed the 14th. Austin was in with the clubhouse lead at 15 under, and O'Meara birdied two of the last three to tie him. Langer got to 16 under with a 25-foot birdie putt at the 14th, then parred in for the 66 and the one-stroke win. What was still driving the 56-year-old?

"Well, it's just I love to compete and I'm still capable of high-quality golf ... and I'm having fun," Langer said. "Why should I quit?"

Boeing Classic

Snoqualmie, Washington

Winner: Scott Dunlap

Scott Dunlap, a Champions Tour rookie, who had chased the little white ball all over the world, gave a quick grammar lesson after taking the lead in the second round of the Boeing Classic. Someone asked, so can you hang on to win? Said Dunlap: "I know I can — it's will I?"

Whatever the verb, Dunlap answered the question the next day with a birdie putt on the first hole of a playoff against Mark Brooks. He had won twice on the Web.com Tour, but three ties for third was the best he'd done in seven fragmented years and 204 starts on the PGA Tour. What did it mean to win at last?

"It means the wait was worth it," Dunlap said.

It looked like business as usual for Dunlap when he opened with a 69. That was three under par at TPC Snoqualmie Ridge, but five off Mike Goodes' lead. But all those years of work and frustration seemed to get wiped out in the second round. Goodes faded, as did Michael Allen, who ran off five straight birdies but double-bogeyed the 10th. Fred Couples, the hometown favorite, and Bernhard Langer, the tour's hottest player, both were struggling. And Dunlap holed out a 150-yard approach for an eagle at the par-four No. 4, then racked up seven birdies for a flawless 63 and a one-stroke lead — his first lead ever entering the final round on the Champions, Web.com or PGA Tours.

Dunlap had to survive a real shootout in the final round. When he bogeyed the fourth and sixth, seven players were within a stroke of the lead. Then he rolled in a 45-foot putt for eagle at No. 8. Brooks, three behind starting the final round, shot 65, and Dunlap made three birdies coming in for a 68 and a tie at 16-under 200. On the first playoff hole, the par-five 18th,

Dunlap missed an eagle from four feet but got the birdie and his first tour win.

"I was very much looking forward to this day," Dunlap said.

Shaw Charity Classic

Calgary, Alberta, Canada

Winner: Fred Couples

The guys were having a high time putting up low numbers in the Shaw Charity Classic, so Fred Couples, in only his ninth start of the season, was entertaining no greater ambition than a comeback from the sore wrist and chronic aching back that had sidelined him for some two months. He had started 68-66 and didn't figure he had a chance. Then in the final round, after a handful of birdies and an eagle, another idea occurred to him.

"It never came into my mind about winning the tournament until really, maybe the 15th, 16th holes," Couples said. At that point, he was well on his way to a Canyon Meadows course record. Tom Pernice, Jr. and Bart Bryant had set it at 62 for the first-round lead. Couples broke it two days later, chipping in from 40 feet for an eagle and a nine-under 61. Then came a playoff against tour rookie Billy Andrade, who tied him at 15-under 195 with an eagle at the 18th for a 62. In the playoff, also at the 18th, after Andrade missed the green, Couples tapped in for a birdie for his second win of the season and 11th on the tour.

"Hats off to Fred, and move on," Andrade said. "When you lose, you lose. But you want to win when you get this close. Unfortunately, I didn't. Life's still great, everything's good."

Couples won in two ways — flawless play and dominating the par-fives. "No bogeys is good," is the way he put it. He'd gone all three rounds without one. And his length helped conquer the course's three par-fives. He played them in nine under, including three eagles.

The tournament was up for grabs most of the way. First Pernice and Bryant led the first round, and Bob Tway, Joe Durant and Joe Daley tied in the second. Then came Couples and Andrade, finishing two ahead of Daley and Steve Lowery. Lowery thought his closing 63 would have a chance. "But you never know," he offered, "when someone's going to come out and shoot a 61 like that."

Quebec Championship

Quebec City, Quebec, Canada

Winner: Wes Short, Jr.

Scott Dunlap was recalling his statement of a few weeks earlier: "...you can play winning golf and not hoist the trophy." Dunlap had just taken the lead with an eagle at the final hole in the Quebec Championship, and that truism was no sooner out of his mouth than along came Wes Short, Jr. to top him with an eagle of his own to snatch the title, scoring his first victory on the Champions Tour.

Dunlap had the tournament just about wrapped up with his eight-under-par 64 and a 14-under total. Then he lost by a shot. Nobody saw Short coming.

He opened with an eagle-birdie 69, four off the lead. He shot 68 in the second round, with five birdies and his only bogey of the tournament, and gained only a stroke. He was no stranger to streaks. He'd shot a 62 in the 3M Championship a month earlier. Still, even he was surprised by his breakout in the final round. He'd ground out eight straight pars, and at the par-five No. 9, came out of a bunker to six feet and holed the birdie putt. "It seemed to open the floodgates," he said. He rolled to birdies at Nos. 10, 12, 14, 16 and 17, and the clutch eagle at the 18th for a 64 and a 15-under 201.

The tournament opened with winless Chip Beck, 57, taking the lead with a 65 and saying, "It's time, isn't it?" Esteban Toledo (66) and Brad Faxon (67) tied at 10-under 134 through the second round.

Short thought the birdie at the 17th had given him the lead or a tie. Then he glanced at the scoreboard and discovered Dunlap had eagled, and that he needed a birdie at the 18th to tie. He hit a hybrid from 251 yards to eight feet. Then he holed the eagle and could reflect that he had played pretty well for 45 holes but didn't have much to show for it.

"But," said Short, "I saved an awful lot for those last nine holes."

Pacific Links Hawai'i Championship

Kapolei, Hawaii

Winner: Paul Goydos

The notion of adversity to a golfer usually means a buried lie in a bunker, a triple bogey and the like. Adversity can take other forms, however, as Paul Goydos discovered, en route to his first Champions Tour victory. This time, it was the shock of the oft-winning Fred Funk scoring a hole-in-one late in a scramble down the final stretch of the Pacific Links Hawai'i Championship.

"I couldn't hit a better putt than I did on 16," Goydos said. "I'm happy how I handled things at 16 after Fred made ace." That was Goydos bouncing back from Funk's ace to get a birdie as he was breaking out of a traffic jam with four straight birdies from the 14th. Goydos scrambled to a bogey at the 18th, to wrap up a card of 66-63-68, a tournament-record 197, 19 under par at Kapolei Golf Club, for a one-shot victory over Funk (69) and Scott Dunlap (65).

The mid-September tournament was a mad dash of low scores, beginning with Tom Pernice, Jr. blitzing the course for a 12-under-par 60. "That's awesome," said Pernice, taking a four-stroke lead on Michael Allen. But he would come back with a 72.

The chase started in the second round, the heat of which was old hat to Funk, owner of nine tour titles. Funk shot a 62 and Goydos a 63 to tie at 15-under 129 for a two-stroke lead. "You've got to make a lot of birdies out here," Funk said, and he did, including seven in an eight-hole stretch from No. 4.

Goydos resolved the issue late in the final round, launching his four-birdie streak with a six-foot putt at the par-five 14th. At the 15th, he fired a 140-yard approach to an inch, then holed a 15-foot putt at No. 16 — this after Funk's ace — and then rolled in a six-footer at the par-five 17th. At the 18th, he fired his approach beyond the green. "You're a little nervy up there," said Goydos, who faced down that adversity, too, and scratched out the bogey that held up for the win.

Nature Valley First Tee Open

Monterey Peninsula, California

Winner: John Cook

Was John Cook really calling himself a slow learner?

Well, not really. It was just a little self-deprecating needle, but he made his point. Cook's ball sat 25 feet from a birdie at Pebble Beach's famed par-five 18th. But all he needed was a par to win the Nature Valley First Tee Open. Who can resist a chance to make a birdie? In this case, Cook. He was content to get his first putt close, then tapped in for the par and notched his 10th Champions Tour victory by a shot.

"I played to make par," said Cook. "I don't often do that, but maybe I've learned something in 40 or 45 years."

It was more than just a victory for Cook. It was a huge relief. Cook last won in early 2013, and this February he was injured in a fall at home and missed 10 weeks. "I was really excited for this year, then [with the injury], I got really down," he said. "I didn't know when I was going to be able to play again."

It all came together in September, in the tournament that brings in 81 First Tee kids from across the country to play with the pros on two courses on California's Monterey Peninsula. Cook opened with a 67 at the par-71 Poppy Hills, birdieing five of the last 10 holes to finish one behind the leader, Blaine McCallister. Then he moved to Pebble Beach and took the second-round lead with a piecemeal 68 — four birdies and a double bogey going out, and two birdies and two bogeys coming in. In the final round, after a birdie at No. 2 and a bogey at No. 5, Cook finished flawlessly, with birdies at Nos. 6, 7 and 13 for the 69, an 11-under 204 and the one-stroke win over Tom Byrum, who derailed his chances for his first tour win with bogeys at the 14th and 17th. "But I am encouraged with how I played," Byrum said.

As for Cook on the final round: "I didn't have my best stuff, but my putting showed up."

SAS Championship

Cary, North Carolina

Winner: Kirk Triplett

You're leading by three with only one hole left to play. How great does that feel? "Everybody watching on TV feels comfortable," Kirk Triplett said. "The guy with the three-shot lead still doesn't feel comfortable."

But, finally, the guy did. Triplett made his sixth birdie of the day at the 17th, then parred the 18th to complete a card of 70-63-69– 202 for a three-stroke victory over Tom Lehman in the SAS Championship at Prestonwood Country Club.

But Triplett had good reason to be edgy. "I was playing with Paul [Goydos] and Tom, and ... they were getting some chances but they weren't converting," Triplett said. "And I just felt like I had a nice cushion. After that, a tough old guy, Tommy Lehman, birdied 16, eagled 17." Triplett weathered the threat and Lehman closed at 70–205.

Guy Boros, son of Hall-of-Famer Julius Boros, found a putter he liked and authored a six-under-par 66 for the first-round lead. "Hopefully, I'll stick with this one quite a while," said Boros, playing in his second Champions Tour event and leading by one over Lehman and Marco Dawson. Lehman found the course much to his liking. "Once you drive it in the fairway, you can get aggressive and start attacking the pins," he said.

In the second round, Triplett found the course a little softer and even more approachable. "I felt you could be a little more aggressive," he said. Accordingly, he went out with three birdies for a 32, and came in with four birdies and a hole-out eagle at the par-four 18th for a bogey-free 63 and a two-stroke lead on Lehman and Goydos, who noted, "I've got a feeling tomorrow, you're going to have to make a lot of birdies."

Triplett wrapped the win with an odd round. He made three bogeys but followed each with a birdie, and closed out with birdies at 11, 12 and 17 and had a luxurious three-stroke lead going to the 18th. It was clear he had his fourth tour win all locked up — clear to everyone but him.

Greater Hickory Kia Classic

Conover, North Carolina

Winner: Jay Haas

Jay Haas had been playing well on the Champions Tour, but nothing like when he was a kid among the 50-and-overs. Then the old spark returned at the Greater Hickory Kia Classic at Rock Barn in October. Haas ignored the fact that he was now 60 and led wire-to-wire for his 17th Champions Tour victory but his first since 2012, a span of 27 months and 49 events.

"Sixty is some sort of benchmark," Haas allowed. "I guess it's just a number."

But it didn't come easily. Haas tied with Joe Durant for the first-round lead with an eight-under-par 63, then led the rest of the way with 67-66 for a convincing 17-under-par 196 and a two-shot win over Durant and Kirk Triplett.

Durant made the finish more interesting than Haas would have liked, birdieing five of the first six holes to tie him. "Then I hit the doldrums," Durant said. "I couldn't make a putt." Haas retook the solo lead at the 12th and went two ahead at the 17th, dropping a 16-foot birdie putt.

Haas suspected he was getting his touch back right from the start. An eagle on the first hole is a good hint. Then he logged four straight birdies from the third hole and added three more on the back nine for seven over a span of 12 holes. A bogey at the 15th cooled him on his way to the 63.

Even so — "It was pretty magical," Haas said. Durant had eight birdies and an eagle, but two bogeys, for his 63. Haas led by two through the second round and said he felt a good round coming on in the final. "Whether it'll be good enough," he added, cautiously, "we'll see."

It was enough. Haas logged four birdies through the 10th, and after a bogey at the 12th, added two more coming in for the 66 and the 196 total and the two-stroke win. He said it gave a charge of confidence to a 60-year-old. "Hopefully," he added, "I won't fall completely off the map when I turn 61 in December."

AT&T Championship

San Antonio, Texas

Winner: Michael Allen

Michael Allen's timing was a bit off, that's all. "Today, I just started out with the goal to get to 15 under," he said. "I thought I could do it a little sooner than I did."

His aim was a bit high, too. He was shooting for the AT&T Championship, the final full-field event on the 2014 Champions Tour, seeking his second win of the year and seventh on the tour. He was nine under and three behind starting the third and final round. This meant he had to shoot a six-under-par 66 and hope the rest of field wouldn't gain ground across the TPC San Antonio. "I knew the course was playing awfully difficult today," he said. "I was hoping to get there somewhere on the back nine."

For Allen, who had started 70-65, "somewhere" turned out to be the last hole, where he dropped a five-foot birdie putt for a bogey-free 66 and a 15-under 201 to win by two over the stoical Marco Dawson, still seeking his first win. "I'm not going to lose any sleep," Dawson had said, after taking the second-round lead. "My attitude now is to play like I'm in the pro-am. It's not life or death out there."

Contrary to the popular sports tenet, winning wasn't the only thing in the AT&T. A good finish also could go a long way. The top 30 on the money list would qualify for the season-ending Charles Schwab Cup Championship the following week. Bernhard Langer, a five-time winner, took the suspense out of it by tying for sixth and earning enough points to win the Schwab Cup and its $1 million annuity. The chase for the last spot was lively, though. Esteban Toledo birdied the last three holes for a 68 and a tie for 12th, moving up to the 30th and last spot and knocking back Rocco Mediate and Mark Calcavecchia.

Allen's spot had been secure. The AT&T had a different importance for him. "You always wonder if you can win again," he said. "It's nice to get over that hurdle."

Charles Schwab Cup Championship

Scottsdale, Arizona

Winner: Tom Pernice, Jr.

If Tom Pernice, Jr. were asked to name his favorite golf hole and his least-favorite (to put it gently), chances are he wouldn't have to leave the Cochise Course at Desert Mountain. In the season-ending Charles Schwab Cup Championship, he all but crashed at the 17th, but he all but won at the 18th.

Pernice ended up scoring his fourth Champions Tour win by beating Jay Haas on the fourth hole of a playoff — at the 18th. It was one of the few times that Haas, a 12-time winner, had been thwarted.

"I played really pretty solid ... never had any real trouble to speak of," Pernice said, "...and my short game held up and carried me through."

In a no-cut tournament limited to the top 30 on the money list, Bernhard Langer had taken the suspense out of things by locking up the Charles Schwab Cup point title — and its $1 million annuity — the week before. And Pernice and Haas were on a collision course from the start. Pernice shot the par-70 course in 65-67-70-67, Haas in 66-62-75-66, and they tied at 11-under 269. Pernice led by one in the first round, and Haas leaped four ahead with the 62 in the second. But he slipped one behind with the third-round 75, which included a double bogey and six bogeys. "Pretty awful," Haas said. In the final round, Haas took the clubhouse lead, holing a 35-foot birdie putt on the final hole for his 66. Pernice, playing in the group behind, birdied from six feet for a 67 to tie.

Oddly enough, Pernice had played the par-three 17th in bogey-par-bogey-bogey, and reversed that performance at the par-five 18th, playing it birdie-par-birdie-birdie.

In the playoff, they birdied the 18th the first time, parred it the next, then parred the 17th. Finally, back at the 18th, Haas holed a 12-foot putt for par, but Pernice blasted out of a bunker and sank a six-footer for birdie and the win.

Said Pernice: "Jay and I have become good friends. I hate for anybody to lose."

European Senior Tour

U.S. Senior PGA Championship

Benton Harbor, Michigan
Winner: Colin Montgomerie

See Champions Tour section.

ISPS Handa PGA Seniors Championship

Colchester, Essex, England
Winner: Santiago Luna

Going into the final round of the ISPS Handa PGA Seniors Championship, Santiago Luna confessed that he didn't expect to win, even though he was just three strokes off the lead. But, as he said later, "When you shoot 64, you are going to have a chance." More than a chance. As things turned out, the 64 propelled the 51-year-old Spaniard to a two-stroke victory at 14-under-par 270 in the senior major.

Luna, who won in just his sixth European Senior Tour start in 2013, trailed by five halfway through the tournament at the Stoke by Nayland Hotel course as Mark James went in front with 66–134, taking over the top spot from Des Smyth, who shot 66 the first day. The lead changed hands again on Saturday as Denmark's Steen Tinning put up a 68 for 203 to move two ahead of James (71) and three ahead of Luna (67), Jamie Spence (68), Andrew Oldcorn (66) and Chris Williams (70).

Tinning, who made up two strokes on Luna on the final three holes of the English Senior Open in winning his second 2013 title, built a four-stroke lead early in the final round. But he fell back with bogeys at the 11th and 12th holes and needed an eagle at the par-five 14th to overtake Luna, who had birdied that hole ahead of him. Luna then eagled himself at the other par-five, the 16th, to seize the lead to stay. He parred in and Tinning bogeyed the final hole for 69–272. Welshman Mark Mouland picked off third place with a closing 64–274.

Bad Ragaz PGA Seniors Open

Bad Ragaz, Switzerland
Winner: Rick Gibson

Usually, when a player grabs a first-round lead with chip-ins and putts from off the greens, the game gets even in subsequent rounds and somebody else steps up to grab the brass ring. Not so in the case of Rick Gibson in the Bad Ragaz PGA Seniors Open.

Gibson, who chipped in once and holed three putts from fringes for an opening, seven-under-par 63, followed with a pair of 66s on the weekend in the Swiss Alps and rolled to his first victory on the European Senior Tour by a whopping, six-stroke margin. He was 15 under par at 195.

Gibson led by just a stroke over American Gary Rusnak after his eight birdie-one bogey opening round, but was four in front of Scotland's Ross Drummond after the first 66 Saturday as Rusnak dropped out of contention with 74. Gibson began Sunday's round quietly with six pars, then rang up six birdies against a lone bogey the rest of the way. Ireland's Denis O'Sullivan matched his 66 to claim second place, a shot in front of Drummond, who shot 69. Five players shared fourth place.

Afterward, an emotional Gibson dedicated the victory to his mother, who passed away in March, and celebrated with his father in western Canada electronically via Skype.

U.S. Senior Open

Edmund, Oklahoma

Winner: Colin Montgomerie

See Champions Tour Section

The Senior Open Championship presented by Rolex

Bridgend, Wales

Winner: Bernhard Langer

Colin Montgomerie went to Royal Porthcawl hoping to win the third senior major of the season in over-50 golf. It didn't happen. He beat 142 of the other 144 in the field but was turned back resoundingly by Bernhard Langer, who shattered records right and left as he rolled to an astounding, 13-stroke, wire-to-wire victory, continuing his dominating play on the senior circuits on both sides of the Atlantic.

An admiring Montgomerie called it "one of the [finest] golfing performances of all time. To finish 18 under par round here is remarkable, remarkable play."

Langer's 13-stroke margin was not only the widest margin by far in Open history (six strokes better than Bob Charles' previous record gap in 1989), but also was the largest margin in the history of European Senior Tour and all senior major championship golf. His 18-under-par 266 was the lowest ever in the 28-year history of the Senior Open.

The 56-year-old German, who won the 2010 Open at Carnoustie in another wire-to-wire dash and lost a heartbreaker a year earlier in a playoff against American Mark Wiebe at Royal Birkdale, built his lead steadily all week at Royal Porthcawl. His opening, six-under-par 65 gave him a two-stroke lead over American Bob Tway. He stretched it to seven shots, then over Montgomerie and England's Chris Williams, with 66–131.

A 68 Saturday moved him eight strokes in front, with Canada's Rick Gibson, the winner of the previous week's Bad Ragaz tournament in Switzerland, moving into the runner-up slot with 66–207. Sunday's final round quickly became a walk in the park when Langer birdied three of the first six holes and strolled home with a 67 for the 266. Montgomerie grabbed the second spot with a closing 69. The win was Langer's fourth of the season, following the Senior Players Championship and two others in America.

SSE Scottish Senior Open

St. Andrews, Fife, Scotland

Winner: Mark Davis

Since 2002 when Mark Davis left the European Tour with two victories on his record, he had been "doing all sorts of things to keep the head above water ... mainly painting and decorating." Not much golf, he conceded.

Obviously, though, he didn't lose his touch. Just 45 days beyond his 50th birthday in his third start on the European Senior Tour, Davis scored an impressive, five-stroke victory in the SSE Scottish Senior Open with a superior, wind-blown final round at Fairmont St. Andrews.

Davis entered the last day in a second-place tie at 140 with Welsh great Ian Woosnam and Spaniard Pedro Linhart. They were three strokes behind Argentinian Cesar Monasterio, also a tour rookie, who had opened the tournament excitingly with a circuit record-tying 61 — nine birdies and an eagle — and followed with a back-to-earth 76 on a windier second day when the best score was a lone 70.

In winning, Englishman Davis shook off a first-hole, three-putt bogey on Sunday, took command with birdies at the fourth, 11th and 13th holes, and finished bogey-bogey-birdie for a 71, the co-low round of the gusty day. Five behind his two-under-par 211 were Linhart (76), David J. Russell (73), Philip Golding (74) and Monasterio, who had five bogeys on the first 11 holes en route to a 79 and his 216.

English Senior Open

County Durham, England

Winner: Cesar Monasterio

Cesar Monasterio wasn't about to let another potential victory get away from him. One week after yielding a three-stroke lead in the final round of the Scottish Senior Open, Monasterio found himself in the same position in the English Senior Open, three shots in front after 36 holes. This time, instead of shooting 79 and winding up five strokes behind rookie winner Mark Davis in Scotland, the Argentinean rolled to a five-stroke victory of his own in just his fifth start on the European Senior Tour.

Monasterio's nine-under-par 63 in the second round, which tied the course record at County Durham's Rockliffe Hall, set up the triumph. The 10-birdie outing established his three-shot margin over Scotland's Ross Drummond (70-65) and five ahead of third-place Englishman Barry Lane (71-66). Monasterio had opened the tournament with 69, two off the pace of England's Jamie Spence.

With Drummond stumbling to a 73 Sunday, Monasterio needed only a

70 to wrap up the easy victory with his 14-under-par 202. Lane matched the 70 and was joined in the runner-up slot by Andrew Oldcorn. The Scot closed with 67 for his 207.

The 50-year-old Monasterio, one of only five players with victories on Europe's regular, challenge and senior circuits, was the third first-time and second rookie winner of the season.

Travis Perkins Masters

Woburn, England

Winner: Colin Montgomerie

It's fair to say that Colin Montgomerie "owns" the Travis Perkins Masters and the Duke's course of Woburn Golf Club. After all, the Hall-of-Famer has won it in both of his first two appearances in the tournament since turning 50 by a overwhelming combined margin of 16 strokes.

The 10-stroke victory this time was Montgomerie's third win of the season and his fourth in just his ninth start on the European Senior Tour. It put the 2014 Order of Merit money title squarely in the sights of a man who was No. 1 on the regular European Tour eight times in a splendid career that lacks only the acquisition of a major title.

It wasn't a true wire-to-wire victory only because the burly Scot, who hit every fairway in a bogey-free round, had to share the opening-day lead at four-under 68 with American Gary Rusnak. Only nine players broke par on a windy Friday.

Despite two bogeys, Montgomerie moved four shots in front of another American, Mike Cunning (73-68), with 69–137 in the second round and sailed home Sunday after breaking free of Cunning's early challenge with five birdies from the sixth hole on. He posted a 67 for his 204, with Andre Bossert (Switzerland), Gordon Manson (Austria) and Tim Thelen (U.S.) sharing second place at 214.

Russian Open

Moscow, Russia

Winner: Colin Montgomerie

Not even his old college roommate was going to stand in the way of Colin Montgomerie as he sought the fourth victory of his splendid European Senior Tour season in the Russian Open.

A final-hole birdie and 68 Saturday put the streaking Montgomerie into the last grouping for the final round with American Tim Thelen, his golfing teammate 28 years ago at Houston Baptist University. Thelen, a two-time tour winner in 2012, had taken the lead with a strong, seven-under-par 65–135, two ahead of Montgomerie and Spain's Miguel Angel Martin.

There was no stopping Montgomerie Sunday. He zoomed past Thelen early with four birdies on the first five holes and went on to a 65 of his own, a 14-under-par 202 and a three-shot victory to go back-to-back with his win in the Travis Perkins the week before. This was in addition to his major victories in the U.S. Senior Open and PGA Championship earlier in the season.

"I'm playing as well as I have ever done right now," Montgomerie observed. "A year ago, I wasn't driving as well as I did when I was winning my Order of Merit titles (seven), but that's not the case any more. I hit 28 fairways out of 28 the last two days and you can't do any better than that.

"I have had a lot of good runs of form over the years, but I think this is right up there with the best of them."

Canadian Rick Gibson, the Bad Ragaz victor in July, finished second with 67–205, and Thelen (71) joined Martin (69), Andrew Oldcorn and Barry Lane (68s) in third place at 206.

Senior Open de Portugal

Porto, Portugal

Winner: Tim Thelen

It's always nice to see old friends, but Tim Thelen must have been happy that Colin Montgomerie chose not to play in the Senior Open de Portugal. For the previous two weeks on the European Senior Tour, Thelen had played second and third fiddle as Montgomerie, his college roommate in Texas, pranced to victory in England and Russia.

With no Montgomerie to contend with in Portugal, Thelen picked off his fourth title on the circuit, holding off a late charge by Spain's Miguel Angel Martin to gather a one-stroke victory with a 12-under-par 204.

The American, winner of three EST events in 2012, shook off a back spasm early, shot an eight-under 64 and surged to the lead in the second round after South Africa's Chris Williams had opened with 63. Thelen's 68-64–132 gave him a three-stroke lead over Greg Turner, Des Smyth and Carl Mason, the all-time career winner on the circuit.

Thelen had to contend with Martin and the weather Sunday. Though playing steadily, Thelen led by just a stroke when, late in the round, the remaining players were called in for forty minutes. When play resumed, he birdied the 17th for the cushion he needed when he bogeyed the final hole. Martin shot 67 for his 203, and Smyth and Mason tied for third with 71s.

WINSTONgolf Senior Open

Vorbeck, Germany

Winner: Paul Wesselingh

The 2014 season had not gone particularly well for Paul Wesselingh following his four-victory performance that brought him the Order of Merit title in 2013. Wesselingh had not finished higher than 14th place in any of his previous starts when he arrived in Vorbeck, Germany, for the WINSTONgolf Senior Open in mid-September.

Yet, he came alive and rained on Bernhard Langer's parade in his homeland, where Langer is revered as the nation's greatest golfer ever. Wesselingh, who never gave back a stroke over the 54 holes, finished eagle-birdie for a final-round 65 that hoisted him into a playoff with Phil Golding (66) and Langer (69), who was enjoying a brilliant season in Europe (Senior Open) and especially in America, where he was the leading money winner with four victories in the books.

With a pair of 66s, Langer had entered the final round at WINSTONgolf tied for the lead with lightly regarded Englishmen Gary Emerson, the first-round leader with 65, and Wraith Grant (67-65). Golding made up three strokes and Wesselingh four to reach the playoff.

It went three extra holes. All three birdied the first, Golding went out at the second with a ball in the water, and Wesselingh produced a tap-in birdie at the third for his sixth victory in his three seasons on the European Senior Tour.

French Riviera Masters

Tourrettes, Provence, France

Winner: Philip Golding

Undaunted by his playoff loss two weeks earlier in Germany, Philip Golding bounced back with a vengeance when the European Senior Tour visited the Mediterranean coast for the French Riviera Masters. Leading all the way, the 52-year-old Englishman rolled to a four-stroke victory. It was his second tour win, but, interestingly, his third professional triumph in France. "There must be something about the French air," he quipped afterward.

Golding was on top of his game the first two days at Terre Blanche Hotel Spa Golf Resort in Provence. Although he blistered the course with a bogey-free, eight-under-par 64, he led by just a stroke over fellow Englishman Gary Emerson. Four early birdies Saturday powered Golding to a four-shot lead over Cesar Monasterio, the English Senior Open winner in August. He headed into the final round at 67–131 as Argentina's Monasterio moved into second place with a 67 of his own.

Golding started slowly Sunday, but birdies at the 11th and 13th "gave me a bit of breathing space" just before an electrical storm forced a two-hour rain delay. He finished on the soggy course with 70–201. Monasterio matched the 70 for 205, closing a shot ahead of Barry Lane (68), Peter Fowler (67) and John Gould (69).

Dutch Senior Open

Amsterdam, The Netherlands

Winner: Ian Woosnam

Maybe there is such a thing as being too good a friend. Ian Woosnam took pal David J. Russell's advice, went for a lesson from a golf biomechanics guru and won the Dutch Senior Open at the expense of, among others, David J. Russell.

"Maybe I should have kept my mouth shut," reflected Russell after he finished second with Philip Golding and George Ryall at The International in

Amsterdam. "If I'd said nothing, I might have been collecting the winner's check."

Woosnam, the revered Welshman with a Masters and 50 other victories on his overall career record, gave due credit to Russell and mentor Jacques Rivet when he finished off a five-stroke victory with an 11-under-par 208. "I guess I owe D.J. a few drinks," he said. "And speaking to Jacques made a massive difference to me."

Golding, maintaining momentum from his French Riviera Masters victory the previous week, led the tournament for two days on his 68-71–139 with Woosnam (71-69) and Ryall (70-70) one behind. Woosnam, who hadn't won on the European Senior Tour since bagging his fourth senior title in 2011, managed the 69 Saturday despite taking a quadruple bogey on the second hole.

Woosnam won going away Sunday, taking the lead at the ninth hole and finishing with birdies on three of the last four holes for the winning 68.

Coca-Cola Australian PGA Seniors Championship

Richmond, New South Wales
Winner: Simon Owen

With two New Zealand PGA Senior Championships already on his record, Simon Owen added the Australian version of the same tournament at the end of November at Richmond Golf Club in New South Wales. It took a playoff birdie to accomplish the feat, though.

Playing in the Coca-Cola Australian PGA Seniors for the first time, Owen jumped off in front with a four-under-par 66, taking a one-stroke lead on Terry Price and two on six others, including Michael Harwood. He fattened the margin to two shots with a 70 Saturday for 136. Price (71), Allan Cooper (69) and Tim Elliott (68) were at 138; Harwood, with 71, at 139. Harwood overtook Owen Sunday as Owen slipped to a 72 while Harwood was shooting 69 for his 208. The other three contenders shot 71s, missing the overtime chance by a stroke.

Owen gambled in the playoff, going for the green with a three wood on the short 18th hole and putting his shot 20 feet from the hole. Harwood laid up, pitched to 10 feet and missed the putt. Owen's two-putt gave him the winning birdie.

"I'm ecstatic to win the tournament," Owen said afterward. "There are some great names on this trophy and it's an honor to now be alongside them."

MCB Tour Championship

Poste de Flacq, Mauritius
Winner: Paul Wesselingh

Paul Wesselingh repeated as the winner of the MCB Tour Championship, but there was nothing repetitious about the way he did it the second time around. Wesselingh coasted to a five-stroke victory and the Order of Merit title on the 2013 European Senior Tour. Twelve months later, the 52-year-old had to survive an incredible six-hole playoff, and that second victory of the 2014 campaign merely lifted him to sixth place on the final money list.

Colin Montgomerie, who finished sixth in the December finale, had clinched the money title long before on the strength of his two major championships, his runner-up finish in a third and two other victories. He banked €624,542.

Wesselingh entered the final round on the Legend Course at Constance Belle Mare Plage a stroke behind David Frost, the 2010 and 2012 Tour Championship winner, but wound up in a playoff against fellow Englishman Barry Lane. Wesselingh three-putted the final green for 69 and nine-under-par 207. Frost shot 71–208 to finish third.

Lane, who shook off the effects of a four-day bout with the flu and a disc problem in his back to lead the first round with a 68, shot 67 Sunday for his 207 despite missing a three-foot birdie putt at the 17th hole and an eight-foot eagle putt on the last green.

Remarkably in the playoff, which tied the record for the longest ever on the senior circuit, the two players matched birdies five times on the par-five 18th hole before Lane missed a four-foot par putt the sixth time around and Wesselingh tapped in for his seventh senior win.

"I feel like I've been through the wringer," Wesselingh expressed as he accepted the trophy. "I'm just delighted and relieved to win. I do feel very proud."

Japan PGA Senior Tour

Kanehide Senior Okinawa Open

Okinawa

Winner: Hatsuo Nakane

Hatsuo Nakane frustrated the bid of Takeshi Sakiyama to repeat as the winner of the Kanehide Senior Okinawa Open, the inaugural event of the Japan Senior Tour season.

Sakiyama, who, like Nakane, had not won on the circuit until his 2013 victory in Okinawa, seemed well on his way to a second straight April win at Kise Country Club when he opened with an eight-under-par 64. He led by three shots over Shinji Ikeuchi, Masami Ho and Australian Gregory Meyer and by four over Nakane and three other players.

However, Sakiyama slipped to an even-par 72–136 the second day and dropped into a tie with Nakane, who shot a second 68 for his 136 and won the subsequent playoff with a birdie on the first extra hole (No. 18). Englishman Paul Wesselingh (68-70), the four-time victor and leading money winner on the 2013 European Senior Tour, tied for third at 138 with Tatsuya Shiraishi (69-69).

Kyoraku More Surprise Cup

Mie

Winner: Seiki Okuda

Seiki Okuda shot the only round in the 60s the last day and it paid off with his second Japan Senior Tour victory in the Kyoraku More Surprise Cup tournament in early May. Three strokes off the pace after 36 holes, Okuda garnered a three-under-par 69 in the final round at Ryosen Golf Club in Mie Prefecture that lifted him into a tie with international veteran T.C. Chen at 214, and he won the subsequent playoff with a par on the second extra hole.

Chen, the noted Taiwanese star, and Australian Gregory Meyer shared the second-round lead at 142, Chen shooting 68 and Meyer 69 Friday to sit a shot in front of Kiyoshi Murota, 11 times a winner on the senior circuit. Okuda had rounds of 74 and 71.

Meyer faded badly Sunday as Chen shot 72 for his 214 that brought on the playoff. Both players parred the first extra hole, but Chen bogeyed the 18th the next time around to Okuda's winning par.

Starts Senior

Ibaraki

Winner: Shinji Ikeuchi

Even though Kiyoshi Murota has compiled a near-record victory total on the Japan Senior Tour, Shinji Ikeuchi seems to have his number. Ikeuchi won his first senior title by a stroke over Murota in the 2010 Komatsu Open and he repeated that feat four years later for his second circuit victory in the Starts Senior tournament at the Starts Kasama Golf Club.

What made the win more surprising was the fact that Murota, with 11 wins on his Japan Senior Tour record, opened the tournament with an eight-under-par 64 and a two-stroke lead over Yutaka Hagawa. Ikeuchi was another shot behind with Nobumasa Nakanishi. However, when Murota managed just a 70–134 the second day, Ikeuchi jumped in front when he followed the 67 with 66 for 133. Still in the picture were Atsushi Takamatsu at 136 and past tournament winners Frankie Minoza and Hajime Meshiai, who shot 66s for 137.

As the final round played out, Ikeuchi matched 70s with Murota for his one-stroke triumph at 203. Minoza came up with a 68 to finish a stroke behind Murota.

ISPS Handa Cup Philanthropy Senior

Kanagawa

Winner: Hideki Kase

Hideki Kase put together three low-scoring rounds and pulled out his second victory on the Japan Senior Tour in the ISPS Handa Cup Philanthropy Senior tournament at the end of June.

Trailing by a shot going into the final day after rounds of 65-67, the 54-year-old Kase, a four-time winner on the regular Japan Tour in his younger days, picked off a one-stroke win with his closing 67 for 199, 17 under par on the Hakone Kohan Golf Course in Kanagawa.

Second-round leader Hatsuo Nakane, who won the season-opening Kanehide Senior Okinawa Open, shot 69 Sunday, finishing in a three-way tie for second with Takashi Miyoshi and Yutaka Hagawa, both multiple winners on the circuit who had 67 cards in the final round for their 200s.

Kase won the Japan Senior PGA Championship in 2010 and the Japan PGA Championship in 1990.

Maruhan Cup Taiheiyo Club Senior

Hyogo

Winner: Gregory Meyer

Gregory Meyer didn't let this one get away. Time and again during recent seasons and particularly earlier in 2014 at the Surprise Cup tournament, the Australian had been in contention and let victory slip away. He finally nailed the elusive win in the Maruhan Cup Taiheiyo Club Senior on the club's Rokko course in early August, scoring a one-stroke victory with a 12-under-par 132.

Meyer seized a three-shot lead when he shot an opening 62, and his following 70 was just enough to edge 50-year-old Toshikazu Sugihara, son of the long-respected Teruo Sugihara and a newcomer on the Japan Senior Tour. Sugihara had rounds of 65 and 68 for his 133.

Fancl Classic

Susono, Shizuoka

Winner: Yutaka Hagawa

It wasn't as spectacular, but Yutaka Hagawa stowed away the Fancl Classic title for a second year in a row on the Japan Senior Tour. Hagawa, a five-time winner on the regular Japan Tour in earlier years, captured the 2013 Fancl Classic by coming from nine strokes behind and winning a playoff. In 2014, Hagawa never trailed but had his hands full all three days at Susono Country Club before posting his two-stroke victory and third on the senior circuit.

His opening 69 gave him a share of the lead with Tatsuya Shiraishi, Tatsuo Oyama and Kiyoshi Murota, the current king of the tour with 11 victories on his record. Hagawa and Murota matched 71s Saturday to remain on top, then tied for the lead with Seiki Okuda, the Kyoraku More Surprise Cup victor in May (72-68–140), and Kasuhiro Takami (73-67), the Fancl winner in 2012. Shiraishi (69-72) and Masahiro Kuramoto (70-71) were right on their heels.

Hagawa's final 69–209 gave him the two-shot win as four players tied for second at 211, Naonori Nakamura with 68, Jong-Duck Kim with 69, Kuramoto with 70 and Takami with 71.

Komatsu Open

Komatsu, Ishikawa

Winner: Tateo Ozaki

Tateo (Jet) Ozaki ended a five-year victory drought on the Japan Senior Tour at the Komatsu Open, as his younger brother Naomichi (Joe) gave him a run for his money. The elder Ozaki, the winner of four previous circuit titles, including the 2007 Senior PGA Championship, led from the start at Komatsu Country Club and survived by a lone stroke an eight-under-par 64 that brother Joe threw at him in the final round.

Tateo Ozaki roared in front with a 65 the first day, taking a two-shot lead over Takeshi Sakiyama, Tsukasa Watanabe, Yoichi Shimizu and Nobumitsu Yuhara. He remained two in front after Saturday's 70–135 with Hajime Meshiai (71-66) and Shimizu (70) in the runner-up position. Naomichi Ozaki (72-67), who scored one of his two senior victories at Komatsu in 2012, trailed by four.

His final-round 67 and 14-under-par 202 were just enough for Tateo to edge Naomichi and his 64 and land his fifth senior title. Masihiro Kuramoto, another of Japan's top-echelon players from the past, finished third at 205.

Japan PGA Senior Championship

Ibaraki

Winner: Naomichi Ozaki

Naomichi (Joe) Ozaki joined older brother Tateo (Jet) as a 2014 winner on the Japan Senior Tour when he ground out a grueling playoff victory in the Japan PGA Senior Championship. A month after Tateo edged him by a stroke in the Komatsu Open for his fifth win, Naomichi picked up his third senior title and first senior major when he prevailed in a three-man, four-hole playoff against Tsukasa Watanabe, the defending champion, and Kiyoshi Murota, the circuit's current top winner with 11 titles.

Those three prominent players came to the fore in the third round at Summit Golf Club in Ibaraki after lesser lights held sway the first two days. Gohei Sato, who led the first day with 66, eventually tied for 54th place. Hiroki Kamide, the second-round leader with 68-67–135 followed with 78 and tied for 30th.

Then on Saturday, Watanabe, gunning for his third PGA Championship and fifth overall title, fired an eight-under-par 64 for 204 and a one-shot lead over Ozaki (67), Murota (65) and visiting Englishman Paul Wesselingh (68). The overtime session on the 18th hole was required Sunday when Ozaki and Murota shot 68s and Watanabe 69 for 273s. Wesselingh took a 71.

The trio matched pars, then birdies the first two times they played No. 18. Watanabe and Ozaki birdied again the third time around, eliminating Murota with his par. Then, Ozaki made yet another birdie against Watanabe's par on the fourth return trip.

Japan Senior Open Championship

Hyogo

Winner: Masahiro Kuramoto

Masahiro (Massy) Kuramoto joined fellow greats Isao Aoki (5 times) and Tsuneyuki Nakajima (3) as multiple winners of Japan's most prestigious senior tournament when he won the Senior Open Championship for the second time at Ono Grand Country Club in early November.

Kuramoto, who had 34 victories in his outstanding career on the Japan Tour, needed the birdie he made at the 72nd hole to fend off the powerful finish of Tsukasa Watanabe, like Kuramoto a four-time winner on the senior circuit.

After starting the final round six strokes behind co-leaders Kuramoto and Kohki Idoki (204s), Watanabe racked up eight birdies on the first 15 holes Sunday and swept into a one-shot lead. He ran out of birdies, though, and Kuramoto, with birdies at the 16th and 18th holes, posted a 69 for a 15-under-par 273 and the one-stroke victory. Thus, Watanabe finished second in both major championships of the season.

The 59-year-old Kuramoto was in good position all week at Ono Grand. Seiki Okuda, who won the early season Kyoraku More Surprise Cup, opened with 64 and led him by two. Kuramoto followed his 66 with 67 Friday and moved a shot ahead of Okuda (70) with his 133. Idoki fired a 67 Saturday to Kuramoto's 71 to set up the tie heading into the final round.

Fuji Film Senior Championship

Chiba

Winner: Kiyoshi Murota

Kiyoshi Murota scored a record-sharing 12th victory on the Japan Senior Tour when he rolled to a three-stroke triumph in the Fuji Film Senior Championship. His final-round 65 gave him a 14-under-par 202.

The dozen wins tied Murota in the career-victory department with Katsunari Takahashi, who, at 63, is still active on the circuit and, in fact, held the first-round lead with 67 before fading to a 36th-place finish.

Murota was three behind Takahashi after his first-round 70, then moved into a five-way tie for second place Saturday. He shot 67 for 137, sitting one behind Englishman Paul Wesselingh (69-67) and deadlocked with Boonchu Ruangkit of Thailand and Yoichi Shimizu (68-69) and Hajime Meshiai and Tsutomu Higa (69-68).

Wesselingh, the 2013 Order of Merit winner on the European Senior Tour, slipped to 71 Sunday as Murota rolled past him to the victory by three over Ruangkit, the European champion in 2011, who closed with 68–205.

Iwasaki Shiratsuyu Senior

Kagoshima

Winner: Masahiro Kuramoto

Back-to-back 66s and a Sunday downpour in the year's closing event at the end of November carried Masahiro (Massy) Kuramoto to his second victory of the Japan Senior Tour season and the money-winning championship. The 12-under-par 132 gave the 59-year-old pro, one of Japan's all-time premier players, a four-stroke victory in the Iwasaki Shiratsuyu tournament.

The ¥12-million prize lifted Kuramoto ¥1 million ahead of Kiyoshi Murota in the race for the No. 1 spot on the money list. His final total was ¥39,292,451.

Yutaka Hagawa and Katsuyoshi Tomori also shot 66 in the opening round on the Kaimon course of Ibusuki Golf Club in Kagoshima, but couldn't match Kuramoto's second 66 Saturday. Hagawa shot 70–136 and Tomori 71–137 to finish two-three when a heavy rain storm forced cancellation of the final round Sunday and gave Kuramoto his fifth victory on the senior circuit.

APPENDIXES

American Tours

Hyundai Tournament of Champions

Kapalua Resort, Plantation Course, Maui, Hawaii
Par 36-37–73; 7,411 yards

January 3-6
purse, $5,700,000

	SCORES				TOTAL	MONEY
Zach Johnson	67	66	74	66	273	$1,140,000
Jordan Spieth	66	70	69	69	274	665,000
Webb Simpson	66	71	68	70	275	382,000
Kevin Streelman	67	71	70	67	275	382,000
Jason Dufner	67	72	69	69	277	276,000
Billy Horschel	72	72	68	66	278	198,750
Dustin Johnson	70	66	69	73	278	198,750
Matt Kuchar	68	68	75	67	278	198,750
Adam Scott	70	70	69	69	278	198,750
Ryan Moore	67	71	72	69	279	170,000
Harris English	70	71	70	69	280	155,000
Brandt Snedeker	70	69	69	72	280	155,000
Woody Austin	72	70	68	71	281	130,000
Brian Gay	70	76	65	70	281	130,000
Gary Woodland	71	70	67	73	281	130,000
Ken Duke	70	69	71	72	282	100,250
Chris Kirk	66	75	68	73	282	100,250
Patrick Reed	70	72	67	73	282	100,250
Michael Thompson	66	71	73	72	282	100,250
Martin Laird	71	72	70	70	283	87,000
Jonas Blixt	76	70	69	70	285	79,333.34
Sang-Moon Bae	69	73	71	72	285	79,333.33
Jimmy Walker	73	73	67	72	285	79,333.33
Scott Brown	71	73	68	75	287	71,500
Bill Haas	71	73	69	74	287	71,500
Boo Weekley	71	74	70	73	288	68,000
Russell Henley	72	72	70	75	289	66,000
John Merrick	71	76	71	74	292	63,000
D.A. Points	72	74	73	73	292	63,000
Derek Ernst	79	76	76	70	301	61,000

Sony Open in Hawaii

Waialae Country Club, Honolulu, Hawaii
Par 35-35–70; 7,044 yards

January 9-12
purse, $5,600,000

	SCORES				TOTAL	MONEY
Jimmy Walker	66	67	67	63	263	$1,008,000
Chris Kirk	64	69	65	66	264	604,800
Jerry Kelly	67	67	66	65	265	380,800
Harris English	66	66	67	67	266	268,800
Marc Leishman	67	64	71	65	267	224,000
Brian Stuard	65	65	71	67	268	201,600
Jeff Overton	68	68	65	68	269	187,600
Matt Every	69	65	69	67	270	119,000
Retief Goosen	66	69	66	69	270	119,000
Charles Howell	71	67	66	66	270	119,000
Zach Johnson	68	67	66	69	270	119,000

	SCORES				TOTAL	MONEY
Matt Kuchar	68	68	68	66	270	119,000
Kevin Na	70	67	67	66	270	119,000
Ryan Palmer	65	70	67	68	270	119,000
Pat Perez	68	67	66	69	270	119,000
Adam Scott	67	66	71	66	270	119,000
Hudson Swafford	70	64	69	67	270	119,000
Hideto Tanihara	66	65	70	69	270	119,000
Will Wilcox	69	66	64	71	270	119,000
K.J. Choi	67	69	69	66	271	54,817.78
Stewart Cink	69	69	66	67	271	54,817.78
Ryuji Imada	67	69	68	67	271	54,817.78
Jason Kokrak	66	67	70	68	271	54,817.78
John Peterson	68	69	65	69	271	54,817.78
Heath Slocum	69	69	65	68	271	54,817.78
Chris Stroud	68	65	70	68	271	54,817.78
Robert Allenby	68	68	65	70	271	54,817.77
Brendon Todd	70	66	66	69	271	54,817.77
Jason Dufner	67	68	67	70	272	38,080
Spencer Levin	69	69	66	68	272	38,080
Boo Weekley	67	67	70	68	272	38,080
Sang-Moon Bae	63	70	70	70	273	30,986.67
John Daly	66	73	64	70	273	30,986.67
Brian Harman	69	66	69	69	273	30,986.67
Michael Putnam	70	68	68	67	273	30,986.67
Brian Gay	71	68	67	67	273	30,986.66
Justin Leonard	68	66	69	70	273	30,986.66
Ricky Barnes	68	69	68	69	274	22,400
Charlie Beljan	68	70	69	67	274	22,400
Brice Garnett	67	71	67	69	274	22,400
David Hearn	68	70	67	69	274	22,400
Billy Hurley	67	69	69	69	274	22,400
Peter Malnati	69	69	70	66	274	22,400
Ben Martin	67	69	68	70	274	22,400
Charlie Wi	69	70	68	67	274	22,400
Chad Collins	71	67	68	69	275	15,523.20
James Hahn	67	68	71	69	275	15,523.20
William McGirt	67	72	68	68	275	15,523.20
Daniel Summerhays	66	71	70	68	275	15,523.20
Tim Wilkinson	71	67	67	70	275	15,523.20
Steven Bowditch	72	66	69	69	276	12,902.40
Greg Chalmers	68	66	69	73	276	12,902.40
Brendon de Jonge	68	71	69	68	276	12,902.40
Russell Henley	73	65	69	69	276	12,902.40
Tim Herron	68	70	66	72	276	12,902.40
Justin Hicks	69	69	70	68	276	12,902.40
D.A. Points	70	69	67	70	276	12,902.40
John Rollins	69	68	70	69	276	12,902.40
Mark Wilson	68	68	71	69	276	12,902.40
Y.E. Yang	73	66	66	71	276	12,902.40
Paul Goydos	74	64	70	69	277	12,040
Seung-Yul Noh	70	66	69	72	277	12,040
John Senden	72	67	68	70	277	12,040
Tyrone van Aswegen	69	69	66	73	277	12,040
Stuart Appleby	70	68	71	69	278	11,648
Morgan Hoffmann	68	69	71	70	278	11,648
Hyung-Sung Kim	70	68	66	74	278	11,648
Scott Brown	71	67	70	71	279	11,368
Robert Streb	70	69	67	73	279	11,368
Tommy Gainey	72	67	70	73	282	11,144
Derek Tolan	70	66	70	76	282	11,144
Miguel Angel Carballo	68	70	72		210	10,696
Ken Duke	68	71	71		210	10,696
Kevin Foley	67	72	71		210	10,696

	SCORES			TOTAL	MONEY
John Huh	71	67	72	210	10,696
Toshinori Muto	70	69	71	210	10,696
Scott Verplank	71	67	72	210	10,696
Eric Dugas	70	68	73	211	10,304
Joe Durant	68	71	73	212	10,192

Humana Challenge

PGA West, Palmer Course: Par 36-36–72; 6,950 yards
PGA West, Nicklaus Course: Par 36-36–72; 6,924 yards
La Quinta CC: Par 36-36–72; 7,060 yards
La Quinta, California

January 16-19
purse, $5,700,000

	SCORES				TOTAL	MONEY
Patrick Reed	63	63	63	71	260	$1,026,000
Ryan Palmer	64	65	70	63	262	615,600
Zach Johnson	65	68	68	62	263	330,600
Justin Leonard	66	67	65	65	263	330,600
Brian Stuard	67	66	66	65	264	228,000
Bill Haas	65	66	67	67	265	198,075
Brendon Todd	65	63	68	69	265	198,075
Chad Collins	68	68	65	65	266	176,700
Stuart Appleby	66	69	67	65	267	148,200
Charlie Beljan	68	64	68	67	267	148,200
Ben Crane	70	64	65	68	267	148,200
Charley Hoffman	64	66	66	71	267	148,200
Matt Every	65	68	69	66	268	103,740
Matt Jones	66	67	66	69	268	103,740
Jerry Kelly	69	65	68	66	268	103,740
Russell Knox	65	70	67	66	268	103,740
Will MacKenzie	67	66	66	69	268	103,740
Keegan Bradley	69	66	65	69	269	74,328
Brendon de Jonge	69	68	66	66	269	74,328
James Driscoll	68	63	66	72	269	74,328
Luke Guthrie	69	67	67	66	269	74,328
Scott Langley	69	68	65	67	269	74,328
Webb Simpson	69	70	67	64	270	57,000
Charlie Wi	65	69	69	67	270	57,000
Roberto Castro	68	73	66	64	271	41,681.25
Martin Flores	69	65	69	68	271	41,681.25
Billy Horschel	72	65	70	64	271	41,681.25
Ryo Ishikawa	66	69	69	67	271	41,681.25
Martin Laird	69	66	68	68	271	41,681.25
Hudson Swafford	65	71	70	65	271	41,681.25
Tyrone van Aswegen	69	67	67	68	271	41,681.25
Johnson Wagner	72	66	68	65	271	41,681.25
Jason Bohn	70	65	66	71	272	30,780
Harris English	67	66	71	68	272	30,780
Rickie Fowler	68	71	67	66	272	30,780
Josh Teater	68	68	70	66	272	30,780
Camilo Villegas	70	66	68	68	272	30,780
Brian Davis	69	71	66	67	273	21,660
James Hahn	70	68	69	66	273	21,660
Spencer Levin	69	68	66	70	273	21,660
Bryce Molder	69	72	63	69	273	21,660
Seung-Yul Noh	68	66	66	73	273	21,660
Jeff Overton	70	67	67	69	273	21,660
Rory Sabbatini	68	67	67	71	273	21,660
Andrew Svoboda	69	69	66	69	273	21,660
Cameron Tringale	68	66	70	69	273	21,660

	SCORES				TOTAL	MONEY
Gary Woodland	69	71	65	68	273	21,660
Steven Bowditch	71	67	68	68	274	13,816.80
Scott Brown	67	68	70	69	274	13,816.80
Brad Fritsch	67	70	67	70	274	13,816.80
Brice Garnett	67	69	68	70	274	13,816.80
Justin Hicks	64	71	70	69	274	13,816.80
Kevin Kisner	66	70	69	69	274	13,816.80
John Merrick	66	70	69	69	274	13,816.80
Kevin Na	68	68	68	70	274	13,816.80
Michael Putnam	68	69	70	67	274	13,816.80
Bo Van Pelt	70	68	67	69	274	13,816.80
Jonathan Byrd	68	69	65	73	275	12,198
Kevin Chappell	70	70	63	72	275	12,198
Stewart Cink	73	63	71	68	275	12,198
Harrison Frazar	69	68	68	70	275	12,198
Charles Howell	73	68	65	69	275	12,198
Davis Love	69	68	69	69	275	12,198
Pat Perez	69	70	66	70	275	12,198
Brandt Snedeker	72	64	69	70	275	12,198
Scott Stallings	68	69	69	69	275	12,198
Daniel Summerhays	64	69	73	69	275	12,198
Lee Williams	70	68	69	68	275	12,198
Blake Adams	70	70	66	70	276	11,172
Chad Campbell	71	68	68	69	276	11,172
Erik Compton	70	66	70	70	276	11,172
Ken Duke	71	70	65	70	276	11,172
Jim Herman	67	68	68	73	276	11,172
John Senden	71	70	66	69	276	11,172
Nicholas Thompson	71	69	67	69	276	11,172
Freddie Jacobson	71	68	68	70	277	10,659
William McGirt	70	70	64	73	277	10,659
David Lingmerth	69	68	69	72	278	10,431
Kevin Stadler	69	66	72	71	278	10,431
Brett Quigley	66	73	68	72	279	10,260
Scott McCarron	72	69	66	73	280	10,146
Brian Harman	69	66	72	74	281	9,975
J.J. Henry	71	70	65	75	281	9,975
Jhonattan Vegas	69	71	67	76	283	9,804

Farmers Insurance Open

Torrey Pines, La Jolla, California — January 23-26
South Course: Par 36-36–72; 7,569 yards — purse, $6,100,000
North Course: Par 36-36–72; 6,874 yards

	SCORES				TOTAL	MONEY
Scott Stallings	72	67	72	68	279	$1,098,000
K.J. Choi	74	70	70	66	280	366,000
Jason Day	66	73	73	68	280	366,000
Graham DeLaet	70	73	69	68	280	366,000
Marc Leishman	66	71	72	71	280	366,000
Pat Perez	67	71	72	70	280	366,000
Charley Hoffman	69	70	75	67	281	190,116.67
Ryo Ishikawa	72	70	69	70	281	190,116.67
Will MacKenzie	72	69	70	70	281	190,116.66
Trevor Immelman	68	74	71	69	282	135,216.67
Russell Knox	71	67	74	70	282	135,216.67
Seung-Yul Noh	68	73	72	69	282	135,216.67
Justin Thomas	68	73	72	69	282	135,216.67
Brad Fritsch	69	70	72	71	282	135,216.66

	SCORES				TOTAL	MONEY
Gary Woodland	65	73	70	74	282	135,216.66
Keegan Bradley	69	72	71	71	283	97,600
Morgan Hoffmann	72	66	72	73	283	97,600
Hideki Matsuyama	72	72	70	69	283	97,600
Nicolas Colsaerts	69	67	75	73	284	76,555
Erik Compton	69	69	74	72	284	76,555
Jordan Spieth	71	63	75	75	284	76,555
Robert Streb	73	69	70	72	284	76,555
Luke Guthrie	76	68	71	70	285	54,290
J.B. Holmes	71	68	75	71	285	54,290
Billy Horschel	70	67	77	71	285	54,290
Rory Sabbatini	74	68	69	74	285	54,290
Bubba Watson	70	73	73	69	285	54,290
Stewart Cink	64	71	79	72	286	38,023.34
Justin Leonard	74	69	73	70	286	38,023.34
Jamie Lovemark	72	67	76	71	286	38,023.34
Sang-Moon Bae	67	76	71	72	286	38,023.33
Chad Collins	78	66	73	69	286	38,023.33
Robert Garrigus	71	71	72	72	286	38,023.33
Brendan Steele	76	67	74	69	286	38,023.33
Brian Stuard	70	73	69	74	286	38,023.33
Y.E. Yang	76	67	74	69	286	38,023.33
Charles Howell	70	72	70	75	287	26,840
Martin Laird	69	71	74	73	287	26,840
Michael Putnam	69	73	75	70	287	26,840
Brendon Todd	69	73	72	73	287	26,840
Kevin Tway	69	70	73	75	287	26,840
Tyrone van Aswegen	66	76	76	69	287	26,840
Stuart Appleby	74	69	72	73	288	20,740
Bill Haas	74	70	71	73	288	20,740
Justin Hicks	71	68	75	74	288	20,740
Matt Jones	75	65	77	71	288	20,740
Kevin Chappell	73	66	73	77	289	15,478.75
Jim Herman	66	75	74	74	289	15,478.75
David Lingmerth	72	70	75	72	289	15,478.75
Hunter Mahan	72	72	73	72	289	15,478.75
John Merrick	69	74	72	74	289	15,478.75
Ian Poulter	75	67	71	76	289	15,478.75
Andres Romero	72	72	67	78	289	15,478.75
Lee Westwood	73	68	75	73	289	15,478.75
Blake Adams	75	69	72	74	290	13,847
Mark Calcavecchia	70	74	71	75	290	13,847
David Lynn	68	73	75	74	290	13,847
Tag Ridings	73	70	73	74	290	13,847
Victor Dubuisson	72	69	74	76	291	13,176
Harrison Frazar	68	74	77	72	291	13,176
D.H. Lee	73	71	75	72	291	13,176
D.A. Points	67	74	75	75	291	13,176
Jhonattan Vegas	68	75	74	74	291	13,176
Nick Watney	70	74	74	73	291	13,176
Chris Williams	71	72	72	76	291	13,176
Matt Bettencourt	71	73	74	74	292	12,627
Cameron Tringale	71	71	76	74	292	12,627
Jonathan Byrd	70	72	77	74	293	12,383
Ben Crane	77	67	73	76	293	12,383
Bryce Molder	77	65	77	75	294	12,200
Nicholas Thompson	72	70	76	77	295	12,017
Charlie Wi	72	70	77	76	295	12,017
Greg Owen	70	74	74	82	300	11,834
Aaron Baddeley	74	71	73	76	220	11,712
Steven Bowditch	68	76	77		221	11,346
Will Claxton	71	73	77		221	11,346
Brice Garnett	75	68	78		221	11,346

	SCORES			TOTAL	MONEY
Tim Herron	70	74	77	221	11,346
Camilo Villegas	72	71	78	221	11,346
Bobby Gates	69	72	81	222	10,919
Tiger Woods	72	71	79	222	10,919
Michael Block	74	69	86	229	10,736

Waste Management Phoenix Open

TPC Scottsdale, Scottsdale, Arizona — January 30-February 2
Par 35-36–71; 7,216 yards — purse, $6,200,000

	SCORES				TOTAL	MONEY
Kevin Stadler	65	68	67	68	268	$1,116,000
Graham DeLaet	67	72	65	65	269	545,600
Bubba Watson	64	66	68	71	269	545,600
Hunter Mahan	66	71	65	68	270	272,800
Hideki Matsuyama	66	67	68	69	270	272,800
Charles Howell	70	69	67	65	271	207,700
Ryan Moore	66	71	64	70	271	207,700
Brendan Steele	66	74	62	69	271	207,700
Harris English	65	67	69	71	272	179,800
Webb Simpson	68	72	67	66	273	167,400
Pat Perez	65	68	70	71	274	155,000
Matt Jones	65	65	72	73	275	130,200
John Mallinger	67	72	67	69	275	130,200
Cameron Tringale	71	67	69	68	275	130,200
Greg Chalmers	65	67	71	73	276	102,300
Morgan Hoffmann	69	66	70	71	276	102,300
Jason Kokrak	66	69	68	73	276	102,300
Scott Piercy	67	67	75	67	276	102,300
Roberto Castro	72	69	70	66	277	63,302
Justin Hicks	71	70	69	67	277	63,302
Martin Laird	67	68	71	71	277	63,302
William McGirt	65	69	73	70	277	63,302
John Merrick	75	65	69	68	277	63,302
Kevin Na	70	70	68	69	277	63,302
Patrick Reed	67	67	71	72	277	63,302
John Rollins	72	67	67	71	277	63,302
Chris Stroud	70	67	68	72	277	63,302
Michael Thompson	72	68	70	67	277	63,302
Ken Duke	70	67	72	69	278	40,300
Spencer Levin	67	69	70	72	278	40,300
Bryce Molder	67	71	70	70	278	40,300
Geoff Ogilvy	71	70	68	69	278	40,300
Nick Watney	69	68	68	73	278	40,300
Jonas Blixt	68	71	72	68	279	33,480
Jason Bohn	70	70	70	69	279	33,480
Bill Haas	69	68	71	71	279	33,480
Ricky Barnes	71	67	67	75	280	27,900
Brian Davis	72	69	70	69	280	27,900
Matt Every	72	66	67	75	280	27,900
Camilo Villegas	70	71	68	71	280	27,900
Gary Woodland	67	72	72	69	280	27,900
K.J. Choi	71	70	69	71	281	21,080
Ben Crane	69	69	69	74	281	21,080
James Driscoll	67	70	73	71	281	21,080
David Lingmerth	72	68	68	73	281	21,080
Phil Mickelson	71	67	72	71	281	21,080
Chris Smith	70	69	71	71	281	21,080
Aaron Baddeley	68	70	73	71	282	15,772.80

	SCORES				TOTAL	MONEY
Erik Compton	67	72	71	72	282	15,772.80
David Lynn	72	66	70	74	282	15,772.80
Ryan Palmer	76	64	70	72	282	15,772.80
Jhonattan Vegas	71	66	75	70	282	15,772.80
Brendon de Jonge	66	73	70	74	283	14,284.80
Robert Garrigus	70	70	70	73	283	14,284.80
Martin Kaymer	69	71	71	72	283	14,284.80
Kevin Streelman	71	68	74	70	283	14,284.80
Brian Stuard	73	68	69	73	283	14,284.80
Nicolas Colsaerts	69	68	74	73	284	13,764
David Hearn	68	70	73	73	284	13,764
J.B. Holmes	73	68	70	73	284	13,764
Sang-Moon Bae	67	73	71	74	285	13,206
Jonathan Byrd	68	73	69	75	285	13,206
Brian Gay	69	71	71	74	285	13,206
Charley Hoffman	70	71	69	75	285	13,206
John Peterson	68	70	74	73	285	13,206
Brandt Snedeker	70	64	72	79	285	13,206
Kiradech Aphibarnrat	66	71	73	76	286	12,710
Fred Funk	69	71	76	70	286	12,710
Steven Bowditch	71	69	75	72	287	12,276
Mark Calcavecchia	70	71	71	75	287	12,276
Derek Ernst	72	69	72	74	287	12,276
Scott Langley	71	70	71	75	287	12,276
Y.E. Yang	64	73	75	75	287	12,276
Ben Curtis	68	72	73	75	288	11,842
Joe Ogilvie	71	70	77	70	288	11,842
Chris Kirk	65	73	75	76	289	11,656
Vijay Singh	69	72	75	76	292	11,532

AT&T Pebble Beach National Pro-Am

Pebble Beach GL: Par 36-36–72; 6,816 yards
Monterey Peninsula CC: Par 36-36–72; 6,838 yards
Spyglass Hill GC: Par 36-36–72; 6,858 yards
Pebble Beach, California

February 6-9
purse, $6,600,000

	SCORES				TOTAL	MONEY
Jimmy Walker	66	69	67	74	276	$1,188,000
Dustin Johnson	68	73	70	66	277	580,800
Jim Renner	65	73	72	67	277	580,800
Kevin Na	72	68	70	69	279	290,400
Jordan Spieth	67	67	78	67	279	290,400
Hunter Mahan	68	68	72	72	280	237,600
Graeme McDowell	71	71	72	67	281	205,700
Pat Perez	69	70	71	71	281	205,700
Tim Wilkinson	67	72	69	73	281	205,700
Chesson Hadley	71	70	70	71	282	165,000
Richard Lee	65	72	72	73	282	165,000
Bryce Molder	72	71	69	70	282	165,000
Brian Davis	68	74	70	71	283	116,600
Victor Dubuisson	73	67	74	69	283	116,600
Scott Gardiner	65	73	77	68	283	116,600
Will MacKenzie	69	74	70	70	283	116,600
Patrick Reed	69	70	75	69	283	116,600
Cameron Tringale	70	73	71	69	283	116,600
Steven Bowditch	68	70	75	71	284	71,775
Roberto Castro	70	73	71	70	284	71,775
Brice Garnett	75	68	68	73	284	71,775
Jason Kokrak	74	68	70	72	284	71,775

	SCORES				TOTAL	MONEY
Phil Mickelson	66	73	71	74	284	71,775
Seung-Yul Noh	72	71	71	70	284	71,775
Daniel Summerhays	69	69	74	72	284	71,775
Michael Thompson	71	68	72	73	284	71,775
Robert Garrigus	67	71	73	74	285	46,860
Padraig Harrington	72	69	72	72	285	46,860
Jim Herman	70	70	71	74	285	46,860
Russell Knox	70	72	70	73	285	46,860
Andrew Loupe	63	73	76	73	285	46,860
Ryan Palmer	72	66	72	76	286	39,050
Wes Roach	67	74	72	73	286	39,050
Robert Streb	67	75	72	72	286	39,050
Stuart Appleby	65	74	76	72	287	29,139
Kevin Chappell	73	68	73	73	287	29,139
James Driscoll	69	71	73	74	287	29,139
David Duval	72	68	74	73	287	29,139
Kevin Foley	68	76	71	72	287	29,139
Jim Furyk	70	70	73	74	287	29,139
Dudley Hart	71	68	73	75	287	29,139
Bronson La'Cassie	70	72	72	73	287	29,139
Dicky Pride	66	72	74	75	287	29,139
Michael Putnam	69	71	75	72	287	29,139
Woody Austin	73	70	69	76	288	18,498.86
Bud Cauley	73	69	72	74	288	18,498.86
Brian Gay	70	70	72	76	288	18,498.86
Matt Jones	68	74	70	76	288	18,498.86
Kevin Stadler	67	73	73	75	288	18,498.86
Blake Adams	69	69	72	78	288	18,498.85
Brendon Todd	70	68	73	77	288	18,498.85
Russell Henley	73	70	72	74	289	15,477
Doug LaBelle	70	74	70	75	289	15,477
George McNeill	67	74	73	75	289	15,477
Andres Romero	71	70	74	74	289	15,477
Aaron Baddeley	69	70	73	78	290	14,784
Alex Cejka	69	71	75	75	290	14,784
Ben Kohles	72	73	69	76	290	14,784
Sean O'Hair	70	71	74	75	290	14,784
Greg Owen	67	74	74	75	290	14,784
J.B. Holmes	68	75	70	78	291	14,256
Chris Kirk	71	68	76	76	291	14,256
Kyle Stanley	74	69	72	76	291	14,256
Kiradech Aphibarnrat	69	74	73		216	13,200
Rafa Cabrera-Bello	74	71	71		216	13,200
Jason Day	68	77	71		216	13,200
Fabian Gomez	72	74	70		216	13,200
Retief Goosen	71	73	72		216	13,200
Lee Janzen	68	73	75		216	13,200
Kevin Kisner	72	69	75		216	13,200
Scott Langley	69	75	72		216	13,200
Jamie Lovemark	73	69	74		216	13,200
John Mallinger	71	71	74		216	13,200
John Peterson	70	72	74		216	13,200
Rory Sabbatini	67	72	77		216	13,200
Will Wilcox	72	69	75		216	13,200

Northern Trust Open

Riviera Country Club, Pacific Palisades, California — February 13-16
Par 35-36–71; 7,298 yards — purse, $6,700,000

	SCORES				TOTAL	MONEY
Bubba Watson	70	71	64	64	269	$1,206,000
Dustin Johnson	66	70	69	66	271	723,600
Jason Allred	73	64	67	68	272	388,600
Brian Harman	67	69	68	68	272	388,600
Charl Schwartzel	69	68	68	68	273	268,000
Matt Every	69	69	69	67	274	216,912.50
William McGirt	69	67	65	73	274	216,912.50
George McNeill	69	68	66	71	274	216,912.50
Bryce Molder	69	69	69	67	274	216,912.50
Harris English	70	69	69	67	275	174,200
Brendan Steele	68	71	67	69	275	174,200
Sang-Moon Bae	67	66	72	71	276	127,300
Charlie Beljan	67	68	68	73	276	127,300
K.J. Choi	69	72	67	68	276	127,300
Charley Hoffman	67	71	68	70	276	127,300
Jordan Spieth	72	66	67	71	276	127,300
Cameron Tringale	68	70	67	71	276	127,300
Aaron Baddeley	69	65	72	71	277	97,150
John Senden	71	70	66	70	277	97,150
Keegan Bradley	68	70	72	68	278	80,846.67
Lee Westwood	69	70	68	71	278	80,846.67
Jimmy Walker	67	71	67	73	278	80,846.66
Kevin Chappell	71	70	69	69	279	57,955
Jim Furyk	68	68	71	72	279	57,955
Robert Garrigus	67	67	73	72	279	57,955
Bill Haas	72	67	67	73	279	57,955
Hideki Matsuyama	70	69	69	71	279	57,955
Kevin Stadler	69	69	74	67	279	57,955
Robert Allenby	71	69	71	69	280	42,600.84
Daniel Summerhays	71	72	66	71	280	42,600.84
Blake Adams	67	70	71	72	280	42,600.83
James Hahn	71	72	65	72	280	42,600.83
David Lingmerth	70	69	70	71	280	42,600.83
Geoff Ogilvy	74	68	69	69	280	42,600.83
Ernie Els	71	70	68	72	281	33,031
Gonzalo Fernandez-Castano	71	70	71	69	281	33,031
John Huh	71	71	72	67	281	33,031
Kevin Streelman	72	69	73	67	281	33,031
Brendon Todd	71	70	69	71	281	33,031
Victor Dubuisson	70	72	68	72	282	26,130
Luke Guthrie	71	69	67	75	282	26,130
J.J. Henry	70	69	71	72	282	26,130
Francesco Molinari	67	73	71	71	282	26,130
Jhonattan Vegas	70	69	71	72	282	26,130
Stuart Appleby	72	71	67	73	283	18,779.15
Justin Rose	70	72	68	73	283	18,779.15
Scott Brown	70	67	74	72	283	18,779.14
Richard Lee	69	72	73	69	283	18,779.14
Davis Love	71	71	73	68	283	18,779.14
Vijay Singh	75	67	70	71	283	18,779.14
Scott Stallings	67	72	72	72	283	18,779.14
Angel Cabrera	69	71	71	73	284	15,467.43
Ken Duke	71	69	69	75	284	15,467.43
J.B. Holmes	67	71	75	71	284	15,467.43
Justin Leonard	70	72	70	72	284	15,467.43
Will MacKenzie	73	69	72	70	284	15,467.43
Hunter Mahan	70	73	71	70	284	15,467.43

	SCORES				TOTAL	MONEY
Billy Hurley	70	71	74	69	284	15,467.42
Erik Compton	74	67	71	73	285	14,539
Jason Gore	71	69	74	71	285	14,539
Matt Jones	67	73	70	75	285	14,539
Marc Leishman	69	74	71	71	285	14,539
David Lynn	70	71	70	74	285	14,539
Ian Poulter	72	70	71	72	285	14,539
Jason Dufner	70	72	76	68	286	13,869
Retief Goosen	73	69	73	71	286	13,869
Martin Laird	70	73	70	73	286	13,869
Tim Wilkinson	71	72	73	70	286	13,869
Ben Crane	72	70	69	76	287	13,534
Graham DeLaet	70	73	72	73	288	13,199
Martin Flores	72	69	73	74	288	13,199
Webb Simpson	70	72	72	74	288	13,199
Harold Varner	69	72	72	75	288	13,199
Michael Putnam	71	72	75	72	290	12,864
Pat Perez	69	72	73	78	292	12,730
Ben Curtis	70	73	74	78	295	12,596
Scott Piercy	71	69	76	83	299	12,462

WGC - Accenture Match Play Championship

The Golf Club at Dove Mountain, Marana, Arizona — February 19-23
Par 36-36–72; 7,849 yards — purse, $9,000,000

FIRST ROUND

George Coetzee defeated Steve Stricker, 3 and 1.
Patrick Reed defeated Graham DeLaet, 1 up.
Jason Day defeated Thorbjorn Olesen, 2 up.
Billy Horschel defeated Jamie Donaldson, 6 and 5.
Brandt Snedeker defeated David Lynn, 20 holes.
Webb Simpson defeated Thongchai Jaidee, 3 and 2.
Henrik Stenson defeated Kiradech Aphibarnrat, 2 and 1.
Louis Oosthuizen defeated Nick Watney, 1 up.
Rickie Fowler defeated Ian Poulter, 2 and 1.
Jimmy Walker defeated Branden Grace, 5 and 4.
Sergio Garcia defeated Marc Leishman, 22 holes.
Bill Haas defeated Miguel Angel Jimenez, 4 and 3.
Charl Schwartzel defeated Kevin Stadler, 3 and 2.
Jim Furyk defeated Chris Kirk, 2 and 1.
Rory McIlroy defeated Boo Weekley, 3 and 2.
Harris English defeated Lee Westwood, 5 and 3.
Jordan Spieth defeated Pablo Larrazabal, 2 up.
Thomas Bjorn defeated Francesco Molinari, 2 and 1.
Matt Kuchar defeated Bernd Wiesberger, 3 and 2.
Ryan Moore defeated Joost Luiten, 1 up.
Jason Dufner defeated Scott Stallings, 19 holes.
Matteo Manassero defeated Luke Donald, 5 and 4.
Justin Rose defeated Scott Piercy, 1 up.
Ernie Els defeated Stephen Gallacher, 19 holes.
Bubba Watson defeated Mikko Ilonen, 2 and 1.
Jonas Blixt defeated Keegan Bradley, 2 and 1.
Peter Hanson defeated Dustin Johnson, 4 and 3.
Victor Dubuisson defeated Kevin Streelman, 5 and 4.
Graeme McDowell defeated Gary Woodland, 19 holes.
Hideki Matsuyama defeated Martin Kaymer, 2 and 1.
Richard Sterne defeated Zach Johnson, 5 and 4.
Hunter Mahan defeated Gonzalo Fernandez-Castano, 3 and 2.

(Each losing player received $48,000.)

SECOND ROUND

Day defeated Horschel, 22 holes.
Coetzee defeated Reed, 21 holes.
Oosthuizen defeated Stenson, 4 and 3.
Simpson defeated Snedeker, 4 and 3.
Garcia defeated Haas, 3 and 1.
Fowler defeated Walker, 1 up.
English defeated McIlroy, 19 holes.
Furyk defeated Schwartzel, 3 and 2.
Kuchar defeated Moore, 2 up.
Spieth defeated Bjorn, 5 and 4.
Els defeated Rose, 20 holes.
Dufner defeated Manassero, 2 and 1.
Dubuisson defeated Hanson, 3 and 1.
Watson defeated Blixt, 2 up.
Mahan defeated Sterne, 2 up.
McDowell defeated Matsuyama, 1 up.

(Each losing player received $99,000.)

THIRD ROUND

Oosthuizen defeated Simpson, 5 and 4.
Day defeated Coetzee, 3 and 1.
Furyk defeated English, 1 up.
Fowler defeated Garcia, 1 up.
Els defeated Dufner, 1 up.
Spieth defeated Kuchar, 2 and 1.
McDowell defeated Mahan, 21 holes.
Dubuisson defeated Watson, 1 up.

(Each losing player received $148,000.)

QUARTER-FINALS

Day defeated Oosthuizen, 2 and 1.
Fowler defeated Furyk, 1 up.
Els defeated Spieth, 4 and 2.
Dubuisson defeated McDowell, 1 up.

(Each losing player received $280,000.)

SEMI-FINALS

Day defeated Fowler, 3 and 2.
Dubuisson defeated Els, 1 up.

PLAYOFF FOR THIRD-FOURTH PLACE

Fowler defeated Els, 19 holes.

(Fowler received $630,000; Els received $510,000.)

FINAL

Day defeated Dubuisson, 23 holes.

(Day received $1,500,000; Dubuisson received $906,000.)

Honda Classic

PGA National, Champion Course, Palm Beach Gardens, Florida
Par 35-35–70; 7,140 yards

February 27-March 2
purse, $6,000,000

	SCORES				TOTAL	MONEY
Russell Henley	64	68	68	72	272	$1,080,000
Russell Knox	70	63	68	71	272	448,000
Rory McIlroy	63	66	69	74	272	448,000
Ryan Palmer	68	66	69	69	272	448,000
(Henley won on first playoff hole.)						
Billy Hurley	70	67	67	69	273	240,000
David Hearn	67	70	70	67	274	208,500
Will MacKenzie	67	68	69	70	274	208,500
Stuart Appleby	69	69	65	72	275	168,000
Luke Donald	67	68	68	72	275	168,000
Sergio Garcia	72	68	68	67	275	168,000
David Lingmerth	69	68	68	70	275	168,000
Keegan Bradley	69	68	66	73	276	94,800
Paul Casey	72	68	69	67	276	94,800
Martin Flores	69	70	68	69	276	94,800
Freddie Jacobson	69	69	67	71	276	94,800
Chris Kirk	69	67	72	68	276	94,800
Matteo Manassero	67	71	71	67	276	94,800
George McNeill	70	67	69	70	276	94,800
Andres Romero	70	68	71	67	276	94,800
Adam Scott	68	69	70	69	276	94,800
Chris Stroud	69	66	73	68	276	94,800
Daniel Summerhays	70	65	69	72	276	94,800
Jhonattan Vegas	70	66	66	74	276	94,800
Matt Every	66	73	65	73	277	45,400
Gonzalo Fernandez-Castano	71	69	68	69	277	45,400
Rickie Fowler	69	69	69	70	277	45,400
Luke Guthrie	67	73	65	72	277	45,400
Chesson Hadley	73	66	69	69	277	45,400
Patrick Reed	71	67	70	69	277	45,400
Brian Stuard	72	68	65	72	277	45,400
Tyrone van Aswegen	67	71	68	71	277	45,400
Nick Watney	71	69	70	67	277	45,400
Derek Ernst	66	69	71	72	278	30,375
Zach Johnson	67	70	68	73	278	30,375
Brooks Koepka	71	68	68	71	278	30,375
Seung-Yul Noh	69	68	72	69	278	30,375
Rory Sabbatini	65	71	68	74	278	30,375
Brendan Steele	69	66	71	72	278	30,375
Josh Teater	70	68	71	69	278	30,375
Nicholas Thompson	68	70	66	74	278	30,375
Jason Kokrak	70	66	70	73	279	22,200
Ted Potter, Jr.	71	66	67	75	279	22,200
Cameron Tringale	69	69	66	75	279	22,200
Camilo Villegas	71	68	69	71	279	22,200
Boo Weekley	68	67	73	71	279	22,200
Thomas Bjorn	69	66	70	75	280	15,600
James Driscoll	68	71	70	71	280	15,600
Graeme McDowell	70	67	72	71	280	15,600
Troy Merritt	68	69	72	71	280	15,600
Carl Pettersson	72	67	68	73	280	15,600
John Senden	72	63	73	72	280	15,600
Lee Westwood	68	65	73	74	280	15,600
Charlie Wi	69	71	68	72	280	15,600
Mark Wilson	67	69	73	71	280	15,600
Jamie Donaldson	65	69	72	75	281	13,680
Charles Howell	72	68	69	72	281	13,680

	SCORES				TOTAL	MONEY
Tim Wilkinson	70	69	67	75	281	13,680
Stewart Cink	69	68	69	76	282	13,320
Derek Fathauer	67	71	69	75	282	13,320
Brian Harman	67	72	69	74	282	13,320
D.A. Points	70	69	70	74	283	13,020
Hudson Swafford	67	71	68	77	283	13,020
Brendon de Jonge	66	64	76	78	284	12,660
Ken Duke	68	71	72	73	284	12,660
Justin Hicks	70	70	71	73	284	12,660
Vijay Singh	69	71	68	76	284	12,660
Trevor Immelman	69	69	72	75	285	12,300
Jeff Overton	69	71	71	74	285	12,300
Ben Crane	69	68	71	78	286	12,120
Mark Calcavecchia	69	70	73		212	11,700
Erik Compton	70	68	74		212	11,700
Davis Love	69	71	72		212	11,700
William McGirt	65	69	78		212	11,700
Scott Brown	71	69	73		213	11,220
Brice Garnett	66	71	76		213	11,220
Jamie Lovemark	69	68	76		213	11,220
Y.E. Yang	71	68	74		213	11,220
Heath Slocum	71	68	75		214	10,920

WGC - Cadillac Championship

Trump National at Doral, Miami, Florida — March 6-9
Par 36-36–72; 7,481 yards — purse, $9,000,000

	SCORES				TOTAL	MONEY
Patrick Reed	68	75	69	72	284	$1,530,000
Jamie Donaldson	74	70	71	70	285	753,000
Bubba Watson	73	72	72	68	285	753,000
Dustin Johnson	69	74	73	72	288	395,000
Richard Sterne	74	73	70	71	288	395,000
Thongchai Jaidee	73	74	74	68	289	248,333.34
Stephen Gallacher	75	75	70	69	289	248,333.33
Bill Haas	73	76	69	71	289	248,333.33
Jason Dufner	69	77	68	76	290	151,250
Hunter Mahan	69	74	71	76	290	151,250
Graeme McDowell	73	71	73	73	290	151,250
Charl Schwartzel	70	76	76	68	290	151,250
Miguel Angel Jimenez	70	77	69	75	291	110,000
Matt Kuchar	69	74	74	74	291	110,000
Joost Luiten	76	72	71	72	291	110,000
Jonas Blixt	79	72	75	66	292	90,666.67
George Coetzee	74	74	73	71	292	90,666.67
Sergio Garcia	74	76	73	69	292	90,666.67
Scott Hend	72	76	73	71	292	90,666.67
Henrik Stenson	73	76	74	69	292	90,666.67
Gary Woodland	72	78	71	71	292	90,666.67
Harris English	69	77	74	72	292	90,666.66
Zach Johnson	70	75	71	76	292	90,666.66
Phil Mickelson	74	75	69	74	292	90,666.66
Luke Donald	70	82	72	69	293	76,000
Rory McIlroy	70	74	75	74	293	76,000
Francesco Molinari	69	75	76	73	293	76,000
Ryan Moore	70	79	69	75	293	76,000
Adam Scott	75	73	72	73	293	76,000
Kevin Streelman	75	74	72	72	293	76,000
Peter Uihlein	73	77	71	72	293	76,000

	SCORES				TOTAL	MONEY
Jimmy Walker	73	77	67	76	293	76,000
Tiger Woods	76	73	66	78	293	76,000
Graham DeLaet	78	72	70	74	294	68,500
Hyung-Sung Kim	72	74	74	74	294	68,500
Hideki Matsuyama	72	77	71	74	294	68,500
Justin Rose	74	77	70	73	294	68,500
Jordan Spieth	73	79	73	69	294	68,500
Lee Westwood	75	79	70	70	294	68,500
Darren Fichardt	73	78	72	72	295	63,500
Branden Grace	75	74	69	77	295	63,500
Chris Kirk	75	71	76	73	295	63,500
Louis Oosthuizen	72	78	71	74	295	63,500
Thomas Bjorn	75	75	73	73	296	60,500
Rickie Fowler	76	75	74	71	296	60,500
Brandt Snedeker	73	73	75	76	297	59,000
Russell Henley	72	78	75	73	298	57,000
Webb Simpson	80	78	70	70	298	57,000
Kevin Stadler	77	76	72	73	298	57,000
Keegan Bradley	74	76	75	74	299	54,500
Billy Horschel	77	78	71	73	299	54,500
Ernie Els	75	78	73	74	300	52,500
Ian Poulter	71	78	73	78	300	52,500
Brendon de Jonge	76	79	74	72	301	51,000
Gonzalo Fernandez-Castano	77	77	77	70	301	51,000
Boo Weekley	75	75	78	73	301	51,000
Steve Stricker	77	78	71	76	302	50,000
Roberto Castro	74	78	78	73	303	49,250
Martin Kaymer	75	80	73	75	303	49,250
Jin Jeong	75	75	78	77	305	48,250
Matteo Manassero	76	76	74	79	305	48,250
Victor Dubuisson	72	81	75	78	306	47,000
Jim Furyk	78	77	75	76	306	47,000
D.A. Points	82	76	74	74	306	47,000
Dawie van der Walt	81	83	71	75	310	46,000
Brett Rumford	83	79	77	74	313	45,500
Kiradech Aphibarnrat	74	82	79	79	314	45,000
Nick Watney	72	75	71		WD	

Puerto Rico Open

Trump International Golf Club, Rio Grande, Puerto Rico — March 6-9
Par 36-36–72; 7,506 yards — purse, $3,500,000

	SCORES				TOTAL	MONEY
Chesson Hadley	68	65	67	67	267	$630,000
Danny Lee	67	68	66	68	269	378,000
Ben Martin	68	67	70	66	271	238,000
Jason Gore	67	69	66	70	272	131,950
Richard Lee	69	68	68	67	272	131,950
Carl Pettersson	71	66	66	69	272	131,950
Wes Roach	69	66	70	67	272	131,950
David Toms	72	64	67	69	272	131,950
Ricky Barnes	68	68	69	68	273	94,500
Jerry Kelly	69	67	67	70	273	94,500
Chris Stroud	73	67	68	65	273	94,500
Jonathan Byrd	69	66	67	72	274	77,000
Andrew Loupe	70	70	65	69	274	77,000
James Driscoll	69	63	75	69	276	59,500
Robert Karlsson	71	67	69	69	276	59,500
Peter Malnati	73	68	69	66	276	59,500

	SCORES				TOTAL	MONEY
Tim Petrovic	68	72	66	70	276	59,500
Robert Streb	69	72	66	69	276	59,500
Martin Flores	72	69	69	67	277	42,420
Ryo Ishikawa	70	69	69	69	277	42,420
Brooks Koepka	72	68	69	68	277	42,420
Scott Langley	72	70	70	65	277	42,420
George McNeill	69	67	68	73	277	42,420
Eric Axley	68	66	72	72	278	29,050
Rafa Cabrera-Bello	69	67	68	74	278	29,050
David Hearn	70	68	69	71	278	29,050
Greg Owen	69	67	71	71	278	29,050
Andrew Svoboda	74	66	68	70	278	29,050
Rafael Campos	74	69	67	69	279	21,306.25
Bud Cauley	69	67	72	71	279	21,306.25
Nicolas Colsaerts	70	69	73	67	279	21,306.25
Brad Fritsch	71	68	67	73	279	21,306.25
Emiliano Grillo	71	71	71	66	279	21,306.25
William McGirt	68	71	69	71	279	21,306.25
Ted Potter, Jr.	71	70	65	73	279	21,306.25
David Skinns	74	66	71	68	279	21,306.25
Cameron Beckman	69	71	71	69	280	15,400
Steven Bowditch	69	70	67	74	280	15,400
Trevor Immelman	74	66	70	70	280	15,400
Seung-Yul Noh	72	70	71	67	280	15,400
Tyrone van Aswegen	69	68	72	71	280	15,400
Y.E. Yang	68	70	71	71	280	15,400
Brian Stuard	66	71	73	71	281	11,223.34
Will Wilcox	71	71	69	70	281	11,223.34
Ryuji Imada	73	67	68	73	281	11,223.33
Ryan Sullivan	69	70	68	74	281	11,223.33
Hudson Swafford	72	68	69	72	281	11,223.33
Lee Williams	71	70	68	72	281	11,223.33
John Daly	74	69	67	72	282	8,638
Jim Herman	69	70	68	75	282	8,638
Kevin Kisner	71	69	69	73	282	8,638
Sean O'Hair	75	67	70	70	282	8,638
Brady Watt	71	69	72	70	282	8,638
Stephen Ames	70	72	71	70	283	8,015
Alex Cejka	69	73	68	73	283	8,015
Joe Ogilvie	74	67	72	70	283	8,015
Michael Thompson	71	69	68	75	283	8,015
Daniel Chopra	74	66	74	70	284	7,665
Harrison Frazar	72	71	71	70	284	7,665
Bronson La'Cassie	71	70	72	71	284	7,665
Edward Loar	69	70	72	73	284	7,665
Jamie Lovemark	73	65	71	75	284	7,665
John Rollins	69	69	71	75	284	7,665
Scott Brown	70	73	70	72	285	7,420
Marco Dawson	70	73	71	72	286	7,245
Fred Funk	71	72	71	72	286	7,245
Jesper Parnevik	69	73	71	73	286	7,245
Vaughn Taylor	72	71	71	72	286	7,245
Jhonattan Vegas	74	68	71	74	287	7,070
Matt Bettencourt	71	71	71	75	288	7,000
Max Homa	73	70	71	75	289	6,930
Brice Garnett	70	72	73		215	6,720
Rod Pampling	70	71	74		215	6,720
Tag Ridings	70	72	73		215	6,720
Chris Smith	69	74	72		215	6,720
Paul Stankowski	73	70	72		215	6,720
Jose Coceres	73	70	73		216	6,510
Tim Clark	72	70	75		217	6,370
Chris DiMarco	75	68	74		217	6,370
Lee Janzen	73	70	74		217	6,370

Valspar Championship

Innisbrook Resort, Copperhead Course, Palm Harbor, Florida — March 13-16
Par 36-35–71; 7,340 yards — purse, $5,700,000

	SCORES				TOTAL	MONEY
John Senden	72	71	64	70	277	$1,026,000
Kevin Na	70	68	68	72	278	615,600
Scott Langley	71	69	69	70	279	387,600
Luke Donald	71	72	67	70	280	235,600
Robert Garrigus	69	66	70	75	280	235,600
Will MacKenzie	73	70	68	69	280	235,600
George McNeill	73	71	67	70	281	190,950
Graham DeLaet	75	68	71	68	282	148,200
Matt Every	68	71	72	71	282	148,200
David Hearn	71	70	70	71	282	148,200
Matteo Manassero	69	70	71	72	282	148,200
Justin Rose	71	68	69	74	282	148,200
Gary Woodland	72	71	70	69	282	148,200
Sang-Moon Bae	72	73	71	67	283	94,050
Jason Dufner	72	73	68	70	283	94,050
Bill Haas	69	73	72	69	283	94,050
Chesson Hadley	75	70	67	71	283	94,050
Charles Howell	71	70	74	68	283	94,050
Jason Kokrak	74	68	68	73	283	94,050
Jim Furyk	71	69	71	73	284	64,068
Freddie Jacobson	70	71	70	73	284	64,068
Carl Pettersson	71	70	71	72	284	64,068
Ted Potter, Jr.	73	71	67	73	284	64,068
Jordan Spieth	71	70	71	72	284	64,068
Ryo Ishikawa	73	72	72	68	285	42,587.15
Cameron Tringale	74	71	70	70	285	42,587.15
Brian Harman	71	70	73	71	285	42,587.14
Charley Hoffman	70	72	67	76	285	42,587.14
Morgan Hoffmann	74	69	71	71	285	42,587.14
Russell Knox	70	73	70	72	285	42,587.14
Josh Teater	73	70	70	72	285	42,587.14
Robert Allenby	73	71	70	72	286	31,540
Jonathan Byrd	70	73	70	73	286	31,540
Erik Compton	72	73	72	69	286	31,540
Ben Crane	70	72	71	73	286	31,540
Justin Hicks	72	72	70	72	286	31,540
John Merrick	70	70	72	74	286	31,540
Chad Collins	73	71	69	74	287	23,940
Harris English	72	69	74	72	287	23,940
James Hahn	69	74	70	74	287	23,940
Matt Kuchar	73	71	69	74	287	23,940
Kevin Streelman	73	69	71	74	287	23,940
Y.E. Yang	73	72	70	72	287	23,940
Woody Austin	71	71	74	72	288	15,891.60
Greg Chalmers	68	72	72	76	288	15,891.60
K.J. Choi	72	72	69	75	288	15,891.60
Ben Curtis	70	74	71	73	288	15,891.60
Tommy Gainey	69	72	72	75	288	15,891.60
Retief Goosen	72	73	64	79	288	15,891.60
Peter Hanson	75	70	69	74	288	15,891.60
Pat Perez	68	71	77	72	288	15,891.60
Nicholas Thompson	76	69	69	74	288	15,891.60
Brendon Todd	70	75	70	73	288	15,891.60
James Driscoll	73	70	68	78	289	13,053
J.B. Holmes	71	74	71	73	289	13,053
Justin Leonard	71	71	71	76	289	13,053
Michael Putnam	69	72	74	74	289	13,053

	SCORES				TOTAL	MONEY
Stuart Appleby	71	73	74	72	290	12,426
Darren Clarke	71	74	73	72	290	12,426
Jerry Kelly	76	68	71	75	290	12,426
D.H. Lee	74	70	70	76	290	12,426
David Lingmerth	73	72	71	74	290	12,426
Brandt Snedeker	72	73	71	74	290	12,426
Michael Thompson	72	69	72	77	290	12,426
Stephen Ames	72	70	72	77	291	11,742
Jason Bohn	71	74	73	73	291	11,742
Nicolas Colsaerts	69	73	76	73	291	11,742
Padraig Harrington	75	70	72	74	291	11,742
Marc Leishman	75	69	74	73	291	11,742
Paul Goydos	75	69	73	75	292	11,229
Davis Love	74	70	71	77	292	11,229
Rory Sabbatini	70	72	72	78	292	11,229
Daniel Summerhays	77	68	71	76	292	11,229
Sean O'Hair	73	71	74	78	296	10,944
John Mallinger	71	73	74	80	298	10,830
Eric Axley	72	70	77		219	10,431
Ricky Barnes	70	72	77		219	10,431
Brian Gay	75	69	75		219	10,431
Tim Herron	73	72	74		219	10,431
Luke Guthrie	70	70	80		220	10,146
Tim Clark	73	72	76		221	9,975
Ken Duke	71	71	79		221	9,975
Boo Weekley	74	71	77		222	9,804
Mark Calcavecchia	73	71	73		WD	

Arnold Palmer Invitational

Bay Hill Club & Lodge, Orlando, Florida — March 20-23
Par 36-36–72; 7,381 yards — purse, $6,200,000

	SCORES				TOTAL	MONEY
Matt Every	69	70	66	70	275	$1,116,000
Keegan Bradley	71	67	66	72	276	669,600
Adam Scott	62	68	71	76	277	421,600
Jason Kokrak	67	71	67	73	278	297,600
Erik Compton	72	68	70	69	279	226,300
Francesco Molinari	67	70	69	73	279	226,300
Henrik Stenson	69	73	69	68	279	226,300
Ryo Ishikawa	65	74	70	71	280	186,000
Brandt Snedeker	67	71	74	68	280	186,000
J.B. Holmes	68	69	72	73	282	148,800
Freddie Jacobson	71	68	70	73	282	148,800
Graeme McDowell	68	77	67	70	282	148,800
Sean O'Hair	71	75	69	67	282	148,800
Kevin Chappell	71	70	71	71	283	102,300
Harris English	69	71	75	68	283	102,300
Lucas Glover	72	74	68	69	283	102,300
Matt Jones	71	71	69	72	283	102,300
George McNeill	71	72	69	71	283	102,300
Kevin Na	70	71	71	71	283	102,300
Brian Davis	70	74	71	69	284	67,166.67
Vijay Singh	72	73	68	71	284	67,166.67
Camilo Villegas	71	73	73	67	284	67,166.67
Gary Woodland	73	71	70	70	284	67,166.67
Ian Poulter	68	71	69	76	284	67,166.66
Brendan Steele	68	74	70	72	284	67,166.66
Chesson Hadley	69	68	69	79	285	45,880

	SCORES				TOTAL	MONEY
Trevor Immelman	69	72	71	73	285	45,880
Brooks Koepka	74	70	72	69	285	45,880
Davis Love	70	73	69	73	285	45,880
Nicholas Thompson	71	73	71	70	285	45,880
Retief Goosen	70	75	68	73	286	37,587.50
Danny Lee	71	72	73	70	286	37,587.50
Marc Leishman	72	74	69	71	286	37,587.50
Chris Stroud	73	69	72	72	286	37,587.50
Aaron Baddeley	70	70	70	77	287	28,636.25
Gonzalo Fernandez-Castano	66	77	74	70	287	28,636.25
Luke Guthrie	71	71	74	71	287	28,636.25
Peter Hanson	75	69	71	72	287	28,636.25
Morgan Hoffmann	67	71	71	78	287	28,636.25
Charles Howell	68	71	72	76	287	28,636.25
Bryce Molder	72	72	69	74	287	28,636.25
Seung-Yul Noh	72	68	74	73	287	28,636.25
Charlie Beljan	72	72	70	74	288	18,476
Jamie Donaldson	67	71	74	76	288	18,476
Billy Horschel	70	74	69	75	288	18,476
Zach Johnson	71	71	73	73	288	18,476
Russell Knox	71	71	72	74	288	18,476
Will MacKenzie	71	75	72	70	288	18,476
John Merrick	65	74	76	73	288	18,476
Sam Saunders	69	71	71	77	288	18,476
Jhonattan Vegas	70	72	75	71	288	18,476
David Hearn	70	72	73	74	289	14,539
David Lingmerth	75	71	69	74	289	14,539
Patrick Reed	69	73	70	77	289	14,539
John Senden	72	74	71	72	289	14,539
Jason Bohn	73	73	72	72	290	14,012
Lee Janzen	72	73	74	71	290	14,012
Cameron Tringale	70	74	75	71	290	14,012
*Zachary Olsen	73	71	72	74	290	
Briny Baird	72	71	74	74	291	13,454
Paul Casey	67	79	72	73	291	13,454
K.J. Choi	70	76	70	75	291	13,454
Chris Kirk	69	72	72	78	291	13,454
Ryan Moore	68	72	78	73	291	13,454
Brian Stuard	72	74	74	71	291	13,454
Stewart Cink	71	70	72	79	292	13,020
Padraig Harrington	70	70	73	80	293	12,772
Rod Pampling	73	72	71	77	293	12,772
Pat Perez	70	70	70	83	293	12,772
Woody Austin	72	71	75	76	294	12,462
Michael Putnam	70	75	74	75	294	12,462
Greg Owen	76	69	74	76	295	12,214
Tim Wilkinson	71	74	77	73	295	12,214
Chad Campbell	69	77	73	77	296	11,966
Justin Hicks	78	68	71	79	296	11,966
Martin Laird	71	72	76	78	297	11,780

Valero Texas Open

JW Marriott, TPC San Antonio, San Antonio, Texas — March 27-30
Par 36-36–72; 7,435 yards — purse, $6,200,000

	SCORES				TOTAL	MONEY
Steven Bowditch	69	67	68	76	280	$1,116,000
Will MacKenzie	69	72	70	70	281	545,600
Daniel Summerhays	72	68	70	71	281	545,600

	SCORES				TOTAL	MONEY
Matt Kuchar	70	72	65	75	282	272,800
Andrew Loupe	67	70	70	75	282	272,800
Jim Furyk	70	74	68	71	283	200,725
Zach Johnson	70	71	70	72	283	200,725
Jerry Kelly	71	71	70	71	283	200,725
Brendon Todd	71	76	68	68	283	200,725
Jordan Spieth	75	70	68	71	284	167,400
Charley Hoffman	70	75	70	70	285	136,400
Kevin Na	70	70	69	76	285	136,400
Geoff Ogilvy	74	69	69	73	285	136,400
Pat Perez	68	71	69	77	285	136,400
Justin Hicks	69	73	72	72	286	111,600
Stephen Ames	74	71	68	74	287	78,740
Martin Flores	71	71	73	72	287	78,740
James Hahn	71	70	76	70	287	78,740
Brian Harman	70	72	75	70	287	78,740
Freddie Jacobson	70	70	73	74	287	78,740
Seung-Yul Noh	69	76	71	71	287	78,740
Carl Pettersson	70	73	71	73	287	78,740
Wes Roach	75	66	72	74	287	78,740
Michael Thompson	70	75	71	71	287	78,740
Jimmy Walker	76	71	71	69	287	78,740
Chad Collins	71	66	73	78	288	45,880
Russell Knox	74	70	71	73	288	45,880
Andrew Svoboda	73	73	67	75	288	45,880
Bo Van Pelt	69	73	71	75	288	45,880
Johnson Wagner	73	73	71	71	288	45,880
Brice Garnett	70	73	71	75	289	36,766
Trevor Immelman	70	71	74	74	289	36,766
Jason Kokrak	71	71	77	70	289	36,766
Justin Leonard	76	69	71	73	289	36,766
William McGirt	72	71	72	74	289	36,766
Cameron Beckman	69	70	77	74	290	28,571.67
Scott Brown	70	74	73	73	290	28,571.67
Brendon de Jonge	73	72	71	74	290	28,571.67
Jamie Lovemark	73	72	72	73	290	28,571.67
Brooks Koepka	71	74	73	72	290	28,571.66
Josh Teater	71	70	77	72	290	28,571.66
Kevin Foley	74	73	70	74	291	22,320
Joe Ogilvie	74	73	71	73	291	22,320
Michael Putnam	72	71	73	75	291	22,320
John Senden	72	73	73	73	291	22,320
Briny Baird	72	72	72	76	292	15,934
Miguel Angel Carballo	69	76	74	73	292	15,934
Ben Curtis	70	75	72	75	292	15,934
Brian Davis	71	72	76	73	292	15,934
Bronson La'Cassie	74	73	70	75	292	15,934
John Mallinger	74	73	70	75	292	15,934
Troy Matteson	72	73	74	73	292	15,934
Troy Merritt	73	72	74	73	292	15,934
Andres Romero	71	74	73	74	292	15,934
Cameron Tringale	71	74	72	75	292	15,934
Greg Chalmers	73	73	74	73	293	13,826
Brian Gay	73	71	73	76	293	13,826
Chesson Hadley	69	73	71	80	293	13,826
Jeff Maggert	72	74	72	75	293	13,826
Ryan Palmer	72	71	68	82	293	13,826
Mike Weir	76	71	72	74	293	13,826
Richard Lee	72	75	73	74	294	13,330
Tim Wilkinson	74	70	74	76	294	13,330
Scott Gardiner	74	69	77	75	295	13,020
Luke Guthrie	74	72	74	75	295	13,020
J.B. Holmes	72	75	72	76	295	13,020

	SCORES				TOTAL	MONEY
Aaron Baddeley	70	71	79	76	296	12,710
John Peterson	74	72	74	76	296	12,710
Charlie Beljan	70	76	74	77	297	12,462
Fred Funk	70	72	77	78	297	12,462
Alex Aragon	70	74	76	78	298	12,276
Stuart Appleby	70	77	74		221	11,966
Alex Prugh	71	73	77		221	11,966
Robert Streb	72	72	77		221	11,966
Charlie Wi	73	73	75		221	11,966
Jim Herman	73	73	76		222	11,656
Tyrone van Aswegen	71	76	77		224	11,470
Camilo Villegas	71	73	80		224	11,470
Branden Grace	72	73	82		227	11,222
John Merrick	72	75	80		227	11,222

Shell Houston Open

Golf Club of Houston, Humble, Texas — April 3-6
Par 36-36–72; 7,441 yards — purse, $6,400,000

	SCORES				TOTAL	MONEY
Matt Jones	68	68	71	66	273	$1,152,000
Matt Kuchar	66	67	68	72	273	691,200
(Jones defeated Kuchar on first playoff hole.)						
Sergio Garcia	67	65	73	70	275	435,200
Cameron Tringale	68	68	69	71	276	307,200
Shawn Stefani	67	69	73	69	278	256,000
Rickie Fowler	70	70	68	71	279	230,400
Brice Garnett	68	71	72	69	280	186,240
Retief Goosen	68	71	71	70	280	186,240
Russell Henley	73	69	72	66	280	186,240
Rory McIlroy	70	71	74	65	280	186,240
Ryan Palmer	70	68	73	69	280	186,240
Erik Compton	66	73	73	69	281	125,440
Ben Curtis	67	70	71	73	281	125,440
J.B. Holmes	66	73	71	71	281	125,440
Phil Mickelson	68	70	72	71	281	125,440
Chris Stroud	68	72	71	70	281	125,440
Martin Flores	68	72	72	70	282	99,200
Lee Westwood	70	72	71	69	282	99,200
Jonathan Byrd	68	74	73	68	283	77,568
Graham DeLaet	70	71	72	70	283	77,568
Jason Gore	67	71	74	71	283	77,568
Freddie Jacobson	68	72	74	69	283	77,568
Charl Schwartzel	67	75	70	71	283	77,568
Luke Donald	71	71	71	71	284	50,651.43
Michael Putnam	68	72	73	71	284	50,651.43
Jim Renner	66	72	74	72	284	50,651.43
Steve Stricker	68	69	76	71	284	50,651.43
Nicholas Thompson	71	69	74	70	284	50,651.43
Jimmy Walker	71	65	77	71	284	50,651.43
Andres Romero	72	69	70	73	284	50,651.42
Kevin Chappell	71	72	76	66	285	37,952
Jon Curran	69	72	69	75	285	37,952
Ryo Ishikawa	69	74	71	71	285	37,952
Hunter Mahan	69	72	71	73	285	37,952
Carl Pettersson	69	74	72	70	285	37,952
James Hahn	71	72	73	70	286	32,960
Brendon de Jonge	71	73	72	71	287	28,160
Bill Haas	65	74	76	72	287	28,160

	SCORES				TOTAL	MONEY
Charley Hoffman	65	76	78	68	287	28,160
John Huh	71	71	72	73	287	28,160
Jeff Overton	73	69	74	71	287	28,160
David Toms	71	71	75	70	287	28,160
Ricky Barnes	70	73	74	71	288	18,373.82
Keegan Bradley	66	77	73	72	288	18,373.82
Angel Cabrera	68	73	75	72	288	18,373.82
Ben Crane	70	74	72	72	288	18,373.82
Brian Gay	71	70	71	76	288	18,373.82
Justin Hicks	67	73	74	74	288	18,373.82
Jeff Maggert	69	73	74	72	288	18,373.82
Brendon Todd	69	74	73	72	288	18,373.82
Camilo Villegas	67	73	73	75	288	18,373.82
Ernie Els	68	76	74	70	288	18,373.81
Hudson Swafford	70	74	76	68	288	18,373.81
John Mallinger	72	72	75	70	289	14,656
John Merrick	74	68	75	72	289	14,656
Kyle Stanley	69	74	74	72	289	14,656
Henrik Stenson	71	72	76	70	289	14,656
Stewart Cink	67	75	74	74	290	14,208
Harrison Frazar	71	71	76	72	290	14,208
Brian Harman	70	71	74	75	290	14,208
Robert Garrigus	74	69	73	75	291	13,760
Davis Love	68	73	78	72	291	13,760
Webb Simpson	68	73	73	77	291	13,760
Michael Thompson	67	73	77	74	291	13,760
Chris Kirk	68	74	75	75	292	13,312
Justin Leonard	70	71	81	70	292	13,312
John Rollins	68	76	72	76	292	13,312
Kevin Kisner	71	70	81	71	293	13,056
Greg Chalmers	69	74	75	76	294	12,864
Tommy Gainey	71	72	77	74	294	12,864
Tyrone van Aswegen	71	73	74	77	295	12,672
J.J. Henry	72	71	78	75	296	12,480
Jhonattan Vegas	67	75	76	78	296	12,480
Stephen Ames	72	71	78	76	297	12,224
Bubba Dickerson	74	70	74	79	297	12,224
Roberto Castro	71	72	83	73	299	12,032

Masters Tournament

Augusta National Golf Club, Augusta, Georgia — April 10-13
Par 36-36–72; 7,435 yards — purse, $8,000,000

	SCORES				TOTAL	MONEY
Bubba Watson	69	68	74	69	280	$1,620,000
Jonas Blixt	70	71	71	71	283	792,000
Jordan Spieth	71	70	70	72	283	792,000
Miguel Angel Jimenez	71	76	66	71	284	432,000
Rickie Fowler	71	75	67	73	286	342,000
Matt Kuchar	73	71	68	74	286	342,000
Lee Westwood	73	71	70	73	287	301,500
Thomas Bjorn	73	68	73	74	288	234,000
Bernhard Langer	72	74	73	69	288	234,000
Rory McIlroy	71	77	71	69	288	234,000
John Senden	72	68	75	73	288	234,000
Kevin Stadler	70	73	72	73	288	234,000
Jimmy Walker	70	72	76	70	288	234,000
Stewart Cink	73	72	76	68	289	148,500
Jamie Donaldson	73	70	76	70	289	148,500

	SCORES				TOTAL	MONEY
Jim Furyk	74	68	72	75	289	148,500
Justin Rose	76	70	69	74	289	148,500
Adam Scott	69	72	76	72	289	148,500
Henrik Stenson	73	72	74	70	289	148,500
Fred Couples	71	71	73	75	290	101,160
Jason Day	75	73	70	72	290	101,160
Bill Haas	68	78	74	70	290	101,160
Chris Kirk	75	72	71	72	290	101,160
Ian Poulter	76	70	70	74	290	101,160
Louis Oosthuizen	69	75	75	72	291	79,200
Steven Bowditch	74	72	74	72	292	66,600
Gonzalo Fernandez-Castano	75	69	74	74	292	66,600
Joost Luiten	75	73	77	67	292	66,600
Hunter Mahan	74	72	74	72	292	66,600
Gary Woodland	70	77	69	76	292	66,600
Russell Henley	73	70	75	75	293	55,800
Martin Kaymer	75	72	73	73	293	55,800
Steve Stricker	72	73	73	75	293	55,800
K.J. Choi	70	75	78	71	294	48,600
Stephen Gallacher	71	72	81	70	294	48,600
Jose Maria Olazabal	74	74	73	73	294	48,600
Brendon de Jonge	74	72	76	73	295	40,500
Billy Horschel	75	72	75	73	295	40,500
Thongchai Jaidee	73	74	75	73	295	40,500
Vijay Singh	75	71	74	75	295	40,500
Brandt Snedeker	70	74	80	71	295	40,500
Lucas Glover	75	69	77	75	296	34,200
Kevin Streelman	72	71	74	79	296	34,200
Darren Clarke	74	74	73	76	297	27,972
Sandy Lyle	76	72	76	73	297	27,972
Thorbjorn Olesen	74	72	76	75	297	27,972
Nick Watney	72	75	76	74	297	27,972
Mike Weir	73	72	79	73	297	27,972
*Oliver Goss	76	71	76	75	298	
Francesco Molinari	71	76	76	76	299	23,400
Larry Mize	74	72	79	79	304	22,680

Out of Final 36 Holes

Sang-Moon Bae	72	77	149
Luke Donald	79	70	149
Victor Dubuisson	74	75	149
Ernie Els	75	74	149
Matthew Fitzpatrick	76	73	149
Sergio Garcia	74	75	149
Marc Leishman	70	79	149
Phil Mickelson	76	73	149
Ryan Moore	77	72	149
Charl Schwartzel	73	76	149
Webb Simpson	74	75	149
Harris English	74	76	150
Zach Johnson	78	72	150
Graeme McDowell	72	78	150
D.A. Points	78	72	150
Ian Woosnam	77	73	150
Ken Duke	75	76	151
John Huh	75	76	151
Dustin Johnson	77	74	151
Hideki Matsuyama	80	71	151
Angel Cabrera	78	74	152
Graham DeLaet	80	72	152
Derek Ernst	76	76	152
Matt Jones	74	78	152
David Lynn	78	74	152
Matteo Manassero	71	81	152
Mark O'Meara	75	77	152
Patrick Reed	73	79	152
Keegan Bradley	75	78	153
Roberto Castro	73	80	153
Branden Grace	84	69	153
Trevor Immelman	79	74	153
Chang-Woo Lee	80	73	153
Jason Dufner	80	74	154
Y.E. Yang	77	77	154
Matt Every	77	78	155
Jordan Niebrugge	81	74	155
Scott Stallings	75	80	155
Garrick Porteous	76	80	156
Boo Weekley	73	83	156
Tim Clark	79	78	157
Peter Hanson	78	81	159
Craig Stadler	82	77	159
Tom Watson	78	81	159
Michael McCoy	78	83	161
Ben Crenshaw	83	85	168

(Professionals who did not complete 72 holes received $5,000.)

RBC Heritage

Harbour Town Golf Links, Hilton Head Island, South Carolina — April 17-20
Par 36-35–71; 7,101 yards — purse, $5,800,000

	SCORES				TOTAL	MONEY
Matt Kuchar	66	73	70	64	273	$1,044,000
Luke Donald	70	69	66	69	274	626,400
Ben Martin	69	68	71	67	275	336,400
John Huh	71	68	68	68	275	336,400
Scott Brown	70	69	71	67	277	220,400
Brian Stuard	69	72	68	68	277	220,400
Brian Harman	69	71	69	69	278	187,050
Jim Furyk	71	66	71	70	278	187,050
William McGirt	66	76	71	66	279	156,600
Rory Sabbatini	69	72	70	68	279	156,600
Russell Knox	69	72	68	70	279	156,600
Stuart Appleby	73	73	67	67	280	110,200
Jordan Spieth	69	74	70	67	280	110,200
Jason Kokrak	71	73	66	70	280	110,200
Matt Every	69	70	70	71	280	110,200
Nicholas Thompson	70	70	68	72	280	110,200
Charl Schwartzel	70	70	68	72	280	110,200
Pat Perez	74	69	74	64	281	75,632
Paul Casey	74	67	72	68	281	75,632
Ryo Ishikawa	77	68	67	69	281	75,632
J.B. Holmes	72	71	69	69	281	75,632
Ted Potter, Jr.	70	69	71	71	281	75,632
Martin Kaymer	73	67	72	70	282	55,680
Graeme McDowell	71	69	72	70	282	55,680
Robert Allenby	69	72	70	71	282	55,680
*Matthew Fitzpatrick	71	71	69	71	282	
Camilo Villegas	72	71	73	67	283	43,790
Chris Kirk	71	72	71	69	283	43,790
Tim Herron	69	72	72	70	283	43,790
Geoff Ogilvy	72	68	71	72	283	43,790
Jonathan Byrd	71	73	73	67	284	34,469
Steve Marino	72	72	72	68	284	34,469
Harris English	68	73	75	68	284	34,469
Jerry Kelly	76	70	67	71	284	34,469
Billy Hurley	70	69	73	72	284	34,469
K.J. Choi	70	67	74	73	284	34,469
Richard Lee	70	69	71	74	284	34,469
Brendon Todd	75	71	71	68	285	23,200
Ricky Barnes	72	73	72	68	285	23,200
Spencer Levin	72	74	70	69	285	23,200
Scott Langley	66	73	75	71	285	23,200
Tim Clark	72	71	71	71	285	23,200
Justin Hicks	75	70	68	72	285	23,200
Kevin Kisner	73	72	68	72	285	23,200
Chesson Hadley	72	67	73	73	285	23,200
Kevin Stadler	71	69	72	73	285	23,200
Charley Hoffman	73	71	68	73	285	23,200
Chris Stroud	71	71	74	70	286	15,335
Andrew Loupe	70	73	72	71	286	15,335
Patrick Reed	71	72	70	73	286	15,335
Bo Van Pelt	69	70	73	74	286	15,335
Ken Duke	72	71	69	74	286	15,335
Boo Weekley	73	73	73	68	287	13,326
David Toms	73	73	72	69	287	13,326
Brice Garnett	73	71	72	71	287	13,326
Charles Howell	69	73	74	71	287	13,326
Shawn Stefani	74	69	71	73	287	13,326

	SCORES				TOTAL	MONEY
Woody Austin	74	71	67	75	287	13,326
Gonzalo Fernandez-Castano	74	71	67	75	287	13,326
Kevin Streelman	69	72	70	76	287	13,326
Zach Johnson	71	73	70	74	288	12,644
Tim Wilkinson	70	71	73	74	288	12,644
Stewart Cink	70	72	72	74	288	12,644
Tommy Gainey	72	74	75	68	289	12,238
Jeff Maggert	70	76	72	71	289	12,238
Ernie Els	72	73	73	71	289	12,238
John Mallinger	69	74	73	73	289	12,238
Mark Anderson	71	75	74	70	290	11,716
Brian Gay	70	74	74	72	290	11,716
Erik Compton	70	75	73	72	290	11,716
James Hahn	72	74	69	75	290	11,716
Billy Horschel	69	74	72	75	290	11,716
Robert Garrigus	71	74	71	75	291	11,368
Brian Davis	71	75	73	73	292	11,078
Brandt Snedeker	72	73	74	73	292	11,078
Trevor Immelman	74	69	75	74	292	11,078
Dudley Hart	73	69	75	75	292	11,078
Briny Baird	72	72	74	78	296	10,788

Zurich Classic of New Orleans

TPC Louisiana, Avondale, Louisiana — April 24-27
Par 36-36–72; 7,425 yards — purse, $6,800,000

	SCORES				TOTAL	MONEY
Seung-Yul Noh	65	68	65	71	269	$1,224,000
Robert Streb	67	66	68	70	271	598,400
Andrew Svoboda	64	68	70	69	271	598,400
Jeff Overton	67	68	67	70	272	326,400
Erik Compton	66	68	72	68	274	248,200
Robert Garrigus	73	69	68	64	274	248,200
Charley Hoffman	68	67	68	71	274	248,200
Keegan Bradley	69	66	65	75	275	197,200
Tommy Gainey	71	66	67	71	275	197,200
Justin Rose	71	67	69	68	275	197,200
Paul Casey	71	68	64	73	276	149,600
Bud Cauley	71	68	66	71	276	149,600
Peter Hanson	65	69	71	71	276	149,600
J.B. Holmes	71	65	69	71	276	149,600
Ben Martin	62	67	73	75	277	119,000
David Toms	73	68	67	69	277	119,000
Mark Anderson	72	65	70	71	278	98,600
Stuart Appleby	67	72	70	69	278	98,600
Rory Sabbatini	69	72	69	68	278	98,600
Cameron Tringale	73	69	66	70	278	98,600
Retief Goosen	72	65	68	74	279	73,440
Brooks Koepka	71	68	67	73	279	73,440
Bronson La'Cassie	70	69	69	71	279	73,440
Daniel Summerhays	72	66	68	73	279	73,440
Robert Allenby	71	68	68	73	280	54,230
David Duval	68	69	70	73	280	54,230
Danny Lee	71	69	65	75	280	54,230
Bo Van Pelt	74	63	73	70	280	54,230
Graham DeLaet	69	68	71	73	281	44,200
Freddie Jacobson	72	69	66	74	281	44,200
Alex Prugh	70	68	70	73	281	44,200
John Senden	70	70	69	72	281	44,200

	SCORES				TOTAL	MONEY
Boo Weekley	71	70	71	69	281	44,200
Sang-Moon Bae	68	72	71	71	282	30,785.46
Greg Chalmers	71	71	71	69	282	30,785.46
Derek Ernst	71	71	71	69	282	30,785.46
David Hearn	71	71	69	71	282	30,785.46
Charles Howell	68	73	70	71	282	30,785.46
Mark Calcavecchia	71	70	69	72	282	30,785.45
Kevin Chappell	72	67	69	74	282	30,785.45
Morgan Hoffmann	70	68	70	74	282	30,785.45
Kevin Kisner	69	68	69	76	282	30,785.45
Charlie Wi	70	71	69	72	282	30,785.45
Will Wilcox	68	68	71	75	282	30,785.45
Chad Collins	66	71	76	70	283	21,080
Tag Ridings	71	70	72	70	283	21,080
Andres Romero	70	71	70	72	283	21,080
Max Homa	71	71	71	71	284	17,544
Troy Merritt	71	69	70	74	284	17,544
Kevin Tway	70	72	69	73	284	17,544
Y.E. Yang	72	70	69	73	284	17,544
Briny Baird	71	69	70	75	285	15,476.80
Ricky Barnes	70	72	69	74	285	15,476.80
Martin Flores	72	68	69	76	285	15,476.80
Andrew Loupe	71	70	71	73	285	15,476.80
Sean O'Hair	71	69	71	74	285	15,476.80
D.A. Points	73	68	69	75	285	15,476.80
Kyle Stanley	71	67	71	76	285	15,476.80
Brendan Steele	73	67	70	75	285	15,476.80
Shawn Stefani	69	72	72	72	285	15,476.80
Tim Wilkinson	70	70	65	80	285	15,476.80
Lucas Glover	71	71	69	75	286	14,416
Fabian Gomez	72	69	66	79	286	14,416
John Merrick	69	72	72	73	286	14,416
Wes Roach	74	67	71	74	286	14,416
Vijay Singh	70	71	68	77	286	14,416
Joe Durant	69	71	67	80	287	13,872
Padraig Harrington	70	72	71	74	287	13,872
Michael Thompson	66	71	75	75	287	13,872
J.J. Henry	68	69	75	76	288	13,396
Doug LaBelle	68	73	72	75	288	13,396
Troy Matteson	72	68	69	79	288	13,396
Jim Renner	75	67	71	75	288	13,396
John Rollins	74	66	73	76	289	13,056

Wells Fargo Championship

Quail Hollow Club, Charlotte, North Carolina — May 1-4
Par 36-36–72; 7,562 yards — purse, $6,900,000

	SCORES				TOTAL	MONEY
J.B. Holmes	70	67	66	71	274	$1,242,000
Jim Furyk	72	69	69	65	275	745,200
Martin Flores	67	68	69	72	276	469,200
Jason Bohn	73	67	67	70	277	331,200
Justin Rose	69	67	71	71	278	276,000
Brendon de Jonge	80	62	68	69	279	239,775
Kevin Kisner	72	66	68	73	279	239,775
Roberto Castro	71	70	69	70	280	200,100
Rory McIlroy	69	76	65	70	280	200,100
Rory Sabbatini	74	68	71	67	280	200,100
Kevin Chappell	73	70	70	68	281	158,700

	SCORES				TOTAL	MONEY
Phil Mickelson	67	75	63	76	281	158,700
Michael Thompson	71	69	69	72	281	158,700
Jonathan Byrd	68	71	70	73	282	120,750
Zach Johnson	71	70	69	72	282	120,750
Geoff Ogilvy	72	67	70	73	282	120,750
Kevin Streelman	72	69	71	70	282	120,750
Charles Howell	69	71	70	73	283	89,976
Martin Kaymer	69	69	70	75	283	89,976
Ryan Moore	70	71	76	66	283	89,976
Kevin Na	69	72	69	73	283	89,976
Gary Woodland	71	72	68	72	283	89,976
Jason Kokrak	75	68	73	68	284	58,157.15
Y.E. Yang	73	72	71	68	284	58,157.15
Stewart Cink	68	70	74	72	284	58,157.14
John Merrick	71	70	70	73	284	58,157.14
Wes Roach	71	71	69	73	284	58,157.14
Robert Streb	71	69	71	73	284	58,157.14
Mark Wilson	72	72	66	74	284	58,157.14
Ricky Barnes	72	72	68	73	285	40,106.25
Scott Brown	71	73	70	71	285	40,106.25
Angel Cabrera	66	69	75	75	285	40,106.25
Derek Ernst	73	68	70	74	285	40,106.25
Chris Kirk	71	70	71	73	285	40,106.25
Martin Laird	69	70	73	73	285	40,106.25
Vijay Singh	69	72	71	73	285	40,106.25
Brendan Steele	72	72	69	72	285	40,106.25
Sang-Moon Bae	72	71	71	72	286	28,980
Bud Cauley	71	71	70	74	286	28,980
Rickie Fowler	74	71	74	67	286	28,980
Scott Langley	70	71	71	74	286	28,980
Hideki Matsuyama	69	72	72	73	286	28,980
Webb Simpson	68	73	70	75	286	28,980
Ernie Els	76	67	67	77	287	20,861
Bill Haas	75	70	70	72	287	20,861
David Hearn	70	74	71	72	287	20,861
Pat Perez	73	71	66	77	287	20,861
Shawn Stefani	69	68	75	75	287	20,861
Andrew Svoboda	72	72	69	74	287	20,861
Retief Goosen	70	70	74	74	288	16,642.80
Danny Lee	71	71	70	76	288	16,642.80
Hunter Mahan	72	73	72	71	288	16,642.80
Ben Martin	71	73	69	75	288	16,642.80
Ted Potter, Jr.	72	73	74	69	288	16,642.80
Robert Allenby	73	72	73	71	289	15,801
Daniel Summerhays	70	72	72	75	289	15,801
Josh Teater	72	73	75	70	290	15,456
Mike Weir	72	71	70	77	290	15,456
Will Wilcox	71	72	73	74	290	15,456
Brian Davis	74	71	75	71	291	14,904
Michael Putnam	73	69	72	77	291	14,904
Heath Slocum	77	68	74	72	291	14,904
Kyle Stanley	74	71	75	71	291	14,904
Cameron Tringale	74	68	79	70	291	14,904
Brian Harman	70	74	78	70	292	14,352
Davis Love	75	68	74	75	292	14,352
Kevin Tway	73	72	75	72	292	14,352
Johnson Wagner	75	70	73	75	293	14,076
Justin Hicks	74	71	74	76	295	13,800
Carl Pettersson	73	71	74	77	295	13,800
Jim Renner	71	74	74	76	295	13,800
Bronson La'Cassie	71	73	77	75	296	13,524
Jim Herman	76	68	72	81	297	13,386

The Players Championship

TPC Sawgrass, Ponte Vedra Beach, Florida — May 8-11
Par 36-36–72; 7,215 yards — purse, $10,000,000

	SCORES				TOTAL	MONEY
Martin Kaymer	63	69	72	71	275	$1,800,000
Jim Furyk	70	68	72	66	276	1,080,000
Sergio Garcia	67	71	69	70	277	680,000
Justin Rose	67	71	71	69	278	440,000
Jordan Spieth	67	66	71	74	278	440,000
David Hearn	70	71	68	70	279	313,000
Rory McIlroy	70	74	69	66	279	313,000
Francesco Molinari	72	70	67	70	279	313,000
Jimmy Walker	75	68	71	65	279	313,000
Lee Westwood	67	71	71	70	279	313,000
Brian Davis	72	67	73	68	280	240,000
Gary Woodland	67	71	70	72	280	240,000
K.J. Choi	74	70	72	65	281	187,500
Chris Kirk	71	73	70	67	281	187,500
George McNeill	71	68	69	73	281	187,500
Steve Stricker	71	70	71	69	281	187,500
Russell Henley	65	71	80	66	282	135,333.34
Justin Hicks	73	70	71	68	282	135,333.34
Morgan Hoffmann	71	70	70	71	282	135,333.33
Matt Jones	70	69	69	74	282	135,333.33
Matt Kuchar	71	71	69	71	282	135,333.33
Brian Stuard	67	76	69	70	282	135,333.33
Marc Leishman	70	72	74	67	283	96,000
Hideki Matsuyama	70	71	72	70	283	96,000
Daniel Summerhays	74	68	69	72	283	96,000
Kevin Chappell	72	68	75	69	284	69,500
Bill Haas	68	71	72	73	284	69,500
Billy Horschel	72	70	75	67	284	69,500
Zach Johnson	69	71	72	72	284	69,500
Ryan Moore	70	74	67	73	284	69,500
John Senden	70	69	68	77	284	69,500
Brendan Steele	69	73	75	67	284	69,500
Bo Van Pelt	71	70	70	73	284	69,500
Erik Compton	72	70	74	69	285	52,750
Russell Knox	72	72	73	68	285	52,750
Scott Langley	71	72	72	70	285	52,750
Henrik Stenson	71	70	70	74	285	52,750
Angel Cabrera	70	74	71	71	286	38,000
Stewart Cink	70	70	70	76	286	38,000
Jamie Donaldson	74	67	74	71	286	38,000
Luke Donald	73	69	75	69	286	38,000
Gonzalo Fernandez-Castano	67	77	72	70	286	38,000
Charley Hoffman	77	67	71	71	286	38,000
Justin Leonard	68	73	70	75	286	38,000
Kevin Na	70	69	76	71	286	38,000
Rory Sabbatini	71	73	69	73	286	38,000
Adam Scott	77	67	69	73	286	38,000
Charlie Beljan	73	69	73	72	287	24,072.73
Jason Dufner	69	74	72	72	287	24,072.73
Martin Flores	70	71	74	72	287	24,072.73
Retief Goosen	72	70	75	70	287	24,072.73
J.J. Henry	74	70	72	71	287	24,072.73
Jeff Maggert	72	71	74	70	287	24,072.73
Pat Perez	68	73	75	71	287	24,072.73
Charl Schwartzel	72	67	77	71	287	24,072.73
Steven Bowditch	72	72	71	72	287	24,072.72
Brandt Snedeker	75	69	67	76	287	24,072.72

	SCORES				TOTAL	MONEY
Bubba Watson	69	72	70	76	287	24,072.72
Dustin Johnson	68	74	72	74	288	22,000
Ryan Palmer	71	73	71	73	288	22,000
John Peterson	73	69	72	74	288	22,000
Scott Brown	68	71	77	73	289	21,500
Graeme McDowell	69	71	77	72	289	21,500
Freddie Jacobson	70	70	75	75	290	21,200
Richard Lee	71	71	76	73	291	20,800
Ian Poulter	74	69	72	76	291	20,800
Scott Stallings	67	77	71	76	291	20,800
Sang-Moon Bae	66	73	79	74	292	20,400
Geoff Ogilvy	69	70	76	78	293	20,200
Brendon de Jonge	69	74	75	76	294	20,000
Kyle Stanley	73	69	76	77	295	19,800
Ernie Els	68	76	75		219	19,400
John Huh	69	72	78		219	19,400
Seung-Yul Noh	76	68	75		219	19,400
Jonas Blixt	71	72	77		220	18,900
John Merrick	72	71	77		220	18,900
Stuart Appleby	71	73	77		221	18,400
Rickie Fowler	71	72	78		221	18,400
John Rollins	73	71	77		221	18,400
Joost Luiten	68	72	82		222	17,900
Chris Stroud	76	67	79		222	17,900
Jeff Overton	70	72	83		225	17,600

HP Byron Nelson Championship

TPC Four Seasons Resort, Irving, Texas — May 15-18
Par 35-35–70; 7,166 yards — purse, $6,900,000

	SCORES				TOTAL	MONEY
Brendon Todd	68	64	68	66	266	$1,242,000
Mike Weir	68	66	67	67	268	745,200
Charles Howell	68	66	69	67	270	400,200
Marc Leishman	66	68	68	68	270	400,200
James Hahn	71	65	65	70	271	262,200
Boo Weekley	67	68	68	68	271	262,200
Graham DeLaet	68	66	68	70	272	207,862.50
Dustin Johnson	69	69	68	66	272	207,862.50
Matt Kuchar	69	67	68	68	272	207,862.50
Gary Woodland	68	67	66	71	272	207,862.50
Charlie Beljan	72	65	70	67	274	146,280
Louis Oosthuizen	68	68	64	74	274	146,280
Charl Schwartzel	73	67	67	67	274	146,280
John Senden	70	70	68	66	274	146,280
Shawn Stefani	74	66	67	67	274	146,280
Paul Casey	71	63	73	68	275	100,050
Morgan Hoffmann	68	66	68	73	275	100,050
John Huh	67	71	66	71	275	100,050
Billy Hurley	70	69	68	68	275	100,050
Kevin Kisner	69	70	70	66	275	100,050
Tyrone van Aswegen	67	68	72	68	275	100,050
Greg Chalmers	71	67	65	73	276	64,055
Padraig Harrington	68	68	66	74	276	64,055
Tim Herron	68	66	74	68	276	64,055
Ryan Palmer	67	68	71	70	276	64,055
Andres Romero	71	66	69	70	276	64,055
Tim Wilkinson	66	71	71	68	276	64,055
*Scottie Scheffler	71	68	69	68	276	

	SCORES				TOTAL	MONEY
Brendon de Jonge	73	68	67	69	277	43,944.38
Brice Garnett	69	70	68	70	277	43,944.38
Brian Harman	72	69	71	65	277	43,944.38
Charlie Wi	73	67	66	71	277	43,944.38
Aaron Baddeley	68	70	67	72	277	43,944.37
Keegan Bradley	70	68	68	71	277	43,944.37
Robert Garrigus	74	64	68	71	277	43,944.37
Martin Kaymer	67	67	71	72	277	43,944.37
Robert Allenby	72	69	70	67	278	30,403.13
Ben Crane	68	70	73	67	278	30,403.13
Peter Hanson	65	73	69	71	278	30,403.13
Jordan Spieth	70	67	73	68	278	30,403.13
Scott Gardiner	70	69	67	72	278	30,403.12
Retief Goosen	70	65	71	72	278	30,403.12
Vijay Singh	69	68	68	73	278	30,403.12
Jimmy Walker	71	68	68	71	278	30,403.12
Carl Pettersson	69	71	67	72	279	22,770
Michael Putnam	70	70	71	68	279	22,770
Rory Sabbatini	70	68	71	70	279	22,770
Kris Blanks	70	69	70	71	280	17,326.67
Chad Campbell	69	72	70	69	280	17,326.67
Jason Dufner	70	70	69	71	280	17,326.67
Bryce Molder	71	70	71	68	280	17,326.67
Sean O'Hair	69	72	71	68	280	17,326.67
David Toms	71	68	72	69	280	17,326.67
Jason Allred	68	70	70	72	280	17,326.66
Ricky Barnes	72	68	68	72	280	17,326.66
Lee Williams	67	71	68	74	280	17,326.66
Ken Duke	70	69	72	70	281	15,663
Brian Gay	71	67	72	71	281	15,663
Angel Cabrera	73	67	68	74	282	15,180
Brian Davis	70	71	70	71	282	15,180
Martin Flores	70	71	69	72	282	15,180
Brad Fritsch	72	69	71	70	282	15,180
J.J. Henry	70	71	68	73	282	15,180
James Driscoll	70	71	66	76	283	14,559
Jamie Lovemark	73	67	71	72	283	14,559
Rod Pampling	68	72	71	72	283	14,559
Chris Thompson	69	69	72	73	283	14,559
Jim Renner	69	71	71	73	284	14,145
Josh Teater	71	69	68	76	284	14,145
Luke Guthrie	69	72	71	73	285	13,938
Patrick Cantlay	70	69	71	76	286	13,731
Alex Prugh	67	71	72	76	286	13,731
Jim Herman	70	68	74	76	288	13,524
Steve Marino	70	69	71	79	289	13,386
Daniel Chopra	70	68	75		213	13,110
Kevin Foley	70	71	72		213	13,110
Ryo Ishikawa	73	68	72		213	13,110
Alex Cejka	67	70	77		214	12,696
Jhonattan Vegas	70	71	73		214	12,696
Will Wilcox	72	68	74		214	12,696
Mark Anderson	73	68	74		215	12,282
Eric Axley	68	73	74		215	12,282
Johnson Wagner	73	68	74		215	12,282
Kyle Stanley	74	66	76		216	12,006

Crowne Plaza Invitational

Colonial Country Club, Fort Worth, Texas — May 22-25
Par 35-35–70; 7,204 yards — purse, $6,400,000

	SCORES				TOTAL	MONEY
Adam Scott	71	68	66	66	271	$1,152,000
Jason Dufner	67	69	69	66	271	691,200
(Scott defeated Dufner on third playoff hole.)						
Freddie Jacobson	67	71	67	67	272	371,200
Nicholas Thompson	69	68	69	66	272	371,200
David Lingmerth	72	69	66	66	273	216,960
Ryan Palmer	69	69	68	67	273	216,960
John Senden	71	68	66	68	273	216,960
Brendon Todd	69	69	67	68	273	216,960
David Toms	72	66	65	70	273	216,960
Kevin Chappell	68	73	63	70	274	153,600
Hideki Matsuyama	69	70	64	71	274	153,600
Michael Thompson	73	66	69	66	274	153,600
Jimmy Walker	67	68	69	70	274	153,600
Brian Davis	68	67	70	70	275	102,400
Graham DeLaet	69	70	68	68	275	102,400
Dustin Johnson	65	70	74	66	275	102,400
Chris Kirk	73	64	67	71	275	102,400
Jordan Spieth	67	69	70	69	275	102,400
Chris Stroud	70	64	69	72	275	102,400
Bo Van Pelt	67	68	70	70	275	102,400
Bud Cauley	70	69	69	68	276	58,453.34
David Hearn	67	69	74	66	276	58,453.34
George McNeill	68	72	68	68	276	58,453.34
Tim Clark	67	68	69	72	276	58,453.33
Bill Haas	70	68	69	69	276	58,453.33
Russell Knox	71	70	66	69	276	58,453.33
Marc Leishman	69	68	67	72	276	58,453.33
Ben Martin	70	68	69	69	276	58,453.33
William McGirt	72	67	67	70	276	58,453.33
Chad Campbell	69	66	68	74	277	37,200
Brendon de Jonge	70	68	70	69	277	37,200
Harris English	66	70	73	68	277	37,200
Brice Garnett	67	66	74	70	277	37,200
Brian Harman	69	67	68	73	277	37,200
Billy Hurley	71	67	70	69	277	37,200
Martin Laird	70	69	69	69	277	37,200
Heath Slocum	69	69	69	70	277	37,200
Robert Allenby	68	70	68	72	278	26,240
Jerry Kelly	70	71	69	68	278	26,240
Danny Lee	71	69	68	70	278	26,240
Louis Oosthuizen	72	68	67	71	278	26,240
Michael Putnam	70	71	68	69	278	26,240
Robert Streb	66	68	74	70	278	26,240
Josh Teater	68	71	70	69	278	26,240
Trevor Immelman	69	71	68	71	279	18,304
Matt Jones	70	67	73	69	279	18,304
Andrew Loupe	75	65	68	71	279	18,304
Bryce Molder	70	70	67	72	279	18,304
Jeff Overton	70	71	70	68	279	18,304
Brandt Snedeker	70	66	73	70	279	18,304
Jim Furyk	69	69	71	71	280	15,061.34
Daniel Summerhays	69	71	73	67	280	15,061.34
Aaron Baddeley	68	67	71	74	280	15,061.33
Ken Duke	67	72	69	72	280	15,061.33
Charley Hoffman	70	68	69	73	280	15,061.33
Tim Wilkinson	66	71	69	74	280	15,061.33

	SCORES				TOTAL	MONEY
Brian Gay	71	69	72	69	281	14,336
J.J. Henry	70	70	68	73	281	14,336
Justin Leonard	69	72	70	70	281	14,336
Ricky Barnes	68	71	73	70	282	13,952
Steve Flesch	71	70	69	72	282	13,952
Hunter Mahan	66	71	70	75	282	13,952
Jeff Curl	71	69	71	72	283	13,440
Tim Herron	72	69	71	71	283	13,440
Sean O'Hair	69	69	70	75	283	13,440
John Rollins	69	72	69	73	283	13,440
Cameron Tringale	70	70	67	76	283	13,440
Scott Langley	71	70	74	69	284	12,992
Kyle Stanley	73	68	73	70	284	12,992
Jonathan Byrd	70	70	73	72	285	12,672
Davis Love	72	69	74	70	285	12,672
Vijay Singh	68	73	69	75	285	12,672
Zach Johnson	70	71	69	76	286	12,416
Briny Baird	71	70	72	74	287	12,288
Boo Weekley	71	69	74	74	288	12,160

Memorial Tournament

Muirfield Village Golf Club, Dublin, Ohio — May 29-June 1
Par 36-36–72; 7,392 yards — purse, $6,200,000

	SCORES				TOTAL	MONEY
Hideki Matsuyama	70	67	69	69	275	$1,116,000
Kevin Na	72	69	70	64	275	669,600
(Matsuyama defeated Na on first playoff hole.)						
Bubba Watson	66	69	69	72	276	421,600
Chris Kirk	66	70	74	68	278	272,800
Adam Scott	69	70	68	71	278	272,800
Ben Curtis	69	71	69	70	279	215,450
Steve Stricker	71	70	70	68	279	215,450
Luke Guthrie	75	69	66	70	280	167,400
Bill Haas	73	67	72	68	280	167,400
Thorbjorn Olesen	71	67	74	68	280	167,400
Charl Schwartzel	72	69	67	72	280	167,400
Brendon Todd	71	68	69	72	280	167,400
Scott Brown	70	69	71	71	281	124,000
Paul Casey	66	66	76	73	281	124,000
Jason Allred	74	68	74	66	282	102,300
Billy Horschel	71	69	68	74	282	102,300
Matt Kuchar	74	69	69	70	282	102,300
Rory McIlroy	63	78	69	72	282	102,300
Jason Dufner	71	69	71	72	283	65,237.78
Ernie Els	70	72	69	72	283	65,237.78
Martin Flores	69	68	75	71	283	65,237.78
Jim Furyk	73	68	72	70	283	65,237.78
Charley Hoffman	69	72	73	69	283	65,237.78
Ryan Moore	68	70	72	73	283	65,237.78
Bo Van Pelt	72	72	66	73	283	65,237.78
Jordan Spieth	69	72	67	75	283	65,237.77
Andrew Svoboda	72	69	68	74	283	65,237.77
K.J. Choi	73	71	72	68	284	38,646.67
Brendon de Jonge	73	69	69	73	284	38,646.67
Robert Garrigus	72	70	70	72	284	38,646.67
David Hearn	71	73	69	71	284	38,646.67
Hunter Mahan	68	70	73	73	284	38,646.67
Daniel Summerhays	74	70	68	72	284	38,646.67

	SCORES				TOTAL	MONEY
Scott Langley	72	66	67	79	284	38,646.66
Kevin Stadler	72	71	68	73	284	38,646.66
Robert Streb	72	67	69	76	284	38,646.66
Aaron Baddeley	69	74	70	72	285	25,420
Keegan Bradley	67	75	70	73	285	25,420
Jason Day	72	69	70	74	285	25,420
Billy Hurley	73	70	74	68	285	25,420
Marc Leishman	71	68	73	73	285	25,420
Justin Thomas	73	68	72	72	285	25,420
Michael Thompson	67	76	72	70	285	25,420
Cameron Tringale	73	70	70	72	285	25,420
Camilo Villegas	71	68	72	74	285	25,420
Dustin Johnson	73	68	72	73	286	18,062.67
Kevin Kisner	69	72	76	69	286	18,062.67
Justin Hicks	73	67	71	75	286	18,062.66
Stewart Cink	71	73	72	71	287	15,148.67
Luke Donald	71	69	73	74	287	15,148.67
David Lingmerth	72	72	70	73	287	15,148.67
Phil Mickelson	72	70	72	73	287	15,148.67
Freddie Jacobson	71	71	71	74	287	15,148.66
Ben Martin	72	72	65	78	287	15,148.66
Michael Putnam	71	73	73	71	288	14,198
Nick Watney	69	71	74	74	288	14,198
Charles Howell	69	75	71	74	289	13,764
Ryo Ishikawa	72	71	71	75	289	13,764
Richard Lee	76	68	76	69	289	13,764
Justin Leonard	68	75	68	78	289	13,764
Gary Woodland	71	68	75	75	289	13,764
Kiradech Aphibarnrat	73	71	70	76	290	13,268
John Huh	73	70	75	72	290	13,268
Carl Pettersson	72	72	73	73	290	13,268
Hyung-Sung Kim	70	72	76	73	291	12,834
Carlos Ortiz	75	68	76	72	291	12,834
Scott Stallings	72	71	77	71	291	12,834
Josh Teater	71	72	76	72	291	12,834
Lucas Glover	70	73	76	73	292	12,400
Pat Perez	71	70	77	74	292	12,400
Chris Stroud	74	68	74	76	292	12,400
Greg Chalmers	71	72	75	75	293	12,090
Mark Wilson	69	74	74	76	293	12,090
Kyle Stanley	74	68	80	76	298	11,904
Gonzalo Fernandez-Castano	73	70	79	77	299	11,718
J.B. Holmes	67	75	81	76	299	11,718

FedEx St. Jude Classic

TPC Southwind, Memphis, Tennessee — June 5-8
Par 35-35–70; 7,239 yards — purse, $5,800,000

	SCORES				TOTAL	MONEY
Ben Crane	63	65	69	73	270	$1,044,000
Troy Merritt	67	66	67	71	271	626,400
Matt Every	69	68	65	70	272	301,600
Carl Pettersson	67	67	69	69	272	301,600
Webb Simpson	71	66	69	66	272	301,600
James Hahn	69	70	67	67	273	181,540
Brian Harman	69	65	67	72	273	181,540
Billy Horschel	67	68	68	70	273	181,540
Ian Poulter	69	68	72	64	273	181,540
Andrew Svoboda	69	66	68	70	273	181,540

	SCORES				TOTAL	MONEY
Phil Mickelson	67	68	67	72	274	139,200
Camilo Villegas	68	64	71	71	274	139,200
Rickie Fowler	70	68	68	69	275	102,466.67
Chesson Hadley	67	69	72	67	275	102,466.67
J.J. Henry	66	70	71	68	275	102,466.67
Ben Martin	69	67	74	65	275	102,466.67
Austin Cook	67	73	65	70	275	102,466.66
Ted Potter, Jr.	68	67	70	70	275	102,466.66
Tim Clark	68	69	67	72	276	70,296
Brooks Koepka	67	70	72	67	276	70,296
Peter Malnati	65	68	70	73	276	70,296
John Peterson	69	68	73	66	276	70,296
Will Wilcox	70	67	68	71	276	70,296
Jason Bohn	67	68	70	72	277	49,445
Paul Casey	70	67	70	70	277	49,445
Dustin Johnson	68	67	75	67	277	49,445
Graeme McDowell	69	68	70	70	277	49,445
Charles Howell	71	68	71	68	278	40,310
Steve Marino	69	70	68	71	278	40,310
George McNeill	69	69	73	67	278	40,310
Charlie Wi	68	71	69	70	278	40,310
Ben Curtis	70	69	71	69	279	28,841.82
Tommy Gainey	69	68	70	72	279	28,841.82
Danny Lee	72	67	67	73	279	28,841.82
William McGirt	73	66	74	66	279	28,841.82
Ryan Palmer	67	72	72	68	279	28,841.82
Heath Slocum	69	70	70	70	279	28,841.82
Cameron Tringale	68	70	70	71	279	28,841.82
Jhonattan Vegas	69	70	70	70	279	28,841.82
Tim Wilkinson	68	68	70	73	279	28,841.82
Retief Goosen	66	66	75	72	279	28,841.81
Scott Stallings	68	72	68	71	279	28,841.81
Luke Guthrie	67	72	70	71	280	20,300
Davis Love	65	70	71	74	280	20,300
Sean O'Hair	69	70	70	71	280	20,300
Chad Campbell	70	68	71	72	281	16,443
Gonzalo Fernandez-Castano	67	70	71	73	281	16,443
Robert Streb	70	70	72	69	281	16,443
Boo Weekley	69	70	70	72	281	16,443
Ryuji Imada	71	69	71	71	282	14,268
Kevin Kisner	65	72	70	75	282	14,268
John Rollins	70	69	69	74	282	14,268
Zach Johnson	64	74	74	71	283	13,240.58
Benjamin Alvarado	68	72	70	73	283	13,240.57
Stuart Appleby	65	74	72	72	283	13,240.57
Woody Austin	68	71	72	72	283	13,240.57
Miguel Angel Carballo	68	70	74	71	283	13,240.57
Stewart Cink	70	66	75	72	283	13,240.57
Jeff Overton	68	71	72	72	283	13,240.57
Freddie Jacobson	67	71	73	73	284	12,644
Martin Laird	70	67	76	71	284	12,644
Greg Owen	70	70	70	74	284	12,644
John Merrick	70	68	77	70	285	12,354
Shawn Stefani	70	67	74	74	285	12,354
Martin Flores	70	70	75	71	286	12,064
Padraig Harrington	68	67	79	72	286	12,064
Jerry Kelly	71	67	73	75	286	12,064
Josh Teater	72	67	75	73	287	11,832
Justin Leonard	68	71	74	75	288	11,658
David Lingmerth	77	63	71	77	288	11,658
John Daly	72	67	76	76	291	11,484

U.S. Open Championship

Pinehurst No. 2, Village of Pinehurst, North Carolina — June 12-15
Par 35-35–70; 7,562 yards — purse, $9,000,000

	SCORES				TOTAL	MONEY
Martin Kaymer	65	65	72	69	271	$1,620,000
Erik Compton	72	68	67	72	279	789,330
Rickie Fowler	70	70	67	72	279	789,330
Keegan Bradley	69	69	76	67	281	326,310
Jason Day	73	68	72	68	281	326,310
Brooks Koepka	70	68	72	71	281	326,310
Dustin Johnson	69	69	70	73	281	326,310
Henrik Stenson	69	69	70	73	281	326,310
Adam Scott	73	67	73	69	282	211,715
Jimmy Walker	70	72	71	69	282	211,715
Brandt Snedeker	69	68	72	73	282	211,715
Jim Furyk	73	70	73	67	283	156,679
Marcel Siem	70	71	72	70	283	156,679
Justin Rose	72	69	70	72	283	156,679
Kevin Na	68	69	73	73	283	156,679
Matt Kuchar	69	70	71	73	283	156,679
Brendon Todd	69	67	79	69	284	118,234
Ian Poulter	70	70	74	70	284	118,234
J.B. Holmes	70	71	72	71	284	118,234
Jordan Spieth	69	70	72	73	284	118,234
Cody Gribble	72	72	72	69	285	98,598
Steve Stricker	70	71	73	71	285	98,598
Billy Horschel	75	68	73	70	286	79,968
Aaron Baddeley	70	71	73	72	286	79,968
Shiv Kapur	73	70	71	72	286	79,968
Rory McIlroy	71	68	74	73	286	79,968
Francesco Molinari	69	71	72	74	286	79,968
Daniel Berger	72	71	78	66	287	59,588
Graeme McDowell	68	74	75	70	287	59,588
Kenny Perry	74	69	74	70	287	59,588
Phil Mickelson	70	73	72	72	287	59,588
Victor Dubuisson	70	72	70	75	287	59,588
Brendon de Jonge	68	70	73	76	287	59,588
Chris Kirk	71	68	72	76	287	59,588
Patrick Reed	71	72	73	72	288	46,803
Ernie Els	74	70	72	72	288	46,803
Sergio Garcia	73	71	72	72	288	46,803
Bill Haas	72	72	71	73	288	46,803
Hideki Matsuyama	69	71	74	74	288	46,803
Louis Oosthuizen	71	73	78	67	289	37,754
Zac Blair	71	74	73	71	289	37,754
Zach Johnson	71	74	72	72	289	37,754
Lucas Bjerregaard	70	72	72	75	289	37,754
Garth Mulroy	71	72	70	76	289	37,754
Danny Willett	70	71	78	71	290	30,828
Webb Simpson	71	72	73	74	290	30,828
Retief Goosen	73	71	71	75	290	30,828
*Matthew Fitzpatrick	71	73	78	69	291	
Billy Hurley	71	74	75	71	291	26,504
Harris English	69	75	75	72	291	26,504
Ryan Moore	76	68	71	76	291	26,504
Seung-Yul Noh	70	72	76	74	292	24,514
Gary Woodland	72	71	75	74	292	24,514
Scott Langley	72	71	75	75	293	23,535
Stewart Cink	72	72	74	75	293	23,535
Fran Quinn	68	74	79	73	294	22,649
Paul Casey	70	75	74	75	294	22,649

	SCORES				TOTAL	MONEY
Nicholas Lindheim	72	73	72	77	294	22,649
Justin Leonard	75	70	75	75	295	22,090
Russell Henley	70	74	82	71	297	21,564
Kevin Tway	72	72	81	72	297	21,564
Alex Cejka	73	71	77	76	297	21,564
Kevin Stadler	77	68	78	75	298	20,775
Clayton Rask	73	71	77	77	298	20,775
Bo Van Pelt	72	72	75	79	298	20,775
Boo Weekley	71	73	80	75	299	20,249
Toru Taniguchi	72	73	88	76	309	19,980

Out of Final 36 Holes

Hunter Mahan	74	72	146
*Cory Whitsett	77	69	146
Rod Pampling	73	73	146
*Hunter Stewart	75	71	146
Jason Dufner	72	74	146
Matt Dobyns	74	72	146
Luke Donald	77	69	146
Matt Jones	74	72	146
Casey Wittenberg	74	72	146
Joost Luiten	70	76	146
Kyoung-Hoon Lee	74	72	146
Shane Lowry	73	73	146
*Brian Campbell	76	70	146
Mark Wilson	70	76	146
Bubba Watson	76	70	146
Angel Cabrera	74	72	146
Hudson Swafford	76	70	146
Andres Echavarria	74	72	146
Thongchai Jaidee	73	73	146
Charl Schwartzel	70	76	146
Miguel Angel Jimenez	72	74	146
David Toms	73	74	147
Nicolas Colsaerts	72	75	147
Luke Guthrie	73	74	147
Stephen Gallacher	73	74	147
Andrea Pavan	75	72	147
Darren Clarke	75	72	147
Jim Renner	74	73	147
Ken Duke	75	72	147
Ryan Blaum	73	74	147
Chris Doak	74	73	147
Geoff Ogilvy	73	74	147
John Senden	71	76	147
Brian Stuard	75	73	148
Lucas Glover	79	69	148
Wen-Chong Liang	74	74	148
Chad Collins	74	74	148
Lee Westwood	75	73	148
David Gossett	76	72	148
Nick Watney	76	72	148
Roberto Castro	74	74	148
Ryan Palmer	74	74	148
Justin Thomas	75	73	148
*Cameron Wilson	78	70	148
Sam Love	76	72	148
Matt Every	76	72	148
Joe Ogilvie	73	76	149
Henrik Norlander	70	79	149
Pablo Larrazabal	71	78	149
Smylie Kaufman	73	76	149
Oliver Fisher	74	75	149
Craig Barlow	74	75	149
Tom Lewis	79	70	149
Anthony Broussard	78	72	150
*Maverick McNealy	74	76	150
Maximilian Kieffer	76	74	150
Kevin Sutherland	75	75	150
Bernd Wiesberger	72	78	150
Graham DeLaet	75	75	150
Niclas Fasth	76	74	150
Hyung-Sung Kim	73	77	150
D.A. Points	77	74	151
Graeme Storm	72	79	151
Y.E. Yang	75	76	151
Brady Watt	77	74	151
Jamie Donaldson	70	81	151
David Oh	75	76	151
Brett Stegmaier	77	74	151
Rob Oppenheim	75	77	152
Steven Alker	76	76	152
Simon Griffiths	72	80	152
Robert Allenby	79	73	152
Gonzalo Fdez-Castano	76	76	152
Kevin Kisner	75	77	152
Aron Price	78	74	152
Kevin Streelman	75	77	152
*Robby Shelton	78	75	153
Nick Mason	78	75	153
Jeff Maggert	73	80	153
Jonas Blixt	77	76	153
Chris Thompson	80	74	154
*Oliver Goss	71	83	154
Donald Constable	82	73	155
*Brandon McIver	82	73	155
Bobby Gates	79	76	155
*Will Grimmer	77	80	157
*Andrew Dorn	79	80	159
Azuma Yano	77	83	160
Kiyoshi Miyazato	81	81	162

(Professionals who did not complete 72 holes received $4,000.)

Travelers Championship

TPC River Highlands, Cromwell, Connecticut — June 19-22
Par 35-35–70; 6,841 yards — purse, $6,200,000

	SCORES				TOTAL	MONEY
Kevin Streelman	69	68	64	64	265	$1,116,000
K.J. Choi	65	65	69	67	266	545,600
Sergio Garcia	65	69	65	67	266	545,600
Aaron Baddeley	67	66	65	69	267	297,600
Ryan Moore	63	68	66	71	268	235,600
Brendan Steele	62	69	71	66	268	235,600
Chad Campbell	64	70	67	68	269	186,775
Harris English	66	64	72	67	269	186,775
Jeff Maggert	64	70	68	67	269	186,775
Carl Pettersson	68	67	66	68	269	186,775
Angel Cabrera	68	70	65	67	270	123,114.29
Bud Cauley	63	70	68	69	270	123,114.29
Marc Leishman	70	68	65	67	270	123,114.29
Brandt Snedeker	65	69	72	64	270	123,114.29
Scott Langley	64	65	70	71	270	123,114.28
Michael Putnam	67	63	69	71	270	123,114.28
Nick Watney	70	66	65	69	270	123,114.28
Stuart Appleby	69	70	68	64	271	78,120
Miguel Ángel Carballo	68	68	72	63	271	78,120
Jason Day	70	69	67	65	271	78,120
Tommy Gainey	70	66	67	68	271	78,120
Chris Stroud	67	67	68	69	271	78,120
Tim Wilkinson	66	68	67	70	271	78,120
Sang-Moon Bae	67	68	67	70	272	57,040
Hudson Swafford	66	71	66	69	272	57,040
Gonzalo Fernandez-Castano	68	68	71	66	273	45,880
Charley Hoffman	67	68	71	67	273	45,880
John Merrick	67	72	67	67	273	45,880
Kevin Tway	71	65	69	68	273	45,880
Tyrone van Aswegen	68	70	67	68	273	45,880
Joe Durant	64	72	71	67	274	32,296.37
Freddie Jacobson	69	69	69	67	274	32,296.37
Jerry Kelly	70	66	71	67	274	32,296.37
Vijay Singh	68	68	70	68	274	32,296.37
Keegan Bradley	66	69	71	68	274	32,296.36
Dustin Johnson	66	66	71	71	274	32,296.36
Matt Kuchar	66	67	72	69	274	32,296.36
Jamie Lovemark	68	63	70	73	274	32,296.36
William McGirt	71	67	66	70	274	32,296.36
Jhonattan Vegas	69	70	65	70	274	32,296.36
Bubba Watson	67	72	67	68	274	32,296.36
Eric Axley	64	67	71	73	275	22,320
Brian Davis	69	70	68	68	275	22,320
Brendon de Jonge	70	66	71	68	275	22,320
Brian Harman	68	67	69	71	275	22,320
Ricky Barnes	73	65	68	70	276	17,186.40
Ken Duke	65	72	71	68	276	17,186.40
Matt Jones	69	69	67	71	276	17,186.40
Patrick Rodgers	66	69	71	70	276	17,186.40
Heath Slocum	66	69	70	71	276	17,186.40
Graham DeLaet	70	68	71	68	277	14,590.67
Retief Goosen	68	69	71	69	277	14,590.67
Brooks Koepka	65	72	71	69	277	14,590.67
Greg Owen	72	65	71	69	277	14,590.67
Jonathan Byrd	70	68	69	70	277	14,590.66
Steve Marino	66	72	70	69	277	14,590.66
John Daly	70	68	70	70	278	13,826

	SCORES				TOTAL	MONEY
Justin Hicks	66	71	69	72	278	13,826
Billy Hurley	71	66	70	71	278	13,826
Johnson Wagner	68	66	74	70	278	13,826
Tim Herron	68	71	69	71	279	13,206
Russell Knox	66	72	70	71	279	13,206
Doug LaBelle	65	71	72	71	279	13,206
Seung-Yul Noh	68	69	72	70	279	13,206
Wes Roach	68	70	71	70	279	13,206
Vaughn Taylor	67	71	71	70	279	13,206
Morgan Hoffmann	68	70	69	73	280	12,586
Troy Merritt	71	66	72	71	280	12,586
Bo Van Pelt	69	68	73	70	280	12,586
Camilo Villegas	71	66	74	69	280	12,586
Brian Gay	70	66	72	73	281	12,214
Andrew Svoboda	67	71	77	66	281	12,214
Kevin Stadler	72	67	72	72	283	12,028
Ben Crane	69	68	68	79	284	11,904
Brice Garnett	67	68	72	78	285	11,718
Billy Mayfair	67	71	71	76	285	11,718
James Hahn	69	70	76	73	288	11,532

Quicken Loans National

Congressional Country Club, Bethesda, Maryland — June 26-29
Par 36-35–71; 7,569 yards — purse, $6,500,000

	SCORES				TOTAL	MONEY
Justin Rose	74	65	71	70	280	$1,170,000
Shawn Stefani	74	68	68	70	280	702,000
(Rose defeated Stefani on first playoff hole.)						
Charley Hoffman	72	72	68	69	281	377,000
Ben Martin	72	68	70	71	281	377,000
Andres Romero	70	72	72	68	282	237,250
Brendan Steele	74	66	71	71	282	237,250
Brendon Todd	72	70	69	71	282	237,250
Brendon de Jonge	71	68	71	73	283	188,500
Billy Hurley	69	73	70	71	283	188,500
Marc Leishman	70	66	73	74	283	188,500
Ricky Barnes	67	69	75	73	284	125,125
Robert Garrigus	73	70	70	71	284	125,125
Billy Horschel	70	68	74	72	284	125,125
Freddie Jacobson	67	71	71	75	284	125,125
Richard Lee	74	68	68	74	284	125,125
Patrick Reed	68	68	71	77	284	125,125
Jordan Spieth	74	70	69	71	284	125,125
Hudson Swafford	69	68	73	74	284	125,125
Stewart Cink	74	69	71	71	285	87,750
John Huh	72	72	70	71	285	87,750
Steven Bowditch	73	71	70	72	286	72,800
Brandt Snedeker	70	70	75	71	286	72,800
Tyrone van Aswegen	68	74	73	71	286	72,800
Angel Cabrera	71	74	69	73	287	52,650
Russell Knox	73	67	78	69	287	52,650
Hunter Mahan	71	73	69	74	287	52,650
Michael Putnam	69	72	72	74	287	52,650
Brady Watt	71	71	71	74	287	52,650
Tim Wilkinson	70	71	72	74	287	52,650
Roberto Castro	71	72	75	70	288	36,977.78
Greg Chalmers	66	78	72	72	288	36,977.78
George McNeill	69	69	77	73	288	36,977.78

	SCORES				TOTAL	MONEY
Webb Simpson	72	73	71	72	288	36,977.78
Daniel Summerhays	70	72	71	75	288	36,977.78
Cameron Tringale	70	71	73	74	288	36,977.78
Nick Watney	69	75	69	75	288	36,977.78
Bill Haas	68	72	71	77	288	36,977.77
Seung-Yul Noh	73	70	66	79	288	36,977.77
Brian Davis	72	73	71	73	289	25,350
Matt Every	71	69	72	77	289	25,350
Retief Goosen	69	71	76	73	289	25,350
J.J. Henry	74	69	74	72	289	25,350
Andrew Loupe	74	70	69	76	289	25,350
Davis Love	72	70	74	73	289	25,350
John Rollins	72	72	71	74	289	25,350
Stuart Appleby	70	67	76	77	290	16,900
Erik Compton	68	73	75	74	290	16,900
Ben Curtis	75	69	71	75	290	16,900
Peter Hanson	72	68	75	75	290	16,900
Charles Howell	71	73	72	74	290	16,900
Trevor Immelman	74	71	71	74	290	16,900
John Merrick	74	71	73	72	290	16,900
Andrew Svoboda	71	72	76	71	290	16,900
Gary Woodland	72	71	69	78	290	16,900
Kevin Chappell	71	72	76	72	291	14,430
Oliver Goss	70	66	76	79	291	14,430
J.B. Holmes	72	72	70	77	291	14,430
Sean O'Hair	73	71	74	73	291	14,430
Geoff Ogilvy	70	72	72	77	291	14,430
Ryan Palmer	73	71	70	77	291	14,430
Carl Pettersson	72	69	76	74	291	14,430
Patrick Rodgers	73	69	73	76	291	14,430
Heath Slocum	72	72	72	75	291	14,430
Jason Bohn	71	71	78	72	292	13,520
K.J. Choi	69	72	75	76	292	13,520
D.H. Lee	73	71	75	73	292	13,520
Spencer Levin	69	74	73	76	292	13,520
Bo Van Pelt	71	71	78	72	292	13,520
James Driscoll	71	74	74	74	293	13,065
Kevin Kisner	75	68	78	72	293	13,065
Scott Brown	72	72	74	76	294	12,740
Morgan Hoffmann	70	68	78	78	294	12,740
Scott Stallings	75	70	68	81	294	12,740
Robert Streb	74	71	75	77	297	12,480
Rory Sabbatini	71	74	77	78	300	12,350

Greenbrier Classic

The Old White TPC, White Sulphur Springs, West Virginia — July 3-6
Par 34-36–70; 7,287 yards — purse, $6,500,000

	SCORES				TOTAL	MONEY
Angel Cabrera	68	68	64	64	264	$1,170,000
George McNeill	70	67	68	61	266	702,000
Webb Simpson	71	69	67	63	270	442,000
Keegan Bradley	67	69	69	66	271	227,035.72
Bud Cauley	69	68	70	64	271	227,035.72
Brendon Todd	71	67	67	66	271	227,035.72
Billy Hurley	68	63	67	73	271	227,035.71
Chris Stroud	66	66	70	69	271	227,035.71
Cameron Tringale	72	66	64	69	271	227,035.71
Will Wilcox	68	69	65	69	271	227,035.71

	SCORES				TOTAL	MONEY
Charlie Beljan	67	69	71	65	272	137,800
Jason Bohn	65	72	68	67	272	137,800
Joe Durant	65	71	66	70	272	137,800
Steve Marino	69	70	66	67	272	137,800
Michael Thompson	66	72	64	70	272	137,800
Sang-Moon Bae	66	74	66	67	273	91,185.72
Danny Lee	65	71	71	66	273	91,185.72
Troy Merritt	66	72	68	67	273	91,185.72
Kevin Chappell	67	65	69	72	273	91,185.71
David Lingmerth	67	68	69	69	273	91,185.71
Jim Renner	65	70	68	70	273	91,185.71
Bubba Watson	68	67	69	69	273	91,185.71
Patrick Cantlay	69	68	69	68	274	62,400
Bill Haas	69	70	65	70	274	62,400
J.B. Holmes	68	68	69	69	274	62,400
Ted Potter, Jr.	70	70	68	67	275	44,236.12
Robert Allenby	67	70	68	70	275	44,236.11
Luke Guthrie	67	69	68	71	275	44,236.11
Scott Langley	68	71	67	69	275	44,236.11
Andrew Loupe	69	69	67	70	275	44,236.11
Patrick Reed	67	69	71	68	275	44,236.11
David Toms	69	69	68	69	275	44,236.11
Camilo Villegas	68	67	67	73	275	44,236.11
Johnson Wagner	68	68	71	68	275	44,236.11
Jonas Blixt	64	73	68	71	276	28,697.50
Brice Garnett	68	66	72	70	276	28,697.50
Davis Love	67	73	65	71	276	28,697.50
Carl Pettersson	71	68	70	67	276	28,697.50
Michael Putnam	67	72	67	70	276	28,697.50
Scott Stallings	70	69	70	67	276	28,697.50
Kyle Stanley	71	68	66	71	276	28,697.50
Shawn Stefani	73	67	67	69	276	28,697.50
Steve Stricker	66	68	68	74	276	28,697.50
Tom Watson	71	68	68	69	276	28,697.50
Chris Kirk	65	69	75	68	277	18,218.58
Richard Lee	71	68	67	71	277	18,218.57
Troy Matteson	72	61	71	73	277	18,218.57
Patrick Rodgers	65	75	68	69	277	18,218.57
Andres Romero	72	68	67	70	277	18,218.57
Heath Slocum	70	69	68	70	277	18,218.57
Josh Teater	69	69	70	69	277	18,218.57
Stephen Ames	69	68	71	70	278	15,158
Charles Howell	67	71	68	72	278	15,158
Justin Leonard	71	67	69	71	278	15,158
Kevin Na	66	70	71	71	278	15,158
Hudson Swafford	72	67	65	74	278	15,158
Jason Gore	70	70	69	70	279	14,300
J.J. Henry	70	70	69	70	279	14,300
Trevor Immelman	69	70	67	73	279	14,300
Bronson La'Cassie	70	66	70	73	279	14,300
Wes Roach	69	71	69	70	279	14,300
Tyrone van Aswegen	67	70	72	70	279	14,300
Tim Wilkinson	68	71	70	70	279	14,300
Brendon de Jonge	70	69	68	73	280	13,585
Gonzalo Fernandez-Castano	68	71	70	71	280	13,585
David Hearn	68	68	68	76	280	13,585
Andrew Svoboda	72	68	69	71	280	13,585
Matt Bettencourt	70	68	68	75	281	13,130
Chad Collins	66	73	70	72	281	13,130
Oliver Goss	70	68	68	75	281	13,130
Robert Streb	68	72	69	73	282	12,870
Gary Woodland	69	70	69	75	283	12,740
Roberto Castro	72	68	69	75	284	12,545

	SCORES				TOTAL	MONEY
Ken Duke	72	67	70	75	284	12,545
Woody Austin	68	72	70		210	12,155
Scott Brown	72	68	70		210	12,155
Martin Flores	70	70	70		210	12,155
Pat Perez	66	69	75		210	12,155
Steven Bowditch	68	70	73		211	11,700
John Daly	68	72	71		211	11,700
Jeff Maggert	69	70	72		211	11,700
Greg Chalmers	69	69	74		212	11,310
Derek Ernst	71	69	72		212	11,310
Scott Gardiner	70	67	75		212	11,310
Jamie Lovemark	68	72	73		213	11,050
D.A. Points	65	75	74		214	10,855
Mark Wilson	68	72	74		214	10,855
Brendan Steele	70	68	77		215	10,660
James Hahn	65	74	78		217	10,530

John Deere Classic

TPC Deere Run, Silvis, Illinois
Par 35-36–71; 7,268 yards

July 10-13
purse, $4,700,000

	SCORES				TOTAL	MONEY
Brian Harman	63	68	65	66	262	$846,000
Zach Johnson	63	67	69	64	263	507,600
Jhonattan Vegas	69	68	63	65	265	272,600
Jerry Kelly	66	68	65	66	265	272,600
Tim Clark	72	63	64	67	266	178,600
Scott Brown	67	70	61	68	266	178,600
Bo Van Pelt	67	69	67	65	268	141,588
Jordan Spieth	71	64	67	66	268	141,588
Johnson Wagner	66	65	69	68	268	141,588
Ryan Moore	66	67	67	68	268	141,588
Steven Bowditch	64	67	70	68	269	112,800
Steve Stricker	68	65	64	72	269	112,800
Kevin Na	68	66	71	65	270	80,571
Bryce Molder	73	65	67	65	270	80,571
Shawn Stefani	73	67	64	66	270	80,571
Chad Campbell	69	71	62	68	270	80,571
David Toms	65	70	67	68	270	80,571
Daniel Summerhays	69	68	65	68	270	80,571
Brad Fritsch	70	68	63	69	270	80,571
Kevin Kisner	68	72	68	64	272	56,713
Troy Merritt	68	70	66	68	272	56,713
D.H. Lee	72	66	66	68	272	56,713
John Rollins	72	68	66	67	273	43,240
Charlie Beljan	71	68	66	68	273	43,240
Charles Howell	66	68	67	72	273	43,240
William McGirt	64	66	69	74	273	43,240
Dicky Pride	70	70	66	68	274	30,628
Luke Guthrie	69	69	69	67	274	30,628
Justin Hicks	66	70	70	68	274	30,628
Glen Day	72	65	69	68	274	30,628
Steven Ihm	73	65	68	68	274	30,628
Tommy Gainey	70	68	67	69	274	30,628
Russell Henley	70	67	68	69	274	30,628
Will MacKenzie	73	65	67	69	274	30,628
Scott Langley	69	70	65	70	274	30,628
*Jordan Niebrugge	71	68	66	69	274	
Greg Chalmers	70	68	71	66	275	20,709

	SCORES				TOTAL	MONEY
Ben Crane	69	70	69	67	275	20,709
Robert Streb	65	69	72	69	275	20,709
Davis Love	69	70	67	69	275	20,709
Nicholas Thompson	67	71	68	69	275	20,709
Alex Prugh	68	68	69	70	275	20,709
Rory Sabbatini	63	70	71	71	275	20,709
Brian Davis	72	68	64	71	275	20,709
David Hearn	71	69	69	67	276	13,872
John Senden	68	69	71	68	276	13,872
Brice Garnett	68	71	68	69	276	13,872
Andres Romero	71	68	68	69	276	13,872
Trevor Immelman	66	71	70	69	276	13,872
Camilo Villegas	70	67	69	70	276	13,872
Brendon de Jonge	65	75	65	71	276	13,872
Richard Lee	70	70	69	68	277	10,998
Stewart Cink	69	66	74	68	277	10,998
Jonathan Byrd	74	66	68	69	277	10,998
Heath Slocum	69	70	68	70	277	10,998
Kevin Chappell	68	69	70	70	277	10,998
Kevin Tway	65	69	72	71	277	10,998
Bud Cauley	67	67	69	74	277	10,998
Chris Stroud	69	71	70	68	278	10,387
Retief Goosen	71	69	69	69	278	10,387
Todd Hamilton	64	69	73	72	278	10,387
Wes Roach	67	69	70	72	278	10,387
Bobby Wyatt	69	71	71	68	279	9,964
Kyle Stanley	71	67	72	69	279	9,964
Mark Wilson	71	69	69	70	279	9,964
Derek Ernst	69	71	68	71	279	9,964
J.J. Henry	68	67	72	72	279	9,964
Ricky Barnes	68	70	72	70	280	9,635
Sean O'Hair	67	70	69	74	280	9,635
Chad Collins	69	71	70	71	281	9,447
Paul Goydos	69	71	66	75	281	9,447
Edward Loar	70	68	72	72	282	9,259
Marc Turnesa	69	71	66	76	282	9,259
Harris English	67	73	74	69	283	9,071
Jamie Lovemark	69	71	71	72	283	9,071
Cameron Beckman	69	69	74	74	286	8,883
John Merrick	71	69	71	75	286	8,883

The Open Championship

See European Tours chapter.

RBC Canadian Open

Glen Montreal Golf Club, Blue Course,
Ile Bizard, Quebec, Canada
Par 35-35–70; 7,153 yards

July 24-27
purse, $5,700,000

	SCORES				TOTAL	MONEY
Tim Clark	67	67	64	65	263	$1,026,000
Jim Furyk	67	63	65	69	264	615,600
Justin Hicks	66	67	70	64	267	387,600
Gonzalo Fernandez-Castano	67	67	69	66	269	235,600
Matt Kuchar	69	65	70	65	269	235,600
Michael Putnam	64	70	69	66	269	235,600
Graham DeLaet	69	63	70	68	270	183,825

	SCORES				TOTAL	MONEY
Dicky Pride	66	71	70	63	270	183,825
Brad Fritsch	72	68	67	64	271	153,900
Kevin Kisner	70	69	68	64	271	153,900
Graeme McDowell	68	65	70	68	271	153,900
Ben Curtis	67	70	70	65	272	101,887.50
Joe Durant	69	66	67	70	272	101,887.50
Ernie Els	70	67	69	66	272	101,887.50
Retief Goosen	69	67	69	67	272	101,887.50
Jamie Lovemark	69	65	67	71	272	101,887.50
Troy Matteson	70	68	67	67	272	101,887.50
Kyle Stanley	65	67	68	72	272	101,887.50
Nick Watney	66	68	71	67	272	101,887.50
Robert Allenby	66	69	72	66	273	64,068
Matt Bettencourt	67	70	68	68	273	64,068
Scott Brown	67	66	69	71	273	64,068
Kevin Chappell	72	67	68	66	273	64,068
Andres Romero	71	68	67	67	273	64,068
William McGirt	69	70	69	66	274	45,457.50
Scott Piercy	72	65	71	66	274	45,457.50
Brandt Snedeker	69	69	67	69	274	45,457.50
Will Wilcox	68	68	69	69	274	45,457.50
Woody Austin	68	70	71	66	275	37,050
Russell Knox	72	66	69	68	275	37,050
Martin Laird	71	66	70	68	275	37,050
Steve Marino	69	69	70	67	275	37,050
Charlie Wi	66	73	66	70	275	37,050
Eric Axley	68	68	71	69	276	26,980
Roberto Castro	69	67	70	70	276	26,980
Stewart Cink	68	69	71	68	276	26,980
Ben Crane	71	69	71	65	276	26,980
Ken Duke	67	71	72	66	276	26,980
Tim Herron	69	67	70	70	276	26,980
Danny Lee	69	65	72	70	276	26,980
Geoff Ogilvy	70	68	70	68	276	26,980
Johnson Wagner	71	67	71	67	276	26,980
Ricky Barnes	70	70	70	67	277	16,986
James Hahn	72	68	68	69	277	16,986
J.J. Henry	67	69	71	70	277	16,986
Morgan Hoffmann	69	69	70	69	277	16,986
Jeff Overton	69	71	69	68	277	16,986
Tim Petrovic	64	66	72	75	277	16,986
Charl Schwartzel	66	72	70	69	277	16,986
Vijay Singh	69	69	70	69	277	16,986
Andrew Svoboda	67	66	72	72	277	16,986
*Taylor Pendrith	65	75	68	69	277	
Joel Dahmen	66	72	68	72	278	13,034
Nathan Green	67	69	71	71	278	13,034
Adam Hadwin	70	69	68	71	278	13,034
David Hearn	67	70	70	71	278	13,034
D.H. Lee	69	70	69	70	278	13,034
Edward Loar	72	64	75	67	278	13,034
Troy Merritt	66	74	70	68	278	13,034
D.A. Points	71	68	69	70	278	13,034
Tim Wilkinson	67	68	75	68	278	13,034
Sean O'Hair	69	70	69	72	280	12,369
Patrick Rodgers	71	66	70	73	280	12,369
Charlie Beljan	67	72	71	71	281	12,141
Greg Chalmers	66	68	76	71	281	12,141
K.J. Choi	72	68	73	69	282	11,799
Jerry Kelly	67	71	72	72	282	11,799
Josh Teater	70	69	68	75	282	11,799
Mike Weir	70	70	71	71	282	11,799
Derek Ernst	70	69	73	72	284	11,457

	SCORES				TOTAL	MONEY
Ryuji Imada	68	72	75	69	284	11,457
Thomas Aiken	70	69	73	73	285	11,286
Jim Herman	70	70	75	73	288	11,172

WGC - Bridgestone Invitational

Firestone Country Club, South Course, Akron, Ohio — July 31-August 3
Par 35-35–70; 7,400 yards — purse, $9,000,000

	SCORES				TOTAL	MONEY
Rory McIlroy	69	64	66	66	265	$1,530,000
Sergio Garcia	68	61	67	71	267	900,000
Marc Leishman	64	69	68	67	268	522,000
Keegan Bradley	68	67	67	69	271	308,000
Patrick Reed	67	68	71	65	271	308,000
Justin Rose	65	67	70	69	271	308,000
Charl Schwartzel	65	69	73	64	271	308,000
Rickie Fowler	67	67	72	67	273	170,000
Graeme McDowell	71	70	66	66	273	170,000
Ryan Moore	65	73	68	67	273	170,000
Adam Scott	69	68	65	71	273	170,000
Matt Kuchar	71	66	72	65	274	115,000
Hideki Matsuyama	70	71	65	68	274	115,000
Brandt Snedeker	68	68	68	70	274	115,000
Thomas Bjorn	69	68	69	69	275	97,500
Jim Furyk	69	68	69	69	275	97,500
Hunter Mahan	71	65	71	68	275	97,500
Phil Mickelson	71	73	69	62	275	97,500
Kevin Stadler	71	70	66	69	276	89,000
Henrik Stenson	71	66	68	71	276	89,000
Lee Westwood	72	71	70	63	276	89,000
Gary Woodland	70	68	68	70	276	89,000
Branden Grace	69	71	67	70	277	82,000
Zach Johnson	70	70	68	69	277	82,000
Kevin Na	71	73	66	67	277	82,000
Ernie Els	71	69	70	68	278	75,200
J.B. Holmes	69	69	67	73	278	75,200
John Senden	74	66	67	71	278	75,200
Jimmy Walker	69	70	70	69	278	75,200
Fabrizio Zanotti	70	71	68	69	278	75,200
Angel Cabrera	73	68	70	68	279	69,500
Victor Dubuisson	72	70	69	68	279	69,500
Harris English	69	69	68	73	279	69,500
Matt Jones	70	70	69	70	279	69,500
Francesco Molinari	67	70	73	69	279	69,500
Webb Simpson	72	69	70	68	279	69,500
Brendon de Jonge	72	69	70	69	280	64,500
Jamie Donaldson	68	70	71	71	280	64,500
Seung-Yul Noh	69	69	70	72	280	64,500
Bubba Watson	69	70	73	68	280	64,500
Bill Haas	71	69	69	72	281	61,000
Russell Henley	72	70	71	68	281	61,000
Chris Kirk	69	73	72	67	281	61,000
Steven Bowditch	69	71	73	69	282	59,000
Miguel Angel Jimenez	69	69	72	73	283	57,500
Brendon Todd	74	70	69	70	283	57,500
Matt Every	74	68	73	69	284	55,500
Stephen Gallacher	74	71	69	70	284	55,500
Jordan Spieth	71	70	73	71	285	54,000
Tim Clark	72	73	70	71	286	52,500

	SCORES				TOTAL	MONEY
Luke Donald	73	70	72	71	286	52,500
David Howell	69	71	71	76	287	49,625
Thongchai Jaidee	70	74	71	72	287	49,625
Ian Poulter	73	73	70	71	287	49,625
Scott Stallings	72	75	68	72	287	49,625
Martin Kaymer	77	68	72	71	288	47,750
Joost Luiten	73	73	71	71	288	47,750
Jonas Blixt	75	72	69	73	289	46,500
Alexander Levy	72	71	77	69	289	46,500
Richard Sterne	75	70	73	71	289	46,500
Louis Oosthuizen	75	73	67	75	290	45,500
Gonzalo Fernandez-Castano	79	71	67	74	291	45,000
Pablo Larrazabal	71	74	77	70	292	44,250
Steve Stricker	74	73	72	73	292	44,250
Brian Harman	72	70	75	76	293	43,750
Jason Dufner	70	74	73	77	294	43,375
Mikko Ilonen	75	74	73	72	294	43,375
Daisuke Maruyama	73	73	73	78	297	43,000
David Lynn	76	72	75	75	298	42,625
Yoshitaka Takeya	74	75	74	75	298	42,625
Kevin Streelman	78	71	78	73	300	42,250
Estanislao Goya	76	77	71	78	302	42,000

Barracuda Championship

Montreux Golf & Country Club, Reno, Nevada — July 31-August 3
Par 36-36–72; 7,472 yards — purse, $3,000,000

	POINTS				TOTAL	MONEY
Geoff Ogilvy	16	7	12	14	49	$540,000
Justin Hicks	9	6	11	18	44	324,000
Jonathan Byrd	7	6	13	11	37	174,000
John Huh	12	7	7	11	37	174,000
Rod Pampling	11	5	9	11	36	120,000
Jason Allred	7	11	14	3	35	104,250
Martin Laird	13	-4	14	12	35	104,250
Ricky Barnes	5	6	12	11	34	84,000
Kyle Stanley	5	11	6	12	34	84,000
Nick Watney	18	8	6	2	34	84,000
Tim Wilkinson	16	5	1	12	34	84,000
Eric Axley	11	4	3	15	33	66,000
Hudson Swafford	9	9	6	9	33	66,000
Chad Campbell	13	-1	7	13	32	54,000
Bryce Molder	10	10	6	6	32	54,000
Robert Streb	10	4	9	9	32	54,000
Miguel Angel Carballo	10	1	7	13	31	43,500
George Coetzee	11	-1	11	10	31	43,500
Joe Durant	9	1	14	7	31	43,500
Tommy Gainey	11	10	3	7	31	43,500
Steve Flesch	1	9	11	9	30	32,400
Morgan Hoffmann	6	3	13	8	30	32,400
David Lingmerth	9	7	12	2	30	32,400
Wes Roach	12	10	0	8	30	32,400
Retief Goosen	5	8	6	10	29	25,200
Brendan Steele	9	11	10	-1	29	25,200
Woody Austin	11	8	3	6	28	20,400
Derek Ernst	11	0	5	12	28	20,400
Lee Janzen	8	7	13	0	28	20,400
Doug LaBelle	11	1	13	3	28	20,400
Billy Mayfair	3	9	11	5	28	20,400

	POINTS				TOTAL	MONEY
Andres Romero	7	7	4	10	28	20,400
Johnson Wagner	10	8	4	6	28	20,400
Kevin Chappell	12	-1	6	10	27	15,480
Brice Garnett	-2	10	15	4	27	15,480
J.J. Henry	5	4	12	6	27	15,480
Kent Jones	5	11	-2	13	27	15,480
Jamie Lovemark	6	5	10	6	27	15,480
John Mallinger	4	5	19	-2	26	12,900
Patrick Rodgers	11	0	11	4	26	12,900
D.J. Trahan	2	6	9	9	26	12,900
Greg Chalmers	3	13	10	-1	25	11,100
Jeff Overton	7	13	0	5	25	11,100
Kevin Tway	8	1	5	11	25	11,100
Oliver Goss	6	3	9	5	23	9,600
Mark Wilson	8	9	2	4	23	9,600
Padraig Harrington	10	7	2	3	22	7,810
Kevin Lucas	11	2	3	6	22	7,810
Troy Matteson	5	3	11	3	22	7,810
Thorbjorn Olesen	10	5	-2	9	22	7,810
Michael Putnam	8	3	16	-5	22	7,810
Marc Turnesa	6	5	6	5	22	7,810
Arjun Atwal	7	10	6	-2	21	6,980
Danny Lee	11	4	0	6	21	6,980
Tim Petrovic	10	2	4	5	21	6,980
Nicholas Thompson	10	5	-1	6	20	6,840
Trevor Immelman	7	1	6	4	18	6,750
Andrew Loupe	8	0	6	4	18	6,750
Jim Herman	10	2	5	0	17	6,630
Bronson La'Cassie	6	3	2	6	17	6,630
Cameron Beckman	7	2	4	3	16	6,420
Charlie Beljan	6	5	5	0	16	6,420
Ben Curtis	7	5	6	-2	16	6,420
Ryuji Imada	4	5	4	3	16	6,420
John Merrick	3	5	8	0	16	6,420
Tim Herron	4	8	3	0	15	6,180
D.H. Lee	11	5	-1	0	15	6,180
John Rollins	12	2	1	0	15	6,180
Len Mattiace	-1	9	7	-1	14	6,000
Rory Sabbatini	-3	13	2	2	14	6,000
Mike Weir	4	10	0	0	14	6,000
Brian Stuard	4	9	-2	0	11	5,880
Chris Smith	8	3	0	-1	10	5,820
Chad Collins	7	4	3	-5	9	5,760

PGA Championship

Valhalla Golf Club, Louisville, Kentucky
Par 35-36–71; 7,458 yards

August 7-10
purse, $10,000,000

	SCORES				TOTAL	MONEY
Rory McIlroy	66	67	67	68	268	$1,800,000
Phil Mickelson	69	67	67	66	269	1,080,000
Rickie Fowler	69	66	67	68	270	580,000
Henrik Stenson	66	71	67	66	270	580,000
Jim Furyk	66	68	72	66	272	367,500
Ryan Palmer	65	70	69	68	272	367,500
Victor Dubuisson	69	68	70	66	273	263,000
Ernie Els	70	70	68	65	273	263,000
Mikko Ilonen	67	68	69	69	273	263,000
Hunter Mahan	70	71	65	67	273	263,000

	SCORES				TOTAL	MONEY
Steve Stricker	69	68	68	68	273	263,000
Jimmy Walker	69	71	68	65	273	263,000
Kevin Chappell	65	74	67	68	274	191,000
Brandt Snedeker	73	68	66	67	274	191,000
Jason Day	69	65	69	72	275	127,888.88
Graham DeLaet	69	68	68	70	275	127,888.88
Brooks Koepka	71	71	66	67	275	127,888.88
Louis Oosthuizen	70	67	67	71	275	127,888.88
Charl Schwartzel	72	68	69	66	275	127,888.88
Adam Scott	71	69	66	69	275	127,888.88
Marc Warren	71	71	66	67	275	127,888.88
Lee Westwood	65	72	69	69	275	127,888.88
Bernd Wiesberger	68	68	65	74	275	127,888.88
Jamie Donaldson	69	70	66	71	276	84,000
Justin Rose	70	72	67	67	276	84,000
Joost Luiten	68	69	69	71	277	78,000
Bill Haas	71	68	68	71	278	71,000
Jerry Kelly	67	74	70	67	278	71,000
Kenny Perry	72	69	69	68	278	71,000
Alexander Levy	69	71	68	71	279	62,000
Thorbjorn Olesen	71	71	70	67	279	62,000
Danny Willett	68	73	66	72	279	62,000
Daniel Summerhays	70	72	68	70	280	53,000
Cameron Tringale	69	71	71	69	280	53,000
Nick Watney	69	69	70	72	280	53,000
Jonas Blixt	71	70	68	72	281	42,520
Sergio Garcia	70	72	66	73	281	42,520
Hideki Matsuyama	71	72	70	68	281	42,520
Vijay Singh	71	68	73	69	281	42,520
Richard Sterne	70	69	72	70	281	42,520
Jason Bohn	71	71	71	69	282	32,000
Brendon de Jonge	70	70	72	70	282	32,000
Luke Donald	70	72	68	72	282	32,000
Brian Harman	71	69	69	73	282	32,000
Ryan Moore	73	68	67	74	282	32,000
Koumei Oda	74	68	71	69	282	32,000
Scott Brown	71	70	70	72	283	24,791.66
Branden Grace	73	70	68	72	283	24,791.66
Matt Jones	68	71	72	72	283	24,791.66
Robert Karlsson	71	69	74	69	283	24,791.66
Marc Leishman	71	71	72	69	283	24,791.66
Shane Lowry	68	74	74	67	283	24,791.66
Graeme McDowell	73	70	71	69	283	24,791.66
Edoardo Molinari	66	73	71	73	283	24,791.66
Geoff Ogilvy	69	71	71	72	283	24,791.66
Pat Perez	71	71	71	70	283	24,791.66
Chris Wood	66	73	70	74	283	24,791.66
Fabrizio Zanotti	71	70	71	71	283	24,791.66
Gonzalo Fernandez-Castano	71	70	72	71	284	20,416.66
Billy Horschel	71	68	69	76	284	20,416.66
Francesco Molinari	71	71	71	71	284	20,416.66
Ian Poulter	68	73	71	72	284	20,416.66
Patrick Reed	70	71	70	73	284	20,416.66
Brendan Steele	71	70	73	70	284	20,416.66
J.B. Holmes	68	72	69	78	287	18,700
Kevin Stadler	71	70	72	74	287	18,700
Chris Stroud	70	73	73	71	287	18,700
Bubba Watson	70	72	73	72	287	18,700
Shawn Stefani	68	75	72	73	288	18,200
Freddie Jacobson	72	69	73	75	289	17,900
Zach Johnson	70	72	70	77	289	17,900
Colin Montgomerie	70	72	72	75	289	17,900
Brendon Todd	70	73	75	75	293	17,700
Rafa Cabrera-Bello	69	71	74	80	294	17,600

Out of Final 36 Holes

Tim Clark	70	74	144
Erik Compton	71	73	144
Tommy Fleetwood	73	71	144
Padraig Harrington	73	71	144
Ryan Helminen	73	71	144
Russell Henley	69	75	144
Charley Hoffman	70	74	144
Martin Kaymer	70	74	144
Scott Piercy	73	71	144
Gary Woodland	72	72	144
Matt Every	73	72	145
Russell Knox	75	70	145
Johan Kok	78	67	145
Anirban Lahiri	72	73	145
Davis Love	72	73	145
Ben Martin	74	71	145
Seung-Yul Noh	68	77	145
Kevin Streelman	69	76	145
Brian Stuard	71	74	145
Tom Watson	72	73	145
Steven Bowditch	74	72	146
Keegan Bradley	74	72	146
Jamie Broce	74	72	146
Paul Casey	74	72	146
Roberto Castro	73	73	146
Stuart Deane	75	71	146
Harris English	74	72	146
Ross Fisher	73	73	146
David Hearn	74	72	146
Ryo Ishikawa	72	74	146
Chris Kirk	74	72	146
Kevin Na	74	72	146
Rory Sabbatini	75	71	146
Hideto Tanihara	74	72	146
Y.E. Yang	75	71	146
Stewart Cink	72	75	147
George Coetzee	73	74	147
Stephen Gallacher	70	77	147
Chesson Hadley	74	73	147
Charles Howell	73	74	147
Webb Simpson	73	74	147
Eric Williamson	74	73	147
Darren Clarke	79	69	148
John Daly	76	72	148
Hyung-Sung Kim	73	75	148
Pablo Larrazabal	79	69	148
George McNeill	73	75	148
Jordan Spieth	71	77	148
Tiger Woods	74	74	148
Miguel Angel Jimenez	72	77	149
Rod Perry	74	75	149
John Senden	75	74	149
Scott Stallings	71	78	149
Thomas Bjorn	75	75	150
Thongchai Jaidee	71	79	150
Will MacKenzie	76	74	150
Steve Schneiter	72	78	150
Bob Sowards	75	75	150
Michael Block	77	74	151
K.J. Choi	72	79	151
John Huh	78	73	151
Jason Kokrak	78	73	151
Shaun Micheel	72	79	151
Brian Norman	78	74	152
Rich Beem	74	79	153
Rob Corcoran	76	77	153
Mark Brooks	78	79	157
Matteo Manassero	80	77	157
Jim McGovern	83	74	157
David McNabb	77	80	157
David Hronek	81	77	158
Jerry Smith	80	78	158
Dave Tentis	79	79	158
Frank Esposito, Jr.	83	78	161
Aaron Krueger	84	77	161
Dustin Volk	81	82	163
Matt Pesta	79	89	168
Kiradech Aphibarnrat	72	72	WD
Ben Crane	74	74	WD
Boo Weekley	80	80	WD
Angel Cabrera	82	82	WD
Jason Dufner			WD

Wyndham Championship

Sedgefield Country Club, Greensboro, North Carolina
Par 35-35–70; 7,127 yards

August 14-17
purse, $5,300,000

	SCORES				TOTAL	MONEY
Camilo Villegas	63	69	68	63	263	$954,000
Bill Haas	68	66	66	64	264	466,400
Freddie Jacobson	68	64	66	66	264	466,400
Heath Slocum	65	65	68	67	265	254,400
Webb Simpson	64	69	66	67	266	193,450
Brandt Snedeker	68	65	66	67	266	193,450
Nick Watney	67	64	65	70	266	193,450
Brad Fritsch	69	63	65	70	267	148,400
Kevin Kisner	69	64	67	67	267	148,400
William McGirt	64	68	71	64	267	148,400
Jhonattan Vegas	67	65	69	66	267	148,400
Scott Langley	65	65	69	69	268	116,600
Scott Piercy	70	64	69	65	268	116,600

	SCORES				TOTAL	MONEY
Sang-Moon Bae	69	68	66	66	269	92,750
Martin Laird	65	66	69	69	269	92,750
Andres Romero	70	66	64	69	269	92,750
Bo Van Pelt	67	65	68	69	269	92,750
Paul Casey	65	69	68	68	270	66,780
Roberto Castro	71	66	65	68	270	66,780
Carl Pettersson	67	65	71	67	270	66,780
D.A. Points	67	65	70	68	270	66,780
Robert Streb	69	66	67	68	270	66,780
David Toms	67	69	67	67	270	66,780
Ricky Barnes	66	69	66	70	271	41,008.75
Tim Clark	67	67	69	68	271	41,008.75
Luke Guthrie	69	69	68	65	271	41,008.75
Andrew Loupe	65	68	70	68	271	41,008.75
Francesco Molinari	69	67	68	67	271	41,008.75
Patrick Reed	71	67	67	66	271	41,008.75
Andrew Svoboda	67	64	70	70	271	41,008.75
Will Wilcox	67	67	67	70	271	41,008.75
Brice Garnett	71	67	68	66	272	29,326.67
J.J. Henry	66	70	68	68	272	29,326.67
John Merrick	70	67	68	67	272	29,326.67
Jeff Overton	70	67	67	68	272	29,326.67
Justin Bolli	67	68	67	70	272	29,326.66
Brian Stuard	66	65	71	70	272	29,326.66
Stuart Appleby	68	69	66	70	273	21,730
Brian Davis	69	65	70	69	273	21,730
Derek Ernst	68	69	69	67	273	21,730
Brooks Koepka	68	68	73	64	273	21,730
Doug LaBelle	72	65	66	70	273	21,730
Josh Teater	67	69	66	71	273	21,730
Johnson Wagner	66	67	70	70	273	21,730
Steve Marino	66	69	69	70	274	16,960
Y.E. Yang	69	68	68	69	274	16,960
Jason Allred	69	66	67	73	275	14,257
Ben Curtis	68	67	73	67	275	14,257
Robert Garrigus	68	68	72	67	275	14,257
Billy Horschel	70	65	72	68	275	14,257
Troy Merritt	70	68	67	71	276	12,472.67
Shawn Stefani	67	67	71	71	276	12,472.67
Charlie Wi	70	66	71	69	276	12,472.67
Mark Wilson	71	67	72	66	276	12,472.67
Kevin Foley	69	68	67	72	276	12,472.66
Retief Goosen	69	69	67	71	276	12,472.66
Steven Bowditch	66	70	70	71	277	11,660
Joe Durant	69	67	71	70	277	11,660
James Hahn	69	69	69	70	277	11,660
Justin Hicks	69	69	69	70	277	11,660
John Huh	70	68	70	69	277	11,660
Michael Putnam	68	67	74	68	277	11,660
Wes Roach	70	68	74	65	277	11,660
Ernie Els	68	69	73	68	278	11,130
Peter Malnati	70	67	74	67	278	11,130
Michael Thompson	70	66	73	69	278	11,130
Tommy Gainey	66	72	67	74	279	10,812
Richard Sterne	69	68	71	71	279	10,812
Hudson Swafford	71	67	73	68	279	10,812
Tim Herron	70	68	69	73	280	10,441
Ryo Ishikawa	70	62	78	70	280	10,441
Nicholas Thompson	70	68	73	69	280	10,441
Bobby Wyatt	67	70	73	70	280	10,441
David Lingmerth	67	70	73	71	281	10,123
Tyrone van Aswegen	72	66	72	71	281	10,123
Lee Janzen	70	68	71	73	282	9,964
Joe Ogilvie	70	68	72	73	283	9,858

PGA Tour Playoffs for the FedExCup

The Barclays

Ridgewood Country Club, Paramus, New Jersey — August 21-24
Par 35-36–71; 7,319 yards — purse, $8,000,000

	SCORES				TOTAL	MONEY
Hunter Mahan	66	71	68	65	270	$1,440,000
Stuart Appleby	73	66	68	65	272	597,333.34
Jason Day	72	64	68	68	272	597,333.33
Cameron Tringale	66	68	72	66	272	597,333.33
Ernie Els	68	68	71	66	273	292,000
Matt Kuchar	68	70	68	67	273	292,000
William McGirt	68	71	68	66	273	292,000
Jim Furyk	66	69	69	70	274	248,000
Rickie Fowler	68	73	67	67	275	208,000
Morgan Hoffmann	70	70	66	69	275	208,000
Kevin Na	70	66	70	69	275	208,000
Patrick Reed	71	66	73	65	275	208,000
Bo Van Pelt	65	71	70	70	276	160,000
Gary Woodland	73	66	69	68	276	160,000
Stewart Cink	69	72	68	68	277	132,000
Gonzalo Fernandez-Castano	70	69	68	70	277	132,000
Bill Haas	70	70	70	67	277	132,000
Adam Scott	69	65	75	68	277	132,000
Erik Compton	68	69	70	71	278	104,000
Ryo Ishikawa	67	73	68	70	278	104,000
Chris Stroud	69	70	69	70	278	104,000
Steven Bowditch	68	72	70	69	279	70,200
Angel Cabrera	71	69	69	70	279	70,200
Paul Casey	66	71	71	71	279	70,200
Charles Howell	66	75	68	70	279	70,200
Zach Johnson	68	70	72	69	279	70,200
Rory McIlroy	74	65	70	70	279	70,200
John Senden	68	71	74	66	279	70,200
Jordan Spieth	70	70	72	67	279	70,200
Kevin Chappell	68	67	71	74	280	46,500
Charley Hoffman	73	69	69	69	280	46,500
Scott Langley	70	68	76	66	280	46,500
Hideki Matsuyama	68	70	72	70	280	46,500
Justin Rose	68	70	70	72	280	46,500
Charl Schwartzel	69	70	71	70	280	46,500
Shawn Stefani	71	70	71	68	280	46,500
Bubba Watson	68	70	71	71	280	46,500
David Hearn	69	72	69	71	281	32,000
John Huh	69	69	74	69	281	32,000
Jerry Kelly	74	68	68	71	281	32,000
Russell Knox	67	69	74	71	281	32,000
Danny Lee	67	71	70	73	281	32,000
Graeme McDowell	70	68	71	72	281	32,000
Andres Romero	72	70	68	71	281	32,000
Henrik Stenson	72	64	77	68	281	32,000
Ben Martin	66	76	70	70	282	21,394.29
Troy Merritt	69	71	72	70	282	21,394.29
Kevin Stadler	74	67	70	71	282	21,394.29
Daniel Summerhays	68	72	72	70	282	21,394.29
Bryce Molder	74	68	68	72	282	21,394.28
Kevin Streelman	75	67	69	71	282	21,394.28
Brendon Todd	66	69	71	76	282	21,394.28
Keegan Bradley	68	73	70	72	283	18,520

	SCORES				TOTAL	MONEY
Chris Kirk	71	68	73	71	283	18,520
Seung-Yul Noh	68	72	70	73	283	18,520
Jeff Overton	72	71	70	70	283	18,520
Sergio Garcia	71	68	71	74	284	17,840
Brian Harman	69	74	68	73	284	17,840
Brendan Steele	71	71	69	73	284	17,840
Lee Westwood	70	73	71	70	284	17,840
Jason Bohn	68	71	74	72	285	17,120
Brendon de Jonge	66	72	72	75	285	17,120
Russell Henley	70	71	73	71	285	17,120
Jason Kokrak	70	71	71	73	285	17,120
Boo Weekley	72	68	71	74	285	17,120
Retief Goosen	69	69	74	74	286	16,560
Jhonattan Vegas	69	74	69	74	286	16,560
Ricky Barnes	68	75	70	76	289	16,240
Vijay Singh	69	73	71	76	289	16,240
Chesson Hadley	74	69	70	78	291	16,000
K.J. Choi	68	75	72		215	15,680
Luke Guthrie	71	72	72		215	15,680
Tim Wilkinson	72	71	72		215	15,680
Brian Davis	73	66	77		216	15,120
Ryan Palmer	69	71	76		216	15,120
Brian Stuard	73	70	73		216	15,120
David Toms	69	73	74		216	15,120
Phil Mickelson	71	72	75		218	14,720
Martin Flores	73	70	76		219	14,560

Deutsche Bank Championship

TPC Boston, Norton, Massachusetts — August 29-September 1
Par 36-35–71; 7,216 yards — purse, $8,000,000

	SCORES				TOTAL	MONEY
Chris Kirk	73	66	64	66	269	$1,440,000
Geoff Ogilvy	70	71	65	65	271	597,333.34
Russell Henley	70	66	65	70	271	597,333.33
Billy Horschel	69	66	67	69	271	597,333.33
Rory McIlroy	70	69	64	70	273	304,000
John Senden	69	71	67	66	273	304,000
Jason Day	66	68	69	71	274	258,000
Martin Kaymer	71	66	70	67	274	258,000
Bill Haas	67	69	70	69	275	185,142.86
Chesson Hadley	66	73	67	69	275	185,142.86
Carl Pettersson	67	73	69	66	275	185,142.86
Robert Streb	73	67	67	68	275	185,142.86
Jimmy Walker	70	70	68	67	275	185,142.86
Seung-Yul Noh	69	68	68	70	275	185,142.85
Webb Simpson	66	70	68	71	275	185,142.85
Jason Kokrak	68	72	70	66	276	112,228.58
Keegan Bradley	65	71	69	71	276	112,228.57
Zach Johnson	71	68	70	67	276	112,228.57
Ryan Palmer	63	71	71	71	276	112,228.57
Adam Scott	73	68	68	67	276	112,228.57
Kevin Stadler	71	70	67	68	276	112,228.57
Brian Stuard	72	71	65	68	276	112,228.57
Rickie Fowler	70	69	67	71	277	76,800
Jim Furyk	72	66	69	70	277	76,800
Ian Poulter	67	73	71	66	277	76,800
Russell Knox	67	70	71	70	278	61,600
Henrik Stenson	70	70	73	65	278	61,600

	SCORES				TOTAL	MONEY
Kevin Streelman	73	67	65	73	278	61,600
Matt Kuchar	69	66	73	71	279	50,866.67
George McNeill	73	68	72	66	279	50,866.67
Bubba Watson	72	71	69	67	279	50,866.67
Gary Woodland	71	70	73	65	279	50,866.67
Ben Crane	69	68	70	72	279	50,866.66
Jordan Spieth	67	70	69	73	279	50,866.66
Jason Bohn	74	68	69	69	280	36,950
K.J. Choi	72	70	70	68	280	36,950
Morgan Hoffmann	72	69	68	71	280	36,950
J.B. Holmes	70	75	68	67	280	36,950
Charles Howell	68	73	71	68	280	36,950
Danny Lee	74	65	73	68	280	36,950
Vijay Singh	72	68	69	71	280	36,950
Scott Stallings	70	74	72	64	280	36,950
David Hearn	70	74	72	65	281	28,800
Charl Schwartzel	72	72	68	69	281	28,800
Steven Bowditch	77	68	72	65	282	23,424
Gonzalo Fernandez-Castano	71	69	68	74	282	23,424
Will MacKenzie	70	73	67	72	282	23,424
Phil Mickelson	74	69	72	67	282	23,424
Chris Stroud	69	69	73	71	282	23,424
Ernie Els	72	71	73	67	283	19,017.15
Brendan Steele	74	71	69	69	283	19,017.15
Kevin Chappell	68	73	68	74	283	19,017.14
Stewart Cink	71	72	69	71	283	19,017.14
Graham DeLaet	71	74	67	71	283	19,017.14
Michael Putnam	71	70	68	74	283	19,017.14
Camilo Villegas	72	69	72	70	283	19,017.14
Luke Donald	69	74	74	67	284	17,600
Billy Hurley	68	74	71	71	284	17,600
Jerry Kelly	71	74	70	69	284	17,600
Hideki Matsuyama	73	69	68	74	284	17,600
Daniel Summerhays	74	71	67	72	284	17,600
Andrew Svoboda	71	72	69	72	284	17,600
Bo Van Pelt	70	73	69	72	284	17,600
Hunter Mahan	73	71	73	68	285	16,960
Brian Harman	72	70	75	69	286	16,640
Scott Langley	71	72	70	73	286	16,640
Marc Leishman	73	72	72	69	286	16,640
Shawn Stefani	69	74	71	73	287	16,320
John Huh	70	75	71	72	288	15,920
William McGirt	71	74	71	72	288	15,920
Jeff Overton	73	69	75	71	288	15,920
Cameron Tringale	72	73	71	72	288	15,920
Ryan Moore	72	71	74	73	290	15,520
Brendon de Jonge	77	67	74		218	15,280
Patrick Reed	68	68	82		218	15,280
Andres Romero	76	69	74		219	15,040
Scott Brown	75	68	77		220	14,880
Matt Jones	69	75	79		223	14,720
Freddie Jacobson	72	72	80		224	14,560
Matt Every	68	73	86		227	14,400

BMW Championship

Cherry Hills Country Club, Cherry Hills Village, Colorado — September 4-7
Par 34-36–70; 7,352 yards — purse, $8,000,000

	SCORES				TOTAL	MONEY
Billy Horschel	68	66	63	69	266	$1,440,000
Bubba Watson	70	66	66	66	268	864,000
Morgan Hoffmann	72	72	62	63	269	544,000
Rickie Fowler	71	66	66	68	271	319,000
Jim Furyk	70	68	67	66	271	319,000
Sergio Garcia	68	64	72	67	271	319,000
Ryan Palmer	69	64	67	71	271	319,000
Rory McIlroy	67	67	72	66	272	232,000
Adam Scott	71	66	69	66	272	232,000
Jordan Spieth	67	70	68	67	272	232,000
Graham DeLaet	68	68	69	68	273	200,000
Angel Cabrera	71	72	66	65	274	162,000
Chesson Hadley	68	70	68	68	274	162,000
J.B. Holmes	71	68	67	68	274	162,000
Charl Schwartzel	72	66	70	66	274	162,000
Kevin Chappell	68	72	70	65	275	124,000
Ernie Els	70	69	69	67	275	124,000
Bill Haas	72	68	67	68	275	124,000
Martin Kaymer	68	70	64	73	275	124,000
Camilo Villegas	70	71	68	67	276	96,533.34
Hideki Matsuyama	69	67	71	69	276	96,533.33
Jimmy Walker	72	67	69	68	276	96,533.33
Ben Crane	70	70	68	69	277	69,200
Russell Knox	74	69	72	62	277	69,200
Seung-Yul Noh	70	71	67	69	277	69,200
John Senden	73	66	70	68	277	69,200
Henrik Stenson	68	69	72	68	277	69,200
Gary Woodland	67	73	68	69	277	69,200
Jerry Kelly	71	73	66	68	278	55,600
Daniel Summerhays	75	68	71	64	278	55,600
Harris English	71	71	67	70	279	48,500
George McNeill	71	69	69	70	279	48,500
Carl Pettersson	73	70	68	68	279	48,500
Cameron Tringale	70	73	68	68	279	48,500
Justin Rose	69	71	70	70	280	43,200
Tim Clark	71	69	70	71	281	36,057.15
Geoff Ogilvy	73	69	69	70	281	36,057.15
Charles Howell	69	72	71	69	281	36,057.14
Chris Kirk	71	70	71	69	281	36,057.14
Graeme McDowell	73	72	69	67	281	36,057.14
Brian Stuard	71	69	71	70	281	36,057.14
Brendon Todd	73	67	72	69	281	36,057.14
Brian Harman	73	71	71	67	282	28,000
Zach Johnson	71	71	71	69	282	28,000
Chris Stroud	69	73	69	71	282	28,000
Stuart Appleby	71	71	70	71	283	22,680
Erik Compton	69	74	73	67	283	22,680
Matt Kuchar	71	73	70	69	283	22,680
Kevin Na	74	69	69	71	283	22,680
Matt Every	68	73	71	72	284	19,680
Ryan Moore	80	69	69	66	284	19,680
Kevin Stadler	74	69	70	71	284	19,680
Charley Hoffman	72	71	73	69	285	18,346.67
Freddie Jacobson	73	71	66	75	285	18,346.67
Marc Leishman	74	69	69	73	285	18,346.67
Webb Simpson	73	72	69	71	285	18,346.67
Matt Jones	73	73	70	69	285	18,346.66

	SCORES				TOTAL	MONEY
Patrick Reed	77	70	71	67	285	18,346.66
Russell Henley	68	74	76	69	287	17,520
Will MacKenzie	75	72	69	71	287	17,520
Hunter Mahan	75	70	71	71	287	17,520
Kevin Streelman	75	70	76	66	287	17,520
Steven Bowditch	72	77	70	69	288	17,040
K.J. Choi	69	74	69	76	288	17,040
William McGirt	71	71	76	73	291	16,800
Jason Bohn	74	71	75	72	292	16,640
Keegan Bradley	71	72			WD	
Phil Mickelson	70	76			WD	
Jason Day	70				WD	

Tour Championship

East Lake Golf Club, Atlanta, Georgia
Par 35-35–70; 7,307 yards

September 11-14
purse, $8,000,000

	SCORES				TOTAL	MONEY
Billy Horschel	66	66	69	68	269	$1,440,000
Jim Furyk	67	69	67	69	272	708,000
Rory McIlroy	69	65	67	71	272	708,000
Chris Kirk	66	68	71	68	273	343,333.34
Jason Day	67	67	70	69	273	343,333.33
Justin Rose	72	66	66	69	273	343,333.33
Ryan Palmer	69	67	69	69	274	275,000
Rickie Fowler	69	68	67	71	275	260,000
Sergio Garcia	69	71	70	66	276	231,666.67
Gary Woodland	71	75	63	67	276	231,666.67
Adam Scott	69	72	65	70	276	231,666.66
Russell Henley	70	68	67	72	277	210,000
Matt Kuchar	68	71	69	70	278	200,000
Bubba Watson	67	73	67	73	280	190,000
Cameron Tringale	68	68	74	71	281	180,000
Bill Haas	68	71	73	70	282	175,000
Brendon Todd	70	75	72	66	283	168,000
Jimmy Walker	73	69	69	72	283	168,000
Kevin Na	70	66	75	73	284	160,000
Patrick Reed	67	74	74	69	284	160,000
Zach Johnson	68	74	72	71	285	154,000
Hideki Matsuyama	71	71	71	73	286	150,000
Martin Kaymer	73	69	73	73	288	143,000
Hunter Mahan	74	72	71	71	288	143,000
Webb Simpson	74	72	72	70	288	143,000
John Senden	72	75	69	74	290	138,000
Morgan Hoffmann	70	73	73	76	292	135,000
Jordan Spieth	71	70	80	71	292	135,000
Geoff Ogilvy	77	77	73	73	300	132,000

Final Standings – PGA Tour Playoffs for the FedExCup

RANK	NAME	FEDEXCUP POINTS	BONUS MONEY
1	Billy Horschel	4,750	$10,000,000
2	Chris Kirk	3,100	3,000,000
3	Rory McIlroy	3,050	2,000,000
4	Jim Furyk	2,450	1,500,000
5	Bubba Watson	2,285	1,000,000
6	Hunter Mahan	1,835	800,000
7	Jimmy Walker	1,668	700,000
8	Matt Kuchar	1,300	600,000
9	Rickie Fowler	1,225	550,000
10	Jason Day	1,200	500,000
11	Justin Rose	850	300,000
12	Adam Scott	835	290,000
13	Sergio Garcia	815	280,000
14	Ryan Palmer	730	270,000
15	Jordan Spieth	698	250,000
T16	Bill Haas	655	242,500
T16	Martin Kaymer	655	242,500
18	Zach Johnson	650	235,000
19	Russell Henley	635	230,000
20	Cameron Tringale	600	225,000
21	Patrick Reed	598	220,000
22	Gary Woodland	595	215,000
23	John Senden	585	210,000
24	Kevin Na	528	205,000
25	Webb Simpson	525	200,000
26	Morgan Hoffmann	518	195,000
27	Brendon Todd	508	190,000
28	Hideki Matsuyama	475	185,000
29	Geoff Ogilvy	470	180,000
30	Dustin Johnson	210	175,000

The Ryder Cup

See European Tours chapter.

Frys.com Open

Silverado Country Club, North Course, Napa, California — October 9-12
Par 36-36–72; 7,203 yards — purse, $6,000,000

	SCORES				TOTAL	MONEY
Sang-Moon Bae	66	69	65	73	273	$1,080,000
Steven Bowditch	73	68	67	67	275	648,000
Retief Goosen	69	71	66	70	276	270,600
Martin Laird	67	67	71	71	276	270,600
Hunter Mahan	70	68	68	70	276	270,600
Hideki Matsuyama	70	67	69	70	276	270,600
Bryce Molder	70	69	69	68	276	270,600
Robert Allenby	70	71	66	70	277	168,000
Jon Curran	68	72	67	70	277	168,000
Brooks Koepka	68	70	67	72	277	168,000
Hudson Swafford	70	69	71	67	277	168,000
Zachary Blair	69	66	69	74	278	117,600
Scott Brown	71	68	72	67	278	117,600
Derek Fathauer	70	71	68	69	278	117,600
Tony Finau	69	73	68	68	278	117,600
Lee Westwood	73	69	69	67	278	117,600
Scott Langley	70	66	69	74	279	93,000

	SCORES				TOTAL	MONEY
David Lingmerth	68	68	70	73	279	93,000
Ryo Ishikawa	71	71	67	71	280	81,000
Byron Smith	73	66	68	73	280	81,000
Kevin Kisner	71	72	70	68	281	62,400
Matt Kuchar	71	68	66	76	281	62,400
Spencer Levin	73	69	67	72	281	62,400
Scott Stallings	71	69	70	71	281	62,400
Brendan Steele	72	70	69	70	281	62,400
Tom Gillis	70	68	72	72	282	44,400
Andres Gonzales	66	74	70	72	282	44,400
Colt Knost	68	71	71	72	282	44,400
Cameron Percy	69	70	70	73	282	44,400
Cameron Tringale	69	69	73	71	282	44,400
Aaron Baddeley	68	73	72	70	283	33,300
Charlie Beljan	68	72	70	73	283	33,300
Brendon de Jonge	72	71	70	70	283	33,300
Jarrod Lyle	72	70	71	70	283	33,300
Jeff Overton	70	71	67	75	283	33,300
Scott Pinckney	71	70	70	72	283	33,300
Robert Streb	74	68	74	67	283	33,300
Cameron Wilson	71	68	74	70	283	33,300
Blayne Barber	73	67	74	70	284	23,400
Chad Campbell	69	72	70	73	284	23,400
Graham DeLaet	71	70	71	72	284	23,400
Max Homa	72	68	72	72	284	23,400
Jerry Kelly	69	72	72	71	284	23,400
John Peterson	70	72	74	68	284	23,400
Kyle Reifers	68	74	73	69	284	23,400
Trevor Immelman	76	67	71	71	285	16,045.72
Marc Leishman	69	73	71	72	285	16,045.72
Daniel Summerhays	71	72	72	70	285	16,045.72
Erik Compton	74	66	69	76	285	16,045.71
Brice Garnett	71	70	70	74	285	16,045.71
Jason Kokrak	70	73	70	72	285	16,045.71
Danny Lee	73	67	72	73	285	16,045.71
Adam Hadwin	70	69	72	75	286	13,890
Mark Hubbard	71	65	75	75	286	13,890
Chez Reavie	73	70	71	72	286	13,890
Shawn Stefani	73	69	73	71	286	13,890
Tim Clark	69	74	70	74	287	13,260
Derek Ernst	72	71	70	74	287	13,260
Chesson Hadley	73	69	74	71	287	13,260
Carlos Ortiz	71	71	73	72	287	13,260
Carl Pettersson	71	69	73	74	287	13,260
Brandt Snedeker	71	71	73	72	287	13,260
Jimmy Walker	75	66	73	74	288	12,840
Harrison Frazar	71	71	71	76	289	12,720
Stuart Appleby	69	70	74	77	290	12,480
Bo Van Pelt	73	70	74	73	290	12,480
Tim Wilkinson	76	67	74	73	290	12,480
Luke Guthrie	68	72	76	75	291	12,120
David Hearn	72	71	78	70	291	12,120
Russell Knox	72	71	73	75	291	12,120
Charles Howell	73	67	75	77	292	11,820
Steve Wheatcroft	75	68	73	76	292	11,820
Sam Saunders	73	69	76	75	293	11,580
Tyrone van Aswegen	68	72	77	76	293	11,580

Shriners Hospitals for Children Open

TPC Summerlin, Las Vegas, Nevada
Par 35-36–71; 7,255 yards

October 16-19
purse, $6,200,000

	SCORES				TOTAL	MONEY
Ben Martin	68	66	62	68	264	$1,116,000
Kevin Streelman	71	67	63	65	266	669,600
Russell Knox	65	67	66	70	268	421,600
Brooks Koepka	69	68	64	68	269	256,266.67
Webb Simpson	69	65	67	68	269	256,266.67
Jimmy Walker	69	69	62	69	269	256,266.66
Tony Finau	68	65	70	67	270	193,233.34
David Hearn	70	66	66	68	270	193,233.33
Scott Piercy	67	67	67	69	270	193,233.33
Scott Brown	70	67	68	66	271	137,433.34
Adam Hadwin	67	72	69	63	271	137,433.34
Spencer Levin	71	63	68	69	271	137,433.33
Hideki Matsuyama	66	71	68	66	271	137,433.33
Brandt Snedeker	67	68	67	69	271	137,433.33
Robert Streb	71	67	67	66	271	137,433.33
Harris English	71	68	66	67	272	102,300
Nick Watney	68	69	69	66	272	102,300
Jason Bohn	68	68	66	71	273	68,014
Alex Cejka	69	68	65	71	273	68,014
Jim Herman	68	72	62	71	273	68,014
Charles Howell	70	69	67	67	273	68,014
Colt Knost	68	72	65	68	273	68,014
Martin Laird	64	70	68	71	273	68,014
Carlos Ortiz	69	70	69	65	273	68,014
John Senden	70	68	68	67	273	68,014
Andrew Svoboda	66	67	67	73	273	68,014
Hudson Swafford	69	67	68	69	273	68,014
Erik Compton	69	70	67	68	274	42,160
John Huh	72	67	68	67	274	42,160
Ryo Ishikawa	72	68	67	67	274	42,160
Jonathan Randolph	68	71	66	69	274	42,160
Kevin Stadler	67	70	67	70	274	42,160
Aaron Baddeley	69	70	70	66	275	30,724.45
William McGirt	68	71	68	68	275	30,724.45
Andrew Putnam	67	65	73	70	275	30,724.45
Brendan Steele	68	70	69	68	275	30,724.45
Jonathan Byrd	69	69	66	71	275	30,724.44
Stewart Cink	64	75	66	70	275	30,724.44
Bill Lunde	68	68	66	73	275	30,724.44
George McNeill	71	63	70	71	275	30,724.44
Sam Saunders	66	72	68	69	275	30,724.44
Tim Clark	68	67	72	69	276	20,495.43
Brendon de Jonge	70	68	69	69	276	20,495.43
Jarrod Lyle	66	71	70	69	276	20,495.43
Bryce Molder	68	70	67	71	276	20,495.43
Carl Pettersson	72	66	71	67	276	20,495.43
Wes Roach	67	67	70	72	276	20,495.43
John Merrick	69	70	65	72	276	20,495.42
Andres Gonzales	70	68	70	69	277	15,301.60
Whee Kim	71	68	70	68	277	15,301.60
Troy Merritt	72	68	67	70	277	15,301.60
Alex Prugh	71	69	66	71	277	15,301.60
Vijay Singh	67	71	67	72	277	15,301.60
Daniel Summerhays	71	68	67	72	278	14,322
Kevin Tway	73	67	68	70	278	14,322
Steven Alker	70	69	70	70	279	13,764
Martin Flores	70	70	68	71	279	13,764

	SCORES				TOTAL	MONEY
Wes Homan	68	72	67	72	279	13,764
Kevin Kisner	70	65	72	72	279	13,764
Kyle Reifers	73	66	69	71	279	13,764
Nick Taylor	71	65	73	70	279	13,764
Bo Van Pelt	66	68	75	70	279	13,764
Derek Ernst	70	69	70	71	280	13,082
Brice Garnett	68	70	70	72	280	13,082
Sean O'Hair	71	69	67	73	280	13,082
Steve Wheatcroft	74	65	70	71	280	13,082
Ken Duke	69	68	72	72	281	12,648
Dudley Hart	74	65	67	75	281	12,648
Tom Hoge	68	72	69	72	281	12,648
Byron Smith	71	69	69	74	283	12,400
J.J. Henry	71	69	68	76	284	12,276
Tommy Gainey	73	65	72		210	12,028
Cameron Percy	68	68	74		210	12,028
Camilo Villegas	70	70	70		210	12,028
Zachary Blair	70	70	71		211	11,594
Padraig Harrington	70	69	72		211	11,594
John Peterson	70	70	71		211	11,594
D.A. Points	68	71	72		211	11,594
Stuart Appleby	74	64	79		217	11,284

McGladrey Classic

Sea Island Golf Club, Seaside Course, St. Simons Island, Georgia — October 23-26
Par 35-35–70; 6,967 yards — purse, $5,600,000

	SCORES				TOTAL	MONEY
Robert Streb	69	66	68	63	266	$1,008,000
Brendon de Jonge	68	64	69	65	266	492,800
Will MacKenzie	65	68	65	68	266	492,800
(Streb defeated MacKenzie on first and de Jonge on second playoff hole.)						
Ken Duke	67	69	66	66	268	220,500
Russell Henley	68	63	68	69	268	220,500
Chris Kirk	68	67	66	67	268	220,500
Kevin Kisner	69	68	66	65	268	220,500
Kevin Chappell	67	67	70	65	269	156,800
Fabian Gomez	67	66	68	68	269	156,800
Andrew Svoboda	66	66	66	71	269	156,800
Mark Wilson	67	66	69	67	269	156,800
Andrew Putnam	68	67	66	69	270	123,200
Hudson Swafford	70	67	66	67	270	123,200
Tony Finau	71	67	67	66	271	100,800
David Lingmerth	68	67	70	66	271	100,800
David Toms	73	66	67	65	271	100,800
James Hahn	71	69	65	67	272	78,400
Ben Martin	70	68	65	69	272	78,400
Sean O'Hair	69	71	64	68	272	78,400
Carl Pettersson	68	67	69	68	272	78,400
Scott Piercy	67	67	68	70	272	78,400
Stuart Appleby	71	67	66	69	273	46,760
Eric Axley	67	70	68	68	273	46,760
Daniel Berger	68	69	69	67	273	46,760
Bill Haas	69	66	69	69	273	46,760
Matt Kuchar	67	70	68	68	273	46,760
John Peterson	66	71	72	64	273	46,760
D.A. Points	70	70	66	67	273	46,760
Rory Sabbatini	67	70	66	70	273	46,760
Nicholas Thompson	70	69	66	68	273	46,760

	SCORES				TOTAL	MONEY
Cameron Tringale	68	68	67	70	273	46,760
Steven Alker	69	67	71	67	274	29,057.78
Zachary Blair	71	68	68	67	274	29,057.78
Tommy Gainey	67	73	68	66	274	29,057.78
Chesson Hadley	66	70	70	68	274	29,057.78
Tom Hoge	70	68	68	68	274	29,057.78
Sung Joon Park	66	71	68	69	274	29,057.78
Daniel Summerhays	68	68	68	70	274	29,057.78
Stewart Cink	69	69	63	73	274	29,057.77
William McGirt	68	67	68	71	274	29,057.77
Robert Allenby	69	71	68	67	275	19,600
Chad Campbell	68	68	71	68	275	19,600
Brian Harman	65	67	73	70	275	19,600
Andrew Loupe	71	69	67	68	275	19,600
Davis Love	71	68	70	66	275	19,600
Webb Simpson	67	70	69	69	275	19,600
Shawn Stefani	66	69	71	69	275	19,600
Aaron Baddeley	67	73	66	70	276	14,074.67
Mark Hubbard	68	67	71	70	276	14,074.67
John Huh	72	68	68	68	276	14,074.67
Jeff Overton	70	69	69	68	276	14,074.67
Erik Compton	65	70	70	71	276	14,074.66
Brendon Todd	67	70	67	72	276	14,074.66
Mark Anderson	70	70	67	70	277	12,544
Jason Bohn	71	67	67	72	277	12,544
Jon Curran	70	70	69	68	277	12,544
Derek Ernst	68	67	70	72	277	12,544
Patton Kizzire	66	71	70	70	277	12,544
Bill Lunde	71	69	67	70	277	12,544
Kyle Reifers	71	68	69	69	277	12,544
Camilo Villegas	67	72	69	69	277	12,544
Cory Whitsett	70	70	66	71	277	12,544
Jerry Kelly	70	68	69	71	278	11,872
Cameron Percy	68	70	70	70	278	11,872
Andy Pope	72	66	70	70	278	11,872
Jason Kokrak	66	72	69	72	279	11,536
Justin Leonard	72	65	72	70	279	11,536
Michael Thompson	65	71	67	76	279	11,536
Roberto Castro	68	72	68	72	280	11,256
Martin Flores	67	73	68	72	280	11,256
Justin Thomas	74	66	67	75	282	11,088

CIMB Classic

See Asia/Japan Tours chapter.

WGC - HSBC Champions

See Asia/Japan Tours chapter.

Sanderson Farms Championship

Country Club of Jackson, Jackson, Mississippi — November 6-9
Par 36-36–72; 7,354 yards — purse, $4,000,000

	SCORES				TOTAL	MONEY
Nick Taylor	67	69	70	66	272	$720,000
Boo Weekley	70	68	70	66	274	352,000
Jason Bohn	68	71	66	69	274	352,000

	SCORES				TOTAL	MONEY
Peter Uihlein	70	71	69	65	275	165,333
Justin Thomas	71	68	69	67	275	165,333
John Rollins	68	66	68	73	275	165,333
William McGirt	68	70	66	72	276	134,000
Robert Streb	67	70	70	70	277	124,000
Blayne Barber	71	71	70	66	278	100,000
Garrett Osborn	70	69	71	68	278	100,000
Carlos Sainz, Jr.	70	70	69	69	278	100,000
Mark Wilson	71	69	68	70	278	100,000
David Toms	68	66	72	72	278	100,000
David Hearn	69	72	71	67	279	66,000
Cory Whitsett	72	69	70	68	279	66,000
Charles Howell	71	69	70	69	279	66,000
Will Wilcox	69	71	68	71	279	66,000
Fabian Gomez	71	68	69	71	279	66,000
Kyle Reifers	71	70	67	71	279	66,000
Jason Kokrak	69	70	71	70	280	50,000
Vaughn Taylor	72	66	71	71	280	50,000
Greg Owen	72	69	69	71	281	41,600
Jerry Kelly	70	73	72	66	281	41,600
Lucas Glover	71	67	67	76	281	41,600
Shawn Stefani	70	68	73	71	282	31,900
John Huh	70	70	68	74	282	31,900
Bo Van Pelt	71	72	73	66	282	31,900
Jonathan Byrd	72	70	66	74	282	31,900
Tom Gillis	69	68	76	70	283	25,433
Chad Collins	70	72	69	72	283	25,433
Daniel Summerhays	72	68	71	72	283	25,433
John Daly	71	72	67	73	283	25,433
Ben Curtis	68	73	69	73	283	25,433
Ben Martin	71	70	69	73	283	25,433
Alex Prugh	68	72	73	71	284	18,475
Tom Hoge	70	70	73	71	284	18,475
Sebastian Cappelen	65	74	72	73	284	18,475
Tim Petrovic	71	69	74	70	284	18,475
Josh Teater	70	70	71	73	284	18,475
Nicholas Thompson	70	72	73	69	284	18,475
Charley Hoffman	70	70	69	75	284	18,475
Russell Knox	72	70	73	69	284	18,475
John Peterson	69	72	72	72	285	12,180
J.J. Henry	72	69	72	72	285	12,180
Chris Smith	72	69	73	71	285	12,180
Oscar Fraustro	69	69	73	74	285	12,180
Andrew Putnam	69	72	73	71	285	12,180
Max Homa	72	70	68	75	285	12,180
Charlie Wi	68	71	75	71	285	12,180
Woody Austin	70	73	72	70	285	12,180
Andres Gonzales	68	73	71	74	286	9,360
Daniel Berger	70	71	73	72	286	9,360
Danny Lee	72	68	74	72	286	9,360
Derek Fathauer	73	70	71	72	286	9,360
Carl Pettersson	72	71	71	72	286	9,360
Jim Herman	69	71	75	71	286	9,360
Mark Hubbard	69	72	76	69	286	9,360
Heath Slocum	69	72	70	76	287	8,880
Scott McCarron	73	69	72	73	287	8,880
Roberto Castro	72	70	76	69	287	8,880
Sean O'Hair	70	71	73	74	288	8,560
Brendan Steele	69	73	72	74	288	8,560
Justin Hicks	72	71	71	74	288	8,560
Jason Gore	70	70	75	73	288	8,560
Jim Renner	71	72	72	73	288	8,560
Michael Thompson	71	68	72	78	289	8,240

	SCORES				TOTAL	MONEY
Rod Pampling	74	68	73	74	289	8,240
Sung Joon Park	72	71	73	73	289	8,240
Greg Chalmers	71	72	71	76	290	7,960
Michael Block	71	72	71	76	290	7,960
Andrew Loupe	72	69	76	73	290	7,960
Jason Allred	71	72	73	74	290	7,960
Padraig Harrington	70	69	76	76	291	7,680
Adam Hadwin	70	72	75	74	291	7,680
Jonathan Randolph	71	72	75	73	291	7,680

OHL Classic at Mayakoba

El Camaleon, Playa del Carmen, Mexico, Par 36-35–71; 6,987 yards

November 13-16 purse, $6,100,000

	SCORES				TOTAL	MONEY
Charley Hoffman	66	68	67	66	267	$1,098,000
Shawn Stefani	66	65	68	69	268	658,800
Andres Gonzales	69	67	66	67	269	353,800
Danny Lee	66	69	67	67	269	353,800
Jerry Kelly	69	66	67	68	270	244,000
Brice Garnett	66	68	71	66	271	219,600
Jason Bohn	66	65	67	74	272	196,725
Tony Finau	65	72	70	65	272	196,725
Blayne Barber	66	68	72	67	273	141,171.43
Ken Duke	69	63	70	71	273	141,171.43
Oscar Fraustro	68	67	69	69	273	141,171.43
Will MacKenzie	65	68	74	66	273	141,171.43
Carlos Ortiz	67	69	69	68	273	141,171.43
Nicholas Thompson	68	65	71	69	273	141,171.43
Fred Funk	69	65	69	70	273	141,171.42
Ricky Barnes	69	69	71	65	274	85,574.29
Jason Kokrak	66	69	72	67	274	85,574.29
Scott Piercy	67	69	73	65	274	85,574.29
Johnson Wagner	69	68	70	67	274	85,574.29
Alex Cejka	66	67	68	73	274	85,574.28
David Hearn	68	65	73	68	274	85,574.28
John Peterson	69	67	70	68	274	85,574.28
Zachary Blair	70	68	68	69	275	52,765
Fabian Gomez	70	66	72	67	275	52,765
Jim Herman	67	69	69	70	275	52,765
Billy Hurley	67	69	71	68	275	52,765
Chris Stroud	69	68	69	69	275	52,765
Justin Thomas	67	70	69	69	275	52,765
Greg Chalmers	68	67	71	70	276	37,133.75
Chad Collins	66	69	72	69	276	37,133.75
Max Homa	68	71	69	68	276	37,133.75
John Huh	69	67	69	71	276	37,133.75
Jeff Overton	71	66	70	69	276	37,133.75
Kyle Reifers	69	67	71	69	276	37,133.75
Daniel Summerhays	69	65	75	67	276	37,133.75
Tim Wilkinson	68	67	72	69	276	37,133.75
Aaron Baddeley	66	70	70	71	277	26,230
Harris English	67	71	69	70	277	26,230
Colt Knost	68	70	69	70	277	26,230
Russell Knox	69	68	70	70	277	26,230
Patrick Rodgers	67	70	70	70	277	26,230
Brendan Steele	68	68	70	71	277	26,230
Robert Streb	67	69	72	69	277	26,230
Ben Curtis	71	68	71	68	278	18,958.80

	SCORES				TOTAL	MONEY
J.J. Henry	70	69	70	69	278	18,958.80
Tom Hoge	70	69	71	68	278	18,958.80
John Rollins	71	65	74	68	278	18,958.80
Steve Wheatcroft	65	69	71	73	278	18,958.80
Robert Garrigus	65	73	72	69	279	15,616
Mark Hubbard	69	66	76	68	279	15,616
Daniel Berger	65	74	74	67	280	14,444.80
Gonzalo Fernandez-Castano	71	67	72	70	280	14,444.80
John Merrick	70	69	73	68	280	14,444.80
Michael Putnam	66	64	77	73	280	14,444.80
Hudson Swafford	65	73	71	71	280	14,444.80
Spencer Levin	71	68	75	67	281	13,603
Sung Joon Park	71	67	76	67	281	13,603
Rory Sabbatini	73	66	76	66	281	13,603
Roger Sloan	68	70	71	72	281	13,603
Nick Taylor	71	68	70	72	281	13,603
Jhonattan Vegas	68	70	70	73	281	13,603
Scott Brown	71	66	73	72	282	13,054
Freddie Jacobson	69	70	70	73	282	13,054
Andrew Putnam	68	70	73	71	282	13,054
Retief Goosen	68	71	75	69	283	12,627
Luke Guthrie	68	71	77	67	283	12,627
Scott Langley	69	70	74	70	283	12,627
D.A. Points	71	66	74	72	283	12,627
Pat Perez	66	73	72	73	284	12,261
Jay Woodson	72	66	74	72	284	12,261
Jason Gore	68	66	79	72	285	12,017
Brian Stuard	69	70	75	71	285	12,017
Derek Fathauer	68	71	77	71	287	11,834
Erik Compton	71	68	74	75	288	11,651
Alvaro Quiros	71	68	71	78	288	11,651
Patrick Cantlay	71	68	76	74	289	11,468

Special Events

CVS Caremark Charity Classic

Rhode Island Country Club, Barrington, Rhode Island — June 23-24
Par 36-35–71; 6,688 yards — purse $1,500,000

	SCORES		TOTAL	MONEY (Team)
Steve Stricker/Bo Van Pelt	62	60	122	$300,000
Peter Jacobsen/Jimmy Walker	62	61	123	200,000
Suzann Pettersen/Jonas Blixt	66	61	127	160,000
Russell Henley/Harris English	64	63	127	160,000
Erik Compton/Brad Faxon	65	63	128	121,666
Hunter Mahan/Jason Dufner	64	64	128	121,666
Bill Haas/Billy Andrade	63	65	128	121,666
Lexi Thompson/Billy Horschel	67	62	129	110,000
Zach Johnson/Matt Kuchar	65	68	133	105,000
Morgan Pressel/Juli Inkster	67	67	134	100,000

PGA Grand Slam of Golf

Port Royal Golf Course, Southampton Parish, Bermuda — October 14-15
Par 36-35–71; 6,821 yards — purse, $1,350,000

	SCORES		TOTAL	MONEY
Martin Kaymer	65	71	136	$600,000
Bubba Watson	67	69	136	300,000
(Kaymer defeated Watson on first playoff hole.)				
Rory McIlroy	69	75	144	250,000
Jim Furyk	72	73	145	200,000

Callaway Pebble Beach Invitational

Pebble Beach GL: Par 36-36–72; 6,828 yards — November 20-23
Spyglass Hills GC: Par 36-36–72; 6,953 yards — purse, $300,000
Del Monte GC: Par 36-36–72; 6,365 yards
Pebble Beach, California

	SCORES				TOTAL	MONEY
Tommy Armour	72	69	66	67	274	$60,000
Lee Janzen	65	68	72	69	274	32,200
(Armour defeated Janzen on first playoff hole.)						
Kevin Sutherland	73	70	68	67	278	16,400
Tommy Gainey	73	70	65	71	279	8,650
Bryce Molder	72	67	76	64	279	8,650
Thomas Pieters	69	71	68	71	279	8,650
Andrew Putnam	69	66	70	74	279	8,650
Arron Oberholser	72	68	72	68	280	6,250
Michael Putnam	69	71	70	70	280	6,250
Blake Adams	72	68	73	69	282	5,200
Todd Fischer	70	68	72	72	282	5,200

	SCORES				TOTAL	MONEY
John Rollins	69	69	71	73	282	5,200
Derek Fathaeur	68	73	72	70	283	4,300
Scott Langley	68	70	76	69	283	4,300
Charlie Wi	71	71	73	68	283	4,300
Brandon Harkins	71	70	73	70	284	3,500
Duffy Waldorf	70	69	73	72	284	3,500
Steve Wheatcroft	71	69	71	73	284	3,500
Billy Andrade	65	73	75	72	285	2,875
Martin Flores	69	73	70	73	285	2,875
Adam Hadwin	69	75	71	70	285	2,875
Robert Streb	72	68	74	71	285	2,875
Tony Finau	63	79	72	72	286	2,500
Rob Oppenheim	69	74	74	69	286	2,500
Jamie Sindelar	71	69	75	71	286	2,500
Mark Brooks	71	72	70	74	287	2,225
Jonathan Byrd	72	68	69	78	287	2,225
Jason Gore	74	68	70	75	287	2,225
Mark Hubbard	71	67	73	76	287	2,225
Justin Thomas	75	67	73	73	288	2,100
Daniel Berger	75	70	68	76	289	2,030
Matt Bettencourt	67	72	76	74	289	2,030
Bobby Clampett	68	76	69	76	289	2,030
Jeff Gove	72	71	72	74	289	2,030
Luke Guthrie	69	68	77	75	289	2,030
Kyle Reifers	67	73	76	73	289	2,030
James Hahn	67	73	74	76	290	1,950
Scott McCarron	72	74	71	73	290	1,950
Kelly Kraft	71	67	76	77	291	1,920
Mina Harigae	74	67	75	76	292	1,900
Andy Miller	74	69	74	78	295	1,900

Hero World Challenge

Isleworth Golf & Country Club, Windermere, Florida — December 4-7
Par 36-36–72; 7,215 yards — purse, $3,500,000

	SCORES				TOTAL	MONEY
Jordan Spieth	66	67	63	66	262	$1,000,000
Henrik Stenson	67	68	68	69	272	400,000
Keegan Bradley	72	66	65	70	273	212,500
Patrick Reed	73	63	69	68	273	212,500
Jason Day	71	67	70	66	274	150,000
Rickie Fowler	67	70	72	68	277	142,500
Justin Rose	72	64	70	71	277	142,500
Zach Johnson	67	71	72	69	279	126,666.67
Matt Kuchar	69	70	70	70	279	126,666.67
Billy Horschel	73	72	67	67	279	126,666.66
Graeme McDowell	68	73	68	71	280	112,500
Bubba Watson	69	68	72	71	280	112,500
Hideki Matsuyama	68	73	71	69	281	109,000
Steve Stricker	67	73	74	69	283	108,000
Jimmy Walker	68	69	75	72	284	107,000
Chris Kirk	70	68	74	73	285	106,000
Hunter Mahan	71	71	71	75	288	102,500
Tiger Woods	77	70	69	72	288	102,500

Franklin Templeton Shootout

Tiburon Golf Course, Naples, Florida
Par 36-36–72; 7,288 yards

December 11-13
purse, $3,100,000

	SCORES			TOTAL	MONEY (Each)
Jason Day/Cameron Tringale	55	64	65	184	$385,000
Harris English/Matt Kuchar	57	66	62	185	242,500
Keegan Bradley/Camilo Villegas	59	67	61	187	130,000
Billy Horschel/Ian Poulter	61	65	61	187	130,000
Jerry Kelly/Steve Stricker	60	68	60	188	95,000
Graeme McDowell/Gary Woodland	59	63	66	188	95,000
Charles Howell/Scott Verplank	61	64	65	190	83,750
Justin Leonard/Rory Sabbatini	60	67	63	190	83,750
Ryan Palmer/Jimmy Walker	59	68	64	191	80,000
Patrick Reed/Brandt Snedeker	61	65	66	192	77,500
Sean O'Hair/Kenny Perry	60	69	65	194	75,000
Retief Goosen/Mike Weir	60	74	67	201	72,500

PNC Father/Son Challenge

Ritz-Carlton Golf Club, Orlando, Florida
Par 36-36–72; 7,023 yards

December 13-15
purse, $1,085,000

	SCORES		TOTAL	MONEY (Won by professional)
Bernhard Langer/Jason Langer	62	59	121	$200,000
Davis Love/Dru Love	64	59	123	80,000
Vijay Singh/Qass Singh	63	61	124	53,625
Curtis Strange/Tom Strange	62	62	124	53,625
Mark O'Meara/Shaun O'Meara	64	61	125	49,000
Sandy Lyle/James Lyle	64	62	126	48,000
Dave Stockton/Ron Stockton	64	63	127	47,000
Hale Irwin/Steve Irwin	63	65	128	45,166.67
Lee Janzen/Connor Janzen	64	64	128	45,166.67
Stewart Cink/Connor Cink	63	65	128	45,166.66
Tom Lehman/Thomas Lehman	67	62	129	44,000
Larry Nelson/Josh Nelson	66	64	130	43,500
Lanny Wadkins/Tucker Wadkins	68	63	131	43,000
Sir Nick Faldo/Matthew Faldo	69	63	132	42,500
Steve Elkington/Sam Elkington	67	66	133	41,500
Johnny Miller/Andy Miller	63	70	133	41,500
Jack Nicklaus/Jack Nicklaus II	67	66	133	41,500
Raymond Floyd/Robert Floyd	65	69	134	40,500
Lee Trevino/Daniel Trevino	67	68	135	40,250
Nick Price/Greg Price	69	67	136	40,000

Web.com Tour

Pacific Rubiales Colombia Championship

Bogota Country Club, Bogota, Colombia — February 13-16
Par 35-36–71; 7,237 yards — purse, $750,000
(Final round cancelled—rain.)

	SCORES			TOTAL	MONEY
Alex Cejka	68	68	63	199	$135,000
Andrew Putnam	68	66	68	202	81,000
Carlos Ortiz	67	69	67	203	51,000
Bill Lunde	66	68	70	204	36,000
Sam Saunders	69	67	69	205	27,375
Justin Thomas	65	69	71	205	27,375
Chris Wilson	69	66	70	205	27,375
Derek Fathauer	72	64	70	206	19,500
Adam Hadwin	69	71	66	206	19,500
Whee Kim	69	70	67	206	19,500
Sebastian Pinzon	68	71	67	206	19,500
Vaughn Taylor	69	68	69	206	19,500
Peter Tomasulo	67	69	70	206	19,500
Tony Finau	69	69	69	207	12,000
Jose Garrido	70	69	68	207	12,000
Andres Gonzales	69	71	67	207	12,000
Matt Hendrix	68	70	69	207	12,000
Hugo Leon	66	74	67	207	12,000
Jonathan Randolph	66	70	71	207	12,000
Manuel Villegas	69	70	68	207	12,000
Chris Baker	72	69	67	208	7,099.69
Blayne Barber	68	73	67	208	7,099.69
Ariel Canete	70	70	68	208	7,099.69
Glen Day	66	72	70	208	7,099.69
Jeff Gove	70	69	69	208	7,099.69
Alexandre Rocha	66	72	70	208	7,099.69
Jon Curran	75	67	66	208	7,099.68
Zack Sucher	72	70	66	208	7,099.68

Chile Classic

Prince of Wales Country Club, Santiago, Chile — March 6-9
Par 36-36–72; 6,903 yards — purse, $650,000

	SCORES				TOTAL	MONEY
Adam Hadwin	67	69	67	69	272	$117,000
Alistair Presnell	70	70	65	68	273	70,200
Henrik Norlander	64	72	70	69	275	33,800
Sung Joon Park	67	72	70	66	275	33,800
Kyle Reifers	68	68	68	71	275	33,800
Bhavik Patel	67	68	72	69	276	21,775
Scott Pinckney	67	70	67	72	276	21,775
Andrew Putnam	67	71	68	70	276	21,775
Franklin Corpening	68	68	70	71	277	17,550
Mark Hubbard	69	73	67	68	277	17,550

	SCORES				TOTAL	MONEY
Jose de Jesus Rodriguez	70	67	69	71	277	17,550
Tom Hoge	69	69	74	66	278	10,589.10
Blayne Barber	70	66	74	68	278	10,589.09
Daniel Berger	71	67	73	67	278	10,589.09
Jorge Fernandez-Valdes	66	66	74	72	278	10,589.09
Andres Gonzales	69	68	70	71	278	10,589.09
Ash Hall	71	69	69	69	278	10,589.09
Fernando Mechereffe	69	72	65	72	278	10,589.09
Garth Mulroy	64	71	70	73	278	10,589.09
Darron Stiles	71	65	72	70	278	10,589.09
Justin Thomas	69	68	71	70	278	10,589.09
Martin Ureta	70	69	69	70	278	10,589.09
Albin Choi	69	70	73	67	279	5,062.91
Andres Echavarria	68	71	70	70	279	5,062.91
Tom Gillis	73	66	70	70	279	5,062.91
Hunter Haas	71	68	71	69	279	5,062.91
Richard Johnson	70	67	71	71	279	5,062.91
Troy Kelly	71	68	70	70	279	5,062.91
Brett Lederer	67	69	74	69	279	5,062.91
Timothy O'Neal	71	70	69	69	279	5,062.91
Jonathan Randolph	72	67	71	69	279	5,062.91
Byron Smith	65	66	75	73	279	5,062.91
Sebastian Vazquez	64	70	72	73	279	5,062.90

Brasil Champions

Sao Paulo Golf Club, Sao Paulo, Brazil — March 13-16
Par 35-36–71; 6,574 yards — purse, $800,000

	SCORES				TOTAL	MONEY
Jon Curran	61	64	65	69	259	$144,000
Alex Cejka	65	66	63	69	263	86,400
Ash Hall	65	64	65	70	264	54,400
Manuel Villegas	67	66	67	66	266	38,400
Oscar Fraustro	67	64	67	69	267	30,400
Casey Wittenberg	66	71	65	65	267	30,400
Daniel Berger	64	64	71	69	268	25,800
Tom Gillis	65	66	68	69	268	25,800
Jonathan Fricke	69	64	66	70	269	21,600
Cameron Percy	68	68	69	64	269	21,600
Andrew Putnam	69	68	66	66	269	21,600
Shane Bertsch	66	68	69	67	270	16,200
Andres Echavarria	67	63	70	70	270	16,200
Mathew Goggin	67	67	66	70	270	16,200
Brad Schneider	66	63	71	70	270	16,200
Steve Allan	69	65	70	67	271	12,000
Richard Johnson	67	69	68	67	271	12,000
Philip Pettitt, Jr.	66	68	65	72	271	12,000
Jose de Jesus Rodriguez	68	63	69	71	271	12,000
Sam Saunders	72	65	65	69	271	12,000
Lucas Lee	69	68	67	68	272	9,600
Gavin Coles	70	68	67	68	273	8,000
Timothy O'Neal	65	71	70	67	273	8,000
Carlos Ortiz	72	64	68	69	273	8,000
Dawie van der Walt	72	64	69	68	273	8,000

Panama Claro Championship

Panama Golf Club, Panama City, Panama — March 20-23
Par 35-35–70; 7,102 yards — purse, $625,000

	SCORES				TOTAL	MONEY
Carlos Ortiz	70	68	66	64	268	$112,500
Jason Gore	70	67	69	66	272	67,500
Daniel Berger	68	68	70	67	273	32,500
Derek Fathauer	72	69	65	67	273	32,500
Aron Price	66	68	69	70	273	32,500
Nick Taylor	69	69	69	67	274	21,718.75
Roland Thatcher	73	64	67	70	274	21,718.75
Steve Allan	71	66	67	71	275	18,125
Mark Hubbard	72	63	70	70	275	18,125
Tim Petrovic	71	67	68	69	275	18,125
Alex Cejka	68	69	70	69	276	13,750
Fabian Gomez	72	68	70	66	276	13,750
Manuel Villegas	69	67	71	69	276	13,750
Steve Wheatcroft	68	70	71	67	276	13,750
Jon Curran	67	68	70	72	277	10,000
James Nitties	70	71	66	70	277	10,000
Andrew Putnam	69	68	68	72	277	10,000
Jonathan Randolph	69	66	71	71	277	10,000
Justin Thomas	70	67	71	69	277	10,000
Steven Alker	69	69	72	68	278	7,025
Chris Epperson	71	67	72	68	278	7,025
Colt Knost	69	71	68	70	278	7,025
Byron Smith	75	66	68	69	278	7,025
Will Wilcox	72	67	71	68	278	7,025
Carlos Franco	72	67	72	68	279	4,966.25
Andres Gonzales	69	68	72	70	279	4,966.25
Philip Pettitt, Jr.	72	67	69	71	279	4,966.25
Shawn Stefani	69	70	73	67	279	4,966.25
T.J. Vogel	72	70	67	70	279	4,966.25

Chitimacha Louisiana Open

Le Triomphe Country Club, Broussard, Louisiana — March 27-30
Par 36-35–71; 7,004 yards — purse, $550,000

	SCORES				TOTAL	MONEY
Kris Blanks	71	66	71	62	270	$99,000
Brett Stegmaier	71	66	65	68	270	59,400
(Blanks defeated Stegmaier on third playoff hole.)						
Jonathan Randolph	66	65	73	67	271	31,900
Kyle Reifers	65	70	66	70	271	31,900
Aaron Goldberg	70	67	67	68	272	18,012.50
Garth Mulroy	70	66	69	67	272	18,012.50
Steve Saunders	72	66	65	69	272	18,012.50
Zack Sucher	68	67	69	68	272	18,012.50
Justin Thomas	69	66	68	69	272	18,012.50
Sebastian Vazquez	69	65	69	69	272	18,012.50
Blayne Barber	69	68	65	71	273	12,650
Ryan Blaum	65	68	71	69	273	12,650
Fabian Gomez	66	67	70	70	273	12,650
Bronson Burgoon	69	65	73	67	274	9,900
Jeff Curl	66	70	69	69	274	9,900
Andres Gonzales	69	68	68	69	274	9,900
Matt Boyd	68	71	65	71	275	6,957.50

	SCORES				TOTAL	MONEY
Jon Curran	71	64	71	69	275	6,957.50
Zack Fischer	68	67	71	69	275	6,957.50
Jason Gore	68	67	72	68	275	6,957.50
Carlos Ortiz	70	66	70	69	275	6,957.50
Roland Thatcher	73	63	70	69	275	6,957.50
Harold Varner	69	68	69	69	275	6,957.50
Brett Wetterich	69	70	66	70	275	6,957.50
Matt Davidson	68	69	72	67	276	4,182.36
Tony Finau	68	67	70	71	276	4,182.36
Hunter Haas	68	68	71	69	276	4,182.36
Ryuji Imada	72	67	69	68	276	4,182.36
Nick O'Hern	69	69	69	69	276	4,182.36
Andres Echavarria	67	67	69	73	276	4,182.35
T.J. Vogel	68	67	69	72	276	4,182.35

El Bosque Mexico Championship

El Bosque Golf Club, Leon, Guanajuato, Mexico — April 10-13
Par 36-36–72; 7,701 yards — purse, $700,000

	SCORES				TOTAL	MONEY
Carlos Ortiz	74	67	66	68	275	$126,000
Justin Thomas	66	70	72	69	277	75,600
Daniel Berger	71	67	74	69	281	29,925
Jason Gore	72	69	67	73	281	29,925
Nathan Green	67	70	70	74	281	29,925
Adam Hadwin	73	71	69	68	281	29,925
Jonathan Randolph	69	70	69	73	281	29,925
Nathan Tyler	71	68	72	70	281	29,925
D.J. Brigman	73	71	65	73	282	18,200
Mark Hubbard	72	71	72	67	282	18,200
Cameron Percy	70	72	69	71	282	18,200
Brad Schneider	66	74	69	73	282	18,200
Roberto Diaz	72	73	68	70	283	12,366.67
Oscar Fraustro	74	68	73	68	283	12,366.67
Hunter Haas	72	69	71	71	283	12,366.67
Alex Prugh	74	70	70	69	283	12,366.67
Colt Knost	71	70	71	71	283	12,366.66
Peter Tomasulo	70	69	73	71	283	12,366.66
Steven Alker	75	68	71	70	284	8,484
Ryan Armour	70	71	74	69	284	8,484
Kelly Kraft	71	71	69	73	284	8,484
Byron Smith	69	75	71	69	284	8,484
Casey Wittenberg	69	73	75	67	284	8,484
Ryan Blaum	70	71	72	72	285	5,898.20
Tony Finau	76	69	73	67	285	5,898.20
Scott Harrington	73	71	72	69	285	5,898.20
Andrew Putnam	72	72	75	66	285	5,898.20
Brett Stegmaier	74	70	69	72	285	5,898.20

WNB Golf Classic

Midland Country Club, Midland, Texas — April 24-27
Par 36-36–72; 7,380 yards — purse, $600,000
(Final round cancelled—wind.)

	SCORES			TOTAL	MONEY
Andrew Putnam	66	66	64	196	$108,000
Richard Johnson	68	69	66	203	52,800
Rod Pampling	66	69	68	203	52,800
Tom Gillis	69	64	71	204	26,400
Mathew Goggin	69	68	67	204	26,400
Jin Park	74	67	64	205	20,100
Sam Saunders	70	68	67	205	20,100
Harold Varner	68	69	68	205	20,100
Matt Fast	73	68	65	206	14,400
Derek Fathauer	71	67	68	206	14,400
Oscar Fraustro	68	69	69	206	14,400
Jeff Klauk	69	70	67	206	14,400
Trevor Murphy	66	71	69	206	14,400
Carlos Ortiz	67	68	71	206	14,400
Roberto Diaz	71	68	68	207	10,200
Andy Pope	73	67	67	207	10,200
Brett Wetterich	72	70	65	207	10,200
Camilo Benedetti	74	69	65	208	8,100
Ryan Blaum	68	72	68	208	8,100
Ryuji Imada	70	70	68	208	8,100
Scott Pinckney	71	68	69	208	8,100
Blayne Barber	74	68	67	209	5,188.67
Andres Gonzales	71	71	67	209	5,188.67
Fernando Mechereffe	68	74	67	209	5,188.67
Henrik Norlander	70	71	68	209	5,188.67
Scott Parel	72	69	68	209	5,188.67
Kyle Reifers	73	68	68	209	5,188.67
Josh Broadaway	70	67	72	209	5,188.66
Albin Choi	68	70	71	209	5,188.66
Hunter Haas	68	70	71	209	5,188.66

South Georgia Classic

Kinderlou Forest Golf Club, Valdosta, Georgia — May 1-4
Par 36-36–72; 7,781 yards — purse, $650,000

	SCORES				TOTAL	MONEY
Blayne Barber	68	72	66	67	273	$117,000
Alex Prugh	70	68	70	67	275	70,200
Carlos Ortiz	67	65	72	72	276	44,200
Ryan Armour	74	66	67	70	277	26,866.67
Greg Owen	72	69	67	69	277	26,866.67
Rob Oppenheim	69	66	70	72	277	26,866.66
Max Homa	67	68	70	73	278	21,775
Trevor Murphy	73	69	71	66	279	18,850
Nathan Tyler	71	68	72	68	279	18,850
Adam Webb	70	70	65	74	279	18,850
Jason Allred	72	69	67	72	280	14,950
Ryan Blaum	72	68	72	68	280	14,950
Zack Sucher	71	70	70	69	280	14,950
Daniel Berger	70	68	73	70	281	11,050
Derek Fathauer	70	73	67	71	281	11,050
Mike Miller	68	71	70	72	281	11,050

	SCORES				TOTAL	MONEY
Andrew Putnam	68	69	72	72	281	11,050
Roger Sloan	70	72	69	70	281	11,050
Andres Gonzales	73	71	69	69	282	7,095.57
Bill Lunde	72	69	74	67	282	7,095.57
Kent Bulle	70	70	70	72	282	7,095.56
Tony Finau	71	72	69	70	282	7,095.56
Jimmy Gunn	70	68	73	71	282	7,095.56
Cameron Percy	72	68	71	71	282	7,095.56
Kyle Reifers	72	69	70	71	282	7,095.56
Roland Thatcher	70	70	72	70	282	7,095.56

BMW Charity Pro-Am

Thornblade Club: Par 35-36–71; 7,024 yards
Green Valley Country Club: Par 36-36–72; 7,030 yards
Reserve at Lake Keowee: Par 36-36–72; 7,112 yards
Greer, South Carolina

May 15-18
purse, $650,000

	SCORES				TOTAL	MONEY
Max Homa	68	65	70	63	266	$117,000
Jonathan Randolph	65	70	69	63	267	70,200
Blayne Barber	63	70	68	67	268	33,800
Jon Curran	68	68	66	66	268	33,800
Kyle Reifers	68	64	70	66	268	33,800
Zack Sucher	67	70	67	65	269	23,400
Gavin Coles	68	66	69	67	270	20,962.50
Matt Davidson	69	65	67	69	270	20,962.50
Dominic Bozzelli	67	69	70	65	271	16,900
Mark Hubbard	66	67	72	66	271	16,900
Justin Lower	69	68	70	64	271	16,900
David Skinns	69	66	68	68	271	16,900
Ryan Blaum	67	66	68	71	272	11,830
Kelly Kraft	65	67	72	68	272	11,830
Cliff Kresge	65	68	71	68	272	11,830
Peter Tomasulo	71	63	72	66	272	11,830
Harold Varner	68	69	69	66	272	11,830
Bronson Burgoon	68	69	68	68	273	8,476
Matt Fast	70	68	68	67	273	8,476
Tony Finau	69	68	69	67	273	8,476
Jimmy Gunn	68	68	68	69	273	8,476
Roger Sloan	68	69	68	68	273	8,476
Franklin Corpening	68	69	70	67	274	6,033.63
Nick Rousey	71	71	65	67	274	6,033.63
Josh Broadaway	67	70	70	67	274	6,033.62
Dawie van der Walt	64	72	69	69	274	6,033.62

Rex Hospital Open

TPC Wakefield Plantation, Raleigh, North Carolina
Par 36-35–71; 7,257 yards

May 22-25
purse, $625,000

	SCORES				TOTAL	MONEY
Byron Smith	70	69	63	66	268	$112,500
Scott Gardiner	69	66	68	69	272	55,000
Harold Varner	67	65	70	70	272	55,000
Brad Fritsch	72	65	70	66	273	25,833.34
Roberto Diaz	68	68	67	70	273	25,833.33

	SCORES				TOTAL	MONEY
Tony Finau	67	71	68	67	273	25,833.33
Ryan Blaum	67	69	69	69	274	20,937.50
Andres Gonzales	70	66	72	67	275	18,125
Hunter Haas	67	68	67	73	275	18,125
Chris Wilson	68	68	72	67	275	18,125
Max Homa	65	68	74	69	276	14,375
Roland Thatcher	68	69	71	68	276	14,375
Justin Thomas	69	71	68	68	276	14,375
Derek Fathauer	71	69	69	68	277	9,687.50
Hugo Leon	72	69	68	68	277	9,687.50
Jin Park	70	69	69	69	277	9,687.50
Alex Prugh	69	70	68	70	277	9,687.50
Carlos Sainz, Jr.	69	69	69	70	277	9,687.50
Peter Tomasulo	68	67	73	69	277	9,687.50
Nathan Tyler	69	68	68	72	277	9,687.50
Steve Wheatcroft	66	75	69	67	277	9,687.50
Camilo Benedetti	70	65	73	70	278	5,690.18
Kris Blanks	68	72	68	70	278	5,690.18
Luke List	69	69	71	69	278	5,690.18
Scott Pinckney	68	69	70	71	278	5,690.18
Ryan Spears	69	67	75	67	278	5,690.18
Manuel Villegas	69	71	69	69	278	5,690.18
Jason Allred	70	68	69	71	278	5,690.17

Cleveland Open

Lakewood Country Club, Westlake, Ohio — June 5-8
Par 36-35–71; 7,022 yards — purse, $600,000

	SCORES				TOTAL	MONEY
Steven Alker	70	70	65	65	270	$108,000
Dawie van der Walt	70	69	65	66	270	64,800
(Alker defeated van der Walt on 11th playoff hole.)						
Si Woo Kim	66	69	71	65	271	40,800
Ryan Armour	69	68	66	70	273	23,625
Jeff Curl	66	67	70	70	273	23,625
Jon Curran	71	66	67	69	273	23,625
Jason Gore	69	68	66	70	273	23,625
Adam Hadwin	72	69	66	67	274	18,000
Byron Smith	71	69	66	68	274	18,000
Mark Hubbard	72	64	70	69	275	14,400
Michael Kim	69	68	69	69	275	14,400
Whee Kim	68	66	68	73	275	14,400
Chase Wright	70	71	66	68	275	14,400
Andres Echavarria	72	68	68	68	276	10,500
Scott Harrington	75	66	66	69	276	10,500
Roland Thatcher	69	72	67	68	276	10,500
Aaron Watkins	69	66	70	71	276	10,500
Daniel Berger	70	70	69	68	277	6,084.47
Max Homa	64	76	69	68	277	6,084.47
Blayne Barber	69	69	70	69	277	6,084.46
Camilo Benedetti	69	68	71	69	277	6,084.46
Derek Fathauer	73	66	70	68	277	6,084.46
Mathew Goggin	71	62	69	75	277	6,084.46
Sung Kang	68	71	73	65	277	6,084.46
Kevin Kim	69	70	69	69	277	6,084.46
Scott Parel	69	68	69	71	277	6,084.46
Sung Joon Park	70	69	68	70	277	6,084.46
Alexandre Rocha	73	68	66	70	277	6,084.46
Ryan Sullivan	68	73	68	68	277	6,084.46
Harold Varner	70	67	69	71	277	6,084.46

Air Capital Classic

Crestview Country Club, Wichita, Kansas — June 19-22
Par 35-35–70; 6,926 yards — purse, $600,000

	SCORES				TOTAL	MONEY
Sebastian Cappelen	66	65	65	66	262	$108,000
Matt Weibring	68	65	66	64	263	64,800
Jeff Gove	68	64	68	66	266	34,800
Cameron Percy	67	67	70	62	266	34,800
Ryan Armour	69	68	65	65	267	21,075
Paul Claxton	65	68	67	67	267	21,075
Andres Gonzales	65	67	66	69	267	21,075
Sung Joon Park	69	66	64	68	267	21,075
*Ollie Schniederjans	64	71	65	67	267	
Blayne Barber	65	67	67	69	268	16,200
Rod Pampling	68	68	65	67	268	16,200
Sam Saunders	65	66	70	67	268	16,200
Rob Oppenheim	69	63	67	70	269	13,800
Matt Fast	66	68	68	68	270	11,600
Tom Hoge	67	67	69	67	270	11,600
Aaron Watkins	63	66	71	70	270	11,600
Shane Bertsch	67	66	70	68	271	9,000
Josh Broadaway	67	68	67	69	271	9,000
Oscar Fraustro	70	66	66	69	271	9,000
Vince India	70	68	69	64	271	9,000
Zack Sucher	72	63	70	66	271	9,000
Derek Fathauer	67	66	70	70	273	6,033
Tom Gillis	66	65	71	71	273	6,033
Hunter Haas	69	69	66	69	273	6,033
Sung Kang	71	67	68	67	273	6,033
Andrew Putnam	67	69	70	67	273	6,033
Justin Thomas	69	66	69	69	273	6,033

United Leasing Championship

Victoria National Golf Club, Newburgh, Indiana — June 26-29
Par 36-36–72; 7,242 yards — purse, $600,000

	SCORES				TOTAL	MONEY
Greg Owen	73	67	72	67	279	$108,000
Ryan Armour	70	67	75	68	280	52,800
Mark Hubbard	69	68	68	75	280	52,800
Tony Finau	71	64	72	74	281	23,625
Fabian Gomez	69	70	72	70	281	23,625
Justin Thomas	70	71	69	71	281	23,625
Matt Weibring	74	67	68	72	281	23,625
Andres Echavarria	68	70	70	74	282	18,000
Henrik Norlander	69	75	68	70	282	18,000
Garrett Osborn	71	74	69	69	283	14,400
Chris Smith	70	68	71	74	283	14,400
Zack Sucher	70	70	72	71	283	14,400
Chase Wright	73	70	70	70	283	14,400
Guy Boros	70	71	71	72	284	11,400
Paul Claxton	76	67	66	76	285	9,900
Scott Harrington	76	64	72	73	285	9,900
Andy Pope	69	72	71	73	285	9,900
David Skinns	73	68	74	70	285	9,900
Albin Choi	74	68	73	71	286	6,348.67
Glen Day	75	69	69	73	286	6,348.67

	SCORES				TOTAL	MONEY
Roberto Diaz	66	75	72	73	286	6,348.67
Adam Hadwin	68	71	73	74	286	6,348.67
Doug LaBelle	74	71	72	69	286	6,348.67
Roger Sloan	73	72	69	72	286	6,348.67
Derek Fathauer	74	71	73	68	286	6,348.66
Alexandre Rocha	68	69	73	76	286	6,348.66
Peter Tomasulo	73	70	67	76	286	6,348.66

Nova Scotia Open

Ashburn Golf Club, New Course, Halifax, Canada — July 3-6
Par 35-36–71; 6,906 yards — purse, $650,000

	SCORES				TOTAL	MONEY
Roger Sloan	67	65	71	70	273	$117,000
Derek Fathauer	70	66	71	66	273	70,200
(Sloan defeated Fathauer on first playoff hole.)						
John Mallinger	70	66	67	73	276	44,200
Kyle Thompson	68	72	68	69	277	26,867
Zack Fischer	74	66	70	67	277	26,867
Henrik Norlander	66	70	72	69	277	26,867
Zac Blair	72	69	67	70	278	18,915
Adam Hadwin	66	73	74	65	278	18,915
Alex Cejka	71	68	68	71	278	18,915
Aaron Goldberg	65	72	68	73	278	18,915
Jose de Jesus Rodriguez	63	69	74	72	278	18,915
Ryan Spears	69	71	71	68	279	13,163
Shane Bertsch	69	71	70	69	279	13,163
Nick Rousey	70	69	71	69	279	13,163
David Skinns	65	70	72	72	279	13,163
Scott Pinckney	71	69	70	70	280	9,119
Tony Finau	70	69	68	73	280	9,119
Kyle Stough	69	73	69	69	280	9,119
Vaughn Taylor	67	70	72	71	280	9,119
Garrett Osborn	67	69	75	69	280	9,119
Peter Tomasulo	68	68	73	71	280	9,119
Zack Sucher	69	66	73	72	280	9,119
Andy Pope	72	69	73	67	281	5,173
Byron Smith	74	66	67	74	281	5,173
Cory Renfrew	73	68	71	69	281	5,173
Chris Smith	73	68	68	72	281	5,173
Manuel Villegas	69	72	70	70	281	5,173
Josh Anderson	67	71	70	73	281	5,173
Justin Shin	69	69	71	72	281	5,173
James Sacheck	65	73	71	72	281	5,173
Ryan Armour	71	71	70	69	281	5,173
Jeff Klauk	71	71	72	67	281	5,173

Utah Championship

Willow Creek Country Club, Sandy, Utah — July 10-13
Par 35-36–71; 6,952 yards — purse, $625,000

	SCORES				TOTAL	MONEY
Andres Gonzales	62	67	65	69	263	$112,500
Adam Crawford	71	61	69	66	267	46,667
Sung-Hoon Kang	67	65	67	68	267	46,667
Travis Bertoni	68	63	68	68	267	46,667

	SCORES				TOTAL	MONEY
Tony Finau	65	67	68	68	268	25,000
Bill Lunde	67	67	72	63	269	22,500
Chase Wright	68	68	67	67	270	18,828
Brett Stegmaier	69	67	66	68	270	18,828
Steve Allan	69	65	67	69	270	18,828
Jeff Curl	69	67	63	71	270	18,828
Scott Piercy	68	69	66	68	271	13,750
Kelly Kraft	67	68	66	70	271	13,750
Zac Blair	68	67	66	70	271	13,750
Aaron Goldberg	67	67	64	73	271	13,750
Max Homa	69	68	69	66	272	9,688
Nicholas Lindheim	67	68	68	69	272	9,688
Vince India	66	70	67	69	272	9,688
Jason Gore	66	69	67	70	272	9,688
Jonathan Fricke	71	66	64	71	272	9,688
Jose Toledo	66	66	68	72	272	9,688
Vaughn Taylor	69	66	70	68	273	6,500
Fabian Gomez	70	67	68	68	273	6,500
Andrew Putnam	73	64	68	68	273	6,500
Steve Wheatcroft	65	66	72	70	273	6,500
John Mallinger	69	66	67	71	273	6,500

Albertsons Boise Open

Hillcrest Country Club, Boise, Idaho — July 17-20
Par 36-35–71; 6,807 yards — purse, $800,000

	SCORES				TOTAL	MONEY
Steve Wheatcroft	64	66	65	65	260	$144,000
Steven Alker	62	66	65	67	260	86,400
(Wheatcroft defeated Alker on first playoff hole.)						
Justin Thomas	68	65	64	65	262	54,400
Andrew Putnam	66	68	65	66	265	33,066.67
Chase Wright	64	66	69	66	265	33,066.67
Zack Sucher	60	67	68	70	265	33,066.66
Matt Davidson	65	70	67	65	267	24,933.34
Daniel Berger	69	66	65	67	267	24,933.33
Bill Lunde	66	61	70	70	267	24,933.33
Joey Garber	69	65	67	67	268	18,400
Fabian Gomez	65	70	67	66	268	18,400
Andres Gonzales	67	66	69	66	268	18,400
Fernando Mechereffe	71	64	66	67	268	18,400
Garth Mulroy	66	69	64	69	268	18,400
Jeff Curl	65	68	67	69	269	12,800
Jamie Lovemark	69	66	66	68	269	12,800
James Nitties	64	72	66	67	269	12,800
Nick Taylor	63	68	70	68	269	12,800
Matt Weibring	68	64	69	68	269	12,800
Ryan Blaum	66	65	69	70	270	8,992
Jason Gore	67	65	67	71	270	8,992
Luke List	69	65	68	68	270	8,992
Timothy O'Neal	64	72	66	68	270	8,992
Steve Saunders	68	64	70	68	270	8,992
Steve Allan	68	68	67	68	271	6,083.43
Blayne Barber	67	68	67	69	271	6,083.43
Zac Blair	65	67	73	66	271	6,083.43
Jeff Gove	66	68	72	65	271	6,083.43
Michael Kim	67	67	69	68	271	6,083.43
Kelly Kraft	67	67	68	69	271	6,083.43
Tom Gillis	65	68	67	71	271	6,083.42

Midwest Classic

Nicklaus Golf Club at LionsGate, Overland Park, Kansas — July 24-27
Par 35-36–71; 7,237 yards — purse, $600,000

	SCORES				TOTAL	MONEY
Zack Sucher	66	63	64	72	265	$108,000
Aaron Watkins	67	65	64	72	268	64,800
Bill Lunde	69	65	66	69	269	40,800
Jonathan Randolph	71	67	65	67	270	28,800
Derek Fathauer	66	70	66	69	271	24,000
Andres Gonzales	69	68	67	68	272	18,780
Jason Gore	68	63	68	73	272	18,780
Tom Hoge	70	71	60	71	272	18,780
Aron Price	68	70	63	71	272	18,780
Kyle Reifers	68	67	68	69	272	18,780
Steve Allan	68	67	73	65	273	12,300
Sebastian Cappelen	65	74	66	68	273	12,300
Zack Fischer	69	67	70	67	273	12,300
Jarrod Lyle	67	69	68	69	273	12,300
Rod Pampling	71	66	64	72	273	12,300
Nick Rousey	69	69	65	70	273	12,300
Shane Bertsch	65	70	66	73	274	8,400
Mark Hubbard	65	71	67	71	274	8,400
Chris Smith	67	69	67	71	274	8,400
D.J. Trahan	67	72	63	72	274	8,400
Harold Varner	70	67	65	72	274	8,400
Darron Stiles	68	71	63	73	275	6,480
Dawie van der Walt	69	71	68	67	275	6,480
Steven Alker	68	68	67	73	276	4,516.80
Adam Crawford	70	70	67	69	276	4,516.80
Brandt Jobe	69	70	70	67	276	4,516.80
Steve LeBrun	70	66	69	71	276	4,516.80
Luke List	70	66	69	71	276	4,516.80
Martin Piller	67	69	66	74	276	4,516.80
Andrew Putnam	69	69	69	69	276	4,516.80
James Sacheck	72	66	65	73	276	4,516.80
Kyle Thompson	71	68	68	69	276	4,516.80
Nathan Tyler	68	71	70	67	276	4,516.80

Stonebrae Classic

TPC Stonebrae, Hayward, California — July 31-August 3
Par 35-35–70; 7,024 yards — purse, $600,000

	SCORES				TOTAL	MONEY
Tony Finau	67	62	63	66	258	$108,000
Daniel Berger	66	65	62	68	261	44,800
Fabian Gomez	66	60	67	68	261	44,800
Zack Sucher	65	68	62	66	261	44,800
Blayne Barber	63	64	68	67	262	21,900
Ashley Hall	65	65	65	67	262	21,900
Colt Knost	65	65	64	68	262	21,900
Max Homa	68	66	63	66	263	18,000
Nicholas Lindheim	63	67	63	70	263	18,000
Tom Hoge	67	66	66	65	264	16,200
Ryan Blaum	63	70	67	65	265	13,800
Bill Lunde	68	66	64	67	265	13,800
Gregor Main	68	65	67	65	265	13,800
Travis Bertoni	65	65	70	66	266	10,500

	SCORES				TOTAL	MONEY
Josh Broadaway	64	67	67	68	266	10,500
Michael Kim	67	64	68	67	266	10,500
Aaron Watkins	69	64	65	68	266	10,500
Bronson Burgoon	66	64	66	71	267	8,400
Michael Hebert	72	65	63	67	267	8,400
Kelly Kraft	63	70	65	69	267	8,400
Cam Burke	65	66	67	70	268	6,480
Justin Shin	68	64	66	70	268	6,480
Vaughn Taylor	68	67	64	69	268	6,480
Peter Tomasulo	67	66	68	67	268	6,480
Hugo Leon	64	68	66	71	269	5,006
Andrew Putnam	65	70	68	66	269	5,006
Kyle Thompson	69	67	67	66	269	5,006

Price Cutter Charity Championship

Highland Springs Country Club, Springfield, Missouri — August 7-10
Par 36-36–72; 7,115 yards — purse, $675,000

	SCORES				TOTAL	MONEY
Cameron Percy	64	68	68	67	267	$121,500
Zac Blair	66	67	69	66	268	44,550
Brandt Jobe	69	68	66	65	268	44,550
Michael Kim	65	66	70	67	268	44,550
Carlos Sainz, Jr.	70	66	65	67	268	44,550
Sebastian Cappelen	70	63	67	69	269	22,612.50
Ryan Spears	69	70	63	67	269	22,612.50
Justin Thomas	72	67	66	64	269	22,612.50
Dominic Bozzelli	68	68	65	69	270	18,900
Nick Taylor	67	70	66	67	270	18,900
Daniel Berger	70	67	65	69	271	13,837.50
Tony Finau	69	69	69	64	271	13,837.50
Mark Hubbard	69	67	66	69	271	13,837.50
J.J. Killeen	67	70	65	69	271	13,837.50
Scott Pinckney	67	65	69	70	271	13,837.50
Chris Wilson	68	66	69	68	271	13,837.50
Glen Day	71	67	65	69	272	8,832.86
Whee Kim	68	66	68	70	272	8,832.86
Aron Price	70	68	67	67	272	8,832.86
Alexandre Rocha	68	64	73	67	272	8,832.86
Brett Stegmaier	68	67	68	69	272	8,832.86
Martin Piller	65	67	68	72	272	8,832.85
Cory Whitsett	67	68	66	71	272	8,832.85
Mathew Goggin	71	67	66	69	273	6,210
Rod Pampling	70	66	67	70	273	6,210

News Sentinel Open

Fox Den Country Club, Knoxville, Tennessee — August 14-17
Par 35-36–71; 7,071 yards — purse, $550,000

	SCORES				TOTAL	MONEY
Martin Piller	65	67	67	63	262	$99,000
Bronson Burgoon	70	68	64	62	264	59,400
Darron Stiles	72	65	65	64	266	37,400
Ryan Armour	69	70	63	65	267	26,400
Vaughn Taylor	68	68	68	64	268	22,000

	SCORES				TOTAL	MONEY
Steve Allan	70	67	65	67	269	18,425
Josh Broadaway	68	68	65	68	269	18,425
Aaron Watkins	70	66	65	68	269	18,425
Jason Gore	70	70	64	66	270	15,400
J.J. Killeen	67	69	64	70	270	15,400
Fabian Gomez	67	66	67	71	271	12,650
Rob Oppenheim	68	70	66	67	271	12,650
D.J. Trahan	70	66	69	66	271	12,650
Zac Blair	72	65	68	67	272	9,900
Bill Lunde	67	67	71	67	272	9,900
Casey Wittenberg	70	69	65	68	272	9,900
Camilo Benedetti	67	66	71	69	273	7,700
Adam Crawford	67	72	69	65	273	7,700
Tyler Duncan	72	67	69	65	273	7,700
Derek Fathauer	71	66	65	71	273	7,700
Billy Mayfair	70	67	67	69	273	7,700
Jon Curran	70	67	69	68	274	4,876.44
Sung Kang	70	70	66	68	274	4,876.44
Garrett Osborn	69	70	66	69	274	4,876.44
Greg Owen	72	66	70	66	274	4,876.44
Aron Price	70	67	68	69	274	4,876.44
Ryan Spears	66	68	70	70	274	4,876.44
Brett Stegmaier	68	71	64	71	274	4,876.43
Cory Whitsett	66	72	64	72	274	4,876.43

WinCo Foods Portland Open

Witch Hollow at Pumpkin Ridge, North Plains, Oregon — August 21-24
Par 36-35–71; 7,017 yards — purse, $800,000

	SCORES				TOTAL	MONEY
Carlos Ortiz	66	63	70	71	270	$144,000
Jason Gore	67	68	70	66	271	70,400
Adam Hadwin	73	65	63	70	271	70,400
Colt Knost	69	71	63	70	273	38,400
Steven Alker	69	70	65	70	274	28,100
Blayne Barber	67	69	70	68	274	28,100
James Nitties	66	67	70	71	274	28,100
Scott Pinckney	67	68	68	71	274	28,100
Travis Bertoni	70	69	68	68	275	20,000
Nicholas Lindheim	66	64	76	69	275	20,000
Gregor Main	66	70	69	70	275	20,000
Aaron Watkins	69	71	67	68	275	20,000
Chris Wilson	72	65	68	70	275	20,000
Alex Cejka	70	71	68	67	276	12,800
Fabian Gomez	70	70	65	71	276	12,800
Matt Hendrix	68	67	71	70	276	12,800
Mark Hubbard	67	65	70	74	276	12,800
Jonathan Randolph	68	72	64	72	276	12,800
Darron Stiles	69	72	64	71	276	12,800
Roland Thatcher	69	68	70	69	276	12,800
Michael Kim	65	71	70	71	277	8,320
Rob Oppenheim	67	68	68	74	277	8,320
Andy Pope	68	70	68	71	277	8,320
Alex Prugh	69	68	71	69	277	8,320
Kyle Reifers	70	69	64	74	277	8,320

Web.com Tour Finals

Hotel Fitness Championship

Sycamore Hills Golf Club, Fort Wayne, Indiana — August 28-31
Par 36-36–72; 7,318 yards — purse, $1,000,000

	SCORES				TOTAL	MONEY
Bud Cauley	66	70	67	65	268	$180,000
Colt Knost	67	67	67	68	269	108,000
Greg Owen	67	67	68	70	272	68,000
David Lingmerth	67	72	71	64	274	41,333.34
Tom Gillis	69	69	70	66	274	41,333.33
Sam Saunders	66	66	70	72	274	41,333.33
Dicky Pride	66	69	71	69	275	32,250
Tyrone van Aswegen	68	67	69	71	275	32,250
Derek Fathauer	66	68	72	70	276	27,000
Nick Taylor	71	68	71	66	276	27,000
Matt Weibring	70	71	71	64	276	27,000
James Driscoll	74	68	68	67	277	19,600
Scott Gardiner	69	70	68	70	277	19,600
John Peterson	70	69	64	74	277	19,600
Martin Piller	68	67	72	70	277	19,600
Andrew Putnam	70	73	67	67	277	19,600
Chad Campbell	69	69	67	73	278	15,500
Kevin Tway	71	64	72	71	278	15,500
Daniel Berger	72	71	66	70	279	11,700
Tony Finau	66	73	70	70	279	11,700
Rod Pampling	71	70	71	67	279	11,700
Carlos Sainz, Jr.	67	71	69	72	279	11,700
Roland Thatcher	67	73	68	71	279	11,700
Will Wilcox	69	73	69	68	279	11,700

Chiquita Classic

River Run Country Club, Davidson, North Carolina — September 4-7
Par 36-36–72; 7,320 yards — purse, $1,000,000

	SCORES				TOTAL	MONEY
Adam Hadwin	63	72	67	68	270	$180,000
John Peterson	65	70	68	69	272	108,000
Tom Hoge	73	63	69	68	273	68,000
Oscar Fraustro	67	71	71	66	275	39,375
Jim Herman	72	67	69	67	275	39,375
Scott Pinckney	66	68	70	71	275	39,375
Kyle Reifers	67	68	70	70	275	39,375
Greg Chalmers	69	65	67	75	276	30,000
Colt Knost	67	70	69	70	276	30,000
Roberto Castro	72	67	67	71	277	26,000
Hudson Swafford	66	73	68	70	277	26,000
Eric Axley	69	74	68	67	278	20,250
Spencer Levin	72	65	69	72	278	20,250
Carlos Sainz, Jr.	70	72	64	72	278	20,250
Will Wilcox	71	70	67	70	278	20,250
Richard Johnson	69	69	70	71	279	13,133.34
Roland Thatcher	70	67	71	71	279	13,133.34
Peter Tomasulo	72	71	67	69	279	13,133.34
Derek Fathauer	66	66	75	72	279	13,133.33

	SCORES				TOTAL	MONEY
James Nitties	71	66	68	74	279	13,133.33
Aron Price	72	66	69	72	279	13,133.33
Alex Prugh	72	67	68	72	279	13,133.33
Sam Saunders	71	66	69	73	279	13,133.33
Heath Slocum	72	69	64	74	279	13,133.33
Steven Alker	70	72	73	65	280	8,565
Chase Wright	71	72	66	71	280	8,565

Nationwide Children's Hospital Championship

The OSU Golf Club, Scarlet Course, Columbus, Ohio — September 11-14
Par 36-35–71; 7,455 yards — purse, $1,000,000

	SCORES				TOTAL	MONEY
Justin Thomas	67	69	72	70	278	$180,000
Richard Sterne	72	69	67	70	278	108,000
(Thomas defeated Sterne on first playoff hole.)						
Whee Kim	71	72	67	69	279	58,000
Sean O'Hair	68	71	73	67	279	58,000
J.J. Henry	74	70	69	67	280	40,000
Blayne Barber	65	74	70	72	281	34,750
Tony Finau	66	72	72	71	281	34,750
Derek Fathauer	63	69	76	74	282	30,000
Patrick Rodgers	70	70	73	69	282	30,000
Adam Hadwin	71	72	70	70	283	26,000
Vaughn Taylor	66	69	74	74	283	26,000
Tag Ridings	67	73	74	70	284	22,000
Sam Saunders	70	70	76	68	284	22,000
Sebastian Cappelen	71	71	71	72	285	15,500
Tom Gillis	70	70	77	68	285	15,500
Jason Gore	70	73	73	69	285	15,500
Jim Herman	71	71	70	73	285	15,500
David Lingmerth	71	72	72	70	285	15,500
Andrew Loupe	64	75	74	72	285	15,500
Sung Joon Park	69	73	70	73	285	15,500
Zack Sucher	70	71	71	73	285	15,500
Tom Hoge	68	74	67	77	286	10,400
Hudson Swafford	70	74	70	72	286	10,400
Chase Wright	69	71	75	71	286	10,400
Steve Marino	71	68	74	74	287	8,565
Alex Prugh	71	69	75	72	287	8,565

Web.com Tour Championship

TPC Sawgrass, Ponte Vedra Beach, Florida — September 18-21
Par 35-35–70; 6,847 yards — purse, $1,000,000

	SCORES				TOTAL	MONEY
Derek Fathauer	65	66	67	68	266	$180,000
Zac Blair	63	65	71	68	267	108,000
Jason Gore	69	65	66	69	269	68,000
Jim Herman	70	67	65	70	272	44,000
Heath Slocum	67	70	67	68	272	44,000
David Lingmerth	68	67	73	65	273	36,000
Travis Bertoni	66	69	68	71	274	30,125
Chad Collins	65	69	70	70	274	30,125
Adam Hadwin	66	69	67	72	274	30,125

	SCORES				TOTAL	MONEY
Sam Saunders	69	68	70	67	274	30,125
Sung Joon Park	65	68	71	71	275	23,000
John Rollins	70	68	68	69	275	23,000
Tyrone van Aswegen	66	69	67	73	275	23,000
Tony Finau	68	72	70	66	276	16,000
Michael Kim	71	68	68	69	276	16,000
Colt Knost	67	69	70	70	276	16,000
Richard Lee	67	68	70	71	276	16,000
Jamie Lovemark	73	66	67	70	276	16,000
Scott Pinckney	65	75	65	71	276	16,000
Alex Prugh	70	69	68	69	276	16,000
Jonathan Byrd	70	69	69	69	277	10,800
Tom Gillis	67	67	70	73	277	10,800
Nick Taylor	68	72	74	63	277	10,800
Justin Thomas	68	71	69	69	277	10,800
Eric Axley	69	71	70	68	278	7,771.67
Shane Bertsch	69	70	70	69	278	7,771.67
Max Homa	74	66	69	69	278	7,771.67
Brett Stegmaier	74	66	71	67	278	7,771.67
Chez Reavie	70	67	70	71	278	7,771.66
Hudson Swafford	69	70	68	71	278	7,771.66

PGA Tour Canada

PC Financial Open

Point Grey Golf & Country Club, Vancouver, British Columbia
Par 36-36–72; 6,801 yards

May 29-June 1
purse, C$150,000

	SCORES				TOTAL	MONEY
Joel Dahmen	66	70	68	68	272	C$27,000
Eugene Wong	66	67	71	69	273	13,200
Brad Clapp	67	69	67	70	273	13,200
Chris Williams	68	73	68	66	275	6,200
Olin Browne, Jr.	71	68	66	70	275	6,200
John Catlin	67	67	71	70	275	6,200
Matt Harmon	69	69	72	66	276	4,212.50
Ryan McCormick	69	70	70	67	276	4,212.50
Andrew Noto	68	72	69	67	276	4,212.50
David Byrne	70	69	69	68	276	4,212.50
Kelvin Day	68	66	72	70	276	4,212.50
Jack Newman	70	71	61	74	276	4,212.50
Matthew Smith	68	70	71	68	277	3,000
Mark Silvers	69	70	69	69	277	3,000
Beon Yeong Lee	72	69	71	66	278	2,325
Sean Shahi	70	69	70	69	278	2,325
Donald Preston	70	71	68	69	278	2,325

	SCORES				TOTAL	MONEY
Jeff Dennis	73	68	68	69	278	2,325
Riley Wheeldon	70	70	68	70	278	2,325
Timothy Madigan	73	67	67	71	278	2,325

Bayview Place Island Savings Open

Uplands Golf Club, Victoria, British Columbia
Par 35-35–70; 6,420 yards

June 5-8
purse, C$150,000

	SCORES				TOTAL	MONEY
Josh Persons	66	65	67	70	268	C$27,000
Brock Mackenzie	63	66	71	69	269	13,200
Timothy Madigan	67	64	69	69	269	13,200
Olin Browne, Jr.	67	68	68	67	270	5,906.25
Wes Homan	69	64	69	68	270	5,906.25
Michael Buttacavoli	68	64	70	68	270	5,906.25
James Allenby	66	69	67	68	270	5,906.25
T.J. Bordeaux	69	67	69	66	271	4,200
Robert Karlsson	69	68	66	68	271	4,200
Daniel Miernicki	71	65	66	69	271	4,200
Garrett Sapp	68	65	67	71	271	4,200
Daniel McCarthy	67	67	72	66	272	3,450
Brandon Harkins	70	69	69	65	273	2,812.50
Christopher Ross	66	70	69	68	273	2,812.50
Joel Dahmen	66	67	71	69	273	2,812.50
Ryan Yip	70	69	65	69	273	2,812.50
Matthew Galloway	70	69	69	66	274	2,030
Jeffrey Corr	69	67	71	67	274	2,030
Michael Gligic	69	69	69	67	274	2,030
Philip Francis	68	67	70	69	274	2,030
Justin Shin	70	67	67	70	274	2,030
Travis Ross	68	69	67	70	274	2,030

Syncrude Boreal Open

Fort McMurray Golf Club, Ft. McMurray, Alberta
Par 36-36–72; 6,886 yards

June 19-22
purse, C$150,000

	SCORES				TOTAL	MONEY
Joel Dahmen	63	66	68	69	266	C$27,000
Richard McDonald	72	64	68	67	271	16,200
Timothy Madigan	70	66	66	70	272	10,200
Ryan Williams	67	65	72	69	273	7,200
Michael Buttacavoli	68	72	65	69	274	5,475
Greg Eason	69	68	69	68	274	5,475
Matt Harmon	71	67	67	69	274	5,475
Seann Harlingten	69	72	65	69	275	4,500
Riley Wheeldon	73	64	66	72	275	4,500
Robert Karlsson	69	67	72	68	276	3,750
Daniel Miernicki	66	72	71	67	276	3,750
Bruce Woodall	67	69	71	69	276	3,750
Devin Carrey	69	67	69	72	277	2,730
Kyle Kallan	71	66	69	71	277	2,730
Beon Yeong Lee	70	65	69	73	277	2,730
Dan McCarthy	75	62	66	74	277	2,730
Benjamin Silverman	68	70	71	68	277	2,730
Julian Etulain	70	69	71	68	278	1,825.72

	SCORES				TOTAL	MONEY
Jay Vandeventer	69	69	72	68	278	1,825.72
Eugene Wong	71	68	70	69	278	1,825.72
Adam Cornelson	68	72	69	69	278	1,825.71
Wes Homan	73	67	68	70	278	1,825.71
Brady Schnell	70	66	70	72	278	1,825.71
Sean Shahi	67	68	71	72	278	1,825.71

SIGA Dakota Dunes Open

Dakota Dunes Golf Links, Saskatoon, Saskatchewan — July 3-6
Par 36-36–72; 7,301 yards — purse, C$150,000

	SCORES				TOTAL	MONEY
Matt Harmon	65	70	63	66	264	C$27,000
William Kropp	71	68	66	62	267	16,200
Robert Karlsson	72	66	65	65	268	10,200
Erik Barnes	70	63	73	63	269	7,200
Matt Marshall	71	71	64	64	270	6,000
Brady Schnell	74	66	67	64	271	5,400
Ted Brown	73	69	66	64	272	4,675
Riley Fleming	71	70	65	66	272	4,675
Chris Williams	70	70	64	68	272	4,675
Clayton Rask	72	67	69	65	273	3,900
Benjamin Silverman	68	71	67	67	273	3,900
Brad Hopfinger	72	67	68	67	274	3,150
Drew Stoltz	63	72	71	68	274	3,150
Ryan Yip	67	73	69	65	274	3,150
John Catlin	69	67	73	66	275	2,625
Emilio Dominguez	73	67	69	66	275	2,625
Tyler Aldridge	74	64	70	68	276	1,962.86
Daniel Balin	71	69	69	67	276	1,962.86
Jeff Corr	68	70	70	68	276	1,962.86
Jeff Dennis	71	72	68	65	276	1,962.86
Greg Eason	74	67	69	66	276	1,962.86
Hunter Hamrick	75	66	73	62	276	1,962.85
Nate McCoy	76	67	65	68	276	1,962.85

PGA Tour Canada Players Cup

Pine Ridge Golf Club, Winnipeg, Manitoba — July 10-13
Par 36-35–71; 6,601 yards — purse, C$150,000

	SCORES				TOTAL	MONEY
Timothy Madigan	70	66	68	71	275	C427,000
Matt Hill	67	68	74	67	276	13,200
Richard McDonald	68	68	71	69	276	13,200
Clark Klaasen	69	71	70	67	277	7,200
Jay Myers	74	67	67	70	278	5,475
Josh Persons	68	67	71	72	278	5,475
Ryan Yip	68	70	71	69	278	5,475
Beon Yeong Lee	71	66	72	70	279	4,650
Chris Killmer	75	69	65	71	280	3,900
Christopher Ross	70	68	72	70	280	3,900
Drew Stoltz	66	69	74	71	280	3,900
Eugene Wong	69	70	72	69	280	3,900
Daniel Balin	73	69	69	70	281	2,900
Stephen Gangluff	69	68	72	72	281	2,900

	SCORES				TOTAL	MONEY
Nate McCoy	69	69	73	70	281	2,900
Erik Barnes	63	70	75	74	282	2,250
David Holmes	71	73	68	70	282	2,250
Brock Mackenzie	65	70	75	72	282	2,250
Clayton Rask	71	71	70	70	282	2,250
Bruce Woodall	72	72	66	72	282	2,250

Staal Foundation Open

Whitewater Golf Club, Thunder Bay, Ontario
Par 36-36–72; 7,293 yards

July 17-20
purse, C$150,000

	SCORES				TOTAL	MONEY
Wes Homan	67	65	68	71	271	C$27,000
Greg Eason	67	65	70	70	272	16,200
Jeff Corr	66	72	67	69	274	10,200
Daniel Miernicki	70	69	70	68	277	7,200
John Catlin	72	71	67	68	278	5,700
Joel Dahmen	68	69	72	69	278	5,700
Ted Brown	70	67	72	70	279	4,518.75
Drew Evans	70	68	69	72	279	4,518.75
Cory Renfrew	71	70	67	71	279	4,518.75
Joshua Stone	65	70	74	70	279	4,518.75
Ryan Brehm	68	69	72	71	280	3,300
Andrew Georgiou	72	70	70	68	280	3,300
Josh Persons	70	68	72	70	280	3,300
Ryan Yip	69	70	71	70	280	3,300
Tyler Brown	70	72	70	69	281	2,475
Dan Buchner	68	75	70	68	281	2,475
Randall Hutchison	70	69	72	70	281	2,475
Robert Karlsson	69	69	74	69	281	2,475
Abraham Ancer	72	71	70	69	282	1,590
Hunter Hamrick	71	71	72	68	282	1,590
Clark Klaasen	71	68	73	70	282	1,590
Garrett Sapp	69	70	72	71	282	1,590
Brady Schnell	68	71	74	69	282	1,590
Sean Shahi	66	73	74	69	282	1,590
Matthew Smith	69	72	66	75	282	1,590
Will Strickler	70	72	69	71	282	1,590
Eugene Wong	69	74	69	70	282	1,590

ATB Financial Classic

Sirocco Golf Club, Calgary, Alberta
Par 36-36–72; 7,185 yards

July 31-August 3
purse, C$150,000

	SCORES				TOTAL	MONEY
Brock Mackenzie	65	63	67	66	261	C$27,000
Steve Carney	64	65	68	68	265	13,200
Joel Dahmen	65	68	68	64	265	13,200
Cory Renfrew	67	67	65	67	266	6,600
Brady Schnell	71	59	67	69	266	6,600
Ted Brown	65	68	68	66	267	5,400
Ryan Brehm	74	64	66	64	268	5,025
Steven Fox	69	64	72	64	269	4,500
Linus Gillgren	65	67	72	65	269	4,500
Sam Ryder	67	64	69	70	270	3,750

	SCORES				TOTAL	MONEY
Benjamin Silverman	68	66	69	67	270	3,750
Ryan Williams	69	67	67	67	270	3,750
Riley Fleming	70	69	68	64	271	2,900
Bo Hoag	68	68	68	67	271	2,900
Jay Myers	68	71	67	65	271	2,900
John Catlin	67	70	66	70	273	2,400
Matt Harmon	69	66	71	67	273	2,400
Jesse Speirs	71	65	67	70	273	2,400
Andrew Georgiou	67	66	70	71	274	1,882.50
Matthew Smith	66	67	69	72	274	1,882.50
Chris Williams	70	69	68	67	274	1,882.50
Eugene Wong	75	65	67	67	274	1,882.50

Forces and Families Open

Hylands Golf Club, Ottawa, Ontario — August 7-10
Par 35-36–71; 6,800 yards — purse, C$150,000

	SCORES				TOTAL	MONEY
Greg Machtaler	69	68	68	62	267	C$27,000
Peter Campbell	66	69	67	66	268	13,200
Jeff Dennis	68	64	70	66	268	13,200
Greg Eason	63	66	70	70	269	7,200
Ryan Brehm	66	67	70	67	270	5,085
Dan Buchner	68	67	69	66	270	5,085
Devin Carrey	71	68	67	64	270	5,085
Kelvin Day	66	70	66	68	270	5,085
Brent Long	69	69	67	65	270	5,085
Ted Brown	70	66	70	65	271	4,050
Olin Browne, Jr.	71	67	67	67	272	3,450
Travis Ross	64	69	71	68	272	3,450
Marcelo Rozo	70	70	65	67	272	3,450
Mike Ballo, Jr.	69	67	67	70	273	2,550
Matt Hill	70	70	66	67	273	2,550
Jordan Krantz	66	69	67	71	273	2,550
Michael McCabe	67	68	70	68	273	2,550
Clayton Rask	66	69	70	68	273	2,550
Alexis Anghert	69	69	66	70	274	1,755
Dan McCarthy	66	67	70	71	274	1,755
Christopher Ross	69	69	69	67	274	1,755
Sam Ryder	64	71	68	71	274	1,755
Ryan Williams	71	68	67	68	274	1,755
Bruce Woodall	70	69	66	69	274	1,755

Great Waterway Classic

Loyalist Golf & Country Club, Kingston, Ontario — August 21-24
Par 35-37–72; 6,584 yards — purse, C$150,000

	SCORES				TOTAL	MONEY
David Bradshaw	66	68	66	67	267	C$27,000
Tommy Cocha	67	69	66	66	268	13,200
Adam Long	67	68	66	67	268	13,200
Michael Gligic	71	64	66	69	270	7,200
Michael Buttacavoli	70	69	66	66	271	5,085
Chris Hemmerich	68	66	66	71	271	5,085
Brock Mackenzie	66	69	71	65	271	5,085

	SCORES				TOTAL	MONEY
Cory Renfrew	68	66	69	68	271	5,085
Brady Schnell	71	68	69	63	271	5,085
Seann Harlingten	69	68	69	66	272	3,900
Christopher Wolfe	71	65	68	68	272	3,900
Ted Brown	66	71	66	70	273	2,850
Dan Buchner	67	67	70	69	273	2,850
Jeff Dennis	67	69	71	66	273	2,850
Greg Eason	68	69	68	68	273	2,850
Andrew Noto	74	65	70	64	273	2,850
Chris Williams	74	65	68	66	273	2,850
Kelvin Day	66	66	70	72	274	1,956
Chris Killmer	68	68	72	66	274	1,956
Clayton Rask	68	68	69	69	274	1,956
Darren Wallace	67	70	71	66	274	1,956
Ryan Yip	69	70	68	67	274	1,956

Wildfire Invitational

Wildfire Golf Club, Peterborough, Ontario — August 28-31
Par 36-36–72; 6,803 yards — purse, C$150,000

	SCORES				TOTAL	MONEY
Nate McCoy	72	65	67	65	269	C$27,000
Michael Gligic	69	68	66	66	269	16,200
(McCoy defeated Gligic on fourth playoff hole.)						
Jay Vandeventer	68	65	69	68	270	10,200
John Ellis	69	69	67	66	271	7,200
Adam Cornelson	63	67	72	70	272	5,700
Max Gilbert	69	68	65	70	272	5,700
Tommy Cocha	67	67	73	66	273	4,365
Jeff Corr	68	66	68	71	273	4,365
Chris Hemmerich	66	68	68	71	273	4,365
Brock Mackenzie	66	65	71	71	273	4,365
Justin Shin	66	68	68	71	273	4,365
Ted Brown	70	69	68	67	274	3,037.50
John Catlin	70	66	70	68	274	3,037.50
Evan Harmeling	64	73	69	68	274	3,037.50
Joe Panzeri	68	64	68	74	274	3,037.50
Tyler Brown	69	71	67	68	275	2,250
Greg Eason	71	68	67	69	275	2,250
Bo Hoag	68	68	69	70	275	2,250
Brady Schnell	68	67	68	72	275	2,250
Chris Williams	67	71	68	69	275	2,250

Cape Breton Celtic Classic

Lakes Golf Club, Ben Eoin, Nova Scotia — September 4-7
Par 36-36–72; 6,904 yards — purse, C$150,000

	SCORES				TOTAL	MONEY
Mark Silvers	70	65	72	66	273	C$27,000
Matt Harmon	66	69	69	69	273	16,200
(Silvers defeated Harmon on first playoff hole.)						
Seann Harlingten	67	71	67	70	275	7,800
Beon Yeong Lee	72	70	68	65	275	7,800
Dan McCarthy	67	66	69	73	275	7,800
Michael Gligic	70	66	66	74	276	5,212.50

	SCORES				TOTAL	MONEY
Chris Williams	67	67	72	70	276	5,212.50
John Catlin	72	69	71	65	277	4,350
Adam Long	67	74	71	65	277	4,350
Russell Surber	68	71	70	68	277	4,350
Paul Ferrier	68	68	71	71	278	3,750
Philip Francis	72	67	70	70	279	3,150
Derek Gillespie	71	70	67	71	279	3,150
Matt Hill	72	68	69	70	279	3,150
Ryan Brehm	69	68	75	68	280	2,475
Adam Cornelson	71	69	70	70	280	2,475
Mackenzie Hughes	72	67	72	69	280	2,475
Greg Machtaler	73	62	72	73	280	2,475
Greg Eason	70	69	73	69	281	1,818
Brandon Harkins	69	69	73	70	281	1,818
Brady Schnell	74	69	67	71	281	1,818
Justin Shin	73	70	71	67	281	1,818
Eugene Wong	68	72	73	68	281	1,818

Tour Championship of Canada

Sunningdale Golf & Country Club, London, Ontario — September 11-14
Par 36-36–72; 7,089 yards — purse, C$150,000

	SCORES				TOTAL	MONEY
Ryan Williams	69	65	72	68	274	C$27,000
Adam Cornelson	69	67	71	68	275	13,200
Clayton Rask	71	66	67	71	275	13,200
Dan McCarthy	71	69	72	64	276	7,200
Mark Silvers	72	71	68	66	277	6,000
Nate McCoy	71	66	72	69	278	5,400
Peter Campbell	71	68	72	68	279	5,025
Ryan Brehm	70	70	70	70	280	4,500
Matt Marshall	68	69	72	71	280	4,500
Erik Barnes	68	67	76	70	281	3,600
Greg Eason	70	68	73	70	281	3,600
Jay Myers	69	70	70	72	281	3,600
Chris Williams	74	71	69	67	281	3,600
Ted Brown	70	68	72	72	282	2,550
John Catlin	71	71	68	72	282	2,550
John Ellis	70	69	73	70	282	2,550
Clark Klaasen	73	66	72	71	282	2,550
Eugene Wong	69	69	73	71	282	2,550
Matt Harmon	70	68	73	72	283	2,025
Sean Shahi	69	70	70	74	283	2,025

PGA Tour Latinoamerica

Arturo Calle Colombian Open

Ruitoque Golf & Country Club, Bucaramange, Colombia — February 20-23
Par 36-34–70 — purse, $150,000

	SCORES				TOTAL	MONEY
David Vanegas	66	68	61	68	263	$27,000
Andres Echavarria	68	69	66	63	266	13,200
Rick Cochran	64	66	67	69	266	13,200
Jordan Russell	69	68	66	64	267	5,655
Daniel Mazziotta	63	68	69	67	267	5,655
Jose Manuel Garrido	66	69	65	67	267	5,655
Nelson Ledesma	69	65	65	68	267	5,655
Manuel Merizalde	68	69	60	70	267	5,655
Timothy O'Neal	67	70	66	65	268	4,350
Jorge Fernandez-Valdes	64	69	71	65	269	3,900
Erik Barnes	67	69	65	68	269	3,900
Chris Parra	68	67	68	67	270	2,940
William Kropp	70	67	66	67	270	2,940
Rafael Becker	68	65	69	68	270	2,940
Cody Paladino	69	68	64	69	270	2,940
Santiago Rivas	68	66	66	70	270	2,940
Cody Gribble	67	67	69	68	271	2,325
Jesus Amaya	67	67	69	68	271	2,325
Christian Espinoza	71	67	70	64	272	1,950
Adam Long	70	67	69	66	272	1,950
Oscar David Alvarez	66	72	68	66	272	1,950

TransAmerican Power Products CRV Open

Las Lomas Club de Golf, Guadalajara, Mexico — March 20-23
Par 35-36–71; 6,800 yards — purse, $150,000

	SCORES				TOTAL	MONEY
Marcelo Rozo	67	65	66	69	267	$27,000
Mauricio Azcue	65	66	68	68	267	8,338
Lucho Dodda	69	67	64	67	267	8,338
Rick Cochran	65	66	70	66	267	8,338
Julian Etulain	69	63	70	65	267	8,338
Roberto Diaz	63	69	68	67	267	8,338
Matt Ryan	67	64	68	68	267	8,338
(Rozo won on second playoff hole.)						
Alex Moon	72	67	64	65	268	4,500
David Chung	67	67	68	66	268	4,500
Gustavo Acosta	65	71	68	65	269	3,600
Austin Graham	67	65	71	66	269	3,600
James Vargas	70	67	66	66	269	3,600
Sebastian Saavedra	67	66	68	68	269	3,600
Rafael Echenique	66	70	69	65	270	2,700
Andrew Mason	68	65	69	68	270	2,700
David Vanegas	66	66	69	69	270	2,700
Armando Villarreal	69	69	68	65	271	1,908
Zac Blair	69	68	67	67	271	1,908

	SCORES				TOTAL	MONEY
Cesar Agustin Costilla	66	72	66	67	271	1,908
Tyler Duncan	66	65	71	69	271	1,908
Jordan Russell	72	65	65	69	271	1,908
Felipe Navarro	64	67	70	70	271	1,908
Adam Long	67	70	64	70	271	1,908
Max Scodro	64	67	69	71	271	1,908

Stella Artois Open

La Reunion Golf Resort, Fuego Maya Course, Antigua, Guatemala — March 27-30
Par 36-36–72; 7,300 yards — purse, $150,000

	SCORES				TOTAL	MONEY
Armando Favela	67	68	68	71	274	$27,000
Nelson Ledesma	72	70	67	66	275	16,200
William Kropp	65	72	71	68	276	7,200
Chris Gilman	72	68	68	68	276	7,200
Martin Trainer	73	69	63	71	276	7,200
Rafael Echenique	69	69	65	73	276	7,200
David Vanegas	69	74	67	67	277	4,838
Mauricio Azcue	70	68	69	70	277	4,838
Brad Hopfinger	69	68	70	72	279	4,350
Eric Atsma	70	69	73	68	280	3,750
Jordan Russell	69	70	72	69	280	3,750
Rafael Campos	71	66	70	73	280	3,750
Cesar Monasterio	69	69	71	72	281	3,150
Max Scodro	73	71	72	66	282	2,550
Liam Logan	69	71	74	68	282	2,550
Adam Long	70	73	71	68	282	2,550
Tyler Duncan	71	69	73	69	282	2,550
David Chung	69	72	69	72	282	2,550
Tommy Cocha	69	75	70	69	283	1,950
Chase Carroll	70	70	72	71	283	1,950
Rodolfo Cazaubon	71	73	67	72	283	1,950

Mundo Maya Open

Yucatan Country Club, El Jaguar Course, Meridia, Mexico — April 3-6
Par 36-36–72; 7,282 yards — purse, $150,000

	SCORES				TOTAL	MONEY
Daniel Mazziotta	69	72	69	68	278	$27,000
Robert Rohanna	72	71	69	70	282	8,338
Peter Campbell	71	70	70	71	282	8,338
Bryan Bigley	73	69	69	71	282	8,338
Rick Cochran	69	67	73	73	282	8,338
Rodolfo Cazaubon	68	71	70	73	282	8,338
Brad Hopfinger	69	70	69	74	282	8,338
Tyler McCumber	72	72	70	70	284	4,650
Nicholas Lindheim	70	69	74	73	286	4,050
Danny Balin	71	70	72	73	286	4,050
Devin Carrey	74	69	68	75	286	4,050
Chris Meyer	67	70	77	73	287	3,038
David Chung	70	71	73	73	287	3,038
Armando Favela	71	72	70	74	287	3,038
Chris Bray	70	72	68	77	287	3,038
Sebastian MacLean	73	70	73	72	288	2,325
Rafael Campos	69	77	69	73	288	2,325

	SCORES				TOTAL	MONEY
Santiago Rivas	72	71	70	75	288	2,325
Matt Ryan	69	75	66	78	288	2,325
Chris Parra	73	71	72	73	289	1,755
James Vargas	71	73	70	75	289	1,755
Zac Blair	73	71	70	75	289	1,755
Mitchell Gregson	73	73	68	75	289	1,755

Abierto OSDE del Centro

Cordoba Golf Club, Cordoba, Argentina
Par 35-36–71; 6,794 yards

April 17-20
purse, $150,000

	SCORES				TOTAL	MONEY
William Kropp	73	66	68	69	276	$27,000
Angel Cabrera	69	72	67	69	277	16,200
Marcelo Rozo	71	69	69	70	279	10,200
Puma Dominguez	69	71	72	69	281	6,600
Fermin Noste	71	66	69	75	281	6,600
Zac Blair	72	70	69	71	282	5,400
Maximiliano Godoy	73	68	73	69	283	4,675
Kent Bulle	72	72	69	70	283	4,675
Erik Barnes	74	71	68	70	283	4,675
Andrew Mason	76	70	71	67	284	3,600
Estanislao Goya	75	71	69	69	284	3,600
Michael Buttacavoli	71	67	75	71	284	3,600
Marco Ruiz	77	68	67	72	284	3,600
David Chung	72	71	72	70	285	2,700
Chris Gilman	69	72	72	72	285	2,700
Finley Ewing	70	74	68	73	285	2,700
Julian Etulain	72	72	72	70	286	2,175
Corbin Mills	71	73	71	71	286	2,175
Sebastian MacLean	73	72	69	72	286	2,175
Pablo Acuna	71	71	70	74	286	2,175

Roberto de Vicenzo Invitational Copa NEC

Club de Golf Uruguay, Montevideo, Uruguay
Par 36-36–72; 6,680 yards

April 24-27
purse, $150,000

	SCORES				TOTAL	MONEY
Ty Capps	66	67	68	71	272	$27,000
Tommy Cocha	68	68	70	66	272	16,200
(Capps defeated Cocha on third playoff hole.)						
Robert Rohanna	71	69	65	68	273	8,700
Rafael Campos	69	67	67	70	273	8,700
Kent Bulle	68	70	67	69	274	5,700
Marcelo Rozo	68	65	69	72	274	5,700
Gato Zarlenga	65	70	71	69	275	4,675
Puma Dominguez	65	67	73	70	275	4,675
Diego Velasquez	69	69	66	71	275	4,675
Santiago Russi	70	69	69	68	276	4,050
Mauricio Azcue	69	68	68	72	277	3,750
Stephan Jaeger	70	67	68	73	278	3,450
Charlie Ford	67	68	76	69	280	2,900
Armando Villarreal	70	68	70	72	280	2,900
Gunner Wiebe	69	66	72	73	280	2,900
Samuel Del Val	68	71	75	67	281	2,400
Juan Cerda	68	70	74	69	281	2,400

	SCORES				TOTAL	MONEY
Russell Surber	65	70	70	76	281	2,400
Rick Cochran	73	66	78	65	282	1,884
Yoshio Yamamoto	70	69	77	66	282	1,884
Liam Logan	73	67	76	66	282	1,884
Tyler McCumber	70	70	69	73	282	1,884

Dominican Republic Open

Teeth of the Dog, Casa de Campo, La Romana, Dominican Republic
Par 36-36–72

May 15-18
purse, US$150,000

	SCORES				TOTAL	MONEY
Michael Buttacavoli	66	70	73	67	276	US$27,000
Rick Cochran	70	64	74	68	276	16,200
(Buttacavoli defeated Cochran on third playoff hole.)						
Julian Etulain	70	69	71	67	277	10,200
Vaita Guillaume	73	70	68	67	278	7,200
Zac Blair	66	71	74	69	280	5,475
William Kropp	71	68	72	69	280	5,475
Sean Jacklin	68	71	71	70	280	5,475
Robert Rohanna	71	68	74	68	281	4,200
Brad Hopfinger	72	69	72	68	281	4,200
Alex Moon	72	69	70	70	281	4,200
Danny Balin	73	68	67	73	281	4,200
Erik Barnes	75	68	69	70	282	3,300
Chris Gilman	68	70	70	74	282	3,300
Patricio Salem	73	71	70	69	283	2,700
Christian Espinoza	72	71	69	71	283	2,700
Michael Schachner	75	68	69	71	283	2,700
Martin Trainer	64	77	73	70	284	2,031
Andrew Johnson	74	67	72	71	284	2,031
Liam Logan	68	71	73	72	284	2,031
Brady Watt	71	70	71	72	284	2,031
David Borda	69	76	67	72	284	2,031
Maximiliano Godoy	66	74	71	73	284	2,031

Lexus Panama Classic

Buenaventura Golf Club, Rio Hato, Panama
Par 36-36–72

May 22-25
purse, US$150,000

	SCORES				TOTAL	MONEY
Julian Etulain	69	67	66	69	271	US$27,000
Gato Zarlenga	68	66	71	68	273	16,200
Jhared Hack	69	73	66	66	274	8,700
Puma Dominguez	70	70	64	70	274	8,700
Tyler McCumber	69	68	70	69	276	6,000
Chas Narramore	70	71	70	67	278	4,695
Peter Campbell	71	71	67	69	278	4,695
Tyler Duncan	69	68	69	72	278	4,695
Marcelo Rozo	69	70	67	72	278	4,695
Zac Blair	69	69	67	73	278	4,695
Bryan Martin	71	70	69	69	279	3,180
Robert Rohanna	70	72	67	70	279	3,180
*Juan Diego Fernandez Mac	73	67	68	71	279	
Juan P. Luna	70	71	67	71	279	3,180
Samuel Del Val	70	72	66	71	279	3,180

	SCORES				TOTAL	MONEY
Erik Barnes	70	70	73	67	280	2,400
Santiago Rivas	71	68	71	70	280	2,400
Brady Watt	70	69	70	71	280	2,400
Jordan Russell	69	70	72	70	281	1,950
Brad Hopfinger	72	68	71	70	281	1,950
Liam Logan	70	69	68	74	281	1,950

All You Need is Ecuador Open

Quito Tenis y Golf Club, Quito, Ecuador — September 25-28
Par 36-36–72; 7,380 yards — purse, US$150,000

	SCORES				TOTAL	MONEY
Tyler McCumber	67	67	71	70	275	US$27,000
Jose Toledo	73	71	66	70	280	9,900
Marcelo Rozo	69	69	71	71	280	9,900
Mitch Krywulycz	67	74	68	71	280	9,900
Mauricio Azcue	73	63	68	76	280	9,900
Jorge Fernandez-Valdes	74	69	72	66	281	5,025
Bryan Bigley	71	73	68	69	281	5,025
Sebastian Vazquez	67	72	70	72	281	5,025
Stephan Jaeger	72	69	72	69	282	4,050
David Chung	69	74	69	70	282	4,050
Martin Trainer	71	68	72	71	282	4,050
Santiago Rivas	77	69	67	70	283	3,300
Adam Long	69	73	68	73	283	3,300
Kent Bulle	68	76	71	69	284	2,775
Gunner Wiebe	71	72	70	71	284	2,775
Joel Lynn	73	72	72	68	285	2,475
Gustavo Acosta	70	72	71	72	285	2,475
David Vanegas	73	73	69	71	286	1,838
Sebastian MacLean	74	72	70	70	286	1,838
Puma Dominguez	71	74	70	71	286	1,838
Vince India	68	76	73	69	286	1,838
Juan P. Luna	68	76	69	73	286	1,838
Tyler Duncan	71	73	68	74	286	1,838
Scott Lamb	71	68	72	75	286	1,838

Arturo Calle Colombian Classic

Pueblo Viejo Country Club, Bogota, Colombia — October 2-5
Par 36-36–72; 7,407 yards — purse, US$150,000

	SCORES				TOTAL	MONEY
Nicholas Lindheim	67	68	67	67	269	US$27,000
Marcelo Rozo	70	68	65	67	270	13,200
Brad Hopfinger	69	70	64	67	270	13,200
Rafael Campos	67	68	66	70	271	7,200
Tommy Cocha	66	70	68	68	272	5,700
Jhonathan Perez	69	67	66	70	272	5,700
Diego Vanegas	66	73	69	65	273	4,838
Alex Moon	66	68	66	73	273	4,838
Nicolas Geyger	68	67	69	70	274	3,471
Federico Cabrera	69	68	67	70	274	3,471
Manuel Inman	69	69	66	70	274	3,471
Ariel Canete	71	65	67	71	274	3,471
Chas Narramore	73	63	67	71	274	3,471
Jhared Hack	69	68	66	71	274	3,471

Women's Tours

David Cannon/Getty Images

A week after Martin Kaymer, Michelle Wie also won the U.S. Open at Pinehurst No. 2.

©Stephen Dunn/Getty Images

Lexi Thompson won her first major title at the last Kraft Nabisco Championship.

Scott Halleran/Getty Images

Inbee Park retained the Wegmans LPGA title.

David Cannon/Getty Images

Mo Martin captured the Women's British Open.

Stuart Franklin/Getty Images

Hyo-Joo Kim, 19, won the Evian Championship.

Stanley Chou/Getty Images

Stacy Lewis was the LPGA Player of the Year.

Sam Greenwood/Getty Images

Lydia Ko, inaugural Race to CME Globe winner.

Dave Sandford/Getty Images

Canadian Pacific Open winner So Yeon Ryu.

Warren Little/Getty Images

Shanshan Feng won the Omega Dubai Ladies Masters for the second time in three years.

David Cannon/Getty Images

Anna Nordqvist won twice on the LPGA.

Warren Little/Getty Images

British Open runner-up Suzann Pettersen.

Hunter Martin/Getty Images

Karrie Webb won a fifth Australian Open.

David Cannon/Getty Images

Sun-Ju Ahn won five times on the Japan LPGA.

Ross Kinnaird/Getty Images

Paula Creamer won the HSBC Champions with a remarkable 75-foot putt.

David Cannon/Getty Images

Charley Hull, 18, was the youngest Ladies European Tour money winner.

Senior Tours

Phil Inglis/Getty Images

Bernhard Langer won the Senior Open at Royal Porthcawl by 13 strokes, one of five victories.

Phil Inglis/Getty Images

Colin Montgomerie was the Senior PGA and U.S. Senior Open champion.

Steve Dykes/Getty Images

Kenny Perry was a major winner again at the Regions Tradition.

Christian Petersen/Getty Images

Jay Haas won the Greater Hickory Kia Classic.

Christian Petersen/Getty Images

Tom Pernice Jr. won twice in the U.S.

Boris Streubel/Getty Images

Paul Wesselingh won twice in Europe.

Hunter Martin/Getty Images

Jeff Sluman won the Legends with Fred Funk.

One of Fred Couples' two wins came at the Shaw Charity Classic in Canada.

Gene Sauers lost a playoff at the U.S. Senior Open.

Michael Allen won the Allianz Championship.

Rick Gibson won the Bad Ragaz PGA Seniors.

	SCORES				TOTAL	MONEY
Rick Cochran	69	65	68	72	274	3,471
Sebastian MacLean	70	67	70	68	275	2,175
Jose Toledo	71	66	69	69	275	2,175
Daniel Mazziotta	69	68	69	69	275	2,175
Mitch Krywulycz	66	70	69	70	275	2,175
Eric Atsma	68	68	69	70	275	2,175
Julio Zapata	73	66	66	70	275	2,175

TransAmerican Power Products CRV Mazatlan Open

Estrella del Mar Golf, Mazatlan, Mexico — October 9-12
Par 36-36–72 — purse, US$150,000

	SCORES				TOTAL	MONEY
Tyler McCumber	71	71	66	70	278	US$27,000
Jorge Fernandez-Valdes	70	67	73	68	278	16,200
(McCumber defeated Fernandez-Valdes on first playoff hole.)						
Julian Etulain	69	69	73	68	279	8,700
James Vargas	73	70	66	70	279	8,700
Robert Rohanna	73	67	69	71	280	6,000
Nicholas Lindheim	72	68	74	68	282	5,025
Jhared Hack	72	71	68	71	282	5,025
David Chung	70	69	71	72	282	5,025
Erik Barnes	76	68	70	70	284	4,200
Cody Paladino	70	71	70	73	284	4,200
Rodolfo Cazaubon	72	75	69	69	285	3,750
Vince India	68	73	73	72	286	3,150
Brock Mackenzie	67	77	69	73	286	3,150
Rafael Campos	72	69	71	74	286	3,150
Alex Moon	69	74	73	71	287	2,400
Stephan Jaeger	76	69	71	71	287	2,400
Sebastian Vazquez	72	73	71	71	287	2,400
Martin Trainer	73	67	75	72	287	2,400
Marcelo Rozo	75	68	72	72	287	2,400
Santiago Rivas	70	70	77	71	288	1,653
Bryan Bigley	72	70	75	71	288	1,653
Cody Gribble	72	69	75	72	288	1,653
David Bradshaw	74	68	71	75	288	1,653
Armando Villarreal	70	69	73	76	288	1,653
Estanislao Guerrero	68	72	70	78	288	1,653

TransAmerican Power Products CRV Abierto Mexicano

Club de Golf Chapultepec, Estado de Mexico, Mexico — October 16-19
Par 36-36–72 — purse, US$150,000

	SCORES				TOTAL	MONEY
Oscar David Alvarez	66	69	67	69	271	US$27,000
Nelson Ledesma	70	69	66	67	272	16,200
Brad Hopfinger	65	73	71	65	274	8,700
Alexandre Rocha	69	69	69	67	274	8,700
Jose de Jesus Rodriguez	68	70	71	67	276	5,475
Brady Schnell	72	67	68	69	276	5,475
Chris Gilman	63	68	69	76	276	5,475
Armando Favela	70	72	66	69	277	4,650
Marcelo Rozo	70	72	67	69	278	4,350
Rodolfo Cazaubon	73	71	69	66	279	3,600
Juan P. Luna	74	69	69	67	279	3,600

	SCORES				TOTAL	MONEY
David Bradshaw	69	71	70	69	279	3,600
Francisco Bide	68	70	70	71	279	3,600
Michael Buttacavoli	73	71	69	67	280	2,550
Scott Lamb	71	72	69	68	280	2,550
Julian Etulain	72	73	70	65	280	2,550
Jacobo Pastor	70	71	67	72	280	2,550
Paul Apyan	74	69	65	72	280	2,550
Sebastian Vazquez	69	71	73	68	281	1,950
Mauricio Azcue	69	71	71	70	281	1,950
Rafael Echenique	74	71	69	67	281	1,950

Bridgestone America's Golf Cup

Olivos Golf Club, Buenos Aires, Argentina,
Par 36-35–71; 6,777 yards

October 23-26
purse, $600,000

	SCORES				TOTAL	MONEY (Team)
Emilio Dominguez/Rafa Echenique	62	61	61	62	246	US$120,000
Daniel Mazziotta/Robert Rohanna	61	63	60	63	247	
Gato Zarlenga/Maxi Godoy	65	61	62	62	250	
Brad Hopfinger/Jordan Russell	64	61	62	64	251	
Alan Wagner/Julian Etulain	61	64	62	65	252	
Jose Toledo/Pablo Acuna	62	64	63	64	253	
Mauricio Azcue/Roberto Diaz	62	61	65	65	253	
Mitch Krywulicz/Jake Younan Wise	62	64	62	65	253	
Rafael Becker/Felipe Navarro	63	63	65	64	255	
Alex Moon/Cody Paladino	65	62	67	62	256	
Angel Cabrera/Federico Cabrera	65	65	62	64	256	

Lexus Peru Open

Los Inkas Golf Club, Lima, Peru
Par 36-36–72

October 30-November 2
purse, US$150,000

	SCORES				TOTAL	MONEY
Julian Etulain	69	65	68	72	274	US$27,000
Robert Rohanna	71	70	69	67	277	13,200
Sebastian Saavedra	70	69	68	70	277	13,200
Pablo Acuna	72	68	70	68	278	6,200
Russell Surber	69	72	66	71	278	6,200
Gustavo Acosta	67	70	68	73	278	6,200
Julio Zapata	72	72	69	66	279	4,213
Sebastian Vazquez	70	69	71	69	279	4,213
Samuel Del Val	71	70	69	69	279	4,213
Mauricio Azcue	69	70	69	71	279	4,213
Armando Villarreal	70	67	70	72	279	4,213
Derek Gillespie	77	66	64	72	279	4,213
Alan Wagner	73	70	71	66	280	2,730
Manuel Villegas	73	70	69	68	280	2,730
Stephan Jaeger	69	68	74	69	280	2,730
Manuel Merizalde	71	70	69	70	280	2,730
Jorge Fernandez-Valdes	71	68	70	71	280	2,730
Chris Gilman	70	70	70	71	281	1,958
Tommy Cocha	73	68	69	71	281	1,958
Francisco Bide	73	70	66	72	281	1,958
Rafael Becker	68	69	71	73	281	1,958
David Chung	67	72	69	73	281	1,958

Abierto do Brasil/Aberto do Atlantico

Gavea Golf & Country Club, Rio de Janeiro, Brazil — November 6-9
Par 33-36–69 — purse, US$150,000

	SCORES				TOTAL	MONEY
Rafael Becker	67	66	67	62	262	US$27,000
Joel Dahmen	68	69	64	64	265	13,200
Ariel Canete	68	64	65	68	265	13,200
(Becker defeated Dahmen and Canete on first playoff hole.)						
Augusto Nunez	71	67	62	68	268	7,200
Jorge Fernandez-Valdes	71	63	71	64	269	5,700
Michael Buttacavoli	71	65	64	69	269	5,700
Maximiliano Godoy	69	69	66	66	270	4,675
Christian Espinoza	66	68	69	67	270	4,675
Julian Etulain	69	68	66	67	270	4,675
William Kropp	70	69	68	64	271	3,750
Nelson Ledesma	70	63	70	68	271	3,750
Tyler McCumber	68	65	67	71	271	3,750
Miguel Carballo	67	68	67	70	272	3,150
Willy Pumarol	69	65	73	66	273	2,475
David Borda	69	70	68	66	273	2,475
David Vanegas	68	70	67	68	273	2,475
Tommy Cocha	67	65	72	69	273	2,475
Danny Balin	64	68	68	73	273	2,475
Oscar David Alvarez	68	67	65	73	273	2,475
Cesar Agustin Costilla	68	71	69	66	274	1,813
Sebastian MacLean	66	66	71	71	274	1,813
Marcelo Rozo	69	65	69	71	274	1,813

Hyundai - BBVA Abierto de Chile

Club de Golf Los Leones, Santiago, Chile — November 13-16
Par 36-36–72; 6,948 yards — purse, US$150,000

	SCORES				TOTAL	MONEY
Jorge Fernandez-Valdes	68	62	71	70	271	US$27,000
Joel Dahmen	67	65	73	68	273	13,200
Armando Favela	66	70	66	71	273	13,200
Brad Hopfinger	71	66	67	70	274	7,200
Tom Berry	70	69	69	67	275	6,000
Cristian Leon	68	70	69	69	276	5,400
Rafael Campos	68	69	72	68	277	4,675
Rafael Becker	68	70	68	71	277	4,675
Tommy Cocha	70	67	68	72	277	4,675
James Vargas	68	70	72	68	278	3,750
Jacobo Pastor	70	71	69	68	278	3,750
Bryan Bigley	69	68	70	71	278	3,750
Daniel Stapff	70	67	72	70	279	3,000
Julio Zapata	66	69	72	72	279	3,000
Maximiliano Godoy	68	72	74	66	280	2,550
Ricardo Celia	72	69	72	67	280	2,550
Ryan Ellerbrock	68	73	71	68	280	2,550
Pablo Acuna	72	69	71	69	281	2,025
Leandro Marelli	69	71	70	71	281	2,025
Matias O'Curry	73	68	69	71	281	2,025
Patricio Salem	68	70	71	72	281	2,025

Personal Classic

Las Praderas Club Campos de Golf, Lugan, Buenos Aires, Argentina — November 27-30
Par 36-36–72 — purse, US$150,000
(Event reduced to 54 holes and completed on Monday—rain.)

	SCORES			TOTAL	MONEY
Fabian Gomez	65	65	62	192	US$27,000
Gustavo Acosta	67	62	70	199	16,200
Nelson Ledesma	67	68	66	201	10,200
Rodolfo Cazaubon	69	66	67	202	6,600
Tommy Cocha	65	66	71	202	6,600
Rafael Echenique	70	71	62	203	4,856
Sergio Acevedo	70	68	65	203	4,856
Ricardo Gonzalez	68	68	67	203	4,856
Juan Ignacio Lizarralde	65	69	69	203	4,856
Christian Espinoza	68	72	64	204	3,750
Daniel Mazziotta	67	72	65	204	3,750
Danny Balin	69	69	66	204	3,750
Alexandre Rocha	69	71	65	205	2,730
Mauricio Molina	67	72	66	205	2,730
Jorge Fernandez-Valdes	71	66	68	205	2,730
Tyler McCumber	71	66	68	205	2,730
Puma Dominguez	69	67	69	205	2,730
Clodomiro Carranza	66	75	65	206	2,100
Robert Rohanna	70	70	66	206	2,100
Manuel Inman	69	71	66	206	2,100

VISA Open de Argentina

Martindale Golf Club, Buenos Aires, Argentina — December 4-7
Par 36-36–72; 7,236 yards — purse, US$150,000

	SCORES				TOTAL	MONEY
Emiliano Grillo	66	68	65	67	266	US$27,000
Brad Hopfinger	65	71	72	64	272	16,200
Fabian Gomez	69	72	67	65	273	10,200
Rafael Becker	68	72	70	65	275	6,200
Marcelo Rozo	65	67	75	68	275	6,200
Tyler McCumber	65	68	72	70	275	6,200
Robert Rohanna	69	73	70	64	276	4,838
Jose Coceres	67	71	71	67	276	4,838
Puma Dominguez	68	76	70	63	277	4,200
Miguel Carballo	69	69	72	67	277	4,200
Jorge Fernandez-Valdes	70	71	74	63	278	3,450
Bryan Bigley	69	71	73	65	278	3,450
Rodolfo Cazaubon	71	69	70	68	278	3,450
Cody Paladino	69	70	74	67	280	2,700
Augusto Nunez	66	74	72	68	280	2,700
Santiago Rivas	69	72	71	68	280	2,700
Francisco Bide	68	71	74	68	281	2,175
Rick Cochran	65	76	72	68	281	2,175
*Alejandro Tosti	69	73	71	68	281	
Clodomiro Carranza	73	71	68	69	281	2,175
Mauricio Molina	68	74	69	70	281	2,175

European Tours

Volvo Golf Champions

Durban Country Club, Durban, KwaZulu-Natal, South Africa — January 9-12
Par 36-36–72; 6,689 yards — purse, $4,000,000

	SCORES				TOTAL	MONEY
Louis Oosthuizen	68	69	71	68	276	€507,655
Branden Grace	74	67	68	68	277	326,349
Tommy Fleetwood	70	67	69	72	278	174,053
Joost Luiten	70	67	70	71	278	174,053
Victor Dubuisson	69	69	69	72	279	116,761
Padraig Harrington	71	71	70	67	279	116,761
Raphael Jacquelin	67	73	70	69	279	116,761
Thomas Aiken	72	72	70	67	281	81,043
Julien Quesne	74	73	66	68	281	81,043
Thomas Bjorn	79	68	67	69	283	64,545
Matteo Manassero	72	67	73	71	283	64,545
Brett Rumford	73	70	68	72	283	64,545
Jamie Donaldson	71	71	68	74	284	58,380
Morten Orum Madsen	71	74	69	70	284	58,380
Miguel Angel Jimenez	76	70	67	72	285	52,941
Charl Schwartzel	74	69	68	74	285	52,941
Marcel Siem	70	71	72	72	285	52,941
Chris Wood	70	71	71	74	286	48,590
Paul Casey	72	75	65	75	287	46,414
Gonzalo Fernandez-Castano	74	73	71	69	287	46,414
Mikko Ilonen	73	73	69	72	287	46,414
Jin Jeong	73	76	68	71	288	43,695
David Lynn	71	74	72	71	288	43,695
Kiradech Aphibarnrat	75	74	71	69	289	40,431
Darren Clarke	69	71	72	77	289	40,431
David Howell	76	69	71	73	289	40,431
Colin Montgomerie	70	74	69	76	289	40,431
Richard Sterne	72	73	73	73	291	37,711
Stephen Gallacher	73	74	72	73	292	36,080
Michael Hoey	72	73	73	74	292	36,080
Simon Thornton	70	72	80	71	293	34,448
Robert Karlsson	74	72	73	75	294	33,360
Dawie van der Walt	71	71	75	78	295	32,272
Peter Uihlein	70	78	70	78	296	31,185
Darren Fichardt	73	71	74	79	297	30,097
Jose Maria Olazabal	73	77	77	73	300	29,009

Abu Dhabi HSBC Golf Championship

Abu Dhabi Golf Club, Abu Dhabi, United Arab Emirates — January 16-19
Par 36-36–72; 7,600 yards — purse, $2,700,000

	SCORES				TOTAL	MONEY
Pablo Larrazabal	69	70	68	67	274	€328,779
Rory McIlroy	70	67	70	68	275	171,338
Phil Mickelson	73	70	63	69	275	171,338
Rafa Cabrera-Bello	67	68	73	68	276	91,138
George Coetzee	68	70	72	66	276	91,138

	SCORES				TOTAL	MONEY
Joost Luiten	68	70	72	68	278	69,044
Johan Carlsson	73	70	71	65	279	59,180
Stephen Gallacher	70	73	68	69	280	46,752
Robert Karlsson	73	67	72	68	280	46,752
Gaganjeet Bhullar	72	68	66	75	281	31,168
Thomas Bjorn	70	67	72	72	281	31,168
Darren Fichardt	70	70	75	66	281	31,168
Peter Hanson	70	70	69	72	281	31,168
Tyrrell Hatton	69	71	70	71	281	31,168
Michael Hoey	69	71	68	73	281	31,168
Thongchai Jaidee	70	70	68	73	281	31,168
Miguel Angel Jimenez	73	68	67	73	281	31,168
Craig Lee	68	67	69	77	281	31,168
Thomas Aiken	70	73	69	70	282	21,765
Matthew Baldwin	67	72	69	74	282	21,765
Tommy Fleetwood	73	65	72	72	282	21,765
Sergio Garcia	76	68	70	68	282	21,765
Paul McGinley	68	72	72	70	282	21,765
Hennie Otto	70	71	69	72	282	21,765
Brandon Stone	71	71	73	67	282	21,765
Andy Sullivan	73	70	69	70	282	21,765
Danny Willett	73	63	76	70	282	21,765
Jose-Filipe Lima	68	75	67	73	283	18,149
Edoardo Molinari	70	71	71	71	283	18,149
Wade Ormsby	69	73	71	70	283	18,149
Ricardo Gonzalez	71	66	74	73	284	15,584
Emiliano Grillo	72	72	70	70	284	15,584
Martin Kaymer	70	71	69	74	284	15,584
Maximilian Kieffer	71	71	72	70	284	15,584
Matteo Manassero	71	73	70	70	284	15,584
Alvaro Quiros	71	70	70	73	284	15,584
Luke Donald	70	73	71	71	285	12,625
Oliver Fisher	69	72	73	71	285	12,625
David Howell	73	71	72	69	285	12,625
Raphael Jacquelin	71	72	70	72	285	12,625
Shiv Kapur	71	72	75	67	285	12,625
Marcel Siem	69	70	73	73	285	12,625
Paul Waring	73	71	74	67	285	12,625
Marc Warren	68	73	70	74	285	12,625
Tom Lewis	71	70	72	73	286	10,258
Colin Montgomerie	73	68	74	71	286	10,258
Eddie Pepperell	70	72	69	75	286	10,258
Romain Wattel	67	75	70	74	286	10,258
Seve Benson	73	70	72	72	287	8,877
Jorge Campillo	72	72	73	70	287	8,877
Alejandro Canizares	71	69	76	71	287	8,877
Darren Clarke	74	69	72	73	288	7,496
Branden Grace	73	70	70	75	288	7,496
Julien Quesne	71	72	74	71	288	7,496
Ricardo Santos	70	72	71	75	288	7,496
Eduardo De La Riva	70	74	72	73	289	6,066
Jamie Donaldson	73	70	73	73	289	6,066
Alexander Levy	74	69	69	77	289	6,066
Thorbjorn Olesen	74	70	71	74	289	6,066
Jeev Milkha Singh	69	75	74	72	290	5,326
Steve Webster	69	73	75	73	290	5,326
Peter Whiteford	74	70	73	73	290	5,326
Nacho Elvira	72	70	74	75	291	4,833
Jin Jeong	70	71	76	74	291	4,833
Richard Bland	71	73	75	73	292	4,143
Magnus A. Carlsson	71	71	77	73	292	4,143
Paul Casey	72	71	73	76	292	4,143
Gareth Maybin	73	70	76	73	292	4,143

	SCORES				TOTAL	MONEY
Chris Wood	71	73	72	76	292	4,143
Damien McGrane	70	72	75	76	293	3,595
Dawie van der Walt	68	73	74	79	294	2,959

Commercial Bank Qatar Masters

Doha Golf Club, Doha, Qatar — January 22-25
Par 36-36–72; 7,400 yards — purse, $2,500,000

	SCORES				TOTAL	MONEY
Sergio Garcia	71	67	69	65	272	€305,232
Mikko Ilonen	68	67	71	66	272	203,486
(Garcia defeated Ilonen on third playoff hole.)						
Rafa Cabrera-Bello	66	65	73	69	273	103,109
Thorbjorn Olesen	68	69	68	68	273	103,109
Thomas Aiken	67	68	70	69	274	60,620
Alejandro Canizares	68	68	73	65	274	60,620
George Coetzee	64	69	73	68	274	60,620
Steve Webster	65	69	70	70	274	60,620
Magnus A. Carlsson	69	71	70	65	275	38,826
Dawie van der Walt	65	72	70	68	275	38,826
Paul Lawrie	67	70	69	70	276	32,599
Romain Wattel	67	68	74	67	276	32,599
Seve Benson	68	71	69	69	277	28,143
Carlos Del Moral	72	68	69	68	277	28,143
Branden Grace	67	69	71	70	277	28,143
Johan Carlsson	69	65	72	72	278	23,772
Simon Dyson	68	69	71	70	278	23,772
Darren Fichardt	69	70	69	70	278	23,772
*Dominic Foos	70	70	70	68	278	
Adrien Saddier	70	71	64	73	278	23,772
Peter Uihlein	70	69	69	70	278	23,772
Matthew Baldwin	68	66	74	71	279	19,871
Gaganjeet Bhullar	67	70	73	69	279	19,871
Peter Hanson	69	67	75	68	279	19,871
Tyrrell Hatton	69	71	71	68	279	19,871
Robert Rock	70	71	71	67	279	19,871
Fabrizio Zanotti	69	69	68	73	279	19,871
Kristoffer Broberg	69	68	70	73	280	16,849
Stephen Gallacher	69	68	75	68	280	16,849
Julien Quesne	71	70	70	69	280	16,849
Alvaro Quiros	69	72	69	70	280	16,849
Henrik Stenson	68	71	74	67	280	16,849
Richard Bland	69	70	71	71	281	14,422
Thongchai Jaidee	68	73	72	68	281	14,422
Shiv Kapur	68	71	71	71	281	14,422
Gary Stal	69	70	71	71	281	14,422
Ernie Els	67	76	71	68	282	12,454
Soren Hansen	73	70	68	71	282	12,454
Brooks Koepka	70	70	70	72	282	12,454
Tom Lewis	68	67	76	71	282	12,454
Hennie Otto	71	71	71	69	282	12,454
Anthony Wall	70	66	76	70	282	12,454
Robert-Jan Derksen	70	72	73	68	283	9,340
Robert Dinwiddie	71	72	72	68	283	9,340
Ross Fisher	66	72	75	70	283	9,340
Craig Lee	72	67	72	72	283	9,340
Stuart Manley	69	70	71	73	283	9,340
Ricardo Santos	72	69	73	69	283	9,340
Marcel Siem	69	73	71	70	283	9,340

	SCORES				TOTAL	MONEY
Jeev Milkha Singh	71	71	73	68	283	9,340
Simon Thornton	70	68	74	71	283	9,340
Danny Willett	71	72	70	70	283	9,340
Chris Wood	73	70	71	69	283	9,340
Francois Calmels	66	70	73	75	284	6,776
Marcus Fraser	74	68	74	68	284	6,776
Robert Karlsson	70	73	71	70	284	6,776
Luke Donald	72	69	74	70	285	5,632
Mark Foster	72	71	73	69	285	5,632
Martin Kaymer	70	70	73	72	285	5,632
Soren Kjeldsen	70	71	74	70	285	5,632
John Daly	67	69	77	73	286	5,036
Michael Hoey	68	70	74	74	286	5,036
Paul McGinley	73	70	72	72	287	4,487
James Morrison	68	73	75	71	287	4,487
Jose Maria Olazabal	69	70	74	74	287	4,487
Eddie Pepperell	69	74	76	68	287	4,487
Chris Doak	69	72	74	73	288	3,846
Nacho Elvira	66	73	76	73	288	3,846
Wade Ormsby	72	70	74	72	288	3,846
Marco Crespi	70	71	77	71	289	3,414
Jose-Filipe Lima	72	70	75	72	289	3,414
Jason Dufner	70	71	78	71	290	2,746
Victor Riu	73	70	74	73	290	2,746
Emiliano Grillo	72	70	77	72	291	2,741
Tommy Fleetwood	73	70	74	75	292	2,738
Lee Slattery	73	70	77	73	293	2,735

Omega Dubai Desert Classic

Emirates Golf Club, Dubai, United Arab Emirates — January 30-February 2
Par 35-37–72; 7,316 yards — purse, $2,500,000

	SCORES				TOTAL	MONEY
Stephen Gallacher	66	71	63	72	272	€303,268
Emiliano Grillo	71	67	69	66	273	202,176
Brooks Koepka	69	65	70	70	274	102,446
Romain Wattel	68	73	67	66	274	102,446
Mikko Ilonen	69	72	70	64	275	60,230
Thorbjorn Olesen	71	68	65	71	275	60,230
Robert Rock	67	70	68	70	275	60,230
Steve Webster	71	70	64	70	275	60,230
Paul Casey	70	72	67	67	276	35,483
Rory McIlroy	63	70	69	74	276	35,483
Edoardo Molinari	65	72	68	71	276	35,483
Bernd Wiesberger	70	70	68	68	276	35,483
Thomas Bjorn	72	70	68	67	277	25,735
Darren Fichardt	69	72	66	70	277	25,735
Soren Hansen	67	71	71	68	277	25,735
Francesco Molinari	69	69	71	68	277	25,735
Brett Rumford	69	70	71	67	277	25,735
Paul Waring	70	70	68	69	277	25,735
Danny Willett	71	65	73	68	277	25,735
Jamie Donaldson	69	68	70	71	278	21,168
Simon Dyson	69	69	73	67	278	21,168
Damien McGrane	66	70	71	71	278	21,168
Jorge Campillo	68	72	70	69	279	18,651
Roope Kakko	69	69	68	73	279	18,651
Joost Luiten	70	69	70	70	279	18,651
Morten Orum Madsen	71	67	72	69	279	18,651

	SCORES				TOTAL	MONEY
Anthony Wall	74	66	69	70	279	18,651
Chris Wood	73	69	70	67	279	18,651
Seve Benson	72	70	70	68	280	14,898
Kristoffer Broberg	71	69	73	67	280	14,898
Eduardo De La Riva	70	70	72	68	280	14,898
Scott Hend	69	72	70	69	280	14,898
Soren Kjeldsen	68	71	71	70	280	14,898
Henrik Stenson	70	67	75	68	280	14,898
Dawie van der Walt	72	70	65	73	280	14,898
Fabrizio Zanotti	72	70	70	68	280	14,898
Robert Karlsson	73	67	71	70	281	12,374
Sihwan Kim	70	69	72	70	281	12,374
Hennie Otto	68	73	69	71	281	12,374
Marcel Siem	72	67	73	69	281	12,374
Matthew Baldwin	66	74	69	73	282	10,372
Rafa Cabrera-Bello	71	69	71	71	282	10,372
Chris Doak	71	68	71	72	282	10,372
Thongchai Jaidee	68	69	71	74	282	10,372
Pablo Larrazabal	74	68	69	71	282	10,372
Gary Stal	74	68	73	67	282	10,372
Tiger Woods	68	73	70	71	282	10,372
Marco Crespi	69	71	69	74	283	8,006
Scott Jamieson	73	69	70	71	283	8,006
Shiv Kapur	72	70	70	71	283	8,006
Colin Montgomerie	70	70	69	74	283	8,006
Seung-Yul Noh	69	72	71	71	283	8,006
Julien Quesne	66	70	77	70	283	8,006
Gregory Bourdy	71	68	73	72	284	5,376
Alejandro Canizares	74	67	74	69	284	5,376
Magnus A. Carlsson	69	69	74	72	284	5,376
Fred Couples	70	71	73	70	284	5,376
Gregory Havret	70	72	72	70	284	5,376
Michael Hoey	70	72	73	69	284	5,376
Maximilian Kieffer	71	70	71	72	284	5,376
Paul Lawrie	68	71	72	73	284	5,376
Alvaro Quiros	69	72	74	69	284	5,376
Richard Sterne	66	73	69	76	284	5,376
Jaco Van Zyl	71	68	71	74	284	5,376
Raphael Jacquelin	69	71	69	77	286	4,094
Justin Walters	69	68	75	74	286	4,094
Carlos Del Moral	70	72	73	72	287	3,639
Alexander Levy	69	72	76	70	287	3,639
Lee Slattery	70	71	70	76	287	3,639
Jose-Filipe Lima	71	71	75	72	289	3,326
Tom Lewis	71	69	78	73	291	2,729

Joburg Open

See African Tours chapter.

Africa Open

See African Tours chapter.

Tshwane Open

See African Tours chapter.

Trophee Hassan II

Golf du Palais Royal, Agadir, Morocco — March 13-16
Par 36-36-72; 6,951 yards — purse, €1,500,000

	SCORES				TOTAL	MONEY
Alejandro Canizares	62	68	69	70	269	€250,000
Andy Sullivan	66	73	72	63	274	166,660
Seve Benson	63	68	74	71	276	84,450
Magnus A. Carlsson	65	71	72	68	276	84,450
Richard Bland	69	70	70	68	277	53,700
Rafa Cabrera-Bello	68	67	75	67	277	53,700
Wade Ormsby	68	71	70	68	277	53,700
David Horsey	72	64	72	70	278	33,700
Tom Lewis	69	74	70	65	278	33,700
Paul Waring	72	69	67	70	278	33,700
Lucas Bjerregaard	69	73	71	67	280	23,950
Jorge Campillo	71	69	70	70	280	23,950
George Coetzee	69	69	74	68	280	23,950
Robert Karlsson	71	67	70	72	280	23,950
Richie Ramsay	72	71	68	69	280	23,950
Brett Rumford	73	71	70	66	280	23,950
Gregory Bourdy	68	69	74	70	281	18,425
Jens Dantorp	73	71	69	68	281	18,425
Robert-Jan Derksen	69	70	67	75	281	18,425
Stephen Dodd	68	73	71	69	281	18,425
Shiv Kapur	70	71	67	73	281	18,425
Marc Warren	66	73	70	72	281	18,425
Tommy Fleetwood	66	72	73	71	282	16,275
James Morrison	69	69	75	69	282	16,275
Kristoffer Broberg	75	70	72	66	283	14,700
Rhys Davies	68	73	71	71	283	14,700
Daniel Im	71	73	69	70	283	14,700
Edoardo Molinari	73	70	74	66	283	14,700
Adrien Saddier	72	72	69	70	283	14,700
Florian Fritsch	72	70	70	72	284	12,900
Richard Green	70	73	69	72	284	12,900
Michael Hoey	68	70	76	70	284	12,900
Robert Dinwiddie	71	71	73	70	285	11,438
Robert Rock	71	68	71	75	285	11,438
Gary Stal	73	71	70	71	285	11,438
Bernd Wiesberger	71	73	70	71	285	11,438
Connor Arendell	65	71	76	74	286	9,900
Simon Dyson	73	70	71	72	286	9,900
Ross Fisher	70	73	71	72	286	9,900
Mikko Ilonen	69	73	73	71	286	9,900
Alexander Levy	70	72	69	75	286	9,900
Danny Willett	72	70	70	74	286	9,900
David Drysdale	73	67	72	75	287	8,250
Nacho Elvira	70	75	68	74	287	8,250
Tyrrell Hatton	73	72	69	73	287	8,250
Soren Kjeldsen	74	70	68	75	287	8,250
Simon Wakefield	72	73	70	72	287	8,250
Marco Crespi	71	74	69	74	288	6,900
Soren Hansen	74	69	75	70	288	6,900
Alexandre Kaleka	72	73	72	71	288	6,900
Marcel Siem	69	69	75	75	288	6,900
Matthew Baldwin	71	74	77	67	289	5,700
Eduardo De La Riva	70	74	76	69	289	5,700
Gregory Havret	72	71	73	73	289	5,700
Mark Tullo	74	69	70	76	289	5,700
Daniel Brooks	72	70	72	76	290	4,612
Daan Huizing	74	70	76	70	290	4,612

	SCORES				TOTAL	MONEY
Maximilian Kieffer	71	72	74	73	290	4,612
Shane Lowry	72	72	73	73	290	4,612
Gaganjeet Bhullar	67	73	74	77	291	3,975
David Howell	72	69	75	75	291	3,975
Roope Kakko	70	73	75	73	291	3,975
Patrik Sjoland	70	74	76	71	291	3,975
Francois Calmels	70	74	73	75	292	3,450
Estanislao Goya	73	69	74	76	292	3,450
Damien McGrane	70	73	76	73	292	3,450
Jose Manuel Lara	72	73	71	79	295	3,150
Duncan Stewart	71	74	74	79	298	2,925
Peter Whiteford	67	78	79	74	298	2,925
Raphael Jacquelin	71	71	79	78	299	2,740
Edouard Dubois	68	75	81	77	301	2,250

EurAsia Cup

See Asia/Japan Tours chapter.

NH Collection Open

La Reserva de Sotogrande Club de Golf, Cadiz, Spain — April 3-6
Par 36-36–72; 7,234 yards — purse, €600,000

	SCORES				TOTAL	MONEY
Marco Crespi	70	73	66	69	278	€100,000
Jordi Garcia Pinto	73	70	71	66	280	52,110
Richie Ramsay	71	72	69	68	280	52,110
Felipe Aguilar	71	69	70	71	281	27,720
Matthew Nixon	72	71	65	73	281	27,720
Kristoffer Broberg	76	70	67	69	282	16,860
Oliver Fisher	71	72	71	68	282	16,860
Adrian Otaegui	71	69	72	70	282	16,860
Marc Warren	72	67	75	68	282	16,860
Bradley Dredge	70	69	78	66	283	11,520
Ricardo Santos	74	70	67	72	283	11,520
Phillip Archer	74	70	73	67	284	9,288
Rhys Davies	72	71	72	69	284	9,288
David Horsey	71	68	73	72	284	9,288
Gary Stal	72	74	73	65	284	9,288
Tjaart van der Walt	70	73	69	72	284	9,288
Daniel Im	72	72	71	70	285	7,920
Damien McGrane	74	69	70	72	285	7,920
Matteo Delpodio	71	73	70	72	286	7,440
Connor Arendell	72	75	70	70	287	6,518
Carlos Del Moral	73	72	72	70	287	6,518
Edouard Dubois	73	73	74	67	287	6,518
John Hahn	74	68	75	70	287	6,518
Lasse Jensen	73	70	74	70	287	6,518
Andrew Johnston	73	72	70	72	287	6,518
Alexander Levy	72	75	72	68	287	6,518
Jamie McLeary	73	70	74	70	287	6,518
Byeong-Hun An	73	73	76	66	288	5,520
Mark Foster	71	77	73	67	288	5,520
Maarten Lafeber	78	69	73	68	288	5,520
Daniel Brooks	73	75	70	71	289	4,890
Estanislao Goya	73	75	69	72	289	4,890
Andrew Marshall	74	73	71	71	289	4,890

	SCORES				TOTAL	MONEY
Kevin Phelan	75	70	73	71	289	4,890
Lucas Bjerregaard	72	73	70	75	290	4,200
Eduardo De La Riva	72	76	73	69	290	4,200
Johan Edfors	76	72	69	73	290	4,200
Sihwan Kim	70	76	70	74	290	4,200
Mikko Korhonen	71	75	71	73	290	4,200
Mikael Lundberg	71	72	78	69	290	4,200
Adrien Bernadet	76	71	78	66	291	3,480
Daniel Gaunt	75	70	73	73	291	3,480
Scott Jamieson	71	72	70	78	291	3,480
Michael Jonzon	74	70	76	71	291	3,480
Chris Paisley	72	72	76	71	291	3,480
Oliver Wilson	75	72	75	69	291	3,480
Jorge Campillo	72	73	77	70	292	2,700
David Drysdale	79	69	70	74	292	2,700
Lorenzo Gagli	71	74	72	75	292	2,700
J.B. Hansen	77	69	74	72	292	2,700
David Howell	71	75	70	76	292	2,700
Jeppe Huldahl	72	73	75	72	292	2,700
Victor Riu	73	74	71	74	292	2,700
Jack Doherty	69	74	77	73	293	2,100
Nacho Elvira	72	76	73	72	293	2,100
Gregory Havret	74	70	76	73	293	2,100
Chris Hanson	72	76	77	69	294	1,830
Simon Wakefield	74	74	71	75	294	1,830
Simon Khan	75	73	73	74	295	1,710
Thomas Norret	73	71	80	71	295	1,710
Lloyd Kennedy	75	72	76	73	296	1,560
Gary Lockerbie	76	70	74	76	296	1,560
Pedro Oriol	75	73	75	73	296	1,560
Jens Dantorp	71	73	73	81	298	1,410
Oscar Stark	74	71	75	78	298	1,410
Simon Thornton	74	73	75	77	299	1,320
Cyril Bouniol	74	73	80	75	302	1,230
Thomas Levet	72	76	77	77	302	1,230

Maybank Malaysian Open

See Asia/Japan Tours chapter.

Volvo China Open

See Asia/Japan Tours chapter.

The Championship

See Asia/Japan Tours chapter.

Madeira Islands Open - Portugal - BPI

Clube de Golf do Santo da Serra, Madeira, Portugal — May 8-11
Par 36-36–72; 6,826 yards — purse, €600,000
(Event shortened to 36 holes—fog.)

	SCORES		TOTAL	MONEY
Daniel Brooks	68	67	135	€75,000
Scott Henry	67	68	135	50,000
(Brooks defeated Henry on first playoff hole.)				
Jordi Garcia Pinto	69	69	138	21,375

	SCORES		TOTAL	MONEY
Julien Guerrier	69	69	138	21,375
Antonio Hortal	69	69	138	21,375
Fabrizio Zanotti	70	68	138	21,375
Johan Edfors	70	69	139	11,610
Michael Lorenzo-Vera	71	68	139	11,610
Martin Wiegele	69	70	139	11,610
Jose-Filipe Lima	69	71	140	8,640
Steven Tiley	72	68	140	8,640
Christopher Mivis	71	70	141	7,121
Adrien Saddier	71	70	141	7,121
Anthony Snobeck	74	67	141	7,121
Tjaart van der Walt	70	71	141	7,121
Bjorn Akesson	72	70	142	5,558
Scott Arnold	71	71	142	5,558
Jens Dantorp	71	71	142	5,558
Bradley Dredge	72	70	142	5,558
Edouard Espana	73	69	142	5,558
Lukas Nemecz	72	70	142	5,558
Chris Paisley	72	70	142	5,558
Brinson Paolini	73	69	142	5,558
Cyril Bouniol	70	73	143	3,900
Tiago Cruz	73	70	143	3,900
Rhys Davies	72	71	143	3,900
Oliver Fisher	72	71	143	3,900
Lorenzo Gagli	72	71	143	3,900
Adam Gee	73	70	143	3,900
Estanislao Goya	73	70	143	3,900
David Higgins	72	71	143	3,900
Lloyd Kennedy	68	75	143	3,900
Tain Lee	72	71	143	3,900
Andrew Marshall	69	74	143	3,900
Pedro Oriol	69	74	143	3,900
Jason Palmer	73	70	143	3,900
Phillip Price	72	71	143	3,900
Pontus Widegren	71	72	143	3,900
Carlos Aguilar	70	74	144	2,655
Connor Arendell	73	71	144	2,655
Ken Benz	72	72	144	2,655
Daniel Gaunt	74	70	144	2,655
Mikael Lundberg	74	70	144	2,655
James Morrison	72	72	144	2,655
Hugo Santos	73	71	144	2,655
Patrik Sjoland	74	70	144	2,655
Sam Walker	72	72	144	2,655
Byeong-Hun An	74	71	145	2,070
Filippo Bergamaschi	73	72	145	2,070
Sam Hutsby	73	72	145	2,070
Pierre Relecom	74	71	145	2,070
Jens Fahrbring	73	73	146	1,547
Michael Jonzon	73	73	146	1,547
David Law	74	72	146	1,547
Jesus Legarrea	74	72	146	1,547
Chris Lloyd	72	74	146	1,547
Ricardo Santos	72	74	146	1,547
Gareth Shaw	73	73	146	1,547
Daniel Vancsik	74	72	146	1,547
Agustin Domingo	72	75	147	1,215
Edouard Dubois	73	74	147	1,215
Callum Shinkwin	72	75	147	1,215
Steven Brown	71	77	148	1,080
*Joao Carlota	69	79	148	
Alastair Forsyth	73	75	148	1,080
Mathias Gronberg	73	75	148	1,080

	SCORES		TOTAL	MONEY
George Woolgar	73	76	149	990
Dara Ford	74	76	150	922
Thomas Linard	74	76	150	922
Matteo Delpodio	74	77	151	838
Damian Ulrich	74	77	151	838
Andrea Rota	74	78	152	675

Open de Espana

PGA Catalunya Resort, Girona, Spain — May 15-18
Par 36-36–72; 7,172 yards — purse, €1,500,000

	SCORES				TOTAL	MONEY
Miguel Angel Jimenez	69	73	69	73	284	€250,000
Richard Green	74	69	69	72	284	130,280
Thomas Pieters	69	69	71	75	284	130,280
(Jimenez defeated Green and Pieters on first playoff hole.)						
Joost Luiten	70	69	74	72	285	75,000
Maximilian Kieffer	75	69	69	73	286	58,050
Richie Ramsay	69	72	71	74	286	58,050
Felipe Aguilar	74	70	69	74	287	34,740
Alejandro Canizares	72	76	69	70	287	34,740
Darren Fichardt	77	66	73	71	287	34,740
Gareth Maybin	73	70	73	71	287	34,740
Chris Wood	73	70	69	75	287	34,740
Richard Bland	73	68	72	75	288	24,300
Daan Huizing	71	76	71	70	288	24,300
Alvaro Velasco	75	73	68	72	288	24,300
Ross Fisher	70	76	67	76	289	18,917
Emiliano Grillo	74	72	69	74	289	18,917
Mikko Korhonen	74	69	73	73	289	18,917
Paul Lawrie	70	72	74	73	289	18,917
Tom Lewis	72	75	69	73	289	18,917
Shane Lowry	72	74	72	71	289	18,917
Paul McGinley	72	72	72	73	289	18,917
Wade Ormsby	72	74	71	72	289	18,917
Danny Willett	70	75	74	70	289	18,917
Niclas Fasth	75	69	77	69	290	15,375
Raphael Jacquelin	73	72	71	74	290	15,375
Francesco Molinari	73	67	75	75	290	15,375
Eddie Pepperell	68	71	79	72	290	15,375
David Drysdale	74	71	76	70	291	12,315
Nacho Elvira	75	72	74	70	291	12,315
Tyrrell Hatton	73	74	71	73	291	12,315
Gregory Havret	71	75	71	74	291	12,315
Mikael Lundberg	72	74	70	75	291	12,315
Matteo Manassero	74	71	74	72	291	12,315
Brinson Paolini	73	75	73	70	291	12,315
Andrea Pavan	74	72	71	74	291	12,315
Julien Quesne	76	71	73	71	291	12,315
Marc Warren	75	70	72	74	291	12,315
Robert-Jan Derksen	69	74	72	77	292	8,850
Agustin Domingo	72	76	72	72	292	8,850
Sergio Garcia	69	74	73	76	292	8,850
David Higgins	73	74	72	73	292	8,850
Jbe' Kruger	70	78	71	73	292	8,850
Michael Lorenzo-Vera	74	72	74	72	292	8,850
Edoardo Molinari	73	72	75	72	292	8,850
James Morrison	71	76	73	72	292	8,850
Mark Tullo	72	74	74	72	292	8,850

	SCORES				TOTAL	MONEY
Romain Wattel	73	75	72	72	292	8,850
Bernd Wiesberger	80	68	74	70	292	8,850
Seve Benson	74	73	72	74	293	6,150
Francois Calmels	74	73	74	72	293	6,150
Magnus A. Carlsson	72	74	68	79	293	6,150
Gonzalo Fernandez-Castano	73	75	71	74	293	6,150
Jordi Garcia Pinto	70	73	74	76	293	6,150
Pedro Oriol	75	73	71	74	293	6,150
Robert Rock	72	75	73	73	293	6,150
Alex Noren	71	72	73	78	294	4,950
Adam Gee	72	75	73	75	295	4,350
J.B. Hansen	75	73	75	72	295	4,350
Alexander Levy	72	75	73	75	295	4,350
Adrian Otaegui	73	71	74	77	295	4,350
Hennie Otto	71	76	76	72	295	4,350
*Renato Paratore	72	75	73	75	295	
Kevin Phelan	76	71	71	78	296	3,825
Graeme Storm	71	76	72	77	296	3,825
Alvaro Quiros	74	67	76	80	297	3,600
Thomas Aiken	74	73	74	77	298	3,225
Jorge Campillo	71	75	79	73	298	3,225
Carlos Pigem	73	71	74	80	298	3,225
Simon Thornton	72	76	76	74	298	3,225
Craig Lee	73	75	71	81	300	2,850
Eduardo De La Riva	73	72	75	81	301	2,412
Carlos Del Moral	74	74	79	74	301	2,412
Jose-Filipe Lima	69	79	76	77	301	2,412
Rafa Cabrera-Bello	69	75	74	85	303	2,244
Gaganjeet Bhullar	71	74	78	83	306	2,240
Ivo Giner	71	74	78	83	306	2,240

BMW PGA Championship

Wentworth Club, Virginia Water, Surrey, England — May 22-25
Par 35-37–72; 7,302 yards — purse, €4,750,000

	SCORES				TOTAL	MONEY
Rory McIlroy	68	71	69	66	274	€791,660
Shane Lowry	64	70	73	68	275	527,770
Thomas Bjorn	62	72	67	75	276	267,425
Luke Donald	71	67	68	70	276	267,425
Simon Dyson	69	74	69	67	279	183,825
Stephen Gallacher	70	75	68	66	279	183,825
Thomas Aiken	68	72	70	70	280	110,010
Pablo Larrazabal	69	71	69	71	280	110,010
Francesco Molinari	71	74	65	70	280	110,010
Marcel Siem	69	71	72	68	280	110,010
Henrik Stenson	68	71	71	70	280	110,010
Chris Doak	69	72	69	71	281	75,169
Martin Kaymer	68	75	69	69	281	75,169
Alexander Levy	71	73	70	67	281	75,169
Joost Luiten	70	71	67	73	281	75,169
Jonas Blixt	68	71	72	71	282	61,655
Rafa Cabrera-Bello	65	73	73	71	282	61,655
Richard Green	70	73	70	69	282	61,655
Marc Warren	73	69	71	69	282	61,655
Fabrizio Zanotti	67	72	73	70	282	61,655
Seve Benson	71	69	73	70	283	52,962
Paul Lawrie	72	71	73	67	283	52,962
Eddie Pepperell	69	73	68	73	283	52,962

	SCORES				TOTAL	MONEY
Chris Wood	73	72	69	69	283	52,962
Justin Rose	70	73	70	71	284	49,400
Mark Foster	72	71	70	72	285	45,838
Ian Poulter	70	72	74	69	285	45,838
Andy Sullivan	70	71	69	75	285	45,838
Anthony Wall	67	76	67	75	285	45,838
George Coetzee	75	70	70	71	286	39,425
Jamie Donaldson	73	69	68	76	286	39,425
Anders Hansen	71	69	74	72	286	39,425
Gregory Havret	69	76	70	71	286	39,425
Romain Wattel	72	74	73	67	286	39,425
David Horsey	68	76	70	73	287	34,675
Miguel Angel Jimenez	72	72	72	71	287	34,675
Lee Westwood	71	71	72	73	287	34,675
Soren Hansen	73	72	73	70	288	29,450
Tyrrell Hatton	75	70	70	73	288	29,450
Mark Hooper	71	71	71	75	288	29,450
Mikko Ilonen	71	71	77	69	288	29,450
Thongchai Jaidee	72	73	74	69	288	29,450
Richie Ramsay	70	72	74	72	288	29,450
Robert Rock	73	73	72	70	288	29,450
Gary Stal	66	76	69	77	288	29,450
Eduardo De La Riva	71	72	78	68	289	21,850
Daan Huizing	72	74	74	69	289	21,850
Raphael Jacquelin	70	75	70	74	289	21,850
Tom Lewis	73	72	71	73	289	21,850
Edoardo Molinari	75	70	72	72	289	21,850
Simon Thornton	74	68	73	74	289	21,850
Paul Waring	72	72	74	71	289	21,850
Bernd Wiesberger	70	71	74	74	289	21,850
Carlos Del Moral	71	75	71	73	290	16,625
Roope Kakko	75	71	72	72	290	16,625
Thorbjorn Olesen	71	73	70	76	290	16,625
Gregory Bourdy	72	73	73	73	291	14,012
Richard Finch	71	72	71	77	291	14,012
Alvaro Quiros	73	72	70	76	291	14,012
Ricardo Santos	72	69	79	71	291	14,012
Branden Grace	70	75	72	75	292	12,588
Padraig Harrington	69	76	74	73	292	12,588
Jorge Campillo	73	73	71	76	293	11,162
Damien McGrane	71	75	74	73	293	11,162
Adrian Otaegui	72	73	75	73	293	11,162
Danny Willett	73	73	72	75	293	11,162
Robert-Jan Derksen	70	76	73	75	294	9,500
Peter Hanson	71	72	80	71	294	9,500
Robert Karlsson	74	70	72	78	294	9,500
Graeme Storm	71	73	73	79	296	8,670
Johan Carlsson	71	75	73	78	297	7,124
Nicolas Colsaerts	77	69	72	79	297	7,124
Oliver Fisher	69	75	84	73	301	7,119
Kristoffer Broberg	73	72	80	81	306	7,116

Nordea Masters

PGA Sweden National, Malmo, Sweden — May 29-June 1
Par 36-36–72; 7,390 yards — purse, €1,500,000

	SCORES				TOTAL	MONEY
Thongchai Jaidee	69	70	68	65	272	€250,000
Victor Dubuisson	69	69	67	67	272	130,280
Stephen Gallacher	67	72	65	68	272	130,280
(Jaidee defeated Dubuisson and Gallacher on first playoff hole.)						
Robert-Jan Derksen	70	71	67	65	273	75,000
Henrik Stenson	69	70	64	71	274	63,600
Robert Karlsson	70	70	72	63	275	45,000
Eddie Pepperell	66	72	65	72	275	45,000
Alvaro Quiros	71	67	66	71	275	45,000
Rafa Cabrera-Bello	68	72	67	69	276	31,800
David Howell	73	70	67	66	276	31,800
Maximilian Kieffer	70	74	67	66	277	25,850
Julien Quesne	72	71	70	64	277	25,850
Romain Wattel	71	70	66	70	277	25,850
Thomas Pieters	73	69	68	68	278	22,950
Thomas Bjorn	70	71	68	70	279	21,150
Darren Fichardt	73	71	68	67	279	21,150
Rikard Karlberg	67	75	68	69	279	21,150
Michael Hoey	69	75	69	67	280	18,650
Craig Lee	68	74	71	67	280	18,650
Edoardo Molinari	71	69	73	67	280	18,650
Eduardo De La Riva	72	72	70	67	281	16,950
Simon Dyson	69	72	70	70	281	16,950
*Marcus Kinhult	71	72	69	69	281	
Tom Lewis	71	71	68	71	281	16,950
Jorge Campillo	68	76	70	68	282	14,700
Chris Doak	70	69	69	74	282	14,700
Bradley Dredge	69	70	67	76	282	14,700
Peter Hanson	69	71	73	69	282	14,700
Raphael Jacquelin	72	70	69	71	282	14,700
Alexander Levy	72	73	71	66	282	14,700
Shane Lowry	71	73	72	66	282	14,700
Felipe Aguilar	70	75	70	68	283	11,512
Jack Doherty	70	74	68	71	283	11,512
Nacho Elvira	73	71	68	71	283	11,512
Niclas Fasth	71	70	70	72	283	11,512
Mikko Ilonen	70	71	71	71	283	11,512
Soren Kjeldsen	70	75	70	68	283	11,512
Pablo Larrazabal	70	72	68	73	283	11,512
Matteo Manassero	74	70	70	69	283	11,512
Oliver Fisher	69	75	69	71	284	9,150
Richard Green	72	69	76	67	284	9,150
Peter Lawrie	75	70	72	67	284	9,150
James Morrison	70	73	66	75	284	9,150
Andrea Pavan	74	71	71	68	284	9,150
Kevin Phelan	71	70	73	70	284	9,150
Paul Waring	68	76	70	70	284	9,150
Lucas Bjerregaard	70	75	70	70	285	7,200
Francois Calmels	73	70	75	67	285	7,200
Johan Carlsson	68	77	71	69	285	7,200
Daniel Im	72	72	74	67	285	7,200
Jose-Filipe Lima	71	74	69	71	285	7,200
Wade Ormsby	69	74	72	70	285	7,200
Bjorn Akesson	71	73	75	67	286	5,700
Scott Jamieson	69	72	73	72	286	5,700
James Kingston	72	70	72	72	286	5,700
Richie Ramsay	72	72	71	71	286	5,700

	SCORES				TOTAL	MONEY
Jens Dantorp	66	73	71	77	287	4,700
Edouard Dubois	70	73	68	76	287	4,700
Daan Huizing	67	78	70	72	287	4,700
Kristoffer Broberg	70	74	68	76	288	4,125
Shiv Kapur	76	68	72	72	288	4,125
Mikael Lundberg	69	75	72	72	288	4,125
Sebastian Soderberg	67	76	74	71	288	4,125
Matthew Baldwin	71	73	73	72	289	3,600
Gregory Havret	71	74	70	74	289	3,600
Jeev Milkha Singh	71	74	70	74	289	3,600
Fredrik Andersson Hed	74	70	74	72	290	3,150
Emiliano Grillo	73	72	71	74	290	3,150
Gareth Maybin	67	75	74	74	290	3,150
Miguel Angel Jimenez	69	73	75	74	291	2,850
Ricardo Gonzalez	69	73	75	75	292	2,740
Stuart Manley	69	74	77	73	293	2,250
Adam Gee	68	75	76	79	298	2,247

Lyoness Open

Diamond Country Club, Atzenbrugg, Austria — June 5-8
Par 36-36–72; 7,433 yards — purse, €1,000,000

	SCORES				TOTAL	MONEY
Mikael Lundberg	67	68	76	65	276	€166,660
Bernd Wiesberger	71	70	66	69	276	111,110
(Lundberg defeated Wiesberger on first playoff hole.)						
Joost Luiten	72	67	66	72	277	62,600
Lee Slattery	70	66	76	66	278	50,000
Miguel Angel Jimenez	70	75	68	67	280	38,700
Fabrizio Zanotti	69	68	72	71	280	38,700
Eduardo De La Riva	73	69	70	69	281	27,500
Daniel Im	70	73	74	64	281	27,500
David Horsey	73	73	65	71	282	20,267
Sihwan Kim	70	68	73	71	282	20,267
Simon Wakefield	70	71	70	71	282	20,267
Matthew Baldwin	68	73	70	72	283	16,650
Adam Gee	67	73	70	73	283	16,650
Jason Knutzon	74	72	69	69	284	14,700
Andrew Marshall	72	71	75	66	284	14,700
Simon Thornton	71	74	67	72	284	14,700
Rhys Davies	68	71	77	69	285	12,100
Florian Fritsch	74	69	74	68	285	12,100
Tyrrell Hatton	72	74	71	68	285	12,100
Berry Henson	68	72	73	72	285	12,100
Jake Roos	73	73	70	69	285	12,100
Anthony Wall	70	73	75	67	285	12,100
Romain Wattel	76	69	71	69	285	12,100
Mikko Korhonen	75	67	74	70	286	10,700
Kenneth Ferrie	71	77	71	68	287	9,500
Soren Hansen	74	70	74	69	287	9,500
Peter Hedblom	74	74	70	69	287	9,500
Scott Henry	69	75	68	75	287	9,500
Rikard Karlberg	73	73	66	75	287	9,500
Ruaidhri McGee	73	70	69	75	287	9,500
Gary Stal	73	74	69	71	287	9,500
Stephen Dodd	70	73	75	70	288	7,333
Richard Finch	68	73	75	72	288	7,333
Daniel Gaunt	75	73	72	68	288	7,333
Estanislao Goya	77	69	74	68	288	7,333

	SCORES				TOTAL	MONEY
Anders Hansen	73	73	73	69	288	7,333
James Morrison	73	70	74	71	288	7,333
Garrick Porteous	74	69	72	73	288	7,333
Brett Rumford	73	70	71	74	288	7,333
*Jordan L. Smith	71	72	74	71	288	
Tjaart van der Walt	70	76	68	74	288	7,333
Richard Bland	69	75	74	71	289	5,800
Alex Haindl	72	69	75	73	289	5,800
Lloyd Kennedy	72	74	72	71	289	5,800
Lukas Nemecz	74	71	73	71	289	5,800
Florian Praegant	70	73	76	70	289	5,800
Victor Riu	69	74	71	75	289	5,800
Robert Dinwiddie	70	75	74	71	290	4,500
Jack Doherty	75	71	76	68	290	4,500
James Heath	76	72	71	71	290	4,500
Michael Hoey	73	74	71	72	290	4,500
James Kingston	72	71	75	72	290	4,500
Ross McGowan	69	74	70	77	290	4,500
Matthew Nixon	70	76	73	71	290	4,500
Leonhard Astl	73	72	74	72	291	3,186
Gaganjeet Bhullar	70	78	72	71	291	3,186
Bradley Dredge	72	73	75	71	291	3,186
J.B. Hansen	73	71	74	73	291	3,186
Tain Lee	71	73	76	71	291	3,186
Thomas Levet	69	73	75	74	291	3,186
Robert Rock	75	70	75	71	291	3,186
Phillip Archer	69	73	75	76	293	2,550
Edouard Dubois	74	73	71	75	293	2,550
Thomas Norret	71	75	76	71	293	2,550
Jeev Milkha Singh	71	76	72	74	293	2,550
Moritz Mayrhauser	75	72	74	73	294	2,250
Ricardo Santos	75	71	79	69	294	2,250
*Lukas Lipold	77	71	77	71	296	
Daniel Vancsik	71	75	73	78	297	2,100
Joakim Lagergren	73	72	84	76	305	2,000

Irish Open

Fota Island Resort, Co. Cork, Ireland — June 19-22
Par 36-35–71; 7,043 yards — purse, €2,000,000

	SCORES				TOTAL	MONEY
Mikko Ilonen	64	68	69	70	271	€333,330
Edoardo Molinari	67	69	69	67	272	222,220
Matthew Baldwin	67	71	66	69	273	103,333
Kristoffer Broberg	69	69	66	69	273	103,333
Danny Willett	73	66	63	71	273	103,333
Magnus A. Carlsson	66	71	68	69	274	65,000
Graeme McDowell	68	66	69	71	274	65,000
Gregory Bourdy	68	71	67	69	275	39,700
Richard Finch	68	72	67	68	275	39,700
Ross Fisher	68	72	70	65	275	39,700
Michael Hoey	68	71	70	66	275	39,700
Gary Stal	70	67	69	69	275	39,700
Chris Wood	69	69	70	67	275	39,700
Adam Gee	68	70	69	69	276	27,114
Padraig Harrington	69	67	71	69	276	27,114
Simon Khan	69	66	70	71	276	27,114
Gareth Maybin	71	65	69	71	276	27,114
Matthew Nixon	70	65	74	67	276	27,114

	SCORES				TOTAL	MONEY
Marcel Siem	66	74	71	65	276	27,114
Fabrizio Zanotti	70	69	65	72	276	27,114
Marco Crespi	68	67	73	69	277	22,000
Ricardo Gonzalez	69	70	68	70	277	22,000
Anders Hansen	67	70	68	72	277	22,000
Roope Kakko	71	66	72	68	277	22,000
Romain Wattel	69	65	70	73	277	22,000
Rafa Cabrera-Bello	72	68	70	68	278	19,600
Oliver Fisher	73	68	66	71	278	19,600
Pablo Larrazabal	72	69	67	70	278	19,600
Matthew Fitzpatrick	72	69	70	68	279	17,500
Sihwan Kim	69	67	74	69	279	17,500
Robert Rock	68	66	74	71	279	17,500
Marc Warren	71	70	68	70	279	17,500
Paul Casey	69	69	69	73	280	15,040
Stephen Dodd	73	69	72	66	280	15,040
Peter Lawrie	69	72	70	69	280	15,040
Ricardo Santos	71	71	66	72	280	15,040
Graeme Storm	69	70	70	71	280	15,040
Alejandro Canizares	72	68	71	70	281	12,800
Estanislao Goya	70	70	70	71	281	12,800
James Heath	70	72	72	67	281	12,800
Daan Huizing	67	71	71	72	281	12,800
Thomas Pieters	72	70	70	69	281	12,800
Jeev Milkha Singh	68	73	69	71	281	12,800
Richard Bland	73	68	68	73	282	10,600
Robert Karlsson	66	76	72	68	282	10,600
Jason Knutzon	73	69	71	69	282	10,600
Alvaro Quiros	70	70	72	70	282	10,600
Steve Webster	70	70	70	72	282	10,600
Gregory Havret	70	68	70	75	283	8,600
David Horsey	72	69	71	71	283	8,600
David Howell	72	67	73	71	283	8,600
Wade Ormsby	70	71	75	67	283	8,600
Anthony Wall	71	71	71	70	283	8,600
Chris Doak	69	70	73	72	284	6,800
Stuart Manley	70	68	72	74	284	6,800
Jose Maria Olazabal	69	73	73	69	284	6,800
Andrea Pavan	71	71	70	72	284	6,800
Johan Carlsson	70	70	72	73	285	5,600
Darren Clarke	72	68	73	72	285	5,600
John G. Kelly	71	71	68	75	285	5,600
Andrew McArthur	71	67	74	73	285	5,600
Sam Walker	72	68	71	74	285	5,600
Darren Fichardt	68	74	72	72	286	4,800
Mikael Lundberg	70	71	74	71	286	4,800
Jake Roos	68	73	72	73	286	4,800
Francois Calmels	73	69	75	70	287	4,200
Hao-Tong Li	69	72	69	77	287	4,200
Adrien Saddier	71	71	74	71	287	4,200
Alastair Forsyth	71	71	72	75	289	3,800
Jack Doherty	71	71	74	74	290	3,325
Justin Walters	68	74	74	74	290	3,325
Tom Lewis	68	72	76	75	291	2,997
*Gary Hurley	72	66	81	73	292	
Patrik Sjoland	69	72	77	74	292	2,994
Michael Miller	73	67	79	80	299	2,991

BMW International Open

Golf Club Gut Larchenhof, Koln, Germany
Par 36-36–72; 7,228 yards

June 26-29
purse, €2,000,000

	SCORES				TOTAL	MONEY
Fabrizio Zanotti	72	67	65	65	269	€333,330
Rafa Cabrera-Bello	64	68	70	67	269	149,140
Gregory Havret	71	65	67	66	269	149,140
Henrik Stenson	68	68	66	67	269	149,140
(Zanotti won on fifth playoff hole.)						
Jamie Donaldson	71	67	65	67	270	71,600
Simon Dyson	69	66	69	66	270	71,600
Thongchai Jaidee	71	66	68	65	270	71,600
Thomas Bjorn	70	66	66	69	271	42,900
Emiliano Grillo	66	66	70	69	271	42,900
Pablo Larrazabal	69	63	67	72	271	42,900
Danny Willett	64	68	71	68	271	42,900
Alex Cejka	68	66	69	69	272	27,960
Oliver Fisher	72	66	65	69	272	27,960
Sergio Garcia	71	66	70	65	272	27,960
Richard Green	72	68	62	70	272	27,960
Alexander Levy	70	67	66	69	272	27,960
Shane Lowry	67	68	70	67	272	27,960
Francesco Molinari	71	66	65	70	272	27,960
Anthony Wall	69	69	68	66	272	27,960
Paul Waring	72	63	69	68	272	27,960
Romain Wattel	67	68	69	68	272	27,960
Paul Casey	73	67	63	70	273	21,100
Mark Foster	70	69	65	69	273	21,100
Anders Hansen	66	72	67	68	273	21,100
Tyrrell Hatton	69	67	70	67	273	21,100
Michael Hoey	66	69	69	69	273	21,100
Robert Karlsson	68	66	68	71	273	21,100
Jens Dantorp	68	68	67	71	274	18,400
Branden Grace	67	67	74	66	274	18,400
Matthew Nixon	69	67	69	69	274	18,400
Eddie Pepperell	72	64	72	67	275	16,900
Julien Quesne	71	68	69	67	275	16,900
Gaganjeet Bhullar	67	70	69	70	276	13,617
Carlos Del Moral	68	68	66	74	276	13,617
David Drysdale	72	68	68	68	276	13,617
Tommy Fleetwood	70	69	69	68	276	13,617
Estanislao Goya	72	67	66	71	276	13,617
J.B. Hansen	70	70	68	68	276	13,617
Craig Lee	69	65	69	73	276	13,617
Wade Ormsby	71	67	69	69	276	13,617
Gary Stal	66	69	70	71	276	13,617
Andy Sullivan	66	69	75	66	276	13,617
Justin Walters	71	69	66	70	276	13,617
Chris Wood	70	70	66	70	276	13,617
James Heath	75	65	67	70	277	10,200
Miguel Angel Jimenez	67	67	73	70	277	10,200
Jbe' Kruger	72	65	69	71	277	10,200
Morten Orum Madsen	70	68	69	70	277	10,200
Sam Walker	67	69	72	69	277	10,200
Alejandro Canizares	70	67	70	71	278	9,000
Adam Gee	71	69	69	70	279	8,000
Mikko Ilonen	68	72	71	68	279	8,000
Maximilian Kieffer	69	71	67	72	279	8,000
Graeme Storm	66	73	69	71	279	8,000
Jorge Campillo	67	71	70	72	280	6,800
Mikko Korhonen	69	71	69	71	280	6,800

	SCORES				TOTAL	MONEY
Victor Dubuisson	71	69	69	72	281	5,900
Damien McGrane	69	71	71	70	281	5,900
*Maximilian Rohrig	73	67	71	70	281	
Adrien Saddier	70	70	69	72	281	5,900
Marcel Siem	70	66	73	72	281	5,900
Ross Fisher	70	70	71	71	282	5,400
Johan Carlsson	68	72	67	76	283	5,000
Jason Knutzon	70	69	71	73	283	5,000
Tom Lewis	67	72	72	72	283	5,000
John Daly	70	67	76	71	284	4,400
Nacho Elvira	67	68	72	77	284	4,400
Andreas Harto	68	66	77	73	284	4,400
Daniel Im	68	70	72	75	285	4,000

Alstom Open de France

Le Golf National, Paris, France
Par 36-35–71; 7,331 yards

July 3-6
purse, €3,000,000

	SCORES				TOTAL	MONEY
Graeme McDowell	70	69	73	67	279	€500,000
Thongchai Jaidee	70	69	69	72	280	260,565
Kevin Stadler	64	68	72	76	280	260,565
Robert Karlsson	73	69	70	69	281	150,000
Matthew Baldwin	70	71	70	71	282	116,100
Jamie Donaldson	67	72	74	69	282	116,100
Michael Hoey	73	66	73	71	283	90,000
Victor Riu	68	67	73	76	284	75,000
Oliver Fisher	69	71	77	68	285	63,600
Fabrizio Zanotti	73	70	75	67	285	63,600
Wade Ormsby	70	75	69	72	286	55,200
Gregory Bourdy	73	72	72	70	287	45,450
Kristoffer Broberg	70	74	72	71	287	45,450
Magnus A. Carlsson	73	72	70	72	287	45,450
Martin Kaymer	72	68	70	77	287	45,450
Damien McGrane	71	69	72	75	287	45,450
Matthew Nixon	71	72	70	74	287	45,450
David Bobrowski	73	70	73	72	288	34,612
Stephen Gallacher	66	73	74	75	288	34,612
Scott Jamieson	69	70	74	75	288	34,612
Shiv Kapur	73	69	76	70	288	34,612
Soren Kjeldsen	72	73	71	72	288	34,612
Joost Luiten	73	69	73	73	288	34,612
Gary Stal	74	68	74	72	288	34,612
Bernd Wiesberger	70	70	71	77	288	34,612
Felipe Aguilar	67	73	77	72	289	26,700
Ross Fisher	72	68	77	72	289	26,700
Matthew Fitzpatrick	69	74	74	72	289	26,700
Mark Foster	69	70	73	77	289	26,700
Mikko Korhonen	72	72	71	74	289	26,700
Francesco Molinari	70	72	74	73	289	26,700
Marcel Siem	65	72	77	75	289	26,700
Andy Sullivan	73	71	72	73	289	26,700
Marc Warren	69	73	73	74	289	26,700
Rafa Cabrera-Bello	70	72	77	71	290	20,400
Estanislao Goya	75	66	74	75	290	20,400
David Howell	72	72	72	74	290	20,400
Roope Kakko	68	74	73	75	290	20,400
Alexander Levy	69	72	72	77	290	20,400
Edoardo Molinari	70	75	75	70	290	20,400

	SCORES				TOTAL	MONEY
Ricardo Santos	71	74	72	73	290	20,400
Steve Webster	73	68	76	73	290	20,400
Kiradech Aphibarnrat	77	66	70	78	291	17,400
Julien Quesne	74	71	68	78	291	17,400
David Lynn	73	69	72	78	292	15,900
Gareth Maybin	73	68	76	75	292	15,900
Lee Slattery	70	73	75	74	292	15,900
Victor Dubuisson	76	68	76	73	293	12,600
Simon Dyson	73	71	75	74	293	12,600
Matt Ford	70	74	70	79	293	12,600
Adam Gee	72	72	73	76	293	12,600
Anders Hansen	71	71	73	78	293	12,600
Jason Knutzon	72	72	76	73	293	12,600
Mikael Lundberg	75	68	74	76	293	12,600
Matteo Manassero	68	73	75	77	293	12,600
J.B. Hansen	72	69	76	77	294	9,400
Daan Huizing	72	73	74	75	294	9,400
Richard Sterne	70	75	73	76	294	9,400
Nicolas Colsaerts	72	72	77	74	295	8,400
Thomas Linard	72	70	73	80	295	8,400
Paul Waring	71	73	78	73	295	8,400
*Julien Brun	73	72	75	77	297	
James Heath	71	73	76	77	297	7,500
Maximilian Kieffer	72	73	75	77	297	7,500
Andrew McArthur	76	67	76	78	297	7,500
Eduardo De La Riva	73	71	75	79	298	6,900
Soren Hansen	74	70	78	77	299	6,450
Patrik Sjoland	73	71	82	73	299	6,450
Alexandre Kaleka	72	73	75	81	301	6,000

Aberdeen Asset Management Scottish Open

Royal Aberdeen, Aberdeen, Scotland — July 10-13
Par 36-35–71; 6,867 yards — purse, £3,000,000

	SCORES				TOTAL	MONEY
Justin Rose	69	68	66	65	268	€627,020
Kristoffer Broberg	65	71	68	66	270	418,009
Marc Warren	67	69	67	70	273	235,509
Stephen Gallacher	72	69	70	63	274	148,039
Tyrrell Hatton	69	71	66	68	274	148,039
Shane Lowry	72	68	68	66	274	148,039
Matteo Manassero	69	72	68	65	274	148,039
Rickie Fowler	71	71	68	65	275	84,522
Scott Jamieson	74	67	70	64	275	84,522
Robert Karlsson	71	71	67	66	275	84,522
Pablo Larrazabal	69	73	66	68	276	64,834
Phil Mickelson	68	73	70	65	276	64,834
Danny Willett	70	71	68	67	276	64,834
Paul Casey	69	71	72	65	277	56,432
Rory McIlroy	64	78	68	67	277	56,432
Luke Donald	67	73	72	66	278	48,832
Ricardo Gonzalez	65	71	71	71	278	48,832
Mikko Ilonen	71	68	69	70	278	48,832
Craig Lee	72	69	66	71	278	48,832
James Morrison	71	72	69	66	278	48,832
John Hahn	71	71	68	69	279	42,512
Alexander Levy	75	69	69	66	279	42,512
Paul Waring	75	66	73	65	279	42,512
Felipe Aguilar	73	71	73	63	280	39,126

	SCORES				TOTAL	MONEY
Thomas Bjorn	70	73	68	69	280	39,126
Adrian Otaegui	71	69	71	69	280	39,126
Lucas Bjerregaard	70	69	73	69	281	32,919
Rafa Cabrera-Bello	72	68	71	70	281	32,919
Mark Foster	71	70	71	69	281	32,919
Padraig Harrington	71	72	71	67	281	32,919
Shiv Kapur	69	75	68	69	281	32,919
Russell Knox	68	74	69	70	281	32,919
Paul Lawrie	74	70	71	66	281	32,919
Marcel Siem	73	69	69	70	281	32,919
David Drysdale	67	76	69	70	282	26,335
Simon Dyson	71	73	68	70	282	26,335
Alastair Forsyth	70	73	70	69	282	26,335
David Howell	68	70	73	71	282	26,335
Miguel Angel Jimenez	74	68	71	69	282	26,335
Simon Khan	70	71	71	70	282	26,335
George Coetzee	73	70	70	70	283	21,820
Ernie Els	73	71	73	66	283	21,820
Soren Kjeldsen	70	70	70	73	283	21,820
Martin Laird	70	73	70	70	283	21,820
*Ollie Schniederjans	71	70	72	70	283	
Jimmy Walker	71	70	73	69	283	21,820
Bernd Wiesberger	74	68	72	69	283	21,820
Niclas Fasth	69	74	73	68	284	18,434
Thongchai Jaidee	71	71	73	69	284	18,434
Mikael Lundberg	71	73	70	70	284	18,434
Thomas Aiken	71	70	74	70	285	14,296
Richard Bland	67	74	72	72	285	14,296
Joost Luiten	73	70	72	70	285	14,296
Gareth Maybin	70	74	69	72	285	14,296
Wade Ormsby	71	73	74	67	285	14,296
Ryan Palmer	70	72	71	72	285	14,296
Gary Stal	68	75	74	68	285	14,296
Graeme Storm	70	72	73	70	285	14,296
Johan Carlsson	71	73	71	71	286	10,534
Magnus A. Carlsson	71	72	72	71	286	10,534
Darren Clarke	69	73	70	74	286	10,534
Michael Hoey	66	74	74	72	286	10,534
Fabrizio Zanotti	70	70	76	70	286	10,534
Carlos Del Moral	70	73	73	71	287	8,465
Matt Ford	75	67	70	75	287	8,465
Greig Hutcheon	70	70	74	73	287	8,465
Tom Lewis	70	71	72	74	287	8,465
Alvaro Quiros	71	71	75	70	287	8,465
Ricardo Santos	73	71	71	72	287	8,465
Gaganjeet Bhullar	75	69	76	68	288	7,004
Maximilian Kieffer	71	73	73	71	288	7,004
J.B. Hansen	71	73	73	72	289	5,640
Damien McGrane	71	72	74	72	289	5,640
Kevin Phelan	69	73	76	71	289	5,640
Tommy Fleetwood	70	70	74	76	290	5,634
Scott Henry	73	71	72	75	291	5,631
Jeev Milkha Singh	70	71	74	77	292	5,628
Matt Jones	71	73	71	80	295	5,625

The Open Championship

Royal Liverpool Golf Club, Hoylake, England — July 17-20
Par 35-37–72; 7,312 yards — purse, £5,400,000

	SCORES				TOTAL	MONEY
Rory McIlroy	66	66	68	71	271	€1,223,450
Rickie Fowler	69	69	68	67	273	577,217
Sergio Garcia	68	70	69	66	273	577,217
Jim Furyk	68	71	71	65	275	351,350
Marc Leishman	69	72	70	65	276	264,140
Adam Scott	68	73	69	66	276	264,140
Edoardo Molinari	68	73	68	68	277	193,556
Charl Schwartzel	71	67	72	67	277	193,556
Victor Dubuisson	74	66	68	70	278	141,376
Shane Lowry	68	75	70	65	278	141,376
Graeme McDowell	74	69	68	67	278	141,376
Dustin Johnson	71	65	71	72	279	106,241
Robert Karlsson	69	71	70	69	279	106,241
Ryan Moore	70	68	73	68	279	106,241
Stephen Gallacher	70	72	70	68	280	86,164
David Howell	72	70	70	68	280	86,164
Francesco Molinari	68	70	75	67	280	86,164
George Coetzee	70	69	74	68	281	77,171
Keegan Bradley	73	71	69	69	282	69,015
Angel Cabrera	76	69	70	67	282	69,015
Chris Kirk	71	74	68	69	282	69,015
Matteo Manassero	67	75	68	72	282	69,015
Phil Mickelson	74	70	71	68	283	57,931
Justin Rose	72	70	69	72	283	57,931
Chris Wood	75	70	73	65	283	57,931
Byeong-Hun An	72	71	69	72	284	47,997
Thomas Bjorn	70	71	76	67	284	47,997
Darren Clarke	72	72	67	73	284	47,997
Brian Harman	72	73	68	71	284	47,997
Ben Martin	71	73	70	70	284	47,997
Jimmy Walker	69	71	71	73	284	47,997
Kristoffer Broberg	70	73	70	72	285	38,899
David Hearn	70	73	71	71	285	38,899
Hunter Mahan	71	73	72	69	285	38,899
D.A. Points	75	69	72	69	285	38,899
Branden Grace	71	72	69	74	286	33,985
Louis Oosthuizen	70	68	76	72	286	33,985
Jordan Spieth	71	75	67	73	286	33,985
Thongchai Jaidee	72	72	72	71	287	26,626
Hideki Matsuyama	69	74	73	71	287	26,626
Koumei Oda	69	77	74	67	287	26,626
Kevin Stadler	73	72	71	71	287	26,626
Henrik Stenson	72	73	73	69	287	26,626
Brendon Todd	73	73	74	67	287	26,626
Marc Warren	71	68	72	76	287	26,626
Gary Woodland	75	69	72	71	287	26,626
Gregory Bourdy	75	69	74	70	288	20,093
Paul Casey	74	71	73	70	288	20,093
Stewart Cink	71	75	73	69	288	20,093
Zach Johnson	71	75	71	71	288	20,093
Jason Dufner	70	74	74	71	289	18,383
Bill Haas	70	72	73	74	289	18,383
Tom Watson	73	73	75	68	289	18,383
Matt Jones	71	74	72	73	290	17,473
Matt Kuchar	73	71	74	72	290	17,473
Kevin Na	76	70	70	74	290	17,473
Kevin Streelman	72	74	69	75	290	17,473

	SCORES				TOTAL	MONEY
Jason Day	73	73	74	71	291	16,752
Jamie McLeary	73	73	75	70	291	16,752
Ryan Palmer	74	71	76	70	291	16,752
Chris Rodgers	73	71	73	74	291	16,752
John Senden	71	74	75	71	291	16,752
Brandt Snedeker	74	72	71	74	291	16,752
Luke Donald	73	73	71	75	292	16,187
Billy Hurley	73	72	76	71	292	16,187
Thorbjorn Olesen	75	71	73	73	292	16,187
Charley Hoffman	74	72	76	71	293	15,873
Brooks Koepka	68	77	74	74	293	15,873
Tiger Woods	69	77	73	75	294	15,685
Martin Kaymer	73	72	72	79	296	15,560
Matt Every	75	71	73	78	297	15,434
Rhein Gibson	72	74	74	78	298	15,309

Out of Final 36 Holes

Kiradech Aphibarnrat	72	75	147	4,768
Rafa Cabrera-Bello	70	77	147	4,768
*Ashley Chesters	70	77	147	
K.J. Choi	72	75	147	4,768
Graham DeLaet	71	76	147	4,768
Oliver Fisher	72	75	147	4,768
Oscar Floren	73	74	147	4,768
Hiroshi Iwata	70	77	147	4,768
Justin Leonard	74	73	147	4,768
Paul McKechnie	76	71	147	4,768
Ian Poulter	73	74	147	4,768
Shawn Stefani	73	74	147	4,768
Yoshinobu Tsukada	69	78	147	4,768
Dawie van der Walt	71	76	147	4,768
Nick Watney	72	75	147	4,768
Lee Westwood	71	76	147	4,768
Erik Compton	71	77	148	3,890
Ben Curtis	74	74	148	3,890
John Daly	77	71	148	3,890
Brendon De Jonge	78	70	148	3,890
*Paul Dunne	75	73	148	
Harris English	72	76	148	3,890
Ross Fisher	74	74	148	3,890
Billy Horschel	73	75	148	3,890
Mikko Ilonen	70	78	148	3,890
Ryo Ishikawa	74	74	148	3,890
Freddie Jacobson	70	78	148	3,890
Miguel Angel Jimenez	75	73	148	3,890
Hyung-Tae Kim	75	73	148	3,890
Hyung-Sung Kim	72	76	148	3,890
*Cheng-Tsung Pan	74	74	148	
Brett Rumford	75	73	148	3,890
John Singleton	78	70	148	3,890
Cameron Tringale	74	74	148	3,890
Bubba Watson	76	72	148	3,890
Boo Weekley	69	79	148	3,890
Danny Willett	74	74	148	3,890
Rhys Enoch	73	76	149	3,890
George McNeill	76	73	149	3,890
Yusaku Miyazato	72	77	149	3,890
Juvic Pagunsan	76	73	149	3,890
Patrick Reed	78	71	149	3,890
Scott Stallings	75	74	149	3,890
Matthew Baldwin	76	74	150	3,263
Jonas Blixt	75	75	150	3,263

	SCORES		TOTAL	MONEY
Gonzalo Fernandez-Castano	74	76	150	3,263
Tommy Fleetwood	74	76	150	3,263
Anirban Lahiri	75	75	150	3,263
Jamie Donaldson	79	72	151	3,263
Chesson Hadley	79	72	151	3,263
Todd Hamilton	77	74	151	3,263
J.B. Holmes	74	77	151	3,263
Masanori Kobayashi	78	73	151	3,263
Victor Riu	74	77	151	3,263
Justin Walters	77	74	151	3,263
Bernd Wiesberger	72	79	151	3,263
Ashun Wu	75	76	151	3,263
Y.E. Yang	75	76	151	3,263
David Duval	73	79	152	3,263
Ernie Els	79	73	152	3,263
Padraig Harrington	74	78	152	3,263
Tyrrell Hatton	75	77	152	3,263
Pablo Larrazabal	75	77	152	3,263
Richard Sterne	73	79	152	3,263
Sir Nick Faldo	76	77	153	3,263
Tomohiro Kondo	76	77	153	3,263
Webb Simpson	76	77	153	3,263
Scott Jamieson	77	77	154	3,263
Paul Lawrie	79	75	154	3,263
Brendan Steele	74	80	154	3,263
Roberto Castro	74	81	155	3,263
Chris Hanson	81	74	155	3,263
Russell Henley	75	80	155	3,263
Jin Jeong	77	78	155	3,263
*Bradley Neil	79	76	155	
Matthew Southgate	80	76	156	3,263
Chris Stroud	79	77	156	3,263
Peter Uihlein	77	79	156	3,263
Dong-Kyu Jang	78	79	157	3,263
Joost Luiten	81	76	157	3,263
Mark Wiebe	79	78	157	3,263
Sandy Lyle	82	84	166	3,263
Bryden Macpherson	90	80	170	3,263
Michael Hoey	75	75	WD	

M2M Russian Open

Tseleevo Golf & Polo Club, Moscow, Russia — July 24-27
Par 36-36–72; 7,491 yards — purse, €1,000,000

	SCORES				TOTAL	MONEY
David Horsey	65	68	70	72	275	€166,660
Damien McGrane	69	71	69	66	275	111,110
(Horsey defeated McGrane on first playoff hole.)						
Scott Jamieson	66	72	69	69	276	62,600
Sam Hutsby	72	67	70	68	277	50,000
Peter Whiteford	66	71	66	75	278	42,400
Krister Eriksson	72	68	71	68	279	32,500
Thomas Pieters	67	68	72	72	279	32,500
Maximilian Kieffer	67	71	73	69	280	23,700
Andrea Pavan	73	70	64	73	280	23,700
Carlos Del Moral	70	71	73	67	281	19,200
Sam Walker	69	71	73	68	281	19,200
Fredrik Andersson Hed	70	69	77	66	282	15,150
Daan Huizing	72	74	69	67	282	15,150

	SCORES				TOTAL	MONEY
Mikko Korhonen	74	71	68	69	282	15,150
Brinson Paolini	72	71	70	69	282	15,150
Haydn Porteous	72	71	70	69	282	15,150
Adrien Saddier	69	73	70	70	282	15,150
Seuk-Hyun Baek	74	70	69	70	283	11,867
Gary Boyd	69	68	72	74	283	11,867
Jorge Campillo	68	76	68	71	283	11,867
Alastair Forsyth	75	70	70	68	283	11,867
J.B. Hansen	69	73	71	70	283	11,867
James Heath	71	72	71	69	283	11,867
Soren Hansen	72	69	69	74	284	10,550
Jamie McLeary	68	72	70	74	284	10,550
Oliver Bekker	67	76	72	70	285	9,200
Gaganjeet Bhullar	67	71	75	72	285	9,200
Javier Colomo	72	68	71	74	285	9,200
Nacho Elvira	69	69	77	70	285	9,200
Adam Gee	70	75	69	71	285	9,200
Andreas Harto	73	70	73	69	285	9,200
Stuart Manley	71	73	71	70	285	9,200
Oskar Henningsson	68	76	73	69	286	7,733
Adrian Otaegui	70	73	68	75	286	7,733
Kevin Phelan	69	70	74	73	286	7,733
David Drysdale	73	69	77	68	287	7,200
Daniel Im	73	72	70	72	287	7,200
Gunn Charoenkul	73	68	74	73	288	6,500
S.S.P. Chowrasia	76	70	72	70	288	6,500
Roope Kakko	71	73	70	74	288	6,500
Rikard Karlberg	67	76	74	71	288	6,500
*Jordan L. Smith	75	70	74	69	288	
Simon Wakefield	70	76	70	72	288	6,500
Bradley Dredge	70	74	75	70	289	5,600
Edouard Dubois	72	68	72	77	289	5,600
Rhys Enoch	70	73	74	72	289	5,600
Carlos Pigem	70	71	78	70	289	5,600
Andreas Andersson	70	73	72	75	290	4,900
Jack Doherty	67	73	78	72	290	4,900
Simon Thornton	70	73	73	74	290	4,900
Johan Carlsson	74	69	78	70	291	4,300
Andrea Maestroni	72	71	75	73	291	4,300
James Morrison	71	73	71	76	291	4,300
Louis de Jager	67	74	75	76	292	3,700
Craig Lee	72	70	74	76	292	3,700
Morten Orum Madsen	71	73	73	75	292	3,700
Joakim Mikkelsen	74	69	78	72	293	3,200
Matthew Nixon	69	76	74	74	293	3,200
Merrick Bremner	79	65	71	79	294	2,950
Jack Wilson	67	74	80	73	294	2,950
Richard Finch	71	73	71	80	295	2,750
Mathias Gronberg	70	70	75	80	295	2,750
John Hahn	72	74	75	75	296	2,600
Peter Erofejeff	74	72	72	79	297	2,450
Phillip Price	70	75	73	79	297	2,450
Liam Bond	73	73	76	76	298	2,300

Made in Denmark

Himmerland Golf & Spa Resort, Aalborg, Denmark — August 14-17
Par 35-36–71; 6,431 yards — purse, €1,500,000

	SCORES				TOTAL	MONEY
Marc Warren	71	70	66	68	275	€250,000
Bradley Dredge	66	68	73	70	277	166,660
Phillip Archer	70	70	71	69	280	93,900
Thomas Bjorn	66	73	73	69	281	63,700
Oliver Fisher	75	65	72	69	281	63,700
Eddie Pepperell	73	68	71	69	281	63,700
Lasse Jensen	72	69	74	67	282	41,250
Thorbjorn Olesen	69	70	72	71	282	41,250
S.S.P. Chowrasia	70	71	71	71	283	27,350
Rikard Karlberg	73	70	71	69	283	27,350
Mikael Lundberg	72	69	71	71	283	27,350
Stuart Manley	73	69	69	72	283	27,350
Gareth Maybin	75	67	68	73	283	27,350
Simon Wakefield	71	67	72	73	283	27,350
Richard Bland	71	74	68	71	284	19,543
David Drysdale	71	68	76	69	284	19,543
Roope Kakko	70	71	73	70	284	19,543
Soren Kjeldsen	71	73	70	70	284	19,543
Craig Lee	73	72	69	70	284	19,543
Tom Lewis	72	70	72	70	284	19,543
David Lipsky	72	71	73	68	284	19,543
Simon Dyson	77	69	70	69	285	15,825
Andreas Harto	70	72	75	68	285	15,825
Daniel Im	72	68	76	69	285	15,825
Shiv Kapur	73	68	74	70	285	15,825
Andrew McArthur	72	72	72	69	285	15,825
Paul Waring	75	66	72	72	285	15,825
Kristoffer Broberg	75	67	75	69	286	13,125
Emiliano Grillo	71	69	74	72	286	13,125
Damien McGrane	73	70	73	70	286	13,125
James Morrison	76	70	70	70	286	13,125
Matthew Nixon	73	67	76	70	286	13,125
Patrik Sjoland	71	70	76	69	286	13,125
Adam Gee	76	70	71	70	287	10,950
Estanislao Goya	77	69	73	68	287	10,950
Wade Ormsby	71	72	76	68	287	10,950
Romain Wattel	73	71	72	71	287	10,950
Steve Webster	76	69	68	74	287	10,950
Robert-Jan Derksen	74	68	74	72	288	9,300
Daniel Gaunt	70	73	74	71	288	9,300
Chris Hanson	72	73	74	69	288	9,300
David Horsey	76	70	73	69	288	9,300
Alexandre Kaleka	78	66	73	71	288	9,300
Adrien Saddier	74	68	73	73	288	9,300
Johan Carlsson	71	70	75	73	289	7,500
Gregory Havret	74	69	74	72	289	7,500
Scott Jamieson	71	75	71	72	289	7,500
Sihwan Kim	70	75	73	71	289	7,500
Moritz Lampert	74	70	77	68	289	7,500
Robert Rock	73	71	75	70	289	7,500
Jack Doherty	74	71	73	72	290	5,700
Kenneth Ferrie	72	70	74	74	290	5,700
Michael Jonzon	75	70	76	69	290	5,700
Mikko Korhonen	71	73	75	71	290	5,700
Garrick Porteous	71	68	78	73	290	5,700
Brandon Stone	73	73	74	70	290	5,700
Felipe Aguilar	66	74	79	72	291	4,425

	SCORES				TOTAL	MONEY
Chris Doak	72	70	74	75	291	4,425
Peter Hedblom	74	67	75	75	291	4,425
Andrea Pavan	71	75	79	66	291	4,425
Jorge Campillo	73	72	74	73	292	3,450
Mark Foster	73	73	73	73	292	3,450
Richard Green	76	69	77	70	292	3,450
Tyrrell Hatton	74	72	73	73	292	3,450
Peter Lawrie	70	75	73	74	292	3,450
Morten Orum Madsen	71	70	76	75	292	3,450
Andrew Marshall	70	76	75	71	292	3,450
Adrian Otaegui	74	72	72	74	292	3,450
Graeme Storm	75	70	78	69	292	3,450
Rasmus Hjelm	73	73	74	73	293	2,370
Jamie McLeary	74	70	73	76	293	2,370
Richie Ramsay	75	70	75	73	293	2,370
Gary Stal	72	72	79	70	293	2,370
Gaganjeet Bhullar	73	70	75	76	294	2,240
Nicolas Colsaerts	70	72	76	76	294	2,240
*Nicolai Kristensen	75	70	79	71	295	
Lee Slattery	71	75	78	71	295	2,235
Carlos Del Moral	75	71	77	73	296	2,228
Andrew Johnston	77	69	76	74	296	2,228
Simon Thornton	76	70	75	75	296	2,228
Peter Uihlein	74	72	72	78	296	2,228
James Heath	77	69	74	77	297	2,220
Jonas Magnusson	75	69	78	76	298	2,217
Victor Riu	73	72	77	78	300	2,214

D+D Real Czech Masters

Albatross Golf Resort, Vysoky Ujezd, Prague, Czech Republic — August 21-24
Par 36-36–72; 7,466 yards — purse, €1,000,000

	SCORES				TOTAL	MONEY
Jamie Donaldson	66	69	71	68	274	€166,660
Bradley Dredge	68	70	66	72	276	111,110
Merrick Bremner	70	68	70	69	277	56,300
Soren Kjeldsen	68	70	68	71	277	56,300
Tommy Fleetwood	72	65	73	70	280	38,700
Eddie Pepperell	70	72	71	67	280	38,700
Stephen Gallacher	70	67	71	73	281	27,500
Sam Walker	69	71	70	71	281	27,500
James Heath	73	70	71	68	282	19,500
Peter Hedblom	70	68	73	71	282	19,500
Scott Jamieson	71	73	74	64	282	19,500
Garrick Porteous	70	67	72	73	282	19,500
Matthew Baldwin	72	71	67	73	283	14,433
Javier Colomo	69	71	71	72	283	14,433
Kenneth Ferrie	68	71	71	73	283	14,433
Craig Lee	69	71	71	72	283	14,433
James Morrison	70	68	72	73	283	14,433
Danny Willett	68	75	72	68	283	14,433
David Lipsky	69	71	69	75	284	11,825
Tim Sluiter	69	73	70	72	284	11,825
Peter Uihlein	70	73	72	69	284	11,825
Paul Waring	68	71	70	75	284	11,825
Felipe Aguilar	73	71	70	71	285	10,100
Gregory Bourdy	69	67	71	78	285	10,100
Daan Huizing	69	74	70	72	285	10,100
Rikard Karlberg	70	72	68	75	285	10,100

	SCORES				TOTAL	MONEY
Paul Lawrie	70	70	71	74	285	10,100
Stuart Manley	71	72	74	68	285	10,100
Kevin Phelan	72	69	73	71	285	10,100
Phillip Archer	69	72	71	74	286	7,811
Edouard Dubois	71	73	70	72	286	7,811
J.B. Hansen	70	69	72	75	286	7,811
Tyrrell Hatton	70	73	71	72	286	7,811
Mikael Lundberg	67	76	68	75	286	7,811
Adrian Otaegui	70	70	72	74	286	7,811
Zane Scotland	74	70	69	73	286	7,811
Lee Slattery	68	69	77	72	286	7,811
Duncan Stewart	70	69	74	73	286	7,811
Francois Calmels	70	72	70	75	287	5,500
S.S.P. Chowrasia	68	75	68	76	287	5,500
Dodge Kemmer	71	70	78	68	287	5,500
Tain Lee	72	68	72	75	287	5,500
Tom Lewis	74	70	73	70	287	5,500
Hennie Otto	70	71	76	70	287	5,500
Andrea Pavan	72	70	69	76	287	5,500
Adrien Saddier	71	72	70	74	287	5,500
Joel Sjoholm	74	70	69	74	287	5,500
Gary Stal	71	73	72	71	287	5,500
Oscar Stark	71	67	76	73	287	5,500
Simon Wakefield	70	74	72	71	287	5,500
Anthony Wall	72	72	71	72	287	5,500
Alastair Forsyth	73	71	70	74	288	3,438
John Hahn	68	69	76	75	288	3,438
Chris Hanson	74	70	75	69	288	3,438
Shiv Kapur	71	70	75	72	288	3,438
Joost Luiten	70	71	73	74	288	3,438
Damien McGrane	73	70	74	71	288	3,438
Patrik Sjoland	72	72	71	73	288	3,438
Andy Sullivan	69	73	69	77	288	3,438
Fredrik Andersson Hed	72	68	75	74	289	2,400
Richard Bland	71	70	74	74	289	2,400
Gary Boyd	72	70	75	72	289	2,400
Nacho Elvira	72	71	70	76	289	2,400
Andreas Harto	73	71	69	76	289	2,400
Keith Horne	68	74	74	73	289	2,400
Roope Kakko	70	70	74	75	289	2,400
Peter Lawrie	72	72	73	72	289	2,400
Haydn Porteous	74	70	69	76	289	2,400
Gaganjeet Bhullar	72	71	71	76	290	1,900
Ben Evans	74	70	76	71	291	1,562
Dylan Frittelli	72	70	75	74	291	1,562
Emiliano Grillo	72	72	73	74	291	1,562
Sihwan Kim	74	67	73	77	291	1,562
Jason Knutzon	70	71	74	76	291	1,562
Jack Doherty	73	69	76	74	292	1,484
Brandon Stone	71	73	75	73	292	1,484
Steve Webster	70	72	68	82	292	1,484
Peter Whiteford	70	70	72	80	292	1,484
James Kingston	76	68	72	77	293	1,474
Gareth Maybin	72	72	77	72	293	1,474
Mark Foster	74	69	74	77	294	1,468
Joakim Lagergren	71	68	76	79	294	1,468
Matthew Nixon	68	74	76	77	295	1,464

Open D'Italia

Circolo Golf Torino - La Mandria, Fiano, Torino, Italy
Par 36-36–72; 7,208 yards

August 28-31
purse, €1,500,000

	SCORES				TOTAL	MONEY
Hennie Otto	67	62	71	68	268	€250,000
David Howell	73	67	67	63	270	166,660
Stephen Gallacher	72	65	69	65	271	93,900
Joost Luiten	69	68	70	65	272	69,300
Richie Ramsay	67	69	66	70	272	69,300
Bernd Wiesberger	66	66	71	72	275	52,500
Simon Dyson	71	68	69	68	276	36,525
Ross Fisher	69	66	70	71	276	36,525
Andreas Harto	70	69	70	67	276	36,525
Lee Slattery	70	68	67	71	276	36,525
James Morrison	70	66	72	69	277	25,850
Andy Sullivan	70	72	66	69	277	25,850
Romain Wattel	73	68	67	69	277	25,850
David Horsey	71	69	72	66	278	21,600
Shiv Kapur	73	69	68	68	278	21,600
Mikko Korhonen	70	67	71	70	278	21,600
Sam Walker	70	72	68	68	278	21,600
Kristoffer Broberg	73	68	72	66	279	17,800
Darren Clarke	72	70	67	70	279	17,800
Carlos Del Moral	70	68	70	71	279	17,800
Darren Fichardt	68	69	71	71	279	17,800
Francesco Molinari	66	72	69	72	279	17,800
Alvaro Quiros	70	72	68	69	279	17,800
Richard Bland	67	71	71	71	280	13,800
S.S.P. Chowrasia	69	72	66	73	280	13,800
Tommy Fleetwood	72	70	67	71	280	13,800
Ricardo Gonzalez	74	66	68	72	280	13,800
Estanislao Goya	71	70	69	70	280	13,800
Sihwan Kim	70	72	69	69	280	13,800
Francesco Laporta	68	72	69	71	280	13,800
Tom Lewis	71	69	73	67	280	13,800
David Lipsky	69	67	73	71	280	13,800
Morten Orum Madsen	68	68	73	71	280	13,800
Robert Rock	69	70	73	68	280	13,800
Fredrik Andersson Hed	74	67	70	70	281	9,750
Merrick Bremner	71	68	70	72	281	9,750
David Drysdale	73	69	71	68	281	9,750
John Hahn	67	73	76	65	281	9,750
James Heath	73	68	70	70	281	9,750
Daan Huizing	69	71	69	72	281	9,750
Craig Lee	70	72	68	71	281	9,750
Wade Ormsby	74	68	70	69	281	9,750
Marcel Siem	73	68	70	70	281	9,750
Marc Warren	69	70	69	73	281	9,750
Peter Whiteford	73	67	71	70	281	9,750
Felipe Aguilar	68	69	76	69	282	7,050
Seve Benson	70	67	72	73	282	7,050
Oliver Fisher	74	67	75	66	282	7,050
J.B. Hansen	69	71	72	70	282	7,050
Gareth Maybin	67	73	74	68	282	7,050
*Benjamin Rusch	73	66	75	68	282	
Adrien Saddier	70	70	72	70	282	7,050
Anthony Wall	71	70	69	72	282	7,050
Jorge Campillo	71	71	73	68	283	5,250
Soren Hansen	71	66	72	74	283	5,250
Maximilian Kieffer	68	70	76	69	283	5,250
Matteo Manassero	73	69	71	70	283	5,250

	SCORES				TOTAL	MONEY
Thomas Pieters	70	68	79	66	283	5,250
Rafa Cabrera-Bello	73	63	75	73	284	4,200
Magnus A. Carlsson	72	70	72	70	284	4,200
Jason Knutzon	70	70	74	70	284	4,200
Edoardo Molinari	71	69	71	73	284	4,200
Alessandro Tadini	72	69	72	71	284	4,200
*Edoardo Raffaele Lipparelli	68	70	71	76	285	
Roope Kakko	69	72	71	74	286	3,675
Damien McGrane	71	71	73	71	286	3,675
Daniel Im	71	71	70	75	287	3,375
Alexander Levy	73	68	68	78	287	3,375
Filippo Bergamaschi	72	69	72	75	288	3,075
Eduardo De La Riva	72	70	73	73	288	3,075
Nacho Elvira	75	67	72	76	290	2,795
Garrick Porteous	71	71	74	74	290	2,795
Gregory Molteni	70	70	74	78	292	2,250

Omega European Masters

Crans-sur-Sierre Golf Club, Crans Montana, Switzerland — September 4-7
Par 36-34–70; 6,262 yards — purse, €2,300,000

	SCORES				TOTAL	MONEY
David Lipsky	67	64	66	65	262	€383,330
Graeme Storm	64	66	64	68	262	255,550
(Lipsky defeated Storm on first playoff hole.)						
Tyrrell Hatton	67	66	65	65	263	129,490
Brooks Koepka	65	65	66	67	263	129,490
Tommy Fleetwood	64	68	63	69	264	89,010
Danny Willett	67	70	64	63	264	89,010
Jamie Donaldson	65	64	69	67	265	69,000
Richie Ramsay	62	66	70	68	266	57,500
Gareth Maybin	64	67	69	67	267	46,613
Lee Slattery	68	68	65	66	267	46,613
Romain Wattel	68	69	65	65	267	46,613
Richard Green	71	64	67	66	268	39,560
Seve Benson	65	67	70	67	269	31,912
Nicolas Colsaerts	68	67	69	65	269	31,912
Anirban Lahiri	70	67	68	64	269	31,912
Shane Lowry	66	65	68	70	269	31,912
Edoardo Molinari	62	70	68	69	269	31,912
Brett Rumford	69	65	71	64	269	31,912
Marc Warren	69	63	71	66	269	31,912
Bernd Wiesberger	66	70	67	66	269	31,912
Ricardo Gonzalez	70	68	68	64	270	25,645
Gregory Havret	68	69	68	65	270	25,645
David Lynn	65	68	69	68	270	25,645
Jyoti Randhawa	72	65	65	68	270	25,645
Emiliano Grillo	66	68	69	68	271	22,885
James Morrison	66	69	67	69	271	22,885
Adrien Saddier	69	67	68	67	271	22,885
Peter Whiteford	68	65	70	68	271	22,885
Felipe Aguilar	66	68	70	68	272	19,123
Marco Crespi	69	69	62	72	272	19,123
Robert-Jan Derksen	66	67	71	68	272	19,123
Victor Dubuisson	65	67	68	72	272	19,123
Soren Hansen	69	67	68	68	272	19,123
Matthew Nixon	66	69	70	67	272	19,123
Julien Quesne	69	66	68	69	272	19,123
Scott Jamieson	70	69	66	68	273	16,100

	SCORES				TOTAL	MONEY
Jason Knutzon	70	69	68	66	273	16,100
Thorbjorn Olesen	69	69	67	68	273	16,100
Peter Uihlein	72	67	65	69	273	16,100
Thomas Bjorn	66	72	68	68	274	13,570
Richard Bland	70	69	68	67	274	13,570
Mikko Ilonen	73	66	65	70	274	13,570
Raphael Jacquelin	65	69	69	71	274	13,570
Peter Lawrie	69	70	62	73	274	13,570
Morten Orum Madsen	70	69	67	68	274	13,570
Adrian Otaegui	68	70	67	69	274	13,570
Mark Foster	69	68	67	71	275	10,350
J.B. Hansen	72	67	65	71	275	10,350
David Howell	69	70	68	68	275	10,350
Matteo Manassero	68	71	66	70	275	10,350
Chapchai Nirat	66	70	73	66	275	10,350
Wade Ormsby	67	67	70	71	275	10,350
Ricardo Santos	67	70	72	66	275	10,350
Matthew Baldwin	68	68	72	68	276	7,636
Michael Hoey	65	68	73	70	276	7,636
Rikard Karlberg	68	68	70	70	276	7,636
Craig Lee	66	70	69	71	276	7,636
Jamie McLeary	66	70	69	71	276	7,636
Nacho Elvira	70	68	68	71	277	6,555
Anders Hansen	67	71	69	70	277	6,555
Francois Calmels	70	68	67	73	278	5,750
Bradley Dredge	70	69	70	69	278	5,750
David Drysdale	66	73	68	71	278	5,750
Mikael Lundberg	67	71	66	74	278	5,750
Hennie Otto	68	69	68	73	278	5,750
Peter Hanson	66	68	73	72	279	4,612
Sihwan Kim	72	66	71	70	279	4,612
Paul Lawrie	70	68	69	72	279	4,612
Martin Rominger	68	70	69	72	279	4,612
Gary Stal	71	66	67	75	279	4,612
John Parry	71	68	69	72	280	3,448
Alvaro Quiros	69	68	69	74	280	3,448
Seuk-Hyun Baek	69	70	68	74	281	3,441
Padraig Harrington	66	71	72	72	281	3,441
Robert Rock	69	69	71	72	281	3,441
Johan Carlsson	70	69	74	70	283	3,430
Rahil Gangjee	72	67	71	73	283	3,430
Jose-Filipe Lima	71	68	72	72	283	3,430
Prom Meesawat	66	73	71	73	283	3,430
Adilson Da Silva	73	65	70	76	284	3,422
Justin Walters	70	68	73	73	284	3,422
Jin Jeong	71	68	77	72	288	3,417

KLM Open

Kennemer Golf & Country Club, Zandvoort, The Netherlands
Par 36-34–70; 6,626 yards

September 11-14
purse, €1,800,000

	SCORES				TOTAL	MONEY
Paul Casey	68	70	62	66	266	€300,000
Simon Dyson	70	66	66	65	267	200,000
Andy Sullivan	67	68	66	67	268	112,680
Eddie Pepperell	69	68	66	66	269	90,000
Johan Carlsson	70	67	70	63	270	59,580
Pablo Larrazabal	68	62	75	65	270	59,580
Joost Luiten	65	70	67	68	270	59,580

	SCORES				TOTAL	MONEY
Romain Wattel	67	65	64	74	270	59,580
Oliver Fisher	70	66	70	65	271	38,160
Richie Ramsay	69	65	65	72	271	38,160
Robert-Jan Derksen	71	67	68	66	272	27,495
Tyrrell Hatton	68	67	72	65	272	27,495
Mikko Ilonen	69	66	70	67	272	27,495
Raphael Jacquelin	71	68	68	65	272	27,495
Brooks Koepka	69	66	70	67	272	27,495
Jbe' Kruger	73	63	70	66	272	27,495
Edoardo Molinari	66	66	71	69	272	27,495
Paul Waring	69	71	65	67	272	27,495
Richard Bland	70	70	67	66	273	21,600
Robert Rock	73	67	65	68	273	21,600
Gary Stal	66	71	65	71	273	21,600
Thomas Aiken	67	68	71	68	274	18,990
Emiliano Grillo	72	66	67	69	274	18,990
Maximilian Kieffer	67	68	68	71	274	18,990
Thomas Pieters	70	66	67	71	274	18,990
Peter Uihlein	66	68	67	73	274	18,990
Chris Wood	69	67	70	68	274	18,990
Tommy Fleetwood	70	67	71	67	275	15,232
J.B. Hansen	72	66	67	70	275	15,232
Padraig Harrington	70	68	70	67	275	15,232
Daniel Im	67	70	70	68	275	15,232
Robert Karlsson	69	69	68	69	275	15,232
Shane Lowry	70	69	67	69	275	15,232
James Morrison	73	67	65	70	275	15,232
Reinier Saxton	71	67	70	67	275	15,232
Magnus A. Carlsson	68	71	70	67	276	12,420
Chris Doak	69	70	68	69	276	12,420
Gonzalo Fernandez-Castano	71	69	66	70	276	12,420
Mikko Korhonen	71	69	67	69	276	12,420
Tom Lewis	70	69	70	67	276	12,420
Gregory Bourdy	73	67	69	68	277	9,900
Nicolas Colsaerts	72	68	66	71	277	9,900
Mark Foster	70	67	73	67	277	9,900
Adam Gee	69	70	69	69	277	9,900
David Howell	68	69	73	67	277	9,900
Alexandre Kaleka	72	67	72	66	277	9,900
Wade Ormsby	70	69	67	71	277	9,900
Andrea Pavan	66	70	67	74	277	9,900
Marc Warren	68	68	71	70	277	9,900
James Heath	69	67	71	71	278	7,920
Thorbjorn Olesen	69	71	69	69	278	7,920
Miguel Angel Jimenez	71	69	66	73	279	7,020
Craig Lee	69	69	68	73	279	7,020
Simon Thornton	68	69	75	67	279	7,020
Nacho Elvira	71	67	69	73	280	5,805
John Hahn	71	66	70	73	280	5,805
Soren Kjeldsen	70	70	71	69	280	5,805
Jose-Filipe Lima	70	67	74	69	280	5,805
Jack Doherty	69	71	68	73	281	5,040
Soren Hansen	68	66	75	72	281	5,040
*Jeroen Krietemeijer	71	69	70	71	281	
John Parry	71	69	69	72	281	5,040
Gaganjeet Bhullar	70	69	75	68	282	4,680
Inder Van Weerelt	69	70	73	71	283	4,500
Byeong-Hun An	72	68	72	72	284	4,050
Wil Besseling	68	72	71	73	284	4,050
Darren Clarke	73	67	70	74	284	4,050
Julien Quesne	70	69	71	74	284	4,050
Roope Kakko	69	69	71	76	285	3,510
Damien McGrane	71	68	73	73	285	3,510

	SCORES				TOTAL	MONEY
Niclas Fasth	70	70	70	76	286	3,280
Marco Crespi	71	69	70	77	287	2,697
Daan Huizing	72	68	76	71	287	2,697
Jeev Milkha Singh	72	68	72	75	287	2,697
Estanislao Goya	67	73	76	72	288	2,691
Jamie McLeary	67	72	74	76	289	2,688

ISPS Handa Wales Open

Celtic Manor Resort, City of Newport, Wales — September 18-21
Par 36-36–72; 7,352 yards — purse, £1,800,000

	SCORES				TOTAL	MONEY
Joost Luiten	65	69	65	71	270	€375,780
Tommy Fleetwood	68	68	68	67	271	195,831
Shane Lowry	68	65	68	70	271	195,831
Nicolas Colsaerts	66	68	71	67	272	82,251
Jamie Donaldson	70	67	68	67	272	82,251
Edoardo Molinari	72	63	68	69	272	82,251
Eddie Pepperell	68	74	63	67	272	82,251
Marc Warren	70	67	67	68	272	82,251
Andrea Pavan	72	69	65	67	273	45,695
Robert Rock	67	71	70	65	273	45,695
Romain Wattel	69	72	64	68	273	45,695
Seve Benson	71	69	68	66	274	34,902
Graeme Storm	71	69	65	69	274	34,902
Anthony Wall	69	71	65	69	274	34,902
Steve Webster	68	72	64	70	274	34,902
Bernd Wiesberger	71	67	71	65	274	34,902
Nathan Holman	70	70	70	65	275	28,138
Thongchai Jaidee	68	67	67	73	275	28,138
Francesco Molinari	71	71	68	65	275	28,138
Richie Ramsay	69	70	70	66	275	28,138
Andy Sullivan	74	66	66	69	275	28,138
J.B. Hansen	69	71	65	71	276	24,463
Gregory Havret	69	67	66	74	276	24,463
Sihwan Kim	70	70	70	66	276	24,463
Ricardo Santos	68	68	69	71	276	24,463
Soren Kjeldsen	69	71	73	64	277	22,096
Patrik Sjoland	69	67	71	70	277	22,096
Peter Uihlein	71	68	68	70	277	22,096
Emiliano Grillo	70	71	70	67	278	20,067
Raphael Jacquelin	76	65	69	68	278	20,067
Victor Riu	72	71	64	71	278	20,067
Gaganjeet Bhullar	71	70	68	70	279	16,769
Kristoffer Broberg	71	70	70	68	279	16,769
Ross Fisher	70	72	68	69	279	16,769
James Morrison	71	69	69	70	279	16,769
Thorbjorn Olesen	71	70	71	67	279	16,769
Phillip Price	71	66	71	71	279	16,769
Julien Quesne	74	68	68	69	279	16,769
Danny Willett	72	67	67	73	279	16,769
Oliver Fisher	69	72	69	70	280	14,655
Bradley Dredge	71	70	68	72	281	13,528
Edouard Dubois	73	70	67	71	281	13,528
John Hahn	70	70	72	69	281	13,528
Robert Karlsson	71	72	70	68	281	13,528
Magnus A. Carlsson	76	67	69	70	282	11,499
Mark Foster	69	69	74	70	282	11,499
David Lynn	72	69	67	74	282	11,499
Thomas Pieters	72	68	71	71	282	11,499

	SCORES				TOTAL	MONEY
Simon Wakefield	68	72	70	72	282	11,499
Johan Carlsson	69	73	71	70	283	9,019
Robert-Jan Derksen	73	66	71	73	283	9,019
Daan Huizing	73	69	68	73	283	9,019
Wade Ormsby	70	71	70	72	283	9,019
Adrian Otaegui	70	69	71	73	283	9,019
Simon Thornton	71	69	70	73	283	9,019
Lucas Bjerregaard	71	68	72	73	284	7,215
Ricardo Gonzalez	74	69	71	70	284	7,215
Thomas Bjorn	71	69	71	74	285	6,651
Paul Casey	70	70	73	72	285	6,651
Phillip Archer	71	71	72	72	286	5,862
Daniel Im	70	72	71	73	286	5,862
Andrew McArthur	66	74	75	71	286	5,862
Lee Slattery	73	70	72	71	286	5,862
Lee Westwood	73	69	68	76	286	5,862
Nacho Elvira	71	70	71	75	287	4,848
Paul Lawrie	72	71	74	70	287	4,848
Damien McGrane	71	72	72	72	287	4,848
Jamie McLeary	68	73	77	69	287	4,848
Greig Hutcheon	72	70	71	75	288	4,196
Chris Wood	73	68	72	75	288	4,196
Craig Lee	68	72	73	76	289	3,382
Niclas Fasth	69	74	69	78	290	3,379
Adam Gee	72	71	72	78	293	3,376
Maximilian Kieffer	71	70	74	80	295	3,373

The Ryder Cup

Gleneagles, Auchterarder, Perthshire, Scotland — September 26-28

Par 454 343 445–36, 344 444 535–36–72; 7,243 yards

FIRST DAY
Morning Fourball

Justin Rose and Henrik Stenson (Europe) defeated Bubba Watson and Webb Simpson, 5 and 4.

Rose	4			2		3				2	4		4	3				
Stenson		4	4		5		4	4	4			4						
Watson	4		4		5	3	4	4										
Simpson		5		3					5	3	4	4	4	4				

Thomas Bjorn and Martin Kaymer (Europe) halved with Rickie Fowler and Jimmy Walker.

Bjorn		4	4		4	3	4	4	4	3	4	4	3	4	4	5		5
Kaymer	3			2					3									
Fowler		5			3	3		4										
Walker	4		4	3			4		3	3	4	4	4	4	4	4	3	4

Jordan Spieth and Patrick Reed (USA) defeated Stephen Gallacher and Ian Poulter, 5 and 4.

Gallacher		4						4	5	3		4	4	4				
Poulter	5		4	3	4	3	4				4							
Spieth	4		4	3	4		3			2		5		4				
Reed		4				2		4	4		3		4					

Keegan Bradley and Phil Mickelson (USA) defeated Sergio Garcia and Rory McIlroy, 1 up.

Garcia			4	2	4			4		3	4	4		3		4		5
McIlroy	3	5				3	5		5				4		4		3	
Bradley		5	4				4			2			5	3	5	3	3	
Mickelson	3			3	4	3		4	4		5	4						4

POINTS: Europe 1½, United States 2½

Afternoon Foursomes

Jamie Donaldson and Lee Westwood (Europe) defeated Jim Furyk and Matt Kuchar, 2 up.

Donaldson/Westwood	4	4	5	3	4	2	4	4	5	3	3	4	4	3	4	5	3	4
Furyk/Kuchar	4	4	4	3	4	3	5	4	5	3	4	4	4	3	4	4	3	5

Rose and Stenson (Europe) defeated Hunter Mahan and Zach Johnson, 2 and 1.

Rose/Stenson	3	4	5	3	4	2	4	5	4	3	3	4	4	4	4	4	3
Mahan/Johnson	4	4	5	3	4	3	3	4	4	3	4	4	4	3	5	4	4

McIlroy and Garcia (Europe) halved with Walker and Fowler.

McIlroy/Garcia	4	4	4	3	6	2	5	3	5	3	4	5	4	4	5	4	2	4
Walker/Fowler	4	4	5	3	5	3	4	3	5	3	3	4	5	4	4	4	3	5

Victor Dubuisson and Graeme McDowell (Europe) defeated Mickelson and Bradley, 3 and 2.

Dubuisson/McDowell	4	4	4	3	4	3	4	5	5	3	4	4	5	4	4	4
Mickelson/Bradley	4	5	4	4	5	3	4	4	4	4	4	5	4	4	4	5

POINTS: Europe 5, United States 3

SECOND DAY
Morning Fourball

Rose and Stenson (Europe) defeated Watson and Kuchar, 3 and 2.

Rose		4	4	3	3			3		2	3		3			4
Stenson	4					3	3		4			3		3	3	
Watson		5	3	3	3		4			2			4	3		5
Kuchar	3					2		4	4		3	4			3	

Furyk and Mahan (USA) defeated Donaldson and Westwood, 4 and 3.

Donaldson			4		4	3		3		3	3	4			4
Westwood	4	4		3			4		4				4	3	
Furyk			3	3	4	3			4	3		4	4		
Mahan	3	4					3	3			3			2	4

Reed and Spieth (USA) defeated Bjorn and Kaymer, 5 and 3.

Bjorn			3	3	5	4	3			3			4		4
Kaymer	3	4						4	5		4	4		4	
Reed				3			3					4	3	3	
Spieth	4	4	4		4	2		4	4	2	4				3

McIlroy and Poulter (Europe) halved with Walker and Fowler.

McIlroy			4			2	4	3	4		4	4	4	3			3	4
Poulter	3	4		3	C					3					3	4		
Walker	4	4	4	3	3		4	4	5		3		3	3				4
Fowler						2				2		4			3	5	3	

POINTS: Europe 6½, United States 5½

Afternoon Foursomes

Donaldson and Westwood (Europe) defeated Johnson and Kuchar, 2 and 1.

Donaldson/Westwood	4	4	4	4	3	3	4	4	4	3	3	4	4	3	4	4	3
Johnson/Kuchar	3	6	4	3	4	4	4	3	5	4	3	4	4	2	4	5	3

Garcia and McIlroy (Europe) defeated Furyk and Mahan, 3 and 2.

Garcia/McIlroy	4	4	5	3	4	2	4	4	4	3	4	5	4	3	4	4
Furyk/Mahan	5	6	4	3	4	2	4	4	4	3	4	5	4	4	4	6

Kaymer and Rose (Europe) halved with Spieth and Reed.

Kaymer/Rose	4	5	4	4	5	4	4	4	4	3	4	4	5	4	4	6	4	4
Spieth/Reed	4	5	5	2	5	3	3	4	5	2	4	5	5	4	5	6	2	5

Dubuisson and McDowell (Europe) defeated Walker and Fowler, 5 and 4.
Dubuisson/McDowell 4 4 4 3 4 3 4 5 5 3 4 4 5 4 4 4
Walker/Fowler 4 5 4 4 5 3 4 4 4 4 4 5 4 4 4 5

POINTS: Europe 10, United States 6

THIRD DAY
Singles

McDowell (Europe) defeated Spieth, 2 and 1.
McDowell 4 5 5 3 5 3 4 3 4 3 3 4 4 3 3 5 3
Spieth 4 4 4 3 4 3 4 3 4 4 4 5 5 3 5 5 3

Reed (USA) defeated Stenson, 1 up.
Stenson 4 4 4 3 4 4 3 4 5 3 4 4 4 3 3 4 3 5
Reed 4 6 4 3 4 2 3 3 6 3 3 3 5 3 6 4 3 4

McIlroy (Europe) defeated Fowler, 5 and 4.
McIlroy 3 3 3 3 3 2 5 4 4 3 4 3 3 4
Fowler 4 5 5 3 4 3 4 4 4 3 4 3 5 4

Rose (Europe) halved with Mahan.
Rose 4 5 4 3 4 3 3 3 4 2 3 5 3 4 4 4 3 4
Mahan 3 4 4 3 3 2 3 4 6 3 4 4 4 3 4 4 3 6

Mickelson (USA) defeated Gallacher, 3 and 1.
Gallacher 4 4 4 3 4 3 4 4 5 2 3 4 4 3 4 5 4
Mickelson 4 5 4 3 3 2 4 3 5 3 4 4 4 3 3 4 3

Kaymer (Europe) defeated Watson, 4 and 2.
Kaymer 3 5 4 3 3 2 5 3 5 3 4 4 3 4 5 3
Watson 3 5 5 4 4 3 4 6 5 3 4 4 3 4 3 4

Kuchar (USA) defeated Bjorn, 4 and 3.
Bjorn 4 5 4 3 5 3 4 3 5 3 3 4 4 3 5
Kuchar 4 4 5 3 4 3 3 2 5 2 4 4 4 3 3

Garcia (Europe) defeated Furyk, 1 up.
Garcia 4 6 3 2 4 3 5 4 4 3 4 3 5 3 3 3 3 4
Furyk 3 6 5 3 3 3 4 4 4 3 4 4 4 3 4 4 3 4

Poulter (Europe) halved with Simpson.
Poulter 5 4 5 4 4 3 3 3 4 3 4 4 3 4 4 4 4 4
Simpson 4 5 5 3 5 2 5 4 5 2 4 4 3 3 4 4 3 5

Donaldson (Europe) defeated Bradley, 4 and 3.
Donaldson 4 5 4 3 4 3 3 4 4 3 3 3 4 4 3
Bradley 4 5 4 3 5 3 4 3 6 3 4 4 4 4 3

Walker (USA) defeated Westwood, 3 and 2.
Westwood 3 4 4 3 4 3 4 3 5 3 3 4 3 4 5 4
Walker 3 4 3 3 4 3 4 3 4 3 3 3 4 4 4 4

Dubuisson (Europe) halved with Johnson.
Dubuisson 4 5 4 3 4 3 4 4 5 3 5 3 4 3 5 4 4 5
Johnson 4 5 4 3 4 3 4 4 5 3 3 4 5 3 4 5 4 4

FINAL POINTS: Europe 16½, USA 11½

Alfred Dunhill Links Championship

St. Andrews Old Course: Par 36-36–72; 7,279 yards
Carnoustie Championship Course: Par 36-36–72; 7,412 yards
Kingsbarns Golf Links: Par 36-36–72; 7,150 yards
St. Andrews & Fife, Scotland

October 2-5
purse, US$5,000,000

	SCORES				TOTAL	MONEY
Oliver Wilson	64	72	65	70	271	€625,787
Tommy Fleetwood	69	73	62	68	272	279,990
Rory McIlroy	73	67	64	68	272	279,990
Richie Ramsay	69	68	68	67	272	279,990
Chris Doak	70	67	70	66	273	159,200
Shane Lowry	66	70	71	67	274	112,642
Louis Oosthuizen	70	74	62	68	274	112,642
Richard Sterne	73	66	68	67	274	112,642
Brooks Koepka	70	73	64	68	275	79,600
Chris Wood	70	69	66	70	275	79,600
Robert-Jan Derksen	73	70	63	70	276	64,706
Mark Foster	68	72	70	66	276	64,706
Marcel Siem	69	71	68	68	276	64,706
David Howell	70	72	68	67	277	54,068
Robert Karlsson	72	68	68	69	277	54,068
Ryan Palmer	69	68	68	72	277	54,068
Bernd Wiesberger	71	71	67	68	277	54,068
Richard Green	68	71	71	68	278	43,930
Soren Hansen	72	68	69	69	278	43,930
Padraig Harrington	66	70	71	71	278	43,930
Raphael Jacquelin	65	70	69	74	278	43,930
Paul Lawrie	69	72	68	69	278	43,930
Thomas Pieters	73	73	65	67	278	43,930
Peter Uihlein	73	69	69	67	278	43,930
Richard Bland	71	71	70	67	279	35,670
George Coetzee	71	67	68	73	279	35,670
Darren Fichardt	73	72	65	69	279	35,670
Branden Grace	76	65	69	69	279	35,670
Alexander Levy	68	68	68	75	279	35,670
John Parry	68	73	68	70	279	35,670
Marc Warren	73	70	68	68	279	35,670
Lucas Bjerregaard	74	68	70	68	280	27,147
Magnus A. Carlsson	74	70	67	69	280	27,147
Ernie Els	71	74	65	70	280	27,147
Nacho Elvira	71	72	68	69	280	27,147
Stephen Gallacher	68	70	69	73	280	27,147
Michael Hoey	72	70	65	73	280	27,147
Thongchai Jaidee	71	71	68	70	280	27,147
Jbe' Kruger	75	71	66	68	280	27,147
Pablo Larrazabal	71	73	68	68	280	27,147
Gary Stal	69	75	68	68	280	27,147
Gregory Bourdy	67	71	71	72	281	19,900
Ryan Evans	67	74	69	71	281	19,900
Emiliano Grillo	72	73	66	70	281	19,900
Gregory Havret	74	71	66	70	281	19,900
Craig Lee	71	71	69	70	281	19,900
Paul McGinley	72	70	69	70	281	19,900
Jamie McLeary	67	72	70	72	281	19,900
Matthew Nixon	70	70	70	71	281	19,900
Brandon Stone	72	67	70	72	281	19,900
Alejandro Canizares	72	71	65	74	282	13,892
Paul Casey	69	73	66	74	282	13,892
Oliver Fisher	74	69	66	73	282	13,892
Maximilian Kieffer	72	70	70	70	282	13,892
Francesco Molinari	74	70	68	70	282	13,892

	SCORES				TOTAL	MONEY
Jason Scrivener	72	72	68	70	282	13,892
Andy Sullivan	70	71	71	70	282	13,892
Nick Dougherty	72	69	71	71	283	10,889
Ricardo Gonzalez	69	70	72	72	283	10,889
Thorbjorn Olesen	71	70	71	71	283	10,889
Ross Fisher	73	73	65	73	284	9,575
Edoardo Molinari	73	68	70	73	284	9,575
Adrian Otaegui	67	75	67	75	284	9,575
Graeme Storm	68	72	70	74	284	9,575
Felipe Aguilar	71	67	72	75	285	8,636
Thomas Aiken	71	70	69	76	286	7,527
Niclas Fasth	72	71	69	74	286	7,527
Shiv Kapur	70	72	70	74	286	7,527
Robert Rock	67	76	67	76	286	7,527
Adrien Saddier	72	73	67	74	286	7,527
Hennie Otto	69	70	70	78	287	5,632
Garrick Porteous	74	67	71	79	291	5,629

Portugal Masters

Oceanico Victoria Golf Course, Vilamoura, Portugal — October 9-12
Par 35-36–71; 7,209 yards — purse, €2,000,000
(Event shortened to 36 holes—rain.)

	SCORES		TOTAL	MONEY
Alexander Levy	63	61	124	€250,000
Nicolas Colsaerts	60	67	127	166,660
Felipe Aguilar	65	64	129	93,900
Richard Bland	66	65	131	63,700
Morten Orum Madsen	65	66	131	63,700
Romain Wattel	67	64	131	63,700
Gregory Bourdy	67	65	132	34,740
Michael Hoey	65	67	132	34,740
Scott Jamieson	63	69	132	34,740
Danny Willett	65	67	132	34,740
Chris Wood	68	64	132	34,740
Thomas Aiken	66	67	133	23,220
Rafa Cabrera-Bello	64	69	133	23,220
Tommy Fleetwood	68	65	133	23,220
Adrian Otaegui	63	70	133	23,220
Paul Waring	67	66	133	23,220
Ricardo Gonzalez	69	65	134	19,050
John Hahn	67	67	134	19,050
Thongchai Jaidee	67	67	134	19,050
Graeme Storm	69	65	134	19,050
Magnus A. Carlsson	69	66	135	15,600
George Coetzee	68	67	135	15,600
Nacho Elvira	67	68	135	15,600
Branden Grace	66	69	135	15,600
Emiliano Grillo	67	68	135	15,600
Thorbjorn Olesen	71	64	135	15,600
Marcel Siem	67	68	135	15,600
Justin Walters	68	67	135	15,600
Marc Warren	69	66	135	15,600
David Drysdale	68	68	136	12,900
Ryan Evans	68	68	136	12,900
Pedro Figueiredo	67	69	136	12,900
Johan Carlsson	67	70	137	9,911
Niclas Fasth	69	68	137	9,911
Ross Fisher	67	70	137	9,911

	SCORES		TOTAL	MONEY
J.B. Hansen	68	69	137	9,911
Simon Khan	67	70	137	9,911
Jbe' Kruger	66	71	137	9,911
Pablo Larrazabal	68	69	137	9,911
Shane Lowry	71	66	137	9,911
Victor Riu	64	73	137	9,911
Adrien Saddier	70	67	137	9,911
Gary Stal	69	68	137	9,911
Peter Uihlein	69	68	137	9,911
Steve Webster	71	66	137	9,911
Peter Whiteford	68	69	137	9,911
Lucas Bjerregaard	68	70	138	6,150
Daniel Brooks	68	70	138	6,150
Marco Crespi	68	70	138	6,150
Eduardo De La Riva	66	72	138	6,150
Robert-Jan Derksen	70	68	138	6,150
Padraig Harrington	72	66	138	6,150
David Horsey	69	69	138	6,150
Roope Kakko	68	70	138	6,150
Soren Kjeldsen	72	66	138	6,150
Andy Sullivan	70	68	138	6,150
Fabrizio Zanotti	71	67	138	6,150
Matthew Baldwin	69	70	139	3,825
Ricardo Gouveia	70	69	139	3,825
Tyrrell Hatton	70	69	139	3,825
Robert Karlsson	69	70	139	3,825
Tom Lewis	72	67	139	3,825
David Lynn	65	74	139	3,825
Paul McGinley	67	72	139	3,825
Matthew Nixon	73	66	139	3,825
Eddie Pepperell	70	69	139	3,825
Jeev Milkha Singh	72	67	139	3,825

Volvo World Match Play Championship

London Golf Club, Ash, Kent, England — October15-19
Par 36-36–72; 7,026 yards — purse, €2,250,000

FIRST ROUND

Graeme McDowell defeated Alexander Levy, 3 and 2.
Joost Luiten defeated Mikko Ilonen, 1 up.
Henrik Stenson halved with George Coetzee.
Thongchai Jaidee defeated Francesco Molinari, 2 up.
Paul Casey defeated Jamie Donaldson, 2 and 1.
Jonas Blixt defeated Patrick Reed, 2 and 1.
Victor Dubuisson defeated Pablo Larrazabal, 3 and 2.
Shane Lowry defeated Stephen Gallacher, 3 and 2.

SECOND ROUND

Dubuisson defeated Lowry, 3 and 2.
Larrazabal defeated Gallacher, 1 up.
Ilonen defeated McDowell, 2 and 1.
Luiten defeated Levy, 4 and 3.
Stenson defeated Molinari, 2 and 1.
Coetzee defeated Jaidee, 2 and 1.
Donaldson defeated Blixt, 3 and 2.
Reed defeated Casey, 2 and 1.

THIRD ROUND

Reed defeated Donaldson, 3 and 2.
Blixt halved with Casey.
Gallacher defeated Dubuisson, 2 and 1.
Larrazabal defeated Lowry, 2 and 1.
Luiten defeated McDowell, 2 up.
Ilonen defeated Levy, 1 up.
Stenson defeated Jaidee, 2 and 1.
Molinari defeated Coetzee, 2 and 1.

(Casey, Jaidee, Lowry and McDowell received €75,000 each; Donaldson, Gallacher, Levy and Molinari received €50,000 each.)

QUARTER-FINALS

Coetzee defeated Reed, 2 and 1.
Ilonen defeated Dubuisson, 2 up.
Luiten defeated Larrazabal, 6 and 5.
Stenson defeated Blixt, 2 up.

(Each losing player received €100,000.)

SEMI-FINALS

Ilonen defeated Luiten, 2 and 1.
Stenson defeated Coetzee, 1 up.

PLAYOFF FOR THIRD-FOURTH PLACE

Luiten defeated Coetzee, 19 holes.

(Luiten received €210,000; Coetzee received €160,000.)

FINAL

Ilonen defeated Stenson, 3 and 1.

(Ilonen received €650,000; Stenson received €333,000.)

Hong Kong Open

See Asia/Japan Tours chapter.

ISPS Handa Perth International

See Australasian Tour chapter.

The Final Series

BMW Masters

Lake Malaren Golf Club, Shanghai, China
Par 36-36–72; 7,607 yards

October 30-November 2
purse, US$7,000,000

	SCORES				TOTAL	MONEY
Marcel Siem	68	66	65	73	272	€918,944
Ross Fisher	70	67	68	67	272	480,504
Alexander Levy	65	66	63	78	272	480,504
(Siem defeated Fisher and Levy on first playoff hole.)						
Jamie Donaldson	68	68	62	75	273	254,942
Justin Rose	72	65	64	72	273	254,942
Nicolas Colsaerts	66	64	73	71	274	179,558
Romain Wattel	66	67	71	70	274	179,558
Emiliano Grillo	66	68	69	72	275	132,138
Ryan Palmer	70	67	68	70	275	132,138
George Coetzee	71	67	67	71	276	102,691
Mikko Ilonen	70	66	69	71	276	102,691
Fabrizio Zanotti	70	68	69	69	276	102,691
Darren Fichardt	69	68	69	71	277	84,022
Joost Luiten	72	69	64	72	277	84,022
Bernd Wiesberger	72	69	66	70	277	84,022
Branden Grace	68	66	71	73	278	72,311
Robert Karlsson	69	70	66	73	278	72,311
Shane Lowry	70	66	71	71	278	72,311
Graeme McDowell	67	69	68	74	278	72,311
Richard Sterne	68	70	70	70	278	72,311
Victor Dubuisson	70	70	68	71	279	64,198
Richie Ramsay	70	68	68	73	279	64,198
Danny Willett	71	70	67	71	279	64,198
Thomas Bjorn	68	67	71	74	280	59,275
David Howell	74	71	66	69	280	59,275
Ernie Els	69	68	69	75	281	55,415
Eddie Pepperell	72	69	70	70	281	55,415
Oliver Fisher	71	69	70	72	282	48,286
Tyrrell Hatton	73	67	71	71	282	48,286
Thongchai Jaidee	71	70	69	72	282	48,286
Edoardo Molinari	70	71	69	72	282	48,286
Thorbjorn Olesen	70	70	70	72	282	48,286
Dong Su	70	69	68	75	282	48,286
Michael Hoey	70	68	72	73	283	41,748
Seung-Hyuk Kim	70	71	69	73	283	41,748
Magnus A. Carlsson	73	72	68	71	284	38,440
Stephen Gallacher	72	69	72	71	284	38,440
Hennie Otto	71	71	70	72	284	38,440
Thomas Aiken	72	68	72	73	285	34,029
Richard Bland	72	68	73	72	285	34,029
Tommy Fleetwood	78	71	67	69	285	34,029
Ze-Yu He	73	71	69	72	285	34,029
Matthew Baldwin	73	71	69	73	286	28,672
Gonzalo Fernandez-Castano	72	68	69	77	286	28,672
Hao-Tong Li	69	71	74	72	286	28,672
Paul McGinley	71	73	71	71	286	28,672
Marc Warren	70	72	72	72	286	28,672
Shao-Cai He	71	71	68	77	287	23,158
Chris Kirk	73	72	68	74	287	23,158
Brooks Koepka	73	72	70	72	287	23,158
Wen-Chong Liang	72	70	73	72	287	23,158
Ian Poulter	74	69	70	74	287	23,158

	SCORES				TOTAL	MONEY
Mu Hu	69	71	74	74	288	19,298
Francesco Molinari	69	74	71	74	288	19,298
Jose Maria Olazabal	71	70	73	75	289	17,723
Simon Dyson	75	72	71	72	290	15,675
Zheng Ouyang	72	66	77	75	290	15,675
Oliver Wilson	68	73	69	80	290	15,675
Felipe Aguilar	70	74	71	76	291	13,115
Kristoffer Broberg	73	69	73	76	291	13,115
Morten Orum Madsen	69	74	71	78	292	10,949
Kevin Stadler	73	71	72	76	292	10,949
Graeme Storm	75	70	72	75	292	10,949
Rafa Cabrera-Bello	74	66	70	84	294	9,295
Alejandro Canizares	78	71	73	72	294	9,295
Ashun Wu	75	70	70	79	294	9,295
Yi Cao	72	71	76	76	295	8,349
Andy Sullivan	76	72	70	77	295	8,349
Mark Foster	75	71	75	75	296	7,719
Maximilian Kieffer	71	69	75	81	296	7,719
David Horsey	73	75	71	78	297	7,089
Pablo Larrazabal	76	72	69	80	297	7,089
Zi-Hao Chen	77	76	73	76	302	6,616
Chen Xiao Duan	78	73	70	82	303	6,301
Yan-Wei Liu	75	76	78	76	305	6,144
Matteo Manassero	74	78	74	80	306	5,986
Miguel Angel Jimenez	77	70	72	88	307	5,829
Tianyi Wu	76	83	80	81	320	5,750

WGC - HSBC Champions

See Asia/Japan Tours chapter.

Turkish Airlines Open

Montgomerie Maxx Royal, Antalya, Turkey — November 13-16
Par 35-37–72; 7,132 yards — purse, US$7,000,000

	SCORES				TOTAL	MONEY
Brooks Koepka	69	67	70	65	271	€930,740
Ian Poulter	64	66	75	67	272	622,302
Henrik Stenson	70	70	70	64	274	351,042
Miguel Angel Jimenez	63	73	71	68	275	220,279
Wade Ormsby	65	71	68	71	275	220,279
Andy Sullivan	67	75	66	67	275	220,279
Danny Willett	67	70	69	69	275	220,279
Marcel Siem	70	69	66	71	276	134,273
Lee Westwood	70	68	67	71	276	134,273
Eddie Pepperell	70	71	67	69	277	112,173
Emiliano Grillo	68	72	71	67	278	93,983
Alexander Levy	68	71	73	66	278	93,983
Peter Uihlein	73	65	70	70	278	93,983
Romain Wattel	67	71	73	67	278	93,983
Brendon de Jonge	65	73	73	68	279	76,930
Victor Dubuisson	77	68	70	64	279	76,930
Stephen Gallacher	67	71	71	70	279	76,930
David Lipsky	69	73	69	68	279	76,930
Chris Doak	69	73	69	69	280	66,259
Jamie Donaldson	72	72	70	66	280	66,259
Branden Grace	67	69	73	71	280	66,259
Tyrrell Hatton	65	72	72	71	280	66,259

	SCORES				TOTAL	MONEY
Hennie Otto	67	69	72	72	280	66,259
Fabrizio Zanotti	72	71	69	68	280	66,259
Jonas Blixt	68	71	72	70	281	53,636
John Daly	69	72	67	73	281	53,636
Ross Fisher	74	70	70	67	281	53,636
Sergio Garcia	75	71	65	70	281	53,636
Shane Lowry	70	66	72	73	281	53,636
Joost Luiten	70	73	71	67	281	53,636
Francesco Molinari	70	71	71	69	281	53,636
Gregory Bourdy	68	73	72	69	282	44,119
Luke Donald	74	73	68	67	282	44,119
Tommy Fleetwood	69	71	77	65	282	44,119
Dawie van der Walt	72	72	68	70	282	44,119
Alejandro Canizares	69	71	73	70	283	39,173
David Horsey	74	70	72	67	283	39,173
Thongchai Jaidee	69	68	74	72	283	39,173
Matthew Baldwin	73	68	72	71	284	32,858
Richard Bland	71	69	73	71	284	32,858
Darren Fichardt	68	73	71	72	284	32,858
Richard Green	71	74	69	70	284	32,858
Scott Jamieson	70	72	72	70	284	32,858
Edoardo Molinari	67	72	71	74	284	32,858
Marc Warren	67	74	75	68	284	32,858
Rafa Cabrera-Bello	72	68	73	72	285	27,604
Robert Karlsson	71	71	70	73	285	27,604
Magnus A. Carlsson	69	70	75	72	286	24,253
Robert-Jan Derksen	69	74	72	71	286	24,253
David Howell	71	71	71	73	286	24,253
David Lynn	69	74	72	71	286	24,253
Nicolas Colsaerts	80	71	70	66	287	20,344
Pablo Larrazabal	70	74	73	70	287	20,344
Bernd Wiesberger	71	71	74	71	287	20,344
George Coetzee	76	71	71	70	288	16,116
Simon Dyson	68	71	75	74	288	16,116
Raphael Jacquelin	68	72	78	70	288	16,116
Matteo Manassero	70	77	72	69	288	16,116
Graeme Storm	75	77	69	67	288	16,116
Oliver Fisher	67	81	71	70	289	11,747
Martin Kaymer	68	72	75	74	289	11,747
Richard Sterne	74	77	73	65	289	11,747
Oliver Wilson	76	70	73	70	289	11,747
Felipe Aguilar	72	74	71	73	290	9,454
Thomas Aiken	70	72	75	73	290	9,454
Darren Clarke	75	70	73	72	290	9,454
Mikko Ilonen	69	72	74	75	290	9,454
Kristoffer Broberg	72	75	72	72	291	8,377
Mark Foster	70	72	78	71	291	8,377
Colin Montgomerie	76	72	72	72	292	7,898
Richie Ramsay	76	70	72	76	294	7,579
Thorbjorn Olesen	77	71	73	74	295	7,260
Morten Orum Madsen	72	76	79	70	297	6,941
Julien Quesne	77	76	75	70	298	6,621
Michael Hoey	82	75	73	73	303	6,462
*Ali Altuntas	79	84	80	76	319	
*Ediz Kemaloglu	81	79	86	74	320	
*Alihan Afsar	82	86	87	75	330	

DP World Tour Championship

Jumeirah Golf Estates, Dubai, United Arab Emirates — November 20-23
Par 36-36–72; 7,675 yards — purse, US$8,000,000

	SCORES				TOTAL	MONEY
Henrik Stenson	68	66	68	70	272	€1,067,152
Victor Dubuisson	71	68	67	68	274	482,604
Rory McIlroy	66	70	70	68	274	482,604
Justin Rose	71	66	68	69	274	482,604
Shane Lowry	66	71	72	66	275	256,122
Tyrrell Hatton	70	68	68	70	276	188,944
Robert Karlsson	71	68	68	69	276	188,944
Louis Oosthuizen	69	71	70	66	276	188,944
Rafa Cabrera-Bello	73	64	65	75	277	147,270
Branden Grace	72	67	68	70	277	147,270
Joost Luiten	70	69	68	70	277	147,270
Jamie Donaldson	72	70	67	69	278	118,456
Tommy Fleetwood	69	74	67	68	278	118,456
Sergio Garcia	73	69	69	67	278	118,456
Thorbjorn Olesen	67	70	69	72	278	118,456
Simon Dyson	73	70	67	69	279	89,643
Pablo Larrazabal	71	69	69	70	279	89,643
Francesco Molinari	73	69	69	68	279	89,643
Richie Ramsay	67	69	75	68	279	89,643
Bernd Wiesberger	72	70	68	69	279	89,643
Hennie Otto	71	68	70	71	280	70,433
Ian Poulter	75	69	70	66	280	70,433
Andy Sullivan	73	69	67	71	280	70,433
Marc Warren	71	71	65	73	280	70,433
Danny Willett	69	67	71	73	280	70,433
George Coetzee	70	70	69	72	281	60,829
Luke Donald	76	66	71	68	281	60,829
Oliver Fisher	72	70	73	66	281	60,829
Alexander Levy	71	72	71	67	281	60,829
Eddie Pepperell	76	69	66	70	281	60,829
Kristoffer Broberg	70	67	72	73	282	51,352
Nicolas Colsaerts	73	72	70	67	282	51,352
Darren Fichardt	72	68	72	70	282	51,352
Stephen Gallacher	72	68	71	71	282	51,352
Thongchai Jaidee	72	72	67	71	282	51,352
Thomas Aiken	76	66	72	69	283	45,461
Thomas Bjorn	71	69	69	74	283	45,461
Romain Wattel	71	70	71	71	283	45,461
Ernie Els	75	67	70	72	284	41,619
Martin Kaymer	72	69	74	69	284	41,619
Marcel Siem	76	66	72	70	284	41,619
Ross Fisher	69	73	67	76	285	36,497
David Howell	71	67	73	74	285	36,497
Miguel Angel Jimenez	71	73	69	72	285	36,497
Brooks Koepka	78	68	70	69	285	36,497
Edoardo Molinari	69	74	69	73	285	36,497
Graeme McDowell	72	70	72	72	286	30,734
Wade Ormsby	73	71	69	73	286	30,734
Charl Schwartzel	72	71	70	73	286	30,734
Lee Westwood	70	71	74	71	286	30,734
Jonas Blixt	70	74	70	73	287	26,252
Richard Sterne	71	74	71	71	287	26,252
Fabrizio Zanotti	73	72	72	70	287	26,252
Emiliano Grillo	68	75	72	73	288	23,691
Mikko Ilonen	74	76	68	74	292	21,770
Oliver Wilson	75	72	72	73	292	21,770
David Lipsky	76	75	70	72	293	19,849

	SCORES				TOTAL	MONEY
Matthew Baldwin	75	74	71	75	295	19,209
Matteo Manassero	75	72	75	75	297	18,568
Michael Hoey	73	78	70	77	298	17,928

Race to Dubai Final Rankings

RANK	NAME	RACE TO DUBAI POINTS	BONUS MONEY
1	Rory McIlroy	7,149,503	US$1,250,000
2	Henrik Stenson	4,981,093	800,000
3	Justin Rose	3,180,388	530,000
4	Jamie Donaldson	3,058,166	400,000
5	Victor Dubuisson	2,966,524	350,000
6	Sergio Garcia	2,861,930	300,000
7	Marcel Siem	2,739,373	250,000
8	Brooks Koepka	2,631,873	200,000
9	Alexander Levy	2,452,757	170,000
10	Shane Lowry	2,173,864	150,000
11	Joost Luiten	2,158,172	140,000
12	Thomas Bjorn	2,122,402	130,000
13	Ian Poulter	2,092,569	120,000
14	Graeme McDowell	2,049,356	110,000
15	Martin Kaymer	2,040,550	100,000

Nedbank Golf Challenge

See African Tours chapter.

Alfred Dunhill Championship

See African Tours chapter.

Challenge Tour

Barclays Kenya Open

Karen Country Club, Nairobi, Kenya — March 6-9
Par 35-35–71; 6,953 yards — purse, €200,000

	SCORES				TOTAL	MONEY
Jake Roos	69	68	71	70	278	€32,000
Adrien Bernadet	70	69	70	70	279	16,000
Lasse Jensen	67	71	71	70	279	16,000
Pedro Oriol	69	69	70	71	279	16,000
Steven Brown	70	72	71	68	281	6,960
Dodge Kemmer	69	73	71	68	281	6,960
Thomas Linard	71	70	71	69	281	6,960
Danie van Tonder	70	69	70	72	281	6,960
Pontus Widegren	69	69	72	71	281	6,960
Oliver Bekker	71	70	68	73	282	4,067
Bernd Ritthammer	74	69	69	70	282	4,067
Greg Snow	70	68	71	73	282	4,067
Jamie Elson	73	69	73	68	283	3,300
Dismas Indiza	73	69	68	73	283	3,300
Maarten Lafeber	72	72	69	70	283	3,300
Sam Little	75	70	67	71	283	3,300
Cyril Bouniol	70	72	72	70	284	2,343
Matt Ford	70	70	72	72	284	2,343
Sam Hutsby	73	66	70	75	284	2,343
Andrew McArthur	71	68	73	72	284	2,343
Oliver Wilson	69	68	78	69	284	2,343
George Woolgar	72	68	75	69	284	2,343
Chris Hanson	73	72	69	71	285	1,820
Jeppe Huldahl	70	71	69	75	285	1,820
Jerome Lando Casanova	70	73	70	72	285	1,820
Niklas Lemke	72	71	69	73	285	1,820
Phillip Price	70	71	71	73	285	1,820
Alvaro Velasco	66	70	72	77	285	1,820

NH Collection Open

See European Tour section.

Challenge de Catalunya

Lumine Golf & Beach Club, Tarragona, Spain — April 24-27
Par 35-36–71; 6,909 yards — purse, €160,000
(Second round cancelled—wind.)

	SCORES			TOTAL	MONEY
Antonio Hortal	68	63	68	199	€25,600
Callum Shinkwin	66	68	68	202	17,600
Connor Arendell	65	67	72	204	10,400
Andrew Johnston	68	69	67	204	10,400
Cyril Bouniol	66	68	71	205	6,507

	SCORES			TOTAL	MONEY
Matt Ford	68	70	67	205	6,507
Jerome Lando Casanova	66	68	71	205	6,507
Byeong-Hun An	67	68	71	206	3,760
Jordi Garcia Pinto	70	68	68	206	3,760
Andrew Marshall	68	69	69	206	3,760
Simon Wakefield	67	70	69	206	3,760
Lorenzo Gagli	68	67	72	207	2,960
Michael Lorenzo-Vera	68	69	70	207	2,960
Juan Antonio Bragulat	68	69	71	208	2,320
Daniel Brooks	69	69	70	208	2,320
Alan Dunbar	66	70	72	208	2,320
Jean-Baptiste Gonnet	70	67	71	208	2,320
Niall Kearney	69	65	74	208	2,320
Mikko Korhonen	70	68	70	208	2,320
Jason Barnes	71	70	68	209	1,527
Filippo Bergamaschi	70	70	69	209	1,527
Wil Besseling	68	73	68	209	1,527
Ben Evans	68	71	70	209	1,527
Lasse Jensen	68	67	74	209	1,527
Nathan Kimsey	69	66	74	209	1,527
Adrien Saddier	64	70	75	209	1,527
Juan Francisco Sarasti	69	69	71	209	1,527
Joel Sjoholm	67	72	70	209	1,527

Madeira Islands Open

See European Tour section.

Turkish Airlines Challenge

National Golf Club, Belek, Antalya, Turkey — May 15-18
Par 36-36–72; 7,085 yards — purse, €175,000

	SCORES				TOTAL	MONEY
Oliver Farr	72	67	77	70	286	€28,000
Dave Coupland	71	70	73	74	288	14,000
Jeppe Huldahl	76	68	71	73	288	14,000
Jerome Lando Casanova	71	71	71	75	288	14,000
Bjorn Akesson	71	71	73	74	289	7,875
Moritz Lampert	74	72	71	72	289	7,875
Chris Hanson	74	71	72	73	290	4,900
Niccolo Quintarelli	72	70	73	75	290	4,900
Bernd Ritthammer	78	66	75	71	290	4,900
Adrien Bernadet	73	75	75	68	291	3,675
Robert Coles	70	75	75	71	291	3,675
Ruaidhri McGee	73	73	72	74	292	3,325
Byeong-Hun An	70	72	75	76	293	2,800
Matteo Delpodio	71	75	74	73	293	2,800
Edouard Espana	72	71	78	72	293	2,800
Thomas Linard	74	74	74	71	293	2,800
Chris Paisley	69	73	74	77	293	2,800
Cyril Bouniol	77	71	72	74	294	2,034
Max Orrin	72	74	72	76	294	2,034
Nicolo Ravano	75	68	73	78	294	2,034
Steven Tiley	75	71	75	73	294	2,034
Wallace Booth	71	72	72	80	295	1,610
Jack Harrison	71	71	75	78	295	1,610
Benjamin Hebert	73	71	74	77	295	1,610
Richard McEvoy	72	72	72	79	295	1,610

	SCORES				TOTAL	MONEY
Martin Rominger	76	70	71	78	295	1,610
Anthony Snobeck	75	74	71	75	295	1,610
Alessandro Tadini	73	73	78	71	295	1,610

Karnten Golf Open

Golfclub Schloss Finkenstein, Godersdorf, Austria — May 22-25
Par 36-35–71; 6,932 yards — purse, €160,000

	SCORES				TOTAL	MONEY
Moritz Lampert	69	66	65	65	265	€25,600
Byeong-Hun An	67	69	64	66	266	17,600
Filippo Bergamaschi	69	66	65	67	267	11,200
Cyril Bouniol	69	67	63	69	268	8,000
Florian Fritsch	65	69	66	68	268	8,000
Jake Roos	67	69	66	66	268	8,000
Wallace Booth	69	68	68	64	269	4,240
Sam Hutsby	72	64	68	65	269	4,240
Paul Maddy	65	68	67	69	269	4,240
Ruaidhri McGee	68	65	69	67	269	4,240
Steven Tiley	72	65	64	69	270	3,200
Adrien Bernadet	65	70	71	65	271	2,720
Jeppe Huldahl	73	60	66	72	271	2,720
Andrew Johnston	67	65	68	71	271	2,720
Niccolo Quintarelli	71	67	67	66	271	2,720
Daniel Vancsik	67	66	68	70	271	2,720
Benjamin Hebert	70	68	66	68	272	1,936
Chris Lloyd	68	67	71	66	272	1,936
Gregory Main	69	69	68	66	272	1,936
Tom Murray	64	70	68	70	272	1,936
Max Orrin	64	74	67	67	272	1,936
Dylan Frittelli	70	65	70	68	273	1,520
Luke Goddard	71	66	65	71	273	1,520
Jerome Lando Casanova	65	67	68	73	273	1,520
Borja Virto	68	66	66	73	273	1,520

D+D Real Czech Challenge

Golf & Spa Kuneticka Hora, Dritec, Czech Republic — May 29-June 1
Par 36-36–72; 7,337 yards — purse, €165,000

	SCORES				TOTAL	MONEY
Thomas Linard	70	68	67	64	269	€26,400
Daniel Gaunt	64	69	70	68	271	18,150
Ross McGowan	70	68	66	69	273	11,550
Chris Lloyd	68	66	69	71	274	9,075
Pontus Widegren	70	67	66	71	274	9,075
Phillip Archer	70	73	68	65	276	4,565
Ken Benz	77	63	69	67	276	4,565
Steven Brown	73	68	69	66	276	4,565
Robert Coles	71	70	67	68	276	4,565
Florian Fritsch	70	68	69	69	276	4,565
Lloyd Kennedy	72	69	67	68	276	4,565
Edouard Espana	70	67	69	71	277	2,888
Benjamin Hebert	71	69	68	69	277	2,888
Jeppe Huldahl	72	67	68	70	277	2,888
Gregor Main	71	71	68	67	277	2,888

	SCORES				TOTAL	MONEY
Wallace Booth	73	67	70	68	278	2,310
Anders Engell	71	72	67	68	278	2,310
Peter Erofejeff	71	69	65	73	278	2,310
Tom Murray	72	68	73	66	279	1,842
Alvaro Velasco	69	72	69	69	279	1,842
Jeff Winther	70	70	66	73	279	1,842
Lorenzo Gagli	73	66	70	71	280	1,502
Sebastian Garcia Rodriguez	70	72	69	69	280	1,502
Max Glauert	68	71	68	73	280	1,502
Jack Harrison	71	67	71	71	280	1,502
Jaakko Makitalo	72	68	69	71	280	1,502
Pierre Relecom	68	73	68	71	280	1,502
Alessandro Tadini	72	67	68	73	280	1,502
Martin Wiegele	71	71	69	69	280	1,502

Fred Olsen Challenge de Espana

Tecina Golf, La Gomera, Canary Islands, Spain — June 5-8
Par 36-35–71; 6,937 yards — purse, €160,000

	SCORES				TOTAL	MONEY
Moritz Lampert	69	66	66	63	264	€25,600
Hugues Joannes	68	67	67	64	266	17,600
Luis Claverie	67	69	68	64	268	10,400
Matteo Delpodio	66	67	66	69	268	10,400
Andrew Johnston	69	66	66	68	269	7,200
Joel Sjoholm	67	62	72	68	269	7,200
Agustin Domingo	68	66	68	68	270	4,240
Nicolo Ravano	68	67	65	70	270	4,240
Diego Suazo	70	69	67	64	270	4,240
Alvaro Velasco	71	66	66	67	270	4,240
Michael Lorenzo-Vera	70	69	66	66	271	3,200
David Law	72	66	66	68	272	2,720
Jason Palmer	66	68	69	69	272	2,720
Neil Raymond	71	70	66	65	272	2,720
Matthew Southgate	70	69	64	69	272	2,720
Alessandro Tadini	70	69	68	65	272	2,720
Sam Hutsby	66	68	71	68	273	2,160
Damien Perrier	65	72	67	69	273	2,160
William Harrold	72	65	70	67	274	1,732
Antonio Hortal	68	68	70	68	274	1,732
Lasse Jensen	72	64	69	69	274	1,732
Pedro Oriol	68	66	69	71	274	1,732
David Borda	68	70	68	69	275	1,504
Max Orrin	66	69	73	67	275	1,504
Jack Senior	67	70	68	70	275	1,504

Najeti Hotels et Golfs Open

Aa St. Omer Golf Club, St. Omer, France — June 12-15
Par 36-35–71; 6,538 yards — purse, €200,000

	SCORES				TOTAL	MONEY
Jordi Garcia Pinto	71	65	71	70	277	€32,000
Carlos Aguilar	73	68	68	71	280	22,000
Lorenzo Gagli	72	71	68	71	282	10,080
Scott Henry	68	74	71	69	282	10,080

	SCORES				TOTAL	MONEY
Lloyd Kennedy	71	70	70	71	282	10,080
Andrea Rota	69	69	72	72	282	10,080
Mark Tullo	72	71	71	68	282	10,080
Berry Henson	72	70	72	69	283	5,600
David Law	68	71	72	73	284	4,400
Daniel Vancsik	72	72	70	70	284	4,400
Pontus Widegren	69	75	71	69	284	4,400
Jack Doherty	73	70	70	72	285	3,200
Pelle Edberg	70	70	71	74	285	3,200
Benjamin Hebert	71	71	70	73	285	3,200
Lasse Jensen	71	73	69	72	285	3,200
Tain Lee	69	71	70	75	285	3,200
Ross McGowan	71	71	68	75	285	3,200
Alessandro Tadini	70	68	74	73	285	3,200
Bjorn Akesson	74	68	70	74	286	2,077
Christophe Brazillier	73	68	72	73	286	2,077
Pedro Figueiredo	71	71	72	72	286	2,077
Joakim Lagergren	69	75	71	71	286	2,077
Chris Paisley	70	73	71	72	286	2,077
Terry Pilkadaris	70	71	72	73	286	2,077
Robert Coles	69	74	74	70	287	1,720
Chris Hanson	68	72	70	77	287	1,720
Eirik Tage Johansen	72	72	73	70	287	1,720
Andrew Marshall	69	75	74	69	287	1,720
Christopher Mivis	75	68	73	71	287	1,720
Joel Sjoholm	72	71	71	73	287	1,720
Oscar Stark	70	70	76	71	287	1,720

Belgian Challenge Open

Cleydael Golf & Country Club, Aartselaar, Belgium — June 19-22
Par 36-35–71; 6,548 yards — purse, €160,000

	SCORES				TOTAL	MONEY
William Harrold	70	63	67	66	266	€25,600
Florian Fritsch	64	68	69	65	266	17,600
(Harrold defeated Fritsch on first playoff hole.)						
Dave Coupland	63	72	67	66	268	10,400
Jason Palmer	66	63	73	66	268	10,400
Joel Stalter	68	64	70	67	269	8,000
Filippo Bergamaschi	69	69	68	66	272	4,672
Michael Jonzon	68	69	67	68	272	4,672
Tain Lee	68	68	70	66	272	4,672
Terry Pilkadaris	66	70	67	69	272	4,672
Andrea Rota	66	72	67	67	272	4,672
Jason Barnes	73	67	67	66	273	2,960
Rodolfo Cazaubon	65	66	70	72	273	2,960
Edouard Espana	68	69	67	69	273	2,960
Alvaro Velasco	67	66	72	68	273	2,960
Connor Arendell	70	68	69	67	274	2,160
Robert Coles	74	65	66	69	274	2,160
Hugues Joannes	66	71	68	69	274	2,160
Chris Paisley	66	69	69	70	274	2,160
Nicolo Ravano	66	71	67	70	274	2,160
Jack Wilson	69	67	68	70	274	2,160
Wallace Booth	70	69	67	69	275	1,498
Pelle Edberg	67	70	70	68	275	1,498
Niall Kearney	71	69	66	69	275	1,498
Robin Kind	66	71	69	69	275	1,498
Jaakko Makitalo	71	68	66	70	275	1,498

	SCORES				TOTAL	MONEY
Richard McEvoy	69	65	68	73	275	1,498
Paul McKechnie	69	69	64	73	275	1,498
Martin Rominger	70	69	71	65	275	1,498

Scottish Hydro Challenge

Macdonald Spey Valley Golf Club, Aviemore, Scotland
Par 35-36–71; 7,100 yards

June 26-29
purse, €250,000

	SCORES				TOTAL	MONEY
Andrew Johnston	66	65	68	66	265	€40,000
Moritz Lampert	69	67	65	67	268	22,500
Terry Pilkadaris	66	67	68	67	268	22,500
Oliver Farr	68	67	68	66	269	13,750
Jack Senior	70	66	68	65	269	13,750
Bjorn Akesson	67	67	68	68	270	7,300
Jamie Elson	68	67	67	68	270	7,300
Edouard Espana	66	68	69	67	270	7,300
Florian Fritsch	69	67	66	68	270	7,300
Mark Tullo	65	71	69	65	270	7,300
Jason Barnes	65	67	69	70	271	4,875
Michael Lorenzo-Vera	66	69	69	67	271	4,875
Maarten Lafeber	70	67	66	69	272	4,375
Taco Remkes	70	65	69	68	272	4,375
Dave Coupland	71	67	69	66	273	3,500
Stephen Dodd	72	66	72	63	273	3,500
Bradley Dredge	67	69	68	69	273	3,500
Xavier Guzman	70	64	68	71	273	3,500
Lasse Jensen	69	68	69	67	273	3,500
Kenneth Ferrie	70	66	69	69	274	2,515
Benjamin Hebert	70	69	69	66	274	2,515
Greig Hutcheon	67	68	68	71	274	2,515
Andrew Marshall	74	64	68	68	274	2,515
Paul McKechnie	70	68	66	70	274	2,515
Byeong-Hun An	69	69	71	66	275	2,225
Paul Dwyer	72	66	69	68	275	2,225
Sam Hutsby	69	69	74	63	275	2,225
Jake Roos	67	69	71	68	275	2,225

Aegean Airlines Challenge Tour

Hartl Resort, Bad Griesbach, Germany
Par 36-36–72; 7,322 yards

July 3-6
purse, €170,000

	SCORES				TOTAL	MONEY
Jake Roos	69	69	67	70	275	€27,200
Jason Barnes	71	71	67	68	277	18,700
Chris Hanson	71	67	67	73	278	10,200
Bernd Ritthammer	71	71	71	65	278	10,200
Alessandro Tadini	72	66	68	72	278	10,200
Bjorn Akesson	66	72	67	74	279	4,964
Robert Coles	72	70	68	69	279	4,964
Jens Fahrbring	70	71	70	68	279	4,964
Andrew Johnston	70	68	72	69	279	4,964
Nathan Kimsey	71	72	70	66	279	4,964
Florian Fritsch	75	64	72	69	280	3,400
Fabian Becker	72	72	69	68	281	2,720

	SCORES				TOTAL	MONEY
Jeppe Huldahl	71	71	69	70	281	2,720
Michael Jonzon	69	70	71	71	281	2,720
Moritz Lampert	70	70	73	68	281	2,720
Jaakko Makitalo	71	68	70	72	281	2,720
Pedro Oriol	70	71	68	72	281	2,720
Max Orrin	69	71	71	70	281	2,720
Jesus Legarrea	69	70	75	68	282	1,898
Sam Little	67	72	72	71	282	1,898
Andrew Marshall	69	72	68	73	282	1,898
Cyril Bouniol	67	72	70	74	283	1,615
Matteo Delpodio	68	71	70	74	283	1,615
Dylan Frittelli	71	70	67	75	283	1,615
Benjamin Hebert	69	75	71	68	283	1,615

D+D Real Slovakia Challenge

Penati Golf Resort, Senica, Slovakia
Par 36-36–72; 6,899 yards

July 10-13
purse, €160,000

	SCORES				TOTAL	MONEY
Andrew McArthur	65	66	68	68	267	€25,600
Sam Hutsby	66	69	65	69	269	17,600
Oliver Farr	68	67	68	67	270	11,200
Alvaro Velasco	68	68	65	70	271	9,600
Robert Coles	65	68	70	69	272	7,200
Pedro Oriol	68	65	72	67	272	7,200
Mark F. Haastrup	67	65	70	72	274	4,480
Andrew Johnston	73	68	62	71	274	4,480
Nathan Kimsey	69	70	69	66	274	4,480
Brandon Stone	71	67	68	69	275	3,520
Florian Fritsch	73	66	68	69	276	2,720
Jean-Baptiste Gonnet	72	70	67	67	276	2,720
Michael Lorenzo-Vera	69	70	68	69	276	2,720
Ross McGowan	66	71	71	68	276	2,720
Tim Sluiter	68	70	69	69	276	2,720
Steven Tiley	68	71	67	70	276	2,720
Mark Tullo	70	72	65	69	276	2,720
Alexander Bjork	71	69	69	68	277	1,802
Edouard Espana	66	76	71	64	277	1,802
Cesar Monasterio	71	69	70	67	277	1,802
Nicolo Ravano	70	66	72	69	277	1,802
Anthony Snobeck	70	69	71	67	277	1,802
Jens Fahrbring	73	66	70	69	278	1,456
Jordan Gibb	68	73	73	64	278	1,456
Hugues Joannes	70	70	66	72	278	1,456
Jaakko Makitalo	66	68	75	69	278	1,456
Lukas Nemecz	71	67	73	67	278	1,456
Martin Wiegele	70	71	67	70	278	1,456

Swiss Challenge

Golf Sempachersee, Lucerne, Switzerland
Par 36-35–71; 7,147 yards

July 17-20
purse, €160,000

	SCORES				TOTAL	MONEY
Pierre Relecom	70	63	68	68	269	€25,600
Niccolo Quintarelli	67	66	69	68	270	17,600

	SCORES				TOTAL	MONEY
Rhys Davies	68	69	67	68	272	10,400
*Mathias Eggenberger	68	68	68	68	272	
George Murray	66	66	70	70	272	10,400
Scott Fallon	68	70	67	68	273	8,000
Charlie Ford	67	69	64	74	274	5,760
Jack Senior	67	71	71	65	274	5,760
Steven Brown	67	70	67	71	275	4,480
Matteo Delpodio	68	68	72	68	276	3,520
Jeppe Huldahl	69	68	69	70	276	3,520
Manuel Trappel	73	67	70	66	276	3,520
Gary Boyd	70	66	68	73	277	2,720
Sean Einhaus	72	68	72	65	277	2,720
Edouard Espana	71	68	68	70	277	2,720
Ricardo Gouveia	69	69	68	71	277	2,720
Bernd Ritthammer	66	66	75	70	277	2,720
Sebastian Garcia Rodriguez	68	71	72	67	278	1,936
Jacobo Pastor	68	70	70	70	278	1,936
Florian Praegant	69	72	66	71	278	1,936
Alessandro Tadini	68	72	68	70	278	1,936
Lionel Weber	72	69	69	68	278	1,936
Niall Kearney	70	71	69	69	279	1,504
Sam Little	74	67	68	70	279	1,504
Ross McGowan	70	71	69	69	279	1,504
Tom Murray	71	71	68	69	279	1,504
Kalle Samooja	71	64	71	73	279	1,504

Le Vaudreuil Golf Challenge

Golf PGA France du Vaudreuil, Le Vaudreuil, France — July 24-27
Par 35-36–71; 6,764 yards — purse, €200,000

	SCORES				TOTAL	MONEY
Andrew Johnston	66	69	69	64	268	€32,000
Byeong-Hun An	69	70	66	67	272	16,000
Connor Arendell	67	70	67	68	272	16,000
Jens Fahrbring	66	66	69	71	272	16,000
*Clement Sordet	67	74	68	63	272	
Edouard Espana	67	70	69	67	273	9,000
Jason Palmer	66	66	71	70	273	9,000
Filippo Bergamaschi	66	66	73	69	274	5,040
Matthew Fitzpatrick	69	69	67	69	274	5,040
Gareth Shaw	66	68	69	71	274	5,040
Callum Shinkwin	66	72	67	69	274	5,040
Lionel Weber	68	69	65	72	274	5,040
Niall Kearney	67	68	71	69	275	3,600
Ben Parker	69	70	67	69	275	3,600
Nicolo Ravano	69	68	66	72	275	3,600
Christophe Brazillier	71	69	68	68	276	2,900
Jordi Garcia Pinto	75	66	64	71	276	2,900
Niklas Lemke	74	68	68	66	276	2,900
Andrew Marshall	67	74	65	70	276	2,900
Ben Evans	69	69	69	70	277	2,165
Thomas Linard	71	69	71	66	277	2,165
Jack Senior	66	68	73	70	277	2,165
Manuel Trappel	70	72	67	68	277	2,165
Jason Barnes	69	68	70	71	278	1,880
Johan Edfors	67	68	67	76	278	1,880
Florian Fritsch	71	69	67	71	278	1,880

Azerbaijan Golf Challenge Open

National Azerbaijan Golf Club, Quba, Azerbaijan — July 31-August 3
Par 36-36–72; 7,011 yards — purse, €300,000

	SCORES				TOTAL	MONEY
Moritz Lampert	72	65	69	66	272	€48,000
Michael Lorenzo-Vera	68	68	69	69	274	33,000
Steven Brown	71	68	70	66	275	19,500
Andrew Johnston	66	72	69	68	275	19,500
Alexander Bjork	68	67	69	72	276	13,500
Andrew Marshall	72	65	69	70	276	13,500
Edouard Espana	65	71	74	67	277	7,950
Daniel Gaunt	70	68	69	70	277	7,950
Benjamin Hebert	72	62	67	76	277	7,950
Alessandro Tadini	70	71	69	67	277	7,950
Gary Lockerbie	68	68	70	72	278	5,850
Jaakko Makitalo	69	69	72	68	278	5,850
Sam Hutsby	71	68	74	66	279	5,100
Tim Sluiter	67	69	71	72	279	5,100
Damian Ulrich	71	71	69	68	279	5,100
Johan Edfors	67	70	73	70	280	4,050
Scott Henry	73	69	70	68	280	4,050
Maarten Lafeber	69	69	74	68	280	4,050
Kieran Pratt	70	71	68	71	280	4,050
Connor Arendell	73	70	69	69	281	2,899
Dave Coupland	70	73	70	68	281	2,899
Ben Evans	66	67	76	72	281	2,899
Paul McKechnie	72	71	71	67	281	2,899
Jocke Rask	69	68	74	70	281	2,899
Anthony Snobeck	69	69	71	72	281	2,899
Duncan Stewart	71	67	72	71	281	2,899
Jeff Winther	65	70	72	74	281	2,899

Norwegian Challenge

Miklagard Golf Club, Klofta, Norway — August 7-10
Par 36-36–72; 7,349 yards — purse, €175,000

	SCORES				TOTAL	MONEY
Benjamin Hebert	65	67	69	72	273	€28,000
Florian Fritsch	64	67	73	71	275	19,250
Cyril Bouniol	68	68	71	69	276	12,250
Wallace Booth	68	73	68	69	278	8,750
Andreas Harto	68	69	70	71	278	8,750
Mark Tullo	71	67	70	70	278	8,750
Scott Arnold	66	74	69	70	279	4,638
Daniel Im	68	70	70	71	279	4,638
Max Orrin	72	70	72	65	279	4,638
Pontus Widegren	70	70	67	72	279	4,638
Agustin Domingo	68	70	67	75	280	3,062
Peter Erofejeff	72	70	69	69	280	3,062
Nathan Holman	66	71	71	72	280	3,062
Tain Lee	70	67	70	73	280	3,062
Richard McEvoy	71	66	70	73	280	3,062
Brandon Stone	71	70	68	71	280	3,062
William Harrold	70	70	68	73	281	2,050
Niall Kearney	67	70	72	72	281	2,050
Paul Maddy	69	70	70	72	281	2,050
Jacobo Pastor	71	67	72	71	281	2,050

	SCORES				TOTAL	MONEY
Nicolo Ravano	73	66	71	71	281	2,050
Joel Sjoholm	74	68	66	73	281	2,050
Connor Arendell	70	68	71	73	282	1,540
Dave Coupland	69	71	71	71	282	1,540
Pelle Edberg	75	67	70	70	282	1,540
Pedro Figueiredo	67	72	73	70	282	1,540
Jocke Rask	71	70	71	70	282	1,540
Jack Senior	70	70	69	73	282	1,540
Anthony Snobeck	70	70	72	70	282	1,540
Matthew Southgate	67	71	73	71	282	1,540
Steven Tiley	68	73	70	71	282	1,540

Vacon Open

Kytaga Golf, Hyvinkaa, Finland — August 14-17
Par 35-36–71; 6,961 yards — purse, €170,000

	SCORES				TOTAL	MONEY
Mark Tullo	68	67	65	64	264	€27,200
Pelle Edberg	71	68	63	65	267	18,700
Charlie Ford	64	68	67	69	268	11,900
Byeong-Hun An	68	68	67	66	269	7,735
H.P. Bacher	67	64	70	68	269	7,735
Guillaume Cambis	65	66	70	68	269	7,735
Pontus Widegren	68	65	70	66	269	7,735
Niklas Lemke	68	66	71	67	272	4,193
Andrea Rota	67	68	68	69	272	4,193
Callum Shinkwin	69	64	70	69	272	4,193
Jeppe Huldahl	67	69	67	70	273	3,315
Maarten Lafeber	67	72	66	68	273	3,315
David Law	69	65	70	70	274	2,890
Charles-Edouard Russo	69	68	66	71	274	2,890
Zane Scotland	70	66	69	69	274	2,890
Max Glauert	70	67	69	69	275	2,380
Jack Hiluta	71	70	67	67	275	2,380
Jocke Rask	72	66	68	69	275	2,380
Eirik Tage Johansen	70	68	69	69	276	1,898
Ruaidhri McGee	69	67	70	70	276	1,898
*Erik Myllymaki	69	68	70	69	276	
Max Orrin	71	64	69	72	276	1,898
Baptiste Chapellan	72	69	67	69	277	1,581
William Harrold	72	69	67	69	277	1,581
Antonio Hortal	66	67	71	73	277	1,581
Michael Lorenzo-Vera	70	70	67	70	277	1,581
Stanislav Matus	70	70	68	69	277	1,581
Jacobo Pastor	70	70	69	68	277	1,581

Rolex Trophy

Golf Club de Geneve, Geneva, Switzerland — August 20-23
Par 36-36–72; 6,727 yards — purse, €232,510

	SCORES				TOTAL	MONEY
Byeong-Hun An	63	69	73	64	269	€26,000
Benjamin Hebert	67	68	65	72	272	19,000
Lasse Jensen	61	70	67	75	273	11,650
Callum Shinkwin	69	69	66	69	273	11,650

	SCORES				TOTAL	MONEY
Sam Hutsby	65	71	71	67	274	9,000
Steven Brown	68	70	69	68	275	7,100
Florian Fritsch	68	67	71	69	275	7,100
Michael Lorenzo-Vera	64	70	71	70	275	7,100
Cyril Bouniol	67	68	74	67	276	5,400
Jerome Lando Casanova	69	70	67	70	276	5,400
Matthew Fitzpatrick	69	68	71	69	277	4,650
Andrew Marshall	71	67	70	69	277	4,650
Dave Coupland	71	71	67	69	278	3,900
Edouard Espana	67	71	69	71	278	3,900
Antonio Hortal	68	73	70	67	278	3,900
Damian Ulrich	67	68	69	74	278	3,900
Andrew Johnston	66	69	72	72	279	3,400
Carlos Aguilar	74	69	70	67	280	3,200
Matteo Delpodio	70	75	67	69	281	2,850
Jordi Garcia Pinto	69	69	72	71	281	2,850
Thomas Linard	71	68	68	74	281	2,850
Mark Tullo	69	68	72	72	281	2,850
Lorenzo Gagli	70	69	70	73	282	2,580
Jake Roos	68	68	72	74	282	2,580
Jason Barnes	70	70	70	73	283	2,520

Northern Ireland Open Challenge

Galgorm Castle, Ballymena, County Antrim, Northern Ireland — August 28-31
Par 35-36–71; 6,930 yards — purse, €170,000

	SCORES				TOTAL	MONEY
Joakim Lagergren	62	71	66	72	271	€27,200
Adrien Bernadet	68	70	68	66	272	18,700
Jerome Lando Casanova	68	71	69	65	273	11,050
Bernd Ritthammer	68	70	69	66	273	11,050
Steven Brown	65	69	72	68	274	6,375
Kenneth Ferrie	68	68	71	67	274	6,375
Charlie Ford	70	70	66	68	274	6,375
Brandon Stone	69	67	69	69	274	6,375
Max Orrin	66	71	68	70	275	4,080
Paul Maddy	69	70	69	68	276	3,570
Tim Sluiter	67	70	68	71	276	3,570
Jonathan Caldwell	65	73	69	71	278	2,890
Mathieu Decottignies-Lafon	70	74	65	69	278	2,890
Dodge Kemmer	66	69	72	71	278	2,890
Niccolo Quintarelli	69	75	64	70	278	2,890
Gareth Shaw	67	72	69	70	278	2,890
Matt Haines	71	71	65	72	279	1,992
Scott Henry	72	69	68	70	279	1,992
Thomas Linard	67	68	72	72	279	1,992
Richard McEvoy	67	73	68	71	279	1,992
Chris Paisley	72	67	72	68	279	1,992
Anthony Snobeck	64	78	68	69	279	1,992
Ken Benz	67	76	70	67	280	1,547
Rhys Davies	68	70	68	74	280	1,547
Edouard Espana	71	70	69	70	280	1,547
Maarten Lafeber	72	72	67	69	280	1,547
Andrew McArthur	69	72	73	66	280	1,547
Joel Sjoholm	68	72	70	70	280	1,547

Open Blue Green Cotes d'Armor Bretagne

Golf Blue Green de Pleneuf Val Andre, Pleneuf, France — September 4-7
Par 35-35–70; 6,447 yards — purse, €200,000

	SCORES				TOTAL	MONEY
Benjamin Hebert	66	66	67	66	265	€32,000
Andrew McArthur	67	69	63	69	268	22,000
Paul Dwyer	67	65	70	68	270	14,000
Ben Evans	63	73	68	67	271	8,400
Oliver Farr	66	69	69	67	271	8,400
Hugues Joannes	64	70	69	68	271	8,400
Niccolo Quintarelli	66	69	67	69	271	8,400
Alessandro Tadini	68	69	62	72	271	8,400
Robert Coles	68	66	69	69	272	3,775
Dave Coupland	64	67	71	70	272	3,775
Johan Edfors	67	69	69	67	272	3,775
Jens Fahrbring	72	67	67	66	272	3,775
Michael Lorenzo-Vera	68	65	67	72	272	3,775
Richard McEvoy	70	66	70	66	272	3,775
Mark Tullo	66	70	72	64	272	3,775
Alvaro Velasco	69	69	66	68	272	3,775
Carlos Aguilar	68	69	67	69	273	2,283
Edouard Espana	68	68	68	69	273	2,283
Pedro Figueiredo	70	67	64	72	273	2,283
Lasse Jensen	74	64	66	69	273	2,283
Paul Maddy	68	67	73	65	273	2,283
Joel Sjoholm	67	69	69	68	273	2,283
Jeff Winther	67	67	70	69	273	2,283
Christophe Brazillier	69	71	65	69	274	1,720
Matt Ford	69	66	69	70	274	1,720
Antonio Hortal	67	69	73	65	274	1,720
Lloyd Kennedy	71	69	69	65	274	1,720
David Law	66	68	74	66	274	1,720
Lukas Nemecz	66	71	66	71	274	1,720
Raymond Russell	70	68	71	65	274	1,720
Brandon Stone	65	73	70	66	274	1,720
Daniel Vancsik	70	66	70	68	274	1,720

Kazakhstan Open

Zhailjau Golf Club, Almaty, Kazakhstan — September 18-21
Par 36-36–72; 7,197 yards — purse, €450,000

	SCORES				TOTAL	MONEY
Sam Hutsby	68	63	71	67	269	€72,000
Andrew Johnston	72	70	65	64	271	49,500
Byeong-Hun An	69	67	71	69	276	31,500
Jocke Rask	71	69	69	68	277	24,750
Alvaro Velasco	67	71	71	68	277	24,750
Ben Evans	71	70	68	69	278	16,200
Mark Tullo	68	75	66	69	278	16,200
Matthew Fitzpatrick	70	68	74	67	279	12,600
Cyril Bouniol	73	69	66	72	280	9,000
Matteo Delpodio	68	72	69	71	280	9,000
Edouard Espana	69	71	71	69	280	9,000
Scott Fallon	68	73	71	68	280	9,000
Lasse Jensen	73	69	68	70	280	9,000
Callum Shinkwin	68	72	70	70	280	9,000
Daniel Vancsik	68	74	70	69	281	7,200

	SCORES				TOTAL	MONEY
Steven Brown	70	71	69	72	282	5,662
Guillaume Cambis	72	69	69	72	282	5,662
Julien Guerrier	72	66	72	72	282	5,662
Joakim Lagergren	69	74	70	69	282	5,662
George Murray	67	71	69	75	282	5,662
Pontus Widegren	68	72	72	70	282	5,662
Jeppe Huldahl	72	71	69	71	283	4,095
Hugues Joannes	75	68	68	72	283	4,095
Thomas Linard	72	70	69	72	283	4,095
Pedro Oriol	68	71	72	72	283	4,095
Mark Pilkington	70	71	72	70	283	4,095
Jake Roos	73	70	69	71	283	4,095
Joel Stalter	71	67	74	71	283	4,095
Damian Ulrich	67	73	72	71	283	4,095

EMC Golf Challenge Open

Olgiata Golf Club, Rome, Italy — October 2-5
Par 35-36–71; 7,566 yards — purse, €180,000

	SCORES				TOTAL	MONEY
Ricardo Gouveia	68	71	69	67	275	€28,800
Florian Fritsch	70	67	69	69	275	19,800
(Gouveia defeated Fritsch on third playoff hole.)						
Edouard Espana	68	73	72	66	279	11,700
Benjamin Hebert	71	67	72	69	279	11,700
Alessandro Tadini	70	71	69	70	280	9,000
Julien Guerrier	68	71	69	73	281	7,200
Matteo Delpodio	70	71	71	70	282	5,400
Matthew Fitzpatrick	75	67	70	70	282	5,400
Pelle Edberg	71	71	71	71	284	4,140
Antonio Hortal	68	72	72	72	284	4,140
Robert Coles	72	73	70	70	285	3,150
Oliver Farr	70	74	68	73	285	3,150
Michael Jonzon	69	73	71	72	285	3,150
Phillip Price	72	70	72	71	285	3,150
Nicolo Ravano	70	76	68	71	285	3,150
Tim Sluiter	71	72	74	68	285	3,150
Lasse Jensen	71	70	73	72	286	2,520
Jason Palmer	68	77	72	70	287	2,160
Niccolo Quintarelli	71	72	74	70	287	2,160
Mark Tullo	70	73	71	73	287	2,160
Alessio Bruschi	74	67	74	73	288	1,768
Jordi Garcia Pinto	74	70	70	74	288	1,768
Maarten Lafeber	72	71	76	69	288	1,768
Thomas Linard	69	76	72	71	288	1,768
Dave Coupland	70	73	73	73	289	1,638
Chris Hanson	74	71	73	71	289	1,638

Shankai Classic

Chongqing Poly Golf Club, Chongqing, China — October 16-19
Par 35-37–72; 7,294 yards — purse, €350,000
(Event shortened to 54 holes—rain and fog.)

	SCORES			TOTAL	MONEY
Johan Edfors	69	66	66	201	€44,416
Michael Lorenzo-Vera	72	67	65	204	30,536
Mu Hu	70	68	67	205	16,656
Bernd Ritthammer	72	66	67	205	16,656
Tim Sluiter	71	67	67	205	16,656
Bjorn Akesson	70	68	68	206	8,606
Matteo Delpodio	71	66	69	206	8,606
Daniel Gaunt	72	67	67	206	8,606
Mark Tullo	65	70	71	206	8,606
Cyril Bouniol	70	68	69	207	5,645
Edouard Espana	69	71	67	207	5,645
Pontus Widegren	70	69	68	207	5,645
Antonio Hortal	69	65	74	208	4,858
Joakim Lagergren	70	72	66	208	4,858
Lasse Jensen	69	69	71	209	4,164
David Law	73	70	66	209	4,164
Tian Yuan	71	69	69	209	4,164
*Zi-Hao Chen	72	68	70	210	
Jeppe Huldahl	71	68	71	210	3,227
Paul Maddy	65	76	69	210	3,227
Steven Tiley	73	68	69	210	3,227
Alvaro Velasco	70	68	72	210	3,227
Rhys Davies	72	68	71	211	2,665
Ben Evans	72	70	69	211	2,665
Matthew Fitzpatrick	72	69	70	211	2,665

Foshan Open

Foshan Golf Club, Shishan, Foshan, China — October 23-26
Par 36-36–72; 7,148 yards — purse, US$350,000

	SCORES				TOTAL	MONEY
Jason Palmer	65	69	69	69	272	US$43,594
Ben Evans	67	72	68	66	273	29,971
Jason Barnes	66	70	69	70	275	16,348
Jens Fahrbring	70	68	69	68	275	16,348
Mark Tullo	69	70	68	68	275	16,348
Pelle Edberg	70	66	70	70	276	7,538
Matthew Fitzpatrick	69	70	72	65	276	7,538
Daniel Gaunt	67	69	70	70	276	7,538
Chris Hanson	68	68	69	71	276	7,538
Andrew McArthur	68	70	70	68	276	7,538
Chris Paisley	68	70	68	70	276	7,538
Ricardo Gouveia	65	72	70	70	277	5,041
Terry Pilkadaris	71	70	67	69	277	5,041
Antonio Hortal	71	72	66	69	278	4,087
Hugues Joannes	70	68	68	72	278	4,087
David Law	70	73	69	66	278	4,087
Paul Maddy	71	68	69	70	278	4,087
Callum Shinkwin	71	70	67	70	278	4,087
Pedro Oriol	68	69	74	68	279	2,883
Max Orrin	68	72	72	67	279	2,883
Bernd Ritthammer	66	69	69	75	279	2,883

	SCORES				TOTAL	MONEY
Tim Sluiter	70	71	72	66	279	2,883
Steven Tiley	72	69	68	70	279	2,883
Byeong-Hun An	73	68	71	68	280	2,534
Andrew Marshall	73	67	69	71	280	2,534

National Bank of Oman Golf Classic

Almouj Golf, The Wave, Muscat, Oman — October 30-November 2
Par 36-36–72; 7,310 yards — purse, US$330,000

	SCORES				TOTAL	MONEY
Max Orrin	71	71	68	71	281	€41,591
Jason Palmer	69	72	74	68	283	28,594
Jason Barnes	65	75	77	68	285	16,896
Mark Tullo	73	73	66	73	285	16,896
Byeong-Hun An	72	65	73	76	286	11,698
Michael Jonzon	74	69	75	68	286	11,698
George Murray	70	73	74	70	287	7,798
Niccolo Quintarelli	72	71	73	71	287	7,798
Robert Coles	75	68	75	70	288	5,719
Nick Dougherty	74	70	76	68	288	5,719
Ricardo Gouveia	69	76	75	68	288	5,719
Oliver Farr	73	71	73	72	289	4,679
Chris Hanson	70	73	74	72	289	4,679
Bernd Ritthammer	70	71	75	73	289	4,679
Dave Coupland	73	72	72	73	290	3,203
Edouard Espana	73	73	73	71	290	3,203
Jens Fahrbring	73	74	71	72	290	3,203
Pedro Figueiredo	70	75	78	67	290	3,203
Daniel Gaunt	72	75	73	70	290	3,203
Andrew McArthur	69	71	73	77	290	3,203
Chris Paisley	69	77	73	71	290	3,203
Tim Sluiter	71	70	79	70	290	3,203
Pontus Widegren	70	69	77	74	290	3,203
Matteo Delpodio	72	74	73	72	291	2,210
Pelle Edberg	69	70	77	75	291	2,210
Matthew Fitzpatrick	73	73	74	71	291	2,210
William Harrold	73	70	76	72	291	2,210
Sam Hutsby	72	73	75	71	291	2,210
Paul Maddy	70	71	76	74	291	2,210
Jake Roos	73	72	77	69	291	2,210
Joel Stalter	74	73	72	72	291	2,210
Alessandro Tadini	73	74	73	71	291	2,210
Jeff Winther	75	73	73	70	291	2,210

Dubai Festival City Challenge Tour Grand Final

Al Badia Golf Club, Dubai, United Arab Emirates — November 5-8
Par 36-36–72; 7,377 yards — purse, €350,000

	SCORES				TOTAL	MONEY
Benjamin Hebert	70	69	68	69	276	€60,085
Jerome Lando Casanova	78	66	68	69	281	39,900
Oliver Farr	69	71	69	73	282	22,517
Byeong-Hun An	72	71	72	68	283	18,083
Hugues Joannes	74	71	69	70	284	14,642
Alessandro Tadini	71	75	67	71	284	14,642

	SCORES				TOTAL	MONEY
Cyril Bouniol	78	68	69	70	285	12,425
Bernd Ritthammer	72	71	69	73	285	12,425
Robert Coles	73	69	70	74	286	9,742
Edouard Espana	70	68	76	72	286	9,742
Jordi Garcia Pinto	72	69	70	75	286	9,742
Andrew Johnston	73	72	69	72	286	9,742
Ben Evans	72	73	70	72	287	7,700
Jens Fahrbring	71	71	72	74	288	5,979
Joakim Lagergren	78	69	70	71	288	5,979
Mark Tullo	68	70	73	77	288	5,979
Pontus Widegren	74	73	68	73	288	5,979
Jason Barnes	71	73	72	73	289	3,996
Daniel Gaunt	76	73	70	70	289	3,996
Jeppe Huldahl	76	74	73	66	289	3,996
Sam Hutsby	76	74	69	70	289	3,996
Lasse Jensen	69	75	68	77	289	3,996
Michael Lorenzo-Vera	74	71	73	71	289	3,996
Andrew Marshall	71	70	72	76	289	3,996
Pedro Oriol	75	71	72	71	289	3,996

Asian Tour

King's Cup

Black Mountain Golf Club, Hua Hin, Thailand — January 16-19
Par 36-36–72; 7,550 yards — purse, US$1,000,000

	SCORES				TOTAL	MONEY
Prayad Marksaeng	68	71	71	66	276	US$180,000
Rikard Karlberg	65	71	74	67	277	110,000
Anirban Lahiri	69	71	71	68	279	51,333.33
Chapchai Nirat	68	73	68	70	279	51,333.33
Prom Meesawat	65	71	72	71	279	51,333.33
Mardan Mamat	71	70	71	68	280	33,300
Scott Hend	72	71	69	69	281	26,500
Angelo Que	66	75	67	73	281	26,500
Daisuke Kataoka	73	69	72	69	283	21,400
Andrew Dodt	71	73	71	69	284	18,275
Joong-Kyung Mo	69	68	70	77	284	18,275
Alex Cejka	70	69	74	72	285	14,590
Carlos Pigem	71	69	73	72	285	14,590
Poosit Supupramai	73	68	72	72	285	14,590
Antonio Lascuna	71	70	72	72	285	14,590
Rahil Gangjee	71	71	71	72	285	14,590
Namchok Tantipokhakul	69	72	77	68	286	11,850
Johan Edfors	70	69	77	70	286	11,850
Thaworn Wiratchant	74	71	71	70	286	11,850
S.S.P. Chowrasia	70	73	72	71	286	11,850
Jyoti Randhawa	70	75	73	69	287	10,300
Pariya Junhasavasdikul	72	70	74	71	287	10,300
Chih-Bing Lam	70	74	72	71	287	10,300
Gunn Charoenkul	72	73	70	72	287	10,300
Wen-Tang Lin	66	72	76	73	287	10,300

SAIL-SBI Open

Delhi Golf Club, New Delhi, India — February 26-March 1
Par 36-36–72; 6,963 yards — purse, US$300,000

	SCORES				TOTAL	MONEY
Rashid Khan	61	69	69	71	270	US$54,000
Siddikur Rahman	67	67	67	69	270	33,000
(Khan defeated Rahman on first playoff hole.)						
Rikard Karlberg	71	70	67	68	276	18,900
Carlos Pigem	69	71	69	68	277	12,430
S.S.P. Chowrasia	68	69	72	68	277	12,430
Martin Rominger	72	63	70	72	277	12,430
Steve Lewton	68	70	68	72	278	8,550
Abhijit Chadha	68	73	69	69	279	6,183.75
Jyoti Randhawa	71	69	70	69	279	6,183.75
Anirban Lahiri	70	66	69	74	279	6,183.75
Mithun Perera	66	68	73	72	279	6,183.75
Rahil Gangjee	71	70	68	71	280	4,280
Chiragh Kumar	69	73	70	68	280	4,280
Arnond Vongvanij	74	69	67	70	280	4,280
Sutijet Kooratanapisan	71	72	69	68	280	4,280

	SCORES				TOTAL	MONEY
Akinori Tani	66	71	71	72	280	4,280
Scott Barr	67	70	72	71	280	4,280
Thanyakon Khrongpha	69	73	69	70	281	3,475
David Lipsky	70	70	71	70	281	3,475
George Gandranata	68	70	71	72	281	3,475
Simon Griffiths	72	68	69	73	282	3,225
Sanjay Kumar	68	70	72	72	282	3,225
Chawalit Plaphol	70	71	70	72	283	2,775
Thaworn Wiratchant	69	73	71	70	283	2,775
Anura Rohana	73	66	69	75	283	2,775
Zamal Hossain	71	72	68	72	283	2,775
Javi Colomo	71	67	71	74	283	2,775
Shamim Khan	68	70	71	74	283	2,775
Pawan Kumar	72	71	70	70	283	2,775
Berry Henson	73	71	69	70	283	2,775

Solaire Open

The Country Club, Laguna, Philippines
Par 35-36–71; 7,256 yards

March 13-16
purse, US$300,000

	SCORES				TOTAL	MONEY
Richard T. Lee	68	70	70	69	277	US$54,000
Chawalit Plaphol	68	72	68	70	278	33,000
Carlos Pigem	69	70	71	69	279	18,900
Masahiro Kawamura	71	69	75	65	280	12,430
Steve Lewton	74	69	70	67	280	12,430
Paul Peterson	72	68	71	69	280	12,430
Andrew Dodt	70	71	70	70	281	7,440
Clyde Mondilla	71	70	67	73	281	7,440
Miguel Tabuena	67	68	70	76	281	7,440
Sam Brazel	66	75	70	71	282	5,482.50
David Lipsky	71	68	71	72	282	5,482.50
Bryce Easton	69	68	74	72	283	4,585
Akinori Tani	69	72	67	75	283	4,585
Jeung-Hun Wang	71	67	68	77	283	4,585
Poom Saksansin	71	69	74	70	284	3,975
Zanie Boy Gialon	68	70	74	72	284	3,975
Simon Griffiths	70	69	71	74	284	3,975
Siddikur Rahman	70	70	71	74	285	3,475
Nick Cullen	68	73	70	74	285	3,475
Sam Cyr	72	69	69	75	285	3,475
Elmer Salvador	72	69	75	70	286	3,135
Kalem Richardson	76	66	72	72	286	3,135
Terry Pilkadaris	70	70	72	74	286	3,135
Angelo Que	70	65	69	82	286	3,135
Dimitrios Papadatos	70	69	77	71	287	2,865
Matthew Griffin	68	69	73	77	287	2,865

EurAsia Cup

Glenmarie Golf & Country Club, Kuala Lumpur, Malaysia — March 27-29
Par 36-36–72; 7,004 yards — purse, US$4,000,000

FIRST DAY
Fourball

Miguel Angel Jimenez and Pablo Larrazabal (Europe) defeated Thongchai Jaidee and Kiradech Aphibarnrat, 2 and 1.
Thomas Bjorn and Thorbjorn Olesen (Europe) defeated Koumei Oda and Hideto Tanihara, 2 up.
Victor Dubuisson and Joost Luiten (Europe) defeated Prayad Marksaeng and Siddikur Rahman, 3 and 2.
Gonzalo Fernandez-Castano and Stephen Gallacher (Europe) defeated Gaganjeet Bhullar and Anirban Lahiri, 4 and 3.
Graeme McDowell and Jamie Donaldson (Europe) defeated Hyung-Sung Kim and Nicholas Fung, 3 and 1.

POINTS: Europe 5, Asia 0

SECOND DAY
Foursomes

Jaidee and Aphibarnrat (Asia) halved with Jimenez and Larrazabal.
Marksaeng and Kim (Asia) defeated Bjorn and Olesen, 4 and 3.
Oda and Tanihara (Asia) halved with Fernandez-Castano and Gallacher.
Lahiri and Siddikur (Asia) defeated Luiten and Dubuisson, 1 up.
McDowell and Donaldson (Europe) defeated Bhullar and Fung, 2 and 1.

POINTS: Europe 7, Asia 3

THIRD DAY
Singles

Jimenez (Europe) defeated Fung, 1up.
Jaidee (Asia) defeated McDowell, 3 and 2.
Aphibarnrat (Asia) defeated Bjorn, 2 and 1.
Marksaeng (Asia) halved with Donaldson.
Kim (Asia) defeated Larrazabal, 4 and 2.
Lahiri (Asia) defeated Dubuisson, 2 and 1.
Bhullar (Asia) defeated Olesen, 4 and 3.
Luiten (Europe) defeated Oda, 1 up.
Tanihara (Asia) halved with Fernandez-Castano.
Siddikur (Asia) defeated Gallacher, 4 and 3.

FINAL POINTS: Europe 10, Asia 10

(Each player received US$200,000.)

Maybank Malaysian Open

Kuala Lumpur Golf & Country Club, Kuala Lumpur, Malaysia — April 17-20
Par 36-36–72; 6,967 yards — purse, US$2,750,000

	SCORES				TOTAL	MONEY
Lee Westwood	65	66	71	68	270	US$458,330
Bernd Wiesberger	69	71	70	67	277	205,066.67
Louis Oosthuizen	72	68	69	68	277	205,066.67
Nicolas Colsaerts	66	69	72	70	277	205,066.67
Danny Willett	70	66	72	70	278	98,450

	SCORES				TOTAL	MONEY
Rikard Karlberg	72	69	67	70	278	98,450
Julien Quesne	68	69	69	72	278	98,450
Pablo Larrazabal	74	68	70	67	279	65,175
Thomas Pieters	75	67	69	68	279	65,175
Anirban Lahiri	72	72	66	70	280	50,966.67
Eduardo De La Riva	69	68	71	72	280	50,966.67
Garth Mulroy	71	68	69	72	280	50,966.67
Alvaro Quiros	73	69	71	68	281	40,535
Jbe' Kruger	68	71	72	70	281	40,535
Jason Knutzon	75	67	69	70	281	40,535
Masahiro Kawamura	68	70	70	73	281	40,535
Andy Sullivan	70	67	66	78	281	40,535
Michael Hoey	67	73	73	69	282	32,633.33
Richard T. Lee	69	76	67	70	282	32,633.33
Scott Hend	70	70	72	70	282	32,633.33
Gregory Bourdy	73	70	69	70	282	32,633.33
Wade Ormsby	70	71	69	72	282	32,633.33
Ricardo Santos	67	71	70	74	282	32,633.33
Prom Meesawat	70	71	74	68	283	27,775
Antonio Lascuna	70	65	77	71	283	27,775
Thongchai Jaidee	72	70	70	71	283	27,775
Richard Bland	73	69	69	72	283	27,775
Tom Lewis	70	71	68	74	283	27,775
Edoardo Molinari	69	73	71	71	284	24,887.50
Scott Jamieson	68	71	70	75	284	24,887.50
Shiv Kapur	76	69	69	71	285	23,237.50
Matteo Manassero	71	72	67	75	285	23,237.50
Justin Walters	71	72	71	72	286	19,834.38
Pariya Junhasavasdikul	73	71	70	72	286	19,834.38
Maximilian Kieffer	70	74	69	73	286	19,834.38
Arnond Vongvanij	70	71	73	72	286	19,834.38
S.S.P. Chowrasia	71	70	71	74	286	19,834.38
Bryce Easton	70	74	72	70	286	19,834.38
Andrew Dodt	76	67	74	69	286	19,834.38
Francesco Molinari	71	74	73	68	286	19,834.38
Carlos Pigem	71	71	73	72	287	16,500
Hennie Otto	79	66	71	71	287	16,500
Adilson Da Silva	72	72	72	71	287	16,500
Prayad Marksaeng	69	72	70	76	287	16,500
Steve Lewton	71	69	74	74	288	14,850
Rahil Gangjee	74	68	70	76	288	14,850
Nicholas Fung	72	71	73	73	289	12,375
J.B. Hansen	72	72	73	72	289	12,375
Simon Dyson	73	71	73	72	289	12,375
David Drysdale	71	71	75	72	289	12,375
Marcel Siem	72	71	74	72	289	12,375
Kheng-Hwai Khor	72	72	74	71	289	12,375
Marc Warren	69	75	75	70	289	12,375
*Gavin Green	74	70	75	70	289	
Chiragh Kumar	74	70	75	71	290	9,900
Marco Crespi	71	73	75	71	290	9,900
Soren Kjeldsen	75	68	71	77	291	8,616.67
Romain Wattel	71	72	75	73	291	8,616.67
Siddikur Rahman	73	70	77	71	291	8,616.67
Simon Thornton	74	68	72	78	292	7,425
Peter Whiteford	73	72	72	75	292	7,425
Craig Lee	69	75	73	75	292	7,425
Robert-Jan Derksen	72	73	75	72	292	7,425
Magnus A. Carlsson	74	69	80	69	292	7,425
Namchok Tantipokhakul	76	69	71	77	293	6,325
Jazz Janewattananond	73	72	73	75	293	6,325
Chawalit Plaphol	74	71	76	72	293	6,325
Anthony Kang	71	74	75	74	294	5,637.50

	SCORES				TOTAL	MONEY
Rashid Khan	72	72	76	74	294	5,637.50
Thaworn Wiratchant	69	75	75	76	295	5,225
Soren Hansen	69	76	76	76	297	5,020
Chinnarat Phadungsil	74	71	77	76	298	4,125.61
Kiradech Aphibarnrat	71	71			WD	4,121.44

CIMB Niaga Indonesian Masters

Royale Jakarta Golf Club, Jakarta, Indonesia — April 24-27
Par 36-36–72; 7,322 yards — purse, US$750,000

	SCORES				TOTAL	MONEY
Anirban Lahiri	70	69	64	68	271	US$135,000
Seuk-Hyun Baek	71	68	68	65	272	64,875
Cameron Smith	68	67	67	70	272	64,875
Kiradech Aphibarnrat	71	69	65	68	273	37,500
Thongchai Jaidee	71	72	67	64	274	23,868.75
Jazz Janewattananond	68	70	69	67	274	23,868.75
Wen-Tang Lin	70	64	72	68	274	23,868.75
S.S.P. Chowrasia	71	66	69	68	274	23,868.75
Rashid Khan	70	70	64	71	275	16,050
Chapchai Nirat	68	68	72	68	276	13,200.33
Bernd Wiesberger	68	71	69	68	276	13,200.33
Gunn Charoenkul	70	69	67	70	276	13,200.33
Dimitrios Papadatos	73	72	66	66	277	10,863
Chan Kim	69	69	70	69	277	10,863
Jyoti Randhawa	72	68	67	70	277	10,863
Marcus Both	69	70	68	72	279	9,938
Jake Higginbottom	68	72	73	67	280	8,888
Namchok Tantipokhakul	71	72	69	68	280	8,888
Danny Chia	69	73	68	70	280	8,888
Chih-Bing Lam	72	68	69	71	280	8,888
Nicholas Fung	67	69	74	71	281	8,175
Tae-Hee Lee	69	73	72	68	282	7,612.50
Thaworn Wiratchant	71	70	72	69	282	7,612.50
Rahil Gangjee	70	70	72	70	282	7,612.50
Antonio Lascuna	73	72	66	71	282	7,612.50

The Championship

Laguna National Golf & Country Club, Singapore — May 1-4
Par 36-36–72; 7,207 yards — purse, US$1,500,000

	SCORES				TOTAL	MONEY
Felipe Aguilar	65	67	72	62	266	US$250,000
David Lipsky	64	68	70	65	267	130,280
Anders Hansen	67	66	67	67	267	130,280
Rahil Gangjee	66	67	71	65	269	75,000
Chris Wood	68	67	68	67	270	63,600
Anirban Lahiri	67	70	68	66	271	48,750
Gregory Bourdy	66	70	67	68	271	48,750
David Drysdale	68	70	70	65	273	33,700
Raphael Jacquelin	69	70	68	66	273	33,700
Tommy Fleetwood	68	67	69	69	273	33,700
Rikard Karlberg	70	68	70	66	274	23,950
S.S.P. Chowrasia	68	68	71	67	274	23,950
Antonio Lascuna	68	69	69	68	274	23,950

	SCORES				TOTAL	MONEY
Seuk-Hyun Baek	66	67	72	69	274	23,950
Terry Pilkadaris	68	70	66	70	274	23,950
Panuphol Pittayarat	63	68	69	74	274	23,950
Prom Meesawat	66	70	72	67	275	19,400
Nacho Elvira	68	69	71	67	275	19,400
Kristopher Broberg	65	69	73	68	275	19,400
Simon Thornton	72	67	69	68	276	17,212.50
Sung-Hoon Kang	68	68	72	68	276	17,212.50
Peter Lawrie	68	72	67	69	276	17,212.50
Arnond Vongvanij	65	69	71	71	276	17,212.50
Ki-Sang Lee	68	69	71	69	277	14,250
Francois Calmels	68	69	72	68	277	14,250
Chinnarat Phadungsil	67	71	69	70	277	14,250
Craig Lee	72	68	66	71	277	14,250
Alexander Levy	70	66	70	71	277	14,250
Scott Hend	67	65	73	72	277	14,250
Johan Edfors	70	67	68	72	277	14,250
Scott Barr	66	72	67	72	277	14,250
Robert-Jan Derksen	68	67	67	75	277	14,250
Marc Warren	69	67	72	70	278	11,600
Roope Kakko	70	67	71	70	278	11,600
Pariya Junhasavasdikul	69	69	71	69	278	11,600
Ross Fisher	73	67	68	71	279	10,800
Wade Ormsby	68	71	70	70	279	10,800
Gary Stal	70	70	69	71	280	9,150
Bernd Wiesberger	71	68	70	71	280	9,150
Sihwan Kim	69	67	73	71	280	9,150
Boonchu Ruangkit	67	69	73	71	280	9,150
Chan Kim	67	68	72	73	280	9,150
Lucas Bjerregaard	68	70	72	70	280	9,150
Jason Knutzon	69	71	71	69	280	9,150
Nicholas Fung	68	71	72	69	280	9,150
Victor Riu	67	71	75	67	280	9,150
Mithun Perera	65	71	73	72	281	7,200
Rafa Cabrera-Bello	66	71	71	73	281	7,200
Chih-Bing Lam	71	67	72	71	281	7,200
Paul Waring	70	69	73	69	281	7,200
Brett Rumford	70	67	70	75	282	6,150
Bio Kim	68	72	71	71	282	6,150
Jorge Campillo	73	67	73	69	282	6,150
Scott Jamieson	64	71	74	74	283	4,778.57
Gareth Maybin	71	67	70	75	283	4,778.57
Adrian Otaegui	69	70	70	74	283	4,778.57
In-Woo Lee	68	69	72	74	283	4,778.57
Andy Sullivan	69	69	72	73	283	4,778.57
Kyong-Jun Moon	66	72	73	72	283	4,778.57
Nick Dougherty	69	70	73	71	283	4,778.57
Soren Kjeldsen	68	71	71	74	284	3,900
Chapchai Nirat	71	69	72	72	284	3,900
Andrew Dodt	70	70	75	69	284	3,900
Gi-Whan Kim	68	71	72	74	285	3,225
Chiragh Kumar	69	70	72	74	285	3,225
Jazz Janewattananond	70	69	73	73	285	3,225
Jeev Milkha Singh	67	72	74	72	285	3,225
Adilson Da Silva	69	71	74	71	285	3,225
Masahiro Kawamura	70	70	75	70	285	3,225
Quincy Quek	64	74	72	77	287	2,740
Fabrizio Zanotti	70	68	74	76	288	2,250.30

ICTSI Philippine Open

Wack Wack Golf & Country Club, Manila, Philippines — May 15-18
Par 36-36–72; 7,222 yards — purse, US$300,000

	SCORES				TOTAL	MONEY
Marcus Both	70	66	76	70	282	US$54,000
Siddikur Rahman	66	73	76	69	284	17,838
Nathan Holman	71	71	72	70	284	17,838
Antonio Lascuna	74	71	69	70	284	17,838
Arnond Vongvanij	74	72	68	70	284	17,838
Jay Bayron	71	72	69	72	284	17,838
Tung-Shu Hsieh	77	68	70	70	285	8,550
Jazz Janewattananond	72	72	72	70	286	6,885
Jeung-Hun Wang	72	68	72	74	286	6,885
S.S.P. Chowrasia	71	71	76	69	287	4,812.50
Prayad Marksaeng	70	75	71	71	287	4,812.50
Daisuke Kataoka	71	75	70	71	287	4,812.50
Thaworn Wiratchant	74	74	67	72	287	4,812.50
Chapchai Nirat	79	67	69	72	287	4,812.50
Chan Kim	66	72	73	76	287	4,812.50
Shih-Chang Chan	75	71	73	69	288	3,795
Settee Prakongvech	70	74	74	70	288	3,795
Gunn Charoenkul	73	70	74	71	288	3,795
Lionel Weber	72	70	75	72	289	3,360
Mithun Perera	71	72	73	73	289	3,360
Anura Rohana	75	70	71	73	289	3,360
Unho Park	72	72	75	71	290	3,000
Anirban Lahiri	75	69	76	70	290	3,000
Abhijit Chadha	75	72	71	72	290	3,000
Miguel Tabuena	75	70	72	73	290	3,000
Jarin Todd	73	71	71	75	290	3,000

Queen's Cup

Santiburi Samui Country Club, Samui, Thailand — June 5-8
Par 36-35–71; 6,832 yards — purse, US$300,000

	SCORES				TOTAL	MONEY
Thaworn Wiratchant	71	68	67	66	272	US$$54,000
Poom Saksansin	66	67	68	72	273	33,000
Donlaphatchai Niyomchon	68	68	70	68	274	16,950
Siddikur Rahman	68	70	64	72	274	16,950
Seuk-Hyun Baek	69	66	71	70	276	12,300
Choo Tze Huang	67	72	71	68	278	8,630
Richard T. Lee	69	71	69	69	278	8,630
Jeung-Hun Wang	72	69	68	69	278	8,630
Pariya Junhasavasdikul	77	68	68	66	279	5,361
Prom Meesawat	71	71	69	68	279	5,361
Rahil Gangjee	73	70	68	68	279	5,361
Antonio Lascuna	69	71	70	69	279	5,361
Chapchai Nirat	72	67	69	71	279	5,361
Jazz Janewattananond	71	74	71	64	280	4,155
Jyoti Randhawa	71	73	68	68	280	4,155
Rattanon Wannasrichan	69	71	70	70	280	4,155
Miguel Tabuena	74	68	71	68	281	3,795
Lionel Weber	72	71	71	68	282	3,475
Tirawat Kaewsiribandit	71	70	71	70	282	3,475
Thanyakon Khrongpha	75	67	70	70	282	3,475
Boonchu Ruangkit	69	76	71	67	283	3,135

	SCORES				TOTAL	MONEY
Joong-Kyung Mo	70	72	73	68	283	3,135
Wolmer Murillo	73	70	69	71	283	3,135
Chawalit Plaphol	73	71	68	71	283	3,135
Michael Tran	72	71	74	67	284	2,865
*Tawan Phongphun	73	72	69	70	284	
Chinnarat Phadungsil	68	70	75	71	284	2,865

Omega European Masters

See European Tours chapter.

Yeangder Tournament Players Championship

Linkou International Golf & Country Club, Chinese Taipei — September 11-14
Par 36-36–72; 7,125 yards — purse, US$500,000

	SCORES				TOTAL	MONEY
Prom Meesawat	67	73	68	69	277	US$90,000
Miguel Tabuena	73	68	65	71	277	55,000
(Meesawat defeated Tabuena on second playoff hole.)						
Antonio Lascuna	68	69	72	69	278	31,500
Paul Peterson	71	71	69	69	280	20,716.67
Daniel Chopra	71	68	69	72	280	20,716.67
Anirban Lahiri	73	66	68	73	280	20,716.67
Cameron Smith	70	67	73	73	283	14,250
Angelo Que	68	71	76	69	284	10,306.25
Rashid Khan	71	70	72	71	284	10,306.25
Lu-Sen Lien	67	71	74	72	284	10,306.25
Wei-Tze Yeh	72	71	65	76	284	10,306.25
Ryan Yip	71	69	70	75	285	7,850
Thaworn Wiratchant	70	69	68	78	285	7,850
Jay Bayron	73	72	69	72	286	6,925
Rikard Karlberg	72	72	68	74	286	6,925
Thanyakon Khrongpha	72	71	67	76	286	6,925
Lionel Weber	76	67	74	70	287	5,657.14
Lian-Wei Zhang	72	69	74	72	287	5,657.14
Kieran Pratt	72	71	72	72	287	5,657.14
Jake Higginbottom	70	72	72	73	287	5,657.14
Berry Henson	72	73	69	73	287	5,657.14
Hao-Sheng Hsu	68	73	72	74	287	5,657.14
Danny Chia	68	74	71	74	287	5,657.14
Simon Griffiths	73	73	70	72	288	4,550
Gunn Charoenkul	69	71	75	73	288	4,550
Sutijet Kooratanapisan	71	71	73	73	288	4,550
Chih-Bing Lam	70	72	73	73	288	4,550
Andrew Dodt	73	73	69	73	288	4,550
Carlos Pigem	75	70	69	74	288	4,550
Jack Munro	70	74	69	75	288	4,550

Worldwide Holdings Selangor Masters

Seri Selangor Golf Club, Petaling Jaya, Selangor, Malaysia — September 18-21
Par 36-35–71 — purse, US$410,000

	SCORES				TOTAL	MONEY
Chapchai Nirat	68	69	69	68	274	US$234,000
Antonio Lascuna	70	70	71	63	274	143,000
(Nirat defeated Lascuna on first playoff hole.)						
Anirban Lahiri	64	68	76	68	276	81,900
Scott Barr	70	69	72	67	278	46,098
Paul Peterson	69	71	71	67	278	46,098
S.S.P. Chowrasia	66	70	73	69	278	46,098
David Lipsky	72	66	69	71	278	46,098
Cameron Smith	68	66	71	73	278	46,098
Carlos Pigem	71	68	72	68	279	24,115
Jazz Janewattananond	70	70	70	69	279	24,115
Jake Higginbottom	72	65	70	72	279	24,115
Sattaya Supupramai	68	70	68	73	279	24,115
Kalem Richardson	72	73	68	68	281	18,828.33
Simon Griffiths	70	68	72	71	281	18,828.33
Chien-Yao Hung	67	73	67	74	281	18,828.33
Jbe' Kruger	71	70	72	69	282	16,445
Ryan Yip	71	70	69	72	282	16,445
Kieran Pratt	69	72	68	73	282	16,445
Chris Rodgers	72	71	69	71	283	14,755
Gi-Whan Kim	73	66	71	73	283	14,755
Thaworn Wiratchant	70	74	70	70	284	13,780
Mardan Mamat	71	68	74	71	284	13,780
Rory Hie	75	68	70	71	284	13,780
Rashid Khan	73	70	72	70	285	11,830
Chan Kim	69	74	71	71	285	11,830
Unho Park	71	72	73	69	285	11,830
Jyoti Randhawa	71	69	73	72	285	11,830
Rattanon Wannasrichan	69	73	71	72	285	11,830
Thitiphun Chuayprakong	74	68	70	73	285	11,830
Lionel Weber	70	70	70	75	285	11,830

Asia-Pacific Diamond Cup

See Japan Tour section.

Mercuries Taiwan Masters

Taiwan Golf & Country Club, Chinese Taipei — October 2-5
Par 36-36–72; 6,923 yards — purse, US$650,000

	SCORES				TOTAL	MONEY
Steve Lewton	70	72	70	71	283	US$130,000
Adilson Da Silva	75	66	72	72	285	61,750
Antonio Lascuna	75	69	69	72	285	61,750
Thaworn Wiratchant	72	73	70	71	286	29,250
Unho Park	72	72	70	72	286	29,250
Chapchai Nirat	75	71	72	70	288	19,500
Javi Colomo	72	74	69	73	288	19,500
Cameron Smith	72	72	70	74	288	19,500
Angelo Que	75	73	71	70	289	12,350
Rahil Gangjee	74	71	70	74	289	12,350
Andrew Dodt	74	70	73	73	290	11,050

	SCORES				TOTAL	MONEY
Wolmer Murillo	76	71	74	70	291	9,425
Sam Brazel	72	74	74	71	291	9,425
Marcus Both	71	73	73	74	291	9,425
Wen-The Lu	74	72	70	75	291	9,425
Simon Griffiths	74	75	72	71	292	7,800
Wei-Chih Lu	73	74	73	72	292	7,800
Sam Cyr	71	74	71	76	292	7,800
Elmer Salvador	74	71	75	73	293	6,808.75
Mong-Nan Hsu	77	70	73	73	293	6,808.75
Prom Meesawat	71	73	74	75	293	6,808.75
Jeung-Hun Wang	73	72	73	75	293	6,808.75
Chien-Yao Hung	75	72	75	72	294	6,110
Wei-Tze Yeh	72	75	75	72	294	6,110
Jazz Janewattananond	73	73	74	74	294	6,110
Lian-Wei Zhang	74	73	73	74	294	6,110
S.S.P. Chowrasia	72	77	70	75	294	6,110

Hong Kong Open

Hong Kong Golf Club, Fanling, Hong Kong — October 16-19
Par 34-36–70; 6,699 yards — purse, US$1,300,000

	SCORES				TOTAL	MONEY
Scott Hend	67	66	67	67	267	US$216,660
Angelo Que	65	69	67	66	267	144,440
(Hend defeated Que on first playoff hole.)						
Kevin Phelan	69	67	67	66	269	81,380
Mark Foster	67	68	66	69	270	65,000
S.S.P. Chowrasia	69	65	70	67	271	43,030
Lucas Bjerregaard	69	68	67	67	271	43,030
Ernie Els	66	65	71	69	271	43,030
Marcus Fraser	67	67	65	72	271	43,030
Eduardo De La Riva	68	67	70	67	272	26,346.67
Raphael Jacquelin	66	67	69	70	272	26,346.67
Cameron Smith	68	65	69	70	272	26,346.67
Wei-Chih Lu	66	68	71	68	273	21,060
Seve Benson	68	66	71	68	273	21,060
Javi Colomo	68	70	64	71	273	21,060
Rahil Gangjee	68	68	72	66	274	17,576
Lee Slattery	68	66	73	67	274	17,576
Richard Bland	70	65	70	69	274	17,576
Adam Groom	67	68	68	71	274	17,576
Jyoti Randhawa	64	70	68	72	274	17,576
Rikard Karlberg	67	70	72	66	275	13,531.82
Peter Whiteford	67	70	71	67	275	13,531.82
Daniel Im	69	68	70	68	275	13,531.82
Charlie Wi	70	68	69	68	275	13,531.82
Shiv Kapur	68	68	70	69	275	13,531.82
Mikko Korhonen	69	67	70	69	275	13,531.82
Daan Huizing	66	68	71	70	275	13,531.82
Prom Meesawat	71	66	68	70	275	13,531.82
Pariya Junhasavasdikul	69	68	68	70	275	13,531.82
Joong-Kyung Mo	68	71	66	70	275	13,531.82
Jbe' Kruger	66	69	66	74	275	13,531.82
Andrea Pavan	70	66	71	69	276	10,790
Matthew Nixon	70	67	69	70	276	10,790
Marcus Both	67	67	71	71	276	10,790
Adilson Da Silva	69	67	74	67	277	9,230
Seuk-Hyun Baek	66	73	69	69	277	9,230
Jeung-Hun Wang	72	67	69	69	277	9,230
Anthony Wall	68	71	68	70	277	9,230

	SCORES				TOTAL	MONEY
Wen-Chong Liang	70	69	68	70	277	9,230
Julien Quesne	67	67	72	71	277	9,230
Gregory Bourdy	67	68	71	71	277	9,230
Jazz Janewattananond	69	69	72	68	278	7,800
Soren Kjeldsen	71	68	70	69	278	7,800
Thaworn Wiratchant	69	68	71	70	278	7,800
Wade Ormsby	67	67	72	72	278	7,800
James Heath	66	73	74	66	279	6,240
Sihwan Kim	67	72	72	68	279	6,240
Tom Lewis	71	68	71	69	279	6,240
J.B. Hansen	70	66	73	70	279	6,240
Stuart Manley	68	71	70	70	279	6,240
Alastair Forsyth	69	66	72	72	279	6,240
Nacho Elvira	66	69	71	73	279	6,240
Andreas Harto	69	69	68	73	279	6,240
Nicholas Fung	69	70	73	68	280	4,810
Mardan Mamat	71	67	71	71	280	4,810
Jack Doherty	68	67	72	73	280	4,810
James Morrison	71	68	73	69	281	3,926
Martin Rominger	72	67	73	69	281	3,926
Chan Kim	67	70	73	71	281	3,926
Paul Waring	73	64	70	74	281	3,926
Craig Lee	71	65	70	75	281	3,926
David Lipsky	68	70	72	72	282	3,445
Jason Knutzon	68	68	73	73	282	3,445
Marco Crespi	71	68	69	75	283	3,250
Jamie McLeary	69	69	77	69	284	3,120
Chi-Huang Tsai	71	68	74	72	285	2,990
Sam Cyr	67	69	71	79	286	2,860

Venetian Macau Open

Macau Golf & Country Club, Macau
Par 35-36–71; 6,624 yards

October 23-26
purse, US$900,000

	SCORES				TOTAL	MONEY
Anirban Lahiri	61	73	67	66	267	US$162,000
Prom Meesawat	68	70	64	66	268	77,850
Scott Hend	62	70	67	69	268	77,850
Adam Groom	65	67	72	66	270	45,000
Berry Henson	69	70	68	65	272	33,435
Unho Park	70	69	68	65	272	33,435
Thaworn Wiratchant	67	70	67	69	273	25,650
Shiv Kapur	73	67	67	67	274	22,050
Kieran Pratt	70	69	68	68	275	19,260
Kiradech Aphibarnrat	71	69	72	64	276	15,840
Thongchai Jaidee	70	70	71	65	276	15,840
Chan Kim	70	69	71	66	276	15,840
Chapchai Nirat	70	68	71	68	277	13,320
Martin Rominger	65	68	73	71	277	13,320
Rattanon Wannasrichan	71	71	73	63	278	11,403
Wei-Tze Yeh	73	69	70	66	278	11,403
Jeung-Hun Wang	71	68	69	70	278	11,403
Jyoti Randhawa	66	74	68	70	278	11,403
Shih-Chang Chan	70	64	70	74	278	11,403
Paul Peterson	71	71	70	67	279	9,795
Charlie Wi	69	70	72	68	279	9,795
Sam Brazel	64	73	68	74	279	9,795
Seuk-Hyun Baek	74	68	73	65	280	9,000
Pariya Junhasavasdikul	69	67	75	69	280	9,000
Adilson Da Silva	69	71	70	70	280	9,000

CIMB Classic

Kuala Lumpur Golf & Country Club, Kuala Lumpur, Malaysia — October 30-November 2
Par 36-36–72; 6,985 yards — purse, US$7,000,000

	SCORES				TOTAL	MONEY
Ryan Moore	68	69	67	67	271	$1,260,000
Kevin Na	69	68	67	70	274	522,666.67
Gary Woodland	71	70	66	67	274	522,666.67
Sergio Garcia	69	68	68	69	274	522,666.66
Sang-Moon Bae	71	68	68	69	276	266,000
Cameron Smith	70	69	69	68	276	266,000
John Senden	72	68	69	68	277	234,500
Billy Hurley	67	67	71	73	278	189,000
Davis Love	68	71	71	68	278	189,000
Prom Meesawat	68	71	70	69	278	189,000
Angelo Que	67	72	69	70	278	189,000
Rory Sabbatini	70	72	70	66	278	189,000
Jonas Blixt	69	69	75	66	279	123,666.67
Danny Lee	69	69	73	68	279	123,666.67
Brian Stuard	67	72	72	68	279	123,666.67
Lee Westwood	72	65	74	68	279	123,666.67
Kevin Chappell	69	68	70	72	279	123,666.66
Brendon de Jonge	70	73	65	71	279	123,666.66
Charl Schwartzel	74	70	68	68	280	94,500
Scott Stallings	69	76	67	68	280	94,500
Jonathan Byrd	70	74	69	68	281	72,800
Hideki Matsuyama	70	70	72	69	281	72,800
Heath Slocum	71	73	70	67	281	72,800
Nicholas Thompson	69	73	70	69	281	72,800
Mike Weir	73	68	72	68	281	72,800
Greg Chalmers	75	68	68	71	282	49,700
Jason Dufner	74	70	69	69	282	49,700
Ryo Ishikawa	69	71	73	69	282	49,700
Michael Putnam	71	72	72	67	282	49,700
Patrick Reed	70	70	68	74	282	49,700
Kevin Streelman	68	68	71	75	282	49,700
Jhonattan Vegas	74	71	70	67	282	49,700
Retief Goosen	74	70	69	70	283	38,675
Jeff Overton	68	69	71	75	283	38,675
Pat Perez	72	73	69	69	283	38,675
Kyle Stanley	76	71	69	67	283	38,675
Paul Casey	73	68	71	72	284	33,600
Billy Horschel	72	68	73	71	284	33,600
Luke Guthrie	73	68	71	73	285	27,300
Rikard Karlberg	65	76	75	69	285	27,300
Marc Leishman	74	72	71	68	285	27,300
David Lingmerth	68	72	73	72	285	27,300
Seung-Yul Noh	68	69	72	76	285	27,300
Chris Stroud	70	74	71	70	285	27,300
Charlie Wi	72	70	72	71	285	27,300
Steven Bowditch	71	73	74	68	286	21,000
Jason Knutzon	72	70	72	72	286	21,000
Steve Lewton	74	69	70	74	287	19,180
Matt Every	69	73	74	72	288	17,686.67
Trevor Immelman	74	70	71	73	288	17,686.67
J.B. Holmes	75	77	70	66	288	17,686.66
Matt Jones	81	69	69	70	289	16,415
Anirban Lahiri	74	72	70	73	289	16,415
Will MacKenzie	69	73	71	76	289	16,415
Tim Wilkinson	68	79	71	71	289	16,415
Stewart Cink	74	73	73	70	290	15,680
Tim Clark	72	74	74	70	290	15,680

	SCORES				TOTAL	MONEY
Brice Garnett	70	75	73	72	290	15,680
James Hahn	74	77	68	71	290	15,680
Troy Merritt	72	75	70	73	290	15,680
Roberto Castro	77	74	71	69	291	15,190
Morgan Hoffmann	72	74	73	72	291	15,190
Robert Allenby	73	73	73	73	292	14,910
Will Wilcox	75	74	72	71	292	14,910
Ricky Barnes	71	77	74	71	293	14,420
Danny Chia	75	74	72	72	293	14,420
Nicholas Fung	73	74	75	71	293	14,420
Chesson Hadley	75	75	74	69	293	14,420
Carlos Ortiz	76	72	75	70	293	14,420
Boo Weekley	75	72	74	73	294	14,000
K.J. Choi	71	74	71	79	295	13,790
Antonio Lascuna	72	72	74	77	295	13,790
Brian Davis	71	75	75	75	296	13,580
*Tianlang Guan	76	71	72	78	297	
David Lipsky	74	73	77	75	299	13,440
Charlie Beljan	76	75	74	76	301	13,300
Seuk-Hyun Baek	81	72	77	73	303	13,160
Graham DeLaet					WD	

WGC - HSBC Champions

Sheshan International Golf Club, Shanghai, China — November 6-9
Par 36-36–72; 7,261 yards — purse, US$8,500,000

	SCORES				TOTAL	MONEY
Bubba Watson	71	67	69	70	277	$1,400,000
Tim Clark	69	70	69	69	277	850,000
(Watson defeated Clark on first playoff hole.)						
Rickie Fowler	69	70	69	70	278	381,666.67
Hiroshi Iwata	73	65	68	72	278	381,666.67
Graeme McDowell	67	67	71	73	278	381,666.67
Ian Poulter	70	67	72	71	280	213,666.67
Thorbjorn Olesen	72	68	69	71	280	213,666.67
Martin Kaymer	69	72	66	73	280	213,666.67
Marc Leishman	72	71	69	69	281	158,000
Jason Dufner	72	70	72	68	282	135,500
Brandt Snedeker	69	74	69	70	282	135,500
George Coetzee	72	73	69	69	283	108,000
Adam Scott	70	72	71	70	283	108,000
Pablo Larrazabal	75	72	69	68	284	89,833.33
Alexander Levy	74	68	71	71	284	89,833.33
Ashun Wu	74	70	69	71	284	89,833.33
Louis Oosthuizen	70	70	72	72	284	89,833.33
Chris Kirk	69	74	69	72	284	89,833.33
Jonas Blixt	71	68	71	74	284	89,833.33
Kevin Na	71	68	79	67	285	81,000
Lee Westwood	70	73	69	73	285	81,000
Ryan Palmer	74	72	72	68	286	77,000
Patrick Reed	71	73	71	71	286	77,000
Tommy Fleetwood	69	75	74	69	287	73,500
Jamie Donaldson	71	77	68	71	287	73,500
Stephen Gallacher	72	72	71	72	287	73,500
Henrik Stenson	70	71	81	65	287	73,500
Anirban Lahiri	74	70	74	70	288	68,500
Sergio Garcia	74	72	73	69	288	68,500
Joost Luiten	77	71	69	71	288	68,500
Ryan Moore	74	71	72	71	288	68,500

	SCORES				TOTAL	MONEY
J.B. Holmes	70	71	73	74	288	68,500
Hunter Mahan	74	68	71	75	288	68,500
Shane Lowry	78	69	74	68	289	65,000
John Senden	73	73	72	72	290	61,500
Jimmy Walker	73	69	75	73	290	61,500
Russell Henley	71	75	74	70	290	61,500
Marc Warren	75	72	69	74	290	61,500
Jordan Spieth	70	74	72	74	290	61,500
Hao-Tong Li	75	72	76	67	290	61,500
Thomas Bjorn	72	75	72	72	291	56,000
Dawie van der Walt	70	72	75	74	291	56,000
Luke Donald	74	72	74	71	291	56,000
Hideki Matsuyama	74	69	73	75	291	56,000
Thongchai Jaidee	71	76	75	69	291	56,000
Ernie Els	74	70	74	74	292	52,500
Mikko Ilonen	75	76	71	70	292	52,500
Justin Rose	72	71	76	74	293	49,300
Marcel Siem	72	72	76	73	293	49,300
Felipe Aguilar	76	74	71	72	293	49,300
Bill Haas	70	74	72	77	293	49,300
Wen-Chong Liang	75	74	73	71	293	49,300
Hennie Otto	74	72	75	73	294	47,000
Matt Jones	75	76	71	72	294	47,000
Scott Stallings	74	76	77	67	294	47,000
Kevin Streelman	77	72	71	75	295	45,250
Gary Woodland	73	75	74	73	295	45,250
Matt Every	75	72	75	73	295	45,250
David Lipsky	78	73	72	72	295	45,250
Brendon Todd	71	74	73	78	296	43,875
Mu Hu	78	71	74	73	296	43,875
Darren Fichardt	74	72	74	77	297	43,500
Hyung-Sung Kim	70	74	75	79	298	43,250
Oliver Wilson	71	70	79	80	300	42,500
Keegan Bradley	72	73	77	78	300	42,500
Lian-Wei Zhang	73	76	74	77	300	42,500
Michael Hendry	76	75	73	76	300	42,500
Charl Schwartzel	74	76	77	73	300	42,500
Ze-Cheng Dou	76	73	74	78	301	41,625
Antonio Lascuna	76	79	73	73	301	41,625
Miguel Angel Jimenez	78	75	73	76	302	41,250
Jason Knutzon	78	74	75	77	304	41,000
Jaco Van Zyl	70	75	83	78	306	40,500
Yoshitaka Takeya	77	78	75	76	306	40,500
Billy Horschel	80	77	79	70	306	40,500
Jin Jeong	85	79	75	80	319	40,000
Victor Dubuisson	76	77			WD	39,500
Brody Ninyette	86				DQ	39,000
Kevin Stadler					WD	39,500
Graham DeLaet					WD	39,500

Panasonic Open India

Delhi Golf Club, New Delhi, India — November 6-9
Par 36-36–72; 6,963 yards — purse, US$300,000

	SCORES				TOTAL	MONEY
S.S.P. Chowrasia	70	71	69	66	276	US$54,000
Mithun Perera	70	67	69	70	276	25,950
Rahil Gangjee	66	68	71	71	276	25,950

(Chowrasia defeated Perera and Gangjee on first playoff hole.)

	SCORES				TOTAL	MONEY
Shubhankar Sharma	73	65	68	71	277	15,000
Akinori Tani	71	72	67	68	278	10,280
Unho Park	69	71	68	70	278	10,280
Siddikur Rahman	70	67	69	72	278	10,280
Jazz Janewattananond	69	70	71	69	279	6,885
Panuphol Pittayarat	70	68	69	72	279	6,885
Rashid Khan	68	70	71	71	280	5,730
Shankar Das	69	71	73	68	281	4,747.50
Atthaphon Sriboonkaew	73	70	68	70	281	4,747.50
Lionel Weber	73	66	69	73	281	4,747.50
Wade Ormsby	68	68	70	75	281	4,747.50
Chiragh Kumar	71	72	72	67	282	4,065
Shamim Khan	72	71	70	69	282	4,065
Martin Rominger	73	70	73	67	283	3,795
Blair Wilson	70	72	73	69	284	3,475
Manav Jaini	71	71	72	70	284	3,475
Tze-Huang Choo	68	73	71	72	284	3,475
Abhinav Lohan	72	72	73	68	285	3,225
Vikrant Chopra	74	68	70	73	285	3,225
Terry Pilkadaris	69	68	76	73	286	3,045
Chikka S.	72	69	71	74	286	3,045
Thaworn Wiratchant	75	72	72	69	288	2,820
Om Prakash Chouhan	69	72	73	74	288	2,820
Zamal Hossain	68	75	70	75	288	2,820

Chiangmai Golf Classic

Alpine Golf Resort, Chiangmai, Thailand — November 13-16
Par 36-36–72 — purse, US$750,000

	SCORES				TOTAL	MONEY
Rashid Khan	68	69	66	68	271	US$135,000
Jyoti Randhawa	68	65	70	69	272	64,875
Thanyakon Khrongpha	69	65	67	71	272	64,875
Kiradech Aphibarnrat	69	70	66	69	274	37,500
Mithun Perera	70	70	67	68	275	27,862.50
Kalem Richardson	71	69	64	71	275	27,862.50
Jason Dufner	69	69	73	66	277	17,531.25
Danny Chia	74	68	68	67	277	17,531.25
Jbe' Kruger	73	66	68	70	277	17,531.25
Scott Barr	68	69	67	73	277	17,531.25
Panuphol Pittayarat	68	75	66	69	278	12,638
Chien-Yao Hung	71	68	66	73	278	12,638
Namchok Tantipokhakul	71	70	68	70	279	11,363
Sutijet Kooratanapisan	70	69	71	70	280	10,613
Brett Munson	73	70	67	70	280	10,613
Miguel Tabuena	70	72	71	68	281	8,537.78
Javi Colomo	73	72	68	68	281	8,537.78
Chikka S.	69	72	71	69	281	8,537.78
Paul Peterson	70	70	71	70	281	8,537.78
Scott Hend	72	69	70	70	281	8,537.78
Joong-Kyung Mo	69	69	72	71	281	8,537.78
George Gandranata	66	72	72	71	281	8,537.78
Terry Pilkadaris	70	71	69	71	281	8,537.78
Wen-Tang Lin	69	71	69	72	281	8,537.78
Mardan Mamat	67	72	71	72	282	7,050
Rory Hie	70	70	70	72	282	7,050
Daisuke Kataoka	70	71	66	75	282	7,050

Resorts World Manila Masters

Manila Southwoods Golf & Country Club, Manila, Philippines — November 20-23
Par 36-36–72 — purse, US$1,000,000

	SCORES				TOTAL	MONEY
Mardan Mamat	65	68	66	69	268	US$180,000
Lionel Weber	70	70	64	70	274	110,000
Prom Meesawat	73	72	63	68	276	63,000
Sam Brazel	67	75	67	69	278	38,200
Chien-Yao Hung	67	71	69	71	278	38,200
Paul Peterson	68	70	69	71	278	38,200
Kiradech Aphibarnrat	66	69	68	75	278	38,200
Nicholas Fung	69	69	68	73	279	24,500
Thaworn Wiratchant	75	70	68	67	280	15,195.45
Akinori Tani	72	69	70	69	280	15,195.45
Scott Hend	73	69	69	69	280	15,195.45
Jeung-Hun Wang	68	65	77	70	280	15,195.45
Chiragh Kumar	72	71	67	70	280	15,195.45
Thitiphun Chuayprakong	71	68	70	71	280	15,195.45
Arie Irawan	71	71	67	71	280	15,195.45
Danny Chia	66	71	71	72	280	15,195.45
Daisuke Kataoka	65	73	70	72	280	15,195.45
Jbe' Kruger	70	73	64	73	280	15,195.45
Berry Henson	74	68	64	74	280	15,195.45
Rattanon Wannasrichan	75	67	71	68	281	10,737.50
Sattaya Supupramai	74	68	70	69	281	10,737.50
George Gandranata	70	70	69	72	281	10,737.50
Shiv Kapur	69	73	67	72	281	10,737.50
Wen-Teh Lu	68	72	75	67	282	9,550
Chris Rodgers	73	69	69	71	282	9,550
Steve Lewton	71	66	73	72	282	9,550
Simon Yates	70	72	67	73	282	9,550

King's Cup

Singha Park Khon Kaen Golf Club, Khon Kaen, Thailand — November 27-30
Par 36-36–72; 7,546 yards — purse, US$500,000

	SCORES				TOTAL	MONEY
Thaworn Wiratchant	68	67	66	67	268	US$90,000
Andrew Dodt	69	65	69	67	270	43,250
Anirban Lahiri	65	67	68	70	270	43,250
Kalem Richardson	66	72	68	67	273	20,716.67
Danthai Boonma	66	70	68	69	273	20,716.67
Paul Peterson	69	68	67	69	273	20,716.67
Rattanon Wannasrichan	71	68	67	68	274	13,250
Panuphol Pittayarat	68	69	66	71	274	13,250
Phachara Khongwatmai	71	71	65	68	275	9,658.33
Prom Meesawat	68	69	67	71	275	9,658.33
Jakraphan Premsirigorn	69	65	69	72	275	9,658.33
Jack Munro	69	71	70	66	276	8,125
Rashid Khan	71	69	71	66	277	7,241.67
Steve Lewton	71	68	70	68	277	7,241.67
Chan Kim	72	66	70	69	277	7,241.67
Daniel Chopra	67	72	72	67	278	5,867.86
Adam Groom	70	66	74	68	278	5,867.86
Mardan Mamat	68	71	70	69	278	5,867.86
S.S.P. Chowrasia	65	71	70	72	278	5,867.86
Phiphatphong Naewsuk	66	71	69	72	278	5,867.86

	SCORES				TOTAL	MONEY
Carlos Pigem	67	69	69	73	278	5,867.86
Sutijet Kooratanapisan	70	68	65	75	278	5,867.86
Supravee Phatam	69	70	72	68	279	4,925
Antonio Lascuna	68	71	71	69	279	4,925
Chinnarat Phadungsil	70	68	70	71	279	4,925
Mathiam Keyser	68	69	68	74	279	4,925

Bank BRI Indonesia Open

Damai Indah Golf, PIK Course, Jakarta, Indonesia — December 4-7
Par 35-36–71 — purse, US$750,000

	SCORES				TOTAL	MONEY
Padraig Harrington	64	66	67	71	268	US$135,000
Thanyakon Khrongpha	67	63	71	69	270	82,500
Nathan Holman	69	63	70	69	271	47,250
Quincy Quek	71	67	68	66	272	37,500
Sattaya Supupramai	73	67	67	67	274	30,750
David Lipsky	72	68	66	69	275	24,975
Jake Higginbottom	71	69	72	64	276	16,642.60
Terry Pilkadaris	69	70	68	69	276	16,642.60
Jyoti Randhawa	71	68	71	66	276	16,642.60
Sam Brazel	68	68	69	71	276	16,642.60
Scott Hend	69	64	75	68	276	16,642.60
Berry Henson	72	69	70	66	277	11,463
Jeung-Hun Wang	70	66	76	65	277	11,463
Jarin Todd	69	64	74	70	277	11,463
Anirban Lahiri	74	66	66	72	278	9,713
Andrew Dodt	70	69	69	70	278	9,713
Sung Lee	70	72	70	66	278	9,713
George Gandranata	69	68	68	73	278	9,713
S.S.P. Chowrasia	68	71	68	72	279	8,175.20
Jordan Irawan	71	67	71	70	279	8,175.20
Danny Chia	68	69	71	71	279	8,175.20
Scott Barr	69	67	70	73	279	8,175.20
Thitiphun Chuayprakong	69	66	73	71	279	8,175.20
Mithun Perera	69	71	71	69	280	7,050
Chinnarat Phadungsil	73	68	68	71	280	7,050
Carlos Pigem	68	69	69	74	280	7,050
Blair Wilson	68	69	74	69	280	7,050
Chris Rodgers	69	68	71	72	280	7,050

Thailand Golf Championship

Amata Spring Country Club, Chonburi, Thailand — December 11-14
Par 36-36–72; 7,453 yards — purse, US$1,000,000

	SCORES				TOTAL	MONEY
Lee Westwood	70	71	72	67	280	US$180,000
Martin Kaymer	71	72	70	68	281	86,500
Marcus Fraser	69	72	70	70	281	86,500
Tommy Fleetwood	71	69	73	70	283	50,000
Scott Hend	70	74	71	69	284	41,000
Thongchai Jaidee	72	71	74	68	285	28,766.67
Jonathan Moore	71	71	72	71	285	28,766.67
Anirban Lahiri	71	73	68	73	285	28,766.67
Sergio Garcia	71	75	71	69	286	21,400

	SCORES				TOTAL	MONEY
Kiradech Aphibarnrat	76	72	71	68	287	17,600
Paul Peterson	71	72	75	69	287	17,600
Terry Pilkadaris	77	69	72	69	287	17,600
Thanyakon Khrongpha	69	77	73	69	288	14,483.33
Bernd Wiesberger	76	74	68	70	288	14,483.33
Charlie Wi	74	72	71	71	288	14,483.33
Kodai Ichihara	78	68	72	71	289	12,950
Daisuke Kataoka	74	73	71	71	289	12,950
Danny Chia	77	74	72	67	290	11,412.50
Berry Henson	73	72	74	71	290	11,412.50
Jeung-Hun Wang	73	72	73	72	290	11,412.50
Unho Park	76	74	68	72	290	11,412.50
Ashun Wu	71	75	75	70	291	10,300
Masahiro Kawamura	72	74	74	71	291	10,300
Hiroshi Iwata	72	78	69	72	291	10,300
Sebastien Gros	75	75	72	70	292	9,250
Bubba Watson	76	70	77	69	292	9,250
Mu Hu	72	74	74	72	292	9,250
Wei-Chih Lu	69	77	73	73	292	9,250
Anthony Kang	72	73	77	71	293	7,725
Shingo Katayama	75	75	73	70	293	7,725
Lionel Weber	75	69	79	70	293	7,725
Sung-Hoon Kang	75	70	74	74	293	7,725
Chinnarat Phadungsil	73	73	78	69	293	7,725
*Tianlang Guan	74	76	69	74	293	
Andrew Dodt	76	72	70	75	293	7,725
Matthew Stieger	76	72	68	77	293	7,725
Simon Griffiths	73	76	66	78	293	7,725

Dubai Open

The Els Club, Dubai, United Arab Emirates — December 18-21
Par 36-36–72 — purse, US$500,000

	SCORES				TOTAL	MONEY
Arjun Atwal	73	65	68	66	272	US$90,000
Jeung-Hun Wang	71	67	68	67	273	55,000
Simon Yates	71	67	69	68	275	31,500
Jake Higginbottom	72	71	69	64	276	22,750
Thaworn Wiratchant	74	69	65	68	276	22,750
Carlos Pigem	70	73	68	66	277	12,680
Daisuke Kataoka	73	66	68	70	277	12,680
Pariya Junhasavasdikul	68	72	67	70	277	12,680
Chapchai Nirat	71	69	67	70	277	12,680
Jbe' Kruger	70	72	64	71	277	12,680
Bryce Easton	69	71	69	69	278	7,912.50
Joong-Kyung Mo	70	71	68	69	278	7,912.50
Gaganjeet Bhullar	69	69	69	71	278	7,912.50
Shiv Kapur	71	66	69	72	278	7,912.50
Unho Park	75	68	69	67	279	6,475
Rattanon Wannasrichan	75	70	67	67	279	6,475
Thitiphun Chuayprakong	70	71	67	71	279	6,475
Darren Clarke	72	71	64	72	279	6,475
Terry Pilkadaris	71	71	70	68	280	5,450
Namchok Tantipokhakul	71	72	68	69	280	5,450
Panuphol Pittayarat	69	72	68	71	280	5,450
Matthew Fitzpatrick	70	71	68	71	280	5,450
Javi Colomo	69	73	67	71	280	5,450
Chawalit Plaphol	71	69	72	69	281	4,550
Christopher Cannon	67	74	71	69	281	4,550

	SCORES				TOTAL	MONEY
Chih-Bing Lam	67	74	70	70	281	4,550
Poosit Supupramai	72	72	67	70	281	4,550
Thammanoon Sriroj	72	72	67	70	281	4,550
Prom Meesawat	71	68	70	72	281	4,550
Joshua White	71	68	70	72	281	4,550

OneAsia Tour

Enjoy Jakarta Indonesia PGA Championship

Damai Indah Golf Club, Jakarta, Indonesia
Par 36-36–72; 7,156 yards

March 27-30
purse, US$1,000,000

	SCORES				TOTAL	MONEY
Michio Matsumura	65	67	67	68	267	US$180,000
Rhein Gibson	69	65	72	62	268	87,500
Juvic Pagunsan	67	64	68	69	268	87,500
Ashun Wu	69	68	64	69	270	50,000
Dong-Seop Maeng	67	69	70	65	271	42,000
Sung-Hoon Kang	67	68	70	67	272	35,650
Hiroshi Iwata	70	66	69	67	272	35,650
Xin-Jun Zhang	72	67	68	66	273	25,820
Yoshikazu Haku	69	66	71	67	273	25,820
Wen-Chong Liang	67	69	70	67	273	25,820
Bio Kim	68	67	70	68	273	25,820
Young-Han Song	69	66	67	71	273	25,820
Seung-Hyuk Kim	70	68	70	66	274	17,150
Hao-Tong Li	67	67	72	68	274	17,150
David Smail	67	68	71	68	274	17,150
Dong-Kyu Jang	67	69	69	69	274	17,150
Yuki Kono	70	66	70	69	275	12,100
Kunihiro Kamii	65	70	70	70	275	12,100
Masahiro Kawamura	72	68	64	71	275	12,100
Toshinori Muto	71	68	64	72	275	12,100
Sang-Hyun Park	67	64	67	77	275	12,100
Il-Hwan Park	69	67	71	69	276	10,500
Matthew Griffin	68	69	73	66	276	10,500
Jun-Seok Lee	73	68	69	66	276	10,500
Nathan Holman	69	67	71	70	277	8,700
Thaworn Wiratchant	69	70	72	66	277	8,700
Akio Sadakata	69	71	66	71	277	8,700
Danny Chia	69	69	68	71	277	8,700

Volvo China Open

Genzon Golf Club, Shenzen, China — April 24-27
Par 36-36–72; 7,145 yards — purse, RMB20,000,000

	SCORES				TOTAL	MONEY
Alexander Levy	68	62	70	69	269	US$539,054.92
Tommy Fleetwood	70	68	67	68	273	359,369.95
Alvaro Quiros	67	68	68	72	275	202,471.05
Francesco Molinari	70	70	69	67	276	161,718.09
Anders Hansen	73	68	73	63	277	115,790.16
Henrik Stenson	71	70	71	65	277	115,790.16
Ian Poulter	69	74	67	67	277	115,790.16
Rafa Cabrera-Bello	70	70	71	67	278	66,627.86
Michael Hoey	69	72	69	68	278	66,627.86
Andy Sullivan	71	68	69	70	278	66,627.86
Simon Dyson	67	71	69	71	278	66,627.86
Mikko Ilonen	69	68	67	74	278	66,627.86
Eduardo De La Riva	73	71	71	64	279	50,779.49
Hennie Otto	70	71	69	69	279	50,779.49
Jbe' Kruger	74	67	72	67	280	44,634.20
Park Il-Hwan	68	72	72	68	280	44,634.20
Nacho Elvira	69	74	68	69	280	44,634.20
Chris Doak	71	68	70	71	280	44,634.20
Gregory Bourdy	71	72	70	68	281	37,712.66
Morten Orum Madsen	73	68	71	69	281	37,712.66
Prom Meesawat	72	69	71	69	281	37,712.66
Julien Quesne	69	71	70	71	281	37,712.66
Adrian Otaegui	68	66	71	76	281	37,712.66
Danny Willett	73	71	71	67	282	31,211.59
David Horsey	68	76	70	68	282	31,211.59
Scott Jamieson	71	68	73	70	282	31,211.59
Emiliano Grillo	70	71	71	70	282	31,211.59
Scott Strange	71	71	70	70	282	31,211.59
Mark Brown	75	69	68	70	282	31,211.59
Raphael Jacquelin	69	67	75	71	282	31,211.59
Terry Pilkadaris	73	71	67	71	282	31,211.59
Maximilian Kieffer	73	71	69	70	283	25,470.60
Lee Slattery	72	72	69	70	283	25,470.60
Richie Ramsay	69	68	74	72	283	25,470.60
Robert-Jan Derksen	70	69	71	73	283	25,470.60
Ricardo Santos	71	73	74	66	284	22,640.53
Ouyang Zheng	72	72	73	67	284	22,640.53
Pablo Larrazabal	71	70	72	71	284	22,640.53
Oliver Fisher	73	70	69	72	284	22,640.53
Romain Wattel	70	74	74	67	285	19,406.17
Tom Lewis	72	69	74	70	285	19,406.17
Marco Crespi	71	69	74	71	285	19,406.17
Jose-Filipe Lima	72	70	71	72	285	19,406.17
Gregory Havret	70	73	70	72	285	19,406.17
Matthew Griffin	71	73	69	72	285	19,406.17
David Drysdale	70	71	75	70	286	16,171.81
Marcel Siem	71	69	75	71	286	16,171.81
Richard Bland	69	75	71	71	286	16,171.81
Masahiro Kawamura	73	69	72	72	286	16,171.81
Felipe Aguilar	71	71	75	70	287	13,584.32
Ashun Wu	69	74	73	71	287	13,584.32
Ji-Man Kang	71	72	70	74	287	13,584.32
Hao-Tong Li	73	69	67	78	287	13,584.32
Tyrrell Hatton	68	71	75	74	288	11,320.27
Jason Dufner	73	71	69	75	288	11,320.27
Wen-Chong Liang	70	74	69	75	288	11,320.27
Edoardo Molinari	71	73	75	70	289	9,703.09

	SCORES				TOTAL	MONEY
Eddie Pepperell	70	72	75	72	289	9,703.09
Gaganjeet Bhullar	71	70	73	75	289	9,703.09
Seve Benson	74	69	76	71	290	8,732.78
Richard Green	70	71	77	72	290	8,732.78
Soren Kjeldsen	72	72	72	74	290	8,732.78
Brett Rumford	68	75	74	74	291	8,085.90
Jorge Campillo	71	70	76	75	292	7,762.47
Simon Khan	69	75	77	72	293	7,277.32
Stuart Manley	70	74	74	75	293	7,277.32
Kang-Chun Wu	73	70	76	75	294	6,792.16
Anthony Wall	72	72	77	74	295	6,468.72

GS Caltex Maekyung Open

Namseoul Golf & Country Club, Seoul, South Korea — May 8-11
Par 36-36–72; 6,943 yards — purse, KRW1,000,000,000

	SCORES				TOTAL	MONEY
Jun-Won Park	72	64	70	67	273	US$191,580.06
Sang-Hyun Park	72	66	68	70	276	114,948.03
Ki-Sang Lee	70	73	69	67	279	58,431.92
Jung-Gon Hwang	69	73	66	71	279	58,431.92
Woo-Hyun Kim	69	68	74	70	281	31,610.71
Il-Hwan Park	70	69	71	71	281	31,610.71
Scott Hend	71	66	72	72	281	31,610.71
Dong-Kyu Jang	69	72	69	71	281	31,610.71
*Nam-Hun Kim	75	66	69	71	281	
Young-Han Song	69	71	74	68	282	20,020.12
Ryan Fox	73	71	70	68	282	20,020.12
Dong-Min Lee	72	70	69	71	282	20,020.12
Do-Kyu Park	71	70	74	68	283	13,650.08
David Oh	75	70	67	71	283	13,650.08
Ho-Sung Choi	68	72	75	69	284	11,039.80
Hyung-Sung Kim	70	72	72	70	284	11,039.80
Seung-Hyuk Kim	68	71	72	73	284	11,039.80
Jeong-Hyup Hyun	70	70	71	73	284	11,039.80
Sung-Kug Park	69	72	76	68	285	9,248.53
Hao-Tong Li	70	72	70	73	285	9,248.53
Seng-Yong Kim	70	73	69	73	285	9,248.53
Gareth Paddison	73	69	70	73	285	9,248.53
Sung-Hoon Kang	72	70	73	71	286	8,381.63
Hyung-Tae Kim	71	72	70	73	286	8,381.63
Gi-Whan Kim	72	74	70	71	287	7,950.57
Jin Jeong	71	72	72	72	287	7,950.57
Tae-Kyu Lee	73	69	73	72	287	7,950.57
K.T. Kim	71	73	73	70	287	7,950.57
Stephen Dartnall	74	70	70	73	287	7,950.57
Kyoung-Hoon Lee	68	66	78	75	287	7,950.57

SK Telecom Open

Sky 72 Ocean Course, Incheon, South Korea — May 15-18
Par 36-36–72; 7,241 yards — purse, KRW1,000,000,000

	SCORES				TOTAL	MONEY
Seung-Hyuk Kim	66	74	67	70	277	US$195,121.95
Tae-Hee Lee	68	68	73	69	278	78,048.79

	SCORES				TOTAL	MONEY
K.T. Kim	70	70	67	71	278	78,048.79
David Bransdon	71	70	69	69	279	46,829.27
K.J. Choi	75	67	70	68	280	39,024.39
Kyoung-Hoon Lee	70	70	69	72	281	33,951.22
Dae-Hyun Kim	72	69	75	66	282	28,097.57
Sang-Hyun Park	72	67	73	70	282	28,097.57
*Nam-Hun Kim	72	73	69	69	283	
David Oh	74	70	69	70	283	22,634.15
Dong-Kyu Jang	75	66	70	72	283	22,634.15
Michael Wright	71	73	70	70	284	17,951.22
Ho-Sung Choi	71	71	71	71	284	17,951.22
Il-Hwan Park	73	70	69	72	284	17,951.22
Jason Scrivener	72	72	67	73	284	17,951.22
Gi-Whan Kim	75	68	72	70	285	14,829.27
Ryan Fox	74	69	73	70	286	11,874.56
Seong-Man Han	71	70	75	70	286	11,874.56
Ji-Hoon Lee	74	70	72	70	286	11,874.56
Mark Brown	76	68	71	71	286	11,874.56
Hyung-Sung Kim	71	70	73	72	286	11,874.56
Dong-Min Lee	70	72	72	72	286	11,874.56
Sang-Hee Lee	75	68	70	73	286	11,874.56
Jason Kang	75	67	74	71	287	8,780.49
Michael Sim	72	71	73	71	287	8,780.49
David McKenzie	73	74	70	70	287	8,780.49
Matthew Griffin	75	70	71	71	287	8,780.49
Garrett Sapp	78	69	68	72	287	8,780.49
Nick Cullen	71	71	72	73	287	8,780.49

Fiji International

Natadola Bay Championship Golf Course, Nadi, Fiji
Par 36-36–72; 7,068 yards

August 14-17
purse, US$1,000,000

	SCORES				TOTAL	MONEY
Steve Jeffress	69	70	69	70	278	US$180,000
Jake Higginbottom	68	69	71	74	282	102,000
Terry Pilkadaris	70	76	69	71	286	57,750
Andrew Dodt	68	71	71	76	286	57,750
In-Hoi Hur	70	72	70	75	287	40,000
Tae-Hoon Kim	74	74	69	71	288	32,333.33
Ryan Fox	69	76	70	73	288	32,333.33
Michael Sim	71	70	71	76	288	32,333.33
Hyo-Won Park	73	72	76	68	289	27,000
Vijay Singh	73	74	70	73	290	23,500
Brad Kennedy	70	71	70	79	290	23,500
Anirban Lahiri	74	69	75	73	291	18,333.33
David Smail	76	71	67	77	291	18,333.33
Cameron Smith	71	68	73	79	291	18,333.33
Joshua Younger	72	75	76	69	292	12,908.33
Richard Lee	74	75	74	69	292	12,908.33
Peter Cooke	70	73	77	72	292	12,908.33
Brendan Jones	70	73	76	73	292	12,908.33
Nathan Holman	69	73	74	76	292	12,908.33
Scott Laycock	74	71	71	76	292	12,908.33
Paul Gow	70	73	76	74	293	10,050
Dimitrios Papadatos	72	72	75	74	293	10,050
Rohan Blizard	70	74	75	74	293	10,050
Lucas Lee	69	71	76	77	293	10,050
Ted Oh	75	73	71	75	294	8,750
Stephen Dartnall	68	78	71	77	294	8,750

Nanshan China Masters

Nanshan International Golf Club, Nanshan, China — October 9-12
Par 36-35–71; 6,540 yards — purse, US$1,000,000

	SCORES				TOTAL	MONEY
Hao-Tong Li	68	65	72	70	275	US$180,000
Jun-Seok Lee	69	69	72	69	279	105,000
Todd Baek	73	69	65	74	281	70,000
Guo-Wu Zhou	68	71	70	73	282	50,000
Nick Gillespie	68	68	74	73	283	42,000
Mu Hu	69	71	72	72	284	35,650
Michael Sim	70	69	69	76	284	35,650
Sang-Yeop Lee	71	73	71	70	285	28,366.67
Jin-Ho Choi	70	73	67	75	285	28,366.67
Yi-Keun Chang	70	71	65	79	285	28,366.67
Panuwat Muenlek	74	71	71	70	286	20,200
Stephen Dartnall	72	70	71	73	286	20,200
Gareth Paddison	69	71	70	76	286	20,200
Garrett Sapp	71	65	71	79	286	20,200
Aaron Townsend	75	70	69	73	287	15,900
Rhein Gibson	67	70	69	81	287	15,900
David McKenzie	72	75	68	73	288	13,200
Xiong-Yi Zhao	71	72	69	76	288	13,200
Rak Cho	71	76	68	74	289	11,060
Scott Laycock	69	73	73	74	289	11,060
Geon-Ha Kim	72	74	67	76	289	11,060
Jeung-Hun Wang	72	73	68	76	289	11,060
Rattanon Wannasrichan	70	74	68	77	289	11,060
Dong Su	70	73	73	74	290	9,325
Rory Hic	72	75	69	74	290	9,325
Ze-Yu He	74	70	73	73	290	9,325
Daniel Woltman	67	76	70	77	290	9,325

Kolon Korea Open

Woo Jeong Hills Country Club, Cheonan, South Korea — October 23-26
Par 36-35–71; 7,215 yards — purse, KRW1,200,000,000

	SCORES				TOTAL	MONEY
Seung-Hyuk Kim	73	68	71	70	282	US$278,678.32
Seung-Yul Noh	73	71	71	69	284	111,471.33
Tae-Hee Lee	72	72	72	69	285	58,522.45
Ho-Sung Choi	67	79	67	72	285	58,522.45
*Jeong Ham	68	72	75	70	285	
Y.E. Yang	72	70	70	74	286	39,014.97
Dong-Seop Maeng	72	74	74	67	287	28,332.30
Soon-Sang Hong	72	70	73	72	287	28,332.30
Ju-Hyuk Park	71	70	72	74	287	28,332.30
Lee-Jun Seok	70	68	78	71	287	28,332.30
Ji-Man Kang	69	69	77	72	287	28,332.30
Gi-Whan Kim	72	72	70	74	288	19,043.02
Sung-Hoon Kang	76	74	68	70	288	19,043.02
Rory Hie	72	72	76	69	289	13,492.68
Yi-Keun Chang	74	70	68	77	289	13,492.68
Jun-Won Park	71	71	73	74	289	13,492.68
In-Choon Hwang	73	69	75	72	289	13,492.68
Bio Kim	77	67	73	73	290	10,868.45
Heung-Chol Joo	72	71	76	71	290	10,868.45
Tae-Hoon Kim	75	74	69	72	290	10,868.45
Dong-Min Lee	74	73	73	71	291	9,893.08
Bong-Sub Kim	72	71	73	75	291	9,893.08

	SCORES				TOTAL	MONEY
Seng-Yong Kim	76	71	69	76	292	9,149.89
Jason Kang	74	70	74	74	292	9,149.89
Jin-Ho Choi	71	71	78	72	292	9,149.89
Yun-Cheol Jeon	67	71	77	77	292	9,149.89

Emirates Australian Open

See Australasian Tour chapter.

Dongfeng Nissan Cup

Foison Golf Club, Guangzhou, China
Par 36-36–72; 7,453 yards

December 5-7
purse, US$1,000,000

FIRST DAY
Fourballs

Wen-Chong Liang and Mu Hu (China) defeated Scott Laycock and Rhein Gibson, 3 and 2.
Ashun Wu and Dong Su (China) defeated Mark Brown and Ryan Fox, 1 up.
Zihao Chen and Cheng Jin (China) defeated Thaworn Wiratchant and Kheng Hwai Khor, 7 and 5.
Daisuke Maruyama and Nobuhiro Masuda (Asia Pacific) defeated Lian-Wei Zhang and Hao-Tong Li, 1 up.
Tian Yuan and Wen-Yi Huang (China) defeated Hyung-Tae Kim and Jun-Seok Lee, 2 and 1.
Rory Hie and Antonio Lascuna (Asia Pacific) defeated Bin Yan and Guang-Ming Yang, 5 and 3.

POINTS: Asia Pacific 2, China 4

SECOND DAY
Foursomes

Huang and Yuan (China) defeated Hie and Lascuna, 1 up.
Kim and Lee (Asia Pacific) defeated Wu and Su, 1 up.
Maruyama and Masuda (Asia Pacific) defeated Li and Hu, 2 and 1.
Chen and Jin (China) halved with Wiratchant and Khor.
Fox and Brown (Asia Pacific) defeated Yan and Yang, 4 and 2.
Laycock and Gibson (Asia Pacific) defeated Zhang and Liang, 3 and 2.

POINTS: Asia Pacific 6½, China 5½

THIRD DAY
Singles

Liang (China) defeated Gibson, 4 and 3.
Hu (China) defeated Hie, 1 up.
Fox (Asia Pacific) defeated Su, 2 and 1.
Wiratchant (Asia Pacific) defeated Yan, 6 and 5.
Wu (China) halved with Brown.
Laycock (Asia Pacific) defeated Huang, 4 and 2.
Masuda (Asia Pacific) defeated Yang, 2 and 1.
Maruyama (Asia Pacific) defeated Yuan, 4 and 3.
Kim (Asia Pacific) defeated Jin, 4 and 3.
Lascuna (Asia Pacific) defeated Zhang, 5 and 4.
Li (China) defeated Lee, 3 and 2.
Khor (Asia Pacific) defeated Chen, 4 and 3.

FINAL POINTS: Asia Pacific 15, China 9

Australian PGA Championship

See Australasian Tour chapter.

PGA Tour China

Mission Hills Haikou Open

Mission Hills, Haikou, Hainan — April 17-20
Par 36-36–72; 7,228 yards — purse, CN¥1,200,000

	SCORES				TOTAL	MONEY
Jeung-Hun Wang	67	63	69	66	265	CN¥216,000
Xin-Jun Zhang	70	73	64	68	275	129,600
Steve Dartnall	73	66	67	70	276	69,600
Raymond Beaufils	74	66	66	70	276	69,600
Quincy Quek	74	69	64	70	277	48,000
Sam Chien	67	71	71	70	279	41,700
Todd Baek	71	71	71	66	279	41,700
Ryan McCarthy	74	68	69	69	280	36,000
Aaron Townsend	73	70	69	68	280	36,000
Nick Gillespie	72	69	74	66	281	32,400
Yi Keun Chang	73	75	69	65	282	30,000
Kuan Po Lin	73	73	70	67	283	21,450
Xin Yang Li	71	71	70	71	283	21,450
Ted Oh	69	74	71	69	283	21,450
Brad McIntosh	70	74	66	73	283	21,450
Do Eun An	73	68	72	70	283	21,450
Zheng Ouyang	70	71	73	69	283	21,450
David McKenzie	69	73	73	68	283	21,450
K.T. Kim	71	70	69	73	283	21,450
Martin Kim	79	68	71	66	284	13,000
Lucas Lee	69	69	71	75	284	13,000
Bio Kim	74	68	69	73	284	13,000
Jamie Arnold	73	70	70	71	284	13,000
David Lutterus	73	68	74	69	284	13,000
Lian-Wei Zhang	71	68	72	73	284	13,000

Buick Open

Dragon Lake Golf Club, Guangzhou, Guangdong — May 1-4
Par 36-36–72; 7,116 yards — purse, CN¥1,200,000

	SCORES				TOTAL	MONEY
Sam Chien	66	67	69	70	272	CN¥216,000
*Ze Cheng Dou	67	69	70	69	275	
Shih Chang Chan	73	72	66	67	278	129,600
Lucas Lee	73	66	73	67	279	81,600
Ze Yu He	70	71	67	73	281	52,800
Hao-Tong Li	70	68	70	73	281	52,800
Anthony Kang	69	68	74	71	282	43,200
Chien Yao Hung	73	74	68	68	283	37,400
Xin-Jun Zhang	67	70	77	69	283	37,400
Wei Tze Yeh	69	71	74	69	283	37,400
Brad McIntosh	69	69	76	70	284	31,200
Raymond Beaufils	71	72	66	75	284	31,200
Jeung-Hun Wang	71	69	74	71	285	22,800
Chris Campbell	71	70	72	72	285	26,400

	SCORES				TOTAL	MONEY
Brett Drewitt	68	70	73	74	285	26,400
Ji Man Kang	69	76	72	69	286	21,600
Tian Yuan	71	73	74	69	287	17,400
Hai Meng Chao	69	72	76	70	287	17,400
Jae Ho Kim	79	68	72	68	287	17,400
Jun Hyuk Lee	71	72	74	70	287	17,400
Dohyun Kim	73	72	70	72	287	17,400
Yi Keun Chang	71	74	71	71	287	17,400

United Investment Real Estate Wuhan Open

Wuhan Yishan Golf Club, Hubei Wuhan — May 15-18
Par 36-36–72 — purse, CN¥1,200,000

	SCORES				TOTAL	MONEY
Brett Drewitt	73	70	67	70	280	CN¥216,000
Xin-Jun Zhang	67	70	73	70	280	105,600
Hao-Tong Li	72	71	68	69	280	105,600
(Drewitt defeated Zhang and Li on second playoff hole.)						
David Lutterus	71	70	72	69	282	47,250
Anthony Kang	72	71	67	72	282	47,250
Scott Barr	70	76	69	67	282	47,250
Ze Yu He	75	69	69	69	282	47,250
Chris Campbell	73	70	72	69	284	37,200
Sam Chien	70	70	73	72	285	34,800
Todd Baek	69	69	74	74	286	30,000
Tian Yuan	74	71	72	69	286	30,000
Shao Cai He	69	72	75	70	286	30,000
Zheng Ouyang	70	68	75	74	287	21,840
Fang Yi Li	73	73	70	71	287	21,840
Bryden Macpherson	75	68	70	74	287	21,840
Nick Gillespie	73	68	76	70	287	21,840
Ji Hoon Kim	76	69	71	71	287	21,840
Ding Feng Liang	71	73	74	70	288	17,400
Raymond Beaufils	71	72	72	73	288	17,400
Ryan McCarthy	77	68	77	67	289	14,480
Gavin Flint	71	71	69	78	289	14,480
Yi Cao	76	72	72	69	289	14,480

Lanhai Open

Lan Hai International Golf Club, Shanghai — June 5-8
Par 36-36–72; 7,346 yards — purse, CN¥1,200,000

	SCORES				TOTAL	MONEY
David McKenzie	68	67	68	69	272	CN¥216,000
Steve Dartnall	67	67	75	68	277	129,600
Quincy Quek	65	70	71	74	280	81,600
Ted Oh	69	73	69	70	281	57,600
Todd Baek	73	73	69	67	282	43,800
Hao-Tong Li	74	69	67	72	282	43,800
Bryden Macpherson	71	71	70	70	282	43,800
*Ze Cheng Dou	70	70	70	72	282	
Jamie Arnold	70	69	71	73	283	37,200
Brett Drewitt	71	72	73	69	285	30,000
Mathew Perry	75	72	73	65	285	30,000
Shih Chang Chan	73	72	68	72	285	30,000

	SCORES				TOTAL	MONEY
Wei Huang Wu	74	67	73	71	285	30,000
Fei Hao Yang	71	67	71	76	285	30,000
Fang Yi Li	73	68	70	75	286	19,800
David Lutterus	69	72	73	72	286	19,800
Shih Hung Lee	70	69	74	73	286	19,800
Gavin Flint	71	71	74	70	286	19,800
Dong Su	70	72	73	71	286	19,800
Geon Ha Kim	73	72	70	71	286	19,800

Earls Beijing Open

Earls Golf Club, Beijing
Par 36-36–72

June 12-15
purse, CN¥1,200,000

	SCORES				TOTAL	MONEY
Xin-Jun Zhang	66	66	70	67	269	CN¥216,000
Mathew Perry	65	70	64	72	271	129,600
Lucas Lee	69	65	67	72	273	69,600
Seongki Lee	65	68	72	68	273	69,600
Mu Hu	71	72	66	66	275	48,000
Jeung-Hun Wang	68	70	70	68	276	43,200
Ryan Haller	70	69	68	70	277	34,920
Fei Hao Yang	72	70	68	67	277	34,920
Hoon Heui Lee	71	67	73	66	277	34,920
Chien Yao Hung	75	69	65	68	277	34,920
Scott Barr	67	71	68	71	277	34,920
Martin Kim	68	74	67	69	278	25,200
Brad McIntosh	71	66	72	69	278	25,200
Lincoln Tighe	68	69	70	71	278	25,200
Brett Drewitt	74	69	68	68	279	19,800
Arnond Vongvanij	73	70	67	69	279	19,800
Aaron Townsend	71	70	71	67	279	19,800
Gunn Charoenkul	70	69	72	68	279	19,800
*Ze Cheng Dou	73	69	67	71	280	
Nathan Leonhardt	73	69	68	70	280	14,040
Guo Wu Zhou	73	70	70	67	280	14,040
Daniel Nisbet	71	73	67	69	280	14,040
Ted Oh	70	72	68	70	280	14,040
Hong Teng Tseng	68	72	72	68	280	14,040
Bryden Macpherson	74	66	68	72	280	14,040

Yulongwan Yunnan Open

Yulongwan Golf Club, Kunming, Yunnan
Par 36-36–72

August 7-10
purse, CN¥1,200,000

	SCORES				TOTAL	MONEY
Gunn Charoenkul	61	70	66	66	263	CN¥216,000
Xin-Jun Zhang	65	65	69	67	266	129,600
Chien Yao Hung	65	69	67	68	269	81,600
T.K. Kim	68	67	69	69	273	49,600
Shao Cai He	66	74	68	65	273	49,600
Anthony Kang	68	66	71	68	273	49,600
Bryden Macpherson	68	72	70	64	274	34,920
Yi Keun Chang	66	70	68	70	274	34,920
Ben Lein	66	71	71	66	274	34,920
Panuphol Pittayarat	69	73	66	66	274	34,920

	SCORES				TOTAL	MONEY
Stephen Dartnall	66	74	67	67	274	34,920
Xin Yang Li	67	68	71	69	275	27,600
Brett Drewitt	72	67	69	68	276	24,000
Scott Barr	67	70	72	67	276	24,000
*Pariya Junhasavasdikul	70	74	72	61	277	21,000
Todd Baek	70	68	65	74	277	21,000
Hao-Tong Li	73	69	67	69	278	16,800
Yongle Huang	70	72	68	68	278	16,800
Marcus Both	72	70	67	69	278	16,800
Rak Hyun Cho	67	76	67	68	278	16,800
Gui Ming Liao	69	73	65	71	278	16,800

Chateau Junding Penglai Open

Chateau Junding Golf Club, Yantai, Shandong — September 4-7
Par 36-36–72 — purse, CN¥1,200,000

	SCORES				TOTAL	MONEY
Todd Baek	66	67	70	68	271	CN¥216,000
Wei Tze Yeh	68	69	71	68	276	105,600
Raymond Beaufils	73	75	66	62	276	105,600
David Lutterus	73	67	68	70	278	57,600
Panuphol Pittayarat	75	69	70	65	279	48,000
Aaron Townsend	70	68	73	69	280	41,700
Bryden Macpherson	73	70	72	65	280	41,700
Lucas Lee	70	70	71	70	281	37,200
Yi Keun Chang	75	71	66	70	282	32,400
Xin-Jun Zhang	69	69	71	73	282	32,400
Gavin Flint	72	73	66	71	282	32,400
Ted Oh	72	69	71	71	283	26,400
Zheng Ouyang	72	71	69	71	283	26,400
David McKenzie	71	70	70	73	284	21,600
Chris Campbell	71	75	72	66	284	21,600
Scott Barr	74	73	68	69	284	21,600
Yi Cao	77	70	69	69	285	18,000
Mu Hu	77	73	69	66	285	18,000
Jae Ho Kim	70	75	69	71	285	18,000
*Cheng Jin	70	72	73	70	285	

Cadillac Championship

Qinghe Bay Golf Club, Beijing — September 11-14
Par 37-35–72; 7,151 yards — purse, CN¥1,200,000

	SCORES				TOTAL	MONEY
David McKenzie	67	71	65	69	272	CN¥216,000
Bryden Macpherson	68	70	67	69	274	129,600
Rak Hyun Cho	66	69	72	68	275	81,600
Scott Laycock	72	66	68	70	276	57,600
*Zi Hao Chen	70	64	72	73	279	
Yi Keun Chang	68	69	72	70	279	45,600
Brett Drewitt	70	71	64	74	279	45,600
Aaron Townsend	69	71	72	68	280	40,200
Hao-Tong Li	68	67	77	69	281	36,000
Dong Su	69	69	71	72	281	36,000
Todd Baek	69	73	73	67	282	31,200
Geon Ha Kim	72	73	70	67	282	31,200

	SCORES				TOTAL	MONEY
David Lutterus	74	71	70	69	284	25,200
Alex Hawley	69	70	79	66	284	25,200
Yi Cao	68	72	75	69	284	23,200
*Cheng Jin	77	67	70	70	284	
Mu Hu	71	72	73	69	285	19,200
Bin Yan	70	71	76	68	285	19,200
Seongki Lee	72	74	70	69	285	19,200
Carl Santos-Ocampo	67	69	77	72	285	19,200
Dohyun Kim	73	69	72	71	285	19,200

Jianye Tianzhu Henan Open

St. Andrews Zhengzhou Golf Club, Zhengzhou, Henan — September 25-28
Par 36-36–72; 7,295 yards — purse, CN¥1,200,000

	SCORES				TOTAL	MONEY
Hao-Tong Li	72	67	68	68	275	CN¥216,000
Shih Chang Chan	67	71	69	76	283	129,600
*Cheng Jin	68	69	71	76	284	
Bryden Macpherson	68	73	70	75	286	57,600
Michael Choi	75	74	69	68	286	57,600
Brett Drewitt	73	65	75	73	286	57,600
Dohyun Kim	73	70	67	76	286	57,600
Chien Yao Hung	76	68	67	76	287	40,200
Hao Sheng Hsu	72	72	72	72	288	31,200
Mu Hu	73	70	69	76	288	31,200
Lucas Lee	73	68	76	71	288	31,200
Ze Yu He	75	69	69	75	288	31,200
Jeung-Hun Wang	72	68	72	76	288	31,200
Anthony Kang	68	74	70	76	288	31,200
David McKenzie	74	72	73	70	289	22,800
Hoon Heui Lee	69	69	75	77	290	21,000
Aaron Townsend	76	71	70	73	290	21,000
Ben Lein	76	68	72	75	291	17,400
Ji-Hoon Lee	72	77	70	72	291	17,400
Todd Baek	75	70	69	77	291	17,400
Thomas Petersson	74	72	69	76	291	17,400

Nine Dragons Open

Nine Dragons Golf Club, Jiaxing, Zhejiang — November 13-16
Par 36-36–72 — purse, CN¥1,200,000

	SCORES				TOTAL	MONEY
*Cheng Jin	72	68	72	69	281	
Sam Chien	71	69	73	69	282	¥216,000
Lucas Lee	75	69	68	71	283	129,600
Jae Ho Kim	71	71	68	74	284	81,600
Hao-Tong Li	73	73	73	66	285	57,600
Raymond Beaufils	74	74	70	68	286	45,600
Alex Hawley	69	74	73	70	286	45,600
Brett Drewitt	73	70	75	70	288	38,700
Bryden Macpherson	71	73	72	72	288	38,700
*Tianlang Guan	73	73	71	73	290	
Todd Baek	72	71	75	73	291	31,200
Dongha Lee	73	72	72	74	291	31,200
Michael Choi	75	71	72	73	291	31,200

	SCORES				TOTAL	MONEY
Ding Gen Chen	70	75	72	74	291	31,200
Gavin Flint	73	73	77	69	292	22,500
Juhyun Hong	73	68	74	77	292	22,500
Quincy Quek	72	74	74	72	292	22,500
Tsung Chieh Wang	74	72	70	76	292	22,500
Jamie Arnold	74	70	74	75	293	18,600
Xiao Ma Chen	76	73	71	73	293	18,600

Hainan Open

Sanya LuHuitou Golf Club, Hainan
Par 36-36–72

November 20-23
purse, CN¥1,200,000

	SCORES				TOTAL	MONEY
Hao-Tong Li	71	68	69	70	278	CN¥216,000
Dohyun Kim	72	75	70	67	284	105,600
Brett Drewitt	69	70	75	70	284	105,600
Ben Lein	75	72	70	69	286	57,600
Ryan McCarthy	76	70	70	73	289	42,150
Mu Hu	75	69	76	69	289	42,150
Sean Yu	75	76	69	69	289	42,150
Raymond Beaufils	74	73	68	74	289	42,150
Todd Baek	72	73	75	70	290	32,400
Dong Su	73	71	74	72	290	32,400
*Cheng Jin	72	72	74	72	290	
Quincy Quek	70	73	74	73	290	32,400
Jihoon Lee	69	76	74	72	291	25,200
Hui Lin Zhang	74	72	74	71	291	25,200
Sam Chien	76	73	72	70	291	25,200
Gavin Flint	76	75	68	73	292	21,000
Kook Hyan Kim	72	75	73	72	292	21,000
Bin Yan	76	75	69	73	293	18,600
Ze Yu He	75	76	69	73	293	18,600
William Liu	76	73	74	71	294	15,600
Fei Hao Yang	75	74	75	70	294	15,600
*Tianlang Guan	74	75	73	72	294	
T.K. Kim	73	70	76	75	294	15,600

CTS Tycoon Championship

CTS Tycoon Golf Club, D&Y Course, Shenzhen, Guangdong
Par 36-36–72

November 27-30
purse, CN¥1,200,000

	SCORES				TOTAL	MONEY
Hao-Tong Li	65	70	73	69	277	CN¥216,000
Raymond Beaufils	73	69	69	71	282	129,600
Mu Hu	69	72	68	75	284	62,400
Lucas Lee	70	71	71	72	284	62,400
Todd Baek	70	74	70	70	284	62,400
T.K. Kim	73	68	72	72	285	41,700
Tsung-Chieh Wang	74	70	71	70	285	41,700
Dong Su	71	71	73	71	286	34,800
Hao-Sheng Hsu	76	68	71	71	286	34,800
Jihoon Lee	69	73	74	70	286	34,800
Tim Stewart	71	73	72	73	289	26,400
Wei-Tze Yeh	71	76	76	66	289	26,400
Thomas Petersson	72	74	70	73	289	26,400

	SCORES				TOTAL	MONEY
Ben Lein	76	69	70	74	289	26,400
Zi-Hao Chen	77	72	72	69	290	20,400
Ryan McCarthy	73	74	74	69	290	20,400
Ze-Cheng Dou	72	74	75	69	290	20,400
*Tianlang Guan	77	73	71	69	290	
Sam Chien	73	72	71	75	291	16,200
Kook-Hyan Kim	72	71	74	74	291	16,200
Sean Yu	71	70	74	76	291	16,200
Hong-Sheng Tseng	75	70	73	73	291	16,200
*Cheng Jin	72	75	74	70	291	

Japan Tour

Enjoy Jakarta Indonesia PGA Championship

See OneAsia Tour section.

Token Homemate Cup

Token Tado Country Club, Nagoya, Mie — April 17-20
Par 35-36–71; 7,109 yards — purse, ¥130,000,000

	SCORES				TOTAL	MONEY
Yusaku Miyazato	71	66	68	65	270	¥26,000,000
Hiroshi Iwata	68	70	67	67	272	13,000,000
Koumei Oda	71	69	68	65	273	8,840,000
Nobuhiro Masuda	69	66	72	67	274	5,720,000
Adam Bland	69	68	68	69	274	5,720,000
Tadahiro Takayama	70	66	69	70	275	4,680,000
Katsumasa Miyamoto	69	72	71	64	276	3,831,750
Yuta Ikeda	67	68	74	67	276	3,831,750
Seung-Hyuk Kim	70	67	72	67	276	3,831,750
Hidemasa Hoshino	68	69	70	69	276	3,831,750
Michael Hendry	69	68	72	68	277	2,886,000
Satoshi Kodaira	71	68	70	68	277	2,886,000
K.T. Kim	68	70	70	69	277	2,886,000
Toru Taniguchi	66	71	75	66	278	2,106,000
Yoshitaka Takeya	71	65	73	69	278	2,106,000
Kunihiro Kamii	70	71	67	70	278	2,106,000
Tomohiro Kondo	68	72	65	73	278	2,106,000
Daisuke Maruyama	67	68	69	74	278	2,106,000
Ryuji Masaoka	71	69	71	69	280	1,360,666
Yujiro Ohori	66	67	77	70	280	1,360,666
Hiroyuki Fujita	71	66	73	70	280	1,360,666
Toshinori Muto	67	66	77	70	280	1,360,666
Seung-Eun Lim	69	71	73	67	280	1,360,666
Ashun Wu	69	69	72	70	280	1,360,666

	SCORES				TOTAL	MONEY
Kiyoshi Miyazato	66	72	72	70	280	1,360,666
Yui Ueda	71	68	70	71	280	1,360,666
Nobuhiro Tsujimura	72	66	68	74	280	1,360,666

Tsuruya Open

Yamanohara Golf Club, Kawanishi, Hyogo
Par 35-36–71; 6,804 yards

April 24-27
purse, ¥110,000,000

	SCORES				TOTAL	MONEY
Hiroyuki Fujita	66	72	66	67	271	¥22,000,000
Sang-Hyun Park	72	67	68	64	271	11,000,000
(Fujita defeated Park on first playoff hole.)						
Hideto Tanihara	67	71	70	64	272	6,380,000
Michael Hendry	67	70	66	69	272	6,380,000
Tomohiro Kondo	72	69	68	65	274	3,836,250
Hyung-Sung Kim	74	68	65	67	274	3,836,250
I.J. Jang	71	66	69	68	274	3,836,250
Shingo Katayama	66	68	70	70	274	3,836,250
K.T. Kwon	68	71	69	68	276	2,992,000
Koumei Oda	70	69	68	69	276	2,992,000
Adam Bland	73	69	70	65	277	2,244,000
Ryoma Iwai	68	70	73	66	277	2,244,000
David Oh	67	71	71	68	277	2,244,000
Han Lee	69	69	67	72	277	2,244,000
Atomu Shigenaga	68	66	68	75	277	2,244,000
Shunsuke Sonoda	70	68	71	69	278	1,672,000
Ryuji Masaoka	71	71	66	70	278	1,672,000
Kyoung-Hoon Lee	72	69	65	72	278	1,672,000
Yoshinori Fujimoto	70	70	73	66	279	1,216,285
Jay Choi	71	71	67	70	279	1,216,285
Seung-Su Han	69	69	70	71	279	1,216,285
Kazuhiro Yamashita	71	70	66	72	279	1,216,285
Akio Sadakata	68	67	70	74	279	1,216,285
Azuma Yano	70	68	68	73	279	1,216,285
Do-Hoon Kim	68	67	69	75	279	1,216,285

The Crowns

Nagoya Golf Club, Wago Course, Togo, Aichi
Par 35-35–70; 6,545 yards

May 1-4
purse, ¥120,000,000

	SCORES				TOTAL	MONEY
Hyung-Sung Kim	64	67	70	68	269	¥24,000,000
I.J. Jang	64	68	72	69	273	12,000,000
Yasuharu Imano	67	69	69	69	274	8,160,000
Hiroshi Iwata	65	69	72	69	275	5,760,000
Brad Kennedy	65	73	71	67	276	4,360,000
Koumei Oda	72	65	70	69	276	4,360,000
Ryo Ishikawa	66	68	70	72	276	4,360,000
Kyoung-Hoon Lee	72	66	73	66	277	3,660,000
Toshinori Muto	68	71	70	69	278	3,024,000
Steven Conran	68	68	72	70	278	3,024,000
Hideto Tanihara	72	67	69	70	278	3,024,000
Toru Taniguchi	67	69	69	73	278	3,024,000
Toru Suzuki	70	72	66	71	279	2,424,000
Sang-Hyun Park	68	73	71	68	280	1,944,000

	SCORES				TOTAL	MONEY
Yusaku Miyazato	67	74	69	70	280	1,944,000
Atomu Shigenaga	68	68	73	71	280	1,944,000
Katsunori Kuwabara	73	69	66	72	280	1,944,000
Tomohiro Kondo	66	68	69	77	280	1,944,000
K.T. Kim	69	68	76	68	281	1,368,000
Wen-Chong Liang	69	68	75	69	281	1,368,000
Satoshi Tomiyama	70	68	73	70	281	1,368,000
Shingo Katayama	72	70	67	72	281	1,368,000
Yoshinori Fujimoto	69	68	71	73	281	1,368,000
Michio Matsumura	60	71	74	76	281	1,368,000
Young-Han Song	70	73	68	71	282	1,056,000
S.K. Ho	73	68	69	72	282	1,056,000

Kansai Open

Rokko Country Club, Nishinomiya, Hyogo — May 22-25
Par 36-36–72; 7,037 yards — purse, ¥60,000,000

	SCORES				TOTAL	MONEY
Koumei Oda	71	66	69	67	273	¥12,000,000
Yoshinori Fujimoto	67	69	66	73	275	6,000,000
Brad Kennedy	70	67	71	68	276	3,120,000
Hiroo Kawai	69	69	69	69	276	3,120,000
Dong-Kyu Jang	69	66	72	69	276	3,120,000
Tetsuji Hiratsuka	67	68	69	73	277	2,160,000
Yasuharu Imano	71	69	70	68	278	1,643,000
Hiroshi Iwata	69	71	69	69	278	1,643,000
Tadahiro Takayama	68	69	71	70	278	1,643,000
S.K. Ho	69	69	70	70	278	1,643,000
Hideto Tanihara	69	72	67	70	278	1,643,000
Katsumasa Miyamoto	71	70	66	71	278	1,643,000
Akio Sadakata	70	68	73	68	279	1,012,000
Jung-Gon Hwang	73	68	70	68	279	1,012,000
K.T. Kim	71	70	68	70	279	1,012,000
Ashun Wu	67	72	69	71	279	1,012,000
Daisuke Kataoka	67	69	70	73	279	1,012,000
Tomohiro Kondo	69	70	68	72	279	1,012,000
Shigeru Nonaka	70	70	72	68	280	663,428
I.J. Jang	68	72	70	70	280	663,428
Min-Gyu Cho	70	71	69	70	280	663,428
Ryuko Tokimatsu	70	72	66	72	280	663,428
K.T. Kwon	71	68	69	72	280	663,428
Yoshitaka Takeya	69	72	67	72	280	663,428
Adam Bland	71	67	69	73	280	663,428

Gateway to the Open Mizuno Open

JFE Setonaikai Golf Club, Kasaoka, Okayama — May 29-June 1
Par 36-36–72; 7,382 yards — purse, ¥110,000,000

	SCORES				TOTAL	MONEY
Dong-Kyu Jang	70	67	67	69	273	¥22,000,000
Juvic Pagunsan	68	73	65	70	276	11,000,000
Hyung-Tae Kim	72	71	68	66	277	6,380,000
Tomohiro Kondo	69	71	70	67	277	6,380,000
In-Hoi Hur	69	69	72	70	280	4,400,000
Yui Ueda	66	72	73	70	281	3,648,333

	SCORES				TOTAL	MONEY
Michael Hendry	69	73	68	71	281	3,648,333
Hiroshi Iwata	66	69	73	73	281	3,648,333
Tadahiro Takayama	69	70	74	69	282	2,772,000
Young-Han Song	72	71	70	69	282	2,772,000
Taichi Teshima	67	68	75	72	282	2,772,000
Nobuhiro Masuda	68	74	68	72	282	2,772,000
Kurt Barnes	69	75	72	67	283	1,974,500
Atomu Shigenaga	73	73	69	68	283	1,974,500
K.T. Kim	74	70	69	70	283	1,974,500
Ashun Wu	69	74	70	70	283	1,974,500
Steven Conran	71	74	70	69	284	1,433,666
Michio Matsumura	70	71	74	69	284	1,433,666
Koki Shiomi	73	73	68	70	284	1,433,666
Jung-Gon Hwang	69	71	74	70	284	1,433,666
Yusaku Miyazato	72	70	71	71	284	1,433,666
K.T. Kwon	73	68	71	72	284	1,433,666
Wen-Chong Liang	75	70	71	69	285	1,048,666
Yoshinobu Tsukada	70	71	76	68	285	1,048,666
Kyoung-Hoon Lee	72	72	70	71	285	1,048,666

Japan PGA Championship

Golden Valley Golf Club, Hyogo — June 5-8
Par 36-36–72; 7,233 yards — purse, ¥150,000,000

	SCORES				TOTAL	MONEY
Taichi Teshima	71	68	69	71	279	¥30,000,000
Kyoung-Hoon Lee	72	69	68	71	280	12,600,000
Koumei Oda	71	71	67	71	280	12,600,000
Dong-Kyu Jang	79	69	67	68	283	7,200,000
Hyung-Tae Kim	69	69	72	74	284	5,700,000
Yusaku Miyazato	73	69	71	71	284	5,700,000
Katsumasa Miyamoto	75	72	72	66	285	4,762,500
Toru Taniguchi	68	71	76	70	285	4,762,500
Yoshinori Fujimoto	74	70	75	68	287	4,080,000
K.T. Kwon	74	74	68	71	287	4,080,000
David Oh	77	69	74	68	288	3,330,000
Hideto Tanihara	75	72	71	70	288	3,330,000
Michio Matsumura	70	73	72	73	288	3,330,000
Han Lee	75	71	74	69	289	2,292,857
Scott Strange	74	71	74	70	289	2,292,857
Hiroyuki Fujita	73	69	76	71	289	2,292,857
Yuta Ikeda	71	75	75	68	289	2,292,857
Shinji Tomimura	72	76	68	73	289	2,292,857
Ho-Sung Choi	72	74	69	74	289	2,292,857
Keiichiro Fukabori	72	69	73	75	289	2,292,857
I.J. Jang	75	69	75	71	290	1,590,000
Tomohiro Kondo	78	70	74	68	290	1,590,000
Jung-Gon Hwang	78	69	70	73	290	1,590,000
Michael Hendry	76	72	69	73	290	1,590,000
Hiroo Kawai	76	67	76	72	291	1,290,000
Hidemasa Hoshino	74	73	75	69	291	1,290,000
Steven Conran	74	68	73	76	291	1,290,000

Japan Golf Tour Championship

Shishido Hills Country Club, West Course, Kasama, Ibaraki — June 19-22
Par 36-36–72; 7,402 yards — purse, ¥150,000,000

	SCORES				TOTAL	MONEY
Yoshitaka Takeya	69	65	69	68	271	¥30,000,000
Sang-Hee Lee	71	68	67	67	273	15,000,000
Hideto Tanihara	67	72	69	68	276	8,700,000
Dong-Kyu Jang	68	66	69	73	276	8,700,000
Prayad Marksaeng	67	70	70	71	278	6,000,000
K.T. Kim	71	68	67	73	279	5,400,000
K.T. Kwon	71	70	72	67	280	4,421,250
Daisuke Maruyama	71	71	70	68	280	4,421,250
Hiroshi Iwata	76	68	65	71	280	4,421,250
Tetsuji Hiratsuka	72	67	70	71	280	4,421,250
Thanyakon Khrongpha	68	68	72	73	281	3,630,000
I.J. Jang	69	72	73	68	282	3,180,000
Kazuhiro Yamashita	71	72	68	71	282	3,180,000
Juvic Pagunsan	71	73	69	70	283	2,655,000
Ryuji Masaoka	71	71	70	71	283	2,655,000
Ho-Sung Choi	71	73	71	69	284	2,148,000
Hyung-Sung Kim	67	72	73	72	284	2,148,000
Hidemasa Hoshino	67	72	73	72	284	2,148,000
Masahiro Kawamura	70	69	72	73	284	2,148,000
Hyun-Woo Ryu	71	74	67	72	284	2,148,000
Tadahiro Takayama	70	71	76	68	285	1,590,000
Yasuharu Imano	68	72	73	72	285	1,590,000
Taichi Teshima	68	72	73	72	285	1,590,000
Scott Strange	70	73	69	73	285	1,590,000
Shota Akiyoshi	72	73	70	71	286	1,230,000
Sang-Hyun Park	74	70	70	72	286	1,230,000
Seung-Hyuk Kim	71	70	72	73	286	1,230,000
Yoshinori Fujimoto	70	71	72	73	286	1,230,000
Masamichi Uehira	68	70	71	77	286	1,230,000

Nagashima Shigeo Invitational

North Country Golf Club, Chitose, Hokkaido — July 3-6
Par 36-35–71; 7,050 yards — purse, ¥200,000,000

	SCORES				TOTAL	MONEY
Ryo Ishikawa	69	71	67	67	274	¥40,000,000
Koumei Oda	69	67	69	69	274	20,000,000
(Ishikawa defeated Oda on third playoff hole.)						
K.T. Kwon	69	74	69	65	277	11,600,000
Kazuhiro Yamashita	67	69	70	71	277	11,600,000
David Oh	65	74	73	66	278	8,000,000
Shunsuke Sonoda	72	69	71	67	279	6,900,000
Kodai Ichihara	71	68	72	68	279	6,900,000
Koki Shiomi	73	70	71	66	280	4,513,333
Toru Taniguchi	69	68	76	67	280	4,513,333
Kurt Barnes	69	74	71	66	280	4,513,333
Ryutaro Nagano	72	72	69	67	280	4,513,333
I.J. Jang	71	72	70	67	280	4,513,333
Scott Strange	68	72	71	69	280	4,513,333
Daisuke Kataoka	72	69	70	69	280	4,513,333
Prayad Marksaeng	73	71	67	69	280	4,513,333
Han Lee	67	71	70	72	280	4,513,333
Hideki Matsuyama	71	71	71	68	281	2,770,000

	SCORES				TOTAL	MONEY
K.T. Kim	69	69	74	69	281	2,770,000
Brad Kennedy	70	73	67	71	281	2,770,000
Yoshinori Fujimoto	67	69	72	73	281	2,770,000
Hiroo Kawai	73	69	70	70	282	2,280,000
Tadahiro Takayama	70	72	70	70	282	2,280,000
Hideto Tanihara	73	70	71	69	283	1,860,000
Hyun-Woo Ryu	72	71	73	67	283	1,860,000
Kiyoshi Murota	72	70	71	70	283	1,860,000
Yosuke Tsukada	68	74	70	71	283	1,860,000

Dunlop Srixon Fukushima Open

Grandee Nasushirakawa Golf Club, Nishigo, Fukushima — July 31-August 3
Par 36-36–72; 6,961 yards — purse, ¥50,000,000

	SCORES				TOTAL	MONEY
Satoshi Kodaira	72	68	64	68	272	¥10,000,000
Yuki Inamori	72	69	67	66	274	2,920,000
Hiroshi Iwata	70	64	73	67	274	2,920,000
Kazuhiro Yamashita	74	67	66	67	274	2,920,000
Ryosuke Kinoshita	68	69	67	70	274	2,920,000
Ryutaro Nagano	68	66	67	73	274	2,920,000
Kazuhiko Hosokawa	74	67	70	64	275	1,473,750
Katsumasa Miyamoto	74	63	71	67	275	1,473,750
Daisuke Kataoka	71	67	68	69	275	1,473,750
Naomi Ohta	71	70	63	71	275	1,473,750
Satoshi Tomiyama	70	70	72	64	276	1,060,000
Atomu Shigenaga	68	69	70	69	276	1,060,000
Wen-Chong Liang	65	75	67	69	276	1,060,000
Thanyakon Khrongpha	69	65	67	75	276	1,060,000
Kodai Ichihara	66	70	73	68	277	718,571
Adam Bland	72	70	66	69	277	718,571
K.T. Kwon	68	69	70	70	277	718,571
Sung-Joon Park	73	69	65	70	277	718,571
Yasuki Hiramoto	68	71	68	70	277	718,571
Koumei Oda	72	65	69	71	277	718,571
Yuki Kono	70	69	67	71	277	718,571
Taichi Teshima	64	71	74	69	278	482,000
Tadahiro Takayama	68	68	72	70	278	482,000
S.K. Ho	69	71	67	71	278	482,000
Yuichiro Nishi	70	68	68	72	278	482,000
Azuma Yano	72	64	68	74	278	482,000

RZ Everlasting KBC Augusta

Keya Golf Club, Shima, Fukuoka — August 28-31
Par 36-36–72; 7,150 yards — purse, ¥110,000,000

	SCORES				TOTAL	MONEY
Hiroyuki Fujita	71	66	74	65	276	¥22,000,000
Wen-Chong Liang	70	70	67	69	276	11,000,000
(Fujita defeated Liang on fifth playoff hole.)						
Yosuke Tsukada	72	69	70	66	277	5,280,000
Toshinori Muto	69	72	68	68	277	5,280,000
Yusaku Miyazato	74	67	67	69	277	5,280,000
Hyung-Sung Kim	65	69	71	72	277	5,280,000
Adam Bland	71	70	72	65	278	3,242,250

	SCORES				TOTAL	MONEY
Sang-Hyun Park	68	71	72	67	278	3,242,250
Yuta Ikeda	69	69	72	68	278	3,242,250
Ryutaro Nagano	71	69	70	68	278	3,242,250
Hiroshi Iwata	71	68	74	66	279	2,552,000
Michael Hendry	72	67	69	71	279	2,552,000
Shota Akiyoshi	71	68	73	68	280	1,800,857
Seung-Hyuk Kim	69	70	73	68	280	1,800,857
Kunihiro Kamii	70	72	70	68	280	1,800,857
Tomohiro Kondo	69	71	75	65	280	1,800,857
Toru Suzuki	69	70	71	70	280	1,800,857
Yuki Inamori	66	73	69	72	280	1,800,857
Shigeru Nonaka	69	69	68	74	280	1,800,857
Jung-Gon Hwang	69	70	72	70	281	1,298,000
Prayad Marksaeng	72	69	70	70	281	1,298,000
Tetsuji Hiratsuka	69	71	69	72	281	1,298,000
Yoshikazu Haku	68	73	72	69	282	865,000
Kazuhiro Yamashita	73	69	72	68	282	865,000
Ryosuke Kinoshita	72	70	70	70	282	865,000
In-Hoi Hur	71	70	71	70	282	865,000
Azuma Yano	74	66	72	70	282	865,000
Kyoung-Hoon Lee	71	71	73	67	282	865,000
Katsumasa Miyamoto	70	69	76	67	282	865,000
Jinichiro Kozuma	70	70	71	71	282	865,000
Juvic Pagunsan	69	70	71	72	282	865,000
Keiichiro Fukabori	71	70	68	73	282	865,000
Yoshitaka Takeya	71	68	68	75	282	865,000

Fujisankei Classic

Fujizakura Country Club, Fujikawaguchiko, Yamanashi — September 4-7
Par 35-36–71; 7,437 yards — purse, ¥110,000,000

	SCORES				TOTAL	MONEY
Hiroshi Iwata	69	69	70	66	274	¥22,000,000
In-Hoi Hur	71	64	72	68	275	11,000,000
Brendan Jones	71	70	68	67	276	7,480,000
Daisuke Kataoka	69	71	69	70	279	4,546,666
Yuta Ikeda	68	69	69	73	279	4,546,666
Hyung-Sung Kim	68	71	69	71	279	4,546,666
Ryuji Masaoka	72	70	72	66	280	3,362,333
Yosuke Tsukada	69	74	68	69	280	3,362,333
Yoshinobu Tsukada	72	67	69	72	280	3,362,333
Yoshinori Fujimoto	70	70	72	69	281	2,882,000
Hyun-Woo Ryu	67	68	75	72	282	2,552,000
Seung-Hyuk Kim	70	64	75	73	282	2,552,000
Taichi Teshima	73	69	71	70	283	1,974,500
Kyoung-Hoon Lee	73	68	71	71	283	1,974,500
Toru Taniguchi	66	76	70	71	283	1,974,500
Tomohiro Kondo	69	70	70	74	283	1,974,500
Ippei Koike	75	68	71	70	284	1,523,500
Akio Sadakata	71	69	73	71	284	1,523,500
I.J. Jang	73	68	71	72	284	1,523,500
Scott Strange	69	71	71	73	284	1,523,500
Toru Suzuki	68	73	73	71	285	1,100,000
Han Lee	70	71	73	71	285	1,100,000
Satoshi Kodaira	70	73	71	71	285	1,100,000
Kazuhiro Yamashita	75	68	73	69	285	1,100,000
Yoshikazu Haku	69	72	75	69	285	1,100,000
Adam Bland	69	69	72	75	285	1,100,000

ANA Open

Sapporo Golf Club, Wattsu Course, Kitahiroshima, Hokkaido
Par 36-36–72; 7,063 yards

September 18-21
purse, ¥110,000,000

	SCORES				TOTAL	MONEY
Katsumasa Miyamoto	68	67	68	67	270	¥22,000,000
Hideto Tanihara	66	68	69	67	270	11,000,000
(Miyamoto defeated Tanihara on first playoff hole.)						
Wen-Chong Liang	71	69	65	67	272	5,720,000
Hyung-Sung Kim	65	71	68	68	272	5,720,000
Yoshinori Fujimoto	70	65	69	68	272	5,720,000
Sang-Hee Lee	66	69	69	69	273	3,960,000
Nobuhiro Masuda	69	72	63	70	274	3,630,000
I.J. Jang	69	70	69	67	275	2,777,500
K.T. Kim	71	69	67	68	275	2,777,500
Taichi Teshima	69	67	70	69	275	2,777,500
Prayad Marksaeng	68	70	69	68	275	2,777,500
Kyoung-Hoon Lee	70	69	66	70	275	2,777,500
Hiroyuki Fujita	70	72	63	70	275	2,777,500
Hidemasa Hoshino	74	69	68	66	277	2,002,000
Sang-Moon Bae	71	71	69	67	278	1,580,857
Ho-Sung Choi	69	70	71	68	278	1,580,857
Ryo Ishikawa	69	71	70	68	278	1,580,857
Tomohiro Kondo	65	74	70	69	278	1,580,857
Tadahiro Takayama	75	67	67	69	278	1,580,857
Yuta Ikeda	68	73	67	70	278	1,580,857
Ippei Koike	65	70	70	73	278	1,580,857
Brendan Jones	71	73	67	68	279	1,034,000
Hyung-Tae Kim	69	75	68	67	279	1,034,000
Kazuhiko Hosokawa	69	72	68	70	279	1,034,000
Shinji Tomimura	67	71	70	71	279	1,034,000
Yasuki Hiramoto	71	73	71	64	279	1,034,000
Masamichi Uehira	70	66	70	73	279	1,034,000

Asia-Pacific Diamond Cup

Otone Country Club, West Course, Ibaraki
Par 35-36–71; 7,117 yards

September 25-28
purse, ¥150,000,000

	SCORES				TOTAL	MONEY
Hiroyuki Fujita	68	71	73	66	278	¥30,000,000
Kiradech Aphibarnrat	71	72	70	67	280	11,850,000
Jason Knutzon	71	71	70	68	280	11,850,000
S.K. Ho	68	70	73	69	280	11,850,000
Kyoung-Hoon Lee	72	68	72	69	281	4,987,500
Seuk-Hyun Baek	70	69	73	69	281	4,987,500
Yoshitaka Takeya	73	67	70	71	281	4,987,500
Yoshinobu Tsukada	71	71	68	71	281	4,987,500
Cameron Smith	66	74	72	70	282	2,313,750
Adam Bland	69	68	74	71	282	2,313,750
Juvic Pagunsan	69	72	70	71	282	2,313,750
Shingo Katayama	71	71	69	71	282	2,313,750
Scott Strange	70	71	70	71	282	2,313,750
Yusaku Miyazato	71	73	66	72	282	2,313,750
Kazuhiro Yamashita	72	69	68	73	282	2,313,750
Wen-Chong Liang	70	69	69	74	282	2,313,750
Hideto Tanihara	73	70	71	69	283	1,431,000
Javi Colomo	70	70	73	70	283	1,431,000
Prayad Marksaeng	69	69	75	70	283	1,431,000

	SCORES				TOTAL	MONEY
Arjun Atwal	69	72	72	70	283	1,431,000
Panuphol Pittayarat	70	72	70	71	283	1,431,000
Michio Matsumura	74	68	71	71	284	1,185,000
I.J. Jang	70	69	73	72	284	1,185,000
Adilson Da Silva	73	67	72	72	284	1,185,000
Masanori Kobayashi	71	69	78	66	284	1,185,000
Hyung-Sung Kim	71	70	70	73	284	1,185,000
Namchoak Tantipokakul	68	74	69	73	284	1,185,000

Top Cup Tokai Classic

Miyoshi Country Club, West Course, Miyoshi, Aichi
Par 36-36–72; 7,315 yards

October 2-5
purse, ¥110,000,000

	SCORES				TOTAL	MONEY
Seung-Hyuk Kim	66	73	72	70	281	¥22,000,000
Jung-Gon Hwang	73	70	69	70	282	9,240,000
Hyung-Sung Kim	69	70	69	74	282	9,240,000
In-Hoi Hur	72	71	67	73	283	5,280,000
Yuta Ikeda	72	71	74	67	284	3,996,666
Yoshinori Fujimoto	69	68	77	70	284	3,996,666
Kazuhiko Hosokawa	71	70	72	71	284	3,996,666
Yoshitaka Takeya	77	69	70	69	285	3,000,250
Sang-Hyun Park	74	67	73	71	285	3,000,250
Taichi Teshima	70	74	70	71	285	3,000,250
Hideto Tanihara	70	70	72	73	285	3,000,250
Do-Hoon Kim	73	73	72	68	286	2,002,000
Prayad Marksaeng	72	75	68	71	286	2,002,000
Koumei Oda	71	67	75	73	286	2,002,000
I.J. Jang	71	75	67	73	286	2,002,000
Nobuhiro Masuda	71	68	73	74	286	2,002,000
Tomohiro Kondo	71	68	72	75	286	2,002,000
Hiroo Kawai	74	68	73	72	287	1,474,000
Ryuichi Oda	70	70	74	73	287	1,474,000
Hidemasa Hoshino	72	72	70	73	287	1,474,000
Tadahiro Takayama	75	71	71	71	288	1,254,000
Yuki Inamori	71	74	72	71	288	1,254,000
Min-Gyu Cho	69	70	73	77	289	1,122,000
Satoshi Kodaira	72	71	75	72	290	924,000
Sang-Hee Lee	73	74	71	72	290	924,000
Brad Kennedy	71	76	71	72	290	924,000
Han Lee	67	74	76	73	290	924,000
Hiroyuki Fujita	71	72	74	73	290	924,000
Akio Sadakata	72	74	70	74	290	924,000

Toshin Golf Tournament

Toshin Golf Club, Central Course, Tomika, Gifu
Par 36-36–72; 7,004 yards

October 9-12
purse, ¥100,000,000

	SCORES				TOTAL	MONEY
In-Hoi Hur	64	63	66	67	260	¥20,000,000
Seung-Hyuk Kim	68	68	61	67	264	10,000,000
Tomohiro Kondo	68	65	68	65	266	6,800,000
Hiroshi Iwata	70	69	64	64	267	3,925,000
Yoshitaka Takeya	69	65	68	65	267	3,925,000
Min-Gyu Cho	68	67	65	67	267	3,925,000

	SCORES				TOTAL	MONEY
Dong-Kyu Jang	68	66	65	68	267	3,925,000
Sang-Hee Lee	69	65	68	66	268	2,830,000
Kazuhiro Yamashita	71	64	66	67	268	2,830,000
Young-Han Song	69	67	65	67	268	2,830,000
Ashun Wu	66	69	69	65	269	2,420,000
Toru Suzuki	67	70	70	63	270	2,020,000
Hidemasa Hoshino	70	64	70	66	270	2,020,000
Do-Hoon Kim	69	67	67	67	270	2,020,000
Ryuji Imada	68	67	68	68	271	1,620,000
Kunihiro Kamii	67	63	71	70	271	1,620,000
Yoshinori Fujimoto	64	67	69	71	271	1,620,000
S.K. Ho	68	71	67	66	272	1,340,000
Koumei Oda	69	68	68	67	272	1,340,000
Ryuichi Oda	65	66	70	71	272	1,340,000
Hiroo Kawai	68	71	67	67	273	1,060,000
Juvic Pagunsan	65	71	69	68	273	1,060,000
Hyung-Sung Kim	68	68	68	69	273	1,060,000
Ryuji Masaoka	67	73	64	69	273	1,060,000
Ho-Sung Choi	68	68	72	66	274	800,000
Wen-Chong Liang	69	69	70	66	274	800,000
Akio Sadakata	71	67	68	68	274	800,000
Tomokazu Yoshinaga	70	69	67	68	274	800,000
Satoshi Tomiyama	66	69	69	70	274	800,000
Daisuke Kataoka	68	69	66	71	274	800,000

Japan Open Championship

Chiba Country Club, Umesato Course, Noda, Chiba
Par 35-35–70; 7,081 yards

October 16-20
purse, ¥200,000,000

	SCORES				TOTAL	MONEY
Yuta Ikeda	64	68	66	72	270	¥40,000,000
Satoshi Kodaira	68	68	69	66	271	18,700,000
Shingo Katayama	68	66	67	70	271	18,700,000
Prayad Marksaeng	63	68	70	72	273	10,000,000
Tomohiro Kondo	68	69	69	68	274	8,400,000
Kiyoshi Murota	70	72	66	67	275	6,500,000
Brad Kennedy	68	70	69	68	275	6,500,000
Shintaro Kai	70	74	67	65	276	4,466,666
Hiroo Kawai	69	71	69	67	276	4,466,666
Yoshinori Fujimoto	71	70	67	68	276	4,466,666
Yoshitaka Takeya	68	71	70	68	277	2,856,000
Min-Gyu Cho	68	71	69	69	277	2,856,000
Hideto Tanihara	69	68	70	70	277	2,856,000
Dong-Kyu Jang	68	69	68	72	277	2,856,000
Ryuko Tokimatsu	65	71	68	73	277	2,856,000
Koumei Oda	68	72	70	68	278	2,000,000
Sang-Hyun Park	68	71	69	70	278	2,000,000
Koichi Kitamura	70	69	68	71	278	2,000,000
Masanori Kobayashi	68	70	69	71	278	2,000,000
Sung-Joon Park	68	69	67	74	278	2,000,000
Hidemasa Hoshino	69	71	70	69	279	1,740,000
Makoto Inoue	72	72	70	66	280	1,640,000
Yasuharu Imano	66	74	71	69	280	1,640,000
Ryuichi Kondo	70	72	68	70	280	1,640,000
Stephen Leaney	71	72	69	69	281	1,520,000
Sang-Hee Lee	67	73	70	71	281	1,520,000
Seung-Hyuk Kim	70	72	68	71	281	1,520,000

Bridgestone Open

Sodegaura Country Club, Chiba
Par 35-36–71; 7,119 yards

October 23-26
purse, ¥150,000,000

	SCORES				TOTAL	MONEY
Koumei Oda	67	65	69	68	269	¥30,000,000
Hiroyuki Fujita	73	68	65	64	270	15,000,000
Yoshitaka Takeya	66	71	69	66	272	7,800,000
Katsumasa Miyamoto	69	68	69	66	272	7,800,000
Shunsuke Sonoda	69	70	66	67	272	7,800,000
Shingo Katayama	73	70	65	65	273	4,788,750
Adam Bland	70	69	68	66	273	4,788,750
K.T. Kim	69	69	67	68	273	4,788,750
Hiroshi Iwata	69	69	67	68	273	4,788,750
Yasuharu Imano	68	69	71	66	274	3,330,000
Koki Shiomi	74	69	66	65	274	3,330,000
Kodai Ichihara	66	73	68	67	274	3,330,000
Brad Kennedy	69	68	69	68	274	3,330,000
Prayad Marksaeng	70	65	71	68	274	3,330,000
Sang-Hee Lee	66	69	72	68	275	2,355,000
Hideto Tanihara	71	66	69	69	275	2,355,000
Ryuichi Oda	71	67	67	70	275	2,355,000
Azuma Yano	65	68	71	71	275	2,355,000
Han Lee	72	69	68	67	276	1,830,000
Tadahiro Takayama	68	70	70	68	276	1,830,000
Kurt Barnes	66	73	69	68	276	1,830,000
Hyun-Woo Ryu	71	68	68	69	276	1,830,000
Yoshinobu Tsukada	69	72	68	68	277	1,267,500
Yosuke Tsukada	71	70	68	68	277	1,267,500
Hidemasa Hoshino	69	69	71	68	277	1,267,500
David Oh	68	72	71	66	277	1,267,500
Akio Sadakata	69	72	67	69	277	1,267,500
Hyung-Sung Kim	71	69	66	71	277	1,267,500
Daisuke Kataoka	70	69	66	72	277	1,267,500
Min-Gyu Cho	72	66	67	72	277	1,267,500

Mynavi ABC Championship

ABC Golf Club, Kato, Hyogo
Par 35-36–71; 7,130 yards

October 30-November 2
purse, ¥150,000,000

	SCORES				TOTAL	MONEY
Ryuichi Oda	68	67	66	62	263	¥30,000,000
Koumei Oda	69	65	70	64	268	12,600,000
Hideto Tanihara	69	66	68	65	268	12,600,000
Yuta Ikeda	66	70	70	65	271	6,600,000
Tomohiro Kondo	67	71	66	67	271	6,600,000
Brendan Jones	70	66	68	68	272	5,175,000
S.K. Ho	66	69	66	71	272	5,175,000
Kyoung-Hoon Lee	66	67	76	64	273	4,245,000
Akio Sadakata	66	69	69	69	273	4,245,000
Jung-Gon Hwang	69	67	68	69	273	4,245,000
Yoshinori Fujimoto	68	70	70	66	274	3,180,000
Kiradech Aphibarnrat	69	72	67	66	274	3,180,000
Taichi Teshima	69	68	69	68	274	3,180,000
Hyun-Woo Ryu	68	70	67	69	274	3,180,000
Hiroshi Iwata	70	66	71	68	275	2,430,000
Tadahiro Takayama	71	70	67	67	275	2,430,000
Young-Han Song	71	65	70	69	275	2,430,000

	SCORES				TOTAL	MONEY
Prayad Marksaeng	71	71	69	65	276	1,950,000
Yosuke Tsukada	75	67	67	67	276	1,950,000
Hiroyuki Fujita	68	70	71	67	276	1,950,000
David Oh	69	70	67	70	276	1,950,000
Ho-Sung Choi	70	69	71	67	277	1,530,000
Min-Gyu Cho	72	71	67	67	277	1,530,000
Yusaku Miyazato	69	69	73	66	277	1,530,000
Hyung-Sung Kim	71	71	67	69	278	1,320,000
Yuki Inamori	70	71	68	69	278	1,320,000

Heiwa PGM Championship

Miho Golf Club, Kasumigaura, Ibaraki — November 6-9
Par 36-35–71; 6,968 yards — purse, ¥200,000,000

	SCORES				TOTAL	MONEY
Tomohiro Kondo	68	66	64	66	264	¥40,000,000
Hideto Tanihara	64	68	68	68	268	14,400,000
Hyun-Woo Ryu	67	65	69	67	268	14,400,000
Yoshinori Fujimoto	68	68	64	68	268	14,400,000
Brad Kennedy	64	72	64	70	270	8,000,000
Taichi Teshima	68	67	70	66	271	7,200,000
Min-Gyu Cho	68	69	69	66	272	5,895,000
Adam Bland	70	65	70	67	272	5,895,000
Katsumasa Miyamoto	69	65	71	67	272	5,895,000
Shunsuke Sonoda	64	69	68	71	272	5,895,000
J.B. Park	68	69	71	65	273	4,640,000
Koumei Oda	66	69	69	69	273	4,640,000
Hiroyuki Fujita	69	67	70	68	274	4,040,000
Atomu Shigenaga	68	70	72	65	275	3,440,000
Daisuke Kataoka	68	69	72	66	275	3,440,000
Yosuke Tsukada	71	68	68	68	275	3,440,000
I.J. Jang	67	72	72	65	276	2,445,000
Jung-Gon Hwang	68	66	74	68	276	2,445,000
Han Lee	71	71	69	65	276	2,445,000
Steven Conran	70	70	68	68	276	2,445,000
Prayad Marksaeng	69	72	67	68	276	2,445,000
Yasuharu Imano	66	72	68	70	276	2,445,000
Shugo Imahira	71	68	67	70	276	2,445,000
Satoshi Tomiyama	67	66	72	71	276	2,445,000
Shingo Katayama	73	70	68	66	277	1,560,000
Tadahiro Takayama	67	71	70	69	277	1,560,000
Toshinori Muto	69	73	66	69	277	1,560,000
Kodai Ichihara	71	65	70	71	277	1,560,000
Nobuhiro Masuda	73	69	71	64	277	1,560,000
Keiichiro Fukabori	68	70	68	71	277	1,560,000
Toru Taniguchi	70	68	67	72	277	1,560,000

Mitsui Sumitomo VISA Taiheiyo Masters

Taiheiyo Club, Gotemba Course, Gotemba, Shizuoka
Par 36-36–72; 7,246 yards

November 13-16
purse, ¥150,000,000

	SCORES				TOTAL	MONEY
David Oh	70	68	68	70	276	¥30,000,000
Toshinori Muto	71	68	69	69	277	15,000,000
Tomohiro Kondo	71	71	69	67	278	8,700,000
Han Lee	74	66	67	71	278	8,700,000
Wen-Chong Liang	72	67	68	72	279	6,000,000
Tadahiro Takayama	72	71	69	68	280	4,788,750
Michio Matsumura	77	67	66	70	280	4,788,750
Kazuhiro Yamashita	68	71	70	71	280	4,788,750
Ashun Wu	71	68	69	72	280	4,788,750
Yosuke Tsukada	67	73	76	65	281	3,330,000
Hidemasa Hoshino	73	70	70	68	281	3,330,000
Sang-Hee Lee	70	73	69	69	281	3,330,000
Yusaku Miyazato	70	73	67	71	281	3,330,000
Hyun-Woo Ryu	71	70	68	72	281	3,330,000
Daisuke Maruyama	71	71	74	66	282	2,355,000
Ryuichi Oda	74	68	71	69	282	2,355,000
Min-Gyu Cho	73	71	68	70	282	2,355,000
Yuta Ikeda	71	70	68	73	282	2,355,000
S.K. Ho	71	70	74	68	283	1,830,000
Hiroshi Iwata	72	71	71	69	283	1,830,000
J.B. Park	70	72	71	70	283	1,830,000
Toru Taniguchi	72	70	71	70	283	1,830,000
Kyoung-Hoon Lee	73	72	70	69	284	1,530,000
Satoshi Tomiyama	75	72	67	71	285	1,260,000
Bubba Watson	67	70	77	71	285	1,260,000
Kazuhiko Hosokawa	72	71	73	69	285	1,260,000
Yuki Kono	71	72	71	71	285	1,260,000
Hideto Tanihara	71	74	69	71	285	1,260,000
Jung-Gon Hwang	72	70	70	73	285	1,260,000

Dunlop Phoenix

Phoenix Country Club, Miyazaki
Par 36-35–71; 7,027 yards

November 20-23
purse, ¥200,000,000

	SCORES				TOTAL	MONEY
Hideki Matsuyama	68	64	67	70	269	¥40,000,000
Hiroshi Iwata	68	69	69	63	269	20,000,000
(Matsuyama defeated Iwata on first playoff hole.)						
Brendan Jones	65	69	68	68	270	11,600,000
Jordan Spieth	69	64	68	69	270	11,600,000
In-Hoi Hur	67	66	70	69	272	8,000,000
Yusaku Miyazato	68	72	69	64	273	6,900,000
Toshinori Muto	68	69	68	68	273	6,900,000
Chris Stroud	67	70	71	66	274	6,100,000
Tadahiro Takayama	74	66	70	66	276	5,440,000
Shingo Katayama	70	66	73	67	276	5,440,000
Brad Kennedy	70	68	69	70	277	4,440,000
Yuki Inamori	64	74	68	71	277	4,440,000
Koumei Oda	66	71	68	72	277	4,440,000
Yosuke Tsukada	70	69	71	68	278	3,240,000
Masahiro Kawamura	67	74	69	68	278	3,240,000
Seung-Hyuk Kim	70	71	69	68	278	3,240,000
Hiroyuki Fujita	70	71	68	69	278	3,240,000

	SCORES				TOTAL	MONEY
Min-Gyu Cho	69	68	69	72	278	3,240,000
Hyung-Sung Kim	68	71	71	69	279	2,680,000
Gonzalo Fernandez-Castano	74	69	68	69	280	2,440,000
Yuta Ikeda	69	65	73	73	280	2,440,000
Steven Conran	67	71	72	71	281	1,880,000
Prayad Marksaeng	70	71	71	69	281	1,880,000
Jung-Gon Hwang	70	70	70	71	281	1,880,000
Ryuichi Oda	71	70	68	72	281	1,880,000
David Smail	69	67	70	75	281	1,880,000
J.B. Park	69	70	68	74	281	1,880,000

Casio World Open

Kochi Kuroshio Country Club, Geisei, Kochi
Par 36-36–72; 7,315 yards

November 27-30
purse, ¥200,000,000

	SCORES				TOTAL	MONEY
Shingo Katayama	70	64	72	65	271	¥40,000,000
Satoshi Tomiyama	67	70	70	67	274	20,000,000
Tomohiro Kondo	70	69	71	67	277	8,516,666
Young-Han Song	71	69	69	68	277	8,516,666
Hyung-Sung Kim	69	70	69	69	277	8,516,666
Thanyakon Khrongpha	69	69	69	70	277	8,516,666
Satoshi Kodaira	68	70	67	72	277	8,516,666
Yasuki Hiramoto	68	69	68	72	277	8,516,666
Hiroyuki Fujita	71	72	69	66	278	4,840,000
I.J. Jang	71	70	70	67	278	4,840,000
Shinichi Yokota	66	70	72	70	278	4,840,000
Toshinori Muto	71	70	67	70	278	4,840,000
Kenichi Kuboya	67	70	69	72	278	4,840,000
Min-Gyu Cho	73	69	70	67	279	2,970,000
K.T. Kim	72	71	68	68	279	2,970,000
Ashun Wu	70	70	71	68	279	2,970,000
Ryuji Masaoka	73	68	70	68	279	2,970,000
Koumei Oda	69	67	74	69	279	2,970,000
Sang-Hyun Park	66	72	72	69	279	2,970,000
Yoshitaka Takeya	71	70	69	69	279	2,970,000
Tadahiro Takayama	67	70	72	70	279	2,970,000
Yusaku Miyazato	72	70	70	68	280	1,880,000
Yuta Ikeda	70	72	69	69	280	1,880,000
Brendan Jones	72	70	71	67	280	1,880,000
Kyoung-Hoon Lee	70	65	73	72	280	1,880,000
Brad Kennedy	73	68	67	72	280	1,880,000
Shugo Imahira	66	71	68	75	280	1,880,000

Golf Nippon Series JT Cup

Tokyo Yomiuri Country Club, Inagi, Tokyo
Par 35-35–70; 7,023 yards

December 4-7
purse, ¥130,000,000

	SCORES				TOTAL	MONEY
Katsumasa Miyamoto	68	67	71	65	271	¥40,000,000
Prayad Marksaeng	70	68	67	67	272	15,000,000
Koumei Oda	64	72	72	66	274	6,508,695
Michio Matsumura	67	72	69	66	274	6,508,695
Sang-Hee Lee	68	67	68	71	274	6,508,695
Toshinori Muto	68	71	65	70	274	6,508,695

	SCORES				TOTAL	MONEY
Yoshinori Fujimoto	71	68	70	66	275	4,261,593
In-Hoi Hur	70	69	68	69	276	3,936,593
Shingo Katayama	72	70	69	66	277	3,247,593
Seung-Hyuk Kim	69	67	70	71	277	3,247,593
Satoshi Kodaira	66	72	67	72	277	3,247,593
Yusaku Miyazato	67	68	69	73	277	3,247,593
Hyung-Sung Kim	69	72	70	67	278	2,467,593
Dong-Kyu Jang	68	71	70	69	278	2,467,593
Ryo Ishikawa	70	67	73	69	279	2,207,593
Hideto Tanihara	70	70	69	71	280	2,077,593
Tadahiro Takayama	74	73	69	66	282	1,882,593
Tomohiro Kondo	70	72	70	70	282	1,882,593
Yoshitaka Takeya	70	72	72	69	283	1,609,592
Kyoung-Hoon Lee	71	71	71	70	283	1,609,592
Taichi Teshima	72	71	70	70	283	1,609,592
I.J. Jang	70	73	72	71	286	1,297,592
Yuta Ikeda	72	71	71	72	286	1,297,592
David Oh	69	70	71	76	286	1,297,592
Hiroshi Iwata	70	70	73	74	287	1,141,592

Australasian Tour

Lexus of Blackburn Victorian PGA Championship

Heritage Golf & Country Club, St. John Course,
Melbourne, Victoria
Par 36-36-72; 7,272 yards

February 6-9
purse, A$100,000

	SCORES				TOTAL	MONEY
Gareth Paddison	67	68	66	71	272	A$15,000
Michael Hendry	68	70	66	69	273	9,500
Jamie Arnold	68	67	68	71	274	7,000
Andrew Martin	71	70	69	66	276	4,550
Kurt Barnes	67	69	69	71	276	4,550
Mark Brown	65	71	71	70	277	3,300
Daniel McGraw	70	70	67	70	277	3,300
*Ben Eccles	68	69	66	75	278	
David Bransdon	73	71	68	68	280	2,483.33
Andrew Evans	73	71	65	71	280	2,483.33
Troy Cox	72	72	65	71	280	2,483.33
Matthew Ballard	72	70	68	72	282	1,900
Paul Sheehan	68	69	70	75	282	1,900
Adam Bland	74	71	67	71	283	1,550
Kim Felton	72	73	64	74	283	1,550
Peter O'Malley	70	72	70	72	284	1,275
Michael Long	68	72	74	70	284	1,275
Luke Humphries	70	68	69	77	284	1,275
Ryan Fox	70	69	68	77	284	1,275
*Lucas Herbert	70	73	68	75	286	
Aaron Townsend	74	71	65	76	286	1,110
Scott Arnold	70	71	69	76	286	1,110
Alex Hawley	68	70	66	82	286	1,110
Peter Wilson	70	72	71	74	287	1,030
Anthony Houston	69	73	71	74	287	1,030
Adam Blyth	72	69	73	73	287	1,030
Max McCardle	70	71	66	80	287	1,030

Coca-Cola Queensland PGA Championship

City Golf Club, Toowoomba, Queensland
Par 33-37-70; 6,332 yards

February 13-16
purse, A$120,000

	SCORES				TOTAL	MONEY
Anthony Summers	61	62	70	63	256	A$18,000
Ryan Fox	61	67	64	67	259	11,400
David Bransdon	61	70	68	62	261	8,400
Brad Kennedy	64	64	67	67	262	5,460
Stephen Dartnall	66	63	65	68	262	5,460
Aaron Townsend	71	65	63	65	264	3,960
Ryan Lynch	66	66	65	67	264	3,960
Clint Rice	66	66	66	68	266	3,360
Andrew Dodt	67	66	69	65	267	2,940
Jamie Arnold	64	73	66	65	268	2,280
Adam Stephens	71	66	68	63	268	2,280
Michael Choi	64	68	68	68	268	2,280
Jason Scrivener	67	68	65	68	268	2,280

	SCORES				TOTAL	MONEY
Daniel Fox	67	69	68	65	269	1,626
*Taylor MacDonald	69	69	66	65	269	
Michael Hendry	67	68	70	64	269	1,626
Mark Brown	68	68	65	68	269	1,626
Kurt Barnes	67	68	65	69	269	1,626
Scott Laycock	73	65	65	67	270	1,353
Kevin Conlong	65	68	69	68	270	1,353
Jared Pender	72	63	66	69	270	1,353
Bradley Hughes	68	65	66	71	270	1,353
Scott Strange	67	64	71	69	271	1,248
Thomas Petersson	65	67	73	66	271	1,248
Terry Pilkadaris	69	66	67	69	271	1,248

Oates Victorian Open

13th Beach Golf Links, Barwon Heads, Victoria — February 20-23
Par 36-36–72; 7,036 yards — purse, A$150,000

	SCORES				TOTAL	MONEY
Matthew Griffin	74	71	68	68	281	A$22,500
Matthew Stieger	74	68	70	69	281	14,250
(Griffin defeated Stieger on third playoff hole.)						
Brett Drewitt	75	66	70	71	282	10,500
Andrew Kelly	70	77	70	67	284	6,825
Terry Pilkadaris	70	70	73	71	284	6,825
Raymond Beaufils	76	70	74	65	285	4,443.75
Adam Bland	75	71	73	66	285	4,443.75
Paul Donahoo	72	73	71	69	285	4,443.75
Steven Jeffress	72	74	70	69	285	4,443.75
Peter O'Malley	74	73	69	70	286	2,730
Brendan Chant	74	73	70	69	286	2,730
Jack Wilson	73	75	67	71	286	2,730
Richard Green	78	69	67	72	286	2,730
Pieter Zwart	76	67	75	68	286	2,730
Alex Hawley	77	70	73	67	287	1,837.50
Samuel Eaves	73	74	72	68	287	1,837.50
Scott Strange	73	72	71	71	287	1,837.50
Josh Younger	74	69	73	71	287	1,837.50
Dimitrios Papadatos	75	71	70	71	287	1,837.50
Kim Felton	74	68	73	72	287	1,837.50
Jun Seok Lee	77	65	74	72	288	1,590
Nick Cullen	71	75	70	72	288	1,590
*Anthony Murdaca	75	69	73	71	288	
Ryan Haller	75	72	72	69	288	1,590
Wayne Perske	73	75	71	70	289	1,470
Rohan Blizard	71	75	71	72	289	1,470
Max McCardle	71	74	73	71	289	1,470
David Klein	72	75	68	74	289	1,470
Christopher Campbell	72	73	73	71	289	1,470

New Zealand Open

The Hills & Millbrook, Queenstown, New Zealand
Par 36-36–72; 7,116 yards

February 27-March 2
purse, NZ$850,000

	SCORES				TOTAL	MONEY
Dimitrios Papadatos	68	69	67	66	270	A$141,169.86
Mark Brown	67	72	66	69	274	79,996.25
David Klein	69	70	69	67	275	52,938.70
Ashley Hall	67	73	66	70	276	34,508.19
Richard Lee	68	67	70	71	276	34,508.19
Ryan Fox	70	69	69	69	277	26,665.42
Terry Pilkadaris	66	73	69	69	277	26,665.42
Andrew Martin	67	75	68	68	278	21,959.76
Adam Blyth	70	65	73	70	278	21,959.76
Scott Strange	66	76	68	69	279	17,515.52
Cameron Smith	70	71	67	71	279	17,515.52
Kieran Muir	70	70	67	72	279	17,515.52
Matthew Giles	72	69	70	69	280	13,724.85
Gareth Paddison	70	71	66	73	280	13,724.85
Rohan Blizard	68	77	70	66	281	10,862.24
Jack Wilson	72	72	70	67	281	10,862.24
Jake Stirling	66	74	70	71	281	10,862.24
Adam Bland	73	70	64	74	281	10,862.24
Craig Palmer	72	70	65	75	282	8,823.12
Nick Gillespie	69	73	73	68	283	8,117.27
Steven Jeffress	71	73	69	70	283	8,117.27
Steven Jones	73	71	68	71	283	8,117.27
Daniel Fox	70	71	68	74	283	8,117.27
Jun Seok Lee	70	74	70	70	284	6,146.77
Ben Campbell	71	74	69	70	284	6,146.77
Brad Shilton	70	70	73	71	284	6,146.77
Paul Spargo	69	74	69	72	284	6,146.77
David Bransdon	67	74	70	73	284	6,146.77
David Smail	72	71	68	73	284	6,146.77
Matt Jager	69	69	70	76	284	6,146.77
Hong Soon Sang	73	67	68	76	284	6,146.77

Fiji International

See Asia/Japan Tours chapter.

Isuzu Queensland Open

Brookwater Golf & Country Club, Brisbane, Queensland
Par 36-36-72; 7,114 yards

August 28-31
purse, A$110,000

	SCORES				TOTAL	MONEY
Andrew Dodt	72	70	72	67	281	A$16,500
Tom Bond	67	73	68	75	283	10,450
Cameron Smith	74	68	73	70	285	4,994
Michael Long	72	72	71	70	285	4,994
Jake Higginbottom	72	67	75	71	285	4,994
Anthony Brown	65	73	74	73	285	4,994
Matthew Griffin	73	70	68	74	285	4,994
*Kade McBride	66	72	79	69	286	
Brett Drewitt	73	74	68	71	286	3,080
Grant Thomas	77	70	71	69	287	2,557.50
Peter Martin	71	72	72	72	287	2,557.50

	SCORES				TOTAL	MONEY
Nick Cullen	71	72	76	69	288	1,980
*Taylor MacDonald	72	76	71	69	288	
Adam Stephens	69	74	74	71	288	1,980
David McKendrick	71	72	73	72	288	1,980
Marcus Cain	76	73	71	69	289	1,452
Scott Laycock	69	74	73	73	289	1,452
Daniel McGraw	72	75	68	74	289	1,452
Max McCardle	75	66	73	75	289	1,452
David Bransdon	67	74	72	76	289	1,452
Matthew Guyatt	75	72	72	71	290	1,221
Ryan Fox	71	71	76	72	290	1,221
Leigh McKechnie	76	74	66	74	290	1,221
Jason Scrivener	74	73	75	69	291	1,133
Michael Sim	76	70	73	72	291	1,133
Jim Cusdin	74	72	73	72	291	1,133
*Shae Wools-Cobb	71	72	74	74	291	
Kim Felton	70	71	73	77	291	1,133

South Pacific Open Championship

Tina Golf Club, Noumea, New Caledonia — September 10-13
Par 36-35–71; 6,442 yards — purse, A$140,000

	SCORES				TOTAL	MONEY
Adam Stephens	67	64	68	70	269	A$21,000
*Luke Toomey	73	64	69	68	274	
Andrew Kelly	74	63	69	68	274	11,550
Kota Kagasaki	72	67	65	70	274	11,550
Benjamin Clementson	71	70	69	65	275	5,495
Jason Scrivener	71	71	67	66	275	5,495
Peter Lee	71	69	68	67	275	5,495
Daniel Valente	66	69	70	70	275	5,495
Tim Hart	68	69	69	70	276	3,920
Mitchell A. Brown	72	64	71	70	277	3,255
Matthew Guyatt	69	66	70	72	277	3,255
Brady Watt	71	67	73	67	278	2,520
David McKendrick	70	68	70	70	278	2,520
Michael Wright	66	68	70	74	278	2,520
Matthew Griffin	71	69	71	68	279	1,897
Max McCardle	72	69	70	68	279	1,897
Brad Shilton	68	65	76	70	279	1,897
Jason Norris	66	67	73	73	279	1,897
Edward Stedman	68	72	71	69	280	1,578.50
Jun Seok Lee	70	70	69	71	280	1,578.50
Jean-Louis Guepy	70	69	69	72	280	1,578.50
Josh Geary	72	69	67	72	280	1,578.50
Matthew Millar	76	68	68	69	281	1,442
R.J. Caracella	70	70	71	70	281	1,442
Anthony Summers	67	71	72	71	281	1,442
Grant Thomas	68	72	70	71	281	1,442
*Blair Riordan	67	70	71	73	281	

John Hughes/Nexus Risk Services WA Open

Cottesloe Golf Club, Perth, Western Australia
Par 36-36–72; 6,716 yards

October 16-19
purse, A$110,000

	SCORES				TOTAL	MONEY
Ryan Fox	64	66	68	67	265	A$16,500
Stephen Dartnall	64	69	69	69	271	10,450
Rhein Gibson	71	65	66	70	272	5,903.33
Daniel Nisbet	65	69	67	71	272	5,903.33
Paul Spargo	66	66	66	74	272	5,903.33
Mathew Perry	68	71	69	67	275	2,805
Josh Younger	71	67	73	64	275	2,805
Kim Felton	69	68	69	69	275	2,805
*Todd Sinnott	65	67	73	70	275	
Daniel Fox	68	68	69	70	275	2,805
Matt Jager	71	65	68	71	275	2,805
Anthony Houston	73	64	67	71	275	2,805
Steven Jones	63	70	69	73	275	2,805
*Minwoo Lee	73	64	68	71	276	
Aaron Townsend	70	67	68	71	276	1,760
Andre Stolz	70	68	67	72	277	1,595
David Bransdon	68	70	66	73	277	1,595
Jason Scrivener	69	71	67	71	278	1,386
Matthew Millar	67	69	70	72	278	1,386
Kalem Richardson	68	69	71	71	279	1,240.25
Gareth Paddison	69	70	69	71	279	1,240.25
Tim Hart	70	68	69	72	279	1,240.25
Andrew Tampion	68	69	68	74	279	1,240.25
Marcus Cain	68	70	71	71	280	1,133
Peter Lee	68	69	71	72	280	1,133
David McKenzie	70	71	69	70	280	1,133
Peter O'Malley	66	70	70	74	280	1,133

ISPS Handa Perth International

Lake Karrinyup Country Club, Perth, Western Australia
Par 36-36–72; 7,143 yards

October 23-26
purse, A$1,750,000

	SCORES				TOTAL	MONEY
Thorbjorn Olesen	64	69	67	71	271	A$291,667.25
Victor Dubuisson	71	67	70	66	274	194,442.50
Mark Foster	67	73	67	69	276	109,550
Matthew Griffin	67	73	70	67	277	63,840
Stephen Dartnall	68	71	68	70	277	63,840
Lucas Bjerregaard	71	70	66	70	277	63,840
David Drysdale	67	68	71	71	277	63,840
James Morrison	72	63	69	73	277	63,840
Wade Ormsby	72	68	72	66	278	31,908.33
Ryan Fox	69	70	72	67	278	31,908.33
Andrea Pavan	71	70	67	70	278	31,908.33
Richard Green	68	68	70	72	278	31,908.33
Peter Uihlein	69	71	65	73	278	31,908.33
Sihwan Kim	66	68	69	75	278	31,908.33
Jason Scrivener	67	74	70	68	279	24,150
Marcus Fraser	68	70	71	70	279	24,150
Mikko Korhonen	71	70	67	71	279	24,150
Charl Schwartzel	68	69	70	72	279	24,150
Brett Rumford	67	72	73	68	280	21,350
Nathan Green	71	71	66	72	280	21,350

	SCORES				TOTAL	MONEY
Richard Bland	68	72	70	71	281	20,037.50
J.B. Hansen	71	68	69	73	281	20,037.50
Matthew Nixon	70	71	69	72	282	18,200
Nick Gillespie	71	71	67	73	282	18,200
Jason Dufner	70	70	69	73	282	18,200
Jason Norris	71	69	68	74	282	18,200
Gary Stal	69	71	67	75	282	18,200
Gregory Bourdy	69	72	71	71	283	16,362.50
Peter O'Malley	72	69	70	72	283	16,362.50
Carlos Del Moral	71	72	69	72	284	14,525
Greg Chalmers	70	73	69	72	284	14,525
James Nitties	69	69	72	74	284	14,525
Jamie McLeary	70	71	69	74	284	14,525
Rhein Gibson	70	70	70	74	284	14,525
Magnus A. Carlsson	67	76	69	73	285	12,425
Kevin Phelan	72	69	72	72	285	12,425
Ryan Haller	71	69	74	71	285	12,425
Anthony Brown	68	75	72	70	285	12,425
Peter Whiteford	66	66	75	78	285	12,425
Stuart Manley	73	68	72	73	286	10,150
Damien McGrane	70	70	73	73	286	10,150
James Heath	72	71	70	73	286	10,150
David McKenzie	70	70	74	72	286	10,150
Ricardo Gonzalez	68	74	72	72	286	10,150
Soren Hansen	72	71	71	72	286	10,150
Steven Bowditch	73	70	72	71	286	10,150
Brody Ninyette	69	74	72	71	286	10,150
Julien Quesne	67	73	72	75	287	7,875
Jack Doherty	69	72	72	74	287	7,875
Soren Kjeldsen	69	71	74	73	287	7,875
Paul Spargo	70	70	74	73	287	7,875
Simon Wakefield	72	67	75	73	287	7,875
John Wade	64	72	75	77	288	6,125
John Parry	69	72	73	74	288	6,125
Nacho Elvira	71	71	74	72	288	6,125
Craig Lee	73	69	75	71	288	6,125
Roope Kakko	72	71	74	71	288	6,125
Steven Jeffress	74	69	69	77	289	4,900
Josh Younger	69	70	74	76	289	4,900
Clint Rice	68	72	70	79	289	4,900
David Bransdon	69	72	73	75	289	4,900
Oliver Goss	68	74	75	72	289	4,900
Daan Huizing	68	73	73	76	290	4,287.50
Tom Lewis	66	74	76	74	290	4,287.50
Michael Long	69	74	73	75	291	3,937.50
Michael Sim	66	77	74	74	291	3,937.50
Nathan Holman	73	68	75	76	292	3,587.50
Daniel Nisbet	71	72	74	75	292	3,587.50
Scott Jamieson	69	74	71	81	295	3,325

WA Goldfields PGA Championship

Kalgoorlie Golf Course, Kalgoorlie, Western Australia — October 30-November 2
Par 36-36–72; 7,399 yards — purse, A$110,000

	SCORES				TOTAL	MONEY
Ryan Lynch	68	69	72	67	276	A$16,500
Peter Cooke	70	66	70	71	277	9,075
Chris Gaunt	67	67	69	74	277	9,075
Ben Campbell	65	71	71	71	278	5,500

	SCORES				TOTAL	MONEY
Daniel Valente	71	68	68	72	279	4,510
*Jarryd Felton	71	65	69	74	279	
Anthony Houston	69	72	72	68	281	3,630
Tim Hart	68	69	71	73	281	3,630
Nathan Green	67	71	74	70	282	2,887.50
Peter Lee	71	71	65	75	282	2,887.50
Craig Hancock	71	71	73	68	283	2,420
Anthony Brown	69	73	72	70	284	1,980
Matthew Ballard	70	69	73	72	284	1,980
Luke Humphries	67	71	71	75	284	1,980
Marcus Cain	69	73	72	71	285	1,490.50
Rhein Gibson	69	74	70	72	285	1,490.50
Andrew Kelly	68	74	69	74	285	1,490.50
Lincoln Tighe	68	71	71	75	285	1,490.50
Tom Bond	71	73	71	71	286	1,298
Michael Choi	71	74	71	71	287	1,182.50
Callan O'Reilly	70	71	76	70	287	1,182.50
James Nitties	68	72	74	73	287	1,182.50
Steven Jones	71	74	73	69	287	1,182.50
Gavin Reed	68	73	73	73	287	1,182.50
Mitchell A. Brown	69	73	72	73	287	1,182.50

Mazda NSW Open

Stonecutters Ridge Golf Club, Sydney, New South Wales — November 13-16
Par 36-36–72 — purse, A$100,000

	SCORES				TOTAL	MONEY
Anthony Brown	71	65	69	69	274	A$15,000
Josh Geary	66	68	68	72	274	9,500
(Brown defeated Geary on second playoff hole.)						
James Nitties	65	66	71	73	275	7,000
*Gunn Yang	69	69	66	72	276	
Rohan Blizard	70	70	69	69	278	4,200
Michael Long	68	68	72	70	278	4,200
Matthew Giles	70	68	68	72	278	4,200
Daniel Valente	71	67	66	75	279	3,100
*Travis Smyth	69	68	71	72	280	
Aaron Pike	71	69	68	72	280	2,483.33
Andrew Kelly	68	70	69	73	280	2,483.33
Ashley Hall	71	68	68	73	280	2,483.33
Ryan Lynch	69	68	72	72	281	1,725
Jake Stirling	69	72	68	72	281	1,725
*Cameron Davis	73	69	67	72	281	
Ben Campbell	69	75	65	72	281	1,725
Matthew Millar	68	67	73	73	281	1,725
Ewan Porter	72	71	72	67	282	1,248
Gavin Reed	77	65	69	71	282	1,248
Michael Foster	71	71	68	72	282	1,248
Gavin Fairfax	71	70	66	75	282	1,248
Nathan Green	67	68	70	77	282	1,248
Andrew Evans	68	72	73	70	283	1,083.33
Harrison Russell	69	69	72	73	283	1,083.33
*Ben Eccles	73	66	69	75	283	
Chris Gaunt	69	68	69	77	283	1,083.33

BetEasy Masters

Metropolitan Golf Club, Oakleigh, Victoria
Par 35-37–72

November 20-23
purse, A$1,000,000

	SCORES				TOTAL	MONEY
Nick Cullen	73	71	66	69	279	A$180,000
Adam Scott	73	68	71	68	280	72,500
Josh Younger	70	70	71	69	280	72,500
James Nitties	72	71	67	70	280	72,500
*Matthew Griffin	71	69	72	69	281	
Aron Price	68	73	71	69	281	34,250
Adam Bland	75	68	69	69	281	34,250
Paul Spargo	70	67	71	73	281	34,250
Rhein Gibson	68	74	75	65	282	26,000
Robert Allenby	70	73	71	68	282	26,000
Anthony Houston	71	68	75	69	283	20,000
Bryden Macpherson	70	71	72	70	283	20,000
Matthew Guyatt	70	69	73	71	283	20,000
*Lucas Herbert	75	70	65	73	283	
Boo Weekley	72	72	70	70	284	16,500
Brett Rumford	74	68	71	71	284	16,500
David McKenzie	72	70	74	69	285	11,975
*Todd Sinnott	67	71	77	70	285	
Steven Bowditch	67	75	73	70	285	11,975
*Ryan Ruffels	75	68	72	70	285	
Tom Bond	70	72	72	71	285	11,975
Stephen Dartnall	72	73	69	71	285	11,975
Peter Wilson	70	71	72	72	285	11,975
Chris Campbell	72	74	66	73	285	11,975
Kristopher Mueck	72	70	76	68	286	8,290
Alistair Presnell	75	71	72	68	286	8,290
Stephen Leaney	73	71	72	70	286	8,290
Brett Rankin	73	71	72	70	286	8,290
Nathan Green	73	71	71	71	286	8,290
Zac Blair	70	75	69	72	286	8,290
Mathew Goggin	71	69	73	73	286	8,290
Matthew Millar	74	70	69	73	286	8,290
Nick O'Hern	76	69	67	74	286	8,290
Geoff Ogilvy	69	71	71	75	286	8,290

Emirates Australian Open

The Australian Golf Club, Sydney, New South Wales
Par 36-356–71

November 27-30
purse, A$1,250,000

	SCORES				TOTAL	MONEY
Jordan Spieth	67	72	69	63	271	A$225,000
Rod Pampling	73	67	69	68	277	127,500
Brett Rumford	70	69	69	70	278	84,375
Greg Chalmers	71	66	71	71	279	60,000
Adam Scott	74	66	69	71	280	50,000
Jake Higginbottom	71	69	72	69	281	38,125
Robert Allenby	71	69	73	70	283	38,125
Ryan Fox	72	72	69	70	283	38,125
Daniel Nisbet	74	72	67	71	284	33,750
Nathan Holman	73	72	73	67	285	25,500
Sung-Hoon Kang	73	70	72	70	285	25,500
Aaron Townsend	73	70	71	71	285	25,500
Josh Younger	71	72	70	72	285	25,500

	SCORES				TOTAL	MONEY
Aron Price	68	75	69	73	285	25,500
Stephen Dartnall	72	71	74	69	286	15,320.31
Stephen Allan	75	71	70	70	286	15,320.31
Steven Bowditch	70	74	71	71	286	15,320.31
Rory McIlroy	69	69	76	72	286	15,320.31
Richard Green	69	71	74	72	286	15,320.31
Boo Weekley	72	71	71	72	286	15,320.31
Alistair Presnell	74	72	68	72	286	15,320.31
David Bransdon	72	70	71	73	286	15,320.31
Conrad Shindler	70	68	81	68	287	11,593.75
*Lucas Herbert	75	71	72	69	287	
John Senden	73	69	75	70	287	11,593.75
Adam Crawford	69	69	76	73	287	11,593.75
James Nitties	71	73	70	73	287	11,593.75

Nanshan NSW PGA Championship

Riverside Oaks Golf Resort, Cattai, New South Wales — December 4-7
Par 36-36–72; 6,767 yards — purse, A$110,000

	SCORES				TOTAL	MONEY
Lincoln Tighe	63	70	68	64	265	A$16,500
Scott Arnold	65	69	62	70	266	10,450
Kristopher Mueck	71	63	70	66	270	7,700
*Troy Moses	67	62	72	69	270	
Clint Rice	66	68	68	69	271	5,005
Grant Thomas	68	66	67	70	271	5,005
Daniel Valente	68	72	67	65	272	3,630
Peter Cooke	68	68	67	69	272	3,630
Jamie Arnold	65	71	71	66	273	2,731.67
*Travis Smyth	71	68	70	64	273	
Anthony Houston	69	68	69	67	273	2,731.67
Richard Gallichan	69	65	71	68	273	2,731.67
Bronson La'Cassie	68	69	68	69	274	1,760
Callan O'Reilly	69	69	67	69	274	1,760
Michael Choi	67	72	65	70	274	1,760
Gavin Reed	67	69	68	70	274	1,760
Matt Jager	69	68	67	70	274	1,760
David Klein	67	67	69	71	274	1,760
Mitchell A. Brown	68	67	73	67	275	1,278.75
Josh Younger	67	70	72	66	275	1,278.75
Matthew Millar	66	67	69	73	275	1,278.75
Ryan Lynch	69	65	66	75	275	1,278.75
Daniel Hoeve	72	65	72	67	276	1,188
David McKendrick	69	67	71	70	277	1,122
Aaron Townsend	68	70	71	68	277	1,122
Luke Humphries	69	65	71	72	277	1,122
Theodore Coroneo	71	67	67	72	277	1,122
Leigh McKechnie	68	67	76	66	277	1,122

Australian PGA Championship

RACV Royal Pines Resort, Gold Coast, Queensland
Par 35-36-71; 6,747 yards

December 11-14
purse, A$1,000,000

	SCORES				TOTAL	MONEY
Greg Chalmers	71	71	71	64	277	A$180,000
Wade Ormsby	68	67	71	71	277	84,750
Adam Scott	68	69	69	71	277	84,750
(Chalmers defeated Ormsby on third and Scott on seventh playoff hole.)						
Michael Hendry	70	71	67	71	279	48,000
Scott Stallings	72	70	68	70	280	40,000
Boo Weekley	66	72	69	74	281	36,000
Matthew Giles	73	69	70	70	282	30,500
Scott Strange	69	66	71	76	282	30,500
John Senden	73	68	73	69	283	26,000
Cameron Smith	74	68	71	70	283	26,000
Marc Leishman	69	71	74	70	284	21,000
Ryan Fox	70	74	69	71	284	21,000
Brad Kennedy	69	73	75	68	285	15,680
Robert Allenby	72	69	72	72	285	15,680
Geoff Drakeford	73	68	72	72	285	15,680
Brendon de Jonge	71	71	70	73	285	15,680
David Bransdon	73	70	68	74	285	15,680
Peter Lonard	70	74	72	70	286	10,607.14
Matthew Guyatt	72	72	70	72	286	10,607.14
Jun-Seok Lee	73	68	72	73	286	10,607.14
Michael Wright	71	73	69	73	286	10,607.14
Brett Rumford	72	71	70	73	286	10,607.14
David Smail	68	71	71	76	286	10,607.14
Jason Scrivener	73	66	68	79	286	10,607.14
Adam Crawford	73	70	73	71	287	7,585.17
Nathan Green	69	73	73	72	287	7,585.17
Nick Cullen	68	71	75	73	287	7,585.17
Craig Hancock	68	71	75	73	287	7,585.17
Josh Geary	70	72	72	73	287	7,585.17
Peter Cooke	70	72	71	74	287	7,585.17
Jarrod Lyle	69	72	70	76	287	7,585.17

African Tours

Joburg Open

Royal Johannesburg & Kensington Golf Club,
Johannesburg, South Africa
Par 36-36–72; 7,656 yards

February 6-9
purse, €1,300,000

	SCORES				TOTAL	MONEY
George Coetzee	65	68	69	66	268	R3,090,750
Tyrrell Hatton	67	69	69	66	271	1,516,450
Jin Jeong	65	69	66	71	271	1,516,450
Justin Walters	64	70	64	73	271	1,516,450
Andy Sullivan	66	72	69	65	272	637,650
Alvaro Quiros	69	68	69	66	272	637,650
Matthew Baldwin	68	69	68	67	272	637,650
Thomas Aiken	70	65	63	74	272	637,650
Danie van Tonder	65	72	69	67	273	421,200
Seve Benson	68	68	70	68	274	321,100
Ross Fisher	69	69	68	68	274	321,100
Robert-Jan Derksen	65	74	67	68	274	321,100
Anthony Wall	69	70	66	69	274	321,100
David Horsey	70	63	70	71	274	321,100
Roope Kakko	70	64	67	73	274	321,100
Jorge Campillo	67	69	71	68	275	243,750
Justin Harding	66	72	69	68	275	243,750
Danny Willett	69	65	71	70	275	243,750
Gregory Bourdy	68	67	70	70	275	243,750
Brandon Stone	68	67	70	70	275	243,750
James Morrison	70	66	69	70	275	243,750
Graeme Storm	71	67	70	68	276	201,825
Adrian Otaegui	71	68	68	69	276	201,825
Drikus van der Walt	66	71	69	70	276	201,825
Peter Karmis	73	65	68	70	276	201,825
Robert Dinwiddie	68	70	68	70	276	201,825
Jaco Van Zyl	70	68	68	70	276	201,825
Dawie van der Walt	69	68	72	68	277	175,500
Emiliano Grillo	68	69	69	71	277	175,500
Gary Stal	66	69	70	72	277	175,500
Ricardo Santos	67	71	72	68	278	156,000
Fabrizio Zanotti	71	68	70	69	278	156,000
Wade Ormsby	68	71	70	69	278	156,000
Jbe' Kruger	68	71	69	70	278	156,000
Louis de Jager	68	70	69	71	278	156,000
Alastair Forsyth	64	70	68	76	278	156,000
Hennie Otto	65	71	74	69	279	134,550
James Heath	66	68	74	71	279	134,550
Heinrich Bruiners	71	68	69	71	279	134,550
Lorenzo Gagli	68	71	68	72	279	134,550
Edoardo Molinari	64	68	72	75	279	134,550
Michael Hollick	69	68	73	70	280	111,150
Alexander Levy	71	67	72	70	280	111,150
Richard Bland	67	71	72	70	280	111,150
Soren Hansen	70	67	72	71	280	111,150
Jason Knutzon	67	71	70	72	280	111,150
Erik van Rooyen	69	70	68	73	280	111,150
Andrew Georgiou	69	65	72	74	280	111,150
Eduardo De La Riva	68	68	73	72	281	87,750
Wallie Coetsee	70	67	72	72	281	87,750

	SCORES				TOTAL	MONEY
Tyrone Ryan	71	65	72	73	281	87,750
Christiaan Basson	71	65	71	74	281	87,750
Craig Lee	65	67	74	75	281	87,750
Adilson Da Silva	69	69	72	72	282	68,640
Garth Mulroy	73	66	71	72	282	68,640
Keith Horne	69	70	71	72	282	68,640
Jean Hugo	66	73	70	73	282	68,640
Edouard Dubois	65	70	73	74	282	68,640
Lucas Bjerregaard	71	68	73	71	283	55,575
Charl Schwartzel	69	70	72	72	283	55,575
Patrik Sjoland	68	71	71	73	283	55,575
Gaganjeet Bhullar	71	67	71	74	283	55,575
Ariel Canete	70	68	69	76	283	55,575
Byeong-Hun An	69	68	68	78	283	55,575
Colin Nel	68	71	71	74	284	48,750
John Hahn	71	67	77	70	285	44,850
Mark Murless	67	72	73	73	285	44,850
Mikael Lundberg	70	69	73	73	285	44,850
Daniel Im	69	70	75	72	286	33,513
Daniel Brooks	69	69	75	73	286	33,513
David Drysdale	71	67	74	74	286	33,513
Dean Burmester	72	67	72	75	286	33,513
Tyrone Mordt	68	71	71	76	286	33,513
Divan van den Heever	70	68	76	74	288	29,092.50
Francesco Laporta	69	70	75	74	288	29,092.50
Soren Kjeldsen	68	71	76	74	289	29,025

Africa Open

East London Golf Club, East London, Eastern Cape, South Africa — February 13-16
Par 35-36–71; 6,616 yards — purse, €1,000,000

	SCORES				TOTAL	MONEY
Thomas Aiken	66	65	66	67	264	R2,377,500
Oliver Fisher	66	63	66	69	264	1,725,000
(Aiken defeated Fisher on first playoff hole.)						
David Horsey	66	64	70	65	265	887,250
John Hahn	65	61	71	68	265	887,250
Jaco Van Zyl	69	65	67	65	266	490,500
Darren Fichardt	66	67	67	66	266	490,500
Richard Bland	64	69	64	69	266	490,500
Emiliano Grillo	68	63	62	73	266	490,500
Keith Horne	68	69	66	65	268	284,250
Damien McGrane	67	69	67	65	268	284,250
Lucas Bjerregaard	64	67	69	68	268	284,250
Ulrich van den Berg	66	68	65	69	268	284,250
Stuart Manley	68	69	65	67	269	223,000
Adrian Otaegui	69	65	68	67	269	223,000
Fabrizio Zanotti	65	66	68	70	269	223,000
J.J. Senekal	66	71	69	64	270	194,250
Wade Ormsby	70	64	69	67	270	194,250
Jean Hugo	68	66	67	69	270	194,250
Jens Dantorp	69	63	68	70	270	194,250
Gregory Bourdy	65	72	69	65	271	162,214.29
Jbe' Kruger	67	69	67	68	271	162,214.29
Ruan de Smidt	68	66	69	68	271	162,214.29
Lee Slattery	67	68	68	68	271	162,214.29
Daniel Im	69	67	66	69	271	162,214.29
Justin Walters	66	69	67	69	271	162,214.29
Ricardo Santos	62	66	73	70	271	162,214.29

	SCORES				TOTAL	MONEY
Charl Coetzee	71	66	70	65	272	131,785.71
James Morrison	66	69	72	65	272	131,785.71
David Drysdale	65	70	71	66	272	131,785.71
Mikko Korhonen	72	63	71	66	272	131,785.71
Matthew Nixon	66	70	69	67	272	131,785.71
Mark Tullo	66	71	66	69	272	131,785.71
Jared Harvey	67	69	66	70	272	131,785.71
Jamie McLeary	69	68	69	67	273	105,000
P.H. McIntyre	69	67	70	67	273	105,000
Robert Dinwiddie	69	68	68	68	273	105,000
Roope Kakko	69	67	69	68	273	105,000
Danie van Tonder	70	66	69	68	273	105,000
Rhys Davies	64	71	70	68	273	105,000
Mark Williams	67	65	71	70	273	105,000
James Kamte	69	64	70	70	273	105,000
Garth Mulroy	64	68	70	71	273	105,000
Gaganjeet Bhullar	67	67	68	71	273	105,000
Brandon Stone	66	71	71	66	274	82,500
Neil Schietekat	69	68	70	67	274	82,500
Simon Wakefield	66	67	72	69	274	82,500
Dawie van der Walt	68	66	70	70	274	82,500
Jose-Filipe Lima	67	67	69	71	274	82,500
Jorge Campillo	70	65	75	65	275	67,500
Sihwan Kim	68	68	71	68	275	67,500
Daniel Brooks	70	67	69	69	275	67,500
Jacques Blaauw	70	65	71	69	275	67,500
Morten Orum Madsen	72	63	68	72	275	67,500
Patrik Sjoland	66	65	76	69	276	52,800
Edouard Dubois	69	67	71	69	276	52,800
Jaco Ahlers	69	68	69	70	276	52,800
Michael Hoey	68	68	70	70	276	52,800
Adam Gee	66	65	73	72	276	52,800
Adrien Saddier	70	66	76	65	277	46,500
Tjaart van der Walt	67	68	70	73	278	44,250
Oliver Bekker	70	67	66	75	278	44,250
Jason Knutzon	71	66	72	70	279	39,750
Adilson Da Silva	68	69	71	71	279	39,750
Sam Walker	67	70	70	72	279	39,750
Victor Riu	66	67	71	75	279	39,750
Heinrich Bruiners	66	71	75	70	282	36,000
Chris Doak	69	67	67	84	287	34,500

Dimension Data Pro-Am

Montagu Golf Course, Fancourt, George, South Africa
Par 36-36–72; 7,342 yards

February 20-23
purse, R3,750,000

	SCORES				TOTAL	MONEY
Estanislao Goya	73	67	67	68	275	R594,375
Lucas Bjerregaard	68	73	69	66	276	257,437.50
Keith Horne	71	66	69	70	276	257,437.50
Jean Hugo	68	67	70	71	276	257,437.50
Adilson Da Silva	67	66	70	73	276	257,437.50
Jaco Van Zyl	67	73	67	70	277	121,687.50
Morten Orum Madsen	67	72	66	72	277	121,687.50
Jack Doherty	68	70	73	67	278	92,250
Hennie Otto	72	71	66	70	279	73,875
Warren Abery	68	72	68	71	279	73,875
Rhys Enoch	77	67	66	69	279	73,875
Michael Hollick	76	66	71	67	280	55,125

	SCORES				TOTAL	MONEY
Jaco Ahlers	71	69	71	69	280	55,125
Justin Harding	72	66	72	70	280	55,125
Wallie Coetsee	69	69	72	70	280	55,125
Jake Redman	69	74	65	72	280	55,125
Trevor Fisher, Jr.	70	68	67	75	280	55,125
Rhys Davies	69	72	69	71	281	45,875
Dawie van der Walt	69	73	69	70	281	45,875
Francois Coetzee	68	69	69	75	281	45,875
Jens Dantorp	69	70	71	72	282	42,187.50
Oliver Bekker	69	68	74	71	282	42,187.50
Jacques Kruyswijk	69	71	75	68	283	39,375
Jbe' Kruger	72	70	71	70	283	39,375
Charl Coetzee	69	71	70	73	283	39,375

Tshwane Open

Copperleaf Golf & Country Estate, Centurion, South Africa
Par 36-36–72; 7,964 yards

February 27-March 2
purse, €1,500,000

	SCORES				TOTAL	MONEY
Ross Fisher	66	65	67	70	268	R3,566,250
Danie van Tonder	66	70	69	66	271	2,072,250
Michael Hoey	69	65	69	68	271	2,072,250
Carlos Del Moral	68	65	71	68	272	1,104,750
Hennie Otto	71	65	69	68	273	929,250
Chris Wood	67	68	72	68	275	671,250
Darren Fichardt	66	68	71	70	275	671,250
Kevin Phelan	68	69	68	70	275	671,250
Merrick Bremner	69	69	67	71	276	486,000
Trevor Fishero	65	69	71	72	277	406,500
Edoardo Molinari	70	65	70	72	277	406,500
Simon Dyson	65	68	71	73	277	406,500
Morten Orum Madsen	67	65	75	71	278	353,250
Robert Rock	70	71	65	73	279	330,750
David Howell	69	69	74	68	280	291,750
Shiv Kapur	67	74	70	69	280	291,750
Matthew Baldwin	72	69	68	71	280	291,750
Keith Horne	74	67	67	72	280	291,750
Jake Roos	69	65	72	74	280	291,750
Oliver Bekker	70	67	69	74	280	291,750
Lucas Bjerregaard	67	71	71	72	281	249,750
Mikko Korhonen	70	68	70	73	281	249,750
Paul Waring	70	70	68	73	281	249,750
Jean Hugo	68	68	76	70	282	222,750
Kristoffer Broberg	67	74	71	70	282	222,750
Thomas Aiken	69	71	70	72	282	222,750
Oliver Fisher	73	68	69	72	282	222,750
Ruan de Smidt	69	71	69	73	282	222,750
Gregory Bourdy	72	69	73	69	283	180,225
Marc Warren	73	68	71	71	283	180,225
Callum Mowat	72	69	71	71	283	180,225
Daniel Brooks	72	67	72	72	283	180,225
Nacho Elvira	71	67	72	73	283	180,225
James Kingston	71	69	70	73	283	180,225
Haydn Porteous	70	70	69	74	283	180,225
Jens Dantorp	70	69	69	75	283	180,225
Heinrich Bruiners	69	70	69	75	283	180,225
James Kamte	72	69	67	75	283	180,225
Ryan Cairns	70	69	74	71	284	141,750
Soren Kjeldsen	72	69	71	72	284	141,750

	SCORES				TOTAL	MONEY
Jaco Van Zyl	71	70	70	73	284	141,750
Alex Haindl	72	68	70	74	284	141,750
Jaco Ahlers	71	66	72	75	284	141,750
Justin Harding	70	67	72	75	284	141,750
Shane Lowry	68	71	70	75	284	141,750
Andy Sullivan	69	69	78	69	285	117,000
C.J. du Plessis	71	69	73	72	285	117,000
Jared Harvey	66	72	74	73	285	117,000
Tyrrell Hatton	70	69	70	76	285	117,000
Tyrone Ferreira	72	69	75	70	286	96,750
Erik van Rooyen	66	72	74	74	286	96,750
George Coetzee	70	70	71	75	286	96,750
Gaganjeet Bhullar	70	65	74	77	286	96,750
Maximilian Kieffer	68	70	71	77	286	96,750
Anthony Wall	68	71	76	72	287	77,062.50
Vaughn Groenewald	71	68	73	75	287	77,062.50
James Morrison	69	70	72	76	287	77,062.50
Ricardo Santos	68	71	71	77	287	77,062.50
Tjaart van der Walt	69	71	74	74	288	68,625
Daan Huizing	68	71	70	79	288	68,625
Doug McGuigan	71	70	75	73	289	64,125
Tyrone Mordt	70	71	74	74	289	64,125
Louis de Jager	71	69	75	75	290	58,500
Jack Doherty	69	71	75	75	290	58,500
Warren Abery	71	70	73	76	290	58,500
Soren Hansen	70	70	76	75	291	52,875
Alejandro Canizares	70	71	75	75	291	52,875
Michael Jonzon	72	69	76	76	293	49,500

Investec Cup

Millval & Lost City Golf Clubs, Sun City, South Africa — March 20-23
Par 36-36–72; 7,401 yards — purse, R1,000,000

	SCORES				TOTAL	MONEY
Trevor Fisher, Jr.	69	70	67	66	272	R163,400
Jacques Blaauw	67	73	67	66	273	117,700
Jaco Van Zyl	71	72	65	66	274	59,950
Keith Horne	70	68	69	67	274	59,950
George Coetzee	68	67	70	71	276	42,600
Jbe' Kruger	68	72	71	66	277	35,450
Dawie van der Walt	74	70	64	69	277	35,450
Jean Hugo	71	69	70	68	278	32,400
Darren Fichardt	73	70	66	70	279	30,300
Adilson Da Silva	75	70	67	69	281	28,800
Jake Roos	75	68	72	67	282	26,700
Merrick Bremner	69	69	71	73	282	26,700
Hennie Otto	73	74	68	68	283	24,100
Ulrich van den Berg	70	73	71	69	283	24,100
Thomas Aiken	74	70	72	68	284	21,400
Morten Orum Madsen	74	75	67	68	284	21,400
Lucas Bjerregaard	65	72	75	72	284	21,400
Andrew Curlewis	75	69	74	67	285	19,800
Richard Finch	76	71	73	67	287	19,200
Danie van Tonder	76	70	73	68	287	19,200
Justin Harding	74	72	74	69	289	18,300
Oliver Fisher	72	74	71	72	289	18,300
Oliver Bekker	76	77	70	67	290	17,700
Ross Fisher	77	71	73	70	291	17,300
Warren Abery	78	73	68	73	292	16,900

Telkom Business PGA Championship

The Country Club, Johannesburg, South Africa — April 3-6
Par 36-36–72; 7,546 yards — purse, R3,750,000

	SCORES				TOTAL	MONEY
Titch Moore	68	69	69	67	273	R594,375
Ulrich van den Berg	65	70	70	68	273	431,250
(Moore defeated van den Berg on fifth playoff hole.)						
J.J. Senekal	70	68	66	70	274	259,500
Danie van Tonder	67	69	71	68	275	157,250
Darren Fichardt	70	68	68	69	275	157,250
Oliver Bekker	65	71	66	73	275	157,250
Tyrone Ferreira	70	67	72	67	276	101,437.50
Merrick Bremner	67	69	70	70	276	101,437.50
Shaun Smith	66	75	70	66	277	68,625
Jacques Blaauw	71	70	69	67	277	68,625
Haydn Porteous	68	73	68	68	277	68,625
Neil Schietekat	72	70	65	70	277	68,625
James Kingston	69	69	67	72	277	68,625
Colin Nel	68	72	73	65	278	51,375
Christiaan Basson	67	73	69	69	278	51,375
Daniel Greene	69	70	68	71	278	51,375
Vaughn Groenewald	70	67	69	72	278	51,375
Rhys West	68	68	69	73	278	51,375
Anthony Michael	70	73	67	69	279	42,975
George Coetzee	66	69	74	70	279	42,975
Wynand Dingle	69	63	75	72	279	42,975
Erik van Rooyen	69	67	71	72	279	42,975
Ruan de Smidt	67	74	66	72	279	42,975
Alex Haindl	71	71	68	70	280	38,812.50
Jean Hugo	69	72	67	72	280	38,812.50

Golden Pilsener Zimbabwe Open

Royal Harare Golf Club, Harare, Zimbabwe — April 10-13
Par 36-36–72; 7,166 yards — purse, R1,800,000

	SCORES				TOTAL	MONEY
Jbe' Kruger	67	69	68	66	270	R285,300
Jacques Blaauw	66	71	66	68	271	207,000
Haydn Porteous	69	66	64	73	272	124,560
Jaco Ahlers	72	67	69	65	273	88,380
Jean Hugo	66	67	70	71	274	74,340
Andrew Curlewis	71	68	67	70	276	58,410
Andrew Georgiou	70	69	66	71	276	58,410
Le Roux Ferreira	65	71	67	74	277	44,280
Trevor Fisher, Jr.	73	69	68	68	278	38,880
Danie van Tonder	70	70	71	68	279	30,456
Alex Haindl	72	69	70	68	279	30,456
Lindani Ndwandwe	72	68	70	69	279	30,456
James Kingston	74	67	67	71	279	30,456
T.C. Charamba	67	71	69	72	279	30,456
Merrick Bremner	71	72	67	70	280	23,340
Doug McGuigan	70	70	69	71	280	23,340
Steve Surry	71	70	68	71	280	23,340
Ulrich van den Berg	68	70	69	73	280	23,340
Colin Nel	71	67	68	74	280	23,340
Steven Ferreira	69	67	69	75	280	23,340
Allan Versfeld	69	72	70	70	281	19,980

	SCORES				TOTAL	MONEY
Daniel Greene	67	69	71	74	281	19,980
C.J. du Plessis	70	70	66	75	281	19,980
*Scott Vincent	73	70	72	67	282	
Titch Moore	70	71	71	70	282	18,090
Vaughn Groenewald	69	70	70	73	282	18,090
Louis de Jager	70	67	71	74	282	18,090
Keith Horne	68	72	68	74	282	18,090

Investec Royal Swazi Open

Royal Swazi Sun Country Club, Mbabane, Swaziland — May 7-10
Par 36-36–72; 6,715 yards — purse, R1,000,000

	POINTS				TOTAL	MONEY
Danie van Tonder	4	12	14	18	48	R158,500
Jared Harvey	4	17	11	16	48	93,200
Jacques Blaauw	11	14	11	12	48	93,200
(Van Tonder defeated Harvey and Blaauw on first playoff hole.)						
Ross Wellington	17	11	6	11	45	50,500
Haydn Porteous	9	14	18	3	44	42,400
Jaco Ahlers	13	10	15	4	42	36,300
Trevor Fisher, Jr.	8	11	13	9	41	30,200
Le Roux Ferreira	14	5	10	11	40	25,100
Wynand Dingle	11	6	10	12	39	19,453
Keith Horne	8	18	3	10	39	19,453
Keenan Davidse	11	8	7	13	39	19,453
James Kingston	14	12	4	9	39	19,453
Dean Burmester	10	6	4	18	38	15,472.67
Wallie Coetsee	11	7	10	10	38	15,472.67
C.J. du Plessis	9	1	19	9	38	15,472.67
Jeff Inglis	5	12	8	11	36	14,306
Peter Karmis	5	12	9	9	35	13,556
Andrew Curlewis	10	7	13	5	35	13,556
Martin du Toit	9	8	4	13	34	12,906
Desvonde Botes	8	10	9	6	33	11,981
Tyrone Ferreira	10	9	7	7	33	11,981
Jean Hugo	6	12	11	4	33	11,981
Bryce Easton	3	8	13	9	33	11,981
Doug McGuigan	14	3	8	7	32	10,756
Allan Versfeld	6	16	11	-1	32	10,756
Alex Haindl	9	15	10	-2	32	10,756
Tyrone Mordt	5	18	16	-7	32	10,756

Mopani Copper Mines Zambia Open

Nkana Golf Club, Kitwe, Zambia — May 15-18
Par 36-36–72; 7,002 yards — purse, US$250,000

	SCORES				TOTAL	MONEY
Wallie Coetsee	65	69	68	71	273	R410,229.70
Justin Harding	68	71	67	68	274	238,373.22
Danie van Tonder	69	68	66	71	274	238,373.22
Francesco Laporta	71	67	70	67	275	116,986.64
Jean Hugo	71	67	64	73	275	116,986.64
Erik van Rooyen	68	69	71	68	276	83,987.09
C.J. du Plessis	70	67	69	70	276	83,987.09
Warren Abery	73	66	69	69	277	59,787.42

	SCORES				TOTAL	MONEY
Theunis Spangenberg	62	72	69	74	277	59,787.42
Jaco Ahlers	72	70	69	67	278	48,528.75
Keenan Davidse	70	69	68	71	278	48,528.75
Adilson Da Silva	70	73	70	67	280	39,664.17
Peter Karmis	71	74	68	67	280	39,664.17
Matthew Carvell	70	72	68	70	280	39,664.17
Jared Harvey	67	69	69	75	280	39,664.17
Jacques Blaauw	74	67	72	68	281	34,164.24
Louis de Jager	70	72	68	71	281	34,164.24
Allan Versfeld	71	71	65	74	281	34,164.24
Gideon Pienaar	73	69	72	68	282	31,058.40
Jacques Kruyswijk	65	72	74	71	282	31,058.40
J.C. Ritchie	72	69	73	69	283	28,729.02
Desne van den Bergh	72	74	68	69	283	28,729.02
Callum Mowat	70	72	68	73	283	28,729.02
Attie Schwartzel	72	71	74	67	284	25,623.18
Jaco Prinsloo	69	77	71	67	284	25,623.18
Tyrone Ferreira	72	69	74	69	284	25,623.18
Pieter Moolman	69	76	70	69	284	25,623.18
Heinrich Bruiners	70	72	69	73	284	25,623.18

Lombard Insurance Classic

Royal Swazi Sun Country Club, Mbabane, Swaziland — May 23-25
Par 36-36–72; 6,715 yards — purse, R900,000

	SCORES			TOTAL	MONEY
Christiaan Basson	69	66	62	197	R142,650
Ruan de Smidt	67	71	64	202	62,842.50
Adilson Da Silva	67	70	65	202	62,842.50
Neil Schietekat	67	67	68	202	62,842.50
Jake Redman	67	66	69	202	62,842.50
Ulrich van den Berg	70	68	65	203	27,480
Jaco Ahlers	69	68	66	203	27,480
Erik van Rooyen	68	69	66	203	27,480
Vaughn Groenewald	69	69	66	204	18,855
Danie van Tonder	64	70	70	204	18,855
Trevor Fisher, Jr.	71	65	69	205	16,745
Divan van den Heever	70	68	68	206	15,575
Riekus Nortje	67	72	68	207	13,662.50
Justin Harding	70	68	69	207	13,662.50
Mark Murless	68	69	70	207	13,662.50
Francesco Laporta	69	67	71	207	13,662.50
Oliver Bekker	71	70	67	208	11,633
Lindani Ndwandwe	69	71	68	208	11,633
Derick Petersen	71	68	69	208	11,633
Jacques Blaauw	68	69	71	208	11,633
Chris Swanepoel	67	67	74	208	11,633
Attie Schwartzel	72	71	66	209	10,220
Jean Hugo	72	69	68	209	10,220
Titch Moore	67	71	71	209	10,220
Keenan Davidse	68	69	72	209	10,220

Zambia Sugar Open

Lusaka Golf Club, Lusaka, Zambia — June 5-8
Par 35-38–73; 7,225 yards — purse, R1,200,000

	SCORES				TOTAL	MONEY
Lyle Rowe	76	69	66	68	279	R190,200
Neil Schietekat	70	70	70	73	283	138,000
P.H. McIntyre	69	72	71	73	285	70,980
Ulrich van den Berg	71	67	72	75	285	70,980
Jared Harvey	68	71	73	75	287	46,020
Haydn Porteous	70	71	70	76	287	46,020
Matthew Carvell	78	66	69	75	288	35,400
Ryan Cairns	72	70	76	71	289	24,096
Titch Moore	72	71	74	72	289	24,096
Adilson Da Silva	74	71	72	72	289	24,096
Toto Thimba	73	76	67	73	289	24,096
Riekus Nortje	70	71	73	75	289	24,096
Louis de Jager	73	71	75	71	290	16,840
Maritz Wessels	74	71	73	72	290	16,840
Derick Petersen	70	70	77	73	290	16,840
Shaun Smith	72	73	72	73	290	16,840
Le Roux Ferreira	72	70	72	76	290	16,840
Jean Hugo	69	70	74	77	290	16,840
Jake Redman	69	74	74	74	291	14,400
Tyrone Mordt	72	71	72	76	291	14,400
Heinrich Bruiners	74	72	75	71	292	13,320
Wallie Coetsee	66	73	80	73	292	13,320
Grant Muller	71	70	74	77	292	13,320
Christiaan Basson	73	76	71	73	293	12,420
Attie Schwartzel	76	69	73	75	293	12,420

Vodacom Origins of Golf - Euphoria

Euphoria Golf Estate & Hydrop, Naboomspruit, Limpopo, South Africa — June 25-27
Par 36-36–72; 7,699 yards — purse, R600,000

	SCORES			TOTAL	MONEY
Danie van Tonder	67	67	70	204	R95,100
Tyrone Ferreira	72	65	68	205	69,000
Ulrich van den Berg	69	67	70	206	48,000
Jared Harvey	72	67	69	208	37,800
Jacques Blaauw	68	69	72	209	28,200
Adilson Da Silva	68	69	73	210	22,800
Justin Harding	66	73	73	212	18,900
Callum Mowat	69	71	73	213	15,600
Heinrich Bruiners	73	67	73	213	15,600
Anthony Michael	72	73	69	214	11,212.50
Keenan Davidse	75	69	70	214	11,212.50
Shaun Norris	69	74	71	214	11,212.50
Charl Coetzee	67	76	71	214	11,212.50
Bryce Easton	72	71	71	214	11,212.50
Morne Buys	71	70	73	214	11,212.50
Le Roux Ferreira	72	69	73	214	11,212.50
Ross Wellington	68	70	76	214	11,212.50
Ockie Strydom	69	75	71	215	8,048.57
Maritz Wessels	74	70	71	215	8,048.57
Jean Hugo	69	73	73	215	8,048.57
Oliver Bekker	70	71	74	215	8,048.57

	SCORES			TOTAL	MONEY
Steven Ferreira	71	70	74	215	8,048.57
Andrew Curlewis	72	69	74	215	8,048.57
Louis de Jager	73	66	76	215	8,048.57
Ruan de Smidt	74	72	70	216	6,780
Chris Swanepoel	69	75	72	216	6,780

Sun City Challenge

Lost City Golf Course, Sun City, South Africa — July 2-4
Par 36-36–72; 6,987 yards — purse, R700,000

	SCORES			TOTAL	MONEY
Dean Burmester	68	67	71	206	R110,950
Haydn Porteous	68	70	69	207	80,500
Merrick Bremner	71	71	66	208	56,000
P.H. McIntyre	69	74	67	210	28,980
Titch Moore	71	71	68	210	28,980
Lindani Ndwandwe	68	73	69	210	28,980
Ulrich van den Berg	70	70	70	210	28,980
Keith Horne	70	68	72	210	28,980
Adilson Da Silva	69	70	72	211	17,150
Jared Harvey	76	69	67	212	15,225
Louis de Jager	69	69	74	212	15,225
Matthew Carvell	72	69	72	213	13,650
Jean Hugo	72	68	73	213	13,650
Neil Cheetham	71	73	70	214	11,993.33
Warren Abery	71	70	73	214	11,993.33
Tyrone Ryan	68	70	76	214	11,993.33
Madalitso Muthiya	76	67	72	215	10,122
Riekus Nortje	73	70	72	215	10,122
Trevor Fisher, Jr.	72	71	72	215	10,122
J.J. Senekal	72	71	72	215	10,122
Toto Thimba	70	73	72	215	10,122
Grant Muller	72	75	69	216	8,225
Colin Nel	71	75	70	216	8,225
C.J. du Plessis	72	74	70	216	8,225
Tyrone Ferreira	73	73	70	216	8,225
Keenan Davidse	72	72	72	216	8,225
Christiaan Basson	73	68	75	216	8,225

Vodacom Origins of Golf - Arabella

Arabella Country Club, Western Cape, South Africa — July 23-24
Par 36-36–72; 6,976 yards — purse, R600,000
(Event shortened to 36 holes—rain.)

	SCORES		TOTAL	MONEY
Jean Hugo	68	69	137	R95,100
Rhys West	67	71	138	69,000
Chris Swanepoel	68	71	139	34,200
Trevor Fisher, Jr.	67	72	139	34,200
Ulrich van den Berg	69	70	139	34,200
Adilson Da Silva	68	71	139	34,200
Jacques Blaauw	67	74	141	18,900
Wallie Coetsee	70	73	143	14,900
Keith Horne	69	74	143	14,900
Jared Harvey	72	71	143	14,900

	SCORES		TOTAL	MONEY
Christiaan Basson	72	72	144	11,412
Charl Coetzee	74	70	144	11,412
Le Roux Ferreira	71	73	144	11,412
Tyrone Ferreira	70	74	144	11,412
Keenan Davidse	74	70	144	11,412
Neil Cheetham	72	73	145	9,570
P.H. McIntyre	67	78	145	9,570
Matthew Carvell	71	75	146	8,200
Warren Abery	74	72	146	8,200
Michael Hollick	72	74	146	8,200
Callum Mowat	75	71	146	8,200
Neil Schietekat	69	77	146	8,200
Tyrone Mordt	72	74	146	8,200
Vaughn Groenewald	74	73	147	6,428.57
James Kamte	70	77	147	6,428.57
Alex Haindl	71	76	147	6,428.57
Heinrich Bruiners	73	74	147	6,428.57
Jake Redman	72	75	147	6,428.57
Danie van Tonder	73	74	147	6,428.57
Jbe' Kruger	72	75	147	6,428.57

Vodacom Origins of Golf - St. Francis

St. Francis Links, Eastern Cape, South Africa — July 30-August 1
Par 36-36–72; 7,283 yards — purse, R600,000

	SCORES			TOTAL	MONEY
Keith Horne	65	71	71	207	R95,100
Erik van Rooyen	68	68	74	210	69,000
Ulrich van den Berg	72	74	69	215	42,900
Wallie Coetsee	70	74	71	215	42,900
Chris Swanepoel	74	70	72	216	25,500
Madalitso Muthiya	69	74	73	216	25,500
Dean Burmester	72	74	71	217	17,700
Ruan de Smidt	72	71	74	217	17,700
Anthony Michael	76	67	75	218	13,600
Jaco Ahlers	74	68	76	218	13,600
Shaun Smith	68	73	77	218	13,600
Colin Nel	74	69	76	219	11,700
Titch Moore	67	75	77	219	11,700
Peter Karmis	75	70	75	220	10,050
Le Roux Ferreira	72	73	75	220	10,050
Vaughn Groenewald	73	70	77	220	10,050
Warren Abery	70	73	77	220	10,050
Michael Hollick	74	72	75	221	8,200
Doug McGuigan	74	72	75	221	8,200
Adilson Da Silva	75	72	74	221	8,200
Tyrone Mordt	70	74	77	221	8,200
Steven Ferreira	73	69	79	221	8,200
Danie van Tonder	69	73	79	221	8,200
Allan Versfeld	69	74	79	222	7,020
Neil Schietekat	68	74	80	222	7,020

Wild Waves Golf Challenge

Wild Coast Sun Country Club, KwaZulu-Natal, South Africa — August 27-28
Par 35-35–70; 6,351 yards — purse, R700,000
(Final round cancelled—rain.)

	SCORES		TOTAL	MONEY
Colin Nel	65	65	130	R110,950
Jared Harvey	69	64	133	68,250
Ulrich van den Berg	68	65	133	68,250
Jaco Ahlers	68	66	134	28,980
James Kamte	65	69	134	28,980
Ockie Strydom	72	62	134	28,980
Tyrone Mordt	67	67	134	28,980
Heinrich Bruiners	67	67	134	28,980
Danie van Tonder	69	66	135	16,450
Andrew McLardy	66	69	135	16,450
Alex Haindl	69	67	136	12,164.44
Mark Murless	70	66	136	12,164.44
Doug McGuigan	69	67	136	12,164.44
Charl Coetzee	69	67	136	12,164.44
Warren Abery	67	69	136	12,164.44
Divan van den Heever	68	68	136	12,164.44
Le Roux Ferreira	68	68	136	12,164.44
Steven Ferreira	67	69	136	12,164.44
Tyrone Ferreira	68	68	136	12,164.44
Jake Redman	69	68	137	8,557.50
P.H. McIntyre	69	68	137	8,557.50
Morne Buys	68	69	137	8,557.50
Grant Muller	70	67	137	8,557.50
Lindani Ndwandwe	73	64	137	8,557.50
Drikus Bruyns	67	70	137	8,557.50
Daniel Greene	69	68	137	8,557.50
J.J. Senekal	72	65	137	8,557.50

Vodacom Origins of Golf - Wild Coast Sun

Wild Coast Sun Country Club, KwaZulu-Natal, South Africa — September 3-5
Par 35-35–70; 6,351 yards — purse, R600,000

	SCORES			TOTAL	MONEY
Louis de Jager	63	68	77	208	R95,100
Haydn Porteous	73	68	67	208	58,500
Jaco Ahlers	71	65	72	208	58,500
(De Jager defeated Porteous and Ahlers on first playoff hole.)					
Andrew Curlewis	78	65	66	209	29,600
C.J. du Plessis	72	67	70	209	29,600
Danie van Tonder	72	66	71	209	29,600
Jacques Blaauw	73	70	67	210	15,240
Christiaan Basson	71	70	69	210	15,240
Grant Muller	75	66	69	210	15,240
Keith Horne	70	69	71	210	15,240
Stuart Smith	67	69	74	210	15,240
Torben Baumann	76	69	66	211	11,115
Warren Abery	72	69	70	211	11,115
Daniel Greene	75	66	70	211	11,115
Jean Hugo	71	69	71	211	11,115
Ulrich van den Berg	74	70	68	212	9,195
Jeff Inglis	74	68	70	212	9,195
Wallie Coetsee	74	66	72	212	9,195

	SCORES			TOTAL	MONEY
Tyrone Mordt	72	67	73	212	9,195
Heinrich Bruiners	70	69	74	213	8,040
Jared Harvey	67	72	74	213	8,040
Colin Nel	73	66	74	213	8,040
Andre Cruse	73	72	69	214	6,790
Bryce Easton	76	69	69	214	6,790
Michael Hollick	73	71	70	214	6,790
Matthew Carvell	71	71	72	214	6,790
James Kamte	68	73	73	214	6,790
Pieter Moolman	72	68	74	214	6,790

Vodacom Origins of Golf - Vaal de Grace

Vaal de Grace Golf Estate, Parys, South Africa — October 1-3
Par 36-36–72; 7,341 yards — purse, R600,000

	SCORES			TOTAL	MONEY
P.H. McIntyre	64	68	68	200	R95,100
Jake Roos	65	67	68	200	69,000
(McIntyre defeated Roos on third playoff hole.)					
Shaun Norris	66	72	66	204	31,140
Steven Ferreira	69	67	68	204	31,140
Jean Hugo	70	66	68	204	31,140
Jaco Ahlers	66	70	68	204	31,140
Tyrone Ferreira	67	67	70	204	31,140
Wallie Coetsee	67	67	71	205	16,500
Francois Coetzee	69	71	66	206	13,600
Rhys West	69	68	69	206	13,600
Jared Harvey	66	70	70	206	13,600
Anthony Michael	66	72	69	207	11,400
Jean-Paul Strydom	71	67	69	207	11,400
C.J. du Plessis	67	67	73	207	11,400
Doug McGuigan	71	68	69	208	9,408
Roberto Lupini	71	68	69	208	9,408
Tyrone Mordt	70	68	70	208	9,408
Christiaan Basson	69	69	70	208	9,408
Justin Turner	67	68	73	208	9,408
Drikus Bruyns	71	70	68	209	8,040
Stuart Smith	73	69	67	209	8,040
Mark Williams	68	71	70	209	8,040
Heinrich Bruiners	72	68	70	210	7,160
Allan Versfeld	69	69	72	210	7,160
Dean Burmester	66	72	72	210	7,160

Sun Boardwalk Golf Challenge

Humewood Golf Club, Port Elizabeth, South Africa — October 8-10
Par 35-37–72; 6,989 yards — purse, R600,000
(Event shortened to 36 holes—wind.)

	SCORES		TOTAL	MONEY
Titch Moore	70	70	140	R95,100
Steve Surry	71	70	141	58,500
Roberto Lupini	68	73	141	58,500
Peter Karmis	73	69	142	33,000
Heinrich Bruiners	73	69	142	33,000
Ryan Tipping	75	68	143	19,400

	SCORES		TOTAL	MONEY
Doug McGuigan	73	70	143	19,400
Ulrich van den Berg	73	70	143	19,400
Derik Ferreira	75	69	144	12,840
Adrian Ford	73	71	144	12,840
Jean Hugo	74	70	144	12,840
Danie van Tonder	74	70	144	12,840
Shaun Norris	72	72	144	12,840
Justin Harding	74	71	145	10,280
Steven Ferreira	73	72	145	10,280
Jake Redman	73	72	145	10,280
Louis de Jager	74	72	146	8,676
Justin Turner	74	72	146	8,676
Alex Haindl	74	72	146	8,676
Colin Nel	74	72	146	8,676
Keith Horne	71	75	146	8,676
Stefan Engell Andersen	75	72	147	7,176
Allan Versfeld	74	73	147	7,176
Chris Swanepoel	73	74	147	7,176
James Kamte	72	75	147	7,176
Bryce Bibby	74	73	147	7,176

BMG Classic

Glendower Golf Club, Johannesburg, South Africa — October 17-19
Par 36-36–72; 7,564 yards — purse, R800,000

	SCORES			TOTAL	MONEY
Merrick Bremner	66	71	67	204	R126,800
Darren Fichardt	68	65	72	205	92,000
Haydn Porteous	69	70	67	206	57,120
Justin Harding	72	67	68	207	40,400
Divan van den Heever	74	66	68	208	31,480
Jean Hugo	68	68	72	208	31,480
Louis de Jager	74	67	68	209	20,613.33
Jaco Ahlers	70	66	73	209	20,613.33
Danie van Tonder	70	66	73	209	20,613.33
Neil Schietekat	71	69	70	210	15,402
Erik van Rooyen	70	70	70	210	15,402
Jacques Kruyswijk	73	71	67	211	12,744
J.C. Ritchie	71	72	68	211	12,744
Dylan Frittelli	72	71	68	211	12,744
Le Roux Ferreira	69	71	71	211	12,744
Andrew Georgiou	73	66	73	212	11,244
Christiaan Basson	70	69	73	212	11,244
Andre Cruse	70	70	73	213	10,484
Oliver Bekker	67	71	75	213	10,484
Jaco Prinsloo	70	72	72	214	9,584
Trevor Fisher, Jr.	69	72	73	214	9,584
Doug McGuigan	73	68	73	214	9,584
Jacques Blaauw	72	69	73	214	9,584
Francesco Laporta	71	73	71	215	8,604
Jack Harrison	71	72	72	215	8,604
Tyrone Mordt	73	69	73	215	8,604
Thomas Aiken	74	66	75	215	8,604

Vodacom Origins of Golf Final

Pezula Championship Course, Western Cape, South Africa — October 29-31
Par 36-36–72; 6,951 yards — purse, R650,000

	SCORES			TOTAL	MONEY
Keith Horne	65	71	67	203	R103,025
Ulrich van den Berg	73	66	65	204	74,750
Dylan Frittelli	69	67	69	205	52,000
Ruan de Smidt	74	69	64	207	25,079.17
Michael Hollick	69	73	65	207	25,079.17
Neil Schietekat	69	70	68	207	25,079.17
Alex Haindl	69	70	68	207	25,079.17
Madalitso Muthiya	66	71	70	207	25,079.17
Erik van Rooyen	69	66	72	207	25,079.17
Tyrone Mordt	70	73	65	208	13,406.25
Mark Williams	71	71	66	208	13,406.25
Jacques Blaauw	66	74	68	208	13,406.25
Dean Burmester	70	69	69	208	13,406.25
Danie van Tonder	69	73	67	209	10,887.50
Jean-Paul Strydom	72	70	67	209	10,887.50
Chris Swanepoel	70	68	71	209	10,887.50
Doug McGuigan	66	70	73	209	10,887.50
Eddie Taylor	68	73	69	210	9,555
Jean Hugo	66	71	73	210	9,555
Wallie Coetsee	72	70	69	211	8,872.50
Steve Surry	75	68	68	211	8,872.50
Heinrich Bruiners	69	74	69	212	7,913.75
Jake Redman	71	70	71	212	7,913.75
Shaun Norris	66	74	72	212	7,913.75
Jaco Ahlers	72	68	72	212	7,913.75

Nedbank Affinity Cup

Lost City Golf Club, Sun City, South Africa — November 4-6
Par 36-36–72; 7,385 yards — purse, R750,000

	SCORES			TOTAL	MONEY
Louis de Jager	68	68	68	204	R118,875
Danie van Tonder	70	68	66	204	69,900
Vaughn Groenewald	70	68	66	204	69,900
(De Jager defeated van Tonder on first and Groenewald on second playoff hole.)					
Jake Redman	69	67	69	205	37,875
Dean Burmester	65	72	69	206	23,400
Oliver Bekker	66	71	69	206	23,400
Trevor Fisher, Jr.	66	70	70	206	23,400
Ulrich van den Berg	68	66	72	206	23,400
Ruan de Smidt	68	64	74	206	23,400
Chris Swanepoel	66	74	67	207	14,925
Madalitso Muthiya	71	70	67	208	13,466.50
Peter Karmis	71	69	68	208	13,466.50
Neil Schietekat	75	67	67	209	10,286.50
Alex Haindl	69	72	68	209	10,286.50
Colin Nel	73	68	68	209	10,286.50
Keenan Davidse	73	67	69	209	10,286.50
Rhys West	72	68	69	209	10,286.50
Jeff Inglis	73	66	70	209	10,286.50
Christiaan Basson	70	68	71	209	10,286.50
Morne Buys	66	71	72	209	10,286.50
Derik Ferreira	69	68	72	209	10,286.50

	SCORES			TOTAL	MONEY
Titch Moore	71	66	72	209	10,286.50
Wynand Dingle	68	72	70	210	8,629
Jared Harvey	71	71	69	211	7,954
Tyrone Mordt	71	69	71	211	7,954
Jean Hugo	71	68	72	211	7,954
James Kamte	69	70	72	211	7,954
P.H. McIntyre	69	70	72	211	7,954

Lion of Africa Cape Town Open

Royal Cape Golf Club, Cape Town, South Africa — November 27-30
Par 36-36–72; 6,818 yards — purse, R1,500,000

	SCORES				TOTAL	MONEY
Jaco Ahlers	71	69	68	68	276	R237,750
Ross McGowan	69	71	68	68	276	138,150
Hennie Otto	66	67	71	72	276	138,150
(Ahlers defeated on Otto on first and McGowan on fourth playoff hole.)						
Jbe' Kruger	72	70	70	65	277	67,800
Thomas Aiken	69	66	71	71	277	67,800
David Drysdale	70	69	68	71	278	53,100
Ryan Tipping	68	70	72	69	279	35,737.50
Tjaart van der Walt	71	70	69	69	279	35,737.50
Justin Harding	71	68	70	70	279	35,737.50
Danie van Tonder	67	68	69	75	279	35,737.50
Adilson Da Silva	69	71	71	69	280	25,950
Justin Walters	71	67	70	72	280	25,950
Christiaan Basson	72	69	71	69	281	21,862.50
Rhys Enoch	68	71	71	71	281	21,862.50
Branden Grace	75	64	71	71	281	21,862.50
Rhys West	71	65	70	75	281	21,862.50
Andrew Georgiou	68	76	70	68	282	16,827.27
Peter Karmis	70	72	70	70	282	16,827.27
Jean Hugo	71	68	72	71	282	16,827.27
Merrick Bremner	71	68	72	71	282	16,827.27
Dean Burmester	71	69	71	71	282	16,827.27
David Frost	71	71	69	71	282	16,827.27
Steven Ferreira	70	73	68	71	282	16,827.27
Jake Redman	69	67	73	73	282	16,827.27
Shaun Norris	76	64	69	73	282	16,827.27
Jacques Blaauw	72	68	68	74	282	16,827.27
Titch Moore	67	68	72	75	282	16,827.27

Nedbank Golf Challenge

Gary Player Country Club, Sun City, South Africa — December 4-7
Par 36-36–72; 7,831 yards — purse, US$6,500,000

	SCORES				TOTAL	MONEY
Danny Willett	71	68	65	66	270	$1,250,000
Ross Fisher	66	70	70	68	274	775,000
Luke Donald	71	63	69	73	276	433,000
Marcel Siem	68	72	71	68	279	348,000
Kiradech Aphibarnrat	72	73	68	68	281	295,000
Miguel Angel Jimenez	70	74	69	69	282	245,000
Jonas Blixt	71	73	70	71	285	172,500
Tim Clark	70	71	72	72	285	172,500

	SCORES				TOTAL	MONEY
Thongchai Jaidee	71	70	71	73	285	172,500
Louis Oosthuizen	70	73	69	73	285	172,500
Shane Lowry	72	72	71	71	286	154,000
Brendon Todd	73	68	75	71	287	148,000
Stephen Gallacher	70	73	72	72	287	148,000
Charl Schwartzel	70	71	75	73	289	140,000
Tommy Fleetwood	74	67	74	74	289	140,000
Lee Westwood	72	70	78	70	290	132,000
George Coetzee	68	74	76	72	290	132,000
Pablo Larrazabal	73	71	71	75	290	132,000
Brooks Koepka	70	74	75	72	291	124,500
Dawie Van der Walt	73	72	69	77	291	124,500
Martin Kaymer	74	75	71	72	292	117,000
Jaco Ahlers	74	75	70	73	292	117,000
Alexander Levy	68	70	76	78	292	117,000
Thomas Bjorn	80	72	68	73	293	110,750
Joost Luiten	72	74	73	74	293	110,750
Kevin Na	77	73	72	73	295	105,750
Marc Warren	75	73	71	76	295	105,750
Mikko Ilonen	76	78	72	72	298	103,000
Danie van Tonder	77	78	76	70	301	101,500
Jamie Donaldson	74				WD	

Alfred Dunhill Championship

Leopard Creek Golf Club, Malelane, South Africa — December 11-14
Par 35-37–72; 7,287 yards — purse, €1,500,000

	SCORES				TOTAL	MONEY
Branden Grace	62	66	72	68	268	R3,566,250
Louis Oosthuizen	69	69	68	69	275	2,587,500
Andrew Johnston	69	67	68	73	277	1,557,000
Trevor Fisher, Jr.	73	67	69	69	278	1,017,000
Danny Willett	66	69	67	76	278	1,017,000
David Drysdale	71	68	71	69	279	730,125
Francesco Molinari	68	65	70	76	279	730,125
Thomas Pieters	71	71	68	70	280	493,500
Tjaart van der Walt	67	67	75	71	280	493,500
Shaun Norris	68	67	73	72	280	493,500
Pedro Oriol	70	72	74	65	281	377,250
Justin Harding	71	70	70	70	281	377,250
Richard Sterne	71	71	67	72	281	377,250
Daniel Brooks	70	72	71	69	282	325,125
Espen Kofstad	70	72	71	69	282	325,125
Andrew Curlewis	72	67	74	70	283	281,250
Louis de Jager	69	67	76	71	283	281,250
Jbe' Kruger	68	69	75	71	283	281,250
Thomas Aiken	71	72	69	71	283	281,250
Danie van Tonder	70	69	70	74	283	281,250
Morten Orum Madsen	70	66	72	75	283	281,250
Hennie Otto	74	67	75	68	284	239,625
Dylan Frittelli	70	70	73	71	284	239,625
Byeong-Hun An	71	69	72	72	284	239,625
Johan Carlsson	70	68	73	73	284	239,625
Charl Schwartzel	69	70	76	70	285	219,375
Renato Paratore	73	68	72	72	285	219,375
Julien Quesne	69	72	75	70	286	197,100
Darren Fichardt	74	68	72	72	286	197,100
Craig Lee	68	72	72	74	286	197,100
Alex Haindl	71	67	73	75	286	197,100

	SCORES				TOTAL	MONEY
Benjamin Hebert	68	70	72	76	286	197,100
Max Orrin	72	71	73	71	287	168,750
Chris Paisley	70	72	73	72	287	168,750
Kevin Phelan	72	71	72	72	287	168,750
Michael Hollick	67	70	76	74	287	168,750
Lee Slattery	71	70	72	74	287	168,750
Christiaan Basson	69	69	74	75	287	168,750
Nacho Elvira	67	71	74	75	287	168,750
Eduardo de la Riva	70	70	77	71	288	146,250
Ulrich van den Berg	70	72	75	71	288	146,250
Kevin Stone	68	71	75	74	288	146,250
Jaco Ahlers	70	69	78	72	289	126,000
John Hahn	70	70	75	74	289	126,000
Chris Swanepoel	68	68	78	75	289	126,000
Jean Hugo	69	71	72	77	289	126,000
Mark Murless	71	68	72	78	289	126,000
Scott Jamieson	68	70	72	79	289	126,000
Magnus A. Carlsson	68	73	76	73	290	101,250
Carlos Del Moral	68	73	75	74	290	101,250
Oliver Bekker	74	67	73	76	290	101,250
Shiv Kapur	71	66	75	78	290	101,250
Lucas Bjerregaard	68	67	66	89	290	101,250
Adilson Da Silva	69	70	82	70	291	81,000
Robert Rock	71	72	78	70	291	81,000
Kristoffer Broberg	70	73	74	74	291	81,000
Martin du Toit	74	67	74	76	291	81,000
Alessandro Tadini	73	68	78	74	293	69,750
Pablo Martin Benavides	73	70	74	76	293	69,750
Ross McGowan	72	70	73	78	293	69,750
Jake Roos	65	72	84	73	294	64,125
Tyrone Ferreira	72	69	73	80	294	64,125
Andrew Georgiou	72	71	78	74	295	58,500
*Bradley Neil	73	70	77	75	295	
Richard McEvoy	75	68	76	76	295	58,500
Jacques Blaauw	71	68	73	83	295	58,500
Steve Surry	71	72	79	74	296	50,625
Rhys West	73	68	79	76	296	50,625
Desvonde Botes	70	73	77	76	296	50,625
Soren Hansen	69	73	75	79	296	50,625
Matt Ford	66	75	78	79	298	45,000
Jason Barnes	69	73	80	77	299	33,750
Lasse Jensen	75	68	83	75	301	33,705
Jason Palmer	70	73	78	82	303	33,660
James Kamte	72	69	85	79	305	33,615

Women's Tours

Pure Silk Bahamas LPGA Classic

Ocean Club Golf Course, Paradise Island, Bahamas
Par 36-37–73; 6,644 yards

January 23-26
purse, $1,300,000

	SCORES				TOTAL	MONEY
Jessica Korda	69	66	72	66	273	$195,000
Stacy Lewis	69	71	68	66	274	120,655
Lizette Salas	72	67	66	71	276	63,581
Paula Creamer	71	65	71	69	276	63,581
Na Yeon Choi	70	68	66	72	276	63,581
Pornanong Phatlum	71	69	69	67	276	63,581
Sandra Gal	71	69	71	66	277	31,543
Lydia Ko	68	70	71	68	277	31,543
P.K. Kongkraphan	69	69	71	68	277	31,543
Christel Boeljon	71	67	73	66	277	31,543
Thidapa Suwannapura	70	71	68	69	278	23,945
Morgan Pressel	70	73	69	66	278	23,945
Amelia Lewis	69	73	66	72	280	19,289
Brittany Lincicome	70	71	71	68	280	19,289
Chella Choi	73	69	67	71	280	19,289
Jenny Suh	71	66	71	72	280	19,289
Michelle Wie	72	65	72	71	280	19,289
Kristy McPherson	73	71	69	69	282	15,220
Hee Young Park	69	72	72	69	282	15,220
Alena Sharp	75	69	70	68	282	15,220
Sandra Changkija	71	72	68	71	282	15,220
Azahara Munoz	70	71	69	72	282	15,220
Jodi Ewart Shadoff	75	68	71	69	283	13,344
Haru Nomura	73	74	70	66	283	13,344
Laura Diaz	74	69	70	71	284	12,386
Angela Stanford	73	73	69	69	284	12,386
Gerina Piller	71	75	68	71	285	11,230
Line Vedel	73	74	70	68	285	11,230
Moriya Jutanugarn	74	72	70	69	285	11,230
Karine Icher	74	73	67	72	286	9,975
Tiffany Joh	73	74	66	73	286	9,975
Pernilla Lindberg	70	71	74	71	286	9,975

ISPS Handa Women's Australian Open

See Australian Ladies Tour section.

Honda LPGA Thailand

Siam Country Club, Pattaya Old Course, Chonburi, Thailand
Par 36-36–72; 6,548 yards

February 18-23
purse, $1,500,000

	SCORES				TOTAL	MONEY
Anna Nordqvist	66	72	67	68	273	$225,000
Inbee Park	71	71	67	66	275	139,933
Catriona Matthew	76	71	65	65	277	101,512
Michelle Wie	67	73	69	69	278	78,527

	SCORES				TOTAL	MONEY
Julieta Granada	71	68	71	69	279	46,044
Gerina Piller	70	73	70	66	279	46,044
Yani Tseng	72	73	66	68	279	46,044
Lexi Thompson	68	74	69	68	279	46,044
Stacy Lewis	71	69	73	66	279	46,044
Suzann Pettersen	69	73	72	66	280	31,028
So Yeon Ryu	69	72	71	69	281	27,771
Azahara Munoz	71	68	74	68	281	27,771
Jenny Shin	72	70	70	70	282	25,128
Sandra Gal	69	70	73	71	283	22,268
Thidapa Suwannapura	73	70	70	70	283	22,268
Angela Stanford	68	73	71	71	283	22,268
Se Ri Pak	72	72	68	72	284	19,460
Na Yeon Choi	75	73	72	64	284	19,460
Karrie Webb	71	70	71	73	285	17,621
Caroline Hedwall	69	73	70	73	285	17,621
Lydia Ko	72	70	69	74	285	17,621
Shanshan Feng	71	72	69	74	286	15,215
Dewi Claire Schreefel	71	73	74	68	286	15,215
Morgan Pressel	70	73	74	69	286	15,215
Cristie Kerr	71	72	68	75	286	15,215
Eun-Hee Ji	70	78	70	68	286	15,215
Mariajo Uribe	75	69	71	72	287	13,560
Brittany Lincicome	74	79	65	70	288	12,756
Brittany Lang	73	69	76	70	288	12,756
Jennifer Johnson	68	73	71	77	289	11,338
Paula Creamer	72	77	72	68	289	11,338
Meena Lee	79	71	69	70	289	11,338
Hee Young Park	71	76	70	72	289	11,338

HSBC Women's Champions

Sentosa Golf Club, Serapong Course, Singapore — February 26-March 2
Par 36-36–72; 6,600 yards — purse, $1,400,000

	SCORES				TOTAL	MONEY
Paula Creamer	67	73	69	69	278	$210,000
Azahara Munoz	69	72	67	70	278	133,681
(Creamer defeated Munoz on second playoff hole.)						
Karrie Webb	66	69	70	74	279	96,976
Inbee Park	70	72	71	68	281	52,477
Angela Stanford	68	69	69	75	281	52,477
Suzann Pettersen	71	70	70	70	281	52,477
Morgan Pressel	71	69	70	71	281	52,477
So Yeon Ryu	71	71	73	66	281	52,477
Teresa Lu	68	70	70	75	283	31,106
Michelle Wie	73	71	69	70	283	31,106
Eun-Hee Ji	71	73	71	69	284	25,689
Na Yeon Choi	71	70	71	72	284	25,689
Chella Choi	73	71	69	71	284	25,689
Ha Na Jang	73	69	71	72	285	22,542
Lydia Ko	73	69	73	71	286	21,224
Karine Icher	72	72	72	71	287	17,956
Se Ri Pak	75	71	72	69	287	17,956
Sandra Gal	75	76	68	68	287	17,956
Caroline Hedwall	67	73	72	75	287	17,956
Brittany Lang	73	74	68	72	287	17,956
Lexi Thompson	71	71	72	73	287	17,956
Gerina Piller	70	75	70	73	288	15,370
Jenny Shin	72	72	73	71	288	15,370

	SCORES				TOTAL	MONEY
Jaye Marie Green	75	70	73	71	289	13,979
Jiyai Shin	74	70	71	74	289	13,979
Anna Nordqvist	73	67	74	75	289	13,979
Pornanong Phatlum	73	75	69	73	290	12,698
Sun Young Yoo	72	73	73	72	290	12,698
Nicole Castrale	73	68	76	74	291	10,832
Mika Miyazato	75	73	69	74	291	10,832
Hee Young Park	75	74	71	71	291	10,832
Ilhee Lee	76	73	69	73	291	10,832
Hee Kyung Seo	76	67	71	77	291	10,832
Amy Yang	70	73	73	75	291	10,832

JTBC Founders Cup

Wildfire Golf Club at JW Marriott Phoenix Desert Ridge Resort & Spa, Phoenix, Arizona
Par 36-36–72; 6,601 yards

March 20-23
purse, $1,500,000

	SCORES				TOTAL	MONEY
Karrie Webb	66	71	69	63	269	$225,000
Stacy Lewis	66	71	67	66	270	85,895
Azahara Munoz	68	71	64	67	270	85,895
Amy Yang	67	69	67	67	270	85,895
Mirim Lee	64	67	70	69	270	85,895
Lydia Ko	67	66	67	70	270	85,895
Pornanong Phatlum	67	71	67	66	271	37,956
So Yeon Ryu	68	67	68	68	271	37,956
Jessica Korda	69	66	66	70	271	37,956
Cristie Kerr	73	69	63	67	272	29,507
Inbee Park	66	69	70	67	272	29,507
Caroline Masson	70	71	66	66	273	24,866
Lizette Salas	69	67	69	68	273	24,866
Michelle Wie	66	70	67	70	273	24,866
Hee-Won Han	68	72	71	63	274	20,276
Jenny Shin	68	71	71	64	274	20,276
Gerina Piller	66	73	67	68	274	20,276
Laura Davies	68	71	66	69	274	20,276
Belen Mozo	70	68	69	68	275	17,402
Jaye Marie Green	70	68	67	70	275	17,402
Paula Creamer	70	70	64	71	275	17,402
Karine Icher	72	68	70	66	276	14,483
Eun-Hee Ji	66	70	74	66	276	14,483
Jodi Ewart Shadoff	67	69	71	69	276	14,483
Candie Kung	70	68	68	70	276	14,483
Morgan Pressel	65	72	67	72	276	14,483
Chella Choi	69	66	68	73	276	14,483
Sun Young Yoo	69	65	68	74	276	14,483
Pernilla Lindberg	66	72	73	66	277	11,424
Katie Futcher	68	72	70	67	277	11,424
Suzann Pettersen	68	72	70	67	277	11,424
Brittany Lang	72	69	68	68	277	11,424
Lexi Thompson	69	69	67	72	277	11,424

Kia Classic

Park Hyatt Aviara Golf Club, Carlsbad, California
Par 36-36–72; 6,593 yards

March 27-30
purse, $1,700,000

	SCORES				TOTAL	MONEY
Anna Nordqvist	73	68	67	67	275	$255,000
Lizette Salas	69	68	69	70	276	155,874
Lexi Thompson	69	70	70	68	277	113,075
Chella Choi	74	65	70	69	278	87,473
Cristie Kerr	68	68	70	73	279	70,406
Inbee Park	69	71	72	68	280	46,511
Se Ri Pak	70	70	71	69	280	46,511
Stacy Lewis	70	66	73	71	280	46,511
Eun-Hee Ji	71	73	65	71	280	46,511
Giulia Sergas	75	68	71	67	281	30,142
Azahara Munoz	69	72	69	71	281	30,142
Gerina Piller	71	73	68	69	281	30,142
Julieta Granada	70	70	70	71	281	30,142
Dori Carter	70	64	74	73	281	30,142
Jenny Shin	73	69	70	70	282	24,748
Mariajo Uribe	67	71	73	72	283	20,183
Ji Young Oh	72	70	71	70	283	20,183
Hee Young Park	77	68	68	70	283	20,183
Michelle Wie	70	73	70	70	283	20,183
Meena Lee	73	70	69	71	283	20,183
P.K. Kongkraphan	72	73	65	73	283	20,183
Shanshan Feng	68	71	69	75	283	20,183
Paula Creamer	67	72	72	72	283	20,183
Ai Miyazato	70	71	73	70	284	16,897
Mi Hyang Lee	68	73	73	71	285	14,544
Mina Harigae	76	69	70	70	285	14,544
Haeji Kang	75	70	67	73	285	14,544
Jenny Suh	72	69	73	71	285	14,544
Paz Echeverria	74	72	66	73	285	14,544
Karrie Webb	75	68	67	75	285	14,544
Ayako Uehara	70	71	67	77	285	14,544

Kraft Nabisco Championship

Mission Hills Country Club, Dinah Shore Course,
Rancho Mirage, California
Par 36-36–72; 6,738 yards

April 3-6
purse, $2,000,000

	SCORES				TOTAL	MONEY
Lexi Thompson	73	64	69	68	274	$300,000
Michelle Wie	67	71	68	71	277	187,584
Stacy Lewis	73	70	69	69	281	136,079
Se Ri Pak	67	70	71	74	282	94,998
Cristie Kerr	69	70	71	72	282	94,998
Shanshan Feng	66	73	72	72	283	69,323
Charley Hull	73	69	66	76	284	51,522
Azahara Munoz	72	70	70	72	284	51,522
Angela Stanford	74	69	69	72	284	51,522
Amy Yang	68	73	71	73	285	41,594
Karrie Webb	73	70	70	73	286	33,911
Gerina Piller	77	65	70	74	286	33,911
Catriona Matthew	72	68	70	76	286	33,911
Caroline Masson	73	72	72	69	286	33,911
Morgan Pressel	70	70	75	71	286	33,911

	SCORES				TOTAL	MONEY
Christina Kim	74	69	72	72	287	24,289
Mi Hyang Lee	72	72	72	71	287	24,289
Tiffany Joh	70	75	70	72	287	24,289
Chella Choi	70	72	69	76	287	24,289
Jee Young Lee	71	75	67	74	287	24,289
Na Yeon Choi	72	71	72	72	287	24,289
Jiyai Shin	69	73	70	75	287	24,289
Anna Nordqvist	71	69	74	73	287	24,289
*Minjee Lee	75	68	73	72	288	
Jessica Korda	73	73	71	71	288	20,335
Mirim Lee	71	72	70	76	289	19,257
*Brooke M. Henderson	77	68	70	74	289	
Hee Young Park	72	72	71	74	289	19,257
Giulia Sergas	73	74	72	71	290	17,125
Lydia Ko	73	70	73	74	290	17,125
Eun-Hee Ji	74	73	69	74	290	17,125
Mo Martin	73	68	74	75	290	17,125
*Alison Lee	75	74	70	71	290	
Sandra Gal	72	70	77	72	291	14,583
Mariajo Uribe	72	72	74	73	291	14,583
Pernilla Lindberg	73	74	69	75	291	14,583
Paula Creamer	72	74	74	71	291	14,583
Inbee Park	74	70	73	75	292	13,146
P.K. Kongkraphan	74	74	68	77	293	11,180
Pornanong Phatlum	71	73	72	77	293	11,180
Jodi Ewart Shadoff	76	70	73	74	293	11,180
Jenny Shin	74	73	70	76	293	11,180
I.K. Kim	74	73	72	74	293	11,180
Alison Walshe	73	74	70	76	293	11,180
Thidapa Suwannapura	73	72	72	76	293	11,180
Karine Icher	75	72	72	75	294	8,909
Jimin Kang	76	69	74	75	294	8,909
Ilhee Lee	78	69	70	77	294	8,909
So Yeon Ryu	70	72	75	77	294	8,909
*Lilia Vu	73	73	73	75	294	
*Su-Hyun Oh	74	74	73	74	295	
Nicole Castrale	71	73	74	77	295	7,805
Austin Ernst	71	74	72	78	295	7,805
Haeji Kang	70	74	71	80	295	7,805
Ha Na Jang	73	73	71	79	296	6,881
Christel Boeljon	73	72	78	73	296	6,881
Meena Lee	74	74	75	73	296	6,881
Sun Young Yoo	74	72	71	79	296	6,881
Brittany Lincicome	77	72	76	72	297	6,265
Sakura Yokomine	75	70	77	75	297	6,265
Sei Young Kim	75	70	76	77	298	5,751
Danielle Kang	76	73	73	76	298	5,751
Carlota Ciganda	73	69	79	77	298	5,751
Caroline Hedwall	71	74	76	78	299	5,170
Juli Inkster	76	70	73	80	299	5,170
Haru Nomura	75	72	75	77	299	5,170
Hee-Won Han	75	73	75	77	300	4,775
Jennifer Rosales	69	74	76	81	300	4,775
Mina Harigae	76	72	77	75	300	4,775
Ai Miyazato	77	71	76	76	300	4,775
Candie Kung	74	70	76	81	301	4,468
Dewi Claire Schreefel	75	74	75	77	301	4,468

LPGA LOTTE Championship

Ko Olina Golf Club, Kapolei, Oahu, Hawaii — April 16-19
Par 36-36–72; 6,383 yards — purse, $1,700,000

	SCORES				TOTAL	MONEY
Michelle Wie	70	67	70	67	274	$255,000
Angela Stanford	72	64	67	73	276	155,874
Inbee Park	70	68	72	67	277	113,075
Hyo-Joo Kim	68	70	69	71	278	87,473
So Yeon Ryu	68	70	72	69	279	64,005
Chella Choi	74	68	70	67	279	64,005
Haru Nomura	73	67	73	68	281	45,231
Amy Anderson	70	72	68	71	281	45,231
Katherine Kirk	73	70	71	68	282	33,602
Katie M. Burnett	71	69	72	70	282	33,602
Cristie Kerr	72	66	70	74	282	33,602
Se Ri Pak	68	71	74	69	282	33,602
Christel Boeljon	71	70	74	69	284	26,341
Julieta Granada	74	72	67	71	284	26,341
Shanshan Feng	73	71	70	70	284	26,341
Ariya Jutanugarn	73	70	71	71	285	23,383
Eun-Hee Ji	77	71	72	66	286	20,448
Na Yeon Choi	75	70	69	72	286	20,448
Brooke Pancake	75	69	73	69	286	20,448
Amelia Lewis	77	66	70	73	286	20,448
Tiffany Joh	73	68	77	68	286	20,448
Amy Yang	74	73	73	67	287	17,260
Lizette Salas	73	71	74	69	287	17,260
Paula Reto	72	69	73	73	287	17,260
Azahara Munoz	73	70	71	73	287	17,260
*So Young Lee	70	70	75	72	287	
Danah Bordner	72	74	70	72	288	14,525
Line Vedel	76	71	72	69	288	14,525
Mariajo Uribe	76	70	71	71	288	14,525
Jenny Shin	73	72	73	70	288	14,525
Christina Kim	74	71	70	73	288	14,525

Swinging Skirts LPGA Classic

Lake Merced Golf Club, San Francisco, California — April 24-27
Par 36-36–72; 6,507 yards — purse, $1,800,000

	SCORES				TOTAL	MONEY
Lydia Ko	68	71	68	69	276	$270,000
Stacy Lewis	69	69	68	71	277	163,551
Jenny Shin	68	74	68	68	278	118,644
Line Vedel	72	71	70	69	282	75,365
Shanshan Feng	74	70	68	70	282	75,365
Inbee Park	73	68	73	68	282	75,365
Hyo-Joo Kim	69	73	72	70	284	47,458
P.K. Kongkraphan	74	68	70	72	284	47,458
Michelle Wie	72	72	71	71	286	35,257
Brittany Lang	71	71	72	72	286	35,257
Cristie Kerr	73	75	70	68	286	35,257
Karine Icher	66	73	73	74	286	35,257
Haeji Kang	72	70	72	73	287	28,474
I.K. Kim	72	71	72	72	287	28,474
Eun-Hee Ji	73	71	74	70	288	24,594
Ashleigh Simon	73	70	73	72	288	24,594

	SCORES				TOTAL	MONEY
Azahara Munoz	76	69	73	70	288	24,594
Hee Young Park	70	73	68	78	289	21,371
Caroline Masson	74	75	72	68	289	21,371
Sun Young Yoo	72	76	69	72	289	21,371
Mina Harigae	75	73	73	69	290	17,806
Ilhee Lee	68	73	76	73	290	17,806
Haru Nomura	75	73	71	71	290	17,806
Alison Walshe	74	69	76	71	290	17,806
Pornanong Phatlum	72	72	71	75	290	17,806
Catriona Matthew	73	69	74	74	290	17,806
Mika Miyazato	72	69	77	72	290	17,806
Suzann Pettersen	70	72	79	70	291	14,909
Mi Hyang Lee	72	76	74	69	291	14,909
Dewi Claire Schreefel	68	76	77	71	292	12,983
Ariya Jutanugarn	73	73	74	72	292	12,983
Karrie Webb	74	73	72	73	292	12,983
Sandra Gal	73	76	71	72	292	12,983
Mirim Lee	76	71	75	70	292	12,983

North Texas LPGA Shootout

Las Colinas Country Club, Irving, Texas
Par 36-35–71; 6,410 yards

May 1-4
purse, $1,300,000

	SCORES				TOTAL	MONEY
Stacy Lewis	71	64	69	64	268	$195,000
Meena Lee	70	64	70	70	274	119,765
Michelle Wie	67	73	68	67	275	86,881
Kim Kaufman	72	66	68	70	276	60,653
Na Yeon Choi	72	69	66	69	276	60,653
Christina Kim	67	69	70	71	277	32,348
Lexi Thompson	70	71	67	69	277	32,348
Cristie Kerr	67	70	69	71	277	32,348
Dewi Claire Schreefel	71	66	72	68	277	32,348
Suzann Pettersen	66	71	68	72	277	32,348
Dori Carter	67	70	68	72	277	32,348
Jennifer Johnson	71	70	65	72	278	22,228
Jenny Shin	69	69	68	72	278	22,228
Amy Anderson	71	72	67	69	279	18,097
Pat Hurst	72	70	67	70	279	18,097
Chella Choi	69	74	67	69	279	18,097
Inbee Park	71	68	68	72	279	18,097
Alena Sharp	73	70	66	70	279	18,097
Stacey Keating	71	71	69	69	280	14,295
Megan Grehan	76	67	69	68	280	14,295
Julieta Granada	71	66	68	75	280	14,295
Natalie Gulbis	70	65	71	74	280	14,295
Pornanong Phatlum	70	68	71	71	280	14,295
Thidapa Suwannapura	70	68	68	74	280	14,295
Karine Icher	73	69	68	71	281	11,606
Tiffany Joh	74	66	70	71	281	11,606
Mina Harigae	74	68	68	71	281	11,606
Sarah Jane Smith	72	70	70	69	281	11,606
Ji Young Oh	73	67	71	70	281	11,606
Jennifer Song	73	69	68	72	282	9,704
Brittany Lang	70	71	70	71	282	9,704
Alison Walshe	72	72	67	71	282	9,704
Jodi Ewart Shadoff	69	72	68	73	282	9,704

Kingsmill Championship

Kingsmill Resort, River Course, Williamsburg, Virginia
Par 36-35–71; 6,379 yards

May 15-18
purse, $1,300,000

	SCORES				TOTAL	MONEY
Lizette Salas	67	68	65	71	271	$195,000
Yani Tseng	68	70	68	69	275	90,642
Lexi Thompson	67	69	70	69	275	90,642
Sarah Jane Smith	68	71	70	66	275	90,642
Lydia Ko	70	68	67	71	276	48,832
So Yeon Ryu	70	69	68	69	276	48,832
Thidapa Suwannapura	67	70	71	69	277	36,786
Pornanong Phatlum	71	69	66	72	278	27,997
Sandra Gal	69	71	69	69	278	27,997
Azahara Munoz	65	71	72	70	278	27,997
Mina Harigae	72	68	70	68	278	27,997
Mi Hyang Lee	74	69	70	66	279	19,641
Jennifer Johnson	70	72	70	67	279	19,641
Brittany Lang	67	68	74	70	279	19,641
Suzann Pettersen	72	68	70	69	279	19,641
Stacy Lewis	70	65	70	74	279	19,641
Alejandra Llaneza	68	69	71	71	279	19,641
Charley Hull	70	69	71	70	280	15,001
Joanna Klatten	69	72	70	69	280	15,001
Katherine Kirk	69	68	68	75	280	15,001
Austin Ernst	65	74	68	73	280	15,001
Chie Arimura	74	70	69	67	280	15,001
Mariajo Uribe	72	65	74	70	281	12,219
Gerina Piller	69	68	75	69	281	12,219
Paz Echeverria	73	65	73	70	281	12,219
Anna Nordqvist	74	68	69	70	281	12,219
Ilhee Lee	72	70	68	71	281	12,219
Sarah Kemp	70	71	72	68	281	12,219
Christina Kim	72	70	67	73	282	9,270
Jenny Shin	69	70	71	72	282	9,270
Cristie Kerr	67	71	72	72	282	9,270
Jennifer Rosales	70	69	70	73	282	9,270
Jane Park	71	71	73	67	282	9,270
Danielle Kang	67	72	72	71	282	9,270
Hee Young Park	66	68	69	79	282	9,270
Angela Stanford	73	68	70	71	282	9,270

Airbus LPGA Classic

Robert Trent Jones Golf Trail, Magnolia Grove, The Crossings,
Mobile, Alabama
Par 36-36–72; 6,521 yards

May 22-25
purse, $1,300,000

	SCORES				TOTAL	MONEY
Jessica Korda	67	67	69	65	268	$195,000
Anna Nordqvist	68	66	66	69	269	120,962
Charley Hull	65	67	71	67	270	70,089
Catriona Matthew	64	67	70	69	270	70,089
Michelle Wie	71	66	66	67	270	70,089
Jenny Shin	67	68	69	67	271	44,703
Jodi Ewart Shadoff	69	67	68	68	272	33,224
Lexi Thompson	70	65	71	66	272	33,224
Eun-Hee Ji	66	70	68	68	272	33,224
Stacy Lewis	66	70	66	71	273	24,139
Brittany Lincicome	69	69	69	66	273	24,139

	SCORES				TOTAL	MONEY
So Yeon Ryu	70	67	67	69	273	24,139
Belen Mozo	70	68	67	68	273	24,139
Chella Choi	69	68	71	66	274	20,398
Julieta Granada	67	70	71	68	276	17,748
Jennifer Johnson	71	69	68	68	276	17,748
Paula Creamer	71	71	66	68	276	17,748
Carlota Ciganda	72	69	69	66	276	17,748
Se Ri Pak	67	69	71	70	277	14,182
Hannah Jun Medlock	73	66	71	67	277	14,182
Paz Echeverria	70	71	67	69	277	14,182
Pornanong Phatlum	69	68	71	69	277	14,182
Haru Nomura	71	65	70	71	277	14,182
Xi Yu Lin	69	68	71	69	277	14,182
Paola Moreno	68	71	66	72	277	14,182
Karine Icher	71	69	69	69	278	10,646
Christina Kim	70	66	70	72	278	10,646
Katherine Kirk	70	67	68	73	278	10,646
Hee Young Park	68	66	73	71	278	10,646
Ariya Jutanugarn	70	71	69	68	278	10,646
Na Yeon Choi	69	69	69	71	278	10,646
Suzann Pettersen	66	70	69	73	278	10,646
Kelly Tan	71	70	71	66	278	10,646

ShopRite LPGA Classic

Stockton Seaview Hotel & Golf Club, Galloway, New Jersey — May 30-June 1
Par 37-34–71; 6,155 yards — purse, $1,500,000

	SCORES			TOTAL	MONEY
Stacy Lewis	67	63	67	197	$225,000
Christina Kim	64	67	72	203	138,527
Gerina Piller	67	67	70	204	72,998
Haeji Kang	68	67	69	204	72,998
Anna Nordqvist	69	65	70	204	72,998
Jennifer Johnson	62	70	72	204	72,998
Julieta Granada	71	66	68	205	42,851
Karrie Webb	69	70	67	206	31,399
Meena Lee	70	70	66	206	31,399
Shanshan Feng	74	65	67	206	31,399
Azahara Munoz	69	71	66	206	31,399
Inbee Park	66	70	70	206	31,399
Joanna Klatten	70	71	66	207	21,590
Suzann Pettersen	70	70	67	207	21,590
Mo Martin	70	71	66	207	21,590
Na Yeon Choi	66	71	70	207	21,590
Haru Nomura	63	73	71	207	21,590
Mina Harigae	68	72	67	207	21,590
Sarah Kemp	67	72	69	208	17,140
Brittany Lincicome	67	70	71	208	17,140
Jodi Ewart Shadoff	68	73	67	208	17,140
Chella Choi	67	71	70	208	17,140
Laura Diaz	67	72	70	209	13,212
Christel Boeljon	71	68	70	209	13,212
Becky Morgan	69	70	70	209	13,212
Paula Creamer	73	70	66	209	13,212
Dori Carter	69	68	72	209	13,212
Line Vedel	74	69	66	209	13,212
Michelle Wie	67	72	70	209	13,212
Kim Kaufman	69	68	72	209	13,212
Hee Young Park	70	70	69	209	13,212
Karine Icher	72	69	68	209	13,212

Manulife Financial LPGA Classic

Grey Silo Golf Course, Waterloo, Ontario, Canada — June 5-8
Par 36-35–71; 6,330 yards — purse, $1,500,000

	SCORES				TOTAL	MONEY
Inbee Park	69	66	65	61	261	$225,000
Cristie Kerr	67	69	65	63	264	136,903
Shanshan Feng	66	65	67	68	266	99,314
Belen Mozo	68	67	68	65	268	69,332
Lydia Ko	71	67	64	66	268	69,332
Stacy Lewis	69	69	68	63	269	46,471
Michelle Wie	65	67	68	69	269	46,471
Suzann Pettersen	70	67	67	66	270	35,229
Chella Choi	70	69	67	64	270	35,229
Anna Nordqvist	69	64	69	69	271	27,320
So Yeon Ryu	68	67	70	66	271	27,320
Caroline Masson	69	67	70	65	271	27,320
Hee Young Park	65	66	72	68	271	27,320
Na Yeon Choi	68	67	68	69	272	23,086
Angela Stanford	71	67	67	68	273	19,638
Line Vedel	69	70	69	65	273	19,638
Catriona Matthew	71	67	70	65	273	19,638
Meena Lee	70	67	68	68	273	19,638
Mirim Lee	69	73	65	66	273	19,638
Candie Kung	70	68	65	71	274	16,340
Marina Alex	68	68	71	67	274	16,340
Julieta Granada	72	69	67	66	274	16,340
Austin Ernst	69	69	70	66	274	16,340
Louise Friberg	72	69	70	64	275	12,320
Thidapa Suwannapura	72	66	67	70	275	12,320
Jee Young Lee	68	68	69	70	275	12,320
Jennifer Johnson	70	68	69	68	275	12,320
Jennifer Rosales	69	72	65	69	275	12,320
Mi Jung Hur	73	68	66	68	275	12,320
Jaye Marie Green	70	68	70	67	275	12,320
Karine Icher	69	71	72	63	275	12,320
Paz Echeverria	68	71	68	68	275	12,320
Danielle Kang	71	68	67	69	275	12,320
Joanna Klatten	70	70	70	65	275	12,320

U.S. Women's Open

Pinehurst Resort & Country Club, Village of Pinehurst, North Carolina — June 19-22
Par 35-35–70; 6,649 yards — purse, $3,250,000

	SCORES				TOTAL	MONEY
Michelle Wie	68	68	72	70	278	$720,000
Stacy Lewis	67	73	74	66	280	432,000
Stephanie Meadow	71	72	69	69	281	271,373
Amy Yang	71	69	68	74	282	191,536
Meena Lee	72	73	70	68	283	149,942
So Yeon Ryu	69	74	70	70	283	149,942
Lexi Thompson	71	68	74	71	284	113,582
Sakura Yokomine	74	68	71	71	284	113,582
Pornanong Phatlum	71	73	69	71	284	113,582
Catriona Matthew	75	69	75	66	285	90,861
Jenny Shin	74	70	73	68	285	90,861
*Brooke Mackenzie Henderson	71	73	72	69	285	

	SCORES				TOTAL	MONEY
Yueer Cindy Feng	73	71	71	71	286	77,640
Na Yeon Choi	71	70	71	74	286	77,640
Lydia Ko	76	71	71	69	287	58,096
Shanshan Feng	77	70	70	70	287	58,096
Brittany Lincicome	77	70	69	71	287	58,096
Hee Young Park	73	73	69	72	287	58,096
Paula Creamer	70	72	72	73	287	58,096
Chella Choi	75	70	69	73	287	58,096
Juli Inkster	71	75	66	75	287	58,096
Julieta Granada	75	71	74	68	288	40,327
Sandra Gal	74	72	73	69	288	40,327
Karine Icher	76	72	71	69	288	40,327
Azahara Munoz	73	71	74	70	288	40,327
Brittany Lang	73	75	69	71	288	40,327
*Minjee Lee	69	71	72	76	288	
Eun Hee Ji	71	75	75	68	289	32,708
Caroline Masson	72	75	73	69	289	32,708
Candie Kung	71	76	75	68	290	27,721
Angela Stanford	71	72	77	70	290	27,721
I.K. Kim	71	74	75	70	290	27,721
Mariajo Uribe	72	70	76	72	290	27,721
Karrie Webb	70	73	70	77	290	27,721
Yani Tseng	77	71	74	69	291	23,555
Rikako Morita	73	75	73	70	291	23,555
Ha Na Jang	76	73	70	72	291	23,555
Jennifer Song	74	72	77	69	292	20,090
Caroline Hedwall	73	76	72	71	292	20,090
Mina Harigae	71	74	74	73	292	20,090
Se Ri Pak	76	69	74	73	292	20,090
Jee Young Lee	73	73	73	73	292	20,090
Lee-Anne Pace	76	73	73	71	293	16,887
Hee Kyung Bae	77	71	73	72	293	16,887
Inbee Park	76	71	73	73	293	16,887
Nikki Campbell	74	75	76	69	294	14,536
Beatriz Recari	73	74	72	75	294	14,536
Sei Young Kim	72	75	72	75	294	14,536
Giulia Sergas	77	72	74	72	295	11,943
Moriya Jutanugarn	72	77	74	72	295	11,943
Laura Diaz	75	72	75	73	295	11,943
Jennifer Johnson	75	74	72	74	295	11,943
Katherine Kirk	69	76	74	76	295	11,943
So-Young Jang	75	72	77	72	296	10,840
Belen Mozo	78	70	73	76	297	10,527
Misuzu Narita	76	70	73	78	297	10,527
Jodi Ewart Shadoff	76	71	78	73	298	10,197
Ashley Knoll	75	74	73	76	298	10,197
*Mathilda Cappeliez	76	70	78	75	299	
Sue Kim	71	73	79	76	299	9,881
Danielle Kang	75	71	76	77	299	9,881
Haeji Kang	74	75	72	78	299	9,881
*Emma Talley	75	73	78	74	300	
Carlota Ciganda	75	72	78	75	300	9,528
Gerina Piller	72	72	80	76	300	9,528
Pernilla Lindberg	72	77	73	78	300	9,528
Ilhee Lee	73	76	77	75	301	9,292
*Chisato Hashimoto	73	76	76	77	302	
Dori Carter	72	77	77	77	303	9,175
*Andrea Lee	79	70	77	77	303	
Sandra Changkija	76	73	75	80	304	9,050

Walmart NW Arkansas Championship

Pinnacle Country Club, Rogers, Arkansas — June 27-29
Par 36-35–71; 6,386 yards — purse, $2,000,000

	SCORES			TOTAL	MONEY
Stacy Lewis	70	66	65	201	$300,000
Lydia Ko	69	68	65	202	141,128
Cristie Kerr	69	66	67	202	141,128
Angela Stanford	68	67	67	202	141,128
So Yeon Ryu	67	67	69	203	83,633
Chella Choi	70	65	69	204	62,852
Suzann Pettersen	68	67	69	204	62,852
Julieta Granada	72	68	65	205	39,188
Meena Lee	70	70	65	205	39,188
Jennifer Rosales	67	71	67	205	39,188
Karine Icher	72	65	68	205	39,188
Mina Harigae	70	66	69	205	39,188
Mi Hyang Lee	71	65	69	205	39,188
Michelle Wie	66	66	73	205	39,188
Hee Young Park	69	70	67	206	27,168
Inbee Park	69	69	68	206	27,168
Na Yeon Choi	68	69	69	206	27,168
Alejandra Llaneza	66	70	70	206	27,168
Jennifer Johnson	69	72	66	207	22,910
Mi Jung Hur	72	68	67	207	22,910
Pornanong Phatlum	67	72	68	207	22,910
Line Vedel	68	68	71	207	22,910
Jennifer Song	72	70	66	208	18,323
Hee-Won Han	69	72	67	208	18,323
Morgan Pressel	71	70	67	208	18,323
Dori Carter	69	71	68	208	18,323
Brooke Pancake	71	69	68	208	18,323
Caroline Hedwall	67	72	69	208	18,323
Mo Martin	68	71	69	208	18,323
Gerina Piller	67	69	72	208	18,323

Ricoh Women's British Open

See Ladies European Tour section.

Marathon Classic

Highland Meadows Golf Club, Sylvania, Ohio — July 17-20
Par 34-37–71; 6,512 yards — purse, $1,400,000

	SCORES				TOTAL	MONEY
Lydia Ko	67	67	70	65	269	$210,000
So Yeon Ryu	68	67	68	67	270	128,069
Cristie Kerr	70	67	68	67	272	92,905
Katherine Kirk	69	68	68	68	273	59,015
Lee-Anne Pace	66	68	68	71	273	59,015
Kelly Tan	68	70	68	67	273	59,015
Mo Martin	67	71	67	69	274	32,044
Pernilla Lindberg	71	68	70	65	274	32,044
Julieta Granada	68	72	68	66	274	32,044
Kris Tamulis	73	69	64	68	274	32,044
Lindsey Wright	67	70	69	68	274	32,044
Ai Miyazato	68	72	67	68	275	23,045

	SCORES				TOTAL	MONEY
Mirim Lee	71	67	68	69	275	23,045
Rebecca Lee-Bentham	68	67	72	68	275	23,045
Candie Kung	70	67	69	70	276	19,259
Karine Icher	73	67	73	63	276	19,259
Lexi Thompson	71	72	66	67	276	19,259
Mariajo Uribe	67	70	71	69	277	15,586
Laura Diaz	62	69	71	75	277	15,586
Brittany Lang	70	66	69	72	277	15,586
Jaye Marie Green	72	68	63	74	277	15,586
Austin Ernst	66	73	66	72	277	15,586
Tiffany Joh	71	72	67	67	277	15,586
Brooke Pancake	69	69	67	72	277	15,586
Brittany Lincicome	69	69	69	71	278	11,950
Jenny Shin	72	70	67	69	278	11,950
Jennifer Rosales	70	69	71	68	278	11,950
Beatriz Recari	70	68	70	70	278	11,950
Stacy Lewis	70	70	68	70	278	11,950
Meena Lee	72	70	66	70	278	11,950
Marina Alex	69	69	69	71	278	11,950

International Crown

Caves Valley Golf Club, Owings Mills, Maryland
Par 71; 6,628 yards

July 24-27
purse, $1,600,000

FIRST DAY
Fourball Matches

Ariya Jutanugarn and Moriya Jutanugarn (Thailand) tied with Belen Mozo and Beatriz Recari (Spain).
Carlota Ciganda and Azahara Munoz (Spain) defeated P. Phatlum and O. Sattaya (Thailand), 3 and 2.
Mamiko Higa and Mika Miyazato (Japan) tied with Caroline Hedwall and Anna Nordqvist (Sweden).
Ai Miyazato and Sakura Yokomine (Japan) defeated Pernilla Lindberg and Mikaela Parmlid (Sweden), 2 up.
Inbee Park and So Yeon Ryu (Korea) defeated Katherine Kirk and Lindsey Wright (Australia), 3 and 2.
Minjee Lee and Karrie Webb (Australia) defeated Na Yeon Choi and I.K. Kim (Korea), 2 up.
Candie Kung and Teresa Lu (Chinese Taipei) defeated Paula Creamer and Cristie Kerr (USA), 4 and 3.
Yani Tseng and Phoebe Yao (Chinese Taipei) defeated Stacy Lewis and Lexi Thompson (USA), 1 up.

POINTS: Chinese Taipei 4, Spain 3, Japan 3, Korea 2, Australia 2, Thailand 1, Sweden 1, United States 0.

SECOND DAY
Fourball Matches

Ariya Jutanugarn and Moriya Jutanugarn (Thailand) defeated Kung and Lu (Chinese Taipei), 3 and 2.
Phatlum and Sattaya (Thailand) defeated Tseng and Yao (Chinese Taipei), 1 up.
Higa and Miyazato (Japan) defeated Lee and Webb (Australia), 3 and 2.
Miyazato and Yokomine (Japan) tied with Kirk and Wright (Australia).
Hedwall and Nordqvist (Sweden) defeated Park and Ryu (Korea), 1 up.
Choi and Kim (Korea) defeated Lindberg and Parmlid (Sweden), 1up.
Kerr and Thompson (USA) defeated Mozo and Recari (Spain), 3 and 2.
Creamer and Lewis (USA) defeated Ciganda and Munoz (Spain), 2 up.

POINTS: Japan 6, Thailand 5, United States 4, Chinese Taipei 4, Korea 4, Spain 3, Sweden 3, Australia 3.

THIRD DAY
Fourball Matches

Hedwall and Nordqvist (Sweden) defeated Lee and Webb (Australia), 5 and 3.
Lindberg and Parmlid (Sweden) defeated Kirk and Wright (Australia), 7 and 5.
Ciganda and Munoz (Spain) defeated Tseng and Yao (Chinese Taipei), 6 and 5.
Mozo and Recari (Spain) defeated Kung and Lu (Chinese Taipei), 1 up.
Park and Ryu (Korea) defeated Higa and Miyazato (Japan), 4 and 3.
Miyazato and Yokomine (Japan) defeated Choi and Kim (Korea), 3 and 2.
Kerr and Thompson (USA) defeated Ariya Jutanugarn and Moriya Jutanugarn (Thailand), 3 and 2.
Phatlum and Sattaya (Thailand) defeated Creamer and Lewis (USA), 1 up.

POINTS: Japan 8, Thailand 7, Spain 7, Sweden 7, Korea 6 (won wildcard playoff), United States 6, Chinese Taipei 4, Australia 3.

FOURTH DAY
Singles Matches

Park (Korea) defeated Hedwall (Sweden), 4 and 2.
Phatlum (Thailand) defeated Kim (Korea), 1 up.
Lindberg (Sweden) defeated Ariya Jutanugarn (Thailand), 6 and 5.
Ciganda (Spain) defeated Choi (Korea), 8 and 6.
Ryu (Korea) defeated Yokomine (Japan), 1 up.
Recari (Spain) defeated Parmlid (Sweden), 3 and 2.
Nordqvist (Sweden) defeated Higa (Japan), 3 and 2.
Mozo (Spain) defeated Moriya Jutanugarn (Thailand), 3 and 2.
Miyazato (Japan) defeated Sattaya (Thailand), 3 and 1.
Munoz (Spain) defeated Miyazato (Japan), 2 and 1.

FINAL POINTS: Spain 15, Sweden 11, Korea 10, Japan 10, Thailand 9. (Eliminated: United States 6, Chinese Taipei 4, Australia 3.)

Meijer LPGA Classic

Blythefield Country Club, Grand Rapids, Michigan — August 7-10
Par 36-35–71; 6,414 yards — purse, $1,500,000

	SCORES				TOTAL	MONEY
Mirim Lee	70	64	67	69	270	$225,000
Inbee Park	66	66	68	70	270	139,217
(Lee defeated Park on second playoff hole.)						
Suzann Pettersen	69	64	69	69	271	100,992
Haru Nomura	70	67	69	68	274	78,125
Amy Yang	68	67	72	68	275	52,465
Sandra Gal	65	72	72	66	275	52,465
Line Vedel	68	69	68	70	275	52,465
Shanshan Feng	69	69	72	66	276	37,730
Kris Tamulis	70	69	71	67	277	32,394
Cristie Kerr	72	72	64	69	277	32,394
Stacy Lewis	70	72	70	66	278	28,582
Lee-Anne Pace	70	70	67	72	279	22,993
Katie M. Burnett	71	68	68	72	279	22,993
Lydia Ko	69	68	71	71	279	22,993
Beatriz Recari	70	69	67	73	279	22,993
Ayako Uehara	72	68	70	69	279	22,993
Paula Creamer	69	70	68	72	279	22,993
Thidapa Suwannapura	71	73	72	64	280	17,561
Sydnee Michaels	69	70	70	71	280	17,561
Gerina Piller	68	70	71	71	280	17,561
Azahara Munoz	68	70	71	71	280	17,561
Xi Yu Lin	71	70	71	68	280	17,561

	SCORES				TOTAL	MONEY
Jodi Ewart Shadoff	69	73	69	70	281	15,397
Giulia Molinaro	71	67	69	74	281	15,397
Lisa McCloskey	74	70	70	68	282	13,758
Brittany Lincicome	74	70	70	68	282	13,758
Angela Stanford	73	70	69	70	282	13,758
Joanna Klatten	73	70	70	69	282	13,758
Brianna Do	69	71	74	69	283	10,048
Catriona Matthew	70	72	71	70	283	10,048
Mariajo Uribe	70	74	71	68	283	10,048
Katherine Kirk	67	70	73	73	283	10,048
Austin Ernst	72	72	68	71	283	10,048
Jane Park	71	70	71	71	283	10,048
Hee Young Park	70	71	70	72	283	10,048
Karine Icher	69	73	72	69	283	10,048
Anna Nordqvist	75	69	71	68	283	10,048
Dewi Claire Schreefel	71	72	68	72	283	10,048
Amy Anderson	71	73	69	70	283	10,048
Jane Rah	72	71	70	70	283	10,048

Wegmans LPGA Championship

Monroe Golf Club, Pittsford, New York — August 14-17
Par 36-36–72; 6,717 yards — purse, $2,250,000

	SCORES				TOTAL	MONEY
Inbee Park	72	66	69	70	277	$337,500
Brittany Lincicome	67	68	71	71	277	207,791
(Park defeated Lincicome on first playoff hole.)						
Lydia Ko	70	69	71	70	280	150,737
Azahara Munoz	71	70	71	70	282	105,231
Anna Nordqvist	69	73	69	71	282	105,231
Shanshan Feng	68	72	71	72	283	58,816
Julieta Granada	75	65	72	71	283	58,816
Suzann Pettersen	71	69	67	76	283	58,816
Mirim Lee	69	71	69	74	283	58,816
Stacy Lewis	71	73	71	68	283	58,816
Jane Park	70	69	72	73	284	41,238
Meena Lee	66	73	71	74	284	41,238
Gerina Piller	72	69	69	75	285	34,129
Jenny Shin	75	71	69	70	285	34,129
Carlota Ciganda	73	73	67	72	285	34,129
So Yeon Ryu	73	71	72	69	285	34,129
Lisa McCloskey	67	75	72	72	286	27,258
Cristie Kerr	68	74	71	73	286	27,258
Mo Martin	72	70	72	72	286	27,258
Caroline Masson	72	73	68	73	286	27,258
Lexi Thompson	66	72	74	74	286	27,258
Sandra Gal	71	73	71	72	287	23,436
Chella Choi	70	74	72	71	287	23,436
Sydnee Michaels	74	69	73	71	287	23,436
Karrie Webb	73	71	71	73	288	20,136
Laura Diaz	73	70	72	73	288	20,136
Danielle Kang	70	73	72	73	288	20,136
Na Yeon Choi	74	68	73	73	288	20,136
Laura Davies	71	72	75	70	288	20,136
Catriona Matthew	69	76	75	69	289	15,862
Angela Stanford	69	75	74	71	289	15,862
Jennifer Song	72	73	71	73	289	15,862
Tiffany Joh	70	72	70	77	289	15,862
Eun-Hee Ji	69	73	73	74	289	15,862

	SCORES				TOTAL	MONEY
Juli Inkster	74	71	74	70	289	15,862
Yani Tseng	70	75	71	73	289	15,862
Lizette Salas	71	75	71	73	290	12,855
Karin Sjodin	73	73	74	70	290	12,855
Sarah Kemp	71	72	74	73	290	12,855
Moriya Jutanugarn	71	74	75	71	291	10,324
Sarah Jane Smith	73	71	74	73	291	10,324
Haeji Kang	72	73	73	73	291	10,324
Xi Yu Lin	71	72	77	71	291	10,324
Beatriz Recari	70	70	72	79	291	10,324
Ilhee Lee	69	73	73	76	291	10,324
Jessica Korda	70	73	73	75	291	10,324
Ashleigh Simon	74	72	68	77	291	10,324
Emma Jandel	69	75	74	74	292	8,032
Candie Kung	74	72	72	74	292	8,032
Paula Reto	70	71	76	75	292	8,032
Haru Nomura	73	72	72	75	292	8,032
Katie M. Burnett	74	70	75	73	292	8,032
Pernilla Lindberg	73	73	70	77	293	6,826
Jennifer Kirby	67	79	71	76	293	6,826
Ayako Uehara	72	74	74	73	293	6,826
Kristy McPherson	71	71	77	74	293	6,826
Brooke Pancake	69	76	70	78	293	6,826
Jennifer Johnson	70	70	77	77	294	5,831
Stacey Keating	72	74	70	78	294	5,831
Becky Morgan	75	71	74	74	294	5,831
Jaye Marie Green	73	73	73	75	294	5,831
Brittany Lang	70	75	73	77	295	5,176
Mi Jung Hur	71	75	76	73	295	5,176
Jimin Kang	74	72	74	75	295	5,176
Jacqui Concolino	73	73	76	73	295	5,176
Erica Popson	73	73	75	74	295	5,176
Kathleen Ekey	72	72	73	78	295	5,176
Katy Harris	72	74	76	75	297	4,777
Mina Harigae	73	73	75	77	298	4,608
Chie Arimura	71	75	73	79	298	4,608
Austin Ernst	71	75	75	78	299	4,495
Dewi Claire Schreefel	74	70	76	80	300	4,436
Thidapa Suwannapura	72	71	78	80	301	4,379

Canadian Pacific Women's Open

London Hunt & Country Club, London, Ontario, Canada — August 21-24
Par 36-36–72; 6,656 yards — purse, $2,250,000

	SCORES				TOTAL	MONEY
So Yeon Ryu	63	66	67	69	265	$337,500
Na Yeon Choi	64	70	66	67	267	202,281
Inbee Park	66	71	65	68	270	146,741
Azahara Munoz	66	71	63	71	271	113,515
Kim Kaufman	69	70	68	66	273	83,061
Danielle Kang	66	68	70	69	273	83,061
Suzann Pettersen	69	68	70	68	275	52,882
Anna Nordqvist	65	69	69	72	275	52,882
Brittany Lincicome	71	65	68	71	275	52,882
Cristie Kerr	67	68	70	70	275	52,882
Pornanong Phatlum	70	69	68	69	276	40,145
Caroline Masson	67	70	72	67	276	40,145
Pernilla Lindberg	68	70	71	69	278	34,183
Karrie Webb	69	72	67	70	278	34,183

	SCORES				TOTAL	MONEY
Mariajo Uribe	69	69	71	69	278	34,183
Line Vedel	71	72	67	69	279	28,868
Karine Icher	71	71	68	69	279	28,868
Mi Hyang Lee	67	69	72	71	279	28,868
Ilhee Lee	71	69	69	71	280	25,029
Haru Nomura	68	69	72	71	280	25,029
Kristy McPherson	70	72	71	67	280	25,029
Felicity Johnson	69	69	71	71	280	25,029
Jacqui Concolino	69	70	71	71	281	20,784
Morgan Pressel	70	69	72	70	281	20,784
Brittany Lang	68	70	70	73	281	20,784
Jenny Shin	70	71	72	68	281	20,784
Stacy Lewis	71	68	71	71	281	20,784
Lizette Salas	70	66	74	71	281	20,784
Xi Yu Lin	66	70	75	71	282	17,055
Chie Arimura	72	71	67	72	282	17,055
Sydnee Michaels	69	70	68	75	282	17,055
Belen Mozo	68	69	74	71	282	17,055

Portland Classic

Columbia Edgewater Country Club, Portland, Oregon — August 28-31
Par 36-36–72; 6,476 yards — purse, $1,300,000

	SCORES				TOTAL	MONEY
Austin Ernst	69	69	69	67	274	$195,000
I.K. Kim	65	67	74	68	274	118,921
(Ernst defeated Kim on first playoff hole.)						
So Yeon Ryu	70	66	70	70	276	76,502
Chella Choi	68	70	70	68	276	76,502
Na Yeon Choi	70	69	70	68	277	41,670
Line Vedel	69	69	69	70	277	41,670
Karine Icher	68	71	72	66	277	41,670
Eun-Hee Ji	71	69	67	70	277	41,670
Paula Reto	67	69	74	68	278	23,262
Xi Yu Lin	68	68	70	72	278	23,262
Mariajo Uribe	69	72	66	71	278	23,262
Mi Jung Hur	70	65	70	73	278	23,262
Ilhee Lee	71	72	67	68	278	23,262
Laura Diaz	67	68	72	71	278	23,262
Lizette Salas	69	72	68	69	278	23,262
Suzann Pettersen	71	67	67	74	279	16,972
Carlota Ciganda	70	65	70	74	279	16,972
Tiffany Joh	71	67	72	69	279	16,972
Jacqui Concolino	68	71	70	71	280	14,194
Anna Nordqvist	67	71	73	69	280	14,194
Morgan Pressel	73	67	70	70	280	14,194
Moriya Jutanugarn	72	72	69	67	280	14,194
Hee Young Park	75	70	65	70	280	14,194
Mina Harigae	67	69	72	72	280	14,194
Kim Kaufman	75	69	70	67	281	11,752
Yani Tseng	70	71	73	67	281	11,752
Jennifer Rosales	70	70	73	68	281	11,752
Brittany Lang	71	71	71	68	281	11,752
Jane Rah	71	71	70	70	282	9,831
Sun Young Yoo	74	70	70	68	282	9,831
Jennifer Song	66	74	72	70	282	9,831
Jaye Marie Green	72	66	72	72	282	9,831
Juli Inkster	68	70	72	72	282	9,831

Evian Championship

See Ladies European Tour section.

Yokohama Tire LPGA Classic

Robert Trent Jones Golf Trail, Capitol Hill-Senator Course, Prattville, Alabama
Par 36-36–72; 6,607 yards

September 18-21
purse, $1,300,000

	SCORES				TOTAL	MONEY
Mi Jung Hur	64	70	67	66	267	$195,000
Stacy Lewis	64	71	70	66	271	119,198
Paula Reto	65	66	70	73	274	86,469
Kris Tamulis	67	73	65	70	275	66,891
Moriya Jutanugarn	68	69	71	68	276	48,945
Jodi Ewart Shadoff	70	71	70	65	276	48,945
Cydney Clanton	66	72	72	67	277	34,588
Alison Walshe	69	68	71	69	277	34,588
Karin Sjodin	66	74	70	68	278	27,736
Kim Kaufman	71	72	70	65	278	27,736
Brittany Lang	71	68	70	71	280	19,847
Chella Choi	70	71	70	69	280	19,847
Ayako Uehara	66	73	70	71	280	19,847
Ilhee Lee	67	74	68	71	280	19,847
Sarah Jane Smith	71	71	72	66	280	19,847
Christina Kim	67	71	75	67	280	19,847
Sun Young Yoo	67	72	72	69	280	19,847
Amy Anderson	68	74	71	67	280	19,847
Sydnee Michaels	72	65	72	72	281	13,729
Perrine Delacour	68	72	69	72	281	13,729
Brittany Lincicome	70	69	74	68	281	13,729
Jane Rah	70	72	70	69	281	13,729
Beatriz Recari	67	73	73	68	281	13,729
Stephanie Meadow	68	74	71	68	281	13,729
Angela Stanford	76	68	70	67	281	13,729
Stacey Keating	71	71	68	71	281	13,729
Thidapa Suwannapura	69	70	72	71	282	11,094
Ai Miyazato	73	67	70	72	282	11,094
Becky Morgan	72	69	71	70	282	11,094
Mika Miyazato	68	72	72	71	283	9,658
Cristie Kerr	74	72	72	65	283	9,658
Alena Sharp	72	74	71	66	283	9,658
Ji Young Oh	68	74	74	67	283	9,658

Reignwood LPGA Classic

Pine Valley Golf Club, Nankou, Beijing, China
Par 36-36–72; 6,596 yards

October 2-5
purse, $2,100,000

	SCORES				TOTAL	MONEY
Mirim Lee	70	68	70	69	277	$315,000
Caroline Hedwall	67	71	68	73	279	192,103
Inbee Park	69	72	68	71	280	111,310
Brittany Lang	70	66	72	72	280	111,310
Haeji Kang	69	72	70	69	280	111,310
Stacy Lewis	66	68	72	75	281	65,209
Mi Hyang Lee	69	76	69	67	281	65,209
Pornanong Phatlum	72	75	67	68	282	49,433

	SCORES				TOTAL	MONEY
Ilhee Lee	69	70	71	72	282	49,433
Chella Choi	71	70	70	72	283	42,596
Yanhong Pan	71	68	73	72	284	36,916
Mariajo Uribe	73	69	72	70	284	36,916
Suzann Pettersen	74	66	70	74	284	36,916
Yuting Shi	74	69	68	74	285	32,394
Caroline Masson	70	68	71	78	287	28,187
Pernilla Lindberg	72	70	71	74	287	28,187
Kelly Tan	74	70	69	74	287	28,187
Belen Mozo	69	69	72	77	287	28,187
Jenny Shin	68	73	72	75	288	22,523
Mi Jung Hur	73	71	67	77	288	22,523
Sun Young Yoo	68	73	69	78	288	22,523
Na Yeon Choi	75	71	69	73	288	22,523
So Yeon Ryu	72	69	70	77	288	22,523
Yani Tseng	69	75	69	75	288	22,523
Sandra Gal	72	69	72	75	288	22,523
Catriona Matthew	72	72	72	73	289	17,901
Austin Ernst	71	71	72	75	289	17,901
Hee Young Park	76	73	68	72	289	17,901
Karine Icher	74	69	74	72	289	17,901
Sydnee Michaels	71	69	75	74	289	17,901

Sime Darby LPGA Malaysia

Kuala Lumpur Golf & Country Club, Kuala Lumpur, Malaysia — October 9-12
Par 35-36–71; 6,246 yards — purse, $2,000,000

	SCORES				TOTAL	MONEY
Shanshan Feng	67	67	69	63	266	$300,000
Pornanong Phatlum	67	67	65	70	269	184,703
Pernilla Lindberg	70	68	69	63	270	107,022
So Yeon Ryu	66	65	72	67	270	107,022
Chella Choi	69	66	68	67	270	107,022
Na Yeon Choi	66	70	68	67	271	68,258
Ilhee Lee	70	66	68	68	272	57,135
Caroline Masson	72	67	66	68	273	43,483
Mi Hyang Lee	67	69	69	68	273	43,483
Sun Young Yoo	70	67	68	68	273	43,483
Lydia Ko	69	64	70	70	273	43,483
Brittany Lang	69	68	71	66	274	32,258
Beatriz Recari	70	67	71	66	274	32,258
Carlota Ciganda	68	69	71	66	274	32,258
Mirim Lee	71	67	67	69	274	32,258
Amy Yang	67	70	71	67	275	25,787
Ayako Uehara	70	63	69	73	275	25,787
Gerina Piller	69	67	73	66	275	25,787
Jenny Shin	67	68	71	69	275	25,787
Jessica Korda	71	70	68	67	276	23,258
Mi Jung Hur	71	67	69	70	277	21,236
Stacy Lewis	65	71	72	69	277	21,236
Anna Nordqvist	69	73	67	68	277	21,236
Azahara Munoz	69	65	73	70	277	21,236
Austin Ernst	71	68	72	68	279	18,961
Eun-Hee Ji	66	67	73	73	279	18,961
Ariya Jutanugarn	69	71	64	76	280	16,862
Sandra Gal	73	65	74	68	280	16,862
Catriona Matthew	68	68	73	71	280	16,862
Mariajo Uribe	74	71	69	66	280	16,862

LPGA KEB - HanaBank Championship

Sky 72 Golf Club, Ocean Course, Incheon, South Korea — October 16-19
Par 36-36–72; 6,364 yards — purse, $2,000,000

	SCORES				TOTAL	MONEY
Kyu Jung Baek	74	69	68	67	278	$300,000
Brittany Lincicome	70	70	72	66	278	157,838
In Gee Chun	76	67	69	66	278	157,838
(Baek defeated Lincicome and Chun on first playoff hole.)						
Inbee Park	71	73	68	67	279	102,670
Michelle Wie	76	70	67	67	280	75,126
Catriona Matthew	69	74	70	67	280	75,126
Hyo-Joo Kim	72	72	71	66	281	56,594
Austin Ernst	76	71	69	66	282	43,072
Ilhee Lee	69	72	71	70	282	43,072
Beatriz Recari	70	70	72	70	282	43,072
Gerina Piller	73	70	71	68	282	43,072
Karine Icher	71	68	73	71	283	30,217
Angela Stanford	74	71	68	70	283	30,217
Sandra Gal	70	71	71	71	283	30,217
So Yeon Ryu	76	69	70	68	283	30,217
Suzann Pettersen	70	71	71	71	283	30,217
Hee-Kyung Bae	70	73	68	72	283	30,217
Cristie Kerr	72	72	69	71	284	22,671
Julieta Granada	71	72	72	69	284	22,671
Katherine Kirk	74	72	69	69	284	22,671
Pornanong Phatlum	73	70	69	72	284	22,671
Mirim Lee	69	74	73	68	284	22,671
Yoon Kyung Heo	72	70	70	72	284	22,671
Minjee Lee	69	78	74	64	285	18,781
Azahara Munoz	72	69	72	72	285	18,781
Eun-Hee Ji	70	73	71	71	285	18,781
Morgan Pressel	73	70	73	69	285	18,781
Seul A. Yoon	73	69	74	70	286	17,028
Lydia Ko	73	69	72	73	287	16,327
Min-Young Lee	75	71	73	69	288	14,524
Ha-Neul Kim	74	72	71	71	288	14,524
Shanshan Feng	71	79	68	70	288	14,524
Mi Jung Hur	72	69	76	71	288	14,524
Chella Choi	70	75	73	70	288	14,524

Blue Bay LPGA

Jian Lake Blue Bay Golf Course, Hainan Island, China — October 23-27
Par 36-367–72; 6,760 yards — purse, $2,000,000
(Event shortened to 54 holes and completed on Monday—rain.)

	SCORES			TOTAL	MONEY
Lee-Anne Pace	67	66	67	200	$300,000
Caroline Masson	67	69	67	203	183,814
Michelle Wie	67	68	70	205	118,248
Jessica Korda	66	67	72	205	118,248
Danielle Kang	68	68	70	206	75,478
Chella Choi	68	66	72	206	75,478
Lydia Ko	69	70	68	207	53,338
Shanshan Feng	67	68	72	207	53,338
Jenny Shin	71	70	67	208	42,771
Brittany Lang	67	68	73	208	42,771
Thidapa Suwannapura	70	72	67	209	32,287

	SCORES			TOTAL	MONEY
Cristie Kerr	68	73	68	209	32,287
Dewi Claire Schreefel	68	72	69	209	32,287
Belen Mozo	72	67	70	209	32,287
Mariajo Uribe	69	70	70	209	32,287
Austin Ernst	71	66	72	209	32,287
Sandra Gal	70	71	69	210	25,562
Ilhee Lee	73	68	69	210	25,562
*Wanyao Lu	69	68	73	210	
Sun Young Yoo	70	70	71	211	23,147
I.K. Kim	68	71	72	211	23,147
Beatriz Recari	70	68	73	211	23,147
Christina Kim	71	71	70	212	18,562
Julieta Granada	70	71	71	212	18,562
Mi Jung Hur	71	70	71	212	18,562
Anna Nordqvist	72	69	71	212	18,562
Morgan Pressel	70	71	71	212	18,562
Line Vedel	70	71	71	212	18,562
Amy Yang	69	72	71	212	18,562
Jodi Ewart Shadoff	67	72	73	212	18,562
Jennifer Johnson	70	69	73	212	18,562

Fubon LPGA Taiwan Championship

Miramar Golf Country Club, Chinese Taipei
Par 36-36–72

October 29-November 2
purse, $2,000,000

	SCORES				TOTAL	MONEY
Inbee Park	64	62	69	71	266	$300,000
Stacy Lewis	67	68	64	69	268	183,381
Lydia Ko	69	65	71	66	271	133,030
Azahara Munoz	68	66	69	69	272	102,909
Amy Yang	70	68	68	68	274	82,830
Shanshan Feng	64	65	70	76	275	67,770
Pernilla Lindberg	69	71	69	67	276	53,212
So Yeon Ryu	66	70	68	72	276	53,212
Eun-Hee Ji	67	71	68	71	277	39,532
Sandra Gal	71	68	69	69	277	39,532
Brittany Lang	70	67	68	72	277	39,532
Mariajo Uribe	71	67	67	72	277	39,532
Mirim Lee	72	62	73	71	278	32,930
Chella Choi	70	66	73	71	280	30,923
Caroline Masson	72	70	67	72	281	26,907
Ilhee Lee	69	72	72	68	281	26,907
Kim Kaufman	71	68	70	72	281	26,907
I.K. Kim	67	71	70	73	281	26,907
*Ssu-Chia Cheng	66	70	75	70	281	
Mina Harigae	72	71	65	74	282	20,749
Mi Hyang Lee	68	70	70	74	282	20,749
Michelle Wie	68	70	72	72	282	20,749
Carlota Ciganda	70	69	70	73	282	20,749
Na Yeon Choi	68	68	73	73	282	20,749
Suzann Pettersen	70	67	74	71	282	20,749
Yani Tseng	69	74	69	70	282	20,749
Belen Mozo	72	68	69	73	282	20,749
Lizette Salas	72	68	69	73	282	20,749
Moriya Jutanugarn	69	67	75	72	283	15,783
Line Vedel	66	68	76	73	283	15,783
Thidapa Suwannapura	70	69	68	76	283	15,783
Yu-Ling Hsieh	73	70	70	70	283	15,783
Pei-Yun Chien	70	72	69	72	283	15,783

Mizuno Classic

See Japan LPGA Tour section.

Lorena Ochoa Invitational

Club de Golf Mexico, Mexico City, Mexico — November 13-16
Par 36-36–72 — purse, $1,000,000

	SCORES				TOTAL	MONEY
Christina Kim	65	69	68	71	273	$200,000
Shanshan Feng	72	67	68	66	273	103,449
(Kim defeated Feng on second playoff hole.)						
Inbee Park	70	70	69	68	277	75,045
Brittany Lincicome	70	71	69	69	279	52,390
So Yeon Ryu	70	69	69	71	279	52,390
Pornanong Phatlum	69	68	71	72	280	38,231
Azahara Munoz	66	71	71	73	281	30,018
Jenny Shin	71	71	71	68	281	30,018
Angela Stanford	73	73	69	68	283	24,071
Lydia Ko	68	69	74	72	283	24,071
Karine Icher	70	73	71	70	284	19,271
Paula Creamer	70	65	76	73	284	19,271
Suzann Pettersen	71	66	75	72	284	19,271
Morgan Pressel	70	72	73	69	284	19,271
Michelle Wie	73	69	71	72	285	15,556
Anna Nordqvist	71	74	71	69	285	15,556
Lexi Thompson	70	72	70	73	285	15,556
Julieta Granada	71	71	71	73	286	14,046
Alejandra Llaneza	71	74	72	70	287	13,253
Lizette Salas	69	72	72	74	287	13,253
Cristie Kerr	76	70	70	72	288	12,347
Austin Ernst	71	73	72	72	288	12,347
Margarita Ramos	75	69	73	72	289	11,668
*Gaby Lopez	72	74	71	72	289	
Caroline Masson	76	72	71	71	290	10,818
Meena Lee	77	71	73	69	290	10,818
Pernilla Lindberg	75	70	74	71	290	10,818
Stacy Lewis	76	70	70	75	291	9,826
Mi Hyang Lee	72	72	74	73	291	9,826
Gerina Piller	69	70	75	78	292	9,062
Catriona Matthew	72	74	72	74	292	9,062
Line Vedel	73	68	76	76	293	8,552
Mo Martin	74	73	70	78	295	8,212
Brittany Lang	78	70	75	74	297	7,872
Juli Inkster	79	71	75	74	299	7,532
Natalie Gulbis	74	71	77	79	301	7,250

CME Group Tour Championship

Tiburon Golf Club, Naples, Florida
Par 36-36–72; 6,949 yards

November 20-23
purse, $2,000,000

	SCORES				TOTAL	MONEY
Lydia Ko	71	71	68	68	278	$500,000
Julieta Granada	66	71	70	71	278	141,743
Carlota Ciganda	70	67	71	70	278	141,743
(Ko defeated Granada on second and Ciganda on fourth playoff hole.)						
Morgan Pressel	72	66	70	72	280	92,200
Sandra Gal	68	71	70	72	281	67,464
Michelle Wie	72	67	72	70	281	67,464
So Yeon Ryu	70	70	70	73	283	47,675
Hee Young Park	70	73	71	69	283	47,675
Brittany Lang	74	68	70	72	284	36,730
I.K. Kim	71	72	71	70	284	36,730
Stacy Lewis	69	74	70	71	284	36,730
Angela Stanford	70	74	67	74	285	27,885
Lizette Salas	75	70	68	72	285	27,885
Shanshan Feng	74	69	71	71	285	27,885
Moriya Jutanugarn	74	67	72	72	285	27,885
Sarah Jane Smith	70	69	76	70	285	27,885
Na Yeon Choi	71	72	73	70	286	22,368
Marina Alex	70	74	71	71	286	22,368
Caroline Hedwall	69	74	73	70	286	22,368
Kim Kaufman	74	70	71	72	287	19,610
Belen Mozo	69	73	73	72	287	19,610
Lexi Thompson	71	72	73	71	287	19,610
Chella Choi	71	69	76	71	287	19,610
Azahara Munoz	73	71	71	73	288	17,181
Inbee Park	71	74	73	70	288	17,181
Karine Icher	72	71	74	71	288	17,181
Christina Kim	71	74	69	75	289	14,716
Mirim Lee	74	70	72	73	289	14,716
Jessica Korda	77	70	70	72	289	14,716
Catriona Matthew	75	68	70	76	289	14,716
Ilhee Lee	71	72	72	74	289	14,716

Ladies European Tour

ISPS Handa New Zealand Women's Open

See Australian Ladies Tour section.

Volvik RACV Ladies Masters

See Australian Ladies Tour section.

ISPS Handa Women's Australian Open

See Australian Ladies Tour section.

Mission Hills World Ladies Championship

Mission Hills, Blackstone Course, Haikou, Hainan, China — March 6-9
Par 36-37–73; 6,206 yards — purse, US$500,000

	SCORES				TOTAL	MONEY
Inbee Park	69	70	62	67	268	€54,470.25
Suzann Pettersen	67	68	66	72	273	36,858.20
So Yeon Ryu	70	67	70	69	276	25,419.45
Ariya Jutanugarn	73	66	67	71	277	19,609.29
*Minjee Lee	68	71	69	69	277	
Yi Chen Liu	71	70	67	70	278	15,396.92
Ha Na Jang	72	70	69	68	279	11,801.89
In Gee Chun	71	69	68	71	279	11,801.89
Trish Johnson	69	68	72	72	281	9,078.38
Ye Na Chung	68	69	68	78	283	8,134.22
Amelia Lewis	73	69	67	75	284	7,335.33
Holly Clyburn	74	74	64	73	285	6,439.59
Shanshan Feng	74	70	69	72	285	6,439.59
Diana Luna	74	64	73	74	285	6,439.59
Nikki Campbell	70	67	73	76	286	5,810.16
Xi Yu Lin	72	72	71	72	287	5,628.59
Joanna Klatten	73	70	66	79	288	5,447.03
Felicity Johnson	77	70	67	76	290	5,156.52
Beth Allen	75	70	70	75	290	5,156.52
Camilla Lennarth	72	68	71	79	290	5,156.52

Lalla Meryem Cup

Golf de l'Ocean, Agadir, Morocco — March 13-16
Par 36-35–71; 6,257 yards — purse, €450,000

	SCORES				TOTAL	MONEY
Charley Hull	68	71	68	62	269	€67,500
Gwladys Nocera	69	68	65	67	269	45,675
(Hull defeated Nocera on first playoff hole.)						
Sophie Giquel-Bettan	67	70	67	69	273	31,500
Hannah Burke	73	70	65	66	274	21,690
Lee-Anne Pace	70	68	70	66	274	21,690

	SCORES				TOTAL	MONEY
Holly Clyburn	70	70	67	69	276	14,625
Sophie Walker	66	71	71	68	276	14,625
Trish Johnson	72	67	70	68	277	10,665
Laura Davies	68	69	71	69	277	10,665
Stacy Lee Bregman	71	71	69	67	278	8,640
Margherita Rigon	69	70	69	70	278	8,640
Joanna Klatten	72	72	66	69	279	7,155
Titiya Plucksataporn	72	70	65	72	279	7,155
Rebecca Codd	69	71	70	69	279	7,155
Ariya Jutanugarn	68	66	72	73	279	7,155
Beth Allen	69	71	72	68	280	6,480
Liz Young	72	69	70	70	281	5,967
Nicole Broch Larsen	71	73	68	69	281	5,967
Valentine Derrey	71	72	65	73	281	5,967
Karolin Lampert	69	72	70	70	281	5,967
Nina Holleder	68	68	74	71	281	5,967

Turkish Airlines Ladies Open

National Golf Club, Belek, Antalya, Turkey
Par 36-37–73; 6,194 yards
(Second round cancelled—rain.)

May 8-11
purse, €250,000

	SCORES			TOTAL	MONEY
Valentine Derrey	73	69	70	212	€37,500
Malene Jorgensen	68	73	73	214	25,375
Charley Hull	70	73	72	215	17,500
Maria Balikoeva	74	70	72	216	12,050
Vikki Laing	71	69	76	216	12,050
Sophie Walker	75	70	72	217	8,125
Klara Spilkova	69	70	78	217	8,125
Sophie Giquel-Bettan	76	71	71	218	6,250
Stephanie Na	74	73	72	219	4,562.50
Alexandra Vilatte	74	73	72	219	4,562.50
Holly Clyburn	74	71	74	219	4,562.50
Noora Tamminen	72	74	73	219	4,562.50
Nikki Campbell	72	72	75	219	4,562.50
Gwladys Nocera	68	79	72	219	4,562.50
Titiya Plucksataporn	76	71	73	220	3,556.25
Felicity Johnson	75	74	71	220	3,556.25
Nicole Broch Larsen	71	74	75	220	3,556.25
Krista Bakker	71	72	77	220	3,556.25
Beth Allen	76	72	73	221	3,225
Julie Greciet	76	71	74	221	3,225
Stacy Lee Bregman	73	73	75	221	3,225

Deloitte Ladies Open

The International, Amsterdam, Netherlands
Par 37-36–73; 6,404 yards

May 23-25
purse, €250,000

	SCORES			TOTAL	MONEY
Kylie Walker	69	72	72	213	€37,500
Malene Jorgensen	74	72	67	213	21,437.50
Nikki Campbell	72	72	69	213	21,437.50
(Walker defeated Jorgensen and Campbell on second playoff hole.)					
Christel Boeljon	77	69	69	215	12,050

	SCORES			TOTAL	MONEY
Camilla Lennarth	75	69	71	215	12,050
Linda Wessberg	73	73	70	216	7,500
Titiya Plucksataporn	73	70	73	216	7,500
Nontaya Srisawang	72	74	70	216	7,500
Krista Bakker	72	74	71	217	5,066.67
Vikki Laing	71	77	69	217	5,066.67
Maria Balikoeva	71	73	73	217	5,066.67
Kim Williams	75	69	74	218	4,300
Sally Watson	74	72	73	219	3,937.50
Klara Spilkova	72	74	73	219	3,937.50
Ann-Kathrin Lindner	75	75	70	220	3,505
Lauren Taylor	74	71	75	220	3,505
Beth Allen	72	73	75	220	3,505
Julia Davidsson	71	78	71	220	3,505
Diana Luna	71	77	72	220	3,505
Florentyna Parker	75	76	70	221	3,075
Gwladys Nocera	74	72	75	221	3,075
Liz Young	73	75	73	221	3,075
Sophie Gustafson	72	77	72	221	3,075
Ariane Provot	72	74	75	221	3,075

Allianz Ladies Slovak Open

Golf Resort Tale, Brezno, Tale, Slovakia — June 19-22
Par 35-37–72; 6,242 yards — purse, €275,000

	SCORES				TOTAL	MONEY
Camilla Lennarth	70	72	69	66	277	€41,250
Melissa Reid	75	68	71	67	281	27,912.50
Hannah Ralph	72	72	73	68	285	17,050
Sally Watson	69	67	75	74	285	17,050
Ann-Kathrin Lindner	72	74	68	72	286	9,102.50
Liz Young	71	71	72	72	286	9,102.50
Klara Spilkova	71	68	74	73	286	9,102.50
Valentine Derrey	69	70	78	69	286	9,102.50
Sophie Sandolo	73	70	71	73	287	6,160
Nicole Broch Larsen	77	73	70	68	288	5,280
Beth Allen	70	74	73	71	288	5,280
Sophie Giquel-Bettan	75	77	66	71	289	4,464.17
Patricia Sanz Barrio	69	78	72	70	289	4,464.17
Kylie Walker	68	78	73	70	289	4,464.17
Stefania Croce	73	73	72	72	290	3,969.17
Pamela Pretswell	71	81	67	71	290	3,969.17
Malene Jorgensen	70	71	79	70	290	3,969.17
Sophie Walker	72	74	70	75	291	3,639.17
Maria Balikoeva	72	69	78	72	291	3,639.17
Lauren Taylor	70	74	73	74	291	3,639.17

Ladies Italian Open

Golf Club Perugia, Perugia, Italy — June 27-29
Par 37-35–72; 6,147 yards — purse, €250,000

	SCORES			TOTAL	MONEY
Florentyna Parker	69	72	68	209	€37,500
Holly Clyburn	69	71	70	210	25,375
Rebecca Hudson	67	73	71	211	17,500

	SCORES			TOTAL	MONEY
Diana Luna	69	72	72	213	13,500
Veronica Zorzi	73	69	72	214	8,950
Pamela Pretswell	72	72	70	214	8,950
Stacy Lee Bregman	70	73	71	214	8,950
Sophie Sandolo	74	68	73	215	5,616.67
Marianne Skarpnord	72	73	70	215	5,616.67
Whitney Hillier	66	75	74	215	5,616.67
Ursula Wikstrom	74	72	70	216	4,308.33
Caroline Afonso	73	69	74	216	4,308.33
Leigh Whittaker	71	75	70	216	4,308.33
Karolin Lampert	73	72	72	217	3,787.50
Georgina Simpson	73	71	73	217	3,787.50
Steffi Kirchmayr	74	70	74	218	3,450
Jade Schaeffer	73	75	70	218	3,450
Sophie Walker	71	75	72	218	3,450
Cassandra Kirkland	70	74	74	218	3,450
Vikki Laing	77	71	71	219	3,000
Carly Booth	76	71	72	219	3,000
Holly Aitchison	74	74	71	219	3,000
Elina Nummenpaa	73	73	73	219	3,000
Louise Larsson	73	71	75	219	3,000
Julie Greciet	72	75	72	219	3,000
Ann-Kathrin Lindner	69	73	77	219	3,000

ISPS Handa Ladies European Masters

Buckinghamshire Golf Club, Denham, Buckinghamshire, England — July 3-6
Par 36-36–72; 6,498 yards — purse, €500,000

	SCORES				TOTAL	MONEY
I.K. Kim	71	68	63	68	270	€75,000
Nikki Campbell	72	68	68	67	275	50,750
Stephanie Meadow	73	71	70	63	277	27,733.33
Lee-Anne Pace	70	69	70	68	277	27,733.33
Caroline Masson	68	74	66	69	277	27,733.33
Ariya Jutanugarn	72	73	66	67	278	13,240
Stacy Lee Bregman	70	71	68	69	278	13,240
Vikki Laing	69	72	69	68	278	13,240
Amelia Lewis	68	71	68	71	278	13,240
Sarah Kemp	67	68	72	71	278	13,240
Hannah Jun	71	71	70	67	279	8,900
*Minjee Lee	71	68	67	73	279	
Amy Boulden	69	69	72	69	279	8,900
Sarah-Jane Smith	72	70	67	71	280	7,733.33
Charley Hull	70	74	68	68	280	7,733.33
Gwladys Nocera	69	70	71	70	280	7,733.33
Sophie Giquel-Bettan	74	71	67	69	281	7,200
Katie Burnett	70	71	72	69	282	6,900
Sally Watson	67	73	69	73	282	6,900
Karrie Webb	73	70	70	70	283	6,500
Diana Luna	69	72	72	70	283	6,500

Ricoh Women's British Open

Royal Birkdale Golf Club, Lancashire, England
Par 35-35–70; 6,458 yards

July 10-13
purse, US$3,000,000

	SCORES				TOTAL	MONEY
Mo Martin	69	69	77	72	287	€348,747.99
Shanshan Feng	73	71	69	75	288	185,825.42
Suzann Pettersen	72	73	68	75	288	185,825.42
Inbee Park	72	72	68	77	289	119,719.46
Angela Stanford	74	72	70	75	291	82,502.32
Eun-Hee Ji	74	70	71	76	291	82,502.32
Jessica Korda	72	72	73	74	291	82,502.32
Julieta Granada	72	70	72	77	291	82,502.32
Laura Davies	75	72	72	73	292	57,604.15
Sun-Ju Ahn	75	67	71	79	292	57,604.15
Marina Alex	72	76	68	76	292	57,604.15
Charley Hull	73	76	66	78	293	40,496.41
Gwladys Nocera	73	70	73	77	293	40,496.41
Anna Nordqvist	72	78	71	72	293	40,496.41
Azahara Munoz	72	72	74	75	293	40,496.41
Stacy Lewis	71	74	70	78	293	40,496.41
Beatriz Recari	74	67	74	79	294	31,231.16
*Emma Talley	72	73	76	73	294	
Amelia Lewis	72	71	71	80	294	31,231.16
So Yeon Ryu	71	70	74	79	294	31,231.16
Giulia Sergas	76	73	72	74	295	25,505.45
Paula Creamer	75	73	71	76	295	25,505.45
Meena Lee	73	75	70	77	295	25,505.45
Erina Hara	73	74	73	75	295	25,505.45
Amy Yang	71	72	72	80	295	25,505.45
Morgan Pressel	70	74	75	76	295	25,505.45
Rikako Morita	75	75	68	78	296	21,731.68
Pornanong Phatlum	73	74	75	74	296	21,731.68
Belen Mozo	77	72	74	74	297	18,153.11
Ayaka Watanabe	76	72	75	74	297	18,153.11
Lee-Anne Pace	75	73	72	77	297	18,153.11
Carlota Ciganda	74	75	73	75	297	18,153.11
*Georgia Hall	73	72	78	74	297	
Jenny Shin	73	72	73	79	297	18,153.11
Lydia Ko	72	76	69	80	297	18,153.11
Jiyai Shin	72	75	71	79	297	18,153.11
Mina Harigae	70	78	74	75	297	18,153.11
Mika Miyazato	78	72	70	78	298	14,574.54
Nikki Campbell	77	72	73	76	298	14,574.54
Brittany Lincicome	76	72	72	78	298	14,574.54
Sophie Giquel-Bettan	76	69	73	80	298	14,574.54
Chella Choi	73	73	72	80	298	14,574.54
Alison Walshe	74	76	74	75	299	12,752.72
Brittany Lang	73	75	74	77	299	12,752.72
Valentine Derrey	79	70	77	74	300	10,670.65
Karine Icher	76	72	71	81	300	10,670.65
Haru Nomura	75	73	76	76	300	10,670.65
Ariya Jutanugarn	75	68	75	82	300	10,670.65
Jeong Jang	73	74	74	79	300	10,670.65
Ai Miyazato	72	73	72	83	300	10,670.65
Thidapa Suwannapura	76	74	73	78	301	8,328.31
Alena Sharp	74	76	76	75	301	8,328.31
Dori Carter	73	76	75	77	301	8,328.31
Christina Kim	79	71	75	77	302	6,506.49
Diana Luna	76	72	75	79	302	6,506.49
Lexi Thompson	72	77	78	75	302	6,506.49
Ayako Uehara	68	79	72	83	302	6,506.49

	SCORES				TOTAL	MONEY
Ji Young Oh	76	73	78	76	303	5,075.06
Jee Young Lee	76	72	76	79	303	5,075.06
Miki Saiki	76	71	73	83	303	5,075.06
Sarah Kemp	70	79	74	80	303	5,075.06
Vikki Laing	78	68	78	80	304	4,164.16
Austin Ernst	76	73	77	78	304	4,164.16
Hannah Jun	75	71	81	77	304	4,164.16
Xi Yu Lin	74	74	75	81	304	4,164.16
Ilhee Lee	76	74	76	79	305	3,643.64
Hee Young Park	76	72	79	79	306	3,435.43
Kristy McPherson	74	76	73	85	308	1,255
Beth Allen	77	73	75	85	310	1,255
Becky Brewerton	77	73	78	85	313	1,255

Ladies German Open

Worthsee Golf Club, Worthsee, Germany
Par 36-36–72; 6,205 yards

July 17-20
purse, €250,000

	SCORES				TOTAL	MONEY
Kylie Walker	64	64	64	71	263	€37,500
Charley Hull	64	70	64	65	263	25,375
(Walker defeated Hull on first playoff hole.)						
Carlota Ciganda	65	70	67	63	265	17,500
Gwladys Nocera	69	70	66	65	270	10,087.50
Sandra Gal	69	67	66	68	270	10,087.50
Amy Boulden	68	68	65	69	270	10,087.50
Yu Yang Zhang	64	67	67	72	270	10,087.50
Celine Herbin	67	68	65	71	271	6,250
Sally Watson	70	66	69	67	272	5,300
Klara Spilkova	67	68	68	69	272	5,300
Sophie Giquel-Bettan	72	70	64	67	273	4,308.33
Liz Young	70	65	68	70	273	4,308.33
Anne-Lise Caudal	65	69	66	73	273	4,308.33
Linda Wessberg	70	65	68	71	274	3,787.50
Dewi Claire Schreefel	68	64	72	70	274	3,787.50
Nikki Campbell	70	70	66	69	275	3,500
Diana Luna	68	70	65	72	275	3,500
Sophia Popov	68	67	70	70	275	3,500
Alexandra Vilatte	72	65	69	70	276	3,225
Rebecca Hudson	70	67	70	69	276	3,225
Valentine Derrey	69	71	68	68	276	3,225

Sberbank Golf Masters

Golf Park Plzen-Dysina, Prague, Czech Republic
Par 36-35–71; 5,859 yards

July 25-27
purse, €250,000

	SCORES			TOTAL	MONEY
Julie Greciet	66	64	66	196	€37,500
Lee-Anne Pace	68	65	65	198	25,375
Amy Boulden	66	68	65	199	17,500
Anne-Lise Caudal	69	70	62	201	10,950
Sophie Giquel-Bettan	67	67	67	201	10,950
Nikki Garrett	66	69	66	201	10,950
Rebecca Hudson	68	67	68	203	6,875
Connie Chen	67	69	67	203	6,875

	SCORES			TOTAL	MONEY
Stacy Lee Bregman	70	71	63	204	5,300
Nikki Campbell	68	70	66	204	5,300
Trish Johnson	68	72	65	205	4,308.33
Gwladys Nocera	68	68	69	205	4,308.33
Pamela Pretswell	66	67	72	205	4,308.33
Maria Balikoeva	72	67	67	206	3,615
Ainil Bakar	70	71	65	206	3,615
Mireia Prat	69	70	67	206	3,615
Noora Tamminen	69	70	67	206	3,615
Ursula Wikstrom	66	65	75	206	3,615
Celine Herbin	73	66	68	207	3,187.50
Diana Luna	70	70	67	207	3,187.50
Ann-Kathrin Lindner	69	71	67	207	3,187.50
Nontaya Srisawang	67	72	68	207	3,187.50

Aberdeen Asset Management Ladies Scottish Open

Archerfield Links, East Lothian, Scotland — August 29-31
Par 36-36–72; 6,346 yards — purse, €250,000

	SCORES			TOTAL	MONEY
Trish Johnson	66	70	73	209	€38,654.40
Gwladys Nocera	73	69	69	211	26,156.14
Rebecca Artis	77	69	66	212	14,293.54
Stephanie Na	72	73	67	212	14,293.54
Sally Watson	71	71	70	212	14,293.54
Anne-Lise Caudal	69	74	71	214	9,019.36
Margherita Rigon	75	73	68	216	7,086.64
Nikki Campbell	72	76	68	216	7,086.64
Liz Young	76	73	68	217	5,772.39
Ann-Kathrin Lindner	73	72	73	218	5,205.46
Rebecca Hudson	73	73	73	219	4,690.07
Kylie Walker	70	77	72	219	4,690.07
Maria Balikoeva	79	72	69	220	3,898.57
Holly Clyburn	76	73	71	220	3,898.57
Nikki Garrett	75	72	73	220	3,898.57
Florentyna Parker	74	74	72	220	3,898.57
Minea Blomqvist	74	72	74	220	3,898.57
Catriona Matthew	73	77	70	220	3,898.57
Nicole Broch Larsen	70	76	74	220	3,898.57
Hannah Burke	74	75	72	221	3,179.97
Marion Ricordeau	74	73	74	221	3,179.97
Beth Allen	74	73	74	221	3,179.97
Stacy Lee Bregman	73	72	76	221	3,179.97
Melissa Reid	71	75	75	221	3,179.97

Helsingborg Open

Vasatorp Golf Club, Helsingborg, Skane, Sweden — September 4-7
Par 36-36–72; 6,318 yards — purse, €250,000

	SCORES				TOTAL	MONEY
Dewi Claire Schreefel	67	70	68	66	271	€37,500
Rebecca Artis	69	70	68	71	278	25,375
Laura Davies	69	76	68	66	279	17,500
Valentine Derrey	69	71	72	70	282	13,500
Felicity Johnson	71	74	71	67	283	10,600

	SCORES				TOTAL	MONEY
Line Vedel	70	70	70	73	283	8,750
Lydia Hall	73	72	71	68	284	5,325
Noora Tamminen	72	69	70	73	284	5,325
Becky Brewerton	71	71	69	73	284	5,325
Sophia Popov	71	70	73	70	284	5,325
Christine Wolf	70	70	69	75	284	5,325
Nikki Garrett	69	74	72	69	284	5,325
Nikki Campbell	69	73	71	71	284	5,325
Nina Holleder	74	73	68	70	285	3,562.50
Ursula Wikstrom	71	71	73	70	285	3,562.50
Johanna Bjork	71	71	73	70	285	3,562.50
Caroline Hedwall	70	70	68	77	285	3,562.50
Louise Friberg	69	71	75	70	285	3,562.50
Camilla Lennarth	68	73	74	70	285	3,562.50
Holly Clyburn	75	70	69	72	286	3,112.50
Louise Larsson	71	71	71	73	286	3,112.50
Amy Boulden	69	76	69	72	286	3,112.50
Malene Jorgensen	69	74	70	73	286	3,112.50

Evian Championship

Evian Golf Club, Evians-les-Bains, France — September 11-14
Par 35-36–71; 6,453 yards — purse, US$3,250,000

	SCORES				TOTAL	MONEY
Hyo-Joo Kim	61	72	72	68	273	€377,212.88
Karrie Webb	65	71	70	68	274	234,597.78
Ha-Na Jang	70	71	68	66	275	150,917.65
Mi Jung Hur	66	69	72	68	275	150,917.65
Na Yeon Choi	70	72	67	67	276	105,964.71
Suzann Pettersen	67	69	74	67	277	86,697.83
Paula Creamer	69	71	72	66	278	72,569.57
Lydia Ko	69	68	72	71	280	60,367.99
Brittany Lincicome	67	65	77	71	280	60,367.99
Anna Nordqvist	71	67	70	74	282	44,012.04
Shanshan Feng	70	70	73	69	282	44,012.04
Lexi Thompson	70	70	71	71	282	44,012.04
Inbee Park	69	72	69	72	282	44,012.04
Moriya Jutanugarn	69	68	75	70	282	44,012.04
Mariajo Uribe	68	70	70	74	282	44,012.04
Ji Young Oh	73	71	71	68	283	32,752.91
Minjee Lee	72	67	73	71	283	32,752.91
Stacy Lewis	70	67	73	73	283	32,752.91
Lizette Salas	69	75	71	68	283	32,752.91
Jodi Ewart Shadoff	72	72	74	66	284	28,513.42
Hee Young Park	72	70	72	70	284	28,513.42
Jenny Shin	71	76	69	68	284	28,513.42
*Jing Yan	71	75	69	69	284	
Jane Park	74	72	67	72	285	25,472.53
Azahara Munoz	70	72	72	71	285	25,472.53
Mina Harigae	69	71	75	70	285	25,472.53
I.K. Kim	69	69	73	75	286	23,183.70
Karine Icher	68	73	72	73	286	23,183.70
Marina Alex	71	74	70	72	287	21,385.46
*Celine Boutier	71	72	76	68	287	
Sakura Yokomine	71	71	75	70	287	21,385.46
Sandra Gal	72	73	73	70	288	19,009.21
Ilhee Lee	69	74	72	73	288	19,009.21
Ayako Uehara	69	73	70	76	288	19,009.21
Julieta Granada	68	72	73	75	288	19,009.21

	SCORES				TOTAL	MONEY
Sun Young Yoo	76	68	70	75	289	15,798.06
Beatriz Recari	72	71	76	70	289	15,798.06
Katherine Kirk	71	70	77	71	289	15,798.06
Amelia Lewis	70	76	68	75	289	15,798.06
Mika Miyazato	69	72	76	72	289	15,798.06
Pernilla Lindberg	73	74	72	71	290	12,586.92
Jennifer Song	71	73	74	72	290	12,586.92
Laura Davies	70	76	71	73	290	12,586.92
Morgan Pressel	70	76	70	74	290	12,586.92
Kris Tamulis	70	71	75	74	290	12,586.92
Jaye Marie Green	69	78	71	72	290	12,586.92
Charley Hull	71	73	70	77	291	10,724.45
Se Ri Pak	69	75	75	72	291	10,724.45
*Emily Kristine Pedersen	69	74	74	74	291	
Mirim Lee	71	76	75	70	292	9,568.44
Caroline Hedwall	70	73	74	75	292	9,568.44
Juli Inkster	69	77	70	76	292	9,568.44
Candie Kung	69	74	71	78	292	9,568.44
Laura Diaz	75	72	71	75	293	7,963.64
Haeji Kang	74	73	71	75	293	7,963.64
Lee-Anne Pace	73	73	76	71	293	7,963.64
Sydnee Michaels	71	76	72	74	293	7,963.64
Christina Kim	71	75	74	73	293	7,963.64
Kristy McPherson	70	77	72	74	293	7,963.64
Amy Yang	68	70	78	77	293	7,963.64
Eun-Hee Ji	75	71	75	73	294	6,583.24
Mi Hyang Lee	72	69	80	73	294	6,583.24
Meena Lee	71	73	77	73	294	6,583.24
Line Vedel	70	72	72	80	294	6,583.24
Florentyna Parker	71	72	76	76	295	6,100.40
In Gee Chun	69	78	70	78	295	6,100.40
Sarah Kemp	71	76	76	73	296	5,844.28
Cristie Kerr	71	74	75	76	296	5,844.28
Gerina Piller	71	73	76	77	297	5,651.62
Dewi Claire Schreefel	68	76	81	78	303	5,523.94
Jessica Korda	72	75	79	78	304	5,393.18
Sarah-Jane Smith	68	78	83	78	307	5,266.28

Tenerife Open de Espana Femenino

Golf Costa Adeje, Tenerife, Spain — September 18-21
Par 36-36–72; 6,341 yards — purse, €350,000

	SCORES				TOTAL	MONEY
Connie Chen	68	70	69	69	276	€52,500
Carlota Ciganda	68	71	70	69	278	35,525
Beth Allen	71	73	68	67	279	24,500
Charley Hull	68	71	71	70	280	18,900
Celine Herbin	73	70	65	73	281	10,836
Nontaya Srisawang	72	74	69	66	281	10,836
Pamela Pretswell	72	73	68	68	281	10,836
Hannah Burke	71	74	68	68	281	10,836
Nikki Campbell	70	73	70	68	281	10,836
Amy Boulden	69	69	69	75	282	6,720
Christine Wolf	68	74	69	71	282	6,720
Nicole Broch Larsen	72	71	66	76	285	5,565
Azahara Munoz	70	75	70	70	285	5,565
Kelsey MacDonald	68	74	74	69	285	5,565
Stacy Lee Bregman	67	75	73	70	285	5,565
Lee-Anne Pace	75	71	69	71	286	4,970

	SCORES				TOTAL	MONEY
Florentyna Parker	72	72	71	71	286	4,970
Holly Clyburn	75	72	70	70	287	4,522
Titiya Plucksataporn	70	72	73	72	287	4,522
Maria Balikoeva	68	69	77	73	287	4,522
Kylie Walker	67	71	71	78	287	4,522
Whitney Hillier	66	77	73	71	287	4,522

Lacoste Ladies Open de France

Chantaco Golf Club, Saint-Jean-de-Luz, Aquitaine, France
Par 35-35–70; 5,965 yards

October 2-5
purse, €250,000

	SCORES				TOTAL	MONEY
Azahara Munoz	67	68	67	67	269	€37,500
Amy Boulden	69	69	66	66	270	21,437.50
Maria Hernandez	65	67	66	72	270	21,437.50
Florentyna Parker	66	67	70	68	271	13,500
Isabelle Boineau	67	68	69	68	272	10,600
Charley Hull	68	67	71	68	274	8,125
Carlota Ciganda	66	67	70	71	274	8,125
Gwladys Nocera	70	71	68	66	275	6,250
*Albane Valenzuela	69	64	70	73	276	
Anne-Lise Caudal	73	70	66	68	277	5,100
Sophie Gustafson	73	66	69	69	277	5,100
Hannah Burke	68	70	70	69	277	5,100
Beth Allen	73	69	66	71	279	4,216.67
Jade Schaeffer	70	70	71	68	279	4,216.67
Noora Tamminen	68	72	67	72	279	4,216.67
Malene Jorgensen	70	67	68	75	280	3,758.33
Liz Young	69	70	72	69	280	3,758.33
Klara Spilkova	68	68	73	71	280	3,758.33
Titiya Plucksataporn	74	68	70	69	281	3,425
Ariane Provot	71	67	71	72	281	3,425
Felicity Johnson	68	68	73	72	281	3,425

Cell C South African Women's Open

San Lameer Country Club, Hibiscus Coast, South Africa
Par 36-36–72; 6,312 yards
(Event shortened to 54 holes—rain.)

October 16-19
purse, €320,000

	SCORES			TOTAL	MONEY
Lee-Anne Pace	71	73	67	211	€48,000
Holly Clyburn	71	70	70	211	32,480
(Pace defeated Clyburn on second playoff hole.)					
Gwladys Nocera	73	70	70	213	22,400
Georgina Simpson	73	72	69	214	12,912
Florentyna Parker	72	74	68	214	12,912
Valentine Derrey	70	73	71	214	12,912
Ann-Kathrin Lindner	70	71	73	214	12,912
Leigh Whittaker	73	67	75	215	7,584
Fabienne In-Albon	70	72	73	215	7,584
Alexandra Vilatte	77	69	71	217	5,736
Minea Blomqvist	74	72	71	217	5,736
Nina Holleder	72	72	73	217	5,736
Charley Hull	68	74	75	217	5,736
Stacy Lee Bregman	75	74	69	218	4,848

	SCORES			TOTAL	MONEY
Steffi Kirchmayr	69	77	72	218	4,848
Katie Burnett	77	71	71	219	4,304
Melissa Reid	76	75	68	219	4,304
Ainil Bakar	74	73	72	219	4,304
Julia Davidsson	74	70	75	219	4,304
Caroline Martens	73	75	71	219	4,304
Sophie Giquel-Bettan	72	71	76	219	4,304

Sanya Ladies Open

Yalong Bay Golf Club, Sanya, China
Par 36-36–72; 6,461 yards

November 14-16
purse, €300,000

	SCORES			TOTAL	MONEY
Xi Yu Lin	68	67	67	202	€45,000
Charley Hull	70	68	69	207	30,450
Huei Ju Shih	71	68	69	208	18,600
Nikki Campbell	69	70	69	208	18,600
*Jienalin Zhang	70	68	71	209	
Yu Yang Zhang	70	68	71	209	12,720
Beth Allen	74	65	71	210	10,500
Ashleigh Simon	72	69	70	211	6,948
Stacy Lee Bregman	71	70	70	211	6,948
Yu Ting Shi	70	72	69	211	6,948
Marion Ricordeau	70	70	71	211	6,948
*Ziyi Wang	68	74	69	211	
Babe Liu	68	69	74	211	6,948
Sarah Kemp	72	69	71	212	4,680
Pei-Yun Chien	71	69	72	212	4,680
Malene Jorgensen	68	72	72	212	4,680
Gwladys Nocera	68	71	73	212	4,680
Tzu Chi Lin	66	76	70	212	4,680
Yan Hong Pan	74	70	69	213	4,027.50
Pamela Pretswell	74	66	73	213	4,027.50
Holly Aitchison	72	69	72	213	4,027.50
Numa Gulyanamitta	70	71	72	213	4,027.50

Xiamen Open

Orient Golf & Country Club, Xiamen, China
Par 37-35–72; 6,305 yards

November 21-23
purse, €250,000

	SCORES			TOTAL	MONEY
*Ssu-Chia Cheng	70	68	68	206	
Marion Ricordeau	72	68	69	209	€37,500
Alexandra Vilatte	70	70	70	210	21,437.50
Beth Allen	69	71	70	210	21,437.50
Joanna Klatten	72	68	71	211	10,950
Xi Yu Lin	71	70	70	211	10,950
Liz Young	69	71	71	211	10,950
Sarah Kemp	72	72	68	212	7,500
Tzu Chi Lin	74	69	70	213	5,925
Vikki Laing	72	67	74	213	5,925
Charley Hull	73	69	72	214	4,250
Cassandra Kirkland	72	73	69	214	4,250
Titiya Plucksataporn	72	69	73	214	4,250
Maria Hernandez	71	72	71	214	4,250

	SCORES			TOTAL	MONEY
Chloe Leurquin	70	68	76	214	4,250
Connie Chen	68	70	76	214	4,250
Pei-Yun Chien	76	69	70	215	3,321.43
Sahra Hassan	72	74	69	215	3,321.43
Pamela Pretswell	72	72	71	215	3,321.43
Wichanee Meechai	71	76	68	215	3,321.43
Yu Ting Shi	71	73	71	215	3,321.43
Li Qing Chen	70	72	73	215	3,321.43
Nikki Garrett	69	70	76	215	3,321.43

Hero Women's Indian Open

Delhi Golf Club, New Delhi, India — December 4-6
Par 37-36–73; 6,102 yards — purse, US$300,000

	SCORES			TOTAL	MONEY
Gwladys Nocera	64	72	72	208	€36,477.75
Hyeon Seo Kang	72	72	69	213	18,279.41
Fabienne In-Albon	71	73	69	213	18,279.41
Hannah Burke	71	71	71	213	18,279.41
Vaishavi Sinha	67	71	76	214	10,311.04
Titiya Plucksataporn	71	74	71	216	7,903.51
Holly Clyburn	67	75	74	216	7,903.51
Holly Aitchison	75	72	70	217	5,463.56
Punpaka Phuntumabamrung	75	71	71	217	5,463.56
Gauri Monga	70	76	71	217	5,463.56
Sophie Walker	74	72	72	218	4,190.89
Sally Watson	73	71	74	218	4,190.89
Carlota Ciganda	71	78	69	218	4,190.89
Tiffany Tavee	76	70	73	219	3,623.46
*Aditi Ashok	74	75	70	219	
Klara Spilkova	74	70	75	219	3,623.46
Ye Seul Lee	73	73	73	219	3,623.46
Leigh Whittaker	75	74	71	220	3,185.72
Janya Morrakotphan	75	71	74	220	3,185.72
Wichanee Meechai	72	76	72	220	3,185.72
Bo-Mi Suh	71	75	74	220	3,185.72
Gursimar Badwal	70	75	75	220	3,185.72
Chloe Leurquin	69	73	78	220	3,185.72

Omega Dubai Ladies Masters

Emirates Golf Club, Majlis Course, Dubai, United Arab Emirates — December 10-13
Par 35-37–72; 6,401 yards — purse, €500,000

	SCORES				TOTAL	MONEY
Shanshan Feng	66	67	66	70	269	€75,000
Carlota Ciganda	69	71	66	68	274	50,750
Caroline Masson	68	71	69	67	275	35,000
Anna Nordqvist	69	69	68	70	276	27,000
Nicole Broch Larsen	71	70	66	71	278	15,480
Malene Jorgensen	74	69	67	68	278	15,480
Liz Young	70	71	69	68	278	15,480
Melissa Reid	70	69	65	74	278	15,480
Charley Hull	67	70	69	72	278	15,480
Klara Spilkova	70	70	71	68	279	10,000
Ashleigh Simon	70	71	69	70	280	8,387.50

	SCORES				TOTAL	MONEY
Pornanong Phatlum	68	72	71	69	280	8,387.50
Minjee Lee	74	68	70	68	280	8,387.50
Gwladys Nocera	69	69	71	71	280	8,387.50
Stacy Lee Bregman	72	70	69	70	281	7,112.50
Lee-Anne Pace	67	73	74	67	281	7,112.50
Sarah Kemp	71	68	71	71	281	7,112.50
Caroline Hedwall	72	71	69	69	281	7,112.50
Katie Burnett	71	69	73	69	282	6,600
Cheyenne Woods	70	69	72	72	283	6,375
Isabelle Boinea	72	72	68	71	283	6,375

Japan LPGA Tour

Daikin Orchid Ladies

Ryukyu Golf Club, Nanjo, Okinawa
Par 36-36–72; 6,473 yards

March 7-9
purse, ¥100,000,000

	SCORES			TOTAL	MONEY
O. Sattaya	69	72	67	208	¥18,000,000
Mamiko Higa	71	71	68	210	6,160,000
Jiyai Shin	71	71	68	210	6,160,000
Ayaka Watanabe	74	68	68	210	6,160,000
Airi Saitoh	71	70	69	210	6,160,000
Rikako Morita	70	69	71	210	6,160,000
Bo-Mee Lee	67	73	71	211	3,500,000
Sun-Ju Ahn	73	71	68	212	2,500,000
Ji-Hee Lee	69	71	72	212	2,500,000
Ritsuko Ryu	70	69	73	212	2,500,000
Mi-Jeong Jeon	72	70	71	213	1,810,000
Kumiko Kaneda	72	71	71	214	1,710,000
Erina Hara	74	71	70	215	1,560,000
Teresa Lu	71	73	71	215	1,560,000
Miki Saiki	74	73	69	216	1,160,000
Mayumi Shimomura	69	76	71	216	1,160,000
Yeon-Ju Jung	72	73	71	216	1,160,000
Nozomi Inoue	71	73	72	216	1,160,000
Riho Fujisaki	72	72	72	216	1,160,000
Mika Miyazato	72	72	72	216	1,160,000

Yokohama Tire PRGR Ladies Cup

Tosa Country Club, Kanan, Kochi
Par 36-36–72; 6,232 yards

March 14-16
purse, ¥80,000,000

	SCORES			TOTAL	MONEY
Yuki Ichinose	70	72	67	209	¥14,400,000
Miki Sakai	75	67	67	209	7,040,000
(Ichinose defeated Sakai on first playoff hole.)					
*Haruka Morita	73	70	67	210	
Bo-Bae Song	69	71	70	210	5,600,000
Asako Fujimoto	69	72	70	211	4,800,000
Junko Omote	75	74	63	212	2,880,000
Mami Fukuda	69	75	68	212	2,880,000
Mi-Jeong Jeon	72	71	69	212	2,880,000
Rumi Yoshiba	71	71	70	212	2,880,000
Sun-Ju Ahn	72	70	70	212	2,880,000
Erina Hara	77	70	66	213	1,488,000
So-Hee Kim	77	69	67	213	1,488,000
Bo-Mee Lee	74	70	69	213	1,488,000
Sakura Yokomine	75	71	68	214	1,272,000
Phoebe Yao	75	69	70	214	1,272,000
Yun-Jye Wei	75	67	73	215	1,152,000
Miki Saiki	75	73	68	216	859,428
Yukari Baba	73	74	69	216	859,428
Risa Ogusu	73	74	69	216	859,428
Ritsuko Ryu	73	73	70	216	859,428
Da-Ye Na	74	72	70	216	859,428
Yumiko Yoshida	75	71	70	216	859,428
Yuki Sakurai	73	72	71	216	859,428

T-Point Ladies

Wakagi Golf Club, Saga
Par 36-36–72; 6,304 yards

March 21-23
purse, ¥70,000,000

	SCORES			TOTAL	MONEY
Rikako Morita	69	68	71	208	¥12,600,000
Erina Hara	70	68	74	212	6,300,000
O. Sattaya	69	74	70	213	4,550,000
Mami Fukuda	67	75	71	213	4,550,000
Yeon-Ju Jung	73	73	68	214	2,548,000
Saiki Fujita	72	73	69	214	2,548,000
Sakura Yokomine	72	71	71	214	2,548,000
Yukari Nishiyama	67	75	72	214	2,548,000
Hiroko Fukushima	69	73	72	214	2,548,000
Hye-Jin Jung	72	75	68	215	1,305,500
*Kana Nagai	73	72	70	215	
Bo-Bae Song	77	67	71	215	1,305,500
Yukari Baba	71	72	72	215	1,305,500
Bo-Mee Lee	70	71	74	215	1,305,500
Haruka Kudo	73	72	71	216	1,099,000
Eun-Bi Jang	73	70	73	216	1,099,000
Mayu Hattori	73	73	71	217	828,333
Misuzu Narita	74	72	71	217	828,333
Shinobu Moromizato	74	74	69	217	828,333
Esther Lee	73	72	72	217	828,333
Ritsuko Ryu	72	76	69	217	828,333
Jiyai Shin	71	73	73	217	828,333

AXA Ladies

UMK Country Club, Miyazaki — March 28-30
Par 36-36–72; 6,470 yards — purse, ¥80,000,000

	SCORES			TOTAL	MONEY
Ayaka Watanabe	66	70	67	203	¥14,400,000
Saiki Fujita	67	67	71	205	7,040,000
Bo-Mee Lee	68	70	69	207	5,600,000
*Asuka Kashiwabara	71	67	70	208	
Rui Kitada	70	69	69	208	4,800,000
Lala Anai	70	69	70	209	4,000,000
Erina Hara	69	69	72	210	3,000,000
Asako Fujimoto	70	71	69	210	3,000,000
Natsuka Hori	71	69	71	211	2,400,000
Rie Tsuji	72	69	71	212	1,574,400
Megumi Kido	71	71	70	212	1,574,400
Shiho Toyonaga	70	74	68	212	1,574,400
Miki Sakai	71	68	73	212	1,574,400
Mami Fukuda	70	70	72	212	1,574,400
O. Sattaya	72	69	72	213	1,144,000
Rikako Morita	68	74	71	213	1,144,000
Junko Omote	73	70	70	213	1,144,000
Megumi Shimokawa	73	70	70	213	1,144,000
Misuzu Narita	70	69	75	214	840,000
Da-Ye Na	71	71	72	214	840,000
Ritsuko Ryu	71	72	71	214	840,000
Nozomi Inoue	72	72	70	214	840,000

Yamaha Ladies Open

Katsuragi Golf Club, Fukuroi, Shizuoka — April 3-6
Par 36-36–72; 6,540 yards — purse, ¥100,000,000

	SCORES				TOTAL	MONEY
Sun-Ju Ahn	70	69	72	72	283	¥18,000,000
Yumiko Yoshida	68	71	71	74	284	8,800,000
Erina Hara	70	71	75	70	286	6,000,000
Yukari Baba	72	73	70	71	286	6,000,000
Ritsuko Ryu	69	69	74	74	286	6,000,000
Esther Lee	75	72	72	68	287	4,000,000
Kaori Ohe	72	75	72	69	288	3,500,000
Rikako Morita	66	75	73	75	289	2,750,000
Bo-Mee Lee	69	71	73	76	289	2,750,000
Hyo-Joo Kim	69	72	72	77	290	2,000,000
Asako Fujimoto	75	72	73	71	291	1,680,000
Saiki Fujita	67	75	74	75	291	1,680,000
Mihoko Iseri	70	71	78	73	292	1,380,000
Risa Ogusu	67	77	74	74	292	1,380,000
Young Kim	70	69	78	75	292	1,380,000
Shiho Oyama	72	70	74	76	292	1,380,000
Ayaka Watanabe	68	81	76	68	293	920,000
Mi-Jeong Jeon	72	72	77	72	293	920,000
Soo-Yun Kang	69	73	76	75	293	920,000
Junko Omote	72	73	73	75	293	920,000
Shinobu Moromizato	70	73	72	78	293	920,000
Hikari Fujita	71	72	71	79	293	920,000

Studio Alice Ladies Open

Hanayashiki Golf Club, Yokawa Course, Miki, Hyogo
Par 36-36–72; 6,477 yards

April 11-13
purse, ¥60,000,000

	SCORES			TOTAL	MONEY
Esther Lee	70	67	70	207	¥10,800,000
O. Sattaya	67	68	73	208	5,280,000
Miki Sakai	74	69	67	210	4,200,000
Mayu Hattori	72	73	66	211	3,600,000
Ritsuko Ryu	70	72	70	212	2,700,000
Hikari Fujita	70	69	73	212	2,700,000
Na-Ri Kim	74	69	70	213	2,100,000
Sun-Ju Ahn	70	76	68	214	1,407,000
Jiyai Shin	72	76	66	214	1,407,000
Phoebe Yao	74	70	70	214	1,407,000
Mi-Jeong Jeon	69	73	72	214	1,407,000
Kaori Ohe	76	69	70	215	1,008,000
Ayaka Watanabe	69	75	71	215	1,008,000
Misaki Hama	73	69	73	215	1,008,000
Aoi Nagata	71	73	72	216	798,000
Megumi Kido	72	72	72	216	798,000
Eriko Tanikawa	74	68	74	216	798,000
Maiko Wakabayashi	70	71	75	216	798,000
Ji-Hee Lee	72	73	72	217	578,000
Natsuka Hori	73	75	69	217	578,000
Nachiyo Ohtani	74	70	73	217	578,000
Yuko Fukuda	74	70	73	217	578,000
Momoko Ueda	71	72	74	217	578,000
Rumi Yoshiba	73	70	74	217	578,000

Vantelin Ladies Open KKT Cup

Kumamoto Kuko Country Club, Kikuyo, Kumamoto
Par 36-36–72; 6,455 yards

April 18-20
purse, ¥100,000,000

	SCORES			TOTAL	MONEY
*Minami Katsu	66	71	68	205	
Bo-Mee Lee	67	70	69	206	¥18,000,000
Ji-Hee Lee	68	72	69	209	8,800,000
Teresa Lu	68	70	72	210	6,500,000
Erina Hara	70	68	72	210	6,500,000
Misuzu Narita	68	69	74	211	4,500,000
Mami Fukuda	70	66	75	211	4,500,000
Kaori Nakamura	69	71	72	212	3,500,000
Mayumi Shimomura	70	74	69	213	2,750,000
Mi-Jeong Jeon	71	71	71	213	2,750,000
Ritsuko Ryu	72	71	71	214	1,842,500
Megumi Kido	71	71	72	214	1,842,500
Ayaka Watanabe	73	69	72	214	1,842,500
Esther Lee	70	70	74	214	1,842,500
Aoi Nagata	73	73	69	215	1,490,000
Yukari Baba	69	70	76	215	1,490,000
O. Sattaya	66	71	78	215	1,490,000
Hikari Fujita	70	74	73	217	1,106,000
Yuko Fukuda	71	73	73	217	1,106,000
Junko Omote	70	72	75	217	1,106,000
Megumi Shimokawa	76	69	72	217	1,106,000
Shiho Oyama	71	71	75	217	1,106,000

Fujisankei Ladies Classic

Kawana Hotel Golf Club, Fuji Course, Ito, Shizuoka
Par 36-36–72; 6,367 yards

April 25-27
purse, ¥80,000,000

	SCORES			TOTAL	MONEY
Phoebe Yao	72	67	68	207	¥14,400,000
Misuzu Narita	72	72	68	212	6,320,000
Mamiko Higa	72	72	68	212	6,320,000
Miki Sakai	70	71	72	213	4,400,000
Eriko Sonoda	69	71	73	213	4,400,000
Ji-Woo Lee	71	71	72	214	3,200,000
Jessica Speechley	74	69	72	215	2,400,000
Mihoko Iseri	70	72	73	215	2,400,000
Esther Lee	71	68	76	215	2,400,000
Rui Kitada	74	72	70	216	1,257,000
Yuko Fukuda	73	72	71	216	1,257,000
Rie Tsuji	73	71	72	216	1,257,000
Teresa Lu	71	72	73	216	1,257,000
Rikako Morita	74	68	74	216	1,257,000
Sayaka Tsuchida	74	68	74	216	1,257,000
Soo-Yun Kang	72	69	75	216	1,257,000
Shiho Oyama	67	72	77	216	1,257,000
Hye-Jin Jung	71	75	71	217	707,200
Ritsuko Ryu	76	68	73	217	707,200
Yumiko Yoshida	70	74	73	217	707,200
Eun-Bi Jang	72	72	73	217	707,200
Kaori Ohe	74	70	73	217	707,200
Asami Kikuchi	74	70	73	217	707,200
P. Chutichai	70	73	74	217	707,200
Shinobu Moromizato	71	71	75	217	707,200
Yun-Jye Wei	68	73	76	217	707,200
Hikari Fujita	71	69	77	217	707,200

Cyber Agent Ladies

Tsurumai Country Club, Ichihara, Chiba
Par 36-36–72; 6,515 yards

May 2-4
purse, ¥70,000,000

	SCORES			TOTAL	MONEY
Yuki Ichinose	68	70	69	207	¥12,600,000
*Haruka Morita	68	68	73	209	
Jiyai Shin	72	65	73	210	6,160,000
Kotono Kozuma	70	69	73	212	4,900,000
*Kotone Hori	69	67	76	212	
*Kana Nagai	72	68	73	213	
Na-Ri Kim	72	71	71	214	3,850,000
Ayaka Watanabe	67	73	74	214	3,850,000
Ritsuko Ryu	71	72	72	215	2,275,000
Young Kim	71	71	73	215	2,275,000
Yuri Fudoh	71	70	74	215	2,275,000
Esther Lee	72	69	74	215	2,275,000
Miki Sakai	74	72	70	216	1,237,600
Misuzu Narita	78	67	71	216	1,237,600
Lala Anai	74	71	71	216	1,237,600
Ha-Neul Kim	75	72	69	216	1,237,600
Riho Fujisaki	72	71	73	216	1,237,600
Yukari Baba	75	70	72	217	882,000
Kaori Ohe	72	71	74	217	882,000
Ji-Hee Lee	72	71	74	217	882,000

	SCORES			TOTAL	MONEY
Ai Suzuki	69	73	75	217	882,000
Mamiko Higa	71	71	75	217	882,000

World Ladies Championship Salonpas Cup

Ibaraki Golf Club, West Course, Tsukubamirai, Ibaraki — May 8-11
Par 36-36–72; 6,630 yards — purse, ¥120,000,000

	SCORES				TOTAL	MONEY
Misuzu Narita	74	72	66	67	279	¥24,000,000
Shanshan Feng	70	70	70	70	280	12,000,000
Mika Miyazato	74	70	70	67	281	9,000,000
Sun-Ju Ahn	73	72	72	67	284	7,200,000
Erina Hara	75	71	69	70	285	6,000,000
Lala Anai	71	72	73	70	286	4,320,000
Ha-Na Jang	75	71	69	71	286	4,320,000
Ayaka Watanabe	72	74	72	69	287	2,505,000
Erika Kikuchi	71	72	73	71	287	2,505,000
Ai Miyazato	73	71	72	71	287	2,505,000
Yeo-Jin Kang	73	67	75	72	287	2,505,000
Miki Sakai	76	68	75	69	288	1,800,000
Mayu Hattori	76	73	70	69	288	1,800,000
Yeon-Ju Jung	72	70	75	71	288	1,800,000
Phoebe Yao	72	69	73	74	288	1,800,000
*Minjee Lee	76	71	73	69	289	
Saiki Fujita	73	73	72	71	289	1,212,000
Kaori Nakamura	76	71	71	71	289	1,212,000
Yuki Ichinose	74	69	73	73	289	1,212,000
Anna Nordqvist	72	73	70	74	289	1,212,000
Hikari Fujita	74	71	69	75	289	1,212,000

Hoken no Madoguchi Ladies

Fukuoka Country Club, Wajiro Course, Asakura, Fukuoka — May 16-18
Par 36-36–72; 6,314 yards — purse, ¥120,000,000

	SCORES			TOTAL	MONEY
Bo-Mee Lee	73	65	69	207	¥21,600,000
Soo-Yun Kang	71	72	68	211	8,040,000
Mayu Hattori	71	72	68	211	8,040,000
Shanshan Feng	74	69	68	211	8,040,000
Mi-Jeong Jeon	70	68	73	211	8,040,000
Na-Ri Lee	75	68	69	212	4,500,000
Lala Anai	73	69	70	212	4,500,000
*Asuka Kashiwabara	69	68	75	212	
O. Sattaya	75	68	70	213	2,820,000
Sakura Yokomine	71	71	71	213	2,820,000
P. Chutichai	73	68	72	213	2,820,000
Momoko Ueda	73	66	74	213	2,820,000
Kotono Kozuma	72	71	71	214	2,100,000
Shiho Toyonaga	73	68	73	214	2,100,000
Yumi Takabayashi	73	72	70	215	1,740,000
Natsuka Hori	71	73	71	215	1,740,000
Hikari Kawamitsu	70	73	72	215	1,740,000
Yui Mukaiyama	72	69	74	215	1,740,000
Yeon-Ju Jung	74	71	71	216	1,236,000
Ayako Uehara	74	71	71	216	1,236,000

	SCORES			TOTAL	MONEY
Yukari Baba	71	72	73	216	1,236,000
Eun-Bi Jang	72	73	71	216	1,236,000
Ji-Woo Lee	71	74	71	216	1,236,000
Haruka Kudo	70	72	74	216	1,236,000

Chukyo TV Bridgestone Ladies Open

Chukyo Golf Club, Ishino Course, Toyota, Aichi — May 23-25
Par 36-36–72; 6,459 yards — purse, ¥70,000,000

	SCORES			TOTAL	MONEY
Sun-Ju Ahn	69	69	70	208	¥12,600,000
Miki Saiki	69	73	69	211	4,025,000
Miki Sakai	72	69	70	211	4,025,000
Ji-Hee Lee	72	69	70	211	4,025,000
Phoebe Yao	68	72	71	211	4,025,000
Ritsuko Ryu	68	72	71	211	4,025,000
Sakura Yokomine	69	71	71	211	4,025,000
Lala Anai	72	70	70	212	1,750,000
Misuzu Narita	70	69	73	212	1,750,000
*Kotone Hori	70	69	73	212	
Na-Ri Kim	72	67	73	212	1,750,000
Yuki Ichinose	73	71	69	213	1,232,000
Ai Suzuki	69	74	70	213	1,232,000
Ji-Min Lee	71	72	70	213	1,232,000
Akane Iijima	68	71	74	213	1,232,000
Yuko Mitsuka	73	71	70	214	917,000
Yukari Baba	71	71	72	214	917,000
Momoko Ueda	71	71	72	214	917,000
*Haruka Morita	74	71	69	214	
Rikako Morita	68	73	73	214	917,000
Junko Omote	73	68	73	214	917,000

Resort Trust Ladies

Kansai Country Club, Miki, Hyogo — May 30-June 1
Par 36-36–72; 6,510 yards — purse, ¥70,000,000

	SCORES			TOTAL	MONEY
Teresa Lu	67	70	64	201	¥12,600,000
Ji-Min Lee	67	70	69	206	6,160,000
Bo-Mee Lee	71	69	67	207	4,200,000
Na-Ri Lee	73	64	70	207	4,200,000
Junko Omote	68	68	71	207	4,200,000
Misuzu Narita	72	71	66	209	2,625,000
Natsuka Hori	71	69	69	209	2,625,000
Ji-Woo Lee	72	71	67	210	1,925,000
Ayaka Watanabe	70	70	70	210	1,925,000
*Kotone Hori	72	68	70	210	
Yuri Fudoh	71	71	69	211	1,118,250
Sun-Ju Ahn	71	71	69	211	1,118,250
Kaori Ohe	71	71	69	211	1,118,250
Mamiko Higa	71	70	70	211	1,118,250
Sakura Yokomine	72	69	70	211	1,118,250
Rikako Morita	68	72	71	211	1,118,250
Ritsuko Ryu	71	69	71	211	1,118,250
Ji-Hee Lee	73	67	71	211	1,118,250

	SCORES			TOTAL	MONEY
Maiko Wakabayashi	72	71	69	212	679,000
Rie Tsuji	73	71	68	212	679,000
Yayoi Arasaki	72	73	67	212	679,000
Yeo-Jin Kang	69	71	72	212	679,000
Mi-Jeong Jeon	69	71	72	212	679,000
Miki Saiki	67	72	73	212	679,000

Yonex Ladies

Yonex Country Club, Nagaoka, Niigata
Par 36-36–72; 6,337 yards

June 6-8
purse, ¥60,000,000

	SCORES			TOTAL	MONEY
Misuzu Narita	68	68	72	208	¥10,800,000
Shiho Oyama	67	70	71	208	4,740,000
Erina Yamato	69	68	71	208	4,740,000
(Narita defeated Oyama and Yamato on first playoff hole.)					
Sun-Ju Ahn	73	65	71	209	3,600,000
Junko Omote	71	71	68	210	2,500,000
Lala Anai	71	69	70	210	2,500,000
Nana Yamashiro	71	68	71	210	2,500,000
Saiki Fujita	70	72	69	211	1,800,000
Soo-Yun Kang	68	73	71	212	1,276,000
Bo-Mee Lee	72	69	71	212	1,276,000
Da-Ye Na	67	72	73	212	1,276,000
Ayaka Watanabe	75	69	69	213	888,000
Kotono Kozuma	72	69	72	213	888,000
Sakura Yokomine	72	69	72	213	888,000
Erina Hara	68	72	73	213	888,000
Teresa Lu	69	71	73	213	888,000
Jiyai Shin	69	71	73	213	888,000
Erika Kikuchi	72	68	73	213	888,000
Shiho Toyonaga	70	74	70	214	618,000
Ai Suzuki	69	72	73	214	618,000

Suntory Ladies Open

Rokko Kokusai Golf Club, Kobe, Hyogo
Par 36-36–72; 6,511 yards

June 12-15
purse, ¥100,000,000

	SCORES				TOTAL	MONEY
Sun-Ju Ahn	69	71	68	66	274	¥18,000,000
Akane Iijima	69	71	70	69	279	8,800,000
Momoko Ueda	70	68	72	70	280	7,000,000
Kaori Ohe	68	71	72	70	281	6,000,000
Yuri Fudoh	70	71	73	68	282	3,875,000
Miki Saiki	71	72	71	68	282	3,875,000
Ji-Hee Lee	71	68	72	71	282	3,875,000
Haruka Kudo	71	67	70	74	282	3,875,000
Shiho Oyama	74	66	74	70	284	2,250,000
*Haruka Morita	70	69	72	73	284	
Na-Ri Lee	68	68	74	74	284	2,250,000
Ayaka Watanabe	71	70	74	70	285	1,710,000
Nana Yamashiro	71	71	73	70	285	1,710,000
O. Sattaya	68	74	69	74	285	1,710,000
*Asuka Kashiwabara	71	72	72	71	286	
Natsu Nagai	70	71	73	72	286	1,360,000

	SCORES				TOTAL	MONEY
Miki Sakai	71	70	73	72	286	1,360,000
Yukari Baba	70	71	73	72	286	1,360,000
Erina Hara	71	72	70	73	286	1,360,000
Esther Lee	72	72	75	68	287	980,000
Megumi Kido	69	70	77	71	287	980,000
Ai Suzuki	73	70	70	74	287	980,000
Yukari Nishiyama	73	73	67	74	287	980,000

Nichirei Ladies

Sodegaura Country Club, Shinsode Course, Chiba — June 20-22
Par 36-36–72; 6,584 yards — purse, ¥80,000,000

	SCORES			TOTAL	MONEY
Jiyai Shin	69	65	70	204	¥14,400,000
Rumi Yoshiba	69	71	68	208	6,320,000
Hikari Fujita	73	65	70	208	6,320,000
Esther Lee	71	67	71	209	4,800,000
Na-Ri Lee	69	71	70	210	3,333,333
Yuri Fudoh	72	68	70	210	3,333,333
Momoko Ueda	71	68	71	210	3,333,333
Shiho Oyama	74	66	71	211	2,400,000
Soo-Yun Kang	77	67	69	213	1,628,000
Yuko Fukuda	73	73	67	213	1,628,000
Bo-Mee Lee	73	69	71	213	1,628,000
Mayu Hattori	74	68	71	213	1,628,000
Hye-Jin Jung	72	72	70	214	1,216,000
Erika Kikuchi	75	69	70	214	1,216,000
Kaori Ohe	71	74	69	214	1,216,000
Megumi Kido	72	69	73	214	1,216,000
Da-Ye Na	73	72	70	215	816,000
Kumiko Kaneda	73	72	70	215	816,000
Haruka Kudo	72	73	70	215	816,000
Saiki Fujita	73	70	72	215	816,000
Kaori Yamamoto	74	69	72	215	816,000
Maiko Wakabayashi	74	69	72	215	816,000
*Megumi Takahashi	72	74	69	215	
Young Kim	71	71	73	215	816,000
Mami Fukuda	70	70	75	215	816,000

Earth Mondahmin Cup

Camellia Hills Country Club, Sodegaura, Chiba — June 26-29
Par 36-36–72; 6,516 yards — purse, ¥140,000,000

	SCORES				TOTAL	MONEY
Miki Sakai	67	71	64	69	271	¥25,200,000
Sun-Ju Ahn	66	69	69	67	271	12,320,000
(Sakai defeated Ahn on second playoff hole.)						
Mi-Jeong Jeon	68	70	64	71	273	9,800,000
Teresa Lu	68	69	66	71	274	8,400,000
Shiho Oyama	68	71	66	70	275	7,000,000
Lala Anai	71	69	68	68	276	5,250,000
Megumi Shimokawa	70	68	69	69	276	5,250,000
Na-Ri Kim	72	68	69	68	277	3,500,000
Jiyai Shin	71	70	66	70	277	3,500,000
Mihoko Iseri	70	68	68	71	277	3,500,000

	SCORES				TOTAL	MONEY
Erina Hara	69	68	74	67	278	2,254,000
Hikari Fujita	71	70	70	67	278	2,254,000
Ji-Hee Lee	69	70	70	69	278	2,254,000
Na-Ri Lee	70	69	68	71	278	2,254,000
Ah-Reum Hwang	71	67	73	68	279	1,834,000
Young Kim	69	71	70	69	279	1,834,000
Misuzu Narita	70	69	72	69	280	1,554,000
Junko Omote	69	73	68	70	280	1,554,000
Rikako Morita	72	71	71	67	281	1,180,666
Ritsuko Ryu	69	74	69	69	281	1,180,666
Kaori Yamamoto	73	69	69	70	281	1,180,666
Mayu Hattori	68	71	70	72	281	1,180,666
Hiroko Azuma	70	69	70	72	281	1,180,666
Airi Saitoh	71	68	68	74	281	1,180,666

Nichi-Iko Ladies Open

Yatsuo Country Club, Toyama — July 4-6
Par 36-36–72; 6,454 yards — purse, ¥60,000,000

	SCORES			TOTAL	MONEY
Yeon-Ju Jung	66	68	65	199	¥10,800,000
Sakura Yokomine	65	70	66	201	5,280,000
Hikari Fujita	71	68	65	204	4,200,000
Megumi Kido	68	70	67	205	2,775,000
Bo-Mee Lee	71	67	67	205	2,775,000
Natsuka Hori	67	70	68	205	2,775,000
Rumi Yoshiba	69	67	69	205	2,775,000
Airi Saitoh	75	65	66	206	1,800,000
Akane Iijima	66	72	69	207	1,350,000
Ritsuko Ryu	67	70	70	207	1,350,000
Erika Kikuchi	72	69	67	208	984,000
Mayumi Shimomura	68	70	70	208	984,000
Hiromi Mogi	70	68	70	208	984,000
Yukari Baba	71	67	70	208	984,000
Young Kim	70	67	71	208	984,000
Maiko Wakabayashi	65	67	76	208	984,000
Teresa Lu	70	71	68	209	714,000
Nana Yamashiro	71	69	69	209	714,000
Yeo-Jin Kang	72	68	69	209	714,000
Mihoko Iseri	70	70	70	210	546,000
Lala Anai	69	72	69	210	546,000
Kaori Nakamura	69	72	69	210	546,000
Yumiko Yoshida	72	68	70	210	546,000
Aya Ezawa	72	68	70	210	546,000
Eun-Bi Jang	68	71	71	210	546,000
Megumi Shimokawa	71	72	67	210	546,000
Na-Ri Lee	69	68	73	210	546,000
Kaori Ohe	70	66	74	210	546,000

Samantha Thavasa Girls Collection Ladies

Eagle Point Golf Club, Ami, Ibaraki — July 18-20
Par 36-36–72; 6,528 yards — purse, ¥60,000,000

	SCORES			TOTAL	MONEY
Misuzu Narita	66	67	67	200	¥10,800,000
Kotono Kozuma	67	69	64	200	5,400,000
(Narita defeated Kozuma on first playoff hole.)					
Na-Ri Lee	66	66	69	201	4,200,000
Jiyai Shin	66	69	67	202	3,600,000
Megumi Kido	69	67	67	203	2,760,000
Hiroko Azuma	67	67	69	203	2,760,000
Yukari Nishiyama	67	69	68	204	1,950,000
Esther Lee	67	68	69	204	1,950,000
Erina Hara	70	67	68	205	1,500,000
Hiromi Mogi	68	71	67	206	1,089,600
Ji-Hee Lee	70	68	68	206	1,089,600
Megumi Shimokawa	69	68	69	206	1,089,600
Asako Fujimoto	68	68	70	206	1,089,600
Rui Kitada	69	67	70	206	1,089,600
Junko Omote	70	69	68	207	762,000
Hikari Fujita	67	71	69	207	762,000
Natsuka Hori	69	69	69	207	762,000
Serena Aoki	71	67	69	207	762,000
Yumiko Yoshida	66	71	70	207	762,000
Kaori Nakamura	66	69	72	207	762,000

Century 21 Ladies

IzuOhito Country Club, Shizuoka — July 25-27
Par 36-36–72; 6,531 yards — purse, ¥60,000,000

	SCORES			TOTAL	MONEY
Bo-Mee Lee	69	66	70	205	¥10,800,000
Keiko Sasaki	70	68	69	207	4,360,000
Sun-Ju Ahn	65	71	71	207	4,360,000
Asako Fujimoto	66	70	71	207	4,360,000
Natsuka Hori	70	72	66	208	2,325,000
Yukari Baba	69	69	70	208	2,325,000
Ritsuko Ryu	71	67	70	208	2,325,000
Kaori Ohe	71	67	70	208	2,325,000
Hikari Fujita	74	68	67	209	1,212,000
Momoko Ueda	71	70	68	209	1,212,000
Yukari Nishiyama	66	73	70	209	1,212,000
Megumi Kido	69	67	73	209	1,212,000
Miki Sakai	69	72	69	210	924,000
Erika Kikuchi	70	67	73	210	924,000
Yun-Jye Wei	67	67	76	210	924,000
Mi-Jeong Jeon	71	70	70	211	684,000
Shiho Oyama	69	71	71	211	684,000
Esther Lee	68	70	73	211	684,000
Kotono Kozuma	73	65	73	211	684,000
Misuzu Narita	70	66	75	211	684,000

Meiji Cup

Sapporo International Country Club, Kitahiroshima, Hokkaido — August 8-10
Par 36-36–72; 6,473 yards — purse, ¥90,000,000

	SCORES			TOTAL	MONEY
Jiyai Shin	70	66	68	204	¥16,200,000
Teresa Lu	67	70	69	206	7,920,000
Lala Anai	69	72	66	207	5,850,000
Saiki Fujita	71	70	66	207	5,850,000
Bo-Mee Lee	70	68	70	208	4,050,000
Erina Hara	71	66	71	208	4,050,000
Ritsuko Ryu	69	70	70	209	2,700,000
Yuri Fudoh	68	70	71	209	2,700,000
Miki Sakai	69	69	71	209	2,700,000
Shiho Toyonaga	72	72	66	210	1,560,000
Soo-Yun Kang	70	73	67	210	1,560,000
Yukari Nishiyama	69	71	70	210	1,560,000
Yumiko Yoshida	71	69	70	210	1,560,000
Yoko Maeda	70	69	71	210	1,560,000
Misuzu Narita	70	67	73	210	1,560,000
Mi-Jeong Jeon	74	70	67	211	1,062,000
Megumi Shimokawa	72	71	68	211	1,062,000
Natsu Nagai	73	70	68	211	1,062,000
Miki Saiki	67	74	70	211	1,062,000
Rikako Morita	71	67	73	211	1,062,000

NEC Karuizawa 72

Karuizawa 72 Golf Club, Karuizawa, Nagano — August 15-17
Par 36-36–72; 6,555 yards — purse, ¥70,000,000

	SCORES			TOTAL	MONEY
Bo-Mee Lee	69	64	70	203	¥12,600,000
Erika Kikuchi	69	68	66	203	5,530,000
Shiho Oyama	68	67	68	203	5,530,000
(Lee defeated Kikuchi and Oyama on first playoff hole.)					
Sun-Ju Ahn	70	69	66	205	3,850,000
Nana Yamashiro	66	70	69	205	3,850,000
Erina Hara	68	71	67	206	2,275,000
Da-Ye Na	73	67	66	206	2,275,000
Megumi Kido	72	64	70	206	2,275,000
Yumiko Yoshida	67	68	71	206	2,275,000
Mayu Hattori	67	72	68	207	1,118,250
Misuzu Narita	68	71	68	207	1,118,250
Ayaka Watanabe	67	71	69	207	1,118,250
Saiki Fujita	69	68	70	207	1,118,250
Na-Ri Kim	65	71	71	207	1,118,250
Yun-Jye Wei	67	69	71	207	1,118,250
Kaori Yamamoto	69	67	71	207	1,118,250
Na-Ri Lee	70	66	71	207	1,118,250
Saki Nagamine	71	69	68	208	691,600
Mi-Jeong Jeon	69	71	68	208	691,600
Miki Saiki	70	69	69	208	691,600
Haruka Kudo	69	69	70	208	691,600
Esther Lee	69	69	70	208	691,600

CAT Ladies

Daihakone Country Club, Hakone, Kanagawa
Par 36-37–73; 6,701 yards

August 22-24
purse, ¥60,000,000

	SCORES			TOTAL	MONEY
Momoko Ueda	70	71	69	210	¥10,800,000
Rikako Morita	67	71	73	211	5,280,000
Bo-Mee Lee	70	72	71	213	4,200,000
Teresa Lu	74	72	68	214	3,600,000
Ayaka Watanabe	72	70	73	215	3,000,000
Asako Fujimoto	74	73	69	216	2,250,000
Esther Lee	72	72	72	216	2,250,000
Hiroko Fukushima	71	76	71	218	1,500,000
Lala Anai	74	72	72	218	1,500,000
Kaori Yamamoto	69	73	76	218	1,500,000
Yeo-Jin Kang	77	73	70	220	936,000
Mamiko Higa	74	76	70	220	936,000
Natsuka Hori	72	75	73	220	936,000
Kaori Ohe	73	74	73	220	936,000
Mayu Hattori	74	73	73	220	936,000
Erina Hara	74	73	73	220	936,000
Sun-Ju Ahn	72	74	74	220	936,000
Megumi Kido	74	78	69	221	553,090
Yumiko Yoshida	75	77	69	221	553,090
Nana Yamashiro	74	75	72	221	553,090
Yukari Baba	77	72	72	221	553,090
Shinobu Moromizato	75	74	72	221	553,090
Eun-Bi Jang	76	73	72	221	553,090
O. Sattaya	72	76	73	221	553,090
Yukari Nishiyama	74	74	73	221	553,090
Junko Omote	74	74	73	221	553,090
Risa Ogusu	74	73	74	221	553,090
Da-Ye Na	74	72	75	221	553,090

Nitori Ladies

Eniwa Country Club, Eniwa, Hokkaido
Par 36-36–72; 6,522 yards

August 29-31
purse, ¥70,000,000

	SCORES			TOTAL	MONEY
Jiyai Shin	67	71	70	208	¥12,600,000
Bo-Mee Lee	71	71	69	211	5,530,000
Saiki Fujita	69	71	71	211	5,530,000
Yumiko Yoshida	71	74	70	215	3,850,000
Shiho Oyama	74	70	71	215	3,850,000
Esther Lee	70	74	72	216	2,800,000
Natsuka Hori	72	74	71	217	1,925,000
Kotono Kozuma	75	70	72	217	1,925,000
Ritsuko Ryu	72	70	75	217	1,925,000
Lala Anai	73	69	75	217	1,925,000
*Hina Arakaki	70	72	75	217	
Momoko Ueda	74	74	70	218	1,148,000
Junko Omote	77	73	68	218	1,148,000
*Megumi Takahashi	73	72	73	218	
Ah-Reum Hwang	73	72	73	218	1,148,000
O. Sattaya	70	73	75	218	1,148,000
Miki Sakai	76	71	72	219	771,000
Hiroko Azuma	75	73	71	219	771,000
Hyun-Ju Shin	72	76	71	219	771,000

	SCORES			TOTAL	MONEY
Erina Hara	70	75	74	219	771,000
Teresa Lu	73	72	74	219	771,000
Soo-Yun Kang	74	70	75	219	771,000
Yukari Nishiyama	70	70	79	219	771,000

Golf 5 Ladies

Mizunami Country Club, Gifu
Par 36-36–72; 6,520 yards

September 5-7
purse, ¥60,000,000

	SCORES			TOTAL	MONEY
Shiho Oyama	65	63	72	200	¥10,800,000
Misuzu Narita	68	66	68	202	5,280,000
Na-Ri Lee	67	71	65	203	3,900,000
Rumi Yoshiba	69	68	66	203	3,900,000
Kotono Kozuma	69	67	68	204	3,000,000
Eun-Bi Jang	71	68	66	205	2,400,000
Ritsuko Ryu	69	69	68	206	1,800,000
Ji-Hee Lee	67	70	69	206	1,800,000
O. Sattaya	69	67	70	206	1,800,000
Kaori Yamamoto	68	69	71	208	1,200,000
Kumiko Kaneda	70	72	67	209	1,014,000
Esther Lee	70	69	70	209	1,014,000
Ah-Reum Hwang	70	68	71	209	1,014,000
Yumiko Yoshida	66	70	73	209	1,014,000
Yukari Baba	70	72	68	210	804,000
Yeon-Ju Jung	69	71	70	210	804,000
Ai Suzuki	70	70	70	210	804,000
Kaori Nakamura	70	72	69	211	624,000
Natsu Nagai	71	69	71	211	624,000
Jiyai Shin	70	69	72	211	624,000

Japan LPGA Championship

Minagi Golf Club, Minagi, Hyogo
Par 36-36–72; 6,645 yards

September 11-14
purse, ¥140,000,000

	SCORES				TOTAL	MONEY
Ai Suzuki	70	67	75	71	283	¥25,200,000
Na-Ri Lee	72	70	74	68	284	9,380,000
Lala Anai	70	71	74	69	284	9,380,000
Misuzu Narita	72	70	72	70	284	9,380,000
Jiyai Shin	71	71	72	70	284	9,380,000
Esther Lee	75	69	74	68	286	5,600,000
Ah-Reum Hwang	70	73	71	73	287	4,200,000
Momoko Ueda	73	71	69	74	287	4,200,000
Kaori Ohe	70	74	69	74	287	4,200,000
Erika Kikuchi	72	74	72	71	289	2,464,000
Ritsuko Ryu	70	77	71	71	289	2,464,000
Eun-Bi Jang	74	74	68	73	289	2,464,000
Erina Hara	76	71	70	73	290	2,086,000
Yoko Maeda	71	73	77	70	291	1,946,000
Kotono Kozuma	72	75	74	71	292	1,456,000
Kaori Nakamura	73	73	74	72	292	1,456,000
Saiki Fujita	75	72	72	73	292	1,456,000
Ayaka Watanabe	70	76	72	74	292	1,456,000
Ji-Hee Lee	71	74	71	76	292	1,456,000
Shiho Oyama	74	72	70	76	292	1,456,000

Munsingwear Ladies Tokai Classic

Shin Minami Aichi Country Club, Minama, Aichi — September 19-21
Par 36-36–72; 6,375 yards — purse, ¥80,000,000

	SCORES			TOTAL	MONEY
Jiyai Shin	68	67	67	202	¥14,400,000
Na-Ri Lee	67	70	66	203	7,040,000
Esther Lee	70	71	64	205	5,200,000
Rui Kitada	66	70	69	205	5,200,000
Na-Ri Kim	67	68	72	207	4,000,000
Sakura Yokomine	70	71	67	208	2,600,000
Megumi Shimokawa	68	71	69	208	2,600,000
Yukari Nishiyama	71	67	70	208	2,600,000
O. Sattaya	72	63	73	208	2,600,000
Erika Kikuchi	72	71	66	209	1,528,000
Misuzu Narita	67	69	73	209	1,528,000
Nana Yamashiro	72	69	69	210	1,136,000
Mi-Jeong Jeon	70	70	70	210	1,136,000
Rumi Yoshiba	67	72	71	210	1,136,000
Momoko Ueda	69	69	72	210	1,136,000
Ji-Min Lee	69	69	72	210	1,136,000
Asako Fujimoto	70	68	72	210	1,136,000
Mami Fukuda	70	64	76	210	1,136,000
Miki Sakai	69	74	68	211	776,000
Miki Saiki	70	73	68	211	776,000

Miyagi TV Cup Dunlop Ladies Open

Rifu Golf Club, Rifu, Miyagi — September 26-28
Par 36-36–72; 6,499 yards — purse, ¥70,000,000

	SCORES			TOTAL	MONEY
Miki Sakai	69	72	67	208	¥12,600,000
Ayaka Watanabe	71	66	72	209	6,160,000
Junko Omote	70	72	68	210	4,200,000
Sun-Ju Ahn	69	70	71	210	4,200,000
Teresa Lu	72	65	73	210	4,200,000
Kaori Ohe	72	72	67	211	2,450,000
Na-Ri Lee	71	72	68	211	2,450,000
Tomoko Kanai	71	71	69	211	2,450,000
Rikako Morita	72	69	71	212	1,750,000
Natsu Nagai	72	73	68	213	1,295,000
Mami Fukuda	72	70	71	213	1,295,000
Erika Kikuchi	72	70	71	213	1,295,000
Natsuka Hori	69	71	73	213	1,295,000
Sakura Yokomine	72	72	70	214	945,000
Momoko Ueda	74	69	71	214	945,000
Mihoko Iseri	71	71	72	214	945,000
Ji-Woo Lee	72	70	72	214	945,000
Yumiko Yoshida	71	70	73	214	945,000
Ritsuko Ryu	72	69	73	214	945,000
Rui Kitada	71	72	72	215	672,000
Misuzu Narita	75	68	72	215	672,000
Ji-Hee Lee	74	71	70	215	672,000
Erina Yamato	69	72	74	215	672,000
Shiho Oyama	70	70	75	215	672,000

Japan Women's Open Championship

Biwako Country Club, Mikami Course, Ritto, Shiga
Par 36-36–72; 6,522 yards

October 2-5
purse, ¥140,000,000

	SCORES				TOTAL	MONEY
Teresa Lu	69	71	73	67	280	¥28,000,000
Na-Ri Lee	74	69	69	69	281	15,400,000
*Kana Nagai	69	71	72	70	282	
Sun-Ju Ahn	69	72	71	71	283	10,780,000
Ai Suzuki	68	71	69	76	284	7,000,000
Shiho Oyama	69	71	74	71	285	4,060,000
Erika Kikuchi	68	70	74	73	285	4,060,000
Hiroko Azuma	67	72	72	74	285	4,060,000
Ah-Reum Hwang	71	69	71	74	285	4,060,000
Jiyai Shin	71	68	71	75	285	4,060,000
Yun-Jye Wei	69	71	68	77	285	4,060,000
Rikako Morita	74	72	70	70	286	2,450,000
Erina Hara	74	73	70	70	287	1,964,666
Bo-Mee Lee	71	71	73	72	287	1,964,666
Chie Arimura	71	67	75	74	287	1,964,666
Kumiko Kaneda	69	73	75	71	288	1,554,000
Kotone Hori	75	69	73	71	288	1,554,000
Sakura Kito	74	71	71	72	288	1,554,000
Mami Fukuda	71	73	74	71	289	1,365,000
Mi-Jeong Jeon	70	69	73	77	289	1,365,000

Stanley Ladies

Tomei Country Club, Susano, Shizuoka
Par 36-36–72; 6,561 yards

October 10-12
purse, ¥90,000,000

	SCORES			TOTAL	MONEY
Sun-Ju Ahn	68	68	66	202	¥16,200,000
Ji-Hee Lee	65	67	72	204	8,100,000
Miki Sakai	69	68	68	205	6,300,000
O. Sattaya	65	73	68	206	4,950,000
Erina Hara	67	70	69	206	4,950,000
Na-Ri Lee	69	71	69	209	2,970,000
Ritsuko Ryu	70	70	69	209	2,970,000
Bo-Mee Lee	70	68	71	209	2,970,000
Misuzu Narita	66	69	74	209	2,970,000
Ai Suzuki	76	66	68	210	1,800,000
*Akiho Sato	70	67	73	210	
Eun-Bi Jang	69	72	70	211	1,548,000
Mami Fukuda	71	70	70	211	1,548,000
Yumiko Yoshida	70	69	72	211	1,548,000
Da-Ye Na	69	69	73	211	1,548,000
Esther Lee	71	67	73	211	1,548,000
Mayu Hattori	72	71	69	212	1,188,000
Rui Kitada	69	72	71	212	1,188,000
Momoko Ueda	69	70	73	212	1,188,000
Asako Fujimoto	72	71	70	213	903,000
Kotone Hori	68	73	72	213	903,000
Yeon-Ju Jung	71	72	70	213	903,000
Kotono Kozuma	74	69	70	213	903,000
Nobuko Kizawa	67	73	73	213	903,000
Sakura Yokomine	70	70	73	213	903,000

Fujitsu Ladies

Tokyu Seven Hundred Club, West Course, Chiba — October 17-19
Par 36-36–72; 6,635 yards — purse, ¥80,000,000

	SCORES			TOTAL	MONEY
Sun-Ju Ahn	64	69	72	205	¥14,400,000
Sakura Yokomine	70	65	70	205	6,400,000
Erika Kikuchi	65	69	71	205	6,400,000
(Ahn defeated Yokomine and Kikuchi on first playoff hole.)					
Teresa Lu	68	71	69	208	4,800,000
Rikako Morita	71	71	67	209	3,386,666
Soo-Yun Kang	71	69	69	209	3,386,666
Mami Fukuda	70	67	72	209	3,386,666
Megumi Kido	70	71	69	210	2,200,000
O. Sattaya	67	69	74	210	2,200,000
Phoebe Yao	69	70	72	211	1,600,000
Miki Sakai	71	69	72	212	1,536,000
Yumiko Yoshida	70	71	72	213	1,376,000
Junko Omote	71	70	72	213	1,376,000
Mihoko Iseri	69	69	75	213	1,376,000
Ai Suzuki	72	71	71	214	1,176,000
Kaori Ohe	70	71	73	214	1,176,000
Lala Anai	73	72	70	215	908,800
Shiho Oyama	72	71	72	215	908,800
Erina Hara	70	72	73	215	908,800
Ah-Reum Hwang	72	70	73	215	908,800
Nana Yamashiro	72	70	73	215	908,800

Nobuta Group Masters Golf Club Ladies

Masters Golf Club, Miki, Hyogo — October 23-26
Par 36-36–72; 6,445 yards — purse, ¥140,000,000

	SCORES				TOTAL	MONEY
Shiho Oyama	65	67	69	68	269	¥25,200,000
Sun-Ju Ahn	66	68	71	66	271	12,320,000
Momoko Ueda	66	69	71	66	272	9,800,000
Yumiko Yoshida	69	69	66	69	273	8,400,000
Kotono Kozuma	74	67	68	66	275	7,000,000
Paula Creamer	69	69	70	68	276	5,250,000
Ayaka Watanabe	70	63	72	71	276	5,250,000
Da-Ye Na	70	71	68	68	277	3,850,000
Teresa Lu	69	68	67	73	277	3,850,000
Bo-Mee Lee	71	68	71	69	279	2,604,000
Yukari Nishiyama	70	65	74	70	279	2,604,000
Kaori Ohe	68	70	70	71	279	2,604,000
Erina Hara	70	68	70	72	280	2,226,000
Yukari Baba	71	70	67	72	280	2,226,000
Jiyai Shin	77	66	70	68	281	1,736,000
Asuka Kashiwabara	70	68	74	69	281	1,736,000
Mami Fukuda	69	73	70	69	281	1,736,000
*Minami Katsu	73	71	72	65	281	
Kumiko Kaneda	69	71	69	72	281	1,736,000
Ai Suzuki	70	68	69	74	281	1,736,000

Hisako Higuchi Morinaga Ladies

Morinaga Takataki Country Club, Ichihara, Chiba
Par 36-36–72; 6,652 yards

October 31-November 2
purse, ¥70,000,000

	SCORES			TOTAL	MONEY
Momoko Ueda	68	69	69	206	¥12,600,000
Junko Omote	69	68	70	207	6,160,000
Erina Hara	69	71	68	208	4,550,000
Yumiko Yoshida	70	69	69	208	4,550,000
Megumi Kido	71	69	69	209	3,150,000
Mika Miyazato	71	69	69	209	3,150,000
Na-Ri Kim	72	69	69	210	2,450,000
Kaori Aoyama	71	71	69	211	1,636,250
Akane Iijima	71	70	70	211	1,636,250
Ai Suzuki	70	70	71	211	1,636,250
Erika Kikuchi	71	68	72	211	1,636,250
Ji-Woo Lee	73	69	70	212	1,190,000
Bo-Mee Lee	71	67	74	212	1,190,000
Erina Yamato	73	72	68	213	1,015,000
Na-Ri Lee	72	70	71	213	1,015,000
Yukari Baba	72	67	74	213	1,015,000
Miki Sakai	72	72	70	214	728,000
Mihoko Iseri	68	75	71	214	728,000
Yui Mukaiyama	71	72	71	214	728,000
Teresa Lu	72	71	71	214	728,000
Esther Lee	69	71	74	214	728,000
Ji-Hee Lee	66	70	78	214	728,000

Mizuno Classic

Kintetsu Kashikojima Country Club, Shima, Mie
Par 36-36–72; 6,506 yards

November 7-9
purse, US$1,200,000

	SCORES			TOTAL	MONEY
Mi Hyang Lee	69	67	69	205	¥20,412,000
Kotono Kozuma	69	67	69	205	10,714,825
Ilhee Lee	69	66	70	205	10,714,825
(Mi Hyang Lee defeated Kozuma and Ilhee Lee on fifth playoff hole.)					
Morgan Pressel	67	72	67	206	3,898,578
Sakura Yokomine	70	69	67	206	3,898,578
Saiki Fujita	70	69	67	206	3,898,578
Karrie Webb	70	68	68	206	3,898,578
Na-Ri Lee	72	65	69	206	3,898,578
Jessica Korda	71	67	68	206	3,898,578
Ayako Uehara	70	68	68	206	3,898,578
Chella Choi	68	68	70	206	3,898,578
Laura Davies	68	67	71	206	3,898,578
Bo-Mee Lee	71	69	67	207	1,985,520
Teresa Lu	73	67	67	207	1,985,520
Harukyo Nomura	70	69	68	207	1,985,520
Misuzu Narita	72	67	68	207	1,985,520
Ai Suzuki	71	64	72	207	1,985,520
Asako Fujimoto	71	71	67	209	1,484,859
Sun-Young Yoo	70	72	67	209	1,484,859
Giulia Sergas	72	71	66	209	1,484,859
Sydnee Michaels	73	69	67	209	1,484,859
Pernilla Lindberg	72	70	67	209	1,484,859
Jiyai Shin	71	70	68	209	1,484,859
Mirim Lee	73	68	68	209	1,484,859

	SCORES			TOTAL	MONEY
Beatriz Recari	71	69	69	209	1,484,859
Amelia Lewis	72	71	67	210	1,157,360
Tiffany Joh	73	69	68	210	1,157,360
Junko Omote	76	68	66	210	1,157,360
Catriona Matthew	71	70	69	210	1,157,360
Angela Stanford	71	68	71	210	1,157,360

Itoen Ladies

Great Island Club, Chonan, Chiba
Par 36-36–72; 6,639 yards

November 14-16
purse, ¥100,000,000

	SCORES			TOTAL	MONEY
Yoko Maeda	68	69	70	207	¥18,000,000
Satsuki Oshiro	69	71	67	207	8,800,000
(Maeda defeated Oshiro on first playoff hole.)					
Momoko Ueda	70	69	69	208	7,000,000
Mami Fukuda	71	72	66	209	4,000,000
Ai Suzuki	67	73	69	209	4,000,000
Ayaka Watanabe	70	70	69	209	4,000,000
Rui Kitada	72	68	69	209	4,000,000
Soo-Yun Kang	73	66	70	209	4,000,000
Erina Hara	68	68	73	209	4,000,000
Junko Omote	69	73	68	210	1,682,857
Misuzu Narita	68	72	70	210	1,682,857
Shiho Oyama	69	71	70	210	1,682,857
Miki Sakai	70	69	71	210	1,682,857
Yeon-Ju Jung	70	68	72	210	1,682,857
Ritsuko Ryu	69	68	73	210	1,682,857
Asako Fujimoto	68	68	74	210	1,682,857
Bo-Mee Lee	70	73	68	211	1,130,000
Yumiko Yoshida	70	70	71	211	1,130,000
Erika Kikuchi	69	70	72	211	1,130,000
Yukari Nishiyama	69	68	74	211	1,130,000

Elleair Ladies Open

Elleair Golf Club, Kagawa
Par 36-36–72; 6,428 yards

November 20-23
purse, ¥100,000,000

	SCORES				TOTAL	MONEY
Sakura Yokomine	69	68	65	68	270	¥18,000,000
Teresa Lu	68	70	68	65	271	7,266,666
Rikako Morita	69	70	66	66	271	7,266,666
Ai Suzuki	71	65	64	71	271	7,266,666
Erina Hara	71	66	69	67	273	4,166,666
Rui Kitada	67	66	71	69	273	4,166,666
Miki Sakai	68	69	66	70	273	4,166,666
Na-Ri Lee	69	67	72	66	274	2,500,000
Yumiko Yoshida	70	67	68	69	274	2,500,000
Sun-Ju Ahn	70	65	68	71	274	2,500,000
Ayaka Watanabe	72	70	66	67	275	1,850,000
Shiho Oyama	68	68	68	71	275	1,850,000
Junko Omote	70	70	69	67	276	1,650,000
Momoko Ueda	65	70	70	71	276	1,650,000
Haruka Kudo	71	68	69	69	277	1,400,000
Mi-Jeong Jeon	67	67	73	70	277	1,400,000

	SCORES				TOTAL	MONEY
Bo-Mee Lee	72	69	66	70	277	1,400,000
Asako Fujimoto	68	72	73	65	278	1,200,000
Megumi Shimokawa	67	70	73	69	279	1,026,666
Yuko Fukuda	71	72	66	70	279	1,026,666
Kaori Aoyama	72	66	70	71	279	1,026,666

Japan LPGA Tour Championship Ricoh Cup

Miyazaki Country Club, Miyazaki
Par 36-36–72; 6,428 yards

November 27-30
purse, ¥100,000,000

	SCORES				TOTAL	MONEY
Teresa Lu	69	67	70	72	278	¥25,000,000
Lala Anai	70	68	67	73	278	14,500,000
(Lu defeated Anai on second playoff hole.)						
Shiho Oyama	72	70	70	70	282	9,000,000
Yeon-Ju Jung	73	68	68	73	282	9,000,000
Ayaka Watanabe	66	72	72	73	283	6,650,000
Kotono Kozuma	68	70	72	74	284	5,720,000
Misuzu Narita	72	68	73	72	285	3,713,333
Momoko Ueda	71	73	69	72	285	3,713,333
Jiyai Shin	71	70	70	74	285	3,713,333
Rikako Morita	71	73	69	73	286	1,790,000
Erina Hara	70	70	72	75	287	1,590,000
Na-Ri Lee	67	75	74	72	288	1,200,000
Saiki Fujita	75	71	69	73	288	1,200,000
Bo-Mee Lee	71	69	71	77	288	1,200,000
Yumiko Yoshida	70	75	72	72	289	785,000
Ji-Hee Lee	72	72	69	76	289	785,000
Miki Sakai	73	72	73	72	290	650,000
Ritsuko Ryu	71	71	77	72	291	515,000
Erika Kikuchi	73	70	76	72	291	515,000
Sun-Ju Ahn	74	68	73	76	291	515,000
O. Sattaya	69	73	72	77	291	515,000
Phoebe Yao	72	71	75	75	293	475,000
Mi-Jeong Jeon	76	71	71	75	293	475,000
*Minami Katsu	74	73	75	72	294	
Esther Lee	73	72	75	74	294	460,000
Ai Suzuki	74	74	74	73	295	450,000
Yoko Maeda	73	71	77	75	296	440,000
Junko Omote	74	73	71	79	297	430,000

Australian Ladies Tour

Moss Vale Classic

Moss Vale Golf Club, New South Wales — January 13-14
Par 73; 5,796 yards — purse, A$30,000

	SCORES		TOTAL	MONEY
Bree Arthur	71	67	138	A$4,500
Stacy Lee Bregman	68	71	139	2,550
Laura Davies	69	70	139	2,550
Danielle Montgomery	72	68	140	1,560
Stacey Keating	70	71	141	1,320
Sarah Kemp	69	72	141	1,320
Hannah Burke	72	70	142	915
Felicity Johnson	70	72	142	915
Chloe Leurquin	71	71	142	915
Kristie Smith	71	71	142	915
Nikki Campbell	73	70	143	810
Breanna Elliott	75	68	143	810
Stacey Tate	74	69	143	810
Jody Fleming	73	71	144	594
Joanna Klatten	73	71	144	594
Courtney Massey	71	73	144	594
Bree Turnbull	75	69	144	594
Liz Young	74	70	144	594
Frances Bondad	72	73	145	457.50
Ginny Brown	71	74	145	457.50
Nancy Harvey	73	72	145	457.50
Vicky Thomas	67	78	145	457.50

Mount Broughton Classic

Mount Broughton Golf Club, Sutton Forest, New South Wales — January 17-18
Par 72; 6,124 yards — purse, A$50,000

	SCORES		TOTAL	MONEY
Daniela Holmqvist	67	67	134	A$7,500
Sarah Kemp	70	66	136	5,000
Trish Johnson	70	67	137	3,250
Joanna Klatten	67	70	137	3,250
Stacey Keating	69	69	138	2,500
Rebecca Artis	69	70	139	1,875
Frances Bondad	72	67	139	1,875
Pamela Pretswell	69	70	139	1,875
Marta Silva	69	70	139	1,875
Lauren Hibbert	71	69	140	1,400
Hannah Burke	68	73	141	1,150
Nikki Campbell	70	71	141	1,150
Rebecca Codd	68	73	141	1,150
Stephanie Na	71	70	141	1,150
Bree Arthur	69	73	142	760
Emma De Groot	72	70	142	760
Chloe Leurquin	68	74	142	760

	SCORES		TOTAL	MONEY
Kristie Smith	71	71	142	760
Jessica Speechley	73	69	142	760
Cherie Alison	70	73	143	531.25
Julia Boland	72	71	143	531.25
Stacy Lee Bregman	69	74	143	531.25
Cathryn Bristow	73	70	143	531.25

Bing Lee Fujitsu General Women's NSW Open

Oatlands Golf Club, Sydney, New South Wales — January 24-26
Par 36-36–72; 5,974 yards — purse, A$100,000

	SCORES			TOTAL	MONEY
Joanna Klatten	70	67	63	200	A$15,000
Nikki Campbell	68	69	66	203	9,900
Hannah Burke	68	68	68	204	6,000
Stephanie Na	68	66	70	204	6,000
*Minjee Lee	68	71	66	205	
Kristie Smith	65	70	70	205	3,675
Lindsey Wright	70	64	71	205	3,675
*Jing Yan	69	69	68	206	
Stacy Lee Bregman	70	68	69	207	2,516.67
Noriko Kubo	69	67	71	207	2,516.67
Kylie Walker	70	67	70	207	2,516.67
Julia Boland	69	70	69	208	2,100
Frances Bondad	69	75	65	209	1,416.67
*Su-Hyun Oh	70	69	70	209	
Jessica Speechley	69	68	72	209	1,416.67
Sally Watson	70	71	68	209	1,416.67
Beth Allen	68	72	70	210	1,300
*Shelly Shin	70	70	70	210	
Laura Davies	69	70	72	211	1,260
Felicity Johnson	68	74	70	212	1,180
Sarah Kemp	72	68	72	212	1,180
Marion Ricordeau	72	67	73	212	1,180
Alexandra Vilatte	67	72	73	212	1,180
Liz Young	71	70	71	212	1,180

ISPS Handa New Zealand Women's Open

Clearwater Golf Club, Christchurch, New Zealand — January 31February 2
Par 36-36–72; 6,170 yards — purse, €200,000

	SCORES			TOTAL	MONEY
Mi Hyang Lee	72	72	63	207	A$30,000
Lydia Ko	69	69	70	208	20,300
Beth Allen	71	68	70	209	11,093.33
Anya Alvarez	70	66	73	209	11,093.33
Seonwoo Bae	68	71	70	209	11,093.33
Bree Arthur	75	70	66	211	6,000
Marion Ricordeau	74	69	68	211	6,000
Sarah-Jane Smith	69	77	65	211	6,000
Hyun Soo Kim	74	66	72	212	4,260
Nikki Campbell	72	72	68	212	4,260
Lorie Kane	74	72	67	213	3,323.33
*Jing Yan	73	69	71	213	
Marta Silva Zamora	72	70	71	213	3,323.33

	SCORES			TOTAL	MONEY
Stacy Lee Bregman	71	75	67	213	3,323.33
Jessica Speechley	70	70	73	213	3,323.33
Kyu Jung Baek	70	69	74	213	3,323.33
Charley Hull	69	73	71	213	3,323.33
*Shelly Shin	76	68	70	214	
Breanna Elliott	75	70	69	214	2,920
Yu Yang Zhang	77	69	69	215	2,600
Felicity Johnson	74	70	71	215	2,600
Cecilia Cho	73	72	70	215	2,600
Linda Wessberg	73	71	71	215	2,600
Christel Boeljon	72	72	71	215	2,600
Vikki Laing	71	72	72	215	2,600

Volvik RACV Ladies Masters

RACV Royal Pines Resort, Ashmore, Queensland
Par 37-36–73; 6,600 yards

February 6-9
purse, €250,000

	SCORES				TOTAL	MONEY
Cheyenne Woods	69	67	71	69	276	€37,500
*Minjee Lee	70	70	69	69	278	
Camilla Lennarth	71	67	72	70	280	21,437.50
Stacy Lee Bregman	69	67	72	72	280	21,437.50
Min-Sun Kim	72	68	73	70	283	12,050
Caroline Hedwall	71	73	73	66	283	12,050
*So Young Lee	71	70	73	69	283	
Belen Mozo	73	73	73	65	284	8,125
Jessica Korda	68	73	74	69	284	8,125
Yani Tseng	73	72	74	66	285	5,616.67
Charley Hull	73	66	76	70	285	5,616.67
Gwladys Nocera	71	73	71	70	285	5,616.67
Vikki Laing	76	71	70	70	287	4,016.67
Alison Whitaker	75	69	69	74	287	4,016.67
Sarah-Jane Smith	72	73	73	69	287	4,016.67
Trish Johnson	71	66	73	77	287	4,016.67
Dewi Claire Schreefel	70	74	74	69	287	4,016.67
Rebecca Artis	70	74	73	70	287	4,016.67
Xi Yu Lin	75	70	69	74	288	3,120
Laura Davies	73	74	73	68	288	3,120
Beth Allen	73	68	76	71	288	3,120
Chella Choi	72	73	73	70	288	3,120
Cathryn Bristow	71	74	72	71	288	3,120
Tiffany Joh	71	72	74	71	288	3,120
Sarah Kemp	70	73	75	70	288	3,120
Yu Yang Zhang	70	70	77	71	288	3,120
Valentine Derrey	69	75	72	72	288	3,120
Katie Burnett	68	71	75	74	288	3,120

ISPS Handa Women's Australian Open

Victoria Golf Club, Victoria
Par 36-36–72; 6,472 yards

February 13-16
purse, US$1,200,000

	SCORES				TOTAL	MONEY
Karrie Webb	71	69	68	68	276	US$180,000
Chella Choi	70	71	62	74	277	110,822
Paula Creamer	68	69	73	68	278	64,213
Karine Icher	69	68	70	71	278	64,213
Lydia Ko	68	68	69	73	278	64,213
Stacy Lewis	71	69	70	69	279	33,068
Amelia Lewis	71	67	69	72	279	33,068
Morgan Pressel	69	68	70	72	279	33,068
Jenny Shin	74	67	66	72	279	33,068
Gerina Piller	75	69	68	68	280	24,573
Azahara Munoz	68	70	73	70	281	21,296
Jessica Speechley	71	67	70	73	281	21,296
Mi Hyang Lee	72	67	68	74	281	21,296
*Minjee Lee	68	67	68	78	281	
Trish Johnson	70	73	68	71	282	17,171
Sarah Kemp	71	68	71	72	282	17,171
Perrine Delacour	70	73	65	74	282	17,171
Caroline Hedwall	68	65	74	75	282	17,171
Sandra Gal	73	69	72	69	283	14,228
Giulia Sergas	68	71	72	72	283	14,228
Jessica Korda	67	70	72	74	283	14,228
Dewi Claire Schreefel	70	68	71	74	283	14,228
Cheyenne Woods	74	65	71	74	284	12,742
Holly Clyburn	68	68	71	77	284	12,742
Mirim Lee	74	68	72	71	285	11,589
Becky Morgan	70	74	69	72	285	11,589
Amy Anderson	72	70	68	75	285	11,589
Beatriz Recari	72	69	74	71	286	8,847
Hee Young Park	67	77	70	72	286	8,847
Dori Carter	70	70	73	73	286	8,847
Hannah Burke	72	72	68	74	286	8,847
Lorie Kane	71	71	69	75	286	8,847
Brooke Pancake	70	70	71	75	286	8,847
Carlota Ciganda	68	70	72	76	286	8,847
Rebecca Lee-Bentham	73	69	67	77	286	8,847
Caroline Masson	72	68	69	77	286	8,847
Marianne Skarpnord	70	69	68	79	286	8,847
Suzann Pettersen	66	68	72	80	286	8,847

Oates Victorian Open

13th Beach Golf Links, Bellarine Peninsula, Victoria
Par 37-37–74; 6,398 yards

February 20-23
purse, A$150,000

	SCORES				TOTAL	MONEY
*Minjee Lee	73	70	68	68	279	
Vikki Laing	76	76	67	66	285	A$22,500
Sarah-Jane Smith	69	71	74	73	287	15,000
Sarah Kemp	78	72	70	68	288	10,500
*Su-Hyun Oh	72	77	67	72	288	
Nikki Campbell	79	67	72	71	289	6,900
Hannah Jun	74	72	74	69	289	6,900
Lindsey Wright	72	76	74	70	292	5,700

	SCORES				TOTAL	MONEY
Emma De Groot	76	75	72	70	293	5,025
Jessica Speechley	78	73	73	70	294	4,425
Laura Davies	72	77	71	76	296	3,900
Trish Johnson	77	72	76	71	296	3,900
Sophie Gustafson	76	73	72	76	297	3,030
Lorie Kane	74	74	76	73	297	3,030
*Elizabeth Elmassian	76	74	74	74	298	
Stacey Keating	73	74	72	79	298	2,400
Ashley Ona	78	70	79	71	298	2,400
Marianne Skarpnord	78	78	73	69	298	2,400
Whitney Hillier	76	76	73	74	299	1,950
Felicity Johnson	76	77	74	72	299	1,950

Senior Tours

Mitsubishi Electric Championship

Hualalai Golf Course, Ka'upulehu-Kona, Hawaii
Par 36-36–72; 7,053 yards

January 17-19
purse, $1,800,000

	SCORES			TOTAL	MONEY
Bernhard Langer	66	64	64	194	$307,000
Fred Couples	65	65	67	197	159,000
Jeff Sluman	66	66	65	197	159,000
Jay Haas	68	66	65	199	111,000
Rocco Mediate	63	70	67	200	91,000
David Frost	68	64	69	201	76,000
Mark O'Meara	66	65	70	201	76,000
Tom Lehman	67	66	69	202	59,000
Tom Pernice, Jr.	65	70	67	202	59,000
Bart Bryant	66	68	69	203	47,500
Fred Funk	65	70	68	203	47,500
Russ Cochran	70	67	67	204	39,000
Dan Forsman	64	73	67	204	39,000
Jay Don Blake	66	72	67	205	34,000
Steve Elkington	65	67	73	205	34,000
Kirk Triplett	70	69	66	205	34,000
Brad Faxon	71	69	66	206	30,000
Loren Roberts	68	72	67	207	28,000
Roger Chapman	67	71	70	208	23,200
John Cook	69	71	68	208	23,200
Mark McNulty	76	67	65	208	23,200
Esteban Toledo	69	72	67	208	23,200
Willie Wood	71	70	67	208	23,200
Hale Irwin	69	69	71	209	18,500
Larry Nelson	70	68	71	209	18,500
John Riegger	71	69	69	209	18,500
Tom Watson	70	69	70	209	18,500
Michael Allen	73	68	69	210	15,750
Nick Price	73	67	70	210	15,750
Olin Browne	72	67	72	211	14,250
Joe Daley	71	70	70	211	14,250
Kohki Idoki	70	70	71	211	14,250
Corey Pavin	70	67	74	211	14,250
Kenny Perry	72	68	72	212	12,500

Allianz Championship

Old Course at Broken Sound, Boca Raton, Florida
Par 36-36–72; 6,807 yards

February 7-9
purse, $1,600,000

	SCORES			TOTAL	MONEY
Michael Allen	60	69	69	198	$240,000
Duffy Waldorf	68	63	67	198	140,800
(Allen defeated Waldorf on second playoff hole.)					
Chien Soon Lu	65	65	69	199	115,200
Tom Lehman	65	67	68	200	95,200
Brad Bryant	66	67	68	201	70,000
Jay Haas	68	64	69	201	70,000

	SCORES			TOTAL	MONEY
Bernhard Langer	70	68	64	202	54,400
Rocco Mediate	69	67	66	202	54,400
Jeff Hart	68	66	69	203	44,800
Colin Montgomerie	67	70	67	204	40,000
Wes Short, Jr.	65	68	71	204	40,000
Mike Reid	68	68	69	205	32,533.34
Olin Browne	68	67	70	205	32,533.33
Gary Koch	67	66	72	205	32,533.33
Mark Calcavecchia	75	67	64	206	24,826.67
Roger Chapman	69	68	69	206	24,826.67
Fred Funk	71	66	69	206	24,826.67
John Inman	70	68	68	206	24,826.67
Scott Dunlap	63	67	76	206	24,826.66
Gene Sauers	67	68	71	206	24,826.66
Tommy Armour	72	66	69	207	18,160
David Frost	68	68	71	207	18,160
Bill Glasson	69	69	69	207	18,160
Jeff Sluman	68	70	69	207	18,160
Russ Cochran	70	69	69	208	14,592
Doug Garwood	70	68	70	208	14,592
Kenny Perry	68	67	73	208	14,592
John Riegger	69	67	72	208	14,592
Rod Spittle	69	69	70	208	14,592
Hale Irwin	67	73	69	209	12,053.34
Steve Elkington	67	74	68	209	12,053.33
Mark McNulty	74	65	70	209	12,053.33

ACE Group Classic

TwinEagles Golf Club, Talon Course, Naples, Florida — February 14-16
Par 36-36–72; 7,300 yards — purse, $1,600,000

	SCORES			TOTAL	MONEY
Kirk Triplett	67	67	66	200	$240,000
Olin Browne	66	69	66	201	117,066.67
Bernhard Langer	64	70	67	201	117,066.67
Duffy Waldorf	67	68	66	201	117,066.66
Jay Haas	68	72	64	204	76,000
Michael Allen	68	71	67	206	60,800
Colin Montgomerie	70	67	69	206	60,800
Mark Calcavecchia	73	69	66	208	45,866.67
Mike Goodes	68	72	68	208	45,866.67
Billy Andrade	71	69	68	208	45,866.66
Tommy Armour	68	72	69	209	32,000
Jim Rutledge	72	73	64	209	32,000
Peter Senior	75	69	65	209	32,000
Wes Short, Jr.	69	73	67	209	32,000
Rod Spittle	70	70	69	209	32,000
Bob Tway	65	72	72	209	32,000
Tom Pernice, Jr.	69	71	70	210	25,600
Bill Glasson	69	69	73	211	21,120
Tom Lehman	70	70	71	211	21,120
Rocco Mediate	70	70	71	211	21,120
Mark O'Meara	70	72	69	211	21,120
Gene Sauers	70	69	72	211	21,120
Roger Chapman	72	73	67	212	15,337.15
Lee Rinker	70	73	69	212	15,337.15
Tom Kite	71	72	69	212	15,337.14
Chien Soon Lu	69	71	72	212	15,337.14
Mark McNulty	68	71	73	212	15,337.14

	SCORES			TOTAL	MONEY
Steve Pate	73	70	69	212	15,337.14
Kenny Perry	70	70	72	212	15,337.14
Steve Elkington	70	76	67	213	11,062.86
Brian Henninger	72	72	69	213	11,062.86
Scott Hoch	70	74	69	213	11,062.86
Gary Koch	73	71	69	213	11,062.86
Tom Purtzer	75	69	69	213	11,062.86
Steve Lowery	68	72	73	213	11,062.85
Jim Thorpe	70	73	70	213	11,062.85

Toshiba Classic

Newport Beach Country Club, Newport Beach, California
Par 35-36–71; 6,584 yards

March 14-16
purse, $1,750,000

	SCORES			TOTAL	MONEY
Fred Couples	65	67	66	198	$262,500
Colin Montgomerie	67	70	62	199	128,042
Steve Pate	68	65	66	199	128,042
Bernhard Langer	63	66	70	199	128,042
Mark O'Meara	71	65	64	200	64,225
Michael Allen	66	67	67	200	64,225
Jeff Hart	65	67	68	200	64,225
Scott Dunlap	68	64	68	200	64,225
Kenny Perry	66	65	69	200	64,225
Loren Roberts	69	66	66	201	43,750
Kirk Triplett	66	67	68	201	43,750
Tom Pernice, Jr.	69	67	66	202	34,562
Jay Haas	68	67	67	202	34,562
Fred Funk	67	68	67	202	34,562
Duffy Waldorf	66	68	68	202	34,562
Russ Cochran	70	66	67	203	27,125
Tom Byrum	68	66	69	203	27,125
Peter Senior	70	63	70	203	27,125
Esteban Toledo	67	65	71	203	27,125
Willie Wood	68	70	66	204	19,500
Gene Sauers	72	66	66	204	19,500
Tommy Armour	69	68	67	204	19,500
Roger Chapman	70	67	67	204	19,500
Joey Sindelar	68	68	68	204	19,500
Tom Watson	71	63	70	204	19,500
Chien Soon Lu	65	66	73	204	19,500
Bart Bryant	69	69	67	205	14,525
David Frost	72	67	66	205	14,525
John Riegger	70	69	66	205	14,525
Wes Short, Jr.	70	65	70	205	14,525
Dan Forsman	69	65	71	205	14,525

Mississippi Gulf Resort Classic

Fallen Oak Golf Club, Biloxi, Mississippi
Par 36-36–72; 7,054 yards

March 21-23
purse, $1,600,000

	SCORES			TOTAL	MONEY
Jeff Maggert	68	69	68	205	$240,000
Billy Andrade	71	65	71	207	140,800
Jay Haas	68	69	71	208	105,200

	SCORES			TOTAL	MONEY
Bernhard Langer	71	69	68	208	105,200
Fred Couples	66	71	72	209	76,000
Bart Bryant	70	71	69	210	47,542.86
Mike Goodes	73	70	67	210	47,542.86
Scott Hoch	71	69	70	210	47,542.86
Steve Pate	73	70	67	210	47,542.86
Jeff Sluman	70	73	67	210	47,542.86
Colin Montgomerie	71	69	70	210	47,542.85
John Riegger	69	70	71	210	47,542.85
Michael Allen	68	72	71	211	28,000
Fred Funk	69	67	75	211	28,000
Tom Lehman	70	69	72	211	28,000
Mark O'Meara	70	68	73	211	28,000
Kenny Perry	68	73	70	211	28,000
Duffy Waldorf	69	69	73	211	28,000
Esteban Toledo	71	72	69	212	21,013.34
Russ Cochran	72	69	71	212	21,013.33
Scott Dunlap	69	72	71	212	21,013.33
Roger Chapman	69	70	74	213	17,240
Anders Forsbrand	69	72	72	213	17,240
Bill Glasson	71	67	75	213	17,240
Tom Pernice, Jr.	72	71	70	213	17,240
Olin Browne	70	70	74	214	14,560
Sandy Lyle	70	73	71	214	14,560
Jim Rutledge	74	69	71	214	14,560
Mark Calcavecchia	72	73	70	215	12,096
Bobby Clampett	73	72	70	215	12,096
Mark McNulty	70	70	75	215	12,096
Gene Sauers	73	68	74	215	12,096
Rod Spittle	72	71	72	215	12,096

Greater Gwinnett Championship

TPC Sugarloaf, Duluth, Georgia
Par 36-36–72; 7,259 yards

April 18-20
purse, $1,800,000

	SCORES			TOTAL	MONEY
Miguel Angel Jimenez	65	70	67	202	$270,000
Bernhard Langer	68	68	68	204	158,400
Jay Haas	71	68	67	206	129,600
Fred Couples	69	68	70	207	107,100
David Frost	72	68	69	209	74,100
Steve Pate	68	71	70	209	74,100
Duffy Waldorf	71	68	70	209	74,100
Chien Soon Lu	71	68	71	210	49,500
Colin Montgomerie	70	72	68	210	49,500
Kenny Perry	68	71	71	210	49,500
Willie Wood	74	70	66	210	49,500
Billy Andrade	72	72	67	211	36,600
Scott Dunlap	73	68	70	211	36,600
Fred Funk	72	69	70	211	36,600
Larry Mize	73	71	68	212	32,400
Bart Bryant	73	71	69	213	27,036
Mark Calcavecchia	73	71	69	213	27,036
Roger Chapman	71	74	68	213	27,036
Peter Senior	72	73	68	213	27,036
Wes Short, Jr.	73	69	71	213	27,036
Russ Cochran	73	71	70	214	18,607.50
Marco Dawson	71	69	74	214	18,607.50
Joe Durant	74	73	67	214	18,607.50

	SCORES			TOTAL	MONEY
Bill Glasson	72	70	72	214	18,607.50
Mike Goodes	72	73	69	214	18,607.50
Joey Sindelar	72	69	73	214	18,607.50
Jeff Sluman	69	75	70	214	18,607.50
Esteban Toledo	72	73	69	214	18,607.50
Michael Allen	72	70	73	215	13,320
Anders Forsbrand	73	70	72	215	13,320
Dan Forsman	76	70	69	215	13,320
Jim Rutledge	75	73	67	215	13,320
Rod Spittle	70	71	74	215	13,320
Bob Tway	73	73	69	215	13,320

Insperity Invitational

The Woodlands Country Club, The Woodlands, Texas
Par 36-36–72; 7,002 yards

May 2-4
purse, $2,000,000

	SCORES			TOTAL	MONEY
Bernhard Langer	66	68	71	205	$300,000
Fred Couples	69	70	67	206	176,000
Colin Montgomerie	71	66	70	207	144,000
Esteban Toledo	67	71	71	209	119,000
Jay Haas	70	70	70	210	87,500
Tom Pernice, Jr.	72	67	71	210	87,500
Bart Bryant	66	72	73	211	68,000
Russ Cochran	71	70	70	211	68,000
Tom Byrum	74	70	68	212	50,000
Fred Funk	68	71	73	212	50,000
Jeff Maggert	68	73	71	212	50,000
Rod Spittle	71	70	71	212	50,000
Michael Allen	71	72	70	213	39,000
Steve Pate	69	70	74	213	39,000
Billy Andrade	72	70	72	214	34,000
Joe Daley	68	75	71	214	34,000
Mark O'Meara	69	70	75	214	34,000
Peter Senior	71	72	72	215	28,066.67
Duffy Waldorf	74	70	71	215	28,066.67
Dan Forsman	70	71	74	215	28,066.66
Mark McNulty	71	71	74	216	23,900
Bob Tway	69	72	75	216	23,900
Larry Mize	73	74	70	217	20,500
Kenny Perry	75	70	72	217	20,500
Gene Sauers	70	72	75	217	20,500
Scott Simpson	72	70	75	217	20,500
Olin Browne	71	74	73	218	16,600
Morris Hatalsky	73	77	68	218	16,600
Rocco Mediate	71	75	72	218	16,600
Joey Sindelar	69	75	74	218	16,600
Jeff Sluman	73	70	75	218	16,600

Regions Tradition

Shoal Creek, Shoal Creek, Alabama
Par 36-36–72; 7,231 yards

May 15-18
purse, $2,200,000

	SCORES				TOTAL	MONEY
Kenny Perry	72	68	69	72	281	$330,000
Mark Calcavecchia	69	69	74	70	282	193,600
Jay Haas	69	70	73	71	283	131,266.67
Tom Lehman	73	71	72	67	283	131,266.67
Olin Browne	69	71	72	71	283	131,266.66
John Cook	71	70	71	72	284	79,200
Rocco Mediate	73	72	69	70	284	79,200
Tom Watson	72	72	73	67	284	79,200
Michael Allen	73	74	69	69	285	49,342.86
Marco Dawson	71	73	71	70	285	49,342.86
Joe Durant	74	73	69	69	285	49,342.86
Bernhard Langer	74	70	70	71	285	49,342.86
Jeff Sluman	72	71	71	71	285	49,342.86
Steve Elkington	70	71	71	73	285	49,342.85
John Inman	72	72	66	75	285	49,342.85
Fred Funk	71	72	73	70	286	33,044
Jeff Hart	73	70	73	70	286	33,044
Colin Montgomerie	72	72	69	73	286	33,044
Corey Pavin	70	74	71	71	286	33,044
Tom Pernice, Jr.	72	70	70	74	286	33,044
Jeff Maggert	73	70	69	75	287	27,060
Chien Soon Lu	69	77	70	72	288	25,520
Roger Chapman	72	77	72	68	289	23,650
Steve Pate	73	74	71	71	289	23,650
David Frost	72	71	71	76	290	20,064
Mike Goodes	74	71	70	75	290	20,064
Gene Sauers	75	74	71	70	290	20,064
Wes Short, Jr.	74	69	73	74	290	20,064
Willie Wood	70	75	73	72	290	20,064
Peter Senior	74	75	75	67	291	17,380
Mike Reid	74	74	73	71	292	15,510
Loren Roberts	74	78	69	71	292	15,510
Rod Spittle	72	75	72	73	292	15,510
Esteban Toledo	74	72	74	72	292	15,510
Doug Garwood	74	76	75	68	293	13,200
Sandy Lyle	75	71	78	69	293	13,200
Mark O'Meara	74	70	74	75	293	13,200
Tommy Armour	77	72	74	71	294	11,880
Bobby Clampett	77	76	69	72	294	11,880
Mark Brooks	73	74	77	71	295	10,780
Bill Glasson	71	74	74	76	295	10,780
John Riegger	71	75	75	74	295	10,780
Tom Byrum	74	71	77	74	296	9,460
Gil Morgan	74	75	72	75	296	9,460
Ian Woosnam	73	72	77	74	296	9,460
Peter Jacobsen	74	81	73	69	297	7,260
Mark McNulty	74	74	70	79	297	7,260
Larry Mize	76	75	74	72	297	7,260
Jerry Pate	79	71	77	70	297	7,260
Nick Price	74	69	75	79	297	7,260
Scott Simpson	75	74	72	76	297	7,260
Duffy Waldorf	73	77	73	74	297	7,260
Brian Henninger	76	75	76	71	298	5,060
Tom Purtzer	74	72	78	74	298	5,060
Jim Rutledge	76	74	75	73	298	5,060
Joey Sindelar	73	76	78	71	298	5,060
Hal Sutton	77	71	74	76	298	5,060

	SCORES				TOTAL	MONEY
Mark Wiebe	72	73	77	77	299	4,400
Scott Dunlap	71	78	75	76	300	3,740
Dan Forsman	73	76	76	75	300	3,740
Gary Hallberg	83	71	74	72	300	3,740
Tom Kite	75	76	73	76	300	3,740
Lee Rinker	73	73	77	77	300	3,740
Brad Faxon	73	81	72	75	301	2,860
Bruce Fleisher	75	75	74	77	301	2,860
Bob Gilder	75	75	74	77	301	2,860
Joe Daley	74	75	79	74	302	2,156
Morris Hatalsky	76	75	76	75	302	2,156
Larry Nelson	78	82	71	71	302	2,156
Bob Tway	76	75	78	73	302	2,156
Wayne Levi	75	77	70	81	303	1,804
Rick Fehr	75	82	71	77	305	1,606
Hale Irwin	77	77	76	75	305	1,606
Steve Lowery	75	76	74	81	306	1,408
Jim Thorpe	80	78	73	75	306	1,408
Anders Forsbrand	77	76	81	73	307	1,276
Bobby Wadkins	75	73	78	83	309	1,188
Jim Gallagher, Jr.	78	71	79	82	310	1,100
Fred Couples	74	77	73		DQ	
Russ Cochran	73	82	82		WD	
Craig Stadler					WD	

Senior PGA Championship

The Golf Club at Harbor Shores, Benton Harbor, Michigan — May 22-25
Par 36-35–71; 6,852 yards — purse, $2,000,000

	SCORES				TOTAL	MONEY
Colin Montgomerie	69	69	68	65	271	$378,000
Tom Watson	70	68	72	65	275	227,000
Jay Haas	69	71	70	67	277	121,500
Bernhard Langer	70	68	69	70	277	121,500
Mark Brooks	68	71	74	65	278	68,000
Bart Bryant	71	67	70	70	278	68,000
Joe Durant	65	75	74	64	278	68,000
David Frost	72	69	69	68	278	68,000
Marco Dawson	72	72	64	71	279	51,000
Jeff Maggert	69	72	72	66	279	51,000
Kiyoshi Murota	73	65	70	71	279	51,000
Russ Cochran	70	69	72	69	280	43,000
Steve Pate	72	67	72	70	281	38,500
Kenny Perry	70	75	66	70	281	38,500
Stephen Ames	71	68	72	71	282	28,167
Mark Calcavecchia	71	72	69	70	282	28,167
Bill Glasson	69	76	68	69	282	28,167
Mike Goodes	70	74	73	65	282	28,167
Peter Senior	70	73	71	68	282	28,167
Jeff Sluman	73	72	67	70	282	28,167
John Cook	70	72	68	73	283	19,500
Gary Hallberg	70	70	70	73	283	19,500
Scott Simpson	71	69	72	71	283	19,500
Joey Sindelar	69	72	72	70	283	19,500
Greg Bruckner	69	71	73	71	284	15,300
Dan Forsman	66	73	75	70	284	15,300
Carl Mason	73	71	70	70	284	15,300
Gene Sauers	73	73	68	70	284	15,300
Duffy Waldorf	70	70	72	72	284	15,300

	SCORES				TOTAL	MONEY
Jim Carter	72	71	68	74	285	12,833
Steve Lowery	69	73	71	72	285	12,833
John Riegger	78	67	70	70	285	12,833
Bobby Clampett	74	72	70	71	287	10,600
Bob Friend	72	72	69	74	287	10,600
Kohki Idoki	76	70	70	71	287	10,600
Nick Job	69	76	68	74	287	10,600
Craig W. Thomas	71	74	70	72	287	10,600
Steen Tinning	72	66	74	75	287	10,600
Joe Daley	72	74	73	69	288	7,667
Frank Esposito, Jr.	69	73	74	72	288	7,667
Brad Faxon	67	74	73	74	288	7,667
Anders Forsbrand	69	73	71	75	288	7,667
Fred Funk	73	73	73	69	288	7,667
Jeff Hart	77	67	71	73	288	7,667
P.H. Horgan	68	75	78	67	288	7,667
Sonny Skinner	72	73	70	73	288	7,667
Willie Wood	71	72	71	74	288	7,667
Billy Andrade	75	70	73	71	289	5,329
Brian Henninger	74	71	73	71	289	5,329
Tom Lehman	70	75	74	70	289	5,329
James Mason	73	72	71	73	289	5,329
Mark McNulty	70	74	69	76	289	5,329
Andrew Oldcorn	74	72	73	70	289	5,329
Wes Short, Jr.	74	70	71	74	289	5,329
Chip Beck	72	74	71	73	290	4,650
Roger Chapman	71	72	74	73	290	4,650
Todd McCorkle	69	76	74	71	290	4,650
Tom Pernice, Jr.	72	70	72	76	290	4,650
Michael Allen	78	68	72	73	291	4,350
Don Berry	73	73	69	76	291	4,350
Philip Golding	70	73	73	75	291	4,350
Mark Mouland	71	75	75	70	291	4,350
Esteban Toledo	72	74	74	71	291	4,350
Bob Gilder	73	73	72	74	292	4,150
Ronan Rafferty	75	71	75	71	292	4,150
Craig Stevens	71	74	71	76	292	4,150
Hale Irwin	75	70	74	74	293	4,038
Tim Parun	72	73	75	73	293	4,038
David J. Russell	72	73	79	69	293	4,038
Gary Wolstenholme	72	70	76	75	293	4,038
Tracy Phillips	72	72	78	72	294	3,963
Stuart L. Smith	71	75	73	75	294	3,963
Jon Corliss	76	70	76	73	295	3,913
Bobby Wadkins	71	75	75	74	295	3,913
Mark Wiebe	73	73	76	74	296	3,875
Angel Franco	72	74	76	75	297	3,850
Rick Fehr	75	70	76	77	298	3,825
Bruce Fleisher	72	73	79	76	300	3,800

Principal Charity Classic

Wakonda Club, Des Moines, Iowa
Par 36-36–72; 6,959 yards

May 30-June 1
purse, $1,750,000

	SCORES			TOTAL	MONEY
Tom Pernice, Jr.	68	67	69	204	$262,500
Doug Garwood	68	65	71	204	154,000
(Pernice defeated Garwood on second playoff hole.)					
Michael Allen	68	66	71	205	95,812.50

	SCORES			TOTAL	MONEY
Mark Calcavecchia	66	69	70	205	95,812.50
Bill Glasson	72	69	64	205	95,812.50
Jay Haas	69	69	67	205	95,812.50
Joe Durant	69	67	70	206	63,000
Bobby Clampett	67	72	68	207	52,500
Tom Lehman	69	68	70	207	52,500
Bart Bryant	71	69	68	208	42,000
Jeff Hart	70	68	70	208	42,000
Duffy Waldorf	70	70	68	208	42,000
Steve Lowery	67	70	72	209	33,250
Chien Soon Lu	71	65	73	209	33,250
John Riegger	68	68	73	209	33,250
Willie Wood	71	69	70	210	29,750
Rick Fehr	69	70	72	211	24,640
Mark McNulty	74	66	71	211	24,640
Rocco Mediate	69	73	69	211	24,640
Mark Mouland	68	73	70	211	24,640
Kirk Triplett	69	71	71	211	24,640
Ben Bates	75	67	70	212	16,115.91
Mark Brooks	71	69	72	212	16,115.91
Roger Chapman	71	69	72	212	16,115.91
Marco Dawson	68	74	70	212	16,115.91
Dan Forsman	71	75	66	212	16,115.91
David Frost	70	71	71	212	16,115.91
Kohki Idoki	73	69	70	212	16,115.91
Wayne Levi	69	71	72	212	16,115.91
Blaine McCallister	71	73	68	212	16,115.91
Jeff Sluman	70	71	71	212	16,115.91
Tommy Armour	69	69	74	212	16,115.90

Big Cedar Lodge Legends of Golf

Buffalo Ridge: Par 35-36–71; 7,002 yards
Top of the Rock: Par 27-27–54; 2,940 yards
Ridgedale, Missouri

June 6-8
purse, $2,400,000

	SCORES			TOTAL	MONEY (Each)
Fred Funk/Jeff Sluman	61	50	48	159	$230,000
Jay Haas/Peter Jacobsen	62	48	50	160	130,000
Craig Stadler/Kirk Triplett	49	64	52	165	102,500
Russ Cochran/Kenny Perry	61	56	49	166	80,000
Morris Hatalsky/Don Pooley	50	66	51	167	55,000
Tom Pernice, Jr./Bob Tway	50	64	53	167	55,000
Bernhard Langer/Tom Lehman	63	56	49	168	40,833.34
Corey Pavin/Duffy Waldorf	63	56	49	168	40,833.34
Steve Elkington/Rocco Mediate	65	51	52	168	40,833.33
Billy Andrade/Tommy Armour	62	56	51	169	34,000
Andy North/Tom Watson	49	65	55	169	34,000
Olin Browne/Steve Pate	64	56	50	170	29,000
Ben Crenshaw/Jerry Pate	54	66	50	170	29,000
Tom Kite/Gil Morgan	55	66	49	170	29,000
Roger Chapman/Hale Irwin	53	66	52	171	24,000
Wayne Levi/Scott Simpson	53	66	52	171	24,000
Michael Allen/David Frost	65	56	52	173	18,250
Dan Forsman/Mike Reid	52	70	51	173	18,250
Andy Bean/Mark McNulty	52	67	54	173	18,250
Joe Daley/Doug Tewell	52	67	54	173	18,250
Mark Brooks/Tom Purtzer	64	54	55	173	18,250
Nick Faldo/Eduardo Romero	49	68	56	173	18,250
Bart Bryant/Brad Bryant	65	59	50	174	14,000

	SCORES			TOTAL	MONEY (Each)
Bob Gilder/Bobby Wadkins	51	67	56	174	14,000
Mark Calcavecchia/Steve Lowery	65	52	57	174	14,000
Larry Mize/Hal Sutton	67	56	53	176	12,750
Mark O'Meara/Nick Price	67	53	56	176	12,750
Loren Roberts/Mark Wiebe	66	55	56	177	11,500
John Cook/Joey Sindelar	65	55	57	177	11,500
John Jacobs/Fuzzy Zoeller	54	66	57	177	11,500
Sandy Lyle/Denis Watson	55	70	58	183	10,500

Encompass Championship

North Shore Country Club, Glenview, Illinois
Par 36-36–72; 7,103 yards

June 20-22
purse, $1,800,000

	SCORES			TOTAL	MONEY
Tom Lehman	65	66	70	201	$270,000
Michael Allen	67	68	67	202	144,000
Kirk Triplett	67	67	68	202	144,000
Doug Garwood	66	71	66	203	107,100
Bart Bryant	67	68	69	204	85,500
Roger Chapman	66	68	72	206	55,800
Russ Cochran	71	71	64	206	55,800
Colin Montgomerie	69	67	70	206	55,800
Kenny Perry	71	67	68	206	55,800
Jeff Sluman	67	70	69	206	55,800
Esteban Toledo	69	70	67	206	55,800
Fred Funk	69	69	69	207	37,800
Tom Pernice, Jr.	69	68	70	207	37,800
Olin Browne	71	68	69	208	29,700
Jose Coceres	68	69	71	208	29,700
John Inman	67	67	74	208	29,700
Sandy Lyle	67	71	70	208	29,700
Blaine McCallister	70	69	69	208	29,700
Mark O'Meara	67	70	71	208	29,700
Brad Bryant	69	71	69	209	19,160
Bobby Clampett	70	69	70	209	19,160
Scott Dunlap	71	67	71	209	19,160
Mike Goodes	71	67	71	209	19,160
Bernhard Langer	71	69	69	209	19,160
Mark McNulty	69	70	70	209	19,160
Larry Mize	69	69	71	209	19,160
Corey Pavin	71	67	71	209	19,160
John Riegger	71	71	67	209	19,160
Steve Elkington	69	69	72	210	13,905
Loren Roberts	69	70	71	210	13,905
Wes Short, Jr.	70	71	69	210	13,905
Joey Sindelar	72	70	68	210	13,905

Constellation Senior Players Championship

Fox Chapel Golf Club, Pittsburgh, Pennsylvania
Par 35-35–70; 6,696 yards

June 26-29
purse, $2,700,000

	SCORES				TOTAL	MONEY
Bernhard Langer	65	64	66	70	265	$405,000
Jeff Sluman	69	67	64	65	265	237,600
(Langer defeated Sluman on second playoff hole.)						
Russ Cochran	70	66	63	67	266	194,400
Kenny Perry	70	63	65	69	267	160,650
Mark McNulty	66	66	71	66	269	128,250
Mark Brooks	66	67	71	66	270	83,700
Jay Haas	69	70	65	66	270	83,700
Corey Pavin	65	69	69	67	270	83,700
Mark O'Meara	67	66	69	68	270	83,700
Bill Glasson	67	64	68	71	270	83,700
Joe Durant	64	68	67	71	270	83,700
Bob Gilder	70	69	69	63	271	54,900
John Cook	69	66	70	66	271	54,900
John Riegger	68	64	69	70	271	54,900
Colin Montgomerie	69	69	66	68	272	43,200
David Frost	64	71	68	69	272	43,200
Doug Garwood	64	67	71	70	272	43,200
Marco Dawson	66	68	68	70	272	43,200
Michael Allen	68	64	69	71	272	43,200
Barry Lane	66	69	68	70	273	34,290
Tom Lehman	67	69	66	71	273	34,290
Kirk Triplett	70	70	69	65	274	27,765
Tom Byrum	69	70	69	66	274	27,765
Dan Forsman	69	69	69	67	274	27,765
Bart Bryant	65	70	71	68	274	27,765
Rocco Mediate	67	70	69	68	274	27,765
Loren Roberts	68	66	71	69	274	27,765
Larry Mize	65	69	72	69	275	21,384
Brad Bryant	67	69	70	69	275	21,384
Steve Pate	65	71	69	70	275	21,384
Jeff Brehaut	70	68	67	70	275	21,384
Tommy Armour	66	70	66	73	275	21,384
Mike Goodes	74	68	68	66	276	18,225
Billy Andrade	67	71	66	72	276	18,225
Willie Wood	70	72	68	67	277	15,862
Joey Sindelar	70	73	68	66	277	15,862
Wayne Levi	71	67	68	71	277	15,862
Esteban Toledo	71	66	68	72	277	15,862
Steve Lowery	70	73	68	67	278	13,230
Gene Sauers	69	72	68	69	278	13,230
Olin Browne	65	71	71	71	278	13,230
Peter Senior	70	70	67	71	278	13,230
Peter Fowler	65	68	71	74	278	13,230
Joe Daley	71	70	70	68	279	11,070
Wes Short, Jr.	65	71	73	70	279	11,070
Bobby Clampett	67	69	69	74	279	11,070
Chien Soon Lu	72	70	70	68	280	9,450
John Inman	70	68	71	71	280	9,450
Brad Faxon	68	72	66	74	280	9,450
Jeff Hart	69	71	72	69	281	8,370
Bob Tway	66	78	70	68	282	7,290
Rick Fehr	71	70	70	71	282	7,290
Dick Mast	69	70	69	74	282	7,290
Jim Rutledge	72	70	74	67	283	6,075
Rod Spittle	69	73	71	70	283	6,075
Bruce Vaughan	71	68	73	71	283	6,075

	SCORES				TOTAL	MONEY
Steve Jones	72	65	74	72	283	6,075
Hal Sutton	74	70	72	68	284	4,995
Morris Hatalsky	70	71	71	72	284	4,995
Scott Dunlap	74	67	70	73	284	4,995
Gene Jones	69	72	68	75	284	4,995
Joel Edwards	74	71	71	70	286	4,050
Mark Wiebe	74	69	72	71	286	4,050
Tom Pernice, Jr.	72	72	69	73	286	4,050
Anders Forsbrand	72	73	75	67	287	2,992
Fred Funk	71	70	76	70	287	2,992
Roger Chapman	73	70	72	72	287	2,992
Sandy Lyle	72	73	70	72	287	2,992
Jeff Freeman	74	67	71	75	287	2,992
Peter Jacobsen	73	71	73	71	288	2,376
Gary Hallberg	70	75	75	70	290	2,133
David Eger	73	68	76	73	290	2,133
Duffy Waldorf	71	76	74	70	291	1,836
Scott Simpson	72	73	76	70	291	1,836
Hale Irwin	73	72	74	73	292	1,620
Mark Mouland	71	75	71	75	292	1,620
Mike Reid	76	71	73	73	293	1,458
Jim Gallagher, Jr.	75	74	74	72	295	1,350
Tom Kite	76	76	71	76	299	1,242
Mark Calcavecchia	70	68	73		WD	
Nick Price	77	73			WD	

U.S. Senior Open

Oak Tree Golf Club, Edmond, Oklahoma
Par 35-36–71; 7,219 yards

July 10-13
purse, $3,500,000

	SCORES				TOTAL	MONEY
Colin Montgomerie	65	71	74	69	279	$630,000
Gene Sauers	69	69	68	73	279	378,000
(Montgomerie defeated Sauers, 12-13, in three-hole playoff.)						
David Frost	71	71	71	70	283	200,762
Woody Austin	72	70	71	70	283	200,762
Jeff Sluman	70	69	72	73	284	122,988
Vijay Singh	69	71	71	73	284	122,988
Marco Dawson	66	76	69	73	284	122,988
Kirk Triplett	69	72	75	69	285	97,907
Joe Durant	71	73	75	67	286	79,080
Peter Senior	73	73	68	72	286	79,080
Scott Dunlap	69	68	72	77	286	79,080
Bernhard Langer	69	69	71	77	286	79,080
Mark Brooks	68	71	76	72	287	64,789
Kenny Perry	75	74	72	67	288	51,796
Lance Ten Broeck	70	69	79	70	288	51,796
Tom Byrum	71	75	72	70	288	51,796
Tom Kite	73	70	73	72	288	51,796
Esteban Toledo	73	70	72	73	288	51,796
Russ Cochran	70	74	71	73	288	51,796
Duffy Waldorf	75	73	72	69	289	38,339
Roger Chapman	79	70	71	69	289	38,339
Steve Pate	72	72	75	70	289	38,339
Loren Roberts	73	72	71	73	289	38,339
John Cook	79	69	76	66	290	31,752
Tom Lehman	72	69	77	72	290	31,752
Bart Bryant	71	73	81	66	291	25,830
Corey Pavin	72	73	75	71	291	25,830

	SCORES				TOTAL	MONEY
*Mike McCoy	74	74	72	71	291	
Sonny Skinner	73	70	75	73	291	25,830
Brad Bryant	73	72	73	73	291	25,830
Michael Allen	73	73	72	73	291	25,830
Rocco Mediate	70	74	71	76	291	25,830
Jerry Haas	78	71	74	69	292	20,443
Barry Lane	74	69	79	70	292	20,443
Bill Glasson	73	73	76	70	292	20,443
Fred Funk	70	77	73	72	292	20,443
Scott Hoch	75	71	72	74	292	20,443
Mark O'Meara	75	74	73	71	293	16,704
Kevin Sutherland	73	72	76	72	293	16,704
Chris Williams	72	72	75	74	293	16,704
Doug Garwood	70	69	79	75	293	16,704
Joey Sindelar	72	71	74	76	293	16,704
Bob Tway	74	73	75	72	294	13,961
John Riegger	77	71	74	72	294	13,961
Steen Tinning	72	75	73	74	294	13,961
*Jeff Wilson	70	76	73	75	294	
Mike Goodes	73	76	74	72	295	12,275
Olin Browne	70	72	76	77	295	12,275
Steve Elkington	74	73	78	72	297	10,780
Willie Wood	74	73	77	73	297	10,780
Rod Spittle	71	78	73	75	297	10,780
Brad Faxon	74	75	77	72	298	9,620
Sam Randolph	75	74	77	72	298	9,620
Gil Morgan	72	76	73	77	298	9,620
Jeff Maggert	76	72	76	75	299	9,131
Bruce Vaughan	75	74	73	77	299	9,131
Hendrik Buhrmann	71	77	78	75	301	8,787
Robin Byrd	77	67	76	81	301	8,787
Jose Coceres	75	74	71	81	301	8,787
Philip Golding	72	74	83	75	304	8,570
Lonnie Nielsen	77	72	79	77	305	8,366
Hal Sutton	77	71	79	78	305	8,366
Damon Gree	74	75	76	80	305	8,366
Billy Andrade	71	77	80	78	306	8,162
Ronnie Black	71	77	78	81	307	8,059
Wes Short, Jr.	73	68	76		WD	2,000

The Senior Open Championship presented by Rolex

See European Senior Tour section.

3M Championship

TPC Twin Cities, Blaine, Minnesota
Par 36-36–72; 7,114 yards

August 1-3
purse, $1,750,000

	SCORES			TOTAL	MONEY
Kenny Perry	65	63	65	193	$262,500
Bernhard Langer	64	67	63	194	154,000
Jeff Maggert	64	67	65	196	104,416.67
Gene Sauers	66	65	65	196	104,416.67
Marco Dawson	63	66	67	196	104,416.66
Mike Goodes	66	68	64	198	70,000
John Cook	69	63	68	200	59,500
Vijay Singh	64	68	68	200	59,500
Steve Elkington	68	67	67	202	40,541.67

	SCORES			TOTAL	MONEY
Paul Goydos	67	68	67	202	40,541.67
Peter Senior	68	68	66	202	40,541.67
Wes Short, Jr.	70	70	62	202	40,541.67
Gary Hallberg	66	65	71	202	40,541.66
Hale Irwin	68	66	68	202	40,541.66
Bart Bryant	69	66	68	203	28,000
Mark Calcavecchia	72	64	67	203	28,000
David Frost	69	65	69	203	28,000
Rocco Mediate	64	71	68	203	28,000
Kevin Sutherland	69	67	67	203	28,000
Scott Dunlap	69	65	70	204	21,000
Tom Pernice, Jr.	69	67	68	204	21,000
Rod Spittle	68	67	69	204	21,000
Duffy Waldorf	68	70	66	204	21,000
Fred Funk	70	70	65	205	16,730
Doug Garwood	66	67	72	205	16,730
Bill Glasson	70	66	69	205	16,730
Blaine McCallister	69	68	68	205	16,730
Mark O'Meara	69	67	69	205	16,730
Brad Faxon	71	67	68	206	13,230
Bob Gilder	68	68	70	206	13,230
Joey Sindelar	69	68	69	206	13,230
Jeff Sluman	67	67	72	206	13,230
Kirk Triplett	67	66	73	206	13,230

Dick's Sporting Goods Open

En-Joie Golf Course, Endicott, New York — August 15-17
Par 37-35–72; 6,957 yards — purse, $1,850,000

	SCORES			TOTAL	MONEY
Bernhard Langer	67	67	66	200	$277,500
Woody Austin	67	69	65	201	148,000
Mark O'Meara	68	67	66	201	148,000
Olin Browne	65	69	69	203	90,650
Marco Dawson	68	69	66	203	90,650
Steve Lowery	66	65	72	203	90,650
Billy Andrade	68	67	69	204	54,020
John Cook	65	67	72	204	54,020
Dick Mast	67	68	69	204	54,020
John Riegger	67	67	70	204	54,020
Kevin Sutherland	71	59	74	204	54,020
David Frost	66	69	70	205	40,700
Wes Short, Jr.	68	67	71	206	37,000
Ben Bates	67	70	70	207	32,375
Bart Bryant	66	72	69	207	32,375
Scott Hoch	69	64	74	207	32,375
Jeff Sluman	67	68	72	207	32,375
Scott Dunlap	67	68	73	208	25,160
Fred Funk	69	68	71	208	25,160
Mark McNulty	68	68	72	208	25,160
Colin Montgomerie	68	67	73	208	25,160
Mark Brooks	68	69	72	209	19,462
Joe Daley	71	66	72	209	19,462
Steve Pate	69	67	73	209	19,462
Rod Spittle	68	67	74	209	19,462
Duffy Waldorf	68	73	68	209	19,462
Tom Byrum	68	71	71	210	15,725
Mark Calcavecchia	68	70	72	210	15,725
Doug Garwood	67	71	72	210	15,725
Jay Haas	71	70	69	210	15,725

Boeing Classic

TPC Snoqualmie Ridge, Snoqualmie, Washington
Par 36-36–72; 7,183 yards

August 22-24
purse, $2,000,000

	SCORES			TOTAL	MONEY
Scott Dunlap	69	63	68	200	$300,000
Mark Brooks	65	70	65	200	176,000
(Dunlap defeated Brooks on first playoff hole.)					
Gene Sauers	66	71	65	202	144,000
Tom Pernice, Jr.	68	69	66	203	119,000
Marco Dawson	69	70	65	204	82,333.34
Woody Austin	67	69	68	204	82,333.33
Doug Garwood	67	66	71	204	82,333.33
Tommy Armour	67	68	70	205	60,000
Joe Durant	68	68	69	205	60,000
Olin Browne	70	67	69	206	48,000
Fred Funk	68	68	70	206	48,000
Rocco Mediate	71	70	65	206	48,000
Michael Allen	68	69	70	207	39,000
Kevin Sutherland	72	69	66	207	39,000
Russ Cochran	70	68	70	208	34,000
Fred Couples	71	71	66	208	34,000
Bernhard Langer	70	71	67	208	34,000
Bart Bryant	71	70	68	209	27,200
Mike Goodes	64	75	70	209	27,200
Steve Lowery	72	71	66	209	27,200
Mark O'Meara	66	72	71	209	27,200
Chip Beck	70	68	72	210	21,040
Bill Glasson	70	70	70	210	21,040
Paul Goydos	71	69	70	210	21,040
Blaine McCallister	70	69	71	210	21,040
Mark McNulty	66	71	73	210	21,040
Mark Calcavecchia	67	75	69	211	16,600
Gary Hallberg	72	71	68	211	16,600
Jeff Hart	70	71	70	211	16,600
Tom Purtzer	72	72	67	211	16,600
Jeff Sluman	66	74	71	211	16,600

Shaw Charity Classic

Canyon Meadows Golf & Country Club,
Calgary, Alberta, Canada
Par 35-35–70; 7,086 yards

August 29-31
purse, $2,250,000

	SCORES			TOTAL	MONEY
Fred Couples	68	66	61	195	$337,500
Billy Andrade	67	66	62	195	198,000
(Couples defeated Andrade on first playoff hole.)					
Joe Daley	64	66	67	197	147,937.50
Steve Lowery	66	67	64	197	147,937.50
Wes Short, Jr.	69	65	64	198	106,875
Woody Austin	65	67	67	199	90,000
Bart Bryant	62	71	67	200	76,500
Paul Goydos	67	66	67	200	76,500
Steve Elkington	65	69	67	201	52,125
David Frost	63	68	70	201	52,125
Doug Garwood	66	66	69	201	52,125
Mark Mouland	69	64	68	201	52,125
Tom Pernice, Jr.	62	70	69	201	52,125

	SCORES			TOTAL	MONEY
Kevin Sutherland	66	68	67	201	52,125
Gary Hallberg	66	65	71	202	37,125
Mark McNulty	65	66	71	202	37,125
Corey Pavin	66	69	67	202	37,125
Duffy Waldorf	71	65	66	202	37,125
Roger Chapman	69	67	67	203	25,875
Joe Durant	64	66	73	203	25,875
Bob Gilder	68	68	67	203	25,875
Bill Glasson	70	67	66	203	25,875
John Inman	66	69	68	203	25,875
Rocco Mediate	68	66	69	203	25,875
Mark O'Meara	66	68	69	203	25,875
Gene Sauers	66	69	68	203	25,875
Michael Allen	65	70	69	204	17,493.75
Russ Cochran	66	68	70	204	17,493.75
Jeff Coston	69	71	64	204	17,493.75
Fred Funk	67	71	66	204	17,493.75
Bernhard Langer	67	65	72	204	17,493.75
Jeff Maggert	70	65	69	204	17,493.75
Jeff Sluman	67	73	64	204	17,493.75
Bob Tway	67	63	74	204	17,493.75

Quebec Championship

La Tempete Golf Club, Quebec City, Quebec, Canada — September 5-7
Par 36-36–72; 7,065 yards — purse, $1,600,000

	SCORES			TOTAL	MONEY
Wes Short, Jr.	69	68	64	201	$240,000
Scott Dunlap	72	66	64	202	140,800
Brad Faxon	67	67	71	205	105,200
Esteban Toledo	68	66	71	205	105,200
Jim Carter	70	68	68	206	70,000
Kirk Triplett	70	68	68	206	70,000
David Frost	70	69	68	207	51,200
Jay Haas	68	69	70	207	51,200
Loren Roberts	67	69	71	207	51,200
Michael Allen	70	70	68	208	31,466.67
Jay Delsing	69	70	69	208	31,466.67
Bill Glasson	70	70	68	208	31,466.67
Mark Mouland	69	70	69	208	31,466.67
Jim Rutledge	71	69	68	208	31,466.67
Jeff Sluman	69	70	69	208	31,466.67
P.H. Horgan	67	71	70	208	31,466.66
Scott Simpson	69	68	71	208	31,466.66
Duffy Waldorf	66	71	71	208	31,466.66
Olin Browne	69	69	71	209	20,400
Fred Funk	68	71	70	209	20,400
Corey Pavin	69	69	71	209	20,400
Rod Spittle	75	68	66	209	20,400
Keith Clearwater	69	70	71	210	15,680
Rick Fehr	72	72	66	210	15,680
Doug Garwood	71	68	71	210	15,680
Gary Hallberg	68	74	68	210	15,680
Lee Janzen	71	67	72	210	15,680
Chien Soon Lu	73	71	66	210	15,680
Tommy Armour	69	72	70	211	12,640
Tom Byrum	70	73	68	211	12,640
James Mason	71	68	72	211	12,640

Pacific Links Hawai'i Championship

Kapolei Golf Course, Kapolei, Hawaii
Par 36-36–72; 7,002 yards

September 19-21
purse, $2,200,000

	SCORES			TOTAL	MONEY
Paul Goydos	66	63	68	197	$330,000
Scott Dunlap	65	68	65	198	176,000
Fred Funk	67	62	69	198	176,000
Russ Cochran	67	66	66	199	130,900
Jeff Maggert	67	66	67	200	104,500
Wes Short, Jr.	67	66	68	201	88,000
Mark Brooks	67	67	68	202	64,240
Doug Garwood	69	63	70	202	64,240
Jay Haas	66	68	68	202	64,240
Corey Pavin	70	61	71	202	64,240
Tom Pernice, Jr.	60	72	70	202	64,240
Michael Allen	64	68	71	203	46,200
Vijay Singh	66	65	72	203	46,200
David Frost	69	66	69	204	33,244.45
Barry Lane	69	68	67	204	33,244.45
Chien Soon Lu	70	69	65	204	33,244.45
Kevin Sutherland	67	69	68	204	33,244.45
Mark Calcavecchia	67	65	72	204	33,244.44
Jim Carter	66	66	72	204	33,244.44
Jeff Hart	67	68	69	204	33,244.44
Larry Mize	70	65	69	204	33,244.44
Mark O'Meara	69	66	69	204	33,244.44
Tommy Armour	70	66	69	205	21,560
Olin Browne	69	65	71	205	21,560
Jose Coceres	68	66	71	205	21,560
Joe Durant	67	68	70	205	21,560
Rocco Mediate	68	65	72	205	21,560
Joey Sindelar	65	69	71	205	21,560
Roger Chapman	69	69	68	206	16,632
Bill Glasson	70	70	66	206	16,632
Hideki Kase	69	68	69	206	16,632
Hal Sutton	68	70	68	206	16,632
Esteban Toledo	70	67	69	206	16,632

Nature Valley First Tee Open

Pebble Beach Golf Links: Par 36-36–72; 6,837 yards
Poppy Hills: Par 36-35–71; 6,879 yards
Monterey Peninsula, California

September 26-28
purse, $1,900,000

	SCORES			TOTAL	MONEY
John Cook	67	68	69	204	$285,000
Tom Byrum	68	68	69	205	167,200
Roger Chapman	70	71	65	206	124,925
Skip Kendall	67	69	70	206	124,925
Woody Austin	70	71	66	207	90,250
Billy Andrade	69	70	69	208	64,600
Fred Funk	69	69	70	208	64,600
Lee Janzen	68	70	70	208	64,600
Kirk Triplett	69	72	67	208	64,600
David Frost	71	71	67	209	43,700
Jay Haas	68	70	71	209	43,700
Loren Roberts	71	73	65	209	43,700
Grant Waite	72	68	69	209	43,700

	SCORES			TOTAL	MONEY
Mark Calcavecchia	72	68	70	210	31,350
Marco Dawson	69	68	73	210	31,350
Paul Goydos	69	69	72	210	31,350
Jeff Hart	71	67	72	210	31,350
Steve Lowery	71	70	69	210	31,350
Wes Short, Jr.	73	68	69	210	31,350
Joe Durant	74	67	70	211	22,800
John Inman	68	72	71	211	22,800
Blaine McCallister	66	73	72	211	22,800
Esteban Toledo	72	69	70	211	22,800
Stephen Ames	74	69	69	212	16,264
Mark Brooks	69	73	70	212	16,264
Olin Browne	72	67	73	212	16,264
Russ Cochran	70	70	72	212	16,264
Steve Elkington	74	70	68	212	16,264
Doug Garwood	71	71	70	212	16,264
Davis Love	71	67	74	212	16,264
Chien Soon Lu	72	72	68	212	16,264
Gene Sauers	73	68	71	212	16,264
Jeff Sluman	69	72	71	212	16,264

SAS Championship

Prestonwood Country Club, Cary, North Carolina — October 10-12
Par 35-37–72; 7,240 yards — purse, $2,100,000

	SCORES			TOTAL	MONEY
Kirk Triplett	70	63	69	202	$315,000
Tom Lehman	67	68	70	205	184,800
Bernhard Langer	73	65	68	206	138,075
Kenny Perry	72	67	67	206	138,075
Paul Goydos	68	67	72	207	86,450
Mark McNulty	72	68	67	207	86,450
Kevin Sutherland	69	68	70	207	86,450
Marco Dawson	67	70	71	208	63,000
David Frost	69	69	70	208	63,000
Michael Allen	73	67	70	210	41,300
Guy Boros	66	70	74	210	41,300
Bart Bryant	72	70	68	210	41,300
Fred Funk	72	64	74	210	41,300
Gary Hallberg	73	68	69	210	41,300
Jeff Hart	73	68	69	210	41,300
Steve Lowery	70	70	70	210	41,300
Corey Pavin	71	71	68	210	41,300
Joey Sindelar	76	65	69	210	41,300
Billy Andrade	72	70	69	211	25,375
Roger Chapman	69	72	70	211	25,375
John Inman	71	69	71	211	25,375
Colin Montgomerie	73	66	72	211	25,375
Mark O'Meara	69	69	73	211	25,375
Tom Pernice, Jr.	72	70	69	211	25,375
Brad Faxon	74	72	66	212	19,152
Anders Forsbrand	72	70	70	212	19,152
Skip Kendall	73	68	71	212	19,152
Gary Koch	69	68	75	212	19,152
Craig Stadler	71	71	70	212	19,152
Tom Byrum	76	66	71	213	15,820
Mark Calcavecchia	77	66	70	213	15,820
Bob Tway	71	73	69	213	15,820

Greater Hickory Kia Classic

Rock Barn Golf & Spa, Conover, North Carolina
Par 35-36–71; 6,874 yards

October 17-19
purse, $1,600,000

	SCORES			TOTAL	MONEY
Jay Haas	63	67	66	196	$240,000
Joe Durant	63	69	66	198	128,000
Kirk Triplett	66	66	66	198	128,000
David Frost	67	65	68	200	95,200
John Cook	67	68	66	201	76,000
Stephen Ames	69	68	65	202	51,840
Doug Garwood	70	66	66	202	51,840
Paul Goydos	68	67	67	202	51,840
Skip Kendall	71	65	66	202	51,840
Wayne Levi	67	66	69	202	51,840
Roger Chapman	65	69	69	203	34,000
Mike Goodes	66	69	68	203	34,000
Jeff Maggert	68	69	66	203	34,000
Jeff Sluman	69	66	68	203	34,000
Bill Glasson	66	68	70	204	27,200
Rocco Mediate	66	70	68	204	27,200
Kevin Sutherland	69	67	68	204	27,200
Mike Reid	70	68	67	205	22,453.34
Jose Coceres	70	67	68	205	22,453.33
Gene Sauers	70	67	68	205	22,453.33
Tommy Armour	69	67	70	206	17,728
Marco Dawson	68	70	68	206	17,728
Jeff Hart	70	67	69	206	17,728
Esteban Toledo	71	67	68	206	17,728
Willie Wood	69	68	69	206	17,728
Michael Allen	67	70	70	207	13,020
Chip Beck	70	67	70	207	13,020
Jeff Freeman	69	71	67	207	13,020
Barry Lane	71	68	68	207	13,020
Chien Soon Lu	67	72	68	207	13,020
Wes Short, Jr.	71	70	66	207	13,020
Rod Spittle	69	75	63	207	13,020
Bob Tway	69	68	70	207	13,020

AT&T Championship

TPC San Antonio, AT&T Canyons Course, San Antonio, Texas
Par 36-36–72; 6,923 yards

October 24-26
purse, $1,950,000

	SCORES			TOTAL	MONEY
Michael Allen	70	65	66	201	$292,500
Marco Dawson	65	67	71	203	171,600
Woody Austin	68	65	71	204	140,400
Scott Hoch	68	67	70	205	104,325
Tom Pernice, Jr.	72	66	67	205	104,325
Jay Haas	67	68	71	206	74,100
Bernhard Langer	71	66	69	206	74,100
Fred Funk	70	67	70	207	53,625
Jeff Maggert	74	65	68	207	53,625
Wes Short, Jr.	67	67	73	207	53,625
Kirk Triplett	67	69	71	207	53,625
Rocco Mediate	72	70	66	208	40,950
Esteban Toledo	69	71	68	208	40,950
Olin Browne	70	72	67	209	33,150

	SCORES			TOTAL	MONEY
Scott Dunlap	66	74	69	209	33,150
Lee Janzen	69	73	67	209	33,150
Steve Pate	73	67	69	209	33,150
Gene Sauers	70	72	67	209	33,150
Guy Boros	67	73	70	210	23,562.50
Bart Bryant	67	74	69	210	23,562.50
John Cook	65	72	73	210	23,562.50
Tom Lehman	67	72	71	210	23,562.50
Kenny Perry	68	70	72	210	23,562.50
Willie Wood	69	72	69	210	23,562.50
Tommy Armour	73	67	71	211	17,387.50
Fred Couples	73	68	70	211	17,387.50
Gary Hallberg	67	76	68	211	17,387.50
Jeff Hart	72	67	72	211	17,387.50
Steve Lowery	68	73	70	211	17,387.50
Peter Senior	67	73	71	211	17,387.50

Charles Schwab Cup Championship

Desert Mountain Club, Cochise Course, Scottsdale, Arizona — October 30-November 2
Par 35-35–70; 6,929 yards — purse, $2,500,000

	SCORES				TOTAL	MONEY
Tom Pernice, Jr.	65	67	70	67	269	$440,000
Jay Haas	66	62	75	66	269	254,000
(Pernice defeated Haas on fourth playoff hole.)						
Kenny Perry	66	68	68	68	270	213,000
Bernhard Langer	66	70	70	65	271	158,000
Colin Montgomerie	71	67	66	67	271	158,000
Olin Browne	68	67	71	67	273	117,000
Fred Couples	71	64	69	70	274	99,000
Wes Short, Jr.	69	67	69	69	274	99,000
Michael Allen	69	66	70	70	275	79,000
Gene Sauers	68	68	69	70	275	79,000
Jeff Maggert	70	69	70	67	276	70,000
Woody Austin	71	67	70	69	277	61,500
Marco Dawson	69	67	69	72	277	61,500
John Cook	71	70	71	66	278	50,500
Fred Funk	74	66	71	67	278	50,500
Paul Goydos	70	67	70	71	278	50,500
Esteban Toledo	71	67	70	70	278	50,500
Bart Bryant	70	71	70	68	279	39,375
Scott Dunlap	69	69	71	70	279	39,375
Joe Durant	66	70	75	68	279	39,375
Tom Lehman	71	70	67	71	279	39,375
David Frost	74	68	69	69	280	33,000
Jeff Sluman	71	70	69	70	280	33,000
Doug Garwood	74	71	68	68	281	30,000
Duffy Waldorf	72	72	71	67	282	29,000
Billy Andrade	68	75	69	71	283	27,000
Kirk Triplett	69	71	74	72	286	26,000
Mark O'Meara	73	74	68	72	287	25,000
Mark Brooks	74	74	71	74	293	24,500
Russ Cochran	68	70	71		WD	

European Senior Tour

U.S. Senior PGA Championship

See Champions Tour section.

ISPS Handa PGA Seniors Championship

Stoke By Nayland Hotel, Golf & Spa, Colchester, Essex, England
Par 35-36–71; 6,887 yards

June 5-8
purse, £235,000

	SCORES				TOTAL	MONEY
Santiago Luna	68	71	67	64	270	€46,304
Steen Tinning	67	68	68	69	272	32,413
Mark Mouland	68	71	71	64	274	21,705
Cesar Monasterio	71	68	69	67	275	15,911
Andrew Oldcorn	73	67	66	69	275	15,911
Paul Eales	68	69	74	65	276	8,719
Marc Farry	72	70	66	68	276	8,719
Philip Golding	73	70	67	66	276	8,719
Andrew Murray	68	71	68	69	276	8,719
Andre Bossert	73	68	68	68	277	5,436
Gary Emerson	70	68	71	68	277	5,436
Barry Lane	71	69	71	66	277	5,436
Jerry Smith	68	70	71	68	277	5,436
Chris Williams	69	67	70	71	277	5,436
Mark James	68	66	71	73	278	4,118
Ronan Rafferty	70	70	68	70	278	4,118
Jamie Spence	70	68	68	72	278	4,118
Tim Thelen	70	72	67	69	278	4,118
Peter Fowler	68	74	71	66	279	3,137
Gordon Manson	71	67	71	70	279	3,137
Des Smyth	66	75	71	67	279	3,137

Bad Ragaz PGA Seniors Open

Golf Club Bad Ragaz, Bad Ragaz, Switzerland
Par 35-35–70; 6,157 yards

July 4-6
purse, €280,000

	SCORES			TOTAL	MONEY
Rick Gibson	63	66	66	195	€42,000
Denis O'Sullivan	70	65	66	201	28,000
Ross Drummond	65	68	69	202	19,600
Luis Carbonetti	72	62	69	203	11,659
Peter Fowler	66	68	69	203	11,659
Gordon Manson	68	66	69	203	11,659
Carl Mason	68	67	68	203	11,659
Jamie Spence	67	68	68	203	11,659
Philip Golding	69	67	68	204	7,000
Mike Harwood	71	66	67	204	7,000
Mark Mouland	71	66	67	204	7,000
Gary Wolstenholme	68	68	68	204	7,000

	SCORES			TOTAL	MONEY
Bob Cameron	68	66	71	205	5,180
Marc Farry	69	67	69	205	5,180
Juan Quiros	70	65	70	205	5,180
Gary Rusnak	64	74	67	205	5,180
Gary Emerson	70	66	70	206	4,340
Jerry Smith	69	68	69	206	4,340
Andrew Murray	69	69	70	208	3,822
Ian Woosnam	71	71	66	208	3,822

U.S. Senior Open

See Champions Tour section.

The Senior Open Championship presented by Rolex

Royal Porthcawl Golf Club, Bridgend, Wales
Par 35-36–71; 6,901 yards

July 24-27
purse, £1,250,000

	SCORES				TOTAL	MONEY
Bernhard Langer	65	66	68	67	266	€248,535
Colin Montgomerie	72	66	72	69	279	165,753
Rick Gibson	70	71	66	75	282	77,018
Barry Lane	72	69	69	72	282	77,018
Tom Pernice, Jr.	78	64	70	70	282	77,018
Scott Dunlap	71	73	65	75	284	48,463
Bob Tway	67	73	68	76	284	48,463
Miguel Angel Jimenez	74	69	74	68	285	35,327
Kirk Triplett	72	72	71	70	285	35,327
Russ Cochran	74	73	67	72	286	28,602
Tom Watson	74	66	69	77	286	28,602
Esteban Toledo	73	72	69	73	287	25,546
Fred Couples	71	71	68	78	288	22,900
Miguel Angel Martin	74	69	69	76	288	22,900
Bruce Vaughan	73	69	73	73	288	22,900
Dan Forsman	72	73	74	70	289	20,044
Jeff Sluman	73	71	67	78	289	20,044
Chris Williams	68	70	71	80	289	20,044
Roger Chapman	75	73	73	69	290	18,349
Steve Pate	75	68	70	77	290	18,349
Olin Browne	72	72	70	77	291	15,813
Peter Fowler	71	72	73	75	291	15,813
David Frost	71	76	71	73	291	15,813
Jeff Hart	71	74	72	74	291	15,813
Mark Mouland	74	69	75	73	291	15,813
Jamie Spence	71	77	75	68	291	15,813
Rod Spittle	76	73	72	70	291	15,813
Paul Wesselingh	75	73	71	72	291	15,813
Michael Allen	75	72	73	72	292	12,713
Marc Farry	76	71	72	73	292	12,713
Fred Funk	74	72	74	72	292	12,713
Mike Goodes	75	70	70	77	292	12,713
David J. Russell	77	71	69	75	292	12,713
Mark Brooks	74	72	71	76	293	10,880
Ross Drummond	72	71	75	75	293	10,880
Chien Soon Lu	76	68	71	78	293	10,880
Philip Walton	72	77	64	80	293	10,880
Willie Wood	76	71	78	68	293	10,880
Joe Daley	75	71	72	76	294	9,135
Marco Dawson	76	71	73	74	294	9,135

	SCORES				TOTAL	MONEY
Gary Hallberg	72	74	71	77	294	9,135
Pedro Linhart	70	69	75	80	294	9,135
Carl Mason	72	72	71	79	294	9,135
Javier Sanchez	74	72	77	71	294	9,135
Gary Wolstenholme	74	73	73	74	294	9,135
Graeme Bell	74	75	71	75	295	7,434
Jim Carter	72	73	72	78	295	7,434
Paul Eales	73	76	74	72	295	7,434
*Chip Lutz	72	72	73	78	295	
Malcolm Mackenzie	73	74	77	71	295	7,434
Andrew Oldcorn	69	78	71	77	295	7,434
Wraith Grant	78	70	70	78	296	5,880
Mike Harwood	74	73	70	79	296	5,880
Kohki Idoki	74	73	72	77	296	5,880
Seiki Okuda	77	71	75	73	296	5,880
Ronan Rafferty	75	73	72	76	296	5,880
Hiroshi Ueda	76	70	75	75	296	5,880
Bob Cameron	73	75	74	75	297	4,523
Angel Franco	74	70	71	82	297	4,523
Bob Gilder	81	68	69	79	297	4,523
Kenny Hutton	71	78	70	78	297	4,523
Wes Short, Jr.	77	72	76	72	297	4,523
*George Zahringer	71	78	68	80	297	
Luis Carbonetti	76	68	75	79	298	3,622
John Cook	73	73	75	77	298	3,622
Santiago Luna	75	71	76	76	298	3,622
Jerry Smith	74	74	77	73	298	3,622
Greg Turner	73	75	66	84	298	3,622
Jean-Francois Remesy	73	70	76	80	299	3,024
Boonchu Ruangkit	73	70	78	78	299	3,024
Katsuyoshi Tomori	72	73	73	81	299	3,024
Richard Backwell	76	73	74	77	300	2,772
Steve Jones	71	73	75	82	301	2,646
Alastair Webster	75	72	81	74	302	2,520
Ian Woosnam	73	74	81	75	303	2,394
Jose Manuel Carriles	79	70	76	80	305	2,268

SSE Scottish Senior Open

Fairmont St. Andrews, Torrance Championship Course,
St. Andrews, Fife, Scotland
Par 35-37–72; 6,804 yards

August 15-17
purse, £250,000

	SCORES			TOTAL	MONEY
Mark Davis	66	74	71	211	€47,328
Philip Golding	72	70	74	216	21,313
Pedro Linhart	68	72	76	216	21,313
Cesar Monasterio	61	76	79	216	21,313
David J. Russell	70	73	73	216	21,313
Gordon Manson	69	73	75	217	11,359
Jerry Smith	66	76	75	217	11,359
Jamie Spence	70	73	74	217	11,359
Simon P. Brown	70	72	76	218	8,519
Des Smyth	70	73	75	218	8,519
Gordon Brand, Jr.	69	73	77	219	5,955
Bob Cameron	71	74	74	219	5,955
Peter Fowler	72	76	71	219	5,955
Mark James	70	73	76	219	5,955
Carl Mason	69	74	76	219	5,955
Jean-Francois Remesy	68	76	75	219	5,955

	SCORES			TOTAL	MONEY
George Ryall	65	78	76	219	5,955
Katsuyoshi Tomori	64	78	77	219	5,955
Paul Curry	71	75	74	220	4,047
Marc Farry	72	74	74	220	4,047
Gary Wolstenholme	71	76	73	220	4,047
Ian Woosnam	68	72	80	220	4,047

English Senior Open

Rockliffe Hall, County Durham, England
Par 36-36–72; 6,987 yards

August 22-24
purse, £200,000

	SCORES			TOTAL	MONEY
Cesar Monasterio	69	63	70	202	€37,504
Barry Lane	71	66	70	207	21,252
Andrew Oldcorn	72	68	67	207	21,252
Ross Drummond	70	65	73	208	11,685
Paul Eales	74	68	66	208	11,685
Jamie Spence	67	71	70	208	11,685
Mark James	70	70	70	210	7,626
Santiago Luna	71	68	71	210	7,626
Andrew Murray	71	69	70	210	7,626
Chris Williams	69	71	70	210	7,626
Andre Bossert	72	69	70	211	5,313
Jose Manuel Carriles	70	68	73	211	5,313
Peter Fowler	73	70	68	211	5,313
Jean Pierre Sallat	75	66	70	211	5,313
Marc Farry	71	72	69	212	3,888
Angel Franco	72	69	71	212	3,888
John Harrison	77	67	68	212	3,888
Pedro Linhart	72	69	71	212	3,888
Miguel Angel Martin	70	71	71	212	3,888
Steen Tinning	72	68	72	212	3,888

Travis Perkins Masters

Woburn Golf Club, Duke's Course, Woburn, England
Par 35-37–72; 6,904 yards

August 29-31
purse, £300,000

	SCORES			TOTAL	MONEY
Colin Montgomerie	68	69	67	204	€56,376
Andre Bossert	74	69	71	214	28,188
Gordon Manson	76	71	67	214	28,188
Tim Thelen	72	71	71	214	28,188
Mike Cunning	73	68	74	215	16,011
Peter Fowler	71	72	72	215	16,011
Jose Manuel Carriles	72	72	72	216	12,779
Barry Lane	73	70	73	216	12,779
Ross Drummond	73	71	73	217	9,020
Rick Gibson	70	73	74	217	9,020
Miguel Angel Martin	72	70	75	217	9,020
Cesar Monasterio	70	72	75	217	9,020
Philip Walton	70	75	72	217	9,020
Mark Davis	75	70	73	218	6,030
Tony Johnstone	79	68	71	218	6,030
Jose Rivero	73	71	74	218	6,030
Eduardo Romero	75	71	72	218	6,030

	SCORES			TOTAL	MONEY
Andrew Sherborne	71	76	71	218	6,030
Des Smyth	76	69	73	218	6,030
Paul Wesselingh	73	73	72	218	6,030

Russian Open

Moscow Country Club, Moscow Region, Russia
Par 36-36–72; 6,877 yards

September 5-7
purse, US$900,000

	SCORES			TOTAL	MONEY
Colin Montgomerie	69	68	65	202	€102,591
Rick Gibson	73	65	67	205	68,394
Barry Lane	73	65	68	206	35,941
Miguel Angel Martin	67	70	69	206	35,941
Andrew Oldcorn	72	66	68	206	35,941
Tim Thelen	70	65	71	206	35,941
Philip Golding	68	73	67	208	23,254
Steen Tinning	68	71	69	208	23,254
Paul Eales	72	68	69	209	18,466
Marc Farry	65	73	71	209	18,466
Andre Bossert	73	68	69	210	15,731
Cesar Monasterio	72	67	71	210	15,731
Angel Franco	69	70	72	211	12,653
Santiago Luna	71	73	67	211	12,653
Jean-Francois Remesy	70	72	69	211	12,653
Eduardo Romero	74	72	65	211	12,653
Ross Drummond	73	68	71	212	10,943
Bob Cameron	71	72	70	213	9,353
Mike Harwood	74	72	67	213	9,353
Boonchu Ruangkit	71	73	69	213	9,353
Andrew Sherborne	70	73	70	213	9,353

Senior Open de Portugal

Vidago Palace, Porto, Portugal
Par 36-36–72; 6,898 yards

September 12-14
purse, €225,000

	SCORES			TOTAL	MONEY
Tim Thelen	68	64	72	204	€33,750
Miguel Angel Martin	72	66	67	205	22,500
Carl Mason	66	69	71	206	14,062
Des Smyth	67	68	71	206	14,062
Angel Franco	71	71	65	207	8,154
Jose Rivero	69	70	68	207	8,154
Steen Tinning	67	71	69	207	8,154
Greg Turner	68	67	72	207	8,154
Chris Williams	63	73	71	207	8,154
Peter Fowler	70	74	65	209	4,995
Cesar Monasterio	68	71	70	209	4,995
Andrew Murray	67	75	67	209	4,995
Gary Rusnak	67	71	71	209	4,995
Jerry Smith	69	69	71	209	4,995
Simon P. Brown	71	67	72	210	3,712
Jose Manuel Carriles	71	71	68	210	3,712
Bill Longmuir	71	70	69	210	3,712
George Ryall	70	69	71	210	3,712
Rick Gibson	73	67	71	211	2,978

	SCORES			TOTAL	MONEY
David J. Russell	69	74	68	211	2,978
Gary Wolstenholme	66	77	68	211	2,978

WINSTONgolf Senior Open

WINSTONopen Course, WINSTONgolf, Vorbeck, Germany — September 19-21
Par 36-36–72; 6,833 yards — purse, €400,000

	SCORES			TOTAL	MONEY
Paul Wesselingh	69	67	65	201	€60,000
Philip Golding	68	67	66	201	34,000
Bernhard Langer	66	66	69	201	34,000
(Wesselingh defeated Golding on second and Langer on third playoff hole.)					
Gary Emerson	65	67	70	202	22,000
Andre Bossert	66	69	68	203	16,160
Wraith Grant	67	65	71	203	16,160
Jean-Francois Remesy	70	64	69	203	16,160
Simon P. Brown	67	66	71	204	11,467
Santiago Luna	67	71	66	204	11,467
Cesar Monasterio	66	68	70	204	11,467
Jose Manuel Carriles	72	69	65	206	9,200
Chris Williams	67	66	73	206	9,200
Marc Farry	72	63	72	207	7,600
Peter Fowler	70	68	69	207	7,600
Andrew Oldcorn	67	71	69	207	7,600
Ross Drummond	68	66	74	208	5,232
Paul Eales	66	71	71	208	5,232
John Gould	69	69	70	208	5,232
Mike Harwood	68	67	73	208	5,232
Gordon Manson	70	69	69	208	5,232
George Ryall	67	69	72	208	5,232
Jerry Smith	66	72	70	208	5,232
Des Smyth	71	70	67	208	5,232
Kevin Spurgeon	71	69	68	208	5,232
Greg Turner	71	67	70	208	5,232

French Riviera Masters

Terre Blanche Hotel Spa Golf Resort, Tourrettes, Provence, France — October 3-5
Par 36-36–72; 6,955 yards — purse, €400,000

	SCORES			TOTAL	MONEY
Philip Golding	64	67	70	201	€60,000
Cesar Monasterio	66	69	70	205	40,000
Peter Fowler	68	71	67	206	22,693
John Gould	70	67	69	206	22,693
Barry Lane	68	70	68	206	22,693
Rick Gibson	68	68	71	207	15,200
Gary Wolstenholme	68	71	68	207	15,200
Simon P. Brown	68	69	71	208	12,000
Tim Thelen	70	70	68	208	12,000
Miguel Angel Martin	67	72	71	210	10,000
Ian Woosnam	74	70	66	210	10,000
Barry Conser	69	72	70	211	8,400
Greg Turner	71	69	71	211	8,400
Gary Emerson	65	72	75	212	6,607
Pedro Linhart	70	71	71	212	6,607

	SCORES			TOTAL	MONEY
Juan Quiros	67	74	71	212	6,607
Gary Rusnak	75	68	69	212	6,607
Steen Tinning	72	69	71	212	6,607
Paul Wesselingh	71	72	69	212	6,607
Domingo Hospital	70	71	72	213	5,120
Ronan Rafferty	70	71	72	213	5,120

Dutch Senior Open

The International, Amsterdam, The Netherlands
Par 37-36–73; 6,966 yards

October 10-12
purse, €200,000

	SCORES			TOTAL	MONEY
Ian Woosnam	71	69	68	208	€30,475
Philip Golding	68	71	74	213	15,238
David J. Russell	75	70	68	213	15,238
George Ryall	70	70	73	213	15,238
Pedro Linhart	72	71	71	214	8,655
Ronan Rafferty	76	68	70	214	8,655
Angel Franco	71	75	69	215	6,197
Santiago Luna	72	72	71	215	6,197
Gordon Manson	74	71	70	215	6,197
Gary Rusnak	72	73	70	215	6,197
Ross Drummond	75	73	68	216	4,470
Barry Lane	72	73	71	216	4,470
Kevin Spurgeon	75	74	67	216	4,470
Luis Carbonetti	72	72	73	217	3,759
Terry Price	72	73	72	217	3,759
Simon P. Brown	73	76	69	218	3,251
Gary Emerson	72	76	70	218	3,251
Mike Harwood	74	72	72	218	3,251
Andre Bossert	79	72	68	219	2,531
Bob Cameron	76	72	71	219	2,531
Marc Farry	72	73	74	219	2,531
Carl Mason	75	69	75	219	2,531
Jerry Smith	77	71	71	219	2,531

Coca-Cola Australian PGA Seniors Championship

Richmond Golf Club, Richmond, New South Wales, Australia
Par 36-36–72

October 29-November 1
purse, A$70,000

	SCORES			TOTAL
Simon Owen	66	70	72	208
Michael Harwood	68	71	69	208
(Owen defeated Harwood on first playoff hole.)				
Allan Cooper	69	69	71	209
Terry Price	67	71	71	209
Tim Elliott	70	68	71	209
Craig Warren	68	73	69	210
George Serhan	73	70	68	211
David Merriman	71	71	69	211
Rodger Davis	71	71	70	212
Craig Owen	70	71	71	212
Michael Clayton	73	70	70	213
Tod Power	68	77	69	214
Peter Hayes	68	72	74	214

	SCORES			TOTAL
Glen Moss	69	71	74	214
Hugh Dolan	69	73	73	215
Stephen Herbert	70	71	74	215
David Good	68	76	72	216
Colin Hunt	70	73	73	216
Elliott Booth	70	71	75	216
David Saunders	68	69	79	216

MCB Tour Championship

Constance Belle Mare Plage, Poste de Flacq, Mauritius — December 12-14
Par 36-36–72; 6,614 yards — purse, €420,000

	SCORES			TOTAL	MONEY
Paul Wesselingh	69	69	69	207	€63,998
Barry Lane	68	72	67	207	42,666
(Wesselingh defeated Lane on sixth playoff hole.)					
David Frost	69	68	71	208	29,866
Jean-Francois Remesy	72	69	68	209	21,375
Andrew Sherborne	70	71	68	209	21,375
Colin Montgomerie	71	71	68	210	17,066
Rick Gibson	71	70	70	211	13,013
Cesar Monasterio	71	69	71	211	13,013
Gary Rusnak	70	71	70	211	13,013
Steen Tinning	71	69	71	211	13,013
Andre Bossert	71	69	72	212	9,386
Philip Golding	75	70	67	212	9,386
Gordon Manson	74	68	70	212	9,386
Mark Mouland	72	77	64	213	7,893
Des Smyth	72	70	71	213	7,893
John Gould	72	71	71	214	6,624
Wraith Grant	75	71	68	214	6,624
Bill Longmuir	71	69	74	214	6,624
George Ryall	71	72	71	214	6,624
Ross Drummond	71	71	73	215	5,291
Miguel Angel Martin	73	73	69	215	5,291
Chris Williams	70	71	74	215	5,291

Japan PGA Senior Tour

Kanehide Senior Okinawa Open

Kise Country Club, Okinawa
Par 36-36–72; 6,881 yards

April 18-19
purse, ¥20,000,000

	SCORES		TOTAL	MONEY
Hatsuo Nakane	68	68	136	3,600,000
Takeshi Sakiyama	64	72	136	1,800,000
(Nakane defeated Sakiyama on first playoff hole.)				
Tatsuya Shiraishi	69	69	138	1,100,000
Paul Wesselingh	68	70	138	1,100,000
Yoichi Shimizu	70	69	139	880,000
Ikuo Shirahama	72	68	140	660,000
Gohei Sato	72	68	140	660,000
Hideki Kase	71	69	140	660,000
Gregory Meyer	67	73	140	660,000
Anthony Gilligan	71	70	141	376,666
Katsunari Takahashi	71	70	141	376,666
Shinji Kuraoka	69	72	141	376,666
Hajime Meshiai	69	72	141	376,666
Katsumi Kubo	68	73	141	376,666
Jong-Duck Kim	68	73	141	376,666
Tsukasa Watanabe	73	69	142	260,800
Junji Kawase	74	68	142	260,800
Yutaka Hagawa	71	71	142	260,800
Satoshi Higashi	71	71	142	260,800
Shinji Ikeuchi	67	75	142	260,800

Kyoraku More Surprise Cup

Ryosen Golf Club, Mie
Par 36-36–72; 7,036 yards

May 9-11
purse, ¥70,000,000

	SCORES			TOTAL	MONEY
Seiki Okuda	74	71	69	214	¥15,000,000
T.C. Chen	74	68	72	214	7,700,000
(Okuda defeated Chen on second playoff hole.)					
Satoshi Higashi	76	69	71	216	3,500,000
Kiyoshi Murota	73	70	73	216	3,500,000
Takeshi Sakiyama	74	72	72	218	2,450,000
Hiroshi Ueda	74	74	72	220	1,925,000
Naomichi Ozaki	73	74	73	220	1,925,000
Frankie Minoza	71	80	70	221	1,302,000
Katsunari Takahashi	72	78	71	221	1,302,000
Kiyoshi Maita	75	75	71	221	1,302,000
Tsutomu Higa	71	76	74	221	1,302,000
Masahiro Kuramoto	73	73	75	221	1,302,000
Hiroshi Makino	75	76	71	222	980,000
*Hiroshi Wada	73	74	75	222	
Atsushi Takamatsu	73	74	75	222	980,000
Gregory Meyer	73	69	80	222	980,000
Tatsuya Shiraishi	75	77	71	223	787,500

	SCORES			TOTAL	MONEY
Hideki Kase	73	77	73	223	787,500
Yoichi Shimizu	73	75	75	223	787,500
Kohki Idoki	75	74	74	223	787,500

Starts Senior

Starts Kasama Golf Club, Ibaraki
Par 36-36–72; 6,936 yards

June 13-15
purse, ¥56,500,000

	SCORES			TOTAL	MONEY
Shinji Ikeuchi	67	66	70	203	¥14,000,000
Kiyoshi Murota	64	70	70	204	6,800,000
Frankie Minoza	71	66	68	205	4,180,000
Takeshi Sakiyama	68	71	67	206	2,145,000
Hajime Meshiai	71	66	69	206	2,145,000
Kohki Idoki	69	70	68	207	1,589,500
Seiki Okuda	70	69	68	207	1,589,500
Nobumitsu Yuhara	69	72	67	208	1,164,250
Hideki Kase	71	69	68	208	1,164,250
Yoichi Shimizu	68	71	69	208	1,164,250
Ikuo Shirahama	70	69	69	208	1,164,250
Yoshitaka Yamamoto	72	71	66	209	822,285
Kiyoshi Maita	73	69	67	209	822,285
Masami Ito	71	70	68	209	822,285
Yuji Takagi	69	71	69	209	822,285
Paul Wesselingh	69	71	69	209	822,285
Satoshi Higashi	70	70	69	209	822,285
Akio Nishizawa	71	69	69	209	822,285
Gregory Meyer	71	72	67	210	589,500
Tsutomu Higa	68	74	68	210	589,500
Masahiro Kuramoto	71	71	68	210	589,500
Hatsuo Nakane	70	69	71	210	589,500

ISPS Handa Cup Philanthropy Senior

Hakone Kohan Golf Club, Kanagawa
Par 36-36–72; 6,488 yards

June 27-29
purse, ¥50,000,000

	SCORES			TOTAL	MONEY
Hideki Kase	65	67	67	199	¥10,000,000
Takashi Miyoshi	65	68	67	200	3,550,000
Yutaka Hagawa	67	66	67	200	3,550,000
Hatsuo Nakane	65	66	69	200	3,550,000
Naomichi Ozaki	64	71	66	201	1,716,666
Tsukasa Watanabe	69	66	66	201	1,716,666
Jong-Duck Kim	68	66	67	201	1,716,666
Ahmad Bateman	68	68	66	202	1,206,250
Ikuo Shirahama	62	73	67	202	1,206,250
Norikazu Kawakami	67	67	68	202	1,206,250
Kohki Idoki	68	65	69	202	1,206,250
Seiki Okuda	69	69	65	203	865,000
Takeshi Sakiyama	68	70	65	203	865,000
Nobumitsu Yuhara	68	68	67	203	865,000
Atsushi Takamatsu	67	68	68	203	865,000
Hiroshi Ueda	64	70	69	203	865,000
Yoshimitsu Fukuzawa	70	70	64	204	712,500
Hitoshi Kato	64	70	70	204	712,500

	SCORES			TOTAL	MONEY
Nobuo Serizawa	67	71	67	205	600,000
Katsumi Kubo	70	69	66	205	600,000
Kiyoshi Murota	66	72	67	205	600,000
Takashi Tsutsumi	71	67	67	205	600,000
Tatsuya Shiraishi	73	67	65	205	600,000
Tsutomu Higa	64	72	69	205	600,000
T.C. Chen	69	64	72	205	600,000

Maruhan Cup Taiheiyo Club Senior

Taiheiyo Club, Rokko Course, Hyogo
Par 36-36–72; 6,825 yards

August 2-3
purse, ¥40,000,000

	SCORES		TOTAL	MONEY
Gregory Meyer	62	70	132	¥8,000,000
Toshikazu Sugihara	65	68	133	3,800,000
Takeshi Sakiyama	69	66	135	2,600,000
Takashi Miyoshi	67	69	136	1,800,000
Tsutomu Higa	71	67	138	1,330,000
Boonchu Ruangkit	70	68	138	1,330,000
Ikuo Shirahama	67	71	138	1,330,000
Satoshi Higashi	66	72	138	1,330,000
Kazuhiro Takami	72	67	139	879,333
Tsukasa Watanabe	71	68	139	879,333
Yoshinori Mizumaki	71	68	139	879,333
Seiki Okuda	70	69	139	879,333
Frankie Minoza	70	69	139	879,333
Nobuo Serizawa	68	71	139	879,333
Yutaka Hagawa	72	68	140	566,285
Masahiro Kuramoto	70	70	140	566,285
Kiyoshi Murota	69	71	140	566,285
Atsushi Takamatsu	68	72	140	566,285
Katsumi Kubo	69	71	140	566,285
Hatsuo Nakane	68	72	140	566,285
Naoyuki Tamura	67	73	140	566,285

Fancl Classic

Susono Country Club, Susono, Shizuoka
Par 36-36–72; 6,911 yards

August 22-24
purse, ¥60,000,000

	SCORES			TOTAL	MONEY
Yutaka Hagawa	69	71	69	209	¥15,000,000
Naonori Nakamura	74	69	68	211	3,675,000
Jong-Duck Kim	70	72	69	211	3,675,000
Masahiro Kuramoto	70	71	70	211	3,675,000
Kazuhiro Takami	73	67	71	211	3,675,000
Katsunari Takahashi	74	69	69	212	1,540,000
Naomichi Ozaki	71	71	70	212	1,540,000
Kiyoshi Murota	69	71	72	212	1,540,000
Satoshi Oide	75	72	66	213	1,000,000
Toshikazu Sugihara	71	72	70	213	1,000,000
Kiyoshi Maita	73	70	70	213	1,000,000
Boonchu Ruangkit	70	72	71	213	1,000,000
Tatsuya Shiraishi	69	72	72	213	1,000,000
Seiki Okuda	72	68	73	213	1,000,000
Gregory Meyer	76	69	70	215	780,000